PIT BOSS
Wood Pellet Grill and Smoker
COOKBOOK

The Biggest Guide for Pit Boss with 1500 Amazing Mouthwatering BBQ Recipes for Beginners and Advanced. Impress Your Friends and Become the Undisputed Pitmaster of Your Neighborhood!

ALEC POOLE

THIS BOOK BY RENOWNED CHEF ALEC POOLE WILL SHOW YOU THE WAY TO BECOME AN UNPARALLELED PITMASTER FROM THE COMFORT OF YOUR OWN HOME!

PIT BOSS

© Copyright 2021 by ALEC POOLE- All rights reserved.

This document is geared towards providing exact and reliable information regarding the topic and issue covered. The publication is sold with the idea that the publisher is not required to render accounting, officially permitted, or otherwise, qualified services. If advice is necessary, legal, or professional, a practiced individual in the profession should be ordered.

- From a Declaration of Principles which was accepted and approved equally by a Committee of the American Bar Association and a Committee of Publishers and Associations.

In no way is it legal to reproduce, duplicate, or transmit any part of this document in either electronic means or printed format. Recording of this publication is strictly prohibited, and any storage of this document is not allowed unless with written permission from the publisher. All rights reserved.

The information provided herein is stated to be truthful and consistent, in that any liability, in terms of inattention or otherwise, by any usage or abuse of any policies, processes, or directions contained within is the solitary and utter responsibility of the recipient reader. Under no circumstances will any legal responsibility or blame be held against the publisher for any reparation, damages, or monetary loss due to the information herein, either directly or indirectly.

Respective authors own all copyrights not held by the publisher.

The information herein is offered for informational purposes solely and is universal as so. The presentation of the information is without a contract or any type of guaranteed assurance.

The trademarks that are used are without any consent, and the publication of the trademark is without permission or backing by the trademark owner. All trademarks and brands within this book are for clarifying purposes only and are owned by the owners themselves, not affiliated with this document.

Table of Contents

Chapter 1: Beef Recipes 23
- 1.1 Marinated Beef Ribs.. 23
- 1.2 Salt & Pepper Beer-Braised Beef Ribs 23
- 1.3 Asian-Style Grilled Beef Skewers.................................. 23
- 1.4 Secret Ingredient BBQ Beef Short Ribs........................... 23
- 1.5 Spicy Smoked Chili Beef Jerky 24
- 1.6 Vietnamese Beef Jerky.. 24
- 1.7 Reuben Sandwich 24
- 1.8 BBQ Beef Tamale Casserole...................................... 24
- 1.9 Coffee Break Smoked Beef Jerky 25
- 1.10 Jalapeño Beef Jerky 25
- 1.11 Roasted Prime Rib with Mustard and Herbs De Provence 25
- 1.12 Grilled Rib Eyes with Hasselback Sweet Potatoes 25
- 1.13 Southwestern Stuffed Peppers 26
- 1.14 Pit Boss Smoky Meatball Subs 26
- 1.15 3 Ingredient Pot Roast 26
- 1.16 Grilled Santa Maria Tri-Tip 26
- 1.17 Espresso Beef Tenderloin (Coriander & Rubbed) 27
- 1.18 Smoked Paleo Beef Jerky 27
- 1.19 Brined Smoked Brisket.. 27
- 1.20 Blue Cheese & Peppercorn Butter over Beef Tenderloin Steaks... 27
- 1.21 Ultimate Loaded Nachos 28
- 1.22 Smoked Burgers... 28
- 1.23 BBQ Beef Ribs... 28
- 1.24 Sweet Mandarin Meatloaf 28
- 1.25 Smoked Beef Cheek Tacos 29
- 1.26 Smoked Brisket.. 29
- 1.27 Beer-Braised Corned Beef & Irish Vegetables............ 29
- 1.28 Roasted Santa Maria Tri-Tip 29
- 1.29 Rosemary Prime Rib... 30
- 1.30 Smoked Corned Beef & Cabbage............................. 30
- 1.31 Diva Q's Herb-Crusted Prime Rib............................. 30
- 1.32 Garlic Parmesan Grilled Filet Mignon 30
- 1.33 Smoked Texas BBQ Brisket..................................... 30
- 1.34 Braised Mediterranean Beef Brisket 31
- 1.35 Smoked Tri-Tip... 31
- 1.36 Sweetheart Steak 31
- 1.37 Grilled Bacon-Wrapped Hot Dogs 31
- 1.38 Smoked Porterhouse Steak 31
- 1.39 BBQ Brisket with Pit Boss Coff 32
- ee Rub 32
- 1.40 BBQ Burnt Ends... 32
- 1.41 Chef's Brisket 32
- 1.42 Korean BBQ Short Ribs... 32
- 1.43 Beef Satay 32
- 1.44 Pit Boss BBQ Double Decker Taco........................... 32
- 1.45 Cocoa Crusted Grilled Flank Steak 33
- 1.46 Tin Foil Dinner 33
- 1.47 Smoked Rib-Eyes with Bourbon Butter 33
- 1.48 Grilled Carne Asada with Grilled Peppers & Onions.. 33
- 1.49 Reverse Seared Rib-Eye Caps................................. 34
- 1.50 Beginner's Smoked Beef Brisket............................... 34
- 1.51 Not Your Mama's Meatloaf...................................... 34
- 1.52 Grilled Tomahawk Steak.. 34
- 1.53 BBQ Brisket Reuben... 35
- 1.54 Beef Tenderloin with Tomato Vinaigrette................... 35
- 1.55 BBQ Beef Short Ribs.. 35
- 1.56 Teriyaki Beef Jerky... 35
- 1.57 Sunday Supper Beef Roast 35
- 1.58 Mexican Grilled Skirt Steak Tacos 36
- 1.59 Grilled Skirt Steak Bulgogi Bowls.............................. 36
- 1.60 Pit Boss Smash Burger 36
- 1.61 Breakfast Brisket Hash Recipe 36
- 1.62 Loaded Reuben Fries with Fontina Cheese............... 36
- 1.63 3-2-1 BBQ Beef Cheeks 37
- 1.64 Grilled Ribeye Shish Kabobs with Chimichurri Sauce.37
- 1.65 Asian-Style Grilled Rib-Eye Steak 37
- 1.66 Grilled Carne Asada Skirt Steak............................... 37
- 1.67 Grilled Flank Steak with Chilean Salsa 38
- 1.68 Wagyu Tri-Tip... 38
- 1.69 Smoked Midnight Brisket... 38
- 1.70 Grilled Butter Basted Rib-Eye 38
- 1.71 Roasted Mustard Crusted Prime Rib......................... 38
- 1.72 Beef Pot Roast... 39
- 1.73 Grilled Triple Cheeseburger..................................... 39
- 1.74 Sweet and Spicy Beef Sirloin Tip Roast.................... 39
- 1.75 Smoked Chili Rib Eye Steaks 39
- 1.76 The Perfect Smoked New York Strip Steak 39
- 1.77 Grilled Thai Beef Skewers....................................... 40
- 1.78 Grilled Sirloin Steaks... 40
- 1.79 Smoked Moink Burger by Scott Thomas 40

1.80 Grilled Rib-Eye Steaks by Doug Scheiding 40
1.81 Chorizo Cheese Stuffed Burgers 40
1.82 Grilled Butter Basted Porterhouse Steak 41
1.83 Slow Smoked Rib-Eye Roast 41
1.84 Smoked Bourbon Jerky 41
1.85 Grilled Korean Short Ribs 41
1.86 Bloody Mary Flank Steak 41
1.87 Smoked Longhorn Cowboy Tri-Tip 42
1.88 Sweet Grilled Shrimp & Spicy Sausage Skewers 42
1.89 Pit Boss Tri-Tip Roast 42
1.90 Pit Boss Bacon-Wrapped Filet Mignon 42
1.91 Pit Boss Filet Mignon 42
1.92 Slow Smoked and Roasted Prime Rib 42
1.93 Grilled Wagyu Burgers 43
1.94 BBQ Brisket Hot Dog 43
1.95 Grass-fed Beef Burgers 43
1.96 Meatloaf Cupcake Bites 43
1.97 BBQ Beef Short Ribs with Pit Boss Prime Rib Rub 43
1.98 Smoked Longhorn Brisket 43
1.99 Grilled Southern Pimento Cheeseburger 44
1.100 Grilled Steak 44
1.101 Dry Brined Texas Beef Ribs by Doug Scheiding 44
1.102 Smoked Corned Beef Brisket 44
1.103 Smoked Peppered Beef Jerky 44
1.104 Classic Beef Chili 45
1.105 Grilled Steak for Two with Cocoa Rub 45
1.106 Cherry BBQ Steak Skewers 45
1.107 Baked Corned Beef Au Gratin 46
1.108 Grilled Loco Moco Burger 46
1.109 Chimichurri Smoked Rib-Eyes 46
1.110 Skirt Steak with Corn & Avocado Salsa 46
1.111 Braised Cincinnati Chili 47
1.112 Beer Brined Corned Beef 47
1.113 Baked Ziti with Italian Sausage 48
1.114 Smoked Carolina Burger 48
1.115 Baked Bacon-Weaved Honey Bourbon-Glazed Meatloaf 48
1.116 Grilled Bacon Cheeseburger 48
1.117 Guinness Shepherd's Pie 49
1.118 Whiskey Bourbon BBQ Cheeseburger 49
1.119 BBQ Brisket Breakfast Tacos 49
1.120 Garlic and Herb Stuffed Prime Rib Roast 50

1.121 Flank Steak Matambre 50
1.122 Braised Brunswick Stew 50
1.123 Smoked T-Bone Steaks 50
1.124 Pit Boss Prime Rib Roast 51
1.125 Reverse Seared NY Strip Steak 51
1.126 Pit Boss NY Strip Steak 51
1.127 Corned Beef Hash 51
1.128 Leftover BBQ Sandwich 52
1.129 Moroccan Ground Meat Kebabs 52
1.130 Hickory Smoked Prime Rib 52
1.131 Grilled Beef Back Ribs 52
1.132 BBQ Meatball Onion Bombs 53
1.133 Grilled Rib-Eye with Green Butter 53
1.134 Smoked Brisket with Pit Boss Coffee Rub 53
1.135 Grilled Balsamic & Blue Steak 53
1.136 Grilled Ribeye Steak Sandwich 54
1.137 Reverse Seared Filet Mignon with Red Wine Reduction 54
1.138 Grilled Tri-Tip with Garlic Mashed Potatoes 54
1.139 Grilled Carne Asada Burrito with Smoked Pico 55
1.140 Smoked Pot Roast 55
1.141 Smoked Beef Back Ribs 55
1.142 Grilled Double Burgers with Texas Spicy BBQ Sauce 55
1.143 Braised Beef Short Ribs with Mashed Potatoes 55
1.144 Brisket Tacos with Smoked Cilantro Cream 56
1.145 Grilled Cleveland Polish Boy 56
1.146 Bourbon-Braised Beef Short Ribs 56
1.147 Pit Boss Smoked Salami 57
1.148 Smoked German Rouladen 57
1.149 Glazed Cajun Meatloaf 57
1.150 Smoked Peppered Beef Tenderloin 58
1.151 Smoked Beef Pastrami 58
1.152 Ribs Smoked Beef Pastrami 58
1.153 Smoked Pastrami Burgers 59
1.154 BBQ Brisket Sandwich Along with Special Sauce 59
1.155 Smoked Teriyaki Jerky 59
1.156 Peppercorn Steaks Grilled with Mushroom Cream Sauce 60
1.157 Short Rib Braised Sandwich 60
1.158 Smoked Whiskey Burgers 60
1.159 French Pit Boss Dip Sandwich 61
1.160 Weekend Pasta Along with Braised Slow Meat Sauce 61

- 1.161 Sweet Mandarin Meatloaf ... 62
- 1.162 BBQ Beef Sandwich ... 62
- 1.163 Gyros ... 62
- 1.164 Smoked Texas-Style Beef Brisket ... 63
- 1.165 Skirt Steak Quesadillas Grilled ... 63
- 1.166 Grilled Skirt Steak with Peach Salsa ... 63
- 1.167 Tuscan Meatloaf ... 64
- 1.168 Short Rib Chili ... 64
- 1.169 NY Grilled Steak Along with Cornbread Salad ... 64
- 1.170 Steak Sweetheart with Lobster Ceviche ... 65
- 1.171 Flat Iron Steaks ... 65
- 1.172 Smoked Pastrami Sandwich ... 65
- 1.173 BBQ Brisket Competition Style ... 66
- 1.174 Garlic & Herb Roasted Prime Rib ... 66
- 1.175 Salt-Crusted Prime Rib ... 67
- 1.176 T-Bone Grilled Steaks Along with Bloody Mary Steak Sauce ... 67
- 1.177 Braised Alarm Chili ... 67
- 1.178 Smoke n Grill Flank Steak ... 68
- 1.179 Pit Boss Frito Pie ... 68
- 1.180 Bacon Roasted & Wrapped Beef Tenderloin ... 68
- 1.181 Chocolate Bark Brisket ... 69
- 1.182 Spice BBQ Beef Short Ribs ... 69
- 1.183 Grilled Beef Sliders ... 69
- 1.184 Pot Smoked Roast Brisket ... 70
- 1.185 Smoked Coffee Break Beef Jerky ... 70
- 1.186 Strip Steak Along with Bacon-Onion Jam ... 70
- 1.187 Beef Stew Old-Fashioned ... 70
- 1.188 Porterhouse Grilled Steak Along with Creamed Greens ... 71
- 1.189 Grilled Italian Meatballs ... 71
- 1.190 Pastrami Short Ribs ... 71

Chapter 2: Pork Recipes ... 73

- 2.1 Muffaletta Sandwich (Pit Boss Smoked) ... 73
- 2.2 Bacon-Draped Introduced in Pork Loin Roast ... 73
- 2.3 Smoked Pork Loin along with Apples and Sauerkraut ... 73
- 2.4 Spicy Mandarin Glaze with BBQ Spareribs ... 73
- 2.5 Rib-Eye Grilled with Hasselback Sweet Potatoes ... 74
- 2.6 Spareribs Sweet Peach ... 74
- 2.7 Dan Patrick Display Chorizo Armadillo Eggs ... 74
- 2.8 Pinwheels Bacon Pork (Kansas Lollipops) ... 74
- 2.9 Roasted Pork Loin Honey-Glazed ... 75
- 2.10 Lynchburg Bacon ... 75
- 2.11 Pit Boss Smoked Sausage ... 75
- 2.12 Grilled German Sausage with a Smoky Pit Boss Twist ... 75
- 2.13 Reverse Seared Bone-In Pork Chops ... 76
- 2.14 Old-Fashioned Roasted Glazed Ham ... 76
- 2.15 Plain Smoked Ribs ... 76
- 2.16 Blueberry Sausage (Grilled) ... 76
- 2.17 Wrapped Asparagus in Grilled Prosciutto ... 76
- 2.18 Pulled Pork Mac & Cheese ... 77
- 2.19 Loin Smoked Pork ... 77
- 2.20 Pork Spareribs BBQ Paleo ... 77
- 2.21 Tenderloin Pork ... 77
- 2.22 Holiday Ham Cider (Glazed & Baked) ... 78
- 2.23 Roast Pork Loin along with Mango Salsa ... 78
- 2.24 Marcona Almonds with Prosciutto Roofed Dates ... 78
- 2.25 Cajun Broil Pit Boss ... 78
- 2.26 Chopped Grilled Pork along with Pineapple-Mango Salsa ... 79
- 2.27 Tenderloin Smoked Pork ... 79
- 2.28 Smoked Ribs BBQ ... 79
- 2.29 Baby Back Ribs Smoked ... 79
- 2.30 Pineapple Skewers & Sticky Teriyaki BBQ Pork ... 79
- 2.31 Moink Burger Smoked by Scott Thomas ... 80
- 2.32 Grilled Bacon-Wrapped Hot Dogs ... 80
- 2.33 Tenderloin Apricot Pork ... 80
- 2.34 Cooked Potato Skins along with Pulled Pork ... 80
- 2.35 Supreme Pizza Baked Deep Dish ... 80
- 2.36 Spicy Bacon Covered Grilled Chicken Skewers ... 81
- 2.37 Onion Ring of Bacon ... 81
- 2.38 Brown Sugar Bacon Bites BBQ ... 81
- 2.39 Pork Tenderloin of Cocoa Crusted ... 81
- 2.40 Bourbon Glazed Ham & Apple ... 81
- 2.41 In a Blanket Everything Pigs ... 82
- 2.42 Potatoes & Smoked Sausage ... 82
- 2.43 Bacon Dog Grilled ... 82
- 2.44 BBQ Pork Chop Seared ... 82
- 2.45 Sausage Stuffing (Classic) ... 82
- 2.46 Double Decker Tacos from Pit Boss BBQ ... 83
- 2.47 Pulled pig from Hawaii ... 83
- 2.48 Banana Bacon Pancakes ... 83
- 2.49 Cabbage Braised-Beer with Bacon ... 83
- 2.50 Grilled Lemons on Aked German Pork Schnitzel ... 83

2.51 Bologna Smoked. 84
2.52 Bacon-Wrapped Water Chestnuts BBQ 84
2.53 Smoked Packed Avocado Recipe 84
2.54 Spicy Pork and Sweet Roast 84
2.55 Egg Cups & Grilled Ham 85
2.56 Breakfast Strata Holiday 85
2.57 Pork Chops Pit Boss 85
2.58 Pork Tenderloin and Lemon Pepper Grilling 85
2.59 Quick Ribs BBQ 85
2.60 Arugula Pesto & Smoked Chorizo 86
2.61 Apricot-Sauced Roasted Ham 86
2.62 Bacon & Cheese & Brie Mac 86
2.63 Smoky Ham & Bean Soup 86
2.64 Smoked Pork Tenderloin 86
2.65 Pork Roast Anytime 87
2.66 Pork Chops with Mustard and Peach Relish 87
2.67 Rendezvous Ribs Smoked 87
2.68 Ham Glazed 87
2.69 Smoked BLT Sandwich 87
2.70 Breakfast Pizza Grilled 88
2.71 Pork Tenderloin Asian-Style 88
2.72 Smoked Baby Back Ribs 88
2.73 Sticky Teriyaki BBQ Pork & Pineapple Skewers 88
2.74 Smoked Moink Burger by Scott Thomas 88
2.75 Apricot Pork Tenderloin 89
2.76 Baked Deep Dish Supreme Pizza 89
2.77 Bacon Onion Ring 89
2.78 BBQ Brown Sugar Bacon Bites 89
2.79 Grilled Bacon Dog 89
2.80 Seared BBQ Pork Chop 89
2.81 Pit Boss BBQ Double Decker Taco 90
2.82 Smoked Bologna 90
2.83 BBQ Bacon-Wrapped Water Chestnuts 90
2.84 Sweet and Spicy Pork Roast 90
2.85 Grilled Pork Chops with Pineapple-Mango Salsa 90
2.86 Smoked Stuffed Avocado Recipe 91
2.87 Grilled Ham & Egg Cups 91
2.88 Holiday Breakfast Strata 91
2.89 Pit Boss Pork Chops 91
2.90 Anytime Pork Roast 91
2.91 Mustard Pork Chops with Peach Relish 91
2.92 Pork Loin Injected Bacon-Draped Roast 92

2.93 Grilled Breakfast Pizza 92
2.94 Asian-Style Pork Tenderloin 92
2.95 Grilled Cleveland Polish Boy 92
2.96 Pit Boss Cajun Broil 92
2.97 Bacon & Brie Mac & Cheese 93
2.98 Roasted Ham with Apricot Sauce 93
2.99 Smoked Chorizo & Arugula Pesto 93
2.100 Pit Boss Roasted Easter Ham 93
2.101 Smoked Bratwurst with Homemade Mustard 93
2.102 BBQ Pulled Pork Sliders 94
2.103 Grilled New York Style Pepperoni Pizza 94
2.104 BBQ Spareribs with Classic Wedge Salad 95
2.105 Smoked Classic Porchetta 95
2.106 Stuffed Pork Crown Roast 95
2.107 Citrus Brined Pork Roast with Fig Mostarda 96
2.108 Smoked BBQ Ribs 96
2.109 Big Game Day BBQ Ribs 96
2.110 Roasted Pork Tenderloin with Herbs and Garlic 97
2.111 Competition Style BBQ Pork Ribs 97
2.112 BBQ Spareribs with Spicy Mandarin Glaze 97
2.113 Braised Pork Chile Verde 97
2.114 Baked Candied Bacon Cinnamon Rolls 98
2.115 Bacon-Rubbed Smoked Ribs Applewood 98
2.116 Baked Potato Skins with Pulled Pork 98
2.117 Pulled Enchiladas Pork with Smoke-Roasted Red
Sauce 99
2.118 Spicy Bacon Wrapped Grilled Chicken Skewers 99
2.119 Grilled Italian Meatballs (Polpette) 99
2.120 Smoked Pit Boss Pulled Pork 100
2.121 Fall-off-the-bone BBQ Ribs 100
2.122 Cocoa-Crusted Pork Tenderloin 100
2.123 Rosemary Roasted Pork Collar 101
2.124 Bacon Weave Smoked Country Sausage 101
2.125 Apple & Bourbon Glazed Ham 101
2.126 Braised Brunswick Stew 101
2.127 Everything Pigs in a Blanket 102
2.128 Simple Smoked Ribs 102
2.129 Smoked Sausage & Potatoes 102
2.130 Smoked Sausage Pancake Sandwich 102
2.131 Classic Sausage Stuffing 103
2.132 BBQ Pulled Pork Pizza 103
2.133 Competition Style BBQ Pulled Pork 103

2.134 Hawaiian Pulled Pig 104
2.135 Maple Bacon Pull-Apart 104
2.136 BBQ Dragged Pork and Pork Belly Bánh Mì 104
2.137 Buffalo & Pork Stuffed Poblano Peppers 105
2.138 Baked Bean Casserole with the Pulled Pork 105
2.139 Baked German Pork Schnitzel with Grilled Lemons 105
2.140 Mini Sausage Rolls 106
2.141 Sausage Pepper Skewers 106
2.142 Baked Pork Belly Mac and Cheese 106
2.143 Bacon Stuffed Smoked Pork Loin 107
2.144 Ultimate BLT Salad 107
2.145 Beer-Braised Cabbage with Bacon 107
2.146 Hawaiian BBQ Baked Beans 107
2.147 Roasted Pork with Balsamic Strawberry Sauce ...108
2.148 Smothered Pork Chops 108
2.149 BBQ Rib Sandwich 108
2.150 Spice-Rubbed Pork Tenderloin 109
2.151 Baked Breakfast Sausage Casserole 109
2.152 Jalapeno Cheddar Smoked Sausages 109
2.153 Smoked Pork Loin with Sauerkraut and Apples ...109
2.154 BBQ Paleo Pork Spareribs 110
2.155 Bacon Pork Pinwheels (Kansas Lollipops) 110
2.156 Gochujang BBQ Pork Ribs Marinated 110
2.157 Home-Cured Bourbon Bacon 110
2.158 BBQ Pulled Pork with Sweet & Heat BBQ Sauce 111
2.159 Applewood Smoked Bacon 111
2.160 BBQ Pork Belly Tacos 111
2.161 Smoked Italian Lasagna Recipe 112
2.162 Holiday Prosciutto-Wrapped Pork Tenderloin 112
2.163 Pernil 112
2.164 Meaty Beer Beans 113
2.165 Baked Ballpark Mac and Cheese 113
2.166 Holiday Smoked Cheese Log 113
2.167 Smoked Ribs with the Coconut Rum BBQ Sauce by Journey South 114
2.168 Grilled Sugar Snap Peas & Smoked Bacon 114
2.169 Double-Decker Pulled Pork Nachos with Smoked Cheese 114
2.170 Smoked Citrus & Polenta Pork Tenderloin 114
2.171 Pit Boss Pulled Pork Sandwiches 115
2.172 Smoked Pork Spareribs 115
2.173 St. Louis BBQ Ribs 115
2.174 Apple Juice BBQ Brined Pulled Pork 116

2.175 Smoked Dry Rubbed Baby Back Ribs 116
2.176 Smoked Bacon Cheese Ball 116
2.177 Smoked Rendezvous Ribs 117
2.178 Bagel Breakfast Sandwich 117
2.179 Western Breakfast Casserole 117
2.180 Baked Bacon Caramel Popcorn 118
2.181 Smoked Porchetta with Italian Salsa Verde 118
2.182 Bacon Chili Cheese Dogs 118
2.183 BBQ Pulled Pork Breakfast Burrito with Smoked Hot Sauce 119
2.184 Bacon Explosion 119
2.185 Cuban Sandwich Cubano 119
2.186 Smoky Ham & Bean Soup 120
2.187 Prosciutto Wrapped Dates with Marcona Almonds 120
2.188 BBQ Quick Ribs 120
2.189 Carolina Pulled Pork Sandwiches (Smoked) 121
2.190 Lemon Pepper Tenderloin (Grilled) 121
2.191 Corn Dog Bites (Baked) 121
2.192 Maple Baked Ham 122
2.193 BBQ St Louis Fashion Ribs with Homemade BBQ Sauce 122
2.194 Competition-Style Spareribs 122
2.195 Brats in Beer 123
2.196 Grilled Combination Pizza 123
2.197 Belly Bourbon Beans of Pork (Baked) 123
2.198 Twice Cut Grilled Pork Chop with Sweet & Sour Peaches 123
2.199 Honey-Glazed Roasted Pork Loin 124
2.200 Hot & Fast Smoked Baby Back Ribs 124
2.201 Bourbon Bacon Stuffing 124
2.202 Baked Peach Cobbler 124
2.203 Smoked Brisket Pot Pie 125
2.204 Baked Eggs in Bacon Nest 125

Chapter 3: Poultry Recipes 126

3.1 Baked Prosciutto-Wrapped Chicken Breast with Spinach and Boursin 126
3.2 The Grilled Chicken Challenge 126
3.3 Grilled Paprika Chicken with Jalapeño Salsa 126
3.4 Duck Confit, Red Onion Jam, and Goat Cheese Crostinis 127
3.5 Baked Game Day Hatch Chile and Bacon Hot Dish .127
3.6 Yogurt-Marinated Chicken Thigh & Beef Tenderloin Kabobs 127

3.7 Pit Boss Mandarin Wings 127
3.8 Smoking' Thai Curry Chicken 127
3.9 Roasted Tin Foil Dinners 128
3.10 Roasted Serrano Wings 128
3.11 BBQ Spatchcocked Chicken 128
3.12 Smoked Chicken Tikka Drumsticks 128
3.13 Roasted Rosemary Orange Chicken 129
3.14 Ancho-Chili Smoked BBQ Chicken Legs 129
3.15 Whole Smoked Chicken 129
3.16 Spatchcocked Chicken with Toasted Fennel & Garlic 129
3.17 Spatchcocked Chile-Lime Rubbed Chicken ... 129
3.18 Grilled Sweet Cajun wings 130
3.19 Roasted Christmas Goose 130
3.20 Spicy Bacon Wrapped Grilled Chicken Skewers 130
3.21 Tandoori Chicken Wings 130
3.22 Whole Chicken 130
3.23 Oktoberfest Pretzel Mustard Chicken 131
3.24 Asian BBQ Chicken 131
3.25 Grilled Chicken Alfredo Pizza 131
3.26 Pit Boss BBQ 1/2 Chickens 131
3.27 Pit Boss BBQ Chicken Breasts 132
3.28 Roasted Teriyaki Wings 132
3.29 BBQ Chicken Bacon Ranch Sandwich 132
3.30 Honey Lime Chicken Adobo Skewers 132
3.31 Baked Cranberry Chicken 133
3.32 Diablo Grilled Chicken Thighs 133
3.33 Kansas City Hot Fried Chicken 133
3.34 Whole Roasted Chicken 133
3.35 Roasted Sheet Pan Chicken 133
3.36 Tomatillo Braised Chicken 134
3.37 Smoked turkey (bacon-wrapped turkey breast) 134
3.38 Texas-style turkey 134
3.39 Boneless stuffed turkey breast 134
3.40 Brie stuffed turkey burgers 135
3.41 Thanksgiving smoked turkey 135
3.42 Maple smoked thanksgiving turkey 135
3.43 Cajun Brined Maple Smoked Turkey Breast 136
3.44 Pit Boss BBQ Chicken Salad 136
3.45 Smoked Chicken Leg & Thigh Quarters 136
3.46 Grilled Greek Chicken with Garlic & Lemon 136
3.47 BBQ Chicken Sandwich 137

3.48 Roasted Garlic Wings 137
3.49 BBQ Chicken Legs 137
3.50 Smoked Texas Spicy Drumsticks 137
3.51 BBQ Game Day Chicken Wings and Thighs 137
3.52 Smoked Spatchcocked Cornish Game Hens 137
3.53 Grilled Sriracha Wings 138
3.54 Chile Chicken Thighs 138
3.55 Buffalo Chicken Thighs 138
3.56 BBQ Chicken Wings with Spicy Honey Glaze 138
3.57 Baked Apricot Glazed Chicken Thighs 138
3.58 Smoked Ditch Chicken 139
3.59 Stuffed Balsamic Chicken 139
3.60 Braised Beer Chicken Stew 139
3.61 Peach & Basil Grilled Chicken Recipe 139
3.62 BBQ Chicken Tostada 140
3.63 Chipotle Honey Wings 140
3.64 Tequila Lime Chicken Thighs 140
3.65 Baked Garlic Parmesan Wings 140
3.66 Spicy BBQ Whole Chicken 141
3.67 Grilled Chicken Fajitas 141
3.68 Pit Boss Crispy Orange Chicken Wings 141
3.69 Bacon Jalapeño Chicken 141
3.70 California Club Chicken 141
3.71 Smoked turkey legs 142
3.72 Sweet heat Cajun spatchcock turkey 142
3.73 BBQ breakfast sausage not so fatty 142
3.74 BBQ dry rubbed turkey drumsticks 142
3.75 Bacon lattice turkey 142
3.76 Bacon-wrapped turkey legs 143
3.77 Texas-style turkey 143
3.78 Hot turkey sandwich 143
3.79 Pepper and onion turkey burger sliders 143
3.80 Smoked turkey legs 143
3.81 Mayo and herb-roasted turkey 144
3.82 Smoked turkey jerky 144
3.83 Injected drunken smoked turkey legs 144
3.84 Homemade turkey gravy 144
3.85 Smoked wild turkey jerky 145
3.86 Traditional smoked thanksgiving turkey 145
3.87 Roasted stuffed turkey breast 145
3.88 Nashville hot turkey melt 145
3.89 Smoked turkey with fig BBQ sauce 146

3.90 Smoked turkey 146
3.91 Pit Boss brined smoked turkey 146
3.92 Dry brine Pit Boss turkey 146
3.93 Roasted herbed turkey breast 147
3.94 Grilled Asian lettuce wrap turkey burger 147
3.95 Smoked bourbon & orange brined turkey 147
3.96 Smoked turkey legs with brown butter and bourbon glaze 147
3.97 Roasted cider brined turkey breast 148
3.98 Beer-brined turkey 148
3.99 Roasted Honey bourbon glazed turkey 148
3.100 Thanksgiving BBQ Turkey 149
3.101 BBQ pulled turkey sandwiches 149
3.102 Pit Boss Smoked Deviled Eggs 149
3.103 Prosciutto Stuffed Chicken Roasted 149
3.104 Pit Boss Ultimate Thanksgiving Sandwich 150
3.105 Chicken Cordon Bleu Baked 150
3.106 Turkey Lettuce Wraps Smoked 150
3.107 Smoked Scotch Eggs 150
3.108 Vietnamese Chicken Wings 151
3.109 Chicken Roasted with Wild Rice & Mushrooms 151
3.110 Bacon-Wrapped Skewers 151
3.111 Tandoori Chicken Burgers 152
3.112 Smoked Creole Jambalaya 152
3.113 Thai Chicken Skewers 152
3.114 Roasted Chicken Enchiladas 152
3.115 Roasted Smoke Chicken along with Herb Butter 153
3.116 Maple Bourbon Drumsticks 153
3.117 Leftover Pit Boss Turkey Soup 153
3.118 Southwest Wild Turkey Egg Rolls 154
3.119 BBQ Chicken Drumsticks 154
3.120 Bacon-Wrapped Chicken Stuffed Breast 154
3.121 Parmesan Chicken Sliders along with Pesto Mayonnaise 154
3.122 Stuffed Bacon-Wrapped Chicken Thighs 155
3.123 Stand Pineapple Chicken 155
3.124 Stuffing Turkey Bacon Balls 155
3.125 Mustard Wings Smoked 156
3.126 Chicken Lollipops 156
3.127 Goddess Green Chicken Legs 156
3.128 Turkey Jalapeño Meatballs 156
3.129 Ultimate Scratch Gravy 157
3.130 BBQ Halved Chickens 157

3.131 Grilled Loaded Chicken Tacos 157
3.132 Cherry Smoked Bomb Chicken 158
3.133 Italian Grilled Chicken Saltimbocca 158
3.134 Andouille, Chicken & Potato Roasted Gumbo 158
3.135 Garlic BBQ Chicken 159
3.136 Buffalo Chicken Dip Baked 159
3.137 Honey Grilled Garlic Wings 159
3.138 Smoke Roasted Chicken 159
3.139 Turkey Cornbread Tamale Pie Baked 160
3.140 White Chicken Chili 160
3.141 Thanksgiving Shepherd's Pie Baked 160
3.142 Sticky Grilled Ginger Chicken Thighs 161
3.143 BBQ Chicken Nachos 161
3.144 Chicken Fajita Skewers Grilled 161
3.145 Beantown Chicken Wings Grilled 161
3.146 Big Game Roast Chicken 162
3.147 Bucket O' Chicken Baked 162
3.148 Jerked Jamaican Chicken Legs 162
3.149 Grilled Hellfire Chicken Wings 163
3.150 Tequila-Lime Wings Roasted 163
3.151 Pickle Brined Chicken Sandwich 163
3.152 Turkey Sliders with Chipotle Tartar Sauce 164
3.153 Grilled Thai Chicken Burgers with Papaya Slaw 164
3.154 Bacon Cheesy Malibu Chicken 164
3.155 Peruvian Roasted Chicken with Green Sauce 165
3.156 Roasted Citrus-Herb Turkey 165
3.157 Roasted Tingle Wings 166
3.158 Lemon Herb Chicken 166
3.159 Smoked Chicken along with Jalapeno Salsa Verde 166
3.160 Smoked Chicken Lollipops along with BBQ Champagne Sauce 166
3.161 Three Ways BBQ Chicken Wings 167
3.162 Cajun Chicken Wings Smoked 167
3.163 Beer Can Chicken Roasted 167
3.164 Roasted Buffalo Wings 168
3.165 Mandarin Chicken Breast 168
3.166 Chicken Smoked with Apricot BBQ Glaze 168
3.167 Grilled Duck Breasts 168
3.168 Bacon Stuffed Weaved Turkey Breast 168
3.169 Baked BBQ Chicken Potato 169
3.170 Roast Citrus Chicken 169
3.171 Smoked Wings 169

3.172 Dry Rub Wings Smoked 169
3.173 Ultimate Smoked Turkey 170
3.174 Baked Crispy Chicken Thighs with Buffalo Sauce ... 170
3.175 Grilled Bacon Chicken Lettuce Wraps 170
3.176 Smoked Korean Wings 170
3.177 Carne Asada Tacos 171
3.178 Machaca Mexican Shredded Beef 171
3.179 Braised Italian Meatballs 171
3.180 Sweet Braised & Sour Brisket 172
3.181 Beef Short Ribs Braised Along with Creamy Grits ... 172
3.182 Chipotle-Lime Poultry Bowls with Guacamole 173
3.183 BBQ Half Chicken with Alabama White Sauce 173
3.184 Smoky Fried Chicken 174
3.185 Ancho-Chile Chicken Legs (Smoked BBQ) 174
3.186 BBQ Chicken Thighs 174
3.187 Competition BBQ Chicken Thighs 174
3.188 Bourbon BBQ Chicken Kabobs 175
3.189 Deli-Style Grilled Turkey Breast 175
3.190 Sweet Cajun Wings 175
3.191 Cajun Brined Smoked Turkey Breast 175
3.192 Chardonnay Chicken with Roasted Root Vegetables 175
3.193 Beer-Braised Chicken Tacos with Jalapeño Relish . 176
3.194 Grilled Asian Chicken Burgers 176
3.195 Roast Chicken & Pimenton Potatoes 177
3.196 Bacon-Wrapped Turkey Legs 177
3.197 Skillet-Roasted Game Bird 177
3.198 Bacon-Wrapped Chicken Wings 178
3.199 Braised Brunswick Stew 178
3.200 Smoked Buffalo Fries 178
3.201 Greek Chicken Pizza 178
3.202 Baked Chicken Pot Pie 179
3.203 Herb Roasted Turkey 179
3.204 Grilled Chicken and Roasted Beet Salad 179
3.205 Smoked Chicken with Chimichurri 180
3.206 Smoked Deviled Eggs 180
3.207 Lemon Chicken Breast 180

Chapter 4: Vegetable Recipes 181
4.1 Vegetables Pan Roasted Sheet 181
4.2 Crushed Cheddar Baby Potatoes Bacon 181
4.3 Bacon with Roasted Beans (Green) 181
4.4 Garlic Herbed Potato Wedges 181
4.5 Grilled Cabbage Steaks with a Bacon Vinaigrette 181
4.6 Roasted Beans (Green) with Bacon 182
4.7 Roasted Garlic Herb Fries 182
4.8 Asparagus Grilled & Spinach Salad 182
4.9 Sweet Grilled Potato Planks 182
4.10 Casserole Green Bean 182
4.11 Marshmallow Casserole Sweet Potato 182
4.12 Chipotle Ketchup with Pit Boss Fries 183
4.13 Mango Coleslaw (Grilled) 183
4.14 Braised Butter Green Beans 183
4.15 Roasted Parmesan Cauliflower 183
4.16 Baked Pit Boss Potato Torte 183
4.17 Baked Winter Squash Au Gratin 184
4.18 Root Vegetables Roasted 184
4.19 Baked Sweet Potato Hash 184
4.20 Broccoli Rabe (Grilled) 184
4.21 Sweet Potato Roasted Steak Fries 184
4.22 Roasted New Potatoes 185
4.23 Smoked Pickles 185
4.24 Pit Boss Potatoes Au Gratin 185
4.25 Garlic Fries (Cheesy & Baked) 185
4.26 Grilled Beer Cabbage 185
4.27 Bacon Asparagus (Wrapped) 186
4.28 Potato Wedges with Garlic and Herbs 186
4.29 Bacon Onion Ring 186
4.30 Baby Carrots Grilled & Fennel with Spanish sauce (Romesco) 186
4.31 Baked Deep Dish Supreme Pizza 186
4.32 Red Mashed Potatoes 187
4.33 Smoked Olives 187
4.34 Sweet Potato Roasted Fries 187
4.35 Baked Potatoes Salt Crusted 187
4.36 Potato Salad (Smoked) 187
4.37 Corn Salsa (Grilled) 188
4.38 Chimichurri Sauce 188
4.39 Grilled Corn with Honey Butter & Smoked Salt 188
4.40 Roasted River Potatoes by Chef Timothy Hollingsworth 188
4.41 Pico De Gallo (Smoked) 188
4.42 Roasted Broccoli with Parmesan 188
4.43 Romaine Caesar Salad (Grilled) 189
4.44 Frypan Potato Cake 189
4.45 Butternut Squash 189

4.46 Ratatouille Salad (Grilled) 189
4.47 Fall Vegetables (Roasted) 189
4.48 Harvest Vegetables (Grilled) 189
4.49 Stuffed Jalapenos 190
4.50 Mashed Potatoes (Roasted) 190
4.51 Pit Boss Smoked Coleslaw 190
4.52 Red Onion Salad and Broccoli (Roasted) 190
4.53 Loaded Tater Tots (Baked) 190
4.54 Chili-Lime Corn (Grilled) 191
4.55 French Onion Dip (Grilled) 191
4.56 Roasted Olives 191
4.57 Hawaiian Sour Grilled 191
4.58 Baby Carrots Grilled and Fennel with Romesco 191
4.59 Salt-Crusted Baked Potatoes 192
4.60 Cold Brew Coffee Smoked 192
4.61 Corn Grilled on the Cob with Garlic and Parmesan 192
4.62 Pico De Gallo Smoked 192
4.63 Pomegranate Lemonade Cocktail Smoked 192
4.64 Smoked Sangria 193
4.65 Smoked Plum and Thyme Fizz Cocktail 193
4.66 Cinnamon Almonds Roasted 193
4.67 Party Mix Pit Boss Chex 193
4.68 Parmesan Roasted Cauliflower 193
4.69 Green Bean Casserole 194
4.70 Broccoli Rabe Grilled 194
4.71 A Classic Smoking Cocktail 194
4.72 Applejack O'Lantern Cocktail Grilled 194
4.73 Corn on The Cob Grilled 194
4.74 Apple Cider Smoked 194
4.75 Asparagus Grilled & Honey-Glazed Carrots ... 194
4.76 Hot Buttered Rum Smoked 195
4.77 Grilled Pit Boss Whole Corn 195
4.78 Asparagus Roasted 195
4.79 Cider Brew Cocktail Spiced 195
4.80 Smoke Salsa Roasted 195
4.81 Roasted Mushrooms with Sherry and Thyme ... 195
4.82 Grilled Zucchini Squash Spears 196
4.83 Pit Boss Mushrooms Smoked 196
4.84 The Old-fashioned Orchard Cocktail 196
4.85 Heirloom Carrots Roasted 196
4.86 Whole Roasted Cauliflower along with Garlic Parmesan Butter 196

4.87 New Potatoes Roasted 196
4.88 Fig Slider Cocktail 197
4.89 Cocktail Batter Up 197
4.90 Peach Sour Cocktail Grilled 197
4.91 Smoked Pit Boss Coleslaw 197
4.92 Watermelon Grilled 197
4.93 Lemon Gremolata 197
4.94 Honey Glazed Pineapple Grilled 198
4.95 Tomatoes Roasted 198
4.96 Green Beans Southern 198
4.97 Grilled Sweet Potato Casserole 198
4.98 Gluten-Free Mashed Potato Cakes 198
4.99 Corn Salad Mexican Street 199
4.100 Green Chile Potatoes Mashed 199
4.101 Grilled Corn Salad 199
4.102 Cauliflower Whole Roasted with Garlic Parmesan Butter 199
4.103 Grilled Peach & Bacon Salad with the Maple Vinaigrette 199
4.104 Sausage & Pesto Lasagna 200
4.105 Smoked Macaroni Salad 200
4.106 Green Beans Roasted with Bacon 200
4.107 Pit Boss Fries with Chipotle Ketchup 200
4.108 Roasted Cauliflower & Broccoli Salad with Bacon 201
4.109 Grilled Burrata Salad with Ripped Croutons ... 201
4.110 Roasted Sweet Potato Fries 201
4.111 Roasted Crispy Potatoes 201
4.112 Roasted Jalapeño Poppers 202
4.113 Roasted Asparagus 202
4.114 Blistered Curry Cauliflower 202
4.115 Baked Salt-Crusted Potatoes 202
4.116 Smoked Pasta Salad 202
4.117 Smoked Pumpkin Soup 203
4.118 Fennel with Romesco & Grilled Baby Carrots ... 203
4.119 Rosemary & Mashed Thyme-Infused Potatoes with Cream 203
4.120 Roasted Hasselback Potatoes 204
4.121 Mashed Red Potatoes 204
4.122 Garlic Duchess Potatoes Baked 204
4.123 Baked Sweet & Savory Yams 204
4.124 Sweet Baked Potato Casserole along with Marshmallow Fluff 204
4.125 Romaine Caesar Salad Grilled 205

4.126 Roasted Wild Salmon Along with Cauliflower Pickled Salad 205

4.127 Breakfast Mini Quiches Baked 205

4.128 Butternut Roasted Squash Soup 205

4.129 Grilled Veggie Burgers along with Lentils & Walnuts 206

4.130 Hummus (Smoked) with Roasted Vegetables 206

4.131 Roasted Root Vegetables 206

4.132 Sweet Potatoes Marshmallow Hasselback 207

4.133 Grilled Corn Salsa 207

4.134 Green Bean Casserole Baked with Pulled Pork 207

4.135 Red Pepper White Roasted Bean Dip 207

4.136 Homemade Smoked Ketchup 208

4.137 Baked Creamed Spinach 208

4.138 Carrots along with Pistachio & Pomegranate Relish Roasted 208

4.139 Smoked Scalloped Potatoes 209

4.140 Famous Chef Curtis' Chimichurri Sauce 209

4.141 Maxi Mac & Cheese 209

4.142 Beer-Braised Cabbage along With Bacon 209

4.143 Southern Grilled Comfort Sweet Potato Fries 209

4.144 Sheet Pan Roasted Vegetables 210

4.145 Buffalo Blue Cheese Grilled Corn 210

4.146 Grilled Veggie Sandwich 210

4.147 Grilled Corn on Cob with some Parmesan and Garlic 210

4.148 Cast Iron Potatoes 211

4.149 Bacon Green Baked Bean Casserole 211

4.150 Pico De Gallo Smoked 211

4.151 Baked Potato Soup Smoked 211

4.152 Brussels (Smoked & Shredded) Sprout Salad 211

4.153 Asparagus Grilled Along with Wild Mushrooms & Fried Shallots 212

4.154 Corned Baked Beef Au Grautin 212

4.155 Smoked 3-Bean Salad 212

4.156 Grilled Artichokes Along with Sauce Gribiche 213

4.157 Fingerling Grilled Potato Salad 213

4.158 Christmas Brussel Sprouts 213

4.159 Cheesy Baked Accordion Potatoes 213

4.160 Smoked Potato Salad 214

4.161 Grilled Peach Salsa 214

4.162 Smoked Loaded Roasted Potato Salad 214

4.163 Grilled Asparagus & Spinach Salad 214

4.164 Sugar Snap Grilled Peas & Smoked Bacon 215

4.165 Grilled Fingerling Potato Salad 215

4.166 Bacon Salad with Beet (Roasted) 215

4.167 Wedge Grilled Salad 215

4.168 Beet (Roasted) & Bacon Salad 216

4.169 Roasted Carrots with Pomegranate Relish and Pistachio 216

4.170 Grilled Wedge Salad 216

4.171 Sherry Root Vegetables Roasted 216

4.172 Whole Pickles (Smoked) 217

4.173 Rosemary and Thyme-Infused Crushed Potatoes along with a Cream 217

4.174 Broil Cajun Pit Boss 217

4.175 Roasted Peach Salsa 217

4.176 Macaroni Salad (Smoked) 218

4.177 Baked Garlic Duchess Potatoes 218

4.178 Mini Quiches Breakfast (Baked) 218

4.179 Baked Savory & Sweet Baked Yams 218

4.180 Scalloped Smoked Potatoes 218

4.181 Baked Spinach Creamed 219

4.182 Baked Pickles along with Buttermilk Dip 219

4.183 Loaded & Baked Potato Salad 219

4.184 Seasonal (Roasted) & Pickled Vegetables 220

4.185 Roasted Creamy Brussel Sprouts 220

4.186 Roasted Jalapeño Poppers 220

4.187 Whole Pickles Smoked 220

4.188 Mango Coleslaw Grilled 221

4.189 Thyme-Infused" Mashed Potatoes & Rosemary with Cream 221

4.190 Stone Fruit Grilled along with Cream & Berries 221

4.191 Cauliflower Roasted 221

4.192 Smoked Deviled Eggs 222

4.193 Smoked Hummus with Roasted Vegetables 222

4.194 Deviled Eggs Smoked 222

4.195 Brussels Shredded Sprout Salad Smoked 222

4.196 Buck Grapefruit Cocktail Grilled 223

4.197 Pumpkin Chocolate Chip Cookies 223

4.198 Cold Smoked Cheese 223

4.199 Tomatoes Roasted 223

4.200 Squash Butternut Macaroni plus Cheese 223

4.201 The Max Burgers 224

4.202 London Broil Grilled Along with Blue Cheese Butter 224

4.203 Filet Mignon Smoked with Sweet Pepper Relish & Baked Ricotta 224

4.204 Cheesesteak Sandwich Grilled 225

4.205 Pit Boss BLT Burgers 225

Chapter 5: Seafood Recipes 226

5.1 Pit Boss Baked Rainbow Trout 226

5.2 Sweet & Spicy Sriracha Salmon 226

5.3 Smoked Chilean Sea Bass 226

5.4 Grilled Shrimp Cocktail 226

5.5 Grilled Salmon with Smoked Avocado Salsa 227

5.6 Grilled Shrimp Brochette 227

5.7 Kimi's Simple Grilled Fresh Fish 227

5.8 Bacon-Wrapped Shrimp 227

5.9 BBQ Roasted Salmon 227

5.10 Vodka Brined Smoked Wild Salmon 228

5.11 Grilled Swordfish with Corn Salsa 228

5.12 Pit Boss Cajun Broil 228

5.13 Grilled Whole Steelhead Fillet 228

5.14 Fried Halibut Fish Sticks 228

5.15 Tuna Burgers 229

5.16 Baked Salmon Cakes 229

5.17 Grilled Blackened Saskatchewan Salmon 229

5.18 Smoked Seafood Ceviche 229

5.19 Prosciutto Wrapped Grilled Shrimp with Peach Salsa
.... 229

5.20 Smoked Salmon Flatbread 230

5.21 Teriyaki Salmon 230

5.22 Baked Tuna Noodle Casserole 230

5.23 Grilled Mussels with Lemon Butter 230

5.24 Mahi-Mahi Shish Kabobs 230

5.25 Baked Whole Fish in Sea Salt 231

5.26 Smoked Salmon Salad 231

5.27 Honey Balsamic Salmon 231

5.28 Grilled Tuna Salad with Smoky & Spicy Mayo 231

5.29 Grilled Fresh Fish 231

5.30 Roasted Yellowtail with Potatoes, Mushrooms & Italian Salsa Verde 232

5.31 Smoked Albacore Tuna 232

5.32 Smoked Crab Legs 232

5.34 Cajun Smoked Shrimp 232

5.35 Seared Lemon Garlic Scallops 232

5.36 Smoked Lobster Scampi 233

5.37 Simple Glazed Salmon Fillets 233

5.38 Garlic Salmon 233

5.39 Smoked Salmon Candy 233

5.40 Grilled Texas Spicy Shrimp 233

5.41 Grilled Saké Shrimp 234

5.42 Pit Boss Smoked Mussels By Dennis The Prescott 234

5.43 Smoky Crab Dip 234

5.44 Pit Boss Crab Legs 234

5.45 Swordfish with Sicilian Olive Oil Sauce 234

5.46 Grilled Shrimp Tacos with Garlic Cilantro Lime Slaw 235

5.47 Oysters Traegefeller 235

5.48 Spicy Shrimp Skewers 235

5.49 Salmon (Balsamic Glaze) 235

5.50 Scallops (Bacon-Wrapped) 236

5.51 Albacore Tuna (Grilled) with Tomato-Potato Casserole 236

5.52 Salmon (Cedar-Plank) with Salsa (Mango) 236

5.53 Shrimp Scampi 236

5.54 Tacos (Shrimp) with Crema (Lime) 236

5.55 Lime Shrimp (Spicy & Grilled) 237

5.56 Shrimp (Garlic & Pesto Bruschetta) 237

5.57 Tartar Sauce (Homemade) & Salmon Cakes 237

5.58 Smoked Tuna Belly Tacos 237

5.59 Sweet Grilled Shrimp & Spicy Sausage Skewers 237

5.60 Smoked Trout Dip 238

5.61 Pit Boss Salmon with Balsamic Glaze 238

5.62 Bacon-Wrapped Scallops 238

5.63 Grilled Albacore Tuna with Potato-Tomato Casserole
.... 238

5.64 Cedar-Plank Salmon with Mango Salsa 238

5.65 Shrimp (Bacon Wrapped) 239

5.66 Salmon (Cedar-Plank) 239

5.67 Salmon (Glazed) Honey-Soy 239

5.68 Grilled Oysters by Journey South 239

5.69 Smoked Trout 239

5.70 Sweet Mandarin Salmon 240

5.71 Roasted Stuffed Rainbow Trout with Brown Butter 240

5.72 Roasted Cod with Meyer Lemon-Herb Butter 240

5.73 Roasted Halibut with Tartar Sauce 240

5.74 Roasted Cod with Meyer Lemon-Herb Butter 240

5.75 Grilled Trout with Citrus & Basil 241

5.76 Seared Bluefin Tuna Steaks 241

5.77 Grilled Crab Legs with Herb Butter 241

5.78 Chinese Shrimp with Sweet Sherry 241

5.79 Grilled Sriracha Salmon with Avocado Pineapple Salsa ... 241
5.80 Pit Boss Jerk Shrimp ... 242
5.81 Whole Vermillion Red Snapper ... 242
5.82 Grilled Ahi Tuna Sliders ... 242
5.83 Grilled Clams in Garlic Butter ... 242
5.84 Citrus Salmon ... 243
5.85 Grilled Soy-Ginger Yellowtail Collar ... 243
5.86 Cedar Plank Salmon with Sweet Thai Chili Sauce Glaze ... 243
5.87 Smoked Sesame Crusted Halibut with Tahini Mayonnaise ... 243
5.88 Pit Boss Grilled Shrimp Scampi ... 243
5.89 Smoked Buttery Shrimp ... 244
5.90 Grilled Salmon in Foil ... 244
5.91 Honey Smoked Tilapia with Cajun Spice Rub ... 244
5.92 Lemon Herb-Grilled Salmon ... 244
5.93 Whole Red Snapper - Stuffed, Sauced and Smoked ... 244
5.94 Smoked Clams Casino ... 245
5.95 Smoked Salmon and Brine Recipe ... 245
5.96 Grilled Shrimp Foil Packets ... 245
5.97 Smoked Prawns Recipe ... 246
5.98 Sweet Chili Lime Pit Boss Grilled Crappie Recipe ... 246
5.99 Lemon Herb Cedar Plank Salmon Recipe ... 246
5.100 Grilled Salmon Burger with Chipotle Mayo ... 246
5.101 Baja-style Grilled Fish Tacos ... 247
5.102 Grilled Salmon Tacos with Smoked Tomato Salsa by Daniel Seidman ... 247
5.103 Roasted Wild Salmon with Pickled Cauliflower Salad ... 247
5.104 Chinese Jumbo Shrimp ... 248
5.105 Bacon Wrapped Shrimp ... 248
5.106 Smoked Fish Chowder ... 248
5.107 Roasted Clambake ... 249
5.108 Smoked Salmon Sandwich ... 249
5.109 Baked Halibut Fish Sticks with Spicy Coleslaw ... 249
5.110 Grilled Soft-Shell Crabs ... 250
5.111 Smoked Albacore Tuna Niçoise Salad ... 250
5.112 Sweet Smoked Salmon Jerky ... 250
5.113 Slow Roasted Wild Salmon with Cheesy Scalloped Potatoes ... 251
5.114 Crab Cakes ... 251
5.115 Grilled Crawfish with Spicy Garlic Butter ... 251
5.116 Grilled White Fish Steaks with Basil Orange Pesto ... 252
5.117 Baked Halibut Sandwich with Smoked Tartar Sauce ... 252
5.118 Pit Boss Smoked Salmon ... 252
5.119 Smoked Whitefish Salad ... 252
5.120 New England Clambake ... 253
5.121 Grilled Oysters with Mignonette ... 253
5.122 Cider Hot-Smoked Salmon ... 253
5.123 Grilled Lobster Tails ... 254
5.124 Red Curry Salmon with Avocado Creme ... 254
5.125 Teriyaki-Glazed Cod with Ginger-Scallion Ramen ... 254
5.126 Smoked Salmon Potato Bake ... 255
5.127 Potato Crusted Salmon with Lemon Butter Sauce ... 255
5.128 Smoked Steelhead Breakfast Sandwich ... 256
5.129 Smoked Creole Jambalaya ... 256
5.130 Smoked Salt Cured Lox ... 256
5.131 Tandoori Shrimp ... 256
5.132 Smoked Trout Hash ... 257
5.133 Cold-Smoked Salmon Gravlax ... 257
5.134 Smoked Shrimp and Grilled Dungeness Crab Cocktail ... 257
5.135 Jalapeño Candied Smoked Salmon ... 258
5.136 Smoked Lobster Rolls ... 258
5.137 Grilled Lobster with Lemon Garlic Butter ... 258
5.138 Smoked Chilean Sea Bass by Doug Sheading ... 258
5.139 Coconut Shrimp Jalapeño Poppers ... 259
5.140 Chicken, Andouille & Roasted Potato Gumbo ... 259
5.141 Tuna Steak with Baby Bok Choy and Carrots ... 259
5.142 Alder Smoked Scallops with Citrus & Garlic Butter Sauce ... 260
5.143 Smoked Salmon Veggie Dip ... 260
5.144 Roasted Halibut in Parchment ... 260
5.145 Roasted Halibut with Spring Vegetables ... 261
5.146 Grilled Halibut Fillets with Lemon and Butter Sauce ... 261
5.147 Grilled Surf & Turf ... 261
5.148 Jamaican Jerk Grilled Halibut with Pico De Gallo ... 261
5.149 Grilled Salmon Steaks with BBQ Corn Salad ... 262
5.150 Spicy Asian BBQ Shrimp ... 262
5.151 Tuna Tacos with Lime & Cilantro Cream ... 262
5.152 Baked Steelhead ... 263
5.153 Pan-Seared Halibut with Green Garlic Pesto ... 263
5.154 Smoked Shrimp and Grits ... 263
5.155 Smoked Seafood Paella ... 263

5.156 Spicy Crab Poppers 264
5.157 West Coast Cioppino Fries 264
5.158 Stuffed Lobster Tail 264
5.159 Roasted Garlic & Clam Pizza 265
5.160 Caribbean Curry Grilled Lobsters with Garlic Lime Asparagus 265
5.161 BBQ Oysters 265
5.162 A.J. Allmendinger's Blackened Salmon 266
5.163 Shrimp scampi 266
5.164 Shrimp tacos with lime crema 266
5.165 Smoked salmon dip with grilled artichoke and cheese 266
5.166 Grilled Shrimp with Cajun dip 267
5.167 Blackened Catfish 267
5.168 Cedar plank salmon 268
5.169 Seared Ahi Tuna Steak 268
5.170 Salmon cakes and homemade tartar sauce 268
5.171 Grilled Mango Shrimp 268
5.172 Mango Thai Shrimp 269
5.173 Crab Stuffed Mushrooms 269
5.174 Fish Tacos 269
5.175 Lemon Smoked Salmon 269
5.176 New England Lobster Rolls 269
5.177 Grilled Lobster Tails 269
5.178 Garlic Shrimp Pesto Bruschetta 270
5.179 Scallops Wrapped in Bacon 270
5.180 Grilled Spicy Lime Shrimp 270
5.181 Cedar Smoked Salmon 270
5.182 Honey-soy Glazed Salmon 270
5.183 Blackened Catfish Tacos 271
5.184 Cajun Crab Stuffed Shrimp & Jicama Corn Salad Recipe 271
5.185 Grilled Seafood Delight with Kickin Corn Maque Choux 271
5.186 Grilled Mahi Fish Tacos with Creamy Chipotle Sauce Recipe 271
5.187 Grilled Salmon with Honey Sriracha Lime Glaze 272
5.188 Grilled Shrimp Bruschetta with Balsamic Glaze 272
5.189 Lemon Ginger Grilled Shrimp Recipe 272
5.190 Lobster Tails and Herb Butter Recipe 272
5.191 Quick Hot Smoked Salmon 273
5.192 Red Snapper Los Grilla 273
5.193 Swine Life's Smoked Parmesan Crusted Salmon 273
5.194 Sugar Cured Salmon 273
5.195 Tequila Lime Shrimp Tacos with Pineapple Pomegranate Salsa 274
5.196 BBQ Salmon with Bourbon Glaze 274
5.197 Smoked New England clam chowder 274
5.198 Bourbon Bacon Stuffing 275
5.199 Baked Peach Cobbler 275
5.200 Smoked Brisket Pot Pie 275
5.201 Baked Eggs in Bacon Nest 275
5.202 Sweet Smoked Salmon Jerky 276
5.203 Prosciutto Wrapped Dates with Marcona Almonds 276
5.204 Sweet Smoked Salmon 276

Chapter 6: Appetizers Recipes 277

6.1 Baked Garlic Bread 277
6.2 Lynchburg Bacon 277
6.3 Chorizo Armadillo Eggs 277
6.4 Bison Summer Sausage & Smoked Wild Boar 277
6.5 Southwestern Filled Peppers 277
6.6 Paprika Chicken Grilled along with Jalapeño Salsa .. 278
6.7 Bacon Cheddar (Smashed) Baby Potatoes 278
6.8 Cooked Taco Skillet Dip 278
6.9 Red Onion Jam, Duck Confit, & Goat Cheese Crostini 278
6.10 Cooked Teff Flatbread along with Zhoug Sauce 279
6.11 Pit Boss Mandarin Wings 279
6.12 Bacon-Wrapped Chicken Wings 279
6.13 Grilled Shrimp Cocktail 279
6.14 Grilled Shrimp Brochette 279
6.15 Roasted Garlic Herb Fries 280
6.16 Grilled Prosciutto Covered Asparagus 280
6.17 Pit Boss Smoked Guacamole 280
6.18 Sweet Potato (Grilled) Planks 280
6.19 Baked Artichoke Dip 280
6.20 Honey & Sage Skillet Cornbread 281
6.21 Pit Boss Fries along with Chipotle Ketchup 281
6.22 Smoked Nuts (Diva Q's Savory) 281
6.23 Pit Boss Chex Party Mix 281
6.24 Buffalo (Baked) Chicken Dip 282
6.25 Sweet Cajun Wings (Grilled) 282
6.26 Potato Skins(Baked) along with Pulled Pork 282
6.27 Deep Dish Supreme Pizza (Baked) 282
6.28 Ultimate Loaded Nachos 282
6.29 Onion Dip 283

6.30 Smoked Trout 283
6.31 Spicy Bacon covered Chicken Skewers (Grilled) 283
6.32 Bacon Onion Ring 283
6.33 Chicken Wings (Tandoori) 283
6.34 Brown Sugar Bacon Bites (BBQ) 284
6.35 Hasselback Potatoes (Roasted) 284
6.36 Old Fashioned Cornbread 284
6.37 Smoked Olives 284
6.38 Breakfast Mini Quiches (Baked) 284
6.39 Jalapeño Poppers (Coconut Shrimp) 285
6.40 Bloody Mary Wings (Grilled) 285
6.41 Beef Satay 285
6.42 (Adobo Skewers) Honey Lime Chicken 285
6.43 Chinese Jumbo Shrimp 285
6.44 Smoked Hummus along with Roasted Veggies 286
6.45 Venison Tater Tot Casserole (Baked) 286
6.46 Sweet Potato Fries (Roasted) 286
6.47 Spicy Cashews & Smoked Sweet 286
6.48 Grilled Corn Salsa 286
6.49 Smoked Seafood Ceviche 286
6.50 Prosciutto Covered Grilled Shrimp along with Peach Salsa 287
6.51 BBQ Bacon-Wrapped Water Chestnuts 287
6.52 Roasted Habanero Wings 287
6.53 BBQ Brisket Hot Dog 287
6.54 Grilled Oysters 288
6.55 Smoked Hummus with Roasted Vegetables 288
6.56 Buffalo & Pork Stuffed Poblano Peppers 288
6.57 Smoked Sweet & Spicy Cashews 289
6.58 Roasted Sweet Potato Fries 289
6.59 Bourbon BBQ Chicken Kabobs 289
6.60 Journey South Oyesters 289
6.61 Baked Potato Skins with Pulled Pork 289
6.62 BBQ Brown Sugar Bacon Bites 290
6.63 Roasted Potatoes by Doug Scheiding 290
6.64 Everything Pigs in a Blanket 290
6.65 Pit Boss Fries with Chipotle Ketchup 290
6.66 Whole Roasted Cauliflower with Garlic Parmesan Butter 290
6.67 Grilled Watermelon with Lime & Smoked Chili Salt ... 291
6.68 Pit Boss English Muffins 291
6.69 Grilled Burrata Salad with Ripped Croutons 291
6.70 Smoke Blended Salsa 291

6.71 Grilled Fruit Skewers with Yogurt Sauce 291
6.72 Roasted Tingle Wings 292
6.73 Smoked Stuffed Avocado Recipe 292
6.74 Smoked Venison Holiday Jerky 292
6.75 Grilled Hummus 292
6.76 Grilled Oysters with Mignonette 293
6.77 Baked Brie 293
6.78 Holiday Smoked Cheese Log 293
6.79 Double-Decker Pulled Pork Nachos with Smoked Cheese 293
6.80 Smoked Homemade Crackers 294
6.81 Smoked Cajun Chicken Wings 294
6.82 Roasted Buffalo wings 294
6.83 Smoked Jalapeño Poppers 294
6.84 Coconut Shrimp Jalapeño Poppers 295
6.85 Reuben Dip 295
6.86 Smoked Dry Rub Wings 295
6.87 Smoked & Loaded Baked Potato 295
6.88 Roasted Potato Poutine 296
6.89 Grilled Sweet Potato Planks 296
6.90 Smoked Beet-Pickled Eggs 296
6.91 Smoked Asparagus Soup 296
6.92 Roasted Red Pepper White Bean Dip 296
6.93 Baked Breakfast Mini Quiches 297
6.94 The Dan Patrick Show Grilled Bloody Mary Wings ... 297
6.95 Competition Style BBQ Pulled Pork 297

Chapter 7: Desserts Recipes 298

7.1 Grilled Stone Fruit with Berries & Cream 298
7.2 Dutch Baby with Bourbon Apples 298
7.3 Christmas Shortbread Cookies 298
7.4 Maple Bacon Donuts 298
7.5 Baked Dutch Baby 299
7.6 Maple Bacon Pull Apart 299
7.7 Donut Bread Pudding 299
7.8 Grilled Season Fruit with Gelato 299
7.9 Dark Chocolate Brownies with Bacon-Salted Caramel 299
7.10 Baked Cast Iron Berry Cobbler 300
7.11 Baked Molten Chocolate Cake 300
7.12 Caramelized Bourbon Baked Pears 300
7.13 Smoked Whipped Cream 300
7.14 Croissant S'mores on the Grill 300

7.15 Marbled Brownies with Amaretto & Ricotta 301
7.16 Baked Irish Creme Cake 301
7.17 Baked Bourbon Monkey Bread 301
7.18 Baked Gluten-Free Banana Bread 301
7.19 Baked Carrot Sheet Cake with Cream Cheese Frosting 301
7.20 Baked Apple Turnover 302
7.21 Pumpkin Pie with Bourbon Whipped Cream 302
7.22 Triple Chocolate Cast Iron Cookie 302
7.23 Baked Honey Cornbread Cake 302
7.24 Strawberry Rhubarb Cobbler 303
7.25 Smoked Cherry Bourbon Ice Cream 303
7.26 Smoked Irish Coffee Pie 303
7.27 Pit Boss Chocolate Chip Cookies 303
7.28 Flourless Chocolate Cake with Raspberry Sauce 304
7.29 Traditional Baked Pumpkin Pie 304
7.30 Baked Cherry Bourbon Pie 304
7.31 Baked Bread Pudding by Doug Scheiding 305
7.32 Baked Cherry Cheesecake Galette 305
7.33 Holiday Brownie Pie 305
7.34 Grilled Stone Fruit with Berries & Cream 305
7.35 Baked Pear Tarte Tatin 306
7.36 Crème Brûlée 306
7.37 Smoked Sweet Potato Soufflé by Diva Q 306
7.38 Tarte Tatin 306
7.39 Oatmeal Chocolate Chip Cookies 307
7.40 Baked Cherry Cobbler 307
7.41 Holiday Roasted Apple Pudding 307
7.42 Grilled Plums with Brown Sugar Balsamic Reduction 307
7.43 Grilled Peaches & Cream Popsicle 308
7.44 Carrot Souffle 308
7.45 Baked Pear & Fig Upside Down Cake 308
7.46 Lava Cake (Chocolate) and Whipped Cream (Smoked) 308
7.47 Baked Cast-Iron Cookie with Smoked Bourbon Whip 309
7.48 Kodiak Cakes Candied Bacon Crumble Brownies 309
7.49 Baked Rhubarb Cobbler 309
7.50 Baked Peach Cobbler 309
7.51 Chocolate Chip Cookies 310
7.52 Smoked Roasted Apple Pie 310
7.53 Cast Iron Pineapple Upside Down Cake 310
7.54 Super Bowl Sundae (Smoked) 310

7.55 Grilled Apple Pie 310
7.56 Baked Apple Bourbon Crisp 311
7.57 Blueberry Bread Pudding 311
7.58 Funfetti Ice Cream Sandwich 311
7.59 Baked Walnut Pumpkin Cookies 311
7.60 Pound Cake 312
7.61 Brownie Pudding of Bread (Baked) 312
7.62 French Toast of Raspberry Casserole (Baked) 312
7.63 Watermelon and Pineapple Creamsicles (Grilled) .. 312
7.64 Bananas Foster 313
7.65 Vegan Pumpkin Muffins of Apple (Gluten-Free) 313
7.66 Beaver Tails 313
7.67 Banana Trifle (Smoked) 313
7.68 Pie (Blueberry) 313
7.69 Chocolate Chip Cookies (Mint) 314
7.70 Cheesecake Frypan Brownie 314
7.71 Cookies of Peanut Butter 314
7.72 Pumpkin Pie (Pit Boss) 314
7.73 Grilled Banana Split with Vanilla Bourbon Ice Cream 314
7.74 Chewy Coconut Gluten-Free Cookies 314
7.75 Grilled Mango with Lime and Coconut 315
7.76 Grilled Seasonal Fruit with Gelato 315
7.77 Baked Caramel Pecan Brownie 315
7.78 Baked Coffee Cake 315
7.79 Baked Peach Cobbler Cupcakes 315
7.80 Baked Strawberry Shortbread 316
7.81 Baked Gluten-Free Banana Bread 316
7.82 Baked Apple Pear Crisp 316
7.83 Baked Apple Pie with Cheddar Cheese 316
7.84 Grilled Honey Bourbon Peaches 317
7.85 Baked Chocolate Brownie Cookies with Egg Nog ... 317
7.86 Mom's Best Baked Pumpkin Bread 317
7.87 Pumpkin Chocolate Chip Cookies 318
7.88 Baked Chocolate Coconut Brownies 318
7.89 Double Chocolate Chip Brownie Pie 318
7.90 Baked Pumpkin Pie 318
7.91 Baked Pumpkin Cheesecake 318
7.92 Baked Chocolate Soufflé with Smoked Whipped Cream 319
7.93 Baked Soft Gingerbread Cookie 319
7.94 Baked Summer Berry Cheesecake 319
7.95 Gluten-Free Baked Fruit Crisps 320

7.96 Scones with Vanilla Bean Glaze 320

7.97 The Dan Patrick Show Smoked Super Bowl Sundae. 320

7.98 Baked Brownie Bread Pudding 321

7.99 Baked Raspberry French Toast Casserole 321

7.100 Grilled Pineapple & Watermelon Creamsicles 321

Chapter 8: Cocktail Recipes 322

8.1 Pit Bossade Cocktail 322

8.2 Smoked Hibiscus Sparkler 322

8.3 Smoked Ice Mojito Slurpee 322

8.4 Smoked Mexican Hot Chocolate 322

8.5 Smoked Barnburner Cocktail 322

8.6 Smoked Mulled Wine 323

8.7 Smoked Cold Brew Coffee 323

8.8 Game Day Micheladas 323

8.9 Smoked Pineapple Hotel Nacional Cocktail 323

8.10 Smoked Plum and Thyme Fizz Cocktail 323

8.11 Smoked Hot Toddy 324

8.12 Smoked Kentucky Mule 324

8.13 Smoked Sangria 324

8.14 Smoky Mountain Bramble Cocktail 324

8.15 Smoked Pomegranate Lemonade Cocktail 324

8.16 A Smoking Classic Cocktail 324

8.17 Grilled Hawaiian Sour 325

8.18 Grilled Applejack O'Lantern Cocktail 325

8.19 Grilled Grapefruit Buck Cocktail 325

8.20 Grilled Jungle Juice 325

8.21 Smoked Margarita 325

8.22 Bacon Old-Fashioned Cocktail 326

8.23 Grilled Peach Mint Julep 326

8.24 Grilled Peach Smash Cocktail 326

8.25 Pit Boss Old Fashioned 326

8.26 Smoked Grape Lime Rickey 326

8.27 Grilled Blood Orange Mimosa 327

8.28 Smoked Jacobsen Salt Margarita 327

8.29 Smoked Apple Cider 327

8.30 Smoked Arnold Palmer 327

8.31 Smoked Berry Cocktail 327

8.32 Pit Boss French 75 Cocktail 328

8.33 Smoke Screen Cocktail 328

8.34 Seeing Stars Cocktail 328

8.35 Maui Waui Cocktail 328

8.36 Smoked Hot Buttered Rum 328

8.37 Smoky Paloma Cocktail 328

8.38 Spiced Cider Brew Cocktail 329

8.39 Smoked Bloody Mary Cocktail 329

8.40 Smoked Irish Coffee 329

8.41 Ryes and Shine Cocktail 329

8.42 Strawberry Basil Daiquiri 329

8.43 Smoked Bloody Mary with Grilled Garnishes 329

8.44 Strawberry Mint Julep Cocktail 330

8.45 Sunset Margarita 330

8.46 Smoked Salted Caramel White Russian 330

8.47 Grilled Frozen Strawberry Lemonade 330

8.48 Smoked Eggnog 331

8.49 Zombie Cocktail Recipe 331

8.50 The Old Orchard Cocktail 331

8.51 The Trifecta Cocktail 331

8.52 Pit Boss Boulevardier Cocktail 331

8.53 Pit Boss Gin & Tonic 332

8.54 Pit Boss Paloma Cocktail 332

8.55 Smoked Raspberry Bubbler Cocktail 332

8.56 Smoked Sangaree Cocktail 332

8.57 Smoked Spring Tea Cocktail 332

8.58 Smoky Scotch & Ginger Cocktail 332

8.59 Smoking Gun Cocktail 333

8.60 Smoking Jacket Cocktail 333

8.61 Pit Boss Smoked Daiquiri 333

8.62 Pit Boss Grilled Tiki Cocktail 333

8.63 Robert Palmer Cocktail 333

8.64 Pit Boss Cocktail 334

8.65 Maipole Cocktail 334

8.66 Strawberry Mule Cocktail 334

8.67 In Pit Boss Fashion Cocktail 334

8.68 Pit Boss 'Que Cocktail 334

8.69 Home Team Cocktail 334

8.70 Garden Gimlet Cocktail 334

8.71 Honey Glazed Grapefruit Shandy Cocktail 335

8.72 Grilled Strawberry Bourbon Lemonade 335

8.73 Smoked Pumpkin Spice Latte 335

8.74 Cran-Apple Tequila Punch with Smoked Oranges .. 335

8.75 Dublin Delight Cocktail 336

8.76 Grilled Piña Colada 336

8.77 Bulldog Margarita 336

8.78 Smoked Lemonade with Pit Boss Simple Syrup 336
8.79 Burnt Orange Julep Cocktail 336
8.80 Cannonball Cocktail 337
8.81 Elite 8 Punch Cocktail 337
8.82 Fig Slider Cocktail 337
8.83 Weizen Up Cocktail 337
8.84 Brush Fire Cocktail 337
8.85 Batter Up Cocktail 337
8.86 Grilled Peach Sour Cocktail 338
8.87 Blackberry Bourbon Smash 338
8.88 Bloody Mary with Grilled Garnishes 338
8.89 Grilled Rabbit Tail Cocktail 338
8.90 Smoked Roasted Apple Pie 338
8.91 Beer & Smoke Cocktail 339
8.92 Smoke and Bubz Cocktail 339
8.93 Grilled Watermelon Punch 339
8.94 Grilled Melancholy Fix Cocktail 339
8.95 Pig in a Hammock 339
8.96 Smoked Texas Ranch Water 340
8.97 Smoked Blood Orange & Rosemary Spritz 340
8.98 Red, White, and Blue Summer Breeze Drink Recipe . 340
8.99 Smoked Lemon Sweet Tea 340
8.100 Smoked Ice Recipe & Cocktail 341

Chapter 9: Baked Goods Recipes 342
9.1 Sausage and Pesto Lasagna 342
9.2 Baked Apple Bourbon Crisp 342
9.3 Pit Boss Fries with Chipotle Ketchup 342
9.4 Baked Honey Cornbread Cake 343
9.5 Baked Salmon Cakes 343
9.6 Baked Mac & Cheese with Jerky Dust 343
9.7 Strawberry Rhubarb Cobbler 344
9.8 Pit Boss English Muffins 344
9.9 Yellow Layer Cake with Smoked Candied Bacon 344
9.10 Salt Crusted Baked Potatoes 345
9.11 Ultimate Pit Boss Cookie 345
9.12 Baked Caramel Pecan Brownie 345
9.13 Baked Candied Bacon Cinnamon Rolls 345
9.14 Homemade Turkey Gravy 346
9.15 Baked Soft Gingerbread Cookie 346
9.16 Smoked Pumpkin Soup 346
9.17 Baked Potato Skins with Pulled Pork 347

9.18 Pulled Pork Enchiladas with Smoke-Roasted Red Sauce 347
9.19 Baked Deep Dish Supreme Pizza 347
9.20 Baked Cornbread Sausage Stuffing 347
9.21 Spicy Bacon Wrapped Grilled Chicken Skewers 348
9.22 Bacon Onion Ring 348
9.23 Oktoberfest Pretzel Mustard Chicken 348
9.24 Rosemary and Thyme-Infused Mashed Potatoes with Cream 348
9.25 Baked Granola 349
9.26 Apple & Bourbon Glazed Ham 349
9.27 Asian BBQ Chicken 349
9.28 Baked Garlic Duchess Potatoes 349
9.29 Baked Sweet and Savory Yams by Bennie Kendrick 350
9.30 Chorizo Cheese Stuffed Burgers 350
9.31 Venison Meatloaf by Nikki Boxler 350
9.32 Old Fashioned Cornbread 350
9.33 Greek Chicken Pizza 351
9.34 Baked Chicken Pot Pie 351
9.35 Baked Coffee Cake 351
9.36 Baked Breakfast Mini Quiches 351
9.37 Dark Chocolate Brownies with Bacon-Salted Caramel 352
9.38 Baked Peach Cobbler Cupcakes 352
9.39 Baked Donut Holes 352
9.40 BBQ Pulled Pork Pizza 353
9.41 Baked Cinnamon Rolls 353
9.42 Baked Dutch Baby 353
9.43 Baked Venison Casserole Tater Tot 354
9.44 Baked Asparagus Pancetta Cheese Tart 354
9.45 Baked Cast Iron Berry Cobbler 354
9.46 Baked Strawberry Shortbread 354
9.47 Banana Bacon Pancakes 355
9.48 Baked Halibut Fish Sticks with Spicy Coleslaw 355
9.49 Salted Apple Cheesecake Galette 355
9.50 Baked Green Bean Casserole with Pulled Pork 355
9.51 Baked Venison Meatloaf with Potato Puree 356
9.52 Baked Cherry Pie 356
9.53 Baked Pretzel Bites & Beer Cheese Dip 357
9.54 Baked German Pork Schnitzel with Grilled Lemons . 357
9.55 Mini Sausage Rolls 357
9.56 Baked Creamed Spinach 358
9.57 Baked Pork Belly Mac and Cheese 358

- 9.58 Caramelized Bourbon Baked Pears 358
- 9.59 Ultimate BLT Salad 358
- 9.60 Beer-Braised Cabbage with Bacon 359
- 9.61 Lynchburg Bacon 359
- 9.62 Baked Cranberry Chicken 359
- 9.63 Baked Tuna Noodle Casserole 359
- 9.64 Baked Macaroni & Cheese 360
- 9.65 Baked Cheesy Corn Pudding 360
- 9.66 Tin Foil Dinner 360
- 9.67 Cast Iron Potatoes 360
- 9.68 Baked Bacon Green Bean Casserole 361
- 9.69 Baked Bourbon Monkey Bread 361
- 9.70 Smoked Baked Potato Soup 361
- 9.71 Not Your Mama's Meatloaf 361
- 9.72 Baked Breakfast Sausage Casserole 361
- 9.73 Baked Winter Squash Au Gratin 362
- 9.74 Baked Queso Blanco Dip 362
- 9.75 Baked Corned Beef Au Grautin 362
- 9.76 Skillet S'Mores Dip with Candied Smoked Pecans 362
- 9.77 Baked Cheesy Accordion Potatoes 363
- 9.78 New England Clambake 363
- .79 Roasted Steak Fries with Homemade Ketchup 363
- 9.80 Baked Ziti with Italian Sausage 364
- 9.81 Baked Bacon-Weaved Honey Bourbon-Glazed Meatloaf 364
- 9.82 Guinness Shepherd's Pie 364
- 9.83 Baked Apple Turnover 365
- 9.84 Grilled Mussels with Lemon Butter 365
- 9.85 BBQ Brisket Breakfast Tacos 365
- 9.86 Sourdough Pizza 365
- 9.87 Baked Brie 365
- 9.88 Holiday Breakfast Strata 366
- 9.89 Baked Cheesy Parmesan Grits 366
- 9.90 Double-Decker Pulled Pork Nachos with Smoked Cheese 366
- 9.91 Artichoke & Spinach Dip 366
- 9.92 Pumpkin Chocolate Chip Cookies 367
- 9.93 Bacon Weaved Stuffed Turkey Breast 367
- 9.94 Baked Pear, Bacon & Brown Butter Stuffing 367
- 9.95 Western Breakfast Casserole 367
- 9.96 Baked Parker House Rolls 368
- 9.97 BBQ Chicken Baked Potato 368
- 9.98 Baked Sweet Potatoes 368
- 9.99 Twice Baked Potatoes 369
- 9.100 Glazed Ham 369
- 9.101 Donut Bread Pudding 369
- 9.102 Baked Bacon Caramel Popcorn 369
- 9.103 The Dan Patrick Show pull-apart Pesto Bread 370
- 9.104 Smoked & Loaded Baked Potato 370
- 9.105 Baked Pumpkin Pie 370
- 9.106 Baked Wood-Fired Pizza 370
- 9.107 Bacon Chili Cheese Dogs 371
- 9.108 BBQ Pulled Pork Breakfast Burrito with Smoked Hot Sauce 371
- 9.109 Pit Boss Baked Corn Dog Bites 371
- 9.110 Baked Heirloom Tomato Tart 372
- 9.111 Pork Belly Bourbon Baked Beans 372
- 9.112 Baked Potatoes & Celery Root Au Gratin 372
- 9.113 Baked Sweet Potato Hash 372
- 9.114 Green Bean Casserole 373
- 9.115 Gyros 373
- 9.116 Smoked Mushrooms 373
- 9.117 Orange & Maple Baked Ham 373
- 9.118 Bacon Weave Mac n' Cheese 374
- 9.119 Baked Sage & Sausage Stuffing 374
- 9.120 Smoky Crab Dip 374
- 9.121 Baked Game Day Hatch Chile and Bacon Hot Dish 374
- 9.122 Steak Fries with Horseradish Creme 375
- 9.123 Strawberry Basil Daiquiri 375
- 9.124 Tuscan Meatloaf 375
- 9.125 Sweet Potato Marshmallow Casserole 375
- 9.126 Scalloped Potatoes with Bacon & Chipotle Cream 376
- 9.127 Pit Bossed Lasagna 376
- 9.128 Tarte Tatin 376
- 9.129 Smoked Trout Hash 377
- 9.130 Thanksgiving Sausage Leek Stuffing 377
- 9.131 Baked Blueberry French Toast Casserole 377
- 9.132 Game Day Cheese Dip 377
- 9.133 Pit Boss Baked Protein Bars 378
- 9.134 Grilled Vegetables with Lemon Herb Vinaigrette ... 378
- 9.135 Drunken Peach Cobbler 378
- 9.136 Baked Artichoke Dip with Homemade Flatbread .. 379
- 9.137 Artichoke & Spinach Dip 379
- 9.138 Baked Maple and Brown Sugar Bacon 379

9.139 Baked S'Mores Donuts	379
9.140 Baked Cherry Cobbler	380
9.141 Sopapilla Cheesecake by Doug Scheiding	380
9.142 Braised Collard Greens & Bacon	380
9.143 Baked Bread Pudding by Doug Scheiding	380
9.144 Easy Garlic Cheese Bombs	381
9.145 Baked Cherry Cheesecake Galette	381
9.146 Pit Boss Duck Poppers	382
9.147 Spring Frittata	382
9.148 Grilled Meat Lover's Pizza	382
9.149 Baked Honey Glazed Ham	382
9.150 Spicy Asian Brussels Sprouts	382
9.152 Grilled Quadruple Cheese Pizza	383
9.153 Baked Garlic Parmesan Wings	383
9.154 Mini Apple Pies	383
9.155 Baked Pimento Bacon Mac & Cheese	384
9.156 Italian Herb & Parmesan Scones	384
9.157 Baked Artichoke Dip	384
9.158 Baked Green Chile Mac & Cheese by Doug Scheiding	385
9.159 Pit Boss Cowboy Beans	385
9.160 Baked Cauliflower Tots	385
9.161 Irish Soda Bread	386
9.162 Veggie Flat Bread	386
9.163 Baked Green Bean Casserole with Crispy Shallots	386
9.164 Baked Otium House Rolls	386
9.165 Baked Meat Bagel	387
9.166 Baked Maple Venison Sausage Quiche	387
9.167 Baked Cheesy Garlic Fries	387
9.170 Ultimate Game Day Dip	388
9.171 Pit Boss Potatoes Au Gratin	388
9.172 Pizza Bites	389
9.173 Baked Cornbread Turkey Tamale Pie	389
9.174 Gluten-Free Baked Fruit Crisps	389
9.175 Pit Boss Wheat Bread	390
9.176 Cider-Glazed Baked Holiday Ham	390
9.177 Baked Thanksgiving Shepherd's Pie	390
9.178 Pull-Apart Dinner Rolls	391
9.179 Pit Boss Baked Rainbow Trout	391
9.180 Ultimate Baked Garlic Bread	391
9.181 BBQ Baked Beans	391
9.182 Cornish Game Hens	391
9.183 Peach Tart	392
9.184 Baked Strawberry Rhubarb Pie	392
9.185 Tater Tot Bake	392
9.186 Baked Pig Candy	393
9.187 Pulled Pork Stew	393
9.188 Baked Buffalo Cauliflower Bites	393
9.189 Butternut Squash Macaroni and Cheese	393
9.190 Baked Loaded Tater Tots	393
9.191 Pit Boss Baked Focaccia	394
9.192 Funfetti Ice Cream Sandwich	394
9.193 Green Bean Casserole Circa 1955	394
9.194 Pretzel Rolls	394
9.195 Baked Rhubarb Cobbler	395

Chapter 1: Beef Recipes

1.1 Marinated Beef Ribs

Total Time: 5 hr 15 Mins, Servings: 8
Ingredients
Beef Ribs Center-Cut 4 rack
Pit Boss Prime-Rib Rub
1 c Red Wine
Olive Oil, ¼ c
2 tbsp. Worcestershire Sauce
2 tbsp. Dijon Mustard
Salt, 1 ½ tsp
1 tsp Black Pepper Coarse Ground
3 Minced clove Garlic
1 small Diced Onion
1 Bay Leaf, Coarsely Crumbled
Instructions
Place your ribs in the non-reactive pan large enough to hold them. You might alternatively use a big resealable bag.
Follow these methods to produce the marinade: In a wide mixing bowl, combine the pepper, olive oil, wine, mustard, salt, & Worcestershire sauce. In a wide mixing dish, combine the garlic, onion, & bay leaf. Toss your meat racks into the marinade & flip them to cover them.
Cover and chill for several hrs or maybe overnight. To guarantee that the meat is evenly marinated, flip the racks several times.
Remove your ribs from the marinade & discard the solids. Either side of ribs may be rubbed with Pit Boss Prime-Rib-Rub.
Preheat your Pit Boss to 250°F for around 15 mins with its lid covered when you're all set to cook.
Place a b1 section of your ribs on your grill grate. Roast for about 2 & 2-1/2 hrs, or till soft. Serve immediately.

1.2 Salt & Pepper Beer-Braised Beef Ribs

Total Time: 3 hr 5 Mins, Servings: 4
Ingredients
2 Rack Meaty Beef Ribs
Sea Salt or Coarse Kosher
Black Pepper Freshly Ground
Granulated Garlic
Beef Stock or Beer, 1 ½ c
BBQ Sauce Pit Boss 'Que
Instructions
1 hr before frying, season your ribs on both sides with salt, granulated garlic, & pepper, then set them in your foil tray.
When you're all set to cook, preheat your Pit Boss to 165°F for approximately 15 mins with its lid closed.
Place your ribs into a pan on your grill grate & smoke them for around 1 hr. Half-fill the pan using malt. Wrap the foil all around the plate firmly.
Steam your ribs for the next 2-3 hrs, or till the meat is meltingly tender, at a temp of 250°F in your Pit Boss.
Carefully remove your foil. Discard the braising oil & serve your ribs with Barbecue Sauce.

1.3 Asian-Style Grilled Beef Skewers

Total Time: 1 Hr 8 Mins, Servings: 6
Ingredients
2 lb Boneless Rib Eye or Flat Iron Steak
Marinade Carne Asada, 1 ½ c
3 Garlic Clove Peeled & Crushed
2 large Thinly Sliced Scallions
2 medium Orange or Yellow Bell Peppers, slice In Chunks
Peanut Sauce Asian-Style
Dry-Roasted Chopped Peanuts, ¼ c
For Garnish Lime Wedges
Instructions
Using a sharp knife, chop the steak into slices on a sharp diagonal. Fill a large bowl halfway with water.
Pour little Carne Asada marinade on the meat, then toss in the garlic & scallions. Keep 1 hr in the freezer.
Before removing the steak from this marinade, scrape some scallions & garlic from it. Thread each piece together with a skewer. Some slices of sliced bell pepper must be put onto every skewer.
Preheat your Pit Boss at 500°F for around 15 mins with its lid covered when you're all set to cook.
Each skewer should be grilled for 3-4 mins each hand, turning once, or unless the core temp reaches 145°F.
Place your skewers on the serving plate & arrange them as desired. Drizzle with some peanut sauce and top with a sprinkling of peanuts. Serve with some lime wedges on the side.

1.4 Secret Ingredient BBQ Beef Short Ribs

Total Time: 3 hr 15 Mins, Servings: 4
Ingredients
6 oz. Chili Sauce
6 oz. BBQ Sauce (Pit Boss 'Que)
1 c Beer Soda High-Quality Root
1 tbsp. Thyme Leaves Fresh
1 large Thinly Sliced in Rings, Sweet Onion
4 lb. Bone-In Ribs
Salt
Black Pepper Freshly Ground
Mashed Potatoes or Polenta, For Serving
Instructions
In a wide mixing bowl, combine the chili sauce, BBQ Sauce, root beer, & thyme leaves.
Spread chopped onions evenly on the bottom of a dish.
On both sides, season the short ribs using pepper & salt. Place sliced potatoes into a thin layer over top of those onions.
Pour an equal coating of chili-root beer sauce over ribs. The plate must be tightly covered in Al foil.
When you're all ready to cook, preheat your Pit Boss at 300°F for approximately 15 mins with its lid closed.
Cook for around 2-3 hrs, or until the ribs become tender but not falling apart on the barbecue grate.
Add a dash of root beer to your pan if the meal isn't saucy enough.
Serve immediately with polenta.

1.5 Spicy Smoked Chili Beef Jerky

Total Time: 4 hr 10 Mins, Servings: 6
Ingredients
1 c Chili Sauce
Beer, 1/3 c
2 tbsp. Soy Sauce
1 tbsp. Worcestershire Sauce
2 tbsp. Morton Tender
1 tbsp. Jalapeño Peppers Minced Pickled
2 lb. Flank Steak, Sliced into one-4th-Inch Thick Slices
Instructions
In a wide mixing bowl, combine the soda, curing flour, Worcestershire sauce, chili sauce, soy sauce, & braised jalapeño peppers.
Half-fill a big resealable bag using beef pieces. Pour some marinade on the beef slices & massage the bag to ensure that all slices are covered. After sealing the container, place it into the freezer for several hrs.
Preheat your Pit Boss at 165°F for around 15 mins with the top covered till ready to use.
Remove the steak from the marinade & discard the remaining marinade. Dry your beef pieces with paper towels.
Arrange the steak in a layer on the smoke shelf.
Smoke your jerky for around 4-5 hrs, or till it's dry & still chewy & flexible when bent.
Even though this jerky is soft, place it into a resealable container.
Allow 1 hr for your jerky to rest at room temp. Refrigerate the jerky after squeezing the air out from the wrapper.
Any chunk beef may be used in this dish.

1.6 Vietnamese Beef Jerky

Total Time: 4 hr 20 Mins, Servings: 6
Ingredients
2 lb. Bottom Round Lean, Sirloin or Rump Roast
2 large Garlic Roughly Chopped
1 stalk Fresh Lemongrass
Fresh Ginger, Roughly Chopped and Peeled, 1 ½
1/2 c Liquid Bragg Aminos or Soy Sauce
3 tbsp. Water
3 tbsp. Sugar
2 tbsp. Fish Sauce
2 tsp Red Chile Flakes
1/2 tsp Salt Pink Curing
Instructions
Remove any visible fat from the meat with a sturdy chef's knife and cut it into tiny slices against the grain. Half-fill a large resealable bag with the mixture.
Follow this method for producing the marinade: In a blender container or a food processor jar, combine the pink cure salt, garlic, Chile flakes, lemongrass, fish sauce, ginger, soy sauce, and water, if using. Pulse the mixture until it is reasonably smooth.
Pour the marinade over the pork slices and massage the bag until they are evenly coated. Refrigerate for at least 8 hrs or overnight in the fridge. Switch this bag once, maybe twice, to re-distribute the juices.
Preheat the Pit Boss to 165°F for 15 mins with the top covered until ready to use.
Drain the meat and pat it dry with paper towels (discard this marinade). Place the meat strips on a grill grate opposite the bars in a single sheet. Add a few more red-Chile flakes to the meat before serving if you want your jerky to be fiery.
Smoke for 46 hrs, rotating once until the jerky is dry but still flexible.
Leave it cool completely before transferring to a clean resealable container. Refrigeration is the only technique to increase the shelf life of your food. The jerky may also be preserved.

1.7 Reuben Sandwich

Total Time: 20Mins, Servings: 4
Ingredients
2 c Mayonnaise
1/2 c Ketchup
Pickle Relish, ¼ c
2 tbsp. Pit Boss Chicken scrub
4 lb. Leftover Thinly Sliced Corned Beef
Sauerkraut, 2 ½
Ten pieces Swiss Cheese
Ten pieces Bread Marble Rye
6 tbsp. Butter, Room Temp
Instructions
Preheat the Pit Boss to 350°F for 15 mins with the lid covered when you're all set to cook.
Meanwhile, preheat the big skillet on a grill grate while your sandwiches are being made.
Whisk together the relish, ketchup, mayonnaise, and Pit Boss Chicken Rub in a mixing bowl until fully combined.
Butter the outsides of the bread. Spread a coating of sauce at the opposite side of your bread & top with sauerkraut, corned meat, & Swiss cheese pieces. On top of it, place another piece of the sauced bread.
Place your sandwiches on the hot Pit Boss grill & cook for 5 mins. With a spatula, flip the sandwiches and heat for another 5 mins, or until toasted with heated meat and melted cheese. Set the sandwiches aside after removing them from the Pit Boss.

1.8 BBQ Beef Tamale Casserole

Total Time: 60 Mins, Servings: 4
Ingredients
3 can Chopped Brisket
1 can Enchilada Sauce
1/2 c Yellow Cornmeal
All-Purpose Flour, 1 ½ c
Salt, ¼ tsp
1 tsp Baking Powder
3 tbsp. Sugar
2 tbsp. Vegetable Oil
Milk, ¼ c
1 Large Egg
1 can Slice and Drained Green Chiles
1 c Mozzarella Shredded Cheese
1 tbsp. For Garnish Sliced Cilantro
Instructions
Preheat your Pit Boss to 375°F for around 15 mins with lid covered when you're all set to cook.
Set aside both cut brisket & enchilada sauce in a shallow bowl.
In a wide mixing bowl, combine baking powder, flour,

sugar, salt, & cornmeal. Stir till the oil becomes crumbly, & add the milk, chiles, & egg, stirring unless everything is completely combined.
Press the cornmeal crust mix into the oiled cast-iron pan.
Bake for approximately 25 mins on your Pit Boss at 375° F, or unless golden brown.
Reduce the Pit Boss's temp to 350°F. Fill your enchilada crust using filling & poke holes in it. Bake for approximately 20 mins, or unless the chicken is cooked & the cheese melt & bubbling.
Enjoy with a sprinkle of cilantro on top.

1.9 Coffee Break Smoked Beef Jerky

Total Time: 5 hr 10 Mins, Servings: 4
Ingredients
1 c Brewed Espresso or Strong Coffee, Chilled
1 c Cola
1/2 c Soy Sauce
Worcestershire Sauce, ¼ c
Brown Sugar, ¼ c
2 tbsp. Morton Tender
Black Pepper Freshly Ground, 1 ½ tsp
1 tbsp. Hot Sauce
2 lb. Trimmed Beef Bottom or Top Round, Flank Steak or Sirloin Tip
Instructions
Prepare ahead of time. This meal requires an overnight marinating period.
In a mixing bowl, combine the hot sauce, pepper, coffee, curing salt, cola, brown sugar, Worcestershire sauce, & soy sauce.
Using a strong knife, slice the beef into 1/4-inch-thick slices across the grain. It's a good idea to get rid of some excess fat or connective tissue.
Half-fill a large resealable bag with beef slices. Brush the beef slices with the marinade, then rub the bag to coat all the slices in the marinade.
After closing the bag, put it in the fridge for several hrs or overnight.
Preheat the Pit Boss to 165°F for about 15 mins with the lid sealed till ready to use.
Remove the steak from the marinade and discard the marinade.
Dry the meat slices among paper towels. Arrange the steak in a single layer on your grill grate.
Smoke for around 4-5 hrs, or till the jerky become crispy when bent in half & yet pliable and chewy.
Transfer the jerky to the resealable container while it's soft. Allow an hr for the jerky to settle at room temp.
Chill the jerky after squeezing the air out of the wrapper. It would keep in the fridge for some weeks.

1.10 Jalapeño Beef Jerky

Total Time: 4 hr 15 Mins, Servings: 8
Ingredients
2 Jalapeños, Seeded and Stemmed
Lime Juice, ¼ c
Soy Sauce, ¼ c
4 tbsp Brown Sugar
1 c Mexican Beer
2 tbsp Morton Tender
2 lb Beef Bottom or Top Round
Sirloin Tip, Wild Game or Flank Steak
Instructions
In a blender, combine the brown sugar, curing salt, jalapenos, soy sauce, and lime juice, and pulse till the jalapenos have been finely sliced.
Using the sharp knife, remove some connective tissue or fat from the meat. Cut the meat in 1/4-inch-thick strips against the grain.
Place the beef pieces in a large resealable container. Fill the resealable bag halfway with the jalapeno mix & halfway with beer. To ensure that the marinade is evenly distributed among the slices, rub the bag. After closing, refrigerate for several hrs or overnight.
When you're all set to cook, preheat the Pit Boss to 180°F for approximately 15 mins with its lid closed. Use Super Smoke if it's available for the finest flavor.
Remove the steak from the marinade and discard the remainder. Dry your beef slices among paper towels. Arrange the steak in a single layer on the grill grate.
Smoke for around 4-5 hrs, or till jerky becomes crispy when bent in half but still malleable & chewy.
Place on the cooling rack and let cool for around 1 hr.
Fill the resealable container halfway with water. Refrigerate the jerky after squeezing the air out of the wrapper. It will keep for many weeks in the refrigerator.

1.11 Roasted Prime Rib with Mustard and Herbs De Provence

Total Time: 3 hr 15Mins, Servings: 8
Ingredients
1 whole B1 Prime-Rib Roast
Olive Oil Extra-Virgin
Kosher Salt
Black Pepper Coarse Ground
2 c Dijon Mustard
2 c Herbs De-Provence
Instructions
Coat the prime rib with olive oil to ensure that the seasoning clings to it. Season the roast well on both sides with salt & pepper. Then, generously season both sides with herb Provence & a consistent coat of Dijon mustard. Allow it to sit in the refrigerator for about 24 hrs, open.
15 mins before beginning to cook, preheat the grill to 325°F with its lid closed. Roast your prime rib fat sides up for 3-12 hrs, or till the core temp reaches 110°F, then transfer to your grill grate or sheet pan.
Remove the prime rib from the grill and lay it aside to rest for an hr. You may obtain a final temp of 130°F for around medium-small by increasing the internal temperature during repose.
Carve the roast before serving. Carve down the bones with a sharp, firm cutting knife, following the curvature of these bones as precisely as possible before breaking through the center, keeping your prime rib straight. Cut each roast into 1" thick pieces after that. Return it to its original position and chop along these bones to carve the bones.

1.12 Grilled Rib Eyes with Hasselback Sweet Potatoes

Total Time: 1 hr 15 Mins, Servings: 4
Ingredients
2 Rib-Eye Bone-In Steaks
Potatoes Hassel back Sweet
4 Potatoes Sweet
Olive Oil Extra-Virgin
Salt & Pepper
Instructions
Remove your steaks from the refrigerator
an hr before cooking to allow them to come down in temp.
Preheat the Pit Boss to 400°F and keep the lid covered until preparing to roast for approximately 15 mins.
With the sharp knife, cut all sweet potatoes crosswise into one-eighth-inch slices, just going 3-4th of the way into the potatoes

to keep them intact. To protect the knife, place chopsticks on both sides of the potatoes.

Arrange the sliced potatoes on the sheet plate. Drizzle with some oil, then season with pepper & salt. Place the tray on the grill after preheating it. Roast for around 50-60 mins, or until the potatoes are browned on the exterior and tender on the inside.

While the potatoes are roasting, prepare the steaks. Scrub the steaks with the oil & season well on both sides with pepper & salt.

When the sweet potatoes are nearly done, put the steaks on the grill & cook till the core temperature reaches 130° F for high, 4-5 mins each side, allowing all sides to sear.

After taking the steaks from the grill, let them rest for approximately 10 mins.

The steaks must be sliced against the grain on both sides. Arrange the steak pieces & potatoes on the plate. Serve with Lemon Gremolata of Amanda for a kick of flavor.

1.13 Southwestern Stuffed Peppers

Total Time: 55 Mins, Servings: 6
Ingredients
6 large Red Bell Pepper
1 lb. Ground Beef
1 small Onion, Diced
2 whole Garlic, Minced
2 tbsp. Pit Boss Cajun Rub
Salsa, Tomato 2/3 c
2 c Rice, Cooked
1 c Black Beans, Drained and Rinsed
1 c Ears Fresh Corn
Grated Colby and Monterey Jack Cheese, 1 1/2 c
Instructions

Clean every pepper well under cold running water. These halves should be broken lengthwise through the stem, then the ribs & seeds should be removed using a knife.

Follow these instructions to make the stuffing: Fry your ground beef in a wide frying pan, dividing it with a wooden spoon.

With the garlic & onion, sauté for around 2-3 mins. With the Pit Boss Cajun Scrub, corn, salsa, black beans, & rice, cook till the flavors are mixed, about 5 mins. Fill every pepper half halfway with filling.

Preheat the grill to 350°F, then seal the cover for around 10-15 mins while preparing the roast.

Place the peppers on your grill grate, fill side up, & hold them there among the rungs. Preheat your grill to 400°F & bake for almost 40 mins.

Spread a thin layer of grated cheese on the peppers. Cook for the next 5 mins, or till the cheese has completely melted.

1.14 Pit Boss Smoky Meatball Subs

Total Time: 55 Mins, Servings: 4
Ingredients
1 large Egg
Buttermilk or Milk, 1/3 c
2 tbsp Worcestershire Sauce
1/2 c Crushed Croutons or Seasoned Breadcrumbs
1 tbsp. Cajun Seasoning
Ground Beef, 1 ½ lb
Minced Onion, ¼ c
Black Pepper Freshly Ground 1 ½ tbsp
2 Minced clove Garlic
1 jar (24 Oz) Marinara Sauce
4 (6 inches) Baguettes or Sub Rolls
Provolone Cheese Grated or Thinly Sliced
Instructions
Shake your eggs in a wide mixing bowl using a fork.

Whisk together all the Worcestershire sauce & milk in a medium bowl. In a wide mixing bowl, combine the Cajun spice & breadcrumbs, then let aside for around 5 mins.

In a different dish, combine the black pepper, garlic, onion, & ground meat. In a large mixing bowl, thoroughly combine the egg & meat mixture.

If the mixture seems to be too dry, add a bit more cream. If the mix is too moist, add more dry breadcrumbs. Form the mixture into spheres the size of golf balls.

Preheat your Pit Boss at 325° F for approximately 15 mins with its lid covered when prepared to roast.

Place your meatballs immediately on your grill grate. Preheat the grill to 350°F & bake your meatballs for around 30–35 mins or fully cooked.

Meanwhile, in a small saucepan, bring some marinara sauce to a boil. After removing the fried meatballs from the platter, cook for around 5-10 mins.

Put 4 sheets of Al foil over the work area & break them apart with your hands. Put the hoagie roll in the center of each. Split the meatballs amongst the buns using the meatballs as a guide.

The meatballs may be topped with Provolone cheese. Cook the sandwiches on your Pit Boss for around 10-12 mins, tightly wrapped in foil.

Remove the meat from your Pit Boss, pan it, and serve.

1.15 3 Ingredient Pot Roast

Total Time: 3 Hrs 10 Mins, Servings: 4
Ingredients
4 lb. Chuck Roast
2 Yellow Onions
2 tsp Kosher Salt
Olive Oil Extra-Virgin, ¼ c
Black Pepper Freshly Ground
Instructions

Preheat the Pit Boss at 400°F for around 15 mins with the lid covered till to roast. Place chuck roast in the 3-4-quart Dutch oven. Salt, pepper, & olive oil are added to half of the onions. The bulk of the components have a representative.

Cover a Dutch oven with a tight cover and put this on your grill. Cook for approximately 2-3 hrs, or until the chuck roast is easily shredded with a fork. Reduce the grill temperature to 350° F if your roast chuck starts heating rather than simmering. Remove the cover from the grill. Allow your meat to cool completely before scraping the fat off the top. Allow the meat to settle before refrigerating overnight & skimming excess fat cap the following day before reheating. It'll last nearly two days in the fridge.

1.16 Grilled Santa Maria Tri-Tip

Total Time: 5 Hrs, Servings: 4
Ingredients
2 tsp Salt
2 tsp Black Pepper
2 tsp Garlic Powder
2 tsp Paprika
1 tsp Onion Powder
1 tsp Rosemary
1 tsp Cayenne Pepper
Beef Tri-Tip Roast (2-1/2 Lb)
Vinegar Red Wine, 1/3 c
Vegetable Oil, 1/3 c
4 Garlic clove
1/2 tsp Dijon Mustard
Instructions
Combine the rosemary, garlic powder, salt, onion powder, paprika, black pepper, & cayenne in a wide mixing bowl.

Place your tri-tip within the baking dish & coat all sides using the scrub. Wrap your dish into plastic wrap & refrigerate for nearly 4 hrs.

Combine smashed garlic, vinegar, vegetable oil, & Dijon mustard in a container. Cover your bottle & whisk it to combine the ingredients.

Preheat your grill at 500°F & leave the lid covered for 15 mins.

After taking your tri-tip from the fridge, put it immediately on your grill grate. Garlic & vinegar should be brushed into mop sauce.

Cook for 15 mins before flipping and basting the meat. For around 30-40 mins, or until the core temp reaches 130°F, flip & baste every 15 mins.

Allow for around 5-10 mins of resting time before cutting.

1.17 Espresso Beef Tenderloin (Coriander & Rubbed)

Total Time: 1 Hr 5 Mins, Servings: 8
Ingredients
1 (4 Lb) Whole Beef Tenderloin
2 tbsp. Olive Oil
Coriander Rub & Espresso
2 tbsp. Ground Espresso
1 tbsp Sugar (Brown)
Coriander (Ground) 1 ½ tsp
Cayenne Pepper Ground, ¼ tsp
1/2 tsp Garlic Powder
1/2 tsp Black Pepper Freshly Ground & Sea Salt
1 tbsp Lemon Zest (Grated)
1 tsp Chives Finely Diced
Instructions

Preheat your Pit Boss at 425°F with its lid covered for approximately 15 mins.

Trim your tenderloin if necessary. Continue by carefully pulling the chain that goes through the center of the tenderloin back with your hands, then trimming this with a sharp knife. Trim any excess fat skin from the meat.

To guarantee uniform cooking, truss a tenderloin. Bind the tenderloin with pre-cut kitchen twine every 2" & tuck the tenderloin's thin end beneath itself.

In a large mixing bowl, whisk together the salt, sugar, spices, espresso, lemon zest, & black pepper.

Coat your tenderloin in olive oil & liberally apply the spice rub, ensuring it reaches into every crevice. When you're ready to grill, use any remaining spice rub over ham, fish, other meats. Place the meat straight on your grill grates & cook for around 45-50 mins, or until a core temp of 130°F is reached.

After taking the meat from the grill, wrap it in foil. Allow for a 15-min rest period. The core temp of a sleeping person may reach 135 degrees Fahrenheit.

Cut all links before slicing & serving together with your favorite side dishes.

1.18 Smoked Paleo Beef Jerkey

Total Time: 4 Hrs 30 Mins, Servings: 6
Ingredients
Coconut Aminos, ¾ c
½ tbsp. Fish Sauce
1 tbsp. Onion Powder
1 tbsp. Garlic Powder
1 tsp Black Pepper
½ tsp Cayenne Pepper
Flank Steak, 2 ½ lb
Instructions

In a mixing bowl, combine the cayenne pepper, onion powder, coconut aminos, fish sauce, black pepper, & garlic powder. To combine, whisk everything together.

The meat should be free of connective tissue & excess fat. Using some sharp knife, cut meat in slices across the grain.

Cuts should be half-filled in a wide resealable bag. Place your beef slices within a bag with the marinade mixture & massage the bag till all these slices are coated.

After closing the container, chill for several hrs or maybe overnight.

Preheat your Pit Boss at 165°F for approximately 15 mins with top closed.

Remove the meat from the marinade & discard the marinade. Place the meat in a fine layer on your grill grate.

Smoke for around 4-5 hrs, or till jerky becomes crispy on the outside but still chewy & malleable once bent in half.

On the cooling rack, allow for 1 hr of cooling.

Seal any leftover jerky within a resealable container to keep it cool.

1.19 Brined Smoked Brisket

Total Time: 7 Hrs 20 Mins, Servings: 4
Ingredients
1 (5-7 Lb) Brisket Flat Cut
1 c Brown Sugar
1/2 c Kosher Salt
Pit Boss Beef Scrub, ¼ c
Instructions

Dissolve the sugar & salt in boiling water. After adding some ice, let it aside to chill. Put your brisket in the brine & wrap this in some plastic wrap. Refrigerate for around 24 hrs after making the brine.

After taking your brisket from the brine, wipe it dry using your paper towel. Beef Pit Boss Scrub must be spread evenly.

Preheat your Pit Boss at 250°F with its lid closed for approximately 15 mins.

Set the fat top of the brisket over your Pit Boss & smoke for approximately 3 hrs.

After 3 hrs, reduce the temp to nearly 275°F & double wrap this brisket into the foil. Cook for around 3-4 hrs, or till the core temp reaches 204°F.

Remove your brisket from the wrapper & cook it for the next 30 mins on your grill.

Allow 15 mins for your brisket to settle before cutting it against some grain.

1.20 Blue Cheese & Peppercorn Butter over Beef Tenderloin Steaks

Total Time: 50 Mins, Servings: 4
Ingredients
8 tbsp. Butter
3 tbsp. Blue Cheese, Crumbled
1 clove Garlic, Minced
1 tbsp Red Wine or Dry Sherry
1 tsp Black & Green Peppercorns Coarse Ground
1 tsp Coarse Salt
1 tbsp. Chopped Chives
Beef Steaks 4 whole
Olive Oil Extra-Virgin
Pit Boss Prime-Rib Scrub
Instructions

In a wide mixing bowl, combine the sherry, blue cheese, butter, garlic, chives, & salt to make flavorful butter. Cover & chill till ready to use, or maybe coil this in a log & freeze into a wax paper, plastic parchment, or wrap, for nearly 6 hrs.

Preheat your Pit Boss grill at 185°F, mainly with its lid closed, approximately 15 mins.

Brush the outsides of your steaks using olive oil & season with Prime Pit Boss Rib Scrub.

Put your steaks straight on your grill grate for approximately 30 mins to smoke.

To serve, arrange the steaks over a plate. Raise the temperature to be high and cook for around 10-15 mins with its lid closed.

Put your smoked steaks back on your grill grate & cook till done to your satisfaction, turning once with tongs.

Cover your steaks with a dollop of Blue Cheese & Peppercorn Butter before transferring them onto a plate.

1.21 Ultimate Loaded Nachos

Total Time: 40 Mins, Servings: 4
Ingredients
1 bag Tortilla Chips
1/2 c Fresh Salsa
1 lb. Cooked & Sliced Kielbasa Sausage
1 c Chicken Breast, Shredded Cooked
1 lb. Tri-Tip Cooked & Cubed
Sliced Scallions, ¼ c
1 small Jar Jalapeños, Sliced
Black Olives, Sliced, ¼ c
Cheddar Cheese, 1 ½ c
1/2 c Sour Cream
1/2 c Guacamole
Cilantro, ¼ c

Instructions
Preheat your Pit Boss at 375°F with its lid shut for approximately 15 mins.

On a large platter, evenly distribute your tortilla chips. First, spread some salsa over the chips & top with Kielbasa sausage, chicken, & tri-tip. The nachos are topped with olives, jalapenos, scallions, & cheese.

Put the pan on your grill & bake for around 10-15 mins, or unless the cheese completely melted & the nachos are done. Toss with some sour cream, guacamole, & cilantro before serving.

1.22 Smoked Burgers

Total Time: 2 hr 15 Mins, Servings: 8
Ingredients
2 lb. Ground Beef
1 tbs Worcestershire Sauce
2 tbsp. Pit Boss Beef Scrub
Instructions
In a wide mixing bowl, combine the Worcestershire sauce, ground beef, and Beef Scrub.

With the beef mix, make 8 hamburger patties.

Once you're all set to cook, set the Pit Boss to 180°F & preheat for around 15 mins with its lid closed. Use the Super Smoke if it's available for the finest flavor.

Smoke the patties for approximately 2 hrs by placing them directly on your grill grate.

After 2 hrs, remove from grill and serve with your preferred toppings.

1.23 BBQ Beef Ribs

Total Time: 8 hrs 10Mins, Servings: 4
Ingredients
2 Rack 3-B1 of Beef Ribs (5-7 Lb)
Cow meat BBQ Rub ¾ c
2 c Beef Broth
Instructions
Preheat your Pit Boss to 275°F for around 15 mins before you plan to cook.

Remove the membrane off the back of a rack of ribs, then flip the ribs meat-side down. Using a paper towel to capture and remove the membrane is one option.

Cover the surface with a thick coat of Meat Church. BBQ holy cow Rep with the second rack, rubbing the steak mainly on all sides and fully covering it. Allow 10 mins for the rub to take effect. Repeat the procedure on the other side of a rack of ribs.

Put the ribs on your Pit Boss with the meat on top. Spritz the ribs with either water or beef broth every hr to keep them moist.

Keep smoking the ribs until they're tender to the touch. To make the process easier, cover your ribs shortly after the meat has reached a core temp of nearly 160 degrees Fahrenheit. Temp in the core often exceeds 210 degrees Fahrenheit.

Remove the ribs from the grill & lay them aside for around 15-20 mins to rest & cool while nicely tented in Al foil. Remove your ribs into two long pieces & serve them fresh or cut the meat off the bones & cube it for additional indulgence.

1.24 Sweet Mandarin Meatloaf

Total Time: 2 hrs 30 Mins, Servings: 6
Ingredients
2 lb. Ground Beef Lean
Twelve pieces Peppered Bacon
1 large Onion, Diced
6 Garlic clove, Minced
1 large Diced Red Pepper
1 c Breadcrumbs
2 Large Eggs
2 tsp Beef Rub Pit Boss
Milk, 2/3 c
1 tsp Worcestershire Sauce
1/2 c Chopped Cilantro
Orange Sauce (Mandarin) 1/3 c
Instructions
Combine the ground beef in a wide mixing bowl & put it aside. In a pan, cook till the bacon bits become finely browned. Remove the bacon with the slotted spoon & set it aside.

Remove all except 2 tbsps of bacon grease from the skillet. In a medium bowl, combine the pepper, salt, onion, & garlic. Continue to sauté till the onion becomes translucent.

Toss the beef mince with breadcrumbs, chopped cilantro, eggs, Worcestershire sauce, Pit Boss Beef Scrub, milk, & Mandarin sauce. Stir everything up well to ensure that everything is well combined.

Refrigerate the beef mix for roughly 2 hrs after wrapping it. With the meat, make a large circle.

Preheat your Pit Boss at 225°F for around 15 mins with the cover covered till ready to use. If the Special Smoke is available, use it for the finest flavor. Place each loaf on the cooling rack placed on top of an Al foil-lined baking sheet.

1 hr of vaping over Pit Boss with its lid closed. After 1 hr of smoking over your Pit Boss, cook until the meatloaf's core temp reaches 160° F on an immediate thermometer.

Allow the meatloaf to rest for around 15-20 mins before scrubbing with additional chopped cilantro. After slicing, serve warm.

1.25 Smoked Beef Cheek Tacos
Total Time: 6 hrs 20 Mins, Servings: 8
Ingredients
3 lb. Trimmed Beef Cheeks
Meat Cow BBQ Scrub
Eighteen oz. Broth or Beef Stock
1 Head of Garlic
1 White Quartered Onion
Twenty Small Corn Tortillas
1 Bunch Cilantro
1 small Chopped White Onion
Cotija Cheese
Lime Slices Fresh
Instructions
Trim some excess fat from the beef thighs. Tacos are more fun to consume.
Holy Cow Meat Church BBQ Rub can be used sparingly, mostly on trimmed buttocks. Enable for almost 15 mins for adhesion.
Set the Pit Boss to 275° F, then preheat about 15 mins with the lid closed when you're ready to cook.
Smoke the buttocks for 2-2 1/2 hrs immediately onto your grill grate. There's no need to spritz; all you need is a fine, thick smoke. The core temperature must be almost 160° F.
Place the cheeks in a half-size steam pan until they've hit a pleasant color. Pour the braising sauce on the cheeks, along with the onions and garlic. In the tub, you should have around 1" of oil. Make sure the buttocks aren't fully underwater. Place the pan back onto your grill for another 4-5 hrs. During the cooking process, flip once. They must be willing to be stabbed with a fork.
Adjust Pit Boss to 200° F, cover with tape, then look back the next morning if you'd like to smoke them overnight.
Cover with onions & cilantro and serve on the corn tortillas. If required, top with fresh limes and Cotija cheese.

1.26 Smoked Brisket
Total Time: 9 Hrs 15 Mins, Servings: 8
Ingredients
2 tbsp. Garlic Powder
2 tbsp Onion Powder
2 tbsp. Paprika
2 tsp Chili Powder
Kosher Salt or Jacobsen Salt, 1/3 c
Coarse Ground, Divided, Black Pepper, 1/3 c
1 Whole (12-14 Lb) Packer Brisket, Trimmed
Beef Broth, 1 ½ c
Instructions
Preheat your Pit Boss at 225°F with its lid closed for approximately 15 mins when prepared to roast. Use the Super Smoke if it's available for the greatest flavor.
Solve the Issue: Combine kosher salt, onion powder, chili powder, paprika, garlic powder, & pepper in a medium bowl. All sides of a brisket may be rubbed with the rub.
Place your brisket on your grill grate. Cook for around 5-6 hrs, or till the brisket reaches a core temp of 160°F. As soon as your brisket reaches a core temp of 160°F, remove this from your grill.
Wrap the meat in Al foil twice & fill the foil packet with beef broth. Return your brisket to a grill and cook for the next 3 hrs, or unless the core temp hits 204°F.

Remove from grill, unwrap the foil, and set aside for around 15 mins to rest. Serve along with a slice of wheat.

1.27 Beer-Braised Corned Beef & Irish Vegetables
Total Time: 7 Hrs 5 Mins, Servings: 6
Ingredients
4 lb. Beef brisket Corned
1 tbsp Brown Sugar
1 tbsp. Pickling Spice
1/2 medium Onion, Chopped
4 Garlic clove Smashed or Minced
Twelve oz. Guinness Beer
Peeled Carrots & Sliced in ¾-Inch Slices 4
1 lb. Red Potatoes Small, Halved, Washed
Cabbage Head sliced Into Wedges 1/2
1 tsp Fresh Thyme
Fresh Slice Parsley
Instructions
When you're all set to cook, warm the Pit Boss at 180°F for approximately 15 mins with its lid closed. Use the Super Smoke if it's available for the greatest flavor.
Place your BBQ beef brisket over the grill & let it smoke for around 3 hrs.
After 3 hrs, raise the Pit Boss temp to 250°F and prepare for approximately 15 mins.
Combine the brown sugar, garlic cloves, pickling spice, corned meat, & onion in a large saucepan.
Fill the bottle with Guinness. Securely cover your pan & cook for around 4-5 hrs, or unless the meat is cooked. Flip your brisket halfway through the cooking duration.
Simmer the broccoli, potatoes, sliced carrots, & thyme for approximately 1 hr, or unless the brisket gets done, then cover & cook for another 30 mins to 1 hr, or unless the vegetables are fork-tender.
Allow your meat to settle for nearly 10 mins before slicing & serving.

1.28 Roasted Santa Maria Tri-Tip
Total Time: 1 Hr 15 Mins, Servings: 4
Ingredients
1 Onion, Roughly Chopped
3 tbsp. Garlic, Chopped
1 bunch Chopped Thyme
Balsamic Vinegar, 1/4 c
1 tbsp Onion Powder
1 tbsp Garlic Powder
Cayenne Pepper, ¼ tsp
Pepper Flakes, ¼ tsp
1/2 c Olive Oil
Salt & Pepper
Beef Tri-Tip Roast (2-1/2 Lb)
1 Red Onion, Finely Diced
1 Jalapeño, Finely Diced
3 Roma Tomatoes, Cored & Finely Diced
1 bunch Cilantro, Roughly Chopped
2 Limes, Juiced
Salt & Pepper
Instructions
Combine all your marinade ingredients in a wide mixing bowl & whisk thoroughly. In a container, apply your marinade to the tri-tip. Freeze for nearly 24 hrs or up to three days after placing this in the fridge.
Preheat your Pit Boss at 165°F for approximately 15 mins with top closed till ready to use.
Remove your tri-tip from the marinade & discard it. Season the tri-tip with pepper and salt, then leave aside for approximately 10 mins.

To smoke your tri-tip, place it over the grill for approximately 90 mins.

In a wide mixing bowl, combine the following ingredients for Pico-de-Gallo. Simply combine all the ingredients in a standard size mixing bowl with some lime juice & salt. Remove the baking sheet from the heat & put it aside.

Remove your tri-tip from Pit Boss & preheat for around 15 mins at 500°F with its lid closed.

Return your tri-tip to a Pit Boss & sear for approximately 10 mins on each side till it reaches a core temp of 125° F.

After taking your tri-tip from the grill, let it cool for approximately 10 mins. Serve with pico-de-Gallo & pieces sliced against the grain.

1.29 Rosemary Prime Rib

Total Time: 1 Hr 10Mins, Servings: 8
Ingredients
8 lb. Whole Rib-Eye Roast
4 tbsp. Olive Oil
4 tbsp. Tri-Color Peppercorns
3 whole Rosemary Sprigs
3 whole Thyme Sprigs
1/2 cup Garlic, Minced
1/2 cup Jacobsen Salt Co. Cherrywood Smoked Salt
Instructions
Set your Pit Boss to SMOKE & keep its lid open for around 5-10 mins. The grill was then turned up to HIGH.

Using a sharp knife, cut each rib loin into half. Both halves must be cooked over high heat using olive oil when they're a nice dark golden color.

Remove the leaves from rosemary & thyme springs. In a large dish, combine cinnamon, rosemary, thyme, broken peppercorns, & garlic.

Olive oil & the rub mix should be rubbed into a rib loin. Gently massage it onto the meat to help it stick.

Roast for around 20-30 mins at max heat, then reduce to 300°F & roast for the next 30-40 mins.

Remove all meat from your Pit Boss & set it aside for nearly 20 mins till ready to slice.

1.30 Smoked Corned Beef & Cabbage

Total Time: 5 Hr 20 Mins, Servings: 6
Ingredients
1 (3-5 Lb) Beef Brisket Corned
1 Chicken Stock
Twelve oz. Beer
Garlic Salt, ¼ tsp
1/2 c Butter
2 c Baby Carrots
1 lb. Fingerling or Baby Potatoes
1 Cabbage Head
2 tbsp. Dill, Fresh Chopped
Instructions
Allow your corned beef to soak into water for around 8 hrs, changing the water every 2 hrs.

Preheat your Pit Boss at 180°F, then cook for around 15 mins with its lid closed.

Remove your brisket from the water & pat this dry. Stick straight onto your grill grate & smoke for approximately 2 hrs.

After taking this brisket from your grill, put it within a roasting pan. Preheat your grill at 325°F with the lid covered.

Season your brisket with some spice packet before covering it into chicken stock & black beer.

Wrap your roasting pan with foil & place it over the stove. Cook for around 2 hrs or till the meat becomes fork-tender.

Remove all foil from the roasting pan & place the potatoes & carrots inside. Vegetables & meat may be seasoned with garlic, salt & butter slices.

Cover with foil & cook for a further hr, or until carrots & potatoes are just tender. Cover & cook on your grill for approximately 20 mins.

After taking the veggies from the pan, put them into a dish or over-serving plate. Serve with cabbage, potatoes, carrots, & sliced meat. Garnish with some fresh dill & thyme, if desired.

1.31 Diva Q's Herb-Crusted Prime Rib

Total Time: 20 Mins, Servings: 4
Ingredients
Rosemary Leaves, Fresh, ¼ c
Parsley Leaves, Fresh Flat-Leaf, ¼ c
Minced Garlic, ¼ c
Canola Oil, ¼ c
3 tbsp Dijon Mustard
2 tbsp. Black Pepper Finely Ground
2 tbsp. Kosher Salt
1 (5-7 Lb) Bone-In Prime-Rib Roast
Instructions
Combine salt, garlic, mustard, canola oil, rosemary, parsley, & pepper in the food processor. Pulse till all your ingredients are combined & the herbs have been finely chopped.

Using a pastry brush, coat your prime rib with some spice mix. Chill your prime rib for around 4 hrs, open within the refrigerator.

Preheat your Pit Boss at 250°F with its lid covered for approximately 15 mins.

Put the bone-in prime rib on your grill, bone-side down. Roast beef for medium-regular roasting, which takes around 5 hrs. Take the core temp every 45 mins after the 2-hr mark.

Remove all your prime ribs from your grill, cover with foil, & let rest for around 15 mins until slicing.

1.32 Garlic Parmesan Grilled Filet Mignon

Total Time: 25 Mins, Servings: 2
Ingredients
4 Mignon Steaks Filet
1 tsp Salt
1 tsp Black Pepper
1 tsp Garlic Salt
1 c Parmesan Cheese
4 Garlic
1 tbsp. Dijon Mustard
Instructions
Preheat your grill at high for approximately 15 mins with its lid covered.

As your grill heats up, season your fillets using salt, garlic salt, & pepper. Mince your garlic & carefully slice your Parmesan into a different container, then combine the two.

Once your grill has achieved temp, put your fillets on it & cook for around 4 mins on each side. Brush your fillets using Dijon mustard after 8 mins, then dip them within Parmesan cheese & minced garlic mix before bringing them to your grill for another 1-2 mins, or till the cheese completely melted.

Allow 5 mins before serving.

1.33 Smoked Texas BBQ Brisket

Total Time: 10 Hrs 15 Mins, Servings: 8
Ingredients
1 (14-18 Lb) Packer Brisket
Meat Cow BBQ Scrub
Meat Gospel BBQ Scrub
Instructions
Trim down fat from all sides of your brisket, being careful not to puncture the meat too deeply. Trim the excess fat off your

arms. Trim your fat side of the brisket to one-fourth of an inch broad.

Meat Church Holy Cow Rub may be applied evenly on both sides. If necessary, apply a light layer of Gospel Meat Holy Church Rub. Allow your brisket to rest at room temp for around 20-30 mins throughout the seasoning process.

Preheat your Pit Boss at 275°F with its lid closed for approximately 15 mins.

Place brisket on your grill grate. Cook for around 5-6 hrs, or till the internal temp reaches 165°F.

Take the brisket out of the pan & wrap it tightly with Brown Pit Boss Paper. Return a wrapped brisket to your grill & cook for around 3-4 hrs, or till the internal temp reaches 204°F.

As soon as your brisket achieves 204°F, remove it from your grill & set it aside to rest for around 30 mins. Unwrap your brisket & cut it against the grain.

1.34 Braised Mediterranean Beef Brisket

Total Time: 1 Day 12 Hrs, Servings: 8
Ingredients
3 tbsp. Dried Rosemary
2 tbsp Cumin Seeds, Ground
2 tbsp. Dried Coriander
2 tbsp. Dried Oregano
2 tsp Ground Cinnamon
1/2 tsp Salt
8 lb. Beef Brisket
1 c Beef Stock
Instructions

Combine all spices & coat your brisket well. Put bubble wrap on top & set away. Chill your covered brisket for around 12-24 hrs. Allow plenty of time to prepare the meal.

Preheat your grill at 180°F with its lid closed for approximately 15 mins till its meat is ready to roast.

Put the brisket on your grill grate, attach the probe of the thermometer, & smoke for around 4 hrs.

After 4 hrs, preheat your grill for 250°F.

Remove brisket from your grill & wrap it into foil with some beef stock till it reaches 160°F into the center. The probe of the thermometer must not be removed. Return a foiled brisket to your grill & cook till it hits 204°F.

Remove the brisket from the grill & wrap it into a foil for nearly 30 mins.

1.35 Smoked Tri-Tip

Total Time: 1 Hr 5 Mins, Servings: 6
Ingredients
Pepper, 1/8 c
1 (3-5 Lb) Tri-Tip
Salt, 1/8 c
Instructions

Preheat your Pit Boss at 225°F with its lid covered for approximately 15 mins.

Season with some salt & pepper. Season your meat using a liberal quantity of pepper & salt mixture on all sides.

Put tri-tip straight on your grill grate & cook for around 60-90 mins, or until the core temp reaches 130°F.

As soon as the tri-tip achieves 130°F, remove this from your grill & wrap it into the foil.

Preheat your Pit Boss at 500°F & cook for around 15 mins with its lid closed.

Remove the foil from your tri-tip & sear for around 4 mins on all sides till your grill reaches temp.

Remove that meat from your grill & set it aside for around 10-15 mins to settle. To serve, cut the meat against the grain.

1.36 Sweetheart Steak

Total Time: 15 Mins, Servings: 2
Ingredients
20 oz. Snake Boneless, River Farms
Rib or Strip Steak Butterflied
2 oz. Jacobsen Salt or Sea Salt
2 tsp Black Pepper
2 tbsp Raw Dark Finely Chopped Chocolate
1/2 tbsp. Olive Oil Extra-Virgin
Instructions

Draw a large heart on a piece of cardboard & shape it to the size of the meat that you've selected. Cut the heart shape out of the cardboard & shape the meat in the heart.

Combine your ingredients over the sliced beef.

Preheat your grill at 450°F, then shut the cover for around 10-15 mins.

Grill these steaks for around 5-7 mins on all sides, or till done to your liking. Turn off the heat on your grill. Leave for a 5-min rest time after each set.

1.37 Grilled Bacon-Wrapped Hot Dogs

Total Time: 35 Mins, Servings: 8
Ingredients
12 Whole Hot Dogs
8 oz. Cheese, Cheddar/Colby
12 sliced Bacon
12 Buns Hot Dog
Instructions

8 cheese slices, sliced. Cut your hot dogs in half & fill them all with a piece of cheese, leaving a "hinge" on one side.

Make a loop with every piece of bacon over all hot dogs & secure with toothpicks.

Preheat your Pit Boss at 350°F & keep its lid closed until you are all set to roast for approximately 15 minutes.

Cook your bacon-wrapped hot dogs for around 20-30 mins on your grill grate, or till the cheese has melted & the bacon had crisped up.

Serve immediately with your favorite toppings on the buns.

1.38 Smoked Porterhouse Steak

Total Time: 55 Mins, Servings: 2
Ingredients
4 tbsp. Butter, Melted
2 tbsp. Worcestershire Sauce
2 tsp Dijon Mustard
1 tsp Pit Boss Coffee Scrub
40 oz. Steak, Porterhouse
Instructions

Preheat your grill at 180°F with its lid closed for approximately 15 mins.

When combined, the butter, Worcestershire sauce, & mustard should be whisked together. Brush the mix on all sides of the steaks. All sides of the steak may be rubbed with Coffee Pit Boss Rub.

Smoke your steaks approximately 30 mins after placing them on your grill grate. Using tongs, transfer the steaks onto the plate.

Preheat your grill after raising the temp to high. Set the temp around 500°F if required for the best results. Re-drizzle your steaks with the butter & Worcestershire sauce mix.

Put your steaks on your grill grate till the temp reaches the desired level. For the medium-small, cook to a core temp of 135°F, adding several mins on all sides. Leave the steaks to cool for around 5 mins before serving.

1.39 BBQ Brisket with Pit Boss Coffee Rub

Total Time: 9 Hrs 15 Mins, Servings: 8
Ingredients
15 lb. Packer Brisket
2 tbsp. Pit Boss Coffee Scrub
Water, 1 ½ cup
2 tbsp. Salt
Instructions
Remove any excess fat from your brisket, leaving a 1/4" cap on the base.
Mix the water, coffee rub, & salt in a big bowl till the salt is nearly dissolved. Per square inch, inject some coffee rub mix into your brisket. On the exterior, season your brisket with remaining rub & salt.
Preheat your Pit Boss to nearly 250°F for approximately 15 mins with the lid covered.
Place your brisket straight on a grill grate & cook for around 6 hrs, or till the core temp hits 160°F.
Cover your brisket with two layers of Al foil & water. Tie a tin foil tightly to keep all liquid confined. Raise the temp of your grill to 275°F. Cook for the next 3 hrs, or till the core temp hits 204°F.
Carve your brisket into small slices after removing it from your grill.

1.40 BBQ Burnt Ends

Total Time: 9 Hrs 10 Mins, Servings: 6
Ingredients
1 Cut Brisket (4-6 Lb)
2 c Beef Broth
12 oz. Pit Boss Texas BBQ Sauce, Spicy
Pit Boss Beef Scrub
Instructions
Preheat your Pit Boss at 250°F with its lid covered for approximately 15 mins.
Put the sauce & broth in a big bowl & set this aside. Rub the Beef Pit Boss Scrub over brisket point to remove any excess fat. Put brisket on your grill grate & cook till the core temp reaches 190°F. After removing that brisket from your grill, cut this into 1" cubes.
Toss these brisket cubes just with some sauce mix into a pan & cover with Al foil. Preheat your grill to its highest setting & cook this pan for around 1 hr.
After tossing in the burned ends, cook for the next hr.

1.41 Chef's Brisket

Total Time: 8 Hrs 10 Mins, Servings: 8
Ingredients
1 (12 Lb) Beef Brisket Whole Packer
Sea Salt Pure Kosher
2 tbsp Garlic Paste
2 tbsp. Onion Powder
Black Pepper
Instructions
Combine the garlic, salt, onion powder, & pepper in a wide dish. Season the meat with some salt & pepper to taste. Refrigerate for at least 8 hrs or overnight.
Preheat your Pit Boss at 225°F with its lid closed for approximately 15 mins.
Put brisket on your grill grate. Smoke your brisket for around 4-5 hrs, till it hits an internal temp of 160-165° F.
After taking cooked brisket from your grill, wrap this in butcher paper. Keep smoking at 225°F for the next 3-4 hrs, or till the brisket reaches a core temp of 203°F, for a total smoke & cook time of 8-10 hrs.

After removing butcher paper-covered brisket from your grill, allow for 1 hr of the rest period.
After the brisket has cooled, slice it into pieces.

1.42 Korean BBQ Short Ribs

Total Time: 20 Mins, Servings: 2
Ingredients
1/2 c Soy Sauce
1/2 c Water
2 tbsp. Rice Vinegar or White Vinegar
2 tbsp. Brown Sugar
1 tbsp. Honey or Granulated Sugar
2 clove Garlic Minced
1 Pear, Peeled Ripe Cored & Coarsely Chopped
One-piece Fresh Ginger, Peeled & Sliced in the Coins
1 Scallion Trimmed & Coarsely Chopped
Sesame Oil 2 tsp
1 tsp Pit Boss Beef Scrub
Beef Ribs, Crosscut 1 ½ lb
Instructions
To combine the pear, garlic, Beef Rub, granulated sugar, soy sauce, ginger, Pit Boss, brown sugar, water, vinegar, scallion, & sesame oil, pulse the ingredients inside a mixer several times.
Arrange your beef ribs in a wide baking dish. Place the meat in some marinade & turn it to coat all sides. Freeze for several hrs in an airtight container.
Preheat your Pit Boss at 500°F for approximately 15 mins with its lid closed.
Remove the meat from the marinade, then discard all marinade.
Cook your meat for around 2-3 mins on all sides over your grill grate.

1.43 Beef Satay

Total Time: 20 Mins, Servings: 6
Ingredients
2 lb. Iron Steak Black Flat
1 bottle Carne of Choice Asada Marinade
2 clove Garlic, Minced
2 Scallions, Chopped
Peanut Sauce
Crushed Peanuts, ¼ c
2 Limes
Instructions
Using a sharp knife, chop your steak into slices on the sharp diagonal. Pouring the Asada Carne marinade over your meat, stir in some garlic & scallions. Put those in a wide mixing bowl.
Remove this meat from the marinade & discard any remaining onion & garlic. The bamboo skewer must be threaded with each piece.
Preheat your Pit Boss at Higher for approximately 15 mins with its lid closed.
Grill satays for around 3-4 mins on all sides, turning once.
Put the satays over top of the chopped avocado into this serving plate. Meanwhile, on one side of a plate, put a small dish of peanut sauce. Serve with some lime wedges on the side.

1.44 Pit Boss BBQ Double Decker Taco

Total Time: 35 Mins, Servings: 6
Ingredients
2 c Sour Cream
16 oz. Refried Beans
2 c Beef Brisket
2 c Pulled Pork

10 Flour Tortillas
10 Crisp Taco Shell
3 Guacamole
2 c Tomato, Salsa
1 c Diced Red Onion
1/2 c Finely Chopped Cilantro
Cheddar Cheese, 1 ½ c
Instructions
Preheat your grill at 325°F & cover for approximately 15 mins till the food begins to cook.
In a wide mixing bowl, combine the sour cream &
refried beans. Place a tray in a pre-heated grill.
Put the leftover brisket & pork in the double layer of foil on your grill. Warm both beans & meats in on your for approximately 25 mins.
To prepare double-decker tacos, add a thin layer of beans over your soft taco shell and tie it across the crispy taco shell's outside.
Toss your brisket & pork into those crisp taco shells with cheese, salsa, guacamole, sour cream, cilantro,
& onion for taste.

1.45 Cocoa Crusted Grilled Flank Steak
Total Time: 25 Mins, Servings: 6
Ingredients
1 tbsp. Cocoa Powder
2 tsp Chili Powder
1 tsp Chili Powder Chipotle
1/2 tsp Garlic Powder
1/2 tsp Onion Powder
Brown Sugar, 1 ½ tbsp
1 tbsp. Kosher Salt
1/2 tsp Black Pepper
1 tbsp Cumin
1 tbsp Smoked Paprika
Olive Oil
Instructions
In a wide mixing bowl, add smoked paprika, brown sugar, cocoa powder, kosher salt, cumin, chipotle, garlic powder, black pepper, chili powder, & onion powder to prepare your cocoa rub.
Brush all sides of flank steak using cocoa rub after sprinkling it with some olive oil.
Preheat the grill to its highest setting for approximately 15 mins with its lid covered.
Cook your flank steaks for 3-5 mins per foot over your grill grate, or till an immediate thermometer detects 135° F.
Allow your flank steak to settle for approximately 10-15 mins after taking it from your grill to allow all juices to return to the meat.
Slice the meat against some grain on some sharp diagonal to serve.

1.46 Tin Foil Dinner
Total Time: 1 Hr 10 Mins, Servings: 4
Ingredients
1 lb. Stew Meat
1 tsp Fish Sauce
1 tbsp. Worcestershire Sauce
Salt & Pepper
1 tbsp. Pit Boss Veggie Scrub
1 small Red Onion, Chopped
2 Green Chopped Bell Pepper
1 clove Garlic, Minced
2 whole Russet Potatoes Peeled & Cubed
4 Thyme Sprig
Eight tbsp. Butter, Sliced in the Cubes
Instructions
Preheat your Pit Boss at 350° F for approximately 15 mins with the top closed.
Place your stew meat in a large mixing bowl. In a mixing bowl, combine Worcestershire sauce & fish sauce. To taste, season with salt, pepper, & Vegetable Pit Boss Rub. To ensure an even delivery, re-mix.
4 ripped pieces of foil laid out on the flat surface. Distribute your potatoes evenly among the four pieces of foil, then add the bell pepper, stew meat, onion, potato, garlic, & thyme to complete. Add 2 tbsp butter to every packet
Fold that foil in half & wrap it across the piece firmly.
Put the packets over the sheet tray & grill. Cook for around 45 mins to an hr, or till potatoes become tender & stew meat is cooked through.
Remove the package from the grill, open it, then, if required, sprinkle it with some herbs.

1.47 Smoked Rib-Eyes with Bourbon Butter
Total Time: 1 Hr 10Mins, Servings: 4
Ingredients
1/2 c Butter
2 Minced clove Garlic
2 tbsp. Bourbon
1 tbsp. Green Onions or Minced Chives
1 tbsp. Minced Parsley
1/2 tsp Salt
1/2 tsp Black Pepper Ground
4 Rib-Eye Steaks (1" Thick)
Pit Boss Prime-Rib Scrub
Instructions
To prepare a Bourbon Butter, whisk together the salt, butter, parsley, garlic, chives, bourbon, and pepper in a large mixing bowl. Make the butter ahead of time and keep it refrigerated till ready to use.
Preheat the Pit Boss at 180° F for 15 mins with the top closed. Use Super Smoke if it's available for the greatest flavor.
Season the steaks with a liberal amount of Pit Boss Prime-Rib Rub.
Place the steaks on the grill grate and cook for 1 hr.
Preheat the Pit Boss to 500° F and place the steaks on a plate. Return these steaks to the grill, turning once, until they reach a core temperature of 135° F for medium-rare, which should take about 6-8 mins each side once the grill is hot.
Place the steaks on a serving dish and top with a pat of bourbon butter right away.
Allow the meat to rest for 3 mins before eating.

1.48 Grilled Carne Asada with Grilled Peppers & Onions
Total Time: 40Mins, Servings: 4
Ingredients
1 c Light beer Mexican
1/2 c Chipotle Peppers
4 clove Garlic, Crushed
1 tbsp. Cumin
2 tbsp. Brown Sugar
2 tbsp. Salt
2 lb. Skirt Steak
1 Grapefruit, Sliced
1 Orange, Sliced
1 Lime, Sliced
2 Lemon, Sliced
2 Bell Green Pepper
2 Yellow Onions, Sliced
Cilantro
Guacamole

Cooked Rice
Beans
Instructions
In a medium baking dish, combine brown sugar, beer, garlic, chipotle pepper in adobo sauce, cumin, and salt. Make a thorough mix.
To seal the skirt steak, toss it in the marinade. Lemon slices should be placed on top of the skirt steak. Refrigerate for 1 hr or overnight marinating. Take the meat out of the marinade and blot it dry.
Preheat the oven to its highest setting for 10 to 15 mins with the lid closed.
Toss some bell peppers in olive oil and cook them right on the grill. Place the onion pieces next to the bell peppers and cook for 10-15 mins, or until the onions and peppers have softened and become a light brown hue.
Cook a skirt steak over a grill grate for 3 to 5 mins per side, or until the outside is finely browned and the internal temperature reaches 125° F for medium fresh. Remove off the grill and set aside for 5 to 10 mins to rest. Cut the meat into strips against the grain using a sharp knife
After removing the peppers and onions from the grill, cut them into strips.
Rice, sliced steak, and beans, as well as ginger, cilantro, and guacamole, are served alongside.

1.49 Reverse Seared Rib-Eye Caps
Total Time: 15 Mins, Servings: 4
Ingredients
Rib-Eye Cap, 1 ½ lb
2 tbsp. Pit Boss Coffee Scrub
2 tbsp. Pit Boss Beef Scrub
Instructions
Remove any excess silver skin and fat from the rib-
eye hat if necessary. Cut the cap into four pieces and wrap each piece into a steak. Tie it with butcher's string to keep it tight.
In a small dish, combine all the rubs. Brush the steaks generously with the rub mixture while the grill heats up.
Preheat the Pit Boss to 225°F for approximately 15 mins with the top closed. Use Super Smoke if it's available for the greatest flavor.
Place your steaks directly on the grill grate and smoke for 30 to 45 mins, or until they reach a core temperature of 120 degrees F.
After taking the steaks from the grill, set them aside to cool. Preheat the grill to 450 degrees Fahrenheit.
Over the grill grate, cook the stakes for 3-4 mins on each side or until the core temperature reaches 130°F.
Before serving, remove the steaks from the grill and set them aside to rest for 5 mins.

1.50 Beginner's Smoked Beef Brisket
Total Time: 30 Mins, Servings: 4
Ingredients
1 (6 Lb) Flat Cut Brisket, Trimmed
Pit Boss Beef Rub
2 c Beef Broth, Beer or Cola
Apple Cider Vinegar, Apple Cider or Apple Juice, ¼ c
2 tbsp. Worcestershire Sauce
Pit Boss Texas Spicy BBQ Sauce
Instructions
Preheat the Pit Boss to 180°F and keep the lid covered for 15 mins until ready to use.
All sides of the meat should be rubbed with Pit Boss Beef Scrub.
In a mixing basin, whisk together all the ingredients.
Place the brisket fat side down on the barbecue grate and smoke for 3-4 hrs, sprinkling with mop sauce every hr.
Raise the temperature of your grill to 225° F and cook for 6-8 hrs, or until an instant thermometer inserted into the thickest part of the meat reads 204° F.
After foiling the beef, let nearly 30 mins for it to rest. Using a small knife, cut the wood into pencil-width strips. On the side, there's BBQ sauce.

1.51 Not Your Mama's Meatloaf
Total Time: 2 hrs 15 Mins, Servings: 6
Ingredients
Meatloaf
1 c Breadcrumbs
1 c Milk
2 tbsp. Onion, Chopped
1/2 tsp Ground Sage
2 tsp Salt
2 Egg, Beaten
2 lb. Ground Beef
Ground Sausage, ¼ lb
1 c BBQ Sauce (Pit Boss 'Que)
1/2 c Apple Juice
Instructions
Preheat the Pit Boss to 225°F for approximately 15 mins with the top closed. Use Super Smoke if it's available for the greatest flavor.
In a mixing dish, combine the sage, breadcrumbs, onion, milk, and salt. Add the beaten eggs and mix well. In a large mixing bowl, thoroughly combine the ground beef and ground bacon. Form the mixture into a loaf by tightly wrapping it around the pan.
To cook the meatloaf, place it on a wire rack on the grill. Cook for another 2 hrs, or until an internal temperature of 160° F is reached.
To create the glaze, combine the Pit Boss' Que-Sauce and apple juice in a mixing bowl. Glaze the meatloaf within 20 mins of its preparation.
Allow the meatloaf to rest for 5-10 mins before slicing.

1.52 Grilled Tomahawk Steak
Total Time: 1 Hr 5 Mins
Cooking Time: 1 Hr
Servings: 4
Ingredients
2 large Tomahawk Steaks
2 tbsp. Kosher Salt
2 tbsp Black Pepper Ground
1 tbsp. Paprika
1/2 tbsp Garlic Powder
1/2 tbsp. Onion Powder
1/2 tbsp. Brown Sugar
1 tsp Ground Mustard
Cayenne Pepper, ¼ tsp
Instructions
In a small mixing bowl, combine both rub ingredients. When the grill is hot, season the steaks generously with the rub and set them aside.
Preheat the Pit Boss at 225° F for 15 mins with the top closed. Use Super Smoke if it's available for the greatest flavor.
Place your steaks directly on the grill grate and cook for 45 to 60 mins, or until the internal temperature reaches 120° F.
Remove the steaks from the grill and set them aside to rest on a cutting board.
Preheat your grill to 450 degrees Fahrenheit.
Cook the stakes directly over the grill grate for 7-10 mins on each side, or until the core temperature reaches 130° F.

Before serving, remove the steaks from the grill and set them aside to rest for 5 mins.

1.53 BBQ Brisket Reuben
Total Time: 55 Mins, Servings: 4
Ingredients
Twelve oz. Cooked Brisket
1/2 c BBQ Sauce, Pit Boss Apricot
1 tbsp. Canola Oil
1 medium Thinly Sliced Yellow Onion
1/2 Cabbage Shredded Heads
Vinegar Apple Cider, 1 ¼ c
1/2 c Beer
Water, ¼ c
1 tbsp Kosher Salt
1 tsp Caraway Seeds
Twelve pieces Rye Bread
Instructions
Set the temp to high, then preheat the skillet for 15 mins with the lid closed.
In a pan on the grill, heat the BBQ Brisket with Pit Boss Apricot Barbecue Sauce for 3-5 mins, or until cooked through. Keep the kraut mushy while it's cooking.
In a pan, heat some canola oil, then add the chopped onion and cook for 2 to 3 mins. Stir in the shredded cabbage for a further 2-3 mins, or until it starts to wilt.
Allow 5-10 mins for the liquid to reduce by half and the cabbage to be completely wilted and cooked through, sometimes stirring, after adding the other ingredients: salt, cider vinegar, water, beer, and caraway seeds.
Layer bread, Swiss cheese, brisket, dressing, kraut, then another bread layer to make the sandwich.

1.54 Beef Tenderloin with Tomato Vinaigrette
Total Time: 50 Mins, Servings: 6
Ingredients
1 whole Beef
Tenderloin Steaks
1 bottle Pit Boss Prime-Rib Scrub
Olive Oil Extra-Virgin, 2/3 c
Salt & Pepper
1 tsp Fresh Thyme
6 Tomatoes Plum
1 tsp Thyme, Minced
2 tbsp. Balsamic Vinegar
Instructions
Preheat the grill to 450°F and bake for 10-15 mins with the lid closed.
Tuck the narrow end of the tenderloin under the roast and secure it with the butcher's cord. After rubbing the beef with olive oil, season it with Prime Rib Scrub or salt and pepper. Place your meat on the shelf in the small roasting pan.
In a hot Pit Boss, roast for approximately 20 mins. Preheat the grill to 350 degrees Fahrenheit (180 degrees Celsius). Cook for another 20 mins, or until the desired doneness is achieved.
Allow for a 5-min rest period before slicing thinly. Serve with thyme sprigs as a garnish.
To make the vinaigrette, purée the tomatoes, balsamic vinegar, olive oil, and thyme leaves in a food processor or blender jar until smooth. Season to taste with salt and pepper or Pit Boss Prime-Rib Scrub.
In a gravy boat, serve the tenderloin with the sauce.

1.55 BBQ Beef Short Ribs
Total Time: 10 Hrs 15 Mins, Servings: 8
Ingredients
4 (4 Bone) Beef Rib Racks
1/2 c Pit Boss Beef Scrub
1 c Apple Juice
Instructions
Use paper towels to obtain a good grip, then pull the membrane off.
All sides of the ribs may be rubbed with Pit Boss Beef Scrub.
Preheat the Pit Boss to 225°F with the lid closed for approximately 15 mins when ready to roast.
Place the ribs on the grill grate bone-side down.
Cook for 8-10 hrs, or until the internal temperature reaches 205° F, mopping or spritzing every 60 mins.
After slicing between the ribs, serve immediately.

1.56 Teriyaki Beef Jerky
Total Time: 5 Hrs 15 Mins, Servings: 8
Ingredients
3 c Soy Sauce
2 c Brown Sugar
3 cloves of Garlic
1-piece Ginger Knob Peeled and Chopped
1 tbsp Sesame Oil
4 lb. Skirt Steak
Instructions
Combine all the ingredients, except the steak, in a food processor or blender and mix until smooth.
Remove the excess fat from the steak before slicing it against the grain in 1/4-inch-long pieces. Combine the marinade and the meat in a large zip lock bag. Refrigerate the bag for nearly 12 hrs or 24 hrs in a tub.
Set the temperature to smoke and preheat for approximately 5 mins before cooking.
Set the Timberline grill to 160° F and press the Super Smoke button. Place the steaks on the grill with a little gap between them. The cooking time is about 5 hrs.
Remove the jerky from the grill and place it on a plate. It's ideal for serving it hot or at room temperature.

1.57 Sunday Supper Beef Roast
Total Time: 3 Hrs 5 Mins, Servings: 6
Ingredients
1 (3 To 3-1/2 Lb) Beef Round, Sirloin Roast or Rump
3 tbsp. Olive Oil Extra Virgin Vegetable Oil
Pit Boss Prime-Rib Scrub
2 c Beef Broth
1 large Potato, Russet
2 Carrots Peeled & sliced
2 Celery Sliced Stalks
1 small Onion Sliced
2 Sprigs Thyme
Instructions
Season the steaks on both sides with pepper and salt, then set aside for 20 mins at room temperature.
Preheat your Pit Boss to 500°F and leave the lid closed for approximately 15 mins. Preheat your grill grate by putting a pan large enough to hold this steak directly on top of it.
Place the steaks over the hottest part of your grill and cover for approximately 5 mins.
After 5 mins, remove the lid and add the butter to the pan; it should melt nearly immediately.
In the skillet, the grill side of the steaks should be facing up. Cook for 5-7 mins, brushing your steaks with butter every min. Cook until the internal temperature reaches 125-130 degrees Fahrenheit.
Remove the steaks from the pan and put them aside for 10 mins to rest. Drizzle the remaining butter over the steaks and serve.

1.58 Mexican Grilled Skirt Steak Tacos
Total Time: 25Mins, Servings: 6
Ingredients
1 c Sour Cream
Nine whole Juiced Lime Wedge
Trimmed Skirt Steak, 2 ½ lb
2 tbsp. Pit Boss Cajun Scrub
6 Flour Tortillas or Whole Corn, Warmed Twelve
1 medium Red Onion Thinly Sliced
1 c Mexican Cheese Shredded
Cilantro Leaves Minced, ¼ c
Instructions
Preheat your grill to 350 degrees Fahrenheit for 15 mins with the lid closed.
In a shallow mixing dish, combine sour cream and the juice from three lime wedges. Maintain a safe distance.
Place a steak on a rimmed baking sheet. 6 lime wedges should be squeezed on both sides of the skirt steaks. The steaks should be evenly coated with Pit Boss Cajun Scrub. Grill for 4-5 mins on each side, turning once, or until the steak reaches your desired doneness.
Allow resting on the cutting board for approximately 2 mins. Wrap the wood in "Cut in Half" strips, on warm tortillas, top with sour lime cream, onion, cilantro, and cheese.

1.59 Grilled Skirt Steak Bulgogi Bowls
Total Time: 40 Mins, Serves: 4
Ingredients
1/2 Pear, Peeled
1/4 Cup Soy Sauce
2 Clove Garlic
1 Inch, Fresh Ginger, Peeled
1 Tbsp Gochujang
1 Tbsp Brown Sugar
1 Tbsp Sesame Oil
2 Lb Skirt Steak, Trimmed
2 Cup Cooked Rice
1 Cup Kimchi
1/2 Cup Thinly Sliced Cucumber
4 Whole Fried Eggs
Sesame Seeds, For Garnish
Thinly Sliced Green Onion, For Garnish
Instructions
In your blender, purée all the marinade ingredients till smooth. Pour the marinade over the skirt steak into a resealable bag. Seal this bag after squeezing out enough air. Refrigerate for around 1 hr or almost four hrs, depending on how long you want to marinate.
In a big bowl, combine all the ingredients for pickled carrots & leave them on the side to pickle for almost 1 hr.
When you are all set to cook, preheat the Pit Boss to 450°F & cook for around 15 mins with the lid covered.
Remove your skirt steak out of the marinade & set it straight on your grill grate, where it will be the hottest. Cook for around 15-20 mins, till caramelized & cooked through, turning halfway through. Remove the steaks from the grill & put them aside for settle.
Divide the kimchi, cucumbers, rice, & carrots into four bowls to make the bowls. Add an egg fried to every bowl and top with some sesame seeds & scallions. Top all bowls with thinly sliced skirt steak cut against the grain.

1.60 Pit Boss Smash Burger
Total Time: 25 Mins, Serves: 4
Ingredients
1 Lb Ground Beef, 80% Lean
1 Tsp Salt
1/2 Tsp Black Pepper
Pit Boss Beef Rub
Butter, Melted
2 Medium White Onions, Thinly Sliced
4 Slices American Cheese
4 Potato Buns, Or White Burger Buns
Ketchup And Mustard, For Serving
2 Cup Shredded Iceberg Lettuce
Sliced Pickles, For Serving
Instructions
Season your ground beef with some Beef Rub or salt & pepper, then shape into balls.
Set the Pit Boss to 450°F & preheat for around 15 mins with the lid covered when you're all set to cook. While your grill preheats, put a skillet (cast iron) on its grate.
Using butter or fat, oil your grill. To begin caramelizing the onions, place them on the grill's corner. Put burger balls over a heated grill & squash them down using a spatula till they're thin & flat.
Cook till the burgers have a nice brown color.
Flip your burger carefully, sprinkle some onions over the top, & top with cheese. Butter the buns & cook them on the grill.
Remove the burgers & buns from your grill & assemble the burgers in the following order: bottom bun, chosen sauce, lettuce, caramelized onions & cheese, lettuce layer, house pickles, extra sauce, & top bun.

1.61 Breakfast Brisket Hash Recipe
Total Time: 25 Mins, Serves: 4
Ingredients
3 Tbsp Canola Oil
1/2 Cup Yellow Onion, Diced
1/2 Cup Green Bell Pepper, Diced
1/2 Cup Red Bell Pepper, Diced
1 Clove Garlic, Minced
2 Cup Hash brown Potatoes, Cooked
2 Cup Brisket, Cooked and Shredded
3 Whole Eggs
Salt And Pepper
Instructions
To pre-heat the grill, set a skillet on it. When you're all set to cook, turn on the Pit Boss & preheat it for 10-15 mins at 450°F.
In a skillet, heat the oil, peppers, & onion till they are transparent.
Cook for the next 3 mins after adding the garlic. Cook the potatoes, brisket, & eggs together. Cook for approximately 10 mins, or unless the brisket should be well heated. Season with some salt & pepper, then toss to combine.

1.62 Loaded Reuben Fries with Fontina Cheese
Total Time: 15 Mins, Serves: 6
Ingredients
1 Cup Smoked Corned Beef, Leftover, Shredded into Bite-Size Pieces
2 Tbsp Butter
2 Clove Garlic, Minced
2 Tbsp Shallot, Minced
2 Tbsp All-Purpose Flour
2 Cup Chicken Stock
1 Tbsp Dijon Mustard
Salt And Pepper
1/2 Cup Fontina Cheese
4 Cup Crispy Fries
1/2 Cup Thousand Island Dressing
Instructions
To prepare the gravy, start by whisking together the

cornstarch, salt, & pepper. In the sauté pan on medium-high heat, melt the butter. Sauté for approximately a min & a half, or till the garlic & shallot are transparent and soft. Cook, constantly stirring, till the flour is aromatic. While whisking, slowly pour in the chicken stock, making sure there are no lumps.
Bring to the low simmer with the Dijon, salt, & pepper. Allow simmering for 5-10 mins, or till gravy coats the slotted spoon. Remove from fire & stir in the warmed corned meat & fontina cheese.
Put the fries over a serving plate & pour some gravy on them. Sauerkraut & Island dressing are served on top.

1.63 3-2-1 BBQ Beef Cheeks

Total Time: 6 hrs 10 Mins, Serves: 8
Ingredients
2 (2 Lb) Beef Cheeks, Silver skin Trimmed
Pit Boss Beef Rub
1/4 Cup Liquid of Choice (Beef Stock, Dark Beer, Etc.)
2 Tbsp Honey, Brown Sugar or Other Sweetener
Instructions
Please ensure the silver skin on your beef cheeks is removed. Season with some Beef Rub Pit Boss generously.
Set the temperature to 180°F & preheat for around 15 mins with the lid covered when you are all set to cook.
Put the beef cheeks straight on your grill grate & cook for approximately 3 hrs, or till they hit a core temp of 165°F. Remove the cheeks from the grill & set them in a shallow rimmed baking pan.
Raise the temp of the grill to 225°F.
Combine liquid & sweetener in a shallow bowl & whisk until sugar is dissolved. Return these cheeks to your grill for another 2 hrs after pouring the mix into a baking dish.
Cover the cheeks with foil after removing them from the grill. Cook for the next hr on the grill, or till the core temp reaches 205°F.
Leave the gas to escape by removing the pan from your grill. Before slicing or shredding, cover in foil once again and set aside for around 30 mins.

1.64 Grilled Ribeye Shish Kabobs with Chimichurri Sauce

Total Time: 35 Mins, Servings: 6
Ingredients
2 c Packed Flat-Leaf Parsley Leaves
Fresh Oregano, ¼ c
6 Garlic clove
Black Pepper
Kosher Salt
1 c Olive Oil
Vinegar Red Wine, ¼ c
1 tsp red pepper flakes
Rib-Eye Steaks (1-Inch-Thick) 3 whole Cut into Cubes
Quartered 2 Small Red Onion
2 c Cherry Tomatoes
Instructions
Finely chop oregano, parsley, and garlic in a mixing dish. Combine the vinegar, olive oil, and pepper flakes in a mixing bowl. After seasoning with salt and pepper, set aside on the counter.
Using wood skewers, skewer rib-eye, skewer onions, and skewer tomatoes before serving. After brushing with olive oil, season with pepper and salt.
Preheat the oven too high for approximately 15 mins before serving. Place the skewers on the grill while it is still hot. Cook for 8 mins on one side, then turn and cook for another 8 mins. Remove from the grill and serve with chimichurri on the side. Serve the chimichurri that was left over.

1.65 Asian-Style Grilled Rib-Eye Steak

Total Time: 2 Hr 10 Mins, Servings: 8
Ingredients
1 tbsp. Dry Mustard
1 tbsp. Brown Sugar
Ten Minced Anchovy Fillets
1 tsp Garlic Powder
2 tsp Onion Powder
2 tsp Black Pepper
2 tbsp. Warm Water
4 (1-Half" Thick) Rib-Eye Steaks
Instructions
In a dish, combine all marinade ingredients to create a paste. After spreading the paste to all surfaces of the steaks, refrigerate for nearly 2 hrs.
Preheat the oven to 500°F and leave the lid covered for 15 mins until ready to cook.
Place the steaks on the grill and cook for 4-5 mins on each side, or until the meat reaches a temperature of 135° F. Remove the steaks from the grill and put them aside for 10 mins rest before serving.
Top with grilled bok choy and grilled garlic if desired.

1.66 Grilled Carne Asada Skirt Steak

Total Time: 60 Mins, Servings: 6
Ingredients
Marinade
3 Oranges, Juiced
2 Lemons, Juiced
4 Limes, Juiced
3 clove Garlic, Minced
1/2 c Cilantro, Chopped
1 Jalapeño Minced
1/2 tbsp. Cumin
Olive Oil, ¼ c
1 tsp Salt
1/2 tsp Pepper
Main
2 lb. Skirt Steak
Pit Boss Prime-Rib Scrub, ¾ c
Instructions
Combine all marinade ingredients in a medium mixing bowl and whisk well to combine for salt dissolving.
Remove any excess fat from the skirt steak and place it in a big resealable container. After you've poured the marinade over the steak, put it in the fridge. Before serving, chill for nearly 2 hrs.
Remove the skirt steak from the marinade and rub it all over with Pit Boss Prime-Rib Scrub. Allow 30 mins for sleep.
Preheat the Pit Boss to 225°F for approximately 15 mins with the top closed. Use Super Smoke if it's available for the greatest flavor.
Place each skirt steak directly over your grill grate for approximately 45 mins to smoke.
Remove the meat from the heat. Preheat the Pit Boss to 500°F

for 15 mins with the top closed.
About 2 mins after the grill reaches temperature, or before the meat reaches a core temperature of 135° F, sear through the steak side.
Allow 10 mins for the meat to rest before cutting it against the grain.

1.67 Grilled Flank Steak with Chilean Salsa
Total Time: 35 Mins, Servings: 6
Ingredients
Olive Oil Extra-Virgin
Pit Boss Prime-Rib Scrub
1 bunch Cilantro
2 Scallions Chopped
1 clove Garlic, Chopped
1 Stemmed Jalapeño Pepper, Seeded & Diced
Vinegar Red Wine, ¼ c
1/2 tsp Ground Cumin
1/2 c Olive Oil Extra-Virgin
Kosher Salt
Black Pepper Freshly Ground
1 Lime, sliced Into Wedges
Instructions
Preheat the grill to high and leave the lid closed for approximately 15 mins. Set the temperature to 500°F if required for better results.
Drizzle a little olive oil over the steak and season with Pit Boss Prime-Rib Rub as needed. Set aside the salsa while you're making it.
Remove the tough, low stems from the cilantro, then thinly chop the remaining cilantro. In a food processor, blend or process the ingredients. Pulse the vinegar, scallions, jalapeño, garlic, and cumin in a food processor until finely chopped.
Place the steak at an angle over the grill grate and cook for 8-10 mins on each side, turning with tongs or until medium-rare.
Allow the meat to rest for 5 mins before cutting thinly on the sharp diagonal, with lime wedges and Chilean salsa on the side.

1.68 Wagyu Tri-Tip
Total Time: 1 Hr 5 Mins, Servings: 8
Ingredients
2 Wagyu Beef Tri-Tip
1 c Pit Boss Prime Rib Rub
Instructions
Preheat the grill to 225°F and bake for 15 mins with the lid closed. Use Super Smoke if it's available for the greatest flavor. While the grill is heated up, trim any excess fat from the tri-tip and season with Pit Boss Prime-Rib Scrub.
Cook the tri-tip on the Pit Boss until the internal temperature reaches 130 degrees Fahrenheit. This may take an hr and a half. When the tri-tip reaches 130° F, remove it from the grill and put it aside.
Preheat the grill to 475 degrees Fahrenheit. After 15 mins, return the tri-tip to the grill and cook for 3 mins on each side. Remove it and slice it.

1.69 Smoked Midnight Brisket
Total Time:12 Hrs 30 Mins, Servings: 6
Ingredients
1 tbsp. Worcestershire Sauce
1 tbsp. Pit Boss Beef Scrub
1 tsp Pit Boss Chicken Scrub
1 tsp Pit Boss Blackened Saskatchewan Scrub
1 (4-6 Lb) Flat-Cut Brisket
1 c Beef Broth
Instructions
Combine the Pit Boss spices and Worcestershire sauce in a mixing bowl. Combine the ingredients and stir them into the beef.
Preheat the Pit Boss at 180° F for 15 mins with the top closed. Use Super Smoke if it's available for the greatest flavor.
Place the brisket on the barbecue for 5-7 hrs, or until the internal temperature reaches 160 degrees Fahrenheit.
Remove off the grill, double wrap in plastic, and return to the grill with 1/2 cup beef broth instead of 1 cup beef broth.
Raise the grill temperature to 225° F and continue to cook the brisket for another 4-5 hrs, or until the internal temperature reaches 204° F.
Remove the steak from the grill and let it aside for almost 30 mins to rest before cutting it through the grain. Serve with your favorite Pit Boss BBQ sauce.

1.70 Grilled Butter Basted Rib-Eye
Total Time: 20 Mins, Servings: 2
Ingredients
2 Bone-In Thick-Cut Rib-Eye Steaks
Kosher Salt
Pepper
4 tbsp. Unsalted Butter
Instructions
Season the steaks on both sides with pepper and salt, then set aside for 20 mins at room temperature.
Preheat your Pit Boss to 500°F and leave the lid closed for approximately 15 mins. Preheat your grill grate by putting a pan large enough to hold this steak directly on top of it.
Place the steaks over the hottest part of your grill and cover for approximately 5 mins.
After 5 mins, remove the lid and add the butter to the pan; it should melt nearly immediately.
In the skillet, the grill side of the steaks should be facing up. Cook for 5-7 mins, brushing your steaks with butter every min. Cook until the internal temperature reaches 125-130 degrees Fahrenheit.
Remove the steaks from the pan and put them aside for 10 mins to rest. Drizzle the remaining butter over the steaks and serve.

1.71 Roasted Mustard Crusted Prime Rib
Total Time:3 hrs 15 Mins, Serves: 6
Ingredients
1 3-B1 Prime Rib Roast
1 Tbsp Black Pepper
2 Tbsp Kosher Salt
2 Tbsp Garlic, Minced to A Paste
1 Cup Whole Grain Mustard
Instructions
In a mixing bowl, combine black pepper, salt, grain mustard, & garlic. Rub the mix across the outside of your roast, being careful to coat each area equally.
Start your Pit Boss, adjust the temp to 450°F, & warm for 10-15 mins with its lid closed.
With ribs towards the rear of your grill, set the roast straight on your grill grate. Close the cover & cook for around 45 mins, or till your roast has an equal coating of browning on the outside. Reduce the temp to 325°F & cook for another 2.5 hrs, or till the core temperature hits 125°F.
Remove the roast from the grill and set aside for 15 mins to settle before slicing. Remove the trussing & bones from the

roast once it has rested, then slice it into 1" pieces.

1.72 Beef Pot Roast
Total Time: 3 Hrs 15 Mins, Serves: 4
Ingredients
1/2 cup Red Wine
3 cup Beef Stock
4 Tbsp Butter, Softened
1 Tbsp Chopped Sage
1 Tbsp Garlic, Minced
1 Cup Chopped Carrots
1 Cup Chopped Red Onion
1 Tbsp Jacobsen Salt Co. Pure Kosher Sea Salt
1 Tsp Ground Black Pepper
1 (3-4 Lb) Chuck Roast
Instructions
When you are all set to cook, preheat the Pit Boss to 325°F for around 15 mins with the lid closed.
Combine the salt, red wine, red onion, beef stock, melted butter, garlic, carrots, sage, & pepper in a big
stock pot. Cover your chuck roast with the lid.
Put each stock pot straight on your grill grate when the grill has reached temp. Cook for around 3 hrs with the lid closed before checking.
When the pot roast achieves a core temp of 203°F & can easily be pulled apart using a fork, it's done.

1.73 Grilled Triple Cheeseburger
Total Time: 20 Mins, Serves: 4 people
Ingredients
4 Lb Ground Beef, 80% Lean
1 Tbsp Pit Boss Beef Rub
12 Slices American Cheese
4 Whole Hamburger Buns
1 Large White Onion, Sliced, For Serving
1 Large Tomato, Sliced, For Serving
Butter Lettuce, For Serving
Pickles, For Serving
2 Tbsp Mayonnaise
1 Tbsp Ketchup
2 Tsp Sweet Pickle Relish
1/2 Tsp Sugar
1/2 Tsp Distilled White Vinegar
Instructions
Form the meat mixture into 12 5-oz patties. Beef Rub Pit Boss should be liberally applied to both sides.
For Special Sauce, combine all the sauce ingredients & put away till all set to use.
Set the Pit Boss to 400°F & preheat for around 15 mins with the lid covered when you're all set to cook.
Place patties on your grill grate & cook for around 4 mins before flipping and cooking for another 2 mins.
Cook for the next 2 mins, or till the cheese completely melted. Put the buns over your grill for toasting if
desired during the final min of cooking.
Remove it all from your grill & assemble burgers over the bread with a specific sauce, three burger patties, lettuce, onions, tomato, & pickles.

1.74 Sweet and Spicy Beef Sirloin Tip Roast
Total Time: 2 Hrs 15 Mins, Serves: 8
Ingredients
3 Lb Beef Sirloin Tip Roast
2 Tbsp Pit Boss Beef Rub
1/2 Cup Pit Boss 'Que BBQ Sauce
1/4 Cup Chili sauce
Instructions
On both sides, season the sirloin roast using Beef Rub Pit Boss. Allow 30 mins for the roast to settle at room temp.
Set the Pit Boss to 275°F & preheat for around 15 mins with the lid covered when you're all set to cook.
Cook your roast for around 75 mins on your Pit Boss, or till the core temperature hits 130°F.
Combine the Pit Boss 'Que & chili sauce in a big bowl. Brush your roast with barbecue chili sauce after it has attained 130°F.
Cook until the core temperature hits 140 degrees Fahrenheit.
Place on the chopping board & tent using foil after removing from your Pit Boss. Allow for a 10-min rest period or till the core temperature hits 145°F.
Piece the roast thinly across your grain & brush every slice with the leftover sauce.

1.75 Smoked Chili Rib Eye Steaks
Total Time: 1 Hr 10 Mins, Serves: 6
Ingredients
4 (10-12 Oz) Rib-Eye Steaks
2 Clove Garlic, Minced
1 Tsp Salt
2 Tbsp Chili Powder
2 Tbsp Worcestershire Sauce
2 Tbsp Extra-Virgin Olive Oil
1 Tsp Brown Sugar, Packed
1 Tsp Ground Cumin
Instructions
In a bowl, make a paste with garlic & salt. Combine the chili powder, brown sugar, olive oil, Worcestershire sauce, & cumin into a large mixing bowl. The mixture should be applied to all sides of your steaks.
Freeze the steaks with the leftover rub for around 4 hrs in a wide resealable bag.
Set your Pit Boss to 225°F & preheat for around 15 mins with the lid closed when you're all set to cook. If the Super Smoke is available, use it for the best taste.
Put these steaks on your grill grate & smoke for around 45 mins. Remove these steaks from the pan and put them aside to settle. Preheat the grill to 500 degrees Fahrenheit for around 15 mins with the lid closed.
Return all steaks to your grill & cook for 3-5 mins from one side & 1-2 mins from the other side, or till the desired doneness.
Allow 5-10 mins for the steaks to rest before serving.

1.76 The Perfect Smoked New York Strip Steak
Total Time: 55 Mins, Serves: 2
Ingredients
2 Tbsp Unsalted Butter
2 Tbsp Extra-Virgin Olive Oil
1 Yellow Onion (Small), Sliced
4 New York Strip Steaks
Salt
Cracked Black Pepper
1 White Button Mushroom Caps
1 Tsp Salt
1/2 Tsp Cracked Black Pepper
Instructions
Set the temperature to 180°F & preheat for around 15 mins with the lid covered when prepared to cook.
In the cast-iron skillet, combine the olive oil, butter, & sliced onions; put immediately on your grill grate along with a seasoned steak.
Smoke for around 30 mins with the lid closed.
Transfer all smoked steaks into a dish and cover with foil.
Increase the heat to high & place the mushrooms in a cast-

iron skillet. Season with some pepper and salt to taste. Cook till the mushrooms & onions are tender.
Return all steaks to your hot grill for a quick sear & 3-4 mins each side for the rare steak.
Top all steaks with grilled onions & mushrooms in the final min of cooking. Leave 6-8 mins for your steaks to settle before cutting.

1.77 Grilled Thai Beef Skewers
Total Time: 4 Hrs 8 Mins, Serves: 4
Ingredients
1/4 Cup Vegetable Oil
1/4 Cup Soy Sauce
1 whole Lime, Juiced
2 Clove Garlic, Minced
2 Tbsp Ginger, Peeled and Minced
1 Tbsp Sugar
1 Tsp Freshly Ground Black Pepper
2 1/2 Lb Beef Sirloin, Trimmed and Cut into 1" Dice
1/2 Whole Red Bell Pepper, Seeded and Diced
1/2 Cup Chopped Dry-Roasted Peanuts, For Garnish
Instructions
Whisk together all the oil, ginger, sugar, soy sauce, garlic, lime juice, & black pepper in a mixing bowl. Pour your marinade over meat in a medium bowl, stirring to coat every piece well. Freeze for 2-4 hrs or up to 24 hrs.
Remove your sirloin cubes from the marinade & wipe them dry using paper towels. Thread the meat onto the skewers, placing the pieces tightly together to reduce skewer heating.
Preheat the grill to 425°F for around 15 mins with the lid covered when prepared to cook.
Place your skewers on your grill grate & cook for 2-4 mins each side until optimum doneness is achieved. Sprinkle with sliced red pepper & chopped peanuts before serving.

1.78 Grilled Sirloin Steaks
Total Time: 15 Mins, Serves: 2
Ingredients
2 Sirloin Steak
1 Tsp Garlic Powder
1 Tsp Onion Powder
1 Tsp Paprika
1 Tsp Chile Powder
1 Tsp Brown Sugar
1 Tbsp Jacobsen Salt Co. Pure Kosher Sea Salt
1 Tbsp Ground Black Pepper
Instructions
Set the Pit Boss to 500°F & preheat for around 15
mins with the lid covered when you're prepared to cook.
Take the steaks out of the fridge & pat them dry.
Combine garlic, Jacobsen Salt, onion, paprika, Chile, brown sugar, & pepper in a wide mixing bowl.
Rub with Jacobsen Salt & spice combination from all sides of your meat.
Put steaks over the outside rim of your grill while it's hot since this is usually the hottest area of the grill. Before inspecting them, shut the cover & wait for 3-4 mins.
Cook your steak until it reaches the required core temperature on one side only (130°F). Cook for around 1 min further once the meat reaches the desired temperature.
Remove the steaks from the pan and set them aside to settle for around 5-10 mins.

1.79 Smoked Moink Burger by Scott Thomas
Total Time: 1 Hr 10 Mins, Serves: 4
Ingredients
1 Lb Ground Sirloin
1/2 Lb Ground Pork
1/4 cup Worcestershire Sauce
1 Tsp Garlic, Minced
Salt
Black Pepper
Instructions
In a mixing dish, combine all the ingredients & stir well. Make 6 patties out of the mixture.
Preheat your grill to 350°F & shut the cover for 10-15 mins.
Cook till the burgers hit a temp of 160° on the inside.
Top with the preferred cheese & serve with the preferred toppings sometime before the burgers are done.

1.80 Grilled Rib-Eye Steaks by Doug Scheiding
Total Time: 25 Mins, Serves: 2
Ingredients
2 (1-1/2-Inch-Thick) Bone-In Rib-Eye Steaks
Canola Oil
Montreal Steak Seasoning
Instructions
Remove the thick outer fat from the steaks & coat both sides using canola oil.
When prepared to cook, preheat the Pit Boss to 325°F with the lid covered for around 15 mins.
Season all sides of your meat using Steak Seasoning Montreal while a grill is heating up. Allow 15 mins for the mixture to come to room temp.
Put the steaks on your grill grate immediately. 6 mins on from each side. Cook for around 14-20 mins, or till steaks achieve a temp of 132°F on the inside.
Take the steaks from your grill & serve right away.

1.81 Chorizo Cheese Stuffed Burgers
Total Time: 55 Mins, Serves: 2
Ingredients
2 Lb Ground Beef, 80% Lean
4 Oz Pit Boss Prime Rib Rub
12 Oz Chorizo
2 Slices Cheddar Cheese
4 Whole Brioche Burger Buns
Tomatoes, Sliced
Red Onion, Sliced
Lettuce, Sliced
Instructions
In a wide mixing bowl, combine 2 lb of meat with Rib Rub Pit Boss Prime.
Make eight 1/4-lb patties out of your ground beef. Form a patty by laying down the cheese slice, put chorizo, and another cheese slice. To bind the two parties together, place another patty over the top & squeeze the end around your burger.
Continue until all four patties are cooked.
Preheat the grill to 325°F and leave the lid covered for 10-15 mins.
Cook your burgers for around 15 mins from each side on your Pit Boss. Top every burger with a Cheddar cheese and melt it if desired. Remove from the Pit Boss & cover with foil to settle for around 10 mins.
Brush your brioche buns using melted butter & toast for around 30-45 secs on your grill while the burgers rest.
Remove the buns from the grill & put the burger together with the toppings.

1.82 Grilled Butter Basted Porterhouse Steak

Total Time: 45 Mins, Serves: 2
Ingredients
4 Tbsp Butter, Melted
2 Tbsp Worcestershire Sauce
2 Tsp Dijon Mustard
Pit Boss Prime Rib Rub
2 (16-20 Oz) Porterhouse Steaks, at least 1-1/2 Inch Thick
Instructions
When prepared to cook, preheat the Pit Boss to 225°F with the lid covered for around 15 mins.
To make the sauce, whisk together all Worcestershire sauce, melted butter, & mustard till smooth.
Using the pastry brush, brush the mix on all sides of your steaks.
Prime Pit Boss Rib Rub should be used on all sides of the steaks.
When your grill has reached the desired temperature, place the steaks on your grate & cook for around 30 mins.
Transfer your steaks to the plate with tongs & raise the temp to 500°F.
Return your steaks to your grill grate once the grill hits 500°F & cook till cooked to your liking. 2-3 mins on every side at 130°F for the medium-rare.
If desired, baste with butter sauce
Worcestershire combination one more.
Allow for around 3 mins of resting time before serving.

1.83 Slow Smoked Rib-Eye Roast

Total Time: 4 Hrs 15 Mins, Serves: 6
Ingredients
1 (4-6 Lb) Rib-Eye Roast
4 Tbsp Yellow Mustard
1 Tbsp Worcestershire Sauce
1 Clove Garlic, Minced
Pit Boss Prime Rib Rub
4 Sprig Fresh Thyme
Instructions
When prepared to cook, preheat the Pit Boss to 250°F with the lid covered for around 15 mins.
Prepare your roast while a Pit Boss heats up. Trim the extra fat from your roast.
Combine the Worcestershire sauce, mustard, & garlic in a medium bowl. Spread the mustard mix across the roast & season well with Prime Pit Boss Rib rub.
Place the thyme sprigs on the roast.
Put the roast straight on your grill grate & smoke for around 3-4 hrs, or till the core temp hits 135°F.
Take the roast off the grill before cutting, tent using foil & set aside for around 20 mins.

1.84 Smoked Bourbon Jerky

Total Time: 6 Hrs 20 Mins, Serves: 6
Ingredients
3 Lb Flank Steak
1 cup Bourbon
1/2 Cup Brown Sugar
1/4 Cup Pit Boss Jerky Rub
1 Can Chipotle Peppers in Adobo Sauce
3 Tbsp Worcestershire Sauce
1/2 Cup Apple Cider Vinegar
Instructions
Flank steak should be rolled up parallel toward the grain. Slice into slices with some grain.
In a small mixing bowl, combine all your marinade ingredients & stir thoroughly. Pour the marinade over the cut flank steak into a wide zip-top bag.
Place in the refrigerator or freezer to marinate.
Set the Pit Boss to 180°F & preheat for around 15 mins with the lid covered when you're all set to cook.
Remove the flanks from the marinade & place them on the jerky rack & straight on the barbecue grate, discarding the marinade.
Smoke for around 6 hrs, or till the jerky becomes dry yet still flexible.
Remove off the grill & set aside to cool for around 1 hr at room temp, gently covered.
Keep refrigerated in a zip-top bag.

1.85 Grilled Korean Short Ribs

Total Time: 8 Hrs 10 Mins, Serves: 4
Ingredients
1/2 Cup Soy Sauce
1 cup Brown Sugar
1/2 Cup Rice Wine Vinegar
1 Tbsp Sesame Oil
2 Clove Garlic
1 Whole Inch Ginger, Peeled and Coarsely Chopped
1 Whole Asian Pear, Peeled and Quartered
1 Whole Red Thai Chili, Deseeded and Chopped
5 Lb Korean Short Ribs
Sesame Seeds
Scallions, Sliced
Instructions
To prepare the marinade, put all your ingredients in the blender pitcher, except the ribs, & puree till smooth. Cover & marinate your short ribs in the freezer overnight.
Set the temp to High & preheat for around 15 mins with the lid covered when prepared to cook. If possible, raise the temperature to 500°F for best results.
Remove the ribs from the marinade & discard them. Cook your ribs for 3-5 mins on each side straight on the barbecue grate.
Remove from the grill & top with some sesame seeds & sliced scallions.

1.86 Bloody Mary Flank Steak

Total Time: 8 Hrs 15 Mins, Serves: 4
Ingredients
2 Cup Pit Boss Smoked Bloody Mary Mix Or V-8 Juice
1/2 cup Vodka
1 Whole Lemon or Lime, Juiced
3 Clove Garlic, Minced
1 Tbsp Worcestershire Sauce
1 Tsp Coarse Ground Black Pepper, Divided
1 Tsp Celery Salt
1 To Taste Hot Sauce
1/2 Cup Vegetable Oil
1 1/2 Lb Flank Steak
Instructions
Combine Bloody Mary Pit Boss Smoked Mix, vodka, celery salt, pepper, lemon juice, Worcestershire sauce, garlic, & hot sauce in a small mixing bowl. Oil should be whisked in.
Pour half of the marinade on your flank steak into a plastic bag. Marinate for at least 24 hrs. Refrigerate the remaining half of the marinade into a closed jar.
Preheat the grill & set the temp to high once you're all set to cook.
Pour your marinade from that jar into a medium saucepan & simmer in half on medium heat. Keep it warm.
Drain your flank steak & toss out the marinade which had been applied to it. Using paper towels, pat your meat dry.
Grill your meat for 7-10 mins on each side, straight on your grill grate.
Transfer your steak to the cutting board & set it aside for 3 mins before slicing across the grain over a sharper diagonal. Serve

with some marinade that has been reheated.

1.87 Smoked Longhorn Cowboy Tri-Tip
Total Time: 4 Hrs 15 Mins, Serves: 6 people
Ingredients
1 (2-3 Lb) Tri-Tip
1/8 Cup Coffee Grounds
1/4 Cup Pit Boss Beef Rub
Instructions
Set the Pit Boss to 180°F & preheat for around 15 mins with the lid covered when you're all set to cook.
Beef Pit Boss Rub & coffee grinds are applied to the tri-tip. Place on your grill grate & smoke for around 3 hrs at 180°F.
Remove your tri-tip from the grill & raise the temp to 275°F.
Return your tri-tip to a grill & cook for around 45-90 mins, till it reaches a core temp of 130-135°F.
Remove the steak from your grill, remove its foil, & set it aside to settle for around 10 mins before slicing.

1.88 Sweet Grilled Shrimp & Spicy Sausage Skewers
Total Time: 40 Mins, Serves: 6
Ingredients
24 Shrimp, Peeled, and Deveined
1/2 Cup Apple Cider Vinegar
1 Tsp Dijon Mustard
1 Tsp Onion Powder
2 Clove Garlic, Minced
3 Tbsp Honey
1/4 Cup Canola Oil
1 Tsp Dried Thyme
Salt And Pepper
8 Italian Pork Sausage, Regular or Spicy
Instructions
Vinegar, mustard, salt, pepper, onion powder, honey, thyme, garlic, & canola oil should all be mixed. Toss in the shrimp & set aside for around 30 mins to marinate.
Sausage links should be sliced in half lengthwise & into chunks.
Set the temp to High & preheat for around 15 mins with the lid covered.
On your skewers, alternate the sausages & shrimps. Place shrimp over grill & cook for around 8-10 mins, or until done.
Remove the steaks from the grill & serve.

1.89 Pit Boss Tri-Tip Roast
Total Time: 4 Hrs 10 Mins, Serves: 6
Ingredients
1 Tri-Tip Roast
Pit Boss 'Que BBQ Sauce
Pit Boss Prime Rib Rub
1/2 Cup Beef Broth
Instructions
Make sure you have enough time to marinade this dish overnight. Refrigerate your tri-tip overnight after marinating it in 'Que Pit Boss BBQ Sauce.
Remove the tri-tip from the marinade & toss it out. Season lightly with Prime Pit Boss Rib Rub.
Set the Pit Boss to 180°F & preheat for around 15 mins with the lid covered.
Smoke your tri-tip for 3-4 hrs on a grill.
Remove the tri-tip from the grill and cover it with Al foil & beef broth. Close the Al foil & raise the temperature of the grill to 350°F.
Return the meat to your grill for another 45 mins. Remove the steak from the grill and set it aside to settle for around 15 mins before slicing.

1.90 Pit Boss Bacon-Wrapped Filet Mignon
Total Time: 25 Mins, Serves: 2
Ingredients
3 (6 Oz) Filet Mignon Steaks
1 Tsp Pepper
1 Tsp Salt
2 Clove Garlic, Minced
3 Tbsp Butter, Softened
3 Slices Bacon
Instructions
Because fillets have little marbling, aim for a deep red hue when choosing beef.
Combine pepper, garlic, salt, &melted butter in a medium bowl. Rub the fillet on all sides. Allow 10 mins for resting.
Set the Pit Boss to 450°F & preheat for 15 mins with the lid covered.
Wrap a piece of bacon around each steak & fasten with the toothpick.
Cook for 5-8 mins on all sides, or unless the fillets achieve a core temp of 130°F for a medium-rare, straight on your grill.

1.91 Pit Boss Filet Mignon
Total Time: 15 Mins, Serves: 2
Ingredients
1 Tsp Salt
1 Tsp Pepper
2 Clove Garlic, Minced
3 Tbsp Butter, Softened
2 Filet Mignon Steaks
Instructions
Combine garlic, salt, pepper, & melted
butter in a mixing bowl. Rub the fillets on all sides. Allow 10 mins for resting.
Set the Pit Boss to 450°F & preheat for around 15 mins with the lid covered.
Cook for around 5-8 mins on all sides, or till the fillets achieve a core temp of 130-135°F for a medium-rare, straight on your grill.

1.92 Slow Smoked and Roasted Prime Rib
Total Time: 4 Hrs 15 Mins, Serves: 8
Ingredients
1 (8-10 Lb) 4-B1 Prime Rib Roast
5 Tbsp Kosher Salt
5 Tbsp Ground Black Pepper
3 Tbsp Fresh Chopped Thyme
3 Tbsp Fresh Chopped Rosemary
Instructions
When prepared to cook, preheat the Pit Boss to 250°F with the lid covered for around 15 mins.
The trim extra fat from the roast as the grill warms up. Combine the other ingredients & brush the mixture all over the roast.
Place that roast on your grill & cook for 4 hrs, or till the core temp reaches 120°F. Check the interior temp each hr or till it hits 120°F. Remove the roast from the grill & set it aside to settle for around 20 mins.
Raise the temperature of the grill to 450°F & preheat it while the roast is cooling. Place your roast back on that grill once it has heated up for around 15 mins, turning halfway through, or till the core temp reaches 130°F for a medium-rare.
Before slicing, remove the roast from the grill & let it cool for around 30 mins.

1.93 Grilled Wagyu Burgers
Total Time: 15 Mins, Serves: 4
Ingredients
2 Lb Wagyu Ground Beef
Salt And Pepper
6 Slices American Cheese
6 Burger Buns
Butter Lettuce
1 Heirloom Tomato, Sliced
1 Red Onion, Sliced
Instructions
Set the Pit Boss to 500°F & preheat for around 15 mins with the lid covered.
Season six burger patties generously with salt & black pepper. Put burger patties straight on your grill grate & cook for around 4 mins once the grill becomes hot.
Cook for another 4 mins from the other side, then top with some cheese through the final min of cooking.
Remove off the grill & set aside for 2 mins to cool.
Heirloom tomato, Butter lettuce, & red onion, as well as any preferred sauces, go inside your burger.

1.94 BBQ Brisket Hot Dog
Total Time: 15 Mins, Serves: 4
Ingredients
6 Whole Hot Dogs
1/2 Lb Leftover Beef Brisket
1/2 Cup Pit Boss Sweet & Heat BBQ Sauce
6 Whole Hot Dog Buns
1/2 Cup Shredded Cheddar Cheese
1 Onion, Diced
2 Whole Jalapeño, Seeded, and Diced
Instructions
When you're all set to cook, fire up the Pit Boss as per the manufacturer's directions. Preheat the grill to 450°F & bake for around 10-15 mins with the lid covered.
Put hot dogs straight on your grill grate & cook for around 7-10 mins, or till warmed through & lightly browned, flipping periodically.
To keep the brisket slices wet, wrap them in Al foil with some BBQ sauce. Put next to hot dogs over a grill grate & cook until warmed through, approximately 5-7 minutes.
Put a hot dog over the bun & top with some brisket, additional BBQ sauce, onion, cheddar cheese, & jalapenos to serve.

1.95 Grass-fed Beef Burgers
Total Time: 40 Mins, Serves: 4
Ingredients
2 Lb Grass-Fed Ground Beef
4 Tsp Kosher Salt
4 Slices Provol1 Cheese
4 Whole Brioche Burger Buns
4 Slices Tomato
Burger Toppings of Your Choice
Instructions
Cut the ground meat into four equal pieces. Remove your meat from the box and form this in burger patties approximately 5 inches wide to avoid overworking it. The meat should not be kneaded. Some kosher salt, split in half on every side, in each burger
When prepared to cook, preheat the Pit Boss to 415°F with the lid covered for around 15 mins.
On your grill grate, arrange the hamburgers. For a medium-rare, cook for around 12 mins. The outside of the meat should be well browned. Your thermometer must read 130°F when inserted into the middle of your burger.

Put provolone slices into burgers & toast buns over the grill. Serve with a side of condiments.

1.96 Meatloaf Cupcake Bites
Total Time: 40 Mins, Serves: 8
Ingredients
1 Tsp Olive Oil
1 cup Onion, Diced
1 Tsp Dried Oregano
2 Clove Garlic, Minced
1 cup Breadcrumbs
1 Tsp Worcestershire Sauce
1 Tsp Salt
Tsp Black Pepper
2 Whole Eggs
Cooking Spray
1 1/2 Lb Ground Beef, 80% Lean
3 Tbsp Chives, Chopped
1 Cup Chili Pit Boss BBQ Sauce
5 Cup Mashed Potatoes
12 Slices Crumbled Cooked Bacon
Instructions
Preheat the grill to 350 degrees Fahrenheit with the lid covered.
In a wide mixing bowl, combine all your ingredients except BBQ sauce. Fold the paper carefully with your hands.
Using cooking spray, coat a muffin or small loaf pan. Fill the cups halfway with the meat mix.
Some BBQ sauce on top of every meatloaf pancake. Preheat grill to 350°F and bake for around 25 mins.
While your meatloaf is baking, make some mashed potatoes. Once your meat is done, use the pastry bag using a big star tip for piping those mashed potatoes over top of every tiny meatloaf.
Bacon & chives are sprinkled on top.

1.97 BBQ Beef Short Ribs with Pit Boss Prime Rib Rub
Total Time: 8 Hrs 15 Mins, Serves: 6
Ingredients
2 (4 Bone) Beef Short Rib Racks
Pit Boss Prime Rib Rub
1 cup Beef Broth
Instructions
Beef ribs should be cleaned and trimmed. Season with Prime Pit Boss Rib Rubs liberally.
When prepared to cook, preheat your Pit Boss at 225°F for around 15 mins with its lid closed.
Place your ribs straight on a grill grate & cook for around 5 hrs, or till an internal temp of 160°F is reached.
Two sheets of the foil stacked on the flat surface. Wrap a rack of the ribs around the middle of foil sheets like a package, leaving one end open. Continue with the remaining rack. Close the package after adding beef broth.
Return the ribs to the grill for another 2-3 hrs or till they reach a temp of 204°F. Then, remove the steak from the grill & let it settle for around 10 mins.
Serve with some favorite sides & cut in individual ribs.

1.98 Smoked Longhorn Brisket
Total Time: 7 Hrs 10 Mins, Serves: 8
Ingredients
1 (12-14 Lb) Whole Packer Brisket, Trimmed
1/4 Cup Pit Boss Prime Rib Rub
2 Tbsp Coffee Grounds
Instructions

When prepared to cook, preheat the Pit Boss to 250°F for around 15 mins with the lid closed.
Using Prime Pit Boss Rib Rub & coffee grounds, rub the brisket.
Put the brisket on your grill grate & smoke for 4-5 hrs, till it hits a core temp of 160°F.
Remove the brisket off the grill & cover it in foil twice. Then, return the wrapped brisket to the grill & cook for another 2-3 hrs, or until it hits a core temp of 204°F.
Remove off the grill, unwrap, & set aside for around 15 mins. Serve by slicing against grains.

1.99 Grilled Southern Pimento Cheeseburger
Total Time: 30 Mins, Serves: 2
Ingredients
8 Oz Cheese, Sharp Cheddar
1/3 Cup Cream Cheese
2 Tbsp Mayonnaise
1/2 Cup Pimento Peppers
1 Pinch Kosher Salt
1 Lb Ground Beef
Salt
Black Pepper
2 Brioche Buns, Halved
Instructions
Mix all the ingredients for making pimento cheese.
Set the temp to High & preheat for around 15 mins with the lid covered.
Season all sides of the burger patties with some salt & pepper.
Cook your patties for around 5 mins on the grill. Cook for a further 5 mins on the other side.
Cook for another 2 mins, or till the cheese has melted.
For 1 min, toast these buns straight on your grill grate.
If preferred, top the burger with some romaine lettuce & tomato.

1.100 Grilled Steak
Total Time: 25 Mins, Serves: 2
Ingredients
2 Steaks, Cut of Your Choice
Pit Boss Prime Rib Rub
Instructions
Prime Pit Boss Rib Rub should be used on both sides of the steaks.
When prepared to cook, preheat the Pit Boss to 425°F with the lid covered for around 15 mins.
Put the steak on your grill & cook until the desired
core temperature is achieved: 120°F for the rare, 135°F for the medium-rare, 145°F for the medium, or 155°F for very well done.

1.101 Dry Brined Texas Beef Ribs by Doug Scheiding
Total Time: 6 Hrs 30 Mins, Servings: 8
Ingredients
2 (9-12 Lb) Uncut Prime or Choice Beef Short Ribs
Kosher Salt
Worcestershire Sauce
Pit Boss Prime Rib Rub
Pit Boss Blackened Saskatchewan Rub
8 Ounce Apple Juice, For Spritzing
8 Ounce Beef Broth
Instructions
Go to your local supermarket or butcher shop and get a pack of uncut short ribs. For two racks of four bones each, the total weight should be about 9-12 pounds.
Using a sharp knife, trim as much fat as possible off the tops of the ribs. Each rack of four bones should have a membrane removed from the bottom.
For the dry brine, sprinkle with salt and cover in plastic wrap within at least six months or overnight in the refrigerator.
When ready to cook, preheat the Pit Boss to 275°F for 15 minutes with the lid closed.
Wipe away any extra mixture of salt from the ribs' tops. Before applying a medium layer of Pit Boss Prime Rib Rub, brush on a thin coating of Worcestershire sauce.
Apply a light layer of Pit Boss Saskatchewan Rub on top. Allow 15-20 mins for the apple juice to soak in.
Arrange the ribs on Pit Boss with a thicker part (if appropriate) towards the rear of the grill.
Smoke the ribs for 4 to 5 hours, spritzing gently with apple juice every 30 minutes to keep them moist, or even the temperature reaches 180°F or the color has a beautiful deep char.
Remove the ribs from the grill and cover them in two sheets of heavy-duty foil with 4-ounces of broth for every rack of ribs, similar to how you would like a brisket.
Return the meat to the Pit Boss for the next hour once the internal temperature reaches 203°F. Remove the item and cut it. Serve right away. Enjoy.

1.102 Smoked Corned Beef Brisket
Total Time: 5 Hrs 15 Mins, Servings: 4
Ingredients
Beef Brisket, 1 (3 Lb)
Fat Cap, 1/4 Inch Thick
Apricot BBQ Sauce, 1 Bottle
Dijon Mustard, 1/4 Cup
Instructions
Take the corned beef brisket out of the package and discard any seasoning packets. Soak the corned beef for min 8 hours in the water, replacing it every 2 hours.
When ready to cook, preheat the Pit Boss to 275°F with the lid closed for fifteen mins.
Place the brisket fat side up on the grill grate and cook for mini 2 hours.
In a medium mixing basin, whisk together the Dijon mustard and Apricot BBQ Sauce.
In the bottom of a disposable aluminum foil pan, pour half BBQ sauce-mustard mixture. Move the brisket to saucepan, fat-side up, using tongs. Pour the remaining BBQ sauce-mustard combination over top of the brisket, spreading it evenly with a spatula. Aluminum foil should be firmly wrapped around the pan.
Return brisket to the grill & cook for a further 2 to 3 hours, or until tender. On an instant-read meat thermometer, the inner temperature should be 203°F.
Remove the meat from the grill and let it rest at room temperature for 15-20 minutes. With a sharp knife, cut across the grain into 1/4-inch slices and serve right away. Enjoy.

1.103 Smoked Peppered Beef Jerky
Total Time: 4 Hrs 15 Mins, Servings: 4
Ingredients
(12 Oz) Can, 1 Bottle
Soy Sauce, 1 Cup
Worcestershire Sauce, 1/4 Cup
Brown Sugar, 3 tbsp
Morton Tender Meat Cure, 1 tbsp
Garlic Salt, 1/2 tsp
Coarse Black Pepper, 4 tbsp
2 Pound beef
Instructions
Plan ahead of time since this dish has to marinate overnight.
Whisk together the beer, Worcestershire sauce, soy sauce,

curing salt, brown sugar, garlic salt, and 2 tsp black pepper in a mixing bowl.
Remove any fat or connective tissue from the meat using a sharp knife. Against the grain, cut the beef into 1/4-inch-thick slices.
Place the meat slices in a big plastic bag that can be resealed. Pour the marinade over the beef slices and knead the bag to coat all of the slices with the marinade. Refrigerate for a few hours to overnight after sealing the bag.
When ready to cook, preheat the Pit Boss to 180°F with the lid closed for 15 min. If Super Smoke is available, use it for the best taste.
Remove the meat slices from the marinade and toss them out. Dry the meat slices with paper towels before liberally seasoning on both sides with the black pepper.
Arrange the meat on the grill grate in a single layer. Smoke for 4 to 5 hours, or when the jerky is dry and still chewy and pliable when bent in half.
While the jerky is still warm, move to a resealable plastic bag. Allow the jerky to rest at room temp for an hour with the bag open.
Squeeze any air out of the bag, seal it, and store the jerky in the refrigerator. It will last for many weeks in the fridge. Enjoy.

1.104 Classic Beef Chili
Total Time: 1 Hr 20 Mins, Servings: 8
Ingredients
Ground Chorizo, 1 Pound
Butter, 2 tbsp
Bell Pepper Green, 1
Ground Beef, 1 Pound
Red Bell Pepper, 1
Garlic Minced, 2 Clove
Tomato Paste, 2 tbsp
Yellow Onion, 1
(15 Oz) Beans, 2 Can
Bay Leaves, 2
(14.5 Oz) Tomatoes, 1 Can
Mexican Oregano, 3 tbsp
(15 Oz) Tomato Sauce, 1 Can
Chili Powder, 3 tbsp
Cumin, 3 tbsp
Salt
Instructions
Preheat the Pit Boss to 350°F for 15 minutes with the lid closed when ready to cook.
In a large Dutch oven, brown the chorizo & ground beef over medium-high heat. Remove any extra fat and put it aside. In a Dutch oven, melt the butter, then add the peppers and onion. Cook for 10 minutes, or until onions are light brown. Add the garlic and cook for another 2 minutes.
Cook until the color of the tomato pastes changes from brilliant red to rust. Combine the tomato sauce, beans, and stewed tomatoes in a large mixing bowl.
Add oregano, chili powder, cumin, and bay leaves to the pot and bring to a boil. To taste, season with salt.
Cook 45-60 minutes with the Dutch oven straight on the grill grate, adding liquid (stock, water, or beer) as required to keep it from drying out.
Garnish with your preferred chili toppings. Enjoy.

1.105 Grilled Steak for Two with Cocoa Rub
Total Time: 1 Hr 40 Mins, Servings: 2
Ingredients
Pit Boss Coffee Rub, 1/2 Cup
Rib-Eye Roast, 1 Whole
Cocoa Powder, 1/8 Cup
Instructions
Begin by roasting a full boneless rib-eye roast. Trim the whole roast of any extra fat or silver skin.
The next step is to carve the roast into the steaks. Begin by cutting the steaks 2-1/2 inches thick from the thickest end of the roast. "Thickness: 4-5 cm If you don't want to cut steaks from a full rib-eye roast, have your butcher cut 2 steaks into 2-inch-thick slices "inch steaks (4-5 cm)
Set aside 2 steaks and keep the rest frozen for later use.
Finely season the steaks with Pit Boss Coffee rub & cocoa powder mixture. Save the rest of the rub for another time.
Allow 45 minutes for the steaks to come to room temperature on the counter.
Preheat the Pit Boss to 225°F (105°C) for 15 minutes with the lid closed when ready to cook.
Season the steaks with salt and pepper and place them on the grill. Cook for a further 20 minutes after flipping the steaks after 20 minutes in the oven. Check the temp of the steaks; it should be between 105 to 110 degrees Fahrenheit (40-43 C).
When the steaks have achieved the appropriate temperature, take them from the grill and set them aside to rest.
Raise the temp to High and warm for 15 minutes with the lid closed. If possible, raise the temperature to 500°F (260°C) for the best results.
Return the steaks to the grill grate & cook for another four minutes. Cook for another four minutes after flipping the steaks.
Check the steaks' interior temperature. For medium-rare steaks, the desired final temp is between 130 and 135°F (50-55°C).
Remove the steaks from the grill after the desired temperature is achieved and set them aside to rest for 5-10 minutes. Enjoy.

1.106 Cherry BBQ Steak Skewers
Total Time: 24 Mins, Servings: 4
Ingredients
Onion Chopped, 1
Butter, 2 tbsp
Ketchup, 1 Cup
Frozen Sweet Cherries Chopped, 2 Cup
Brown Sugar, 2/3 Cup
Garlic Minced, 2 Clove
Apple Cider Vinegar, 1/4 Cup
Ground Mustard, 2 tsp
Pepper, 1/2 tsp
Worcestershire Sauce, 1 tbsp
Olive Oil
Pit Boss Rib Rub
Flank Steak, 1 1/2 Pound
Scallions, Chopped
Instructions
Saute onion in butter in a large pot until soft. Cook for a further minute after adding the garlic. Combine the remaining ingredients in a mixing bowl. Cook, stirring periodically, for 20 minutes over medium-low heat, or until cherries are soft and sauce thickens.
Slice flank steak into 16 pieces using a sharp knife. Cut the meat in half lengthwise to begin (along the grain). After that, cut steak in half and across the grain, next fourths, then eighths.
Using a Pit Boss skewer, carefully pierce each slice of beef lengthwise into the middle. Smash each steak skewer with a meat pounder or a small cast iron pan until it is approximately 12 inches thick.
Drizzle beef skewers with olive oil & season with the Prime Rib Rub on both sides.
When ready to cook, increase the temp to High & preheat for

10 to 15 minutes with the lid closed.
Cook the steak skewers for 1 to 2 minutes on each side, firmly on the grill grate.
Remove skewers from the grill and set aside for 5-10 mins before serving.
Smash the cherries in the sauce using a spoon or a masher. Finish with a sprinkle of chopped scallions and a brushing of cherry barbecue sauce. Enjoy.

1.107 Baked Corned Beef Au Gratin
Total Time: 1 Hrs 5 Mins, Servings: 6
Ingredients
Butter Softened, 2 tbsp
Whole Milk, 1/2 Cup
Black Pepper
All-Purpose Flour, 2 tbsp
Onion and Thinly Sliced, 1
Heavy Cream, 1 1/2 Cup
Garlic Minced, 4 Clove
Kosher Salt, 1 tsp
Russet Potatoes, 3 Pound
Beef Brisket Flat, 1 Pound
Instructions
When you're ready to cook, fire up the Pit Boss grill. Until the fire has been created, smoke with the lid open (4 to 5 minutes).
Preheat the grill to 450 °F for 10-15 minutes with the lid closed.
Coat the base of a 9-inch cast-iron pan with melted butter.
Mix cream, flour, milk, salt, minced garlic, and freshly ground black pepper to taste in a separate basin.
In a pan, combine 1/3 of onions, potatoes & corned beef. 1/3 of the cream mixture should be poured over the potatoes. Repeat the process twice more, finishing with the cream mixture.
Wrap in foil and bake for 30 minutes in the Pit Boss. Remove the foil and bake the potatoes for another 20
minutes, or until bubbling and golden brown.
Sprinkle the grated cheese over the potatoes & bake for another 3-5 mins, or until the cheese has melted. Enjoy.

1.108 Grilled Loco Moco Burger
Total Time: 30 Mins, Servings: 4
Ingredients
Ground Beef, Ounce
Beef Gravy, Cup
Kosher Salt, 3 tbsp
Black Pepper, 2 tbsp
Rice Cooked, 2 Cup
Hawaiian Pasta Salad, 2 Cup
Eggs, 4
Burger Buns
Instructions
Preheat the Pit Boss to 375°F for 15 minutes
with the lid closed when ready to cook.
Form ground beef into patties by dividing it into four 6-ounce pieces. Using salt and pepper, season the patties.
Arrange patties on the grill and cook for six minutes, flipping halfway through.
Check the patties' interior temperature. Burgers are done once they reach a temperature of 165°F on the inside.
Heat the gravy and rice while the patties are cooking. Over easy, scramble the eggs.
To put the burger together, start with the bottom bread, 1/4 cup pasta salad, 1/4 cup rice, gravy, hamburger patty, fried egg, and the top bun.
Serve immediately. Enjoy.

1.109 Chimichurri Smoked Rib-Eyes
Total Time: 1 Hr 15 Mins, Servings: 2
Ingredients
Rib-Eye Steaks, 2 Whole
Fresh Italian Parsley, 1 Cup
Crushed Red Pepper, 1/2 tbsp
Olive Oil, 1/2 Cup
Pit Boss Prime Rib Rub
Red Wine Vinegar, 2 tbsp
Garlic Peeled, 4 Clove
Ground Black Pepper, 1/4 tsp
Cumin, 1/2 tsp
Salt, 1 tsp
Instructions
When you're ready to cook, turn on the Pit Boss's Smoke setting. Season both sides of the rib-eyes liberally with Prime Rib Rub. Smoke the steaks for 1 hour on the grill grate.
After that, the steaks have smoked for 1 hour, transfer them to a plate and prepare your Pit Boss to 450 degrees F.
To get a nice sear, place steaks on hot grill grates after the Pit Boss has warmed.
Cook for 6 to 8 minutes on each side, or until done to your satisfaction, after flipping the steaks once.
To make the chimichurri, combine all of the ingredients in a blender. Season to taste with additional salt and also red pepper flakes if desired.
Arrange the steaks on a serving dish. Allow 3 minutes for the meat to rest before serving. Serve the rib-eyes with chimichurri on the side. Enjoy.

1.110 Skirt Steak with Corn & Avocado Salsa
Total Time: 30 Mins, Servings: 6
Ingredients
Lime, 1
Tequila, 1/4 Cup
Skirt Steak, 2 Pound
Triple sec, 1 tbsp
Vegetable Oil, 1/4 Cup
Beans Black, 1 Cup
Tomato Diced, 1
Corn, Kernels, 1 1/2 Cup
Red Onion, 1 Cup
Garlic Minced, 2 Clove
Cilantro Chopped, 2 tbsp
Jalapeño, 1 Whole
Lime Juiced, 1 Whole
Rice Wine Vinegar, 1 tbsp
Jacobsen Kosher Sea Salt, 2 tsp
Flour Tortillas
Ground Cumin, 1 tsp
Avocado Diced, 1
Salt & Pepper
Instructions
Peel the lime and remove the zest before juicing it. In a small bowl, combine the zest and juice. Stir in the triple sec, tequila, and salt until the salt crystals are completely dissolved. Add the oil and whisk to combine. Add the meat to a cover with plastic wrap and seal. Freeze for several hours or overnight after sealing.
Prepare the salsa the day before the steak is to be served. In a mixing bowl, combine the corn, tomatoes, beans, garlic, onions, and jalapeño. Combine the lime juice, balsamic vinegar, cumin, and cilantro in a mixing bowl. With a rubber spatula, gently fold in the avocado. Salt and black pepper to taste. If not serving right away, cover and chill.
Begin the Pit Boss grill and adjust the temperature to 500 °F and warm for 10-15 minutes with the lid closed.

Pat the steak dries with the paper towels after removing it from the marinade. 5 minutes each side on the grill or when the steak is cooked to your satisfaction.
Transfer to a chopping board and let aside for at least 2 minutes. Thinly slice on the diagonal. Serve with tortillas & salsa on the side. Enjoy.

1.111 Braised Cincinnati Chili
Total Time: 1 Hr 20 Mins, Servings: 6
Ingredients
Olive oil, 1 tsp
Ground Beef, 2 Pound
Garlic, 1 Clove
Spaghetti Uncooked, 1 Pound
Onion Chopped, 2
Chili Powder, 2 tsp
Apple Cider Vinegar, 2 tsp
Worcestershire Sauce, 2 tsp
Dried oregano, 1 tsp
Ground Cloves, 1/2 tsp
Tomato Paste, 2 tsp
Ground Allspice, 3/4 tsp
Chicken Broth, 2 Cup
Brown Sugar, 2 tsp
Tomato Sauce, 2 Can
Salt
Black Pepper
Beans
Instructions
In a medium Dutch oven, heat the olive oil over medium-high heat till it begins to simmer. Cook, occasionally stirring, until the onions are cooked and transparent, approximately 5 minutes. Cook until the ground meat is browned.
Cook until garlic, chili powder, oregano, allspice, and cloves are aromatic, about 2 minutes. Cook until the color of the tomato paste has turned to a rusty orange.
Combine the broth, vinegar, tomato sauce,
Worcestershire sauce and brown sugar in a large mixing bowl. Season to taste with salt and pepper.
When ready to cook, preheat the oven to 350°F with the lid covered for 15 minutes.
Transfer the Dutch oven to the grill, covered. Cook for 25-30 minutes, or until the sauce has thickened and is boiling.
Bring a big saucepan of water to boil while the chili cooks. Cook until the pasta is al dente. Strain and set aside.
To serve, spoon chili over spaghetti noodles and top with kidney beans, diced onion, and shredded cheese. Enjoy.

1.112 Beer Brined Corned Beef

Total Time: 5 Hrs 15 Mins, Servings: 8
Ingredients
Dark Lager Apple Juice, 3 Bottle (12 Oz)
Cold Water, 3 Quart
Kosher Salt, 1 1/2 Cup
Pickling Spice, 5 tbsp
Fat Cap, 1/4 Inch
Onion Sliced, 1 Medium
Garlic Smashed, 5 Clove
Morton Tender Meat Cure, 1 1/2 Cup
Brown Sugar, 1/2 Cup
Packer Brisket, 1 (9-12 Lb)
Pit Boss Prime Rib Rub
Instructions
To make the brine, mix 3 quarts of cold water, kosher salt, curing salt, and brown sugar, and in a large stockpot or food-safe bucket. Stir until sugar crystals and the salt has dissolved, using a long-handled spoon.
Combine the pickling spice, onion, and garlic in a mixing bowl. Remove the brine from the heat and put it in the refrigerator. Place the meat in the brine & weigh it down to fully immerse it. Brine the brisket in the refrigerator for 3 to 4 days, stirring once a day.
Drain the brine from the brisket and discard it. Under cold running water, thoroughly rinse the brisket.
Finish with a sprinkling of Pit Boss Prime Rib Rub.
When you're ready to cook, preheat the Pit Boss to 250°F with the lid closed for almost 15 mins.
When the Pit Boss is ready, put the beef brisket firmly on the grill grate & cook until the internal temperature reaches 160°F (about 4-5 hours).
Wrap the meat in two layers of foil and cover with 1-1/2 cup water. Return to the Pit Boss and cook until the meat reaches a temperature of 204°F on the inside (about 3 to 4 hours).
Set aside for 30 minutes to allow flavors to meld. To serve, cut the meat into 1/4-inch-thick slices against the grain and place them on a dish or plate. Enjoy.

1.113 Baked Ziti with Italian Sausage

Total Time: 50 Mins, Servings: 6
Ingredients
Grated Mozzarella Cheese, 2 Cup
Ziti, 1 Pound
Garlic Minced, 1 tsp
Spaghetti Sauce, 1 Jar
Red Pepper Flakes, 1 Pinch
Italian Sausage, 1 Pound
Salt & Pepper
Parmesan Cheese, 1/4 Cup
Instructions
Preheat the oven to High (450°F) with the lid closed when ready to cook (10-15 minutes).
In a large mixing bowl, combine the cooked pasta, garlic, spaghetti sauce, red pepper flakes, and salt & pepper to taste. Toss. In a large mixing bowl, combine the spaghetti, Sausage, and cheese.
Using non-stick cooking spray, coat 9 *13* 2-inch baking dish. Pour 1/2 of the pasta combination into the baking dish you've prepared. Half of the mozzarella should be sprinkled on top. Fill the dish with the remaining pasta, level down the top, and top with the remaining mozzarella.
Bake in Pit Boss for 20 minutes, or until cheese is nicely browned and bubbling.
Remove from the oven and top with parmesan cheese. Enjoy.

1.114 Smoked Carolina Burger

Total Time: 1 Hr, Servings: 2
Ingredients
Ground Beef, 2 1/2 Pound
Dried oregano, 1 tsp
Chili Powder, 2 tbsp
Paprika, 1 tsp
Cumin, 1 tsp
Brown Sugar, 1 tsp
Garlic Powder, 1/2 tsp
Onion Powder, 1/2 tsp
Salt, 1/2 tsp
Black Pepper, 1 tsp
San Marzano Tomatoes, 1 Can (14 Oz)
Cayenne Pepper
Beef Stock, 1 Cup
Cheddar Cheese, 4 Slices
Sesame Seed Buns, 4
Mayonnaise, 1/2 Cup
Distilled White Vinegar, 2 tsp
Sour Cream, 1/2 Cup
Kosher Salt, 1 tsp
Green Cabbage, 1/2 Head
Purple Cabbage, 1/2 Head
Celery Seed, 1 tsp
Shredded Carrots, 2
Instructions
Preheat a cast-iron pan over medium heat to prepare the chili. Cook until the ground meat is browned and cooked thoroughly. Bring the remaining ingredients to a boil. Reduce the heat to low and cook for 20-30 minutes, or until the liquid has reduced and thickened.
Cut the meat into 4 equal pieces and set aside. Make even patties using the mixture.
When ready to cook, increase the temperature to High & preheat for 15 minutes with the lid closed.
Place the burgers, depression-side down, straight on the grill grate. Cook for at least 6 mins before flipping and turning the grill to 180°F. If Super Smoke is available, use it for the best taste.
Cook for another 7 minutes, or when a thermometer placed in the middle of the burger reads 140°F.
Add cheese to the burgers in the final few mins of cooking and toast the buns on the grill.
In a medium mixing bowl, combine mayonnaise, sour cream, salt, pepper, vinegar, and celery seed. Toss in the cabbages and carrots to mix.
To construct the burgers, place 1 piece of cheese, chili, and slaw on each patty. Enjoy.

1.115 Baked Bacon-Weaved Honey Bourbon-Glazed Meatloaf

Total Time: 1 Hr 15 Mins, Servings: 6
Ingredients
Carrot Diced, 1
Mushrooms Diced, 4 Ounce
Ground Beef, 3 Pound
Stalk Celery Diced, 1
Red Onion Diced, 1/2
Olive Oil
Cooked Bacon, Crumbled, 6 Slices
Garlic, 2 Clove
Sprig Leaves, 4
Worcestershire Sauce, 2 tsp
Egg, 1
Condensed Tomato Soup, 1/2 Cup
Salt, 1 1/2 tsp
Pepper, 1/2 tsp
Breadcrumbs, 1 Cup
Thin Bacon, 1 Pound
Pit Boss BBQ Sauce
Instructions
Preheat Pit Boss to 225°F and cook for 15 minutes with lid covered until ready to cook. If Super Smoke is available, use it for the best taste.
Toss carrots, celery, mushrooms, and onions with olive oil in a mixing dish. To soften the veggies, cover the bowl with plastic wrap & microwave for approximately 2 minutes.
Allow veggies to cool before mixing them with ground beef, thyme, egg, garlic, bacon, salt, pepper, Worcestershire sauce, tomato soup, and breadcrumbs in a large mixing bowl.
Shape the batter into a loaf and set it on a wire rack set over a foil-lined baking tray.
Use the bacon to weave a bacon weave on a big piece of parchment paper.
Gently turn the meatloaf over and place the weave on the top of the paper. Remove the parchment paper from the pan.
Cook the meatloaf for 45 minutes on the grill. Remove the meatloaf from the grill and raise the temperature to 325 degrees Fahrenheit. Allow Pit Boss to warm for 10 minutes with lid closed.
Once the grill has reached temperature, return the meatloaf to it and cook for approximately an hour, or until an instant-read thermometer reads 160 degrees F.
Drizzle meatloaf with the barbecue sauce to caramelize during the final 15 minutes (after it gets about 140°F).
Remove the steak from the grill and let it aside for 15 mins before slicing. Enjoy.

1.116 Grilled Bacon Cheeseburger

Total Time: 1 Hrs 5 Mins, Servings: 2
Ingredients
Bacon, 8 Slices
Ground Beef, 3/4 Pound
Cheddar Cheese, 1/2" Cubes, 4
Salt
Swiss Cheese, 1/2" Cubes, 4
Bacon Ground, 3/4 Pound

Pepper
Mozzarella Cheese, 1/2" Cubes, 4
Sliced Pickles
Romaine Lettuce Leaves
Hamburger Buns, 4
Tomatoes
Instructions
Preheat the Pit Boss to 350°F for 15 minutes with the lid closed when ready to cook.
Cook bacon strips on the grill grate for 20 to 25 minutes, or until rendered & crispy but not burned. Remove the steaks from the grill and put them aside.
Preheat the grill to high and shut the lid for 10 minutes.
In a large mixing bowl, combine the ground bacon, ground beef, salt & pepper to taste. Make 8 equal-sized balls out of the mixture.
Place the three kinds of cheese cubes in the middle of each ball and fill them with meat thoroughly. Form the balls into 1/4" thick hamburger patties. Remove the burgers off the grill when they are done to your liking.
Grill the buns for 1 minute. Top burgers with lettuce, onions, tomatoes, pickles, & bacon strips on buns. Add your favorite condiments on the top. Enjoy.

1.117 Guinness Shepherd's Pie

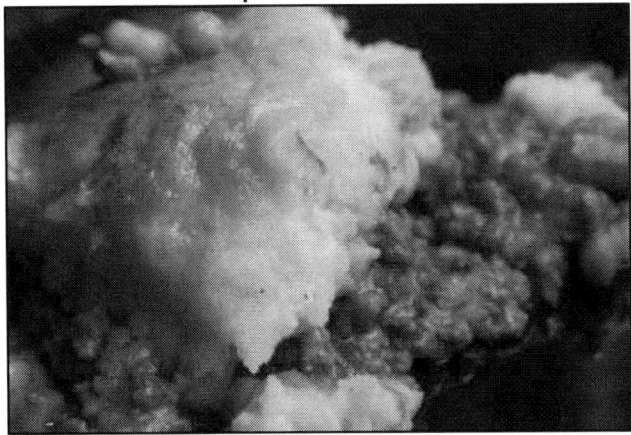

Total Time: 1 Hr 45 Mins, Servings: 4
Ingredients
Russet Potatoes, 6
Worcestershire Sauce, 1 tbsp
Onion Diced, 1
Ground Beef, Pound
Tomato Sauce, 1 1/2 Cup
Garlic Minced, 4 Clove
Vegetables Frozen, 4 Cup
Fresh thyme, 1 tsp
Guinness Extra Stout, 1Cup
Salt & Pepper
Butter, Sticks
Shredded Cheddar Cheese, 1 1/2 Cup
Cup Milk
Instructions
For the potatoes bring a big saucepan of water to a boil. Allow this to heat while you prepare the meat combination.
Cook the onion and garlic in a large skillet. Cook until the meat or lamb is browned. The grease should be removed.
Toss in the veggies and tomato sauce. Cook, often stirring, for 4-5 minutes.
Season with salt & pepper to taste, then add the Guinness, Worcestershire sauce, and thyme. Boil till the liquid has thickened and reduced by half (about 15 minutes).
Cook the potatoes for 15-20 minutes, or until tender but not mushy, in boiling water. Drain and set aside to cool. Using the butter, milk, and salt, and black pepper to taste, mash the potatoes.
Divide the meat mixture into two plates after the meat mixture has finished cooking and also the potatoes have been mashed. The cheese is placed on top of the mashed potatoes.
When ready to cook, preheat the Pit Boss to 350 ° F for 10 to 15 minutes with the lid closed.
Bake for 30-45 minutes, or until cheese has melted and potatoes are golden brown. Serve immediately. Enjoy!

1.118 Whiskey Bourbon BBQ Cheeseburger

Total Time: 1 Hr 5 Mins, Servings: 4
Ingredients
Ground Beef, 3 Pound
Bacon, 1 Pound
Brown Sugar, 1/2 Cup
Hot Sauce, 1
Cheddar Cheese, 4 Slices
Pit Boss Rub
Bourbon Whiskey, 1/2 Cup
Instructions
In a medium mixing bowl, add ground beef with Pit Boss Rub & mix well, take care, and not overwork or overheat the meat. Quarter the ground beef and place each quarter on a 6" cake ring. Form the meat into a patty by pressing it down.
Poke approximately 40 holes about 34% of the way through each burger with a skewer. Drizzle spicy sauce over the patties after coating them in brown sugar. Pour whisky over each burger and set it aside for approximately a half-hour in the fridge.
When ready to cook, preheat the grill to 225°F with the lid covered for 10-15 minutes.
Take the burgers out of the cake rings and set them aside. When the grill is hot, put the bacon & burgers directly on the grate and cook until the internal temperature of the burgers reaches 165 degrees Fahrenheit. Top with the cheddar cheese to melt in the final 10 mins of cooking.
Remove the burgers & bacon from the grill & customize your burger. Enjoy.

1.119 BBQ Brisket Breakfast Tacos

Total Time: 40 Mins, Servings: 6
Ingredients
Leftover Beef Brisket, 4 Pound
Shredded Cheddar Cheese, 2 Cup
Green Bell Pepper, 1
Yellow Bell Pepper, 1
Extra-Virgin Olive Oil, 1/2 Teaspoon
Eggs, 10
Milk, 1/2 Cup
Salt & Pepper
Flour Tortillas
Instructions
Preheat the Pit Boss grill to 375 degrees Fahrenheit when you're ready to cook. Preheat for 10-15 mins with the lid closed.
Wrap leftover brisket in two layers of foil and reheat it on the grill.
Brush the interior of a cast iron pan with oil and warm for 10 minutes on the grill. When the pan is heated, add the diced peppers and cook, occasionally turning, until they are done to your liking.
Whisk together milk, eggs, salt, and pepper to taste while the peppers are cooking. Scramble the scrambled eggs in the skillet. When the eggs are nearly done, add the cheese to the skillet.

Remove the eggs and beef from the grill. Serve the eggs in a tortilla with beef on top. If desired, top with guacamole or salsa. Enjoy.

1.120 Garlic and Herb Stuffed Prime Rib Roast
Total Time: 3 Hrs 15 Mins, Servings: 6
Ingredients
Butter Softened, 3 tbsp
Garlic Chopped, 5 Clove
Prime Rib Roast, 3 Pound (8 Lb)
Parsley Minced, 4 tbsp
Rosemary Chopped, 1 tbsp
Kosher Salt, 2 tbsp
Thyme Leaves, 4 tbsp
Black Pepper, 1 tbsp
Instructions
Combine butter, parsley, garlic, thyme & rosemary in a small bowl.
Make 2 slits in the prime rib. "Fill each slit halfway with butter herb mixture.
Liberally season the outside of the roast with black pepper & kosher salt. Allow 30 minutes to come to room temperature before cooking.
When ready to cook, turn on the Pit Boss grill, set the temperature to High, and preheat for 10 to 15 minutes with the lid closed.
Place the roast on the grill grate with the ribs towards the rear of the grill. Close the cover and cook for 45 minutes or until the roast has an equal coating of browning on the outside.
Lower the heat to 325°F and continue to cook for another 2 1/2 hours, or till the temperature reaches 125°F.
Remove the roast from the grill and set aside for 15 minutes to rest before slicing.
Remove the trussing and bones from the roast when it has rested, and slice it into 1-inch-thick slices "pieces of one-inch Enjoy.

1.121 Flank Steak Matambre
Total Time: 2 Hrs 20 Mins, Servings: 6
Ingredients
Flank Steak, 2 Pound
Dried oregano, 1 1/2 tsp
Extra-Virgin Olive Oil
Pit Boss Rib Rub
Worcestershire Sauce, 2 tbsp
Provolone Cheese, 8 Ounce
Spinach, 4 Ounce
Red Bell Pepper, 1/2
Kielbasa Sausage, 7 Ounce
Carrot Peeled, 2 Large
Instructions
Place the flank steak between two pieces of plastic wrap on a chopping board. Using a scaloppini pounder or meat pounder, pound the meat to an equal 1/4-inch thickness.
Leave the outer piece of the plastic wrap and throw it away. Brush the meat with Worcestershire sauce (the side facing up), then season with oregano & Pit Boss Rib Rub. Starting with the long side nearest to you, spread the sliced cheese over the surface of the meat; leave 2 inches on the opposite end free of cheese and other toppings.
Arrange the sausage strips, bell pepper strips, spinach leaves & carrot strips in rows parallel to the long side closest to you on the meat. Roll the meat tightly like a jelly roll. Toothpicks are used to keep it in place. If desired, trim any scraggly ends. At 2-inch intervals, tie the beef roll using butcher's thread.
Take the toothpicks out. Season the meat with Pit Boss Rib Rub after rubbing it with olive oil on the exterior. Twist the ends of a big sheet of heavy-duty aluminum foil to seal the roll. Make a few small holes with a knife to enable the steam to escape.
Preheat the Pit Boss grill to 325 degrees Fahrenheit when you're ready to cook. Place the foil-covered roll directly on the grill grate and roast for 2 to 2-1/2 hours, or until the meat is extremely tender.
Place the roll on a cutting board and then let it aside to rest for a few minutes. Before cutting the meat lengthwise into 1/2-inch-thick pieces, remove the foil and threads. Enjoy.

1.122 Braised Brunswick Stew
Total Time: 2 Hrs 30 Mins, Servings: 4
Ingredients
Butter, 8 tbsp
Diced Tomatoes, 45 Ounce (28 Oz)
Large Onion, 1
Celery, 2
Garlic Minced, 4 Clove
Green Bell Pepper, 1
Smoked Paprika, 1 tsp
Okra, 1 Cup
Cayenne Pepper, 1/2 tsp
BBQ Sauce, 1 Cup
Pulled Pork, 1 Pound
Worcestershire Sauce, 1 tbsp
Pulled Chicken, 1 Pound
Chicken Broth, 1 Cup
Lima Beans, 10 Ounce
Apple Cider Vinegar, 1 tbsp
Beef Brisket, 1 Pound
Corn, 10 Ounce
Salt
Black Pepper
Hot Sauce
Instructions
In a big cast-iron Dutch oven, melt the butter over medium heat. 5 to 8 minutes until the bell pepper, onion and celery are tender and transparent.
Cook for 2 minutes after adding the garlic. Allow boiling for 5 minutes after adding the Paprika, Worcestershire sauce, cayenne, barbecue sauce, and tomatoes. In a separate bowl, combine the smoked chicken or pork from a prior grilling session. Smoked beef brisket from a prior grilling session may be added now. Bring the chicken broth to a boil, then remove from the heat.
Meanwhile, warm the Pit Boss to 300°F with the lid covered for 15 minutes.
Cover the Dutch oven with a cover and gently place it on the grill grate. Cook for an hour and a half, adding additional broth as needed. The stew mustn't be overly soupy.
Add corn, lima beans & okra, if using, and simmer for another 30 minutes, or until the veggies are cooked, with the lid off. Season with salt & black pepper to taste, depending on how salty the smoked meats are, and much more cayenne pepper if you want it hotter.
To brighten the taste, add vinegar. Serve immediately in dishes with a side of spicy sauce. Enjoy.

1.123 Smoked T-Bone Steaks
Total Time: 50 Mins, Servings: 4
Ingredients
T-Bone Steaks, 4 (14-16 Oz Each)
Pit Boss Rib Rub
Black Pepper
Butter, 4 tbsp
Instructions
Season the steaks with Pit Boss Rib Rub on both sides.

When ready to cook, preheat the Pit Boss to 225°F with the lid closed for 15 minutes. If Super Smoke is available, use it for the best taste.

Place steaks on grill grate & smoke for 35-45 minutes, or until an instant-read thermometer inserted into the thickest portion of the steak registers 115°F. Take the steaks off the grill.

Preheat the grill to 500°F and cook for 15 minutes with the lid covered.

When the grill is hot, sear the steaks for 3-4 minutes on each side, or until they achieve a medium-rare internal temperature of 135°F.

Remove off the grill and spread a pat of butter on top. Allow 5 minutes for the steaks to rest before slicing. *Cook times may vary based on the temperature of the oven and the ambient temperature. The Pit Boss App has this and over a thousand more Pit Boss recipes.

1.124 Pit Boss Prime Rib Roast

Total Time: 4 Hrs 5 Mins, Servings: 8
Ingredients
1 5-7 Bone Rib Roast
Pit Boss Rib Rub
Instructions
Evenly coat the roast with Pit Boss Prime Rib Rub and cover it in plastic wrap. Refrigerate for a minimum of 24 hours.

When ready to cook, preheat the Pit Boss to 500°F with the lid closed for 15 min.

Cook the prime rib for 30 minutes, fat side up, straight on the grill grate. Starting with a higher heat setting will aid in the development of a crispy, rendered crust.

Lower the grill temp to 300°F after 30 minutes. Cook for another 3–4 hours, or until the internal temperature reaches 120°F for rare, 130°F for medium-rare, 140°F for medium, or 150°F for well done. Using an instant-read thermometer, start monitoring the temperature in 30 min intervals throughout the cook. Cooking time may vary depending on the size of your roast and the temperature you want it to finish at.

Remove from the grill and set aside to cool for 30 minutes before carving. Enjoy.

1.125 Reverse Seared NY Strip Steak

Total Time: 1 Hr 15 Mins, Servings: 4
Ingredients
Strip Steaks, 4 (1-1/2 Inch Thick)
Butter, 4 tbsp
Pit Boss Beef Rub
Instructions
Preheat Pit Boss to 225°F and cook for 15 minutes with lid covered until ready to cook. If Super Smoke is available, use it for the best taste.

Season the steaks with the Beef Rub while the grill is getting ready.

Grill the steaks for 60 minutes or till they reach a temp of 105-110 degrees Fahrenheit.

Remove the steaks from the grill and allow them to rest on the counter. Preheat the grill to 500°F and cook for 15 minutes with the lid covered.

Return the steaks to the grill and sear them for another 4 minutes. Now add 1 tablespoon of butter to each steak after flipping.

Continue to sear for 4 minutes more and check the interior temperature. For medium-rare, the finish temperature should be 130°F to 135°F.

Remove steaks from the grill after the desired temperature is achieved. Allow 5 minutes for resting. Enjoy.

1.126 Pit Boss NY Strip Steak

Total Time: 20 Mins, Servings: 2
Ingredients
Pit Boss BBQ Sauce, 1 Cup
Pit Boss Beef Rub
Strip Steaks, 14 Ounce
Instructions
In a shallow casserole dish, add Pit Boss Sweet & Heat BBQ Sauce and whisk to blend.

Dip strip steak into the mixture, ensuring that it is uniformly coated on both sides. Resealable plastic bag and marinate for three hours to overnight in the refrigerator.

Take the steak out of the marinade & season generously with Pit Boss Beef Rub. Allow 45 minutes for the steaks to come to the temperature before cooking.

When ready to cook, preheat the Pit Boss to 500°F for 15 minutes with the lid closed.

Place the steaks towards the front of the grill grate & cook for 4-5 mins, or until the internal temperature reaches 130°F for medium-rare.

Remove the steaks from the grill & set them aside to rest for 5 minutes. To serve, cut against the grain. *Cook times may vary based on the temperature of the oven and the ambient temperature. The Pit Boss App has this and over a thousand more Pit Boss recipes.

1.127 Corned Beef Hash

Total Time: 45 Mins, Servings: 6
Ingredients
Butter, 3 tbsp
Salt & Pepper
Vegetable Oil, 1 tbsp
Poblano Pepper, 1 Whole
Potatoes, 4 Cup
Onion Diced, 1
Garlic Minced, 1 Clove
Worcestershire Sauce, 2 tsp
Cooked Beef, 3 Cup
Cream or Beef Stock, 4 tbsp
Fried or Poached Egg, 4 Whole
Mustard, 1 tsp
Hot Sauce, 1 1/2 tsp
Flat-Leaf Parsley, 2 tbsp
Instructions
Preheat your Pit Boss to 375°F and cook for 10 to 15 minutes with the lid covered.

In a large well-seasoned cast-iron pan or non-stick skillet, oven-proof handle, melt the butter & oil together over medium-high heat. Place the potatoes in a single layer on the baking sheet. Add salt and pepper to taste. Fry the potatoes until golden brown, tossing them with a spatula as required.

Cook for 3 mins after adding the onion & poblano pepper. Cook for another minute after adding the garlic. (If the mixture looks dry, add a tablespoon of butter.)

Combine the potatoes and onions in a large mixing basin. The skillet should not be emptied. Stir in the corned meat, cream, Worcestershire sauce, spicy sauce, and mustard until everything is well combined.

Season to taste with additional spicy sauce, mustard, salt & black pepper if necessary.

Using the back of a big spoon or spatula, compact the hash into the pan.

Place the pan on the grill grate and cook for 25-30 minutes, or until the surface of the hash is crispy and well browned.

Garnish with parsley & lay the eggs on the top before serving with more spicy sauce on the side.

1.128 Leftover BBQ Sandwich

Total Time: 55 Mins, Servings: 4
Ingredients
Steaks, 3 Pound
Garlic Minced, 4 Clove
Extra-Virgin Olive Oil, 1 tbsp
Chopped Shallot, 1/2 Cup
Unsalted butter, 1 tbsp
Brandy, 1/4 Cup
Demi-Glace, 1/4 Cup
All-Purpose Flour, 1 tbsp
Beef Stock, 3 Cup
Butter Chilled, 1 tbsp
Worcestershire Sauce, 1 tbsp
Salt, 1 1/2 tsp
Pepper, 1 tsp
Mayonnaise, 1/2 Cup
Lemon Juiced, 1 tsp
Sour Cream, 1/2 Cup
Garlic Minced, 1 tsp
Butter, 1/2 Cup
Prepared Horseradish, 1/2 Cup
Ciabatta Loaf, 6
Pepper Jack Cheese, 6 Slices
Instructions
Thinly slice any remaining meat. Remove from the equation.
To make the au jus, heat a normal saucepan over medium-high heat. In 7 to 8 minutes, sauté the shallots & garlic in the olive butter and oil until gently caramelized. Mix in the flour until you have a loose paste. Stir in the demi-glace, beef stock, and Worcestershire sauce after deglazing with the brandy.
Bring to the boil, lower to low heat and continue to cook for another 25 mins. Turn off the heat.
Strain off the garlic & shallots from the soup and transfer the liquid to the saucepan. Melt the butter and spread it evenly throughout the sauce. To taste, season with salt and black pepper. Keep yourself warm.
Horseradish Mayo: In a medium mixing bowl, combine all of the ingredients. Refrigerate.
When ready to cook, increase the temp to High and preheat for 15 min with the lid closed.
Put the soft butter and minced garlic in a mixing bowl. Brush cut sides of ciabatta buns with butter, then toast them on both sides under the grill until crispy. Spread horseradish mayo on top.
Pile the beef on the bottoms of the ciabatta buns, cover it with cheese, and serve it with au jus on the side for dipping. Enjoy.

1.129 Moroccan Ground Meat Kebabs

Total Time: 50 Mins, Servings: 2
Ingredients
Ground Lamb, 1 1/2 Pound
Minced Cilantro Leaves, 3 tbsp
Onion Minced, 2/3 Cup
Ground Coriander, 1/2 tsp
Fresh Mint, 1 tbsp
Ground Cumin, 1 tbsp
Paprika, 1 tsp
Salt, 1 tsp
Ground Cinnamon, 1/4 tsp
Garlic Minced, 2 Clove
Pita Bread
Instructions
Combine all of the ingredients in a big mixing bowl, except the pita bread, in a large mixing basin. Form into meatballs with a diameter of approximately 2 inches. Using a bamboo skewer, skewer each meatball, then soak your hands with cool water and form the meat into a cigar shape approximately the size of a man's thumb. Freeze for a minimum of 30 minutes, or even overnight, if possible.
When ready to cook, preheat the oven to 350 degrees Fahrenheit with the lid covered for 10-15 mins.
Grill the kebabs for 25-30 minutes, rotating once or until the meat thermometer reads 160 degrees within.
If preferred, warm pita bread on a grill before serving.

1.130 Hickory Smoked Prime Rib

Total Time: 4 Hrs 15 Mins, Servings: 6
Ingredients
4-Bone Rib Roast, 1 (8-10 Lb)
Dried thyme, 2 tsp
Dijon Mustard, 3 tbsp
Garlic Mashed, 4 Clove
Prepared Horseradish
Worcestershire Sauce, 2 tbsp
Dried rosemary, 2 tsp
Pit Boss Rib Rub
Instructions
Trim any fat cap on the roast that is more than 1/4-inch-thick with a sharp knife, or have your butcher do it for you. Butcher's string should be used to tie the roast between bones. This prevents the meat's eye from detaching from the cap.
Combine the Worcestershire sauce, Dijon mustard, thyme, garlic, and rosemary in a small bowl. Before using, carefully cut the dried rosemary needles if they are lengthy.
Spread the mustard mixture all over the exterior of the roast and season liberally with Pit Boss Rib Rub on both sides. Refrigerate for up to eight hours, uncovered.
When ready to cook, preheat the Pit Boss to 250°F with the lid closed for 15 mins. Place the fat side up the prime rib on the grill grate. Roast for 4 hours or even the meat temperature reaches 125°F to 130°F for rare or 135°F for medium-rare (the point of the temperature probe should be in the middle of the flesh).
Transfer the meat to a chopping board with a deep hole, so the fluids don't escape, and tent it loosely with foil. Allow 30 minutes for the meat to rest.
Remove the string before carving. Remove the rack of bone with a sharp knife, following the curve of the flesh. Carve the meat into 1/2-inch-thick slices across the grain. If desired, top with horseradish. Enjoy.

1.131 Grilled Beef Back Ribs

Total Time: 2 Hrs 15 Mins, Servings: 8
Ingredients
Beef Back Ribs, 4 Rack (2 Lb Each)
Red Wine, 1 Cup
Olive Oil, 1 Cup
Worcestershire Sauce, 1 tbsp
Dijon Mustard, 1 tbsp
Salt, 1 1/2 tsp
Coarse Black Pepper, 1 tsp
Garlic Minced, 3 Clove
Small Onion, 1
Bay Leaf, 1
Pit Boss Rib Rub
Instructions
Loosen a thin papery membrane off the bone-side of the ribs if your butcher hasn't already done so by pushing the point of a butter knife beneath the membrane over a central bone. To obtain a stronghold, use paper towels, then pull the membrane away.
Place the ribs in a nonreactive pan that can hold them.
To make the marinade, whisk together the wine,

Worcestershire sauce, olive oil, salt, Dijon mustard, and pepper in a mixing bowl. Combine the garlic, onion, and bay leaf in a mixing bowl.
Drizzle the marinade and over meat racks and flip them to coat them. Freeze for several hours or overnight, covered.
Rotate the racks a few times to ensure that the meat is uniformly seasoned. Take the ribs out of the marinade and discard the solids.
Rub Pit Boss Rib Rub on both sides of the ribs.
When ready to cook, preheat the Pit Boss to 250°F with the lid closed for 15 mins.
Place the rib's bone side down on the grill grate. Cook for 2 hours, or until the vegetables are soft. Serve right away. Enjoy.

1.132 BBQ Meatball Onion Bombs
Total Time: 1 Hr 10 Mins, Servings: 4
Ingredients
Yellow Onion, 2 Whole
Onion Diced, 1/4 Cup
Parsley Chopped, 1/4 Cup
Ground Beef, 1 Pound
Spicy Ketchup, 1 tbsp
Soy Sauce, 1 tsp
Chopped Mushrooms, 1/4 Cup
Brown Sugar, 1 tbsp
Pit Boss Rib Rub, 1 tbsp
Worcestershire Sauce, 1 tsp
Bacon Package, 1 Whole
Panko Breadcrumbs, 1/4 Cup
Pit Boss BBQ Sauce
Instructions
Preheat the grill to 225°F and pre-heat with the lid covered when ready to cook (10-15 minutes).
Start by removing the rough outer peel from the onions by cutting off the bottoms and tops. Cut the onion in half and begin peeling the layers apart; put aside the onion skins.
Combine ground beef, parsley, Worcestershire sauce, chopped onion, mushroom, ketchup, brown sugar, Pit Boss Rib seasoning, soy sauce, and bread crumbs in a large mixing dish. Hand-mix the ingredients.
To make an onion-sealed meatball, put a small quantity of meatloaf mixture in one of the onion layers pieces, and press an additional piece on top of the mixture. Continue layering your onions until all of your meatloaf combinations are gone. The number of onion bombs you make will be determined by the size of the onions you use.
Wrap each bomb with around three pieces of bacon. To prevent the bacon from unraveling during cooking, secure it with toothpicks. Place directly on the grill grates.
Smoke on the Pit Boss for 1 hour.
Raise the temperature to 350°F and continue to cook for the next 20-30 minutes, or until the internal temperature reaches 160°F. Allow 10 minutes for your preferred Pit Boss BBQ sauce to caramelize before brushing it on the bombs. Allow sitting for 5 minutes after removing from the grill. Enjoy.

1.133 Grilled Rib-Eye with Green Butter
Total Time: 1 Hr 15 Mins, Servings: 6
Ingredients
Green Butter
Butter, 1 Stick
Minced Garlic, 1/2 tsp
White Pepper, 1 Pinch
Flat-Leaf Parsley, 1 1/2 tbsp
Lemon Juiced, 1/2
Main
Kosher Salt, 1/4 Cup
Ground Black Pepper, 1/4 Cup
Onion Powder, 3 tbsp
Rib-Eye Steaks, 3 (2 Inch Thick)
Instructions
Preheat Pit Boss to 225°F and cook for 15 minutes with lid covered until ready to cook.
To make the green butter, combine all of the ingredients in a mixing bowl and chill till ready to use.
Combine the salt, pepper, and onion powder in a mixing bowl. Place the steaks on the grill after rubbing the mixture on them. Cook until the steaks reach a temperature of 120°F on the inside. This should take between 75 and 90 minutes.
Take the steaks from the grill and cover them with foil. Raise the temp to 500°F and warm for 15 minutes with the lid closed. Return the steaks to the grill when it is hot, cooking for 3 to 4 minutes on each side and topping with a tbsp of green butter after the initial flip.
If preferred, top with more green butter. Enjoy.

1.134 Smoked Brisket with Pit Boss Coffee Rub
Total Time: 9 Hrs 20 Mins, Servings: 8
Ingredients
Beef Brisket, 1 (15 Lb)
Beef Broth, 15 Ounce
Pit Boss Coffee Rub, 1/4 Cup
Salt, 4 tbsp
Instructions
Preheat Pit Boss to 225°F and cook for 15 minutes with lid covered until ready to cook. If Super Smoke is available, use it for the best taste.
Remove any extra fat from the brisket.
To create the beef broth injection, whisk together 2 tsp Pit Boss Coffee Rub, 2 tbsp, and salt beef broth, in a small mixing dish until the salt is completely dissolved. Inject the brisket in a checker pattern by placing the needle straight to the grain approximately 1 inch apart across the whole brisket. As you push the plunger, pull it back out. To confine the mess, inject in a high-sided aluminum pan or bus tub & hold your palm over the area where you're injecting.
Season the brisket's outside with the remaining rub and salt.
Place the brisket straight on the grill grate and cook for 6 hours or when the temp reaches 160 degrees Fahrenheit.
Tightly wrap the brisket in foil or butcher paper in two layers. Return the grill to its original position.
Continue to cook for another 3 hours, or when the temp reaches 204°F. Remove the brisket from the grill and poke a hole in the foil to allow steam to escape.
After 10 minutes, close the aperture and let the meat rest for 60 min before slicing. Cut and enjoy.

1.135 Grilled Balsamic & Blue Steak
Total Time: 22 Mins, Servings: 2
Ingredients
Olive Oil, 3 tbsp
Pit Boss Rib Rub, 1 tbsp
Garlic Minced, 4 Clove
Balsamic Vinegar, 6 tbsp
Butter, 1/4 Cup
Crumbled Blue Cheese, 1/4 Cup
Top Round Broil Steak, 1 1/2 Pound
Red Onion, 2 Whole
Tomatoes Sliced, 2 Whole
Instructions
Whisk together the olive oil, Prime Rib Rub, balsamic vinegar, rosemary, thyme, and 3 garlic cloves in a large mixing bowl. Place the steak in a big plastic bag with a zipper. Pour the sauce over the steak, close the bag and marinate for at least

4 hours or overnight in the refrigerator.

Take the steak out of the fridge 45 mins before grilling to allow it to come to room temperature.

In a small bowl, mix the butter, 1 garlic clove, blue cheese, and mix thoroughly. Place in the refrigerator until ready to serve.

When ready to cook, preheat the oven to high (450°F) with the lid closed (10 to 15 minutes).

For medium-rare, place the steak towards the front of the grill grate for 6 minutes on each side to sear it. Remove from the fire and set aside for 10-15 minutes to cool.

Brush the tomato and onion slices with olive oil, season with salt and pepper, and put at the front of the grill until small grill marks appear, then move to the center for another 4 minutes. Serve the steak with the grilled tomatoes and onions, a sprinkle of more rosemary, and a dollop of blue cheese butter, cut against the grain. Enjoy.

1.136 Grilled Ribeye Steak Sandwich

Total Time: 30 Mins, Servings: 4
Ingredients
Tomatillos, 1
Green Onion, 1 Stalk
Cilantro Leaves, 1 Head
Garlic Minced, 1/2 tbsp
Mustard, 1 tbsp
Fresh Horseradish, 1 tsp
Vegetable Oil, 2/3 Cup
Salt & Pepper, 1 Pinch
Beef Rib-Eye, 2
Ciabatta Buns, 6
Pit Boss Rib Rub, 1/2 tbsp
Fresh Arugula
Instructions

Unwrap the tomatillo and put it in a saucepan of boiling water; cook for 3 minutes. Remove from the water and set aside.

In a food processor or blender, combine the cilantro, green onion, tomatillo, and garlic. Combine the oil, mustard, 1/4 cup tomatillo cooking water, Pit Boss Prime Rib Rub, horseradish, and salt & pepper in a large mixing bowl.

Blend all of the ingredients until smooth; save aside 1/2 cup of the sauce for later.

Coat the remaining sauce generously on the steaks (8 oz each) and marinate for 1-4 hours.

When ready to cook, preheat the Pit Boss at 500 degrees F for 10 to 15 minutes with the lid closed.

Grill steaks for 10 minutes on one side, then turn and cook for another 5 minutes. Allow sitting for 5 minutes after removing from the grill.

Thinly slice the steaks and put them on top of the ciabatta buns. Dressing and a tiny handful of arugula on top. Enjoy.

1.137 Reverse Seared Filet Mignon with Red Wine Reduction

Total Time: 35 Mins, Servings: 2
Ingredients
Mignon Steaks, 2 Filet
Pit Boss Rib Rub
Bacon, 2 Slices
Red Wine Reduction
Butter, 1 tbsp
Red Wine, 1/2 Cup
Beef Stock, 1/2 Cup
Shallot, Sliced, 1
Cold Butter, 1 tbsp
Chopped Rosemary, 1 tsp
Salt
Instructions

Preheat Pit Boss to 225°F and cook for 15 minutes with lid covered until ready to cook. If Super Smoke is available, use it for the best taste.

Wrap a piece of bacon around each fillet and fasten with a toothpick. Pit Boss Rib Rub should be used generously.

Place the steaks immediately on the grill grate & cook until they reach an internal temperature of 115°F, approximately 20 minutes.

Take the steaks from the grill and put them aside. Preheat the grill to 500 degrees Fahrenheit for 10 minutes.

To make the Red Wine Reduction Sauce, melt 1 tbsp butter and sauté shallots in a sauté pan over medium heat until transparent. Bring the red wine & beef stock to a low simmer. Reduce the heat to low and continue to cook until the liquid has been reduced by half. Remove from heat, add rosemary, & whisk in 1 tbsp cold butter. To taste, season with salt.

Return the steaks to the grill once the grill has been warmed and sear for 5-7 mins on each side, or when the internal temperature reaches 125°F for medium-rare.

Remove from the grill and let aside to rest for 5–7 minutes before serving.

Toss the steaks with a tablespoon of red wine reduced sauce and serve with your favorite sides. Enjoy.

1.138 Grilled Tri-Tip with Garlic Mashed Potatoes

Total Time: 1 Hrs 40 Mins, Servings: 4
Ingredients
Cloves Garlic, 3
Tri-Tip, 1 (2-3 Lb)
Kosher Salt
Parmesan Cheese, 2 tbsp
Olive Oil, 1 tbsp
Black Pepper
Large Potatoes, 4
Heavy Cream, 1 1/2 Cup
Pit Boss Coffee Rub
Gruyere Cheese, 1/4 Cup
Sour Cream, 1/2 Cup
Instructions

Preheat the Pit Boss to 400°F for 15 minutes with the lid closed when ready to cook.

Place the garlic cloves in the middle of a sheet of foil paper, drizzle with olive oil, then fold up the edges to enclose. Place the garlic straight on the grill grate & roast for 20 to 30 minutes. The garlic will be a bit brown and extremely tender when you unwrap the foil. Reserve.

Lower the temperature of the grill to 225°F. If Super Smoke is available, use it for the best taste.

Trim fat off tri-tip, season on both sides with salt and pepper, then coat with Pit Boss Coffee Rub.

Place the beef directly on the grill grate and cook for 1 1/2 hours, or when the temp reaches 105°F to 110°F. Remove the steaks from the grill and put them aside.

Bring a big saucepan of salted water to a boil while the tri-tip is cooking. Add the potatoes to the boiling water after cutting them into ½-inch cubes. Cook until the vegetables are fork-tender. Strain.

Preheat the grill to 500°F and cook for 15 mins with the lid covered. Return the tri-tip to the grill once it has pre-heated and sear for 5 mins on each side, or until the interior temperature reaches 140°F. Remove off the grill and set aside for 15-25 minutes to cool.

Mash the potatoes & garlic together in a bowl. Heat the cream in a sauce pan; once heated, add the cheeses and stir to incorporate. Add the cream mixture to the potatoes and season with salt and black pepper to taste. Fold in sour cream last. Cut the tri-tip against the grain into small slices. Serve with mashed potatoes with garlic. Enjoy.

1.139 Grilled Carne Asada Burrito with Smoked Pico

Total Time: 40 Mins, Servings: 6
Ingredients
Tomatoes, 5
Jalapeño, 1
Red Bell Pepper, 1
Onion Diced, 1
Lemon Juiced, 1/2
Pit Boss Beef Rub, 4 tbsp
Kosher Salt, 1/2 tsp
Black Pepper, 1/2 tsp
Lime Juiced, 1 Whole
Cilantro, 3 tbsp
Flank Steak, 3 Pound
Instructions
Combine the tomatoes, jalapeño, onion, bell pepper, lime juice, lemon, salt & pepper, and 3 tablespoons cilantro in a mixing bowl.
When you're ready to cook, turn on the Pit Boss grill to smoke and keep the lid open until the fire is formed (4-5 minutes). Preheat the grill to 165 degrees F for 5-10 minutes with the lid closed.
Spread pico de gallo equally on the cookie sheet and cook for 20 minutes on the grill. Remove the steaks from the grill and place them in the refrigerator to cool.
Preheat the grill to 450 degrees F for 10 to 15 minutes with the lid closed.
Season the flank steak on all sides with the Pit Boss Beef rub. Cook the steak for 4-5 minutes on the grill. Cook until the temp of the steak reaches 140 degrees F. Flip the steak and continue cooking when the internal temperature reaches 140 degrees F. Before slicing, remove the steak from the grill and let it rest for 10 minutes.
Thinly slice the meat against the grain. Tortillas, sour cream, cooled pico de gallo, cilantro, and guacamole are used to make burritos. Enjoy.

1.140 Smoked Pot Roast

Total Time: 6 Hrs 15 Mins, Servings: 4
Ingredients
Garlic Powder, 1 tsp
Onion Powder, 1 tsp
Kosher Salt, 1 tsp
Black Pepper, 1 tsp
Chuck Roast, 1 (3 Lb)
Braise
Red Bliss Potatoes, 2 Cup
Carrots, 2 Cup
Pearl Onions, 2 Cup
Ancho Chile Powder, 1 tsp
Sherry or Red Wine, 1 Cup
Fresh Rosemary, 1 tbsp
Fresh Thyme, 1 tbsp
Chipotle Pepper, 2 Dried
Beef Stock, 2 Cup
Instructions
In a small mixing bowl, combine the onion powder, garlic powder, salt, and pepper. Rub the mixture all over the roast.
When ready to cook, preheat the Pit Boss to 180°F with the lid closed for at least 15 mins. If Super Smoke is available, use it for the best taste.
Smoke the entire roast for an hour and a half. Remove the roast off the grill and raise the temperature to 275 degrees Fahrenheit.
In a large Dutch oven, combine the potatoes, smoked chuck roast, carrots, ancho chile powder, onions, sherry wine, thyme, chipotle peppers, rosemary, and stock.
Place the Dutch oven in the Pit Boss with the cover on. Cook the roast for 4-5 hours at 275°F, or until extremely tender.
Serve with roasted veggies of your choice or squashed potatoes & gravy. Enjoy.

1.141 Smoked Beef Back Ribs

Total Time: 8 Hrs 15 Mins, Servings: 6
Ingredients
Beef Back Ribs, 2 Rack
Pit Boss Beef Rub, 1/2 Cup
Instructions
Cut the thin papery membranes off the bone-side of ribs, if your butcher hasn't already done so, by pushing the point of a butter knife beneath the membrane over a central bone. To obtain a strong hold, use paper towels, then pull the membrane away.
Rub Pit Boss Beef Rub on both sides of the ribs.
When ready to cook, preheat the Pit Boss to 225°F for 15 minutes with the lid closed.
Place the ribs bone side down on the grill grate. Cook for 8-10 hours, or until temp reaches 205 degrees Fahrenheit.
Remove the ribs from the grill and set aside for 20 minutes to rest before slicing & serving. Enjoy.

1.142 Grilled Double Burgers with Texas Spicy BBQ Sauce

Total Time: 45 Mins, Servings: 4
Ingredients
Ground Beef, 3 Pound
Pit Boss BBQ Sauce, 1 Cup
Bacon, 1/2 Pound
Cheddar Cheese, 8 Slices
Pit Boss Beef Rub, 4 tbsp
Burger Buns, 4 Whole
Sliced Pickles
Instructions
Form eight 1/3-pound patties from ground beef. Pit Boss Beef Rub should be used on both sides of each burger.
When ready to cook, preheat the Pit Boss to 350°F with the lid closed for 15 mins.
To make the bacon, place slices of bacon directly on the grill grate then cook for 15 -20 minutes, or until crispy.
Preheat the Pit Boss to 450 degrees Fahrenheit.
Place the burger patties on the grill grate & cook for 4 mins or until done to your liking.
Place a piece of cheddar cheese on top of each burger and cook, covered, until the cheese melts.
To serve, put the Pit Boss Texas BBQ Sauce on the bottom buns and top with the pickles and patties, then repeat with the BBQ sauce, pickles, burger, BBQ sauce, and bacon. Finish with a top bun. Enjoy.

1.143 Braised Beef Short Ribs with Mashed Potatoes

Total Time: 5 Hrs 15 Mins, Servings: 4
Ingredients
Bone-In Beef, 4
Vegetable Oil, 1 tbsp
Sea Salt, 3/4 tsp
Black Pepper, 1/2 tsp
Medium Carrot, 4
Medium Onion, 1
Garlic, 2 Clove
Tomato Purée, 1 Cup
Demi-Glace, 1/2 Cup

Thyme Sprigs, 2 Sprig
Bay Leaf, 1
Red Wine Vinegar, 1 tbsp
Balsamic Vinegar, 1 tbsp
Russet Potatoes, 4 Large
Butter, 6 tbsp
Half-And-Half, 2 Cup
Instructions
Preheat the oven to high for 15 minutes with the lid covered when you're ready to cook.
Preheat a big cast iron dutch oven on the grill for 15 minutes with the lid covered.
Pat the beef dry using paper towels. In a hot dutch oven, add vegetable oil and brown the meat on both sides, rotating with tongs, for approximately 8 minutes. Place on a platter and season with 1/4 teaspoon sea salt & 1/4 teaspoon pepper.
In a dutch oven, add the chopped carrots, garlic onion, and simmer, turning periodically, until softened, approximately 10 minutes. 1 cup puréed tomatoes cooking time is 20 minutes. Cook for another 30 minutes, stirring per 10 minutes or till the sauce thickens, with the lid off the dutch oven (but the grill covered).
Toss in the demi-glacé, bay leaf, thyme, vinegar, 1/2 tsp of sea salt, 1/4 tsp pepper, and the beef, as well as any liquids that have collected on the dish. Reduce the grill temperature to 325°F and cover the dutch oven with a lid. Cook for 4 hours, or until the meat is very soft.
While the meat is braising, puncture the potatoes a few times with a fork and put them aside. Place the potatoes on the grill great next to the dutch oven for the final 1-1/2 hours of cooking.
Remove the Dutch oven from the grill, as well as the potatoes. Allow potatoes to cool slightly before cutting them in half lengthwise and scraping the flesh into a huge saucepan with a fork.
Using a potato masher, mash the ingredients until it is largely smooth. Set aside after adding the butter and half-and-half, seasoning liberally with salt and black pepper to taste.
Remove the meat from the saucepan and brush each rib with some of the braising liquid. Serve with mashed potatoes and toppings of your choice. Enjoy.

1.144 Brisket Tacos with Smoked Cilantro Cream
Total Time: 1 Hr, Servings: 8
Ingredients
Leftover Beef Brisket
Sour Cream, 8 Ounce
Cilantro Leaves, 1 Bunch
Jalapeño, 4 Whole
Garlic, 2 Clove
Lime Juiced, 3 Whole
Kosher Salt, 1 tsp
Corn or Flour Tortillas, 30 Whole
Pico De Gallo
Crumbled Queso Fresco
Hot Sauce
Lime, cut Into Wedges
Instructions
You may use spare brisket or this Pit Boss Smoked Brisket recipe. The brisket should be thinly sliced. Cover with foil and then keep heated in the pan with the drippings.
When ready to cook, preheat the oven to 180°F with the lid covered for 15 minutes. If Super Smoke is available, use it for the best taste.
To make the Smoked Cilantro Cream, spread the sour cream on a sheet pan and broil it. 30 minutes of smoking Remove the steaks from the grill and raise the temperature to 350°F.
In a blender, combine cilantro, garlic, jalapenos, lime juice, smoked sour cream, and salt. Blend till smooth, then chill until ready to use.
Wrap a total of 10 tortillas in foil each foil packet. Grill for 10-15 minutes, or until warmed through.
Layer brisket, smoked cilantro cream, pico de gallo, queso fresco, & cilantro leaves on tacos. Serve with lime wedges and your favorite spicy sauce. Enjoy.

1.145 Grilled Cleveland Polish Boy
Total Time: 15 Mins, Servings: 2
Ingredients
Russet Potatoes, 2 Pound
Salt
Mayonnaise, 1/2 Cup
Canola Oil
Sour Cream, 1/2 Cup
Pit Boss BBQ Sauce, 1/2 Cup
Salt, 1 tsp
Pepper, 1/2 tsp
White Vinegar, 2 tbsp
Celery Seed, 1/2 tsp
Purple Cabbage, 1/2 Whole
Shredded Carrot, 2 Whole
Shredded Green Cabbage, 1/2 Whole
Olympia Provisions, 4 Whole
Hot Dog Buns, 4 Whole
Instructions
To prepare the fries, peel the potatoes and cut them into 1/4-inch-thick matchsticks in a basin of cold water. In a cast-iron saucepan, pour 3-4 inches of oil and heat to 275 - 300 degrees F. Drain and pat the fries dry. Fry the potatoes in small batches until they are tender and pale, approximately 3 to 5 minutes. Increase the temperature of the oil to 350-375 degrees and drain on paper towels. Working in tiny batches, add the fries and fry for 1-3 minutes, or until crisp and brown. Using a paper towel, absorb excess liquid and season with salt to taste.
To prepare the coleslaw, whisk together the mayonnaise, vinegar, sour cream, pepper, salt, and celery seed in a small mixing bowl. Toss the cabbages and carrots with the mayo mixture in a medium mixing dish. To mix, stir everything together. Remove from the equation.
When ready to cook, preheat the oven to 350 °F and cook for almost 10-15 minutes with the lid covered.
Grill the sausages for 8-10 minutes, or until well heated, rotating once. On buns, place sausages, French fries, Pit Boss BBQ sauce, and coleslaw. Enjoy.

1.146 Bourbon-Braised Beef Short Ribs
Total Time: 3 Hrs 15 Mins, Servings: 4
Ingredients
Yellow Mustard, 1/2 Cup
Worcestershire Sauce, 2 tbsp
Molasses, 1 tbsp
Beef Short Ribs, 12
Pit Boss Rib Rub
Mop Sauce
Beef Broth, 1 Cup
Soy Sauce, 3 tbsp
Bourbon, 2 tbsp
Instructions
Preheat Pit Boss to 250°F and cook for 15 minutes with lid covered until ready to cook.
Whisk together mustard, Worcestershire sauce, and molasses in a tiny mixing basin.
Now Spread mustard slather sauce all over each rib. Pit Boss Rib Rub is used to season the ribs.
Make the mop sauce: In a food-safe spray bottle, mix the beef

broth, soy sauce, and bourbon.
Place the short ribs immediately on the grill grate, bone-side down. Cook for 2 to 2-1/2 hours, or when the temp of each rib reaches 165°F when tested with an instant-read meat thermometer, basting every 30 mins with the mop sauce.
Place the ribs on a big piece of heavy-duty aluminum foil to keep them warm. Bring the foil up to the edges and pour in any remaining mop sauce. Bring the foil's opposing sides together & fold several times to enclose the ribs firmly. Return the ribs to the barbecue grate, foil-wrapped.
Cook the ribs for another 1 hour or until temp reaches 195°F. Leave the ribs wrapped in foil for 15 minutes before gently opening them. (Be aware of leaking steam.) Drizzle the ribs with the juices after transferring them to a dish or plates.

1.147 Pit Boss Smoked Salami
Total Time: 2 Days 8 Hrs, Servings: 8
Ingredients
Ground Sirloin, 1 Pound
Black Peppercorn, 1 tsp
Worcestershire Sauce, 1 tbsp
Ground Black Pepper, 1 tbsp
Morton Tender Meat Cure, 1 tbsp
Red Pepper Flakes, 1 tsp
Honey, 1 tsp
Mustard Seeds, 2 tsp
Instructions
Plan ahead of time! This dish requires an overnight stay. Combine the meat, curing salt, pepper, mustard, Worcestershire sauce, peppercorns, and red pepper flakes in a large glass bowl. Distribute the seasonings evenly across the meat.
Cover with a resealable plastic bag and freeze for 1 day.
Place two pieces of wide plastic wrap on top of each other, on your working area after the meat has cured for one day. Turn the meat over and place it in the center of the plastic wrap. Make a long log out of the meat.
Wrap the plastic wrap over one side of the log and level down the edges. To work out any bubbles, apply equal pressure throughout the length of the tube. To make a tight seal, pull plastic wrap firmly over the opposite side and overlap the corners. With both hands, roll the sausage forward as well as backward. Squeeze the ends of plastic wrap firmly after the sausage is pretty consistent in width. Refrigerate for at least one day.
When ready to cook, preheat the oven to 180°F with the lid covered for 15 mins.
Remove the sausage from the package and sprinkle with honey. Place straight on the grill grate, cover the lid, & smoke for 6-8 hours, or until a meat thermometer registers 170°F within the sausage.
Set aside to cool fully before slicing & serving the sausage. Enjoy.

1.148 Smoked German Rouladen
Total Time: 2 Hrs 25 Mins, Servings: 4
Ingredients
Beef Eye of Round, 2 Pound, and Sliced 1/4 Inch Thick,
Cracked Black Pepper, 1/2 tsp
Stone Ground Mustard, 4 tbsp
Onions Sliced, 2 Large
Dill Pickle Spears, 1 Jar (16 Oz)
Thick-Cut Bacon, 1 Pound
Jacobsen Salt Kosher Sea Salt, 1 tsp
Braising Liquid
Beef Stock, 2 1/2 Cup
Bay Leaf, 1 Whole
Garlic Smashed, 2 Clove
Worcestershire Sauce, 1 1/2 tbsp
Corn-starch, 2 tbsp
Heavy Cream, 1 Cup
Cold Water, 4 tbsp
Instructions
Using a meat mallet, pound each slice of beef thin between two pieces of plastic wrap. 1/2 tbsp mustard, generously apply on one side of each fillet on each steak, arrange onions, bacon, and pickle spears.
Form a tight roll by wrapping the sirloin around the bacon, onions, and pickles. To keep the roll together, use toothpicks or string. Season to taste with salt and freshly cracked black pepper.
When ready to cook, preheat the Pit Boss to 165°F for 15 minutes with the lid closed.
Smoke the rolls for 30 minutes by placing them directly on the grill grate. Close the lid and raise the Pit Boss temp to 325°F after removing the steak rolls from the grill.
While you make the braising liquid, let the Pit Boss warm. Mix the beef stock, bay leaf, Worcestershire sauce & crushed garlic cloves in a large baking dish.
Put steak rolls to the Pit Boss & sear them for 3-5 minutes on each side.
Carefully remove the steak rolls from Pit Boss and place them in the braising liquid. Preheat the grill and place the pan on it. Cook for 1-2 hours, once the meat is completely tender. Now remove the steak from a dish and place it on a separate plate, covered in foil.
Preheat the oven to 350 degrees Fahrenheit and the baking dish to 350 degrees Fahrenheit. In a separate dish, mix the corn starch and 4 tbsp cool water. Slowly stir the corn-starch combination and heavy cream into the baking dish's juices. Bring the gravy to a boil for 1-2 minutes, stirring continuously.
Immediately return the rolls to the heated gravy and serve. Enjoy.

1.149 Glazed Cajun Meatloaf
Total Time: 2 Hrs 20 Mins, Servings: 4
Ingredients
Cooking Spray
Finely Diced Onion, 1/2 Cup
Vegetable Oil, 2 tbsp
Finely Diced Celery, 1/2 Cup
Green Onions, 3 Medium
Garlic Minced, 2 Clove
Diced Green Bell Pepper, 1/2 Cup
Jalapeño Peppers, 2 Medium
Beef Broth, 1/2 Cup
Ketchup, 1/2 Cup
Worcestershire Sauce, 2 tbsp
Dry Breadcrumbs, 1 Cup
Frank's Red Hot, 2 tbsp
Louisiana-Style Rub, 1 1/2 tbsp
Creole-Style Mustard, 1 tbsp
Black Pepper, 1 tsp
Ground Pork, 1/2 Pound
Andouille, 1/2 Pound
Ground Beef, 1 1/2 Pound
Large Egg, 1
Glaze
Louisiana-Style Sauce, 1 tbsp
Ketchup, 1 Cup
White Vinegar, 1 tbsp
Brown Sugar, 3 tbsp
Creole-Style Mustard, 2 tsp
Instructions
Use foil to line a wide baking sheet. Cooking sprays a wire

cooling rack and place it on top of a baking sheet.

Saute the onion, celery, green onion, bell pepper, jalapenos, and garlic in the oil in a large frying pan until the veggies soften, approximately 5 mins.

In a big mixing bowl, combine the beef broth, Louisiana-style rub, ketchup, spicy sauce, Worcestershire sauce, mustard, and pepper. Remove the pan from the heat and set it aside to cool fully.

Mix the ground beef, pork, and andouille sausage in a bowl and mix. Combine the breadcrumbs, egg, and cooled vegetable mixture in a mixing bowl. With your hands, mix gently yet thoroughly until everything is fully mixed.

Form an 8-inch-long, 1-2-inch-high rectangular loaf. It should be placed on top of a cooling rack.

When ready to cook, preheat the Pit Boss to 165°F for 15 mins with the lid closed.

Place the meatloaf pan on the grill grate & smoke it for 1 hour. Preheat the Pit Boss to 325 degrees Fahrenheit & bake meatloaf for almost 1 hour.

Make the glaze in the meanwhile. In a small saucepan, combine the brown sugar, ketchup, white vinegar, spicy sauce, and mustard. Cook for 5-10 mins on low heat.

Using a pastry brush, spread the glaze thoroughly over the meatloaf.

Continue cooking the meatloaf for another 30 minutes, or until an instant-read thermometer reads 160°F in the thickest portion of the meatloaf.

Set aside for 10 mins before slicing & serving the meatloaf. Enjoy.

1.150 Smoked Peppered Beef Tenderloin

Total Time: 1 Hr 15 Mins, Servings: 4
Ingredients
Beef Tenderloin Roast, 1
Dijon Mustard, 1/2 Cup
Garlic Minced, 2 Clove
Bourbon, 2 tbsp
Jacobsen Sea Salt
Ground Green & Black Peppercorns
Instructions

Place the tenderloin on a plastic wrap sheet.

In a small bowl, combine the mustard, garlic, and bourbon. Apply the sauce on the tenderloin in an equal layer. Wrap in the plastic and let aside for 1 hour at room temperature.

Remove the tenderloin from the plastic wrap & season liberally on both sides with salt and powdered green and black peppercorns.

When ready to cook, preheat the Pit Boss to 180°F with the lid closed for almost 15 min. If Super Smoke is available, use it for the best taste.

Smoke the tenderloin for 60 minutes straight on the grill grate. Remove tenderloin from the grill and place it on a plate to cool. Preheat the grill to 400 degrees Fahrenheit. Put tenderloin back on the grill after it has heated up. Roast for 20 to 30 minutes, determines the thickness of the tenderloin until the temp reaches 130°F. Don't overcook the food.

Allow for a 10-minute rest before slicing. Enjoy.

1.151 Smoked Beef Pastrami

Total Time: 8 Hrs 30 Mins, Servings: 8
Ingredients
Water, 6 Quart
Kosher Salt, 1 1/2 Cup
Coriander Seeds, 2 tbsp
Brown Sugar, 2/3 Cup
Pink Curing Salt, 1 1/2 tsp
Granulated Sugar, 3/4 Cup
Pickling Spice, 1 tbsp
Garlic Crushed, 8 Clove
Beef Brisket, 1 (7 Lb)
Yellow Mustard Seeds, 1 tsp
Black Peppercorns, 1/4 Cup
Instructions

In a large saucepan, mix 6 quarts of water, granulated & brown sugars, kosher salt, pink salt, mustard seeds, pickling spice, and garlic. Simmer, stirring periodically, until the sugars and salts have dissolved over fairly high heat. Allow the brine to chill in a big basin. Chill until ready to serve.

Poke holes around the brisket with a metal skewer. Fill a big roasting pan halfway with brine. Cover the pan with plastic wrap and add the brisket. Refrigerate the brisket after weighing it down using heavy plates to maintain it immersed in the brine. Allow 5 days for the brisket to cure, turning it one a day.

Drain the brisket and wipe it dry with the paper towels after removing it from the brine. Place the brisket on a rack placed on a rimmed baking sheet, fat side up. Refrigerate for 24 hours, uncovered.

Remove the brisket from the fridge and bring it to room temperature.

When ready to cook, preheat the Pit Boss to 225°F for 15 minutes with the lid closed.

Coarsely crush the peppercorns and coriander seeds in a spice grinder. Apply the peppercorn-coriander mixture on the fat side of the brisket.

Place the brisket in the middle of the grill grate, seasoned side up. Close the cover and smoke at 225° F unless an instant-read thermometer placed in the thickest portion reads 160° F. (about 3 to 4 hours).

Take the steaks off the grill and cover them in foil, ensuring sure they are well sealed. Return to the grill and cook for another 3 to 4 hours, or until temp of 204° F is reached when a thermometer is put into the thickest portion of the meat.

Remove from the grill and rest for a minimum of 30 mins in foil before slicing. Allow cooling fully before refrigerating and slicing if you want cold pastrami. Enjoy.

1.152 Ribs Smoked Beef Pastrami

Total Time: 8 hours 30 Mins, Servings: 8
Ingredients
Water, 6 Quart
Kosher Salt, 1 1/2 Cup
Granulated Sugar, 3/4 Cup
Brown Sugar, 2/3 Cup
Pickling Spice, 1 tbsp
Pink Curing Salt, 1 1/2 tsp
Garlic (Crushed), 8 Clove
Flat Cut Beef Brisket, 1 (7 Lb)
Yellow Mustard Seeds, 1 tsp
Black Peppercorns, 1/4 Cup
Coriander Seeds, 2 tbsp
Instructions

Mix 6 quarts of water in a large saucepan, kosher Salt, granulated & brown sugars, pink Salt, pickling spice, mustard seeds, and garlic with kosher salt, pink Salt, pickling spice, brown sugars, mustard seeds & garlic. Simmer, stirring periodically, until the salts & sugars have dissolved over fairly high heat. Allow the brine to chill in a big basin. Chill until ready to serve.

Poke holes all over the brisket with a metal skewer. Fill a big roasting pan halfway with brine. Cover the pan with plastic wrap and add the brisket. Refrigerate the brisket after weighing it down using heavy plates to keep it buried in the brine. Allow 5 days for the brisket to cure, turning it once a day.

Drain the brisket and wipe it dry with paper towels after

removing it from the brine. Place the brisket on a rack positioned on a rimmed baking sheet, fat side up. Refrigerate for 24 hours, uncovered.

Remove the brisket from the fridge and bring it to room temperature.

When ready to prepare, preheat the Pit Boss to 225°F for 15 minutes with the lid closed.

Coarsely crush the peppercorns and coriander seeds in a spice grinder. Apply the peppercorn-coriander mixture on the fat side of the brisket.

Place the brisket in the center of the grill grate, seasoned side up. Close the cover and smoke at 225° F till an instant-read thermometer placed in the thickest section reads 160° F. (about 3 to 4 hours).

Take the steaks off the grill and cover them in foil, making sure they are well sealed. Return to the grill and cook for another 3 - 4 hours, or until a core temperature of 204° F is reached when a thermometer is put into the thickest portion of the meat.

Remove from the grill and rest for at least 30 mins in foil before slicing. Allow cooling fully before refrigerating and slicing if you want cold pastrami. Enjoy.

1.153 Smoked Pastrami Burgers

Total Time: 55 Mins, Servings: 6
Ingredients
Ground Chuck (80% Lean), 2 Pound
Pit Boss Beef Rub
Mayonnaise, 1/2 Cup
Pit Boss BBQ Sauce, 1/3 Cup
Pickle Juice, 2 tsp
Pastrami (Sliced), 1 Pound
Cheddar Cheese, 8 Slices
8 Buns
Instructions
Preheat the grill to 180°F and close the cover for 15 minutes when ready to cook.

Season your ground beef with "Pit Boss" Beef Rub and divide it into 8 equal-sized patties. Place the chicken straight on the grill grate, cover, & smoke for 30 minutes.

Make the fry sauce while the burgers are cooking. Combine the mayo, BBQ sauce, & pickle juice in a small bowl. Combine all ingredients in a mixing bowl, cover, and chill till ready to use.

Take the burgers off the grill and increase the temperature to High. Return the burgers to the grate when the grill has preheated. Cook the burgers on high for 4-five min on one side before flipping.

Add the pastrami to the griddle in 8 separately portioned heaps while flipping the burgers. Cook for another 4-5 minutes with the lid closed.

Carefully lay the pastrami on top of the burgers, followed by a piece of cheese. You may even toss the buns on the grill to toast them if desired. Close the lid and heat until the cheese has melted & the burgers are done to your liking. The interior temperature of a well-done burger should be 175°F.

Place the burgers with pastrami on the bottom bread. Slather the top bun with the fry sauce, then layer on your favorite burger toppings and serve right away. Enjoy.

1.154 BBQ Brisket Sandwich Along with Special Sauce

Total Time: 8 hours 30 Mins, Servings: 8
Ingredients
Brisket (Trimmed), 1 (6-8 Lb)
Favorite BBQ Rub
Brioche Buns (Halved), 10 Large
For Serving Iceberg Lettuce
For Serving Sliced Pickles
Mustard, 1/4 Cup
Ketchup, 1/2 Cup
Pit Boss BBQ Sauce of Choice, 1/2 Cup
Mayonnaise, 3/4 Cup
Chopped Pickles, 1/4 Cup
Instructions
Allow 8 - 12 hours of cooking time for a 6 - 8-pound brisket, or 90 minutes per pound. For brisket, a remote probe thermometer is essential.

Rub the brisket liberally with your favorite rubs, such as Pit Boss Beef Rub or Pit Boss Rib Rub, or just pepper and salt.

Cover with plastic wrap. Allow wrapped brisket to rest in the refrigerator for 12 to 24 hours.

When ready to cook, preheat the Pit Boss to 180°F with the lid closed for about 15 minutes. If Super Smoke is available, use it for the best flavor.

Place the brisket on the grill grate fat side down, insert the thermometer probe, & smoke for 4 hours.

Raise the temperature of the Pit Boss to 250°F after 4 hours. Remove the brisket from the grill & cover it in foil when the internal temperature reaches 160°F.

Replace the probe. Return the foiled brisket to the grill and cook till it reaches a temperature of 204°F.

Remove the brisket from the pan and let it rest for at least thirty min in the foil.

To prepare the unique sauce, combine all the mustard, ketchup, Pit Boss BBQ sauce, mayonnaise, and sliced pickles. Spread the sauce on the buns.

After the brisket has rested, slice it, and serve it on buns with iceberg lettuce & additional pickles. Enjoy.

1.155 Smoked Teriyaki Jerky

Total Time: 4 hours 15 Mins, Servings: 4
Ingredients
Soy Sauce, 1/2 Cup
Mirin Or Sweet Cooking Wine, 1/4 Cup
Sugar, 2 tbsp
Fresh Ginger (Each ¼ Inch Thick), 3 Coins
Garlic (Crushed), 1 Clove
Onion Powder, 1/2 tsp
Black Pepper, 1/2 tsp
Beef Bottom or Top Round, Sirloin Tip, Wild Game or Flank Steak (Trimmed), 2 Pound
Instructions
Combine ginger, mirin, sugar, soy sauce, garlic, onion powder, and black pepper in a mixing bowl.

Cut the meat into 1/4-inch-thick slices against the grain using a sharp knife. If the meat is partially frozen, this is considerably easier to do. Any excess fat or connective tissue should be removed.

Place the beef pieces in a big resealable plastic bag & pour over the marinade. Massage the bag to coat all the slices with the marinade. Refrigerate for several hours or overnight after sealing the bag.

When ready to cook, preheat the Pit Boss to 180°F with the lid closed for 15 minutes.

Take the steak out of the marinade and throw away the marinade.

Place the beef slices on the grill grate in a single layer after drying them between paper towels.

Smoke for 4 to 5 hours on the Pit Boss, or till the jerky is dry but still pliable when bent.

Transfer the jerky to a plastic bag and let it aside at room temperature for an hour.

Squeeze out the air in the bag & store the jerky in the fridge. Enjoy.

1.156 Peppercorn Steaks Grilled with Mushroom Cream Sauce

Total Time: 2 hours, Servings: 4
Ingredients
Dijon Mustard, 1/2 Cup
Garlic (Minced to A Paste), 2 Clove
Bourbon Or Strong Cold Coffee, 2 tbsp
Worcestershire Sauce, 1 1/2 tbsp
Beef Steaks (Preferably Beef Tenderloin), 4 Whole
Kosher Salt
Coarse Ground Black & Green Peppercorns
Olive Oil, 1 tbsp
Cremini Mushrooms (Thinly Sliced), 16 Ounce
Garlic (Minced), 1 Clove
White Wine, 1/2 Cup
Chicken Stock, 1/2 Cup
Heavy Cream, 1/2 Cup
Salt n Pepper
Instructions
Combine the mustard, garlic, bourbon, and Worcestershire sauce in a small bowl. To mix the ingredients, whisk them together.

Place the tenderloin steaks on a big piece of plastic wrap & spread the mixture equally over them. Wrap the plastic wrap tightly around the tenderloin on both sides. Allow 60 minutes for the mixture to come to room temperature.

Remove the plastic wrap from the tenderloin and season generously on all sides with Salt & peppercorns. Pat the peppercorns into the meat with your hands.

When ready to cook, preheat the Pit Boss to 180°F with the lid closed for about 15 minutes. If Super Smoke is available, use it for the best flavor.

Place the steaks on the grill grate directly and smoke for 60 min. Take the steaks from the grill and set them aside.

Preheat the Pit Boss to 500°F and cook for 15 minutes with the top covered.

When the Pit Boss is hot, return the steaks to the grill and cook for 20 - 30 minutes, depending on the thickness of the steak, or until an instant-read meat thermometer reads 130°F. Do not overcook the food.

To make the Mushroom Cream Sauce in a large sauté pan over medium heat, heat the olive oil. Sauté the sliced mushrooms until softened and gently browned, being careful not to crowd the pan. Add the garlic and cook for another minute. Bring the white wine & chicken stock to a boil with the mushrooms. Reduce the heat to low and whisk in the cream after 5 - 7 minutes of simmering. Season with salt n pepper to taste. Remove the pan from the heat and set it aside.

Arrange the steaks on a serving dish & cover with foil. Remove the foil and let the meat rest for ten min before slicing it into thin slices.

Spoon the sauce straight onto the steaks to serve. Enjoy.

1.157 Short Rib Braised Sandwich

Total Time: 4 hours 25 mins, Servings: 10
Ingredients
Beef Short Ribs, 2 1/2 Pound
Pit Boss Rib Rub
Olive Oil, 1 tbsp
Onion (Diced), 1
Carrots, 2 Large
Stalk Celery (Diced), 2
Garlic, 2 Clove
Cup Red Wine
Cup Beef Stock
Balsamic Vinegar, 1 tbsp
Bay Leaves, 2 Dried
Thyme Sprigs, 3 Sprig
Butter, 2 tbsp
Yellow Onion, 2
Rosemary Sprigs, 1 Sprig
Sherry Vinegar, 1 tbsp
Salt
Black Pepper
Provolone Cheese
Ciabatta Buns, For Serving
Mayonnaise
Mustard
Instructions
Liberally season short ribs with the Pit Boss Prime Rib Rub.

When ready to cook, preheat the Pit Boss to 225°F for 15 minutes with the lid closed.

Smoke the ribs for 1 hour straight on the grill grate.

In a medium Dutch oven, heat 2 tablespoons of olive oil over medium heat while the ribs are smoking.

Add the onion, carrots, & celery to the pan and cook for 5 minutes, or until the onion is transparent. Sauté for another 30 seconds after adding the garlic.

Bring the red wine, stock, and vinegar to a low boil. Add the herbs and the smoked short ribs on top. Replace the cover on the Dutch oven and set it back on the grate.

Cook the short ribs for 3-4 hours at 225°F, or until a fork/skewer/thermometer inserts with little to no resistance. It should be easy to shred the meat with two forks.

Remove the short ribs from the liquid and remove the Dutch oven from the grill. Remove any bone and rough tissue/cartilage from the meat using two forks.

Strain the particles from the braising liquid, skim the fat off the surface, and return the liquid to the saucepan. Bring to a low simmer & reduce by half over medium heat. It should be thicker than the starting point.

Keep the shredded beef heated in the saucepan while you create the caramelized onions.

Melt 2 tbsp butter in a medium sauté pan over medium-high heat for the caramelized onions. Sauté for 15-20 minutes, until gently browned, caramelized, and soft, with Salt & pepper to taste. Add the sherry vinegar and simmer for another 5 minutes, scraping the bottom of the pan with a wooden spoon to get all the browned pieces.

To assemble the sandwiches, cut the ciabatta buns in half & apply mayonnaise on one side and mustard on the other. On top of the mustard, layer shredded meat, provolone, caramelized onions, and top bread. Enjoy.

1.158 Smoked Whiskey Burgers

Total Time: 1 hour 30 mins, Servings: 2
Ingredients
Pineapple Rings in Their Juices, 1 Can (20 Oz)
Vegetable Oil, 1 tbsp
Diced Yellow Onion, 1/4 Cup
Kosher Salt
Garlic (Minced), 3 Clove
Whiskey, 3 tbsp + ¼ cup

Brown Sugar, 1 Cup
Ginger, 1 tsp
Low Sodium Soy Sauce or Tamari, 1/2 Cup
Water, 1/3 Cup
Hot Sauce (Optional), 1 tsp
Ground Sirloin (80% Lean), 1 Pound
Salt, 1 tsp
Pit Boss Beef Rub, 1 tbsp
Cheddar Cheese, 4 Slices
Hamburger Buns, 4
For Additional Toppings: Grilled Pineapple, Caramelized Onions & Bacon
Instructions
Preheat Pit Boss to 225°F and cook for 15 minutes with lid covered until ready to cook.
Remove the pineapple juice from the can by straining it. One cup of some pineapple juice should be enough. Reserve the liquid for the sauce and set aside the rings for grilling (if preferred).
Heat the oil in a large saucepan over moderate heat for the Whiskey Sauce. Add the onions and a liberal sprinkle of salt, and simmer, turning periodically, until the onions are translucent & tender, approximately 5 minutes. Cook for another minute after adding the garlic. Pour in the whiskey and wait 30 seconds for the alcohol to burn out.
Whisk together the brown sugar and ginger, then add pineapple juice, soy sauce, and 1/3 cup water, whisking constantly. Bring to a boil, then lower to low heat and cook for 10 minutes, or till the sauce thickens enough to coat the back of a spoon.
To make the burgers, pour the whiskey and 1 tsp into the ground meat and mix gently with your hands.
Divide the mixture into four equal pieces. To make your patties, gently flatten each piece. Make sure you do not overwork the meat. On each side, lightly season with Pit Boss Beef Rub.
Cook the burger patties on the grill for 25 to 30 minutes with the lid closed.
After 30 minutes, coat the burgers liberally with the whiskey glaze & increase the heat to 450°F. Cook the burgers for 4–6 minutes on each side.
When the burgers are almost done, top them with the cheddar cheese & cook for another 2 to 3 minutes, or until the internal temperature reaches the required level. Place the hamburger buns directly on the grill grate & toast for 2 to 3 minutes, or until the cheese has melted.
To serve, brush the bottom of each bun with additional whiskey glaze, top with your burger, and then add your favorite toppings like grilled pineapple pieces, bacon, and caramelized onions. Enjoy.

1.159 French Pit Boss Dip Sandwich
Total Time: 1 hour 20 mins, Servings: 6
Ingredients
Manhattan Roast, 1 (2 To 2-1/2 Lb)
Pit Boss Beef Rub
Kosher Salt
Hoagie Rolls, 2
Mayonnaise
Provolone Cheese, 6 Slices
Yellow Onion (Thinly Sliced), 2
Butter, 1 tbsp
Salt
Beef Stock, 1 Quart
Thyme, 1 Sprig
Rosemary, 1 Sprig
Peppercorns, 4
Garlic, 2 Clove
Instructions
Preheat the Pit Boss to 500°F and cook for 15 minutes with the lid covered when ready to cook.
Liberally season the roast with Pit Boss Beef Rub and Salt.
Place the roast directly on the grill grate & cook for 30 minutes, or until the outside begins to brown and caramelize.
Reduce the grill temperature to 325°F and cook the roast for another 30 minutes, or till the core temperature reaches 125°F.
Remove the roast from the grill and set aside for 15 minutes to rest before slicing.
Using a meat slicer or a very sharp knife, finely slice the meat once it has rested. Remove the meat and set it aside.
To make onions, liquify the butter in a sauté pan with the onions & cook over medium heat. Season with salt & heat, turning regularly, till the onions are caramelized and browned. If the bottom of the pan begins to stick before the onions are fully cooked, add 1 tablespoon of water and scrape off the browned pieces with a wooden spoon before continuing to cook. Remove from the fire after softened and caramelized, and put aside until ready to assemble the sandwiches.
To make the au jus, combine all the ingredients in a saucepan and bring to a simmer. Cook for 30 - 45 minutes, then season with Salt and filter off the solids.
Toast the buns on the grill for 5 - 10 minutes, cut-side down, until lightly toasted.
To assemble the sandwiches, lay them on a sheet tray with the toasted side up. Apply mayonnaise to the bread, then layer thinly sliced meat, caramelized onions, and cheese on top.
Place the dish straight on the grill grate and cook until the cheese is melted, about 5 minutes at 500°F.
Serve the sandwiches with au jus on the side. Enjoy.

1.160 Weekend Pasta Along with Braised Slow Meat Sauce
Total Time: 3 hours 30 mins, Servings: 8
Ingredients
Chicken Livers (Finely Minced), 1/2 Pound
Extra-Virgin Olive Oil, 1/4 Cup
Ground Beef Chuck, 2 Pound
Ground Pork Shoulder, 1 Pound
Ground Lamb, 1 Pound
Kosher Salt
Black Pepper (Freshly Ground)
Unsalted Butter, 4 tbsp
Finely Diced Pancetta, 1/2 Pound
Onion (Minced), 1 Large
Carrots (Finely Chopped), 2 Large
Stalk Celery (Finely Chopped), 4
Cloves Garlic (Minced), 4 Medium
Fresh Minced Sage Leaves, 1/4 Cup
Parsley Leaves, Fresh Minced, Divided, Plus More for Serving, 1/2 Cup
Dry White/ Red Wine, 2 Cup
Chicken Stock, 1 Quart
Crushed Tomatoes, 1 Can (28 Oz)
Whole Milk, 1 Cup
Bay Leaves, 2 Whole
Heavy Cream, 1 Cup
Finely Grated Parmesan Cheese, 3 Ounce Add More for Serving
Pasta Of Choice, 1 Pound
Instructions
Preheat the Pit Boss to 325°F for 15 minutes with the lid closed when ready to cook.
Place the chicken livers in a cup that is just big enough to contain the head of an immersion blender and mix until smooth. In a large Dutch oven, heat the olive oil over high heat till it shimmers.
Toss in the ground beef, pork, and lamb. Season with Salt

& pepper & simmer, tossing with a wooden spoon to break up the meat. Cook till golden brown.

Remove the pan from the heat and add the puréed chicken livers. In a large skillet, melt butter and pancetta over medium-high heat. Cook, stirring often, for approximately 8 minutes, or until the fat has rendered, but butter & pancetta have not browned.

Combine the onion, carrots, celery, garlic, sage, and 1/4 cup parsley in a large mixing bowl. Cook, occasionally turning until the veggies are softened but not browned, about 8 minutes.

Combine all ingredients in a Dutch oven with the meat mixture. Preheat the Dutch oven to high. Cook, constantly stirring, for another 10 minutes or until most of the liquid has evaporated from the pan. Cook, constantly stirring until the wine has mostly evaporated.

Combine the stock, tomatoes, milk, and bay leaves in a large mixing bowl. Salt & pepper to taste. Bring the sauce to a low simmer before transferring it to the Pit Boss.

Cook, uncovered, for 3 hours, or until the liquid has nearly entirely reduced and the sauce is rich and thick.

Skim out most of the fat, leaving roughly 1 cup behind. 1/4 cup parsley, heavy cream, and Parmesan cheese on the burner bring to a boil, frequently stirring to emulsify.

Season with Salt & pepper to taste. Keep yourself warm.

A large pot of salted water now cooks the pasta according to directions even al dente. After that drain 1/2 cup of water and set aside. Return the pasta to the saucepan and toss in just enough sauce and 1/2 cup of the saved cooking liquid to coat the pasta.

Cook, tossing and turn slowly over high heat till sauce is thick and pasta is covered for approximately 30 seconds.

Immediately transfer to a serving dish and serve. Garnish with more flat-leaf parsley and freshly grated Parmesan.

1.161 Sweet Mandarin Meatloaf

Total Time: 2 hours 30 mins, Servings: 6
Ingredients
Lean Ground Beef, 2 Pound
Peppered Bacon, 12 Slices
Onion (Diced), 1 Large
Garlic (Minced), 6 Clove
Red Bell Pepper (Diced), 1 Large
Breadcrumbs, 1 Cup
Eggs, 2 Large
Pit Boss Beef Rub, 2 tsp
Milk, 2/3 Cup
Worcestershire Sauce, 1 tsp
Chopped Cilantro, 1/2 Cup Add More for Garnish
Mandarin Orange Sauce, 1/3 Cup
Instructions
In a large mixing bowl, place the ground beef and put it aside. Cook the bacon pieces in a pan until they are gently browned. With a slotted spoon, remove the bacon and set it aside.

Remove all of the bacon fat from the skillet except 2 tablespoons. Combine the onion, garlic, and pepper in a mixing bowl. Cook until the onion is transparent, about 5 minutes.

Combine the breadcrumbs, eggs, Pit Boss Beef Rub, milk, Worcestershire sauce, chopped cilantro, and 1/3 cup Mandarin sauce with the ground beef. To combine all of the ingredients, whisk them together thoroughly.

Refrigerate the beef mixture for at least 2 hours, covered. Make a big round out of the meat.

When ready to cook, preheat the Pit Boss to 225°F for 15 minutes with the lid closed. If Super Smoke is available, use it for the best flavor. Carefully lay the loaf on a cooling rack set on top of a baking sheet lined with aluminum foil.

Smoke for 1 hour on the Pit Boss with the lid closed. After an hour of smoking, increase the Pit Boss temperature to 300°F and cook until an instant-read thermometer reads 160°F for the meatloaf's internal temperature.

Carefully transfer the meatloaf to a dish and let it aside for 15 to 20 minutes before sprinkling with chopped cilantro. Cut into slices and serve. Enjoy.

1.162 BBQ Beef Sandwich

Total Time: 6 hours 10 mins, Servings: 4
Ingredients
Chuck Roast, 1 (4-6 Lb)
Pit Boss Coffee Rub, 1/4 Cup
Beef Broth, 1 Cup
Hamburger Buns, 6
White Onion (Sliced), 1
Dill Pickles
Pit Boss Special Sauce, 1/2 Cup
Pit Boss Sweet & Heat BBQ Sauce
Instructions
Preheat Pit Boss to 250°F and cook for 15 minutes with lid covered until ready to cook.

Trim the chuck roast of any extra fat. Pit Boss Coffee Rub should be applied on the roast. Place the roast on the Pit Boss & cook for 3-1/2 hours, or until the internal temperature of the roast reaches 160°F.

Remove the roast from the grill and cover it in two layers of aluminum foil. Add the beef broth and return the roast to the grill. Cook for another 1-1/2 hours, monitoring the temperature along the way. When the core temperature hits 204°F, the roast is done. If the core temperature has not been achieved after 30 minutes, check it again.

Remove the roast from the grill and shred or pull the flesh. Return the drippings to the meat to help it stay moist.

Place sliced onions, pickles, Pit Boss Special Sauce, & Pit Boss Sweet & Heat BBQ Sauce on top of the pulled roast on buns.

1.163 Gyros

Total Time: 1 hour 15 mins, Servings: 6
Ingredients
Garlic (Chopped), 3 Clove
Greek Tzatziki Sauce
Marjoram (Dried Leaves), 1 tbsp
Onions, 1 Medium
Ground Beef, 1 Pound
Greek Seasoning, 2 tbsp
Dried Oregano, 1 tbsp
Ground Lamb and Ground Beef, 1 Pound
Cayenne Pepper, 1/4 tsp
Pita Bread
Instructions
Using non-stick cooking spray, coat a loaf
pan. Aluminum foil a brick or a heavy container from the pantry; place the bread pan and the block aside.

In the bowl of a food processor, combine the garlic and onion and pulse until finely chopped. Scrape into a colander or mesh strainer and press on the sediments for 15 minutes to drain. The food processor bowl should not be washed.

Combine the ground beef, lamb, oregano, marjoram, Souvlaki Rub, & cayenne in a food processor bowl. Return to the bowl with the onion-garlic combination and pulse until a paste forms.

Press firmly into the loaf pan that has been prepared. If preferred, cook the beef until it reaches this stage, then cover with plastic wrap & refrigerate for several hours or overnight.

When ready to cook, preheat the Pit Boss grill to 325 degrees Fahrenheit with the lid closed for 10 - 15 minutes.

Bake the gyro meat in a water bath for 60 to 75 minutes, or until it reaches 165 degrees Fahrenheit.

Carefully remove from the water bath, drain any excess fat, and place on a cooling rack.

To compress the meat, place the foil-covered block on top of it. Remove the meat from the loaf pan after 15 to 20 minutes & thinly slice with an electric knife / a sharp serrated knife.

Assemble the gyros using the above-mentioned serving components, concluding with tzatziki sauce.

1.164 Smoked Texas-Style Beef Brisket

Total Time: 18 hours 30 mins, Servings: 6
Ingredients
Brisket, 1 (12-15 Lb)
Pit Boss Coffee Rub, 1 Cup
Butcher BBQ Brisket Injection, 2/3 Cup
Water, 2 Cup
Canola Oil, 2 tbsp
Apple Juice, 1 1/2 Cup
Pit Boss Rib Rub, 1 Cup
Black Pepper, 4 tbsp
Instructions
Trim the fat "cap off" the top of the brisket and discard the silver skin. Trim away any brown spots, such as those on the brisket's side. To demonstrate the direction of cuts after cooking, make a long cut with the grain on the flat (thin side) of the brisket & a short cut on the flat again. Trim the bottom fat cap to a thickness of about 1/4 inch.

Combine the Butcher BBQ Prime Brisket Injection and the water in a mixing bowl. Inject into the brisket in a checkerboard pattern with the grain. Rub canola oil all over the brisket, then spritz with apple juice and let aside for 30 minutes.

Combine both Pit Boss rubs & generously season the brisket. Season with black pepper on top.

When ready to cook, preheat the Pit Boss to 180°F with the lid closed for fifteen min. If Super Smoke is available, use it for the best flavor.

Place the brisket fat side down on the barbecue grate and cook for 8 to 12 hours. After the first three hours, spritz with apple juice every 30 - 45 minutes.

After 8 hours, take your temperature by putting your finger about two-thirds of the way into the thickest portion of your arm. It should be between 150- and 160-degrees Fahrenheit. Wrap the brisket in two sheets of aluminum foil, leaving one end uncovered, after it reaches 160°F. Seal the foil packet with the leftover brisket injection. Preheat the grill to 225°F and lay the wrapped brisket directly on the grill grate. Cook for 3 to 4 hours more, or until the internal temperature reaches 204°F.

Remove off the grill and chill for at least 2 hours in a cooler wrapped in a towel. When ready to serve, cut slices against the grain approximately the thickness of a pencil. Separate the cooking liquid from the fat and pour the juices over the sliced brisket pieces if desired. Enjoy.

1.165 Skirt Steak Quesadillas Grilled

Total Time: 25 mins, Servings: 4
Ingredients
Chili Powder, 2 tbsp
Kosher Salt, 2 tsp
Ground Cumin, 1 tsp
Chipotle Chile Powder, 1/2 tsp
Cayenne Pepper, 1/2 tsp
Lime Zest, 1 tsp
Skirt Steak, 1 1/2 Pound
Flour Tortillas, 12 Whole (4 Inch)
Vegetable Oil, 1
Pepper Jack Cheese (Shredded), 1/2 Cup
Instructions
In a separate bowl, mix together the chili powder, cumin, Salt, chipotle powder, cayenne, and lime zest for the skirt steak.

Rub the spice mixture all over the skirt steak and marinate for at least 20 - 25 minutes in a zip-top bag.

When you're ready to cook, fire up the Pit Boss according to the manufacturer's directions. Preheat the oven to 400 ° F and bake for 10 to 15 minutes with the lid covered.

Grill the skirt steak for 3-4 minutes on each side. Allow for 20 minutes of resting time before cutting into bite-sized pieces.

Fill the tortillas with cheese and cooked skirt steak for the quesadillas. To avoid burning, cook on a grill pan or in a sauté pan with additional oil.

Garnish with guacamole, sour cream, or salsa if desired. Enjoy.

1.166 Grilled Skirt Steak with Peach Salsa

Total Time: 38 mins, Servings: 2
Ingredients
Skirt Steak, 2 Pound
Onion Powder
Sea Salt
Black Pepper (Freshly Ground)
Olive Oil (Extra-Virgin)
Sherry Vinegar
Peach, 6
Diced Roma Tomatoes, 2 Whole
Jalapeño (Minced), 2 Whole
Bell Peppers, 1/4 Cup
Red Onion (Diced), 1/4 Cup
Cilantro (Finely Chopped), 2 tbsp
Lime (Juiced), 1
Ancho Chile Powder, 1/4 tsp
Honey, 1 tbsp
Salt n Pepper
Instructions
Season the steaks on both sides with onion powder, sea salt, & freshly cracked black pepper, then drizzle with olive oil and a dash of sherry vinegar. Allow 30 minutes to one day for the meat to marinate.

When you're ready to cook, fire up the Pit Boss and set the temperature to 500 degrees Fahrenheit. Preheat for 10 - 15 minutes with the lid closed.

Halve or quarter the peaches, remove the pits, and place cut-side down on the grate. 2 mins per side on the grill, or until they start to caramelize.

Take the peaches from the grill. Allow it cool before dicing and tossing with the remaining salsa ingredients. Season with salt and honey to taste. Allow at least 10 minutes for the salsa flavors to meld.

Cook the steaks straight on the hot grill grate for about 2 minutes on each side, or until done to your liking.

When the steaks are done, take them from the Pit Boss & cover them in aluminum foil; set aside for 15 minutes. Remove the meat from the foil and set aside the foil and liquids. Thinly slice the meat across the grain. Serve the skirt steak with the grilled peach salsa and the juices from the skirt steak. Enjoy.

1.167 Tuscan Meatloaf

Total Time: 1 hour 40 mins, Servings: 6
Ingredients
Eggs, 6
Onion (Diced), 1
Extra-Virgin Olive Oil, 2 tbsp
Red Bell Pepper (Diced), 1
Green Bell Pepper (Diced), 1
Garlic (Minced), 3 Clove
Milk, 1/2 Cup
Parmesan Cheese, 1 Cup
Italian Seasoned Breadcrumbs, 2/3 Cup
Italian Herbs (Dried), 1 tbsp
Salt, 1 tsp
Freshly Ground Black Pepper, 1 tsp
Ground Beef, 1 Pound
Ground Pork, 1 Pound
Italian Pork Sausage (Regular or Spicy), 1/2 Pound
Marinara Sauce (For Serving), 1 1/2 Cup
Instructions
Cover 4 eggs with 1" of cold water in a pot and bring to a boil for 6 minutes over medium-high heat.
Place in a basin of cold water to cool. Remove the peelings and set them aside.
Meanwhile, cook the onion & bell peppers in olive oil in a frying pan over medium heat.
Add the garlic & simmer for another 1 to 2 minutes, then remove from the heat and set aside to cool.
In a large mixing basin, whisk together the remaining two eggs. Combine the milk, parmesan, breadcrumbs, herbs, plus Salt & pepper in a large
mixing bowl.
Combine the meats & half of the onion/pepper combination in a large mixing bowl. Mix gently with your hands, taking care not to overmix.
Roll the meat between wax paper sheets into an 8 by 5" rectangle using a rolling pin. The leftover onion/pepper combination should be distributed lengthwise through the center of the meat.
Place 3 to 4 hard-cooked eggs on top of the onion/pepper mixture, end to end. Pinch all of the seams closed by bringing the beef rectangle's edges up over the eggs and veggies. Place on a rimmed baking sheet or in a loaf pan, seam side down.
Preheat the Pit Boss grill to 350 degrees Fahrenheit when ready to cook. Preheat for 10 - 15 minutes with the lid closed.
Bake the meatloaf for 1 hour, or till an instant-read meat thermometer is placed in the center of the loaf registers 165 ° F.
Pour the marinara sauce over the top of the meatloaf if desired and bake for another 10 to 15 minutes. Allow it cool for a few minutes before slicing & serving. This dish is equally delicious when served cold.

1.168 Short Rib Chili

Total Time: 4 hours 15 mins, Servings: 4
Ingredients
Dried Ancho Chiles (Stemmed & Seeded), 2 Whole
Beef Stock, 1 1/2 Quart
Chipotle Peppers in Adobo, 2
Dried Guajillo Chiles, 2 Whole
Boneless Beef Short Ribs, 4 Pound
Salt n Pepper
Chile De Arbol, 2 Whole
Vegetable Oil, 2 tbsp
Spanish Onion (Diced), 1 Large
Garlic (Chopped), 4 Clove
Cinnamon Stick, 1
Bay Leaves, 2
Jalapeño (Finely Chopped), 1
Mexican Oregano, 1 tsp
Roasted Ground Cumin, 1 tsp
Bottle Beer, 1
Corn Tortillas
For Serving Fresh Cilantro
Roasted Ground Coriander, 1 tsp
Shredded Cheddar Cheese
Sliced Lime
Chopped Onion
Instructions
Preheat Pit Boss to 225°F and cook for 15 minutes with lid covered until ready to cook. If Super Smoke is available, use it for the best flavor.
Heat a pan over medium heat on the stovetop & add the dried chilies. Toast for 5 minutes in a dry skillet, turning periodically until aromatic. Add a cup of stock to the pan, bring to a boil, and then remove from heat.
Blend the chiles and stock, as well as the adobo chilies and their sauce, in a blender. Close the cover and let the chiles steam while you finish the rest of the process.
Season the short ribs well with Salt and pepper.
Heat the vegetable oil in a large Dutch oven over high heat on the stovetop until it is extremely hot. Four minutes on each side, sear the ribs on any and all sides until well browned. To avoid overcrowding the pan, do this in batches.
Transfer the ribs to a cutting board & cut them into bite-sized pieces once they've been seared. (Cutting the ribs after searing allows for a deeper sear and more tender meat since less moisture is lost.) Remove the meat and set it aside.
Blend on high until smooth after the chiles with the stock have steamed, then put aside.
Reduce the heat to medium and, if needed, add additional oil to the pan. Cook, stirring periodically, for 5 - 7 minutes, or until the onions are softened. Stir in the garlic, chopped jalapeno, bay leaves, oregano, cumin, cinnamon stick, and coriander for another minute or so, when the spices begin to adhere to the base of the pot.
Pour in the beer and heat to a boil while scraping the pan's bottom. Allow half of the beer to reduce before adding the blended chilies and stock. Return the chopped short ribs to the pot.
Pour in enough stock to cover the meat. Depending on the size of your Dutch oven, you may need to modify the quantity of stock used. Bring to a boil, then move the Dutch oven to the Pit Boss with caution.
Grill the chili for about 3 hours, uncover it until the beef is very soft.
If preferred, add 4 or 5 torn-up corn tortillas to help thicken the chili.
Garnish with chopped cilantro, shredded cheddar cheese, and lime. Enjoy.

1.169 NY Grilled Steak Along with Cornbread Salad

Total Time: 1 hour 5 mins, Servings: 4
Ingredients
Flour, 3/4 Cup
Baking Powder, 1 1/2 tsp
Cornmeal, 3/4 Cup
Sugar, 1/4 Cup
Baking Soda, 1 tsp
Green Onion, 1/2 Cup

Buttermilk, 1 1/4 Cup
Eggs, 2 Large
Lemon (Juiced), 1
Unsalted Butter (Melted & Cooled), 1/4 Cup
Strip Steaks, 2
Jalapeño (Minced), 2 tsp
Salt n Pepper
Avocado (Sliced), 1
Red Onion (Sliced), 1
Heirloom Tomatoes, 2
Green Bell Peppers (Sliced), 1
Olive Oil, 1 tbsp

Instructions

Start the Pit Boss grill when ready to cook, set the temperature to 350 ° F, and warm for 10 - 15 minutes with the lid closed.
To prepare the cornbread (which should be done the day before), follow these steps: Butter a metal baking pan that measures 13x9x2. In a large mixing basin, combine flour, cornmeal, sugar, salt, baking powder, & baking soda. Green onions and jalapeno are added last.
In a medium mixing basin, whisk together the buttermilk and eggs, then add the melted butter. Stir in the buttermilk mixture until all of the dry ingredients are well combined (do not overmix). Transfer batter to prepared pan (batter will barely come up the edges of the pan by approximately 3/4 inch).
Grill cornbread for 25 minutes, or until the top is gently browned and a toothpick inserted in the middle comes out clean. Allow cornbread to cool fully before
serving. Flip the pan upside down onto a clean cutting board to remove the cornbread. Tap the bottom of the pan to release the cornbread. Remove the skillet from the oven and cut the corn bread into 12"x 12" pieces. Place the cubes on a baking sheet and let them dry overnight.
Season the steaks well with Salt & pepper on both sides. Start the Pit Boss grill on Smoke when you're ready to cook.
Cook the stakes for 30 minutes on the grill or until the core temperature reaches 120 degrees F.
Remove the steaks from the grill and adjust the temp to High, allowing the grill to warm for 10 minutes with the lid closed.
Return the steaks to the hot grill and cook for 3-4 minutes on each side, or until an internal temperature of 130 degrees for medium-rare is reached. Remove the steaks from the grill & set them aside to cool.
Combine tomatoes, avocado, onion, pepper, & dry cornmeal while the steaks are resting. Season with Salt & pepper and drizzle with olive oil and lemon juice. To serve, top each dish with a generous mound of salad and steaks. Enjoy.

1.170 Steak Sweetheart with Lobster Ceviche

Total Time: 50 mins, Servings: 2
Ingredients
Butterflied Into Heart Shape, Strip Steak or Rib Steak (Boneless), 1 (20 Oz)
Kosher Sea Salt (Jacobsen Salt Co.), 2 tsp
Black Pepper, 2 tsp
Raw Dark Chocolate, 2 tbsp
Olive Oil, 1/2 tbsp
Lemon Juice, 1 Cup
Jalapeño (Diced), 1/2
Lobster Tail Meat, 1/2 Pound
Lime Juice, 1/3 Cup
Cilantro Leaves Chopped, 1/2 Bunch

Instructions

To make the Sweetheart Steak, draw a huge heart on a piece of cardboard the size of the steak you want to use. Cut a heart form out of cardboard, then trim the meat into a heart shape. In a small dish, combine the Salt, pepper, chocolate, and olive oil. Toss on top of the sliced meat.
Remove the flesh from the uncooked lobster tail and cut it.
Combine the lemon juice, lime juice, and jalapeno in a separate medium bowl.
Toss in the lobster flesh, making sure it's fully immersed. Soak the lobster for 30 minutes. The lobster meat is cooked with citric acid.
When ready to prepare, preheat the oven to 350°F for 15 minutes with the lid closed.
Grill lobster in shell for 3 - 5 minutes at 350°F if you like completely cooked flesh. Toss with lemon juice, lime juice, jalapeno, and cilantro after removing from the grill (optional).
Preheat the Pit Boss to 500°F and cook for 15 minutes with the top covered.
Cook the steak straight on the grill grate for 5 - 7 minutes per side, or till the desired doneness is attained. Remove the grill from the heat.
Set aside for 5 minutes to cool. Over steak, serve lobster ceviche. Enjoy.

1.171 Flat Iron Steaks

Total Time: 55 mins, Servings: 4
Ingredients
Tri-Tip Steaks or Flat Iron Steaks, 2 Pound
Worcestershire Sauce, 4 tbsp
Pit Boss Prime Rib Rub
Butter, 6 tbsp
Onion (Thinly Sliced), 1 Half
Salt
Garlic (Minced), 1 tbsp
Dried Oregano, 1 tsp
Tomato Paste, 1/4 Cup
Dry Red Wine, 1/2 Cup
Pepper

Instructions

When you're ready to cook, turn on the Pit Boss's Smoke setting. Allow the steaks to marinade for 30
mins at room temp after seasoning both sides with Worcestershire sauce. Both sides of the steaks should be dusted with Pit Boss Prime Rib Rub. Place on the grill for 45 minutes to smoke. Meanwhile, in a large saucepan over moderate heat, melt 2 tablespoons of butter. Add the onions & cook for 5 minutes, or until they are soft. Season with Salt and pepper.
Add the garlic and oregano & cook for 30 seconds, or until fragrant. Cook, frequently stirring, for 2 minutes after adding the tomato paste. Add the wine and
whisk to combine. Cook, stirring periodically until the sauce has reduced by half, about 10 minutes.
Turn off the heat in the skillet. Into a small bowl, strain the sauce, pushing on the particles to obtain as much liquid as possible. Remove the particles from the sieve and discard them. Whisk in the sauce a bit at a time with the remaining 4 tbsp of butter, cut into tiny 1/2-inch (1-cm) pieces. Season the sauce with salt n pepper to taste.
Remove the steaks from the grill once they've completed smoking and raise the temp to High. Allow 15 minutes for the grill to heat up, then lay the smoked steaks on the hot grill grate & cook for 2 mins per side, or until the meat is done to your liking.
Place the steaks on a chopping board and cover with foil to keep them warm. Allow for a 10-minute rest period before slicing across the grain. Drizzle the sauce all over the steaks. Enjoy.

1.172 Smoked Pastrami Sandwich

Total Time: 9 hours 45 mins, Servings: 8
Ingredients

Water, 3 L
Pink Peppercorns, 1 1/2 tbsp
Mustard Seeds, 1 1/2 tbsp
Bay Leaf, 1 Whole
Cloves, 1 tbsp
Red Pepper Flakes, 1 tbsp
Cinnamon, 2 Stick
Fennel Seed, 3 tbsp
Black Peppercorn, 3 tbsp
Optional - Pink Curing Salt, 1/2 tsp
Brown Sugar, 2 Cup
Brisket, 1 (5 Lb)
Loaf Sliced Rye Bread, 1 Whole
Iceberg Lettuce (Shredded), 1 Head
Red Onion (Thinly Sliced), 1 Medium
Thousand Island Dressing, 1 Cup
Brown Sugar, 2/3 Cup
Kosher Salt, 2/3 Cup
Black Pepper, 2/3 Cup
Ground Coriander, 1/2 Cup
Ground Juniper Berries, 1 tbsp
Red Pepper Flakes, 1/2 tbsp
Instructions
Plan ahead of time! This recipe calls for 3 days of brining and overnight chilling.
To make the brine, combine all of the ingredients in a large mixing bowl. Bring 3 liters of water to a boil, along with the sugar and Salt. Cook until the salt and sugar has completely dissolved. Remove the pan from the heat and stir in the remaining brine ingredients. Allow the brine to cool fully before using.
Place the brisket in a "nonreactive container" that is large enough to accommodate the brisket as well as the brine. The brisket should be brined all over, and then the remaining brine should be poured over it to ensure it is thoroughly immersed. Refrigerate for up to three days.
Drain the brine from the brisket and pat it dry. Rub the rub ingredients over the brisket.
When ready to cook, preheat the Pit Boss to 180°F with the lid closed for fifteen min. If Super Smoke is available, use it for the best flavor.
Smoke the brisket for 6 hours straight on the grill grate.
Increase the temperature of the Pit Boss to 300°F and cook for another 3 hours.
Continue to cook the brisket in foil until it reaches a core temperature of 195°F.
Remove the brisket from the Pit Boss & open the foil to allow steam to escape, which will halt the cooking process.
Refrigerate for at least one night.
Cut pastrami into 1/8-inch slices against the grain the next day.
Layer rye bread, Thousand Island dressing, iceberg lettuce, red onion, and pastrami in a sandwich. Enjoy.

1.173 BBQ Brisket Competition Style

Total Time: 10 hours 30 mins, Servings: 8
Ingredients
Whole Packer Brisket, 1 (12-16 Lb)
Water, 3 Cup
Butcher BBQ Beef Injection, 1/4 Cup
White Pepper, 1 tsp
Onion Powder, 1 tsp
Garlic Powder, 1 tsp
Beef Bouillon, 1 tbsp
Meat Injector
Kosher Salt, 1 Cup
Black Pepper, 3/4 Cup
Pit Boss Coffee Rub
Beef Broth, 2 Cup
Instructions
Preheat Pit Boss to 225°F and cook for 15 minutes with lid covered until ready to cook. If Super Smoke is available, use it for the best flavor.
Remove all of the fat from the top of the brisket, leaving 1/4 inch of fat on the bottom.
After that combine 3 cups of water, pepper, Butcher Beef Injection, garlic powder, onion powder & beef bouillon in a medium mixing basin. Using an injector, inject a 1" checkerboard pattern across the top of the brisket.
Season the brisket with Salt and pepper, as well as a generous application of Pit Boss Coffee Rub.
Smoke the brisket for 4 hours on the barbecue. Check the core temperature of the brisket after 4 hours; it should be 160°F. If the temperature isn't right, wait 30 minutes and check again.
Wrap the brisket in a double layer of heavy-duty "aluminum foil" when the temperature hits 160°F. Return the foil package containing the brisket to the grill with 2 cups beef broth.
Increase the temperature of the grill to 250°F and cook for another 4 hours.
Start monitoring the interior temperature after 7 hours. The final temperature should be 204°F. Check it every 30 minutes if it isn't up to temperature. Depending on the size of the brisket, the total cooking time should be between 8 and 10 hours.
Remove the brisket
from the grill when it reaches a core temperature of 204°F and covers it in a towel.
Allow resting for 1 hour on the counter, wrapped in plastic, before slicing across the grain. Enjoy.

1.174 Garlic & Herb Roasted Prime Rib
Total Time: 3 hours 30 mins, Servings: 8
Ingredients
Boneless Prime Rib Roast, 1 (6 Lb)
Garlic (Coarsely Chopped), 5 Clove
Red Wine Vinegar, 2 tbsp
Fresh Parsley (Coarsely Chopped), 1/2 Cup
Fresh Rosemary Needles, 1 tbsp
Olive Oil or Vegetable Oil, 1/2 Cup
Pit Boss Prime Rib Rub
Beef Broth (Preferably Low Sodium & Divided), 4 Cup
Salt n pepper
Instructions
Tie the roast with butcher's twine at 2-inch intervals.
Combine the garlic, vinegar of red wine, parsley, & rosemary in a blender jar or small food processor. Pulse in a few teaspoons of oil to finely cut the garlic and herbs. In a tiny stream, drizzle in the remaining oil until the mixture is thoroughly combined.
Place the roast in a big resealable plastic bag and pour the herb mixture over it, covering both sides of the roast.
Marinate the meat for 2 hours in the refrigerator.
Take the roast out of the plastic bag and toss out the marinade. Allow the roast to come to room temperature

before liberally seasoning it with Pit Boss Prime Rib Rub on all sides.
In a roasting pan, now place the roast remember that the fat side is up on a rack. In the bottom of the pan.
When ready to prepare, preheat the Pit Boss to 400°F for 15 minutes with the lid closed.
Place the pan on the grill grate with the prime rib & cook for 30 minutes.
After 30 minutes, decrease the temperature to 225°F and continue to cook for another 2 to 3 hours, or until the core temperature of the roast reaches 130°F for medium-rare.
Transfer roast to a cutting board & let aside for 20 minutes, gently covered with foil.
To make the Beef Au Jus, deglaze the roasting pan with "2 cups" beef stock over medium heat. Scrape all the brown pieces off the bottom of the pan using a wooden spoon.
Strain the just into a small saucepan and skim off any fat that comes to the top, discarding the particles. Taste and adjust the heat to medium if necessary (if the jus tastes a little weak, reducing will concentrate the flavor). Season the jus to taste with salt n pepper as needed. Before serving, reheat the dish.
Carve the roast into thick slices & serve with beef au jus on the side. Enjoy.

1.175 Salt-Crusted Prime Rib
Total Time: 3 hours 10 mins, Servings: 8
Ingredients
Pure Kosher Sea Salt of Jacobsen Salt Co., 1 1/2 Cup
Coarse Ground Black Pepper, 3/4 Cup
Head Garlic (Peeled), 1
Rosemary, 1/2 Cup
Chile Powder, 2 tbsp
Extra-Virgin Olive Oil, 3/4 Cup
6-Bone Prime Rib Roast, 1 (15-16 Lb)
Instructions
Combine salt n pepper, garlic cloves, rosemary, and Chile powder in a food processor and pulse until fine. Pulse in the olive oil to make a paste.
Place the prime rib roast, bone-side up, on a cutting board and coat with 1 tablespoon of the salt paste.
Place the meat in a large roasting pan with the bone side down. Apply the salt paste to the fatty surface, pressing it in place to help it stick. Allow 1 hour for the prime rib to come to room temperature.
When ready to cook, preheat the Pit Boss to 450°F for 15 minutes with the lid closed.
Roast the prime rib for 1 hr. or until the crust has been browned somewhat. Reduce the temperature to 300°F
and continue roasting for another 2 hours and 15 minutes, or till an "instant-read" thermometer placed into the middle of the roast (but not touching the bone) reads 125°F for medium-rare.
Place the roast on a broad carving board & let aside for 30 minutes to rest.
Carefully remove the salt crust off the meat & set it aside in a dish. Remove extra salt with a brush.
Run a long sharp carving knife along with the bones, using them as a guide, to remove roast in 1 piece even though keeping the rib rack intact. Leave 1/2 inch of flesh on the bone, or more if you're saving it for leftovers.
Carve prime rib roast into 1/2-inch-thick slices and serve with a side of crumbled salt crust.

1.176 T-Bone Grilled Steaks Along with Bloody Mary Steak Sauce
Total Time: 1 hour 15 mins, Servings: 2
Ingredients
T-Bone Steaks, 2 Large
Kosher Salt, 1 tbsp
Black Pepper, 1 tbsp
Extra-Virgin Olive Oil, 2 tbsp
White Onion (Finely Diced), 1/2
Garlic (Minced), 1 Clove
Lemon (Juiced), 1
Soy Sauce, 1 tbsp
Brown Sugar, 2 tbsp
Mustard, 1 tbsp
Smoked Pit Boss Bloody Mary Mix, 1 Cup
Instructions
Preheat Pit Boss to 225°F and cook for 15 minutes with lid covered until ready to cook. If Super Smoke is available, use it for the best flavor.
Salt and pepper the steaks and lay them immediately on the grill grate. When an "instant-read" thermometer is placed into the thickest portion of the steak, it should read 125°F after 60 - 90 minutes of smoking.
To make the steak sauce, combine all of the ingredients in a mixing bowl. In a medium saucepan, heat the olive oil over medium heat. Add the onion and garlic & cook for 5 minutes, or until the onions
are transparent and gently browned. Reduce heat to a low simmer and add the other ingredients. Cook for 20 to 30 minutes, or till the mixture has thickened and decreased.
Take the steaks off the grill and raise the temp to 500°F.
Sear the steaks for 5 mins on a hot grill. Remove the steaks from the grill and set them aside to rest for 10 minutes before adding.
Warm or at room temperature, serve steak with sauce on the side. Enjoy.

1.177 Braised Alarm Chili
Total Time: 4 hours 30 mins, Servings: 8
Ingredients
Shoulder Or Stew Meat Beef (Chopped into 3/4 Inch Cubes), 4 Pound
Salt To Taste, 2
Black Pepper to Taste, 2
Olive Oil, 3 tbsp
Stout Beer, 2 Bottle
Onion (Diced), 2 Small
Red Onion (Diced), 1 Small
Garlic (Minced), 6 Clove
Jalapeño (Seeded & Diced), 2 Whole
Poblano Pepper (Seeded & Diced), 1 Whole
Red Bell Pepper (Diced), 1 Whole
Green Bell Pepper (Diced), 1 Whole
Black Beans (Strained & Rinsed), 2 Can 15 Oz
Kidney Beans (Strained & Rinsed), 2 Can 15 Oz
Plum Tomatoes with the Juices, 2 Can 28-Oz
Tomatoes With Juices (Chopped), 2 Can 28 Oz
Crushed Tomatoes, 2 Can 28-Oz
Chipotle Peppers in the Adobo Sauce (Diced), 2 Can
Chili Powder, 1/2 Cup
Cup Cumin
Dried Oregano, 1/4 Cup
Ground Cinnamon, 1 tbsp
Tomato Paste, 2 tbsp
Optional - Bar of Chocolate, 1/2 Whole
Instructions
Preheat the grill to 325 degrees Fahrenheit when ready to cook.
Preheat a Dutch oven on the stovetop. Season meat generously with Salt & pepper on all sides.
In a Dutch oven, heat the olive oil and brown the beef on both sides, working in 2 batches to avoid crowding the pan.

Once the meat has been browned, pour the beer into the Dutch oven & cover till it comes to a boil.

Add olive oil, onion, and garlic to a separate frying pan & sauté till slightly browned & transparent. Cook for approximately 10 minutes or until the peppers begin to soften. Combine the onions & peppers with the meat and beer. The beans, tomatoes, chipotle peppers, and spice are then added. Cover with a cover and bring to a low simmer.

Place the Dutch on the Pit Boss grill & cook for 3 hours at 325°F, uncovered, or until the meat is very tender.

Stir in the tomato paste. If necessary, season with Salt and pepper.

Finely slice the chocolate bar & toss it into the chili just before serving. Serve immediately. Enjoy.

1.178 Smoke n Grill Flank Steak

Total Time: 3 hours 20 mins, Servings: 4
Ingredients
Red Wine, 1/4 Cup
Vegetable Oil, 1/4 Cup
Black Pepper, 1 tsp
Kosher Salt, 1 tsp
Soy Sauce, 1/8 Cup
Worcestershire Sauce, 1/8 Cup
Garlic (Crushed), 10 Clove
Limes (Squeezed), 2 Whole
Flank Steak, 2 Pound
Cilantro (Finely Chopped), 1 Bunch
Garlic (Crushed), 6 Clove
Olive Oil (Extra-Virgin), 3/4 Cup
Red Wine Vinegar, 1/4 Cup
Lime (Juiced), 1
Diced Red Onion, 1 tbsp
Black Pepper, 1 tsp
Kosher Salt, 1/2 tsp
Instructions
Combine the red wine, vegetable oil, salt, soy sauce, black pepper, garlic, Worcestershire sauce, and lime juice in a large mixing bowl.

Combine it with the meat in a bag. Place it in the refrigerator for 8 hours.

When ready to prepare, preheat the Pit Boss to 225°F for 15 minutes with the lid closed.

Smoke for at least 3 hours. Remove the steak from the grill, cover with foil, and set aside for 10-15 minutes.

Increase the Pit Boss's temperature to 450°F and let the grill warm.

In a blender, mix cilantro, garlic, olive oil, red wine vinegar, lime juice, red onion, pepper, & Salt as the grill warms up.

Return the steak to the Pit Boss once the grill is hot enough. 3 mins per side on the grill You'll want to sear it to obtain some lovely grill marks and char.

Remove the steak from the grill and cut it into pencil-thin slices against the grain. Chimichurri sauce is served on the side. Enjoy.

1.179 Pit Boss Frito Pie

Total Time: 4 hours 15 mins, Servings: 8
Ingredients
Yellow Onion (Chopped), 1 Medium
Green Bell Pepper, 2 Medium
Orange Pepper (Diced), 1 Medium
Diced Tomatoes, 2 Can (14.5 Oz)
Kidney Beans (Drained & Rinsed), 1 Can (15.5 Oz)
Pinto Beans, 1 Can (15 Oz)
Dark Chili Powder, 4 tbsp
Onion Powder, 2 tbsp
Garlic Powder, 1 tbsp
Jacobsen Salt Co. Pure Kosher Sea Salt, 3 tbsp
Coarse Ground Black Pepper, 3 tbsp
Leftover Smoked Brisket, 3 Pound
Sour Cream (For Serving), 4 Cup
Fresh Chives (For Serving), 4 tbsp
Fritos Corn Chips (For Serving), 12 Small Bags
Instructions
Preheat Pit Boss to 375°F and cook for 15 minutes with lid covered when ready to cook.

Sprinkle Salt and pepper over the onions and peppers. Cook until transparent on a sheet pan in the Pit Boss, about 14 to 20 minutes.

Drain the tomatoes & kidney beans & place them in a 10-inch cast-iron saucepan while the peppers are cooking. Half of the liquid
from the pinto beans should be drained and added to the saucepan.

In a large mixing bowl, combine chili powder, kosher salt, ground pepper, onion powder, & garlic powder.

Add the brisket to the saucepan, cut into 1-inch cubes. Combine the cooked peppers & onions in a mixing bowl. As needed, add more water.

Reduce the temperature to 250°F in the Pit Boss & cook for 4 hours, stirring every 30 mins. During the cooking process, add water as needed.

Taste after 4 hours and season with Salt & pepper as needed. Assemble a bag of Fritos Corn Chips for each guest when ready to serve. Open the package, then pour the chili over the chips, sour cream, and chives on top. Enjoy.

1.180 Bacon Roasted & Wrapped Beef Tenderloin

Total Time: 1 hour 10 mins, Servings: 4
Ingredients
Beef, Loins 4 Pound
Pit Boss Beef Rub, 4 Ounce
Bacon, 8 Strips
Pit Boss Coffee Rub, 4 Ounce
Instructions
When you're ready to cook, fire up the Pit Boss according to the manufacturer's
directions. Preheat the oven to 275 degrees F and bake for 10 to 15 mins with the lid covered.

Lightly season the tenderloin with the beef rub before

wrapping it with bacon. Re-season with a second coat of coffee rub.

Cook the tenderloin for 30 minutes on the grill. Check the interior temperature; 120 degrees F is the ideal temperature. If the target temp. has not been reached, continue to cook, monitoring every 5 minutes until it is.

Remove the tenderloin from the grill and raise the temperature to 450°F (500 degrees Fahrenheit if using a WiFIRE enabled grill). Return tenderloin to grill after 10 minutes and sear for 5 minutes. Check the interior temperature once more; it should be 135 degrees F at this point.

If the final temperature hasn't been achieved, flip the tenderloin & sear for another 5 minutes, or until it reaches 135 degrees F.

Remove the tenderloin from the grill and set it aside for 10 minutes to rest before slicing & serving. Enjoy.

1.181 Chocolate Bark Brisket
Total Time: 12 hours 10 mins, Servings: 8
Ingredients
Beef Brisket (Fat Trimmed to 1/4" Thickness), 1 Whole
Pure Kosher Sea Salt by Jacobsen Salt Co., 1/3 Cup
Garlic Powder, 2 tbsp
Onion Powder, 2 tbsp
Black Pepper (Freshly Ground), 1/3 Cup
Instructions
Chef Tip: Request a brisket that is as uniformly thick as possible, with the surrounding fat cut to 1/4" thick to keep the meat from drying out while cooking. You'll want to prepare ahead of time to have your brisket special ordered (the brisket already sold at the meat counter is typically not whole).

Season the meat a day ahead of time. Season the beef all over with Salt, garlic, onion powder, & pepper in a small bowl.
When you're ready to cook, prepare your grill by setting the temperature to 225-250°F (about 10-15 minutes). Place the brisket, fat side up, in the center of the grill grate. Chef Tip: Resist the desire to open the grill frequently; this may result in temperature fluctuations. Every 45 mins or so, check the pellets. To guarantee an accurate reading, we recommend using a stand-alone
thermometer. Pass it through the grill's space between the lid & the base. Start rotating the brisket every 3 hours when it reaches an internal temp of 160-165°F and turns as required if the top or bottom
is coloring quicker than the other.

Chef Tip: Wrap the brisket in foil till it reaches a temperature of 203°F on the inside. The key is to infuse the meat with a smokey taste, which should take 5-6 hours on the grill. After then, it's only a matter of getting the meat cooked through.

The brisket is done when it reaches an internal temp of 203°F. Allow one hour for the brisket to rest. For this period, you should wrap it in plastic wrap and then foil. Cut into slices and serve. Enjoy.

1.182 Spice BBQ Beef Short Ribs
Total Time: 4 hours 8 mins, Servings: 4
Ingredients
Chinese Five-Spice Powder, 2 tbsp
Fine Sea Salt, 1 tsp
Sugar, 14 tsp
White Pepper (Freshly Ground), 2 tsp
Bone-In Beef Short Ribs, 4 Pound
Hoisin Sauce, 1 Cup
Dry Sherry, 1/3 Cup
Soy Sauce, 1/3 Cup
Ketchup, 1/4 Cup
Unseasoned Rice Vinegar, 2 tbsp
Garlic (Minced), 2 Clove
Ginger (Peeled & Minced), 1 tbsp
Scallions (Minced), 2 Whole
Instructions
Plan ahead of time! This dish necessitates an overnight stay. In a small mixing bowl, combine all the rub's components.

Rub all sides of the ribs liberally with the rub. Refrigerate the ribs overnight, wrapped in plastic wrap.

When you're ready to cook, preheat the oven to 180°F for 15 minutes. Smoke the short ribs for 2 hours directly on the grill grate.

Take the ribs from the grill & set them aside. Raise the temp. to 250 degrees F. Cook for another 2 hours after wrapping the ribs in foil. (If the foiled ribs are still not tender, return them to the grill till they are.)

In a medium saucepan, mix all of the sauce ingredients while the ribs are smoking. Cook, often stirring, over low heat till the sauce thickens slightly, about 10 mins. Remove the pan from the heat & allow it cool.

When the ribs are done, slather them all over with sauce, remove the foil and return the ribs to the grill to finish cooking. (About 10 minutes)

Garnish with the remaining sauce & a sprinkling of minced chives. * Have fun! Cooking times will vary based on the temperature of the set and the ambient temperature.

1.183 Grilled Beef Sliders
Total Time: 4 hours 8 mins, Servings: 4
Ingredients
Olive Oil, 3 tbsp
Yellow Onion (Thinly Sliced), 2 Whole
Salt n Pepper
Kosher Salt
Ground Chuck (80% Lean), 2 Pound
Cheddar Cheese
For Serving Slider Buns
Iceberg Lettuce (Shredded)
Caramelized Onions
Mayonnaise
Ketchup
Mustard
Instructions
In a large sauté or frying pan, heat 2 tbsp olive oil over medium heat for the
caramelized onions. Add the onions & a sprinkle of salt to taste. Cook until the onions begin to caramelize & break down, stirring often.

Reduce the heat to low & simmer, turning regularly, for another 25-30 minutes, or until the onions are very caramelized and delicious. If required, season with additional salt. Allow cooling before using, then keep in an airtight jar in the refrigerator for up to 3 days.

To prepare the burgers, season with 2 tsp kosher salt and 1/2 tsp pepper per pound of beef. Gently mix the ground beef with your hands to incorporate the Salt, being careful not to overwork it.

Form the meat into patties weighing 2 to 3 ounces each. Brush a tiny quantity of the leftover oil on both sides.

When ready to cook, increase the temperature to High & preheat for 15 minutes with the lid closed.

Place the burgers on the grill & cook for 2-3 minutes before turning and grilling for another 2-3 minutes, or
until done to your liking. If using cheese, do so after the burgers have been turned.

Set the sliders aside for a few minutes to let the juices spread evenly. While the burgers are resting, toast the buns on the grill with the split side down for 1-2 minutes.

Add the shredded lettuce, caramelized onions, & other

condiments to the burgers. To make it more interesting, mix in some Pit Boss Summer Shandy Rub or use the Pit Boss BBQ Sauce instead of ketchup. Enjoy.

1.184 Pot Smoked Roast Brisket
Total Time: 4 hours 5 mins, Servings: 6
Ingredients
Coca-Cola, 1 (12 Oz)
Chili Sauce, 1 Heinz Bottle
Mix Packet Onion Soup, 1
Flat Cut Beef Brisket, 4 Pound
Instructions
In a mixing bowl, combine the Coke, Heinz chili sauce (found in the condiment department of the supermarket store), and dry onion soup mix.
Trim the fat off the brisket, leaving about 1/4 inch of fat on top. Place the brisket in a large baking pan and cover with the Coke-chili sauce mixture. (If using a bigger piece of brisket or the entire brisket, the sauce mixture may need to be doubled.)
Place the Pit Boss on Smoke and leave the lid open for 4 to 5 minutes, or until the fire is created. Heat the Pit Boss to 300 ° F. for 10 to 15 minutes with the top closed.
Place the brisket pan on the grill & cook for 3 - 4 hours, or until it is tender. (Place a fork in it and twist it with minimal effort to see whether it's ready!)
Allow the brisket to rest in its juices for 30 mins to an hour before slicing & serving.

1.185 Smoked Coffee Break Beef Jerky
Total Time: 5 hours 10 mins, Servings: 4
Ingredients
Strong Brewed Coffee or Espresso (Chilled), 1 Cup
Cola, 1 Cup
Soy Sauce, 1/2 Cup
Worcestershire Sauce, 1/4 Cup
Brown Sugar, 1/4 Cup
Morton Tender Home Quick Meat Cure, 2 tbsp
Black Pepper (Freshly Ground), 1 1/2 tsp
Hot Sauce, 1 tbsp
Bottom Round/Trimmed Beef Top, Flank Steak/Sirloin Tip, 2 Pound
Instructions
Plan ahead of time! The marinating period for this dish is overnight.
Mix the coffee, soy sauce, cola, Worcestershire sauce, brown sugar, curing salt, pepper, & spicy sauce together in a mixing bowl.
Cut the meat into 1/4-inch slices (thick) against the grain using a sharp knife. (If the meat is partially frozen, this will be easier.)
Any excess fat & connective tissue should be removed.
Place the beef slices in a big zip-top bag. Pour the marinade over the beef slices and knead the bag to coat all of the slices with the marinade.
Refrigerate for several hours or overnight after sealing the bag. When ready to prepare, preheat the Pit Boss to 165°F for 15 minutes with the lid closed.
Take the steak out of the marinade and throw away the marinade.
Using paper towels, dry the meat pieces. Arrange the meat on the grill grate in a single layer.
Smoke for 4 - 5 hours, or till the jerky is dry and still chewy and pliable when bent in half.
While the jerky is still warm, transfer to a bag. Allow the jerky to rest at room temperature for an hour. Squeeze any air out of the bag and store the jerky in the refrigerator. It will last for several weeks in the fridge. Enjoy.

1.186 Strip Steak Along with Bacon-Onion Jam
Total Time: 1 hour 10 mins, Servings: 2
Ingredients
NY Strip Steaks, 2 Whole
Prime Pit Boss Rib Rub
Bacon (Cut into the Small Pieces), 1/2 Pound
Sweet Onion, 1 Small
Brown Sugar, 1/4 Cup
Strong Coffee (Freshly Brewed), 3 tbsp
Apple Juice, 1/4 Cup
Balsamic Vinegar, 1/2 tbsp
Olive Oil, Extra-Virgin
Instructions
Take the steaks out of the fridge 30 minutes before cooking to enable them to come to room temperature. Pit Boss Prime Rib Rub should be used on all sides of the steaks.
When you're ready to cook, preheat your Pit Boss to 350°F with the lid covered for 10 - 15 mins.
Place the diced bacon on the heated grill grate in a cast iron pan. Cook for 10 - 15 minutes, or till the fat has rendered from the bacon.
Drain all except 1 tbsp of the bacon grease from the pan after removing the bacon.
Add the onions to the cast iron pan & simmer for approximately 10 minutes on the Pit Boss, or until softened. After that, add the brown sugar and continue to simmer for another 15 - 20 minutes to allow the onions to caramelize.
Add the coffee, apple juice, or water, & cooked bacon, and simmer, stirring periodically, for another 20 minutes, or until the onions are extremely thick and "jimmy."
Pour in the balsamic vinegar & set it aside in a dish. (Refrigerate any remaining bacon-onion jam.) Always allow this bacon-onion jam to come to room temperature before eating it.)
Preheat the Pit Boss on High for 10 - 15 minutes, with the cover closed.
Drizzle the steaks lightly with olive oil & cook for 4 - 5 mins on each side on the Pit Boss for medium-rare, or till done to your liking.
Now, remove them from the grill once they've finished cooking and let them rest for approximately 10 mins before slicing.
Drizzle the bacon-onion jam over each steak, and you've got yourself a winner. Enjoy.

1.187 Beef Stew Old-Fashioned
Total Time: 4 hours 30 mins, Servings: 6
Ingredients
Chuck Roast (Cut into 4 Inch Chunks), 2 1/2 Pound
Flour, 3 tbsp
Pit Boss Prime Rib Rub, 2 tsp
Vegetable Oil, 2 tbsp
Red Wine, 1/2 Cup
Low Sodium Beef Broth, 3 Cup
Onion (Halved & Sliced Lengthwise), 1 Whole
Garlic (Minced), 2 Clove
Tomato Paste, 1 tbsp
Worcestershire Sauce, 2 tsp
Bay Leaf, 1 Whole
Dried Thyme, 1 1/2 tsp
Carrots (Peeled & Cut into 1 Inch Pieces) 4 Whole
Boiling Potatoes (Peeled & Cut into Chunks), 3 Medium
Optional - Instant Potato Flakes (Mashed), 3 tbsp
Parsley (Chopped), 1
Instructions
In a big resealable plastic bag, combine the flour & Pit Boss Prime Rib Rub. Toss in the meat cubes to coat them.
In a Dutch oven, heat the vegetable oil until it shimmers. Brown the meat in batches, turning it over to brown on all sides.

Scrape up any brown pieces with a wooden spoon & add the wine and beef broth to the pan if used. Combine the garlic, onion, tomato paste, Worcestershire sauce, bay leaf, and thyme in a large mixing bowl. Cover the
Dutch oven with the lid.
When you're ready to cook, preheat the Pit Boss grill to 300 ° F with the lid closed for 10 - 15 minutes.
Place the grill grate over the Dutch oven. After 2 hours, add the carrots & potatoes to the stew.
Cook for a further 2 hours or till the meat & veggies is soft.
Stir in 2 to 3 tablespoons mashed potato flakes if the gravy needs thickening.
Arrange on a serving platter and top with chopped parsley.

1.188 Porterhouse Grilled Steak Along with Creamed Greens

Total Time: 1 hour 5 mins, Servings: 4
Ingredients
Porterhouse Steak, 2
Kosher Salt
Black Pepper (Cracked)
Butter, 6 tbsp
Garlic (Minced), 2 Clove
Shallot (Thinly Sliced), 1
Heavy Cream, 1 Cup
Ground Nutmeg, 1 Pinch
Salad Greens (Mixed), 3 Pound
Instructions
Season the steaks thoroughly with Salt & pepper on both sides.
When you're ready to cook, turn on the Pit Boss and warm it for 10-15 minutes at 225°F.
Grill the steaks straight on the grill for 45 minutes or till the internal temperature reaches 120°F.
Remove the steaks from the grill and raise the temperature to 450-500 degrees Fahrenheit. Allow the grill to warm for 10-15 minutes with the lid closed.
Return the steaks to the hot grill & cook for about 5-6 minutes on each side, or until an
internal temperature of 130 ° F for medium-rare is reached.
Remove the steaks from the grill & set them aside to cool.
To make the Creamed Greens, melt 2 tablespoons butter in a skillet over high heat till it foams. Cook, occasionally turning, until the garlic & shallot are cooked and brown, about 5 minutes over medium-low heat.
Add remaining cream, bring to a boil, and cook for approximately 10 minutes, or until slightly thickened. Toss in the nutmeg and season with salt to taste. Purée with a hand blender until smooth.
Melt the remaining 4 tbsp butter in a large saucepan over high heat until it foams. Cook, stirring regularly until the greens are cooked but still brilliant green, approximately 5 minutes.
Add the cream mixture & season with Salt. Reduce the heat to low, cover, and continue to cook for another 5 minutes.
Season to taste with nutmeg and salt and serve immediately.
To serve, cut the steaks into thin slices and place them on top of the leaves. Enjoy.

1.189 Grilled Italian Meatballs

Total Time: 50 mins, Servings: 4
Ingredients
Cubed White Bread, 1 1/2 Cup
1/4 Cup Milk
Extra-Virgin Olive Oil, 1 tbsp
Strips Bacon, 2
Onion, 1/2 Cup
Garlic (Minced), 1 Clove
Ground Chuck (80% Lean), 1 1/2 Pound
Ground Pork, 1/2 Pound
Parmesan Cheese, 1 Cup
Parsley (Minced), 2 tbsp
Kosher Salt, 1 tsp
Black Pepper, 1/2 tsp
Basil (Dried), 1/2 tsp
Oregano (Dried), 1/4 tsp
Instructions
Combine the bread & milk in a mixing dish and let aside for 5 minutes.
Remove the milk from the bread by wringing it out. Return the bread to the bowl after discarding the milk.
Melt 1 tablespoon of olive oil in a frying pan over medium heat. Combine the bacon, onion, & garlic in a large mixing bowl. Cook for 5 mins, or till the onion is transparent and the bacon grease has started to render. Allow cooling before adding to the bread mixture.
Combine the ground chuck, ground pork, Parmesan cheese, parsley, salt, pepper, basil, & oregano in a large mixing bowl. Combine the ingredients with your hands, using a gentle touch.
Drizzle olive oil on your hands and roll the meat mixture into 1-1/2" balls.
In the meantime, turn on the Pit Boss grill to Smoke and leave the lid open till the fire is ready (4 to 5 minutes). Preheat the oven to 350°F and bake for 10 to 15 minutes with the lid covered.
Place the meatballs on the grill grate in an even layer. Grill for 25 - 30 minutes, till a meatball reaches 160 degrees Fahrenheit on the inside. Allow 5 minutes for the meatballs to rest. Serve with hot marinara or other sauce skewered on toothpicks and short bamboo skewers. If desired, garnish with fresh basil leaves.

1.190 Pastrami Short Ribs

Total Time: 3 hours 15 mins, Servings: 4
Ingredients
Cold Water, 2 Quart
Morton Coarse Kosher Salt, 1/3 Cup
Pink Curing Salt, 1 tsp
Brown Sugar, 1/4 Cup
Garlic (Peeled & Smashed), 4 Clove
Pickling Spices (Roughly Crushed with the Meat Mallet), 4 tbsp
Coriander Seeds, 3 tbsps
Black Peppercorns (Cracked), 3 tbsp
Yellow Mustard Seeds, 2 tsp
Olive Oil (Extra-Virgin), 2 tbsp
Ginger Ale, 1 L
Instructions
To make the brine, combine 2 quarts of cold water, kosher salt, pink Salt, and brown sugar in a large mixing basin. Stir until all of the salt & sugar crystals are gone. Add the short ribs after stirring in the garlic and pickling spices.
Cover and chill for about 48 hours, stirring to disperse spices twice a day.
When ready to cook, drain the ribs and wipe dry on paper towels, removing any particles.
To make the rub, finely grind coriander seeds, peppercorns, and mustard seeds in a small resealable bag.
Drizzle olive oil on all sides of the ribs and coat lightly. Apply the rub on the meaty sides of the ribs and gently massage the spices in.
When ready to cook, preheat the Pit Boss to 165°F for 15 minutes with the lid closed.
Place the short ribs directly on the barbecue grate, bone-side down, & smoke for 2 hours.
Place the ribs in a roasting pan and set them aside. Fill the bottom of the pan with enough ginger ale to reach slightly

over the "top edges" of the bones. Wrap the foil around the dish securely.

Raise the grill temp to 300 °F & continue to cook the ribs for another 1 to 1-1/2 hours or until they are tender. Remove from the oven, allow to cool, and serve.

Chapter 2: Pork Recipes

2.1 Muffaletta Sandwich (Pit Boss Smoked)
Total Time: 3 Hr, Servings: 2
Ingredients
Smoked Mortadella, 1/3 Lb
Four Ciabatta Rolls Or 1 Ciabatta Loaf Large
Lb Salami 1/3, Cut Thin
Mozzarella Cheese 1/4 Lb, Cut Thin
Provol 1 Cheese 1/4 Lb, Cut Thin
Ham or Lb Prosciutto 1/3, Cut Thin
Lb Spicy Salami 1/3 As Capocollo, Pepperoni or Soppressata
Olive Salad
Castelvetrano Olives 1 Cup or Additional Green Olive of Your Choice, Rough and Sliced
Cup Spanish 1/2, French, or Other Green Olives of Your Choice
Drained and Chopped 1/2 Cup Jarred Roasted Red Peppers
Finely Chopped 2 Clove Garlic
Drained and Chopped 3 Tsp Capers
Finely Chopped Fresh Oregano 1 Tsp
Freshly Cracked Black Pepper and Sea Salt
High-Quality Olive Oil 1/3 Cup
Red Wine Vinegar 3 Tsp
Instructions
Preheat the Pit Boss to 165°F and cook for 15 mins with the top covered until ready to use.
Place the unsliced mortadella loaf on the grill to smoke for two and a 1/2 hrs. Allow cooling completely before thinly slicing.
While the mortadella is cooking, combine the ingredients for the olive salad and marinate. Complete the following steps a day ahead of time before constructing the sandwich.
To create the sandwich, cut the ciabatta bread in 1/2 horizontally. Divide the olive salad, including the oil and liquid, evenly between the two halves.
On the bottom 1/2 of a baguette, stack the following ingredients: smoked mortadella, salami, provolone, mozzarella, spicy salami, and prosciutto. Close the sandwich and wrap it firmly in plastic wrap to allow all the flavors to combine and the liquids to soak a significant portion of the bread.
Set aside in the refrigerator for 1 hr. To serve cold, remove the sandwich from the freezer, discard the plastic wrap, and cut it into four pieces.

2.2 Bacon-Draped Introduced in Pork Loin Roast
Total Time: 3 Hrs 15 Mins, Servings: 4
Ingredients
Apple Juice 1 Cup
Cup Water 1/4
1 Tsp Salt
1 Tsp Worcestershire Sauce
Center-Cut Pork Loin 3 Lb (3 Lb.)
Sweet Rub Pit Boss
Slices Bacon 10
Instructions
In a small mixing bowl, combine apple juice, water, salt, and Worcestershire; whisk to remove salt crystals. Plunge the injector into the sauce and withdraw the needle to draw up the liquid. Using a large needle, inject the meat generously.
Rub the beef with the Pit Boss Sweet Rub.
For 10 to 15 mins, preheat your grill to 225 degrees Fahrenheit. Place the bacon pieces on top of the loin and drape them over it. Place the roast directly on the grill grate and smoke for 3 to 4 hrs, or until an instant-read thermometer registers 145 degrees Fahrenheit.
Before slicing and serving, place the pork on a cutting board and leave aside for 10 mins to rest.

2.3 Smoked Pork Loin along with Apples and Sauerkraut
Total Time: 2 Hrs 10 Mins, Serving: 4
Ingredients
1 Pork Loin Roast (2 To 2-1/2 Lb.)
Poultry Rub & Pit Boss Pork
1 Lb Sauerkraut
Cored and cut, Peeled 2 Large Cooking Apples
1 Thinly Sliced Large Sweet Onion
Brown Sugar, 1/3 Cup
1 Cup Dark Beer
2 Tsp Butter
2 Whole Bay Leaves
Instructions
When you're ready to cook, preheat the Pit Boss to 180 degrees Fahrenheit for 15 mins with the lid closed. Use Super Smoke if it's available for the greatest flavor.
On both sides, season the pork loin with Pit Boss Pork & Salt & Pepper or Poultry Rub. Place the roast on the grill grate, cover, and cook for 1 hr.
In a large Dutch oven or glass baking dish, layer the sauerkraut, butter, bay leaves, beer, onions, brown sugar, and strawberries. Place the smoked pork loin directly on top of the sauerkraut mixture. Cover the plate with a cap or a piece of foil.
Return the pan to the Pit Boss and crank the temperature up to 350 degrees Fahrenheit. Close the top and continue to roast the pork for another hr or until an instant-read meat thermometer register 160°F.
Allow the roast to rest on a chopping board for a few mins. Meanwhile, carefully toss the sauerkraut mixture on a serving dish. On top of the roast pork pieces, layer the sauerkraut and apples.

2.4 Spicy Mandarin Glaze with BBQ Spareribs
Total Time: 5 Hrs 15 Mins, Serving: 6
Ingredients
Membrane Removed Racks Spareribs 3 Large
Yellow Mustard 3 Tsp
1 Tsp Worcestershire Sauce
Honey 1 Cup
Brown Sugar 1/2 Cup
Poultry Rub & Pit Boss Pork
Dr. Pepper 24 Ounce
Mandarin Orange Sauce 1/2 Cup
Sesame Oil 1 Tsp
Soy Sauce 1 Tsp
Garlic Powder 1 Tsp
Instructions
Preheat the Pit Boss to 225 degrees Fahrenheit with the lid closed for 15 mins when ready to roast. Use Super Smoke if it's available for the greatest flavor.
In a small bowl, combine Worcestershire sauce and yellow mustard. Both sides of the ribs should be rubbed with the Worcestershire and mustard mixture. Place directly on the grill grate and smoke for 3 hrs.
After removing the ribs from the Pit Boss, place them in an Al foil pan. After pouring honey over the ribs,

sprinkle them with brown sugar and Pit Boss Pork & Poultry Rub. Drizzle the ribs with Dr. Pepper. Cover with foil and raise the temperature to 275 degrees Fahrenheit on the Pit Boss. Ribs should be cooked for at least two hrs.

Set the foil pan aside after removing it from the grill. Increase the Pit Boss's temp to 450 degrees Fahrenheit. In a large bowl, combine the soy sauce, sesame oil, mandarin sauce, & garlic powder. Remove your ribs from the foil pan & brush them with the glaze. Place the ribs, straight on your grill grate for 8-10 mins. Remove the ribs from the Pit Boss.

2.5 Rib-Eye Grilled with Hasselback Sweet Potatoes

Total Time: 1 hour 15 mins, Servings: 4
Ingredients
Rib-Eye Steaks (Bone-In), 2 (1-1/2 To 2 Lb)
Sweet Potatoes, 4
Olive Oil (Extra-Virgin)
Salt n Pepper
Instructions
Take the steaks off from the refrigerator one hour before cooking to enable them to come to room temp.
When ready to prepare, preheat the Pit Boss to 400°F for 15 minutes with the lid closed.
Now, cut each sweet potato crosswise into 1/8" slices with a sharp knife, barely cutting 3/4 of the way through the potatoes to keep them intact. Optional: use chopsticks on either side of the potato to keep your knife from cutting all the way through. Arrange the sliced potatoes on a baking sheet. Drizzle with oil and season with Salt and pepper to taste. Preheat the grill and put the pan on it. Roast for 50 to 60 minutes, or till the potatoes are browned on the exterior and soft in the interior.
Prepare the steaks where the sweet potatoes are cooking. Rub each steak with oil and season well with Salt and pepper on both sides.
When the sweet potatoes are almost done, put the steaks on the grill and cook until the core temperature reaches 130°F for medium-rare, 4 - 5 minutes on each side, allowing each side to sear.
Take the steaks from the grill & set them aside to rest for 10 minutes.
Cut the steaks against the grain with a sharp knife. Arrange the potatoes and steak slices on a plate. For added taste, serve with Amanda's Lemon Gremolata.
Enjoy.

2.6 Spareribs Sweet Peach

Total Time: 5 Hrs 10 Mins, Serving: 6
Ingredients
Pork Spareribs 4 Rack
Poultry Rub & Pit Boss Pork
Apple Juice, For Spritzing
Butter 1 Tsp
Chopped 1 Medium Onion
Peach PreServings 1 1/2 Cup
Corn Syrup 1 Cup Light
Apple Cider Vinegar 1/2 Cup
Bourbon 1/2 Cup
Worcestershire Sauce 1 Tsp
Grated Ginger 1 Tsp
Dry Mustard 1 Tsp
1 Minced Clove Garlic
Instructions
Using damp paper towels, remove any excess fat from the ribs. Both sides of the ribs may be seasoned with the Poultry Rub & Pit Boss Pork.
Preheat the Pit Boss to 275 degrees Fahrenheit with the lid closed for 15 mins when ready to cook. Use Super Smoke if it's available for the greatest flavor.
Cook the ribs bone-side down on a rib rack or directly on your grill grate for 3 hrs, sprinkling with apple juice every 30 to 45 mins.
Meanwhile, melt the butter in a medium saucepan over medium-high heat. Sauté the onion slices until they are golden brown. Combine the peach pre-Servings, vinegar, bourbon, corn syrup, and Worcestershire sauce in a large mixing bowl. Before everything is fully mixed, add the ginger, mustard, and garlic. Cook for 15 mins, stirring occasionally, or until the sauce thickens. Set the sauce aside.
After 3 hrs, reduce the Pit Boss temperature to 165 degrees Fahrenheit. Smoke the ribs for 1 1/2 to 2 hrs, sprinkling with apple juice
every 30 mins.
Finally, preheat the Pit Boss to 275 degrees Fahrenheit for 10 mins. Remove the ribs from the grill and generously coat them with peach sauce.

2.7 Dan Patrick Display Chorizo Armadillo Eggs

Total Time: 55 Mins, Serving: 8
Ingredients
Cream Cheese 4 Ounce, Softened
Shredded Cheddar Cheese 1/2 Cup
Chopped Cilantro 1
Halved and Seeded 6 Whole Jalapeño
Ground Pork 2 Lb
Poultry Rub & Pit Boss Pork 2 Tsp
Instructions
Preheat the Pit Boss to 300 degrees Fahrenheit for 15 mins with the lid covered.
In the bowl of a stand mixer, beat cream cheese, cheddar, and cilantro using the paddle attachment until thoroughly combined. Split each jalapeño 1/2 in 1/2 and fill with the cheese mixture.
1/4 cup chorizo, flattened into a 1/4-inch-wide disc. Wrap the sausage around the cheese-stuffed jalapeno in the center of the tortilla to make an egg shape.
Balls of chorizo Pork and poultry rubs are used to season the dish.
Heat the chorizo balls on your grill grate for around 30 mins, often turning, until they are finely roasted and cooked through.

2.8 Pinwheels Bacon Pork (Kansas Lollipops)

Total Time: 30 Mins, Serving: 4
Ingredients
Pork Loin 1 Whole
Pepper and Salt
Greek Seasoning All Purpose Cavender's
Bacon 4 Slices
Heat BBQ Sauce & Pit Boss Sweet
Instructions
Preheat the Pit Boss to 450 degrees Fahrenheit and cook for

around 15 mins with the lid closed.
Remove some of the pork loin's silver skin or fat. Then, with a sharp knife, cut the pork loin lengthwise into four long strips.
Lay the pork flat and season it with salt, pepper, and Cavender's All Purpose Greek Seasoning. Flip the pork strips over and layer bacon on the unseasoned hand.
Begin rolling the pork strips tightly on the inside, with the bacon-wrapped side facing out.
Insert a skewer around the pork roll to keep it in place. Cook the pork rolls on the grill grate for 15 mins.
Pit Boss Sweet & Heat BBQ Sauce should be brushed on the pork. Then, coat the opposite side of each skewer until it's time to turn it over.
Depending on the thickness of the pork, add another 5 to 10 mins to the cooking time.

2.9 Roasted Pork Loin Honey-Glazed
Total Time: 1 Hr 10 Mins, Servings: 6
Ingredients
1 (3 Lb.) Pork Loin Roast
1 Onion, Chopped.
Garlic Chopped 2 Clove.
1 (12 Oz) Beer Bottle, If Possible, A German Lager
Honey 1/4 Cup
Coarse-Grained Mustard 2 Tsp
Caraway Seeds 1 Tsp
Fresh Dried Thyme 1 Tsp
Kosher Salt 1 Tsp Kosher Salt
Ground Black Pepper 1 Tsp
Poultry Rub & Pit Boss Pork
Instructions
Combine the bacon, onion, and garlic in a large resealable container.
In a mixing cup, combine the beer, sugar, mustard, caraway seeds, thyme, salt, and pepper. Pour the sauce over the meat and onion.
In the refrigerator, chill for several hrs or overnight.
Remove the pork from the marinade and combine it with the marinade in a saucepan. In a roasting pan, season the pork fat-side up with Pit Boss Pork & Poultry Rub.
Meanwhile, bring the marinade to a boil over medium-high heat and reduce it by 1/2.
Preheat the Pit Boss to 350°F for 15 mins with the lid closed when ready to cook.
Place the roasting pan with the meat inside straight on the grill grate. Roast for 1 hr with the fat side up and exposed.
Continue to roast for another 30 to 60 mins, basting twice or three times with the reduced marinade, or until the pork reaches 145 degrees Fahrenheit and is well coated.
Remove the roast from the oven and set aside to rest for 7 to 10 mins before slicing and serving with the pan juices. Have fun with it.

2.10 Lynchburg Bacon
Total Time: 30 Mins, Serving: 4
Ingredients
Country-Style Bacon 1 Lb
Tennessee Whiskey 1 Cup, Such as Apple Juice or Jack Daniel's
Poultry Rub 1 Pit Boss & Pork
All-Purpose Flour 3/4 Cup
Brown Sugar 1/3 Cup
Freshly Ground Black Pepper 1 Tsp
Instructions
Put the bacon strips in a large resealable container and cut them into thin slices.
Combine the whiskey with the Pit Boss Pork & Poultry Rub and stir thoroughly (or apple juice). Apply the whiskey over the bacon pieces and wipe the bag over them to completely coat them.
Set aside for 30 mins.
On wax paper, sift together the flour, brown sugar, and black pepper. Put the mixture in a second resealable bag.
Drain the bacon and add a couple of slices to the flour mixture at a time.
Shake the bag to coat each item evenly, then lay them out in a single layer on a baking sheet.
Preheat the Pit Boss to 375 degrees Fahrenheit with the lid closed for 15 mins when ready to cook.
Preheat the grill to 350°F and bake the bacon for 20 to 25 mins, or until golden brown and crisp.

2.11 Pit Boss Smoked Sausage
Total Time: 2 Hr 30 Mins, Serving: 4
Ingredients
Ground Pork 3 Lb
Ground Mustard 1/2 Tsp
Onion Powder 1 Tsp
Garlic Powder 1 Tsp
Pink Curing Salt 1/2 Tsp
Salt 1 Tsp
Black Pepper 4 Tsp
Ice Water 1/2 Cup
Hog Casings, Rinsed in Cold Water and Soaked
Instructions
In a medium mixing dish, combine the meat and spices and toss thoroughly.
Pour cold water over the meat and mix well with your hands until everything is well combined.
Fill a sausage stuffer halfway with the mixture and stuff it according to the manufacturer's directions. Overfilling the casing will cause it to rupture.
After all the meat has been filled, measure the length of the chain you want to use and squeeze and twist it a few times or tie it. Repeat the procedure for each connection.
Preheat the Pit Boss to 225°Farhenite with the lid covered for 15 mins until ready to cook. Use Super Smoke if it's available for the greatest flavor.
Cook directly on your grill grate for 1-2 hrs, or until the internal temperature reaches 155°Farhenite. Allow the sausage to rest for a few mins before slicing. Have fun with it.

2.12 Grilled German Sausage with a Smoky Pit Boss Twist
Total Time: 2 Hrs 20 Mins, Serving: 8
Ingredients
Jacobsen Salt 2 Tsp Co. Pure Kosher Sea Salt
the Sausage Maker Instacure 1 1 Tsp
Ground Nutmeg 1 Tsp
Ground Mace 2 Tsp
Ground Ginger 1 Tsp
Ground Pork 4 Lb, Lean 80%
Ground Beef or Ground Veal 1 Lb
Large Eggs 2
Nonfat Dry Milk Powder 1 Cup
Instructions
Combine salt, Instacure #1, nutmeg, mace, and ginger in a large pitcher or small tub. In a mixing dish, whisk together the milk and eggs. Blend everything until it's smooth. Pour the egg mixture over the ground beef and fold in gently. With your hands, mix in
the milk powder until it is equally distributed.
Cut the meat into long sausage links.
Preheat the Pit Boss to 225 degrees Fahrenheit with the lid covered for 15 mins when ready to cook.

Cook 2 hrs or until the core temperature reaches 175 degrees Fahrenheit. Serve immediately or store refrigerated until ready to use.

2.13 Reverse Seared Bone-In Pork Chops

Total Time: 50 Mins, Serving: 4
Ingredients
Four Chops Bone-In Pork
Poultry Rub & Pit Boss Pork
Butter 2 Tsp
2 Sprig Thyme
1 Sprig Rosemary
Instructions
Preheat the Pit Boss to 180 degrees Fahrenheit & cook for around 15 mins with the top covered until ready to use.
Season the pork chops well with Pit Boss Pork & Poultry Rub. Place immediately on the grill grate and smoke for 30 to 40 mins, or until an instant-read thermometer registers an interior temperature of 130 degrees Fahrenheit.
Remove the chops from the grill and put them aside for 10 mins to rest.
While the pork chops rest, preheat the grill to 500 degrees Fahrenheit by putting a cast iron skillet on your grill grate for about 10 mins.
Melt the butter in a cast-iron pan and toss in the herb sprigs. Place the pork chops in the basin with the melted butter. Sear for 3 to 4 mins on each side, or until the chop's outside is browned, and the core temperature in the thickest part reaches 140°F.
Remove the chops from the pan and put them aside for 5 mins to enable the internal temperature to reach
145 degrees Fahrenheit.

2.14 Old-Fashioned Roasted Glazed Ham

Total Time: 1 Hr 15 Mins, Serving: 8
Ingredients
Fully Cooked Bone-In Spiral Sliced Ham 1 (10 Lb.)
On cup Pineapple Juice
Brown Sugar 1/2 Cup
1 Cinnamon Stick
Fourteen Whole Cloves
1 Fresh Whole Pineapple
Ten Fresh Sweet Cherries
Instructions
Preheat the Pit Boss to 325°F for around 15 mins, then shut the lid until ready to use.
Wipe the ham with a paper towel after rinsing it with cold water.
In a saucepan, combine brown sugar, pineapple juice, four cloves, and a cinnamon stick. Bring the water to a low boil. Reduce the heat to low and simmer for another 15 mins, or until the pineapple juice has thickened into a syrup and has been reduced by half.
1/2 of the coating should be sprayed on the ham and the creases of the cut pieces. Set aside the remaining half of the glaze for another day.
Cut pineapple into 2-inch squares as required, then lay over ham, pinning it in place with clove and cherry.
In a large baking dish, place the ham fat side up. On the Pit Boss, cook for 1 to 14 hrs.
Carefully remove the ham from the Pit Boss and wipe away any remaining glaze.
Return the ham to the Pit Boss for another 15 to 20 mins of steaming until the internal temperature reaches 160 degrees Fahrenheit.
Allow the ham to rest for 15–20 mins before eating.

2.15 Plain Smoked Ribs

Total Time: 8 Hrs 15 Mins, Serving: 6
Ingredients
Baby Back Ribs 3 Rack
3/4 Cup Poultry Rub & Pit Boss Pork
Pit Boss 'Que BBQ Sauce 3/4 Cup

Instructions
By removing the membrane off the rear of the ribs, you may get rid of some excess fat.
1/4 cup Poultry Rub & Pit Boss Pork per rack on both sides of the ribs
Preheat the Pit Boss to 180°F with the lid closed for 15 mins when ready to cook.
Smoke the ribs over an open flame for 3 to 4 hrs.
When the internal temperature of the ribs hits 160°F-165°F, remove them from the grill and increase the temperature to 350°F.
On a large sheet of heavy-duty Al foil, spread 1/4 cup Pit Boss' Que BBQ Sauce, then place a rack of ribs on top, meat side down, and firmly wrapped. Continue to the next rack.
Return the wrapped ribs to the grill for 45 mins, or until they reach an internal temperature of 204 degrees Fahrenheit.
Before slicing the steak, remove it from the grill and put it aside for 20 mins.

2.16 Blueberry Sausage (Grilled)

Total Time: 55 mins, Servings: 6
Ingredients
2 tbsp Olive oil
Delicately sliced yellow onion 1/2 cup
Salt 1 pinch
Ground dark meat pork, turkey, or combination 2-lb
Dried cranberries or dried blueberries 1/2 cup
Fennel seed 2 tsp
Sliced rosemary 2 tsp
Gently beaten 1 egg
Lemon zest 1 tsp
Freshly black pepper 1/2 tsp
Instructions
In a medium-sized frypan, heat the olive oil over medium-high heat. With a sprinkle of salt, toss in the onion slices. Cook, stirring continuously, for about five to seven mins, or until onions are translucent. Relax and take a break from the sun.
Combine the remaining ingredients in a large mixing cup. Add the onions and mix well. Mix the items while washing your hands to ensure that they are equally spread. Refrigerate the mixture for 30 mins or up to 24 hrs.
Preheat the Pit Boss to 325°F and cook with the cover closed for 15 mins.
Remove the sausage from the refrigerator and form the meat mixture into 18 patties.
Place the grill on high and cook for 2 to 3 mins each hand, or until the internal temperature reaches 165°F-175°F. Have a good time.

2.17 Wrapped Asparagus in Grilled Prosciutto

Total Time: 40 Mins, Serving: 6
Ingredients
2 Bunch Asparagus
Four Ounce Prosciutto
Olive Oil
Pepper and Salt
1 Medium Lemon, Zested
Divided Balsamic Vinegar 2 Tsp
Toasted Pine Nuts 3 Tsp, For Serving

Instructions
Preheat your Pit Boss at 400°F and keep the lid covered unless ready to cook for 15 mins.
Rinse the asparagus and wipe it dry with a paper towel after washing it. The bottom third of the asparagus stalks should be removed and discarded.
Place 4-5 stalks on a baking sheet wrapped in prosciutto. Season the asparagus with salt, pepper, and lemon zest after drizzling it with olive oil.
Cook with the baking sheet on the grill. After 5 mins, shake the pan again to flip the asparagus and sprinkle with 1 Tbsp balsamic vinegar.
Return to the grill for another 5-8 mins, or unless the prosciutto turns crispy & the asparagus becomes tender.
Arrange the asparagus on a serving dish and sprinkle it with the remaining balsamic vinegar.

2.18 Pulled Pork Mac & Cheese
Total Time: 50 Mins, Serving: 6
Ingredients
Vegetable Oil 1 Tsp
Kosher Salt 1/2 Tsp
Elbow Macaroni 1 Lb
Milk 4 Cup
Butter 8 Tsp
Flour 1/2 Cup
Grated Gruyere Cheese 4 Cup
Grated Extra-Sharp Cheddar Cheese 2 Cup
Salt 1 Tsp
Freshly Ground Black Pepper 1/2 Tsp
Nutmeg 1/2 Tsp
Fresh White Breadcrumbs 1 1/2 Cup
Instructions
Preheat the grill to 375 degrees Fahrenheit for 10-15 mins before cooking. Fill a large saucepan halfway with salted boiling water
with the oil. Cook the macaroni according to the package directions, which should take around 6-8 mins. Drain the water completely.
Heat the milk in a small pot but do not boil it.
In a second large 4-quart saucepan, melt six tablespoons of butter and stir in flour. Cook for around 2 mins over low heat, stirring frequently. When whisking, pour in the boiling milk and cook for another min or two until the sauce thickens and soothes.
Remove the saucepan from the heat and add the Gruyere, nutmeg, 1 Tsp salt, pepper, and Cheddar cheeses. In a large mixing bowl, combine the fried macaroni noodles and any leftover pulled pork. Layer the fried macaroni and leftover pulled pork in a 3-quart baking dish or pan.
Spread the remaining 2 tablespoons of butter over the top, along with the new breadcrumbs.
Bake for 30–35 mins, or until the sauce thickens and the breadcrumbs color. Serve immediately with a sprinkle of cheese and a drizzling of barbeque sauce. Have fun with it.

2.19 Loin Smoked Pork
Total Time: 3 Hrs 5 Mins, Serving: 6
Ingredients
Pork Loins 1
Pit Boss Rub
Instructions
Pork loin is seasoned with Pit Boss Rub.
Preheat your grill at 180 degrees Fahrenheit and cover it for 15 mins until ready to roast.
Put the pork loin on your grill grates on a diagonal and cook for 3-4 hrs.

Preheat your grill at 350 degrees Fahrenheit & cook for 20-30 mins.
Remove the steaks from the grill & slice them into 1-1/2" steaks to serve.

2.20 Pork Spareribs BBQ Paleo
Total Time: 4 Hrs 15 Mins, Serving: 4
Ingredients
Rub
Kosher Salt 4 Tsp
Coarse Ground Black Pepper 2 Tsp
Paprika 4 Tsp
Garlic Powder 2 Tsp
Onion Powder 2 Tsp
Chipotle Chile Powder 1 Tsp
Main
Rack St. Louis-Style Ribs 2
BBQ Sauce
Organic Tomato Sauce 15 Fluid Ounce
Water 1/2 Cup
Apple Cider Vinegar 1/2 Cup
Honey 1/3 Cup
Onion Powder 2 Tsp
Coarse Ground Black Pepper 1 1/2 Tsp
Ground Mustard 1 Tsp
Paprika 1 Tsp
Instructions
Preheat your Pit Boss at 225°F and keep the cover closed unless ready to cook for 15 mins.
In a small dish, combine all rub ingredients.
Remove the membrane from the back of the ribs and massage both sides with the rub. Allow your ribs to cool for 15-20 mins.
Place the ribs on the grill bone-side down & cook for around 4-5 hrs. Check the interior temperature of the ribs; a temp of 202°F is excellent. Cook for another 30 mins, or unless the desired temp is reached.
While the ribs are cooking, make the sauce. To create the sauce, mix all the ingredients in a pot and cook on the stovetop until heated.
Brush a thin layer of sauce on both sides of the ribs & continue to cook for the next 10 mins to thicken the sauce.
Remove the ribs from the grill and put them aside for 10 mins to rest before slicing.

2.21 Tenderloin Pork
Total Time: 30 Mins, Serving: 2
Ingredients
Pork Tenderloin 1 Lb
1/3 Cup Apple Juice or Kentucky Bourbon
Low Sodium Soy Sauce 1/4 Cup
Brown Sugar, Packed 1/4 Cup
Dijon Mustard 2 Tsp
Worcestershire Sauce 2 Tsp
Ground Black Pepper 1 Tsp
Chopped Medium Onion 1
Minced Clove Garlic 2
Instructions
Remove all silver skin off the tenderloins
using a sturdy knife. Half-fill a large plastic bag with the meat. In a wide resealable container, whisk together the whiskey, soy sauce, brown sugar, vinegar, Worcestershire sauce, and pepper to create the marinade. In a mixing bowl, combine the onion and garlic. After pouring the sauce over the tenderloins, refrigerate for 8 hrs or overnight.
Preheat the Pit Boss to 400°F for 15 mins with the lid closed when ready to cook.

Scrape some strong components from the dirt and remove the meat from the marinade.
Remove the marinade from the meat and discard it.
Cook the tenderloins for 6 to 8 mins each hand on the grill grate, or until the core temp reaches 145 degrees Fahrenheit. The pork would always be somewhat yellow in the center. If you prefer your pork well-done, cook it to 160°F.
Remove the tenderloins from the pan and put them aside on a chopping board. Allow it to rest for a few mins before slicing into 1/2-inch diagonal slices.

2.22 Holiday Ham Cider (Glazed & Baked)
Total Time: 2 Hrs 15 Mins, Serving: 6
Ingredients
3 Apples, Cored and Cut into Thick Slices
1 Large Ham
4 Cup Apple Cider, Divided
Bourbon 1/4 cup
Dijon Mustard 1/4 cup
Maple Syrup or Honey 1/4 cup
Ground Cinnamon 1/2 Tsp
Ground Cloves 1/4 Tsp
Allspice or Ground Nutmeg 1 Pinch
Instructions
Preheat the Pit Boss to 325°F for 15 mins, then shut the lid till ready to use.
Line a roasting pan with heavy-duty foil to make cleaning easier.
Arrange apple slices at the bottom of the roasting tray to create a natural roasting rack. Cover the sliced apples with the remaining 1 cup apple cider and place the ham on top.
Preheat the oven to 350°F and place the roasting pan directly on the grill grate for 1-1/2 hrs.
For the glaze, combine the remaining 3 cups of apple cider and bourbon in a small saucepan and bring to a boil over medium-high heat. Cook until the liquid has been reduced to one-third of its original volume. In a mixing dish, combine the garlic, nutmeg, cinnamon, mustard, and honey.
If preferred, glaze the ham with the cider (apple) solution & cook for another 30 mins, or until an internal temperature of 140°F is achieved when a thermometer is inserted into the thickest part of the meat.
Remove the ham from the grill and set it aside to cool down for 20 mins before eating.
Warm the remaining sauce, if necessary, then serve with the ham. Have fun with it.

2.23 Roast Pork Loin along with Mango Salsa
Total Time: 55 Mins, Serving: 6
Ingredients
Pork Loin Boneless 6 Lb (5-6 Lb.)
Chili Powder 1 Tsp
Granulated Garlic 1 Tsp
Onion Powder 1 & ½ Tsp
Smoked Paprika 2 Tsp
Cayenne Pepper ¼ Tsp
Salt 1/4
Black Pepper 1/4 Tsp
Pineapple, Crush, or Chunks 1 Cup
Diced Mango 1 Cup
Fresh Strawberries 1 Cup
Minced Cilantro Leaves 1 Tsp
Pepper 1/2 Tsp
Garlic Powder 1/2 Tsp
Instructions
Put the pork loin aside after brushing it with the rub mixture.
Preheat the grill to 450 degrees Fahrenheit for 10-15 mins with the lid covered until you're ready to cook.
Place the pork loin on your grill and sear it all over for a few mins, flipping it every few mins and closing the cover in between turns. Then, reduce the temperature to 350°F. Cook till a beef reaches an internal temp of 150°F.
Remove the steaks from the grill and put them aside for 10 to 15 mins to rest. Then, using a 1/2" thick slicer, cut into 1/2" thick slices. Serve with a dollop of salsa on top.

2.24 Marcona Almonds with Prosciutto Roofed Dates

Total Time: 15 mins, Servings: 8
Ingredients
24 Whole Medjool Dates
1 Small (Salted) Container Marcona Almonds
8 Ounce Prosciutto
2 tbsp Olive Oil
2 For Zesting Washed & Dried Limes
Flake Salt for Serving
Honey for Serving
Instructions
Preheat the Pit Boss to 200°C and cover it for fifteen mins.
Using a large cast-iron pan, preheat the grill. Cut a
split lengthwise across the top of each date with the small paring knife. Get rid of the pit. 1 or 2 Marcona almonds may be used in lieu of the pits, and the dates can be pressed back together with your fingers to cover them.
Prosciutto should be cut into 24 pieces lengthwise. Place 1 at the end of the prosciutto to cover each date, then wrap your prosciutto over the date to completely cover it, leaving a little bit of the date visible on each corner.
2 tsp olive oil in a hot cast-iron skillet Place your dates within pan & cook, turning as required, for 3-5 mins, or until the prosciutto is charred on both sides. Once the prosciutto becomes crispy, gently remove the skillet from your grill.
Squeeze the limes into the pan to extract some citrus zest and add it to olive oil & dates. Arrange the dates on a serving dish. Serve with a sprinkling of flake salt, extra virgin olive oil, and butter.

2.25 Cajun Broil Pit Boss
Total Time: 1 Hr 30 Mins, Serving: 8
Ingredients
Olive Oil 2 Tsp
Red Potatoes 2 Lb
Seasoning Old Bay
Corn Ears 6, Each Sliced into Thirds
Smoked Kielbasa Sausage 2 Lb
Large Shrimp with Tails 3 Lb, Stripped
Butter 2 Tsp
Instructions
Preheat the Pit Boss to 450 degrees Fahrenheit & cook for around 15 mins with the lid covered until ready to use.
Drizzle 1/2 cup olive oil over the potatoes and season with Old

Bay seasoning to taste. Place immediately on the grill brace. Roast the vegetables for 20 mins, or until they are soft.

Drizzle the remaining olive oil over the corn and season with Old Bay seasoning to taste. On the grill plate, arrange the corn and kielbasa next to the potatoes. Roasting time: 15 mins

Season the shrimp with Old Bay seasoning. Cook directly on the barbecue grate with the other items for 10 mins, or until brilliant pink and cooked through.

After taking everything from the grill, transfer everything to a large mixing bowl. Add the butter and season with Old Bay seasoning to taste. Toss to coat and serve immediately.

2.26 Chopped Grilled Pork along with Pineapple-Mango Salsa

Total Time: 50 Mins, Serving: 4
Ingredients
Bone-In Pork Chops Thick-Cut 3 (16 Oz)
Poultry Rub & Pit Boss Pork 2 Tsp
Peeled and Diced Mango 1
Peeled, Cored, and Diced Pineapple 1/2
Diced Red Bell Pepper 1
Seeded and Diced Jalapeño 1
Diced Red Onion 1/2
Finely Chopped Cilantro 2 Tsp
Lime, Juiced 1.
Minced Garlic Clove 1
Pepper and Salt
Pit Boss Apricot BBQ Sauce 1/4 Cup
Instructions
Set aside for 30 mins after brushing both sides of the pork chops with Poultry Rub & Pit Boss Pork.

Combine all the ingredients for the Mango-Pineapple Salsa in a medium mixing bowl. Remove the procedure from the equation.

Preheat the Pit Boss to 500 degrees Fahrenheit with the lid closed for 15 mins when ready to cook.

Cook the chops on both sides of the grill for 7-10 mins. After tossing, rub pork chops with Pit Boss Apricot BBQ Sauce and cook until internal temperature reaches 145°F for medium-well.

Serve with salsa as a garnish.

2.27 Tenderloin Smoked Pork

Total Time: 3 Hrs 5 Mins, Serving: 4
Ingredients
Apple Juice 1/2 Cup
Honey 3 Tsp
3 Tsp Poultry Rub & Pit Boss Pork
Brown Sugar 1/4 Cup
Thyme Leaves 2 Tsp
Black Pepper 1/2 Tsp
Silver skin Removed Pork Tenderloins 2 (1-1/2 Lb.)
Instructions
In a large mixing cup, add the honey (warmed), apple juice, Pit Boss Pork Poultry Rub, thyme leaves, brown sugar, and black pepper to create the marinade. Whisk the ingredients together to combine them.

Place the pork loins in the container with the marinade. After turning the pork to coat it, cover the bowl with plastic wrap. Marinate for 2-3 hrs in the refrigerator.

Preheat the Pit Boss to 225°F for 15 mins with the lid closed when ready to cook. Use Super Smoke if it's available for the greatest flavor.

Place the tenderloins directly on your grill plate & smoke for around 2-3 hrs, or until the internal temp reaches 145 degrees Fahrenheit.

Before slicing, remove the steak from the grill & put it aside to rest for 5 mins.

2.28 Smoked Ribs BBQ

Total Time: 5 Hrs 25 Mins, Serving: 4
Ingredients
Rack St. Louis-Style Ribs 2
Pit Boss Big Game Rub 1/4 Cup
Apple Juice 1 Cup
Pit Boss BBQ Sauce
Instructions
By patting the back of the ribs dry, you may remove the membrane.

Apply an equal layer of rub to the front, back, & sides of the ribs. Allow 20 mins to sit or almost 4 hrs if chilled.

Preheat the Pit Boss to 225°F for 15 mins with the lid closed when ready to cook. Use Super Smoke if it's available for the greatest flavor.

Place the ribs, bone side down, on the grill. Fill a spray bottle with apple juice and spray the ribs after 1 hr of preparation. Spray every 45 mins after that.

After 4-1/2 hrs, check the ribs' core temp. They're done when the ribs' core temperature reaches 201°F. If not, wait 30 mins before trying again.

Apply a thin layer of your favorite Pit Boss BBQ Sauce to the front and back of the ribs until they're done. Allow 10 mins for the sauce to solidify before serving. After the sauce has set, remove the ribs from the grill and put them aside for 10 mins. Serve with extra

sauce and ribs that have been cut in half between the bones.

2.29 Baby Back Ribs Smoked

Total Time: 3 Hrs 15 Mins, Serving: 4
Ingredients
3 Rack Baby Back Ribs
Kosher Salt
Crushed Black Pepper
Instructions
After removing the membrane off the backside of the ribs, season all sides with salt and pepper.

Preheat the Pit Boss to 225°F for 15 mins with the lid closed once ready to cook.

Cook with the meat side up for 2 hrs. Cook for an additional hr, turning the ribs until the beef side is on the bottom. Have fun with it.

2.30 Pineapple Skewers & Sticky Teriyaki BBQ Pork

Total Time: 3 Hrs 10 Mins, Serving: 2
Ingredients
Pork Sirloin 1 Lb
Fresh Pineapple 18 Pieces
Scallions 6
Wooden Skewers 6
Carne Asada Marinade of Choice 1 Cup
Instructions
Thread a pork block, a pineapple chunk, and a sliver of green onion onto the thin side of a skewer; continue with 3-4 pieces of pork per slicer.

Replace the skewers and repeat with the remaining skewers. In a glass pan or pie dish, spray the marinade over the skewers, turning them to coat both sides. After covering in plastic wrap, refrigerate for 1 to 3 hrs.

Raise the temperature to be high and preheat for 15 mins with the lid covered when ready to cook.

Remove the skewers from the skewers and discard the marinade. Place the skewers on the grill grate and cook for 10

mins, turning once, or until the pork is fully cooked.
Place the skewers on a dish or plate and serve them straight away with steamed rice.

2.31 Moink Burger Smoked by Scott Thomas
Total Time: 1 Hr 10 Mins, Serving: 4
Ingredients
Ground Sirloin 1 Lb
Ground Pork 1/2 Lb
Worcestershire Sauce 1/4 Cup
Minced Garlic 1 Tsp
Black Pepper
Salt
Instructions
Combine all the ingredients in a mixing cup. Form the mixture into six patties.
Preheat the grill to 350 degrees F and cover it for 10-15 mins until you're ready to cook.
Cook until the burgers reach an internal temperature of 160 degrees Fahrenheit.
After a few mins, top the burgers with your favorite cheese and serve with your favorite toppings.

2.32 Grilled Bacon-Wrapped Hot Dogs
Total Time: 35 Mins, Serving: 8
Ingredients
Hot Dogs 12 Whole
Colby/Cheddar Cheese 8 Ounce
Sliced Bacon 12
Hot Dog Buns 12
Instructions
Using a sharp knife, cut the cheese into 8 big pieces. Next, cut the hot dogs lengthwise and fill each with a piece of cheese, leaving a "hinge" on the one hand.
Wrap a piece of bacon in a loop around each hot dog and secure it with toothpicks.
Preheat the Pit Boss to 350°F for 15 mins with the lid closed when ready to cook.
Cook the bacon-wrapped hot dogs for 20-30 mins on your grill grate, or until the cheese melts and the bacon crisps.
Transfer to the buns and serve immediately with your favorite condiments.

2.33 Tenderloin Apricot Pork
Total Time: 55 Mins, Serving: 4
Ingredients
Tenderloin Pork 2 Lb
Pit Boss Big Game Rub 3 Ounce
Pit Boss Apricot BBQ Sauce 1 Cup

Instructions
Remove any excess fat and silver skin from the pork tenderloin. After seasoning the pork tenderloin with Pit Boss Big Game Rub, let it rest for 30 mins.
Switch on the Pit Boss's Smoke setting when you're ready to cook. Place the pork tenderloins on the grill and smoke for 45 mins, or until the temperature is reached.
Preheat your grill for around 15 mins on high with the lid closed after removing the tenderloins from the grill.
Grill each side of the pork tenderloin for 90 seconds or until a core temperature of 145 degrees Fahrenheit is achieved after the Pit Boss has reached a high temperature.
Before taking the meat from the grill, spray it with Apricot BBQ Pit Boss Sauce. Allow 20 mins in a pan or on a chopping board to rest before serving. Enjoy it.

2.34 Cooked Potato Skins along with Pulled Pork
Total Time: 1 Hr 15 Mins, Serving: 6
Ingredients
Baker Style Whole Potato 4
Vegetable Oil
Russet Potatoes 4
Melted Butter 2 Tsp
Pulled Pork 3 Cup
4 Tsp Heat BBQ Sauce & Pit Boss Sweet
Mozzarella Cheese 1 Cup
Cheddar Cheese 1 Cup
Salt
Canola Oil
For Serving Chopped Green Onion
For Serving Chopped Bacon
For Serving Sour Cream

Instructions
Preheat the Pit Boss to 450 degrees
Fahrenheit & cook for around 15 mins with the lid covered until ready to use.
Season the potatoes evenly with canola oil and salt and pepper. Place the potatoes directly on your grill plate & cook for around 45 mins, or until they are soft when a fork pricks them in the middle.
Hollow out the insides of the potatoes, leaving 1/4 inch of potato skin on the exterior. Brush the insides of the skins with melted butter and place them on a baking pan. Cook for a further 5 to 6 mins on the grill, or until golden brown.
In a mixing dish, combine the Pit Boss Sweet, pulled pork, mozzarella cheese, Heat BBQ Sauce, and cheddar cheese.
Cover the skins in the mixture and return to the Pit Boss with the lid covered only if the cheese needs to melt.
Before serving, toss with sliced onions, sausage, and sour cream.

2.35 Supreme Pizza Baked Deep Dish
Total Time: 45 Mins, Serving: 4
Ingredients
Pizza Dough Ounce
Olive Oil Extra-Virgin
Pizza Sauce 1/2 Cup
Mozzarella Cheese 2 Cup
Fresh Oregano 1 Tsp
Fresh Basil 1 Tsp
Parmesan Cheese
Mild Italian Sausage Lb
Green 1/2 Bell Pepper 1
Diced Onion 2 Tsp
Red 1/2 Bell Pepper 1
Fresh Mushrooms

Sliced Pepperoni
Black Olives
Instructions
Preheat your grill on higher for 15 mins with the lid covered once you're ready to cook.
Cover a stainless-steel skillet with olive oil. Cover the bottom & up the sides of the pan with dough and push it out halfway.
Pour the sauce over the dough and top with all the toppings to make the pizza. On top of the mozzarella and freshly grated parmesan, sprinkle basil and oregano.
Bake for 25-30 mins, or until the cheese and sauce have melted, and the crust has become golden brown.
Allow for a 5- to 10-min rest period before slicing.

2.36 Spicy Bacon Covered Grilled Chicken Skewers

Total Time: 3 Hrs 20 Mins, Serving: 6
Ingredients
Ranch 1/2 Cup
Garlic Powder 1/2 Tsp
Chili Sauce 2 Tsp
Dried Oregano 1/2 Tsp
Cubed Chicken Breast 16 Ounce
Sliced Whole Red Onion 1
Sliced 1 Whole Green Bell Peppers
Sliced Bacon Strips 8
Instructions
In a large mixing bowl, combine ranch dressing, Chile sauce, oregano, and garlic powder. Toss in the cubed chicken and stir to combine. Allow the chicken to marinate in the refrigerator for 1-3 hrs.
Raise the temperature to be high and preheat for 15 mins with the lid covered when ready to cook.
Slide an onion wedge, a tomato, a piece of bacon, and chicken onto Pit Boss skewers to begin mounting. Before the bacon is wrapped around the chicken pieces, alternate the bacon and chicken. Finish each skewer with a pepper and onion wedge. Do not overcrowd the skewer to ensure fast and uniform roasting. Replace the skewers and repeat with the remaining skewers.
To prevent the skewers from burning and to make flipping them easier, arrange them on the grill grate with a piece of foil beneath their ends.
Cook for 5 mins on each hand, quarter-turning halfway through, for a total of 20 mins, or until the chicken reaches 165°F. Take the skewers out of the mix.

2.37 Onion Ring of Bacon

Total Time: 1 Hr 10 Mins, Serving: 6
Ingredients
Bacon 16 Slices
Sliced 2 Whole Vidalia Onion
Chili Garlic Sauce 1 Tsp
Yellow Mustard 1 Tsp
Honey 1 Tsp
Instructions
Before all the bacon is gone, wrap a piece around each onion ring. Because some onion slices are thicker than others, forming a rectangle with two bacon pieces is required.
Poke a skewer into the bacon-wrapped onion slice to keep the bacon from unraveling during cooking.
Preheat the grill to 400 degrees Fahrenheit when ready to serve. Close the cover and cook for 10-15 mins.
Combine the yellow mustard and chili garlic sauce in a shallow mixing cup; whisk in the sugar.
Cook the skewers for 90 mins on the grill brace, turning halfway through.

2.38 Brown Sugar Bacon Bites BBQ

Total Time: 40 Mins, Serving: 2
Ingredients
Brown Sugar 1/2 Cup
Ground Fennel 1 Tsp
Kosher Salt 2 Tsp
Ground Black Pepper 1 Tsp
Diced 1 Pork Belly Lb
Instructions
Fold a piece of Al foil in half & crimp the edges to create a rim. With a fork, pin gaps in the bottom of the foil. Some of the bacon fat will render, and the bacon bits will crunch.
Preheat the grill to 350 degrees Fahrenheit with the lid covered for 15 mins when ready to roast.
In a large mixing bowl, combine the ground fennel, brown sugar, black pepper, and salt. To mix, stir everything together.
In a large mixing bowl, toss the sliced pork belly until evenly coated. Place the pork pieces on a baking sheet coated with foil.
Cook for 20-30 mins on the grill, or until the pieces are crispy, colored and bubbling.

2.39 Pork Tenderloin of Cocoa Crusted

Total Time: 55 Mins, Serving: 4
Ingredients
Pork Tenderloin 1
Ground Fennel 1/2 Tsp
Cocoa Powder Unsweetened 2 Tsp
Smoked Paprika 1 Tsp
Kosher Salt 1/2 Tsp
Black Pepper 1/2 Tsp
Extra-Virgin Olive Oil 1 Tsp
Thinly Sliced Green Onions 3
Instructions
Using a paring knife, remove the silver skin & connective tissue from the loin. To prepare a paste, combine the remaining ingredients in a shallow mixing basin. After applying the paste, chill the pork loin for 30 mins.
Raise the temperature to high and preheat for 15 mins with the lid covered when ready to cook.
Sear the meat on all sides on the front burner of the grill. After the pork has been seared, reduce the temp to 350 degrees Fahrenheit and move it to the center of the grill.
Cook for the next 10-15 mins, or until the core temp of the pork reaches 145°F for mild to medium doneness.
After cooking, take it from the grill & set it aside for at least 8-10 mins before slicing. Serve with a garnish of green onions.

2.40 Bourbon Glazed Ham & Apple

Total Time: 1 Hr 15 Mins, Serving: 6
Ingredients
Large Ham 1
Apple Jelly 1 Cup
Dijon Mustard 2 Tsp
Bourbon 2 Tsp
Fresh Lemon Juice 2 Tsp
Ground Cloves 1/2 Tsp
Cider or Apple Juice 2 Cup
Instructions
Preheat the Pit Boss to 325 degrees Fahrenheit for 15 mins with the lid covered until ready to use.
Place the ham directly on your grill plate until it is hot. It takes 30 mins to prepare the dish.
In the meanwhile, melt the apple jelly in a small saucepan over medium-low heat. Remove the apple cider, vinegar, whiskey, lemon juice, and ground cloves from the heat and set them

aside.
After 30 mins, glaze the ham with the apple bourbon mixture. Cook for another 30 mins, or until a thermometer inserted into the thickest part of the beef registers a core temperature of 135°F.
Remove the ham from the grill and allow it to cool for 20 mins before eating. Reheat any remaining sauce & serve with ham if desired.

2.41 In a Blanket Everything Pigs
Total Time: 40 Mins, Serving: 4
Ingredients
Poppy Seeds 2 Tsp
Dried Minced Onion 1 Tsp
Minced Garlic 2 Tsp
Sesame Seeds 2 Tsp
Salt 1 Tsp
Pillsbury Original Crescent Rolls Can 8 Ounce (8 Oz)
Dijon Mustard 1/4 Cup
Beaten Egg 1 Large
Instructions
Preheat your Pit Boss for 10-15 mins at 350 degrees Fahrenheit with the lid covered until you're ready to roast.
In a large mixing bowl, combine the dried minced onion, salt, sesame seeds, poppy seeds, and dried minced garlic.
Each crescent roll dough triangle should be cut in thirds lengthwise, resulting in three short strips.
Brush the dough strips with a light coating of Dijon mustard. On one end of the dough, roll up the tiny hot dogs.
Place them seam side down on a prepared baking pan. Season with the seasoning mix after rubbing with egg wash.
In a Pit Boss, bake for 12-15 mins, or until golden brown.
Serve with a mustard or dipping sauce of your choice.

2.42 Potatoes & Smoked Sausage
Total Time: 55 Mins, Serving: 4
Ingredients
Hot Sausage Links 2 Lb
Fingerling Potatoes 2 Lb
Fresh Thyme 1 Tsp
Butter 4 Tsp
Instructions
Preheat your Pit Boss to 375°F and keep the lid covered until ready to cook for 15 mins.
Put your sausage links on the grill to give them some color. This should take approximately 3 mins on either hand.
To achieve uniform cooking, split the potatoes into bite-size pieces about the same size as the sausage. Then, before combining the thyme and butter in a Pit Boss cast iron pan, chop the thyme and butter.
Remove the sausage from the oven and place it in your cast iron pan, breaking it up into bite-size pieces.
Reduce the grill's temperature to 275°F and cook the cast iron for 45 mins to an hr, or until the potatoes are fully cooked.
Cut into 1 of the potatoes with a butter knife after 45 mins to check whether it is done. Reduce cooking time by covering cast iron with a lid or foil. Place the food on the table.

2.43 Bacon Dog Grilled
Total Time: 50 Mins, Serving: 4
Ingredients
Hot Dogs 16
Bacon Slices 16
Sliced Vidalia Onion 2
Velveeta Cheese
Hot Dog Buns 16

Pit Boss 'Que BBQ Sauce
Instructions
Preheat the Pit Boss to 375°F and keep the lid covered for 15 mins.
Cook for 10 mins on each side directly on the grill grate after tying bacon strips around the hot dogs.
Around the same time as the hot dogs, cook the onions for 10-15 mins.
Combine Pit Boss's Que sauce, grilled hot dogs, cheese sauce, and hot dog buns in a large mixing bowl. Serve with a side of veggies.

2.44 BBQ Pork Chop Seared
Total Time: 1 Hr 10 Mins, Serving: 6
Ingredients
Pork Chops 6
Poultry Rub & Pit Boss Pork
Instructions
Preheat the Pit Boss to 275 degrees Fahrenheit with the lid covered for 15 mins.
Poultry Rub & Pit Boss Pork should be generously applied to pork chops. Allow 15 mins for sleep.
On the grate, roast pork chops for 30 mins, then turn and cook for the next 30 mins.
Raise the temp to 500 degrees Fahrenheit after removing the pork chops from the grill.
When the grill is hot, return the pork chops to it and cook for 3 mins on each side, or until they reach a core temp of 145 degrees Fahrenheit.
Remove the steaks from the grill and set them aside to rest for 10 mins before serving.

2.45 Sausage Stuffing (Classic)
Total Time: 1 Hr 15 Mins, Serving: 8
Ingredients
Butter 2 Tsp
Extra-Virgin Olive Oil 2 Tsp
Diced Celery 1 Cup
Diced 1 Yellow Onion Cup
Uncooked Ounce Sausage 8
Tart Cherries, Dried 1/2 Cup
Pieces Pecans 1/2 Cup
For Garnish Chopped Herbs 1/2 Cup
Cubed Bread 8 Cup
4 Chicken Stock Cup
Instructions
Preheat the grill on high for 15 mins with the lid covered.
Using a large cast-iron plate, preheat the grill. The
celery and onions are then added, followed by the butter and olive oil. Cook for 15-20 mins, or until the vegetables are soft.
Substitute the sausage for the veggies in the pan. Cook until the mixture is crumbly and no longer pink in color. Remove the pecans, cherries, and herbs from the grill and toss them in with the rest of the ingredients.
In a large mixing bowl, toss the bread with the celery and onions, as well as the sausage and spice mixture. Drizzle in the stock slowly, mixing with your hands to ensure that all the bread is coated. If the bread is too dry, add a bit more stock.
Cover the stuffing with foil and place it on a greased 9x13-inch baking pan. Set aside 1/2 of the stuffing for use with the bird if desired.
Cook for 30 mins on the grill or until fully warmed. Remove the foil and bake for a further 15-20 mins, or until the crust is crisp on top but soft in the center.

2.46 Double Decker Tacos from Pit Boss BBQ

Total Time: 35 Mins, Serving: 6
Ingredients
Sour Cream 2 Cup
Refried Beans 16 Ounce
Leftover Beef Brisket 2 Cup
Leftover Pulled Pork 2 Cup
Flour Tortillas 10
Crisp Taco Shell 10
Guacamole 3
Tomato Salsa 2 Cup
Diced 1 Red Onion Cup
Finely Chopped Cilantro 1/2 Cup
Cheddar Cheese 1 1/2 Cup
Instructions
Preheat the grill to 325°F and cover it for 15 mins.
In a mixing bowl, combine 1/2 cup sour cream and refried beans. Place on an oven-safe tray in a preheated grill.
In a double layer of Al foil, place the remaining brisket and pork on the grill. For approximately 25 mins, warm the meats and beans.
Spread a thin layer of hot beans on a soft taco shell and wrap it over a crisp taco shell to create double-decker tacos.
Toss the brisket and pork into the crisp taco shell with cilantro, sour cream, tomato, vinegar, guacamole, and cheese to taste.

2.47 Pulled pig from Hawaii

Total Time: 5 Hrs 15 Mins, Serving: 4
Ingredients
Bone-In Pork Shoulder 7 Lb
Jacobsen Salt Co. Pure Kosher Sea Salt 3 Tsp
Whole Banana Leaves 2
Ground Black Pepper
Instructions
Season the pork shoulder with Jacobsen Salt & pepper.
Use a banana leaf to cover your work surface. If you were wrapping a present, bring up the ends and put the pork shoulder in the middle. To surround the meat, fold the ends of the second banana leaf at a right angle to the first. Wrap the whole box with Al foil. Refrigerate for at least 1 night before serving.
Preheat the Pit Boss to 300°F for 15 mins with the lid closed before cooking.
Place the coated pork on the grill grate right away and cook for 5-6 hrs, or until it's falling-apart tender and the internal temperature hits 190 degrees F.
Place the wrapped meat on a chopping board and leave aside for 20 mins. Then, carefully unwrap the pork and preserve any liquids that have been collected in the foil.
Remove any fat from the pork before shredding it into pieces and shreds.

2.48 Banana Bacon Pancakes

Total Time: 30 Mins, Serving: 6
Ingredients
Buttermilk 1 Cup
Large Eggs 1
Vanilla Extract 1/2 Tsp
Melted Butter 2 Tsp
Vegetable Oil
Cornmeal 2 Tsp
Sugar 2 Tsp
Cup All-Purpose Flour
Baking Powder 1 Tsp
Baking Soda 1/2 Tsp
Salt 1/2 Tsp
Crumbled Cooked Bacon 6 Slices
Diced Bananas 2
Instructions
When prepared to cook, preheat the grill to 350 degrees Fahrenheit and shut the cover for 15 mins.
In a mixing basin, whisk together the egg, buttermilk, and vanilla extract. Everything should be well combined. Next, whisk together the melted butter and egg yolks in a separate dish.
In a separate large mixing bowl, combine the sugar, baking powder, baking soda, cornmeal, flour, and salt. Whisk the ingredients together to combine them.
Make a well in the middle of the dry mixture and pour in the wet ingredients.
The batter should be reasonably smooth after whisking. The pancakes will turn rough if the batter is over-mixed. In a mixing dish, combine the bananas and crumbled bacon.
Spray the grill with nonstick cooking spray. Place the skillet on the grill and heat (about 4-5 Mins). On the griddle, 1/4 cup batter should be poured.
Cook the bottom of the pancake until it bubbles, becomes golden, and is hard enough to move.
On the opposite side, cook for another min or so. Finally, place the food on the table.

2.49 Cabbage Braised-Beer with Bacon

Total Time: 45 Mins, Serving: 4
Ingredients
Bulk Unsliced Lb Bacon 1/4
Diced Yellow Onion 1 Cup
Diced Small Apple 1 Cup
Sliced Green Cabbage 2 Lb
Ground Black Pepper
Light Beer 12 Ounce
Salt
Instructions
Heat the grill (Pit Boss) to 325 degrees Fahrenheit (160 degrees Celsius) with the lid covered for ten to fifteen mins before cooking.
Preheat a large, heavy pot or Dutch oven on the stovetop over medium heat. Cook until the bacon is crisp, approximately 10 mins (about 5 Mins). Transfer to a tray lined with paper towels.
Return the saucepan to a low-medium heat setting. After adding the onion, cook for 5 mins, or until golden brown. Before adding the cabbage, stir in the apple. For 3 mins, stir in a large quantity of salt and a sprinkle of black pepper.
Pour in the beer and bring to a simmer over medium-high pressure. Cover and transfer the pot to the Pit Boss as soon as possible.
Preheat oven to 325°F and bake for 10 mins. Cook for the next 10-15 mins, or until the cabbage is tender and the liquid has evaporated, without the cover.
Toss the cabbage with the saved bacon.

2.50 Grilled Lemons on Aked German Pork Schnitzel

Total Time: 40 Mins, Serving: 2
Ingredients
Pork Chops 16 Ounce
Black Pepper
Garlic Powder 1 Tsp
Salt
Paprika 1 Tsp
Eggs 2
Panko Breadcrumbs 1 Cup

Flour 1/2 Cup
Halved Whole Lemon 2
Instructions
Preheat the grill to a high temperature for 15 mins with the lid covered until ready to use.
Placing the pork chops between two pieces of plastic wrap, one on top of the other is a good idea. Lb them using a meat mallet. Season with a liberal quantity of salt and pepper on both sides.
Combine the garlic powder and paprika in a mixing bowl. In a separate bowl, whisk the eggs. In a third dish, place the breadcrumbs.
Dredge the pork cutlets in rice, shaking off any excess, followed by shells, and lastly, breadcrumbs. Place the breaded pork cutlets on a wire rack over a lightly greased baking sheet.
Bake for 15 mins on one side, then turn and bake for 5 mins on the other. As you open the grill to flip the pork, place sliced lemons straight on the grill grate, flesh side down.
Remove the grill pan from the heat and garnish with fried lemon slices.

2.51 Bologna Smoked.
Total Time: 4 Hrs 5 Mins, Serving: 4
Ingredients
Bologna Log 1 Lb
Worcestershire Sauce
Brown Sugar 1/4 Cup
Yellow Mustard 1 Tsp
Soy Sauce 1 Tsp
Instructions
With a sharp knife, score the bologna log, being careful not to slice too deeply.
In a large mixing bowl, combine the brown sugar, vinegar, soy sauce, and Worcestershire sauce.
Brush the bologna with the mixture once it has been well mixed.
Preheat the Pit Boss to 225°F for 15 mins with the lid covered.
3–4 hrs of smoking the bologna
Take the steaks from the grill and put them aside to cool.
Serve with sandwiches, cut into thin pieces. Have fun with it.

2.52 Bacon-Wrapped Water Chestnuts BBQ
Total Time: 50 Mins, Serving: 6
Ingredients
Bacon 1 Lb
Water Chestnuts 2 Can
Brown Sugar 1/3 Cup
Mayonnaise 1/3 Cup
Pit Boss Texas Spicy BBQ Sauce 1/3 Cup
Instructions
Start the Pit Boss grill when you're ready to cook. Smoke with the lid opens before the
fire starts (4 to 5 mins). Preheat the grill to 350 degrees Fahrenheit and bake with the lid covered for 10-15 mins.
Line a rimmed baking dish with Al foil. Each bacon slice should be divided into thirds or half. Wrap each water chestnut with a piece of bacon large enough to surround it and secure it with a toothpick.
Arrange the bacon-wrapped chestnuts in a single layer on the Preparation baking sheet. Preheat the oven to 350°F and bake for 20 mins. Fire up the grill.
Combine the brown sugar, mayonnaise, and Pit Boss Spicy Barbecue Sauce in a mixing cup. Cook the chestnuts in the sauce for another 10-15 mins on the grill. Place on a serving plate and serve.

2.53 Smoked Packed Avocado Recipe
Total Time: 45 Mins, Serving: 8
Ingredients
Whole Avocados 6
Leftover Pulled Pork 3 Cup
Shredded Monterey Jack Cheese 1 1/2 Cup
Tomato Salsa 1 Cup
Finely Chopped Cup Cilantro 1/4
Whole Quail Eggs 8
Instructions
Preheat your grill to 375 degrees Fahrenheit and roast for 10-15 mins with the lid covered.
Remove the avocado pits and, if possible, any of the avocado flesh from the center.
In a mixing bowl, combine the salsa, cilantro, bacon, and cheese. Arrange the avocados on top of the meat mixture and grill them. It takes 25 mins to prepare the dish.
With a spoon, make a divot or "nest" for the quail egg. Break the quail egg carefully into the "nest" & cook for the next 5-8 mins, or until the egg is done to your taste.
Remove the burgers from the grill and place them on a plate to serve.

2.54 Spicy Pork and Sweet Roast
Total Time: 1 Hr 15 Mins, Serving: 2
Ingredients
Loins Pork 2 Lb
Seeded Habanero Peppers 2/3
Coconut Milk 2/3 Can
Chinese Five-Spice Powder 1/3 Tsp
Paprika 2/3 Tsp
Curry Powder 2/3 Tsp
Lime Juice 2/3 Tsp
Minced Garlic 2/3 Tsp
Freshly Grated Ginger 2/3 Tsp
Instructions
Combine all your ingredients, except the bacon, in a mixing dish. Allow the pork to marinate in the marinade overnight.
Preheat the Pit Boss to 300°F for 15 mins with the lid open.
On a heated plate, cook the pork. Cook for 1-2 hrs, or unless the core temperature hits 145-150°F.
Pork Tenderloin Spice-Rubbed
Total Time: 2 Hrs 20 Mins, Serving: 4
Ingredients
Whole Cedar Planks 2
Dried Oregano 1 Tsp
Black Pepper 1/2 Tsp
Cumin 2 Tsp
Ancho Chile Powder 1 Tsp
Smoked Paprika 1 Tsp
Kosher Salt 1 Tsp
Garlic Powder 1/4 Tsp
Brown Sugar 1 Tsp
Dry Mustard 1/4 Tsp
Pork Tenderloin 2 Lb
Olive Oil
Instructions
Prepare ahead of time. An overnight stay is required for this recipe. First, soak the cedar boards in water for almost 2 hrs.
Combine all the dry spices and brown sugar in a shallow mixing cup.
Brush the tenderloins with olive oil before applying the spice mixture. Allow 30 mins for recuperation.
Preheat the grill to 350 degrees Fahrenheit for 10-15 mins with the lid covered when ready to roast.
Cook for 3 mins after placing the cedar boards on the grill and closing the door. Place pork tenderloin on each plank's hot

side and flip.
Grill the tenderloins for 15-20 mins, or until an instant-read thermometer registers 145°F on the interior.
Before serving, wrap the tenderloins in foil and put them aside for 5 mins.

2.55 Egg Cups & Grilled Ham
Total Time: 40 Mins, Serving: 6
Ingredients
Pieces Ham 12
Eggs 12
Whipping Cup Cream
Pepper and Salt
Shredded Cheddar Cheese 1 Cup
Chopped Chives
Instructions
Preheat the Pit Boss to 350°F for 15 mins, then shut the lid.
Coat the wells of a muffin pan with cooking spray. Cut the ham into pieces that are just big enough to go into each muffin nicely.
Place the ham slices on the grill grate as soon as possible & cook for around 5-10 mins per hand, or until well browned. Fire up the grill.
In a mixing dish, whisk together the eggs & hard whipped cream. To taste, season with
salt & pepper.
Cook the eggs for 12-15 mins, or until they are fully cooked. Sprinkle with cheese in the final few mins of preparation if desired.
Cut the ham and egg cups carefully and serve right away with chives or cilantro, if preferred.

2.56 Breakfast Strata Holiday
Total Time: 45 Mins, Serving: 4
Ingredients
Sliced Bread 6
Breakfast Sausage 1 Lb
Mustard 1 Tsp
Shredded Cheddar Cheese 1 Cup
Beaten Egg 4
Whole Milk 1 1/2 Cup
1/2-And-1/2 3/4 Cup
Salt 1/2 Tsp
Pepper 1/4 Tsp
Ground Nutmeg 1 Pinch
Worcestershire Sauce 1 Tsp

Instructions
When you're ready to roast, fire up the Pit Boss grill and set the temp to 350
degrees Fahrenheit. Close the cover and preheat for 10-15 mins.
Remove the crust of the bread and place it in the bottom of a 9-by-13-inch baking pan. After browning the sausage, drain the excess fat.
Combine the sausage and mustard in a mixing bowl. Spread a thin layer of sausage on the bread and top with cheese.
Before pouring over the cheese and sausage, whisk together the other ingredients (pepper, Worcestershire sauce, salt, eggs, nutmeg, and milk).
On the Pit Boss, bake for 25-30 mins. Before serving, reheat the dish.

2.57 Pork Chops Pit Boss
Total Time: 35 Mins, Serving: 2
Ingredients
Pork Chops 2 (1-1/2 Inch Thick)
Sea Salt or Kosher
Pit Boss Blackened Saskatchewan Rub
Instructions
In a mixing dish, combine the Pit Boss Blackened Saskatchewan and salt. It's possible to rub pork chops.
Preheat the Pit Boss to 450°Fahrenheit for 15 mins with the lid covered.
Cook the pork chops for 30 mins on the grill grate, rotating halfway through.
Remove the steaks from the grill and put them aside to cool for around 5 mins.

2.58 Pork Tenderloin and Lemon Pepper Grilling
Total Time: 40 Mins, Serving: 4
Ingredients
Zested Lemons 2
Minced Clove Garlic 1
Freshly Minced Parsley 1 Tsp
Lemon Juice 1 Tsp
Black Pepper 1/4 Tsp
Kosher Salt 1/2 Tsp
Olive Oil 2 Tsp
Pork Tenderloin 1 (2 Lb.)
Instructions
In a wide bowl, combine everything except the tenderloin.
Remove all silver skin and excess fat from the tenderloin.
Put the pork in a large resealable plastic bag and seal it. After pouring the marinade over the tenderloin, zip it up. Refrigerate for a minimum of 2 hrs, but no more than 8 hrs.
Preheat the Pit Boss to 375°F for 15 mins with the lid closed.
Remove the tenderloin from its container and discard the marinade.
When the grill is hot, place the tenderloin directly on your grate & cook for 15-20 mins, rotating halfway through, or until the core temp reaches 145°F.
Before slicing, remove the pan from the heat and set it aside to cool for 5-10 mins.

2.59 Quick Ribs BBQ
Total Time: 3 Hrs 10 Mins, Serving: 6
Ingredients
Baby Back Ribs 3 Rack
Poultry Rub & Pit Boss Pork
1 As Needed Pit Boss Texas Spicy BBQ Sauce
Instructions
Poultry Rub & Poultry Rub lightly coats all sides of the ribs. Ribs should be refrigerated overnight after being covered.
Preheat the Pit Boss to 500 degrees Fahrenheit with the lid closed for 15 mins when ready to cook.
On a hot plate, cook the ribs for 15 mins, uncovered.
Reduce the temperature of the grill to 325°F and cook the ribs for another 2 hrs.
Check after 2 hrs to see if the meat has pulled back 1/4 to 1/2 inch from the end of the bones; if it hasn't, cook for another 15 mins and check again. They're done when the core temp of the ribs reaches 201°F.
When the ribs are done, glaze them with Pit Boss Texas Spicy Barbecue sauce. Cook for an additional 10 mins to thicken the sauce.
Remove the steaks from the grill and set them aside to cool for 10 mins.
To eat, split the ribs between the bones and top with more BBQ sauce.

2.60 Arugula Pesto & Smoked Chorizo
Total Time: 40 Mins, Serving: 4
Ingredients
Fresh Arugula 4 Cup
Clove Garlic 1
Grated Parmesan Cheese 1/2 Cup
Pine Nuts 1/2 Cup
Extra-Virgin Olive Oil 1/4 Cup
Grapeseed Oil 1/4 Cup
Sea Salt
Freshly Ground Black Pepper
Water
Instructions
To prepare the pesto, purée the arugula, garlic, almonds, and cheese in a food processor or blender bowl. While the processor is running, drizzle in the oil. Season the mixture with salt and pepper to taste. If the pesto is too thick, thin it down with water.
Preheat the Pit Boss to 375°F for 15 mins with the lid closed when ready to cook.
Smoke the sausages whole for 20 mins, or until the internal temperature reaches 170°F.
Allow 10 mins for the sausage links to cool before cutting them into large 1-1/2" pieces. Finish with arugula pesto and transfer the sausage to a serving dish.

2.61 Apricot-Sauced Roasted Ham
Total Time: 2 Hrs 15 Mins, Serving: 8
Ingredients
Main
Snake River Farms Kurobuta Whole Bone-In Ham 1 (8-10 Lb.)
For the Glaze
Pit Boss Apricot BBQ Sauce 1 Bottle
Horseradish 1/4 Cup
Dijon Mustard 2 Tsp
Instructions
Preheat the Pit Boss to 325°F for 15 mins, then shut the lid.
Arrange the ham in a large foil-lined roasting pan. Preheat the grill to high and cook for 90 mins with the pan.
In a saucepan over medium heat, combine the Pit Boss Apricot Sauce, horseradish, and mustard to make the glaze. Remove from the oven and keep warm.
After 90 mins, brush the glaze over the ham. Cook for a further 30 mins, or until an internal temperature of 135°F is achieved when a thermometer is inserted into the thickest part of the ham.
Before carving the ham, remove it from the grill and put it aside to rest for 20 mins.
Drizzle with the remaining glaze as required.

2.62 Bacon & Cheese & Brie Mac
Total Time: 1 Hr 15 Mins, Serving: 8
Ingredients
Whole Milk 32 Ounce
Onion Powder 1 Tsp
2 Tsp Garlic Powder
Brie Cheese 24 Ounce
Cheddar Cheese 1 Cup
Shredded Mozzarella Cheese 1 Cup
Diced Whole Jalapeño 2
Pepper and Salt
Corn Starch 2 Tsp
Cooked Bacon 1 Lb
Cooked Penne 16 Ounce
Instructions
In your double boiler, heat the milk until it is slightly sweetened, then add the brie, cheddar, onion, garlic powder, and 1 cup mozzarella cheese.
After the cheese has melted, add the salt, pepper, and jalapenos.
Make a slurry with the corn starch and water, then mix it into the sauce to thicken it. Last, add the fried bacon and penne.
In an oiled cast-iron pan, toss the mac and cheese with the remaining mozzarella cheese.
Preheat the grill to 350 degrees Fahrenheit with the lid covered.
Cook the mac and cheese for 15-20 mins on your Pit Boss, or till golden and bubbling.

2.63 Smoky Ham & Bean Soup
Total Time: 5 Hrs 10 Mins, Serving: 8
Ingredients
Lb Pork Neck 1 1/2
Pepper and Salt
Diced Large Yellow Onion 1
Hot Sauce 2 Tsp
Olive Oil
Northwest Beans 2 Can
Cornstarch 1 Tsp
Chicken Stock 1 Quart
Bacon 3 Slices
Chopped Parsley 1 Tsp
Instructions
Set your Pit Boss to the "Smoke" setting.
Season the pork collar with pepper and salt. Place the pork on the grill plate and smoke it for 2 hrs or longer, depending on the level of smoke you want.
In a large saucepan of oil or butter, caramelize sliced onions over medium heat. Season the onions with salt and pepper.
After the onions have beautifully caramelized, add the pork collar, salt, and spicy sauce to the bowl. Fill the pan with enough water to completely immerse the meat. Bring the soup to a boil, then turn it down to a low heat setting.
Enable 3-4 hrs for the cap to be removed to allow part of the water to evaporate. After 3
hrs of cooking, remove the pork, and set it aside to cool. Remove the bone meat and shred it after it has cooled.
Return the shredded pork and Northwest beans to the stock and cook on low.
Combine the water and corn starch in a mixing bowl, then pour over the stock. Reduce the heat to low and often whisk until the sauce thickens. As a garnish, add sliced bacon and parsley to the soup.

2.64 Smoked Pork Tenderloin
Total Time: 3 Hrs 5 Mins, Servings: 4
Ingredients
1/2 Cup Apple Juice
3 Tbsp Honey
3 Tbsp Pit Boss Pork & Poultry Rub
1/4 Cup Brown Sugar
2 Tbsp Thyme Leaves
1/2 Tbsp Black Pepper
2 (1-1/2 Lb) Pork Tenderloins, Silver skin Removed
Instructions
To make the marinade, combine the thyme leaves, apple juice, brown sugar, honey, Poultry rub, Pit Boss Pork, & black pepper in a big mixing bowl. To mix the ingredients, whisk them together.
Toss your pork loins with marinade in that mixing bowl. Cover the bowl using plastic wrap after turning the pork to coat it. Place in the freezer for 2-3 hrs to marinate.
When you are all set to cook, preheat the Pit Boss to 225°F with

the lid covered for around 15 mins. If Super Smoke is available, use it for the best taste.
Put the tenderloins straight on your grill grate & smoke for 2-3 hrs, or unless the core temp reaches 145°F.
Remove the steak from the grill & set aside for 5 min before slicing.

2.65 Pork Roast Anytime
Total Time: 6 Hrs 5 Mins, Serving: 6
Ingredients
Pork Roast 6 (4-6 Lb.)
Poultry Rub & Pit Boss Pork
Apple Juice 1/4 Cup
Instructions
Preheat the Pit Boss to 180°F and close the lid for 15 mins.
Rub both sides of the pork roast with Pit Boss Pork & Poultry Rub.
In an Al foil pan, pour apple juice on top of the roast. On the grill, smoke the roast for 1 hr.
Remove the roast from the grill and warm the Pit Boss to 275°F with the lid closed for 15 mins.
Continue to cook the roast for another 2 hrs, uncovered. Then, return to the grill for another 3 hrs, or until the interior temperature reaches 205 degrees Fahrenheit for the first 2 hrs. Allow 10 mins for the dish to rest before serving. As a side dish, roasted potatoes, carrots, onions, and apples.

2.66 Pork Chops with Mustard and Peach Relish
Total Time: 50 Mins, Serving: 4
Ingredients
Whole Pork Chops 4
Poultry Rub & Pit Boss Pork
Diced Whole Peaches 3
Blueberries 1/2 Cup
Thinly Sliced Whole Shallot 1
Fresh Chopped Basil 1/4 Cup
Olive Oil 3 Tsp
Cardamom 1/2 Tsp
Honey 2 Tsp
Pepper and Salt
Whole Grain Mustard 1/2 Cup
Instructions
Brush both sides of the pork chops with the Pork & Poultry Shake, then leave aside at room temperature for 30 mins to an hr.
To make the peach-blueberry relish, combine the cardamom, vinegar, shallots, blueberries, basil, olive oil, peaches, and honey in a separate cup. Season with salt and pepper to taste, as well as honey if preferred. Using vinegar, liberally smear the chops.
Increase the temp to high (450°F) and preheat for 10-15 mins with the lid covered when ready to cook.
Cook the pork chops for 5 mins on one side and 5-10 mins on the other, or until an instant-read thermometer registers 140-145 degrees Fahrenheit.
Serve the chops with a side of peach-blueberry relish.

2.67 Rendezvous Ribs Smoked
Total Time: 2 Hrs 15 Mins, Serving: 4
Ingredients
Apple Cider Vinegar 1/2 Cup
Water 1/2 Cup
Pit Boss BBQ Sauce 1/2 Cup
Poultry Rub & Pit Boss Pork 2 Tsp
Baby Back Pork Ribs 3 Rack, Membrane Removed
1 Pork Poultry Rub & As Needed Pit Boss
Instructions
In a mixing bowl, combine the vinegar, water, barbecue sauce, Poultry Rub, and Pit Boss Pork. Place the sauce on the grill, along with a barbecue mop or basting brush.
Preheat the Pit Boss to 325°F for 15 mins with the lid closed when ready to cook.
Place the ribs on the grill grate with the meat side up.
Begin mopping after 30 mins of grilling. Mop the floor every 15 mins. After 2 hrs, check the ribs for doneness.
In the center of a rack, between the bones, place a toothpick. The ribs are handled in an environment with little to no resistance (or close to it). If the ribs aren't to your liking, keep cooking them in 30-min intervals and mopping after 15 mins. Move the ribs to a chopping board and finish with the mop sauce once they're done. Finely strewn Poultry Rub & Pit Boss Pork.
Remove the ribs from the oven and set them aside for a few mins before slicing them into 1/2 slabs or individual ribs.

2.68 Ham Glazed
Total Time: 2 Hrs 15 Mins, Serving: 8
Ingredients
Kurobuta Ham 1 Whole
Orange Juice 2 Cup
Chicken Stock 2 Cup
Butter 4 Tsp
Ground Cloves 1 Tsp
Ground Ginger 1 Tsp
Fresh Rosemary 1 Tsp
Orange Zest 1 Tsp
Jacobsen Salt Co. Pure Kosher Sea Salt 1 Tsp
Ground Black Pepper 1 Tsp
Instructions
Preheat the grill to 350°F until you're ready to roast.
While you're waiting for the grill to heat up, take the ham out of the fridge and pat it dry.
In a stock container, combine orange juice and chicken stock.
In a separate shallow dish, combine the rosemary, orange zest, melted butter, ginger clove, salt, and pepper. This will produce a paste that you can use to cover the ham.
Put the ham in the stockpot. When the stockpot is ready, place it on the grill.
Before examining, bake for 2 hrs with the lid closed. The temperature inside the oven should be 145 degrees Fahrenheit.
If you want a beautiful color outside the ham, you may put it straight on the grill grates. Serve by cutting into slices.

2.69 Smoked BLT Sandwich
Total Time: 35 Mins, Serving: 4
Ingredients
Thick-Cut Bacon 2 Lb
Mayonnaise 1/2 Cup
Texas Toast 8 Slices
Butter Lettuce 2 Head
Sliced Heirloom Tomato 3
Instructions
Preheat the Pit Boss to 350°F for 15 mins, then shut the lid.
While the grill is hot, place the bacon slices directly on the grill plate and cook for 15-20 mins, or until crispy.
To prepare the sandwich, spread mayo over two pieces of bread. On one piece of bread, layer lettuce leaves, tomatoes, and bacon, then top with the other.

2.70 Breakfast Pizza Grilled
Total Time: 55 Mins, Serving: 6
Ingredients
Olive Oil 2 Tsp
Butter 2 Tsp
Sweet Onions Sliced 2
1 Pizza Dough Ham
Pesto Sauce 1 Cup
Asiago Cheese 1 Cup
Fresh Arugula 2 Cup
Soft Boiled Large Eggs 4
Instructions
Melt the butter and olive oil in a large skillet and roast the onions for about 30 mins, frequently stirring, until soft and evenly browned.
Preheat the grill too high for 15 mins with the lid closed.
Cook the pizza dough and ham slices for 2-3 mins on
each side directly on the grill. Remove the pizza and ham from the grill.
Spread the pesto on the dough, then layer the onions, sliced ham, and asiago cheese on top. Return the pizza to the grill for an additional 5-8 mins, or until the cheese has melted and the dough has cooked through.
On top of the fried pizza, scatter the arugula and scrambled eggs.
If needed, season with kosher salt, crushed black pepper, and olive oil. Serve and have a good time.

2.71 Pork Tenderloin Asian-Style
Total Time: 55 Mins, Serving: 6
Ingredients
Whole Pork Tenderloin 2, 8-10 Oz Each
Canola Oil 2 Tsp
Samba Olenek 2 Tsp
Sesame Oil 1 Tsp
Minced Garlic 1 Tsp
Fresh Ginger 1 Tsp
Fish Sauce 1 Tsp
Soy Sauce 1 Tsp
Brown Sugar 1/4 Cup
Instructions
Using a fine paring knife, remove the silver skin from the pork tenderloin.
In a large mixing dish, combine all the ingredients. Allow the tenderloins to marinate in the marinade in the refrigerator for 30 mins.
Preheat the oven to high (450 degrees) with the lid closed when ready to serve (10-15 Mins).
Place the loins towards the front of the grill and flip them occasionally to avoid black grill marks all over. Then, shift them to the
middle of the grill to continue cooking. Cook for a further 7-10 mins for a medium-rare tenderloin. When they're done cooking, take them from the grill and set them aside for 10 mins before slicing.

2.72 Smoked Baby Back Ribs
Total Time: 3 Hrs 15 Mins, Servings: 4
Ingredients
3 Rack Baby Back Ribs
Kosher Salt
Cracked Black Pepper
Instructions
Season both sides of the ribs with pepper and salt after peeling the membrane off the rear side.
When you are all set to cook, preheat the Pit Boss to 225°F with the lid covered for around 15 mins. If Super Smoke is available, use it for the best taste.
Cook for around 2 hrs. Cook for a further hr, flipping the ribs. Enjoy!

2.73 Sticky Teriyaki BBQ Pork & Pineapple Skewers
Total Time: 3 Hrs 10 Mins, Servings: 2
Ingredients
1 Lb Pork Sirloin
18 Pieces Pineapple, Fresh
6 Scallions
6 Wooden Skewers
1 Cup Carne Asada Marinade, Of Choice
Instructions
Thread your pork cube, a bit of pineapple, & a slice of onion through the thinner side of your skewer; repeat the process, using 3 & 4 chunks of pork for each skewer. Rep with the remaining skewers.
Pour this marinade on the skewers in a pie dish, rotating them to cover both sides. Freeze for 1-3 hrs after wrapping in plastic wrap.
Set the temp to high & preheat for around 15 mins with the lid covered.
Drain & discard the marinade from the skewers. Place the skewers over your grill grate & cook for around 10 mins, or unless the pork has cooked through, rotating once.
Move cooked skewers to the plates & serve with steaming rice right away.

2.74 Smoked Moink Burger by Scott Thomas
Total Time: 1 Hr 10 Mins, Servings: 4
Ingredients
1 Lb Ground Sirloin
1/2 Lb Ground Pork
1/4 cup Worcestershire Sauce
1 Tsp Garlic, Minced
Salt
Black Pepper
Instructions
In a mixing dish, combine all the ingredients & stir well. Make six patties out of the mixture.
Preheat the grill to 350°F & shut the cover for 10-15 mins.
Cook till the burgers attain a temp of 160°F on the inside.
Top with preferred cheese & serve with preferred toppings a few moments before the burgers are done.

2.75 Apricot Pork Tenderloin

Total Time: 55 Mins, Servings: 4
Ingredients
2 Lb Pork Tenderloin
3 Ounce Pit Boss Big Game Rub
1 Cup Pit Boss Apricot BBQ Sauce
Instructions
Trim your pork tenderloin of any extra fat & silver skin. Allow 30 mins for your pork tenderloin to rest after being seasoned with Big Game Pit Boss Rub.
Start your Pit Boss on the Smoke setting. Place your pork tenderloins over the grate & smoke for around 45 mins after it hits temperature.
Remove the tenderloins from the grill and warm on high for around 15 mins with the lid closed.
Grill every side of your pork tenderloin for approximately 90 seconds or unless it achieves a core temp of 145°F after the Pit Boss hits high temperature.
Brush the meat in Apricot BBQ Pit Boss Sauce before removing it from the grill. Allow for around 20 mins of resting time on a chopping board before serving.

2.76 Baked Deep Dish Supreme Pizza

Total Time: 45 Mins, Servings: 4
Ingredients
Extra-Virgin Olive Oil
Ounce Pizza Dough
1/2 Cup Pizza Sauce
2 cup Mozzarella Cheese
Parmesan Cheese
1 Tsp Fresh Oregano
1 Tsp Fresh Basil
Lb Mild Italian Sausage
1 1/2 Green Bell Peppers
2 Tbsp Onion, Diced
1 1/2 Red Bell Pepper
Mushrooms
Pepperoni, Sliced
Black Olives
Instructions
When you are all set to cook, preheat the grill on high for around 15 mins with the lid covered.
Olive oil (Extra virgin) should be used to coat a pan (cast iron). Fill the pan 1/2way with dough and push this out through its bottom & up the edges.
To make the pizza, put the sauce over top of the crust & top with all the toppings. Next, sprinkle oregano & basil on top of the mozzarella & grated parmesan.
Bake for around 25-30 mins, or unless the cheese & sauce are bubbling & the crust becomes golden brown.
Allow for around 5-10 mins of resting time before slicing.

2.77 Bacon Onion Ring

Total Time: 1 Hr 10 Mins, Servings: 6
Ingredients
16 Slices Bacon
2 Whole Vidalia Onion, Sliced
1 Tbsp Chili Garlic Sauce
1 Tbsp Yellow Mustard
1 Tsp Honey
Instructions
Wrap a slice of bacon over each onion ring unless all the bacon has gone. A few onion slices are thicker than others, necessitating the use of two chunks of your bacon to form a ring.
To prevent your bacon from unraveling during cooking, poke a skewer thru the onion slice, which is bacon-wrapped.
Preheat the grill to 400°F and leave the lid covered for 10-15 mins.
Meanwhile, combine the chili garlic sauce & yellow mustard; stir in the honey.
Place the skewers on your grill grate & cook for around 90 mins, turning 1/2way through.

2.78 BBQ Brown Sugar Bacon Bites

Total Time: 40 Mins, Servings: 2
Ingredients
1/2 Cup Brown Sugar
1 Tbsp Fennel, Ground
2 Tsp Kosher Salt
1 Tsp Ground Black Pepper
1 Lb Pork Belly, Diced
Instructions
Make a rim by folding a sheet of Al foil into 1/2 & crimping the edges. Poke holes in the bottom of that foil with a fork. It would render part of your bacon fat, & the bacon bits would crisp.
Preheat the grill to 350°F for around 15 mins with the lid covered.
Combine the salt, ground fennel, brown sugar, & black pepper in a wide mixing bowl. To mix, stir everything together. Toss the chopped pork belly within the mixture unless well coated. Place the pork slices on a foil-lined baking sheet.
Place on your grill & cook for 20-30 mins, or unless the pieces become crispy, glazed, & bubbling.

2.79 Grilled Bacon Dog

Total Time: 45 Mins, Servings: 4
Ingredients
16 Hot Dogs
16 Slices Bacon, Sliced
2 Vidalia Onion, Sliced
16 Hot Dog Buns
Pit Boss 'Que BBQ Sauce
Velveeta Cheese
Instructions
Preheat your Pit Boss to 375°F for around 15 mins with the lid covered.
Wrap bacon slices around your hot dogs & cook for around 10 mins on all sides directly on your grill grate. Cook the onions for around 10-15 mins at the same time with hot dogs.
Spread 'Que Pit Boss sauce, hot dogs, grilled, cheese sauce, & grilled onions over buns of hot dog. Serve with veggies on top.

2.80 Seared BBQ Pork Chop

Total Time: 1 Hr 10 Mins, Servings: 6
Ingredients
6 Pork Chops
Pit Boss Pork & Poultry Rub

Instructions
Set the Pit Boss to 275°F & preheat for around 15 mins with the lid covered when you're all set to cook.
Coat pork chops liberally using Pit Boss Poultry & Pork Rub. Allow 15 mins for resting.
Cook for around 30 mins with the pork chops straight on your grate, then turn & cook for the next 30 mins.
Remove your pork chops off the grill & raise the temp to 500°F. Place your pork chops again on your grill for around 3 mins on every side.
Before serving, remove it from your grill & let it cool for around 10 mins.

2.81 Pit Boss BBQ Double Decker Taco
Total Time: 35 Mins, Servings: 6
Ingredients
2 cup Sour Cream
16 Ounce Refried Beans
2 Cup Leftover Beef Brisket
2 Cup Leftover Pulled Pork
10 Flour Tortillas
10 Taco Shell, Crisp
3 Guacamole
2 Cup Salsa, Tomato
1 cup Red Onion, Diced
1/2 Cup Cilantro, Finely Chopped
1 1/2 cup Cheddar Cheese
Instructions
Preheat the grill at 325°F & shut the cover for 15 mins.
Combine sour cream & refried beans in a mixing bowl. Place on a hot grill in the oven-safe dish.
Place the leftover brisket & pork on the grill in 2 layers of Al foil. Warm the beans & meats for around 25 mins.
Spread a small layer of hot beans on the tender taco shell & wrap it around the exterior of the crispy taco shell to make tacos double-decker.
Toss the brisket & pork with cilantro, guacamole, sour cream, salsa, onion, & cheese for taste into the crispy taco shell.

2.82 Smoked Bologna
Total Time: 4 Hrs 5 Mins, Servings: 4
Ingredients
1 Lb Bologna Log
1/4 Cup Brown Sugar
1 Tbsp Yellow Mustard
1 Tsp Soy Sauce
Worcestershire Sauce
Instructions
Score your bologna log with a sharp knife, taking care not to cut too deeply.
Brown sugar, soy sauce, mustard, & Worcestershire sauce should all be combined in a bowl.
Rub this all around the bologna after it's been blended.
When prepared to cook, preheat the Pit Boss to 225°F with the lid covered for 15 mins.
Bologna should be smoked for 3-4 hrs.
Remove off the grill & set aside to cool.
Serve with some sandwiches after slicing.

2.83 BBQ Bacon-Wrapped Water Chestnuts
Total Time: 40 Mins, Servings: 6
Ingredients
1 Lb Bacon
2 Can Water Chestnuts
1/3 Cup Brown Sugar
1/3 cup Mayonnaise
1/3 Cup Pit Boss Texas Spicy BBQ Sauce
Instructions
When you're all set to cook, fire up your Pit Boss grill. Unless the fire has been created, smoke with its lid open. Next, preheat your grill to 350°F and bake for around 10-15 mins with its lid covered.
Al foil should be used to line the rimmed baking pan. Each slice of bacon should be cut into 1/2. Wrap a slice of bacon big enough to surround every water chestnut & fasten it with the toothpick.
Arrange your bacon-wrapped chestnuts over the lined baking sheet into a single layer. Preheat grill to 350°F and bake for around 20 mins. Turn on your grill.
In the mixing bowl, combine the brown sugar, mayonnaise, & Spicy Barbecue Pit Boss Sauce. Return these chestnuts to your grill for another 10-15 mins of baking into the sauce. Then, move to a serving dish.

2.84 Sweet and Spicy Pork Roast
Total Time: 1 Hr 15 Mins, Servings: 2
Ingredients
2 Lb Pork, Loins
2/3 Habanero Peppers, Seeded
2/3 Can Coconut Milk
1/3 Tsp Chinese Five-Spice Powder
2/3 Tbsp Paprika
2/3 Tsp Curry Powder
2/3 Tbsp Lime Juice
2/3 Tbsp Garlic, Minced
2/3 Tsp Freshly Grated Ginger
Instructions
In a mixing dish, combine all your ingredients except the pork. Allow the pork to marinate overnight in the marinade.
When you are all set to cook, preheat your Pit Boss to 300°F for 15 mins with the lid closed.
Preheat the grill and place the meat on it. Cook for around 1-2 hrs, or unless an internal temp of 145 to 150°F is reached.

2.85 Grilled Pork Chops with Pineapple-Mango Salsa
Total Time: 50 Mins, Servings: 4
Ingredients
3 (16 Oz) Thick-Cut, Bone-In Pork Chops
2 Tbsp Pit Boss Pork & Poultry Rub
1 Mango, Peeled, and Diced
1/2 Pineapple, Peeled, Cored, and Diced
1 Red Bell Pepper, Diced
1 Jalapeño, Seeded, and Diced
1/2 Red Onion, Diced
2 Tbsp Cilantro, Finely Chopped
1 Lime, Juiced
1 Clove Garlic, Minced
Salt And Pepper
1/4 Cup Pit Boss Apricot BBQ Sauce
Instructions
Refrigerate your pork chops for around 30 mins after coating each side with Pit Boss Poultry & Pork Rub.
In a big mixing bowl, combine all your ingredients.
Set the Pit Boss to 500°F & preheat for around 15 mins with the lid covered when you're all set to cook.
Cook your chops for 7-10 mins from each side over the grill. Brush the pork chops using Apricot BBQ Pit Boss Sauce after turning & cooking until internal temp reaches 145°F for a medium-well.
Serve with a side of salsa.

2.86 Smoked Stuffed Avocado Recipe

Total Time: 45 Mins, Servings: 8
Ingredients
6 Whole Avocados
3 Cup Leftover Pulled Pork
1 1/2 cup Monterey Jack Cheese, Shredded
1 Cup Salsa, Tomato
1/4 Cup Cilantro, Finely Chopped
8 Whole Quail Eggs
Instructions
Preheat the grill to 375°F and leave the lid covered for 10-15 mins.
Remove all pits from your avocados and, if necessary, part of your avocados from the middle.
Combine the cheese, salsa, pork, & cilantro in a mixing dish. Place the pork mix over top of the avocados & cook them. The cooking time is 25 mins.
Make a "nest" for a quail egg using a spoon. Carefully break a quail egg in the "nest" & cook for 5-8 mins more, or unless the egg is done to your liking.
Remove the skewers from your grill and place them on a serving platter.

2.87 Grilled Ham & Egg Cups

Total Time: 40 Mins, Servings: 6
Ingredients
12 Pieces Ham
12 Eggs
Cup Cream, Whipping
Salt And Pepper
1 Cup Shredded Cheddar Cheese
Chives, Chopped
Instructions
Preheat your Pit Boss to 360°F for around 15 mins with the lid covered.
Coat the muffin tin's wells with some cooking spray. Slice the ham into pieces that are just a little larger than every other muffin well.
Cook for 5-10 mins each side, or unless beautiful grill marks emerge, by placing your ham slices straight on a grill grate.
Combine the eggs & whipping cream in a mixing bowl. Season with salt & pepper to taste.
Bake for 12-15 mins, or unless the eggs have fully cooked. If preferred, sprinkle with some cheese in the final few mins of cooking.
Remove cooked ham & egg cups with care & serve immediately with chopped cilantro or chives. Enjoy!

2.88 Holiday Breakfast Strata

Total Time: 45 Mins, Servings: 4
Ingredients
6 Slices Bread
1 Lb Ground Breakfast Sausage
1 Tsp Mustard
1 Cup Shredded Cheddar Cheese
4 Egg, Beaten
1 1/2 Cup Whole Milk
3/4 Cup 1/2-And-1/2
1/2 Tsp Salt
1/4 Tsp Pepper
1 Pinch Ground Nutmeg
1 Tsp Worcestershire Sauce
Instructions
Start your Pit Boss grill & adjust the temp to 350°F when you're all set to cook. Preheat for 10-15 mins with the lid closed.
Remove the crust of the bread & place it in the base of a baking pan. Drain any extra fat from the sausage after browning it.
Combine mustard & sausage in a mixing bowl. Spread the meat equally over the bread & top with cheese.
After combining the other ingredients, pour on the cheese & sausage.
Bake for 25-30 mins on your Pit Boss. Warm the dish before serving.

2.89 Pit Boss Pork Chops

Total Time: 35 Mins, Servings: 2
Ingredients
2 Pork Chop
Blackened Saskatchewan Pit Boss Rub
Sea or Kosher Salt
Instructions
Salt & Blackened Pit Boss Saskatchewan are rubbed together. Pork chops should be rubbed.
Set the Pit Boss to 450°F & preheat for around 15 mins with the lid covered.
Cook the pork chops straight on the grill grate for around 30 mins, turning 1/2way through.
Remove off the grill & set aside for 5 mins to cool.

2.90 Anytime Pork Roast

Total Time: 6 Hrs 5 Mins, Servings: 6
Ingredients
6 (4-6 Lb) Pork Roast
Pit Boss Pork & Poultry Rub
1/4 Cup Apple Juice

Instructions
Set the Pit Boss to 180°F & preheat for around 15 mins with the lid covered. If Super Smoke is available, use it for the best taste.
All sides of the pork roast should be rubbed with Pit Boss Poultry & Pork Rub. Place the roast in an Al foil pan & cover it with apple juice. Place your roast on the grill for around 1 hr to smoke.
Remove the roast from the grill & preheat the Pit Boss to 275°F with the lid closed for 15 mins.
Cover and cook the roast for another 2 hrs. Then, wrap the pan in Al foil & return this to your grill for another 3 hrs, or unless the core temp reaches 205°F.
Leave 10 mins for resting before serving. With potatoes, carrots, roasted onions, & apples on the side.

2.91 Mustard Pork Chops with Peach Relish

Total Time: 45 Mins, Servings: 4
Ingredients
4 Whole Pork Chops
Pit Boss Pork & Poultry Rub
3 Whole Peaches, Diced
1/2 Cup Blueberries
1 Whole Shallot, Thinly Sliced
1/4 Cup Fresh Chopped Basil
3 Tbsp Olive Oil
1/2 Tsp Cardamom
2 Tsp Honey
Salt And Pepper
1/2 Cup Whole Grain Mustard
Instructions
Season your pork chops from both sides using the Pork & Poultry Shake, then set aside for around 30 mins at room temp.
In a bowl, combine the peaches, cardamom, vinegar, blueberries, shallots, olive oil, basil, & honey to prepare a peach-blueberry relish. The season for taste with

some salt & pepper, as well as extra honey if desired. Using mustard, slather your chops all around.
When prepared to cook, increase the temp to high (450°F) & preheat for around 10-15 mins with the lid closed.
Cook your pork chops over high heat for around 5 mins on the one side & 5-10 mins on the other side.
Serve the chops with some peach-blueberry relish on the side.

2.92 Pork Loin Injected Bacon-Draped Roast
Total Time: 3 Hrs 15 Mins, Servings: 4
Ingredients
1 cup Apple Juice
1 Tsp Salt
1 Tsp Worcestershire Sauce
¼ Cup Water
1 (3 Lb) Center-Cut Pork Loin
Pit Boss Pork & Poultry Rub
10 Slices Bacon

Instructions
For dissolving all salt crystals, mix apple juice, Worcestershire sauce, salt, & water in a wide bowl.
To withdraw the liquid, plunge your injector in the sauce & retract its needle. Then, liberally inject your meat.
Pit Boss Poultry & Pork Rub should be applied thoroughly over your meat.
Set the Pit Boss to 225°F & preheat for around 15 mins with the lid covered.
Using bacon slices, drape your loin. Place the roast straight on your grill grate & smoke it for 3-4 hrs.
Before carving & serving, transfer your pork to the cutting board & set it aside for around 10 mins.

2.93 Grilled Breakfast Pizza
Total Time: 55 Mins, Servings: 6
Ingredients
2 Tbsp Olive Oil
2 Tbsp Butter
2 Sweet Onions, Sliced
1 Pizza Dough
Ham
1 cup Pesto Sauce
1 cup Asiago Cheese
2 Cup Fresh Arugula
4 Large Eggs, Soft Boiled
Instructions
In a big skillet, melt both butter & olive oil, then sauté the onions for about 30 mins, turning periodically, till they are tender & uniformly colored.
Set the temp to high & preheat for around 15 mins with the lid covered.
Directly on your grill, cook your pizza dough & ham slices for around 2-3 mins from each side. Then, take the pizza & ham from your grill.
On your dough, spread some pesto, then add the sliced ham, onions, & asiago cheese. Bring this pizza to your grill for another 5-8 mins, or unless the cheese melt & its dough is done.
Arrange the arugula & boiled eggs on top of the baked pizza. Season with black pepper, kosher salt, & olive oil, if preferred.
Serve

2.94 Asian-Style Pork Tenderloin
Total Time: 55 Mins, Servings: 6
Ingredients
2 Whole (12-14 Oz) Pork Tenderloins, Silver skin Removed
2 Tbsp Canola Oil
2 Tbsp Sambal Oelek
1 Tsp Sesame Oil
1 Tsp Garlic, Minced
1 Tsp Fresh Ginger
1 Tsp Fish Sauce
1 Tsp Soy Sauce
1/4 Cup Brown Sugar
Instructions
Remove all silver skin off your pork tenderloin with a paring knife.
Combine all the ingredients in a mixing bowl. Allow your tenderloins to marinate in the marinade for around 30 mins in the fridge.
Set the thermostat to high (450°) & preheat the grill with the lid covered.
Place your loins towards the front of your grill and flip them occasionally until black grill marks appear all over. To finish cooking, move them to the center of your grill. For the medium tenderloin, cook for additional 7-10 mins. Remove these from your grill after they're done grilling & let them settle for 10 mins before slicing.

2.95 Grilled Cleveland Polish Boy
Total Time: 15 Mins, Servings: 2
Ingredients
2 Lb Russet Potatoes, Peeled and Thinly Sliced
Canola Oil
Salt
1/2 cup Mayonnaise
1/2 Cup Sour Cream
2 Tbsp White Vinegar
1 Tsp Salt
1/2 Tsp Pepper
1/2 Tsp Celery Seed
1/2 Whole Shredded Green Cabbage
1/2 Whole Purple Cabbage, Shredded
2 Whole Shredded Carrot
4 Whole Olympia Provisions Kasekrainer
1/2 Cup Pit Boss Sweet & Heat BBQ Sauce
4 Whole Hot Dog Buns
Instructions
To prepare the fries, follow these steps: Place peeled potatoes in a wide bowl having cold water and cut them into long thick matchsticks. In a saucepan, pour oil & heat to 275-300°F. Drain & pat the fries dry. Fry your potatoes in tiny batches unless they are tender & pale, approximately 3-5 mins. Increase the temp of the oil to 350-375° & drain on the paper towels. Working in tiny batches, add your fries & fry for 1-3 mins, or unless crisp & brown. Using the paper towel, absorb excess liquid & season with some salt for taste.
To prepare the coleslaw, whisk together the mayonnaise, sour cream, salt, pepper, vinegar, & celery seed in a mixing bowl. Next, toss the cabbages & carrots with the mayo mix in a wide mixing bowl. To mix, stir everything together.
Preheat the grill to 350°F & leave the lid covered for 10-15 mins. Grill the sausages for 8-10 mins, or unless well cooked, rotating once on buns, place sausages, French fries, BBQ Pit Boss sauce, & coleslaw. Enjoy!

2.96 Pit Boss Cajun Broil
Total Time: 1 Hr 30 Mins, Servings: 8
Ingredients
2 Tbsp Olive Oil
2 Lb Red Potatoes
Old Bay Seasoning

6 Ears Corn, Cut into Thirds
2 Lb Smoked Kielbasa Sausage
3 Lb Large Shrimp with Tails, Deveined
2 Tbsp Butter
Instructions
Set the Pit Boss to 450°F & preheat for around 15 mins with the lid covered.
Drizzle some olive oil over the potatoes & season gently with Bay seasoning. Place on your grill grate immediately. Roast for 20 mins, or unless the vegetables are soft.
Drizzle the leftover olive oil over the corn & season gently with Bay seasoning. Place the corn & kielbasa beside the potatoes on your grill grate. Do 15 mins of roasting.
Bay seasoning is used to season the shrimp. Cook for around 10 mins, or unless brilliant pink & cooked through, straight on your barbecue grate with the other ingredients.
Transfer everything to a bowl. Season with additional Bay seasoning for taste after adding the butter. Toss to cover, then serve right away.

2.97 Bacon & Brie Mac & Cheese
Total Time: 1 Hrs 15 Mins, Servings: 8
Ingredients
32 Ounce Whole Milk
1 Tbsp Onion Powder
2 Tsp Garlic Powder
24 Ounce Brie Cheese
1 cup Cheddar Cheese
1 cup Shredded Mozzarella Cheese
2 Whole Jalapeño, Diced
Salt And Pepper
2 Tbsp Cornstarch
1 Lb Cooked Bacon
16 Ounce Cooked Penne Pasta
Instructions
Heat some milk in a boiler until it's
boiling, then add the onion, cheddar, brie, garlic powder, & mozzarella cheese.
Add fresh jalapenos, salt, & pepper when the cheese has completely melted.
To thicken your sauce, make the slurry with some corn starch & water, then stir it into the sauce. Add some cooked bacon & penne last.
Top the mac & cheese with the leftover mozzarella cheese in an oiled pan.
Preheat the grill to 350°F with the lid covered.
Cook your mac & cheese for 15-20 mins on your Pit Boss, or unless golden & bubbling.

2.98 Roasted Ham with Apricot Sauce
Total Time: 2 Hrs 15 Mins, Servings: 8
Ingredients
1 (8-10 Lb) Kurobuta Whole Bone-In Ham
1 Bottle Pit Boss Apricot BBQ Sauce
1/4 Cup Horseradish
2 Tbsp Dijon Mustard
Instructions
When prepared to cook, preheat the Pit Boss to 325°F with the lid covered for 15 mins.
In a wide roasting pan coated with Al foil, place the ham. Preheat the grill to high & cook the pan for around 90 mins.
To make the glaze: Combine the Apricot BBQ Pit Boss Sauce, horseradish, & mustard in a wide saucepan on medium heat. Remove from the grill & keep warm.
Brush some glaze over the ham after almost 90 mins. Cook for the next 30 mins, or unless a core temp of 135°F is reached when a thermometer is put into the middle portion of your ham.
Before slicing, remove the ham from the grill & let it cool for around 20 mins.
If desired, drizzle with the leftover glaze.

2.99 Smoked Chorizo & Arugula Pesto
Total Time: 40 Mins, Servings: 4
Ingredients
4 Cup Fresh Arugula
1 Clove Garlic
1/2 cup Parmesan Cheese, Grated
1/2 Cup Pine Nuts
1/4 Cup Extra-Virgin Olive Oil
1/4 cup Grapeseed Oil
Sea Salt
Freshly Ground Black Pepper
Water
Instructions
Into the bowl of a blender, puree the cheese, arugula, garlic, & nuts to prepare the pesto. Drizzle some oil in while the machine is running. For taste, season the mix with some salt & pepper. Thin down the pesto using water if it's too thick.
Preheat your Pit Boss to 375°F for around 15 mins with the lid covered.
Smoke your sausages for 20 mins, or till they reach 170°F on the inside.
Allow 10 mins for your sausage links to rest before cutting into big pieces. Then, transfer your sausage to the serving dish and top with some arugula pesto.

2.100 Pit Boss Roasted Easter Ham
Total Time: 1 Hr 10 Mins, Servings: 8
Ingredients
1 (6-7 Lb) Bone-In Ham
1 Cup Pit Boss Sweet & Heat BBQ Sauce
2 cup Brown Sugar
1/2 Cup Pineapple Juice
Instructions
When prepared to cook, preheat the Pit Boss to 225°F with the lid covered for 15 mins. If Super Smoke is available, use it for the best
taste.
Cook the ham for around 60 mins on the grill.
Combine the brown sugar, Pit Boss Heat & Sweet BBQ Sauce, & pineapple juice when the ham continues frying.
During the final 30 mins of cooking, baste the ham in the sauce every 10 mins. Then, remove the ham from the grill & set it aside to serve.

2.101 Smoked Bratwurst with Homemade Mustard
Total time 1 Hour 10 Minutes, Serving: 4
Ingredients
Bratwurst, 4
Apple Cider Vinegar, 3 Tbsp
Cold Beer, 1 Cup
Salt
Yellow Mustard Seeds & Brown, 1/2 Cup
Hot Dog, 4 Buns
For Serving Sauerkraut
Instructions
Preheat Pit Boss to 225°F and cook for 15 minutes with lid covered until ready to cook.
Cook for 1 hour on the grill with the bratwurst.
While the brats are cooking, crush the mustard seeds into a coarse powder in a spice grinder. Combine mustard seeds, beer, vinegar, and salt in a small dish. Set aside after

thoroughly mixing. If it seems a bit runny at first, do not worry; the mustard seeds will absorb moisture as they settle.

After 1 hour, remove the brats from the grill and raise the Pit Boss temperature to 500°F. Allow 15 minutes to warm with the lid closed.

Return the brats to the grill and cook until the internal temperature reaches 160°F, about 5-7 minutes.

To assemble the bratwursts, put them on the buns and top with mustard and sauerkraut. Enjoy.

2.102 BBQ Pulled Pork Sliders

Total Time: 10 Hours 15 Minutes, Serving: 8 people
Ingredients
Pickles
Persian Cucumbers, 1 Pound
Salt, 1/2 Cup
Sugar, 1/2 Cup
Garlic, 6 Clove
Bay Leaves, 4 Whole
Black Peppercorn, 4 Tbsp
White Peppercorn, 2 Tbsp
Fennel Seed, 4 Tbsp
Whole Coriander, 1 Tbsp
Red Pepper Flakes, 1 Tbsp
Fresh Dill, 1 Bunch
White Wine Vinegar, 2 Cup
Ice Water, 2 Cup
Special Sauce
Mayonnaise, 2 Tbsp
Ketchup, 1 Tbsp
Sweet Pickle Relish, 2 Tbsp
Sugar, 1/2 Tbsp
Distilled White Vinegar, 1/2 Tbsp
Mustard, 1 Tbsp
Pit Boss Apricot BBQ Sauce, 1 Tbsp
main
1 (8-10 Lb.) Bone-In Pork Butt
3/4 Cup Pit Boss Pork & Poultry Rub, Plus More as Needed
1 Cup Pit Boss Apricot BBQ Sauce
24 Whole Slider Buns, For Serving
Instructions
Once ready to cook, preheat the Pit Boss to 165°F with the lid shut for fifteen min. If Super Smoke is available, use it for the best taste.

Homemade Pickles: Plan on bringing these pickles overnight. Place the cucumbers, whole and cleaned, on the grill grate and smoke for 30 to 45 mins.

Take the meat out of the Pit Boss and thinly slice it. Remove from the heat and let it aside until the brine is ready.

Bring salt, garlic, sugar, peppercorns, fennel, bay leaves, coriander, vinegar, and red

pepper flakes to a boil in a medium saucepan. Simmer for 5-10 mins, then turn off the heat and steep for a further 20 minutes. Allow brine to cool in 2 cups of cold water before adding fresh dill.

Once the brine has cooled, pour it over the cucumbers and weigh them down with a few plates to fully immerse them. Allow 24 hours before using.

Mix mustard, ketchup, Apricot BBQ Sauce, sweet pickle relish, mayonnaise, sugar, & distilled vinegar for the Special Sauce. Stir occasionally. Keep it refrigerated until you're ready to use it.

To make the pulled pork, season both sides of the pork butt with Pit Boss Pork & Poultry Rub and set aside to rest for 45 minutes at room temperature.

When ready to cook, preheat the Pit Boss to 225°F with the lid closed for 15 minutes. If Super Smoke is available, use it for the best taste.

Place the fat-side down pork butt on the grill grate and smoke for 3 hours.

Place the pork butt in a disposable Aluminum foil pan big enough to accommodate it and cover it with foil. Raise the temperature on the Pit Boss to 275°F and continue roasting for another 3 to 5 hours, or until an instant-read meat thermometer placed in the thickest portion of the flesh, but not touching bone, reads 200°F.

Transfer the pork roast to a clean disposable pan and set aside for 20 minutes to rest.

Strain the liquids from the pan's bottom into a gravy separator. Pull the pork into pieces with your hands (ideally wearing lined, heavy-duty rubber gloves to protect your hands from the heat). Discard the bone, as well as any fat lumps, including the cap. Transfer each piece to a large mixing basin and shred it. Drizzle with the leftover pig juice and season with more Pit Boss Pork & Poultry Rub. Any fat that has

risen to the top should be discarded. Mix in the Pit Boss Apricot BBQ Sauce well.

Stuff the slider buns with the pork mixture. Pickles and a special sauce are served on top. Enjoy!

2.103 Grilled New York Style Pepperoni Pizza

Total Time: 1 Day 15 Minutes, Serving: 4 people
Ingredients
Peeled Tomatoes (28 Oz) Whole, 1 Can
Olive Oil Extra-Virgin, 4 Tbsp
Unsalted Butter, 1 Tbsp
Grated or minced, 2 Clove Garlic.
Dried Oregano, 1 Tbsp
Red Pepper Flakes
Kosher Salt
Basil Sprig, 2
Medium Yellow Onion, 1
Sugar, 5 1/2 Tbsp
Salt
Cup Bread Flour, 4 1/2
Instant Yeast, 2 Tbsp
Lukewarm Water, 15 Ounce
Bread Flour
Cornmeal
Pizza Peel
Grated Mozzarella Cheese, 1 Pound
Pepperoni Sliced, 1 Pound
Instructions
To make the pizza sauce, puree the tomatoes and the juice in a stick blender. The puree should never be entirely smooth, and there must still be some tomato pieces. Remove from the equation.

In a small saucepan, mix butter and oil and cook over medium-low heat until butter melts.

Add the oregano, garlic, pepper flakes, and a big sprinkle of salt & cook, constantly stirring, for 3 minutes, or till fragrant but not browned.

Combine the basil sprigs, tomatoes, onion halves, & sugar in a mixing bowl. Bring to simmer, and then lower to the lowest heat setting & cook, stirring periodically, until the liquid has been reduced by half (about 1 hour).

Toss out the onions and basil stalks. Season with salt to taste. Allow cooling completely before storing in an airtight jar in the refrigerator for up to two weeks.

In a food processor, combine flour, sugar, 2 Tbsps. salt, and yeast. Pulse 3–4 times until the ingredients are uniformly distributed.

Pour in the olive oil and water. Run the food processor for approximately 15 seconds or until the mixture forms a ball that rides around the bowl above the blade. Continue processing for another 15 seconds.

Take On the dough ball on a lightly floured board and knead it by hand once or twice until it forms a smooth ball.

Separate the dough into three equal pieces and put each in a 1-gallon (4 L) zip-top bag. Allow at least one day, and up to five days, for the dough to rise in the refrigerator.

Retrieve dough from the refrigerator minimum of 2 hours before baking and roll into the balls by gathering dough in the direction of the bottom and pressing close. Each one should be floured well and placed in a separate sized mixing basin. Cover firmly with plastic wrap and set aside to rise until approximately doubled in volume at room temperature.

Once ready to cook, preheat the grill on high for 15 minutes with the lid covered. If using a pizza stone, place it on the grill grates.

Place one dough ball on a lightly floured surface. Gently push the dough into a rough 8" (20 cm) circle, leaving 1" (3 cm) higher on the outside than the rest. Stretch dough into a 12" to 14" (30 to 35 cm) circle, approximately 1/4" (1 cm) thick, by hanging it over knuckles. Place on a pizza peel that has been dusted with cornmeal.

Spread about 2/3 of the sauce evenly over the crust's surface, leaving a 1/2" (0.5 cm) to 1" border around the edge. Dispersed 1/2 of the cheese evenly over the sauce and top with pepperoni.

Place pizza on the baking stone and bake for 15 to 20 minutes, or until cheese is melted (little browned) and crust is golden brown and puffy.

2.104 BBQ Spareribs with Classic Wedge Salad

Total Time: 4 Hours 15 Minutes, Serving: 4 people
Ingredients
St. Louis-Style Ribs Trimmed & Membrane Removed, 1 Rack
Pit Boss Pork & Poultry Rub, 3 Tbsp
Apple Juice, For Spritzing
Pit Boss Sweet & Heat BBQ Sauce, 1 Bottle
Iceberg Lettuce, 1 Head
Cherry Tomatoes, Halved, 8 Ounce
Cooked Bacon, Crumbled, 4 Slices
Chopped Chives, 1/2 Tbsp
Dressing
Mayonnaise, 1/3 Cup
Sour Cream, 1/4 Cup
Milk, 3 Tbsp
Red Wine Vinegar, 2 Tbsp
Salt, 1/4 Tbsp
Pepper, 1/4 Tbsp
Instructions

Apply Pit Boss Pork and Poultry Rub on both ends of the ribs.

Once ready to cook, preheat the Pit Boss to 250°F for 15 minutes with the lid closed. If Super Smoke is available, use it for the best taste.

Place the ribs meat-side up on the barbecue grate or the Pit Boss rib rack, bones resting against the rack. 3 hours in the oven Brush the ribs with fruit juice after the first hour. After that, spray with apple juice every hour.

Spray the ribs with Pit Boss Sweet & Heat BBQ Sauce on both sides after cooking for 3 to 4 hours. Put the sauce on the grill for another 30 minutes to an hour to "tighten" it.

Take the ribs from the grill once the sauce has thickened.

To make up the clothing, combine mayonnaise, sour cream, milk, vinegar, salt, and pepper in a mixing dish.

Remove the core from the lettuce head and cut it into wedges.

Toss the wedges on a dish with the dressing and tomatoes. Bacon crumbles and chives are sprinkled on top.

Carve the rib racks into individual ribs and serve with the wedge salad. Enjoy!

2.105 Smoked Classic Porchetta

Total Time: 3 Hours 30 Minutes, Serving: 8 people
Ingredients
Garlic, Minced, 4 Clove
Rosemary, Chopped, 2 Tbsp
Salt, 2 Tbsp
Black Pepper, 1 Tbsp
Red Pepper Flakes, 1 Tbsp
Skin-On Pork Belly, 6 Pound
Salt
Black Pepper
Center-Cut Pork Loin, 3 Pound (3 Lb)
Instructions

To make the garlic combination, combine chopped garlic, thyme, salt, pepper, and red pepper flakes in a medium mixing bowl.

Put the belly skin side up on the clear work area and crosshatch the skin. Sprinkle the meat side of the belly with salt, pepper, and half of the garlic mixture.

Arrange the trimmed pork loin in the middle of the belly and massage with the remaining garlic mixture, seasoning to taste. Form a cylindrical shape with the pork belly by rolling it around the loin and tying it firmly with cooking twine at 1" intervals. Season the skin with salt and pepper, then place it in the refrigerator, uncovered, overnight to dry.

Whenever ready to cook, preheat the oven to 180°F with the lid covered for 15 minutes.

Put the porchetta straight on the grill grates, seam side down, and burn for 1 hour.

After such an hour, raise the grill temperature to 325°F and roast for approximately 2-1/2 hours, or until the body temperature reaches 135°F. Tent with foil if the outside starts to burn before the required interior temperature is achieved.

Get Rid of the steak from the grill and set it aside for thirty min before cutting. Appreciate!

2.106 Stuffed Pork Crown Roast

Total Time: 30 Minutes 3 Hours, Serving: 2 people
Ingredients
Kurobuta Pork Crown Roast, 1 (12 To 14 Ribs)
Your Favorite Stuffing, Totalised According to The Package Directions, Or Homemade, 8 Cup
Apple Juice Or Cider, 1 Cup
Apple Cider Vinegar, 2 Tbsp
Dijon Mustard, 2 Tbsp
Brown Sugar, 1 Tbsp
Garlic, Minced, 2 Clove
Fresh Chopped Thyme or Rosemary, 2 Tbsp
Salt, 1 Tbsp
Coarse Ground Black Pepper, 1 Tbsp
Olive Oil, 1/2 Cup
Instructions

In a small roasting pan, place the pork on a level rack. Wrap a tiny strip of foil around the end of each bone.

To make the marinade, combine the following ingredients in a mixing bowl. Raise the apple cider to a simmer and decrease by half over high heat. Stir in the vinegar, mustard, brown sugar, garlic, thyme, salt, and pepper after removing the pan from the heat. Whisk in the oil slowly.

Spread the marinate to the steak with a pastry brush, covering all sides. Wrap with plastic wrap and set aside for 60 minutes to enable the meat to come to room temperature. Spray the marinade over the steak and place it in the refrigerator, wrapped, till ready to cook.

While placing the meat on the grilled, let it come to room temperature.

Once ready to cook, preheat the Pit Boss to 425°F with the lid closed for fifteen min.

Place the roasting pan on the grill grates with the meat, and cook for thirty min. Reduce the temperature of the Pit Boss to 325°F after 30 minutes.

Cover the crown with filling, mounding it at the top, loosely. Wrap foil around the filling. Alternatively, the stuffing may be baked separately from the roast in a separate pan. Send Back the meat to the oven for another 90 mins of roasting.

Remove the pig filling and continue roasting for another 30 to 90 minutes, or until the internal temperature reaches 150°F. Note: If the temperature probe meets the bone, you'll receive a false reading.

Remove the roast from the grill and set aside for 15 minutes to rest. Remove the foil from the bones but keep the butcher's rope on the roasts until it's time to cut. Place on a heated serving dish.

Chop between both the bones to serve. Relish!

2.107 Citrus Brined Pork Roast with Fig Mostarda

Total Time: 40 Minutes, Serving: 6 people
Ingredients
Salt, 1/2 Cup
Brown Sugar, 1/4 Cup
Garlic Clove, 3
Dried Bay Leaves, 2
Peppercorns, 6
Halved, 1 Lemon.
Dried Fennel Seed, 1/2 Tbsp
Red Pepper Flakes, 1/2 Tbsp
Apple Juice, 1/2 Cup
Orange Juice, 1/2 Cup
Ice Water, 1
Pork Loins, 5 Pound
Extra-Virgin Olive Oil, 2 Tbsp
Salt
Black Pepper
Butter, 2 Tbsp
Small Shallot, Thinly Sliced, 1
Garlic, Minced, 1/2 Tbsp
Cognac, 1 Cup
Sugar, 1 Cup
Black Figs, Stemmed & Quartered, 10 Ounce
Dijon Mustard, 1/2 Tbsp
Salt
Black Pepper
Instructions

When creating the brine, mix the salt, brown sugar, garlic cloves, bay leaves, black peppercorns, lemon, fennel seeds, red pepper flakes, apple, and orange juice in a moderate stock pot. Bring About to a low boil, reduce to low heat and cook until the salt and sugar dissolve.

Pour the sauce over the cold water and place it in the refrigerator to chill fully.

When the brine is cold enough to handle, pour it over the pig roast and weigh it down if required to immerse it fully. Refrigerate for at least one night to brine.

Drain the brine from the roast, rinse it, and pat it dry. Season the roast with salt and pepper after rubbing it with olive oil.

Once ready to cook, increase the heat to High & heat for fifteen min with the lid closed.

Put the pork roasts straight on the grill grates and cook for 20-25 mins, or until the outside is lightly browned and an instant-read thermometer placed into the thickest portion of the roast registers 140°F. Allow 10 minutes to settle before slicing.

Preheat a sauté pan over medium heat for the fig mostarda. Melt the butter in the pan. Sauté the shallot for 2 minutes, or until tender. Sauté for another 30 seconds after adding the garlic. Bring the cognac to a simmer, then add the sugar.

Add the figs and mustard and simmer for approximately 20 minutes, just until the liquid is reduced and syrupy. Set aside after seasoning with salt and pepper to taste.

To serve, thinly slice the pork roast and arrange it on a serving dish. Spread the fig mostarda on top. Relish.

2.108 Smoked BBQ Ribs

Total Time: 5 Hrs. 25 Minutes, Serving: 4 people
Ingredients
St. Louis-Style Ribs, 2 Rack
Pit Boss Big Game Rub, 1/4 Cup
Apple Juice, 1 Cup
Pit Boss BBQ Sauce
Instructions

Get Rid of the crust off the back of the ribs by patting them dry.

Massage the front, back, and side of ribs with an equal layer of rub. Allow for twenty minutes of sitting time, or up to four hours if chilled.

Once ready to cook, preheat the Pit Boss to 225°F with the lid closed for fifteen min. If Super Smoke is available, use it for the best taste.

Put the ribs on the grill, bone side down. After 1 hour of cooking, fill a spray bottle with apple juice and spray the ribs. After that, spray every 45 mins.

Test the interior temperature of the ribs after 4-1/2 hours. When the internal temperature of the ribs hits 201°F, they are done. If not, wait another 30 minutes and try again.

Brush a little coating of your preferred Pit Boss Barbecue Sauce on the front and backside of the ribs after they are done. Allow 10 minutes for the sauce to solidify. Remove the ribs from the grill once the sauce has set and let them rest for ten min. Serve with additional sauce and ribs sliced in between bones. Enjoy!

2.109 Big Game Day BBQ Ribs

Total Time: 3 Hours 25 Minutes, Serving: 6 people
Ingredients
St. Louis-Style Ribs, 2 Rack
Pit Boss Big Game Rub, 1/4 Cup
Peach Nectar, 1 Cup
Apricot BBQ Sauce, 1 Cup
Instructions

Rinse the ribs and wipe them dry. Remove the membrane from the rear of the ribs.

Once ready to cook, preheat the Pit Boss to 275°F with the lid closed for fifteen min.

Apply a thin layer of rubbing to the back and sides of the ribs. Allow five min for resting. Flip the rib over, apply a thick layer of rub to the top, and let aside for fifteen min to "sweat."

Put the ribs directly on the barbecue grate, bone side down, and roast for 2 to 2-1/2 hrs. Check for doneness; the meat should be leaning away from the bones, and the core temperature should be 160°F.

Take the ribs from the grill and place them on front of a piece of foil, meat side down. Wrap foil firmly over the ribs to form a package and pour 1/2 cup peaches nectar over them.

Give Back the ribs to the grill, bone side up, another 30 to 45 mins, or until cooked but not falling-apart tender.

Take the ribs from the oven and marinate the front and back. To set the sauce, return the ribs to the Pit Boss for fifteen min.

Remove from the oven, set aside for 15 minutes to cool before slicing and serving. Enjoy!

2.110 Roasted Pork Tenderloin with Herbs and Garlic

Total Time: 35 Minutes, Serving: 4 people
Ingredients
Tenderloins (1 Lb. Each), 2 Pork
Clove Garlic, 6
Lemon, 1
Stripped, Plus More for Garnish, 2 Sprig Fresh Thyme
Sprig Fresh Rosemary, Stripped, Plus More for Garnish, 1
Soy Sauce, 1 Tbsp
Coarse Salt, 2 Tbsp
Recently Ground Black Pepper, 1 1/2 Tbsp
Red Pepper Flakes, 1 Pinch
Extra-Virgin Olive Oil, 1/4 Cup

Instructions
Cut both tenderloins of excess fat or silver
skin with a sharp knife.
Mix the lemon juice garlic, zest, rosemary, soy sauce, thyme, salt, pepper, & red pepper flakes throughout the bowl of mini-food processing or a blending jar.
Grind the garlic & herbs until they're finely minced. Whereas the machine is running, slowly trickle in the olive oil until paste forms.
Apply garlic paste to both tenderloins, being sure to cover all sides. Before grilling, wrap the pork firmly in plastic wrap and freeze for almost 8 hours.
Once ready to cook, preheat the Pit Boss to 500°F for fifteen min with the lid closed.
Place the tenderloins on the grill grates directly and cook for 15 minutes.
Turn the tenderloins with tongs and continue to roast until the temperature reached at least 145°F in the thickest section of the meat.
Allow the meat to rest for five min before slicing. Enjoy!

2.111 Competition Style BBQ Pork Ribs

Total Time: 5 Hours 30 Minutes, Serving: 6
Ingredients
St. Louis-Style Ribs, 2 Rack
Pit Boss Poultry & Pork Rub, 1 Cup
Brown Sugar, 1/8 Cup
Butter, 4 Tbsp
Agave, 4 Tbsp
Pit Boss Sweet & Heat BBQ Sauce, 1 Bottle
Instructions
Heat Pit Boss to 225°F and cook for fifteen min with lid covered until ready to cook. If Super Smoke is available, use it for the best taste.
Cut the membrane from the rear of the ribs. On both sides, sprinkle with Pit Boss Poultry & Pork Rub. Allow 15 to 20 minutes for the ribs to rest.
Put the ribs bone-side downwards on the grill and cook for 3 hours. Make the brown sugar wrap while the ribs are cooking. Half the brown sugar, half the butter, and half the agave on top of a double sheet of Aluminum foil (about the same size as the rack of ribs). Continue with the second rack.
After 3 hours, wrap one rack of ribs in brown sugar, butter, and agave, meat side down. Continue with the
second rack. Preheat the grill to 250°F and put the wrapped ribs on the grill, meat side down.
Test the core temperature after another 1-1/2 hours of cooking. The ideal temperature range is 204°F to 205°F. Cook for another 30 minutes if the temperature hasn't reached room temperature.
Take the ribs from the grill and place them in a foil package. Return the ribs to the grill, uncovered, for another 10 minutes.
Take from the grill and baste the meat and bones with Pit Boss Sweet & Heat BBQ Sauce before returning to the grill for another 10 minutes. Serve the ribs sliced. Enjoy!

2.112 BBQ Spareribs with Spicy Mandarin Glaze

Total Time: 5 Hour 15 Minutes, Serving: 6 people
Ingredients
Racks Spareribs, Membrane Removed, 3 Large
Yellow Mustard, 3 Tbsp
Worcestershire Sauce, 1 Tbsp
Honey, 1 Cup
Brown Sugar, 1 1/2 Cup
Pit Boss Poultry & Pork Rub
Dr. Pepper, 24 Ounce
Mandarin Orange Sauce, 1 1/2 Cup
Sesame Oil, 1 Tbsp
Soy Sauce, 1 Tbsp
Garlic Powder, 1 Tbsp
Instructions
Heat Pit Boss to 225°F and grill for fifteen min with lid covered until cooked. If Super Smoking is available, use it for the best taste.
Mix Worcestershire sauce and yellow mustard in a small dish. Apply the Worcestershire and mustard mixture on both sides of the ribs. Smoke for 3 hours by placing firmly on the grill grate.
Take the ribs from the Pit Boss and put them in a foil pan. Cover the ribs with
brown sugar and Pit Boss Poultry & Pork Rub after pouring honey over them. Drizzle Dr. Pepper on the ribs. Cover with foil and raise the temperature to 275°F in the Pit Boss. Ribs should be cooked for 2 hours.
Take the foil pan from the grill. Raise the temperature of the Pit Boss to 450°F. Combine the mandarin sauce, sesame oil, soy sauce, and garlic powder in a
separate bowl. Remove the ribs from the foil pan and glaze them. Place the ribs directly on the grill grate, meat side down, for 8 to 10 minutes.
Take the ribs out of the Pit Boss. Enjoy!

2.113 Braised Pork Chile Verde

Total Time: 2 Hours 20 Minutes, Serving: 6 people
Ingredients
Pork Shoulder (2-3 Lb.), 1
All-Purpose Flour 1 Tbsp
Salt
Black Pepper
Pound Tomatillos, 1
Jalapeños, 2
Skinned and cut into 1 Inch Chunks, 1 Medium Yellow Onion
Clove Garlic, 4
Olive Oil, Divided, 4 Tbsp
Extra-Virgin Olive Oil, 2 Tbsp
Chicken Stock, 2 Cup
Green Chiles, 2 Can
Dried Oregano, 1 Tbsp
Cumin, 1 Tbsp
Juiced, 1/2 Lime.
Cilantro, Chopped, 1/4 Cup
Instructions
Inside a medium mixing bowl, toss the pork shoulder with flour and add salt and pepper.
Preheat the Pit Boss to 500°F and shut the lid for fifteen min until ready to cook.
Preheat the grill for twenty minutes by placing a big cast iron pan immediately on the lowest rack.
Arrange tomatillos, jalapenos, onion, and garlic on a parchment-lined sheet tray. Sprinkle with salt after drizzling 2

tbsp olive oil over the veggies. Toss to coat.
Add the pork shoulder to the cast iron pan with the remaining two tbsps. of olive oil. Evenly distribute the meat.
Close the lid and place the sheet tray on the top rack. Allow the pork to simmer for 20 minutes without opening the cover or stirring it. The bottom of the pork should be a uniform brown hue, and the vegetables should be softened and gently browned.
Take the veggies from the grill after twenty minutes and place them in the pitcher of a blender. Puree until completely smooth. Pour the pureed vegetables, chicken stock, green chiles, oregano, and cumin into the pan with the pork. This is a perfect time to use our Turbo-Temp® technology if you have one of the new D2 grills. The D2® powertrain goes into high gear when you lift the lid and mix the roasted vegetables, chicken stock, spices, and pork shoulder, bringing the grill back up to temperature quicker than ever before.
Close the grill cover and lower the temperature to 325°F. Cook for 60 to 90 minutes, or until the liquid has been reduced and the meat is fork-tender. If the liquid has decreased too much before the pork is tender, add half cup more chicken stock at a time until the meat can be broken apart with a fork.
Remove the lid from the grill and top with chopped cilantro and lime juice. Served in a bowl with burritos, tacos, or anything you like. Enjoy!

2.114 Baked Candied Bacon Cinnamon Rolls
Total Time: 45 Minutes, Serving: 6 people
Ingredients
Slices Bacon, Sliced, 12
Brown Sugar, 1/3 Cup
Pre-Made Cinnamon Rolls
Cream Cheese, 2 Ounce
Instructions
Heat the Pit Boss to 350°F for fifteen min with the lid shut when ready to cook.
Dip 8 of the bacon pieces in brown sugar, ensuring sure both sides are covered.
Arrange the brown sugared bacon slices and the other bacon pieces on a cooling rack set on a large baking sheet.
Cook the bacon for 15-20 mins on the Pit Boss until the fat has rendered, but the bacon is still flexible. Reduce the temperature to 325°F in the Pit Boss.
Unwrap and open the cinnamon buns. Put one slice of sugared brown bacon on top of one of the unrolled rolls and wrap it back up while the bacon is still heated. Carry on with the rest of the rolls in the same manner.
Brush an 8" × 8" cooking dish or cake pan with non-stick cooking spray and place cinnamon rolls in it. Heat the oven to 325°F and bake the cinnamon rolls for 10 to 15 mins, or until brown. Halfway through the cooking period, rotate the pan half a turn.
So, in the meantime, soften your cream cheese and combine it into the supplied cream cheese frosting. Roast the bacon and crumble it into the cream cheese icing. Drizzle warm cinnamon buns with icing. Warm it up and enjoy it.

2.115 Bacon-Rubbed Smoked Ribs Applewood
Total Time: 6 Hours 15 Minutes, Serving: 4 people
Ingredients
Baby Back Pork Ribs, 2 Rack
Bacon Grease, 3/4 Cup
Pit Boss Poultry & Pork Rub
McCormick Maple Seasoning
Apple Cider, 3/4 Cup
Apple Cider Vinegar, 5 Tbsp
Dijon Mustard, 2 Tbsp
Worcestershire Sauce, 1 Tbsp
Brown Sugar, 14 Tbsp
Cup Honey
Ketchup, 1/2 Cup
Paprika, 1/4 Tbsp
Cumin, 1/4 Tbsp
Coriander, Dried, 1/4 Tbsp
Ancho Chile Powder, 1/4 Tbsp
Instructions
Preheat the oven to 180°F and leave the lid closed for 15 minutes when ready to cook. Apply approximately 1/4 cup of the bacon grease on all sides of the ribs; this works best if the fat has fully cooled.
Rub the Pit Boss Pork and Poultry Rub and McCormick Smokehouse Maple Seasoning all over the ribs.
In a pot on the fire, boil the apple cider, vinegar, Dijon mustard, 1/4 cup bacon fat, Worcestershire sauce, and brown sugar. This is what you'll use for basting the ribs every hour while they're smoking.
Place the ribs on the barbecue grate, meat-side up, and smoke for 3 hours, basting every hour with the mop sauce.
Transfer the ribs to baking sheet after they have smoked for 3 hours. Raise the temperature of the grill to 225°F.
Tear four sheets of heavy-duty Aluminum foil into long strips. Pull up the edges to keep the liquid
contained and top with a rack of ribs. Half of the brown sugar is sprinkled over the rack, followed by half of the honey and half of the remaining mop sauce. To prevent leaking, place another sheet of foil on top and firmly crimp the edges. Carry on with the remaining rack of ribs in the same manner.
Return the foiled ribs to the grill and cook at 225°F for about 2 hours.
Make the Bacon Barbecue Sauce although ribs are cooking. In a pot on the fire, mix all ingredients; heat to combine the sauce components; remove heat before mixture boils.
Carefully remove the foil from the ribs and coat them with bacon barbecue sauce on both sides. Remove the foil and throw it away.
Place the ribs directly on the grill grate and cook for another hour or until the sauce "tightens." Before serving, let the ribs rest for a few minutes. Enjoy!

2.116 Baked Potato Skins with Pulled Pork
Total Time: 1 Hour 15 Minutes, Serving: 6 people
Ingredients
Whole Potato, Baker Style, 4
Vegetable Oil
Salt
Russet Potatoes, 4
Canola Oil
Butter, Melted, 2 Tbsp
Pulled Pork, 3 Cup
Pit Boss Sweet & Heat BBQ Sauce, 4 Tbsp
Mozzarella Cheese, 1 Cup
Cheddar Cheese, 1 Cup
Chopped Green Onion, For Serving
Chopped Bacon, For Serving
Sour Cream, For Serving
Instructions
Heat Pit Boss to 450°F and cook for fifteen min with lid covered until ready to cook.
Drizzle canola oil over the potatoes and season equally. Put the potatoes straight on the grill grates and cook for 45 mins, or until a fork pricks them in the centre and they are tender.
Halve the potatoes and empty the insides, leaving 1/4 inch of potato skin on the outside. Place the skins on a baking pan and brush the insides with melted butter. Return to the grill and cook for a further 5 to

6 minutes, or until golden brown.
Combine the pulled pork, Pit Boss Sweet & Heat BBQ Sauce, mozzarella, and cheddar cheese in a large mixing bowl.
Soak the skins with the mixture and return to the Pit Boss, lid closed, for just long enough for the cheese to melt.
Toss with chopped onions, bacon, and sour cream before serving. Enjoy!

2.117 Pulled Enchiladas Pork with Smoke-Roasted Red Sauce

Total Time: 60 Minutes, Serving: 4 people
Ingredients
Garlic Head, 1
Tomatoes on Vine 1 1/2 Pound
Onion, Halved, 1
Flour Tortillas, 6
Monterey Jack Cheese, 1 Cup
Chile Powder 2 Tbsp
Cumin, 2 Tbsp
Hot Sauce
Pulled Pork, 3 Cup
Shredded Cheddar Cheese, 1 Cup
Instructions
Preheat Pit Boss to 375°F and cook for 15 minutes with lid covered when ready to cook.
Remove the top of the garlic head and cover it in Aluminum foil. Directly on the barbecue grate, place wrapped garlic, onion halves and tomatoes on the vine. Cook, occasionally stirring, for 10-15 minutes, or till tomato skins have split & garlic and onion have softened.
Cut Down the tomatoes after the vine and remove the garlic wrap. Add the onions and tomatoes to the blender, squeeze softened garlic out of its peel. In a blender, combine the cumin, chile powder, salt, and hot sauce. Allow the steam to escape by holding the lid at an angle. Blend until the sauce has reached a silky consistency. If the sauce is too thick, add a tbsp of water at a time until it reaches the required consistency.
Spread a thin layer of sauce over the bottom of a 9x13 baking dish. In a large mixing bowl, combine 1/4 cup enchilada sauce with the pulled pork. To mix, gently toss with a spoon.
Spoon about a third of a cup of the pulled pork mixture onto each tortilla, along with a couple of tbsps. of cheese. Place the tortilla in the baking dish seam-side down. Continue with the rest of the tortillas and meat until the pan is filled.
Top with shredded cheese and the leftover enchilada sauce. Take On the pan quickly on the grill grate and bake for 25 minutes, or until the sauce is bubbling and the cheese is fully melted. Enjoy!

2.118 Spicy Bacon Wrapped Grilled Chicken Skewers

Total Time: 3 Hours 20 Minutes, Serving: 6 people
Ingredients
Ranch, 1/2 Cup
Garlic Powder, 1/2 Tbsp
Chile Sauce, 2 Tbsp
Dried Oregano, 1/2 Tbsp
Chicken Breast, Cubed, 16 Ounce
Whole Red Onion, Sliced, 1
Whole Green Bell Peppers, Sliced, 1
Bacon, Sliced, 8 Strips
Instructions
Combine ranch dressing, garlic powder, oregano, and chile sauce in a large mixing basin. Throw in the cubed chicken and toss well to coat. Allow the chicken to marinade for 1 to 3 hours in the refrigerator.
When ready to cook, increase the temperature to High and preheat for 15 minutes with the lid closed.
Begin constructing Pit Boss skewers by sliding an onion wedge, a pepper, a piece of bacon, and chicken onto the skewers. Alternate the bacon and chicken until the bacon is woven around the chicken pieces. Finish with a pepper and onion wedge on each skewer. To ensure quick and uniform grilling, do not overcrowd the skewer. Rep with the remaining skewers. Arrange the skewers on the grill grate with a piece of foil beneath the skewers' ends to protect them from flaming to get rotating them easier.
Cook for 5 minutes each side, quarter-turning halfway through, for a maximum of 20 mins, or till chicken reaches a temperature of 165°F. Take out the skewers. Enjoy!

2.119 Grilled Italian Meatballs (Polpette)

Total Time: 50 Minutes, Serving: 4 people
Ingredients
Cubed White Bread, 1 1/2 Cup
Milk, 1/4 Cup
Extra-Virgin Olive Oil, 1 Tbsp
Bacon, 2 Strips
Onion, 1/2 Cup
Clove Garlic, Minced, 1
Ground Chuck, 80% Lean, 1 1/2 Pound
Ground Pork, 1/2 Pound
Parmesan Cheese, 1 Cup
Parsley, Minced, 2 Tbsp
Kosher Salt, 1 Tbsp
Black Pepper, 1/2 Tbsp
Basil, Dried, 1/2 Tbsp
Dried Oregano, 1/4 Tbsp
Instructions
Mix the milk and bread in a mixing dish and let aside for five min. Remove the milk from the bread by wringing it out. Return the bread to the bowl after discarding the milk.
Melt 1 tbsp of olive oil in a frying pan over medium heat. Combine the bacon, onion, and garlic in a large mixing bowl. Cook for five min, or until the onion is transparent and the bacon grease has started to render. Allow cooling before adding to the bread mixture.
Combine the ground chuck, ground pork, Parmesan cheese, parsley, salt, pepper, basil, and oregano in a large mixing bowl. Mix the materials with your hands, using a gentle touch.
Drizzle olive oil on your hands and roll the meat mixture into 1-1/2-inch balls.
Meanwhile, preheat the Pit Boss grill until the fire has created smoke with the lid open (4 to 5 minutes). Preheat the oven to 350°F and bake for 10 to 15 minutes with the lid covered.
Place the meatballs on the grill grate in an even layer. Grill for 25 to 30 mins, or until a meatball reaches 160 degrees Fahrenheit on the inside. Allow 5 minutes for the meatballs to rest. Serve with hot marinara or other sauce skewered on toothpicks or short bamboo skewers. If necessary, garnish with fresh basil leaves.

2.120 Smoked Pit Boss Pulled Pork

Total Time: 9 Hours 10 Minutes, Serving: 8 people
Ingredients
Bone-In Pork Shoulder, 1 (6-9 Lb.)
Pit Boss Poultry & Pork Rub
Apple Cider, 2 Cup
Pit Boss 'Que BBQ Sauce
Instructions
Preheat Pit Boss to 250°F and cook for 15 minutes with lid covered until ready to cook.
The trim extra fat from the pork butt as the Pit Boss heats up. Season both sides with Pit Boss Poultry & Pork Rub and set aside for 20 minutes.
Place the pork butt fat side up on the grill grate and cook for 3 to 5 hours, or until the internal temperature reaches 160°F.
Take the pork from the grill and set it aside.
Place four big sheets of Aluminum foil on huge baking sheet and stack them on upper of each other, confirming that they are broad enough to cover the pork butt on all sides completely. If you don't have enough foil pieces, overlap them to make a larger foundation. Place the pig butt in the middle of the foil and pull up the sides a little before pouring the apple cider on top of it. Wrap the foil around the pork firmly to prevent the cider from escaping.
Return the foil-wrapped pork butt to the grill, fat side up, and cook until the internal temperature of the thickest portion of the flesh reaches 204°F, approximately 3 to 4 hours more, depending on the size of the pig butt.
Take the burgers off the grill. Allocate the pork to rest in the foil package for 45 minutes.
Carefully remove the pork from the foil and drain any remaining liquid into a fat separator.
Shred the pork in a large dish, removing and discarding the bone and any extra fat. Return the separated liquid to the meat and season with more Pit Boss Big Game Rub to taste. Taste and season with Pit Boss 'Que BBQ Sauce or your preferred BBQ sauce, if desired.
Serve on its own, in your favorite dishes, or as a sandwich filling. Refrigerate leftover pork for up to 4 days in an airtight container. Enjoy!

2.121 Fall-off-the-bone BBQ Ribs

Total Time: 2 Hours 10 Minutes, Serving: 6 people
Ingredients
Rib Rub
Brown Sugar, 2/3 Cup
Paprika, 1/2 Cup
Garlic Powder, 1/3 Cup
Onion Powder, 2 Tbsp
Chili Powder, 2 Tbsp
Cayenne Pepper, 1 Tbsp
Ground Black Pepper, 1 Tbsp
Freshly Ground White Pepper, 1 Tbsp
Dried Oregano, 1 1/2 Tbsp
Ground Cumin, 1 1/2 Tbsp
Baby Back Ribs, 4 Rack
main
Cup Apple Juice, 1/2
White Grape Juice, 1/2 Cup
Honey
Pit Boss BBQ Sauce
Instructions
In a mixing basin, combine all the rub ingredients and stir thoroughly. Massage both sides of the ribs with a generous amount of rub.
When ready to cook, preheat the Pit Boss to 275°F with the lid closed for 15 minutes.
Arrange the ribs on the grill, cover, and cook for 45 minutes. In a small dish, mix the apple and grape juices and put them aside.
Take the ribs off the grill and lay them bone-side down on a big sheet of heavy-duty Aluminum foil or a large disposable foil pan. Over the ribs, pour the liquid mixture.
Drizzle each slab with a large quantity of honey. Wrap the foil over the ribs fully and seal the edges. Restore the ribs to the grill for another hour of cooking.
Place the ribs straight on the grill grate after removing them from the foil. Increase the temperature to 350°F and cook for another 30 minutes.
Drizzle your preferred Pit Boss BBQ Sauce over the ribs and simmer for an additional 5 minutes to allow the sauce to solidify. Place the ribs on a chopping board to cool. Serve by slicing into single-serving portions.

2.122 Cocoa-Crusted Pork Tenderloin

Total Time: 55 Minutes, Serving: 4 people
Ingredients
main
Tenderloin, 1 Pork
Fennel, Ground, 1/2 Tbsp
Unsweetened Cocoa Powder, 2 Tbsp
Smoked Paprika, 1 Tbsp
Kosher Salt, 1/2 Tbsp
Black Pepper, 1/2 Tbsp
Extra-Virgin Olive Oil, 1 Tbsp
Green Onions, Thinly Sliced, 3
Instructions
Cut the silver skin and blood vessels from the loin using a paring knife. Combine the other ingredients in a small bowl and mix to make a paste. Chill the pork loin for thirty min after applying the mixture.
Once ready to cook, increase the temperature to High and preheat for fifteen min with the lid closed.
Put the meat on the grill's front burner and sear it on both sides. Reduce the temperature to 350°F and transfer the pork to the middle of the grill once it has been seared.
Cook for another 10 to 15 minutes, or until the internal flesh temperature reaches 145°F for medium to medium-well.

Take it from the grill after cooking and let it rest for at least 8 - 10 mins before slicing. Serve with green onions as a garnish. Enjoy!

2.123 Rosemary Roasted Pork Collar
Total Time: 8 Hours 30 Minutes, Serving: 6
Ingredients
main
Fresh Rosemary, 3 Tbsp
Whole Shallot, Thinly Sliced, 3
Garlic, Minced, 2 Tbsp
Ground Coriander, 2 Tbsp
Bourbon, 1/2 Cup
Whole Apple Ale, 1
Vegetable Oil, 3 Tbsp
Jacobsen Salt Co. Pure Kosher Sea Salt, 2 Tbsp
Black Pepper, 1 Tbsp
Pork Collar, 4 Pound
Instructions
In a big zip lock bag, mix the shallots, rosemary, coriander, garlic, bourbon, apple ale, canola oil, pepper and salt.
Slice the collar into 2" slabs and marinate in the fridge overnight.
When ready to cook, increase the flame to High and preheat for fifteen min with the lid closed.
Put the collar on the grill for 5-6 mins or until grill marks appear. Reduce the heat to 325°F, pour the remaining marinade over the meat, and simmer for another 20 to 25 minutes.
Sauté on medium to medium-high heat, taking care not to overcook. The main warmth of the beef should be 160°F. Remove the steaks from the barbecue and serve. Enjoy!

2.124 Bacon Weave Smoked Country Sausage
Total Time: 2 Hours 15 Minutes, Serving: 4 people
Ingredients
main
Pound Sausage, Uncooked
Pit Boss Poultry & Pork Rub
Bacon, 8 Slices
Instructions
Make the sausage into some kind of loaf shape with your hands. Sprinkle with Pit Boss Pork and Poultry Shake to taste.
Once geared up to cook, preheat the oven to 180°F with the lid covered for fifteen min.
Directly place the sausage loaf on the grill grates and smoke for 1-1/2 hours.
Assemble the bacon weave on wax paper while the sausage is cooking. To begin, arrange four slices of bacon on wax paper so that they are touching. The fifth slice of bacon should be placed such that it spans the others. Every other slice of bacon should be tucked beneath the fifth piece of bacon. Fold the two pieces of bacon below the fifth piece of bacon back on top of each other.
Place the sixth slice of bacon on top of the two that were folded back. Fold the bacon that was most recently beneath the previous piece of bacon back, two pieces at a time, until your weaving is complete, then put the next piece of bacon on top. Remove from
the equation. Remove the sausage from the grill after it has smoked for 1-1/2 hours and warm your Pit Boss to 350°F with the lid closed.
Wrap the sausage loaf in the bacon weave while the grill is heating up. Place the centre of the weave on top of the sausage loaf and squeeze the bacon around it.
Finish the weave on the underside of the sausage by flipping the sausage and bacon over. Across the bottom, alternate the bacon ends and tuck the ends around each other.

Return the sausage to the grill and cook for another 25-30 minutes, or until the internal temperature reaches 160°F. Enjoy!

2.125 Apple & Bourbon Glazed Ham
Total Time: 1 Hour 15 Minutes, Serving: 6 people
Ingredients
Main
Large Ham, 1
Apple Jelly, 1 Cup
Dijon Mustard2 Tbsp
Bourbon, 2 Tbsp
Fresh Lemon Juice, 2 Tbsp
Ground Cloves, 1/2 Tbsp
Apple Juice or Cider, 2 Cup
Instructions
Preheat Pit Boss to 325°F for fifteen min with the lid shut when ready to cook.
Put the ham straight on the grill grates once the grill is hot. The cooking time is 30 minutes.
Dissolve the apple jelly in a small pot over medium-low heat in the meantime. Turn off the heat and put aside the apple juice, mustard, bourbon, lemon juice, and crushed cloves.
Cover the ham with the apple bourbon mixture after thirty min. Cook for another thirty min, or until a core temperature of 135°F is reached when a thermometer is put into the thickest portion of the meat.
Remove the ham from the grill and set it aside for 20 minutes to rest before serving. If preferred, reheat the leftover sauce and serve with ham. Enjoy!

2.126 Braised Brunswick Stew
Total Time: 2 Hours 30 Minutes, Serving: 4 people
Ingredients
main
Butter, 8 Tbsp
Onion, 1 Large
Green Bell Pepper, Diced, 1
Celery, 2
Clove Garlic, Minced, 4
Pound Pulled Chicken
Smoked Paprika, 1 Tbsp
Cayenne Pepper, 1/2 Tbsp
Worcestershire Sauce
Tomatoes, 45 Ounce (28 Oz)
'Que BBQ Sauce
Pound Pulled Pork
Cup Chicken Broth
Lima Beans, Frozen, 10 Ounce
Pound Beef Brisket
Apple Cider Vinegar
Corn, 10 Ounce
Okra, Frozen, 1 Cup
Black Pepper
Salt
Hot Sauce
Instructions
In a big cast-iron Dutch oven, melt the butter over medium heat. 5 to 8 minutes till the bell pepper, onion, and celery are tender and transparent.
Cook for 2 minutes after adding the garlic. Allow boiling for 5 minutes after adding the cayenne, paprika, tomatoes, Worcestershire sauce and barbecue sauce. In a separate bowl, combine the smoked pulled chicken and pork from a prior grilling session. Smoked the beef brisket from a prior grilling session may be added now. Bring the chicken gumbo to a boil, then remove from the heat.
Meanwhile, warm the Pit Boss to 300°F with the lid covered for

15 minutes.
Cover the Dutch oven with a cover and gently place it on the grill grate. Cook for an hour and a half, adding additional broth as needed. The stew mustn't be overly soupy.
Stir corn, lima beans, and okra, if using, and simmer for another thirty min, or until the veggies are cooked, with the lid off. Flavor with black pepper & salt for taste, and additional pepper if you want it hotter.
To enhance the tastes, add vinegar. Serve immediately in dishes with a side of spicy sauce. Enjoy!

2.127 Everything Pigs in a Blanket
Total Time: 35 Minutes, Serving: 4 people
Ingredients
main
Poppy Seeds, 2 Tbsp
Dried Minced Onion, 1 Tbsp
Garlic, Minced, 2 Tbsp
Sesame Seeds, 2 Tbsp
Salt, 1 Tbsp
Pillsbury Original Crescent Rolls, 8 Ounce (8 Oz)
Dijon Mustard, 1/4 Cup
Large Egg, Beaten, 1
Instructions
Preheat your Pit Boss at 350 ° F for 10 to 15 minutes with the lid covered when you're ready to cook.
Combine poppy seeds, dried minced onion, dried minced garlic, salt, and sesame seeds in a large mixing bowl. Remove from the equation.
Slice each crescent roll dough triangle in thirds horizontally, resulting in three tiny strips of each roll.
Lightly brush the dough strips with Dijon mustard. Roll up the tiny hot dogs on one end of the dough.
Arrange them on a Totalared baking sheet, seam side down. Spray with egg wash and then season with the seasoning mix.
Bake for 12 to 15 mins in a Pit Boss until nicely browned.
Offer with your favorited mustard or dipping sauce. Enjoy!

2.128 Simple Smoked Ribs
Total Time: 4 Hours 15 Minutes, Serving: 6 people
Ingredients
main
Baby Back Ribs, 3 Rack
Pit Boss Poultry & Pork Rub, 3/4 Cup
Pit Boss 'Que BBQ Sauce, 3/4 Cup
Instructions
Remove any extra fat from the rear side of the ribs by peeling the membrane.
Season all edges of the ribs with 1/4 cup Pit Boss Poultry & Pork Rub per rack.
Once ready to cook, preheat the Pit Boss to 180°F with the lid closed for fifteen min.
Barbecue the ribs for 3 to 4 hrs on the barbecue.
Take the ribs from the grill when temp reaches 160°F to 165°F and raise the Pit Boss temperature to 350°F.
Spread 1/4 cup Pit Boss 'Que BBQ Sauce on a big sheet of heavy-duty Aluminum foil, then lay a rack of ribs on top, meat-side down, and firmly wrapped. Carry on with the next rack.
Return the wrapped ribs to the grill and cook for 45 mins, or until the internal temperature reaches 204 degrees Fahrenheit.
Take the steak from the grill and set it aside for 20 mins before slicing. Enjoy.

2.129 Smoked Sausage & Potatoes
Total Time: 1 hour 5 mins, Serving: 4
Ingredients
main
Hot Sausage, 2 Pound
Fingerling Potatoes, 2 Pound
Garden-fresh Thyme, 1 Tbsp
Butter, 4 Tbsp
Instructions
Heat the Pit Boss to 375°F for fifteen min with the lid closed when ready to cook.
To obtain some color on your sausage links, place them on the grill. On each side, this should take approximately 3 minutes.
While the sausage cooks, chop the potatoes into bite-size pieces that are all around the same size to ensure equal cooking. Chop the thyme and butter before mixing everything in a Pit Boss cast iron pan.
Remove the sausage from the grill, slice it into bite-size pieces, and place it in your cast iron skillet.
Reduce the grill's temperature to 275°F and cook the cast iron for 45 minutes to an hour, or until the potatoes are completely cooked.
After 45 mins, check your potatoes by biting into one with a butter knife to check whether it's done. Coat cast iron with a lid or foil to reduce cooking time. Serve. Cherish!

2.130 Smoked Sausage Pancake Sandwich
Total Time: 1 hour 5 min, Serving: 6
Ingredients
main
Ground Pork, 1 Pound
Egg White, 1
Fresh Thyme, 1/2 Tbsp
Fennel, Ground, 1/2 Tbsp
Onion Powder, 1/2 Tbsp
Salt, 3 1/2 Tbsp
Ground Nutmeg, 1/4 Tbsp
Pit Boss Pork & Poultry Rub, 1/2 Tbsp
Maple Syrup, 8 Tbsp
Black Pepper, 1/2 Tbsp
Whole Wheat Flour, 6 Cup
Sugar, 1/2 Cup
Baking Powder, 2 Tbsp
Baking Soda, 1 Tbsp
Milk, 5 Cup
Whole Egg, 1
Vegetable Oil, 1 Tbsp
Instructions
In a mixing dish, combine all of the components for the maple sausage. Chill for 15 mins before adding.
Once ready to cook, preheat the grill to 180°F with the lid covered for fifteen min. If Super Smoke is available, use it for the best taste.
Form the pig mixture into eight circular patties, cook for 30 minutes, and serve.
Remove the smoked sausage patties from the grill and place them on a plate to cool.
Preheat the grill on high for 15 minutes with the lid covered. If possible, raise the temperature to 500°F for best results. While the grill is heating up, place a big cast iron pan or cast-iron skillet on it.
To make the pancakes, combine the dry ingredients in a large mixing basin while the skillet warms up. Mix in the milk, egg, canola oil, and maple syrup until everything is well mixed.
Place a few butter pads in the hot skillet and coat evenly. Fill the skillet with 1/4 cup pieces of the pancake mix. Overcrowding is avoided by fitting as many people as feasible

at once.
Cook for 5 minutes, or until bubbling, with the lid closed. When it starts to bubble, turn it and cook for another 2 to 3 minutes. Allow cooling on a platter.
To make the smoked sausage patties, place them directly on the grill grate and cook for 3 mins on each side, or until golden brown.
Assemble your sandwiches by layering the sausage and pancakes between the bread slices. If preferred, top the sandwich with a fried egg and cheese. Drizzle with maple syrup and a pat of butter on top. Enjoy!

2.131 Classic Sausage Stuffing
Total Time: 1 Hour 15 Minutes, Serving: 8 people
Ingredients
main
Butter, 2 Tbsp
Extra-Virgin Olive Oil, 2 Tbsp
Celery, Diced, 1 Cup
Yellow Onion, Diced, 1 Cup
Sausage, Uncooked, 8 Ounce
Cherries, Dried, Tart, 1/2 Cup
Finely Chopped Pecans, 1/2 Cup
Chopped Herbs, For Garnish, 1/2 Cup
Bread, Cubed, 8 Cup
Chicken Stock, 4 Cup
Instructions
Once ready to cook, preheat the grill on high for 15 mins with the lid covered.
Preheat the grill with a big cast iron pan. After that, add the celery and onions, followed by the butter and olive oil. Cook for 15-20 mins, or until soft.
Take the vegetables from the pan and add the meat. Cook until the mixture is crumbly and the color is no longer pink. Take the cherries, pecans, and herbs from the barbecue and stir them in.
Toss the bread with the celery and onions, as well as the sausage and herb combination, in a large mixing dish. Slowly drizzle in the stock, mixing with your hands to ensure that the bread is uniformly covered. Add a bit extra stock if the bread seems dry.
Transfer the stuffing to a greased 9x13-inch baking pan and cover with foil. If you wish, save aside half of the stuffing for use in the bird.
Set on the grill and cook for thirty min, or until well warmed. Remove the cover and continue to cook for another 15-20 mins, or until the bread is crisp on top but soft in the centre. Enjoy!

2.132 BBQ Pulled Pork Pizza
Total Time: 1 Hour 15 Minutes, Serving: 6 people
Ingredients
main
Water, 1 1/2 Cup
Active Dry Yeast, Divided, 2
Sugar, 2 Tbsp
Olive Oil, 1/4 Cup
Salt, 1 Tbsp
Flour, 4 Cup
Cornmeal, 2 Cup
Pit Boss Sweet & Heat BBQ Sauce, 2 Cup
Mozzarella Cheese, 3 Cup
Pulled Pork, 1 Pound
Pit Boss Prime Rib Rub
Red Onion, Sliced
Cilantro, Finely Chopped
Instructions
When making bread, fill a basin halfway with warm water, add yeast and then mix gently. Allow resting for five minutes or till it foams up. Combine the oil, sugar, and salt in a mixing bowl. Mix in the flour till the dough resembles a ball.
Lightly grease a big mixing bowl and put the dough inside. Allow dough to double in size by covering it with plastic wrap and letting it rest for at least an hour (approximately one hour). Knead the dough four to five times on a lightly floured board. Allow 15 minutes for resting.
While the dough is resting, warm the Pit Boss to 450 degrees F (500 Fahrenheit if using a WI FIRE-enabled grill) with the lid covered for 10-15 minutes.
Generously dust your work surface with cornmeal. Cut the dosh in half and spread out into circles on top of the cornmeal to a thickness of about 1/4 inch.
Evenly distributed 1 cup Pit Boss Sweet Heat BBQ sauce on each round of pizza dough. Add 1/2 cup of cheese. Now chop pulled pork into small pieces and put it on top of the cheese.
Now cover the pizzas with a coating of Pit Boss Prime Rib Rub. Using a pizza peel or the bottom edge of a
sheet pan, transfer pies to the grill.
Bake for 15 to 25 mins, turning the pizza every 5 mins. Get Rid of the pizza from the oven and set it aside for 5 mins before slicing. Sliced red onion and chopped cilantro go on top. Enjoy!

2.133 Competition Style BBQ Pulled Pork
Total Time: 10 Hours 25 Minutes, Serving: 8 people
Ingredients
main
Bone-In Pork Butt, 1 (8-10 Lb.)
Pit Boss Pork & Poultry Rub, Divided, 1 Cup
Apple Juice, Divided, 2 3/4 Cup
Butcher BBQ Pork Injection, 1/4 Cup
Meat Injector
Instructions
Preheat Pit Boss to 225°F and cook for 15 minutes with lid covered until ready to cook. If Super Smoke is available, use it for the best taste.
The trim extra fat from the meat as the grill warms up.
Combine half of the Pit Boss Pork & Poultry Rub, 2 cups apple juice, and butcher's pork
injection in a small dish. Using an injector, thoroughly inject pork butt throughout.
Apply a coat of Pit Boss Meat & Poultry Rub to the pork. Allow 20 minutes for the meat to rest.
Cook the meat for 4-1/2 to 5-1/2 hours on the barbecue. Test the core temperature of the pork after 4-1/2 hours. It should be between 155- and 165-degrees Fahrenheit. If not, wait 30 minutes and check again.
Wrap the pork in a double layer of heavy-duty Aluminum foil when the temperature hits 155-165°F. Place the pork in a foil packet with 3/4 cup of the saved apple juice and return to the grill.
Increase the temperature of the grill to 250°F and cook for another 3 to 4 hours. After 3 hours, check the interior temperature. In the thickest portion of the pork, the temperature should be between 204°F and 206°F. Check the temperature of the pork every 30 minutes until it reaches 204-206°F.
Depending on the amount of pork, the total cooking time should be between 8 and 10 hours.
Remove the pork from the grill and open the foil package for 10 minutes to allow the steam to escape. Re-seal the bag and set it aside for 45 mins to an hour.
After cooling, drain the liquid out of the foil and use a fat separator to remove the fat from the broth. Pull the flesh away

from the bone. Toss the removed meat with 2 cups of broth. If required, add more broth to reach the appropriate moisture level. Enjoy!

2.134 Hawaiian Pulled Pig
Total Time: 5 Hours 15 Minutes, Serving: 4 people
Ingredients
main
Bone-In Pork Shoulder, 7 Pound
Jacobsen Salt Co. Pure Kosher Sea Salt, 3 Tbsp
Ground Black Pepper
Whole Banana Leaves, 2
Instructions
Sprinkle Jacobsen Salt and pepper over the pork shoulder. Cover your work surface with a banana leaf. Draw up the ends as if you were wrapping a present and place the pork shoulder in the middle. Draw up the ends of the second banana leaf at a right angle to the first to surround the meat. Wrap Aluminum foil around the whole box. Refrigerate for at least one night.
Once ready to cook, preheat the Pit Boss to 300 ° F for fifteen min with the lid closed.
Put the covered pork straight on the grill grates and cook for 5 to 6 hrs, just until the pork is starting to fall tender and the internal temperature reaches 190 ° F.
Move the pork to a chopping board and set aside for 20 minutes, still wrapped. Unwrap the pork carefully and preserve any liquids
that have been collected in the foil.
Remove any lumps of fat or bone from the pork and shred them into pieces and shreds. Enjoy!

2.135 Maple Bacon Pull-Apart
Total Time: 55 Minutes, Serving: 8 people
Ingredients
main
Bacon, Sliced, 12 Slices
Biscuits, Homestyle, Canned, 2 Can
Maple Syrup, 1 Cup
Brown Sugar, 1 Cup
Butter, 1 Cup
Water, 1/2 Cup
Ground Cinnamon, 2 Tbsp
Instructions
Preheat the Pit Boss on High for fifteen min with the lid covered when you're ready to cook.
Cook the bacon for 5-8 mins on one side, based on thickness, then turn and cook for another 5-8 mins. Set aside crumbled bacon.
Take the biscuits out of the container and cut each one into four halves, then peel each half in two. Remove from the equation.
In a pan, combine the brown sugar, syrup, butter, and water; bring to a boil, then lower heat & simmer for 1 min. Add the cinnamon and mix well. Toss biscuit quarters with crumbled bacon and syrup to coat.
Toss biscuit quarters with crumbled bacon and syrup to coat.
Pour into a smeared Bundt pan and spread out evenly.
Lower the heat to 350 ° F on the grill and put the pan on it.
Cook for 30 to 35 minutes, or until the biscuits are done, with the lid closed.
Remove the pan first from barbecue and place it on a serving dish.
Serve immediately. Enjoy!

2.136 BBQ Dragged Pork and Pork Belly Bánh Mì
Total Time: 15 Hours, Serving: 4 people
Ingredients
main
Pork Belly, 4 Pound
Cup Salt
Cup Brown Sugar
Black Pepper, 2 Tbsp
Apple Juice, 1 1/2 Cup
To Taste Salt, 2
Sesame Oil, 2 Tbsp
Onion, 1/2 Cup
To Taste Black Pepper, 1
Clove Garlic, Minced, 3
Bone-In Pork, 10 Pound
Ginger, Minced, 2 Tbsp
Tomato Sauce, 3/4 Cup
Soy Sauce, 2 Tbsp
Water, 34 Tbsp
Rice Vinegar, 5 Tbsp
Thai Chili Sauce, 1/4 Cup
Carrots, 3 Whole
Sugar, 2 Tbsp
Mayonnaise, 1 Cup
Sriracha, 2 Tbsp
Jalapeño, 2 Whole
Juiced Full Lime, 1
Daikon, 1 Whole
Whole Baguette, 1
English Cucumber, 1
Cilantro, Leaves Picked, 1 Clump
Instructions
For such Pork Belly, score the fat in a carried-out order pattern on the pork belly (about 1/4" deep). Rub the pork belly with a mixture
of salt, brown sugar, and black pepper. Refrigerate overnight after covering.
Whenever ready to cook, preheat the grill on high for 15 minutes with the lid covered.
Cook for 30 minutes on the grill grate with the pork belly directly on it.
Reduce the heat to 275°F and simmer for another 2 hours, or until a spear inserted into the deepest portion glides in and out easily.
For the Pulled Pig, trim any extra fat from the pork butt, leaving 1/4" of the fat cap intact. In a small dish, mix 1 cup apple juice, brown sugar, and 1 Tbsp salt, stirring until the sugar & salt are almost dissolved.
Inject the apple juice mixture into pork butt each square inch or so. Season the pork butt with the remaining salt & black pepper on the outside.
Once ready to cook, preheat the Pit Boss to 250°F for fifteen min with the lid closed.
Put the pork butt straight on the grill grates and cook for 6 hours, or until the core temperature reaches 160 degrees Fahrenheit. Wrap the pork butt in two pieces of Aluminum foil and pour 1/2 cup apple juice over it. To keep the apple juice contained, wrap the tin foil firmly.
Raise the temperature to 275°F and return the pork butt to the grill in a pan big enough to catch any drips. Cook for 3 hours more, or until the internal temperature reaches 205°F.
Remove the bone from the grill and toss it out. Remove any extra fat or tendons from the pork and shred it. If required, season with more salt and pepper.
To make the pulled pork sauce, heat sesame oil in a small skillet over medium-high heat. Add the onion and cook for 1 to 2 minutes, or until transparent. Sauté garlic and ginger for 30 seconds, or until aromatic. Combine the tomato sauce, soy

sauce, water, vinegar, and chilly sauce in a mixing bowl. Cook for 5 minutes before turning off the heat. Pour over the shredded pork and toss to combine. Reserve.

To Totalize the pickled veggies, put warm water, sugar, salt, and rice vinegar in a mixing bowl and whisk until the sugar and salt dissolve. Wrap and chill for at least 4 hrs after pouring the mixture over the matchstick veggies.

To make the Sriracha Mayo, whisk together all the ingredients. On each side of the cut baguette, spread approximately 2 tbsps. of mayonnaise.

Arrange sliced cucumber, jalapenos and onion on the sandwich. Fill with pickled carrots, sliced pork belly, cilantro and daikon, then top with a piece of the pulled pork. Serve right away. Enjoy!

2.137 Buffalo & Pork Stuffed Poblano Peppers

Total Time: 1 hour 4 Mins, Serving: 4
Ingredients
main
Medium Poblano Pepper, 6
Extra-Virgin Olive Oil, 2 Tbsp
Garlic, Minced, 1 Tbsp
Fresh Parsley, 1/4 Cup
Yellow Onion, Diced, 1 Medium
Vegetable Oil, 2
Ground Buffalo, 1/2 Pound
Ground Pork, 1/2 Pound
Salt, 3/4 Tbsp
Black Pepper, 1/2 Tbsp
Red Pepper Flakes
Rice, Cooked, 2 Cup
Tomato Sauce, 8 Ounce
Instructions
Preheat the Pit Boss on High for fifteen min with the lid covered when you're ready to cook.
Drizzle olive oil over all but one of the poblano peppers and season with salt and pepper. Toss to coat completely.
Grill peppers for ten min, or till the skin is brown and blistered, directly on the grill grates. Take the steaks from the grill and put them aside to cool.
Preheat a cast-iron pan on the grill for 20 mins with the lid covered.
Cut parsley, onion, and leftover poblano pepper and mince garlic.
Halve the peppers lengthwise. With a spoon, scrape out the ribs and seeds.
Add the onions and diced poblano pepper, followed by the oil. Cook for 3 mins or until soft. Pork, buffalo, garlic, parsley, salt, black pepper, and pepper flakes are added to the pan.
Cook, tossing with a heavy wooden spatula to break up the lumps, till the meat is browned, approximately 6 minutes. Mix in the rice and tomato sauce well.
Take from fire and season with salt and pepper to taste. Reduce the grill's temperature to 350 degrees F.
Stuff the peppers with rice mixture and bake them in a skillet. Put a pan on the grill and cook peppers for 25 to 30 mins, or until very tender and filling is cooked through.
Take off the grill and set aside for 10 mins before serving. Enjoy!

2.138 Baked Bean Casserole with the Pulled Pork

Total Time: 1 Hour 15 Minutes, Serving: 6 people
Ingredients
main
Green Beans, Fresh, 2 Pound
Kosher Salt
Extra-Virgin Olive Oil, 2 Tbsp
Cremini Mushrooms, Sliced and Divided, 1 Pound
Butter, 6 Tbsp
Fresh Thyme, 4 Sprig
All-Purpose Flour, 2 Tbsp
Whole Milk, 1 1/4 Cup
1 Cup Heavy Cream, 4
Clove Garlic, Minced
Parmesan Cheese, 1/2 Cup
Ground Black Pepper
Leftover Pulled Pork, 1 Pound
French's Original Crispy Fried Onions, 3/4 Cup
Instructions
Preheat the Pit Boss to 375°F for fifteen min with the lid closed when ready to cook.
Sauté green beans in a large saucepan of boiling salted water, working in batches, until brilliant green and halfway tender, approximately 3 mins each batch. Drain and set aside to cool. Trim the ends of the stems.
In a large frying pan, heat 1 tbsp of oil over medium-high heat. Sauté, occasionally stirring, until half of the mushrooms are golden brown, approximately 2 minutes. Toss and cook for another 3 minutes, or until both sides are browned.
Put 2 tbsp butter and two thyme sprigs into the pan. Cook for another 4 minutes, occasionally turning until the butter has browned and the mushrooms are dark brown and soft. Transfer to a dish and season with salt. Repeat with remaining butter, salt, and oil, as well as the mushrooms and thyme.
In a sizable saucepan, melt the remaining 2 tsp butter. Cook, whisking regularly until the roux is golden brown and nutty smelling, approximately 4 mins. In a separate bowl, whisk together the milk and cream.
Raise the temperature to medium-low and cook, often whisking, until the sauce is thick and boiling, approximately 5 mins. Get Rid of the pan from the heat and stir in the garlic and parmesan cheese. Salt & pepper to taste.
In a 2-quart baking dish, layer green beans, pulled pork & mushrooms. Pour the sauce over the top.
Cover firmly with foil and bake for 25-30 minutes, or until sauce is boiling. Discover and bake for another 15-20 minutes, or until the top and sides of the dish are gently browned.
Topping with the fried onions and bake for another 3 minutes, or even onions are aromatic and slightly darker. Allow 10 minutes for the sauce to solidify before serving. Enjoy!

2.139 Baked German Pork Schnitzel with Grilled Lemons

Total Time: 40 Minutes, Serving: 2 people
Ingredients
main
Pork Chops, 16 Ounce
Salt
Black Pepper
Garlic Powder, 1 Tbsp
Paprika, 1 Tbsp
Eggs 2
Panko Breadcrumbs, 1 Cup
Flour, 1/2 Cup
Lemon, Halved, 2 Whole
Instructions
Preheat the oven to high for 15 mins with the lid covered when you're ready to cook.
Put pork chops over two pieces of plastic wrap, one on top of the other. Using a meat mallet, pound them to a thickness of 1/4 to 1/8 inch. Season both sides with a liberal amount of salt and pepper.
In a mixing dish, combine the garlic powder and paprika. Whisk the eggs in a separate dish. Place the breadcrumbs in a third bowl.
Dredge the pork cutlets in flour, brushing off any excess, then

in eggs, and last in breadcrumbs. Place the breaded pork cutlets on a wire rack over a baking sheet that has been gently greased.

Cook In the Oven for 15 mins on one side, then turn and bake for a further five min on the other. Put sliced lemons on the grill grates flesh side down whenever you open the grill to turn the pork.

Remove from the grill and top with grilled lemon slices. Enjoy!

2.140 Mini Sausage Rolls
Total Time: 35 Minutes, Serving: 4 people
Ingredients
main
3/4 Cup Dry Mustard
Distilled White Vinegar, 3/4 Cup
Honey, 1/2 Cup
Egg Yolk, Beaten, 4
Sausage, Uncooked, 2 Pound
Ground Sage
Diced Small, 1 Small Onion
Frozen Puff Pastry, 17 1/2 Ounce
Instructions
Make the mustard: In a small mixing dish, combine the mustard and vinegar. To develop the tastes, cover with plastic wrap and let at room temperature overnight. Add the honey and egg yolks to the

mustard mixture in a small heavy pot. Cook, whisking continuously until the sauce has thickened, approximately 7 minutes. Allow cooling before refrigerating until ready to serve.

Mix the sausage and onion well in a medium mixing dish. Shape each sheet of frozen puff pastry - two per box - into an 11 by 10-1/2-inch rectangular on a lightly floured work surface. Cut each rectangle into three strips, each 3-1/2 inches wide, using a pizza cutter or knife. Wet your hands and form a tube-like shape out of part of the sausage. It should go in the middle of one of the puff pastries strips.

Fold the pastry across the sausage and use a little beaten egg to seal the seams. Using the leftover sausage and puff pastry, repeat the process. Place all of the rolls on the work area, seam side down, and gently brush the tops with the egg.

Slice the rolls into 1-1/2-inch-long pieces and place them on a parchment-lined rimmed baking sheet. Between each roll, leave approximately an inch. Once ready to cook, preheat the grill to 350°F with the lid covered for 15 minutes.

Cook the sausage rolls for approximately 25 mins, or until the dough is nicely browned and the meat is cooked through. Represent with honey mustard on the side.

2.141 Sausage Pepper Skewers
Total Time: 35 Minutes, Serving: 6 people
Ingredients
main
Andouille Sausage, 12 Ounce
Red Onion, Carved, 1/2 Whole
Green Bell Peppers, Carved, 1 Whole
Yellow Bell Peppers, Carved, 1 Whole
Olive Oil
Pit Boss Cajun Shake
Minced Tomatoes, 1/2 Cup
Peppers in Adobo Sauce, Chopped, 1/2 Tbsp
Cracked Black Pepper, 1/4 Tbsp
Honey, 1 Tbsp
Ancho Chile Powder, 1/4 Tbsp
Garlic Powder, 1/4 Tbsp
Onion Powder, 1/4 Tbsp
Jacobsen Salt Co. Pure Kosher Sea Salt, 1/4 Tbsp
Instructions

Infuse wooden skewers in water for 30 mins before cooking if using them.

Preheat the Pit Boss on high for 10 to 15 mins with the lid covered.

Chop the pepper, onion, and sausage into small pieces. Different the meat and veggies on the skewer.

Pour olive oil over each skewer and sprinkle with Pit Boss Cajun Rub on both sides.

Cook the skewers directly on the grill grate for approximately 5 minutes. Sauté for a further five min after flipping the skewers.

Spicy Ketchup Dipping: Combine sauce ingredients in a small serving dish and set aside.

Remove the skewers from the grill and serve them with a spicy dipping sauce. Enjoy!

2.142 Baked Pork Belly Mac and Cheese
Total Time: 3 Hours 30 Minutes, Serving: 6 people
Ingredients
main
Grind Pork Belly, 3
Salt, 4 Tbsp
Brown Sugar, 4 Tbsp
Black Pepper, 1/2 Tbsp
Elbow Macaroni, 1 Pound
Olive Oil, 1 Tbsp
Butter, 3 Tbsp
Onion, Diced, 1/2 Whole
Garlic, Minced, 1 Tbsp
Flour, 3 Tbsp
Whole Milk, 1 1/2 Cup
Shredded Cheddar, Mozzarella or Swiss Cheese, 3 Cup
Ground Nutmeg, 1/2 Tbsp
Cayenne Pepper, 1/4 Tbsp
Instructions
Season the pork belly with salt, sugar, and black pepper. Cover pork belly evenly with the mixture. Allow resting in the fridge overnight, covered.

Once ready to cook, preheat the oven on High for 10 to 15 mins with the lid closed.

Put the pork belly in a frying pan and cook it. Simmer for 30 mins on high, or until a little color has formed.

Reduce the heat to 250°F and cook for another 1-2 hours, or until the pork belly is tender.

Allow the pork belly to cool to room temperature before serving. When cold enough to handle, wrap in plastic and refrigerate until completely cooled (at least a couple of hours).

Macaroni and Cheese: Boil a big pot of salted water. Sauté until the noodles are soft. Drain and set aside over medium-high heat, heat another large saucepan. Combine the olive oil, butter, and onion in a mixing bowl. Cook until the vegetables are soft.

As the onion is soft, add the garlic and cook until fragrant. In a separate bowl, sift in the flour and mix to combine. Cook the roux until it smells like popcorn and is golden in color.

Mix in the entire milk while whisking. Please ensure any lumps are worked out. Simmer, occasionally stirring, until the mixture has thickened. Remove the pan from the heat and add the cheese, nutmeg, and cayenne pepper. Stir in the noodles until everything is well combined.

Cut the pork belly into large pieces or slices and cook on the grill just until heated.

Pour mac and cheese into a dish and sprinkle with pork belly to serve. Enjoy!

2.143 Bacon Stuffed Smoked Pork Loin

Total Time: 1 Hour 20 Minutes, Serving: 4 people
Ingredients
main
Pork Loin, Butterflied, 3 Pound
Pit Boss Pork & Poultry Rub
Walnuts, Chopped, 1/4 Cup
Craisins, 1/3 Cup
Fresh Oregano, 1 Tbsp
Fresh Thyme, 1 Tbsp
Asparagus, Ends Trimmed, 6 Pieces
Bacon, Sliced, 6 Slices
Parmesan Cheese, Grated, 1/3 Cup
Bacon Grease
Instructions
On your work area, lay down two big lengths of butcher's twine. Put pork loin butterflied perpendicular to thread.
Rub the Pit Boss Pork and Poultry rub all over the interior of the pork loin.
Arrange all of the ingredients in a line on one end of the loin, starting with the chopped nuts, craisins, oregano, thyme, and asparagus.
Put the bacon and parmesan cheese over the top.
Carefully wrap up the pork loin, starting at the end with all of the contents and securing both ends with butcher's twine.
Sprinkle the exterior of the pork loin with additional Pork and Poultry Shake and roll it in the leftover bacon grease.
When you're ready to cook, preheat the oven to 180°F with the lid covered for fifteen min. Smoke the filled pork loin for 1 hour immediately on the grill grate.
Retrieve the pork loin and preheat the oven to 350 degrees Fahrenheit.
Return the loin to the Pit Boss and cook for 30 to 45 minutes, or until an instant-read thermometer registers 135 degrees Fahrenheit.
Transfer the pork loin to a dish and cover it with Aluminum foil to keep it warm. Allow for fifteen min of resting time before cutting and serving. Enjoy!

2.144 Ultimate BLT Salad

Total Time: 35 Minutes, Serving: 4 people
Ingredients
main
Bacon, Lardons, 8 Ounce
French Country Bread, 1 Loaf
Butter, Unsalted, 3 Tbsp
Kosher Salt, 1 1/2 Tbsp
Ground Black Pepper, 1/4 Tbsp
Finely Chopped Shallot, 1 Tbsp
Apple Cider Vinegar, 1/4 Cup
Buttermilk, 1/2 Cup
Mayonnaise, 3/4 Cup
Parmesan Cheese, 1/2 Cup
Sugar, 1/8 Tbsp
Black Pepper, 1/4 Tbsp
Romaine Lettuce Heart, 2
Heirloom Tomato, 4
Instructions
Once you are ready to cook, fire up the Pit Boss according to the manufacturer's directions. Preheat the oven to 375 degrees F and bake for 10 to 15 mins with the lid covered.
In a cast-iron pan, put bacon lardons (slab bacon sliced into matchsticks approximately 1/2-inch-thick by 1-inch-long) immediately on the grill grate. Cook, stirring periodically, for 15-20 mins, or till the fat is rendered and lardons are crispy. Drain and discard the fat and put aside the lardons.
Mix melted butter with 1-inch pieces of French bread. Distribute out on a baking tray and add salt and pepper. Cook for 10-15 minutes, or until the bread is crisp and lightly browned, directly on the grill grate.
Mix shallot and vinegar in a small dish and let aside for 5 minutes. To emulsify, whisk in the buttermilk. Mix in the mayonnaise, parmesan cheese, salt, sugar, and pepper. Remove from the equation.
Mix lettuce, tomatoes (cut into wedges), bacon, and croutons in a large mixing dish. Toss in the dressing to coat.
Arrange on a serving dish and sprinkle with more parmesan cheese, if preferred. Enjoy!

2.145 Beer-Braised Cabbage with Bacon

Total Time: 45 Minutes, Serving: 4 people
Ingredients
main
Bacon, Bulk Unsliced, 1/4 Pound
Yellow Onion, Diced, 1 Cup
Apple, Diced Small, 1 Cup
Green Cabbage, 2 Pound
Salt
Ground Black Pepper
Beer, Light, 12 Ounce
Instructions
Once ready to cook, preheat the Pit Boss grill to 325 ° F (160 degrees Celsius) with the lid closed for 10 to 15 mins.
Preheat a big heavy pot or Dutch pan over medium heat on the stovetop. Bake until the bacon is crisp (about 5 mins). Move to a paper towel-lined plate.
Return the saucepan to a medium-low heat setting. Cook for 5 minutes, or until golden brown, after adding the onion. Stir in the apple before adding the cabbage. Stir in a large amount of salt and a pinch of black pepper for 3 minutes.
Over medium-high heat, pour in the beer and bring to a boil. Cover and transfer the pot to the Pit Boss right away.
Bake for 10 mins at 325 ° F (160 degrees Celsius). Remove the cover and continue to simmer for another
10-15 minutes, or until the cabbage is soft and the liquid has gone.
Toss in the saved bacon with the cabbage. Enjoy!

2.146 Hawaiian BBQ Baked Beans

Total Time: 4 Hours, Serving: 8 people
Ingredients
main
Bacon, 8 Slices
Pineapple, Fresh, 1/2 Whole
Onion, Diced, 1/2 Yellow
Red Bell Pepper, 1/2
Seeded and diced, 1 Jalapeño.
Clove Garlic, 2
Pit Boss 'Que BBQ Sauce, 3/4 Cup
Beer, 1 Cup
Brown Sugar, 1/2 Cup
Yellow Mustard, 2 Tbsp
Molasses, 2 Tbsp
Chili Powder, 1 Tbsp
Cumin, 1 Tbsp
Beans, Pinto (Canned), 3 Can
Leftover Pulled Pork, 3 Cup
Panko Breadcrumbs, 1 1/2 Cup
Instructions
When you're ready to cook, fire up the Pit Boss according to the manufacturer's directions. Preheat the stove to 350 degrees F and bake for 10-15 minutes with the lid covered.
Place the pieces of bacon in a cast iron pan on the Pit Boss. Cook the bacon over medium heat for approximately 20

minutes or until the fat has rendered.

While the bacon is cooking, put the pineapple spears on grill grate & cook till caramelized, approximately 5-8 minutes on each side. Remove the steaks from the grill and dice them. Remove from the equation.

Using tongs, remove the bacon strips and drain them on paper towels. Remove all except 1 tbsp of bacon grease from the pan and set aside. Place the bacon in a bowl and crumble it.

Return the cast iron skillet to the grill, along with one tbsp of bacon grease, and add the onion, bell pepper, jalapeno, and garlic. Remove off the grill after 8-10 minutes, tossing regularly, until softened.

Reduce the grill's temperature to the Smoke setting (set to Super Smoke using a WI FIRE-enabled grill).

Mix the Pit Boss 'Que barbecue sauce, apple cider, mustard, brown sugar, molasses, cumin and chili powder in a big roasting pan—a disposable one works nicely. Stir in sautéed veggies, beans, 2/3 of crumbled bacon, pulled pork, & chopped pineapple after mixing everything.

Put uncovered on the grill and burn for 1 1/2 hours, tossing periodically to ensure that all food is exposed to the smoke.

Raise the grill temperature to 300 ° F after the beans have smoked for 1-1/2 hours and cook till the baked beans are hot and bubbling and the sauce has thickened, approximately 1 hour.

Now mix grilled pineapple into baked beans & cook for about 1 hour, or until the beans are bubbling, hot, and thickened.

In a separate bowl, combine the panko crumbs, 4 tbsp bacon fat, and the remaining crumbled bacon bits. (If you do not have any bacon grease, the melted butter will suffice.) For the final 20 minutes of cooking, evenly sprinkle the breadcrumbs over the top of the beans. Enjoy!

2.147 Roasted Pork with Balsamic Strawberry Sauce

Total Time: 45 Minutes, Serving: 2 people
Ingredients
main
Pork Tenderloin, 2 Pound
Salt And Pepper
Dried Rosemary, 2 Tbsp
Extra-Virgin Olive Oil, 2 Tbsp
Fresh Strawberries, 12 Large
Balsamic Vinegar, 1 cup
Sugar, 4 Tbsp
Instructions
Warm the Pit Boss to 350°F for 15 mins with the lid closed when ready to cook.

Clean and pat dry the pork. Season with salt, pepper, and rosemary on both sides.

Warm the oil in large Dutch ovens pan over high heat until it is nearly smoking. Caramelize the tenderloin on each side for approximately two min, or until the coating is nicely browned.

Place the pan in the Pit Boss and cook for 20 minutes, or until the pork is no longer pink and the internal temperature reaches 150°F.

Take the pork from the grill and set it aside to rest for 5-ten min. Heat the skillet over medium heat and rapidly sear the strawberries on both ends for less than a min. Take the berries out of the pan.

Remove the browned pieces off the bottom of the pan with balsamic vinegar.

Bring About to a boil, then lower to a low heat setting. Stir in the sugar until it dissolves. When the sauce has reduced by half, and the texture is thick, it is ready.

Arrange the cooked strawberries on top of the pork slices. Drizzle with balsamic vinegar sauce before serving. Enjoy!

2.148 Smothered Pork Chops

Total Time: 50 Minutes, Serving: 4 people
Ingredients
main
All-Purpose Flour, 1/2 Cup
Cornmeal, 1/4 Cup
Kosher Salt, 2 Tbsp
Base Black Pepper, 1 1/2 Tbsp
Total Milk, 1/2 Cup
Egg Yolk Large, 1
Peanut or Canola Oil, 1 1/2 Cup
Bone-In Single-Cut Pork Slices (6-8 Oz), 4 Whole
Instructions
Once you're ready to cook, preheat the Pit Boss grill to 250 ° F. with the lid closed for 10 to 15 mins.

Combine flour, cornmeal, salt, and pepper in a mixing bowl. Place the mixture on a dish and set aside.

Combine milk and egg yolk in a medium mixing basin. To mix the ingredients, whisk them together.

Using a frying thermometer, heat the oil in a cast-iron skillet on the fire to 375 degrees F. Reduce the heat to medium-high.

Drop Down the pork chops in the egg and milk mixture, then press them into the flour mixture plate, flipping and repeating on the other side. Remove any extra flour with a shake.

Carefully lower the pork chops into the heated oil. Fry until both sides are a beautiful golden brown. Approximately 2 minutes per side.

Transfer the pork chops to a baking sheet and continue grilling them on the grill. The interior temperature of the chops should be 145 degrees F.

To create the gravy, mix all ingredients in a large mixing bowl. All except 1 tbsp of the oil from the cast iron should be poured away. Cook, occasionally turning, until the onion is transparent but not cooked, approximately 4 minutes in the cast iron pan. Scatter flour in the pan and cook, constantly turning, for approximately 3 minutes, or until the flour is uniformly spread and roasted throughout the onion.

Whisk in the broth and milk until smooth. Bring About to a boil, reduce to low heat and continue to stir until the gravy has achieved the desired thickness, approximately two min. Season with salt and pepper to taste.

Place the chops on a serving dish after removing them from the grill. Represent with gravy smothered over the top. Enjoy!

2.149 BBQ Rib Sandwich

Total Time: 3 Hours 15 Minutes, Serving: 2 people
Ingredients
Main
Baby Back Pork Ribs, 3 Rack
Cracked Black Pepper
Kosher Salt
Pit Boss 'Que BBQ Sauce, 1 Cup
Hoagie Rolls, 4
Jar Pickles, 1
Yellow Onion, Thinly Sliced, 1
Instructions
Remove the membrane from the rear of the ribs. Spice with salt and cracked black pepper to taste.

When ready to cook, preheat the Pit Boss to 225°F for 15 minutes with the lid closed.

Cook for two hours with the meaty side up, turn the ribs and cook for another hour with the meaty side down.

Erase the ribs from the grill and place them skeletal side up on a baking sheet. Cut along the middle of each bone with a sharp knife and remove bones with your fingers.

Return the ribs to their original position and brush with half of the Pit Boss 'Que BBQ Sauce. Return to the grill for 5-10 minutes

to allow the sauce to solidify. Remove the steaks from the grill and put them aside.
Trim the rib racks to the same length as the hoagie rolls. Put the rib on the bottom bun after splitting the hoagie buns in half.
Add pickles, onions, and additional BBQ sauce to the top bun. Enjoy!

2.150 Spice-Rubbed Pork Tenderloin
Total Time: 2 Hours 20 Minutes, Serving: 4 people
Ingredients
main
Cedar Planks, 2 Whole
Dried Oregano, 1 Tbsp
Black Pepper, 1/2 Tbsp
Cumin, 2 Tbsp
Ancho Chile Powder, 1 Tbsp
Smoked Paprika, 1 Tbsp
Kosher Salt, 1 Tbsp
Garlic Powder, 1/4 Tbsp
Brown Sugar, 1 Tbsp
Dry Mustard, 1/4 Tbsp
Pork Tenderloin, 2 Pound
Olive Oil
Instructions
Schedule! This dish necessitates an overnight stay. Soak the cedar boards for at least two hours and up to overnight.
In a small mixing bowl, combine all of the dry spices and brown sugar.
Spray the tenderloins with olive oil and spread the spice mixture all over them. Allow for 30 minutes of resting time.
While ready to cook, preheat the oven to 350 degrees F for 10 to 15 mins with the lid closed.
Place the cedar planks on the barbecue, cover the lid, and cook for three minutes. Put a pork tenderloin on the hot side of each plank and flip.
Grilled the tenderloins for 15 to 20 mins, or until an instant-read thermometer reads 145 degrees F on the inside.
Cover the tenderloins with foil and set them aside for 5 mins before serving. Enjoy!

2.151 Baked Breakfast Sausage Casserole
Total Time: 1 Hour 15 Minutes, Serving: 8 people
Ingredients
main
Olive Oil or Vegetable Oil, 1 Tbsp
Middling Red or Green Bell Peppers, Diced, 2
Middling Yellow Onion, Diced, 1
Kosher Salt, Divided, Plus More as Needed, 3 Tbsp
Thick-Cut Bacon, 1 Pound
Field Breakfast Sausage, 1 Pound
Sliced Hash Browns or Tater Tots, Defrosted, 2 Pound
Grated Medium Cheddar Cheese, Divided, 3 Cup
Eggs Large, 10
Milk, 1/2 Cup
Freshly Field Black Pepper, 1 Tbsp
Instructions
Preheat the Pit Boss to 350°F for 15 minutes with the lid closed when ready to cook. Place a cast-iron pan on one side of the grill and warm with the lid covered while the grill preheats.
Place 1 tbsp olive oil in the cast iron pan after it has been warmed. Combine the chopped peppers, onion, and 1 tbsp salt in a mixing bowl. Cook until soft, approximately 20 minutes, stirring every 5 to 7 minutes with the lid covered.
Place the bacon on the grill at the same time and cook until crispy, approximately 25 to 30 minutes. Bacon should be drained on paper towels before being chopped into bite-size pieces.

Remove the peppers and onions from the pan when cooking and adding the sausage. Cook the sausage until it is crumbled and just cooked through, approximately 8 to 10 minutes total, raising the grill cover to stir it every few minutes.
Toss hash browns with the cooked bacon, cooked sausage, cooked peppers, salt, pepper, onions, and 1-1/2 cup cheese in huge mixing dish. Mixing well & pour into a 9x13-inch baking dish.
Whisk together the eggs, milk, 2 tbsp salt, and 1 tbsp freshly ground pepper in a separate dish. Allow 5 minutes for the eggs to soak into the other ingredients after
pouring the egg mixture equally over the other ingredients in the baking dish. The remaining cheese should be sprinkled on top.
Wrap the dish in foil and place it on the grill. Bake for 45 mins, then uncover the foil and bake for another fifteen min, or until the cheese is bubbling and the mixture is set. Enjoy!

2.152 Jalapeno Cheddar Smoked Sausages

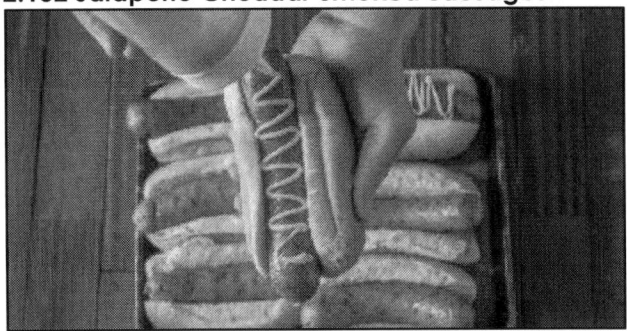

Total Time: 3 Hours 20 Minutes, Serving: 6 people
Ingredients
main
Hog Casings
Ground Pork, 2 Pound
Jalapeños, Seeded and Diced Small, 5 Medium
Shredded Sharp Cheddar Cheese, 1/2 Cup
Kosher Salt, 1/2 Tbsp
Black Pepper, 1 Tbsp
Granulated Garlic, 1 Tbsp
Onion Powder, 1 Tbsp
Instructions
Wash your hog casing in water as directed on the box. Make your sausage while the casings are soaking.
Pulse all the ingredients together in the bowl of a food processor. Don't overwork the meat; it should be a bit sticky, and all of the spices should be thoroughly integrated.
Fill your sausage stuffer with the sausage combination and stuff the casings according to the manufacturer's instructions. Make careful to fill the case to the desired length before adding the links. If you overstuff them, they'll explode when it's time to make the connections.
Hang the sausages to air dry for an hour or so at room temperature before transferring to the refrigerator to dry overnight.
Once ready to cook, preheat the Pit Boss to 180°F with the lid closed for fifteen min. If Super Smoke is available, use it for the best taste.
Smoke the sausages for 2 to 3 hrs, or until they reach a core temperature of 155°F, immediately on the grill grate. Enjoy!

2.153 Smoked Pork Loin with Sauerkraut and Apples
Total Time: 2 Hours 10 Minutes, Serving: 5
Ingredients

main
Pork Loin Roast, 1 (2 To 2-1/2 Lb.)
Pit Boss Pork & Poultry Rub
Sauerkraut, 1 Pound
Cooking Apples, Peeled, Cored and Sliced, 2 Large
Sweet Onion, Thinly Sliced, 1 Large
Brown Sugar, 1/3 Cup
Dark Beer, 1 Cup
Butter, 2 Tbsp
Bay Leaves, 2 Whole
Instructions
Preheat Pit Boss to 180°F and cook for 15 minutes with lid covered until ready to cook. If Super Smoke is available, use it for the best taste.
Season the pork loin with Pit Boss Pork & Poultry Rub or salt and pepper on both sides. Place the roast on the grill grate directly, cover, and smoke for 1 hour.
Place the cabbage, apples, onions, brown sugar, beer, butter, and bay leaves in a large Dutch pan or glassware baking dish. Straight on top of the sauerkraut combination, place the smoked pork loin. Using a lid or a sheet of foil, cover the pan.
Put the pan to the Pit Boss and raise the temperature to 350°F. Close the top and continue to roast the pork for another hour or until an immediate pizza stone register 160°F.
Set aside the roast on a chopping board to rest. Meanwhile, toss the sauerkraut mixture gently and serve on a serving dish. Layer the
sauerkraut and apples on top of the roast pork slices. Enjoy!

2.154 BBQ Paleo Pork Spareribs
Total Time: 4 Hours 15 Minutes, Serving: 4 people
Ingredients
Rub
Kosher Salt, 4 Tbsp
Ground Black Pepper, 2 Tbsp
Paprika, 4 Tbsp
Garlic Powder, 2 Tbsp
Onion Powder, 2 Tbsp
Chipotle Chile Powder, 1 Tbsp
main
St. Louis-Style Ribs, 2 Rack
BBQ Sauce
Ounce Organic Tomato Sauce, 15 Fluid
Water, 1/2 Cup
Apple Cider Vinegar, 1/2 Cup
Honey, 1/3 Cup
Onion Powder, 2 Tbsp
Ground Black Pepper, 1 1/2 Tbsp
Ground Mustard, 1 Tbsp
Paprika, 1 Tbsp
Instructions
Preheat Pit Boss to 225°F for fifteen min with the lid closed until ready to cook. If Extra Smoke is available, use it for the best taste.
Mix all rub ingredients in a bowl dish.
Eliminate the membrane from the back of the ribs and massage the rub on both sides. Allow 15 to 20 mins for the ribs to rest.
Place the ribs bone-side down on the grill and cook for 4 to 4-1/2 hours. Check the ribs' interior temperature; the ideal temperature is 202°F. Cook for a further thirty min or until the heat reaches the desired level.
Make the sauce although ribs are cooking. To make the sauce, mix all ingredients in a saucepan and cook through the stovetop.
Brush a thin coating of sauce on both surfaces of the ribs and simmer for another 10 minutes to allow the sauce to thicken.
Take the ribs from the grill and set them aside to rest for ten min before slicing. Enjoy!

2.155 Bacon Pork Pinwheels (Kansas Lollipops)
Total Time: 30 Minutes, Serving: 4 people
Ingredients
main
Pork Loin, 1 Whole
Salt And Pepper
Cavender's All Purpose Greek Seasoning
Bacon, 4 Slices
Pit Boss Sweet & Heat BBQ Sauce
Instructions
Preheat the Pit Boss to 450°F and shut the cover for fifteen min before cooking.
Remove any silvery skin or fat from the pork loin. Slice the pork belly lengthwise into four long strips using a sharp knife.
Sprinkle the pork with salt, pepper, and Cavender's All Purpose Greek Seasoning, then lay it flat. On the unseasoned side, flip the pork strips over and add bacon.
Begin wrapping the pig strips firmly, with the bacon on the inside.
Secure the pig roll in place with a skewer all the way through. Cook for 15 minutes on the grill grate with the pork rolls.
Drizzle the meat with Pit Boss Sweet & Heat BBQ Sauce. Coat the opposite side of each skewer after turning it over.
Depending on the size of your pork, cook for yet another 5 to 10 mins. Enjoy!

2.156 Gochujang BBQ Pork Ribs Marinated
Total Time: 5 Hours 30 Minutes, Serving: 4 people
Ingredients
main
Chopped Red Onion, 2 Large
Sesame Oil, 1/4 cup
Garlic, 3 Tbsp
Asian Pear, 2 Whole
Ginger, Minced, 3 Tbsp
Gochujang, 1 Cup
Ketchup, 1/2 Cup
Salt, 2 Tbsp
Toma rind Concentrate, 1 Cup
Brown Sugar, 4 Tbsp
St. Louis-Style Ribs, 3 Rack
Instructions
In a blender, purée the red onions and Asian pears until smooth.
Warm sesame oil and garlic in a big heavy-bottomed pan over medium-high heat. Toast till deep brown on both sides.
Mix the onion/pear purée and the minced ginger. Cook until the liquid has been reduced by a fourth (from 4 cups to 3 cups).
Stir in the other ingredients and season with salt to taste. To get the appropriate degree of heat, adjust the quantity of chili flake gochujang.
Marinate the ribs overnight in the marinade. Any leftover should be used to coat the ribs with while they're cooking.
Once ready to cook, preheat the oven to 225°F and cook for 10-15 mins with the lid covered.
Cook the ribs immediately on the grill for four hours, monitoring them halfway through. Brush the ribs with the leftover marinade and return to the grill for the final hour. Enjoy!

2.157 Home-Cured Bourbon Bacon
Total Time: 6 Hours 30 Minutes, Serving: 8 people
Ingredients
main

Pork Belly, Well-Chilled, 1 (2-1/2 Lb.)
Kosher Salt, 1/4 cup
Pink Curing Salt, 1 Tbsp
Bourbon, Divided, 1 Cup
Garlic Powder, 1 Tbsp
Brown Sugar, 1/2 Cup
Coarse Black Pepper, 3 Tbsp
Onion Powder, 1 Tbsp
Instructions
Round off the pork belly with a serrated knife even you have a rectangle piece about 12'' long and 6-7 inches broad. (You may use the trimmings to the flavor beans, collard greens, soups, and other dishes by curing and smoking them with the bacon.)
Place the pork belly on such a baking sheet that has been coated with parchment. Brush or spray bourbons on all surfaces, saving the remainder.
To make dry brine, combine all the ingredients in a large mixing bowl. Combine kosher & pink curing salts well in a small dish. Brown sugar, garlic powder, black
pepper and onion powder are added. Spread the dry brine over the pork belly on both sides and massage its in.
Place the pork in a large plastic baggie with any leftover brine. Refrigerate the bag on the sheet pan (if it spills) for seven days, turning it every day to disperse the brine and collected juices.
Clean the pork thoroughly under cold water on Day 7 and wipe dry with paper towels. Keep it chilled until you are eager to smoke it.
Once ready to cook, preheat the Pit Boss to 180°F with the lid closed for fifteen min. If Super Smoke is available, use it for the best taste.
Spread or spray the reserved bourbon all over the pork belly and place it on the barbecue grate. Smoke for 3 to 4 hours, keeping the temperature between
70- and 100-degrees Fahrenheit. Reapply the bourbon regularly.
Raise the Pit Boss temperature to 200°F and continue to smoke the pork for 1 1/2 to 2 hours, or until an instant-read meat thermometer reads 150°F.
Place the bacon on a wire rack to cool fully, removing any fat beads with paper towels. Put everything in a fresh resealable bag.
Refrigerate overnight before slicing with a long, sharp knife or a meat cutter. Chill for up to 2 weeks or freeze for up to 3 months after repackaging the bacon. Cook before you eat. Enjoy!

2.158 BBQ Pulled Pork with Sweet & Heat BBQ Sauce
Total Time: 9 Hours 15 Minutes, Serving: 4 people
Ingredients
main
Bone-In Pork Butt, 10 Pound
Pit Boss Pork & Poultry Rub, 2 Tbsp
Apple Juice, 1 1/2 Cup
Brown Sugar, 4 Tbsp
Salt, 1 Tbsp
To Taste Salt, 1
To Taste Pit Boss Pork & Poultry Rub, 1
As Needed Pit Boss Sweet & Heat BBQ Sauce, 1
Instructions
Trim all extra fat from the pig butt, leaving 1/4" of the fat cap intact. In a small dish, combine 2 tbsps. Pork and Poultry rub, brown sugar, apple juice and salt, stirring
until the sugar & salt are almost dissolved. Inject the apple juice mixture into pork butt each square inch or so. Apply the leftover rub to the pork butt's exterior.
While ready to cook, preheat the grill to 225°F with the lid covered for 15 minutes.
Place the pig butt firmly on the grill grate and cook for 6 hours, just until the air temp reaches 160
degrees Fahrenheit.
Cover the pork butt with two layers of foil and 1/2 cup apple juice. To keep the apple juice contained, wrap the tin foil firmly. Raise the temperature to 275°F and return the pork butt to the grill in a pan big enough to catch any drips. Cook for 3 hours more, or until the internal temperature reaches 205°F.
Take the bone from the grill and remove it. Cut Off any extra fat or tendons from the pork and shred it. If necessary, season with more Pork and Poultry Rub and salt.
Serve with Sweet & Heat BBQ sauce. Enjoy!

2.159 Applewood Smoked Bacon.
Total Time: 2 Hours 10 Minutes, Serving: 8 people
Ingredients
main
Kosher Salt, 1/2 cup
Brown Sugar, 1/2 Cup
Black Pepper, 1 Tbsp
Pork Belly, Skin Removed, 2 Pound
Instructions
In a mixing dish, combine the salt, brown sugar, and black pepper.
Spread the bacon cure mix all over the pork belly. Get Rid of as much air as possible and place it in a plastic bag.
Refrigerate for at least eight days. Turn the pork belly over every two days to ensure that the fluids are evenly distributed on both sides of the meat.
Take the pork belly from the fridge after eight days. Rinse the pork belly well, ensuring that all of the cure is removed, then pat dry.
When ready to cook, preheat the Pit Boss to 180°F with the lid closed for 15 minutes. If Extra Smoke is available, use it for the best taste.
In a jelly roll pan, pour a layer of ice, then put a rack on top of the ice, followed by the pork belly. The ice will keep the pork belly from becoming too hot while it is being smoked.
Place the ice pan and the pork belly rack immediately on the barbecue grate. Smoke the pork belly for 2 to 3 hours, or until it reaches a temperature of around 150°F on the inside.
Cover the bacon in plastic wrap and put it in the freezer for 30 to 60 mins, or until the bacon is almost frozen and the flesh is firm, after smoking the pig. This makes cutting a lot easier.
Thinly slice the bacon to the desired thickness. Use alone or in your favorite recipes. Enjoy!
When you are ready to cook, preheat the oven to 400°F with the lid covered for 15 minutes.
Put bacon slices immediately on the grill grates and cook for 8 to 10 mins, rotating once or twice, until desired crispness is achieved.
Transfer to a platter lined with paper towels to preserve crispiness

2.160 BBQ Pork Belly Tacos
Total Time: 2 Hours 30 Minutes, Serving: 6 people
Ingredients
main
Salt, 6 Tbsp
Brown Sugar, 4 Tbsp
Black Pepper, 1/2 Tbsp
Pork Belly, Skin Removed and Scored, 4 Pound
Carrots, Peeled and Julienned, 2 Whole
Red Onion, Thinly Sliced, 1 Whole
Persian Cucumbers, 2 Whole
Rice Wine Vinegar, 1/4 Cup

Water, 3/4 Cup
Sugar, 3 Tbsp
Red Pepper Flakes, 1 Tbsp
As Needed Flour Tortillas, 1
As Needed Cilantro, Finely Chopped, 1
Instructions
Put salt, sugar, and black pepper in a mixing bowl for the pork belly. Sprinkle pork belly evenly with the mixture. Allow resting in the fridge overnight, covered.
Once ready to cook, increase the heat to High and preheat for fifteen min with the lid closed.
Put the pork belly in a frying pan and cook it. Cook for thirty min, or until a tinge of color appears.
Lower the heat to 250°F and simmer for another 1-2 hours, or until the pork belly is cooked.
Remove the steak from the grill and set it aside for 30 minutes before slicing.
To make the pickled slaw, mix the carrots, onion, and cucumber in a medium mixing basin. In a small bowl, whisk together the vinegar, water, salt, sugar, and red pepper flakes until the sugar is dissolved. Pour the carrot mixture over the top and place it in
the refrigerator, ensuring sure the veggies are thoroughly immersed. Let at least 30 mins in the refrigerator before serving.
To make the tacos, cut the pork belly into 1/4" pieces once it has rested. Top each tortilla with pickled slaw and a piece or two of pork belly. Garnish with a sprinkling of fresh cilantro leaves. Enjoy!

2.161 Smoked Italian Lasagna Recipe
Total Time: 2 Hours, Serving: 8 people
Ingredients
main
Italian Pork Sausage, 1 Pound
Head of Garlic in Foil and Drizzled with Olive Oil, 1 Whole
Onion, Sliced into Rings, 1 Medium
Canned Diced Tomatoes, 2 Cup
Tomato Sauce, 1 Can (15 Oz)
Fresh Chopped Parsley, 3 Tbsp
Fresh Chopped Basil, 1 Tbsp
Sugar, 1 Tbsp
Container Ricotta Cheese, 1 (15 Oz)
Grated Parmesan Cheese, Divided, 1/2 Cup
Fresh Chopped Oregano, 1 Tbsp or Dried Oregano, 1-1/2 Tbsp
Lasagne Noodles, 12 Oven-Ready
Mozzarella Cheese, 2 cups
Parmesan Cheese, 1/4 cup
Instructions
Heat Pit Boss to 180°F and simmer for fifteen min with lid covered until ready to cook. If Super Smoke is available, use it for the best taste.
Put the sausages on the grill and cook for thirty min after the Pit Boss has started smoking (optional).
Take the sausage from the grill and raise the temperature to 375°F.
Transfer the sausage, together with the cut onions and garlic head, to the grill. 5–7 mins on each side on the grill for the sausage and onions. Fry the garlic for a total of approximately 25 mins.
Combine tomatoes, tomato sauce, 2 tbsps. parsley, basil, and sugar in a 10-inch pan. Bring to low heat and cook, stirring periodically. Reduce to low heat and continue to cook, uncovered, for 45 mins or until somewhat thickened.
Thinly slice the grilled onions and slice the cooked sausage. Toss them in with the sauce. Remove the garlic from the skin after it's browned and soft, then finely chop it. Add to the sauce right away.
Combine ricotta cheese, 1/4 cup Parmesan cheese, leftover 1 tbsp parsley, and oregano in a medium mixing dish.
Pour 1 cup of the sauce mixture into a 9x13 inch (3 quart) glass muffin pan that hasn't been oiled. Add four noodles on the top. One cup of the egg mix, a cup of the sauce mixture, 1 cup of the cream cheese, 1 cup of a sauce mixture, 1 cup of the complex mixtures, 1 cup of the sauce mixture, 1 cup of the sauce 2/3 cup mozzarella cheese is sprinkled over the top. Continue with four noodles, leftover cheese mixture, 1 cup sauce mixture, and 2/3 cup mozzarella cheese. Rest of the noodles and sauce mixture on top.
Top with the leftover mozzarella and Parmesan.
Bake for 30 mins at 375°F with the lasagna covered in Aluminum foil. Remove the lid and bake for another 15 mins, or until hot and bubbling. Allow for a 15-min rest before cutting.

2.162 Holiday Prosciutto-Wrapped Pork Tenderloin
Total Time: 40 Minutes, Serving: 4 people
Ingredients
main
Pork Tenderloin, 2 Pound
Olive Oil, 2 Tbsp
Rosemary, Minced, 2 Tbsp
Garlic, Minced, 1 Tbsp
Salt, 1 Tbsp
Pepper, 1 Tbsp
Butcher's Twine
Prosciutto, 1/2 Tbsp
Bacon, 1/2 Pound
Instructions
Trim the tenderloin of extra fat and silver skin and put it aside.
In a slight bowl, whisk all together with the olive oil, rosemary, garlic, salt, and pepper.
Rub the tenderloins with the rub and put them aside. Lay four or five 8-inch lengths of butcher's twine horizontally on the work surface, two inches apart.
Place a couple of perpendicular slices of bacon or pancetta on top of the string.
On top of the bacon/pancetta, place one slice of prosciutto ham.
On top of the prosciutto, place the tenderloin.
Place one to two additional slices of prosciutto ham on top of the pork, followed by bacon or pancetta; pull twine ends up and over the meat. Tighten the tie but not to the point of squeezing the tenderloin.
Do the same thing with the second tenderloin.
Preheat the Pit Boss grill to high heat. Allow 10-15 minutes for the grill to heat up. Place the tenderloins directly on the grill grate and roast for 16-18 minutes, rotating once, until a thermometer inserted into the thickest part of the loin registers 145 degrees F.
Remove from the grill and set aside for at least 5 mins before slicing and removing the strings. Season with salt & pepper and a drizzle of extra virgin olive oil.

2.163 Pernil
Total Time: 3 Hours 10 Minutes, Serving: 8 people
Ingredients
main
Boneless Pork Shoulder, 7 Pound
Orange, Juiced, 2
whole Lime, Juiced, Two
Cilantro, 3/4
Kosher Salt, 2 Tbsp
Cumin, 1 Tbsp
Dried Oregano, 1 Tbsp
Pit Boss Prime Rib Rub, 1 Tbsp

Clove Garlic, 4
Olive Oil, 1/2 Cup
Instructions
Make deep vertical and horizontal incisions in a vertical gradient along the pork shoulder using a sharp knife.
Halve the oranges and squeeze the juice into a dish. 2 limes should be zested using a little grater. Lime juice should be added to the bowl of orange juice.
Tear about 3/4 of the coriander head and add it to the dish as well. 1 tsp Pit Boss's Prime rib, 2 tbsp kosher salt, 1 tsp cumin, 1 tsp dried oregano. Set aside four garlic cloves and 1/2 cup olive oil to mix everything.
Once your marinade is thoroughly combined, coat all of the pork and set it aside for one hour at room temperature.
Just after the pork has a marinade for an hour, set the Pit Boss to "Smoke" and leave the lid open until the fire is ready (4 to 5 minutes).
Once your grill is warmed and ready, reduce the temperature to 300 degrees and put your meat on it.
Bake your pork for 3 hours at 300 degrees. Remove the grill from the heat and set it aside for 10 minutes.
Thinly slice your meat and serve over rice.
Garnish the pork with cilantro and the leftover lime juice. Enjoy!

2.164 Meaty Beer Beans
Total Time: 2 Hours 25 Minutes, Serving: 8 people
Ingredients
main
Bacon, 1 Pound
Red Bell Pepper, Diced, 2
Yellow Onion, Diced, 1
Pre-Cooked Sausage Links, Diced, 3 Cup
Garlic Powder, 1/2 Tbsp
Onion Powder, 1 Tbsp
Smoked Paprika, 1 Tbsp
Cumin, 1 Tbsp
Black Pepper, 1/2 Tbsp
Chile Powder, 1 Tbsp
Worcestershire Sauce, 1 Tbsp
Mustard Yellow, 1 Tbsp
Sugar Brown, 1/4 Cup
Chopped Chipotle Peppers in Adobo Sauce, 1 Chile from 1 Can
Apple Juice 1 cup
Beer 24 Ounce
Pinto Beans, Drained and Soaked, 2 (16 Oz)
Instructions
Preheat Pit Boss to 450°F and cook for fifteen min with lid covered until ready to cook. Preheat a deep-dish Broiler pan straight on the grill grate for 15 minutes with the lid covered.
Chop the bacon and place it in the preheated Dutch oven. Cook the bacon until it is crispy brown, then remove it from the pan and drain all except 2 tbsps. of oil.
Toss the bell pepper, onion, and sausage with the reserved bacon oil in the Dutch oven. Cook until onions and peppers are transparent and tender. Toss the bacon back into the pan.
Combine the garlic powder, onion powder, smoked paprika, cumin, black pepper, chili powder, Worcestershire sauce, yellow mustard, brown sugar, beer, pinto beans, apple juice, and chipotle chili in a large mixing bowl. Stir everything together well.
Bring the beans to a low boil. Reduce heat to 275°F and simmer for 2-1/2 to 3 hours, or until sauce has thickened, adding additional liquid as needed or covering with a lid once the level has been decreased. Enjoy!

2.165 Baked Ballpark Mac and Cheese
Total Time: 1 hour 5 Minutes, Serving: 2 people
Ingredients
main
Elbow Macaroni or Cavatappi Noodles, 1 Pound
Butter, 2 Tbsp
Yellow Onion, Diced, 1/2 Whole
Garlic, Minced, 2 Clove
All-Purpose Flour, 2 Tbsp
Milk, 2 1/2 Cup
Salt And Pepper
Ketchup, 2 Tbsp
Mustard, 1 Tbsp
Shredded Cheddar Cheese, 2 Cup
Shredded Gruyere Cheese, 1 Cup
Frankfurters, 4
Instructions
Over high heat, bring a large pot of salted water to a boil. Fry the noodles until they are al dente, as directed on the box. Set aside after straining and rinsing with cold water to halt the cooking.
Melt butter in a medium saucepan over medium heat. Add the onion and cook until it is soft. Sauté for another minute, or until garlic is aromatic. Cook for another minute after adding the flour.
Slowly drizzle in the milk while whisking constantly, and simmer until thickened (should coat the back of a spoon). Season with salt and pepper to taste, then stir in the mustard and ketchup.
Remove the saucepan from the heat and stir in 1 1/2 cups cheddar and 1/2 cup gruyere cheese. Remove from the equation.
Once ready to cook, increase the temperature to High and preheat for fifteen min with the lid closed.
Grill the franks for 4-6 minutes, rotating periodically, until lightly browned and warmed thoroughly. Confiscate the steaks from the grill and slice them.
Stir in the cut franks and noodles to cover them in the cheese sauce.
Reduce the temperature of the grill to 350°F.
Transfer the mac and cheese to a cast-iron skillet, cover with the remaining cheese and bake for 20-25 minutes, or until golden brown and the cheese has melted.
For serving, split the mac and cheese into four bowls and top with extra chopped franks, ketchup, and mustard if preferred. Enjoy!

2.166 Holiday Smoked Cheese Log
Total Time: 1 Hour 10 Minutes, Serving: 8 people
Ingredients
main
Cream Cheese, 16 Ounce
Shredded Cheddar Cheese, 3 Cup
Worcestershire Sauce, 1 Tbsp
Hot Sauce, 1 Tbsp
Bacon, 8 Slices
Green Onion, 2
Coarsely Chopped Pecans, 1 cup
Instructions
Mix the cream cheese (room temperature) and the cheddar cheese in a mixing bowl with an electric mixer or a big spoon. Combine the Worcestershire sauce and spicy sauce in a mixing bowl. Recombine the ingredients.
Toss in the cooked and crumbled bacon, as well as the green onions. Mix until everything is well mixed.
Freeze for 4 hours, just until the cheese mixture is hard enough to shape, by covering the bowl with plastic wrap. Form it into a log and sprinkle the toasted nuts on top.

Cover with plastic wrap. To keep the cheese log from becoming too mushy although it is smoking, freeze it overnight. Preheat the Pit Boss to 180 degrees Fahrenheit the following day for 10-15 minutes.
Remove the frozen cheese log from the freezer and unwrap it. Place on a sheet pan and smoke for 1 hour. Make sure it doesn't become too soft by keeping an eye on it.
Transfer the cheese logs to a serving dish and serve with crackers of your choice. (Refrigerate the cheese for an hour or two if it's too soft.)

2.167 Smoked Ribs with the Coconut Rum BBQ Sauce by Journey South
Total Time: 6 Hours 20 Minutes, Serving: 8 people
Ingredients
main
Pit Boss 'Que BBQ Sauce, 1 Bottle
White Rum, 2 Cup
Coconut Milk, 2 Can
Tomato, 2 Chopped.
Clove Garlic, 2
St. Louis-Style Ribs, 3 Rack
Pit Boss Rub, 4 Tbsp
Butter, 6 Tbsp
Brown Sugar, 1 1/2 Cup
Agave, 1 1/2 Cup
Instructions
To make the BBQ sauce, preheat the Pit Boss according to the manufacturer's instructions. Preheat the oven to 350 ° F. and bake for 10 to 15 mins with the lid covered.
Chop the tomatoes and garlic, then mix all ingredients in a cast-iron skillet. To mix, stir everything together. Cook for 45 to 60 mins with the pan straight on the grill grate. Remove the grate from the grill and place it in a blender. Puree until completely smooth.
Save the sauce until you're ready to use it on the ribs.
Reduce the temperature of the grill to 250 ° F for the ribs. Remove the membrane and trim the ribs. Season ribs with Pit Boss Rub and put rib side down on barbecue grate or Pit Boss rib rack with bone resting on the rack. 3 hours in the oven
On the table, stack two pieces of tin foil big enough to cover one rack of ribs. Place 3 tbsps. butter, 1/2 cup brown sugar, and 1/2 cup agave nectar in the middle of the foil.
Put the spines on top of the brown sugar mixture, meat side down, and wrap firmly. Rep with the last two racks.
Place all ribs meat side down on the grill grate (no rack) and cook for another 1-1/2 to 2 hours or until the core temperature reaches 203°F.
Eliminate the ribs from grill & baste them with half cup of Coconut Rum BBQ sauce on each rack. Return to the grill for another 10 minutes to enable the sauce to thicken.
Take the ribs from the grill and slice them. Enjoy!

2.168 Grilled Sugar Snap Peas & Smoked Bacon
Total Time: 35 Minutes, Serving: 4 people
Ingredients
main
Sugar Snap Peas, 2 Pound
Salt and Pepper, 1
Bacon, 1 Pound
Extra-Virgin Olive Oil, 2 Tbsp
Butter, 2 Tbsp
Garlic Minced, 1 Clove
Bourbon, 1/4 cup
Shallot, 2 Medium
Maple Syrup, 2 Tbsp
Instructions
Preheat the Pit Boss to 350°F for fifteen min with the lid closed when ready to cook.
Now toss peas with the olive oil in a medium bowl & season with salt and black pepper to taste.
Cover the barbecue grate with a grill mat or tray to keep peas from falling through.
Put peas on grill mat and cook for 10 minutes, or until cooked but still brilliant green.
Cook bacon slices next to peas on the grill for 15-20 minutes, or until fat is rendered and slightly crunchy.
Melt butter in a skillet over medium-high heat while the bacon and peas simmer.
Add the shallot and garlic and heat until the shallot and garlic are soft and cooked through. Cook until the bourbon has been reduced by half. Toss in the maple syrup and season with salt and pepper to taste. Remove from the equation.
Take the bacon from the skillet and cut it into 1/2-inch pieces. Combine the bacon, grilled sugar snap peas, and maple bourbon mixture in a mixing bowl. Enjoy!

2.169 Double-Decker Pulled Pork Nachos with Smoked Cheese
Total Time: 1 hour, Serving: 4 people.
Ingredients
main
Pepper Jack Cheese, 8 Ounce
Cheese, Sharp Cheddar, 8 Ounce
Tortilla Chips
Leftover Pulled Pork, 2 Cup
Black Olives
Jalapeño, Diced.
Cilantro
Instructions
Preheat the Pit Boss to 165 degrees Fahrenheit when ready to cook. Preheat for 10-15 mins with the lid closed.
Place the frozen cheese on a rack on top of an ice-filled pan. To help the cheese smoke more rapidly, chop it into smaller pieces, maybe 2 or 3 chunks per block.
Toast the cheeses for 45 to 60 mins and then set them aside to cool. Set aside the shredded cheeses (about 1 cup of each).
Preheat the Pit Boss to 350 degrees and cook for 10 to 15 minutes with the lid covered.
Arrange the tortilla chips on a large baking sheet and sprinkle with the shredded, smoked cheeses equally. Cook for approximately 10 minutes, or until the cheese is melted and bubbling, on the Pit Boss barbecue grate.
Take the pan off the Pit Boss and begin putting together the double-decker nachos. Build the nachos with a bottom layer of cheesy chips, a layer of pulled pork, and cheesy chips on top. Add your favorite nacho toppings to finish it off. Warm the dish before serving.

2.170 Smoked Citrus & Polenta Pork Tenderloin
Total Time: 3 Hours 15 Minutes, Serving: 4 people
Ingredients
main
Dark Brown Sugar, 1 cup
Smoked Paprika, 1/2 Tbsp
Ground Cumin, 1/2 Tbsp
Dried Fennel Seed, 1/2 Tbsp
Cayenne Pepper, 1/2 Tbsp
Garlic, 3 Clove
Grapefruit, Zested, Supreme, 1
Salt, 1/2 Tbsp
Tenderloin Pork, 1
Chicken Stock 1/2 Cup
For Serving 1/2 Polenta or Mashed Potatoes

Olive Oil Spray
Mustard Dijon, 1/4 cup
Olive Oil Extra-Virgin, 1/4 Cup
Honey, 1/4 Cup
Mixed Salad Greens, 2 Cup
Instructions
Once ready to cook, turn on the Pit Boss and adjust the timer to 225 ° F Preheat for 10 to 15 mins with the lid closed.
In a food stuff processor, puree half cup brown sugar, cumin, paprika, fennel, garlic, cayenne, grapefruit zest, all grapefruit segments, and salt until very smooth. Transfer mixture to a large mixing bowl, reserving 1/4 cup for grapefruit sauce.
Place pork tenderloin in the basin and coat thoroughly on both sides. Wrap in plastic wrap and set apart at temp for 15 minutes.
In a BBQ-safe saucepan or dish, mix 1/4 cup leftover marinade with 1/2 cup chicken stock to make the grapefruit sauce. Place the burgers on the Pit Boss grill.
Cook the tenderloin for about 3 hours on the Pit Boss, or until it reaches a core temperature of 145 degrees F.
Next, cut 1/2-inch polenta discs into slices. Spray the tops with olive oil melted butter, then sprinkle Dijon mustard on each disc and evenly distribute the remaining 1/2 cup brown sugar. At the two-hour point, equally arrange the polenta discs on the grill for about 1 hour, or until the edges are crispy.
Vinaigrette: Combine grapefruit juice, olive oil, and honey in a large mixing bowl. Remove from the equation.
Remove the pork tenderloin from the grill when it reaches 145 degrees F and let it rest for ten min before slicing into 1/2-inch medallions.
Put pork slices on top of polenta pieces to serve. Drizzle vinaigrette over greens. Enjoy!

2.171 Pit Boss Pulled Pork Sandwiches
Total Time: 11 Hours 15 Minutes, Serving: 8 people
Ingredients
major
Shoulder Bone-In Pork, 1 (5-7 Lb.)
Poultry Rub & Pit Boss Pork
Spray Bottle 2 Cup Apple Juice
Pit Boss BBQ Sauce
Hamburger, 10 Buns
For Serving, Coleslaw
Instructions
Season both sides of the pork roast with Pit Boss Poultry rub and Pork.
Once ready to cook, preheat the Pit Boss to 225°F with the lid closed for fifteen min. If Super Smoke is available, use it for the best taste.
Place the roast fat-side up on the grill grate and smoke for 3 hours. After the first hour, sprinkle the roasts with apple juice every hour.
Move the pork to the throwaway Aluminum foil pan big enough to retain the roast after 3 hours. Increase the grill temperature to 250°F and cook for another 6 to 8 hours, or until an instant-read meat thermometer placed in heaviest part of the flesh, but not touching bone, reads 203°F. Cover the pork sloppily with Aluminum foil if it begins to brown too much.
Shift the pork roast to a cutting board and set aside for 20 minutes to rest. Fill a gravy separator halfway with the juices from the bottom of the pan. Anything fat that has risen to the top should be discarded.
Pull the pork into pieces with your hands (ideally wearing lined, heavy-duty rubber gloves to protect your hands from the heat). Discard the bone, as well as any fat lumps, including the cap. Transfer each piece to a large mixing basin and shred it.
Season with more rub and wet with the pork
liquid you set aside. Mix your preferred Pit Boss BBQ sauce with the pulled pork.
To serve, pile the pork mixture into hamburger buns and top with coleslaw. Enjoy!

2.172 Smoked Pork Spareribs
Total Time: 4 Hours 15 Minutes, Serving: 8 people
Ingredients
main
Pork Spareribs, 2 Rack (6 Lb.)
Pit Boss Pork & Poultry Rub, 3 Tbsp
Pit Boss BBQ Sauce, 9 Ounce
Apple Juice, 1 Cup
Instructions
Preheat Pit Boss to 250°F and cook for fifteen min with lid covered until ready to cook. If Extra Smoke is available, use it for the best taste.
Strip the silver skin off the back of the ribs and trim any extra fat if your butcher has not already done so.
Rub the ribs with Pit Boss Pork & Poultry rub on both sides.
Place the racks of spareribs bone-side down upon on grill grates and cook for 4 hours. Spray the ribs with apple juice after the first hour. After that, keep spraying with apple juice every hour.
After 2 hours, begin monitoring the temperature. After 3 to 4 hours, the interior temperature should be 203°F.
Whenever the internal temperature reaches 203°F, rub both sides of the rib with your favorite Pit Boss BBQ sauce. Send Back the ribs to the grill and cook for another 30 to 60 mins to let the sauce thicken.
To serve, split each slab in half or into single ribs and serve with a side of extra BBQ sauce. Enjoy!

2.173 St. Louis BBQ Ribs
Total Time: 4 Hours 20 Minutes, Serving: 4 people
Ingredients
main
St. Louis-Style Ribs, 2 Rack
Pit Boss Pork & Poultry Rub, 1/4 Cup
Apple Juice, 1 cup
Pit Boss Sweet & Heat BBQ Sauce, 1 Bottle
Instructions
Remove the membranes from the rear of the ribs and trim the ribs. Rub the front back of the ribs with an equal layer of rub. Allow for 20 minutes of sitting time or up to four hours if refrigerated.
Once ready to cook, preheat the Pit Boss to 225°F with the lid closed for fifteen min.
Place the ribs on the barbecue grate, bone side down. Fill a spray bottle halfway with apple juice and evenly coat the ribs.
Remove the ribs from the grill after 3 hours and cover them in Aluminum foil. Leave a hole at one end of the foil and pour in the remaining apple juice (about 6 oz) before securely wrapping it.
Send Back the ribs to the grill, meat side down, and smoke for another 3 hours.
Check the core temperature of the ribs after 1 hour. When the core temperature of the ribs hits 203 degrees Fahrenheit, they are done.
Remove the ribs from the foil when they're done and apply a small sauce coating over the ribs' front and back.
Return to the grill and simmer for another 10 minutes to allow the sauce to thicken.
Remove the ribs from the grill once the sauce has set and let them rest for ten min. Slice the ribcage in between the bones to serve. Enjoy!

2.174 Apple Juice BBQ Brined Pulled Pork
Total Time: 11 Hours 20 Minutes, Serving: 6 people
Ingredients
Brine
Apple Juice, 4 cups
Brown Sugar, Packed, 1 cup
Black Peppercorn, 1 Tbsp
Kosher Salt, 1/4 cup
Cold Water, 2 Cup
Lemon, Sliced, 1.
Orange, Sliced, 1.
Sprig Thyme Fresh, 2
Sprig Fresh Rosemary, 2
main
Bone-In Pork Shoulder, 1 (10-12 Lb.)
Pit Boss Pork & Poultry Rub
Pit Boss 'Que BBQ Sauce
Hamburger Buns, 10
Coleslaw
Green Cabbage, 1 Cup
Shredded Carrot, 1/2 Cup
Onion, Thinly Sliced, 1/2 Red
Mayonnaise, 1/2 cup
Sour Cream, 1/2 Cup
White Wine Vinegar, 2 Tbsp
Sugar, 1 Tbsp
Salt
Pepper
Instructions
Plan of time; this dish brines overnight & roasts all day, but results are good worth the effort.
Bring Together all the brine ingredients in a large mixing bowl with 2 cups water and
bring to a boil over normal heat. Then cook till salt and sugar have properly dissolved.
Then Remove from the heat & whisk in 2 cups ice until completely dissolved. Allow brine to cool fully before using.
In a nutrition bucket or foods storage container, pour over the pig butt. Ascertain that the pork is completely immersed in the brine. Refrigerate overnight, covered.
Once ready to cook, preheat the Pit Boss to 225°F with the lid closed for fifteen min. If Super Smoke is available, use it for the best taste.
Take the pork roast from the marinade and set it aside while the grill warms up. Inject some of the leftover brine into the pork using a meat injector approximately every 2 inches throughout the whole roast. Set aside the remainder of the brine in a dish. During the cooking process, this will be your mop sauce.
Cover the roast with Pit Boss Pork & Poultry Rub on both sides.
Place the pork roast fat-side up on the grill grate and smoke for 3 hours, wiping every hour after the first hour with the apple juice brine.
Place the pork roast in a disposable Aluminum foil pan that is big enough to accommodate it.
Preheat the grill to 250 degrees Fahrenheit and put the pan immediately on the grilling grate. Cook for another 6 to 8 hours, or until an instant-read thermometer inserted into the thickest part of the meat reads 204°F to 206°F without touching the bone. Covering the pork loosely with Aluminum foil if it begins to brown too much. Place the pork roast on a chopping board and set aside for at least 20 minutes to rest.
Strain the liquids from the pan's bottom into a gravy separator. Pull the pork into pieces with your hands. Discard the bone, as well as any fat lumps, including the cap. Transfer each piece to a large mixing basin and shred it. Season the pulled pork with more rub and moisten with the pork liquid you set aside.
To make the coleslaw, whisk together mayonnaise, vinegar, sour cream, sugar, salt & black pepper in a small mixing dish. Merge the cabbage, carrot, and onion in a separate medium bowl. Stir the mayonnaise mixture into the cabbage mixture to coat it.
Toss the pulled pork with Pit Boss 'Que BBQ Sauce and combine thoroughly or serve the barbecue sauce on the side. Serve with coleslaw and the pork mixture on hamburger buns. Enjoy.

2.175 Smoked Dry Rubbed Baby Back Ribs
Total Time: 5 Hours 15 Minutes, Serving: 4 people
Ingredients
Rub
Dark Brown Sugar, 1/4 Cup
Sea Salt, 1/4 Cup
Pimentón (Spanish Smoked Paprika), 1/4 Cup
Black Pepper, 2 Tbsp
Granulated Onion, 2 Tbsp
Granulated Garlic, 2 Tbsp
Ground Cumin, 1 Tbsp
Ground Cinnamon, 1/2 Tbsp
Ground Nutmeg, 1/4 Tbsp
main
Baby Back Ribs, 4 Rack (8-10 Lb. Total)
Pit Boss 'Que BBQ Sauce, 2 Cup
Pit Boss 'Que BBQ Sauce
Instructions
To make the rub, whisk together all of the rub ingredients in a small dish.
Remove the thin silver skin off the bone-side of the ribs if your butcher hasn't already done so by pushing the point of a butter knife or screwdriver beneath the membrane over a central bone. Take the membrane off using paper towels to obtain a stronghold.
Rub equally sides of the ribs with the rub. For each side, you'll need approximately 1-1/2 tbsps. of rub.
When ready to cook, preheat the Pit Boss to 250°F with the lid closed for 15 minutes.
Place the ribs on the grill grate bone-side down. Cook the ribs in the smoker until they are browned, and tender, and the internal temperature reaches 203°F.
Allow the ribs to rest after removing them from the barbecue grate.
Raise the Pit Boss's temperature to 375°F and let it warm.
Spray the ribs with Pit Boss 'Que BBQ Sauce and cook for 6 to 8 minutes on each side, or until the sauce has thickened.
To serve, cut any rack into half or individual ribs. Enjoy.

2.176 Smoked Bacon Cheese Ball

Total Time: 45 Minutes, Serving: 8 people
Ingredients
main
Cream Cheese, Room Temperature, 1 Pound
Sour Cream, 1/4 Cup
Bacon, Sliced, 1/2 Pound

Green Onions, Thinly Sliced, 4 Tbsp
Shredded Cheddar Cheese, 1 Cup
Garlic Powder, 1 Tbsp
To Taste Salt, 1
Instructions
Preheat the grill to 180°F and shut the cover for fifteen min when ready to cook.
In a medium baking dish, combine the cream cheese and sour cream and broil.
Burn for 20 mins or until you achieve the appropriate amount of smoke.
Remove the grill from the heat and raise the temperature to 350°F.
Whenever the grill is hot, put bacon slices directly on the grate for 15-20 minutes, or until crispy and fat has rendered.
Turn off the heat and set it aside to cool at room temperature.
In a food processor bowl, combine the smoked cream cheese, sour cream, cheddar cheese, green onion, garlic powder, and salt while the bacon is cooling.
Pulse until well mixed, then transfer to plastic cover. Produce the cheese mixture into a ball and firmly cover it in plastic wrap. Refrigerate until well cold.
Cut the bacon into tiny pieces and scatter the chopped chives on a dish. Take the cheese ball out of the refrigerator, unwrap it, and roll it in the bacon mixture.
Arrange the cheese ball on a platter and serve with crackers of your choosing. Enjoy.

2.177 Smoked Rendezvous Ribs
Total Time: 2 Hours 15 Minutes, Serving: 4 people
Ingredients
main
Apple Cider Vinegar, 1/2 Cup
Water, 1/2 Cup
Pit Boss BBQ Sauce, 1/2 Cup
Poultry Rub & Pit Boss Pork, 2 Tbsp
Membrane Removed 3 Rack Baby Back Pork Ribs.
As Needed Pit Boss Pork & Poultry Rub, 1
Instructions
Mix vinegar, water, barbecue sauce, and Pit Boss Pork & Poultry Rub in a bowl and mix. Place the sauce, as well as a BBQ mop or basting brush, on the grill.
Once ready to cook, preheat the Pit Boss to 325°F for 15 minutes with the lid closed.
Place the ribs meat-side up on the grill grate.
After 30 minutes of grilling, begin cleaning. Every 15 min, mop the floor. Test the ribs for doneness after two hrs.
Place a toothpick in the middle of a rack between the bones. The ribs are done if
there is little or no resistance (or close to it). If you do not like the ribs, keep grilling them in 30-minute intervals, mopping every fifteen minutes.
Whenever the ribs are finished, move them to a cutting board and finish with the mop sauce. Pit Boss Pork and Poultry Rub gently sprinkled.
Remove the ribs from the oven and rest for several minutes before cutting them into a half slab or single ribs. Enjoy.

2.178 Bagel Breakfast Sandwich
Total Time: 35 Minutes, Serving: 2 people
Ingredients
main
Bacon, 6 Slices
Everything Bagels, 2
Butter 2 Tbsp
For Serving, 2 Slices Your Choice of Cheese
Eggs 4

Instructions
Once you are ready to cook, fire up the Pit Boss according to the manufacturer's directions. Preheat the oven to 400 degrees F, lid covered, for 10-15 mins.
To make the bacon: Put the bacon slices immediately on the grilling grate and cook for 8-10 mins, rotating once or twice to get the required crispness.
Transfer to a dish lined with paper towels to preserve crispy. Cut the bacon pieces in half using a sharp knife.
Preheat the grill to 350 degrees F and set a 10-inch cast-iron pan on the lowest grill grate, cover, and let cook for 10 minutes.
Cover the cut side of the bagels with 1 tbsp melted butter while the pan is cooking.
Place the greased side of the bagel halves on the grill grates and toast for approximately two minutes, or until golden brown. Toss the
bagels around. On the bottom half of the bagel pieces, place a slice of cheese.
Close the cover and wait one minute for the cheese to melt. Place the bagels on the top warming rack or remove them from the grill.
Pour the last tbsp of butter into the cast iron pan. Add the eggs, season with salt and pepper, and cook until they're done to your liking, turning after a minute if needed.
To assemble the sandwiches, layer three bacon pieces on top of the cheese-covered bagel slices, then gently top with two eggs.
Finish with the last toasted bagel piece. Serve right away. Enjoy.

2.179 Western Breakfast Casserole
Total Time: 55 Minutes, Serving: 8 people
Ingredients
main
Bread, Cubed, 6 Slices
Whole Eggs, 6
Milk, 1 Cup
Ground Mustard, 3/4 Tbsp
Salt, 3/4 Tbsp
Black Pepper, 3/4 Tbsp
Chorizo, 6 Ounce
Ground Turkey, 6 Ounce
Onion, Chopped, 1/2 Whole
Red Bell Pepper, 1/2 Whole
Anaheim Chile, Chopped, 1/2 Whole
Cooked and chopped, 4 Slices Bacon.
Baby Spinach, 1 cup
Swiss Cheese, 1 cup
Cheese, Sharp Cheddar, 1 Cup
Jalapeño Cheddar Cheese, Grated, 1 Cup

Instructions
Heat the stove to 350 ° F and leave the lid covered for 10 to 15 mins whenever ready to cook.
Coat a 9-inch-by-13-inch baking sheet with non - stick cooking spray. In the bottom of the pan, arrange the bread cubes in a single layer. Cast aside the eggs, milk, ground mustard, salt, and black pepper that have been whisked together.
Cook the chorizo and minced turkey in a pan on heat until fully done.
Sauté the onion and peppers in the pan until they are soft.
Sauté for another minute with the garlic and fried bacon, then add the spinach and simmer until it wilts.
Spread half of the meat and vegetable combination, part of the egg mixture, and half of the cheeses on the bread. Repeat the layering until all of the ingredients are utilized.
Bake at 350°F for 35-40 mins, or until well cooked, uncovering

for the final 5-10 minutes to allow the cheese to brown slightly on top. Enjoy.

2.180 Baked Bacon Caramel Popcorn
Total Time: 1 hour 10 Minutes, Serving: 6 people
Ingredients
main
Bacon, 1 Pound
Popcorn Kernels, 1 cup
Unsalted Butter, 2 Stick
Salt, 1/2 Tbsp
Brown Sugar, Packed, 2 cups
Kentucky Bourbon, 1/4 cup
Baking Soda, 11 Tbsp
Vanilla, 2 Tbsp
Instructions
Preheat the Pit Boss to 350°F for fifteen min with the lid closed when ready to cook.
Cook for 15 to 20 mins, or until fat is rendered and bacon is gently browned, by placing bacon strips immediately on the grill grate. Remove the chicken from the grill and cut it into 1/2-inch pieces. Remove from the equation.
Pop popcorn kernels in a popcorn maker while the grill cools. Set aside popped kernels and bacon in a large mixing basin.
Melt butter, salt, and sugar in a medium saucepan over medium-high heat. Bring the mixture to a boil, reduce to low heat and continue to simmer until an instant-read thermometer registers 275°F. Remove from heat quickly and mix in the whiskey, vanilla, and baking powder. Because it will bubble up and emit steam, proceed with care.
Lower the heat to 225°F and let the grill cool for 10 to 15 minutes.
Toss the bacon and popcorn in the caramel sauce to coat. Popcorn should be spread out on a big sheet pan lined with parchment paper.
Place the sheet tray immediately on the grill grate and cook for 15 to 20 mins at 225°F, keeping an eye on the caramel to ensure it does not burn.
Remove the popcorn from the grill and place it on a parchment-lined counter. Allow it cool for thirty min or until the caramel has hardened. Enjoy.

2.181 Smoked Porchetta with Italian Salsa Verde
Total Time: 3 Hours 30 Minutes, Serving: 8 people
Ingredients
main
Dried Fennel Seed, 3 Tbsp
Red Pepper Flakes, 2 Tbsp
Sage, Minced, 2 Tbsp
Rosemary, Minced, 1 Tbsp
Garlic, Minced, 3 Clove
Lemon Zest
Orange Zest
Salt And Pepper
Skin-On Pork Belly, 6 Pound
Salt And Pepper
Shallot, Thinly Sliced, 1 Whole
Parsley, Minced, 6 Tbsp
Freshly Minced Chives, 2 Tbsp
Fresh Oregano, 1 Tbsp
White Wine Vinegar, 3 Tbsp
Kosher Salt, 1/2 Tbsp
Olive Oil, 3/4 Cup
Dijon Mustard, 1/2 Tbsp
Fresh Lemon Juice

Instructions
To make the herb combination, combine fennel seeds, red pepper flakes, sage, rosemary, garlic, citrus zest, salt, and pepper in a medium mixing bowl.
Scratch a crosshatch pattern on the pork belly skin side up on a clean work surface. Season the meat side of the pork belly with salt, pepper, and half of the herb mixture.
Arrange the chopped pork loin in the belly's middle and massage with the remaining herb mixture. Salt & pepper to taste.
Form a cylindrical shape with the pork belly by rolling it around the loin and tying it firmly with kitchen twine at 1" intervals.
Season the exterior with salt and pepper, then place it in the refrigerator, uncovered, overnight to dry.
When you're ready to cook, fire up the Pit Boss grill and choose the Smoke setting.
Put the pig on the rack, seams side down on a baking sheet and bake with a rack.
Smoke for 1 hour by placing the pan directly on the grill grate. Raise the grill temperature to 325°F and roast for 2 1/2 hours, or until the internal temperature of the meat reaches 135°F. Tent with foil if the outside starts to burn before the required interior temperature is achieved.
Remove the steak from the grill and set it aside for 30 minutes before slicing.
To Totalize the Italian salsa, merge shallot, chives, parsley, vinegar, salt, & oregano in a medium mixing bowl. After whisking in the olive oil, add the mustard and lemon juice.
Serve with Italian salsa verde on the side.

2.182 Bacon Chili Cheese Dogs
Total Time: 55 Minutes, Serving: 2 people
Ingredients
main
Bacon, 4 Slices
Onion, Chopped, 1 Medium
Ground Beef, 1 Pound
Garlic, Minced, 2 Clove
Tomato Paste, 1 Tbsp
Tomato Sauce, 1 Can
Stewed Tomatoes, 1 Can
Chili Powder, 1 Tbsp
Smoked Paprika, 1/2 Tbsp
Cumin, 1 1/2 Tbsp
Cracked Black Pepper, 1/2 Tbsp
Worcestershire Sauce, 1 Tbsp
Ground Nutmeg, 1/8 Tbsp
Yellow Mustard, 2 Tbsp
Salt And Pepper
Dogs, Beef, 4 Hot
Dog Buns, 4 Hot
Butter
Sour Cream
Jalapeño, Thinly Sliced
Shredded Cheddar Cheese, 1/2 Cup
Instructions
Once you are ready to cook, fire up the Pit Boss according to the manufacturer's directions. Heat the stove to 350 degrees F and bake for 10-15 minutes with the lid covered.
Place the bacon in a pot and cook for about 20 minutes on the Pit Boss, or until the fat has rendered. All except 1 tbsp of bacon grease should be poured away.
Add the chopped onion and simmer for another five min, or until transparent. Cook, breaking up the ground beef with a spoon and stirring periodically, until the ground beef is brown, approximately 10 minutes longer.
Drain most of the oil, return to high heat, and stir in the tomato paste. Microwave for a further 2-3 mins, or until the color

changes from brilliant red to rust.
Boil for fifteen min or until thickened, adding tomato sauce, stewed tomatoes, chili powder, smoked paprika, cumin, black pepper, Worcestershire sauce, nutmeg (optional) mustard. If necessary, season with salt and pepper.
Toss the hot dogs on the grill while the chili cooks to create some beautiful grill marks.
Remove the chili and dogs from the grill once they have finished cooking and place the buttered buns on top to toast gently.
Assemble your chili dogs, slathering them with bacon chili and topping them with cheddar cheese, sour cream, and jalapenos. Enjoy.

2.183 BBQ Pulled Pork Breakfast Burrito with Smoked Hot Sauce

Total Time: 2 Hours 10 Minutes, Serving: 2 people
Ingredients
main
Peppers, 30 Hot
Clove, 1/2 Garlic
White Onion, 2
Extra-Virgin Olive Oil, 4 Tbsp
Salt, 6 Tbsp
Black Pepper, 2 Tbsp
Sugar, 4 Tbsp
Water, 2 Cup
White Vinegar, 1/2 Cup
Leftover Pulled Pork, 1 Cup
Tortillas, 2 Flour
Eggs, 8
Salt And Pepper
Shredded Cheddar Cheese, 1/2 Cup
Sour Cream, 1/2 Cup
Instructions
When you're ready to cook, fire up your Pit Boss according to the manufacturer's directions. Preheat the grill to 225 degrees F (Super Smoke if using a WI FIRE-enabled grill) for 5 minutes with the lid closed.
Toss peppers, garlic, and onion (quartered) in olive oil, salt, and pepper (the desired combination, stems and desired number of seeds removed). Place on a sheet tray and spread out. Smoke for 2 hours on a sheet tray directly on the grill grate. Transfer to a blender after removing from the grill. Puree the sugar, water, and vinegar until smooth.
Pour the mixture into a medium stockpot over medium heat and bring to a boil. Cook for around thirty min, or until the sauce has thickened.
Cool in the refrigerator before transferring to a storage container.
To assemble the burrito, warm the pulled pork and put it in the tortilla's center. Season scrambled eggs with salt and pepper on a non-stick pan. On top of the pulled pork, scramble the eggs.
Add cheese, sour cream, and smoked hot sauce on the top. Enjoy your burrito in a roll.

2.184 Bacon Explosion

Total Time: 2 Hours 25 Minutes, Serving: 4 people
Ingredients
main
Bacon, 1 Pound
Pit Boss Rub
Vegetable Oil, 2 Tbsp
Butter, 2 Tbsp
Red Bell Pepper, Seeded and Diced, 1 Whole
Green Bell Pepper, Diced, 1 Whole
Red Onion, Diced, 1 Small
Hash Browns, Frozen, 2 Cup
To Taste Salt and Pepper, 1
Ground Pork Sausage, 1 Pound
Instructions
Begin by laying down your bacon weave in a 5 x 5 grid. (Detailed instructions for
making a bacon weave may be found here.) Make careful to build your bacon explosion on wax paper or tin foil.
Drizzle a bit of your BBQ rub over the bacon weave. Set aside the leftover bacon bits once they've been chopped up.
In a big heated pan, melt 2 tbsp butter and olive oil together, then add your cut veggies, hash browns, and chopped bacon from the previous step.
Season with salt to desired.
Cook, stirring periodically, for 15-20 minutes, or until the veggies are softened, the hash browns are golden brown, and the bacon is fully cooked.
Get Rid of the pan from the heat and put it aside.
To make the bacon weave, evenly distribute the ground sausage on the bacon weave using the back of a spoon. The thickness of your sausage layer should be approximately 1/2 inch.
Top your sausage with the hash browns, onions, peppers, and bacon combination.
Roll the sausage around the side and top of the veggies, pressing the seams tight on each end while lifting one side of the sausage.
Pull the bacon weaving upward over the sausage roll with wax paper or foil. Make a seam down the bottom and on either end by overlapping the bacon weave.
Once you're ready to cook, preheat the Pit Boss to 180 degrees Fahrenheit. Place the roll on the grill grate seam side down and smoke for 1 hour.
Raise the temperature to 250°F and continue to cook until the internal temperature reaches 175°F (takes approximately one additional hour.)
Serve with your favorite condiment after slicing into 1-inch-thick wheels. Pit Boss's BBQ sauces are our favorites. Enjoy.

2.185 Cuban Sandwich Cubano

Total Time: 40 Minutes, Serving: 4 people
Ingredients
main
Center-Cut Pork Loin3 Pound (3 Lb.)
Garlic, Smashed, 4 Clove
Dried Oregano, 1 Tbsp
Coarse Black Pepper, Divided, 1 Tbsp
Salt, 1 Tbsp
Extra-Virgin Olive Oil, 1/2 Cup
Orange Juice, 2/3 Cup
Lime Juice, 1/3 Cup
Onion, Chopped, 1 Small
Onion, Sliced, 1 Large
Water, 1/2 Cup
Hoagie Rolls, 4
Yellow Mustard
Dill Pickles, For Sandwiches
Swiss Cheese, 1/2 Pound
Ham, Cooked, 3/4 Pound
Instructions
Make incisions across the underside of the pork loin using a thin sharp knife.
On a chopping board, mash the garlic, salt, oregano, and pepper with the flat of a hefty knife. (Alternatively, a mortar and pestle or a small food processor may be used.) To create a coarse paste, scrape it into a small bowl and mix in the olive oil.

Rub the paste all over the meat's exterior, forcing it into the slits with the handle of a Tbsp or your fingers. Fill a big resealable plastic bag halfway with meat. Combine the orange juice, lime juice, and onions in a mixing bowl. Chill for at least 8 hours or up to 24 hours before serving.

Eliminate the pork from the bag and place it in a large roasting pan or Dutch oven with the marinade. On the bottom, equally, distribute the onions, then place the pork on top. Pour 1/2 cup of water into the pan's bottom. Using a lid or heavy-duty foil, seal the container firmly.

Preheat the Pit Boss grill to 300 degrees Fahrenheit when you're ready to cook. Preheat for 10 to 15 mins with the lid closed.

Roast the pork for five hours, or until an immediate meat thermometer register 170°F internal temperature. (Cook the pork until the temperature reached 190 degrees F if you want to shred or pull it.)

Add additional water or orange juice as required if the bottom of the pan starts to dry up. Allow the juices to cool before serving. If you choose the skin to crisp up, remove the cover or foil for the final hour of cooking.

Set aside for 20 mins before cutting or removing the meat. Before serving, spoon the onion and liquids over the pork. Assemble sandwiches.

2.186 Smoky Ham & Bean Soup

Total Time: 5 Hours 10 Minutes, Serving: 8 people
Ingredients
main
Pork Neck, 1 1/2 Pound
Salt And Pepper
Yellow Onion, Diced, 1 Large
Olive Oil
Hot Sauce, 2 Tbsp
Northwest Beans, 2 Can
Corn-starch, 1 Tbsp
Chicken Stock, 1 Quart
Bacon, 3 Slices
Parsley, Chopped, 1 Tbsp
Instructions
Set your Pit Boss to Smoke mode.
Add pepper and salt over the pork neck. Place the pork on the barbecue grate and smoke it for 2 hours or longer, depending on your taste for smoke. Cool pork.

In a big saucepan with oil or butter, caramelize chopped onions over medium heat. Using salt and pepper, season the onions.

Add pork neck, salt, and spicy sauce to the saucepan once the onions have caramelized. Load the container with sufficient water to cover up the meat completely. Bring the soup to a boil, then reduce to low heat.

Leave the lid off for 3-4 hours to allow some water to evaporate. Remove the pork after 3 hours of simmering and let it cool. Pull the pork from the bone and shred it after it has cooled.

Return the shredded pork to the stock, along with the Northwest beans, and cook on medium.

Combine the water and corn starch, then add to the stock. Stir continuously and reduce the temperature if it begins to thicken. Add chopped bacon and parsley to the soup as a garnish. Serve and have fun.

2.187 Prosciutto Wrapped Dates with Marcona Almonds

Total Time: 15 Minutes, Serving: 8 people
Ingredients
main
Medjool Dates, 24 Whole
Container Marcona Salted Almonds, 1 Small
Prosciutto, 8 Ounce
Olive Oil, 2 Tbsp
Washed and Dried for Zesting, 2 Limes
Honey, For Serving
Flake Salt, For Serving
Instructions
Preheat the Pit Boss to 400°F for 15 minutes with the lid closed when ready to cook.

Preheat the grill by placing a big cast iron pan on it. Cut a longitudinal split across the top of each date with a tiny paring knife. Get rid of the pit. Replacing the pits with 1 to 2 Marcona almonds, press the dates together with your fingertips to seal them.

Cut the prosciutto lengthwise into 24 pieces. Wrap each date by placing one at the bottom of a strip of prosciutto and rolling the prosciutto around it to cover it, leaving a little of the date visible on either end.

In a hot cast iron pan, drizzle 2 tbsp olive oil. Place the dates in the pan and heat, rotating as required,
until the prosciutto is seared on both sides, approximately 3 to 5 minutes total. Carefully remove the skillet from the grill after the prosciutto is crispy.

Squeeze the limes over the pan to soak the citrus zest into the olive oil and onto the dates. On a serving plate, arrange the dates. Serve with flake salt, a drizzle of extra virgin olive oil, and honey. Enjoy.

2.188 BBQ Quick Ribs

Total Time: 3 Hours 10 Minutes, Serving: 6 people
Ingredients
main
Baby Back Ribs, 3 Rack
Pit Boss Pork & Poultry Rub
As Needed Pit Boss Texas Spicy BBQ Sauce, 1
Instructions
Lightly coat both sides of the ribs with Pit Boss Pork & Poultry Rub. Ribs should be covered and refrigerated during the night. While you're ready to cook, preheat the Pit Boss to 500°F with the lid covered for fifteen min.

Cook the ribs for fifteen min on a hot grill, unattended.

Reduce the grill temperature to 325°F and roast the ribs for another 2 hours.

After 2 hours, check that the flesh has pulled back 1/4 to 1/2 inch from the end of the bones; if it hasn't, simmer for another 15 minutes and check again. Whenever the internal temperature of the ribs hits 201°F, they are done.

Glaze the ribs with Pit Boss Texas Spicy BBQ sauce when they're done. Cook for a further 10 minutes to let the sauce thicken. Take from the grill and set aside for 10 minutes to cool.

Before serving, slice the ribs between the bones and top with more BBQ sauce. Enjoy.

2.189 Carolina Pulled Pork Sandwiches (Smoked)

Total Time: 8 Hours 20 Minutes, Serving: 6 people
Ingredients
main
Bone-In Ham, 1 (6-7 Lb.)
Pit Boss Pork & Poultry Rub
Apple Cider Vinegar, 1 cup
Beer, 1 Cup
Fresh Lemon Juice, 2 Tbsp
Worcestershire Sauce, 1 Tbsp
Red Pepper Flakes, 1 Tbsp
Buns
Vinegar Sauce
Apple Cider Vinegar
Cup Ketchup, 1/2
Brown Sugar, 1/4 Cup
Salt, 5 Tbsp
Red Pepper Flakes, 2 Tbsp
Freshly Ground Black Pepper, 1 Tbsp
Freshly Ground White Pepper, 1 Tbsp
Carolina Coleslaw
Cabbage, Cored and Shredded, 1/2 Large
Red Onion, Diced, 1/4 Cup
Shredded Carrots, 1/4 Cup
Instructions
Season the pork butt on both sides with Pit Boss Pork & Poultry Rub.

Refrigerate the pork for 8 hours after wrapping it in plastic wrap.

To make the mop sauce, whisk together apple cider vinegar, beer, lemon juice, Worcestershire sauce, and spicy red pepper flakes in a nonreactive bowl. Remove from the equation.

When ready to cook, preheat the Pit Boss to 180°F with the lid closed for 15 minutes.

Remove the pork butt from the plastic wrap and put it straight on the grill grate. Smoke for 3 hours, mopping every hour after the first hour with the mop sauce.

Raise the grill temperature to 250°F and roast the pork for another 3 hours, mopping every hour until the internal temperature reaches 160°F.

Continue to cook the pig butt until it reaches a final internal temperature of 204°F, wrapped in foil.

Wrap the pork in thick bath towels and put it in an insulated fridge for an hour (while still in the foil).

Combine the apple cider vinegar, 1-1/2 cups water, ketchup, brown sugar, salt, hot red pepper flakes, black pepper, and white pepper in a mixing bowl. Stir until the salt crystals, and sugar crystals have completely dissolved. Season to taste, and if necessary, add additional sugar or strong red pepper flakes. Allow for flavor development by setting aside for an hour.

Carolina Coleslaw: Toss the shredded cabbage with approximately 1 cup of vinegar sauce in a mixing dish. 1/4 cup chopped red onion and a handful of shredded carrots.

Pork Belly with Coleslaw: Remove the bone & any unpleasant pieces of fat/ gristle from the still-warm

pork and cut it into chunks. Lay the pork in the roasting pan after shredding it (disposable is okay). Moisten your meat with juices collected in a foil and a little amount of a vinegar sauce. Serve the meat with coleslaw on the buns. Enjoy.

2.190 Lemon Pepper Tenderloin (Grilled)

Total Time: 40 Minutes, Serving: 4 people
Ingredients
main
Zested, 2 Lemons.
Clove Garlic, Minced, 1
Freshly Minced Parsley, 1 Tbsp
Lemon Juice, 1 Tbsp
Black Pepper, 1/4 Tbsp
Kosher Salt, 1/2 Tbsp
Olive Oil, 2 Tbsp
Pork Tenderloin, 1 (2 Lb.)
Instructions
Mix everything but the tenderloin in a small basin.
Trim the tenderloin of any silver skin and extra fat.
Place the pork in a big resealable bag and lock it. Zip the tenderloin shut after pouring the marinade over it. Refrigerate for at least 2 hours but no more than 8 hrs.

When ready to cook, preheat the Pit Boss to 375°F with the lid closed for fifteen min.

Take the tenderloin out of the bag and throw away the marinade.

Once the grill is hot, put the tenderloin right on the grate & cook for 15-20 mins, turning halfway through, till the temperature reached 145 degrees F.

Take the pan from the heat and set it aside to cool for 5 to 10 mins before slicing. Enjoy

2.191 Corn Dog Bites (Baked)

Total Time: 45 Minutes, Serving: 10 people
Ingredients
main
Milk, Room Temperature, 1 Cup
Active Dry Yeast, 4 Tbsp
Granulated Sugar, 1/4 Cup
All-Purpose Flour, 2 cups
Yellow Cornmeal, 1/2 Cup
Baking Soda, 1 Tbsp
Mustard Powder, 1/2 Tbsp
Vegetable Oil, 1/4 Cup
Cayenne Pepper, 1/2 Tbsp
Kosher Salt, plus 1 Tbsp
Beef Frankfurters, 15 Cocktail
Lightly Beaten1 Egg
Dried Minced Garlic, 1 Tbsp
Ketchup And Mustard, For Serving
Instructions
In a mixing dish, mix the milk, yeast, and sugar. Put down for five min, or until foam appears.

Combine all-purpose flour, cornmeal, baking soda, mustard powder, oil, cayenne pepper, and one teaspoon salt in a large mixing bowl.

Stir with a spoon until well mixed, then knead into a dough with your hands.

Place dough in a bowl and cover with plastic wrap, allowing it to rise and double in size for approximately 45 minutes.

When ready to cook, preheat the Pit Boss to 375°F with the lid closed for 15 minutes.

Take Over the dough out of the bowl and divide it into 15 pieces.

Using a rolling pin, spread out each piece of dough into 3" × 3" pieces on a floured work surface.

Place each hot dog in the center of the dough sheet. To

create 15 tiny corn dog
bites, roll them in the dough and seal the edges.
Place corn dog bites on a parchment-lined baking sheet and gently coat each one with a beaten egg. Add the remaining salt and dry minced garlic to each mouthful.
Place sheet tray on the grill grate and bake for 30 minutes, or until golden brown.
Serve with ketchup, mustard, or your favorite dipping sauce. Enjoy.

2.192 Maple Baked Ham
Total Time: 1 Hour 20 Minutes, Serving: 8 people
Ingredients
main
Ham, 1 (14-16 Lb.)
Whole Cloves
Pure Maple Syrup, 1/2 Cup
Brown Sugar, 1/2 Cup
Apple Juice, 1/2 Cup
Brown Mustard, 1 Tbsp
Ground Cinnamon
Ground Ginger
Instructions
Preheat the Pit Boss to 325°F for fifteen min with the lid closed when ready to cook.
Slice a diamond pattern into the ham throughout, cutting to a depth of approximately 3/4 inch. Each "X" in the diamond design should be filled with a clove.
Combine the maple syrup, apple juice, brown sugar, cinnamon, brown mustard, & ginger in a skillet and cook over medium heat, occasionally stirring, until the brown sugar has melted. Remove from the oven and keep warm.
Place the ham in a big roasting pan with Aluminum foil on the bottom. Preheat the grill and cook the pan for 1 1/2 hours.
Remove the ham from the grill and brush it with the saved glaze. Cook for another
thirty min, or until an inner temperature of 135°F is reached when a thermometer is put into the thickest portion of the meat.
Take the ham from the grill and let it rest for 20 mins, wrapped in foil, before serving. If preferred, reheat the leftover sauce and serve with ham. Enjoy.

2.193 BBQ St Louis Fashion Ribs with Homemade BBQ Sauce
Total Time: 5 Hours 5 Minutes, Serving: 6 people
Ingredients
main
St. Louis-Style Ribs of pork, Trimmed, 2 Rack (7 Lb.)
Pit Boss Pork & Rub of Poultry, 1/4 Cup
Juice of Apple, 1/2 Cup
Sweet & Flavorful BBQ Sauce, 1 Cup
Pineapple Juice, 2/3 Cup
Water, 1/2 Cup
Ketchup, 1/2 Cup
Apple Cider Vinegar, 1/4 Cup
Brown Sugar, Firmly Packed, 1/4 Cup
Tamari or Soy Sauce, 2 Tbsp
Worcestershire Sauce, 1 Tbsp
Smoked Paprika, 1 Tbsp
Fennel Seed, 1 Tbsp
Kosher Salt, 1 Tbsp
Granulated Garlic, 1/2 Tbsp
Instructions
Preheat Pit Boss to 180°F and cook for fifteen min with lid covered until ready to cook. The
Pit Boss Pig & Poultry Rub should be used on both sides of the ribs. Spot the ribs on the grilling grate and smoke for 3 hours, meat-side up.
Move the ribs to a cookie sheet after they have smoked for three hours. Raise the temperature of the grill to 225°F. Take three large sheets of heavy-duty Aluminum foil and tear them apart. Pull up the edges to
keep the liquid contained and top with a rack of ribs. Over the ribs, pour the apple juice. To prevent leaking, place another sheet of foil on top and firmly crimp the edges. Place one final sheet of foil on top of the last rack of ribs and crimp all of the corners together to prevent leakage.
Take Back the blocked ribs to the grill and cook at 225°F for about 2 hours.
In a minor pan, mix all ingredients for the BBQ sauce. To mix the ingredients, whisk them together. Bring About to a short boil over medium-high heat. Lower the heat to low and continue to cook until the sauce has thickened to your liking, approximately 20 minutes. It makes about 1-1/2 cup BBQ sauce.
Gently remove the foil from the rib and cover them with the BBQ sauce on both sides. Place the ribs directly on the grill grate and cook for 10 minutes or until the sauce thickens on the ribs. Leave to cool slightly before serving.
Cut into slices and serve with extra sauce on the side. Enjoy.

2.194 Competition-Style Spareribs
Total Time: 4 Hours 30 Minutes, Serving: 4 people
Ingredients
main
St. Louis-Style Ribs, 2 Rack
Pit Boss Pork & Poultry Rub
Dark Brown Sugar, 1 cup
Honey, Preferably Clover, 1/4 Cup
Unsalted Butter, 8 Tbsp
Pit Boss BBQ Sauce, 1 1/2 Cup
Apricot BBQ Sauce, 1/2 Cup
Instructions
Preheat Pit Boss to 180°F and cook for fifteen min with lid covered until ready to cook.
Cut each rack's end bones away. After that, cut any extra fat to a thickness of about 1/4 inch. Strip the membrane from the ribs'
backside.
Season both sides generously with Pit Boss Pork & Poultry Rub, then lay meat side up on the grill. 2 hours of smoking
Remove the ribs off the grill for the time being. Preheat the grill to 225°F and cook for 5 to 10 mins with the lid covered.
Combine 1/4 cup dark brown sugar, 1 tbsp honey, and 2 tbsp butter cut into tiny pieces on a big sheet of heavy-duty Aluminum foil.
Place the ribs in the brown sugar mixture flesh side down. Brown sugar, honey, and butter should be sprinkled over the bone side of the ribs. Carry on with the second set of ribs in the same manner. Return the foil on the grill, flesh side down, for another 2 hours.
Check for tenderness by gently opening the foil and putting a toothpick between the meat's two center-most ribs. You should feel some resistance, but the toothpick should go in rather smoothly. If your ribs are already sensitive, you may go to the following stage and save time. Cook time will be increased if they are still tough.
Collect the juices from the foil and put them aside; the glaze will be made with it later. Place the ribs back on the grill grate after removing them from the foil.
In a small dish, mix the Pit Boss BBQ Sauce of your choice with the Pit Boss Apricot BBQ Sauce and spread generously on both sides of the ribs. Cook for 20 minutes to solidify the sauce if the ribs were already tender after foiling. Cook the ribs for an hour

or longer if they were tough. Because each rack of ribs has a distinct amount of marbling and fat, they will all cook differently. After they have been sauced and returned to the grill, these ribs usually take an hour to cook.

Remove the ribs from the grill once they have completed cooking and let them rest for 15 minutes before slicing.

Scoop the fat from the top of the pork liquid (collected from the foil) and discard.

Spread the sticky sweet glaze liberally over the sliced ribs with a basting brush. It will give things a gleaming appearance.

2.195 Brats in Beer

Total Time: 1 Hour 10 Minutes, Serving: 5
Ingredients
main
Beer, 4 Can (12 Oz)
Onions, Peeled and Sliced into Rings, 2 Large
Butter, 2 Tbsp
Uncooked Bratwurst, 10
Hot Dog Buns, 10
Mustard, For Serving
Instructions

Fill a big saucepan halfway with beer. Toss in the onions and butter. On the flame, get to a low boil.

Once ready to cook, preheat the Pit Boss to 350°F for 15 mins with the lid closed.

Solely on a single side of the Pit Boss, place a deep disposable Aluminum foil pan. Pour the beer and onions from the saucepan onto the grill pan with care.

Place the brats on the grill grate on the other side. Grill the brats for 25 mins, often flipping with tongs until cooked through.

Place the brats in the beer mixture and firmly cover them with Aluminum foil.

Simmer the brats for 45 mins to an hour, or until the onions are soft.

Graze the chopped sides of the buns with butter and toast them on the grill.

Remove a brat from the mixture and place it on a bun to serve. Onions and mustard go on top. Enjoy.

2.196 Grilled Combination Pizza

Total Time: 30 Minutes, Serving: 4 people
Ingredients
main
Hot Italian Ground Sausage, 8 Ounce
Pizza Dough, 1 Pound
Semolina Flour, To Dust Pizza Peel
Pizza Sauce, 1/2 Cup
Mozzarella Cheese, 1/2 Cup
Mushrooms, Sliced.
Black Olives, Sliced
Green Bell Pepper, Diced
Red Onion, Thinly Sliced
Parmesan Cheese
Instructions

In a sauté medium saucepan, saute the Italian sausage until gently brown and cooked through. Get Rid of of the saucepan from the heat, drain the fat, and discard it. Remove from the equation.

On a lightly floured surface, roll out pizza dough to desired shape and thickness. Transfer to a semolina flour-dusted pizza peel.

Transfer to a semolina flour-dusted pizza peel.

Disseminated pizza sauce on the dough, leaving a half inch border all the way around.

Drizzle cheese on topmost of the sauce, then add the sausage, black olives, mushrooms, pepper, red onion, and Parmesan cheese.

When ready to cook, preheat the Pit Boss to 350°F with the lid closed for 15 minutes.

If used, slide the pizza straight from the peel onto the grill grate or pizza stone.

Cook for 15 to 20 mins, or until the cheese is melted and the crust is gently browned. Enjoy.

2.197 Belly Bourbon Beans of Pork (Baked)

Total Time: 6 Hours 15 Minutes, Serving: 8 people
Ingredients
main
Pork Belly, 3 Pound
Poultry Rub & Pit Boss Pork, 2 Tbsp
Unfiltered Apple Juice, 2 Cup
Apple Cider Vinegar, 1/2 Cup
Brown Sugar, Separated, 3/4 Cup
Bourbon, 1/2 cup
Pinto Beans, Drained and Rinsed, 3 (16 Oz)
Kidney Beans, Rinsed and Drained, 2 (16 Oz)
Pit Boss 'Que BBQ Sauce, 2 Cup
Yellow Mustard, 2 Tbsp
Finely Chopped Yellow Onion, 1/2 Cup
Instructions

Sprinkle the pork belly on both sides with Pit Boss Pork & Poultry Rub.

Once ready to cook, preheat the Pit Boss to 180°F for 15 minutes with the lid closed. If Super Smoke is available, use it for the best taste.

Put the salted pork belly fat-side up upon on barbecue grate and cover the lid once the grill is smoking. 2 hours of smoking

Mix apple juice, apple cider vinegar, 1/2 cup brown sugar, and bourbon in a large Dutch oven. Following two hours of smoking, remove the pulled pork from the grill and put it in the Dutch oven. Return to the grill, cover the casserole dish with the lid and heat it to 275°F. Sauté for another 2 hrs, or till the pork is soft and readily shredded with a fork.

Remove the extra liquid from the Dutch oven and put it aside. Remove any extra fat from the pork belly before shredding it. Combine the beans, BBQ sauce, 1/4 cup brown sugar, mustard, and 1/2 cup of the cooking liquid that has been set aside.

Bring to the grill and cover with the lid. Cook for another 2 hrs. We adore our beans thick, although feel free to put in more BBQ sauce as needed if you love a thinner sauce. Toss with your favorite BBQ food as a side dish. Enjoy.

We prefer our bean thick, but if you prefer a thinner sauce, feel free to add more BBQ sauce as needed. Serve with your preferred BBQ food as a side dish. Enjoy.

2.198 Twice Cut Grilled Pork Chop with Sweet & Sour Peaches

Total Time: 1 Hour 16 Minutes, Serving: 4 people
Ingredients
main
West Whiskey High, 1 1/2 Cup
Orange Juice 1 Cup
Sherry Vinegar, 3/4 Cup
Madeira, 1/2 cup
Honey, 1/2 Cup
Black Pepper, 1 Tbsp
Olive Oil, 2 Tbsp
Peaches, Halved, 4 Whole
Onion, Sliced, 2 Whole
Scallions, 2 Whole

Pit Boss Pork & Poultry Rub, 3 Tbsp
Double-Cut Pork Chops, 4 Large
Instructions
When you're ready to cook, fire up the Pit Boss grill, adjust the timer to 375 ° F, and preheat for 10 to 15 mins with the lid closed.
To make the Whiskey Reduction, bring the whiskey, orange juice, sherry, Madeira, honey, and black pepper to a boil in a saucepan. Lessen to low heat and cook for nearly an hour, or until thick and syrupy. Reserve.
Preheat a cast-iron pan over medium-high heat for the peaches. Pour in the olive oil. In a pan, cut side down, place the peaches, onion pieces, and sliced scallions. Griddle them until the peaches and onions are caramelized, and the scallions are just starting to soften, approximately 20 minutes, rotating the onions and scallions as required. When ready to serve, set aside and reheat.
Season pork chops liberally with Pork and Poultry Rub before serving. Cook for 25 minutes on each side, or until the internal temperature reaches 140°F, directly on the grill grate. Get Rid of the steak from the grill and set it aside for 5 minutes before slicing.
To serve, arrange the pork chops, peaches, onions, and scallions on a platter and sprinkle with the whiskey reduction.
*Cook durations may vary based on the temperature of the oven and the ambient temperature.

2.199 Honey-Glazed Roasted Pork Loin
Total Time: 1 Hour 10 Minutes, Serving: 6 people
Ingredients
main
Pork Loin Roast, 1 (3 Lb.)
Onion, Diced, 1.
Garlic, Minced, 2 Clove
Bottle Beer, Preferably A German Lager, 1 (12 Oz)
Honey, 1/4 Cup
Coarse-Grained Mustard, 2 Tbsp
Caraway Seeds, 1 Tbsp
Fresh Dried Thyme, 1 Tbsp
Kosher Salt, 1 Tbsp
Ground Black Pepper, 1 Tbsp
Pit Boss Pork & Poultry Rub
Instructions
In a big, sealed bag, combine the pork, onion, and garlic.
Add beer, honey, mustard, caraway seeds, thyme, salt, and pepper in a mixing bowl. Over the meat and onion, pour the sauce.
Chill over several hours or overnight in the refrigerator.
Take the pork from the marinade and place it in a saucepan with the marinade. Sprinkle the pork fat side up in a roasting pan with Pit Boss Pork and or Poultry Rub.
Next, over medium-high heat, heat the marinade to a boil and reduce it by half.
Once ready to cook, preheat the Pit Boss to 350°F for 15 minutes with the lid closed.
Place the pan right on the grill with the meat inside. Roast for 1 hr, fat-side up, uncovered. Resume to cook for 30-60 mins, baste 2-3 moments with the reduced sauce, or until the core temp of the pork reaches 145°F & the flesh is beautifully coated.
Eliminate from the stove and rest for 7 to 10 minutes before slicing and serving with the pan juices. Enjoy.

2.200 Hot & Fast Smoked Baby Back Ribs
Total Time: 3 Hours 20 Minutes, Serving: 6 people
Ingredients
main
Baby Back Ribs, 3 Rack
Pit Boss Pork & Poultry Rub
Apple Juice, 2 cups
Instructions
Preheat the Pit Boss to 300°F and cook for fifteen min with the lid covered until ready to cook.
Trim any extra fat from the membrane at the rear of the ribcage.
Rub the Pit Boss Pork & Poultry Rub on the front and back of the ribs. Allow 10 minutes for resting on the counter.
Grill the ribs for 30 minutes directly on the grill.
Fill a spray bottle with apple juice while the ribs are cooking.
After the first 30 minutes of cooking, spray the ribs with apple juice
every 30 minutes for the next 2-1/2 hours.
Check the ribs' interior temperature. The ideal temperature is 202 degrees Fahrenheit. If the required temperature has not been achieved after twenty minutes, check it every 20 minutes until it does.
Take the ribs from the grill and set them aside to rest for ten min before slicing and serving. Enjoy.

2.201 Bourbon Bacon Stuffing
Total Time: 1 Hr 10 mins, Serving: 8
Ingredients
Butter, 1/2 Cup
Bacon, 1/2 Pound
Celery, 2 Stalk
Fresh Rosemary, 1 tbsp
Bourbon, 1/2 Cup
Thyme Leaves, 1 tbsp
Onion, 1 Large
Garlic, 1 Clove
4 Egg
Pumpernickel Bread, 1 Loaf
Chicken Stock, 1 Quart
Instructions
In a big, deep pan, fry the bacon until it is uniformly browned over medium heat. Using paper towels, absorb any excess liquid. Set aside the leftover bacon fat in a separate dish.
Melt the butter in the same skillet over medium heat. Cook, occasionally stirring, until the onion, diced
celery, garlic, rosemary, and thyme are soft and translucent, approximately 5 minutes. Stir in the bacon fat that has been set aside.
In a large mixing bowl, put the pumpernickel bread cubes. Combine the eggs & onion mixture in a mixing bowl. Toss to distribute the ingredients properly.
In a mixing dish, combine the chicken stock plus bourbon. Put the chicken stock combination over bread mixture and adjust the consistency as needed. Mix all the ingredients evenly with your hands.
Grease a 9x13-inch baking dish lightly and pour the stuffing mixture equally into it.
Begin the Pit Boss in Smoke with the lid open till it fire is created when you're ready to cook. Preheat the oven to 350 °F and bake for 10 minutes with the lid covered.
Cooked for 45 minutes in the Pit Boss with the stuffing. Warm the dish before serving. Enjoy!

2.202 Baked Peach Cobbler
Total Time: 60 mins, Serving: 8
Ingredients
Yellow Peaches, 3 Pound
Butter, 2 tbsp
Sugar In Raw, 1 tbsp
Pit Boss Smoked Syrup, 1/4 Cup

Flour, 2/3 Cup
Cinnamon
Sugar, 1/2 Cup
Egg, 1 Whole
Salt to taste
Baking Powder, 3/4 tsp
Unsalted Butter, 1/2 Cup
Vanilla, 1/2 tsp
Instructions
Bring the Pit Boss to 350°F and heat for 15 minutes when you're ready to cook. 2 tablespoons melted butter inside a cast iron skillet Blend pear in Smoked Simple Syrup in a normal bowl and put in the preheated cast iron pan.
Now combine cinnamon, flour, baking powder, & salt in a small basin; put aside. Blend the butter and half a cup of sugar in a separate dish. Combine the egg and vanilla essence in a mixing bowl.
Now mix in flour mixture gradually. Spread the batter over top of the peaches and finish with a sprinkling of
raw sugar.
Preheat the grill to 350°F and bake the cast iron for 40 - 45 minutes. * Have fun! Cooking times will vary based on the temperature of the set and the ambient temperature.

2.203 Smoked Brisket Pot Pie
Total Time: 1 Hr, Serving: 8
Ingredients
Carrots, 2 Whole
Garlic, 1 Clove
Frozen Peas, 1/2 Cup
Cornstarch
1 Egg
Salt & Pepper
Beef Stock, 2 Cup
Butter, 2 tbsp
Yellow Onion, 1 Whole
Chopped Brisket, 2 Cup
Pearl Onions, 1 Cup
Frozen Pastry Dough, 1 Sheet
Instructions
In a medium stockpot, melt the butter. Add the carrots to the heated butter and cook for 10 to 15 minutes, until gently browned.
Cook for 5 to 7 minutes, or until the onion is soft and transparent. Sauté for another 30 seconds, or until the garlic is aromatic.
Combine the peas, onions, and chopped brisket in a mixing bowl. Bring the beef stock to a low simmer.
Simmer until the liquid has thickened enough just to cover the slotted spoon and has been reduced. Unless the sauce does not thicken, add a corn-starch slurry until it does. To taste, season with salt.
Fill an oven-safe baking dish halfway with the brisket mixture. Make incisions in the top of the pastry dough to allow air to escape.
In a separate bowl, whisk together the egg and brush the egg wash over the pastry.
Set the Pit Boss to 350°F and preheat for 15 minutes with the lid covered when you're ready to cook.
Bake for 45 minutes, or until the top is gently browned and bubbling, straight on the grill grate.
Allow 10 minutes for cooling before serving. Enjoy!

2.204 Baked Eggs in Bacon Nest
Total Time: 40 mins, Serving: 4
Ingredients
Eggs, 6 Whole
Bacon, 6 Strips
Pepper, 1/4 tsp
Salt, 1/4 tsp
Instructions
Once ready to cook, preheat the oven to 375 ° F and cook for 10-15 minutes with the lid covered.
Cook for 15 minutes upon that grill grate with bacon slices immediately on it. Move to a towel to absorb excess moisture. Using cooking spray, generously coat a muffin tin. One piece of bacon is used to line each muffin cup, and then one egg is cracked into each cup. Season salt and pepper to taste in each cup.
Cook for 15-10 min on the grill till the bacon gets crisp, the whites are barely set, and the yolk still is runny. Enjoy!

Chapter 3: Poultry Recipes

3.1 Baked Prosciutto-Wrapped Chicken Breast with Spinach and Boursin

Total Time: 1 Hr 25 Mins, Servings: 4
Ingredients
1 tbsp. Olive Oil
Ten oz. Washed & Dried Baby Spinach Leaves
2 Whole Packs (5.2 Oz) Herbs Gournay Cheese & Boursin Garlic
2 lb. Boneless, Skinless Chicken Breasts
Mrs. Dash Garlic & Herb Seasoning Blend
14 slices Prosciutto
Instructions
Heat the olive oil in a sauté pan. Cook for 3-5 mins, or unless the spinach has wilted. Using a filter, remove any excess liquid. Combine the spinach and cheese in a mixing bowl; after fully mixing, set aside.
Butterfly the chicken breast to open it like a book. Cover it with plastic wrap and use a meat mallet to lb it out finely. The chicken is additionally seasoned with Mrs. Dash spice.
A 2-foot-long sheet wrapping should be placed on a clean, flat surface. Prosciutto slices should be slightly overlapping and double-wide on the table. Place the chicken on top of the prosciutto, leaving a 1-inch border all the way around.
The spinach mixture should be used to cover the chicken. Roll it up firmly to form a log. After tying the ends firmly, please place them in the refrigerator. Refrigerate for 2-3 hours, or overnight in the fridge.
Preheat the Pit Boss to 300°F with the lid closed for 12 mins when ready to cook.
Carefully remove the wrapper and place it straight on the grill plate. Bake for 1 hour and 15 mins, or until the internal temperature reaches 162°F to 165°F. Remove the meat from the Pit Boss and set it aside for 15 mins before slicing.

3.2 The Grilled Chicken Challenge
Total Time: 1 Hr 5 Mins, Servings: 4
Ingredients
1 (4 lb.) Whole Chicken
Pit Boss Chicken Rub
Instructions
Preheat your Pit Boss to 375°F for 15 mins with the lid covered.
Clean the chicken completely by washing and patting it dry (remove & discard giblets). Season the whole bird, including the cavity, with Pit Boss Chicken Rub (or similar rub of choice). On your grill grate, cook the chicken for about 1 hour and 10 mins. Remove the chicken breast from the grill when the internal temperature reaches 160°F. The temperature may rise to 165°F as the chicken sleeps. Cooking durations vary depending on the size of the chicken, so keep an eye on the temperature.
Allow 15-20 mins for the bird to rest before the internal temperature of the breast reaches 165°F.

3.3 Grilled Paprika Chicken with Jalapeño Salsa
Total Time: 55 Mins, Servings: 6
Ingredients
Main
6 whole Chicken Legs (Thigh and Drumstick)
2 tbsp. Olive Oil
1 tbsp. Smoked Paprika
1 tsp Ground Coriander
1 Lime, Zested
Sea Salt, 1 ½ tsp
1 tsp Freshly Cracked Black Pepper
Jalapeño Salsa
4 medium Jalapeños
4 Garlic clove, Peeled
6 spring Fresh Cilantro
2 Green Onions
1 tbsp. Fresh Squeezed Lime Juice
2 tbsp. Pure Maple Syrup
1/2cupDistilled White Vinegar
1 tsp Sea Salt
Instructions
To begin, prepare the chicken. In a large mixing cup, combine the chicken, smoked paprika, olive oil, coriander, pepper, lime zest, and sea salt. Cover with plastic wrap and refrigerate for 4 hours (minimum 1 hr).
Preheat the Pit Boss to 350°F with the lid closed for 15 mins when ready to cook.
Place the chicken directly on the grill grates, skin side up. Cook for 40-48 mins, or until the chicken reaches an internal temperature of 165°F and is perfectly
grilled.
While the chicken is cooking, make the jalapeno salsa. Place the peppers on the grill grates next to the chicken and cook until charred all over, about 25-35 mins. Remove the leaves from the jalapenos, then combine the peppers with the other salsa ingredients in a blender. Pulse the mixture until it's nearly smooth. Season for taste and adjust seasoning as needed. Drizzle a liberal quantity of soft and spicy jalapeño salsa on top of your delicious chicken.

3.4 Duck Confit, Red Onion Jam, and Goat Cheese Crostinis

Total Time: 50 Mins, Servings: 6
Ingredients
2 tbsp. Butter
3 Red Onions, Sliced
2 Garlic clove, Minced
Sugar, ¼ cup
Sea Salt and Freshly Cracked Black Pepper
Dry Red Wine, ¼ cup
1 tbsp. Apple Cider Vinegar
1 Lemon, Zested
4 Ready-To-Cook Duck Confit Legs
1 Baguette, Sliced Thin
Olive Oil
½ cup Crumbled Herb Goat Cheese
Pomegranate Arils, ¼ cup
Instructions
Preheat the Pit Boss to 350 degrees Fahrenheit & cook for around 15 mins with the cover closed.
In a saucepan over low heat, melt the butter; after melted, add the onions, sugar, garlic, and a touch of salt. Mix thoroughly, cover, and cook for 20-30 mins, or unless softened & caramelizing. After removing the pan from the oven, stir in the red wine, lemon zest, and vinegar. Take it out of the equation.
Preheat the oven to 350 degrees Fahrenheit and grease a baking pan. Switch the duck wings on the grill, skin-side up. Cook for 8-12 mins, or until the skin starts to crisp and the flesh separates easily with a fork. Shred the meat with two forks.
Meanwhile, brush each baguette slice with olive oil and season with salt and pepper. Place the bread on the grill and cook until it has grill marks and is golden brown.
On crostini, layer shredded duck, goat cheese, red onion jelly, pomegranate seeds, and toasted baguette.

3.5 Baked Game Day Hatch Chile and Bacon Hot Dish

Total Time: 55 Mins, Servings: 4
Ingredients
2 tbsp. Unsalted Butter
All-Purpose Flour, ¼ cup
2 can (Fifteen oz.) Cream of Chicken Soup
2 cup Whole Milk
2 medium Onions, Grilled and Chopped
1 lb. Boneless, Skinless Chicken Thighs, Chopped
1/2 cup Chopped Hatch Chiles
Dried Thyme, ¼ tsp
Salt & Pepper
1 cup Smoked Bacon, Chopped
1 lb. Frozen Tater Tots
Instructions
Preheat the Pit Boss to 400°F and shut its lid for 20 mins.
In a medium saucepan, melt the butter, then stir in the flour. With a separate dish, dissolve the chicken broth in the milk and pour it into the pan. Mix the paste continuously till it thickens.
In a large mixing bowl, combine the onions, thyme, chicken, pepper, chilies, and salt. Allow for 10-15 mins of cooling time or until the chicken is fully cooked.
Season with salt and pepper to taste after adding the smoked bacon.
Pour the mixture into a casserole pan. Toss the tater tots on top of the mashed potatoes.
Preheat oven to 350°F and bake for 30–35 mins, or until brown. Serve right away.

3.6 Yogurt-Marinated Chicken Thigh & Beef Tenderloin Kabobs

Total Time: 30 Mins, Servings: 4
Ingredients
Marinade
2 cup Full-Fat Plain Greek Yogurt
1 cup Chopped Cilantro
2 whole Lime, Juiced
3 Garlic clove, Minced
1 tsp Turmeric
1 tsp Curry Powder
1 tsp Ground Cumin
Salt And Pepper
Main
1 lb. Beef Tenderloin, Diced Large
1 lb. Skin-On Chicken Thighs, Cut into Large Strips
Instructions
To prepare the marinade, combine all the ingredients in a mixing bowl. Split the marinade into two bowls. In separate pans, marinate the chicken and beef tenderloin. Cover each bowl with plastic wrap and marinate overnight in the refrigerator.
Preheat the Pit Boss to 360°F and keep the lid covered for 15 mins.
As the grill warms up, skewer the meat and chicken individually.
Place the skewers directly on the grill plate once the grill is hot and cook for 3 to 5 mins, turning halfway through. Cook for 10-15 mins for the chicken and 20-25 mins for the beef, or until the desired doneness is achieved.
Remove off the grill and leave aside for 5 mins to cool.

3.7 Pit Boss Mandarin Wings

Total Time: 35 Mins, Servings: 2
Ingredients
1 Bottle (12 Oz) Mandarin Orange Sauce
Pit Boss Beef Rub
Pit Boss Chicken Rub
2 lb. Chicken Wings, Flats
Drumettes Separated
Instructions
Over the chicken wings, drizzle the mandarin sauce. Pit Boss Beef Rub and Pit Boss Chicken Rub are applied to the wings. Allow for a 35-min marinating period.
Preheat the Pit Boss to 350°F and shut its cover for 12 mins.
Grill the wings for 30 mins on the grill plate.

3.8 Smoking' Thai Curry Chicken

Total Time: 1 Hr 20 Mins, Servings: 6
Ingredients
Soy Sauce, ¼ cup
3 tbsp. Dark Brown Sugar, Packed
2 tbsp. Fresh Lime Juice
2 tbsp. Oil
2 tsp Curry Powder
½ tsp Cardamom
2 Garlic clove, Minced
1 tsp Lemon Grass
1 tsp Fresh Minced Ginger
1 Jalapeño or Thai Red Chile Pepper
Pepper, Coarsely Chopped
3 lb. Boneless, Skinless Chicken Breasts
Fresh Cilantro, For Garnish
Fresh Coconut Flakes, For Garnish
Instructions
Combine all the marinade ingredients in a mixing dish.

In a big zip lock bag, combine the marinade and the chicken breasts. For 1–4 hours, marinate the chicken.
Preheat the Pit Boss to 450°F with the lid closed for 18 mins when ready to cook.
Take the chicken out of the marinade and put it straight on the grill tray.
Cook for around 12 mins on each side.
Allow the chicken to rest for 5 mins before serving.
Before serving, toss with cilantro and coconut flakes. Have fun with it.

3.9 Roasted Tin Foil Dinners
Total Time: 40 Mins, Servings: 4
Ingredients
4 Boneless, Skinless Chicken Breast
Pit Boss Chicken Rub
1/2 lb. New Potatoes, Quartered
8 oz. Cremini Mushrooms, Cleaned & Quartered
Salt & Pepper
1/2 lb. Green Beans, Ends Trimmed
1 medium Lemon, Cut into ¾ Inch Slices
Instructions
Preheat the Pit Boss to 400°F for 15 mins with the lid closed.
Season the chicken breasts on both sides with salt, pepper, & Chicken Pit Boss Rub. Wrap the potatoes, mushrooms, and chicken firmly in foil, seasoning it with salt & pepper.
Cook for around 15 mins on your grill grate using the foil pack.
Remove the foil pack from the grill and toss in the green beans, lemon, and season with salt and pepper to taste. Return to the Pit Boss and cook for another 10 mins.
Remove the tray from the Pit Boss, open the package, and eat.

3.10 Roasted Serrano Wings
Total Time: 55 Mins, Servings: 4
Ingredients
4 lb. Chicken Wings
1 Can Beer or 12 oz.
2 tsp red pepper flakes
Pit Boss Chicken Rub
1 lb. Fresh Serrano Chile Peppers
4 Garlic clove
1 tsp Fresh Oregano
1 tsp Fresh Basil
1/2 tsp Celery Salt
Freshly Cracked Black Pepper, ¼ tsp
1 cup Distilled White Vinegar
Instructions
Combine the wings, red pepper flakes, and soda in a large mixing cup. Chill for 12-25 hours before grilling.
Remove the wings from the brine and pat them dry. Make drumettes & flats out of the wings. Remove the tops and throw them away.
Season generously with Pit Boss Chicken Rub.
Preheat the Pit Boss to 325°F with the lid closed for 15-20 mins when ready to cook.
Arrange the wings & serrano peppers straight on your grill grate. After 10 mins, flip the peppers and grill for another 5-10 mins, or until the skin is browned and the peppers are completely softened.
After removing the peppers from the grill, flip the chicken wings. As you make the spicy sauce, continue to heat the wings for another 20-25 mins.
Remove the stems from the Chile peppers, discard them, and then purée the peppers in a food processor with garlic, celery, oregano, salt, basil, and black pepper.
Start the food processor and slowly drizzle in the vinegar until the mixture is smooth and processed.
Fill a small bowl halfway with sauce and put it on the grill.
Before returning to the Pit Boss for the last 5 mins, drizzle each wing with sauce.

3.11 BBQ Spatchcocked Chicken
Total Time: 55 Mins, Servings: 2
Ingredients
1 whole Chicken
Pit Boss Chicken Rub, ¼ c
Olive Oil
1/2 cup Pit Boss Sweet & Heat BBQ Sauce
Instructions
Preheat the grill to 375°F and shut the cover for 18 mins.
Break the bird apart on both sides around the backbone through the ribs, then use large shears or a knife to remove the backbone.
Cut the breastbone to flatten the bird once it has opened, allowing it to cook more easily. Brush the chicken with olive oil and season with Pit Boss Chicken Rub on both sides.
Cook for 30–40 mins.
In the final few minutes of cooking time, spray the chicken with BBQ sauce and roast for another 2 minutes before the glaze sets. Before carving the steak, remove it from the grill and put it aside to rest for 5 mins.

3.12 Smoked Chicken Tikka Drumsticks
Total Time: 55 Mins, Servings: 6
Ingredients1 tbsp. Smoked Paprika
1 tbsp. Garam Masala
1 tbsp. Ground Cumin
1 tbsp. Ground Coriander
1 tsp Turmeric
1 tsp Ground Cayenne Pepper
1/2 medium Yellow Onion, Diced
1 whole Thumb-Sized Piece of Ginger Peeled And Roughly Chopped
6 Garlic clove, Chopped
2 cup Greek Yogurt
1/2 Lemon, Juiced
1/2 cup Extra-Virgin Olive Oil
12 whole Chicken Drumsticks
1 tbsp. Curry Powder
1 tbsp. Lime Juice
1 pinch Coarse Sea Salt
To Taste Cilantro
1/2 small Red Onion, Thinly Sliced
1 whole Lime, Cut into Wedges
2 whole Green or Red Chiles, Sliced
Instructions
To prepare the marinade in a food processor, pulse the cloves, ginger, garlic,
onion, milk, lemon juice, oil, and salt until smooth.
Place the chicken in a large mixing basin, pour in the marinade, and massage the meat until thoroughly coated. After covering in plastic wrap, refrigerate overnight (minimum 14 hrs).
Preheat the grill on high for 15 mins with the lid covered until you're ready to cook.
Place the chicken directly on the grill and cook for 45-50 mins, or until crispy and perfectly wood-fire cooked.
While the chicken is cooking, combine all the yogurt ingredients in a small mixing dish and whisk well. Refrigerate until ready to serve.
Top with fresh lime wedges, curry lime yogurt, and chopped chilies if you want it extra spicy.

3.13 Roasted Rosemary Orange Chicken

Total Time: 55 Mins, Servings: 4
Ingredients
1 (3-4 Lb.) Chicken, Backbone Removed Marinade
Olive Oil, ¼ c
2 Oranges, Juiced
1 Orange, Zested
2 tsp Dijon Mustard
3 tbsp. Rosemary Leaves, Chopped
2 tsp Kosher Salt
Instructions
Rinse and pat dry your chicken after cleaning it.
In a mixing dish, combine the following ingredients to create the marinade. In a medium mixing bowl, combine olive oil, fresh orange juice (approximately 1/4 cup), Dijon mustard, orange zest, rosemary, and salt. To combine the components, stir them together.
Place the chicken in a baking dish large enough to allow it to open fully in one piece. Make sure the chicken is well covered in the marination.
Cover with plastic wrap and refrigerate for at least 2 hours or overnight, rotating halfway through.
Preheat the Pit Boss to 350°F with the lid closed for 20 mins when ready to cook.
Remove the chicken from the marination and place it on the Pit Boss skin-side down.
Before turning, cook for another 20-35 mins, or until the skin is browned. Continue to cook the chicken for 5-15 mins more, or until the internal temperature of the breast reaches 165°F and the temperature of the thighs reaches 175°F. Allow for a 5-min rest period before cutting.

3.14 Ancho-Chili Smoked BBQ Chicken Legs

Total Time: 10 Hrs, Servings: 4
Ingredients
1 tbsp. Ancho Chile Powder
2 tbsp. Brown Sugar
1/2 tbsp. Ground Espresso
1/2 tsp Ground Cumin
1 Lime, Zested
1 tbsp. Kosher Salt
2 tbsp. Olive Oil
8 Chicken Legs
1/2 cup Pit Boss BBQ Sauce
1 whole Lime, Cut into Wedges
Flat-Leaf Parsley, Chopped
Instructions
In a shallow mixing bowl, combine the ancho chili powder, cumin, brown sugar, lime zest, espresso, & salt. Massage the olive oil into the chicken thighs.
Drizzle the dry rub over the chicken and thoroughly massage it in. After covering, refrigerate for 1 night.
Preheat the grill to 180°F for 20 mins with the lid closed when ready to cook.
On the grill grate, smoke the chicken legs for 1 hour.
Raise the temperature to 360 degrees F. Cook for another hour, or unless the juices flow clear, and the chicken reaches an internal temperature of 165°F.
Cook the chicken with the barbecue sauce all over when 10 mins are remaining in the cooking time. Finish with a sprig of parsley and a squeeze of fresh lime.

3.15 Whole Smoked Chicken

Total Time: 3 Hrs 10 Mins, Servings: 6
Ingredients
Brine
1/2 cup Kosher Salt
1 cup Brown Sugar
1 (3 To 3-1/2 Lb.) Whole Chicken
Main
1 tsp Garlic, Minced
Pit Boss Big Game Rub
1 Lemon, Halved
1 medium Yellow Onion, Quartered
3 whole Garlic Clove
5 Thyme Sprigs
Instructions
In a wide mixing bowl, combine the ancho chili powder, cumin, brown sugar, lime zest, espresso, & salt. Massage the olive oil into the chicken thighs.
Drizzle the dry rub over the chicken and thoroughly massage it in. After covering, refrigerate for 1 night.
Preheat the grill to 180°F for 20 mins with the lid closed when ready to cook.
On the grill grate, smoke the chicken legs for 1 hour.
Raise the temperature to 360 degrees F. Cook for another hour, or unless the juices flow clear, and the chicken reaches an internal temperature of 165°F.
Cook the chicken with the barbecue sauce all over when 10 mins are remaining in the cooking time. Finish with a sprig of parsley and a squeeze of fresh lime.

3.16 Spatchcocked Chicken with Toasted Fennel & Garlic

Total Time: 55 Mins, Servings: 6
Ingredients
6 lb. Whole Chicken
1 tbsp. Toasted Fennel Seed
2 Garlic clove, Minced
1 tbsp. Salt
1/2 tbsp. Pepper
Instructions
By cutting down all the backbone's ends, you may remove the backbone from the bird.
After that, turn the bird over and cut through the keel bone in the center. Therefore, the chicken would be able to lay flat.
When you're ready to roast, turn on the Pit Boss's smoke mode and keep the lid open until the fire is roaring (4-5 mins). Preheat the grill to 450 degrees Fahrenheit and bake for 10-20 mins with the lid covered.
As the grill heats up, massage the fennel, salt, garlic, and pepper into the chicken and set aside to come to room temp. Place the chicken skin-side down on the grill. Cook for 5–10 mins, or until grill marks form on the surface. Cook till the core temp of the chicken reaches 160 degrees.

3.17 Spatchcocked Chile-Lime Rubbed Chicken

Total Time: 1 Hr 10 Mins, Servings: 4
Ingredients
3 tbsp. Chili Powder
2 tbsp. Extra-Virgin Olive Oil
2 tsp Lime Zest
3 tbsp. Lime Juice
1 tbsp. Garlic, Minced
1 tsp Ground Coriander
1 tsp Ground Cumin
1 tsp Dried Oregano
Kosher Salt, 1 ½ tsp
1 tsp Ground Black Pepper, Freshly
1 pinch Cinnamon
1 (3-1/2 To 4 lb.) Whole Chicken
Cilantro, Lime Juice, and Salsa, For Serving
Instructions

In a bowl, combine chili powder, oil, lime zest and juice, cumin, garlic, salt, coriander, oregano, pepper, and cinnamon to create a paste.

To spatchcock the bird, break the backbone by cutting both sides of the backbone. Then flatten the bird with your hand to break the breastbone.

Apply a generous amount of the seasoning rub beneath and over the skin, as well as on the interior of the bird. Combine all the ingredients in a baking dish. After covering with a wrapping sheet, refrigerate for the whole night or the entire day.

Preheat the Pit Boss to 450°F with the lid on for 15 mins.

Cook for around 65-70 mins, or until an internal temperature of 165°F is reached.

Before slicing, place on a serving plate and leave aside for 5–8 mins. Serve with a squeeze of lime and a sprinkling of cilantro on top.

3.18 Grilled Sweet Cajun wings

Total Time: 45 Mins, Servings: 4
Ingredients
2 lb. Chicken Wings
Poultry Rub & Pit Boss Pork
Cajun Shake (Pit Boss)
Instructions
Drizzle Sweet Pit Boss Rub and Cajun Pit Boss Rub on the meat. Shake the wings a little.

Preheat the Pit Boss to 350°F for 15 mins with the lid closed.

Grill for around 25 mins, or till golden brown and juicy in the center.

3.19 Roasted Christmas Goose

Total Time: 2 Hrs 30 Mins, Servings: 8
Ingredients
Goose, 5 ½ lb
2 Lemons
2 Limes
2 tsp Salt
2 Thyme Sprigs
2 Sage Sprigs
1 medium Apple, Green
3 tbsp. Honey
Instructions
Preheat your grill on high for 15 mins with the lid covered.

Tie the breast and leg muscles together in a crisscross pattern. It would help render fat more quickly during cooking.

Scrape the lemons and limes into a large mixing basin. 2 tsps salt + 2 tsps lemon zest; limes may be sliced into slices.

Season the goose cavity with sea salt and massage the citrus paste into the skin and cavity.

Fill the cavities of the geese with sage, lime and lemon, thyme, & apple slices. On the grill grate, cook the geese for 40 mins. Reduce the temperature to 325°F and butter the geese.

Cook for 1-2 hours, or until a thermometer inserted into the center of the breast registers 160 degrees Fahrenheit.

Remove off the grill, cover in foil, and put aside for 1/2 an hour to cool down.

3.20 Spicy Bacon Wrapped Grilled Chicken Skewers

Total Time: 3 Hrs 20 Mins, Servings: 6
Ingredients
Ranch 1/2 c
1/2 tsp Garlic Powder
1/2 tbsp. Chili Sauce
1/2 tsp Dried Oregano
16 oz. Chicken Breast, Cubed
1 whole Red Onion, Sliced
1 whole Green Bell Peppers, Sliced
8 Strips Bacon, Sliced
Instructions
In a wide mixing cup, combine ranch dressing, chili sauce, garlic powder, & oregano. Toss in the cubed chicken and toss well to coat. Allow the chicken to rest in the refrigerator for 1-3 hours.

Preheat the grill too high for 20 mins with the lid closed.

Putting the onion wedges, tomato, a piece of bacon, and chicken on the Pit Boss skewers. Before weaving the bacon around the chicken pieces, alternate the bacon and chicken. Finish each skewer with a pepper and onion wedge. Do not clog the skewer to promote quicker and more uniform cooking. Replace the skewers and repeat with the remaining skewers.

Place the skewers on the grill plate with a piece of foil beneath the skewers' ends to prevent them from burning.

Cook for 5 mins on each side, rotating once, for a total cooking time of 20 mins. Take the skewers out of the mix.

3.21 Tandoori Chicken Wings

Total Time: 60 Mins, Servings: 4
Ingredients
1/2 cup Yogurt
1 whole Scallion, Minced
1 tbsp. cilantro Leaves, Minced
2 tsp Ginger, Minced
1 tsp Masala
Salt 1 ½ tsp
1 tsp Ground Black Pepper
Chicken Wings, 1 ½ lb
2 tbsp. Mayonnaise
2 tbsp. Cucumber
2 tsp Lemon Juice
1/2 tsp Cumin
Cayenne Pepper, 1/8 tsp
Instructions
Combine the milk, cilantro, scallions, gram masala, ginger, pepper, and salt in the jar of a blender and process until smooth. Pour the sauce over the chicken and massage it all over the wings in the bag. Remove the excess marinade from the wings and drain it. Refrigerate it for 6-8 hours before serving.

Preheat the grill to 350°F and keep the door closed for 10-20 mins while preparing to roast. Brush and lubricate the grill plate.

Arrange the wings in an equal layer on the grill plate. Cook for 40-50 mins, or until the meat is cooked through and no longer pink, and the skin is golden and crunchy. Turn the wings once or twice while cooking to keep them from sticking to the grill grate.

Meanwhile, combine all the sauce ingredients in a mixing bowl; put away and refrigerate until ready to use.

When the wings are done, transfer them to a tray.

3.22 Whole Chicken

Total Time: 4 Hrs 15 Mins, Servings: 4
Ingredients
Brine
Salt, ¾ cup
2 tbsp. Brown Sugar
2 Garlic clove
2 spring Thyme
2 spring Rosemary
Main

1 (5-6 lb.) Chicken Free-Range
1 Lemon, Halved
1 Bulb Garlic, Halved
2 tbsp. Olive Oil
1 tbsp. Lemon Zest
Seasoning
4 tsp Kosher Salt
4 tsp Dehydrated Garlic Flakes
Onion Flakes tsp
1 tsp Dried Thyme
1 tsp Smoked Paprika
2 tsp Dried Parsley
2 tsp Cracked Black Pepper
1 tsp Crushed Coriander Seeds
Instructions
First, prepare the brine. In a large kettle, combine 4
cups water, sugar, garlic, salt, and herbs, and bring to a simmer. Reduce the
heat to low and whisk the water until
the salt has dissolved.
8 glasses of water should be poured over the top. After immersing the chicken in the brine, keep it refrigerated overnight.
In a dish, combine all the marination ingredients, cover, and set aside.
Preheat the Pit Boss to 225°F and leave the lid closed for 18 mins until ready to use.
After taking the chicken from the brine, wipe it dry using paper towels.
2 tbsps olive oil sprinkled over the bird 1 tbsp marinade & 1 tsp lemon zest, spread all over the chicken Fill the cavity of the bird with both halves of the garlic bulb as well a lemon.
On a prepared grill, cook until the chicken reaches an internal temperature of 170 degrees Fahrenheit. It will take between two and three hours to finish.

3.23 Oktoberfest Pretzel Mustard Chicken
Total Time: 40 Mins, Servings: 4
Ingredients
Pretzel Sticks, ¼ lb
3 tbsp. Dijon Mustard
3 tbsp. Apple Cider or Brown Ale
1 tbsp. Honey
Fresh Thyme, Plus More for Garnish, 1 ½ tsp
4 Boneless, Skinless Chicken Breasts
Instructions
In a spice grinder, crush the pretzel sticks until they're the consistency of panko breadcrumbs, or crumble them by hand in a zip lock bag.
In a shallow, wide basin, combine the crumbs.
In a separate shallow dish, combine the beer or apple cider, mustard, sugar, and thyme.
On top of a sheet tray, place a wire rack. After dipping the chicken breast in the mixture
and dredging it in pretzel crumbs to evenly coat it, place it on the wire rack.
Coat the tops of the chicken breasts with cooking oil.
Preheat the Pit Boss to 370°F with the lid closed for 20 mins.
Bake for 20-25 mins on a hot plate on the Pit Boss, or until the chicken breasts are fully cooked, and a thermometer hit 165°F. Allow the chicken to rest for 5 mins. Garnish with thyme if desired.

3.24 Asian BBQ Chicken
Total Time: 1 Day 1 Hr, Servings: 4
Ingredients
1 whole Chicken
Pit Boss Asian BBQ Rub
1 whole Ginger Ale
Instructions
Rinse the chicken and pat it dry after washing it in cold water. Spread Asian BBQ Pit Boss rub all over the chicken, including the interior. In a wide bag, cover and chill for 12-24 hours.
Preheat the Pit Boss to 375°F for 15 mins with the lid closed.
Taking a couple of ginger ale cans out of the fridge. Place the can of soda in a secure place. Take the chicken out of the fridge and place it on top of the Coke can. The bottom of the container and the chicken legs must form a tripod to keep the chicken straight.
Cook for 40-60 mins, or until the skin becomes golden brown and the internal temperature of the chicken reaches 165°F on an instant-read thermometer in the center of your hot grill.
To remove the chicken from the thr1, preheat the oven to 350°F.

3.25 Grilled Chicken Alfredo Pizza
Total Time: 1 Hr 15 Mins, Servings: 4
Ingredients
Pit Boss Pork & Poultry Rub
8 tbsp. Butter
2 Garlic clove, Minced
2 cup Heavy Cream
1/2 cup Parmesan Cheese
1/2 tsp Black Pepper
1 pinch Ground Nutmeg
2 whole Pizza Dough, Cooked
2 whole Bell Peppers, Mixed Colors
Mozzarella Cheese, 1 ½ c
2 tsp Basil, Dried
Instructions
Preheat the Pit Boss to 400°F and keep the lid covered for around 15 mins.
Pork & Poultry Rub Pit Boss Rub the chicken breasts with the mixture. Cook for around 15-20 mins on the grill, turning once. Remove the steaks from the grill and let them cool slightly before chopping them into cubes. Switch on the grill.
Meanwhile, make the Alfredo sauce as follows: Melt the butter in a medium saucepan over medium heat. After adding the garlic, cook for 3 mins. Cook for 10 mins, or until the sauce has thickened, before adding the cream. In a mixing dish, combine 1/2 cup grated Parmesan, nutmeg, and pepper. If the mixture is too thin, cook it for a few mins longer.
Separate the cut chicken and peppers between two pizzas. Set the pizzas on a baking pan and bake them. Each crust may be topped with Alfredo sauce. A tsp dried basil on top of 3/4 cup mozzarella cheese. Over the tops, more Parmesan cheese may be sprinkled.
On the grill grate, bake the pizzas for 10-12 mins. Allow for a few mins of cooling before cutting into slices.

3.26 Pit Boss BBQ 1/2 Chickens
Total Time: 1 Hr 15 Mins, Servings: 2
Ingredients
1 (3 To 3-1/2 lb.) Fresh Young Chicken
Leinenkugel's Shandy Rub (Pit Boss)
BBQ Sauce of Apricot (Pit Boss)
Instructions
Place the chicken breast-side down on the cutting board, with the neck facing away from you. Cut along one side of the backbone as close to a bone as possible. So, pull it out and rerun it on the opposite backbone side.
To split up the white cartilage at the top of the chicken's breastbone, cut through it with a knife. Cut the breastbone on each side and remove it from your fingers. Using a knife, cut

the chicken in half across the center. Turn the chicken over to expose the skin side. On each half of the bird, reattach the wings.
Pit Boss Leinenkugel's Summer Shandy Season Rub both ends together.
Preheat the Pit Boss to 375ºF for 20 mins with the top closed when ready to cook.
Cook for around 60-90 mins, or until the core temp reaches 160ºF, with the chicken skin side up on the barbecue grate. Spread the BBQ sauce all over the chicken's skin and continue to cook for another 10 mins. Remove off the grill and put aside for 5 mins to cool before eating.

3.27 Pit Boss BBQ Chicken Breasts
Total Time: 50 Mins, Servings: 4
Ingredients
4 Whole Chicken Breast
Olive Oil, ¼ c
1 tsp Freshly Pressed Garlic
1 tbsp. Worcestershire Sauce
Pit Boss Fin & Feather Rub
1/2 cup Pit Boss Sweet & Heat BBQ Sauce
1/2 cup Pit Boss 'Que BBQ Sauce
Instructions
In a wide mixing bowl, combine the olive oil, Worcestershire sauce, garlic, and Pit Boss Fin & Feather rub. Chicken breasts should be brushed with the mixture.
In a separate dish, combine equal parts Pit Boss Sweet & Heat and Pit Boss 'Que BBQ sauce.
Preheat the grill to 500ºF with the top covered for 20 mins.
Cook the chicken for 20-30 mins on the grill plate or until the thickest part of the breast reaches 160ºF. Use the BBQ sauce to glaze the chicken.
Remove off the grill and leave aside for 5 mins to cool before slicing.

3.28 Roasted Teriyaki Wings
Total Time: 5 Hrs, Servings: 6
Ingredients
Large Chicken Wings, 2 ½ lb
1/2 cup Soy Sauce
Water, ¼ c
Brown Sugar ¼ c
2 tbsp. Rice Wine Vinegar
2 Scallions
1 Garlic clove, Minced
2 tsp Sesame Oil
2 tbsp. Fresh Ginger, Smashed
1 tbsp. Lightly Toasted Sesame Seeds
Instructions
To form three parts, cut the wings in half at the joints. Save the wingtips for chicken stock or throw them away.
In a large Ziplock bag or a mixing cup, combine the drumettes and flats.
In a mixing dish, combine all the ingredients for the marinade. In a saucepan, combine soy sauce, 1/4 cup water, vinegar, brown sugar, garlic, scallions, sesame seed, and ginger.
Bring to a simmer, then lower to low heat and cook for another 10 mins.
Allow cooling completely before applying to chicken wings. After closing the container, chill it for several hours or overnight.
Drain and discard the marination from the wings.
Preheat the Pit Boss to 350ºF with the top covered for 10 mins when ready to cook.
Cook for 40- 50 mins, or until the flesh is no longer pink at the bone and the skin has become golden brown and crunchy.
Turn the wings once throughout the cooking period to prevent them from sticking to the grill grate.
Remove the grill from the heat source. Serve with sesame seeds on top.

3.29 BBQ Chicken Bacon Ranch Sandwich

Total Time: 1 Hr 15 Mins, Servings: 8
Ingredients
1 whole Chicken
2 tbsp. Pit Boss Pork & Poultry Rub
Bacon, ½ lb.
Ciabatta Buns, For Serving
Butter Lettuce, For Serving
Sliced Tomato, For Serving
Avocado Wedges, For Serving
Sliced Havarti Cheese, For Serving
Pit Boss 'Que Sauce, For Serving
Ranch Dressing, For Serving
Instructions
Preheat the Pit Boss to 350 degrees Fahrenheit and cook for 15 mins with the cover closed.
Before adding the poultry Rub and Pit Boss Pork, season the entire chicken with pepper and salt.
Grill the chicken for 60-90 mins, or until an internal thermometer reads 160ºF in the breast and 170ºF in the thigh.
While the chicken is cooking, season 1 side of the bacon with Poultry Rub & Pit Boss Pork. Cook for 25-35 mins, or until bacon is crisp, right next to the chicken on the grill dish.
Remove the chicken from the grill and allow it to cool to room temperature before serving.
While assembling the sandwich, remove the dark flesh from the chicken breast and cut it into 1/2-inch pieces.
Top the ciabatta buns with Pit Boss 'Que Sauce, butter lettuce, sliced beef, pork, avocado, cheese, tomato, and ranch dressing.

3.30 Honey Lime Chicken Adobo Skewers
Total Time: 30 Mins, Servings: 6
Ingredients
4 Chicken Breast, Diced
1 tbsp. Vegetable Oil
2 tsp Garlic, Minced
2 tsp Onion Powder
Rice Vinegar, ¾ c
Soy Sauce, ¼ c
3 tbsp. Honey
2 whole Lime, Juiced
Salt
Black Pepper
8 Pit Boss Skewers
Instructions
Combine all the ingredients, including the chicken, in a wide mixing bowl.
Freeze the mixture overnight, covered.
Preheat your Pit Boss on high for 15 mins with the lid covered.

Cook the marinated chicken on skewers on the Pit Boss, turning halfway through until done (12-15 mins).
Serve with grilled lime wedges as a garnish.

3.31 Baked Cranberry Chicken
Total Time: 1 Hr 15 Mins, Servings: 4
Ingredients
6 Whole Chicken Breast
4 tbsp. Butter
1/2 tsp Salt
Black Pepper, ¼ tsp
1/2 cup Onion, Diced
1/2 cup Thinly Sliced Celery
1 Can Cranberry Sauce, Whole Berry (16oz)
1 cup Pit Boss 'Que BBQ Sauce
Instructions
Season your chicken with salt & pepper. Melt butter in a large pan and brown the chicken on both sides. Fill a greased baking dish halfway with the mixture.
Sauté celery and onion till crispy in the chicken and butter drippings. In a mixing dish, combine the cranberry and barbecue sauces. After fully combining, cook for another 2-3 mins. In an equal layer, pour the sauce over the chicken.
Preheat your Pit Boss to 350°F for 15 mins with the lid closed. Cover & bake at 350°F for 1-2 hours, or until chicken water runs clear. Spoon the sauce over the meat every 12 mins throughout the baking period.
Put the chicken pieces on a serving platter and pour the sauce over them all.

3.32 Diablo Grilled Chicken Thighs
Total Time: 45 Mins, Servings: 2
Ingredients
Pit Boss Cajun Shake
Ancho Chile Powder
Black Pepper
4 Chicken Thighs
Olive Oil, ¼ c
2 Garlic clove
1 & 1/2 Onion, Diced
1 Jalapeno, Sliced into Rings
1 pinch Salt
1/2 cup Water
1 can, 14 oz. San Marzano Tomatoes, Crushed
2 tbsp. Capers, Drained
1/2 cup Chopped Flat-Leaf Parsley
Instructions
Preheat the grill too high for 15 mins with the lid covered.
Season each side of the chicken thighs with the Cajun Shake, black pepper, and ancho or chipotle chili powder. On the grill grate, cook the marinated chicken thighs for 5 mins on each side.
Add the garlic, jalapeño, onion, pinch of salt, and bell pepper to the pan while the chicken is cooking and simmer for approximately 2-3 mins to sauté the onions & peppers.
Scrape the drippings from the pan with a wooden spoon as you deglaze it with 1/2 cup water. Cook for around 5 mins longer, or unless the liquid has been reduced by half.
Add the chicken thighs, tomatoes with juices, and capers to the saucepan, cook for 5 mins, or unless the sauce thickens.
After removing the pan from the heat, stir in the parsley. Serve with extra fresh parsley on the side.

3.33 Kansas City Hot Fried Chicken
Total Time: 1 Hr 25 Mins, Servings: 4
Ingredients
1 whole Chicken, Cut into Pieces
Buttermilk, 1 ½ c
2 tbsp. Hot Sauce
4 cup All-Purpose Flour
1 tsp Salt
1/2 tsp Black Pepper
1/2 tbsp. Red Pepper Flakes
12 oz. Bacon, Uncooked, Chopped
Vegetable Oil
Instructions
Preheat the grill to 180 degrees Fahrenheit & cover for around 20 mins before roasting.
For 10 mins, smoke the 4 chicken pieces.
Combine buttermilk and spicy sauce in a wide mixing cup and set aside to cool completely.
Set aside the dry ingredients and bacon in a separate dish.
Remove the chicken from the pan and chill it for about an hour in an ice-cold buttermilk mixture.
Preheat the oil in a frying pan to 370°F.
After removing the chicken from the marinade, coat it in the dry ingredients mixture and cook it for 10-15 mins. Pickled hot peppers go well with this dish.

3.34 Whole Roasted Chicken
Total Time: 1 Hr 10 Mins, Servings: 4
Ingredients
1 whole Fresh Young Chicken
1 bottle Pit Boss Chicken Rub
Water
1/2 tbsp. Kosher Salt
1 tbsp. Chopped Sage
1 tbsp. Chopped Thyme
1/2 cup Butter, Softened
1/2 tbsp. Coarse Ground Black Pepper
Instructions
Remove the chicken from the package and pat it dry.
To create the brine, combine water and chicken rub in a mixing bowl. Place the chicken, brine, and jar in a wide enough jar to completely submerge the chicken.
Refrigerate for 5-12 hours before serving.
Preheat the Pit Boss to 375°F with the lid closed for 15 mins.
Remove the chicken from the brine without cleaning it.
In a mixing bowl, combine the thyme, pepper, sage, butter, and salt. Using the butter paste, cover the chicken's exterior. Any remaining butter should be stuffed into the cavity of the bird.
Place the chicken directly on the grill pan and cook until the internal temperature reaches 165°F.
Ensure that the interior temperature of the breast is 165 degrees Fahrenheit. Allow 10-20 mins for the chicken to rest once it has been cooked.

3.35 Roasted Sheet Pan Chicken
Total Time: 3 Hrs 40 Mins, Servings: 4
Ingredients
1 bunch Cilantro
1 bunch Fresh Parsley
Basil Leaves, ¼ c
Fresh Mint Leaves, ¼ c
2 Garlic clove
Red Pepper Flakes, ¼ tsp
1 tsp Salt and Pepper
3 whole Lime, Juiced
Extra-Virgin Olive Oil 5/8 c
2 lb. Chicken, Thighs and Drumsticks
1/2 lb. Baby Carrots with Tops
1 whole Red Onion, Cut into 1/8'S

1 Lime Juice, Taste
Instructions
To prepare the puree, in a blender, combine cilantro, mint, parsley, garlic, basil, cinnamon, red pepper flake, lime juice, and 1/2 cup olive oil until smooth. Serve with a portion of the marination, pour the remainder over the chicken, and refrigerate for 2-3 hours.
Preheat the grill on high for 15 mins with the lid covered until you're ready to cook.
Place the chicken on a baking sheet after removing it from the marination. Cook for 25 mins, or unless the chicken begins to brown on the outside.
Toss 2 tbsp. Oil, carrots, & red onion. Season with some salt & pepper for taste. After spreading the chicken on a sheet tray, place it on the grill.
Cook for another 15-20 mins, or until the carrots and onion have begun to brown and the chicken thigh has reached an internal temperature of 160°F.
When the internal temperature of the chicken reaches 165°, remove it from the oven and let it rest for 8-10 mins.
Pour some lime juice & set aside the marination.

3.36 Tomatillo Braised Chicken
Total Time: 2 Hrs 20 Mins, Servings: 4
Ingredients
2 tbsp. Olive Oil
1/2 tsp Kosher Salt
3 tbsp Lime Juice
2 tbsp. Cilantro, Diced
1 pinch Kosher Salt
8 Skin-on, bone-in Chicken Thighs
6 BONE-In, Skin-On Chicken Breasts
Salt & Pepper
1/2 cup Chicken Stock
2 cups Salsa Verde
1 lb. Washed and husked Tomatillos
White onion, 1/4
3 Jalapeno Halved and seeded
Instructions
Preheat the grill to 350 degrees Fahrenheit for 15 mins, then cover and keep warm.
Toss tomatillos, jalapenos, and onions with olive oil and 1/2 tsp salt in a large mixing cup. Transfer to a grilling bucket or baking tray after tossing until evenly coated.
Grill the vegetables for 5-10 mins, rotating them slightly before softening and grilling. Remove the vegetables from the grill as soon as they are done.
Allow them to chill in the same container at room temperature to collect their juices.
Combine the cooled vegetables and juices, as well as lime juice, coriander, and a pinch of salt, in a mixer. Pulse until the paste resembles salsa in consistency. Taste and adjust seasonings as needed, adding more lime juice or salt as needed.
Rinse and dry the chicken thoroughly. Season with salt and pepper on all sides.
Cook for 10-15 mins, or until the meat is nicely browned and crispy, with the skin inverted on the grill. Cook for another 5 mins before transferring the chicken to the pan.
Combine grilled chicken wings, chicken stock, and salsa Verde in an oven / cast iron skillet. Place the pan on your grill grate, covered.
Cook for 1.5-2 hours, or until chicken is fork tender.

3.37 Smoked turkey (bacon-wrapped turkey breast)

Total Time: 30 mins, Servings: 6
Ingredients
Breast
Salt
Pit Boss special Rub
Instructions
Turn your pit master pellet grill on to smoke mode and let it run for approximately 10 mins with the lid open to pre-heat it at 250°F. If you're using a charcoal or gas grill, make sure it's set to medium and indirect heat.
Place the Tarkett directly on the grill grate and smoke it for 2-3 hours, or until the core temp reaches 165°F

3.38 Texas-style turkey
Total Time: 4 Hrs 15 mins, Servings:6
Ingredients
1/2 cup Coarse black pepper
1 lb Butter
1/2 cup kosher Salt
1 Brined turkey
Instructions
Preheat your grill to 300 degrees Fahrenheit.
Season the turkey with black pepper & kosher salt.
Grill till the core temp reaches 145° F.
Coat the turkey with 1 lb of sliced butter, then place it in the roasting pan.
Return to the grill and cook until the core temp of the thigh & breast hits 165° F.
Allow 30 mins between carving & serving to allow the meat to rest.

3.39 Boneless stuffed turkey breast
Total Time: 1 Hrs 40 mins, Servings: 6
Ingredients
1 Bay leaf
1/2 tsp Black pepper
3 tbsp Butter divided
1 minced Celery rib,
cracked black pepper
4 oz Cremini mushrooms
1/2 cup Dried cranberries
2 minced Garlic cloves
Honeysuckle white® turkey breast, Boneless 1 pack
1/2 cup Marsala wine
1 tbsp Olive oil
1 Rosemary sprigs

1/2 tsp Rubbed sage
1/2 tsp Salt
To taste, sea salt
6 oz Stuffing mix
1.25 cup Turkey stock divided
1 chopped yellow onion
Instructions
Turn on the smoke mode on your pit master grill and let it run for approximately 10 mins with the lid open to get it to 325° F. Whether you're using a charcoal barbecue or a gas grill, set the temperature medium low.
Melt butter and olive oil in a large pan over medium heat. Cook, stirring continuously, for 3 mins, or until the celery and onions are soft.
After combining the garlic and mushrooms, cook for approximately 5 mins, or until the mushrooms are gently browned.
Deglaze with marsala liquid, scraping some browned bits from the pan's bottom with a wooden spoon.
After adding the sage, black pepper, dried cranberries, and salt, cook for approximately 2 mins before removing from the heat.
Fold the stuffing into the vegetable mixture, then gently drizzle in the turkey stock, stirring continuously until the stuffing is well absorbed.
Place the skin-side down turkey breasts on a large chopping board and butterfly them. Season with pepper and salt, then pour a spoonful of filling over the top, leaving a 1" gap.
Begin rolling the turkey breast with the least amount of skin on the side the least amount skin. Use butcher's string to truss your turkey breast and preserve the stuffing. Season with pepper and salt and cook in the remaining butter in a skillet. Sprinkle a little rosemary on top, then pour the remaining 14 cups of stock and 1 bay leaf all over the turkey. Place on the grill.
Cook the turkey for 1-1 1/2 hours, or until the internal temperature reaches 165° F.
Remove the filled turkey breast from the grill and set it aside to rest for approximately 15 mins before slicing and serving with the remainder of the stuffing.

3.40 Brie stuffed turkey burgers
Total Time: 40 mins, Servings: 9
Ingredients
Blueberry spread (jalapeno)
Seven oz Bar brie cheese
Burger buns
Sweet burger seasoning (onion) of Pit boss
2 Red Bell peppers
Spinach
3 lbs Turkey ground
Instructions
Brie should be cut into 1/2-inch-wide by 1-inch-high pieces.
3 lbs ground turkey, liberally seasoned with onion burger spice in a mixing bowl. Season the turkey with spices and a little more if required.
Divide the meat into third-lb balls once the spice has been mixed into the ground turkey. Half of the burger patty should go on the bottom of the burger press, followed by three cheese slices in the center.
Place 1/2 of your burger patty on top of the cheese. Push the burger two times using the burger button, and you're done. Flipping the button to drop your burger.
Remove the burgers from the grill and begin creating your masterpiece. You may use any retain you like since the sweet & spicy jam adds a lot of heat to the burger.

3.41 Thanksgiving smoked turkey
Total Time: 8 Hrs, Servings: 6 - 8
Ingredients
1 Turkey brining kits
12 lbs Turkey
1-gallon Water, cold
4 cs+ 1-gallon Water, warm
Instructions
To thaw the turkey, place it in the fridge or freezer.
Render the brine by putting 4 cs of water into a large stockpot with the brine mixture after the turkey has been defrosted as well.
With the mixture, bring 1 tank of cold water to a boil.
Place the turkey in a brine bag and cover it with the brine mix. Refrigerate each lb of turkey for 1 hour.
Clean the turkey with cold water after bringing it home and put it on a pan.
Season each bird with the brine packet seasoning. Pre-heat your pit management
smoker to 275 degrees after the turkey has
been seared as well.
Place the turkey in the smoker with the digital thermometer in the lowest part of the breast. Cook at 275°F until the breast and thigh flesh reaches a core temperature of 165-170°F.
Remove each turkey from the smoker, let it cool, & then slice it into desired pieces.

3.42 Maple smoked thanksgiving turkey
Total Time: 6 Hrs 20 Mins, Servings: 8
Ingredients
1 cup Butter
1/2 cup Maple syrup
2 tbsp Pit boss champion chicken seasoning
1 Turkey (pre-brined)
Instructions
Preheat the grill to 250 degrees Fahrenheit.
Combine melted butter & maple syrup in a wide mixing bowl. Fill the marinade compressor halfway with syrup & butter, then use the needle to pierce the meat while pushing the nozzle to inject the taste. The marinade may be injected into the thigh, breast, & wings' densest areas.
Spread the room-temp butter & champion chicken powder all over the turkey, being careful to get it under the skin.
Place the turkey in an Al pan on the grill to catch all of the drippings.
When the breast and thigh flesh reaches 165-170° F, remove the turkey from the grill and put it aside to rest for 15 mins before carving.

3.43 Cajun Brined Maple Smoked Turkey Breast

Total Time: 3 Hrs 5 Mins, Serving: 4
Ingredients
For the Brine
1- gallon Water
Canning And Pickling Salt, ¾ c
3 tbsp. Minced Garlic
3 tbsp. Dark brown sugar
2 tbsp. Worcestershire Sauce
2 tbsp. Cajun Seasoning
Main
1 (5-6 lb.) BONE-In Turkey Breast
3 tbsp. Extra-Virgin Olive Oil
2 tbsp. Cajun Seasoning
Instructions
In a wide food-safe tub or bucket filled with 1-gallon water, combine all the brine ingredients. Stir continuously until all the salt has dissolved.
Put the turkey breast in the brine & lb it down until it is fully submerged. Refrigerate for 1–2 days before covering and bringing to room temperature.
Remove the turkey breast from the brine & pat it flat. With your fingers, drizzle the oil (olive oil) over the bird, careful to cover both areas. Cajun spice may be used in large quantities.
Preheat the Pit Boss to 225°F with the lid covered for 18 mins.
Place the turkey breast directly on the grill, cover, and cook for 3 hours. After 3 hours, increase the temperature to 403°F and cook for another 30 mins.
Before slicing the turkey breast, remove it from the grill and put it aside for at least 12 mins. Serve by slicing the cake into pieces.

3.44 Pit Boss BBQ Chicken Salad

Total Time: 1 Hr 15 Mins, Servings: 4
Ingredients
Main
Pit Boss Chicken Rub
1 whole Chicken
Burger Buns
Celery, Finely Chopped, ¼ c
Green Onion, Thinly Sliced, ¼ c
Coarsely Chopped Pecans, ¼ c
1/2 cup Mayonnaise
1/2 cup Pit Boss Sweet & Heat BBQ Sauce
1 tsp Salt
1 tsp Ground Black Pepper
1 tsp Garlic Powder
Instructions
When you're prepared to cook, turn on the Pit Boss and set the temp to 500°F. Close the cover and preheat for around 12-15 mins.
Chicken should be lightly seasoned using Chicken Pit Boss Rub. Tuck the wings in & secure the legs with cooking twine (optional).
Grill the chicken for 1 hour and 10 mins, or until the core temp hits 165 degrees.
Remove the grill from the heat and put it aside to cool. In a large mixing basin, draw and shred the chicken until it has cooled.
In a mixing dish, combine the shredded chicken and the other ingredients.

3.45 Smoked Chicken Leg & Thigh Quarters

Total Time: 2 Hrs 10 Mins, Servings: 6
Ingredients
8 Chicken Legs (Thigh and Drumstick)
3 tbsp. Olive Oil
Pit Boss Pork & Poultry Rub
Instructions
Combine the chicken pieces in a wide mixing dish. Toss the chicken slices in enough oil to coat each piece, then season to taste with Pit Boss Pork & Poultry Rub. Rub the chicken pieces to help the oil and spices permeate the flesh. After covering it, put it in the fridge for at least 1-2 hours.
Preheat the Pit Boss to 180°F with the top closed for 15 mins when ready to cook. Use Super Smoke if it's available for the greatest flavor.
Remove the chicken from the fridge and re-add any remaining oil to the pan.
Place the chicken on the grill and smoke it for 1 hour. Raise the temperature of the Pit Boss to 350°F. Continue roasting the chicken for another 50-60 mins, or until the thickest part of a thigh reaches 165°F or the bird becomes golden brown, and the juices flow clear. Before eating, remove the chicken from the grill & set it aside to rest for 8-10 mins.

3.46 Grilled Greek Chicken with Garlic & Lemon

Total Time: 1 Hr 20 Mins, Servings: 4
Ingredients
2 whole Roasting Chicken, 3.5-4lbs Each Cut into 8 Pieces
2 whole Lemons, Quartered
1/2 cup Extra-Virgin Olive Oil
4 clove Garlic, Minced
Oregano, Fresh, 1 ½ c
Pit Boss Chicken Rub 1 as needed
Broth, Chicken
Instructions
Put the chicken pieces on a single sheet on a large roasting pan. Squeeze the lemon juice over the meat, careful not to catch any seeds in your fingers as you do so. Combine the chicken and lemon rinds in a mixing bowl. Using your hands, liberally apply the olive oil on the surface.
Garlic cloves should be rubbed all over the bird. Season the chicken with the Pit Boss Chicken Rub or pepper and salt, then fresh oregano. Pour chicken broth into the tub.
Preheat the Pit Boss to 350°F for 15 mins with the lid closed.
Cook the chicken for 1 hour or until the juices are clear.
Place on a plate or in bowls and drizzle with any of the liquids. Allow for 3 mins of resting time before serving.

3.47 BBQ Chicken Sandwich
Total Time: 55 Mins, Servings: 2
Ingredients
4 whole Chicken, Thighs – Boneless Skinless
Pit Boss Chicken Rub
1 cup Shredded Green Cabbage 1
1/2 cup Shredded Carrot
Red Onion, Thinly Sliced ½ medium
1/2 cup Mayonnaise
1/2 cup Sour Cream
2 tbsp. White Wine Vinegar
1 tsp Sugar
Salt And Pepper
4 whole Burger Buns
Instructions
Preheat the grill to 350°F and bake for 10-12 mins with the lid closed.
Coat the chicken thighs with Pit Boss Chicken Rub in an even layer.
Place the chicken thighs on the grill grate and cook for 25-30 mins, or until they reach an internal temperature of 165°F.
Remove off the grill and set aside to cool while you prepare the coleslaw.
In a shallow cup, combine mayonnaise, whipped cream, mustard, sugar, salt, and pepper. In a medium mixing bowl, combine the cabbage, carrots, and onion. Cover the cabbage mixture with the mayonnaise mixture.
Assemble the sandwich by stacking the coleslaw and desired toppings.

3.48 Roasted Garlic Wings
Total Time: 40 Mins, Servings: 6
Ingredients
1 whole Bulb Garlic
2 lb. Chicken Wings
Salt & Pepper
2 tbsp. Olive Oil
1/2 cup Mayonnaise
1 tbsp. Parmesan Cheese
1/2 tsp Fresh Basil
1/2 tsp Dried Oregano
1 tbsp. Corn Syrup.
1 tsp Lemon Juice
Instructions
Preheat the grill to 450 degrees Fahrenheit and keep the lid closed for 10-15 mins.
Place the garlic on top of the chicken after wrapping it in foil. Before cooking, season the chicken with salt and pepper. Glue the foil sides together.
Cook the foil pack for 35 mins on the grill. Halfway through the cooking time, flip the chicken.
Combine all sauce ingredients in a mixing basin. Until the roasted garlic is done, add 6 garlic cloves to the sauce. Add extra as needed.
Put the chicken on a dish and pour the sauce over it.

3.49 BBQ Chicken Legs
Total Time: 1 Hr 5 Mins, Servings: 6
Ingredients
8 Chicken Drumsticks
2 tbsp. Pit Boss Chicken Rub
1 cup Pit Boss Apricot BBQ Sauce
1 cup Pit Boss 'Que BBQ Sauce
1 cup Apple Jelly, Melted
Instructions
Season the drumsticks with Chicken Pit Boss Rub after drying them with a soft towel.
Preheat the grill to 180°F with the lid closed for 12 mins.
On the grill grate, smoke the chicken legs for 30 mins.
Raise the grill's temperature to 350 degrees Fahrenheit and cook for another 30 mins.
While the drumsticks are cooking, combine the two BBQ sauces & the jelly in a small pan. On medium heat, bring to a low boil, then remove from the heat and put aside.
Brush the BBQ sauce on the chicken legs. Cook for another 12 mins, till a thermometer, hits 165 degrees Fahrenheit.

3.50 Smoked Texas Spicy Drumsticks
Total Time: 1 Hr 15 Mins, Servings: 6
Ingredients
8 Chicken Drumsticks
Salt
Pepper
1 cup Pit Boss Texas Spicy BBQ Sauce
Instructions
Dry the drumsticks with a clean towel and season with pepper & salt.
Preheat the grill to 180°F with the lid covered for 20 mins.
On the grill grate, smoke the chicken legs for 30 mins.
Raise the temperature of the grill to 350°F and cook for another 30 mins.
Brush each drumstick with the Texas Spicy BBQ Sauce and continue to cook for another 15-30 mins, or until a thermometer inserted into the center indicates 165°F.

3.51 BBQ Game Day Chicken Wings and Thighs
Total Time: 60 Mins, Servings: 6
Ingredients
Ten Chicken Thighs
Thirty Chicken Wings
1/2 cup Olive Oil
1/2 cup Pit Boss Chicken Rub
Instructions
Combine the thighs and wings in a large mixing basin. Combine the olive oil & Chicken Pit Boss Rub in a large mixing bowl. Refrigerate it for 4-8 hours, covered.
Preheat the Pit Boss to 375°F with the lid covered for 12 mins.
Cook for around 45 mins on your grill grate with the chicken. Check the internal temperature of the chicken; it should be done at 165°F, but a finishing temperature of 180°F in dark flesh produces a firmer texture.
Remove the chicken from the grill when it reaches the appropriate temperature and put it aside to rest for 4-10 mins before serving.

3.52 Smoked Spatchcocked Cornish Game Hens
Total Time: 60 Mins, Servings: 2
Ingredients
4 Cornish Game Hens 4
4 oz. Pit Boss Big Game Rub
Instructions
Place the game hen on a chopping board.
Cut the backbone from the neck to the tailbone using poultry shears to remove it.
The inside of the bird may be seen once the backbone has been severed. Cut a small slit in the cartilage at the base of the breastbone to reveal the keel bone. Grab the bird by the ribs and open it up like a book, all the way down to the board. It is possible to remove the keel bone. Cut small holes in the bird's flesh behind the legs and tuck the drumsticks into them to hold them in place.
Pit Boss's Season the Big Game Rub both ends together.

Preheat the Pit Boss to 275°F for around 15 mins with the lid closed.
Cook the game chickens on the Pit Boss skin-side up until the internal temperature reaches 160°F.
After removing from the Pit Boss, transfer to a board and cover with foil. Allow for 10 mins of resting time before serving.

3.53 Grilled Sriracha Wings
Total Time: 60 Mins, Servings: 4
Ingredients
2 lb. Chicken Wings
2 tbsp. Pit Boss Chicken Rub
2 tsp Garlic Powder
1 tbsp. Sesame Oil
5 tbsp. Butter, Melted
Dark brown sugar, 1/3 c
Sriracha, ¼ c
2 tbsp. Soy Sauce
2 tbsp. Lime Zest
1 tbsp. Garlic, crushed
1 tbsp. Ginger, Crushed
1 tbsp. Lime Juice
1 tbsp. Cilantro, Finely Chopped
1 tbsp. Toasted Sesame Seeds
Instructions
Before you start cooking, preheat the Pit Boss to 325°F for 15 mins.
In a wide mixing bowl, combine the legs, Chicken Pit Boss Rub, sesame oil, and garlic powder. Toss to coat evenly.
Put the wings on your grill grate & cook for around 25- 30 mins, or until the internal temperature of the chicken reaches 160°F.
Turn the heat up to High and remove the wings from the grill after they have achieved an internal temperature of 160°F.
While the wings are cooking, combine all the sauce ingredients except the cilantro and sesame seeds.
When the grill is hot, sprinkle 1/2 of the sauce mixture over the fried wings and cook for another 12-15 mins, or unless the sauce has set.
Serve the wings with the remaining sauce on the hand and chopped cilantro and sesame seeds on top.

3.54 Chile Chicken Thighs
Total Time: 40 Mins, Servings: 4
Ingredients
2 tbsp. Soy Sauce
Honey, ¼ c
2 clove Garlic, Minced
Red Pepper Flakes, ¼ tsp
4 Boneless, Skinless Chicken Thighs
2 tbsp. Olive Oil
2 tsp Pit Boss Chicken Rub
Ancho Chile Powder
Coarse Ground Black Pepper, ¼ tsp
Instructions
Preheat the Pit Boss to 400°F with the lid closed for 12-15 mins when ready to cook.
Combine the butter, soy sauce, garlic, and red pepper chili flakes in a small cup. Remove it from the
equation.
Sprinkle both sides of the chicken thighs with oil (olive oil) and season with Pit Boss Chicken Rub and pepper, then ancho chili powder.
Cook the marinated chicken thighs for 15 mins per hand on the grill, or until a thermometer reads 165°F.
Over the top, drizzle a chili-Honey glaze. Remove the steaks from the grill. Serve with a hand full of sauce.

3.55 Buffalo Chicken Thighs
Total Time: 25 Mins, Servings: 4
Ingredients
6 BONE-In, Skin-On Chicken Thighs
Pit Boss Pork & Poultry Rub
2 cup Buffalo Wing Sauce
8 tbsp. Butter
Blue Cheese Crumbles, For Serving
Ranch Dressing, For Serving
Instructions
Preheat the Pit Boss to 450 degrees Fahrenheit & cook for around 15 mins with the lid closed.
Before putting the chicken thighs directly on the barbecue grate, liberally season them with Pit Boss Pork & Poultry Rub.
Cook for 8–10 mins, turning halfway.
In a small skillet, heat the wing sauce and butter over medium heat, stirring constantly.
Toss the fried chicken thighs in the wing sauce and butter mixture and turn to coat both sides evenly.
Cook the marinated chicken thighs for another 4-5 mins on the grill.
Finish with a sprinkling of blue cheese and ranch dressing, if desired.

3.56 BBQ Chicken Wings with Spicy Honey Glaze
Total Time: 40 Mins, Servings: 4
Ingredients
4 lb. Chicken Wings
6 oz. Pit Boss Chicken Rub
2 tbsp. Corn Starch
1 cup Honey
1 cup Sriracha
1/2 cup Soy Sauce
2 tbsp. Sesame Oil
3 tbsp. Unsalted Butter
2 tbsp. Sesame Seeds
Instructions
When you're prepared to cook, turn on the Pit Boss grill, set the temperature to 375 degrees Fahrenheit, and shut the lid for 10-15 mins to warm.
While the grill is heating, dry the chicken wings with a soft towel. Spread the Pit Boss Chicken Rub & cornstarch mixture on all sides of the wings.
Cook the wings for 35 mins on a hot grill, rotating halfway through.
While the wings are frying, heat the honey, soy sauce, Sriracha, sesame seeds oil, and unsalted butter on the burner.
Check the temperature of the wings after 35 mins of cooking. A minimum internal temperature of 165°F is required. A temperature of 170-180 F yields a decent result.
Toss the wings with the heated sauce in a large mixing bowl until they're done.
Serve the wings on a plate with sesame seeds on top.

3.57 Baked Apricot Glazed Chicken Thighs
Total Time: 35 Mins, Servings: 4
Ingredients
6 Boneless, skin-on chicken thighs
Salt and pepper
1 cup Pit Boss Apricot BBQ Sauce or Apricot Jam
3 tbsp Chicken broth
2 tbsp. Soy sauce
Red pepper flakes, ¼ tsp
3 tbsp Lemon juice
1/2 tsp Lemon zest
Kosher salt, 1/4 tsp

Black pepper, ¼ tsp
Chopped parsley, ¼ cup
Instructions
Before you start cooking, preheat the Pit Boss grill to 350 degrees Fahrenheit. Preheat the oven for ten to fifteen mins with the lid closed.
Brush the chicken pieces with black pepper and salt and place them immediately on the grill. Cook for 10-15 mins, or until browned.
In a large cast-iron pan, brown the chicken thighs. Combine the glaze ingredients in a shallow bowl and pour over the chicken thighs.
Cook for another 15-20 mins on the grill, or until the meat is cooked through and the sauce has thickened, basting the thighs as needed.
Remove from the grill and sprinkle with chives or parsley before serving.

3.58 Smoked Ditch Chicken
Total Time: 1 Hr 15 Mins, Servings: 2
Ingredients
3 whole Pheasant
Blackened Pit Boss Saskatchewan Rub
3 tbsp Smoky Okie's Rooster Booster Rub
1 White Onion
1 Red Bell Pepper
4 tbsp Olive Oil
Salt and Pepper
1 whole Uncle Ben's Rice Pilaf, Complete Box
Instructions
Before roasting, preheat the grill to 275 degrees Fahrenheit and keep the lid covered for 10-15 mins.
After washing and rinsing the pheasant thighs and breasts, place them in a large,
zippered bag. You may use a lot of Saskatchewan Rub & Rooster Booster. After a good shake, set away.
With a sharp knife, slice onions into thin slices. Remove the seeds and quarter the peppers. Brush the peppers and onions with olive oil and season with salt and pepper. Place the veggies on one side of the grill and cover with tin foil; let the vegetables simmer for at least an hour before adding the pheasant since the pheasant is thin and cooks quickly.
Place the pheasant on the grill after allowing the veggies to steam for at least an hour and keep the grill temperature at 275 degrees Fahrenheit. Preheat the grill to 350 degrees Fahrenheit and bake for 30-45 mins.
Preheat the grill and serve the pheasant and veggies over rice pilaf.

3.59 Stuffed Balsamic Chicken
Total Time: 40 Mins, Servings: 4
Ingredients
4 Skinless, Boneless Chicken Breasts
2 cups Cherry Tomatoes, Diced
½ cup Fresh Diced Basil
Diced Garlic 3 cloves
1 tbsp. Olive Oil
Salt & Pepper
1 tbsp Lemon Juice
3 tbsp Balsamic Glaze-bottled
Fresh Basil
Instructions
Pit Boss should be turned on. Smoke is produced when the lid is opened before the fire is lit (4-5 mins).
Preheat the stove to 350 degrees F with the lid covered for 10-15 mins.
Allow the chicken to dry after rinsing it.
Cut a large pocket in each chicken breast with a sharp knife.
Toss chopped tomatoes, garlic, mozzarella, 1 tbsp olive oil, basil, pepper, salt, and lemon juice.
Fill each chicken breast equally with the tomato mixture.
Place the chicken on a foil-lined baking sheet.
Season the chicken with salt and pepper and drizzle with olive oil and balsamic glaze.
1 cup cherry tomatoes, sprinkled over the chicken
Grill for 25 mins, or unless the chicken is fully roasted, with the baking sheet directly on your grate.
Serve the chicken with additional fresh basil on top.

3.60 Braised Beer Chicken Stew
Total Time: 1 Hr 20 Mins, Servings: 4
Ingredients
3 Whole Chicken Halves, 3.5lbs
2 tbsp. Extra-Virgin Olive Oil
1 large Onion, Diced
2 cloves Minced garlic
1 full Green Bell Pepper, Diced
1 small Baby Carrots, Packet
1 can Tomato, Chopped
12 Fluid Oz Beer
Potatoes 12 small
2 tsp Salt
2 tbsp Pit Boss Chicken rub
Instructions
Preheat the grill on high for 15 mins with the lid covered before using.
Preheat Pit Boss over high heat with a large Dutch oven tray.
In a mixing pot, combine rice, 1 tsp salt, Pit Boss Chicken Scrub, and black freshly ground pepper. Thoroughly coat the chicken in the flour mixture.
Heat the oil in a large Dutch oven and add the chicken pieces. Cook for 15 mins on each side, or until golden brown on both sides. Remove the chicken from the pan and place it on a plate.
Sauté the garlic, onions, and green bell peppers in a Dutch oven for several mins. Add the carrots and continue to cook for another 3 mins. After adding the tomatoes and 1 tsp of salt, roast for 5 mins. In a mixing bowl, combine the beer and potatoes.
Add the chicken pieces to the stew, cover, and continue to cook for another 40 mins. Before serving, reheat the dish.

3.61 Peach & Basil Grilled Chicken Recipe
Total Time: 2 Hrs 30 Mins, Servings: 4
Ingredients
4 Skinless & Boneless Chicken Breasts
4 Peaches, cut in 1/2 and sliced
Olive Oil
1/2 cup Peach, Preserved
1/2 cup Olive Oil
Apple Cider Vinegar, ¼ cup
2 tbsp Lemon Juice
2 tbsp Dijon Mustard
1 clove Garlic, Minced
Frank's Red-Hot Sauce
1/2 tsp Sriracha Salt
Pepper, ¼ tsp
1/2 cup Fresh sliced Basil
Instructions
Clean & dry the chicken before storing it. Peaches that have been gently doused with olive oil should be set aside.
Combine all marinade ingredients in a mixing bowl. For frying, 1/4-1/2 cup is left aside. Soak the chicken for at least 2 hours in a tight plastic bag with the remaining marinade.

Remove the chicken from the marinade and discard it.
Preheat Pit Boss to 350°F for 15 mins with lid closed when ready to cook.
For around 25-30 mins, roast the chicken and peaches. Turn the chicken halfway through the cooking time. Baste the chicken with the remaining marinade for the final 5 mins. The chicken is done when the inside thermometer registers 170°F. Remove the peaches from the pan after they are completely cooked. Remove the chicken from the pan, sprinkle it with fresh basil, and leave it aside for 2 mins.
Cut each peach half into halves and serve with the chicken.
Note: The marinade may be quadrupled and used as a chicken sauce. Please bring all of the ingredients to a boil before removing them to thicken.

3.62 BBQ Chicken Tostada
Total Time: 60 Mins, Servings: 4
Ingredients
4 Skinless chicken thighs-full
Salt & pepper
Corn tostadas 8 whole
Refried beans
Lettuce
Coarsely chopped green onion
Chopped cilantro
Guacamole
Instructions
When roasting, preheat the grill to 350 degrees F and keep the lid closed for 10 mins.
As the grill warms up, trim the excess fat and skin off the chicken thighs.
Season with a touch of salt & pepper.
Grill the chicken thighs on the grill grate for 35 mins.
When the chicken is done, a thermometer placed into the cavity should register 175 deg F. Remove off the grill and put aside for 10 mins before shredding.
While the chicken rests, cook tostadas for 5 mins.
Tostadas should be topped with refried beans, chopped cabbage, shredded beef, peppers, fresh green onions, coriander, and guacamole.

3.63 Chipotle Honey Wings
Total Time: 35 Mins, Servings: 4
Ingredients
Saskatchewan Rub (Blackened) of Pit Boss
Sweet Rub (Pit Boss)
3 can Chipotle Peppers in Adobo Sauce
4 tbsp. Unsalted Butter
1 tbsp Honey
2 tbsp. Fresh Extracted Lime Juice
Avocado Crema
Ranch Dressing or Blue Cheese
Cut into Slices Lime
2 lb flat chicken wings
Drumettes separated.
Instructions
Preheat the grill to 350 degrees Fahrenheit with the lid closed for 10-15 mins.
Brush both sides of the chicken flats and drumettes with a combination of Blackened Saskatchewan Pit Boss rub and Sweet Rub on a baking sheet.
On the grill grate, roast chicken wings for 30 mins.
In the meanwhile, in a skillet over low heat, melt the butter with the chipotles.
After the butter has melted, puree the mixture with an electric mixer. In a mixing dish, combine lime juice and honey.
Toss the wings in a dish with the chipotle Honey-lime glaze and heat until done.
Drizzle the wings with ranch, avocado, crema, or cheese dressing.

3.64 Tequila Lime Chicken Thighs
Total Time: 55 Mins, Servings: 6
Ingredients
12 whole bone-in, skinned chicken thighs
2 tsp Ancho Chile seasoning
2 tsp Sugar
Garlic granules, 1 ½ tsp
Cumin powder, 1 ½ tsp
Black pepper, freshly crushed, 1 ½ tsp
Kosher salt, 3/4 tsp.
1 tbsp. Chili powder
Olive oil (extra-virgin) 1 ½ tsp
4 tbsp. Honey
Pineapple Juice (4 tbsps)
3 tbsp. Tequila
Red chili flakes, ¼ tsp
Cayenne pepper, 1 ½ tsp
Melted butter, 1 ½ tsp
Lime juice, freshly squeezed, 1 ½ tsp
Instructions
When you're prepared to cook, turn on the Pit Boss and warm it to 375 degrees F for 10-15 mins.
Combine the dry ingredients in a medium mixing cup. In a large mixing bowl, thoroughly toss the chicken. Pour the oil into the bowl and stir it in well to coat all the components.
Place the chicken on the grill grate, flesh side down, and steam for 15 mins on the first side.
Combine the glazed ingredients in a small pot. Bring to a low simmer under medium pressure. Cook until the mixture has thickened and reduced by about a third (for approximately 3 mins). Keep the syrup soft while you wait for the glaze to dry.
After 15 mins in the oven, rub the chicken thighs with the sugar mixture. Shift the bird to the opposite side. Brush the opposite face with even more glaze and grill for another 10 mins, or until an instant thermometer reads 165 degrees Fahrenheit.

3.65 Baked Garlic Parmesan Wings
Total Time: 50 Mins, Servings: 4
Ingredients
5 lb. Chicken Wings
Pit Boss Chicken Rub, 3 ½ tbsp
1 Cup Butter
Garlic, chopped ten cloves
1/2 Cup Butter-unsalted
Minced garlic, Finely Chopped ten cloves
1 cup Crushed Parmesan Cheese
3 tbsp Minced Parsley
Instructions
Preheat your Pit Boss to 450 degrees Fahrenheit & cook for around 15 mins with the lid closed.
In a wide mixing bowl, toss wings with Chicken Pit Boss Rub.
Cook for 20 mins on this grill grate with the wings on it right away. After turning the wings, heat for another 20 mins.
Check the core temp of the wings; they should be between 165–180°F when done.
While the chicken is cooking, make the garlic sauce by combining the butter, garlic, and remaining paste in a medium saucepan and heating over a low flame. Cook for 8-10 mins, stirring occasionally.
Place the wings in a large mixing bowl after removing them from the grill. In a mixing cup, combine the legs, Parmesan cheese, garlic sauce, and parsley.

3.66 Spicy BBQ Whole Chicken

Total Time: 3 Hrs 15 Mins, Servings: 4
Ingredients
1 whole Chicken
6 Thai Chiles
2 tbsp Sweet Paprika
1 Scotch Bonnet Spice
2 tbsp Sugar
3 tbsp Salt
1 White Onion
5 Garlic clove
4 cups Grapeseed Oil
Instructions
In your blender, combine the Thai chiles, salt, paprika, sugar, Scotch bonnet pepper, onion, garlic, and grapeseed oil until smooth.
Strangle the chicken in the marinade and place it in the freezer to rest overnight.
Preheat the Pit Boss to 300°F with the cover shut for 15 mins before starting.
Place the chicken breast side up on the grill for 90 mins, or until the core temperature of the breast reaches 165°F.
Before carving the steak, remove it from the grill and let it aside for 10-15 mins. Serve with a side dish of your choice.

3.67 Grilled Chicken Fajitas

Total Time: 1 Hr 20 Mins, Servings: 2
Ingredients
2 Skinless, Boneless chicken breasts
1/2 tbsp. Cumin
Chili powder
1 Lime, juiced
Salt & pepper
1 tbsp. Extra virgin olive oil
4 Tortillas
1 Sliced yellow onion (small)
1 Green bell pepper (sliced)
1 Red bell pepper (sliced)
Instructions
In a Ziploc bag, combine the chicken breasts, cumin, chili powder, salt, pepper, and lime juice. Please marinate it for 1 hour in the refrigerator.
Raise the Maximum levels & preheat for around 15 mins with the lid closed when you're ready to cook.
Put the fajita skillet on your grate to pre-heat the grill for 30 mins. Combine the onions and peppers in a skillet with olive oil, season with pepper & salt, then cover to keep warm.
Cook for 10 mins, or unless the chicken is well cooked.
Cook for 10-15 mins on the grill grate beside the skillet, rotating halfway through before internal temperature reaches 165°F.
After removing the roasted chicken from the grill, allow it to rest for a few mins before carving.
Place sliced meat, peppers, and onions on a fajita tray, along with tortillas and desired toppings.

3.68 Pit Boss Crispy Orange Chicken Wings

Total Time: 1 Hr 20 Mins, Servings: 2
Ingredients
2 Lb Chicken Wings
Kosher Salt
1/2 cup Chicken Broth
1 tbsp Corn Starch
1 cup Quick Squeezed Orange Juice
1 large Orange Zest
2 tbsp Soy Sauce
Brown Sugar, 1/3 cup
1 tsp Ground Ginger
1 tbsp Asian Chili-Garlic Paste
Black pepper, ¼ tsp
Instructions
When you're ready to start, preheat a Pit Boss to 350°F for around 15 mins. Place chicken wings, skin side up, on a hot plate over a sheet tray lined with paper towels. Wipe with paper towels to rinse. After seasoning the wings with kosher salt, chill them for 1 hour.
To prepare the sauce, combine corn starch and chicken stock in a mixing bowl.
Combine the remaining ingredients in a small saucepan and bring to a boil over medium heat.
Stir in the chicken slurry & corn starch after the sauce has reached a boil. Cook till the sauce thickens, about 5 mins. Take the pan off the heat and set it aside.
Grill the wings for around 45 mins, or until the core temp reaches 170°F & the skin is gently browned.
Remove the wings from the grill and combine them with the orange sauce in a mixing dish. Toss before the wings have absorbed much of the sauce.

3.69 Bacon Jalapeño Chicken

Total Time: 1 Hr 15 Mins, Servings: 2
Ingredients
6 Bacon
1 whole Chicken
4 tbsp Butter
Pit Boss rub
2 sliced Seeded Jalapeno
3 tsp Cajun Seasoning
Instructions
In a wide mixing dish, combine melted butter, sliced jalapenos, and 1 tsp Cajun seasoning. Bacon may be chopped and added to the mixture.
Preheat the Pit Boss to 500 degrees Fahrenheit before starting. With the cover shut, preheat for around 15 mins.
Spread 1/2 of the melted butter beneath the surface of the chicken breasts and smear it around to distribute it evenly.
Rub the ribs with a mixture of Cajun spice and Pit Boss Rub on the outside.
Cook for 1 hour, or until the chicken reaches a core temperature of 140°F, directly on the Pit Boss.
Cook until the chicken reaches 165°F, then spread the leftover bacon butter all over the outside.

3.70 California Club Chicken

Total Time: 1 Hr 35 Mins, Servings: 2
Ingredients
4 Skinless, Boneless Chicken Breasts
4 tbsp Olive Oil
Salt and Pepper
4 tsp Ground Cumin
8 Bacon slices
4 tbsp Lime Juice
8 slices Swiss Cheese
2 sliced Avocados
4 tbsp Picante Sauce
Instructions
Preheat the oven to 350°F and slice the chicken breasts into 1/2" thick slices. Coat both sides of the chicken with olive oil, salt, cumin, and pepper to taste, and let the spices soak in for an hour.
Preheat the grill to 350°F for 10-15 mins with the lid covered until you're ready to start cooking.
Remove the grill from the heat, cook the bacon on a baking sheet for 20 mins, or until the fat has rendered and the bacon

is still absorbent.
Drizzle lime juice on each side of the chicken before frying and increase the temperature
to maximum. Cook for 10 mins with the cover closed.
Cook the chicken breasts on the grill for 8 mins, then flip and cook for another 2 mins, or until an instant thermometer registers 165 degrees F.
Remove the chicken off the grill and place it on a plate with 2 bacon pieces on top, sliced avocado, and Swiss cheese on each piece.
When the cheese has melted, return the chicken to the Pit Boss for another min of cooking.
Serve the chicken on a plate with a dollop of Picante sauce on top.

3.71 Smoked turkey legs
Total Time: 2 Hrs 40 mins, Servings: 4
Ingredients
1 cup Chicken stock
2 tbsp Pit boss blackened sriracha rub
4 Turkey legs (drumsticks)
Instructions
On the grill, turn on the smoke setting. Allow it to run for 10 mins with the lid open.
Preheat the grill to 225 degrees Fahrenheit. If you're using a charcoal or gas grill, make sure the heat is set to medium and indirect.
Combine 2 tsp. Blackened sriracha rub and turkey reserve in a mixing bowl.
Place the turkey legs on the sheet tray and fill each with seasoned stock. Season the outsides of the thighs with the remaining blackened sriracha.
Place the turkey legs on the grate of the smoking cabinet and cook for 1 1/2 hours.
Raise the temp to 325° F and continue cooking the turkey legs for another 45-60 mins, or until the core temperature reaches 170° F.
Take the turkey off the grill and let it rest for 10 mins before serving.

3.72 Sweet heat Cajun spatchcock turkey
Total Time: 3 Hrs 30 mins, Servings: 7
Ingredients
16 oz Cajun butter
Pit boss sweet heat rub
1 Brined turkey
Instructions
Preheat the grill to 300 degrees Fahrenheit.
Heat massage the turkey well and infuse it with Cajun butter.
Put the thighs & breasts on the grill & cook till they reach a temp of 165 degrees F.
Allow for 30 mins of resting time before serving.

3.73 BBQ breakfast sausage not so fatty
Total Time: 55 mins, Servings: 4-6
Ingredients
0.25 cup BBQ sauce
1 tbsp Brown sugar
4 oz Cheddar cheese, slice into sticks
Cracked black pepper
6 eggs scrambled
4 oz Ham, diced
1 pack Shady farms turkey sausage (ground)
Ten oz Turkey bacon
Instructions
Turn your grill on smoke mode and let it run for approximately 10 mins with the lid open to get it to 375° F. Whether you're using a charcoal or gas grill, set the temperature to medium to high.
Make a bacon weaving using a piece of plastic wrap and your favorite turkey bacon. Fan out its shady brook turkey sausage in an even sheet using your fingers.
Place the mashed eggs in the middle of the sausage, followed by half of your cheese
sticks, ham, then the remaining cheese sticks.
Begin rolling the "not so fatty" by lifting one end of the plastic wrap lightly. Remove the plastic wrap from the roll and knot the bacon ends together using toothpicks if required.
Place in a skillet and season with sugar and cracked pepper. Cook on the grill for 30 mins or until the internal temperature reaches 155° F.
Cook for another 5 mins, basting with BBQ sauce before it sets, or until the internal temperature reaches 165° F.
Remove the steak from the grill and set it aside to rest for 5 mins before slicing and serving.

3.74 BBQ dry rubbed turkey drumsticks
Total Time: 2 Hrs 10 mins, Servings: 6
Ingredients
1/2 tbsp Black pepper
1 tbsp Brown sugar
1/2 tsp Cayenne pepper
1/2 tbsp Coriander, ground
1/2 tbsp Granulated garlic
Honeysuckle white® turkey drumsticks 1 pack
1 tbsp Kosher salt
2 tbsp Olive oil
Instructions
Turn your grill on smoke mode and let it run for approximately 10 mins with the lid open to get it to 225° F. If you're using a charcoal or gas grill, make sure it's set to medium-low, indirect heat.
On a sheet pan, season turkey legs with granulated garlic, salt, brown sugar, cayenne, pepper, & ground coriander. Drizzle with some olive oil.
Put the turkey legs in a smoker for 12 hours, checking the temperature at the core every 1 hour.
Raise the temp to 325° F and cook the turkey legs for another 25-30 mins, or until the internal temperature reaches 170° F.
Remove the turkey drumsticks from the grill and let them rest for almost 10 mins before serving.

3.75 Bacon lattice turkey
Total Time: 3 Hrs 30 mins, Servings: 7
Ingredients
2 apples
Bacon
2 celery, stick (parsley, rosemary, thyme) herb mix
1 onion, sliced
Pepper
Pit boss grills champion chicken seasoning
1 brined turkey
Instructions
Preheat your grill to 300 degrees Fahrenheit.
Ensure that the giblets and guts of the turkey have been removed.
A paper towel may be used to clean and dry the turkey's exterior and interior parts.
Fruit & vegetables may be put inside the turkey after being chopped into large pieces.
Use a liberal amount of chicken spice to coat the whole turkey.
Arrange bacon in a lattice design on a flexible cutting board.

Cover the breasts with the turkey's top.
To taste, season with black pepper and champion chicken.
Allow the turkey to rest for 30 mins

3.76 Bacon-wrapped turkey legs
Total Time: 3 Hrs 10 mins, Servings: 8
Ingredients
Water 1 -gallon
0.25 cup Pit Boss rub
Morton's tender quick home meat cure 3 c
1/2 cup Brown sugar
6 Black peppercorns
2 Bay leaves
8 Turkey legs
8 Bacon slices
Instructions
Brining the turkey legs overnight is required, so plan. In a large stockpot, combine peppercorns, water, brown sugar, curing salt, Pit Boss rub, and bay leaves.
Bring the sugar granules and salt to a boil over high heat to dissolve them. Remove the pan from the heat and fill it with water and ice. Check to check whether the brine is about room temperature, if not hotter.
Ensure that the turkey legs are completely submerged in the brine.
After 24 hours, drain your turkey legs and discard the brine. Rinse the legs in cold water and dry them well with paper towels to remove the brine.
Preheat the Pit Boss to 250 degrees Fahrenheit and cook for 15 mins with the lid covered.
Place the turkey legs directly on the grill grate.
After 2 1/2 hours, wrap a piece of bacon over each leg and continue cooking for 30-40 mins.
The legs should be roasted for no more than 3 hours, or until an instant meat thermometer shows a core temperature of 165° F. Serve and has a good time.

3.77 Texas-style turkey
Total Time: 6 Hrs 15 mins, Servings:6
Ingredients
1/2 cup Coarse black pepper
1 lb Butter
1/2 cup kosher salt
Turkey 1 brined
Instructions
Preheat your grill to 300 degrees Fahrenheit.
Season the turkey with kosher salt and black pepper to taste.
Cook until the core temp reaches 145° F or the skin has browned to your liking on the grill.
Coat the turkey with 1 lb of sliced butter and place it in the roasting pan.
Return the breast and thigh to the grill & cook until the core temp reaches 165° F.
Allow 30 mins for the meat to rest before cutting and serving.

3.78 Hot turkey sandwich
Total Time: 15 mins, Servings:4
Ingredients
8 Bread slice
1 cup Gravy prepared
2 cs Leftover turkey, shredded
Instructions
Turn on the flame broiler on your grill. Before starting a fire in a burn pot, turn the grill to "smoke" with the lid open. Preheat the grill to 400 degrees Fahrenheit.
Place the grill rack on the preheated grill grates and thinly spread the shredded turkey to reheat for about 10 mins.
Make the sauce from scratch or reheat it. You'll want to have the gravy hot and primed as soon as the turkey is re-cooked and the bread is toasted.
Place each piece of bread on the flame broiler to toast it.
When all of the ingredients are heated, scoop 1/2 cup of shredded turkey over the piece of toasted bread, gently cover with gravy, then top with another piece of toasted bread.

3.79 Pepper and onion turkey burger sliders
Total Time: 45 mins, Servings:5
Ingredients
1 minced sweet onion
1 Anaheim pepper
Bacon cheddar Pit boss burger seasoning
Spinach
16 oz Ground turkey
Instructions
Turn the grill to smoke mode until the flame ignites.
Season the ground turkey liberally with the pit manager cheddar bacon burger seasoning in a mixing dish.
Toss in the chopped Anaheim pepper.
A third of a sweet onion, diced, may be added to the meal.
Mix with your hands till the meat seems to be evenly cooked & the veggies are well mixed.
After cutting the meat into 3oz cubes, toss or scatter the leftovers.
With the pit boss 3 in 1 burger button, you can create the perfect patty. Depending on the thickness of the patties, cook them on the grill for 15 to 20 mins. Flip it every 5 mins or so.
Place your buns on the grill if you want them to be toasted.
Remove the turkey sliders from the grill and top with spinach; the rest of the dish seems delicious.

3.80 Smoked turkey legs
Total Time: 5 Hrs 30mins, Servings: 4
Ingredients
1 cup of Pit Boss rub
1/2 cup Morton tender
1/2 cup Brown sugar
1 tbsp Allspice berries, crushed
1 tbsp Grains de-poivre-noir entiers
2 Bay leaves
2 tsp Liquid smoke
4 Turkey's legs
Instructions
In a large stockpot, combine bay leaves, warm water, peppercorns, the rub, allspice, brown sugar, curing salt, and liquid smoke.
Bring the water to a boil over high heat to remove the salt grains. Cool To room temperature. Refrigerate with 1/2-gallon ice water and 4 cups ice.
Put some turkey legs in the brine, making sure they are completely immersed. Within 24 hours, drain the turkey legs and discard the brine.
Rinse the legs in cold water and dry them well with paper towels to remove the brine. Brush away any aromatic spices that have stuck to the surface.
Preheat the Pit Boss to 250°F for approximately 15 mins with the top closed.
Place your turkey legs directly on the grill grate.
Smoke for approximately 4-5 hours, or until an instant meat thermometer detects an internal temperature of 165°F. You will receive an erroneous reading if the probe comes into touch with a bone.

The turkey's legs should be nicely browned. Don't be concerned if the flesh under the skin looks pinkish: it's a chemical reaction to the cure and smoking.
Serve immediately.

3.81 Mayo and herb-roasted turkey
Total Time: 4 Hrs 20 mins, Servings: 8
Ingredients
1.25 cup Mayonnaise
1/2 cup fresh herbs, chopped
Honey
2 Turkey
Pepper & salt
1/2 cup butter
1/2 bunch Thyme, fresh
1/2 bunch Bay leaf
1/2 bunch sage, fresh
1 Onion, quartered & peeled
4 Roughly chopped carrots
4 Roughly chopped celery stalks
2 cup Chicken stock
Instructions
Preheat the Pit Boss at 425°F for approximately 15 mins with the top closed.
In a mixing dish, combine mayonnaise and herbs. Before thoroughly mixing, whisk in the sugar or honey.
Remove the giblets from the turkey's cavity and save them for stock or other use. Remove the paper towel and pat it dry.
Spread the herbed mayonnaise mixture liberally over the turkey wings, thighs, and breasts. Season everything, including the hollow, with pepper and salt.
Fill the bird's cavity with bay leaf, fresh thyme, butter, and fresh sage, if desired. Truss the legs and wings using kitchen twine.
Place the celery, onion, and carrots in a roasting pan or broadsheet pan until ready to use. Fill the pan halfway with stock and put the chicken on top. Cook the turkey for 30-45 mins on a grill or until the skin is golden brown.
When the turkey is almost done, lower the grill temperature to 350°F. Cook until the breast core temp reaches 160°F and the thickest part of the thigh hits 175°F. When the turkey is removed from the oven, it may continue to cook till the breasts reach a final temperature of 165° F.
Remove the steak from the grill and put it aside to rest for approximately 10-15 mins before cooking. Carve it up and devour it.

3.82 Smoked turkey jerky
Total Time: 12 hrs, Servings: 6
Ingredients
1/2 cup Soy sauce
0.25 cup Water
2 tbsp Honey
2 tbsp Asian garlic chili sauce
2 tbsp Lime juice
1 tbsp Morton
4 lb Turkey breast, Boneless
Instructions
In a wide mixing bowl, combine the curing salt, soy sauce, lime juice, water, chili garlic paste, & honey. With a tiny knife, cut the turkey along the grain, which will help it stay together tighter as it dries. It is necessary to remove any extra fat, connective tissue, & membrane.
Turkey slices should be half-filled in a large resealable plastic bag. Toss the turkey slices in the marinating mixture and massage the bag to ensure that all pieces are coated. After closing the container, chill it for several hours or overnight.
Preheat the oven to 180°F and leave the lid covered for 15 mins to pre-heat.
Remove the turkey from the marinade and discard it. Dry each turkey slice with a paper towel. Arrange the veggies on the grill grate on a single sheet.
Smoke for 2-4 hours, or until crispy but still malleable and chewy when bent in half.
Transfer the jerky to a resealable plastic container while it is still soft. Allow 1 hour for the jerky to rest at room temperature. Refrigerate the jerky after squeezing the air out of the wrapper. It would keep in the fridge for a few weeks.

3.83 Injected drunken smoked turkey legs
Total Time: 45 mins, Servings: 4
Ingredients
1 bottle Frank's red-hot sauce
1/2 cup butter
1 cup Brown sugar
1/2 cup bourbon or whiskey
3 Minced garlic cloves
1 tsp Cajun seasoning
1/2 cup Chicken stock
6 large Turkey's legs
Instructions
Except for the turkey legs, combine all ingredients in a large saucepan. Bring the saucepan to low heat and keep it there. Allow it to marinade for nearly 24 hours in the refrigerator. Allow the marinade to cool before putting it into a resealable bag with the turkey legs.
When removing the turkey legs from the bag, save the marinate.
Bring half of the marinade to a boil, then set aside half for basting.
The chicken reserve may be used to dilute half of the marinade. Fill a meat injector halfway with the chicken stock/marinade mixture and inject it into the meaty parts of the turkey leg several times. Before the turkey legs swell up, inject the marinade into them.
Preheat your Pit Boss at 250 degrees Fahrenheit & cook for around 15 mins with the lid covered.
Place these turkey legs on the grill grate and cook for 1-3 hours, depending on the size of the turkey legs, or until an instant-read thermometer registers 165° F. Baste the legs with the boiling, stored marinade every 45 mins.

3.84 Homemade turkey gravy
Total Time: 3 Hrs 20 mins, Servings: 8
Ingredients
1 Turkey, neck
2 large Onion
4 stalks Celery
4 Fresh large carrots
8 Smashed garlic cloves
8 Thyme springs
4 cup Chicken broth
1 tsp Salt
1 tsp Black pepper cracked
1 stick butter
1 cup all-purpose flour
Instructions
Preheat the grill to 350°F with the lid closed for almost 15 mins.
In a deep roasting pan, combine the thyme, turkey neck, garlic, onion, carrot, and celery. Season with salt and pepper, as well as 4 cups chicken stock.
Place the prepped turkey on a rack in the roasting pan in the Pit Boss.
Cook for 3-4 hours, or until the breast reaches a temperature of 160°F. The turkey may now begin to cook till it achieves a

core temp of 165° F after being taken from the grill.
Reduce the heat to low and pour the drippings into the saucepan.
Whisk the butter and flour together in a bigger pot until golden brown. This will take around 8 mins of continuous stirring.
Then mix the drippings into the roux and bring to a boil. Season with pepper and salt to taste, then serve right away.

3.85 Smoked wild turkey jerky
Total Time: 2 Hrs 20 mins, Servings: 6
Ingredients
1/2 cup Soy sauce
0.25 cup Water
2 tbsp Honey
2 tbsp Asian chili garlic sauce
2 tbsp Lime juice
2 lb Boneless, skinless turkey breast
Instructions
In a wide mixing bowl, combine water, soy sauce, curing salt, honey, lime juice, and garlic chili paste.
Round the turkey crosswise into 1/4-inch-thick strips with a fine knife, which will help it stay together long as it dries.
It is necessary to remove any extra fat, connective tissue, or membrane.
Half-fill a large resealable bag with turkey slices. Toss the turkey slices in the marinating mixture and massage the bag to ensure that all pieces are coated. After closing the container, refrigerate for several hours or overnight.
Preheat the Pit Boss to 165° F and leave the lid closed for 15 mins to pre-heat. Use super smoke if it's available for the greatest flavor.
Remove the turkey from the marinade and discard it.
Dry each turkey slice using both paper towels.
Arrange the veggies on the grill grate on a single sheet.
Continue to smoke for another 2-4 hours, or until the jerky is crispy but still chewy and malleable when bent in half.
Transfer the jerky to a resealable bag while it is still soft.
Allow 1 hour for the jerky to rest at room temperature.
Refrigerate the jerky after squeezing the air out of the wrapper. It would keep in the fridge for a few weeks.

3.86 Traditional smoked thanksgiving turkey
Total Time: 4 Hrs 15 mins, Servings: 8
Ingredients
1/2 lb Butter
6 Minced garlic cloves
8 Fresh thyme springs
1 Fresh rosemary spring
1 tbsp cracked black pepper
1/2 tbsp Kosher salt
Twenty lb Turkey, birds
Instructions
Preheat your grill at 300 degrees Fahrenheit & cook for 15 mins with the lid closed.
In a shallow baking dish, combine kosher salt, melted butter, black pepper, minced garlic, chopped rosemary, and thyme leaves.
Remove the skin from the turkey's breast to create a hollow to stuff the butter-herb mixture. Cover the whole breast with a 1/4-inch layer of the butter mixture.
Season the whole turkey with black pepper and kosher salt. If desired, fill the cavity of your bird with a traditional stuffing recipe. Preheat the grill to 300° F for approximately 15 mins with the lid closed.
On the grill, smoke the turkey for 3-4 hours. Check your core temperature, which should be 175 degrees Fahrenheit at the thigh bone and 160 degrees Fahrenheit at the breast. When the turkey is removed from the oven, it may continue to cook until the breasts reach a final temperature of 165° F.
Allow 10-15 mins for the dish to rest before serving.

3.87 Roasted stuffed turkey breast
Total Time: 60 mins, Servings: 6
Ingredients
1 Turkey breast Boneless
5 Chopped thick-cut bacon slices
0.75 cup Assorted mushrooms
1 bunch Chopped scallions
0.1 cup White wine
3 tbsp Panko breadcrumbs
Black pepper
Salt
Instructions
Preheat the Pit Boss to 375 degrees Fahrenheit and cook for 15 mins with the lid closed.
Cut each turkey breast horizontally, taking care not to cut all the way through. Place the breasts flat on the table, open.
On medium heat, cook bacon until crispy in a pan. Remove the bacon from the pan and place it on a plate to cool. Before browning the mushrooms, sauté them in bacon oil. After adding the scallions, cook for another 2 mins. Cook the white wine until it is completely gone. After combining the breadcrumbs and bacon, season with pepper and salt.
After the turkey breast has cooled, pour the stuffing over it and carefully massage it in to ensure it sticks. Allow the filling to chill in the refrigerator for 15-20 mins. Roll the turkey breasts tightly and tie them together using butcher's twine at 1" intervals. Tuck the ends of the turkey breasts under and tie them together lengthwise with twine.
Season the outside of the turkey breast with pepper and salt. On the grill, cook for approximately 40 mins. Check your core temperature; it should be 165 degrees Fahrenheit. As soon as the turkey reaches the desired temperature, remove it from the grill and set it aside to rest for approximately 10 mins. Serve by cutting into slices.

3.88 Nashville hot turkey melt
Total Time: 35 mins, Servings: 6
Ingredients
Nashville hot sauce
 1 stick salted butter
 2 tbsp Sugar dark brown
 2 tbsp Fire Honey
 1 tbsp Rub-a-dub
 0.25 cup Cayenne pepper
Main
 8 Biscuits
 Hot sauce, Nashville
 2 lb Cooked & sliced turkey breasts
 8 slices Cooked applewood bacon, thick-cut
 16 slices Cheese, pepper jack
 16 Bread
 Jalapeño jelly
Instructions
Preheat your Pit Boss at 400 degrees Fahrenheit & cook for 15 mins with the lid closed.
Combine all of the ingredients for the Nashville hot sauce in a small pot. Before the chocolate is completely melted, heat it.
Place melts in the following sequence on a pan or sheet tray: biscuit split in half, Nashville warm sauce poured on each half, chopped turkey, fried pork, jack pepper cheese, and Biscuit.
Cook the melts in the Pit Boss for 15-20 mins, or until the cheese is melted and the biscuits are completely toasted.
Carefully cut the cast iron using heatproof gloves. Allow 3-5

mins to cool before topping with butter and bread pickle chips; add more Nashville hot sauce or jalapeno jelly for a kick.

3.89 Smoked turkey with fig BBQ sauce
Total Time: 6 hrs, Servings: 4
Ingredients
1 Water gallon
1/2 cup Sugar
2 Bay leaves dried
2 large Thyme sprigs
6 Peppercorns
1/2 cup Salt
6 Turkey's thighs
1/2 cup Ras-el hanout
6 tbsp Olive oil extra-virgin
1 cup Pit Boss apricot BBQ sauce
4 Fresh figs
Instructions
Bring the brine ingredients to a boil at high pressure on the stovetop, after thoroughly combining, set aside to cool until the salt and sugar have dissolved.
Place some turkey thighs in the brine and let them sit for almost 4 hours or overnight. Remove the meat from the brine, thoroughly clean it, and dry it.
Preheat your grill at 250° F for approximately 15 mins with the lid covered. Use super smoke if it's available
for the greatest flavor.
Rub the turkey thighs with the Ras-el-hanout and 1 tbsp of olive oil each. Place the thighs on the grill grate with their backs to the grill. Smoking for 2 hours
To make the fig BBQ sauce, combine the figs and Pit Boss apricot barbecue sauce in a small saucepan over medium heat. Cook for 20 mins, or until the figs are completely softened, adding 3 tbsps water as needed. Any remaining figs should be removed and discarded.
After the turkey thighs have stopped smoking, remove them from the grill and pre-heat on high for approximately 15 mins with the lid closed. Return the thighs to the grill when it's hot and roast them, often basting with fig BBQ sauce until the thighs are thoroughly caramelized, and the internal temperature reaches 165° F.
Remove the turkey thighs off the grill and baste them again with the remaining BBQ sauce.

3.90 Smoked turkey
Total Time: 7 Hrs 20 mins, Servings: 6
Ingredients
1 Frozen or fresh turkey, giblets removed, thawed
1 cup Pit Boss rub
1.5 cup minced garlic
1 cup Sugar
1/2 cup Worcestershire sauce
2 tbsp Canola oil
Instructions
Verify that the turkey has thawed fully & that all giblets have been removed. 3 gallons of water in a 5-gallon nonmetal bucket
In a mixing bowl, whisk together the Worcestershire sauce, Pit Boss rub, sugar, and garlic until the sugars are completely dissolved.
Place the turkey breast side down in the brine bucket. Make sure your turkey is completely submerged in the water.
After closing the bucket, keep it refrigerated overnight.
Remove the turkey from the brine and pat it dry. Brush canola oil all over the outside of the turkey breast and place it facing up on the disposable Al roasting pan.

Preheat your grill at 225°F & cook for approximately 15 mins with the lid closed. Use super smoke if it's available for the greatest flavor.
Smoke your turkey for approximately 2 1/2 to 3 hours on a barbecue.
Cook for 3 1/2-4 hours, or until the core temperature of the breast reaches 165°F in the densest area, after increasing the grill temperature to 350°F.
Remove the meat from the grill and allow it to rest for 30 mins before carving.

3.91 Pit Boss brined smoked turkey
Total Time: 2 Hrs 20 mins, Servings: 8
Ingredients
Brine
8 Water quart
1 cup Kosher salt
0.3 cup Brown sugar
1/2 cup Molasses
1/2 tsp Garlic salt
1/2 tsp Onion powder
1 tsp Salt
1 tsp Pepper
Seven Sage, leaves, fresh
Main
1 Turkey breast
2 tbsp Butter
Rub
Poultry rub or Pit Boss pork
Instructions
Make preparations ahead of time. An overnight stay is required for this recipe.
In a large bag, combine sage leaves, water, spices, kosher salt, molasses, and brown sugar to create the brine.
Brings to a boil under medium pressure. Cook, constantly stirring, until the sugar and salt have completely dissolved. Take the pan off the heat and add the ice cubes. Mix until nearly all of the sugar has dissolved. Ensure that the brine has completely cooled.
Submerge the turkey breast in the brine by weighing it down with a couple of plates. Refrigerate for almost 24 hours with a lid, bubble wrap, or foil on top.
Preheat the oven to 375°F and leave the cover shut for approximately 15 mins before serving.
Meanwhile, after removing the turkey from the brine, clean it inside and out. Remove the turkey's skin
using paper towels. Apply a thin coating of butter to the skin. Using your hands, massage the rub all over the turkey.
On the grill, cook the turkey breast for 2-3 hours or until the core temperature reaches 165° F in the densest region of the breast.
Enable 15 mins for the turkey to rest after taking it from the grill to allow the fluids to redistribute before carving and serving.

3.92 Dry brine Pit Boss turkey
Total Time: 6 Hrs 5 mins, Servings: 6
Ingredients
1 Farm turkey, fresh
1 tsp Kosher salt for each lb of turkey
Fresh thyme
Fresh sage
Fresh rosemary
Fresh parsley
Instructions
Combine parsley, thyme, sage, and rosemary in appropriate amounts with kosher salt. Rub the spice kosher salt mixture all over the turkey, including into the cavity.
Place the turkey in a container or cover it in plastic wrap and

seal it firmly. Refrigerate the turkey for at least two days before serving. Remove the turkey from the box or untie the plastic wrap on the third day. Return the turkey to the freezer for another 24 hours, uncovered.

Preheat the Pit Boss to 120 degrees Fahrenheit for approximately 15 mins with the top closed.

Place each turkey breast on the grill, breast side up. On the grill, cook the turkey for 3-4 hours.

After 3-4 hours, increase the grill temp to 325° F & cook the turkey till it reaches a core temp of 165° F.

3.93 Roasted herbed turkey breast

Total Time: 2 Hrs 20 mins, Servings: 8
Ingredients
Main
0.75 cup Kosher salt
0.3 cup Brown sugar
1 turkey breast BONE-in, skin-on
1 cup Water
Herb butter
8 tbsp Butter
0.25 cup fresh herbs, chopped
1 Minced garlic clove
1 tbsp Lemon juice fresh
1 tsp Lemon zest fresh
1/2 tsp Black pepper freshly ground
Instructions

It's a good idea to get rid of some of the excess fat in your breasts. In a large stockpot, combine 1-gallon water, brown sugar, and kosher salt. Before the sugar and salt crystals are completely dissolved, stir vigorously.

After bringing the turkey, keep it refrigerated for 6-8 hours or overnight. If necessary, weigh down the turkey with a bag of ice to keep it submerged.

Remove the turkey from the brine and wipe dry with paper towels. Place each breast on a roasting rack in a small roasting pan. Pour water over the rim of the pan.

In an oven mixing bowl, combine the salt, butter, chopped herbs, lemon zest, lemon juice, garlic, and pepper to create the herb butter.

Preheat your Pit Boss at 325°F for approximately 15 mins with the top closed.

Using your fingers or the edge of the wooden spoon, loosen the fat beneath the beef breast. By evenly spreading the butter, you may get rid of some air pockets.

Melt the remaining 4 tbsp herb butter in a microwave-safe bowl over medium to low heat. Brush a little of the melted butter around the turkey breast.

Fry the turkey for 2-3 hours, or till golden brown & the thickest part of the breast hits 165°F. 1-2 hours later, baste with the remaining butter. Allow 15 mins for the meat to rest before cutting.

3.94 Grilled Asian lettuce wrap turkey burger

Total Time: 30 mins, Servings: 4
Ingredients
Main
3 tbsp Mayonnaise
1 tbsp Sriracha
1 lb ground turkey
1/2 cup Panko breadcrumbs
0.25 cup finely chopped cilantro
3 Minced garlic cloves
2 chopped Scallions
3 tbsp Soy sauce
1 tbsp Sesame oil
1 tbsp grated ginger
1 tsp Red-pepper flakes
1 Head lettuce, Boston
1 Tomato sliced
1 Red onion sliced
Instructions

Set the temp to the highest setting and pre-heat for 15 mins with the lid covered until ready to use.

Combine mayonnaise and sriracha in a small container and put them aside to make a sriracha mayo.

Combine all of the burger ingredients in a large mixing bowl with your hands till almost mixed.

Scoop about a third of an lb of mix and form it into a patty. Continue with the remaining meat mixture if it hasn't all been eaten.

Grill your burgers for 5-7 mins on each side, or until an instant-read thermometer reads 165°F when inserted.

Place one piece of lettuce in the middle of the burger. Add diced tomato and red onion, as well as a dollop of heated mayo, on the top.

Wrap it in lettuce like a burrito.

3.95 Smoked bourbon & orange brined turkey

Total Time: 3 Hrs 20 mins, Servings: 8
Ingredients
1 Turkey rub-kit and Pit Boss orange-brine
4 Water quart
1 cup Bourbon
1 Turkey, thawed/fresh
1 tbsp butter melted
1 tbsp Grand mariner
Orange flavored liquor
Instructions

Mix 1 quart of water + 1 tbsp of orange brine
seasoning. 5 mins at a rolling boil. Remove the saucepan from the heat & add 3 quarts of cold water to the whiskey in the pot. Refrigerate the ingredients till it has completely chilled.

Put your turkey breast-side down in a large container. Pour the brine mixture over the chicken and let it sit until it cools. Fill the container with cold water until the bird is completely immersed. Refrigerate for at least 24 hours.

Remove the turkey from the brine and toss the brine away. Pat the turkey dry with paper towels.

Brush the outside of the turkey with a butter-Grand Marnier mixture. The outside of the bird is seasoned with Pit Boss turkey scrub.

Preheat the Pit Boss to 225 degrees F for approximately 15 mins with the top closed. Use super smoke if it's available for the greatest flavor.

Smoke the turkey breast side up for approximately 2 hours.

Raise the grill temperature to 350°F and roast the turkey for 2-3 hours, depending on its size, or until the thickest part of the thigh reaches 165°F.

Allow a resting time of 20-30 mins before serving.

3.96 Smoked turkey legs with brown butter and bourbon glaze

Total Time: 2 Hrs 10 mins, Servings: 2
Ingredients
0.6 Water gallon
0.3 cup Sugar
1.3 Bay leaves
1.3 Sprig thyme
3.3 Peppercorns
1.3 cup Kosher salt
2.6 Turkey's legs
3 tbsp Olive oil
0.3 cup Garlic powder & kosher salt mixture

1.3 tbsp Rosemary chopped
0.1 cup Bourbon
0.1 cup Maple syrup
2.6 tbsp Butter browned
Instructions
Bring all of the brine ingredients to a rolling boil under high pressure. Combine the salt and sugar before they are completely dissolved. Allow the brine to settle for a while.
Brine for at least 3 weeks or overnight using these identical turkey legs. Remove the turkey legs from the brine, wash them, and flatten them.
Start the Pit Boss, set the temperature to 250°F, and cook for 10-15 mins with the lid
closed.
After coating the drumsticks with the garlic-salt mixture & a tbsp of olive oil apiece, place them immediately on the grill grate. Smoking for 2 hours
Whisk in the chopped rosemary for a min before adding the whiskey and maple syrup. Over low heat, stir the mixture till it has reduced to 1/2 its original volume and is syrupy.
When the turkey drumsticks have stopped
smoking, remove them from the grill and raise the temperature to high.
Return the drumsticks to the Pit Boss after the grill has reached temperature and roast until completely caramelized and the legs have reached a core temperature of 165° F, frequently basting with a brown sugar glaze.
Remove off the grill, brush with additional glaze, and garnish with sliced herbs, a sprinkling of chilies, and a lemon slice.

3.97 Roasted cider brined turkey breast
Total Time: 4 Hrs 20 Mins, Servings: 6
Ingredients
6 cup Apple cider
2 Smashed garlic cloves
0.3 cup Brown sugar
1 tbsp allspice
0.3 cup Kosher salt
3 Bay leaves
1 Turkey's breast
Unsalted butter, 5/8 cup
1/2 cup plus 2 tbsp Softened unsalted butter
Poultry rub & Pit Boss pork
Instructions
In a huge bowl, combine bay leaves, apple cider vinegar, salt, garlic cloves, allspice, and brown sugar to make the brine. Cook for 5 mins on the stovetop, stirring often.
Remove the pan from the heat and whisk in the ice water until it is completely cool. If necessary, add more water to the brine before the turkey is fully
immersed. Cover and refrigerate overnight.
Reduce the remaining apple cider to a saucepan for 30-45 mins to make the cider glaze. Set aside to cool completely after whisking in the butter.
Reduce the leftover apple cider in the pot over 30-45 mins to create the cider glaze. Set aside to cool completely after whisking in the butter.
After the turkey has brined overnight, drain and clean it. 2 tbsp softened butter, spread with your fingers beneath the surface of the breast.
Apply the Pit Boss pork and poultry rub to the turkey breast carefully.
Preheat your Pit Boss at 325°F for approximately 15 mins with the top closed.
Cook your turkey for 3-4 hours, or unless the core temp reaches 160°F.
Only use the cider glaze on the turkey for the first 20 minutes of cooking and every 45 minutes after that. If the breast gets too dark, cover it with foil.
Allow 30 mins for the meat to rest before cutting.

3.98 Beer-brined turkey
Total Time: 3 Hrs 25 mins, Servings: 6
Ingredients
Main
1 Turkey
1 Peeled & quartered onion
4 Rosemary sprig fresh
4 Thyme sprig fresh
4 Parsley sprig fresh
4 Sage sprig fresh
3 Bay of leaves
2 pieces Celery, chopped
1 Apple, sliced into wedges
1 tbsp Olive oil
Brine
3 bottles apple cider
1.5 cup Kosher salt
1 cup Sugar dark brown
3 clove Smashed garlic
1 tbsp Black peppercorns
Instructions
If the turkey is frozen, allow it to defrost for
three days before serving. Remove any giblets if there are any.
To create the brine, combine the beer, water, salt, and brown sugar in a large 5-gallon bucket, then whisk until the sugar & salt crystals are fully dissolved using a large wooden spoon. Garlic and peppercorns may now be added.
The brine should be poured over the bird. To keep it immersed, use a strong resealable bag or pot lid ice packs. Refrigerate for almost 8 hours or overnight in the fridge.
Remove the bird from the brine. Dry your turkey well inside and out with paper towels. Drop the brine and toss it away.
Place the apple, onion, herbs, celery, and bay leaves in the main cavity, then tie the legs together using the butcher's twine. The bird's wings should be stretched behind its head. The bird's exterior should be greased.
Place the turkey on the shelf in a large roasting pan. If you don't want to save the drippings, put the turkey directly over the grill grate.
Preheat the Pit Boss to 350° F for approximately 15 mins with the top closed.
Place the turkey roasting pan on the grill grate and cook for 2-1/2 to 3 hours, or until a temperature probe inserted into the densest part of the thigh registers 165° F.
Allow the turkey to rest for 20 mins before cutting.

3.99 Roasted Honey bourbon glazed turkey
Total Time: 4 Hrs 30 Mins, Servings: 8
Ingredients
1 Turkey
0.25 cup Pit Boss fin & feather rub
1/2 cup Bourbon
1/2 cup Honey
0.25 cup Brown sugar
3 tbsp Apple cider vinegar
1 tbsp Dijon mustard
Salt & pepper
Instructions
Preheat your grill at 375 degrees Fahrenheit for 15 mins. Form a truss using both turkey legs. Season the exterior of your turkey as well as the cavity with Pit Boss feather and fin rub.
Cook the turkey directly over the grill grate for 20-30 mins at 375° F, or until the skin begins to brown.
Reduce the temperature to 325° F after 30 mins and continue

to cook for 3-4 hours, or until an instant-read thermometer inserted into the densest part of both breasts registers 165° F. Bring all of the ingredients for the whiskey glaze to a simmer in a small saucepan. Reduce the heat to low and simmer for 15-20 mins, or until the sauce has thickened enough to cover the spoon's base. Take the pan off the heat and set it aside.

In the final 10 mins of preparation, rub the glaze over the turkey and roast until it is dry, around 10 mins. Remove the meat from the grill and put it aside for 10-15 mins to rest before carving.

3.100 Thanksgiving BBQ Turkey

Total Time: 4 Hrs 30 mins, Servings: 8
Ingredients
1 Turkey
1 Pit Boss orange-brine & turkey rub-kit
1.5 cup Texas spicy divided BBQ sauce
1/2 cup butter
Instructions
Follow the directions on the turkey Pit Boss rub & orange brine pack to brine the turkey the day before you want to roast it.
On the cook's day, remove the turkey from the brine, clean it, and pat it dry.
Combine the Pit Boss Texas spice BBQ sauce and room temperature honey in a mixing bowl.
Gently peel the skin off the breasts and legs with your fingers, being sure to keep it connected and in one piece.
Spread a thin coating of BBQ butter under the skin. Season the bird's exterior generously with the turkey rub from the Pit Boss turkey rub & orange brine kit.
Preheat your Pit Boss at 400 degrees Fahrenheit & cook for around 15 mins with the lid covered.
Place the turkey directly on the grill grate and roast for approximately 30 mins, then reduce the grill temperature to 300° F.
Cook for another 3-4 hours, or until the breast's core temp reaches 160° F.
During the final twenty mins of cooking, coat your turkey with the leftover spicy BBQ Texas sauce, then steam before all glaze sets.
Allow the bird to rest for 20-25 mins before cutting.

3.101 BBQ pulled turkey sandwiches

Total Time: 2 Hrs 15 mins, Servings: 6
Ingredients
6 Turkey's thighs
Poultry rub Pit Boss pork
1.5 cup Chicken broth
1 cup Pit Boss 'que BBQ sauce
1 Split Kaiser buns
Instructions
Both sides of your turkey thighs may be seasoned with the poultry rub and Pit Boss pork.
Preheat the oven to 180°F and bake for 15 mins with the lid closed.

Place the turkey thighs directly over the grill grate for approximately 30 mins to smoke.
Transfer the thighs to a roasting pan or Al foil. Pour the soup around the thighs. To retain the heat in a pan, cover it with a lid or foil.
Preheat your grill at 325 degrees Fahrenheit with the lid closed. Grill the thighs till they reach a core temp of 180° F.
Remove the pan from the heat but leave it on. Allow the turkey thighs to cool somewhat before proceeding with the treatment.
Fill a jar with the drippings and put it aside. Remove the skin and discard it.
After shredding the turkey flesh with your fingers, return it to the roasting pan.
Place your favorite Pit Boss barbecue sauce, as well as some of the drippings in a bowl.
After covering the sheet with foil, reheat the BBQ turkey over Pit Boss for 20-30 mins.
Serve with toasted buns if desired.

3.102 Pit Boss Smoked Deviled Eggs

Total Time: 1 hour, Servings: 8
Ingredients
Eggs, 12 Large
Jalapeño, 2 Whole
Bacon, 2 Slices
Mayonnaise, 1/2 Cup
White Vinegar, 2 tsp
Mustard, 2 tsp
Chili Powder, 1/2 tsp
Paprika, 1/2 tsp
Salt, 1/4 tsp
Paprika, 1 As Needed
Chives (Chopped), 2 tbsp
Instructions
Boil a big kettle of water for 9 minutes, then add the eggs. Remove the item and rinse it with cold water. When the eggs are cold enough to handle, peel them and cut them in half.
When ready to prepare, preheat the grill to 180°F with the lid covered for 15 minutes.
Place the jalapeño peppers and eggs (yolk side up) on the grill. Allow 45 minutes to smoke after closing the grill.
In the meantime, fry the bacon until it is crispy. Allow to cool before chopping into small pieces.
Remove the jalapenos and eggs from the Pit Boss.
6. Remove the tops from the jalapenos, slice them in half, scoop out the seeds with a spoon, and dice them very finely. scoop the yolks (Carefully) from the eggs into a medium dish. Combine the jalapeño peppers, 1 tablespoon bacon pieces, mayonnaise, chili powder, mustard, vinegar, paprika, & salt in a mixing bowl. Mash the ingredients together with a fork and season to taste. If necessary, season with additional salt.
Fill out each egg white with roughly 2-3 teaspoons of the yolk mixture, using a piping bag with the biggest tip or a teaspoon. Add a sprinkling of paprika, bacon pieces, and chopped chives on top. Enjoy.

3.103 Prosciutto Stuffed Chicken Roasted

Total Time: 50 min, Servings: 2
Ingredients
Boneless (Skinless Chicken Breast), 2 Whole
Salt n Pepper
Dijon Mustard, 2 tbsp
Prosciutto, 2 Slices
Mozzarella Cheese, 4 Pieces
Tomatoes (Sliced), 1 Large
Basil Leaves, 4 Large

Olive Oil, 2 tbsp
Toothpicks
Instructions
Preheat the oven to 225° F. and cook for 10-15 minutes with the lid covered.
While the grill is heating up, cut every chicken breast in half with a sharp knife. Using a meat tenderizer, pound each half-open.
Season every breast half to taste with salt and pepper. Both sides should be rubbed with mustard. On the interior of the breast, place a slice of prosciutto, a slice of cheese, a slice of tomato, and a basil leaf. Drizzle a little extra virgin olive oil on the top.
Secure the chicken breast with toothpicks by folding it back in half. Olive oil the outside of the filled breast.
Place on the grate immediately. Cook for 6 - 7 mins per side, or till the internal temperature of the chicken reaches 160 degrees F.

3.104 Pit Boss Ultimate Thanksgiving Sandwich
Total Time: 11 min, Servings: 2
Ingredients
French Country Bread, 1 Loaf
Dijon Mustard
Turkey Gravy
Mayonnaise
White Cheddar Cheese
Stuffing
Smoked Turkey
Berry Cranberry Sauce, 16 Oz
Instructions
Half a loaf of French bread and toast it on grill grate if preferred. On both half of the bread, spread mayonnaise & Dijon mustard.
Combine the remaining smoked turkey & gravy in a mixing bowl. Place one half of the bread on top of the other.
In this sequence, layer the remaining ingredients: cheddar cheese, cranberry sauce and stuffing.
Place the second half of the bread on top of the sandwich. To serve, cut in half. Enjoy.

3.105 Chicken Cordon Bleu Baked
Total Time: 1 hour, Servings: 4
Ingredients
Chicken Breasts (Boneless, Skinless), 4 (4-5 Oz)
Prosciutto Or Ham, 8 Slices
Swiss Cheese, 8 Slices
All-Purpose Flour, 1/3 Cup
Salt
Black Pepper, Freshly Ground
Breadcrumbs (Preferably Panko), 1 Cup
Parmesan Cheese (Grated), 1/4 Cup
Butter (Melted), 2 tbsp
Fresh Thyme Leaves, 2 tsp
Eggs, 2
Instructions
Spray a baking sheet with (nonstick) cooking spray or line it with parchment paper. Remove from the equation.
Place each chicken breast between 2 pieces of plastic wrap and butterfly it.
Evenly pound the chicken with flat side of a meat mallet until it is 1/4-inch thick, being cautious not to tear it.
Place a (fresh) piece of plastic wrap on top of each chicken breast. Season the chicken with salt and pepper, then layer 1 to 2 pieces of cheese, prosciutto or ham, then 1 to 2 additional slices of cheese on each breast.
Fold the chicken breast in half and roll it up like a tortilla. Fold your bottom of the "breast up" about an inch, then fold in the sides, using the "bottom piece" of plastic wrap as a guide. Roll it up firmly. To shape & compress the chicken, wrap it in plastic wrap & tightly twist the ends. Carry on with the remaining chicken breasts in the same manner.
Chill for 1 hour in the refrigerator.
Season the flour with salt & pepper & place it in a shallow dish while the chicken chills.
Combine breadcrumbs, Parmesan cheese, butter, and thyme in a mixing bowl. Put in a "second shallow dish" and season with salt n pepper.
In a separate third dish, whisk the eggs.
Arrange flour, eggs, and breadcrumbs in this sequence on your work surface. Next to the breadcrumbs, place the prepared baking sheet.
Remove the chicken breasts from the plastic wrap. Coat each one gently in flour before dipping it in the egg. Finally, roll the dough in breadcrumbs, pressing them down to ensure they stick. Arrange the vegetables on the baking sheet.
When ready to cook, preheat the Pit Boss to 375°F with the lid closed for 15 minutes.
Place the chicken on the baking sheet on the grill. Bake for 30 to 40 minutes, or until the chicken is cooked through and the coating is golden brown.
Slice crosswise into pinwheels with a sharp serrated knife or serve whole. Enjoy.

3.106 Turkey Lettuce Wraps Smoked
Total Time: 10 hours, Servings: 6
Ingredients
Turkey Breast (Bone-In, Skin-On), 7 Pound (6-7 Lb)
Water, 4 Quart
Kosher Salt, 1/2 Cup
Brown Sugar, 1/3 Cup
Mayonnaise, 1 Cup
Olive Oil (Extra-Virgin), 1 Cup
Salt
Pepper
Lemon Juice, 1/2
Chives (Fresh), 1 Bunch
Fresh Parsley, 1 Bunch
Instructions
Trim the turkey breast of any excess fat. Combine the water, kosher salt, & brown
sugar in such a large stockpot or other food-safe container and whisk until the salt and sugar crystals dissolve.
Marinate the turkey in the brine for 6 to 8 hours or overnight. Weight the turkey with a couple of plates if necessary to keep it immersed. Using paper towels, absorb any excess liquid. Remove the brine and discard it.
When ready to prepare, preheat the Pit Boss to 325°F for 15 minutes with the lid closed.
Roast the turkey for about 2 to 2-1/2 hours, or till an instant read thermometer inserted into the "thickest portion" of the flesh registers 160 degrees Fahrenheit. Allow 15 minutes for the turkey breast to rest before chilling for 1 hour.
Chive-parsley mayo: In a blender, combine mayonnaise, salt, olive oil, pepper, lemon juice, chives, and parsley. Blend until a vivid green color emerges, then put aside.
Take the turkey breast out of the fridge and slice it. Lettuce, red onion, carrots, and chive parsley mayo are served on the side. Enjoy.

3.107 Smoked Scotch Eggs
Total Time: 2 hours, Servings: 4
Ingredients
Flour, 1/2 Cup

Pit Boss Pork & Poultry Rub, 2 1/2 tsp
Hard Boiled Eggs (Quartered), 4 Whole
Ground Breakfast Sausage, 1 Pound
Beaten Egg, 1
Breadcrumbs, 1 Cup
Mayonnaise, 1 Cup
Dijon Mustard, 1/4 Cup
Green Leaf Lettuce
Pickles
Instructions

In a small shallow dish, combine the flour and 2 tablespoons of the Pit Boss Pork & Poultry rub.

Briefly cover the eggs with seasoned flour after lightly wetting them with water. Wet your hands & split the sausage into four balls of roughly similar size. Make each ball into such an oval by flattening it. Cover each egg with sausage and smooth the seams to enclose the egg evenly. If necessary, rewet your hands. Dredge each sausage-covered egg in the bread crumbs after dipping it in the beaten egg and allowing any excess drip off.

Refrigerate the eggs for 1 to 2 hours, uncovered. Start the Pit Boss grill on Smoke when you're ready to cook.

Place the eggs on the grill grate & let them smoke for an hour. Remove the steaks from the grill & set them aside. Preheat the grill to 375 degrees Fahrenheit. Return the eggs on the grill grate & bake for thirty min after the grill has reached the desired temperature. Allow to cool somewhat before slicing each egg into the quarters with a sharp knife.

In a small mixing dish, combine the mustard, mayonnaise, mustard, and the remaining 2 tablespoons of Pit Boss Pork & Poultry Rub while the eggs bake. Leaf lettuce should be used to cover a serving dish. Arrange the quartered eggs on a serving dish with the dipping sauce and pickles, if preferred.

3.108 Vietnamese Chicken Wings

Total Time: 2 hours, Servings: 4
Ingredients
Chicken Wings, 2 Pound
Garlic (Minced), 1 1/3 tbsp
Shallot (Finely Chopped), 1/8 Cup
Ginger (Minced), 1/8 Cup
Scallion Whites (Chopped), 2 tbsp
Lemongrass Bottoms (Roughly Chopped), 1/3 Cup
Brown Sugar (Packed), 2 tbsp
Fish Sauce
Lime Juice, 2 tbsp
Peanut Oil, 2 tbsp
Salt, 2/3 tsp
Peanuts, Dry-Roasted (Chopped), 1/8 Cup
Cilantro (Finely Chopped), 1/8 Cup
Instructions

Remove the tips of the wings by splitting them at the junction. Using paper towels, gently dry the wings after rinsing them in cold water. Place in a large mixing basin and set aside.

In a food processor, puree the garlic (roughly diced), shallots, ginger, fish sauce, lemongrass, brown sugar, scallions, lime juice, & peanut oil until smooth. Place the wings in a large (resealable) plastic bag with the marinade. Refrigerate for at least one night.

When you're ready to cook, turn on the Smoke setting on your Pit Boss grill. Preheat for 5 minutes with the lid closed.

Take the wings out of the marinade and set them aside. Keep the marinade in a small saucepan & bring to a boil before removing from the heat. Brush the wings with this while they're cooking.

Season the wings with 1 teaspoon salt & smoke for thirty min on the grill.

Raise the temperature of the grill to 350 degrees F after 30 minutes and roast for 45 to 50 minutes, flipping halfway through & brushing on the reserved sauce.

Remove the wings from the grill and arrange them on a serving plate with the peanuts & cilantro on top. Enjoy.

3.109 Chicken Roasted with Wild Rice & Mushrooms

Total Time: 2-hour 20 min, Servings: 2
Ingredients
Chicken, 1 Whole
Salt
Pepper
Butter, 2 tbsp
Onion (Chopped), 1 Medium
Bacon (Diced), 4 Strips
Wild Rice, 1 Cup
Mushrooms (Sliced), 1
Salt
Cup Water, 2 1/4
Parsley (Chopped), 2 tbsp
Instructions

Preheat the Pit Boss to 375°F for 15 minutes with the lid closed when ready to cook.

Season the chicken on the interior and outside with salt & pepper.

Melt 2 tablespoons butter in a large saucepan over medium heat. Cook for 3-5 minutes, or until onions are tender. Cook, stirring constantly, until the bacon & onions are browned. Combine the rice, mushrooms, salt, & pepper in a mixing bowl. Bring the mixture to a boil with 2-1/4 cups of water. Reduce to a low heat, cover, and cook for 25 minutes, or till rice has absorbed all of the liquid. Mix with some fresh parsley.

Loosely fill cavities with rice mixture. Butcher's string should be used to tie the chicken legs together

Place chicken directly on grill grate and cook for 1 hour 15 minutes, or till an immediate thermometer inserted into the thickest part of the breast registers 160°F and the thigh registers 170°F.

Remove the chicken from the grill and set it aside for 10 minutes to rest.

Remove the filling from the cavity of the bird and place it on a dish before slicing the chicken. Serve with the chicken pieces over rice filling right away. Enjoy.

3.110 Bacon-Wrapped Skewers

Total Time: 15 min, Servings: 2
Ingredients
Pork Tenderloin, 1 Pound
Rosemary, 2 tsp
Thyme, 2 tsp
Garlic (Minced), 2 Clove
Chicken Breasts, 1 Pound
Lime (Juiced), 2
Extra-Virgin Olive Oil, 3 tbsp
Salt n Pepper
Bacon, 12 Strips
Instructions

Toss the rosemary, garlic, thyme, chicken cut into half pieces, olive oil, pork cut into 1" pieces, lime juice, pepper and salt together in a large mixing basin. Refrigerate for 30 minutes after covering and marinating.

When you're ready to cook, fire up your Pit Boss & set the temperature to 500 degrees Fahrenheit. Preheat for 10-15 minutes with the lid closed.

While the Pit Boss heats up, cut the bacon into thirds, wrap the chicken pieces in bacon, and alternate the chicken and pork on the skewers.

Place them in the Pit Boss's front and rear to obtain grill marks (4-5 minutes), then transfer them to the middle to complete cooking (5-6 minutes), then remove and serve.

3.111 Tandoori Chicken Burgers
Total Time: 1 hour 5 min, Servings: 4
Ingredients
Plain Yogurt (Preferably Greek Or Sour Cream), 1/2 Cup
Mayonnaise, 2 tbsp
Finely Diced Cucumber, 2 tbsp
Lemon Juice, 2 tsp
Ground Cumin, 1/2 tsp
Salt, 1 1/2 tsp
Cayenne Pepper, 1/8 tsp
Chicken (Ground), 1 1/2 Pound
Scallions (Minced), 1
Minced Cilantro Leaves, 1 tbsp
Ginger (Minced), 2 tsp
Garam Masala, 1 tsp
Freshly Ground Black Pepper, 1 tsp
Instructions
To make the sauce, whisk together the mayonnaise, yogurt, cucumber, lemon juice, cumin, salt, and cayenne pepper in a small mixing dish. Cover and chill until ready to serve.
Use cooking parchment or greased foil to line a rimless baking sheet.
Make the burgers: In medium mixing dish, place the chicken. Combine the yogurt, scallions, cilantro, garam masala, ginger, salt, & pepper in a mixing bowl. The mixture will be moist and loose, so mix
softly yet completely with your hands.
Wet your hands with cold water & make four equal-sized patties on the paper or foil immediately. (If not used right away, cover & store in the refrigerator.)
When you're ready to cook, turn on the Pit Boss grill to Smoke and leave the lid open till the fire is ready (4 to 5 minutes).
Carefully slide or raise the parchment paper onto the grill grate with the burgers within. (There will be no direct contact between the meat and the grill grate.) 30 minutes of smoking
Raise the temperature to 325°F and continue to cook the burgers for another 30 minutes, or till the internal temp reaches 165°F.
Now, remove the hamburgers from the parchment paper & serve with pita breads, lettuce, onion, tomato, and the sauce on the side. Enjoy.

3.112 Smoked Creole Jambalaya
Total Time: 1 hour 15 min, Servings: 4
Ingredients
Shrimp (Peeled, Deveined, & Chopped), 20 Medium
Chicken Thighs (Boneless & Diced), 4 Ounce
Chopped Tomato, 2 Cup
Andouille Sausage, 5 Ounce
Creole Seasoning, 1 tbsp
Chopped Onion, 1/4 Cup
Chopped Green Or Red Bell Pepper, 1/4 Cup
Celery (Finely Chopped), 1/4 Cup
Garlic, 3 Clove
Bay Leaves, 3
Worcestershire Sauce, 1 tsp
Hot Sauce, 1 tsp
Rice (Short Grain), 3/4 Cup
Chicken Stock, 3 Cup
Salt n Pepper
Instructions
Set the Pit Boss to Smoke mode.
On a large baking sheet, spread out the chopped shrimp & diced chicken. Place the chopped tomatoes on a second baking sheet.
Place both baking sheets on the Pit Boss, with the andouille sausage, and smoke for 30 minutes.
Turn the heat to High and remove the meats and tomatoes from the Pit Boss. Place a dutch oven or a big pan on the grill grate & shut the lid for 10 to 15 minutes to warm.
Slice the Andouille sausage & combine it with the chicken & shrimp with the Creole spice once the meat has smoked.
Pour a few teaspoons of olive oil into the Pit Boss pan, then add the chopped onion, pepper, and celery and cook for about 5 minutes.
Combine the garlic, bay leaves, smoked tomatoes, Worcestershire, & spicy sauces in a mixing bowl. Stir in the rice, then gradually pour in the broth.
Cook, stirring periodically, till the rice absorbs liquid & becomes soft, about 15 minutes.
Add the shrimp, chicken, and sausage when the rice is barely soft. Cook for another 10 to 20 minutes, or until the meat is done.
Season with salt, pepper, and Creole spice to taste. Serve and take pleasure in.

3.113 Thai Chicken Skewers
Total Time: 40 min, Servings: 4
Ingredients
Chicken Breast (Boneless, Skinless), 2 Pound
Cilantro Leaves, 1 Cup
Coconut Milk (Unsweetened), 1/2 Cup
Lime Juice, 3 tbsp
Garlic (Chopped), 2 Clove
Ginger (Peeled & Coarsely Chopped), 1" Small
2 tbsp Brown Sugar
Thai Red Curry Paste, 1 tbsp
Cumin, 1 tsp
Black Pepper, 1 tsp
Peanut Sauce
Instructions
Cut the chicken into 1/2-inch broad strips lengthwise. (It's simpler if you partially freeze the chicken first.) Place the strips in a plastic bag that may be resealed.
Blend the cilantro, coconut milk, Garlic, lime juice, brown sugar, curry paste, cumin, & pepper until smooth in a blender jar.
Refrigerate for about 1 hour after pouring over the chicken strips.
Remove the chicken from the marinade and discard it. Using bamboo skewers, thread the chicken strips. When ready to cook, preheat the Pit Boss grill to 400 degrees Fahrenheit with the lid covered for 10 to 15 minutes.
Arrange the skewers on the grill grate in two rows. To keep the skewers from burning, place a piece of aluminum foil beneath the exposed ends. Grill the chicken for 4 to 5 minutes each side, rotating once, until cooked through.
Toss with peanut sauce and serve right away. Enjoy.

3.114 Roasted Chicken Enchiladas
Total Time: 1 hour 15 min, Servings: 4
Ingredients
Chicken, 1 Whole (3-4 Lb)
Olive Oil, 3 tbsp
Salt
Pepper
Olive Oil
Onion (Diced), 1 Small
Diced Green Chiles, 1 Can (4 Oz)
Flour Tortillas, 8 Large

Enchilada Sauce, 2 Can (15 Oz)
Black Beans (Rinsed & Drained), 1 Can (15 Oz)
Shredded Mexican Blend Cheese, 3 Cup
Sour Cream
Cilantro (Finely Chopped), 1/4 Cup
Instructions
Preheat the Pit Boss to 350°F for 15 minutes with the lid closed when ready to cook.
Season the chicken with salt & pepper after rubbing it with olive oil.
Cook for 1 hour, or till chicken reaches a core temperature of 165°F, directly on the grill grate.
Remove from the grill and set aside for 10 minutes to cool.
Remove the chicken from the bone and shred it with a fork.
Heat the oil over medium heat. After that add onion & cook stirring periodically, for 3 mins.
Season with salt & pepper, then add the green chilies. Cook, stirring periodically, for 6-8 minutes. Remove the pan from the heat and stir in the shredded chicken.
Set up an assembly line with tortillas, enchilada sauce & beans, chicken mixture, & cheese to build the enchiladas. surface and sprinkle two teaspoons of sauce over it. Place a line of beans along the center of the tortilla,
then top with a scoop of the chicken mixture & 1/3 cup cheese.
Place the tortilla in a (greased) 9" x 13" baking dish and roll it up. Rep with the rest of the ingredients.
On top of the tortillas, spread the remaining enchilada sauce and the remaining shredded cheese.
Place the baking dish straight on the grill, still at 350°F, close the lid, and cook for 20 minutes uncovered.
Remove from the oven and serve right away. Serve with sour cream & chopped fresh cilantro as a garnish. Enjoy.

3.115 Roasted Smoke Chicken along with Herb Butter
Total Time: 1 hour 15 min, Servings: 4
Ingredients
Butter (Room Temperature), 8 tbsp
Scallions (Minced), 1
Garlic (Minced), 1 Clove
Fresh Herbs (Thyme, Rosemary, Sage Or Parsley, Basil, Oregano, Minced), 2 tbsp
Pit Boss Chicken Rub, 1 1/2 tbsp
Fresh Lemon Juice, 1/2 tbsp
Chicken, 1 (4 To 4-1/2 Lb)
Pit Boss Chicken Rub
Instructions
Combine butter, fresh herbs, minced scallions, garlic, Pit Boss Chicken Rub,
and lemon juice in a small bowl. Using a wooden spoon, thoroughly combine the ingredients.
Remove any giblets from the chicken's cavity. Cold running water should be used to wash the bird both inside and out. Using paper towels, thoroughly dry the area.
Rub the Pit Boss Bird Rub well into the cavity of the chicken.
Gently loosen cooked skin around the chicken breast & spread equally with a few tablespoons of herb butter. Using the leftover herb butter, smear the exterior of the chicken.
Tuck the chicken wings into the rear of the chicken. Butcher's twine should be used to tie the legs together.
If preferred, add additional Pit Boss Bird Rub to the exterior of the chicken and sprigs of fresh herbs to the cavity of the chicken.
When ready to cook, preheat the Pit Boss to 400°F with the lid closed for fifteen min.
When the grill is hot, put the chicken breast side up on the grill grate. Cook for 1 - 1-1/4 hours, or until an internal temperature of 165°F has been reached. If the breast and legs of the chicken are browning too rapidly, lightly cover them with foil & continue to cook.
Remove from the grill & set aside for 15 minutes to cool before carving. Serve. Enjoy.

3.116 Maple Bourbon Drumsticks
Total Time: 1 hour 20 min, Servings: 4
Ingredients
Chicken Drumsticks, 24 Whole
Onion Powder, 2 tbsp
Garlic Powder, 2 tbsp
Ground Coriander, 1 tbsp
Salt, 2.16 tbsp
Black Pepper, 2 tsp
Orange Juice Concentrate, 6 Ounce
Fluid Bourbon, 8 Ounce
Fluid Maple Syrup, 8 Ounce
Sugar, 1/8 Cup
Instructions
When ready to cook, turn on the Pit Boss and adjust the temperature to 180°F. Preheat for 10-15 minutes with the lid closed.
Season the drumsticks generously with onion powder, garlic powder, powdered coriander, salt, and black pepper while the grill is heating up.
Put the coated drumsticks on the grill for 1 hour to smoke. Prepare the glaze by mixing the orange juice concentrate, bourbon, maple syrup, sugar, & salt while the chicken is smoking. Combine all of the ingredients and reduce by 1/3.
After the chicken has smoked for about 1 hour, preheat the grill to 325°F and roast the drumsticks for another 30 minutes, or until the internal temperature reaches 160°F.
5. Turn the grill to high and remove the drumsticks. Toss the drumsticks in the glaze & return to the grill for another 10 to 12 minutes, or until grill marks appear. Serve.

3.117 Leftover Pit Boss Turkey Soup
Total Time: 5-hour 15 min, Servings: 4
Ingredients
Whole Turkey, 1 (12 Lb)
Water, 16 Cup
Celery (Thinly Sliced), 2
Carrot (Diced), 4
Quartered Red Onion, 2
Flat-Leaf Parsley, 10 Sprig
Peppercorns, 1 tbsp
Fresh thyme, 2 tsp
Leftover Shredded Turkey, 2 Cup
Diced Celery, 3 Stalk
Chopped Red Onion, 1
Sprigs Of Fresh Herbs (Like Rosemary, Sage, Parsley & Thyme)
Salt n Pepper
Instructions
Remove all flesh from a turkey carcass and place it in a container.
Discard the turkey carcass bones and throw them in a big saucepan. Add the turkey skin or other non-edible "bits" to the mixture. Make the stock the day after the turkey is cooked for the greatest flavor. Turn the heat to high and add the cold water; come to a boil.
Once the stock has reached a boil, add the other ingredients and reduce the heat to a low enough for the bubbles to barely breach the surface. Allow for 3 - 4 hours of simmering time, stirring periodically. When the broth is reduced to 7 - 8 cups of stock, it tastes the finest.
Strain the stock into a big bowl through a fine-mesh sieve; if

your sieve isn't fine, line it beforehand with cheesecloth. Discard the bones and vegetables that went into the stock (all their flavor is now in the stock). Refrigerate the stock for several hours, ideally overnight, before using it to make soup the next day or freezing it; take careful to skim off any hardened fat before using it to make soup or freezing it.

When you're ready to create the soup, boil up the homemade stock with the vegetables and diced turkey on the burner. Bring to a boil, then reduce to a low heat and cook for 30-45 minutes, or until carrots are soft.

Add preferred herbs & salt n pepper to taste in the last 10 minutes. If you wish to add the leftover cooked pasta or rice, do so shortly before serving to warm it up. To serve, ladle soup into individual bowls. Enjoy.

3.118 Southwest Wild Turkey Egg Rolls

Total Time: 55 min, Servings: 4
Ingredients
Olive Oil (Extra-Virgin), 2 As Needed
White Onion (Chopped), 1/2 Cup
Poblano Pepper (Chopped1), Whole
Minced Garlic, 4 Clove
RO*TEL Original - Tomatoes & Green Chilies (Diced), 1 Can
Black Beans (Rinsed & Drained), 1/2 Cup
Leftover Cooked Wild Turkey, 2 Cup
Dry Taco Seasoning, 3 tbsp
Water, 1/3 Cup
Egg Roll Wrappers, 12 Whole
Instructions
In a large pan, heat the olive oil over medium-high heat. Sauté the onions and peppers for 2-3 minutes, or until tender. Cook for 30 seconds after adding the garlic, then add the Rotel & black beans. Reduce the heat to a low setting and continue to cook.

Combine taco seasoning and 1/3 cup water in a mixing bowl and toss to cover meat thoroughly. Add to the veggie mixture and toss well to combine. Add 2 tbsp water if it appears to be dry. Cook until the food is well warm.

Remove the pan from the heat and place the mixture in the refrigerator. If you don't let the mixture cool fully before filling the egg rolls, the wrappers will shatter.

Spoon a tablespoon of the mixture into each wrapper and securely wrap it. Continue with the remaining wrappers.

When ready to cook, preheat the grill on high for 15 minutes with the lid covered.

Brush each egg roll with oil or butter & set on the Pit Boss grill grate immediately. Cook for about 20 minutes per side, or until the exterior is crispy.

Remove from Pit Boss & set aside to cool. Serve. Enjoy.

3.119 BBQ Chicken Drumsticks

Total Time: 2 hours 15 min, Servings: 4
Ingredients
Chicken Drumsticks, 8
Pit Boss Chicken Rub, 2 tbsp
Pit Boss 'Que BBQ Sauce, 1/2 Cup
Instructions
Season each drumstick with salt and pepper and set aside for 20 minutes.

When ready to cook, preheat the Pit Boss to 275°F for 15 minutes with the lid closed.

Cook for 1 hour, hanging the drumsticks on the leg hanger (alternatively, place straight on the grill grate, flipping halfway through).

Place the drumsticks in a pan after removing them from the hanger (or grate).

Cook for another 45 minutes, or until the beef reaches an internal temp of 190 degrees F, covered with foil.

Remove the foil and coat all of the drumsticks in the pan with the sauce.

Cook for a further 15 minutes to allow the sauce to thicken.

Take the meat out of the Pit Boss and set it aside for 15 mins before serving. Enjoy.

3.120 Bacon-Wrapped Chicken Stuffed Breast

Total Time: 1 hours, Servings: 4
Ingredients
Olive Oil, 1 tbsp
Fresh Baby Spinach, 8 Ounce
Garlic (Minced), 1 Clove
Grated Smoked Gouda / Swiss Cheese, 1 Cup
Diced Ham, 1/2 Cup
Salt
Pepper
Chicken Breast (Boneless, Skinless), 4
Pit Boss Pork & Poultry Rub
Bacon, 8 Slices
Instructions
Heat the olive oil, spinach, & garlic in a pan over medium heat.

Allow to cool before carefully wringing out any extra water from the spinach.

Chop the spinach coarsely and place it in a medium mixing dish. Combine the cheese and ham in a mixing bowl. Season to taste with salt and pepper.

When ready to prepare, preheat the Pit Boss to 350°F for 15 minutes with the lid closed.

Cut a deep slit down the side of every chicken breast with a small sharp knife, stopping approximately 1/2 inch from the other side.

Stuff each chicken breast generously with the spinach mixture. Season the chicken breasts on the exterior with Pit Boss Pork and or Poultry Rub.

Completely coat the exterior of each filled chicken breast with bacon spirals. Use toothpicks to hold the bacon if required.

Place the chicken breasts straight on the grill grate & cook till the bacon is crisp & golden brown & the internal temp of the chicken breast reaches 165°F, flipping once or twice.

Set aside for 3 minutes the chicken breasts. Serve after removing any toothpicks. Enjoy.

3.121 Parmesan Chicken Sliders along with Pesto Mayonnaise

Total Time: 40 mins, Servings: 4
Ingredients
Ground Chicken, 2 Pound
Parmesan Cheese, 1 Cup
Worcestershire Sauce, 1 tbsp
Black Pepper
Mayonnaise, 1 Cup
Pesto Sauce, 2 tbsp
Roma Tomatoes, 3
Red Onion (Sliced), 1
Baby Spinach
Instructions
Preheat oven to 350°F. Line a baking sheet with the plastic wrap. Combine the ground chicken, Parmesan, Worcestershire, and a couple pinches of black pepper in a large mixing basin. Use cold water to wet your hands and use them to combine the items.

Divide the meat mixture into half, then shape each half into six 2-inch patties. Refrigerate the patties for at least 1 hour after placing them on the baking sheet and covering them with another layer of plastic wrap.

In a small mixing bowl, whisk together the mayonnaise and pesto. Cover and chill until ready to serve.

When you're ready to cook, turn on the Pit Boss grill to Smoke and leave the lid open till the fire is ready (4 to 5 minutes). Preheat the oven to 300 degrees Fahrenheit with the lid covered for 10 - 15 minutes.

Arrange the chicken patties on the grill grate & cook, rotating once, for about 30 minutes, or until the patties are cooked through (165F).

To serve, place a chicken patty on the bottom of a slider bun and a dollop of pesto mayonnaise on top. As desired, add tomato, onion, & spinach. If desired, a frilled toothpick can be used to replace the top of the bun & skewer.

3.122 Stuffed Bacon-Wrapped Chicken Thighs

Total Time: 1 hour 5 mins, Servings: 4

Ingredients
Olive Oil, 1 tbsp
Butter, 1 tbsp
Onion (Diced), 1/4 Cup
Minced Garlic, 1 Clove
Diced Package Baby Portobello Mushrooms, 8 Ounce (8 Oz)
Prepared Wild Rice, 1 Cup
White Wine, 1/2 Cup
Grated Parmesan Cheese, 1/3 Cup
Salt
Pepper
Chicken Thighs (Boneless, Skinless), 8
Bacon, 8 Strips

Instructions
Melt the butter & olive oil in a large pan over medium heat. Cook, stirring occasionally, until the onions are tender and beginning to brown, about 5-6 minutes.

Add the garlic & mushrooms & simmer for another 3-5 minutes, or until the mushrooms soften and release their juices. Turn the heat to high and stir in the wild rice.

Pour the wine into the heated pan and stir the stuffing mixture while scraping the bottom of the pan with a spatula. This removes all of the delicious browned

pieces from the bottom of the pan, concentrating the filling's taste. Remove the skillet from the heat & add the cheese, along with a pinch of salt and pepper.

To put the chicken together, start by placing two strips of bacon across each other. Season the chicken thighs with salt and pepper to taste. Place a chicken thigh on the bacon's junction. Fill the middle of the chicken thigh with about "1/3 cup" of the filling mixture. Place a second chicken thigh on top of the filling in the opposite direction as the first, so that when the bacon is pulled together over the top, the thighs do not overlap but instead interlock to form a seal around the filling. Using toothpicks, secure each end of the bacon around the chicken thighs. Reassemble the chicken thighs and filling with the remaining chicken thighs & filling.

When you're ready to cook, fire up the Pit Boss grill. Until the fire has formed, smoke with the lid open (4-5 minutes). Close the cover and raise the temperature to 325 degrees Fahrenheit. Allow 10-15 minutes for
the grill to heat up.

Close the cover and place the completed chicken straight on the grill grate. Grill for 25 minutes, then turn and cook for another 25-35 minutes, or until an internal temperature of 165 degrees F is reached.

Take the steaks from the grill and let them aside to rest for 5-10 minutes before serving. Big eaters can usually finish one whole cowboy griller, but we were more than satisfied after splitting one between two of us. Enjoy.

3.123 Stand Pineapple Chicken

Total Time: 1 hour 30 mins, Servings: 4

Ingredients
Pineapple, 1
Chicken, 1 Whole
Brown Sugar (Packed), 1 Cup
Smoked Paprika, 1/4 Cup
Kosher Salt, 3 tbsp
Coarse Ground Black Pepper (Divided), 2 tbsp
Chili Powder, 2 tbsp
Granulated Onion, 2 tbsp
Granulated Garlic, 2 tbsp
Chipotle Chile Powder, 2 tsp
Ground Cumin, 1 tsp
Ground Coriander, 1 tsp
Ground Thyme, 1 tsp
Pineapple (Peeled, Cored & Cut into Rings), 1/2
Chopped Red Onion, 1/2 Cup
Chopped Cilantro, 1/4 Cup
Salt

Instructions
Remove the pineapple's top. To make the pineapple stand level, cut a slice off the bottom.

Cut the skin and any "eyes" from the pineapple with a big, sharp knife while the
pineapple is standing straight on a chopping board. Cut vertical slices of pineapple flesh all the way around the core, stopping 2" from the pineapple's base. You'll be left with the pineapple's vertical core on a 2" base, which will serve as the chicken's "stand." The pineapple should be saved for the salsa.

When ready to cook, preheat the Pit Boss to 300°F for 15 minutes with the lid closed.

Lightly season the chicken both inside and out with the rub. Place the chicken on the pineapple stand and invert it.

Cook the chicken for thirty min on the grill. Rotate the chicken and cook for another 30-40 minutes, or till the internal temp of the breast reaches 160°F and the thigh reaches 175°F.

In the meantime, make the pineapple salsa. Combine the pineapple, red onion, cilantro, and salt in a mixing bowl.

Remove the pineapple stand and the chicken from the grill. Before serving with the salsa, gently tent the chicken with foil and let aside for 10 minutes. Enjoy.

3.124 Stuffing Turkey Bacon Balls

Total Time: 30 mins, Servings: 8

Ingredients
Cranberry Sauce, 1 Can (16 Oz)
Jalapeño (Diced), 1
Prepared Stuffing, 3 Cup
Shredded Cooked Turkey, 1 Cup
Bacon, 6 Slices

Instructions
Combine cranberry sauce & jalapenos in a small saucepan. Bring to a boil over medium-high heat, then turn down to a low heat. Remove from the heat and set aside to cool for 4-5 minutes.

When you're ready to cook, fire up the Pit Boss grill. Until the fire has formed, smoke with the lid open (4
to 5 minutes). Preheat the oven to 375 degrees F and bake for 10 to 15 minutes with the lid covered.

Start by putting about 1/4 cup of stuffing into the palm of your hand. Make an indentation with your thumb. Fill the indentation with a heaping spoonful of shredded turkey, then wrap the filling around the indentation to make a ball.

Wrap half a slice of bacon around the filling ball and secure with a toothpick if required. Continue till all the bombs have been produced.

Place the stuffing balls straight on the grill grate when ready to cook and cook for 25-thirty min, rotating once. Crispy bacon is preferred.

Toss with cranberry-jalapeno jelly and serve. Enjoy.

3.125 Mustard Wings Smoked
Total Time: 1 hour 5 mins, Servings: 6
Ingredients
Spicy Brown Mustard, 1/2 Cup
Apple Cider Vinegar, 1 Cup
Soy Sauce, 1/2 Cup
Honey, 2 tbsp
Miso, 1 tbsp
Molasses, 1/2 Cup
Chicken Wings, 5 Pound
Canola Oil, 1/4 Cup
Salt n Pepper
Lemon Wedges
Instructions
Combine the mustard, vinegar, soy sauce, molasses, honey, and miso in a medium pot. Bring the water to a boil. Cook, stirring periodically, until thickened & reduced to 1 cup, about 15 mins over medium heat.

When ready to cook, preheat the Pit Boss grill to 500 degrees Fahrenheit. Preheat for 10 - 15 minutes with the lid closed.

Toss the chicken wings with the oil in a large mixing bowl and season generously with salt n pepper.

Place the wings on the hottest area of the grill and cook for 15 minutes, or till cooked through and lightly browned. So that your wings don't burn, turn them often.

Lower the grill temperature to 225 degrees Fahrenheit (and activate Super Smoke if available). Add another 30 minutes of smoking time to the wings.

Transfer the wings to a clean big dish with tongs. Return the wings to the grill after tossing them with the sauce.

Raise the temperature to 350 degrees F and cook for another 10 to 15 minutes, or until the chicken is coated and gently browned in places.

Arrange the wings on a serving dish and top with chopped herbs. Serve with lemon slices on the side. Enjoy.

3.126 Chicken Lollipops
Total Time: 1 hour 5 mins, Servings: 6
Ingredients
Chicken Drumsticks, 18 Medium
Pit Boss Pork and Poultry Rub
Butter, 1 Stick
BBQ Sauce Pit Boss 'Que
Optional - Louisiana Brand Hot Sauce
Instructions
A sharp knife & a pair of kitchen shears are required to convert ordinary chicken legs into lollipops. Begin by cutting all the way around the leg, just below the knuckle, with a sharp knife or a pair of kitchen shears, cutting through the skins and tendons. Pull/cut the remaining skin & cartilage off the knuckle by pushing the meat down to the big end. You could also wish to remove

the little bone against the leg. Easily remove the tendons that protrude from the top of the bone using your fingers or shears. Use Pit Boss Pork and or Poultry Rub to season the chicken. To protect the bone of

the drumsticks from becoming black, wrap them in a tiny piece of aluminum foil. Enable the chicken to remain in the fridge for an hour to allow the flavor to penetrate.

When ready to prepare, preheat the Pit Boss to 180°F for 15 minutes with the lid closed. If Super Smoke is available, use it for the best flavor.

Place the "chicken lollipops" on the grill grate for 30 minutes to smoke.

Increase the grill temp to 350°F after removing the chicken and let it to warm for 15 minutes with the lid closed. Place the stick of butter in a baking pan or an aluminum pan on the grill to melt while the grill heats up. (The chicken does not need to be completely covered with butter.) It just keeps the drumsticks wet and, of course, adds a buttery finish.)

Arrange the popsicles in the pan so that the bones are straight up. Allow the chicken to simmer for about 40 mins, or until an instant-read thermometer reads 165°F on the inside.

Meanwhile, in a small saucepan over low heat, warm up the Pit Boss BBQ Sauce. Add a few squirts of spicy sauce to taste if you want it to have that Louisiana bite. Reduce the heat to keep it warm after it begins to thin merely. If the sauce has to be thinned, add a little amount of the butter from the pan until it achieves a consistency that is thick enough to stick to the drumsticks but not sticky.

Toss the lollipops in the BBQ sauce, making sure they're fully coated. If you want a consistent look and shine on the lollipops, brush the BBQ sauce on the bones as well.

Preheat the Pit Boss to 450 degrees Fahrenheit. Put the chicken straight on the grill grate and cook for another 10 minutes, or until the internal temp reaches 175°F. Make sure the lollipops don't burn by keeping an eye on them. On the outside, you want a beautiful caramelization of the BBQ sauce with a crisp skin to add some texture. Enjoy.

3.127 Goddess Green Chicken Legs
Total Time: 45 mins, Servings: 4
Ingredients
Chicken Legs, 2 Pound
Ready-made "Green Goddess" Dressing, 2 Cup
Parsley (Chopped), 1/4 Cup
Paprika, 1 tbsp
Instructions
In a big resealable plastic bag, place the chicken legs. Combine the Green Goddess dressing, parsley, and paprika in a mixing bowl. Over the chicken legs, pour the sauce. Refrigerate for 2 - 8 hours before serving.

Prepare your grill to 350°F & preheat for 10 - 15 minutes when you're ready to cook. Drain the chicken legs and set aside. Place

the legs straight on the grill grate & cook for 40 - 50 minutes, or till golden brown & cooked through, rotating once. Serve right away.

3.128 Turkey Jalapeño Meatballs
Total Time: 35 mins, Servings: 8
Ingredients
Milk, 1/4 Cup
Breadcrumbs, 1/2 Cup
Ground Turkey, 1 1/4 Pound
Garlic Salt, 1/2 tsp
Onion Powder, 1 tsp
Salt, 1 tsp
Ground Black Pepper, 1/2 tsp
Worcestershire Sauce, 1/4
Cayenne Pepper, 1 Pinch
Beaten Egg, 1 Large
Jalapeño (Seeded & Diced), 1 Whole
Whole Berry Cranberry Sauce, 1 Cup (16 Oz)
Orange Marmalade, 1/2 Cup
Chicken Broth, 1/2 Cup
Salt n Pepper
Instructions
Combine the milk & bread crumbs in a separate small dish.

Combine the turkey, garlic salt, pepper, salt, onion powder, Worcestershire sauce, cayenne pepper, egg, and jalapenos in a large mixing bowl.

Combine the bread crumb milk mixture in the mixing basin. Refrigerate for approximately 1 hour after covering with plastic.

When ready to prepare, preheat the grill to 350°F with the lid covered for 15 minutes.

Form the turkey mixture into 1-tblsp. meatballs and arrange them in a single layer on a parchment-lined baking sheet.

Cook meatballs until they begin to brown, turning once or twice, until they achieve an internal temp of 175 degrees F and are browned on both sides (about 20 minutes).

Glaze: In a small saucepan on the stovetop, combine the cranberry sauce, marmalade, chicken stock, and jalapenos and simmer over medium heat. Cook until all of the ingredients are well combined.

Brush the meatballs with cranberry glaze halfway through the cooking time.

Serve meatballs with cranberry glaze on the side on a serving dish. Serve right away. Enjoy.

3.129 Ultimate Scratch Gravy

Total Time: 10 hours 20 mins, Servings: 8
Ingredients
Chicken Bones & Chicken Feet, 4 Pound
Olive Oil, 1 tbsp
Diced Carrot, 2
Yellow Onion, Quartered 1
Celery (Chopped), 2
Apple Cider Vinegar, 1 tbsp
Fresh Parsley
Fresh Thyme, 2 Sprig
Head Garlic, 1
Leaves, 2 Bay
Black Peppercorn, 2 tbsp
Instructions

Preheat the oven to 450 degrees Fahrenheit and cook for 15 minutes with the lid covered.

Lightly butter a large sheet tray with 1 tbsp olive oil and equally distribute chicken feet and bones. Roast for 90 minutes, turning the bones regularly, until golden brown.

While these are roasting, mix the onion, celery, and carrots with the remaining olive oil on a second sheet tray. Roast for 25

minutes, or until gently caramelized, alongside the bones.

Scrape off all of the browned pieces from the sheet pan and place it in a large roasting pan.

Stir in the apple cider vinegar, parsley, & thyme. Fill the pan with enough cold water to cover the ingredients, including the roasted veggies, garlic, bay leaves, & peppercorns.

Preheat the grill to a temperature of 250 degrees Fahrenheit. Place the roasting pan on tempo the grill grate, partially covered with a lid or foil. Cook for 6-8 hours, scraping extra oil from the top as needed.

Gently fish out the bones with a big slotted spoon or spider skimmer and discard. When all of the big bits have been removed, pour the stock into another large roasting pan using a fine mesh screen.

Return the pan to the grill for another 3-4 hours, or until the sauce has reduced & thickened enough to coat the back of a spoon. Enjoy.

3.130 BBQ Halved Chickens

Total Time: 4 hours, Servings: 8
Ingredients
Butcher BBQ Bird Booster Honey Flavor, 6 tbsp
Water, 2 Cup
Fresh Young Chicken, 1 Whole (5 Lb)
Canola Oil, 2 tbsp
Pit Boss Pork & Poultry Rub, 1/4 Cup
Pit Boss 'Que BBQ Sauce, 1/3 Cup
Pit Boss Apricot BBQ Sauce, 1/3 Cup
Apple Cider Vinegar, 1/3 Cup
Instructions

To make the injection mixture, combine 2 cups of water with the butcher's BBQ honey. Allow at least 30 minutes for the injection to settle before straining it through a fine mesh strainer.

Place the chicken on a chopping board, breast side down, with the neck pointing
away from you.

From the neck to the tail, cut down one side of the backbone, staying as near to the bone as possible. Rep on the opposite side of the backbone, then take it out.

To burst the bird open, cut through the white cartilage at the point of the breastbone. Cut down either side of the breast bone, then pull it out with your fingers.

Inject one full tube into the leg, one full tube into the thigh, and two full tubes into the breasts. Place the chicken skin side up on a sheet tray & refrigerate for 3 hours, uncovered.

Apply canola oil to the skin and liberally season with Pit Boss Pork & Poultry Rub.

When ready to serve, preheat the oven to 325°F with the lid covered for 15 minutes.

Place the chicken skin side up on the grill grate and cook for 1 1/2 hours, or until the core temperature reaches 160 degrees Fahrenheit.

Combine the barbecue sauce, apricot sauce, honey, and vinegar in a mixing bowl. Cook for another 5 minutes after brushing the glaze all over the chicken skin.

Remove off the grill & allow it to cool for 5 minutes before slicing. Enjoy.

3.131 Grilled Loaded Chicken Tacos

Total Time: 4 hours, Servings: 8
Ingredients
Grilled Chicken
2 Pound Boneless, Skinless Chicken Breast
Olive Oil, 2 tbsp
Chili Powder, 2 tsp
Smoked Paprika, 1 tsp
Ground Cumin, 1/2 tsp
Ground Cayenne Pepper, 1/4 tsp
Kosher Salt, 1 1/2 tsp
Black Pepper, 1 tsp
Pico de Gallo
Plum Tomatoes (Diced), 1 1/2 Pound
Red Onion (Diced), 1 Medium
Chopped Cilantro, 1/2 Cup
Juiced Lime, 1
Kosher Salt

Guacamole
Avocados, 2 Whole
Fresh Squeezed Lime Juice, 1 tbsp
Red Onion (Finely Diced), 1/4 Cup
Cilantro Leaves (Finely Chopped), 2 tbsp
Kosher Salt
Spiked Sour Cream
Sour Cream, 1/2 Cup
Chili Powder, 1 tsp
Fresh Squeezed Lime Juice, 1 tbsp
Kosher Salt
Toppings
Tortillas, 12 Flour
Lime (Cut into Wedges), 1
Jalapeño (Sliced into Rings), 1
Fresh Cilantro
Hot Sauce

Instructions

To make the marinade, combine together the chicken breasts, olive oil, spices, zest, salt, & pepper in a freezer bag. Refrigerate for the at least 4 hours before serving (overnight is best).

When ready to cook, preheat the oven to 450°F with the lid covered for 15 minutes.

Place the chicken breasts on a hot grill and cook for 25 to 30 minutes, covered, until crispy and golden and the internal temperature reaches 165°F.

Prepare the Pico, guacamole, & spiked sour cream while the chicken is on the grill.

To make the Pico, mix together the chopped tomatoes, red onion, cilantro, and 1 lime juice in a small dish. Season with salt and pepper to taste, then
put aside.

To make the guacamole, peel the avocados & carefully remove the pits. In a mixing bowl, mash the avocado with the lime juice till smooth, but leave a few pieces for texture. After that, add the red onion and cilantro and toss everything together well. Season with salt and pepper to taste.

To make the spiked sour cream, whisk together all of the ingredients in a small mixing dish.

Take the cooked chicken from the grill and set it aside for 5 minutes before slicing it into thin strips.

Toss the sliced grilled chicken with fresh Pico, guacamole, & a dollop of spiked sour cream over warm tortillas. Serve with lime wedges and spicy sauce, then top each taco with sliced jalapeno and fresh cilantro. Enjoy.

3.132 Cherry Smoked Bomb Chicken

Total Time: 2 hours 20 mins, Servings: 4
Ingredients
Cold Water, 1 Quart
Kosher Salt, 1/3 Cup
Sugar, 1/2 Cup
Cherry Tomatoes, 10 Ounce
Habanero Peppers (Seeded), 3
Garlic, 4 Clove
Ground Allspice, 1/2 tsp
Chicken Legs (Thigh And Drumstick), 4
Thyme, 1 1/2 tsp
Ground Cumin, 1 tsp
Black Pepper, 1 tsp
Cayenne Pepper, 1/2 tbsp
Vegetable Oil, 3 tbsp
Thai Sweet Chile Sauce, 1/2 Cup

Instructions

In a saucepan over low heat, combine water, kosher salt, & sugar; simmer for 4 to 5 minutes, or till sugar and salt dissolve. Allow to cool to room temp before serving.

In a blender, puree the cherry, habanero peppers, tomatoes, & allspice with the salt & sugar until smooth.

Score each piece of chicken 2 - 3 times on the skin side, about 1/8 inch deep. Place the chicken pieces in a big dish or a container with a cover. Make sure all
of the chicken pieces are coated with tomato brine. Refrigerate for 4 to 6 hours before serving.

Take the chicken pieces out of the pan and place them on a plate or a baking sheet coated with paper towels. Using extra paper towels, pat the chicken pieces dry.

When you're ready to cook, turn the Pit Boss on Smoke and leave the lid open till a fire form (4-5 minutes).

In a small bowl, combine the thyme, black pepper, cumin, cayenne pepper, & oil.

Brush each piece of chicken with the thyme-oil mixture. (Don't use too much oil or you'll get major flare-ups!)

Smoke the chicken for 30 to 1 hour on the Pit Boss barbecue grate.

Increase the temp to 350 degrees F & continue to roast the chicken till an instant-read meat thermometer reads 165 ° F in the
thickest part of a thigh, about 50 - 60 minutes.

Transfer the "chicken quarters" to a dish and brush with the Thai sweet Chile sauce on each piece. Transfer the chicken to a dish and let aside for 10 minutes on each side. Enjoy.

3.133 Italian Grilled Chicken Saltimbocca

Total Time: 50 mins, Servings: 4
Ingredients
Chicken Breasts, 6
Olive Oil
Pit Boss Pork & Poultry Rub
Prosciutto Slices, 6 Slices
Sage Leaves, 10
Parmesan Cheese, 1 Cup

Instructions

Preheat the Pit Boss to 350°F (175°C) for 15 minutes
with the lid closed when ready to cook.

Carefully butterfly every chicken breast with a sharp knife.

Lightly season the exterior of each breast with Pit Boss Pork & Poultry Rub.

Add a piece of prosciutto to the wrap. Garnish with sage leaves and Parmesan cheese.

Place the chicken on a baking sheet or straight on the grill grate, angled away from the bars.

Roast till the chicken is well done, about 25 to 30 minutes, or until an inside temperature of 165°F is
reached (75 C).

Remove from the oven and set aside for 2 mins before serving. More fresh sage & parmesan cheese can be sprinkled over top. Enjoy.

3.134 Andouille, Chicken & Potato Roasted Gumbo

Total Time: 3 hours 45 mins, Servings: 6
Ingredients
Andouille Sausage (Cut Into 2 Inch Slices), 1 Pound
Red Potatoes, 1 Pound
Butter, 1/2 Cup
Onion (Coarsely Chopped), 1 Large
Red Bell Pepper (Coarsely Chopped), 1
Thinly Sliced Celery, 1 Cup
Garlic (Minced), 2 Clove
Cajun Seasoning, 2 tsp
Ground Red Pepper, 1/8 tsp
All-Purpose Flour, 1 Cup

Container Chicken Broth, 1 (48 Oz)
Chicken Breasts (Boneless, Skinless), 2 Pound
Small Red Potatoes, 1 Pound
Olive Oil
Salt n Pepper
Instructions
Preheat the Pit Boss to 425°F for 15 minutes with the lid closed when ready to cook. Allow a cast iron Dutch oven to warm on the grill for 20 minutes.
In a Dutch oven, brown sausage for ten min, stirring every 2 minutes. Remove the sausage from the pan, drain it, and wipe it dry with paper towels.
Reduce the temperature of the grill to 375°F. Return the cast iron pot to the grill and let it to warm once more.
Add onion, bell pepper, garlic, celery, Cajun spice, and ground red pepper to melted butter in cast iron saucepan. Cook for 10 minutes, stirring periodically. Cook for another ten min with the lid covered after adding the flour.
Whisk in the chicken broth in a slow, steady stream. Combine the chicken & browned sausage in a large mixing bowl. Cook for 1 hour in a covered Dutch oven.
Halve the potatoes and place them on a baking pan. Toss with a drizzle of olive oil and a pinch of salt and pepper to coat. Remove from the equation.
After 1 hour, remove the lid from the grill and stir the gumbo. Place the potatoes next to the gumbo on the grill. Cook for another hour on both.
Remove the gumbo and potatoes from the grill. Remove the chicken from the gumbo & shred it using two forks into large pieces, then return it to the gumbo.
To serve, pour gumbo over baked potatoes in serving dishes. Enjoy.

3.135 Garlic BBQ Chicken
Total Time: 45 mins, Servings: 6
Ingredients
Olive Oil, 4 tbsp
Freshly Pressed Garlic, 4 Clove
Worcestershire Sauce
Chicken Breasts, 4 Whole
Chicken Legs, 4 Whole
Pit Boss Blackened Saskatchewan Rub
Honey Pit Boss Bourbon BBQ Sauce, 1 Cup
Pit Boss BBQ Sauce, 1 Cup
Texas Pit Boss Spicy BBQ Sauce, 1 Cup
Instructions
Preheat the oven too high for 15 minutes when you're ready to cook. Combine the olive oil, garlic cloves, & Worcestershire sauce in a mixing bowl.
Rub the oil mixture into all the chicken breasts and legs, then season with the Pit Boss Saskatchewan rub on both sides.
In a mixing dish, combine the three barbecue sauces, using equal portions of each.
Cook the seasoned chicken pieces on the grate for 20-30 minutes, depending on the size of the breast or
leg. Cook until the internal temperature of the meat reaches 165°F.
During the last 5 minutes of cooking, drizzle the BBQ sauce mixture on top. Allow to sit for 5 minutes after removing from the grill. Have fun. Cooking times will vary based on the temperature of the set and the ambient temperature.

3.136 Buffalo Chicken Dip Baked
Total Time: 40 mins, Servings: 6
Ingredients
Cream Cheese (Softened), 8 Ounce
Sour Cream, 1/2 Cup
Mayonnaise, 1/2 Cup
Dry Ranch Seasoning, 2 tbsp
Kosher Salt, 1 tsp
Frank's Red-Hot Sauce, 1/2 Cup
Cooked Chicken (Shredded), 2 Cup
Cheddar Cheese (Shredded), 1 Cup
Mozzarella Cheese (Shredded), 1 Cup
Blue Cheese, 1/2 Cup
Cooked Bacon (Crumbled), 4 Strips
For Serving - Crackers, Chips, Crostini Or Sliced Vegetables
Instructions
Preheat the Pit Boss to 350°F for 15 minutes with the lid closed when ready to cook.
Toss together cream cheese, mayonnaise, sour cream, ranch dressing, salt, and hot sauce in a medium mixing basin or the bowl of a stand mixer.
Combine the cheddar, mozzarella, and shredded chicken in a mixing bowl. Transfer to an ovenproof dish & top with crumbled bacon and blue cheese.
Cook for 20 - 30 minutes, till the top is golden brown and the dip is bubbling, by placing the dish straight on the grill grate.
Toss with chips, crackers, crostini, or sliced veggies before serving. Enjoy

3.137 Honey Grilled Garlic Wings
Total Time: 1 hour 20 mins, Servings: 4
Ingredients
Chicken Wings, 2 1/2 Pound
Pit Boss Pork & Poultry Rub
Butter, 4 tbsp
Garlic (Minced), 3 Clove
Honey, 1/4 Cup
Hot Sauce, 1/2 Cup
Blue Cheese or Ranch Dressing, 1 1/2 Cup
Instructions
Begin by cutting through the joints to split the wings into three parts. Save the wing tips to form a stock or discard them.
Arrange the remaining pieces on a rimmed baking sheet coated with parchment paper or nonstick foil.
Pit Boss Pork and or Poultry Rub should be used liberally.
When ready to prepare, preheat the Pit Boss to 350°F with the lid closed for fifteen min.
Cook for 45 to 50 minutes, or until the wings are no pinker at the bone, on a baking sheet direct on the grill grate.
Melt butter in a plastic container to prepare the sauce. Sauté for 2 to 3 minutes after adding the garlic. Cook for a few minutes, until the honey and spicy sauce are thoroughly mixed. While the wings are cooking, keep the sauce warm.
After 45 minutes, flip the wings with tongs to cover them in the spicy honey-garlic sauce.
Return the wings to the grill & cook for another 10-15 minutes to allow the sauce to solidify.
Toss with ranch or blue cheese dressing before serving. Enjoy.

3.138 Smoke Roasted Chicken
Total Time: 1 hour 20 mins, Servings: 4
Ingredients
Butter, 8 tbsp
Garlic (Minced), 1 Clove
Scallions Minced, 1
Fresh Herbs (Such As Rosemary, Thyme, Sage Or Parsley) 2 tbsp
Pit Boss Chicken Rub
Lemon Juice
Chicken, 1 Whole
Vegetable Oil
Instructions
Combine garlic, scallions, butter, minced fresh herbs, 1-1/2 tsp

rub, and lemon juice in a small bowl. Using a wooden spoon, thoroughly combine the ingredients.
Remove extra giblets from the chicken's cavity. Cold running water should be used to wash the bird both inside and out. Using paper towels, thoroughly dry the area.
Rub a large quantity of Chicken Rub into the chicken's cavity. Gently loosen the skin around the chicken breast and spread a few tablespoons of herb butter equally beneath the skin.
Using the leftover herb butter, smear the exterior of the bird. Tuck the chicken wings into the rear of the chicken. Butcher's string is used to tie the legs together.
If preferred, add additional Bird Rub to the exterior of the chicken and sprigs of fresh herbs to the cavity of the chicken. When ready to cook, increase the temperature to High & preheat for 15 minutes with the lid closed.
Brush vegetable oil on the grill grate. Close the cover and place the chicken breast-side up on the grill grate.
Lift the cover after the chicken has cooked for 1 hour. Cover the breast & legs with aluminum foil if the chicken is browning too rapidly.
Replace the top and continue to roast the chicken until an instant-read meat thermometer inserted into the thickest section reads 165°F (about 15 to 20 minutes more).
Remove the chicken from the grill and set it aside for 5 minutes to rest. Serve. Enjoy.

3.139 Turkey Cornbread Tamale Pie Baked
Total Time: 1 hour, Servings: 6
Ingredients
Turkey (Shredded), 2 Cup
Ears Corn, 2
Black Beans (Drained & Rinsed), 15 Ounce
Yellow Bell Pepper (Diced), 1
Orange Bell Pepper, 1
Jalapeño, 2
Cilantro, 2 tbsp
Green Onions, 1 Bunch
Cumin, 1/2 tsp
Paprika, 1/2 tsp
Chipotle Sauce, 7 Ounce
Enchilada Sauce, 15 Ounce (15 Oz)
Shredded Cheddar Cheese (Divided), 1/2 Cup
All-Purpose Flour, 1 Cup
Cornmeal, 1 Cup
Sugar, 1 tbsp
Baking Powder, 2 tsp
1/2 tsp Salt
3 tbsp Butter
Buttermilk, 1 Cup
Egg, 1 Large
Instructions
To make the filling, put all of the ingredients in a mixing bowl. Place in the bottom of a 10-inch pan that has been coated with butter.
To make the cornbread topping, whisk together the flour, cornmeal, sugar, baking powder, & salt in a mixing dish. In a small saucepan, melt the butter. Remove the butter from the heat & whisk in the milk and egg until thoroughly combined. If the mixture becomes too heated, the egg will curdle.
Stir together the dry ingredients & the milk-egg combination. Don't overmix the ingredients.
To assemble the Tamale Pie, place the shredded turkey filling in the bottom of a butter-greased 10-inch pan. Smooth the cornbread topping to the edges of the pan.
When ready to cook, preheat the oven to 375°F with the lid covered for 15 minutes.
Cook for 45-50 minutes, or till the cornbread is lightly browned & cooked through, directly on the grill grate. Enjoy.

3.140 White Chicken Chili
Total Time: 1 hour, Servings: 6
Ingredients
Chicken Broth, 8 Cup
Chicken (Grilled), 5 Cup
Great Northern Beans (Drained), 45 Ounce (15 Oz)
Salsa Verde, 3 Cup
Ground Cumin, 2 tsp
Onion Powder, 1/2 tbsp
Garlic Powder, 1/2 tbsp
Salt n Pepper
Diced Avocado, 2
Sour Cream, 1/2 Cup
Cilantro (Chopped), 1/8 Cup
Instructions
When ready to cook, preheat the grill according to the manufacturer's recommendations. Preheat the oven to 400 degrees F & bake for 10 to 15 minutes with the lid covered.
In a Dutch oven or oven-safe stock pot, combine all chili ingredients. Toss everything together and season with salt and pepper to taste.
Place the Dutch oven on the grill about 4 hours, covered.
Remove the Dutch oven from the heat and serve the chili with the toppings. Enjoy.

3.141 Thanksgiving Shepherd's Pie Baked
Total Time: 1 hour 10 mins, Servings: 6
Ingredients
Canola Oil, 2 tbsp
Chopped Onion, 1 Cup
Garlic (Minced), 2 Clove
Kosher Salt, 1 tsp
Freshly Ground Black Pepper, 1/2 tsp
All-Purpose Flour, 2 tbsp
Tomato Paste, 2 tsp
Leftover Gravy, 1 Cup
Chicken Broth, 1 Cup
Worcestershire Sauce, 1 tsp
Fresh Chopped Rosemary, 2 tsp
Fresh Chopped Thyme, 1 tsp
Leftover Turkey, 1 1/2 Pound
Leftover Green Beans, 1 Cup
Leftover Stuffing, 1 Cup
Leftover Mashed Potatoes, 2 Cup
Instructions
Preheat the Pit Boss to 400°F for 15 minutes with the lid closed when ready to cook.
In a medium sauté pan, heat the canola oil over medium-high heat. When the oil begins to shimmer, add the onion & cook for 3 to 4 minutes, or until softened and gently browned. Stir in the garlic until everything is well combined. Salt & pepper to taste.
Drizzle the flour over the onions and toss to coat, then cook for another minute. Combine the tomato paste, leftover gravy, chicken stock, Worcestershire sauce, rosemary, and thyme in a large mixing bowl. To mix, stir everything together. Bring to a boil, then turn off the heat. Cover and cook for 10 to 12 minutes, or until the sauce has slightly thickened.
Combine the leftover turkey, green beans, and stuffing in an 11x7-inch glass baking dish and distribute evenly.
Spread the mashed potatoes on top, starting around the borders to make a seal & smooth with a rubber spatula to prevent the contents from bubbling up. Bake for 25 minutes, or until the potatoes start to brown, directly on the grill grate. Before serving, chill for at least 15 minutes on a cooling rack. Enjoy.

3.142 Sticky Grilled Ginger Chicken Thighs

Total Time: 35 mins, Servings: 4
Ingredients
Grated Onion, 1/2 Cup
Peanut Oil, 1/2 Cup
Rice Vinegar, 1/3 Cup
Water, 2 tbsp
Freshly Grated Ginger, 2 tbsp
Ketchup, 2 tbsp
Soy Sauce, 4 tsp
Sugar, 2 tsp
Lemon Juice, 2 tsp
Minced Garlic, 1/2 tsp
Chicken Thighs, 6
Limes (Sliced), 2
Stalk Green Onion (Thinly Sliced), 3
Sesame Seeds, For Garnish
Instructions
In a large mixing basin, combine all the marinade ingredients and put aside. Place the chicken thighs in a resealable bag & top with 3/4 of the dressing.
Marinate for at least 1 hour in the refrigerator.
When ready to cook, preheat the Pit Boss to 450°F with the cover closed for fifteen min.
Place the skin-side down marinated chicken thighs on the grill grate. Cook for 10 minutes, then turn and cook for another 10 minutes, or until the core temperature reaches 165 ° F. During the last Ten minutes of cooking, baste with the remaining marinade.
Add lime slices to the top of the chicken and simmer for another 5 minutes. To serve, place on a serving dish and garnish with sliced green onions & sesame seeds. Enjoy.

3.143 BBQ Chicken Nachos

Total Time: 55 mins, Servings: 4
Ingredients
Chicken Breasts (Boneless, Skinless), 1 1/4 Pound
Poultry Rub & Pit Boss Pork
Pit Boss 'Que BBQ Sauce, 1/2 Cup
Tortilla Chips, 1 Bag
Mexican Blend Cheese (Shredded), 3 Cup
Sliced Pickled Jalapeños, 1/4 Cup
Black Olives (Sliced and Drained), 1/2 Cup
Scallions (Thinly Sliced), 3
Guacamole, 1/2 Cup
Sour Cream, 1 Cup
Cherry Tomatoes (Halved), 1/2 Cup
Instructions
Rub the Pit Boss Pork & Poultry Rub all over the chicken breasts. When ready to cook, preheat the Pit Boss to 350°F with the lid closed for 15 minutes.
Arrange the chicken breasts on the grill grate & cook for 25 to 30 minutes, rotating once halfway through the cooking time, or until an instant-read meat thermometer reads 165 degrees F.
Place on a cutting board & set aside for 3 minutes to cool. If you're cooking nachos right away, leave the grill on.
Remove the chicken from the bone and shred it. Place the chicken in a mixing dish and cover with 1/2 cup Pit Boss 'Que BBQ Sauce. To ensure a uniform coating, carefully stir the ingredients together. If not preparing the nachos right now, set aside or cover and refrigerate.
Arrange the tortilla chips on a rimmed baking sheet or pizza plate in a single layer. Half of the cheese & a few jalapenos should be distributed evenly. On each chip, spoon the barbecued chicken mixture. If desired, garnish with black olives and additional pickled jalapenos. Over the chips, equally distribute the remaining cheese.
Place the baking sheet on the grill grate and close the lid. Bake for 12 to 15 minutes, or till the chips are crisp & the cheese is melted.
Transfer the nachos to a dish or tray using a spatula. Scallions, guacamole, sour cream, and cherry tomatoes go on top. Enjoy.

3.144 Chicken Fajita Skewers Grilled

Total Time: 5 hours 10 mins, Servings: 4
Ingredients
Cilantro (Roughly Chopped), 1/2 Cup
Fresh Squeezed Lime Juice, 1/3 Cup
Extra-Virgin Olive Oil, 1/3 Cup
Garlic (Peeled), 4 Clove
Dark Brown Sugar, 1 tbsp
Kosher Salt, 1 tsp
Ground Cumin, 1 1/2 tsp
Ancho Chile Powder, 3/4 tsp
Chicken Breasts (Cut Into 1 Inch Cubes), 2 Pound
Ed Onion, (In 3 Layer Segments, Cut Into 1-1/2 Inch Cubes,) 1 Large
Green Bell Pepper, (Cut Into 1-1/2 Inch Pieces)
Red Bell Pepper, 1 Large
Instructions
In a blender, puree the cilantro, olive oil, garlic, lime juice, salt, cumin, and ancho Chile powder brown sugar until smooth.
Arrange the chicken cubes in big plastic bag with a zipper. Pour the mixture over the chicken cubes, cover the bag, and marinate for 1-5 hours in the refrigerator.
Remove the chicken from the marinade and toss out any remaining liquid. Alternate threading the chicken, pepper, and onion squares onto the skewers.
Preheat the oven too high for 15 minutes when you're ready to cook. Place skewers towards the front of grill grate till grill marks appear, then move to the middle until the internal temperature of the pork hits 160°F (about 10-12 mins).
Take the skewers off the grill. Allow for a 5-minute rest period. Serve and have fun! Cooking times will vary based on the temperature of the set and the ambient temperature.

3.145 Beantown Chicken Wings Grilled

Total Time: 1 hours, Servings: 8
Ingredients
Chicken Wings, 3 Pound
Vegetable Oil, 1/4 Cup
Pit Boss Pork & Poultry Rub, 1 1/2 tbsp
Irish Stout, 1 Cup
Butter, 1/2 Cup
Apple Jelly, 2 tbsp
Frank's RedHot Sauce, 1 Cup
Instructions
Rinse and wipe dry the chicken wings underneath cold running water. Cut the wings into three pieces through the

joints using a sharp knife. Save the wing tips for chicken stock or discard them.

In a large mixing bowl, combine the remaining "drumettes" and "flats." Toss the wings with your hands to uniformly coat them in the oil and Pit Boss Pork & Poultry mix.

To make the beer sauce, bring the beer to a boil in a small saucepan over high heat and reduce it by half. Reduce heat to low and whisk in the butter until it is completely melted. Combine the apple jelly & spicy sauce in a mixing bowl. Keep yourself warm.

When ready to cook, preheat the oven to 350°F with the lid covered for 15 minutes.

Place the wings on the grill grate in an even layer. Cook for 45 - 50 minutes, flipping once halfway through, or till the chicken is no longer pink at the bone. Pour the beer sauce over the wings in a large clean dish and toss to coat. Serve right away.

3.146 Big Game Roast Chicken
Total Time: 1 hour 15 mins, Servings: 4
Ingredients
Chicken, 1 Whole
Big Pit Boss Game Rub
Instructions
Preheat the Pit Boss to 375°F for 15 minutes with the lid closed when ready to cook.

Remove the bird's neck & gizzards from the cavity. Using a paper towel, clean the exterior and interior of the bird. Butcher tie the chicken legs together and tuck the wings.

Rub the Pit Boss Big Game Rub all over the interior and exterior of the bird.

Cook the chicken for 60 minutes on the grill grate. Check the temp of the bird in the thickest portion of the leg after an hour. The temperature should be around 165 –

180-degrees Fahrenheit. If the temperature hasn't reached the desired level, check every 15 minutes. Check the temp of the breast once the leg has reached the desired internal temperature. Before the breast is done, it must achieve a core temperature of 165°F.

Allow 15 - 20 minutes for the bird to rest before slicing. Enjoy.

3.147 Bucket O' Chicken Baked
Total Time: 8 hours 50 mins, Servings: 8
Ingredients
Water, 1 Gallon
Kosher Salt, 1 3/4 Cup
Brown Sugar, 1/2 Cup
Rosemary, 4 Sprig
Thyme, 4 Sprig
Bay Leaves, 6
Black Peppercorn, 4 tbsp
Garlic, 1 Head
Orange Zest, 1
Ice Water, 1/2 Gallon
Chickens (Cut Into 10 Pieces Each), 2 Whole (3 1/2 Lbs.)
All-Purpose Flour, 4 Cup
Granulated Garlic, 1/4 Cup
Onion Powder, 1/4 Cup
Black Pepper, 1 tbsp
Paprika, 1 tbsp
Cayenne Pepper, 2 tbsp
Buttermilk, 1 Quart
Canola Oil
Pit Boss Chicken Rub
Instructions
To make the brine, in a medium stockpot, combine all of the brine ingredients except the ice water & bring to a boil over medium-high heat. Cook until the sugar and salt have completely dissolved.

Fill a large container with ice water large enough to accommodate all of the brine & chicken. Pour the boiling brine over the ice water and swirl until the ice melts and the brine cools.

Place the chicken pieces in the brine and, if required, weigh them down with a stack of plates.

Cover and place in the refrigerator overnight to brine. Rinse the chicken in cold water after removing it from the brine.

Pat dry and place on a sheet tray fitted with a cooling rack. Allow the chicken to remain in the refrigerator for about 1 hour or until the skin is totally dry.

In a medium mixing basin, combine all remaining coating ingredients except the buttermilk and stir thoroughly. In two medium basins, divide the coating in half.

Season buttermilk with salt and pepper in a separate medium bowl.

When ready to cook, increase the temp to High & preheat for 15 minutes with the lid closed.

While the grill preheats, place a cast iron pan with 1-1/2" canola oil on the grill grate.

Dredge the chicken in the first dish of coating, then dip it in the buttermilk and shake off the excess.

Transfer to the second coating basin and shake to remove any excess. Put on another sheet tray that has been coated with cooking spray and lined with a cooling rack.

Bake chicken for 30-40 minutes, or till the internal temperature reaches 150°F, on a sheet pan directly on the grill grate close to the cast iron of oil.

As the chicken pieces warm up, place 2 or 3 at a time in the hot oil to crisp the coating & finish frying.

When the core temperature of the chicken reaches 165°F, remove it from the oil and lay it on a sheet tray fitted with a cooling rack to let the excess oil drain out and preserve the crisp coating.

As soon as the pieces are removed from the oil, season them with Pit Boss Chicken Rub or kosher salt. Carry on with the rest of the chicken pieces in the same manner.

Toss with preferred sides or sauces before serving. Enjoy.

3.148 Jerked Jamaican Chicken Legs
Total Time: 1 hour 20 mins, Servings: 4
Ingredients
Scallions (Chopped), 1 Bunch
Garlic (Chopped), 2 Clove
Scotch Bonnet Pepper
Lime, Juiced 1 Whole
Soy Sauce, 2 tbsp
Vegetable Oil, 1 tbsp
Brown Sugar, 1 tbsp
Fresh thyme, 2 tsp
Salt, 1 tsp
Ground Allspice, 1 tsp
Black Pepper, 1 tsp
Ground Nutmeg, 1/2 tsp
Ground Cinnamon, 1/2 tsp
Water
Onion (Cut Into Chunks), 1 Small
Instructions
To make the marinade, mix all of the ingredients in a blender container, except the
chicken legs. Pulse the mixture until it is liquefied. If the blender blades aren't spinning, add a tbsp or two of water.

Arrange the chicken legs in a single layer in a large glass baking dish. Put the legs in a big resealable plastic bag if you like.

Pour the marinade so over chicken legs & toss them around to coat them evenly. Refrigerate the dish for 6 hours or overnight, covered in plastic wrap.
When you're ready to cook, fire up the "Pit Boss" according to the manufacturer's directions. Preheat the grill to 165 degrees Fahrenheit (Super Smoke when using a WiFIRE-enabled grill) for 5 minutes. Place the chicken legs on the grill grate for 30 minutes to smoke.
Preheat the grill to 350 degrees Fahrenheit and let it sit for 10 minutes. Cook for 45 minutes to an hour, or until a meat thermometer inserted into the thickest part of the leg and not touching the bone registers 165°F. Enjoy.

3.149 Grilled Hellfire Chicken Wings
Total Time: 55 mins, Servings: 4
Ingredients
Chicken Wings, 3 Pound
Cayenne Pepper, 1 tsp
Vegetable Oil, 2 tbsp
Brown Sugar, 2 tsp
Salt, 1 tsp
Hot Sauce, 1/2 Cup
Black Pepper (Freshly Ground), 1 tsp
Paprika, 1 tbsp
Onion Powder, 1 tsp
Cilantro Leaves, 1/2 Cup
Granulated Garlic, 1 tsp
Celery Seed, 1 tsp
Unsalted Butter, 8 tbsp
Jalapeño Peppers, 4
Instructions
Remove the tips of the wings and discard them. Each wing should be cut in half through the joint, resulting in a meaty drumette & a flat. Pour the oil over the chicken and transfer it to a large mixing bowl.
Prepare the Rub: Combine paprika, salt & black pepper, sugar, cayenne, granulated garlic, onion powder, and celery seed in a small mixing dish.
Toss the chicken wings lightly with your hands to cover them with the seasoning.
When ready to cook, preheat the Pit Boss to 350°F for 15 minutes with the lid closed.
Cook the wings for 35 - 40 minutes on the grill, or till the skin is crisp & golden brown & the chicken is fully cooked. Halfway through the cooking time, turn once more.
To make the sauce, melt the butter in a small saucepan over medium-low heat. Cook for 3 - 4 minutes after adding the jalapenos. Combine the cilantro and spicy sauce in a mixing bowl.
Toss the wings in the sauce to coat them. Enjoy.

3.150 Tequila-Lime Wings Roasted
Total Time: 45 mins, Servings: 6
Ingredients
Chicken Wings, 3 Pound
Ancho Chile Powder, 2 tsp
Brown Sugar, 2 tsp
Granulated Garlic, 1 tsp
Cumin, 1 tsp
Kosher Salt, 1 tsp
Chili Powder, 1 tsp
Vegetable Oil, 2 tbsp
Honey, 1/4 Cup
Pineapple Juice, 1/4 Cup
Tequila, 3 tbsp
Hot Sauce, 1 1/2 tbsp
Butter, 1 1/2 tbsp

Fresh Lime Juice, 1 1/2 tbsp
Instruction
When ready to cook, preheat the Pit Boss to 500°F with the lid closed for fifteen min.
Remove the entire chicken wings if you bought them whole. Remove the tip & separate the drumettes & wings from each other if you buy entire chicken wings. Allow them to air dry. Save the wingtips for chicken stock or discard them. Separate the drumettes & wings from each other with a point. Allow them to air dry. Save the wing
tips for chicken stock or discard them.
In a medium mixing bowl, mix all of the dry rub ingredients. Whisk in the oil until it is completely combined. Toss in the chicken wings and coat well.
To make the glaze, whisk together all of the glaze ingredients in a small pot. Over medium heat, bring to a boil. Cook for approximately 3 minutes, or until the mixture has reduced by about 1/3 and is thickening.
While you're waiting for the glaze to dry, keep the syrup heated.
Place the wings straight on the grill grate and cook for 20 minutes, rotating once, until the temperature reaches 155°F to 160°F.
Brush the wings with the glaze & cook for another 5 to 10 minutes, or until the core temperature reaches 165°F to 175°F. Serve immediately. Enjoy.

3.151 Pickle Brined Chicken Sandwich
Total Time: 45 Mins, Servings: 8
Ingredients
Skinless chicken thighs boneless, 8
Pickle juice, 2 cups.
Canola oil
Flour, 1 cup
Tapioca flour, 1/2 cup
Salt
Frank's red sauce, 2 tbsp
Egg, 1
Sesame seed buns, 4
Brown sugar, 1/2 tbsp
Shredded cabbage slaw
Buttermilk, 1 cup
Mayonnaise
Butter (melted), 1/2 cup
Pit Boss smoked pickles
Frank's red-hot sauce, 1/2 cup
Cayenne pepper, 2 tbsp
Garlic powder, 1 tbsp
Paprika, 1 tbsp
Black pepper, 1 tbsp
Instructions
Mix pickle juice & chicken thighs in a medium mixing basin. If required, weigh the thighs to ensure that they are fully immersed. Allow to brine overnight in the refrigerator.
Once ready to cook, preheat the Pit Boss to 450°F for 15 minutes with the lid closed. While the grill is heating up, put a cast iron pan on the grilling grate and pour with canola oil (approximately 1/2-inch deep).
Drain the pickle brine from the chicken thighs and pat them dry.
Mix both flours and a sprinkle of salt in a medium mixing bowl. To combine, whisk everything together well.
Blend the buttermilk, spicy sauce, egg, and a sprinkle of salt in a separate bowl. To mix, whisk everything together well.
Salt and pepper the chicken thighs. The thighs should be dipped in flour, then buttermilk, and finally back into the flour. Repeat with the remaining thighs and place on a wire rack to cool.

Bake chicken for fifteen min or until core temperature reaches 150°F on a wire rack
immediately on the grill grate close to the cast iron of oil.
Once the chicken pieces have reached room temperature, place 2 or 3 at a time in the hot oil to crispy the covering and finish frying.
To make the Butter Hot Sauce, melt the butter in a medium bowl with the hot sauce, brown sugar, cayenne, garlic powder, paprika, and black pepper while the chicken is cooking. Remove from the equation.
When the internal temperature of the chicken reaches 165°F, remove it from the oil and dip it in the butter hot sauce mixture.
Assemble the sandwiches by layering the buns, mayonnaise, pickles, cabbage slaw, and hot chicken on top. Enjoy.

3.152 Turkey Sliders with Chipotle Tartar Sauce
Total Time: 55 Minutes, Serving: 4
Ingredients
Mayonnaise, 1/2 cup
Green onions (sparsely sliced), 2 wholes
Pickle relish, 2 tbsp
Chipotle peppers in adobo, 1 whole + 2 tbsps. Sauce from can
Adobo sauce, 1 tbsp
Milk, 2 tbsp
Onion (shredded), 2 tbsp
Poultry rub & Pit Boss pork, 1 1/2 tbsp
Worcestershire sauce, 1 tbsp
Dijon mustard, 2 tbsp
White breadcrumbs fresh, 1/2 cup
Ground turkey, 1 1/2 pound
Sesame slider buns, 12 wholes
Plum tomatoes, red onion, & arugula (finely sliced)
Instructions
To prepare the Chipotle Tartar Sauce, whisk together the mayonnaise, green onion, pickle
relish, chipotle chile, adobo sauce, and Pit Boss Pork & Poultry Rub in a small mixing dish. To mix the ingredients, whisk them together. If not serving right away, cover and chill.
To prepare the sliders, mix mayonnaise, milk, chopped onion, Worcestershire sauce, mustard, and Pit Boss Pork and Poultry Rub in a medium mixing bowl. Add the bread crumbs and mix well.
Add chopped turkey and mix it in with mayonnaise and bread crumb mix with moist fingertips and a gentle touch. If necessary, re-wet your hands and shape the mixture into 12 patties. Make a large depression in the middle of each using your
thumbs. (If making ahead, cover and chill.)
Whenever ready to cook, preheat the oven to 300 degrees Fahrenheit with the lid covered for 10 to 15 mins.
Grill the sliders for 30 to 35 mins, or until they are cooked through, and an instant-read meat thermometer registers 160 degrees.
Place the sliders on the buns' bottom halves. Add the Chipotle Tartar Sauce, preferred condiments, and the
top half of the bread to the top. Serve with the leftover Tartar Sauce right away. Enjoy.

3.153 Grilled Thai Chicken Burgers with Papaya Slaw
Total Time: 50 Minutes, Serving: 6
Ingredients
Sliced green papaya, 6 ounces
Red onion (thinly carved), 1/2
New lime juice, 3 tbsp
Fish sauce, 1 tbsp
Brown sugar, 1 tbsp
Ground chicken thigh meat, 1 pound
Panko or gluten-free breadcrumbs, 1/2 cup
Coconut cream, 1/4 cup
Fresh chopped cilantro, 1/2 cup
Garlic (minced), 2 clove
Ground ginger, 1/2 tbsp
Salt, 2 tbsp
Black pepper, 1 tbsp
Ground cumin, 1 tbsp
Fresh lime juice, 2 tbsp
Freshly grated lime zest, 2 tbsp
Vegetable oil, 1 tbsp
Leaves butter lettuce / 4 hamburger buns, 8 large
Mayonnaise, 1/2 cup
Curry powder, 1 1/2 tbsp
Instructions
To make the papaya slaw, combine the
papaya, onion, 3 tablespoons lime juice, fish sauce, and brown sugar in a medium mixing bowl. Cover and chill for up to 3 hours, or until ready to use.
In a large mixing bowl, thoroughly combine ground chicken, breadcrumbs, coconut cream, cilantro, garlic, ginger, salt, pepper, cumin, lime zest, and 2 tablespoons lime juice. Refrigerate for 20 minutes before serving.
Adjust the consistency of the mixture with breadcrumbs or coconut milk if it looks too wet or dry.
In a small mixing dish, combine mayonnaise and curry powder. Remove from the equation.
When ready to cook, preheat the Pit Boss to 450°F with the lid closed for 15 minutes.
Form the chicken mixture into four equal patties using your hands. Brush both sides of each burger with vegetable oil.
Cook for 4 to 5 minutes on each side, or until the burgers achieve an internal temperature of 165°F. Allow it rest for a few minutes before serving after removing from the grill.
Serve each burger with curry mayonnaise and pickled papaya slaw on a lettuce leaf. Serve with a second lettuce leaf as a garnish.
Alternatively, put the patties, curry mayonnaise, and papaya slaw on standard hamburger buns. Enjoy.

3.154 Bacon Cheesy Malibu Chicken
Total Time: 45 Minutes, Serving: 4
Ingredients
Boneless chicken thighs skinless, 6
Pit Boss chicken rub
Butter, 4 tbsp
Pineapple juice, 1/2 cup
Dijon mustard, 1 tbsp
Honey, 1 tbsp
Molasses, 1 tbsp
Worcestershire sauce, 1 tbsp
Ancho chile powder, 1 tbsp
Thick-cut bacon, 12 slices
Pineapple, 12 slices
Swiss cheese, 12 slices
Instructions
Preheat the oven to 350°F and pound the chicken thighs between two pieces of plastic wrap until they are uniformly thick.
Rub Pit Boss Chicken Rub on both sides of each thigh. Refrigerate for at least one hour after covering.
In a medium mixing bowl, whisk together melted butter, pineapple juice, molasses, honey, Worcestershire sauce, Dijon mustard, & ancho chile powder even smooth, then put separately.
When ready to cook, preheat the Pit Boss to 400°F for 15 minutes with lid closed.

Remove the chicken thighs from the refrigerator and set up a rolling station on the counter with bacon, Swiss cheese slices, pineapple slices, & chicken thighs.
Place a piece of cheese on each chicken thigh and roll it up. Then, around each wrapped chicken thigh, place two pineapple slices.
Gently wrap two pieces of bacon around each thigh roll-up, securing the bacon with toothpicks.
Place all of the rolled and wrapped chicken thighs immediately on the grill grate.
After 15 minutes of cooking (or until the bacon begins to render and curl), brush the thighs with the glaze.
Flip the roll-ups over and brush the glaze on the other side. Cook for another 15 to 20 minutes, or until the bacon is crisp and an instant-read thermometer reads 165°F for the chicken thigh.
Take the chicken thighs out of the Pit Boss and brush them with the leftover glaze. Remove the toothpicks before serving. Enjoy.

3.155 Peruvian Roasted Chicken with Green Sauce
Total Time: 1 Hours 30 Minutes, Serving: 6
Ingredients
Lemon (juiced), 1
Coldwater, 1 quart
Whole chicken, 4 pounds
Lime, 3 juiced.
Garlic (minced), 3 clove
Aji Amarillo paste, 2 tbsp
Huaca Tay paste, 2 tbsp
Vegetable oil, 1/4 cup
Paprika, 1 tbsp
Granulated sugar, 2 tbsp
Ground cumin, 2 tbsp
Kosher salt, 1 1/2 tbsp
Freshly ground black pepper, 1 tbsp
Green onion, 4 wholes
Romaine lettuce leaves, 4
Clove garlic (chopped), 2
Jalapeño (seeded & chopped), 2
Cilantro leaves, 1/2 cup
Mayonnaise, 3/4 cup
Sour cream, 1/4 cup
Mint leaves fresh, 4
Salt n pepper
Instructions
In a big resealable plastic bag, mix the lemon juice and water and put in the sink or a large mixing basin. Allow the chicken to soak in the acidulated water while you prepare the marinade.
Prepare the marinade by combining all of the ingredients in a mixing bowl. Add the lime juice, aji Amarillo, garlic, and huacatay pastes (or 4 mint leaves) in a blender jar or the bowl of a small food processor, along with the oil, paprika, sugar, cumin, salt and black pepper. Process until the mixture is reasonably smooth.
Press the chicken dry after draining it. Place the chicken in a resealable plastic bag and seal it. Pour the marinade over the chicken and massage it into the bag to ensure that it is uniformly coated. Refrigerate for at least eight hours and up to twenty-four hours.
Prepare the Green Sauce up to 2 hours before you want to cook the chicken. Make it while the chicken roasts by combining all of the sauce ingredients in a blender jar or the bowl of a small food processor and processing until smooth. Season to taste, then season with additional salt and pepper if necessary. The sauce should have a lot of taste. If not used right away, cover and chill.
When ready to cook, preheat the Pit Boss grill to 375 degrees Fahrenheit with the lid closed for 10 to 15 mins.
Take the chicken out of the marinade and toss it out. Knot the legs together with butcher's thread and tuck the wings behind the back. Place the chicken on the grilling grate immediately. Grill for 70 to 80 mins, or until the skin is crisp and golden, and the room temperature of the thigh is 165F when measured with an instant-read meat thermometer.
Place the chicken on a serving dish or a chopping board. Allow 10 minutes for the chicken to rest.

3.156 Roasted Citrus-Herb Turkey
Total Time: 4 Hours, Serving: 8
Ingredients
Salt, 1 cup
Brown sugar, 1/2 cup
Lemons (quartered), 2
Fresh thyme, 6 sprig
Fresh rosemary, 4 sprig
Turkey, 1 (10-13 lb)
Onion (cut into eighths), 1 large
Oranges (quartered), 2
Celery (finely chopped), 4 stalks
Carrot (roughly chopped), 4 large
Leaves, 2 bay
Fresh thyme, 6 sprig
Olive oil, extra-virgin
Kosher salt, 2 tsp
Black pepper, 1/2 tsp
Chicken or turkey, 2 cups
Butter (softened), 2 sticks
Garlic, 1 clove
Thyme leaves, 4 sprigs
Ground Black Pepper, 1 tsp
Instructions
Make the brine: In a big 5-gallon bucket or clean cooler, dissolve the salt & sugar in 1 gallon of cold water. Combine the lemons, thyme, oranges, and rosemary in a large mixing bowl. If you have a large turkey and want additional brine, use 1 cup salt & 1/2 cup of sugar per gallon of water.
Remove the turkey's neck, giblets, and liver from the cavity and set aside for the gravy.
Place the turkey in the brine, cover, & chill for at least 24 hours or overnight.
Rinse the turkey thoroughly under cold running water after removing it from the brine. Inside and out, pat dry with paper towels.
To make the herb butter, combine all of the ingredients in a large mixing bowl and well combine. Keep it aside until you're ready to utilize it.
To spatchcock the turkey, take out the backbone first. Break the breastbone to open the turkey. Tuck the turkey wings under the spatchcock after flattening the turkey breast side up.
Next, gently press your palm inside the skin to release it from the breast and create a pocket. Make a thick, uniform coating of herb butter under the skin of each chicken breast.
Arrange turkey in a roasting pan with celery, carrots, onions, herbs, stock, salt, and pepper. Season with salt and pepper after brushing with oil.
When ready to cook, preheat the Pit Boss to 350°F with the lid closed for 15 minutes.
Roast the turkey for 2 to 3 hours, or until the internal temperature of the breast reaches 160°F. The skin should be golden in color and crisp to the touch.
Allow 20 minutes for resting before cutting. Enjoy.

3.157 Roasted Tingle Wings
Total Time: 40 mins, Serving: 6
Ingredients
Jalapeño, 3 Whole
Trappe's Red Devil Cayenne Pepper Sauce, 1 tbsp
Pit Boss Texas Spicy BBQ Sauce, 1/2 Cup
Pit Boss Saskatchewan Rub (Blackened), 2 tbsp
Honey, 1/2 Cup
Worcestershire Sauce, 1 tbsp
Water, 1/4 Cup
Instructions
To make the sauce, combine all of the ingredients in a blender, except the wings, and blend until smooth.
Pour the sauce into a "resealable plastic bag" & toss the wings around in it to fully coat them. Marinate for a minimum of 1 hour and up to 24 hours.
Preheat the oven to 350 ° F & cook for 10-15 minutes with the lid covered.
Cook for 30 minutes, or until wings achieve an internal temp of 165 degrees F, immediately on the gill grate. Enjoy.

3.158 Lemon Herb Chicken
Total Time: 40 mins, Serving: 6
Ingredients
Chicken Breasts, 6 Whole
Chopped Thyme, 1 tbsp
Rosemary (Chopped), 1 tbsp
Fresh Chopped Basil, 1 tbsp
Lemon (Juiced), 2 Whole
Lemon Zest, 1 tbsp
Salt, 1 tsp
Black Pepper, 1 tsp
Extra-Virgin Olive Oil, 3 tbsp
Instructions
Combine all ingredients in a large mixing dish & coat the chicken breasts. Cover and chill for 1 hour.
Preheat the oven to high with the lid closed (10-15 mins).
Cook the chicken for 8 minutes each side on a hot grill or until it reaches an internal temperature of 165 degrees Fahrenheit.
Take the chicken from the grill & set it aside for 10 minutes to rest. Serve by slicing into strips.

3.159 Smoked Chicken along with Jalapeno Salsa Verde
Total Time: 40 mins, Serving: 6
Ingredients
Kosher Salt, 2 tbsp
Coffee Grounds, 1/4 Cup
Sugar, 1/4 Cup
Crushed Chile Flakes, 4 tbsp
Paprika, 2 tbsp
Garlic Powder, 1 tbsp
Powder of Onion, 1 tbsp
Coriander Seeds, 1 tbsp
Cracked Black Pepper, 1 tbsp
Cumin, 1 tbsp
Ground Fennel, 1 tsp
Mustard Seeds, 1 tsp
Chicken (Cut into Pieces), 8 Pieces
Jalapeño, 3
Garlic, 3 Clove
Olive Oil
Cilantro, 1 Bunch
Fresh Parsley, 1 Bunch
Lemon (Juiced), 1
Lemon Zest, 1

Instructions
To prepare the rub, put all of the ingredients in a mixing dish and well incorporate. Cover and place in the refrigerator until ready to use.
Season the chicken with the dry rub and place it on a baking pan or wire rack. Coat the chicken well with your hands, being sure to get into all of the crevices and beneath the skin if possible.
Refrigerate the chicken for at least 2 hours & up to overnight, uncovered.
Salsa Verde: Remove the seeds from the jalapenos and combine with the garlic and a splash of olive oil in a food processor. Pulse everything together until it's extremely finely chopped, nearly paste-like. Pulse in the cilantro and parsley until they are coarsely chopped.
Slowly trickle in olive oil while the food processor is running until smooth, and the required consistency is achieved. Squeeze in the lemon juice and zest, season with salt & pepper to taste, and transfer to a mixing bowl.
Refrigerate until ready to use, then remove while chicken is cooking.
Remove the chicken from the refrigerator 45 minutes before cooking.
When ready to cook, preheat the Pit Boss to 225°F for 15 minutes with the lid closed.
Place the chicken skin side up on the grill and cook for 1 1/2 to 2 hours, or until the internal temperature reaches 155°F.
Transfer the chickens to a tray and turn the grill to high. Allow the grill to warm for another ten min before repositioning the chicken, skin side up.
Cover the grill and cook the chicken till it reaches a temperature of 165°F on the inside. Remove.
Allow 10 minutes for the chicken to rest before serving.
To serve, slather the chickens with the jalapeno salsa verde. Enjoy.

3.160 Smoked Chicken Lollipops along with BBQ Champagne Sauce
Total Time: 2 hours, Serving: 8
Ingredients
Pit Boss BBQ Sauce, 1 Bottle
Champagne, 1 Cup
Chicken Drumsticks, 18 Whole
Taste Pit Boss Chicken Rub, 1
Butter Sticks 1 Whole
Instructions
To make the Champagne BBQ Sauce, put the champagne & BBQ sauce in a saucepan. Bring to a low simmer, stirring periodically, over medium heat.
Reduce heat to low & cook for 10 minutes, or until sauce thickens. Remove the pan from the heat and set it aside.
For the Chicken Lollipops: A sharp knife & a pair of kitchen shears are required to convert normal chicken legs into lollipops. Begin by cutting all the way around the leg, just below the knuckle, with a sharp knife or a pair of kitchen shears, cutting through the skins and tendons. Pull/cut the remaining skin & cartilage off the knuckle by pushing the meat down to the big end. You could also wish to remove the little bone against the leg. Trim away the tendons that protrude from the top of the bone using your fingers or shears.
Use Pit Boss Chicken Rub to season the chicken lollipops. To protect the bones of the drumsticks from becoming too black, wrap them in a tiny piece of aluminum foil.
Marinate the chicken for an hour in the refrigerator.
When ready to cook, preheat the grill to 180°F with the lid covered for 15 minutes.
Place the chicken lollipops on the grate for 30 minutes to smoke.

Remove the chicken from the grill & preheat the oven to 350 degrees Fahrenheit.
In a baking pan or an aluminium pan, place the stick of butter. Arrange the lollipops in
the pan, butter side up, with the bones sticking straight up. Allow the chicken to simmer for 40 minutes, or until an instant-read thermometer reads 165°F on the inside.
Warm the barbecue sauce in a small pot on the stove over low heat while the lollipops are cooking. Reduce the heat to merely keep it warm after it begins to thin. If the sauce has to be thinned, add a little amount of the butter from the pan until it achieves a consistency that adheres to the drumsticks. Make sure the lollipops are fully coated with barbecue sauce.
Remove the chicken from the grill when it reaches an internal temperature of 165°F and raises the grill temperature to High. Close the cover and preheat the grill.
Cook the chicken directly on the grill grate for about 10 minutes, or until the internal temperature reaches 175°F. Make sure the lollipops don't burn by keeping an eye on them.
Remove from the grill and serve with 3-2-1 Baby Back Ribs right away. Enjoy.

3.161 Three Ways BBQ Chicken Wings
Total Time: 45 mins, Serving: 4
Ingredients
Chicken Wings
Chicken Wings, 8 Pound
Cornstarch, 2 tbsp
Pit Boss Chicken Rub, 6 Ounce
Salt
Franks Red-Hot Sauce
Frank's Red-Hot Sauce, 1/2 Cup
Spicy Brown Mustard, 1/4 Cup
Unsalted Butter, 6 tbsp
Sriracha Wing Sauce
Sriracha, 1/2 Cup
Soy Sauce, 1/4 Cup
Sesame Oil, 2 tbsp
Honey, 1/2 Cup
Instructions
Preheat oven to 375°F with lid covered for 15 minutes when ready to cook.
Dry the "chicken wings" with a paper towel while the grill is heating up. In a large mixing bowl, combine the wings, cornstarch, Pit Boss Chicken Rub, and salt to taste. Coat both sides of the "chicken wings" with the mixture.
Cook the wings for 35 minutes on the grill, rotating halfway through. After 35 minutes, check the interior temperature of the wings. Internal temp should be at least 165 ° F. Internal temperature of 175-180°F, on the other hand, will provide a superior texture.
Meanwhile, prepare the Franks Red-Hot Sauce by combining Franks Red, mustard, and butter in a small skillet over medium heat. Cook, stirring periodically until the butter has melted and the sauce has reached room temperature. Set your wings aside and check on them.
To make the Sriracha Wing Sauce, mix soy sauce, sriracha, honey and sesame seed oil in a small saucepan over medium heat. Cook, stirring periodically even sauce is barely warmed through, whisking to incorporate. Remove from the equation.
Take the wings off the grill. Toss 1/3 of the chicken in a large mixing dish with the Franks Red sauce. Toss the remaining 1/3 of the salad with the Sriracha sauce. If preferred, season the remaining third of the
wings with more Pit Boss Chicken Rub. Serve and have fun.

3.162 Cajun Chicken Wings Smoked
Total Time: 1 hour 5 mins, Serving: 6
Ingredients
Baking Powder, 1 tbsp
Dried Thyme, 1/2 tsp
Paprika, 1 tsp
Cumin, 1/4 tsp
Kosher Salt, 1/4 tsp
Cayenne Pepper, 1/8 tsp
Dried Oregano, 1/4 tsp
Chicken Wings, 3 Pound
Butter, 1/4 Cup
Garlic Powder, 1/2 tsp
Black Pepper, 1/4 tsp
Louisiana-Style Sauce, 1/4 Cup
Onion Powder, 1/2 tsp
Worcestershire Sauce, 1 tbsp
Instructions
Rub: Combine onion powder, paprika, garlic powder, thyme, oregano, cumin, salt, pepper, and cayenne in a small bowl.
Clean the chicken wings by rinsing them and patting them dry with paper towels. Toss the wings in a large mixing basin with the rub to evenly coat them.
Place a wire rack inside a baking pan coated with aluminium foil. Arrange the wings in a single layer, leaving a little gap between them. Refrigerate the baking sheet with the wings for 8 hours to overnight.
When ready to prepare, preheat the oven to 180°F with the lid covered for 15 minutes.
Cook the wings for 30 minutes in the smoker.
Raise the temperature of the grill to 350°F after 30 minutes and roast for 40 - 50 minutes.
In a small saucepan, mix butter, hot sauce, and Worcestershire sauce while the wings are on the grill. Bring to a low simmer over medium heat & stir until everything is well mixed.
Turn the heat down to low & keep the wings warm until they're done.
Place the wings in a large mixing basin. Toss in the sauce to coat the wings completely.
Serve immediately with carrot and celery sticks, blue cheese, ranch, or other favorite dipping sauces on a plate. Enjoy.

3.163 Beer Can Chicken Roasted
Total Time: 1 hour 5 mins, Serving: 6
Ingredients
Chicken, 1 Whole (3-5 Lb)
Pit Boss Chicken Rub
Beer, 1 Can
Instructions
Season the chicken with "Pit Boss Chicken Rub" all over, including the cavity.
Tuck the wing tips behind your back.
Preheat Pit Boss to 350°F for 15 minutes with lid covered when ready to cook.
Pour the beer into the can and place the chicken on top. Make sure the whole beer can is in the cavity of the bird, except for
the bottom 1-1/2 inch. Tip: You may also lay the beer can straight on the grill grates and then top it with the chicken.
Place the entire chicken on the barbecue grate, along with the beer can. Cook for 60 - 75 minutes, till the thickest portion of the breast, registers 165°F on an instant-read thermometer.
Transfer to a sheet tray & set aside to rest for 5 - 10 minutes.
Place the bird on its back & remove the beer can before cutting. Carve and savour.

3.164 Roasted Buffalo Wings

Total Time: 40 mins, Serving: 4
Ingredients
Chicken Wings, 4 Pound
Corn-starch, 1 tbsp
Pit Boss Chicken Rub
Kosher Salt
Frank's Red-hot Sauce, 1/2 Cup
Spicy Mustard, 1/4 Cup
Unsalted Butter, 6 tbsp
Instructions
Preheat the Pit Boss to 375ºF for 15 minutes with the lid closed when ready to cook.
Dry the "chicken wings" with a paper towel while the grill is heating up. In a large mixing bowl, combine
the wings, corn-starch, Pit Boss Chicken Rub, and salt to taste. Coat both of the sides of the chicken wings with the mixture. Place the wing on the grill when it's hot & cook for 35 mins total, rotating halfway during the cooking time.
After 35 minutes, check the interior temperature of the wings. Internal temp should be at least 165 º F. Internal temperature of 175-180ºF, on the other hand, will provide a superior texture.
To make the Buffalo Sauce, combine the Franks Red-Hot, mustard, and butter in a saucepot. Combine all ingredients in a mixing bowl and cook on the burner until well heated. Whereas the wings are cooking,
keep the sauce warm.
Remove the wings from the grill and set them in a medium mixing basin. Turn the wings with tongs to cover them with the buffalo sauce.
Return to the grill for a further 10-15 minutes to let the sauce to solidify. Wings should be served with a ranch / blue cheese dressing. Enjoy.

3.165 Mandarin Chicken Breast

Total Time: 30 mins, Serving: 4
Ingredients
Kosher Salt, 1/2 Cup
Brown Sugar, 1/4 Cup
Soy Sauce, 1/2 Cup
Chicken Breasts (Boneless & Skinless), 8 (6 Oz)
Sweet Chili Sauce
Steamed Rice
Thinly Sliced Scallions
Instructions
In a large mixing basin, combine 2 quarts of water, salt, brown sugar, & soy sauce. Stir until the sugar and salt are completely dissolved.
Soak chicken breasts in brine for 2 hours, then cover and chill. Remove the chicken from the pan, rinse it, and wipe it dry with paper towels. Remove the brine and discard it.
When ready to prepare, preheat the Pit Boss to 350ºF with the cover closed for fifteen min.
Put the chicken breasts on the grate & cook for 25 to 30 mins, or till an instant-read thermometer reads 170ºF inside. Midway through the cooking time, turn the chicken breasts.
During the last few minutes of cooking, brush the chicken breasts with the sweet chili sauce.
Serve immediately with steamed rice on a tray or plate. To serve, top the chicken breasts with (thinly) sliced scallions. Enjoy.

3.166 Chicken Smoked with Apricot BBQ Glaze

Total Time: 1 hour 15 mins, Serving: 4
Ingredients
Chickens (Halved), 2 Whole
Pit Boss Chicken Rub, 4 tbsp
Pit Boss Apricot BBQ Sauce, 1 Cup
Instructions
Preheat the Pit Boss to 375ºF for 15 minutes with the lid closed when ready to cook.
Season chicken with Chicken Rub & lay flesh side up on the grill. Cook for 1 hour, or until the internal temperature of the breast reaches 160ºF, and the leg reaches 175ºF.
Brush every chicken half with a little of the Apricot BBQ glaze & cook for another 10 minutes on the grill.
Remove the chicken from the grill & set it aside for 5-10 minutes to rest. Remove the leg from each half and cut each breast in half, leaving four legs and eight breast pieces. Serve with veggies or sides of your choice. Enjoy.

3.167 Grilled Duck Breasts

Total Time: 1 hour 15 mins, Serving: 4
Ingredients
Boneless Duck Breasts, 4 Whole (6 Oz)
Pit Boss Big Game Rub, 1/4 Cup
Instructions
Score the skin of the duck with a sharp knife in a 1/4" diamond pattern.
Season the duck on both sides with Pit Boss Big Game Rub.
Preheat the Pit Boss to 275ºF (135ºC) for 15 minutes with the lid closed when ready to cook.
Put the duck breasts on the grill, meat side down. Cook for ten min with the lid closed.
Increase the heat to High & cook for another ten min with the skin side on the grate, or until the internal temperature reaches about 130ºF (50-55 C).
Remove off the grill and set aside for 5 minutes. Serve in thick slices, sliced against the grain. Enjoy.

3.168 Bacon Stuffed Weaved Turkey Breast

Total Time: 1 hour 20 mins, Serving: 8
Ingredients
Celery (Diced), 1/2 Cup
Stuffing Mix, 14 Ounce
Chopped sage, 2 tbsp
Pit Boss Chicken Rub, 4 tbsp
Dried Sweetened Cranberries, 1/2 Cup
Apple Cider, 2 Cup
Thick-Cut Bacon, 20 Strips
Instructions
To make the stuffing, combine all of the ingredients in a large mixing basin and toss to combine.
On a cutting board, make a bacon weave & spread it down in a 5x5 pattern.

Butterfly each of the turkey breasts with a long, thin knife. Close each breast after filling it with a sufficient quantity of stuffing. Carefully wrap the turkey breast in Totalared bacon weave and fasten with toothpicks. Rep with the other breast.
Preheat the Pit Boss grill to 375 degrees Fahrenheit when you're ready to cook. Preheat for 10 - 15 minutes with the lid closed.
Place the breasts on a rimmed baking sheet, seam side down. Place immediately on the grill.
Transfer the bacon-wrapped turkey breasts to the Pit Boss and cook for 45 minutes to an hour, or till an instant read thermometer inserted into stuffing registers 165 degrees F.
Cover the bacon with foil if it becomes too black. Cut into slices and eat.

3.169 Baked BBQ Chicken Potato

Total Time: 1 hour 10 mins, Serving: 4
Ingredients
Russet Potatoes, 4
Chicken Breasts, 2
Garlic (Minced), 2 Clove
Olive Oil (Extra-Virgin), 2 tbsp
Worcestershire Sauce, 2 tsp
Poultry Rub & Pit Boss Pork
BBQ Pit Boss Apricot Sauce
Salt n Pepper
Butter
Sour Cream
Any type of cheese
Chives (Chopped)
Instructions
When ready to cook, turn on the Pit Boss & set the temperature to 500 degrees F. Preheat for 10 to 15
minutes with the lid closed.
Scrub the potatoes and use a fork or skewer to poke numerous holes in them. Cook for 1 hour - 1 hour 15 minutes on the grill, or until they are tender.
In the meantime, totalize the chicken by rubbing it with minced garlic, drizzled with olive oil & Worcestershire sauce, and seasoned with Pit Boss Pork & Poultry Rub.
Place the chicken on the grill after the potatoes have been cooking for around 30 minutes.
Cook the chicken for 20 - 30 minutes, or till an instant-read thermometer reads 165 degrees on the inside.
When the chicken is done, remove it from the pan and lay it aside to allow the fluids to redistribute before slicing. Keep an eye on the potatoes & remove them when they're done.
Remove the chicken breasts from the pan. Add a liberal quantity of Pit Boss Apricot BBQ Sauce to the mixture.
To assemble, slice open cooked potatoes and stuff with your chosen toppings, seasoning generously with salt and pepper.
To serve, top each potato with a mound of barbeque chicken and a sprinkling of chives. Enjoy.

3.170 Roast Citrus Chicken

Total Time: 1 hour 20 mins, Serving: 4
Ingredients
Whole Chicken, Pound
Cinnamon Stick, 2
Fresh Ginger, 1 Pieces
Butter, 4 tbsp
Orange (Sliced), 1
Red Onion (Sliced), 1
Onion (Sliced), 1
Garlic, 5 Clove
Thyme Sprigs, 3 Sprig
Salt
Pepper
Zest, 1 Orange
Instructions
Preheat the Pit Boss to 375°F for 15 minutes with the lid closed when ready to cook.
Rinse the chicken in cold water and place it on a
baking sheet.
Combine half of the butter with the coarsely crushed dry spices and ginger. Spread the butter spice mixture beneath the chicken's skin.
Stuff 1 orange, together with the white onion, red onion, garlic cloves, & thyme, inside the chicken.
Season the exterior of the chicken with salt and pepper and rub with the remaining butter. Place the chicken straight on the grill grate after zesting the second orange.
Roast for 1 to 1-1/2 hours at 375°F, or until internal temperature reaches 160°F.
Allow 15 minutes for resting before cutting. Enjoy.

3.171 Smoked Wings

Total Time: 1 hour, Serving: 6
Ingredients
Chicken Wings, 24
Italian Dressing, 12 Ounce
Pit Boss Chicken Rub, 3 Ounce
Pit Boss 'Que BBQ Sauce, 5 Ounce
Chili Sauce, 3 Ounce
Instructions
Clean all of the wings and place them in a resealable bag. Toss the wings in the resealable bag with the Italian dressing. Place in the refrigerator for 6 - 12 hours to marinate.
When ready to cook, preheat the Pit Boss to 225°F with the cover closed for fifteen min. If Super Smoke is available, use it for the best flavor.
Remove the wings from the marinade and brush off any excess. Before putting the wings on the Pit Boss, season all sides with the Pit Boss Chicken Rub and set aside for 15 minutes.
Combine the BBQ & chili sauces in a small bowl. Remove from the equation.
Cook the wings until they reach an internal temp of 160°F. Remove the wings from the pan and toss them in the chili barbecue sauce.
Preheat the grill to 375 degrees Fahrenheit. Place the wings on the Pit Boss after they've reached room temperature & sear both sides until the internal temperature reaches 165°F.
Take the wings from the grill and set them aside to rest for five min. Serve with you favorite wing sauce or dressing on the side. Enjoy.

3.172 Dry Rub Wings Smoked

Total Time: 1 hour 15 mins, Serving: 4
Ingredients
Salt, 1/4 Cup
Brown Sugar, 1/4 Cup
Pit Boss Rub, 1/4 tsp
Garlic, 4 Clove
Dried Thyme, 1 tsp
Red Pepper Flakes, 1 tbsp
Smoked Paprika, 1/4 tsp
Chicken Wings, 2 Pound
Brown Sugar, 1/4 Cup
Granulated Onion, 1/2 tsp
Chipotle Chile Pepper, 1/4 tsp
Garlic Powder, 1/4 tsp
Instructions
To make the brine, whisk together the brine ingredients in a large mixing basin or container with 4 cups water till the brown sugar & salt have dissolved.

Place the wings in the brine. Allow the wings to brine for 24 hours, covered and refrigerated.

Take the wings out of the brine, clean them, and pat them dry. When ready to prepare, preheat the Pit Boss to 180°F with the lid closed for fifteen min. If Super Smoke is available, use it for the best flavor.

To make the rub, combine all of the dry rub ingredients in a small dish. Rub all sides of the wings with the rub.

Smoke the wings for 60 - 90 minutes on the grill grate. Remove the steaks from the grill.

Preheat the grill to 450°F with the lid covered for 15 minutes. Return the wings to the grill & cook for 3 - 5 minutes on each side, or until golden brown and crisp.

Take the wings off the grill & serve right away. Enjoy.

3.173 Ultimate Smoked Turkey

Total Time: 4 hour 20 mins, Serving: 8
Ingredients
Turkey, 1 (18-20 Lb)
Orange Brine And Turkey Rub Kit, 1 Pit Boss
Pit Boss Pork & Poultry Rub, 1/2 Cup
Butter (Softened), 1/2 Pound
Instructions

The day before, brine the turkey as per the instructions on the Pit Boss Turkey Brine Kit box. Remove the meat from the brine, rinse it, and pat it dry.

Rub 2 teaspoons Pit Boss Pork & Poultry Rub into the cavity, saving the remainder for the outside.

Stuff the softened butter into a pocket created by removing the skin from the breast of the turkey. Apply a quarter-inch layer of butter to the whole breast.

Rub the leftover rub on the bird's exterior.

Chill for at least 1 hour after transferring to the fridge.

Take the bird out of the fridge & tuck the wing tips back around the bird.

When ready to prepare, preheat the Pit Boss to 225°F for 15 minutes with the lid closed. If Super Smoke is available, use it for the best flavor.

Place the turkey in a roasting pan on the grill grate immediately. Cook until the meat reaches a temperature of 100-110°F on the inside.

Raise the grill temperature to 350°F and cook until an instant read thermometer inserted in the thickest part of the breast registers 160°F (check every 30 minutes after the grill temperature is raised), about 3 to 4 hours total cook time. Once removed

from the grill, the turkey will continue to cook until the breast reaches a final temperature of 165°F.

Take the chicken from the grill & set it aside to rest for at least 30 mins before cutting it. Enjoy.

3.174 Baked Crispy Chicken Thighs with Buffalo Sauce

Total Time: 35 mins, Serving: 2
Ingredients
Buttermilk, 1 Cup
Beaten, 1 Egg.
Boneless, Skinless Chicken Thighs 2 Pound
Panko Breadcrumbs, 2 Cup
Garlic Powder, 1 tsp
Salt, 1 tsp
Freshly Ground Black Pepper, 1 tsp
Dark Brown Sugar, 1 Cup
Frank's Red-Hot Buffalo Wing Sauce, 1/2 Cup
Wasser, 5 tbsp
Instructions

Combine the buttermilk, egg, and chicken thighs in a gallon resealable bag. Refrigerate for 2 hrs after sealing the top.

When ready to cook, preheat the Pit Boss to 375°F for 15 minutes with the lid closed.

Gently mix the panko "breadcrumbs", garlic, salt, and pepper on a large dish. Remove the thighs one at a time from the buttermilk

mixture and put them in the seasoned breadcrumbs using tongs. Make sure the breadcrumbs are evenly distributed throughout the chicken. Place on a foil or parchment paper-lined sheet tray.

Bake the "breaded chicken" for 15 - 18 mins, till it reaches 175°F on the inside.

Make the brown sugar, buffalo sauce while the chicken is baking. Combine the brown sugar, buffalo sauce, and water in a medium saucepan over medium-high heat. Bring to a rolling boil for approximately 5 minutes, stirring constantly, then remove from the heat. Fill a pitcher or a measuring glass with a pourable spout with the mixture.

Brush the "brown sugar" buffalo sauce on the chicken thighs. Enjoy!

Toss with the "brown sugar" buffalo sauce and serve. Enjoy.

3.175 Grilled Bacon Chicken Lettuce Wraps

Total Time: 35 mins, Serving: 2
Ingredients
Olive Oil, 2 tbsp
Onion, 2 Medium
Bacon, 8 Strips
Shallot, 1 Thinly Sliced
Egg Yolk, 1
Dijon Mustard, 3/4 tsp
Lemon Juice, 1 tsp
Kosher Salt
Black Pepper
Chicken Breasts, 4
Instructions

Preheat the oven to High for 15 minutes with the lid covered when you're ready to cook.

In a frying pan, heat 2 tbsp olive oil over medium heat. Toss in the onions to coat them in oil. Cook for 40 minutes, stirring every 10 minutes and scraping

the bottom of

the pan. Remove the pan from the heat and set it aside.

Cook the bacon in the pan over medium heat until crisp. Remove the bacon from the pan and set aside the fact. Saute the shallots until they are transparent. Allow time for cooling.

In a blender, combine the egg yolk, lemon juice, mustard, salt, pepper, & bacon fat with the shallots to produce Bacon Fat Mayo. Blend for 2 minutes or until the mixture is emulsified.

Season both sides of the chicken breasts with salt & pepper. Cook for 20 minutes, turning once, directly on the grill grate. Grill chicken until a thermometer placed into the thickest portion of the flesh registers 165°F.

Remove the chicken from the grill and set it aside for 5 minutes to rest. Cut the slices into strips. Lettuce, bacon, avocado, tomato, caramelized onion, & bacon fat mayo are served on the side. Enjoy.

3.176 Smoked Korean Wings

Total Time: 4 hours, Servings: 4
Ingredients
Water, 1 Gallon
Sea Salt, 1 Cup
Sugar, 1/2 Cup
Lemon, 1 Halved
Halved Garlic, 1 Head
Thyme, 4 Sprig

Peppercorns, 10
Chicken Wings, 3 Pound
Olive Oil, 3 tbsp
Gochujang Hot Pepper Paste, 1/2 Cup
Soy Sauce, 1/4 Cup
Honey, 1/3 Cup
Rice Wine Vinegar, 2 tbsp
Fresh Squeezed Lime Juice, 2 tbsp
Toasted Sesame Oil, 2 tbsp
Butter (Melted), 1/4 Cup
Garlic (Minced), 4 Clove
Ginger (Peeled & Grated), 1 tbsp
Instruction
To make the brine, combine one gallon of water, salt, & sugar in a stockpot and stir thoroughly. Bring to a boil, then remove
from the heat and add the lemon, garlic, thyme, & peppercorns, stirring constantly. Allow it cool to room temp before submerging the wings. Refrigerate for 2 - 4 hours, covered.
When ready to cook, preheat the oven to 375°F and cook for 15 minutes with the lid covered.
Take the wings out of the brine and pat them dry using a paper towel. Remove the brine and discard it.
Toss the wings in the olive oil to fully cover them.
Place the wings straight on the grill grate and cook for 45 to 60 minutes, or until they reach a core temperature of 165°F.
To make the sauce, whisk together all of the sauce ingredients in a mixing bowl until smooth. Remove from fire and put aside after the sauce has just risen to a simmer over medium heat.
Toss 2/3 of the sauce with the cooked wings.
Garnish with fresh cilantro, lime wedges, & additional dipping sauce. Enjoy.

3.177 Carne Asada Tacos
Total Time: 30 mins, Servings: 4
Ingredients
Flank Steak, 2 Pound
Cilantro (Chopped), 1/2 Cup
White Vinegar, 2 tbsp
Garlic (Minced), 4 Clove
Lime Juice, 1/4 Cup
Vegetable Oil, 1/4 Cup
Kosher Salt, 1 tbsp
Black Pepper, 1 tbsp
Sugar, 1 tsp
Crema Mexicana or Sour Cream, 1/2 Cup
Lime Zest, 1/2 tsp
Fresh Squeezed Lime Juice, 2 tsp
Instructions
Plan ahead of time! This dish needs an overnight preparation time. Combine vinegar, garlic, cilantro, lime juice, Salt, pepper, oil, and sugar in a medium mixing bowl; whisk when salt & sugar are dissolved. Turn the flank steak to cover it in the sauce thoroughly. Cover and marinate for 4-24 hours in the refrigerator, turning the meat regularly.
When you're ready to cook, preheat the oven too high for 10-15 minutes. Remove the meat from the marinade and discard it. Straight on the grill grate, place the meat. Grill for 15 - 20 minutes, covered.
Transfer steak to a chopping board and cover loosely with foil; set aside for 10 minutes (keep grill on high to reheat tortillas later). Cut the steak into thin strips against the grain, then cut the strips into 2-inch pieces.
Toss the steak pieces in a dish with any liquids that have accumulated on the cutting board.
Now combine grated lime zest, sour cream and lime juice to make Crema.

To assemble, preheat the grill & warm the tortillas. Place a layer of salsa, Carne Asada, & crema on top.
Garnish with chopped cilantro. Enjoy.

3.178 Machaca Mexican Shredded Beef
Total Time: 4 hours 20 mins, Servings: 4
Ingredients
Beef Chuck Roast, Boneless (Cut into 1-1/2 Inch Cubes), 3 Pound
Worcestershire Sauce, 1/4 Cup
Pit Boss Prime Rib Rub
Onion (Diced), 1 Large
Red Bell Pepper (Seeded & Diced), 1 Whole
Poblano Pepper (Steamed, Seeded & Diced), 1 Whole
Jalapeño Pepper (Stemmed, Seeded & Diced), 1 Whole
Garlic (Minced), 3 Clove
Tomatoes (Diced) & Green Chilies, 1 Can
Beef Broth, 1 1/2 Cup
Lime Juice (Fresh Squeezed), 1 Whole
Chili Powder, 1 tbsp
Ground Cumin, 2 tsp
Mexican Oregano, 1 1/2 tsp
Salt n Pepper
Instructions
Coat the chuck roast in Worcestershire sauce on all sides in a roasting pan (or a strong disposable foil pan). Pit Boss Prime Rib Rub should be used liberally.
Prepare oven to 180°F & preheat for 15 mins when ready to cook. Place the meat immediately on the grill grate after removing it from the roasting pan. 1 hour of smoking Remove the roasting pan from the oven and set it away; you'll need it later.
Meanwhile, sauté the onions, poblano pepper, bell pepper, jalapeño, and garlic in the oil in a large skillet or frying pan over medium heat till softened, approximately 5 minutes.
Bring to a boil over high heat with the tomatoes, beef broth, lime juice, chilli powder, cumin, oregano, & salt n pepper.
Lower the heat to low and cook the tomato mixture for 20 mins. Season to taste with additional chilli powder, cumin, or salt n pepper if necessary. Place the smoked chuck roast in the roasting pan that was set aside.
Raise the Pit Boss's temperature to 300°F. Cut the roast into 4 or 5 about equal-sized pieces. Cover the meat securely with a lid or heavy-duty foil after carefully pouring the hot tomato sauce over it. Preheat the grill and place the roasting pan on the grate. Roast for 2 1/2 to 3 hours, rotating the meat pieces once or twice in the juices. (To avoid steam burns, raise the cover or foil with tongs.) If
the pan appears to be drying out, add extra beef broth. When the flesh is very soft and easily torn apart, it is ready.
Allow the meat to cool somewhat before shredding with two forks. Return to the tomato mixture, cool, cover, & refrigerate if not serving right away. (Machaca can be prepared up to three days ahead of time)

3.179 Braised Italian Meatballs
Total Time: 2 hours 30 mins, Servings: 4
Ingredients
Ground Beef, 1 Pound
Ground Pork, 1 Pound
Prosciutto (Finely Diced), 4 Ounce
Fresh White Breadcrumbs, 1 Cup
Kosher Salt, 2 tsp
Fennel Seed, 2 tsp

Dried Oregano, 1 tsp
Whole Milk Ricotta, 1 Cup
Milk, 1/2 Cup
Egg (Whisked), 3 Whole
Crushed Tomatoes, 1 Whole (28 Oz)
Olive Oil (Extra-Virgin)
Basil Leaves, 1/2 Cup

Instructions
Prepare the oven to 375°F & preheat for fifteen min when ready to cook. Combine ground beef, pork, prosciutto, breadcrumbs, 2 teaspoons salt, fennel seed, and oregano in a large mixing basin.
Incorporate the ricotta, milk, & eggs in a separate mixing dish and whisk to combine.
Mix the meats, breadcrumbs, Salt, & herbs together using freshly cleaned hands until the mixture is completely mixed and the herbs are equally integrated.
Gently put the liquid mixture over the meat, continuing to blend with your hands. Even when well combined, the mixture will be sticky. Allow for a 10-minute rest period. Form 1 2-inch patty and fry in a small sauté pan till cooked through, about 2 mins per side, to verify the mixture's flavour before cooking the full batch. Taste the meat mixture & adjust the seasoning as required.
Use parchment paper or Pit Boss butcher paper to line a large baking sheet. Alternatively, gently oil a baking sheet and make meatballs the size of golf balls using clean hands or an ice cream scoop. Place them on the baking sheet with enough space between them, so they don't contact. About 48 meatballs should be made from this mixture.
Put the baking sheet straight on the grill & cook for 20 minutes, rotating once, until the meatballs are cooked through when sliced in half. Remove off the grill, repeat with the second batch if required.
Lower the temperature of the grill to 300°F.
Place all of the meatballs in a large roasting pan after they've cooled enough to handle. Over the top, pour the smashed tomatoes. Drizzle 3 tbsp olive oil over the top and season with an extra teaspoon of Salt.
Wrap aluminium foil around the pan securely. Place on the grill & cook, covered, for 60-90 min, or until the meatballs are fork tender and the tomatoes have been absorbed some of the meatballs' flavour.
10. Remove the meatballs from the grill & top with basil leaves. The meatballs may also be roasted, cooled, and refrigerated up to a day ahead of time, then brought to room temperature & simmered in tomato sauce before serving. Enjoy! * Cooking times will vary based on the temperature of the set and the ambient temperature.

3.180 Sweet Braised & Sour Brisket
Total Time: 7 hours 10 mins, Servings: 8
Ingredients
Brisket Snake River Farms, 7 Pound
Prime Pit Boss Rib Rub
Kosher Salt
Butter, 2 tbsp
Yellow Onion (Thinly Sliced)
Garlic (Thinly Sliced), 2 Clove
Oregano (Dried), 1 tsp
Thyme (Dried), 1 tsp
Paprika, 1 tsp
Cayenne Pepper
Salt n Pepper
Beef Stock, 1 1/2 Cup
Ketchup, 1 Cup
Brown Sugar, 1/4 Cup

Instructions
Preheat the oven too high for 15 minutes when you're ready to cook. Using Pit Boss Prime Rib Rub & kosher Salt, generously season the brisket.
Cook the brisket fat side down on the barbecue grate for 30-45 minutes, or until the fat is caramelized & gently browned.
Melt the butter in a "sauté pan" over medium heat while the brisket is cooking. Cook for 5-6 minutes, stirring periodically until the onion is gently caramelized. Cook for another minute after adding the garlic.
Cook for 30 seconds until the thyme, oregano, paprika, cayenne, salt, & pepper are aromatic.
Scrape up any browned pieces with a wooden spoon & deglaze the pan with beef stock. Bring the ketchup & brown sugar to a low boil.
Place the brisket in a baking dish after removing it from the grill. Cover the brisket with foil and pour the onion mixture over it.
Lower the heat to 225°F on the grill and set the baking dish immediately on the grate. Braise the brisket for 5 to 6 hours, or until fork-tender.
Remove the foil from the grill and let it vent. Allow cooling at ambient temperature before refrigerating overnight (this step is
unimportant but will result in a juicier and more flavorful brisket).
Remove the meat from the fridge the next day and preheat the grill to 350°F. Return the brisket to the grill to reheat. Remove the brisket from the grill when it is heated & the sauce has caramelized for about 45 mins.
Now, remove the brisket from the sauce, slice it, and serve with the leftover sauce. (Cook times will vary based on the temperature of the oven and the ambient temperature.)

3.181 Beef Short Ribs Braised Along with Creamy Grits
Total Time: 3 hours 30 mins, Servings: 2
Ingredients
Black Pepper n Salt
Beef Short Ribs, 4
Olive Oil, 2 tbsp
Onion (Diced), 2/3 Medium
Carrot (Diced), 2/3 Medium
Stalk Celery (Diced), 2/3
Garlic, 4 Clove
Thyme, 2 2/3 Sprig
Bay Leaves, 1 1/3 Whole
Balsamic Vinegar, 1 1/3 tbsp
Red Wine, 2 2/3 Cup
Beef Broth, 4 Cup
Flat-Leaf Parsley, 2 2/3 Sprig
Salt n Pepper
Grits, 2/3 Cup
Water, 2/3 Cup
Whole Milk, 1/2 Cup
Heavy Cream, 1/8 Cup
Butter, 2 2/3 tbsp

Instructions
When ready to cook, preheat the Pit Boss to 500°F with the cover closed for fifteen min.
Season short ribs generously with salt n pepper. Sear for 5 mins per side on a Pit Boss, or until beautifully browned.
Remove the Pit Boss from the grill & lower the temperature to 350°F.
Heat the olive oil in huge Dutch oven. Combine carrot, onion, celery, thyme sprigs, garlic and bay leaves in a large mixing bowl.
Cook, occasionally stirring, for 6 - 8 mins, or until the veggies start to the caramelize. Combine balsamic vinegar & wine in

a mixing bowl.

Raise the temperature of the Pit Boss to 500°F and lower the liquid by half. Bring the beef stock to a boil, then remove from the heat. In & around the meat, add short ribs & parsley sprigs. Aluminium foil or a lid should be used to cover the dish securely.

Lower the temperature on the Pit Boss to 350°F, set the Dutch oven on top, and braise for about 3 hours, or till the meat is extremely soft. Allow the ribs to rest in their juices for 10 minutes before removing them from the saucepan.

Strain the soup, pushing down with a spoon to remove all of the juices from the veggies. Remove the solids and throw them away. Reduce the sauce over moderate flame till it has thickened somewhat. Season with Salt and pepper to taste.

Return the short ribs to the sauce & keep heated until serving time.

To make the grits, in a medium saucepan over medium heat, combine the water, milk, cream, butter, and Salt.

Add the grits while whisking & continue to whisk to eliminate any lumps. Bring to a gentle boil, then lower to medium-low heat until the grits are barely bubbling. Cook for 10 - 15 minutes, or until the grits are al dente and the liquid has been absorbed. If necessary, add extra water until the grits are fully cooked. To taste, season with Salt and pepper.

To serve, put the short ribs on a bed of grits & drizzle with the remaining braising liquid. Enjoy.

3.182 Chipotle-Lime Poultry Bowls with Guacamole

Total Time: 60 Minutes, Serving: 2 people
Ingredients
Chicken Marinade
Fresh Squeezed Lime Juice, 1/4 Cup
Chipotle Peppers in Adobo Sauce, 3 Tbsp
Minced Red Onion, 3 Tbsp
Fresh Mint Leaves, 2 Tbsp
Honey, 1 Tbsp
Dried Oregano, 1 Tbsp
Cumin, 1 Tbsp
Garlic, Peeled, 3 Clove
Kosher Salt, 1 Tbsp
Freshly Ground Black Pepper
Avocado, Canola or Grapeseed Oil, 1/2 Cup
main
Boneless, Skinless Chicken Thighs, 6 Whole
Guacamole
Ripe Avocados, 2 Entire
Kosher Salt, 1 Tbsp
Limes, Juiced, 2 Entire
Minced Red Onion, 2 Tbsp
Sliced Cilantro, 2 Tbsp
Bowls
Shredded Romaine Lettuce, 6 Cup
Black Beans, Rinsed, Drained and Warmed, 1 Can (15 Oz)
Grilled or Fresh Corn Kernel, 1 Cup
Cut Cherry Tomatoe, 1 Cup
Crushed Chips of Tortilla or Strips, 1 Cup
Chopped Jack Cheese or Crushed Cotija Cheese, 1/2 Cup
Chopped mint, 2 Tbsp
Instructions
In a food processor or blender, combine the lemon juice, chipotle, onion, mint, spices, honey, & garlic to create the marinade. Flavor with kosher salt & freshly ground pepper. Pulse until the mixture is pretty smooth. Add the oil and puree while the engine is still running to incorporate all of the components. Taste and season with more salt if required.

To marinate the chicken thighs, place them in a glass dish or a big resealable bag. Half of the marinade should be added to the chicken and well coated. Keep Cold for at minimum 2 hrs, or up to 8 hrs, covered. Half of the marinade should be set aside.

To prepare the guacamole, mash the avocados and season with kosher salt in a large mixing basin. Blend the avocados with a fork, pastry blender, or potato masher until nearly smooth or to your preferred guacamole consistency. Combine the lime juice, red onion, and cilantro in a mixing bowl. To mix, stir everything together. If required, season with additional salt. Place a sheet of plastic wrap immediately on top of the guacamole to keep the color fresh. Make sure the whole surface of the guacamole is covered. Set away until needed (or up to 1 hour).

When ready to cook, preheat the Pit Boss to 400°F for 15 minutes with the lid closed.

When the grill is hot, put the chicken thighs directly on the grate, allowing excess marinade to drip into the bowl before placing it on the grill. Cook for 20 to 30 minutes, or until the chicken reaches 165°F on the inside.

Remove the chicken from the grill and let it rest for 10 minutes before chopping it.

Put all of the lettuce in a large mixing basin to construct the bowls. Drizzle a couple of teaspoons of the marinade over the top. Taste and adjust the spice level with a bit more oil if required. Place 1/4 of each of the remaining bowl ingredients in clusters around the lettuce in each of the four bowls. Add the chicken, a dollop of guacamole, and a drizzle of the marinade on top. Enjoy.

3.183 BBQ Half Chicken with Alabama White Sauce

Total Time: 1 Hour 15 Minutes, Serving: 4 people
Ingredients
main
Fresh Young Chicken, 1 (3 To 3-1/2 Lb.)
Pit Boss Chicken Rub
Alabama White Sauce
Mayonnaise, 3/4 cup
Apple Cider Vinegar, 1/3 Cup
Lemon Juice, 1/8 Cup
Apple Juice, 1/4 Cup
Garlic Powder, 1 Tbsp
Totalized Horseradish, 1 Tbsp
Coarse Black Pepper, 1 Tbsp
Mustard Powder, 1 tbsp
Kosher Salt, 1/4 tbsp
Ground Cayenne Pepper, 1/2 tbsp
Instructions
Place the entire chicken on a chopping board, breast-side down, with the neck facing away from you. From the neck to the tail, cut down one side of the backbone, keeping as near the bone as possible. Rep on the other side of the backbone, then take it out.

Slice through the white cartilage at the tip of the chicken's breastbone to burst it open. Cut along each side of the breastbone, then pull it out with your fingers. Split the chicken in half by flipping it over and cutting along the middle, skin-side up. Reattach the wings to each side of the bird. Pit Boss Chicken Seasoning on both sides of each half Rub

When ready to cook, preheat the Pit Boss to 375°F with the lid closed for 15 minutes.

Whereas the grill is heating up, combine the remaining white sauce ingredients.

Add the chicken skin-side up on the grill grate and cook for 60 to 90 minutes, or until the internal temperature of the breast reaches 160°F.

Remove the lid halves to a sheet pan once the breasts have reached 160°F, pour the white sauce over the bottom and top of the chicken halves, and return to the grill for 10 mins. Cut Off the chicken from the pan and set it aside to rest for 10 minutes. Cut and savour.

3.184 Smoky Fried Chicken
Total Time: 3 Hours 15 Minutes, Serving: 6 people
Ingredients
main
Whole Fryer Chickens,2 (3 To 3-1/2 Lb.)
Vegetable Oil
Kosher Salt and Black Pepper
Buttermilk, 1 Quart
Frank's Red-hot or Crystal Hot Sauce, 2 Tbsp
Brown Sugar, 1 Tbsp
All-Purpose Flour, 2 1/2 Cup
Garlic Powder, 2 Tbsp
Onion Powder, 2 Tbsp
Pit Boss Pork Rub, 1 Tbsp
Fresh Black Pepper
Grape Or Peanut Seed Oil, For Frying
Instructions
Preheat the Pit Boss to 200°F and cook for 15 minutes with the lid covered when ready to cook. If Super Smoke is available, use it for the best taste.
Rinse the hens well under cold running water, both inside and out. Allow airing to dry. Put on a cooking sheet with a rim.
Season the outsides of the birds with salt and pepper after rubbing them with vegetable oil. Arrange the birds directly on the grill grate and smoke for 2-half hours, or till an immediate-read meat thermometer
reaches 150°F in a thickest part of a thigh.
Remove the smoked birds from the oven and place them on a clean baking sheet to cool.
Cut the birds into 20 pieces (four drumsticks, four thighs, four wings, and eight breast quarters) (remove the four breast halves, then cut each in half).
Separate the chicken into two sealed bags.
Meanwhile, whisk together the buttermilk, spicy sauce, and brown sugar in a large mixing basin until the sugar crystals dissolve.
Flow half of the combination into each bag of chicken. Refrigerate for 1 hour after sealing.
Combine the flour, garlic powder, poultry seasoning, onion powder, and 2 tbsp each of kosher salt and black pepper in a separate bowl. Remove from the equation.
In a Dutch oven, deep cast-iron skillet, or heavy saucepan, heat 2 inches of peanut or grapeseed oil to 375°F over medium-high heat (a real fried chicken expert would use melted lard).
Cut Off the chicken pieces from the pan and drain them. Dredge each one in the flour mixture one at a time.
Fry the chicken in batches (do not crowd the pan) until golden brown, approximately 6 minutes for the breast pieces and 8 minutes for the thighs, wings, and drumsticks, flipping with tongs as required.
Before serving, drain on paper towels. Enjoy.

3.185 Ancho-Chile Chicken Legs (Smoked BBQ)
Total Time: 2 Hours 20 Minutes, Serving: 4 people
Ingredients
main
Ancho Chile Powder, 1 Tbsp
Brown Sugar, 1 Tbsp
Ground Espresso, 1/2 Tbsp
Ground Cumin, 1/2 Tbsp
Lime Zest, 1 Tbsp
Kosher Salt,1 Tbsp
Cracked Black Pepper, 1/2 Tbsp
Olive Oil, 2 Tbsp
Chicken Legs, 8
Pit Boss BBQ Sauce or Your Favorite BBQ Sauce, 1/2 Cup
Fresh Lime, For Serving, 1
Flat-Leaf Parsley, For Serving
Instructions
Combine the chile powder, espresso, brown sugar, lemon zest, cumin, & salt in a small mixing bowl. Olive oil should be massaged all over the chicken legs. Pour a dry rub on the chicken and massage it in well. Refrigerate overnight after covering.
When ready to cook, preheat the Pit Boss to 180°F with the lid closed for 15 minutes. If Super Smoke is available, use it for the best taste.
Smoke the chicken legs for 1 hour on the barbecue grate.
Raise the temperature of the Pit Boss to 350°F. Cook for a further hour, or until the juices flow clear and the chicken reaches 165°F on the inside.
When there are 10 minutes left in the cooking time, baste the chicken with the barbecue sauce all over. Garnish with flat-leaf parsley and a squeeze of fresh lime. Enjoy.

3.186 BBQ Chicken Thighs
Total Time: 1 hour 10 Minutes, Serving: 4 people
Ingredients
main
Skin-On Chicken Thighs, 6 Bone-In
Salt And Ground Black Pepper
Pit Boss Big Game Rub
Instructions
Preheat the Pit Boss to 350°F for 15 mins with the lid closed when ready to cook.
Trim extra fat and skin off chicken thighs while the grill is heating up. Season with a little seasoning of salt and pepper before sprinkling with Pit Boss Big Game Rub.
Grill the chicken thighs for 35 minutes on the grill grate. Check the internal temp; chicken is ready at 165°F, although there is sufficient fat to keep them moist at 180°F, & the texture is better.
Take the steaks from the grill and set them aside to rest for 5 minutes before serving. Enjoy.

3.187 Competition BBQ Chicken Thighs
Total Time: 2 Hours 30 Minutes, Serving: 8 people
Ingredients
main
Bone-In Thighs, 20 (1/2 Lb. Each)
Low Point Sodium Broth of Chicken, 2 1/2 Cup
Big Game Rub of Pit Boss, 1/3 Cup
Butter, Molten, 3 Stick
Apricot BBQ Sauce of Pit Boss, 3 Cup
Instructions
Remove the skin of the thighs and set it aside. Remove the fat off either side of the chicken thighs with kitchen shears.
Remove 1/4 inch of bone knuckle from the bottom and top of the chicken thighs. Trim the thighs to make them all the same size. Reserved skin should be cut to suit the freshly trimmed thighs.
Reattach the skin to the thighs. When all of the thighs are done, inject 1 tbsp of low point sodium chicken broth in every side of the thigh & set aside for 60 mins to rest.
Season the tops of the thighs with Big Game Rub while they're resting.
Refrigerate or store in a cold cooler until ready to use.
In a big disposable pan, place the thighs and add the melted butter as a braising liquid.

Once ready to cook, preheat the Pit Boss to 250°F for 15 minutes with the lid closed.
Place the whole disposable chicken pan on the grate and bake for an hour.
Cook for another hour, or until the internal temperature reaches 165°F, after wrapping the top of the disposable pan with Aluminum foil.
When the chicken thighs have reached an internal temperature of 165°F, remove them with tongs and dip them in hot Pit Boss Apricot BBQ sauce.
Return to a clean disposable pan and continue to cook for another 20 minutes.
When ready to serve, remove off the grill and set aside for 10 minutes. Enjoy.

3.188 Bourbon BBQ Chicken Kabobs
Total Time: 35 Minutes, Serving: 4 people
Ingredients
main
Chicken Breasts, Cut into 1 Inch Cubes, 3 Pound
Pit Boss Texas Spicy BBQ Sauce, 1/2 Cup
Pit Boss Apricot BBQ Sauce, 1/2 Cup
Bourbon, 1/4 cup
Honey, 2 Tbsp
Garlic, 1 Tbsp
Onion Powder, 1 Tbsp
Instructions
In a 2-quart resealable bag, mix all ingredients and marinate in the refrigerator overnight.
Thread skewers with marinated chicken pieces.
When ready to cook, preheat the Pit Boss to 450°F for 15 minutes with the lid closed.
For a beautiful char, place the skewers at the front of the grill. After that, transfer them to the middle of the grill & cook for another 8-10 minutes, or even the chicken reaches the temp of 165°F. Enjoy.

3.189 Deli-Style Grilled Turkey Breast
Total Time: 2 Hours 11 Minutes, Serving: 4 people
Ingredients
main
Boneless Turkey Breast, 1 (4-5 Lb.)
Pit Boss Pork & Poultry Rub
Instructions
Preheat the Pit Boss to 325°F for 15 minutes with the lid closed when ready to cook.
Remove the turkey breast from the packaging while the grill warms up. Remove the outer layer of the skin. Pit Boss Pork & Poultry Rub should be evenly applied to the breast.
Cook for 1 hr and 45 mins directly on the grill grate.
Check the turkey's internal temperature; it should be 165°F. If the temperature has not reached the required level, check it every 15 minutes until it does.
Remove the turkey from the grill when it reaches 165°F and let it sit for 1-1/2 hours to cool.
Refrigerate the turkey breast after wrapping it in plastic wrap. Allow it to chill for at least 12 hours in the refrigerator.
To serve, slice it thinly with a sharp knife or deli slicer. Enjoy.

3.190 Sweet Cajun Wings
Total Time: 35 Minutes, Serving: 4 people
Ingredients
main
Chicken Wings, 2 Pound
Pork and Poultry Rub of Pit Boss
Cajun Shake of Pit Boss

Instructions
Drizzle Pit Boss Honey Rub & Cajun Shake
over wings.
Once prepared to cook, preheat the Pit Boss to 350°F for 15 mins with the lid closed.
Bake for 30 mins, or until the exterior is golden brown and the interior is moist, and an instantaneous-read thermometer registers 165°F. Serve and have fun.

3.191 Cajun Brined Smoked Turkey Breast
Total Time: 3 Hours 5 Minutes, Serving: 4 people
Ingredients
For the Brine
Water, 1 Gallon
Canning And Pickling Salt, 3/4 Cup
Minced Garlic, 3 Tbsp
Dark Brown Sugar, 3 Tbsp
Worcestershire Sauce, 2 Tbsp
Cajun Seasoning, 2 Tbsp
main
Bone-In Turkey Breast, 1 (5-6 Lb.)
Extra-Virgin Olive Oil, 3 Tbsp
Cajun Seasoning, 2 Tbsp
Instructions
Bring Together all salt-water ingredients in a big food-safe bucket with 1 gallon of water. Stir constantly until the salt is completely dissolved.
Put the breast in the brine & pound it down to thoroughly immerse it. Refrigerate for one to two days after covering and brining.
Drain the brine from the turkey breast and pat it dry. Drizzle the olive oil over the chicken with your hands, being sure to coat all surfaces. Cajun seasoning
should be used generously.
When ready to cook, preheat the Pit Boss to 225°F with the lid closed for 15 minutes.
Cook for 3 hours by placing the turkey breast directly on the grill grate and closing the lid.
Increase the temperature to 425°F
after 3 hours and continue to cook for another 30 minutes, or until a thermometer inserted into the thickest portion of the breast registers 165°F.
Take the turkey breast from the grill and set it aside for at least 15 minutes before slicing. Cut into slices and serve. Enjoy.

3.192 Chardonnay Chicken with Roasted Root Vegetables
Total Time: 1 Hour 15 Minutes, Serving: 6 people
Ingredients
Mop Sauce
Dried Thyme, 1 Tbsp
Ground Fennel Seed, 1/4 Tbsp
Finely Ground Black Pepper, 1 Tbsp
Chopped Preserved Lemon, 2 Tbsp
Olive Oil, 1/4 Cup
Truffle Salt, 1 Tbsp
main
Whole Chicken, 1 (3-5 Lb.)
Chardonnay, Divided, 4 Cup
Roasted Butternut Squash and Yukon Gold Potatoes
Butternut Squash, Cut into 1/2 Inch Cubes, 1 Pound
Four medium Yukon Gold Potatoes, Cut into 1/2 Inch Cubes
Olive Oil, 1/8 Cup
Melted Bacon Grease, 1 Tbsp
Garlic Salt, 1/2 Tbsp
Ground Black Pepper, 1/2 Tbsp

Roasted Brussels Sprouts with balsamic glaze
Brussels Sprouts, Halved, 1 Pound
Melted Bacon Grease, 1 Tbsp
Garlic Salt, 1/2 Tbsp
Ground Black Pepper, 1/2 Tbsp
Balsamic Glaze, 2 Tbsp
Wine country Chardonnay Sauce
Butter, 4 Tbsp
Chicken Broth, 1 cup
Chopped Yellow Onion, 1/3 Cup
Instructions
Begin by making the mop sauce. Place the preserved lemon in a medium mixing bowl and chop it until it forms a paste. (If preserved lemon isn't available, use 2 tsp lemon juice and 1 tsp lemon zest instead.) Whisk in the remaining ingredients until they are emulsified.
Place chicken on a sheet pan and brush with mop sauce (reserving 4 to 5 tbsps. for basting), rubbing
between skin and meat and moving back to the thighs and legs' edges (be cautious not to separate the edge of the skin from the bird). In the middle of a sheet pan, place the Pit Boss Chicken Throne with 1 cup chardonnay. Tuck the wing tips back and cross the legs in front of the chicken on the chicken throne.
In the same dish as the mop sauce, combine the potatoes and butternut squash. Over the top, drizzle olive oil and bacon fat, then season with garlic salt and black pepper. Toss to coat evenly. Position the rooster on the sheet pan and gently arrange it around it.
Repeat with the Brussels sprouts, transferring them to the same dish as the mop sauce. Drizzle the bacon grease over the top and toss to coat the Brussels evenly. Toss in the garlic, salt and black pepper, pour the balsamic over the top and toss one more. Remove from the equation.
When ready to cook, preheat the Pit Boss to 425°F for 15 minutes with the lid closed.
Transfer the sheet pan to the Pit Boss with care. Cook for 30 minutes with the remaining 3 cups of Chardonnay along the edge of the sheet pan.
Make the Chardonnay Sauce while the chicken is cooking. Melt the butter in a small pot. Once the butter gets melted, add the onions and cook for 5 minutes, or until the onions are transparent. Bring About the chicken stock to a boil and reduce it by half.
Add the wine, return to low heat, and reduce by half again. If desired, season with salt or extra butter. Maintain a warm temperature until ready to serve.
Add the Brussels sprouts to the sheet pan after the chicken has cooked for 30 minutes. Bake until the chicken reaches an internal temperature of 165°F (about 1 hour) and the veggies are fully cooked. Remove the sheet tray from the grill with care and set the chicken on the throne to rest for 20 minutes.
Carefully take the chicken from the throne and slice it into eight pieces with a sharp knife.
Strain the sauce and serve with the chicken and veggies through a filter. Enjoy.

3.193 Beer-Braised Chicken Tacos with Jalapeño Relish
Total Time: 60 Minutes, Serving: 8 people
Ingredients
Jalapeño Relish
Seeded and diced, 3 Jalapeño
Finely Diced Red Onion, 1/4 Cup
Garlic, Minced, 1 Clove
White Wine Vinegar, 2/3 Cup
Water, 1/3 Cup
Sugar, 1/2 Tbsp
Salt, 1/2 Tbsp
Pickled Cabbage
Shredded Red Cabbage, 2 Cup
White Wine Vinegar, 1/2 Cup
Salt, 2 Tbsp
Sugar, 2 Tbsp
main
Boneless, Skinless Chicken Thighs, 2 Pound
Olive Oil, 1 Tbsp
Salt, 1 Tbsp
Black Pepper, 1 Tbsp
Flour Tortillas, 12 Small
Cotija Cheese, 1/4 cup
Chopped Cilantro, 1/4 Cup
Your Favorite Hot Sauce
Braising Liquid
Butter 1 Tbsp
Yellow Onion, Chopped Small, 1/2
Jalapeño, Planted and Cut, 1
Garlic, Crushed, 1 Clove
Chili Powder, 1 Tbsp
Garlic Powder, 1 Tbsp
Adobo Sauce, plus 1 Chipotle Pepper in Adobo Sauce, 4 Tbsp
Limes, Juiced, 2.
Model Beer, 1 Can (12 Oz)
Instructions
In a non-reactive bowl, mix all of the ingredients for the jalapeno relish and put them aside.
Add all ingredients in a semi bowl and leave aside to create the pickled cabbage.
Refrigerate the relish and pickled cabbage for at least a couple of hours, preferably overnight.
Pepper chicken thighs with salt and pepper to taste. In a Dutch oven, warm 1 tablespoon olive oil on medium-high heat. Brown the chicken thighs in batches, skin-side down. Take the pan from the heat and put it aside.
Melt 1 tbsp of butter in the Dutch oven over medium-high heat. When the butter has melted, add the onion and jalapeno and cook for 3 to 5 minutes, or until the onion is transparent. Sauté for 30 seconds, or until garlic is aromatic. Chili powder, garlic powder, chipotle pepper, adobo sauce, and lime juice should all be added. Return the chicken thighs to the Dutch oven and add the beer.
Preheat Pit Boss to 350°F for 15 minutes with lid covered when ready to cook. Place the Dutch oven under the grill for 30 minutes, or until the chicken is cooked and falling apart. Shred the chicken after removing it from the braising liquid.
To assemble the tacos, spread the shredded chicken on a tortilla, then layer on jalapeno relish, cornbread, cotija cheese, coriander, and spicy sauce. Enjoy.

3.194 Grilled Asian Chicken Burgers
Total Time: 50 Minutes, Serving: 4 people
Ingredients
main
Protected Cooking Spray
Ground Chicken, First White & Dark Meat
Panko Breadcrumbs, Combined with More as Required,1 cup
Chopped Coarsely or else Shredded Parmesan Cheese, 1 Cup
Pepper, Stopped, Seeded & Diced Small, 1 Standard Fresh Jalapeño
Scallion, Whites & Greens Minced, 2 Stalk
Garlic, Crushed, 2 Clove
Chopped Cilantro Leaves, Heavily Packed, 1/4 Cup
Mayonnaise, Along with More for Helping, 2 Tbsp
Thai Sweet Chile Sauce, 2 Tbsp
Soy Sauce, 1 Tbsp
Fresh Pounded Gingery, 1 Tbsp

Lemon Juice, 2 Tbsp
Lemon Zest, 2 Tbsp
Salt, 1 Tbsp
Ground Black Pepper, 1 Tbsp
Split, Lightly Buttered and Toasted or Grilled, For Serving, 8 Entire Hamburger Buns
Large Ripe Tomato, Thinly Carved, For Plateful, 1
Fresh Arugula or Spinach Leaves, For Plateful
Large Red Onion, Thinly Cut up, For Plateful, 1
Instructions
Spray rimmed baking sheet with non-stick cooking spray and line with Aluminum foil. Remove from the equation.
Toss the chicken with the panko, jalapeno, garlic, Parmesan, scallion, mayonnaise, cilantro, chile sauce, ginger, soy sauce, lemon juice, lemon zest, salt, & pepper in a large mixing bowl. Make a claw with your fingers and carefully massage the meat mixture until all ingredients are thoroughly mixed. Add more panko if the mixture is too moist to shape into patties.
Wet your hands under cool running water, then shape the meat into eight patties, each approximately 3/4-inch-thick and an inch bigger in diameter than the buns.
Make a broad, shallow indentation in the top of each with your thumbs or a tbsp. Place them on the baking sheet that has been Totalized. Use non-stick cooking spray to coat the tops.
Cover with plastic wrap and chill if not using straight away.
When ready to cook, preheat the Pit Boss to 350°F for 15 minutes with the lid closed.
Place the burgers on the grill grate, depression-side down.
Remove and remove the foil from the baking sheet so you can transfer the sliders to a clean surface once they're done.
Grill the burgers for approximately 25 to 30 minutes, rotating once or until a clean metal spatula slid beneath them easily released them from the grill grate. When using an instant-read meat thermometer, the interior temperature should be 160°F. (For an exact reading, stick the probe into the side of the burger.)
Meanwhile, spread mayonnaise on the cut sides of the grilled buns and top with a tomato slice and arugula leaves on one half of each bun.
Place a cooked burger on top, red onions if desired, and replace the top half of the bread.
Serve right away. Enjoy.

3.195 Roast Chicken & Pimenton Potatoes

Total Time: 1 Hour 15 Minutes, Serving: 8 people
Ingredients
main
Chicken, 2 Whole
Garlic, Minced, 6 Clove
Salt, 2 Tbsp
Pimentón (Spanish Smoked Paprika), 3 Tbsp
Extra-Virgin Olive Oil, 6 Tbsp
Fresh Thyme, 2 Bunch
Yukon Gold Potatoes, 3 Pound
Salt
Ground Black Pepper
Lemon, Halved, 2.
Chopped Flat-Leaf Parsley, 1/2 Cup
Instructions
Eliminate giblets, if any, & rinse the chickens, within and outside, under chilly running water. Dry fully with paper towels.
Bind the legs jointly with the butcher's string and tuck the wings behind the backs.
Make the spice paste: In a small bowl, combine the garlic, salt, and pimento and
blend well. Stir in 3 tbsp of olive oil. Smear the mixture all over the outside of the chickens. Tuck one bunch of thyme inside the main cavity of each bird. Spot on a rimmed cooking sheet and refrigerate, uncovered, for at least 6 hours or overnight.
Place the scrubbed potatoes in a large bowl and season with salt and pepper. Drizzle with the remaining 3 tbsp of oil and toss to coat. Spread the potatoes in a large roasting pan or on a large, rimmed baking sheet.
Arrange the chicken side by side on top of the potatoes. Squeeze the lemons over the chickens and add the rinds to the potatoes.
Once ready to bake, start the Pit Boss and set the temperature to 400-450F (205-230 C). Preheat, lid shut down, for 10 to 15 mins.
Roast the chickens, potatoes, and lemons for 30 minutes. Stir the potatoes.
Reduce the temperature to 350F (175 C) and continue to roast till the meat thermometer inserted into the thickest part of the thighs registers 165F (75 C), about 40 minutes more.
Organize the potatoes & lemons on a big platter.

3.196 Bacon-Wrapped Turkey Legs

Total Time: 3 Hours 10 Minutes, Serving: 8 people
Ingredients
main
Water, 1 Gal
Cup Rub Pit Boss, 1/4
Morton Tender Fast Home Meat Cure, 3 cups
Sugar Brown, 1/2 Cup
Black Peppercorns, 6 Whole
Bay Leaves, 2 Whole
Turkey Legs (1-1/2 Lb. Each), 8
Bacon 8 Slices
Instructions
Plan to brine the turkey legs overnight. Merge one gallon of water, Pit Boss Rub, curing salt,
brown sugar, peppercorns, and bay leaves in a large stockpot.
Bring the water to a boil around high heat, constantly stirring, to dissolve the salt and sugar granules. Get Rid of the pan from the temperature and add 1/2 gallon of water and ice to it. Check to see whether the brine is at least room temperature, if not colder. (The brine may need to be refrigerated for an hour or so.)
Place the turkey legs in the brine, ensuring sure they are fully immersed.
Drain the turkey legs and discard the liquid after 24 hours. Remove the brine from the legs by rinsing them in cold water and drying them well with paper towels.
When ready to cook, preheat the Pit Boss to 250°F for 15 minutes with the lid closed.
Place the turkey legs on the grill grate immediately.
After 2-1/2 hours, wrap a slice of bacon over each leg and cook for an additional 30 to 40 minutes.
Cook the legs for 3 hours or until an instant-read meat thermometer registers 165°F internal temperature. Serve and have fun.

3.197 Skillet-Roasted Game Bird

Total Time: 1 Hour 10 Minutes
Serving: 6 people
Ingredients
main
Game Birds or Equivalent, 4 Pound (1 Lb.)
Butter, 4 Tbsp
Salt
Black Pepper
Lemon, Halved, 2 Whole
Fresh Parsley, 1 Bunch

Fresh Thyme, 1 Bunch
Fresh Rosemary, 1 Bunch
Instructions
Preheat the grill to high for 15 minutes with the lid covered when ready to cook. While the grill is heating up, place a big cast-iron skillet on it.
While the grill heats up, spread 2 tbsps. butter all over the game birds and season inside and out with salt and pepper. Stuff each bird's cavity with half a lemon, a sprig of parsley, thyme, and rosemary.
Simply tie the legs of the birds together using thread to truss them. In a cast-iron skillet, melt the remaining 2 tbsps. of butter. Place the birds in a heated cast iron pan and roast for 45 to 60 minutes, or until the internal temperature reaches 165 degrees F.
Set aside for 10 minutes before turning. Enjoy.

3.198 Bacon-Wrapped Chicken Wings
Total Time: 1 Hour 30 Minutes, Serving: 6 people
Ingredients
main
Whole Chicken Wings, 2 Pound
Beer, 24 Ounce
Red Pepper Flakes (Optional), 2 Tbsp
Cajun Seasoning
Bacon, 1 Pound (10 To 12 Slices)
Instructions
Set aside 12 to 24 hours to brine the wings for this recipe. Trim the tips off the wings and toss them in the trash or save them for homemade stock.
Trim the skin flap between the flat and drumette to make the wing straighter and simpler to wrap.
In a large mixing bowl, combine the wings, beer, and red pepper flakes (if desired).
Before grilling, chill for 12 to 24 hours.
Pat the wings dry after removing them from the brine. Cajun seasoning should be used generously.
Wrap a piece of bacon around each wing. If required, toothpicks may be used to keep it in place.
When ready to cook, preheat the Pit Boss to 400°F for 15 minutes with the lid closed.
Fry for thirty min by placing the wings straight on the barbecue grate and closing the lid.
Flip the wings and cook for another 30 minutes, or until the bacon is crisp and the chicken is completely cooked (at least 165°F on the inside). Take it out of the Pit Boss, plate it, and eat it.

3.199 Braised Brunswick Stew
Total Time: 2 Hours 30 Minutes, Serving: 4 people
Ingredients
main
Butter, 8 Tbsp
Large Onion, 1
Green Bell Pepper, Diced, 1
Celery, 2
Garlic, Minced, 4 Clove
Smoked Paprika, 1 Tbsp
Cayenne Pepper, 1/2 Tbsp
Worcestershire Sauce
Diced Tomatoes, 45 Ounce (28 Oz)
Cup Pit Boss 'Que BBQ Sauce
Pound Pulled Pork
Pound Pulled Chicken
Pound Beef Brisket
Cup Chicken Broth
Lima Beans, Frozen, 10 Ounce
Corn, 10 Ounce
Okra, Frozen, 1 Cup
Salt
Black Pepper
Tbsp Apple Cider Vinegar
Hot Sauce
Instructions
In a big cast-iron Dutch oven, melt the butter over medium heat. For 5 to 8 minutes, sauté the onions, bell pepper, and celery until tender and translucent.
Cook for 2 mins after adding the garlic. Allow boiling for 5 minutes after adding cayenne, paprika, tomatoes, Worcestershire sauce and barbecue sauce. In a separate bowl, combine smoked pulled chicken & pork from a prior grilling session. Smoked the beef brisket from a prior grilling session may be added now. Bring About the chicken gumbo to a boil, then cut off from the heat.
Meanwhile, warm the Pit Boss to 300°F with the lid covered for 15 minutes.
Cover the Dutch oven with a cover and gently place it on the grill grate. Cook for an hour and a half, adding additional broth as needed. The stew mustn't be overly soupy.
Add the lima beans, corn, and okra, if using, and simmer for another thirty min, or until the veggies are cooked, with the lid off. Flavor with salt and pepper to taste, depending on how salted your smoked meats are, and additional cayenne pepper if you want it hotter.
To enhance the tastes, add vinegar. Serve immediately in dishes with a side of spicy sauce. Enjoy.

3.200 Smoked Buffalo Fries
Total Time: 45 Minutes, Serving: 4 people
Ingredients
main
Chicken Breasts, 4
Salt
Black Pepper
Blue Cheese Dressing, 2 cups
Frank's Red-hot Sauce, 1/2 cup
Celery, 1
Russet Potatoes, 6
Oil, For Frying
Instructions
Preheat the Pit Boss to 325°F for fifteen min with the lid closed when ready to cook.
Period both sections of the chicken breasts with salt and pepper. Smoke for 25-30 minutes, or until the internal temperature reaches 165 degrees. Remove the item and put it away.
In a mixing dish, combine blue cheese dressing and spicy sauce; put aside.
Keep chopped celery (2" long sticks) soaking in cold water until ready to serve.
Slice potatoes into 14-inch sticks, similar to French fries.
In a Dutch oven or deep saucepan, heat the oil to 375 degrees and carefully put the potatoes in. Fry until golden brown, then drain on a paper towel-lined sheet pan. Use kosher or sea salt to season. Continue until all the potatoes are done. Place them in the oven to keep warm until ready to serve.
Arrange fries on a plate or wood board coated with butcher's paper to construct. Drizzle the franks sauce
mixture evenly, then top with the pulled chicken. Serve immediately with celery as a garnish. Enjoy.

3.201 Greek Chicken Pizza
Total Time: 40 Minutes, Serving: 6 people

Ingredients
main
Chicken Breasts, 3
Extra-Virgin Olive Oil
Pit Boss Fin & Feather Rub
Pizza Dough, 1
Fresh Oregano
Extra-Virgin Olive Oil, 3 Tbsp
Tomatoes, Sliced, 2 Medium
Spinach, Fresh, 1 Cup
Olives, Kalamata, 2 Ounce
Feta Cheese, 1/4 cup
Instructions
Lightly coat the chicken breasts with olive oil on both sides. Season with Pit Boss Fin & Feather Rub on both sides.
When ready to cook, preheat the Pit Boss to 375°F for 15 minutes with the lid closed.
Place the chicken breasts directly on the grill grate and cook for about 20 minutes, turning halfway through, or until an instant-read thermometer reads 165 degrees F on the inside.
Cut Off the lid from the pan and set it aside to rest for 10 min. Across the grain, thinly slice the chicken breasts.
Preheat the Pit Boss to (400 degrees F) or High for 5 to 10 mins with the lid closed.
In the meanwhile, layout the pizza dough to the desired thickness.
Splash with olive oil and sprinkle with fresh oregano on both sides.
Grill the top side of the pizza dough first, right on the grill grate. On each side, cook for 3 to 5 minutes.
Remove the dough from the Pit Boss when cooking and sprinkle olive oil on top.
Arrange spinach, olives, tomatoes, sliced chicken, and feta cheese on the pizza dough in an even layer. Serve. Enjoy.

3.202 Baked Chicken Pot Pie
Total Time: 50 Minutes, Serving: 4 people
Ingredients
main
Butter, 2 Tbsp
Yellow Onion, Chopped, 1 Small
Celery, Diced, 1 Stalk
Flour, 2 Tbsp
Chicken/Turkey Stock, If Possible Homemade, 2 Cup
Cream or Milk, 1/2 Cup
Dry Sherry (optional), 2 Tbsp
Frozen Peas & Carrots, Thawed, 1 half Cup
Pork and Poultry Rub, 1/2 Tbsp
Dried Out Thyme Leaves, 1/4 Tbsp
Roasted Skinless Chicken or Turkey, Diced, 4 Cup
Salt And Pepper
Frozen Puff Pastry, 1 Page
Flour, For Dusting
thumped with 1 Tbsp Water, 1 Egg
Instructions
Preheat the Pit Boss to 400°F for 15 minutes with the lid closed when ready to cook.
In a big pan over medium heat, melt the butter. Cook, occasionally stirring, for 3 to 5 mins, or until the onion is transparent. Toss with flour and toss to coat.
Gradually pour in the chicken stock, stirring to remove any lumps. Bring the milk or cream to a low boil. Permit boiling for a few mins until the liquid has thickened slightly and coats the back of a spoon. Add
the dry sherry to the mix.
Boil for 5 to 10 mins with the Pit Boss Pork and or Poultry Rub, thyme, peas and carrots, and chicken. Season with salt to taste.

Spray a cast iron pan and fill it halfway with the pot pie filling. On a lightly floured countertop, unroll the puff pastry sheet. Allow defrosting for a few minutes.
Crimp any overhanging puff pastry onto the top of the cast iron. To allow the steam out, make many tiny holes in the middle and gently brush with the egg wash.
Cook In the Oven for 30 mins, or until the puff pastry is golden brown and the filling is boiling. Serve right
away. Enjoy.

3.203 Herb Roasted Turkey
Total Time: 3 Hours 15 Minutes, Serving: 6 people
Ingredients
Herb Butter
Butter, Room Temperature, 8 Tbsp
Chopped Mixed Herbs, Such as Parsley, Sage, Rosemary and Marjoram, 2 Tbsp
Black Pepper, 1/4 Tbsp
Kosher Salt, 1 Tbsp
main
Turkey, Fresh or Thawed, 1 (12-14 Lb.)
Butter, Melted, 3 Tbsp
Pit Boss Pork & Poultry Rub
Chicken or Turkey Broth, 2 Cup
Instructions
In a small mixing basin, whisk together the 8 tbsp softened butter, mixed herbs, salt, and black pepper with a spoon until fluffy. (You can prepare the herbed butter ahead of time and keep it refrigerated for up to a
week; bring it to room temperature before using.)
If preferred, take any giblets from the bird cavity and preserve them for preparing gravy. Washing the turkey well underneath cold running water, both inside and out. Using paper towels, pat dry.
In a roasting pan, place the turkey on a roasting rack. Tie the legs together with the butcher's thread and tuck the wings behind the back.
Gently press some of the herbed butter beneath the turkey skin onto the breast halves with your fingertips or the handle of a wooden spoon, being careful not to break the skin. Massage the herbed butter into the skin to ensure that it is properly distributed. Spread melted butter on the exterior of the bird and season with Pit Boss Pork and Poultry Rub.
Put the chicken stock into the roasting pan's bottom.
Once ready to cook, preheat the Pit Boss to 325°F with the lid closed for fifteen min.
Place the turkey in the roasting pan immediately on the grill grate. Three hours to roast the turkey. Add the meat thermometer probe hooked on the thickest
portion of the thigh but avoid contacting the bone. Sauté until the internal temperature reaches 165 degrees Fahrenheit. The skin on the turkey should be crisp and nicely browned. If the temperature is lower than that, or if your turkey isn't browning to your satisfaction, continue roasting it for another thirty minutes, then check the temperature.
Continue until the turkey is completely cooked.
Carefully move the turkey to a chopping board and rest for 20 to 30 minutes. If you use Aluminum foil to tend it, the skin will lose its crispiness. If preferred, create gravy using the drippings that have collected in the bottom of the roasting pan. Etch and serve the turkey.

3.204 Grilled Chicken and Roasted Beet Salad
Total Time: 1 Hour 14 Minutes, Serving: 4
Ingredients
main

Red Beets, Scrubbed and Trimmed, 1 Large
Extra-Virgin Olive Oil
Salt
Cracked Black Pepper
Garbanzo Beans, Drained, 1 Can
Chicken Breasts, 2
Pit Boss Blackened Saskatchewan Rub, 1 Tbsp
Goat Cheese, 4 Ounce
Baby Greens, 4 Cup
Balsamic Vinegar
Extra-Virgin Olive Oil
Instructions
Once ready to cook, preheat the grill on high for 15 mins with the lid covered.
Take a piece of foil big enough to wrap around the beet completely. Put the unpeeled beets on the foil, drizzle with a little olive oil, season with salt and pepper, and then wrap the foil over the beet.
Grill the wrapped beet for 25-30 mins, or until cooked, directly on the grill grate. Remove off the grill, gently unwrap, and set aside to cool.
When the beet is cold enough to handle, remove the skin of the exterior and discard it. Set aside the beets, which have been sliced or diced into 1" pieces.
Spray the garbanzo bean with olive oil and add salt and pepper to taste on a baking sheet, grill-friendly skillet, or cast-iron pan.
Toast the garbanzo beans on the Pit Boss for 25-30 minutes, or until golden brown and crispy. Allow cooling after removing from the grill.
Coat the chicken liberally with Blackened Saskatchewan rub and grill for fifteen min, or until an interior temperature of 165°F is reached. Permit the chicken to rest for 10 mins after removing it from the grill. Set aside after slicing into strips.
Arrange the cut chicken, beets, and dollops of goat cheese on a bed of young greens in a large, shallow dish. Garbanzo beans, salt, and cracked pepper are sprinkled on top. To taste, drizzle balsamic vinegar and olive oil. Serve and have fun.

3.205 Smoked Chicken with Chimichurri
Total Time: 55 Minutes, Serving: 6 people
Ingredients
main
Chicken Legs, 6
Tbsp Extra-Virgin Olive Oil
Paprika, 1 Tbsp
Coriander Seeds, Crushed in A Mortar and Pestle, 1 Tbsp
Lime Zest
Salt, 1 1/2 Tbsp
Black Pepper, 1 Tbsp
Fresh Parsley, 1 Cup
Cilantro Leaves, 1 cup
Halved and Seeds Removed, 1 Jalapeno
Medium Onion, Spanish, Finely Diced, 2
Clove Garlic, 3
Lime Juice, 3 Tbsp
Red Wine Vinegar, 2 Tbsp
Instructions
Toss the chicken legs in a large mixing basin with olive oil, coriander, paprika, salt, lemon zest, and pepper. Cover and marinate in a fridge overnight for optimum flavor.
While ready to cook, preheat the oven to high and shut the cover for 15 minutes.
Place the chicken skin side up on the grill grate. Cook for 40-45 minutes, or until an instant-read thermometer register 165°F.
*Mention: This chimichurri recipe yields additional deliciousness that may be used over grilled steak, seafood, sandwiches, and more. To create the Chimichurri, pulse all of the ingredients in the base of a food processor until thick and creamy.
Mix the grilled chicken legs with chimichurri, a dab of fresh lime juice, and a fresh salad of your choice. Enjoy.

3.206 Smoked Deviled Eggs
Total Time: 45 Minutes, Serving: 4 people
Ingredients
main
Hard-Boiled Eggs, Cooked and Peeled, 7
Mayonnaise, 3 Tbsp
Diced Chives, 3 Tbsp
Brown Mustard, 1 Tbsp
Apple Cider Vinegar, 1 Tbsp
Hot Sauce
Salt And Pepper
Cooked Bacon, Crumbled, 2 Tbsp
Paprika
Instructions
Preheat Pit Boss to 180°F and cook for 15 minutes with lid covered until ready to cook. If Super Smoke is available, use it for the best taste.
Straight on the barbecue grate, place cooked & peeled eggs to smoke for thirty min.
Retrieve the eggs from the grill and set them aside to cool. Scoop the egg yolks into a gallon zip-top bag after slicing the eggs lengthwise.
Fill the bag with mayonnaise, chives, mustard, vinegar, spicy sauce, salt, and pepper. Close the bag and knead all of the materials together with your hands until totally smooth.
Pour the yolk solution into one of the bag's corners
and cut a tiny piece off. Fill the hard-boiled egg whites with the yolk mixture. Paprika and crumbled bacon go on top of the devilled eggs. Refrigerate until ready to serve. Enjoy.

3.207 Lemon Chicken Breast
Total Time: 25 Mins, Servings: 6
Ingredients
Marinade
1 Garlic clove, Coarsely Chopped
2 tsp Honey
2 tsp Kosher Salt
1 tsp Freshly Ground Black Pepper
2 spring Fresh thyme leaves
1 Lemon, Zest and Juice
1/2 cup High-Quality Olive Oil or Vegetable Oil
Main
6 (6 Oz) Chicken Breasts Boneless, Skinless
1 Lemon, Cut into Wedges, For Serving
Instructions
To prepare the marinade, combine the garlic, sugar, thyme, salt, lemon juice, pepper, and zest in a shallow mixing bowl. Combine the
salt and Honey in a mixing bowl and whisk until completely dissolved. Slowly and steadily mix in with the oil.
In a large resealable plastic bag, spray the marinade over the chicken breasts and massage the bag to distribute the marinade evenly.
Refrigerate for 4 hours before serving.
Preheat the Pit Boss to 400°F for 20 mins with the top closed when ready to cook.
Drain and discard the marinade from the chicken breasts.
Put the chicken breasts on your grill pan and cook until the internal temperature reaches 165°F.
Grill the lemon wedges, cut sides down for 12 mins with the chicken if required.
Place the chicken and lemon wedges on a serving platter.

Chapter 4: Vegetable Recipes

4.1 Vegetables Pan Roasted Sheet

Total Time: 35 Mins, Servings: 4
Ingredients
1 Small Head Yellow Cauliflower (Stemmed and incised 2 Inch Florets)
1 Small Head Purple Cauliflower (Stemmed and incised 2 Inch Florets)
4 Cups Butternut Squash
3 tbsp. Olive Oil
2 Cups Shiitake or Oyster Mushrooms (Cut and Rinsed)
Black Pepper Freshly Ground
2 tsp. Kosher Salt
Parsley Flat-Leaf Chopped, 1/4 Cup
Instructions
Preheat your Pit Boss at 450°F & cook for about fifteen mins with the lid closed, or till done.
Place all the veggies in a large mixing bowl. Season with kosher salt & black pepper, then drizzle with olive oil.
With your hands, toss the veggies till they are evenly coated. Place the veggies on baking pans with enough room between them.
With the sheet pans, cook for approximately 15 mins on a Pit Boss. Remove the cover and simmer for another 5-15 mins, or unless the vegetables are browning around the edges.
Serve immediately after garnishing with parsley. The vegetables are also delicious at room temp.

4.2 Crushed Cheddar Baby Potatoes Bacon
Total Time: 60 Mins, Servings: 6
Ingredients
2 lbs. Baby Potatoes
1 tsp. Garlic Powder
1 tsp. Onion Powder
Olive Oil, 1/3 Cup
1 tbsp. Smoked Paprika
2 Cups Cheddar Cheese (Shredded)
1 tbsp. Dried Chives
1 lb. Bacon (Crumbled Cooked)
1 Small Bunch Spring Onion (Chopped),
Sour Cream, 1/4 Cup
Instructions
Microwave baby potatoes till fork soft, then cool to room temp.
In a wide mixing bowl, combine the chives, olive oil, onion powder, garlic powder, & paprika. Toss the potatoes in the mix to coat them. Place the potatoes on a parchment paper or silicone-lined baking sheet. Smash the potatoes with a spatula or your fingers to flatten them.
Preheat your Pit Boss at 450°F with the lid closed for at least 15 mins when prepared to cook.
Grill the potatoes, rotating once, for 20-30 mins, or till crispy & golden. On top, there's cheddar, onions, and bacon. Cook for another 10 mins, or unless the cheese is completely melted. Remove from the grill and serve right away with more green onions and sour cream, if desired. Enjoy.

4.3 Bacon with Roasted Beans (Green)
Total Time: 25 Mins, Servings: 4
Ingredients
Green Beans, 1 1/2 lbs. (Ends Trimmed)
4 Strips Bacon, Cut into desirable Pieces
4 tbsp. Olive Oil (Extra-Virgin)
2 Garlic Clove, Crushed
1 tsp. Kosher Salt
Instructions
Preheat your Pit Boss at 350°F and keep the lid covered for 15 mins.
In a wide mixing bowl, combine the ingredients & distribute them evenly on the sheet tray.
Put the tray straight on your grill, grate the bacon, & cook for around 20 mins, or unless the bacon becomes crispy, and the beans get slightly browned.

4.4 Garlic Herbed Potato Wedges
Total Time: 55 Mins, Servings: 6
Ingredients
6 Large sized Potatoes (Sliced into Wedges)
3 tbsp. Olive Oil
Garlic 6 Cloves, Peeled and Smashed
1 tbsp. Thyme (freshly Chopped)
1 tbsp. Rosemary (freshly chopped)
Black Pepper
Sea Salt
Instructions
Preheat your Pit Boss to 350 deg Fahrenheit & cook for around 15 mins with the cover shut.
Using parchment paper, line a wide baking sheet. Season the potato wedges with fresh black pepper & sea salt, then drizzle with olive oil. Add the thyme, garlic, rosemary, & season with fresh black pepper & sea salt. To mix, toss everything together. Bake for at least 40-45 mins, or unless golden brown & cooked through.

4.5 Grilled Cabbage Steaks with a Bacon Vinaigrette
Total Time: 20 Mins, Servings: 4
Ingredients
Lean Bacon 3 Strips (1/4 or quarter Inch Strips)
2 tbsp. Sherry Vinegar
Shallot 1 Large, Minced
1 tbsp. Mustard Whole Grain
1 Head Green Cabbage
2 tbsp. Olive Oil Add More if Required
1 tsp. Chopped Thyme
Steaks Thick Slices, approx. Six
Pepper & Salt
Instructions
Preheat your Pit Boss to 450 deg Fahrenheit & cook for around 15 mins
with the lid covered.

To make the vinaigrette, cook the bacon in a large pan with 2 tablespoons olive oil over medium-high heat unless crisp. Remove the bacon, vinegar, shallot, thyme, and mustard from the heat & set aside.
Season the cabbage steaks with pepper & salt after drizzling olive oil over them. Grill the cabbage steaks straight on your grill grate for 5 mins on each side.
Remove the cabbage steaks from the grill and serve with the bacon vinaigrette on the side.

4.6 Roasted Beans (Green) with Bacon
Total Time: 25 Mins, Servings: 4
Ingredients
4 Tbsp. Olive Oil (Extra-Virgin)
1 Tsp. Kosher Salt
2 Garlic Clove, Minced
Green Beans, 1 1/2 Lb, Ends Trimmed
4 Strips Bacon, Cut in Small Pieces
Instructions
Preheat the Pit Boss to 350°F and keep the lid covered for 15 mins.
In a mixing bowl, combine the ingredients and distribute them evenly on a sheet tray.
Cook for 20 mins, or unless the bacon is crisp and the beans are slightly browned, with the tray directly on your grill grate. Enjoy.

4.7 Roasted Garlic Herb Fries
Total Time: 55 Mins, Servings: 4
Ingredients
1 Tsp. Chopped Parsley, For Garnish
2 Tbsp. Avocado Oil
4 Whole Russet Potatoes
1 Tsp. Salt
1 Tsp. Chopped Rosemary Fresh
2 Garlic Clove, Minced
2 Tsp. Flake Salt
1 Tsp. Fresh Chopped Thyme Fresh
Instructions
Preheat the Pit Boss to 425°F & keep the lid covered for 15 mins.
Cut potatoes into fries (a mandolin comes in useful here) and soak for 15 to 30 mins in cold water with 1 teaspoon salt.
Combine the oil, rosemary, thyme, and garlic in a large mixing bowl. Using paper towels, wipe the potatoes dry after removing them from the cold water.
Toss the potatoes in the oil mixture and place them in a single layer on 2 to 3 parchment-lined baking pans. Drizzle the flake salt over the fries.
Cook the baking sheets for 30 mins on the grill, then flip the fries and cook for another 15 mins, or unless
golden and crispy. On top, parsley should be sprinkled.
Serve as a nacho foundation and side dish with your favorite dipping sauce.

4.8 Asparagus Grilled & Spinach Salad
Total Time: 0 Mins, Servings: 8
Ingredients
4 Oz Fluid Apple Cider Vinegar
8 Oz Fluid Pit Boss Bourbon Honey BBQ Sauce
2 Oz Pit Boss Beef Rub
4 Oz Candied Pecans
4 Oz Feta Cheese
2 Bunch Asparagus, Ends Trimmed
3 Oz Fluid Olive Oil (Extra-Virgin)
20-4 Oz Spinach, Fresh
Instructions
This festive roasted salad combines vibrant greens, zesty spices, and candied pecans. This delicious salad is a wonderful place to start if you're aiming to eat more greens.
Increase the temp to High and preheat for 15 mins with the lid covered when ready to cook.
Combine the asparagus, Beef Pit Boss Shake, and olive oil in a mixing bowl. Place the asparagus on the barbecue grate using the Pit Boss Grilling Basket.
On the grill, cook for about 10 mins. Remove the asparagus from the pan once it is done.
Arrange the heated asparagus on top of the spinach dish.
Serve with candied pecans, salad dressing, and feta cheese. Enjoy.

4.9 Sweet Grilled Potato Planks
Total Time: 5 Mins, Servings: 6
Ingredients
1 Tsp. Salt
1/2 Tsp. Onion Powder
1 Tsp. Pepper
5 Large Sweet Potatoes
1 Tbsp. Canola Oil
Instructions
Sweet potatoes should be peeled and washed before being sliced into 8 lengthwise.
Toss them with a little oil, pepper, onion powder, and salt in a mixing bowl.
Preheat the Pit Boss to 500°F with the lid closed for at least 15 mins when you're ready to cook.
Place the sweet potatoes directly on the grill. It's worth noting that placing them towards the front and rear of the grill will provide a nice sear.
Switch them to the center of the grill once they've acquired beautiful grill marks and cook for another 15 to 20 mins. Serve the food to your guests.

4.10 Casserole Green Bean
Total Time: 35 Mins, Servings: 6
Ingredients
Onions
1 Cup Grated Sharp Cheddar Cheese
Butter 1/2 Stick
1 Tsp. Lawry's Seasoned Salt
Pepper
1 Small Onion
2 Can Cream of Mushroom, Soup
1 Can French's Original Crispy Fried
1/2 Cup Sliced Button Mushrooms
4 can Drain, Green Beans
Instructions
When all set to cook, preheat the Pit Boss to 375°F and cook for 15 mins with the lid closed.
Melt the butter in the cast iron pan and cook the onions and mushrooms, turning occasionally, unless tender.
Stir in the green beans and mushroom soup cream slowly.
Season with salt and pepper, then top with fried onions and grated cheese (cheddar).
Bake for at least 25 mins.

4.11 Marshmallow Casserole Sweet Potato
Total Time: 1 Hr 10 Mins, Servings: 6
Ingredients
1 Tsp. Cracked Black Pepper
1 Marshmallow, Miniature
5 Yams
Vanilla

1 Tsp. Kosher Salt
Butter, 1 1/2 Stick
1/2 Cup Brown Sugar
Instructions
Preheat your grill to 375°F and bake for 15 mins with the lid covered.
Prick the yams' skin a few times with a fork. Place on a foil tray or baking sheet inside the Pit Boss and roast for 50 mins, or unless very tender.
Peel the skin off using your hands when it's soft and cut it into cubes. Place sweet potatoes in a deep cast-iron skillet or baking dish.
Combine 1 stick brown sugar, vanilla, butter, salt, and pepper in a stiff whisk. Cover the potatoes with the mixture and 1 bag of marshmallows.
Apply the remaining butter to the top of the dish in an equal layer.
Return the marshmallows to the Pit Boss for another 15 mins or unless golden.

4.12 Chipotle Ketchup with Pit Boss Fries
Total Time: 30 Mins, Servings: 4
Ingredients
Chipotle Ketchup
4 can Chipotle Peppers, in Adobo Sauce
1 Whole Lime, Juiced
1 Tbsp. Olive Oil
1 Cup Tomato Ketchup
1 Tbsp. Sugar
1 Tsp. Onion Powder
1 Tsp. Garlic Powder
1 Tbsp. Cumin
1 Tbsp. Chili Powder
Main
6 Whole Gold Yukon Potatoes, Cut them into Thick Strips
1 Tbsp. Beef Pit Boss Rub
Flat-Leaf Parsley, 1/4 Cup, Finely Chopped
2 Tbsp. Butter, Melted
Instructions
Cut the chipotle peppers and combine them with the other ingredients in the chipotle ketchup in a mixing bowl.
To let the flavors blend, chill the mixture for at least 1 hour.
Preheat the Pit Boss to 450°F for 15 mins with the lid closed when ready to cook.
Toss the melted butter, potatoes, and Pit Boss Beef Rub together in a mixing bowl to coat.
Place the fries on a baking sheet and bake for 10 to 15 mins, or unless crispy to your preference. Remove the fries from the grill and toss them in a mixing dish with the parsley.
Serve in handfuls with plenty of chipotle ketchup on the side.

4.13 Mango Coleslaw (Grilled)
Total Time: 20 Mins, Servings: 6
Ingredients
Mangoes 2 Ripe
Green Cabbage 1/2 Head, Shaved
Chopped Cilantro 1/2 Cup
Chicken Pit Boss Rub 1 Tsp.
Red Cabbage 1/2 Head, Shaved
Dressing
2 Tbsp. Olive Oil
1 Tbsp. Brown Sugar
1 Lime, Zested
1 Tbsp. Fish Sauce
3 Tbsp. Lime Juice
Instructions
Preheat the Pit Boss to 450°F & cook for 15 mins, covered.
Remove the pit and peel from the mangoes by cutting them in half. Brush the chicken with a light layer of Chicken Pit Boss Rub.
Cook the mangoes for 5 mins in the Pit Boss. On the other hand, cook for another 5 mins. Remove the steaks from the grill and thinly slice them.
In a medium mixing dish, combine sliced mangoes, cabbage, and cilantro. Toss everything together.
Mix the olive oil, brown sugar, fish sauce, lime juice, and lime zest in a small cup to create the dressing. To coat the slaw, toss it in the dressing.
Place the slaw in a serving dish and, if desired, sprinkle with chopped cilantro. Enjoy.

4.14 Braised Butter Green Beans
Total Time: 1 Hr 5 Mins, Servings: 6
Ingredients
Fresh Ground Black Pepper
20-4 Oz Green Fresh Beans Thin, Frozen/ trimmed Green Beans, Softened
Coarse Salt or Pit Boss Veggie Rub
8 Tbsp. Butter, Melted
Instructions
Preheat the Pit Boss to 325°F for 15 mins, with the lid covered.
Place the green beans on a baking sheet in a single layer and drizzle with melted butter. With tongs, spread out the beans in the pan and season with Pit Boss Veggie Rub and black pepper.
Roast the beans for 1 hour, tossing and tonging them every 20 mins or more. Wilted, tender, and lightly browned beans are required. Transfer to a serving dish and serve while still hot. Enjoy.

4.15 Roasted Parmesan Cauliflower
Total Time: 60 Mins, Servings: 4
Ingredients
1 Head Cauliflower, Cut into Florets
1 Medium Onion, Sliced
Salt
Black Pepper
4 Garlic Clove, Unpeeled
4 Tbsp. Olive Oil
1 Tsp. Fresh Thyme
1/2 Cup Parmesan Cheese, Grated
Instructions
Preheat the Pit Boss to 400°F and keep the lid covered for 15 mins.
On a baking pan, combine the cauliflower, thyme, garlic, onion, olive oil, pepper, and salt.
Cook on a hot grill pan unless cauliflower is crisp and almost soft (around 25 mins).
Cook for a further 10 to 15 mins on Pit Boss with the cauliflower and Parmesan cheese. The cauliflower should be bubbly and the Parmesan crunchy. Serve immediately and enjoy.

4.16 Baked Pit Boss Potato Torte
Total Time: 50 Mins, Servings: 6
Ingredients
3 Garlic Clove, Crushed
1 Cup Parmesan Cheese, Grated
Pepper & salt
2 Tbsp. Rosemary, Chopped
6 Gold Yukon Potatoes, 1/4 Inch Thick Sliced
2 Stick of Butter, Melted
Instructions

Preheat the Pit Boss to 375°F and keep the lid covered for 15 mins.

While the Pit Boss is heating up, peel and slice the potatoes. Melt the butter and toss in the crushed garlic.

Begin stacking the torte in a 12-inch cast-iron pan with butter. Layer potatoes, rosemary, Parmesan, a butter-garlic mixture, and continue stacking unless the pan is full around 4 to 5 layers.

In a Pit Boss pan, bake for 20 to 25 mins, or unless the potatoes are fully cooked. If the top of the torte starts to brown, reduce the heat to 325°F unless it is done cooking. Serve right away and enjoy.

4.17 Baked Winter Squash Au Gratin
Total Time: 55 Mins, Servings: 8
Ingredients
2 Cups Heavy Cream
3 Cups Gruyere Cheese (Shredded)
Pepper and Salt
3 Yellow Potatoes, Cubed and Peeled
4 Garlic Cloves, Diced
1 Acorn Squash (Peeled, Seeded and Cubed)
1 Butternut Squash (Peeled, Seeded and Cubed)
2 tbsps. Butter
Instructions
When prepared to cook, preheat Pit Boss to 375 deg Fahrenheit and cook for 15 mins with lid closed.

In a small saucepan, heat the cream, constantly stirring, unless it reaches a moderate simmer. Season with pepper, garlic, salt, and Gruyere cheese that has been smashed. Stir unless all the cheese has melted.

2 tbsp butter, melted in a baking dish (9x13 inch). In a large mixing dish, combine butternut, acorn, and
potato squash. Mix in the cheese sauce well. Grill the mixture in the baking dish that has already been prepared.

Cook for 45 mins, or unless squash and potatoes are fork tender. After taking the
steak from the grill, set it for 10 mins to cool before Serving. Have fun with it.

4.18 Root Vegetables Roasted
Total Time: 45 Mins, Servings: 6
Ingredients
1 Bunch Golden Beets, Cleaned and Trimmed
1 Bunch Red Beets, Cleaned and Trimmed
1 Large Yam, Peeled
1 Large Red Onion, Peeled
1 Butternut Squash, Seeded and Peeled
3 tbsps. Thyme Leaves (Fresh)
1 Cinnamon Stick
1 Large Carrot, Peeled
4 Garlic Cloves, Peeled
3 tbsp. Olive Oil (Extra-Virgin)
Black Pepper
Salt
2 tbsp. Honey
Instructions
Preheat the Pit Boss to 450°F and cook for 15 mins with the lid covered.

Cut the vegetables into half-inch pieces using a thin knife. In a large mixing bowl, toss the veggies with olive oil, thyme leaves, garlic cloves, and cinnamon stick.

Line a baking dish with foil and set it aside. Season the veggies with pepper and salt and arrange them in a single layer on the baking dish.

On the Pit Boss, roast the veggies for 45 mins or unless tender. When the vegetables are tender, transfer to a serving dish and drizzle with honey. Serve right away.

4.19 Baked Sweet Potato Hash
Total Time: 55 Mins, Servings: 4
Ingredients
1 lb. Sweet Potatoes, Peeled and Diced
8 Oz Oyster Mushrooms
1/2 Red Onion, Diced
2 tbsps. Olive Oil (Extra-Virgin)
2 tbsps. Thyme Leaves
1 Pinch Salt
Garlic, Crushed
1/2 tsp. Smoked Paprika
5 Eggs
Black Pepper
Goat Cheese, 1/4 Cup
1/2 tsp. Paprika
2 tbsp. Chopped Herbs, For Garnish
Instructions
Preheat the grill on High for 15 mins with the lid covered. While the grill is heating up, place a large cast-iron or flameproof pan on the grate to warm.

Heat the grill before adding the sweet potatoes, onions, mushrooms, and oil, as well as a liberal sprinkle of salt. Cook for 20 mins, stirring once to coat the veggies after each stirring.

Close the grill and add the minced garlic, paprika, thyme leaves, and a sprinkling of ground black pepper. Cook for another 10 mins, or unless the potatoes and onions are golden brown and soft.

Make five holes in the veggies and break an egg into each. Cook for another 10 mins or unless the whites are almost set on the grill.

On top, scatter chopped herbs, paprika, and crumbled goat cheese. Have fun with it

4.20 Broccoli Rabe (Grilled)
Total Time: 25 Mins, Servings: 4
Ingredients
4 Bunch Broccoli Rabe
4 Tbsp. Olive Oil (Extra-Virgin)
1 Lemon, Halved
Kosher Salt
Instructions
Preheat the Pit Boss to 450°F and cook for 15 mins with the lid covered.

On a platter or in a big mixing bowl, drizzle olive oil over the broccoli rabe. With your hands, thoroughly combine the ingredients, evenly coating the veggies with oil. Add a pinch of salt to taste.

Arrange broccoli rabe (in single layer configuration) on the grill's bottom. Close the cover and cook for 5
to 10 mins. You want some color and a little char on the mainline. Cook for a few mins more on the opposite side.

Drizzle fresh lemon juice over broccoli rabe on a serving plate. Add more lemon slices to the edge as a garnish.

4.21 Sweet Potato Roasted Steak Fries
Total Time: 50 Mins, Servings: 4
Ingredients
3 Sweet Potatoes
4 tbsps. Olive Oil (Extra-Virgin)
2 tbsps. Chopped Fresh Rosemary
Pepper and Salt
Instructions
Preheat the Pit Boss to 450°F and cook for 15 mins with the lid covered unless the timer goes off.

In a wide bowl, toss potatoes with salt, olive oil, rosemary, and pepper. Place on the baking sheet and grill. Cook for 15 mins, then flip and cook for another 40-45 mins, or unless golden brown and well done.
Serve with your favorite dipping sauce.

4.22 Roasted New Potatoes
Total Time: 40 Mins, Serving: 4
Ingredients
2 Lb Small Potatoes
3 Tbsp Melted Butter
2 Tbsp Olive Oil
2 Tbsp Mustard Seeds Entire
Pepper And Salt
2 Tbsp Fresh Minced Chives
2 Tbsp Fresh Minced Parsley
Instructions
Place the potatoes in a colander and rinse them under cold water. Move to a rimmed baking sheet large enough to hold them in a distinct layer after drying on paper towels.
Drizzle the seeds over the potatoes after they've been brushed with olive oil and butter (mustard). Season with salt and pepper.
Adjust the Pit Boss temp to 400°F and warm for 15 mins with the lid covered.
Place the baking sheet with the potatoes on your grill grate. Roast for 25 mins, stirring the pan once or twice, unless the potatoes are cooked, and the skins are wrinkled.
Place the potatoes on a plate or in a dish. Garnish with parsley and chives. Enjoy.

4.23 Smoked Pickles
Total Time: 1 Day 1 Hr, Serving: 4
Ingredients
1 Lb Persian Cucumbers
1 Cup Salt
1/2 Cup Sugar
6 Garlic Clove
4 Bay Leaves Entire
4 Tbsp Black Peppercorn
2 Tbsp White Peppercorn
4 Tbsp Fennel Seed
1 Tbsp Whole Coriander
1 Tbsp Red Pepper Flakes
2 Cup Wine Vinegar (White)
2 Cup Ice Water
Instructions
Preheat your grill to 180°F and cook for 15 mins with the lid covered. Place the whole, cleaned cucumbers on the grill's grate and smoke for 30 to 45 mins. Remove off the grill and cut into the desired shape (spears or coins). Set aside unless the brine is ready.
Bring all the other ingredients, except the ice water and dill, to a boil in a normal saucepan over medium-high heat. Simmer for 5 to 10 mins, then remove from heat and steep for a further 20 mins. To cool down, pour the brine over cold water.
Once the brine has cooled, pour it over the cucumbers and weigh them down with plates to ensure they are completely immersed. Allow one day before using. Serve as a part of Pit Boss's Picnic Spread (Ultimate). Enjoy.

4.24 Pit Boss Potatoes Au Gratin
Total Time: 1 Hr 20 Mins, Serving: 6
Ingredients
1/2 Cup Heavy Cream
1/2 Cup Whole Milk
2 Tbsp Flour
4 Garlic Clove Chopped
1 Tsp Salt
Fresh Black Pepper (Ground)
2 Tbsp Softened Butter
4 Russet Potatoes, Entire Cleaned
1 Cup Sharp Cheddar Cheese (Grated)
Instructions
Preheat your grill to 500 deg Fahrenheit and cook for 15 mins with the lid covered.
Combine salt, milk, minced garlic, heavy cream, flour, and fresh black pepper (ground) to taste in a normal mixing bowl. Cut potatoes as thinly as possible and as evenly as possible. Completely cover the bottom of the baking dish with softened butter. Place a fourth of the potatoes in the bottom of the baking dish. Pour 1/3 of the cream mixture over the potatoes. Repeat
twice more, finishing with the cream mixture.
Cover with foil and bake for 30 mins under the grill.
Remove the cover and continue baking for another 20 mins, or unless the potatoes are golden brown and bubbling. Place the grated cheese on top of the potatoes and bake for another 3 to 5 mins, or unless the cheese has melted. Enjoy.

4.25 Garlic Fries (Cheesy & Baked)
Total Time: 30 Mins, Serving: 4
Ingredients
4 Yukon Golden Potatoes
2 Tbsp Olive Oil (Extra-Virgin)
1 Tbsp Minced Garlic
1/2 Tsp Red Pepper Flakes
2 Tsp Onion Powder
1 Tsp Salt
1 Tsp Pepper
2 Cup Cheddar Cheese
Sour Cream
Chopped Chives
Instructions
Each potato should be cut into eight wedges. Combine the pepper, salt, red pepper flakes, garlic, onion powder, and oil in a larger mixing bowl. Toss the potato wedges with a thin coating.
Preheat grill to 500°F and cook for 15 mins with the lid covered. Place wedges on a hot grill and cook for 8 mins on each side. Transfer the cooked potatoes to an oiled cast iron fry pan or grill and sprinkle with cheddar cheese.
Return the cheesy potatoes to the grill for another 5 mins or unless the cheese has melted. Glaze with chives, serve warm with a side of sour cream, and enjoy.

4.26 Grilled Beer Cabbage
Total Time: 55 Mins, Serving: 4
Ingredients
2 Head Cabbage
1 Tbsp Olive Oil (Extra-Virgin)
1 Tsp Salt
1 Tsp Fresh Black Pepper (Ground)
Fourteen Oz Fluid Guinness Extra Stout
Instructions
Cabbage should be cleaned and cored. Season with salt and pepper and drizzle with olive oil. In a cabbage, rub.
Preheat your grill to 180°F and cook for 15 mins with the lid covered.
Place the cabbages on your grill grate and smoke for 15 to 20 mins. Remove the cabbage from the grill and slice it thickly.
In a cast-iron skillet, place sliced cabbage. Return the cabbage to the grill after pouring the beer on it.

Raise the temp to 375°F and cook for 30 mins, or unless the cabbage is tender. It goes well with meat (corned). Enjoy.

4.27 Bacon Asparagus (Wrapped)
Total Time: 30 Mins, Serving: 4
Ingredients
1 Bunch of Asparagus
1 Tbsp Olive Oil
1/2 Tsp Garlic Powder
1/2 Tsp Onion Powder
Salt & Pepper
1 Sliced Lb Bacon
Instructions
Lightly coat the asparagus with olive oil. Lightly season the asparagus with salt, pepper, garlic powder, and onion powder. Wrap 1 small piece of sliced bacon around each asparagus spear.
Adjust the temp to High (450F) and preheat your grill with the lid closed when ready to cook (10-15 mins).
Place the asparagus wrapped in bacon on the grill and cook for 15 to 20 mins, or unless the bacon becomes crispy. Enjoy.

4.28 Potato Wedges with Garlic and Herbs

Total Time: 60 Mins, Serving: 6
Ingredients
6 Large Russet Potatoes Slice into Wedges
3 Tbsp Olive Oil
6 Crushed Garlic Clove & Peeled
1 Tbsp Fresh Chopped Rosemary
1 Tbsp Fresh Chopped Thyme
Freshly Cracked Black Pepper and Sea Salt
Instructions
Preheat the Pit Boss to 350°F and cook for 15 mins with the lid covered. Preheat the grill to 350 deg Fahrenheit. Using parchment paper, line a large baking sheet. Drizzle the olive oil over the potato wedges, then sprinkle with the garlic, rosemary, and
thyme, as well as sea salt and freshly cracked black pepper. To combine, toss everything together.
Preheat your grill to 400°F and bake for 40–45 mins, unless potatoes are golden brown and cooked through.

4.29 Bacon Onion Ring
Total Time: 1 Hr 10 Mins, Servings: 6
Ingredients
Sixteen Slices Bacon
1 tbsp. Chili Garlic Sauce
2 Vidalia Onion (Whole), Sliced
1 tsp. Honey
1 tbsp. Yellow Mustard
Instructions
Wrap a piece of bacon around each onion ring unless you've used up all the bacon. Because some onion slices are thicker than others, forming a ring with two bacon pieces is required. Poke a skewer through the bacon-folded onion slice to prevent the bacon from unraveling during cooking.
Preheat your grill to 400 deg Fahrenheit and cook for 10 to 15 mins with the lid covered.
Combine the yellow mustard, Chile hot garlic sauce, and yellow mustard in a small bowl; stir in the honey.
Cook the fillets for 90 mins on a grill, rotating halfway through. Have fun with it.

4.30 Baby Carrots Grilled & Fennel with Spanish sauce (Romesco)
Total Time: 55 Mins, Servings: 8
Ingredients
1 lb. Fingerling Potatoes, Halved and Washed Lengthwise
1 lb. Regular Carrots or Thin Rainbow Carrots
Olive Oil
2 Fennel Bulbs, Cores and Stalks Removed and Split
1 tbsp. Rosemary Leaves or Thyme
Kosher Salt
Instructions
Preheat the Pit Boss to 500 deg Fahrenheit with the lid closed for 15 mins.
Peel the carrot peaks and cut them into 1-inch lengths. Fennel bulbs should be sliced into thick half-inch slices lengthwise. Combine the fennel, potato, and carrot pieces in a mixing dish. Season with salt (to taste) and continue to cook in olive oil. Toss the veggies in the oil to evenly coat them.
Place the veggies on a baking sheet and arrange them. Sprinkle a couple of herb sprigs over the vegetables as well.
Place the pan directly on the grill and cook for 35-45 mins, rotating occasionally, or unless the vegetables are browned and softened. Allow cooling before adding the Romesco Smoked Sauce.

4.31 Baked Deep Dish Supreme Pizza
Total Time: 45 Mins, Servings: 4
Ingredients
Olive Oil (Extra-Virgin)
Pizza Dough Oz
2 Cups Mozzarella Cheese
1/2 Cup Pizza Sauce
Parmesan Cheese
1 tsp. Fresh Basil
1 tsp. Fresh Oregano
1 lb. Italian Sausage
2 tbsps. Onion, Cubed
1 1/2 Bell Pepper, Green
Fresh Mushrooms
1 1/2 Bell Pepper, Red
Pepperoni, Divided
Black Olives
Instructions
Preheat the grill on High for 15 mins with the lid covered.
Coat a ten to twelve-inch-diameter stainless-steel pan with extra virgin olive oil. Fill the
pan halfway with dough and push it out along the sides, up and down.
Pour the sauce over the dough and top with all the toppings to create the pizza. On top of the freshly cut parsley and mozzarella, sprinkle basil and oregano.
Bake for 25-30 mins, or unless the cheese and sauce are bubbling, and the dough is gently browned.
Allow for a 5- to 10-min rest period before slicing.

4.32 Red Mashed Potatoes
Total Time: 55 Mins, Servings: 4
Ingredients
8 Large Red Potatoes
Black Pepper
Salt
Cup Butter, 1/4
1/2 Cup Heavy Cream
Instructions
Preheat your grill to 180°F and keep the lid covered for 15 mins.
Red potatoes are quartered by slicing them in half lengthwise and then in half again. Season the potatoes with pepper and salt.
Increase the grill's temp to its highest setting and preheat it. Place potatoes on a grill grate and cook unless the grill is hot. To achieve equal color dispersion, flip the potatoes every fifteen mins. Continually cook the potatoes in this way unless they are readily chewable.
When the potatoes are soft, mash them with milk, butter, pepper, and salt to taste.

4.33 Smoked Olives
Total Time: 30 Mins, Servings: 4
Ingredients
1 lb. Mixed Olives
1 Whole Lemon Zest
1 Whole Orange Zest
1 Quart Olive Oil (Extra-Virgin)
1/2 tbsp. Flakes Red Pepper
4 Whole Thyme Sprigs
1/2 tbsp. Fennel Seed (Dried)
3 Whole Bay Leaves (Dried)
4 Whole Rosemary Sprigs
Instructions
Turn on a Pit Boss grill and set the temp to smoke.
Place the olives on a roasting pan and cook them on the grill. Smoke the olives for 20 to 30 mins, or unless a woodsmoke flavor emerges.
Remove the olives from the heat when they have achieved the desired degree of smokiness and put them aside to cool. Unless the mixture has cooled, combine the smoked olives, lemon and orange zest, fennel, chili pepper flakes, thyme, bay leaves, thyme, and rosemary. In an airtight container, keep the olives submerged in water.
Serve with your favorite side dishes or as part of the Pit Boss Supreme Picnic Spread.

4.34 Sweet Potato Roasted Fries
Total Time: 35 Mins, Servings: 4
Ingredients
4 Whole Sweet Potatoes
3 tbsps. Olive Oil (Extra-Virgin)
1 tbsp. Salt
1 tsp. Black Pepper
1 Cup Mayonnaise
2 Whole Chipotle Peppers (In Adobo Sauce)
2 Whole Lime, Juiced
Instructions
Preheat the grill for a maximum of 15 mins with the lid covered when it's time to cook.
Combine the potatoes, salt, pepper, and olive oil on a baking sheet. Cook for 20 to 30 mins over the barbeque grate, often turning, unless the potatoes are crispy and golden brown.
Blend the chiles, lime juice, and mayonnaise in a food mill unless smooth while the potatoes are cooking.

4.35 Baked Potatoes Salt Crusted

Total Time: 1 Hr 15 Mins, Servings: 4
Ingredients
3 tbsps. Canola Oil
6 Cleaned and Dried Russet Potatoes
1 tbsp. Kosher Salt
Sour Cream
Butter
Bacon Bits
Fresh Chives
Cheddar Cheese
Instructions
Toss potatoes in canola oil, then season liberally with salt in a large mixing bowl. Preheat the Pit Boss to 450 deg Fahrenheit with the lid closed for 15 mins.
Bake the potatoes for 30 to 40 mins on the barbeque grate or soft when pierced with forks in the center. Serve filled with the toppings of your choice.

4.36 Potato Salad (Smoked)
Total Time: 55 Mins, Servings: 4
Ingredients
1 tbsp. Salt
2 tbsp. Olive Oil
1/2 tsp. Black Pepper
2 lbs. New Potatoes (Small)
Sea Salt (Kosher)
2 Cup Mayonnaise
4 tbsp. Sriracha
1 tbsp. Chopped Basil Fresh
Chives, Parsley
Instructions
When you're all set to cook, start your Pit Boss grill smoking. Toss potatoes with olive oil after seasoning with pepper and salt. Put on a sheet pan and place directly on your grill grate to smoke for 15-20 mins.
Remove the chicken off the grill, increase the temp to High, & preheat for around 10-15 mins with the lid covered.
Cook for another 20-25 mins on the grill, or unless the potatoes are soft. After they've been prepared, set them aside to cool. While the potatoes are cooking, mix the Sriracha and mayonnaise. Once the potatoes have cooled, toss them with the parsley, Sriracha mayonnaise, & chives. Enjoy.

4.37 Corn Salsa (Grilled)
Total Time: 45 Mins, Servings: 6
Ingredients
4 Large Corn Husks, Finely Chopped
1 Diced Red Onion
4 Tomatoes (Chopped)
1 tsp. Onion Powder
1 tsp. Garlic Powder
Jalapeño (Diced, Grilled and Seeded)
1 Lime, Juiced
Black Pepper
Salt
Instructions
When prepared to cook, preheat the Pit Boss for a maximum of 15 mins with the lid closed.
Remove the husk from the corn and grill it unless it is completely done. Remove the corn from the cob.
In a mixing bowl, toss the corn with the other ingredients and refrigerate unless ready to serve. Serve with snacks or as a side dish with your favorite fiesta fare.

4.38 Chimichurri Sauce
Total Time: 15 Mins, Servings: 4
Ingredients
2 Whole Lemon, Halved
4 Garlic Cloves, Diced
2 Medium Italian Parsley Flat-Leaf, Rinsed and Chopped
1/2 tsp. Black Pepper
Wine Vinegar (Red) 1/4 Cup
Olive Oil (Extra-Virgin) 1/4 Cup
1 tsp. Salt
Instructions
When prepared to cook, preheat the Pit Boss to 450 deg Fahrenheit and cook for 15 mins
with the lid closed.
Cook for 5 mins, or unless grill marks appear, by placing lemon halves directly on your grill grate.
Squeeze the lemons after removing them from the grill. Combine all the ingredients in a blender or food processor and puree unless smooth or leave somewhat lumpy for texture.
Add extra olive oil to taste if you want a milder flavor. Serve as a dip or a side dish.

4.39 Grilled Corn with Honey Butter & Smoked Salt
Total Time: 25 Mins, Servings: 4
Ingredients
6 Pieces Corn, Husked
1/2 Cup Butter
2 tbsps. Olive Oil
1/2 Cup Honey
1 tsp. Black Pepper
1 tbsp. Smoked Salt (Jacobsen Co. Cherrywood)
Instructions
Preheat the grill too High for about 15 mins, with the lid covered.
Grill the corn, flipping it periodically, after brushing it with oil. After about 10 mins, the corn should be grilled through and gently sautéed around the edges.
Cream the honey and butter together in a mixing bowl for 1 min, or unless smooth and creamy.
Remove the corn from the bowl and place it on top. * Have fun. Season with smoked salt and pepper before serving. The amount of time it takes to cook varies based on the grill temp and the temp differential.

4.40 Roasted River Potatoes by Chef Timothy Hollingsworth
Total Time: 55 Mins, Servings: 4
Ingredients
1 lb. Potatoes, Halved
2 Bell Pepper (Green), Diced
1 Cup Garlic, Peeled
2 Bell Pepper (Red), Diced
1 lb. Italian Spicy Sausage, Sliced
3 Yellow Onion, Quartered
1 Bunch Fresh Thyme
1 Bay Leaf
1 tbsp. Paprika
Salt
1 tbsp. Cayenne Powder
Black Pepper
Instructions
When prepared to cook, preheat the grill too High for about 15 mins with the lid covered.
Combine all the ingredients in a large mixing bowl.
Twice wrap the mixture with foil. Arrange foil over the Pit Boss's top.
Cook for about 30 mins on high, turning the foil wrapping halfway through.

4.41 Pico De Gallo (Smoked)
Total Time: 40 Mins, Servings: 4
Ingredients
1 Jalapeño, Diced
3 Cups Roma Tomatoes, Diced
1/2 Bunch Cilantro, Finely Chopped
1/2 Red Onion, Diced
2 Lime, Juiced
Olive Oil
Salt
Instructions
When prepared to cook, preheat the Pit Boss to 180 deg Fahrenheit and cook for 15 mins with the lid closed. Use Super Smoke if it's available to get the greatest taste.
On a medium baking sheet, spread the chopped tomatoes in a thin layer. Place the baking sheet directly on the grill to smoke for 30 mins.
Toss all tomatoes with salt, olive oil, and lime juice to taste in a mixing bowl unless they're done.

4.42 Roasted Broccoli with Parmesan
Total Time: 25 Mins, Servings: 6
Ingredients
6 Cup Fresh Broccoli, Slice into Bite-Sized Pieces
2 Tbsp Lemon Juice
2 Tbsp Olive Oil
1 Garlic Clove, Minced
Salt, 1/4 Tsp
Black Pepper, 1/4 Tsp
Grated Parmesan Cheese, 1/4 Cup
Instructions
Broccoli should be placed in a large zip-top bag. Sprinkle the lemon juice, salt, oil, pepper, & garlic
over the broccoli and toss to coat. Allow 30 mins for cooling. Preheat the grill to 325°F for 15 mins. Place it in Pit Boss's Grilling Basket to prevent the broccoli from sticking or falling through your grill grate. Broccoli should be cooked for 8 to 10 mins or unless crisp-tender, then topped with parmesan cheese.

4.43 Romaine Caesar Salad (Grilled)

Total Time: 10 Mins, Servings: 4
Ingredients
Dressing
1 Cup Mayonnaise
2 cloves Garlic
1 tsp. Dijon Mustard
Parmesan Cheese, 1/4 Cup (For Serving to add more)
Pepper
1 tsp. Worcestershire Sauce
Salt, 1/4 tsp.
Olive Oil (Extra-Virgin) 1/4 Cup
Main
2 Head Romaine Lettuce
Canola Oil
For Serving: Croutons
Instructions
In your food processor, combine the garlic, mayonnaise, Dijon mustard, Worcestershire sauce, Parmesan cheese, pepper, & salt, then gently drizzle in the olive oil till smooth. Keep refrigerated till ready to use.
Cut the Romaine in 1/2 lengthwise, keeping the edges intact, to keep it from falling apart.
Clean the romaine lettuce by rinsing & drying it. Preheat your Pit Boss at 500°F with the lid covered for
approximately 15 mins.
Brush the halves of Romaine with canola oil & place them cut edge down on the grill for a few seconds, just unless light grill streaks form.
Toss in the dressing, croutons, and Parmesan cheese.

4.44 Frypan Potato Cake

Total Time: 50 Mins, Servings: 4
Ingredients
8 Tbsp Butter, Melted
2 Lb Russet Potatoes Peeled & Thinly Cut
3 Tbsp Kosher Salt
2 Tbsp Fresh Black Pepper (Ground)
Thyme
Instructions
Preheat the grill to 375°F and cook for 15 mins with the lid covered.
Melt the butter and brush it all over the bottom of the cast-iron frypan. Fill in a mid with potato pieces that are vertical around the outer edges.
Drizzle additional melted butter over the top of the layers and season with salt and pepper.
Grill the frypan for 35-40 mins, or unless the potatoes are fork-tender and golden brown. Drizzle fresh thyme over the top of the potatoes.

4.45 Butternut Squash

Total Time: 50 Mins, Servings: 4
Ingredients
1 Butternut Squash, Entire
Veggie Rub (Pit Boss)
Saskatchewan Rub (Blackened) of Pit Boss
Olive Oil
Instructions
Squash halves should be cut in half and lightly coated with an olive oil combination, Pit Boss Veggie Shake, & Pit Boss Blackened
Saskatchewan.
Cover with foil and 1/2 cup water. Preheat grill to 450°F and cook for 10-15 mins with the lid covered.
Cook the squash for 45 mins on the grill. Remove the meat from the grill and unwrap it. Enjoy.

4.46 Ratatouille Salad (Grilled)

Total Time: 45 Mins, Servings: 4
Ingredients
1 Sweet Potatoes, Entire
1 Whole Red Onion, Chopped
1 Zucchini, Entire
Entire Squash One
1 Tomato, Diced
Vegetable Oil
Salt & Pepper
Instructions
Heat the grill too High for 10-15 mins with the lid covered. Each vegetable should be sliced to a thickness of 14 inches. Brush veggies with oil and season with Pit Boss's Veggie Shake or salt and pepper.
Grill the sweet potato, zucchini, onion, and squash for 20 mins or unless soft. Midway through, take a left. During the final 5 mins of cooking, add tomato slices to the grill.
Vegetables may be changed up in appearance by stacking them upright.

4.47 Fall Vegetables (Roasted)

Total Time: 35 Mins, Servings: 6
Ingredients
1/2 Lb Potatoes
2 Tbsp Olive Oil
Salt & Pepper
1/2 Lb Butternut Squash, Chopped
1/2 Lb Brussels Sprouts (Fresh)
1 Pint Mushrooms, Cut
Instructions
Start the grill according to the grill directions. Preheat grill to 400°F and bake for 10 to 15 mins with the lid covered.
Spread out the potatoes and squash on the sheet pan and toss with salt, olive oil, and pepper. Place directly on the grate and cook for 15 mins. Toss in the brussels sprouts and mushrooms to coat.
Grill for another 15 to 20 mins, or unless the vegetables are lightly browned and cooked through. As needed, adjust the seasoning. Enjoy.

4.48 Harvest Vegetables (Grilled)

Total Time: 55 Mins, Servings: 4
Ingredients
6 Corn Ears Husked
2 Green Bell Pepper, Cut
2 Red Bell Peppers, Cut
2 Orange Bell Peppers, Cut
1 Lb Fresh Green Beans
2 Tbsp Olive Oil
1 Tbsp Kosher Salt
2 Garlic Clove Chopped

2 Tbsp Chopped Thyme
2 Tbsp Chopped Rosemary
1 Lb Cherry Tomatoes
1 Cup Tattered Parmesan Cheese
Instructions
Preheat the grill to 375°F and cover for 15 mins. For 10 mins, grill corn on the cob. Remove the corn from the grill and cut it from the cobb.
In a safe dish, combine all the ingredients except the cherry tomatoes and parmesan cheese. Cook for 25 mins with the veggies on the grill. Cook for a further 5 mins after adding the cherry tomatoes and parmesan cheese. Warm the veggies before serving.

4.49 Stuffed Jalapenos
Total Time: 1 Hr 10 Mins, Serving: 8
Ingredients
40 Jalapeño Entire
8 Oz Cheese Cream Room Temp
1 Cup Cheddar Grated (Sharp)
1 Tsp Poultry Rub & Pit Boss Pork 1/2
2 Tbsp Sour Cream
Fourteen oz. Entire Cocktail Sausages
20 Entire Slices of Smoked Bacon, Cut in Half
Instructions
The peppers should be washed and dried. Slice the stem ends off with a knife (paring), then carefully scrape the seeds and ribs out of each pepper with the same knife or a small metal spoon. Set aside.
Combine the grated cheese, Poultry Rub, cream cheese, sour cream, and Pit Boss Pork in a small bowl.
Transfer the mixture to a resealable solid plastic bag and use the scissors to cut a half-inch off one of the bottom curves. Fill each pepper with a pinch of the cream cheese mixture, filling them halfway.
Fill each pepper with 1 sausage. Wrap a slice of bacon around the outside of each 1 and secure with 1 or 2 toothpicks.
Arrange peppers on a baking pan coated
with foil. When you're ready to cook, fire up the grill and smoke the peppers for 1 to 1 1/2 hours.
Raise the heat to 350 deg Fahrenheit and continue to grill for another 20 to 30 mins, or unless the bacon begins to turn fat and crisp.

4.50 Mashed Potatoes (Roasted)
Total Time: 45 Mins, Servings: 8
Ingredients
Heavy Whipped Cream, 1 1/2 Cup
5 lbs. Potatoes Yukon Gold
Softened Butter, 1 1/2 Stick
Temp
White Pepper
Kosher Salt
Instructions
Preheat your Pit Boss at 300°F with the lid covered for approximately 15 mins.
Cut the potatoes into half-inch cubes after peeling them. In a shallow baking dish, cover the potatoes with 1/2 a cup of water. Preheat the grill to 400°F and bake for around 40 mins, or unless the potatoes become soft.
In a medium saucepan, combine the butter and
cream. Over medium heat, cook till the
butter has melted.
After a few mins, remove the potatoes from the heat and drain the water.
Mash the potatoes on a plate using a masher. Then, using a masher, gently incorporate the butter and cream mixture. The potatoes will get gluey if you overwork them. Season with salt & pepper for taste.

4.51 Pit Boss Smoked Coleslaw
Total Time: 35 Mins, Serving: 8
Ingredients
Main
1 Head Tattered Purple Cabbage
1 Head Tattered Green Cabbage
1 Cup Shredded Carrots
2 Scallions Lightly Sliced
Dressing
1 1/2 Cup Mayonnaise
Wine Vinegar (White) 1/8 Cup
1 Tsp Celery Seed
1 Tsp Sugar
Salt & Pepper
Instructions
Adjust the Pit Boss temp to 180°F and warm for 15 mins with the lid covered. If a Super Smoke is available, use it to get the best taste.
Carrots and cabbage should be spread out on a tray (sheet) and placed directly on your grill grates. Smoke for 20 to 20-5 mins, or unless cabbage absorbs the desired quantity of smoke.
Remove off the grill and place immediately in the refrigerator to chill. Begin preparing the dressing while the cabbage is cooling.
To make a dressing, combine all the ingredients in a small bowl and whisk well.
Pour the dressing over the smoked cabbage and carrots in a bigger bowl. To adequately coat, mix everything.
Transfer to a serving plate and top with scallions.

4.52 Red Onion Salad and Broccoli (Roasted)
Total Time: 35 Mins, Serving: 6
Ingredients
2 Head Fresh Broccoli
2 Tbsp Olive Oil
Salt & Pepper
1 Red Medium Sliced Onion
Olive Oil
1 Cup Cherry Tomatoes
1/2 Tbsp Rice Vinegar
2 Fresh Broccoli
2 Tbsp Fresh Parsley
Instructions
Set the temp to high and shut the lid for 15 mins when ready to grill.
Toss broccoli with 2 tbsp salt, pepper, and olive oil in a mixing bowl. Grill on a sheet pan (foiled) unless blackened, turning occasionally.
Brush the sliced onion with olive oil and place it on the grill's front rack to sear. Remove and cut into 1/4" thick slices.
Toss the tomatoes with the remaining olive oil and rice vinegar in a larger mixing dish. Toss again with the salt, grilled onions, and pepper to taste.
Arrange the broccoli on the plate and top with the tomato mixture. Serve with a parsley glaze. Enjoy.

4.53 Loaded Tater Tots (Baked)
Total Time: 35 Mins, Serving: 6
Ingredients
2 Lb Frozen Tater Tots
1 Can Black Beans
1/2 Cup Leftover Chili

1 Cup Leftover Queso
1 Red Onion Delicately Diced
1/2 Cup Cilantro Chopped
1/2 Cup Sour Cream
1 Jalapeño Sliced

Instructions

Preheat grill to 375°F & cook for 15 mins with the lid covered.
Place frozen tots on a sheet tray and place immediately on your grill grate.
Grill for 20–20–5 mins, or unless tots are crispy.
Serve with a side of spicy chili, beans, and queso. Replace the grate on the grill for another 15 mins.
Remove from the grill and serve with cilantro, red onion, jalapeno, and sour cream on the side. Enjoy.

4.54 Chili-Lime Corn (Grilled)

Total Time: 50 Mins, Serving: 8

Ingredients

Twelve Ears of Corn
1 Tsp Chili Powder
1/2 Tsp Onion Powder
1 Tsp Summer Shandy (Leinenkugel's Pit Boss) Rub
2 Lime Juiced
1 Tbsp Lime Zest

Instructions

Soak the corn ears in water for 4 to 8 hours while still in their husks.
Preheat your grill to 350°F and cook for 15 mins with the lid covered.
Place corn directly on your grill grates. Cook for 45 mins total, flipping the corn every 15 mins.
In a grill-safe dish, combine butter, onion powder, lime juice, lime zest, Summer Shandy rub, and chili powder. Grill for 10 mins. Remove the corn and butter from the grill.
Pull the back of the corn husk out, but not off, and remove the corn silk. Scrub the corn with melted lime-chili butter, using a corn husk as a handle. Enjoy.

4.55 French Onion Dip (Grilled)

Total Time: 45 Mins, Serving: 8

Ingredients

2 Tbsp Butter
2 Tbsp Olive Oil
3 Lb (Quartered)Thinly Cut Yellow Onions
2 Tsp Kosher Salt
1 Tsp Fresh Thyme
Fresh Black Pepper (Ground)
1 Cup Sour Cream
1 Cup Mayonnaise
2 Tsp Lemon Juice (Fresh)

Instructions

Set the temp to high and warm for 15 mins with the lid closed. When the grill is heated up, place a large cast-iron pan on the grate.
In a pan, melt the butter and olive oil after the grate has reached the desired temp. Combine the onions and 2 teaspoons of salt in a large mixing bowl.
Mix, then shut the grill and cook, stirring every 5 mins, for 25 to 30 mins, or unless the onions are very tender and dark brown.
Cook for another 3 mins after adding the thyme. Remove the onions from the heat, season with freshly crushed pepper, and set aside to cool.
Combine the lemon juice, sour cream, and mayonnaise in a mixing dish. Add the onions and stir to combine (grilled). Taste and season with additional pepper and salt as needed. Serve with vegetables of your choice or kettle chips. Enjoy.

4.56 Roasted Olives

Total Time: 55 Mins, Serving: 4

Ingredients

2 Cup Mixed Olives
3 Sprig Rosemary (Fresh)
2 Minced Clove Garlic
2 Tbsp Orange Zest
Olive Oil (Extra-Virgin) 1/3 Cup
2 Tbsp Orange Juice
1/2 Tsp Red Pepper Flakes

Instructions

In a glass grill-safe baking dish or pie plate, combine the olive oil, olives, zest (orange), pepper flakes (red), garlic, rosemary, and orange juice. Cover the dish with foil.
Adjust the temp to 300°F and preheat for 15 mins with the lid closed.
Cook the olives for 45 mins, stirring once or twice.

4.57 Hawaiian Sour Grilled

Total Time: 35 Mins, Serving: 2

Ingredients

2 Sliced and Trimmed Whole Pineapple
1/2 Cup Palm Sugar
3 Oz Bourbon
2 Oz Grilled Pineapple Juice
2 Oz Pit Boss Smoked Simple Syrup
Ten Oz Lemon Juice
For Garnish, 2 Grilled Pineapple Chunk
For Garnish, 2 Pineapple Leaf

Instructions

Preheat the Pit Boss to 350°F with the lid closed for 15 mins.
For the Pineapple Juice from Grilled Pineapple, follow these steps: Over the pineapple slices, sprinkle palm sugar. Then, directly on your grill grate, cook for 8 mins on each side.
Take the steaks from the grill and put them aside to cool. You may save aside a few pieces for garnish. Run the leftover pineapple pieces through a centrifugal juicer to extract the juice.
To prepare the drink, combine the whiskey, grilled pineapple juice, simple syrup, and lemon juice to a cocktail strainer halfway filled with ice. Shake the bottle hard and fast. Strain twice in a cold coupe bottle. As a garnish, serve with grilled pineapple pieces and a pineapple leaf.

4.58 Baby Carrots Grilled and Fennel with Romesco

Total Time: 35 Mins, Serving: 8

Ingredients

Lb Slender Rainbow Carrots 1 or Normal Carrots with Tops On Removed and Halved Stalks and Cores 2 Fennel Bulbs Lengthwise Washed and Halved Fingerling Potatoes 1 Lb
Olive Oil 1/4 Cup
Kosher Salt
Rosemary Leaves or Thyme 1 Tbsp

Instructions

Preheat your Pit Boss to 500°F for 15 mins with the lid closed when ready to cook.
Cut the carrot tops to a circumference of 1 inch. Chop the carrots and cut them in half if they're too large, so they're just about 1/2 inch thick. Fennel bulbs may be sliced half-inch thick lengthwise. Combine the onions, fennel, and potato slices in a large mixing cup. Season with salt and pepper and drizzle with olive oil. Toss the veggies in the liquid unless they are completely covered.
Place the veggies on a baking sheet and arrange them. Toss in a few herbs' sprigs with the veggies.

Place the pan directly on the grill plate and cook for 35 to 45 mins, or unless the veggies are browned and softened, stirring occasionally. Allow cooling before adding the Smoked Romesco Sauce.

4.59 Salt-Crusted Baked Potatoes

Total Time: 1 Hr 15 Mins, Serving: 4
Ingredients
Dried and Scrubbed Russet Potatoes 6
Canola Oil 3 Tbsp
Kosher Salt 1 Tbsp
Sour Cream
Cheddar Cheese
Fresh Chives Butter
Bacon Bits
Instructions
With a wide mixing bowl, toss the potatoes in canola oil and season liberally with salt.
Preheat the Pit Boss to 450 deg Fahrenheit with the lid closed for 15 mins when ready to cook.
Place the potatoes on the grill plate right away and bake for 30-40 mins or soft when pierced in the middle with a fork. Serve with a heaping sprinkling of your favorite toppings.

4.60 Cold Brew Coffee Smoked

Total Time: 2 Hrs 15 Mins, Serving: 8
Ingredients
Coarse Ground Coffee 12 Oz
Milk or Heavy Cream
Sugar
Instructions
Half-fill a plastic jar with coffee grinds, then carefully pour 3-1/2 cups of water over the top. Connect the remaining grounds, then pour another 3-1/2 cup of water over the top in a circular motion.
Press the grinds into the water with the back of a spoon. After covering and putting it in the refrigerator, chill for 18 to 24 hours.
Remove from the refrigerator and pour into a clean tub using a fine mesh strainer or a double layer of cheesecloth.
Preheat the Pit Boss to 180°F with the lid closed for 15 mins when ready to cook. Use Super Smoke if it's available for the greatest flavor.
Pour the cold brew into a small baking dish and place it immediately on your grill grate. Depending on how much smoke you want, smoke for 1 to 2 hours.
Remove the steaks from the grill and place them in an ice bath to cool. Drink alone, with cream or sugar, or as part of a coffee recipe.

4.61 Corn Grilled on the Cob with Garlic and Parmesan

Total Time: 35 Mins, Serving: 6
Ingredients
4 Tbsp Butter, Melted
Minced Garlic 2 Clove
Pepper and Salt
8 Ears 8 Ears
Shaved Parmesan 1/2 Cup
Chopped Parsley 1 Tbsp
Instructions
Preheat your Pit Boss to 450°F with the lid closed for 15 mins. Combine the butter, garlic, salt, and pepper in a medium mixing bowl.
By pulling back the corn husks, you may remove the silk. The corn can be smeared
with half of the garlic butter paste.
Fold the husks in half and place them immediately on your grill grate. Cook for 25 to 30 mins, turning halfway through, or unless corn is tender.
Remove and discard the husks from the grill. Sprinkle the remaining butter, Parmesan, and parsley over the corn on a serving platter.

4.62 Pico De Gallo Smoked

Total Time: 40 Mins, Serving: 4
Ingredients
Diced Roma Tomatoes 3 Cup
Diced Jalapeño 1
Diced Red Onion 1/2
Finely Chopped Bunch Cilantro 1/2
Lime Juiced 2
Olive Oil
Salt
Instructions
15 mins before you're ready to cook, preheat your Pit Boss to 450°F with the lid closed.
In a medium mixing bowl, combine the butter, pepper, salt, and garlic.
Remove the silk from the corn husks by pulling them back. 1/2 of the garlic butter paste may be used to coat the corn.
The husks should be folded in half and laid flat on your grill grate. Cook for 25 to 30 mins, or unless corn is cooked, rotating halfway through.
Remove the husks from the grill and toss them out. On a serving dish, sprinkle the remaining sugar, Parmesan, and parsley over the corn.

4.63 Pomegranate Lemonade Cocktail Smoked

Total Time: 50 Mins, Serving: 2
Ingredients
Pomegranate Ice Cubes
POM Juice 32 Oz
Pomegranate Seeds 2 Cup
Main
Vodka 3 Oz
Lemonade 8 Oz
For Garnish Lemon Wheel
For Garnish Fresh Mint
Instructions
Preheat your Pit Boss to 225°F with the lid closed for 15 mins. Use Extra Smoke if it's available for the greatest flavor.
Make the Smoked Pomegranate Ice Cubes by following these instructions: 1 small POM juice bottle and 1 cup pomegranate seeds in a shallow sheet tray. On the Pit Boss, smoke for 45 mins. Remove the grill from the heat and place it on a cooling rack. Fill the ice molds with the flaming POM juice and place them in the freezer.
Frozen pomegranate cubes should be kept in a mason jar

unless ready to consume. Pour the vodka and lemonade over the ice cubes.
Add a lemon rim and mint leaves to finish.

4.64 Smoked Sangria
Total Time: 55 Mins, Serving: 6
Ingredients
Medium-Bodied Red Wine 1 (750 Ml.)
Grand Marnier, 1/4 Cup
Pit Boss Smoked Simple Syrup, 1/4 Cup
1 Cup Fresh Cranberries
1 Sliced Whole Apple
Sliced Whole Limes 2
Cinnamon Stick 4
Soda Water
Instructions
Preheat the Pit Boss to 180°F with the lid closed for 15 mins when ready to cook. Use Super Smoke if it's available for the greatest flavor.
In a shallow dish, combine the Pit Boss Smoked Simple Syrup, cranberries, red wine, and Grand Marnier and place it immediately on your grill grate.
The liquid consumes smoke for 30 to 45 mins, or unless the required amount of smoke has been consumed. Take the steaks from the grill and put them aside to cool.
Pour the mixture into a large pitcher and let it settle for a while. Cinnamon sticks, limes, cut apples, and ice are combined in a pitcher.
Top with soda water if desired.

4.65 Smoked Plum and Thyme Fizz Cocktail
Total Time: 1 Hr 5 Mins, Serving: 2
Ingredients
Main
6 Fresh Plums
4 Vodka Fluid Oz
1 1/2 Fresh Lemon Juice Fluid Oz
2 Oz Thyme Simple Syrup and Smoked Plum
4 Fluid Oz Club Soda
2 Slices for Garnish Smoked Plum
2 For Garnish Sprig Fresh Thyme
Thyme and Plum Simple Syrup
Sprig Thyme 8
Pit Boss Smoked Simple Syrup 2 Cup
Instructions
Preheat the Pit Boss to 180°F with the lid closed for 15 mins. Use Super Smoke if it's available for the greatest flavor.
Cut the plums in halves and drain the pit. Place the plum halves directly on your grill grate and smoke for 25 mins.
After 25 mins, quarter the plums on the grill to make the Plum and Thyme Easy Syrup. Pit Boss Smoked Simple Syrup, plums, and thyme sprig 1 cup Pit Boss Smoked Simple Syrup, plums, and thyme sprigs 45 mins after inhaling the mixture Take the meat off the grill, drain it, and set it aside to cool.
Combine the alcohol, fresh lemon juice, and smoked plum and thyme simple syrup in a mixing bowl.
Pour in the ice and shake vigorously. Strain over ice, top with club soda and serve with a thyme sprig and a smoked plum strip as garnish.

4.66 Cinnamon Almonds Roasted
Total Time: 1 Hr 5 Mins, Serving: 4
Ingredients
1 Whole Egg White
1/2 Cup Granulated Sugar
1/2 Cup Brown Sugar
1 Tbsp Ground Cinnamon
1 Pinch Salt
1 Lb Almonds
Instructions
Whisk the egg white in a small cup unless it is foamy. In a mixing cup, combine all the cinnamon, sugars, and salt. Toss the almonds in the egg white solution and make sure they're well covered.
Arrange almonds in a single layer on a foil dish coated with parchment paper.
Preheat the Pit Boss to 225°F with the lid closed for 15 mins when ready to cook. Use Super Smoke if it's available for the greatest flavor.
On a sheet pan directly on your grill grate, roast the almonds for 90 mins. Unless the coating is fully dry, stir every 10 mins or so.
Allow for a few mins of chilling before serving.

4.67 Party Mix Pit Boss Chex
Total Time: 1 Hr 15 Mins, Serving: 8
Ingredients
6 Tbsp Butter
2 Tbsp Worcestershire Sauce
1 1/2 Tbsp Seasoned Salt
Garlic Powder 3/4 Tbsp
Onion Powder 1/2 Tbsp
Corn Chex Cereal 3 Cup
Rice Chex Cereal 3 Cup
Wheat Chex Cereal 3 Cup
Salted Mixed Nuts 1 Cup
Bite-Size Pretzels 1 Cup
Regular Bagel Chips or Cup Garlic 1, Smashed into Bite-Sized Pieces
Instructions
Preheat the grill to 250 deg Fahrenheit and cover it for 10 to 15 mins before cooking.
Melt butter in a large roasting pan on the grill. In a mixing bowl, combine Worcestershire sauce and spices. Stir in the remaining ingredients unless they're evenly distributed.
Cook at 250°F for 1 hour, stirring after 15 mins.
Allow cooling completely on a paper towel. Keep in an airtight container or Ziploc bag.

4.68 Parmesan Roasted Cauliflower
Total Time: 20 Mins
Cooking Time: 40 Mins
Serving: 4
Ingredients
Cauliflower 1 Head, Slash into Florets
Sliced Onion 1 Medium
Unpeeled Garlic 4 Clove
Olive Oil 4 Tbsp
Black Pepper
Salt
Fresh Thyme 1 Tbsp
Grated Parmesan Cheese 1/2 Cup
Instructions
Preheat your Pit Boss to 400 deg Fahrenheit and leave the lid closed for 15 mins unless you're ready to cook.
On a baking sheet, combine the cauliflower, thyme, tomato, garlic, pepper, salt, and olive oil.
On a hot grill, cook cauliflower unless robust and nearly soft (about 25 Mins).
After adding the Parmesan cheese, finish cooking the cauliflower on the Pit Boss for another 10 to 15 mins. The Parmesan should be crispy, and the cauliflower should be fluffy.

4.69 Green Bean Casserole

Total Time: 25 Mins, Serving: 6
Ingredients
Butter 1/2 Stick
Onion 1 Small
Sliced Button Mushrooms 1/2 Cup
Drained Green Beans 4 Can
Mushroom Cream Soup 2 Can
Lawry's Seasoned Salt 1 Tbsp
French's Original Crispy Fried Onions 1 Can
Pepper
Grated Sharp Cheddar Cheese 1 Cup
Instructions
Preheat your Pit Boss to 375°F and cook for 15 mins with the lid covered unless ready to serve.
Melt the butter in a cast-iron skillet and sauté the onions and mushrooms, often turning, unless softened.
In a large mixing bowl, combine the cleaned green beans and the cream of mushroom soup.
Finish with fried onions and shredded cheddar cheese after seasoning with coarse pepper and salt.
Preheat grill to 350°F and bake for 25 mins.

4.70 Broccoli Rabe Grilled

Total Time: 25 Mins, Serving: 4
Ingredients
Extra-Virgin Olive Oil 4 Tbsp
Broccolini Or Broccoli Rabe 4 Bunch
Kosher Salt
Halved Lemon 1
Instructions
Preheat your Pit Boss to 450°F with the lid closed for 15 mins when ready to cook.
On a plate or in a mixing cup, drizzle the olive oil over the broccoli rabe. With your hands, thoroughly combine the ingredients, evenly coating the veggies with oil. Add a sprinkle of salt to taste.
Place a single layer of broccoli rabe on the lower grill grate. Close the cover and cook for 5 to 10 mins. You want some color and a tiny char on the first line. After stirring, cook for a few more mins.
Place the broccoli rabe on a serving dish and squeeze half a lemon over it.
On foot, garnish with additional lemon wedges.

4.71 A Classic Smoking Cocktail

Total Time: 1 Hr 5 Mins, Serving: 2
Ingredients
Angostura Orange Bitters 2 Bottle
Sugar Cubes 10
Champagne 8 Oz
Twist Lemon
Instructions
Preheat your Pit Boss to 180°F with the lid covered for 15 mins when ready to cook. Use Extra Smoke if it's available for the greatest
flavor.
In a small mixing bowl, combine the following ingredients to create the Smoked Orange Bitters. In a small pan, combine 1 bottle of Angostura orange bitters, a splash of water, and 4 sugar cubes.
With the skillet on your grill grate, smoke for 60 mins. After the smoked bitters have cooled, return them to the container.
Place a sugar cube in each Champagne flute and soak it in the smoked bitters.
Combine champagne and a lemon twist in a fluted bottle.

4.72 Applejack O'Lantern Cocktail Grilled

Total Time: 40 Mins, Serving: 2
Ingredients
Sliced Orange 2
Dogfish Head Pumpkin Ale 12 Oz
Pit Boss Smoked Simple Syrup 1 Oz
Apple Brandy 2 Oz
Lemon Juice 1 Oz
Orange Juice 1 Oz
Instructions
Preheat your Pit Boss to 500°F with the lid closed for 15 mins. Place the orange wheels directly on the grill plate and cook for 20-30 mins, or unless the fruit caramelizes, to create the grilled oranges. Take the steaks from the grill and put them aside to cool.
Combine the ingredients in a chilled Collins bottle. As a garnish, serve with a half-grilled orange wheel studded with 3 cloves.

4.73 Corn on The Cob Grilled

Total Time: 45 Mins, Serving: 6
Ingredients
main
Ears Fresh Corn 8 Whole
Pepper
Pit Boss Veggie Rub
Salt
Olive Oil
Butter
Instructions
Preheat your Pit Boss on High for 15 mins with the lid closed.
By pulling back the corn husks, you may remove the silk. After rubbing the corn with olive oil, season it with a Vegetable rub, salt, and pepper.
Close the husks and place them on your grill grate. Cook, occasionally stirring, for 25-30 mins, or unless corn is tender. Serve sweet with butter.

4.74 Apple Cider Smoked

Total Time: 35 Mins, Serving: 2
Ingredients
Apple Cider 32 Oz
Cinnamon Sticks 2
Cloves 4 Whole
Star Anise 3
Orange Peel 2 Pieces
Lemon Peel 2 Pieces
Instructions
Preheat your Pit Boss on High for 15 mins with the lid closed.
By pulling back the corn husks, you may remove the silk. After rubbing the corn with olive oil, season it with a Vegetable rub, salt, and pepper.
Close the husks and place them on your grill grate. Cook, occasionally stirring, for 25-30 mins, or unless corn is tender. Serve sweet with butter.

4.75 Asparagus Grilled & Honey-Glazed Carrots

Total Time: 55 Mins, Serving: 4
Ingredients
Woody Ends Removed Bunch Asparagus 1
Carrots Peeled 1 Lb
Olive Oil 2 Tbsp
Sea Salt
Honey 2 Tbsp
Zest Lemon
Instructions

Rinse all veggies with a cold spray. Drizzle olive oil over asparagus and season with salt and pepper to taste. Season the carrots with a sprinkle of salt and drizzle with honey. Preheat the Pit Boss to 350°F for 15 mins with the lid closed when ready to cook.

Cook the carrots for 10-15 mins on the grill first, then add the asparagus and cook for another 15 to 20 mins, or unless the asparagus is cooked to your liking.

Serve with a sprinkle of fresh lemon zest on top of the asparagus.

4.76 Hot Buttered Rum Smoked

Total Time: 35 Mins, Serving: 4
Ingredients
Water 2 Cup
Brown Sugar 1/4 Cup
Melted Butter 1/2 Stick
Cinnamon Ground 1 Tbsp
Nutmeg Ground 1/4 Tbsp
Cloves Ground
Salt
Rum 6 Oz
Instructions
Preheat your Pit Boss to 180°F with the lid covered for 15 mins. Use Super Smoke if it's
available for the greatest flavor.

In a small baking dish, combine 2 cups of water with all ingredients except the rum and put directly on the grill pan. 30 mins without cigarette smoke

Remove the burgers from the grill and place them in a blender pitcher with the rest of the ingredients. To make the mixture bubbly, process it for a few mins.

Fill one of the four bottles with 1.5 oz. Rum. Distribute the heated butter mixture evenly among the four glasses.

Add a cinnamon stick and freshly grated nutmeg on top.

4.77 Grilled Pit Boss Whole Corn

Total Time: 35 Mins, Serving: 4
Ingredients
Onions 3 Green
Butter Softened 6 Tbsp
Chili Powder 1 Tbsp
Toasted Sesame Seeds 1 Tbsp
Ears Corn 4
Instructions
Preheat your Pit Boss to 325°F with the lid closed for 15 mins.

Place the green onions on the grill, grate them, and cook for 15 mins, or unless they are lightly browned. Place the steaks on a plate and set them aside.

Remove the butter from the refrigerator and allow it to soften. Sesame-Chile Butter: Burnt green onions are chopped and combined in butter with chili pepper and sesame seeds. In a mixing cup, combine all the ingredients.

Grill for 25 to 35 mins, occasionally rotating, unless the husks are blackened, and the kernels are tender with some browned and burned areas.

Before shucking corn, allow it to cool somewhat. Serve with a side of Sesame-Chile Butter.

4.78 Asparagus Roasted

Total Time: 35 Mins, Serving: 4
Ingredients
1 Bunch Asparagus
Olive Oil 2 Tbsp
Pit Boss Veggie Rub
Instructions

Toss the asparagus with the Veggie Rub and olive oil, making sure to cover all sides. 2. Preheat the Pit Boss to 350°F for 15 mins with the lid closed.

On the grill pan, cook asparagus for 15-20 mins straight.

4.79 Cider Brew Cocktail Spiced

Total Time: 30 Mins, Serving: 2
Ingredients
Lemons 8 to Yield 1 Cup Grilled Lemon Juice
Bottle Rye Whiskey 2 Bottle (750ml)
Fresh Apple Cider 2 Quart
Pit Boss Smoked Simple Syrup 2 Cup
Fernet-Branca 6 Oz
Angostura Bitters 2 Tbsp
For Garnish Orange Peel Twists
Cinnamon Sticks
Dry Ice, Optional
Instructions
Preheat your Pit Boss to 500°F with the lid covered for 15 mins. Split the lemons in half and chop them down on your grill grate to make the grilled lemon juice. Cook for about 20 mins, or unless the sugars begin to caramelize and grill marks emerge. Set aside to chill after juicing.

In a punch bowl or large tub, combine all ingredients except the orange peel twists and dry ice. Refrigerate for 1 to 4 hours after covering.

Dry ice blocks and a twist of orange peel for garnish.

4.80 Smoke Salsa Roasted

Total Time: 1 Hr 5 Mins, Serving: 6
Ingredients
Peppers 2 Bell
Beefsteak Tomatoes 4
Jalapeños 2
Clove Garlic 3
Green Onions 3
Limes 2
Cilantro 1 Bunch
Instructions
Preheat your Pit Boss to 450°F with the lid closed for 15 mins.
To expose the insides of bell peppers, onions, jalapenos, garlic, and green onion, cut them in half. Place directly on the grill for 2 mins.

Reduce the temp to 275 deg Fahrenheit and roast the veggies for 1 hour. Puree the roasted carrots, cilantro, and lime juice in a blender unless smooth. Serve with chips or a variety of other foods.

4.81 Roasted Mushrooms with Sherry and Thyme

Total Time: 45 Mins, Serving: 4
Ingredients
Unsalted Butter 4 Tbsp
Extra-Virgin Olive Oil 2 Tbsp
Minced Shallot 1
Fresh Mushrooms 2 Lb
Salt
Dry Sherry 1/4 Cup
Fresh Thyme 1 Tbsp
Instructions
Preheat the grill on High for 15 mins with the lid covered. Preheat the grill and set a wide cast iron pan on top of it. To melt the butter, add it to the pan and cover it for 5 mins. Combine the olive oil, shallot, and a liberal sprinkle of salt in a mixing bowl. Cook for 5 mins, covered, or unless the shallot is softened.

Before washing and slicing the mushrooms, remove the stems.

Stir in the mushrooms, cover, and cook for 15 mins, stirring once or twice.
Cover and continue to cook for another 10 mins after adding the sherry and thyme. Before serving, remove off the grill and sprinkle with additional fresh thyme.

4.82 Grilled Zucchini Squash Spears
Total Time: 15 Mins, Serving: 4
Ingredients
Zucchini 4 Medium
Olive Oil 2 Tbsp
Sherry Vinegar 1 Tbsp
Thyme 2, Leaves Pulled
Pepper and Salt
Instructions
Trim the ends of the zucchini and wash it. Each 1 should be divided in half lengthwise and then into thirds.
Combine the spears and the remaining ingredients in a medium Ziplock bag. Toss and thoroughly blend the zucchini to cover it.
Preheat the grill to 350°F with the lid closed for 15 mins.
Place the spears cut side down on your grill grate after removing them from the bag.
Cook for 3-4 mins on each side, or unless grill marks appear, and zucchini is tender.
Remove from the grill and top with additional thyme leaves, if desired.

4.83 Pit Boss Mushrooms Smoked
Total Time: 60 Mins, Serving: 4
Ingredients
Whole Cleaned Baby Portobello 4 Cup
Canola Oil 1 Tbsp
Onion Powder 1 Tbsp
Granulated Garlic 1 Tbsp
Salt 1 Tbsp
Pepper 1 Tbsp
Instructions
Combine all the ingredients in a mixing cup.
Preheat the grill to 180 deg Fahrenheit and place the mushrooms straight on your grill for 30 mins to smoke.
Raise the temp of the grill to high and continue to roast the mushrooms for another 15 mins. Before serving, reheat the dish.

4.84 The Old-fashioned Orchard Cocktail
Total Time: 25 Mins, Serving: 2
Ingredients
Sliced Apple 2
Granulated Sugar 2 Tbsp
Cinnamon 1 Tbsp
Rye Whiskey 3 Oz
Pit Boss Smoked Simple Syrup 1 1/2 Oz
Fresh Lemon Juice 1 Oz
Angry Orchard Cider 4 Oz (Hard)
Instructions
Preheat your Pit Boss to 500°F with the lid covered for 15 mins.
Combine apple slices, cinnamon, and granulated sugar in a mixing bowl.
Cook for 20-25 mins on the grate with apple slices. Remove the pan from the heat and let it cool.
In a cocktail shaker, combine the bourbon, Pit Boss Smoked Simple Syrup, and fresh lemon juice.
Add ice and shake for 15 seconds to combine flavors.
Fill a beer glass halfway with ice and top with Angry Orchard Cider.

As a garnish, place a baked apple-cinnamon slice on top.

4.85 Heirloom Carrots Roasted
Total Time: 45 Mins, Serving: 4
Ingredients
Heirloom Carrots 12
High-Quality Olive Oil 3 Tbsp
Jacobsen Salt Co. Pure Kosher Sea Salt 1 1/4 Tbsp
Freshly Ground Black Pepper 1/2 Tbsp
Minced Parsley 2 Tbsp
Instructions
Preheat the Pit Boss to 425°F for 15 mins with the lid closed.
If the carrots are thick, cut them in half lengthwise; otherwise, keep them whole. In a mixing cup, toss them with olive oil, salt, and pepper.
Spread out in a single layer on a sheet pan and roast on the Pit Boss for 20 mins, or unless browned and soft.
Toss the carrots with minced parsley. Serve after seasoning with salt and pepper to taste.

4.86 Whole Roasted Cauliflower along with Garlic Parmesan Butter
Total Time: 55 Mins, Serving: 4
Ingredients
Head Cauliflower 1 Whole
Olive Oil 1/4 Cup
Pepper and Salt
Melted Butter 1/2 Cup
Shredded Parmesan Cheese 1/4 Cup
Minced Garlic 2 Clove
Chopped Parsley 1/2 Tbsp
Instructions
Preheat the Pit Boss to 450°F for 15 mins with the lid closed.
Season the cauliflower with salt and pepper after drizzling it with olive oil.
Place the cauliflower on the grill right away in a cast-iron pan and cook for 45 mins, or unless golden brown and tender.
While the cauliflower is cooking, mix the melted butter, Parmesan, garlic, and parsley in a shallow cup.
During the final 20 mins of preparation, caramelize the cauliflower with the melted
butter mixture.
Remove the cauliflower from the grill and top with more Parmesan and parsley, if desired.

4.87 New Potatoes Roasted
Total Time: 40 Mins, Serving: 4
Ingredients
2 Lb Small New Potatoes
3 Tbsp Melted Butter
2 Tbsp Olive Oil
2 Tbsp Whole Mustard Seeds
Pepper and Salt
2 Tbsp Freshly Minced Chives
2 Tbsp Freshly Minced Parsley
Instructions
In a colander filled with cold water, wash the potatoes. After drying on paper towels, transfer to a rimmed baking sheet large enough to hold them in a single layer.
Before sprinkling the mustard seeds on top, drizzle the potatoes with olive oil and butter. Season with salt and pepper to taste.
Preheat the Pit Boss to 400°F for 15 mins with the lid closed.
Place the baking sheet with the potatoes on the grill plate.
Roast for about 25 mins, turning the pan once or twice unless the potatoes are tender and wrinkled slightly.
Potatoes should be placed in a dish or on a serving plate. On

top, chives and parsley are added.

4.88 Fig Slider Cocktail
Total Time: 25 Mins, Serving: 2
Ingredients
2 Halved Peach
4 Oranges
Sugar
2 Tbsp Orange Fig Spread
Honey
1 Oz Fresh Lemon Juice
4 Oz Bourbon
3 Oz Honey Orange Juice (Grilled & Glazed)
Instructions
Preheat the Pit Boss to 325°F with the lid closed for 15 mins.
Remove the pit from the peach and cut it in half. Each orange may be split into two halves. Glaze the cut sides of the peaches and oranges with honey, then cook them directly on your grill grate before the honey caramelizes and the fruit develops grill marks.
Brush the second orange with granulated sugar on both sides before slicing it into wheels. Cook for 15 mins on the rim or grill marks form, then transfer to the grill plate.
In a mixing tin, combine grilled peaches, whiskey, orange fig spread, fresh lemon juice, and honey-glazed orange juice.
To combine the juices and fig spread, give it a thorough shake. Strain the mixture using clean ice. As a garnish, place a grilled orange wheel on top.

4.89 Cocktail Batter Up
Total Time: 1 Hr 10 Mins, Serving: 2
Ingredients
2 Whole Nutmeg
4 Oz Michter's Bourbon
3 Tbsp Pumpkin Puree
1 Oz Pit Boss Smoked Simple Syrup
2 Large Egg
Instructions
Preheat the Pit Boss to 180°F with the lid covered for 15 mins when ready to cook the nutmeg. Use Super Smoke if it's available for the greatest flavor.
Grill the nutmeg in its whole on a sheet plate. After 1 hour of smoking, remove the meat from the grill and place it on a cooling rack.
In a shaker, combine all ingredients and shake vigorously without ice. Now, use ice in the shaker, give it a good shake, and pour it into a chilled highball bottle.
Finish with grated smoked nutmeg on top.

4.90 Peach Sour Cocktail Grilled
Total Time: 35 Mins, Serving: 2
Ingredients
2 Sliced Peach
2 Tbsp Sugar
1 1/2 Oz Pit Boss Smoked Simple Syrup
4 Oz Bourbon
6 Dash Lab Bitters (Apricot & Vanilla)
2 For Garnish Sprig Thyme (Fresh)

Instructions
Preheat the Pit Boss to 325°F with the lid closed for 15 mins.
Drizzle granulated sugar over peach slices and put them on the grill pan right away. Cook for 20 mins or unless grill marks form on top. Take the steaks from the grill and put them aside to cool.
In a tin, muddle the peaches with the Pit Boss Smoked Simple Syrup. The peaches may produce around an oz of juice during the muddling process. After that, add the other ingredients and give it a good shake.
Fill a container halfway with ice and top with fresh thyme.

4.91 Smoked Pit Boss Coleslaw
Total Time: 35 Mins, Serving: 8
Ingredients
Main
1 Head Shredded Purple Cabbage
1 Head Shredded Green Cabbage
1 Cup Shredded Carrots
2 Thinly Sliced Scallions
Dressing
1 1/2 Cup Mayonnaise
White Wine Vinegar, 1/8 Cup
1 Tbsp Celery Seed
1 Tbsp Sugar
Pepper and Salt
Instructions
Preheat the Pit Boss to 180°F with the lid closed for 15 mins.
Place the cabbage and carrots on your grill grates on a sheet pan. The cabbage has been consuming smoke for 20 to 25 mins, or unless the appropriate amount of smoke has been absorbed.
Remove the steaks from the grill and set them aside to cool. While the cabbage is cooling, make the dressing.
In a small cup, mix all the ingredients for the dressing.
Toss the smoked carrots and cabbage with the dressing in a large mixing dish. Toss well to coat.
Serve on a serving plate with scallions on top.

4.92 Watermelon Grilled
Total Time: 40 Mins, Serving: 4
Ingredients
8 Slices Seedless Watermelon
Sea Salt
2 Tbsp Honey
Instructions
Season the watermelon slices on both sides with salt.
Standing the watermelon wedges on their sides on a rack over a sink or pan for 1/2 an hour will soak them.
Preheat your Pit Boss to 500°F with the lid covered for 15 mins. After the watermelon slices have cooled, clean them under cold running water. Place each piece between two folded paper towels and gently but firmly press to remove excess water.
Apply a little coating of honey on both sides of the watermelon.
Place the watermelon slices on the grill pan and cook for 5 mins, or unless grill marks form and the fruit has softened somewhat.
Remove off the grill and season with freshly squeezed lime juice and sea salt.

4.93 Lemon Gremolata
Total Time: 1 Hr 10 Mins, Serving: 4
Ingredients
2 Tbsp Honey
2 Tbsp White Wine Vinegar
Finely Chopped Shallot, 1/4 Cup
Finely Chopped Fresh Parsley, 1/4 Cup
Delicately Chopped Salted Almonds, 1/2 Cup (Roasted)
2 Tbsp Diced Preserved Lemon
1 Tbsp Lemon Juice
1/2 Cup Olive Oil (Extra-Virgin)

Kosher Salt
Fresh Black Pepper (Ground)
Instructions
In a medium mixing cup, whisk together the vinegar and honey unless the honey is completely dissolved. After adding the shallot, cook for 5 mins.
In a mixing bowl, combine the parsley, lemon, lemon juice, peanuts, and oil. Season with salt and pepper to taste. Serve immediately or store in an airtight container in the refrigerator for up to a week.

4.94 Honey Glazed Pineapple Grilled
Total Time: 40 Mins, Serving: 4
Ingredients
2 Tbsp Ground Cinnamon
1/2 Cup Brown Sugar
1 Whole Peeled Pineapple
1 Cup Honey
Instructions
Preheat your Pit Boss to 500°F with the lid covered for 15 mins.
In a medium mixing cup, combine the cinnamon and sugar. Deeply coat the pineapple with the paste.
Drizzle honey over the pineapple and make sure it's well covered.
Grill pineapple for 30 mins on the grill plate, turning halfway through.
Remove from the grill and sprinkle with additional honey if desired. Serve by cutting into slices.

4.95 Tomatoes Roasted
Total Time: 3 Hrs 5 Mins, Serving: 2
Ingredients
3 Large Ripe Tomatoes
1/2 Tbsp Kosher Salt
1 Tbsp Coarse Ground Black Pepper
Sugar, 1/4 Tbsp
Basil or Tbsp Thyme, 1/4
Olive Oil
Instructions
On a rimmed baking sheet, place parchment paper.
Preheat the Pit Boss to 225°F with the lid covered for 15 mins.
After removing the stem end, cut the tomatoes into half-inch-thick slices.
Combine the salt, pepper, sugar, and thyme or basil in a small mixing cup.
Spill olive oil into the well of a dinner plate.
Spray one side of each tomato slice with olive oil and place it on the baking sheet. Sprinkle the seasoned mixture on top of the tomato slices.
Roast the tomatoes for about 3 hours, or unless the fluids have stopped running and
the borders have constricted, by placing the pan straight on the grill plate. Remove it off the grill & enjoy it.

4.96 Green Beans Southern
Total Time: 60 mins, Servings: 6
Ingredients
1 tbsp unsalted butter
2 cups chicken broth
2 lbs green beans end cracked off, and long beans cracked in 1/2
seasoning Hickory bacon
bacon raw 4 slices
2 cups water
Instructions
Preheat your Pit Boss to 350 deg Fahrenheit. Whether you're using a gas or charcoal grill, set the temp to medium. Place a cast-iron tray on the grill to preheat it. Place the 4 bacon strips in the pan after completing preheating and cooking for 15 mins, or unless the bacon has crisped up.
Remove the bacon from the pan and save it for later. To the barbecue pan and drippings, add the water, green beans, chicken stock, and Hickory Bacon flavor to taste. Cook for 1 hour, or unless the beans are cooked, on the grill with the lid covered.
Chop the bacon on a chopping board and throw it with the butter into the beans. Allow the beans to steam for another min, then remove from the heat and serve.

4.97 Grilled Sweet Potato Casserole
Total Time: 90 mins, Servings: 4
Ingredients
Brown sugar, 1/4 cup
Softened Butter.
4 oz Chopped pecans.
1/2 tsp cinnamon
6 oz Mini marshmallows.
2 tsp Pit boss Tennessee apple butter rub.
4 sweet potatoes
Instructions
Preheat your grill to 400 deg Fahrenheit in the Pit Boss. Whether you're using a gas or charcoal grill, set the temp to medium-high.
Clean the potatoes by rinsing and washing them, then patting them dry with a paper towel.
Coat the outsides of the potatoes liberally with melted butter and set aside. Smoke the sweet potatoes directly on your grill grate for 1 to 12 hours, depending on their size.
When the sweet potatoes are tender, remove them from the grill. Brown sugar and Tennessee Apple Butter are sprinkled on top; then, more butter is poured. Slice the sweet potato in half and press on the ends to create a hole. Layer butter and marshmallows in each sweet potato with sliced nuts, cinnamon, and brown sugar.
Return to the grill for another 5 mins, covered, or unless the marshmallows are finely browned. Then, remove it from the grill and serve right away.

4.98 Gluten-Free Mashed Potato Cakes
Total Time: 50 mins, Servings: 6
Ingredients
1/2 cup bacon bits
2 tbsp butter
1 cup cheddar jack cheese shredded.
Whisked 1 egg.
gluten-free flour, 1/3 cup
3 cups mashed potatoes
1 tsp pit boss hickory bacon rubs
4 scallions minced.
2 tsp spicy mustard
Instructions
In a mixing dish, combine mashed potatoes, scallions, bacon bits, cheddar jack cheese, mustard, and beaten egg. 1 tablespoon flour, whisked together Hickory Bacon from Pit Boss In a separate dish, rub the meat. Combine the dry and wet ingredients in a mixing bowl. After covering it, chill it for 30 mins. Remove the mixture from the refrigerator and divide it into 12 balls to put on a greased sheet pan. Lb each potato ball with the bottom of a cup to create a 12-inch-thick patty. Set aside some Hickory Bacon for a final sprinkle. In your Pit Boss Platinum Sequence KC Combo or Pit Boss Griddle, preheat the skillet on medium low. If using a gas or charcoal grill, preheat a cast-iron pan over medium heat.

In a pan, melt the butter and oil, then layer the mashed potato cakes on top. Cook for 2 to 3 mins each hand, or unless golden brown on both sides.
Turn off the heat in the skillet. When still heated, top with sour cream, saved bacon pieces, and scallions.

4.99 Corn Salad Mexican Street
Total Time: 20 Mins, Servings: 4
Inredients
1 tbsp chopped cilantro.
4 corn cobs
1/2 cup
1 lime juiced.
2 tbsp mayo
1 tbsp paprika smoked
1 tbsp pit boss champion chicken seasoning
sour cream, 1/4 cup
Instructions
Preheat your Pit Boss Grill to 350 deg Fahrenheit (180 deg Celsius). Grill for approximately 10 mins, or unless the corn cobs are slightly crispy on both sides. Remove off the grill and set aside to cool.
Remove the corn kernels off the cob and place them in a separate container. In a separate bowl, whisk together the smoked paprika, cilantro, lime juice, Champion Chicken spice, sour cream, and mayonnaise unless smooth. In a mixing dish, combine the corn and feta cheese and consume right immediately.

4.100 Green Chile Potatoes Mashed
Total Time: 60 Mins, Servings: 4
Ingredients
1 stick butter unsalted
1 Drained green chiles can
Entire warm milk, 1/4 - 1/2
Competition rub (smoked) of Pit boss
2 tbsp Competition seasoning (smoked) of Pit boss
3 lbs Peeled & cut russet potatoes.
Instructions
Place your potatoes in a large saucepan and cover with cold water to prepare the mashed
potatoes. Bring to a boil over medium heat for 30-35 mins, or unless fork-pierced potatoes are tender. Drain and re-insert the potatoes.
Combine the potatoes in a large mixing bowl. Combine the drained green chiles, Competition Smoked Seasoning, sugar, and 1/4 cups heated milk in a large mixing bowl. Mash the ingredients unless it is smooth and free of lumps. If the potatoes are too thick, add a tablespoon of milk unless they achieve the desired consistency.

4.101 Grilled Corn Salad
Total Time: 20 Mins, Servings: 6
Ingredients
Ear's corn, 6
Crema Mexicana, 1 cup
Ancho or guajillo chile powder, 1 tsp
Roasted garlic, 2 cloves
Chopped cilantro, 1 cup
Lime juiced, 1 whole
Lime zested, 1 whole
Salt
Cotija cheese, 1/2 cup
Instructions
Preheat Pit Boss to 450°F and cook for 15 minutes with lid covered until ready to cook.
Brush the grill grate using oil and cook the corn, rotating once or twice. Corn must be cooked through and lightly browned on the outside after approximately 10 minutes.
Take the corn from the grill and remove the kernels off the cob by keeping it upright and slicing downwards.
Toss the grilled corn kernels with some of the remaining ingredients in a mixing dish. To serve, garnish the corn with chopped cotija cheese and cilantro. Enjoy.

4.102 Cauliflower Whole Roasted with Garlic Parmesan Butter

Total Time: 1 hour, Servings: 4
Ingredients
Head cauliflower, 1 whole
Olive oil, 1/4 cup
Salt & pepper
Butter (melted), 1/2 cup
Parmesan cheese (shredded), 1/4 cup
Clove garlic (minced), 2
Chopped parsley, 1/2 tbsp
Instructions
Preheat Pit Boss to 450°F and cook for 15 minutes with lid covered until ready to cook.
Drizzle olive oil over the cauliflower and season generously with salt & pepper.
Place the cauliflower in a "cast iron skillet" on the grill grate & cook for 45 minutes, or until golden brown & tender in the center.
In a small bowl, merge the (melted) butter, parmesan, garlic, & parsley while the cauliflower is cooking.
Baste the "cauliflower" with the (melted) butter mixture during last 20 mins of cooking.
Remove the "cauliflower" from the grill &, if preferred, sprinkle with more parmesan and parsley. Enjoy.

4.103 Grilled Peach & Bacon Salad with the Maple Vinaigrette
Total Time: 30 min, Servings: 4
Ingredients
Peaches (ripe but firm), 2 whole
Maple syrup, 1 tbsp
Arugula, 2 cup
Feta cheese, 1/4 cup
Toasted pecans, 1/4 cup
Bacon (cooked & chopped), 1/4 cup
Olive oil, 3 tbsp
Shallots (finely chopped), 1 small
Maple syrup, 2 tbsp
Apple cider vinegar, 1 tbsp
Curry powder, 1 tsp
Salt, 1/2 tsp
Instructions
Preheat Pit Boss to 425°F & cook for 15 mins with lid covered

until ready to cook.

Halve the peaches & remove the pit. Place cut-side down on the grill grate and brush with maple syrup. Cook for 15–20 minutes, or till grill marks develop on the surface. Remove the steaks from the grill and set them aside to cool.

Whisk together the dressing ingredients in a small dish and leave aside.

In a large mixing basin, combine all salad ingredients. Grilled peaches should be sliced and placed on top.

Toss the Salad with the maple curry dressing & season to suit. Serve and have fun.

4.104 Sausage & Pesto Lasagna
Total Time: 1 hour 40 min, Servings: 8
Ingredients
Olive oil, 2 tsp
1 Bulk Italian sausage, 1/2 pound
Basil tomato pasta sauce/marinara, 2 jar (25 Oz)
Kosher salt
Shredded mozzarella cheese (divided), 4 cups.
Whole milk ricotta (drained), 15 ounces
Grated parmesan cheese (divided), 3/4 cup.
Black pepper (freshly grounded)
Egg (whisked), 1 large.
Package lasagna noodles (12 short/9 long noodles), 1 whole
Prepared pesto, 1/2 cup
Instructions
Preheat the Pit Boss to 400°F for 15 minutes with the lid closed when ready to cook.

Heat the olive oil in a big pan over medium heat. Add the sausage to the pan and distribute it about the bottom, allowing it to get brown before flipping it. Cook, stirring constantly, until the chicken is fully cooked, about 5 - 8 minutes. Remove a few tbsps of tomato sauce to coat the bottom of the "lasagna pan". Combine the sausage and tomato sauce in a saucepan and cook for 10 - 15 mins, or till the flavors have melded. If required, season with salt.

Prepare the cheese filling while the sauce is simmering. Combine 3 cups mozzarella, ricotta, and 1/2 cup grated Parmesan cheese in a moderate mixing basin. To combine, stir everything together. If necessary, season with a sprinkle of salt & freshly ground pepper. Incorporate the egg into the mixture by stirring it in.

In a small mixing bowl, combine the leftover cup of mozzarella & the remaining (1/4 cup) Parmesan. Remove from the equation.

Spread the reserved tbsp. of tomato sauce across the lower part of an 8x12 / 9x13 inch baking dish to start assembling the lasagna. Place four lasagna noodles crosswise on a baking sheet, allowing each other to overlap slightly if required. (If the noodles you're using don't span the entire length of the pan, start by layering three noodles lengthwise.)

Spoon half of the "ricotta cheese mixture" across the noodles in spoonfuls. To produce a reasonably uniform coating, spread it out uniformly with a spatula. 1/3 of meat sauce should be poured over the cheese & distributed evenly with a spatula.

Repeat with a third of the meat sauce, the remaining "ricotta mixture", all of the pesto, and another layer of noodles. Add the last layer of noodles, followed by the remaining sauce, making sure the noodles are well covered.

Top the lasagna with the leftover mozzarella & Parmesan cheeses.

Wrap a piece of "aluminum foil" around the pan and secure it. Put it on a baking sheet & bake for about 45 minutes on the Pit Boss. Raise a corner of the foil & cut into the lasagna with a knife. If the noodles are readily punctured, remove the cover and bake for another 5 - 10 minutes, or until bubbling. Whether not, cover it again & simmer for 5–10 minutes more before testing to see if it's done.

Allow 10 to 15 minutes for the lasagna to cool before slicing. Serve right away. Enjoy.

4.105 Smoked Macaroni Salad
Total Time: 35 min, Servings: 4
Ingredients
Elbow macaroni, 1 pound
Red onion (diced), 1/2 small
Green bell pepper (diced), 1
Shredded carrots, 1/2 cup
Mayonnaise, 1 cup
White wine vinegar, 3 tbsp
Sugar, 2 tbsp
Salt
Black pepper
Instructions
Boil a large stock pot of salted water over medium heat & cook pasta according to the package directions. Cook until the pasta is al dente, then drain and rinse under cool water.

When ready to cook, preheat the Pit Boss to 180°F with the lid closed for about 15 minutes. If Super Smoke is available, use it for the best flavor.

Place a sheet tray on on grill grate & spread out the cooked spaghetti on it. Cook for 20 minutes, then take from the heat and place in the refrigerator to chill.

Prepare the dressing whereas the pasta is cooling. Whisk together the mayonnaise, sugar, & white wine vinegar in a medium mixing bowl. To taste, season with salt & pepper.

In a large mixing bowl, add chopped vegetables, smoked pasta, and dressing once the pasta has cooled.

Refrigerate for 20 mins before serving, covered in plastic wrap. Enjoy.

4.106 Green Beans Roasted with Bacon
Total Time: 25 min, Servings: 4
Ingredients
1 green bean (trimmed ends), 1/2 pound
Bacon (cut into small pieces), 4 strips
Extra-virgin olive oil, 4 tbsp
Garlic (minced), 2 clove
Kosher salt, 1 tsp
Instructions
Preheat the Pit Boss to 350°F for 15 minutes with the lid closed when ready to cook.

Combine all ingredients in a mixing bowl and distribute equally on a sheet tray.

Put the tray on the grill grate & cook for 20 minutes, or till the bacon is crispy & the beans are gently browned. Enjoy.

4.107 Pit Boss Fries with Chipotle Ketchup
Total Time: 25 min, Servings: 4
Ingredients
Chipotle Peppers in the Adobo Sauce, 2 Can
Olive Oil, 1 tbsp
Onion Powder, 1 tsp
Garlic Powder, 1 tsp
Tomato Ketchup, 1 Cup
Sugar, 1 tbsp
Cumin, 1 tbsp
Chili Powder, 1 tbsp
Lime (Juiced), 1 Whole
Yukon Gold Potatoes (Cut into some Thick Strips), 6 Whole
Butter (Melted), 2 tbsp
Pit Boss Beef Rub, 1 tbsp

Flat-Leaf Parsley (Finely Chopped), 1/4 Cup
Instructions
Chop the "chipotle peppers" and then put them in a mixing bowl with the rest of the chipotle ketchup ingredients.
Chill the mixture for about 1 hour to let the flavors meld (making it at least one day ahead of the time is better if you can swing it).
When you are ready to cook, preheat the Pit Boss to 450°F for 15 minutes with the lid closed.
In a mixing bowl, combine the potatoes, melted butter, and Pit Boss Beef Rub, stirring to coat.
Arrange the fries on the baking sheet & bake for 10 - 15 minutes, or till they are crispy to your liking. Remove the "fries" from the grill & toss with parsley in a mixing bowl.
Serve by the handful, with lots of chipotle ketchup on the side.

4.108 Roasted Cauliflower & Broccoli Salad with Bacon
Total Time: 55 min, Servings: 4
Ingredients
Cauliflower florets (broccoli florets/combination), 12 cup
Extra-virgin olive oil, 3 tbsp
Kosher salt, 2 tsp
Thick-cut bacon, 4 ounce
Mayonnaise, 1/2 cup
Honey, 2 tsp
Red wine vinegar, 2 tbsp
Kosher salt & black pepper (freshly ground)
Dried currants, 1/4 cup
Red onion (thinly sliced), 1/4 medium
Instructions
Preheat the Pit Boss to 325°F for 15 minutes with the lid closed when ready to cook.
In a big mixing bowl, combine the cauliflower & broccoli florets. Drizzle with olive oil, season with salt, and toss to coat evenly.
Arrange florets on a big baking sheet that will fit upon on grill, then set on the grill and roast for 25 to 35 minutes, until caramelized and crispy. During the roasting process, stir once.
Remove from the oven and set aside to cool for a few minutes.
Cook the bacon for 15 to 20 minutes, until crispy, right on grill grate next to baking sheet with the broccoli.
Remove the meat from the grill & crumble or chop by hand.
To make the dressing, combine the mayonnaise and honey in a mixing bowl. Whisk in the red wine vinegar & season with a large sprinkle of salt and freshly ground pepper after everything is mixed.
Combine the roasted vegetables, currants, and sliced red onion in a mixing bowl. Sprinkle in bacon, saving a little amount for sprinkling on top. Taste the dish to make sure it's well-seasoned. Enjoy.

4.109 Grilled Burrata Salad with Ripped Croutons
Total Time: 1 hour, Servings: 6
Ingredients
Tomatoes, 20 Whole
Stalk Asparagus, 20
Avocado Oil, 1/2 Cup
Flake Salt & Pepper
1 Loaf French Bread, ½
Cup Butter, ¾
Garlic Salt, 1 Tsp
Arugula, 4 Cup
Truffle Oil, 2 Tbsp
Burrata Rounds, 3 Whole
Balsamic Reduction, 4 Tsp
Instructions
When ready to prepare, preheat the Pit Boss to 500°F with the lid closed for at least 15 mins.
Toss the tomatoes & asparagus with a fair quantity of salt & pepper and avocado oil. Place the tomatoes & asparagus on grill grates once the grill is hot and cook for 20 to 25 minutes, or till the asparagus is cooked & the tomatoes are blistered.
Cut the "French bread" into silver dollar-sized (or bigger) chunks. Place the bread on a sheet pan and toss it with the butter & garlic salt. Place the sheet
pan on highest level of the grill & toast the bread for 20 to 30 mins, until its browns.
Arrange the "arugula" on the bottom of the serving plate and sprinkle with the truffle oil. Arrange the asparagus and tomatoes on the dish in a circular pattern. Intersperse the burrata rounds about the
platter, then top with bunches of broken bread croutons.
Finish with a sprinkling of flake salt and a drizzle of balsamic reduction and over entire platter.

4.110 Roasted Sweet Potato Fries
Total Time: 45 min, Servings: 4
Ingredients
Sweet Potatoes (Peeled, Washed & Cut Into), Fries 4 Whole
Olive Oil (Extra-Virgin), 3 tbsp
Salt, 1 tbsp
Black Pepper, 1 tsp
Mayonnaise, 1 Cup
Chipotle Peppers In the "Adobo Sauce", 2
Limes (Juiced), 2
Instructions
Preheat the Pit Boss to 400°F for 15 minutes with the lid closed when ready to cook.
Toss the potatoes in olive oil & season with salt and pepper before spreading them out on a sheet pan.
Place the sheet pan mainly on grate & cook for 20 to 30 mins, till the potatoes are golden and crispy, turning periodically.
Puree the mayonnaise, chilies, & lime juice in blender till smooth while potatoes are cooking.
Drizzle chipotle mayo over the fries or serve on the side for dipping. Enjoy.

4.111 Roasted Crispy Potatoes
Total Time: 40 min, Servings: 6
Ingredients
Tri-color potatoes, 2 pounds
Lemon (zested), 1/2
Fleur de sel, 1 tbsp
Peanut oil (for deep frying)
Onion, 1 tbsp
Kosher salt & black pepper
Aleppo pepper (minced), 1 tbsp
Instructions
Preheat the Pit Boss to 350°F for 15 minutes with the lid closed when ready to cook.
Arrange the entire potatoes on a parchment-lined rimmed baking sheet. Bake on Pit Boss until a sharp, skinny knife pierces them with minimal resistance, around 30 - 45 mins, depending on their size.
Set aside to cool at room temperature. Flatten the potatoes with your hand, breaking the skin a little.
Meanwhile, in a massive, heavy Dutch oven & other deep pot, pour the oil 3" to 4" deep & heat over medium-high heat till it reaches 400°F.
While the oil is getting heated, combine the lemon zest & fleur de sel in a small bowl. Remove from the equation.
Fry the potatoes until they are uniformly golden all over, about three minutes, in batches if required. Using a spider or a

slotted spoon, remove them and set them in a large mixing basin.

Adjust heat as needed between batches to bring the oil temperature back to 400°F. Add the red onion & season to taste with both the lemon zest & fleur de sel combination, Aleppo pepper, kosher salt, and black pepper, whereas the potatoes are still heated. Gently toss to coat.

Serve immediately, garnished with fresh parsley. Enjoy.

4.112 Roasted Jalapeño Poppers

Total Time: 45 min, Servings: 2
Ingredients
Center-Cut Bacon (Divided), 8 Slices
Cream Cheese, 2 Cup
Sharp Cheddar Cheese (Shredded), 2 Ounce
Green Onions (Minced), 1/2 Cup
Fresh Lime Juice, 2 tsp
Tomato (Seeded, Chopped), 4 tbsp
Fresh Chopped Cilantro, 4 tbsp
Kosher Salt, 1/2 tsp
Cloves Garlic (Minced), 2 Small
Jalapeños, 12 Whole
Instructions
Preheat the Pit Boss to 350°F for 15 minutes with the lid closed when ready to cook.

Put 2 slices of bacon directly on the grill & cook for 10 - 15 minutes, turning halfway through, till the cooked through & crispy. Remove the steaks off the grill and leave the grill turned on. When the bacon is cold enough to handle, roughly cut it.

Combine cheddar cheese, cream cheese, chopped bacon, green onions, garlic, salt, lime juice, cilantro, & tomatoes in the bowl of a stand mixer. With a paddle, mix on a medium speed till everything is incorporated. Fill a piping bag halfway with the mixture.

Cut out the tops off the jalapenos & use a tiny paring knife to remove the seeds & ribs.

Pipe the mixture into each pepper, leaving a 1/4 inch of space between the filling and the pepper's top. Return the tops to each pepper.

Flatten the remaining six pieces of bacon with a rolling pin till they are 1/8 inch thick. Each slice should be cut in half. Each pepper should be wrapped with half a bacon slice and secured with a toothpick.

Fill the Pit Boss Jalapeno Popper Tray with the peppers. Cook for 30 - 40 mins, or

till the peppers are soft, the bacon is crispy, and the cheese is melted, directly on grill. Enjoy.

4.113 Roasted Asparagus

Total Time: 35 min, Servings: 4
Ingredients
Asparagus, 1 bunch
Olive oil, 2 tbsp (add more as needed)
Pit Boss veggie rub
Instructions
Toss asparagus with "olive oil" and "Pit Boss Veggie Rub", making sure all pieces are evenly coated.

When ready to prepare, preheat the Pit Boss to 350°F for fifteen min with the lid closed.

Grill asparagus for 15-20 minutes straight on the grill grate. Take it out of the Pit Boss and enjoy it.

4.114 Blistered Curry Cauliflower

Total Time: 35 min, Servings: 4
Ingredients
Head Cauliflower, 1 Whole
Olive Oil (Extra-Virgin), 2 Tbsp
Garlic (Grated), 1 Clove
Curry Powder, 1 Tsp
Ground Turmeric, 1/2 Tsp
Kosher Salt, 1/2 Tsp (add More As Needed)
Black Pepper (Freshly Ground), 1/2 Tsp (add More As Needed)
Salted Almonds (Chopped & Roasted), 1/3 Cup
Currants (Rehydrated & Drained), 1/4 Cup
Fresh Mint (Chopped), 1/4 Cup
Lime Zest, 2 Tsp
Sherry Vinegar, 3 Tbsp
Dijon Mustard, 1 Tbsp
Garlic Peeled, 3 Clove
Parsley Leaves (Loosely Packed), 2 Cup
Mint/Basil Leaves, (Loosely Packed), 2 Cup
Olive Oil (Extra-Virgin), 3/4 Cup
Black Pepper
Kosher Salt
Instructions
Preheat Pit Boss to 450°F & cook for 15 minutes with lid covered until ready to cook.

Cut the "cauliflower florets" into 1/2-inch pieces after removing its core from the head.

In a large mixing bowl, combine the oil, cauliflower, garlic, turmeric, curry powder, salt, and pepper. Toss the cauliflower until it is uniformly covered. Spread all cauliflower out evenly on the large baking sheet, being careful not to overcrowd it.

Put the "sheet pan" on the grill grate & roast for 15 to 20 minutes, rotating halfway through, till the cauliflower is soft and golden brown.

In the meantime, create the Haas Sauce, often known as chimichurri. In the food processor, combine the vinegar, mustard, and garlic cloves. Pulse a few times to mix the ingredients & break up the garlic.

Add the herbs & pulse till finely chopped, scraping down the sides once. Pour in olive oil and pulse till the herbs are roughly minced and the sauce has thickened. If preferred, season with up to 1 tsp of salt & a pinch of pepper. If you want a lighter sauce, add a tbsp of water or more olive oil.

Toss the cauliflower with the currants, almonds, mint, & lime zest once it has been removed from the grill. Salt & pepper to taste. With a drizzle of Haas Sauce, serve hot or at room temperature. Enjoy.

4.115 Baked Salt-Crusted Potatoes

Total Time: 1 hour 15 min, Servings: 4
Ingredients
Russet Potatoes (Scrubbed & Dried), 6
Canola Oil, 3 tbsp
Kosher Salt, 1 tbsp
Butter
Sour Cream
Chives, Fresh
Bacon Bits
Cheddar Cheese
Instructions
Toss the potatoes in the canola oil & season well with salt in a large mixing basin.

When ready to prepare, preheat the Pit Boss to 450°F with the lid closed for about 15 minutes.

Bake the potatoes straight on the grill grate for at least 30-40 minutes, or until tender when poked with a fork in the center.
Serve with a heaping helping of your favorite toppings. Enjoy

4.116 Smoked Pasta Salad

Total Time: 50 min, Servings: 8
Ingredients
Mozzarella cheese, 8 ounces
Spicy salami (like capocollo) soppressata/pepperoni, 1 pound
Roasted red peppers (sliced), 1 jar
Cherry tomatoes (sliced), 3 cups
Black olives, 3/4 cup
Flat-leaf parsley (chopped), 1/4 cup
Red onion (diced), 1
Jarred pepperoncini peppers (thinly sliced)
Rotini pasta, 1 pound
Red wine vinegar, 1/2 cup
Olive oil (extra-virgin), 1/2 cup
Garlic (minced), 3 cloves
Honey, 1 tbsp
Italian seasoning (finely crumbled), 1 tbsp
Black pepper
Kosher salt
Instructions
Preheat oven to 180°F and leave the lid closed for fifteen min when ready to cook. If Super Smoke is available, use it for the best flavor.
Arrange all of the ingredients on a sheet tray, except the pasta. Place the tray on the grill for 10 minutes to smoke. Remove the steaks from the grill and set them aside.
Bring a big saucepan of water to a rolling boil over high heat. To the water, add a heaping tablespoon of salt. Cook the dry pasta according to the package directions for al dente.
When the pasta is cooking, mix together all of the vinaigrette ingredients in a small dish and put them aside.
Drain the pasta and rinse it in a strainer with cold water. Remove the excess water from the pasta and set it in a large bowl.
Chop all of the salad ingredients into small pieces. Combine all of the ingredients in a mixing bowl with the pasta. Toss the Salad in the vinaigrette to evenly coat it. As needed, season with salt & pepper.
Allow chilling in the refrigerator for 30 mins before serving. Enjoy.

4.117 Smoked Pumpkin Soup
Total Time: 2 hours 15 min, Servings: 6
Ingredients
Whole pumpkin, 5 pound
Butter, 3 tbsp
Onion (diced), 1
Garlic (minced), 2 cloves
Brown sugar, 1 tbsp
Paprika, 1 tsp
Ground cinnamon, 1/4 tsp
Ground nutmeg, 1/8 tsp
Ground allspice, 1/8 tsp
Apple cider, 1/2 cup
Chicken broth, 5 cups
Whipped cream, 1/2 cup
Fresh parsley
Instructions
Cut the pumpkins into quarters using a strong knife. Remove the seeds & stringy threads using a spoon. If desired, extract the seeds from fibers & reserve the seeds for roasting.
When ready to cook, heat Pit Boss grill to 165 degrees Fahrenheit with the lid closed.
Place the pumpkin quarters immediately on the grill grate, skin-side down. 1 hour of smoking
Preheat the oven to 300°F & roast the pumpkin for 90 minutes, or until it is soft and easily punctured with a fork. Allow cooling before removing the pumpkin meat from the skin.
In a 4-quart saucepan or stockpot, melt the butter over medium-high heat.
Cook the garlic and onions for approximately 5 minutes, or until tender and transparent.
Combine the smoked paprika, brown sugar, cinnamon, nutmeg, & allspice in a large mixing bowl. Add additional apple cider right away and simmer for a few minutes, or till the mixture gets reduced & syrupy.
Combine the pumpkin & chicken broth in a mixing bowl. Allow 20 - 30 minutes for the soup to boil.
Puree the soup in a blender or with a hand-held immersion blender until smooth. Season to taste with salt and pepper. If the sauce is too thick, add more chicken broth.
To serve, ladle the soup into the bowls & top with heavy cream. If preferred, garnish with a bunch of parsley.

4.118 Fennel with Romesco & Grilled Baby Carrots
Total Time: 1 hour 15 min, Servings: 8
Ingredients
Regular carrots with tops on or slender rainbow carrots, 1 pound
Fennel bulbs, stalks & cores removed & halved, 2
Fingerling potatoes (washed & halved lengthwise), 1 pound
Olive oil, 1/4 cup
Kosher salt
Thyme/rosemary leaves, 1 tbsp
Instructions
When ready to prepare, preheat the Pit Boss to 500°F with lid closed for about 15 minutes.
Cut the tops of the carrots to 1" in length. Peel the carrots & cut them in half if they're too big, so they're all approximately 1/2 inch thick. Fennel bulbs should be cut lengthwise into the 1/2" thick slices. In a large mixing basin, combine the carrots, fennel, and potato pieces. Drizzle using olive oil & season with a good
pinch of salt. Toss to evenly coat the veggies with the oil.
Arrange the veggies on a baking sheet. Add a few herbs sprigs to the veggies as well.
Put the pan directly on the grate and cook, occasionally stirring, for 35 - 45 minutes, or till the vegetables are browned & softened. Cool before serving with some Smoked Romesco Sauce. Enjoy.

4.119 Rosemary & Mashed Thyme-Infused Potatoes with Cream
Total Time: 1 hour 20 min, Servings: 6
Ingredients
4 russet potatoes, 1/2 pound
Water, 1/2 cup
Heavy cream, 1 pint
Sprig rosemary (fresh), 2
Sprig fresh thyme, 3 add more for garnish
Sage leaves, 6
Black peppercorn, 6 whole
Garlic (peeled & chopped), 2 clove
Unsalted butter (softened), 2 stick
Kosher salt
Ground black pepper
Instructions
Preheat the Pit Boss to 350°F for 15 minutes with the lid closed when ready to cook.
Peel and wash the potatoes before cutting them into 1-inch cubes for the mashed potatoes. Cook for about one hour until its fork tender in an (oven-safe) dish with 1/2 cups water.
In a small saucepan, mix the cream, herbs, peppercorns, and garlic cloves while the potato is boiling. Put on the grill, cover, and let for 15 minutes to steep.

Strain the cream to exclude the herbs & garlic, then return it to a saucepan & keep it heated on the fire.

Drain, then rice the potatoes in a large stockpot with a potato ricer and food mill. 2/3 of cream should be poured slowly, followed by 1 stick of butter and a spoonful of salt. To get the correct consistency, add extra cream, butter, and salt as needed.

Serve warm or keep warm in a slow cooker tuned to the lowest heat or over a water bath. Enjoy.

4.120 Roasted Hasselback Potatoes
Total Time: 2 hours 30 min, Servings: 6
Ingredients
Russet potatoes, 6 large
Bacon, 1 pound
Butter, 1/2 cup
Salt
Black pepper
Cheddar cheese, 1 cup
Scallions, 3 whole
Instructions
Place 2 wooden spoons from either side of the potato to chop it (this will prevent the knife from going all the way through). Slice the potato into thin chips, leaving approximately 1/4" of the bottom intact.

Freeze the bacon slices for thirty min before cutting into little stamp-sized pieces. Place them between each slice in the crevices.

In a big cast iron pan, place the potato. Hard butter slices should be placed on top of the potato. Salt & pepper to taste. When ready to prepare, preheat the Pit Boss to 350°F for 15 minutes with the lid closed.

Cook for two hours with the iron straight on the grill grate. More butter on top of the potatoes, then baste every 30 minutes with melted butter.

Sprinkle with cheddar cheese in the last ten min of grilling and return to the grill to melt.

Toss with chives/scallions to finish. Enjoy.

4.121 Mashed Red Potatoes
Total Time: 55 min, Servings: 4
Ingredients
Red potatoes, 8 large
Salt
Black pepper
Heavy cream, 1/2 cup
Butter, 1/4 cup
Instructions
Preheat oven to 180°F and leave the lid closed for fifteen min when ready to cook.

Quarter red potatoes by slicing them in half lengthwise and then in half again. Using salt and pepper, season the potatoes. Turn the heat up to High & preheat the oven. Set the potatoes straight on the grate once the grill grate is heated.

Flip the potatoes every 15 minutes to achieve even color distribution. Carry on in this manner until the potatoes are the fork-tender.

Mash potatoes with some cream, butter, salt, & pepper to taste until soft. Warm it up and enjoy it!

4.122 Garlic Duchess Potatoes Baked
Total Time: 1 hour 30 min, Servings: 8
Ingredients
Yukon Gold Potatoes, 12 Medium
Salt
Egg Yolk, 5 Large
Garlic (Minced), 2 Clove
Heavy Cream, 1.24 Cup
Sour Cream, 3/4 Cup
Butter (Melted), 10 tbsp
Black Pepper
Instructions
Fill a big saucepan halfway with water and add the potatoes. Season with salt and pepper. Over medium-high heat, bring to a boil.

Reduce heat to low and cook for 25 - 35 minutes, till a paring knife easily slips into potatoes. Drain and set aside to cool.

When ready to prepare, preheat the Pit Boss to 450°F for 15 minutes with the lid closed.

In a large mixing bowl, whisk together the garlic, egg yolks, cream, sour, butter, & pepper. Season with salt & pepper.

Peel potatoes and press flesh into basin with egg mixture using a ricer or food mill. Carefully fold in egg mixture, taking care not to overmix it.

Transfer it to a 3-quart baking dish & bake for 30–40 minutes, or till golden brown & slightly puffed. Enjoy!

4.123 Baked Sweet & Savory Yams
Total Time: 1 hour 30 min, Servings: 6
Ingredients
Yams, 3 medium
Olive Oil (Extra-Virgin), 3 tbsp
Honey
Goat Cheese
Brown Sugar, 1/2 Cup
Pecans (Finely Chopped), 1/2 Cup
Instructions
Preheat the oven to 350°F and leave the lid covered for 15 minutes when ready to cook.

While the Pit Boss heats up, wash the yams & punch a few holes all over them. Wrap the yams in foil to keep them warm. Bake for 45-60 minutes, or until the meat is tender when pierced with a knife. Since you want to be able to cut every yam into rounds, you don't want to overcook them and make them too soft.

When the yams are cool enough to handle, cut them into 1/4" circles. Place each round on a sheet tray and lightly coat with olive oil.

Sprinkle brown sugar on top of each serving. Place an appropriate amount of the goat cheese on every round using a teaspoon. After that, sprinkle chopped pecans on top. Finally, sprinkle each circle with Bee Local honey.

Add additional brown sugar & honey to taste, depending about how sweet you prefer your yams.

Return your sheet tray to the Pit Boss & cook for another 20 mins with the lid closed. Enjoy!

4.124 Sweet Baked Potato Casserole along with Marshmallow Fluff
Total Time: 1 hour 10 min, Servings: 6
Ingredients
Sweet potatoes, 3 pound
Milk, 1/2 cup
Brown sugar, 1 cup
Eggs, 3
Butter, 4 tbsp
Salt, 1/2 tsp
Egg white, 3
Salt, 1 pinch
Ground cinnamon, 1 pinch
Instructions
Preheat the Pit Boss to 375°F for 15 minutes with the lid closed when ready to cook.

Rinse, dry, and puncture the sweet potatoes before placing them whole on the grill. Cook for 45 minutes, or until the potatoes are fork-tender. Remove the chicken from the grill and skin it.

When peeled, mash the sweet potato with the brown sugar, milk, eggs, butter, and salt in a large mixing dish. Cook for about 35 minutes in some kind of a baking dish with mashed potatoes.

Prepare the fluff while the potatoes are baking. Bring a small saucepan of water to a boil, then place bowl of the stand mixer or the other big stainless-steel bowl on top of the water to create a double boiler.

In a mixing bowl, whisk together the Three egg whites, brown sugar (2/3 cup), a sprinkle of salt, & a pinch of cinnamon till the sugar dissolves & the mixture is warm to the touch.

Move the bowl from the stove to your stand mixer & beat the whites on moderate flame with the whisk attachment until glossy and firm peaks form about 5-8 minutes.

When the casserole is done baking, use a "rubber spatula" to spread the fluff over the "sweet potato" mixture. To make dramatic peaks, use the "back" of the spatula.

Return to the grill for another 5-7 mins, just until the fluff becomes golden & the peaks are just beginning to burn. Take it off the grill and enjoy it!

4.125 Romaine Caesar Salad Grilled

Total Time: 10 min, Servings: 4
Ingredients
Garlic, 2 clove
Dijon mustard, 1 tsp
Parmesan cheese, 1/4 cup add more for serving
Mayonnaise, 1 cup
Worcestershire sauce, 1 tsp
Salt, 1/4 tsp
Pepper
Olive oil (extra-virgin), 1/4 cup
Head romaine lettuce, 2
Canola oil
Croutons, for serving
Instructions
To make the dressing in a food processor or blender, combine the Parmesan cheese, Dijon mustard, garlic, Worcestershire sauce, mayonnaise, salt, & pepper, then gently drizzle in the olive oil until smooth. Refrigerate.
To keep the romaine from falling apart, cut it in half lengthwise, keeping the ends intact.
Rinse and dry the romaine lettuce. When ready to prepare, preheat the Pit Boss to 500°F with the lid closed for about 15 minutes.
Brush Romaine halves (with canola oil) & lay cut side down on the grill for a few seconds, just until light grill marks appear.
Add dressing, Parmesan, and croutons to the top. Enjoy.

4.126 Roasted Wild Salmon Along with Cauliflower Pickled Salad

Total Time: 1 hour 10 min, Servings: 6
Ingredients
Head cauliflower (cut into florets), 1
Golden raisins, 1/2 cup
Jarred pepperoncini peppers, 8 pieces
Red bell pepper, 1 large
Yellow onion, 1 small
Sugar, 1/3 cup
Peppercorns, 2 tbsp
Red wine vinegar, 3/4 cup
Dried bay leaves, 3 whole
Dried oregano, 2 tbsp
Thyme leaves, 2 tbsp
Olive oil (extra-virgin), 3/4 cup
Garlic (thinly sliced), 3 cloves
Fresh parsley, 1 tsp
Fresh dill, 1 tsp
Lemon juice, 3 tsp
Salt
Black pepper
Skin-on salmon fillet, 3 pounds (1-1/2 to 2 lb)
Instructions
Boil a big pot of (salted) water for the pasta. Cook for 2-4 minutes, or until cauliflower is soft. Transfer the cauliflower to the bowl of ice water with a slotted spoon. Carry on with the bell peppers.
Drain veggies and combine with pepperoncini, raisins, & onions in a mixing bowl. In a medium bowl over medium-high heat, heat the oil and garlic. Cook until the mixture is aromatic. Add sugar, vinegar, peppercorns, bay leaves & bring to a boil. Cook for 1-2 minutes, or until the sugar has dissolved. Combine oregano and thyme in a bowl and pour over vegetables. Toss to blend. Allow sitting for 10 minutes at room temperature before chilling.
When ready to prepare, set temp. To 375°F & preheat, lid covered for 15 minutes.
Combine olive oil, parsley, garlic, dill, and lemon juice in a small bowl. Brush the mixture all around the salmon and season to taste with salt and pepper.
Place the salmon directly on the grill grate and cook for 20 to 25 minutes, or till an instant-read thermometer is placed and in the thickest part of the flesh registers 145°F and the meat readily flakes. Remove the grill from the heat.
Serve immediately with a salad of pickled cauliflower. Enjoy.

4.127 Breakfast Mini Quiches Baked

Total Time: 30 min, Servings: 8
Ingredients
Cooking spray
Olive oil (extra-virgin), 1 tbsp
Yellow onion (diced), 1/2
Spinach (fresh), 3 cup
Eggs, 10
Shredded cheddar (mozzarella/swiss cheese), 4 ounce
Fresh basil, 1/4 cup
Kosher salt, 1 tsp
Black pepper, 1/2 tsp
Instructions
Lightly coat a 12-cup muffin pan with cooking spray.
Warm the oil in a small pan over medium heat. Cook, often turning until the onion is softened, approximately 7 minutes. Cook for another minute or until the spinach has wilted.
Allow cooling on a cutting board before chopping the mixture to break up the spinach.
When ready to prepare, preheat the grill to 350°F with the lid closed for fifteen min.
Whisk the eggs in a large mixing bowl until frothy. Combine the cooled onions &spinach, cheese, basil, 1 tsp salt, and 1/2 tsp pepper in a mixing bowl. To mix, stir everything together. Evenly distribute the egg mixture among the muffin cups.
Place the dish on the grill & bake for 18 to 20 minutes, or till the eggs have swelled up, are set, & are beginning to color.
Serve right away, or cool completely on a wire rack before storing in a sealed jar for up to four days. Enjoy.

4.128 Butternut Roasted Squash Soup

Total Time: 1 hour 20 min, Servings: 4
Ingredients
Butternut squash, 2 pound

Olive oil (extra-virgin)
Pit Boss veggie rub
Apples, 1/2 whole
Onion (diced), 1/2 whole
Butter, 1 tbsp
Sage leaves, 4
Salt, 2 tsp
Black pepper, 1/2 tsp
Chicken broth, 1 1/2 cup
Water, 1 cup
Heavy cream, 1/3 cup
Ground nutmeg, 1/4 tsp
Pumpkin seeds, 1/2 cup
Bacon bits, 1/4 cup
Sour cream, 2 tbsp
Instructions
When ready to prepare, preheat the grill on high for 15 minutes with the lid covered.
Cut two big sheets of aluminum foil & place one squash half on each. Drizzle oil over each half's sliced side and season with Veggie rub.
Cook for 45 - 50 minutes, or when the squash is tender & the flesh is scoopable, on the grill grate.
Peel, core, and chop the apple into moderate dice in the meanwhile. The onion should be diced into medium-sized pieces. In a large pot or Dutch oven, melt the tbsp of butter over medium heat. Season with salt and pepper and simmer, occasionally turning, until the apple, onion, & sage are cooked for about 7 minutes. Turn off the heat & set the pan aside.
Place the baking pan on a wire rack to cool till the squash is cold enough to handle. Scoop the meat into the pot with the apples and onions that have been sautéed; discard the skins. Stir in the broth, water, & seasonings to taste, then bring to the boil over moderate flame.
Reduce the heat to low and continue to cook, stirring periodically & breaking up any large chunks of squash, for approximately 15 minutes, with the lid closed.
Turn off the heat, remove all of the sage leaves, and mix in the cream & nutmeg if using. Purée the soup in stages in a blender until smooth, covering the area with towel after removing the tiny cap from the blender lid (the pour lid) (this permits steam to escape & stops the lid from popping off). Alternatively, puree the mixture with an immersion blender until smooth.
Season with salt n pepper if necessary. Serve with a sprinkling of pumpkin seeds, bacon, & sour cream, if desired. Enjoy

4.129 Grilled Veggie Burgers along with Lentils & Walnuts

Total Time: 30 min, Servings: 4
Ingredients
Dried Green Lentils, 3/4 Cup
Ground Flaxseed, 1 tbsp
Onion (Diced), 1
Olive Oil (Extra-Virgin), 2 tbsp
Garlic (Minced), 2 Clove
Salt
Black Pepper
Breadcrumbs, 3/4 Cup
Ground Cumin, 1 tsp
Paprika, 1 tsp
Toasted Walnuts, 1 Cup
Hamburger Buns, 6
Instructions
A medium saucepan of water should be brought to a boil. Cook the lentils for around 15 minutes or until they are tender. Drain the water and set it aside.
Combine the flaxseed and 4 tbsp of water in a small dish. Allow 5 minutes for the mixture to rest.
Add the onion & olive oil to a medium sauté pan over medium heat. Cook for 4 to 6 minutes, or until onion is transparent. Cook for yet another 30 seconds after adding the garlic and a sprinkle of salt and pepper.
In the bowl of a food processor, combine the onion and garlic combination, 3/4 cup lentils, flaxseed, cumin, breadcrumbs, paprika, & toasted walnuts.
Pulse until the mixture is smooth & well-combined. If the mixture is dry, gradually add 1 tbsp of water until it comes together. In a separate bowl, combine the remaining lentils.
Place the lentil mixture on a parchment-lined dish in 4 to 6 patties. Refrigerate for at least 30 min or up to 24h after making the patties.
When you're ready to cook, fire up the Pit Boss as per the manufacturer's directions. Preheat the oven to 425°F and cook for 10-15 minutes with the lid covered.
Grill the vegetable burgers for 8–10 minutes on each side, turning halfway.
Burgers should be served on toasted hamburger buns with lettuce, tomato ketchup, & mayonnaise on top. Enjoy.

4.130 Hummus (Smoked) with Roasted Vegetables

Total Time: 55 min, Servings: 4
Ingredients
Chickpeas, 1 1/2 cup
Tahini, 1/3 cup
Garlic (minced), 1 tbsp
Olive oil (extra-virgin), 6 tbsp
Salt, 1 tsp
Lemon juice, 4 tbsp
Red onion (sliced), 1.
Butternut squash, 2 cups
Cauliflower (cut into florets), 2 cups.
Fresh brussels sprouts, 2 cups
Portobello mushroom, 2 wholes
Salt
Black pepper
Instructions
Preheat the grill to 180°F and close the cover for 15 minutes when ready to cook.
Drain & rinse the chickpeas, then lay them out on a sheet tray to make the hummus. Place tray on grill grate & smoke for 15-20 minutes, or until desired degree of smoke is achieved.
Combine the smoked chickpeas, olive oil, garlic, tahini, salt, & lemon juice into the bowl of a food processor and process until well combined but not entirely smooth. Place in a dish and set aside.
Preheat the grill and raise the temperature to High.
Drizzle the vegetables with olive oil & spread them out on a sheet tray. Roast the vegetables on a sheet tray in grill for 15-20 minutes, or until gently browned & cooked through.
To serve, spread hummus on a serving plate or bowl & top with roasted vegetables.
Serve with the pita bread & a drizzle of olive oil. Enjoy.

4.131 Roasted Root Vegetables

Total Time: 1 hour, Servings: 6
Ingredients
Red beets (scrubbed & trimmed), 1 bunch
Golden beets (scrubbed & trimmed), 1 bunch
Butternut squash (peeled & seeded), 1
Yam (peeled), 1 large
Carrot (peeled), 1 large
Red onion (peeled), 1 large
Garlic (peeled), 4 clove

Fresh thyme leaves, 3 tbsp
Cinnamon stick, 1
Olive oil (extra-virgin), 3 tbsp
Salt
Black pepper
Honey, 2 tbsp

Instructions

Preheat the Pit Boss to 450°F and cook for 15 minutes with the lid covered when ready to cook.

Thinly slice the veggies into 1/2-inch pieces. Toss the veggies with the thyme leaves, garlic cloves, olive oil, and cinnamon stick in a large mixing basin.

Prepare a baking sheet by lining it with foil. Spread the veggies in a single layer on the baking sheet and season well with salt & pepper.

Roast the veggies for 45 mins or till cooked on the Pit Boss. Transfer to a serving plate and sprinkle honey on top when tender. Serve immediately. Enjoy.

4.132 Sweet Potatoes Marshmallow Hasselback

Total Time: 1 hour 10 min, Servings: 6

Ingredients

Sweet potatoes, 4 large
Butter, 8 tbsp
Salt
Brown sugar, 1/2 cup
Ground nutmeg, 1/4 tsp
1 cup toasted pecans, toasted marshmallows & sprigs (fresh) of thyme for garnish

Instructions

Preheat the Pit Boss on High for 15 minutes with the lid covered when you're ready to cook.

Place a sweet potato horizontally between both the handles of two wooden spoons on a clean, level surface. Thinly slice the potato, leaving 1/4" at the bottom unsliced. The spoon handle will prevent you from completely slicing the potato. Continue with each potato.

Sandwich the potato pieces together with a (thin) slice of butter. Add brown sugar, kosher salt, & nutmeg to taste. Place the potatoes on a grill pan & bake for an hour. The potatoes should be cooked all the way through and have a crispy top. Top each potato with a dab of marshmallow sauce or marshmallow sauce.

To create marshmallow sauce, melt micro marshmallows with 1 tablespoon butter on the pan over medium heat till smooth. If desired, sprinkle with more brown sugar.

Return the pan to the grill for 5-10 minutes more, or when the marshmallows have melted and the brown sugar on top has caramelized. Take it out of the oven and eat it.

4.133 Grilled Corn Salsa

Total Time: 40 min, Servings: 6

Ingredients

Corn Husks, 4 Large
Tomato (Chopped), 4
Cilantro (Chopped), 1/2 Cup
Red Onion (Diced), 1
Garlic Powder, 1 tsp
Onion Powder, 1 tsp
Jalapeño (Seeded, Diced & Grilled), 1
Lime (Juiced), 1
Salt
Black Pepper

Instructions

Preheat the Pit Boss on High for 15 minutes with the lid covered when you're ready to cook.

Grill the corn until it is completely roasted, then remove the "husk" and chop the kernels off the cob.

Toss the corn with both the remaining ingredients in a bowl and chill until ready to serve. Serve with some chips or as a complement to your favorite fiesta dish. Enjoy.

4.134 Green Bean Casserole Baked with Pulled Pork

Total Time: 1 hour 15 min, Servings: 6

Ingredients

Green beans (fresh), 2 pound
Kosher salt
Olive oil (extra-virgin), 2 tbsp
Cremini mushrooms (sliced & divided), 1 pound
Butter, 6 tbsp
Sprig fresh thyme, 4
All-purpose flour, 2 tbsp
Whole milk, 1 1/4 cup
Heavy cream, 1 cup
Garlic (minced), 4 clove
Parmesan cheese, 1/2 cup
Ground black pepper
Leftover pulled pork, 1 pound
French's original - crispy fried onions, 3/4 cup

Instructions

Preheat the Pit Boss to 375°F for 15 minutes with the lid closed when ready to cook.

Cook the green beans in a big saucepan of boiling salted water, working in batches, until brilliant green and halfway tender, about 3 mins per batch. Drain and set aside to cool. Trim the ends of the stems.

In a large skillet, heat 1 tablespoon of oil over medium-high heat. Cook, occasionally stirring until half of mushrooms are golden brown, approximately
2 minutes. Toss and cook for another 3 minutes, or until both sides are browned.

Add 2 tbsp butter & 2 thyme sprigs to the pan. Cook for another 4 minutes, turning periodically until the butter has browned and the mushrooms are dark brown & soft. Transfer to a dish and season with salt. Repeat with the remaining butter, salt, and oil, as well as the mushrooms and thyme.

In a big saucepan over medium-low heat, melt the remaining 2 tablespoons butter. Cook, whisking periodically until the roux is golden brown & nutty smelling, about 4 minutes. In a separate bowl, whisk together the milk and cream.

Increase the heat to medium-low and cook, often whisking, until the sauce is thick & boiling for approximately 5 minutes. Remove the pan from the heat and stir in the garlic and parmesan cheese. Salt & pepper to taste.

In a 2-quart baking dish, layer pulled pork, green beans, & mushrooms. Pour the sauce over top.

Cover securely with foil & bake for 25-30 minutes, or until sauce is boiling. Uncover and bake for another 15-20 minutes, or until the top and sides of the dish are gently browned.

Top with fried onions and bake for another 3 minutes, or till onions are slightly darker & aromatic. Allow 10 minutes for the sauce to solidify before serving. Enjoy.

4.135 Red Pepper White Roasted Bean Dip

Total Time: 45 min, Servings: 4

Ingredients

Garlic, 4 whole
Olive oil (extra-virgin), 4 tbsp
Red bell pepper, 2
Fresh dill, 3 tbsp
Flat-leaf parsley (chopped), 3 tbsp
Cannellini beans (mashed), 2 can
Lemon juice, 4 tsp

Salt, 1/2 tsp
Instructions
Roasting the red peppers and garlic:
When ready to prepare, preheat the oven to 400 ° F (205 ° C) with the lid closed for fifteen min.
Peel the garlic husk's outer layers away. Remove the top of the garlic bulb to reveal each clove. Apply olive oil to the top of the garlic head & massage it in. Wrap the garlic cloves in foil to thoroughly encase it. On the
Pit Boss, place the garlic head & two red peppers (washed & dried).
Roast the peppers for around 40 minutes and the garlic for 25-30 minutes. Every 10 minutes rotate the pepper a quarter turn till the exterior is blistered & browned.
Remove the peppers from the grill and place them in a mixing dish. Leave the bowl covered in plastic wrap for 15 minutes. The steam would loosen the skins, allowing them to slide off like a barbecued drumstick.
Remove the skin off the pepper. Cut the stems off & scrape out the seeds, and you're good to go.
Allow the garlic to cool before removing the single cloves as needed.
Take a dip:
Combine the (roasted) red peppers, 4 garlic cloves, dill, parsley, drained & olive oil, rinsed beans, lemon juice, and salt in a blender.
Puree the dip until it is smooth & creamy. You may have to scrape along the edges of the mixer a few times. If it's not mixing well or appears to be overly thick, add additional olive oil/lemon juice. (If you think it needs more acid or brightness, add additional lemon juice.) Enjoy.

4.136 Homemade Smoked Ketchup
Total Time: 1 hour 5 min, Servings: 8
Ingredients
Olive oil (divided), 2 tbsp
Whole peeled tomatoes, 2 cans (28 oz)
Garlic, 3 clove
Yellow onion (peeled & quartered), 1
Tomato paste, 2 tbsp
Apple cider vinegar, 1/4 cup
Worcestershire sauce, 2 tbsp
Ground cloves, 1/8 tsp
Cayenne pepper, 1/4 tsp
Brown sugar, 4 tbsp
Salt
Instructions
Preheat Pit Boss to 225°F and cook for 15 minutes with lid covered until ready to cook. If Super Smoke is available, use it for the best flavor.
Toss the tomatoes with 1 tablespoon of olive oil and lay them out on a baking sheet.
Smoke for 60 minutes by placing the tray on the grate. Remove the steaks from the grill & set them aside.
In a separate saucepan, heat the remaining olive oil over medium heat. Cook for 1 minute after adding the onion and garlic.
Stir in the tomato paste and simmer for another minute, or until it becomes a rusty color.
Add smoked tomatoes & apple cider vinegar and Worcestershire sauce to deglaze the pan.
Using a wooden spoon, stir to scrape up all of the pieces from the bottom of the pan. Bring to a simmer with the ground cloves & cayenne pepper.
Cook for 20 minutes, or until it coats the spoon's back.
Stir in the brown sugar until it is completely combined.
Puree the ingredients in a blender until it is completely smooth.
Season with salt and pepper to taste.

Cool in a storage container before transferring to the refrigerator.
Serve with hamburgers, hot dogs, and fries as a side dish. Enjoy.

4.137 Baked Creamed Spinach
Total Time: 1 hour 5 min, Servings: 8
Ingredients
Butter, 2 tbsp
Shallot (finely chopped), 1
Garlic, 2 clove
Red pepper flakes, 1 tsp
Heavy cream, 1/2 cup
Ground nutmeg, 1 tsp
Salt
Black pepper
Package frozen spinach (thawed & drained), 2 (10 oz)
Sour cream, 3/4 cup
Parmesan cheese, 1/2 cup
Romano cheese, 1/2 cup
Panko breadcrumbs, 1/2 cup
Instructions
Melt butter in the saucepan over moderate heat & cook shallot and garlic. Cook for approximately 3 minutes. Cook for another 2 minutes after adding the Chile flakes.
Bring the cream and nutmeg to a boil. Season with salt & pepper to taste.
Stir in the spinach & sour cream, & season to taste. Remove the pan from the heat and whisk in the cheeses.
Pour the mixture into a baking dish & sprinkle the panko on top.
When ready to prepare, preheat the grill to 375°F with the lid covered for 15 minutes.
Bake for 25-30 minutes, until the top, is golden and bubbling, directly on the grate. Enjoy.

4.138 Carrots along with Pistachio & Pomegranate Relish Roasted
Total Time: 40 min, Servings: 6
Ingredients
Rainbow carrots, 2 bunch
Kosher salt, 2 tsp
Fennel seed, 2 tsp
Sugar, 1 tsp
Coriander, 1 tsp
Cumin, 1/2 tsp
Olive oil (extra-virgin), 2 tbsp
Garlic (grated / finely chopped), 2 clove
Lime (zested), 1
Extra-virgin olive oil, 1/3 cup
Pomegranate seeds, 1/2 cup
Chopped pistachios, 1/2 cup
Chopped mint, 1/4 cup
Flat-leaf Italian (chopped) parsley, 1/4 cup
Salt
Lime (juiced), 1
Instructions
Preheat Pit Boss to 450°F and cook for 15 minutes with lid covered until ready to cook.
Thoroughly wash the carrots to eliminate any dirt, but leave the skins on. In a small bowl, combine the spices, sugar, and salt. Toss the carrots in 2 tablespoons olive oil to evenly coat, then add the garlic & spice combination. Toss to evenly coat. Arrange on a big sheet tray & roast for 30 minutes on the Pit Boss, rotating once. Remove the carrots from the grill when they can easily be punctured with a fork. Lastly, grate the lime zest over top.
To prepare the Pistachio & Pomegranate Relish, follow these steps: 1/3 cup) olive oil, pomegranate seeds, pistachios, herbs,

lime juice, and a large sprinkle salt are mixed. Season to taste, and if required, add additional spice.
Arrange the carrots on even a serving dish when ready to serve. Pour a large quantity of the Parsley and Pomegranate Relish and over carrots' center, and serve the remainder on the side. Enjoy.

4.139 Smoked Scalloped Potatoes
Total Time: 1 hour 10 min, Servings: 6
Ingredients
2 Tablespoon Butter, Softened
1 cup Heavy Cream
1/2 Cup Milk
2 Tablespoon Flour
2 Clove Garlic, Chopped
4 Russet Potatoes, Peeled And Thinly Sliced
Kosher Salt
Coarse Ground Black Pepper
1/2 Cup Grated Medium Cheddar Cheese
1/2 Cup Grated Sharp White Cheddar
Instructions
Preheat the Pit Boss to 375 ° F. & cook for fifteen min with the lid covered when ready to cook.
Coat the bottom & sides of a 9-inch cast-iron pan with butter.
In a mixing dish, combine the flour, milk, cream, & garlic.
In a pan, layer 1/4 of the potatoes, season with salt and pepper, then pour 1/4 of the "sauce mixture" over the potatoes. Rep three times more.
Cook potatoes for 50 minutes on the grill.
Evenly sprinkle both kinds of cheese over the potatoes & cook for a further 10 minutes, or until fork-tender.
Take the burgers from the grill and serve. Enjoy.

4.140 Famous Chef Curtis' Chimichurri Sauce
Total Time: 10 min, Servings: 4
Ingredients
Lemon (halved), 2 whole
Flat-leaf Italian parsley (washed & chopped), 2 medium
Garlic (diced), 4 clove
Red wine vinegar, 1/4 cup
Black pepper, 1/2 tsp
Olive oil (extra-virgin), 1/4 cup
Salt, 1 tsp
Instructions
Preheat Pit Boss to 450°F and cook for 15 minutes with lid covered until ready to cook.
Cook for 5 minutes, or till grill marks emerge, by placing lemon halves straight on the grill grate.
Remove the lemons from the grill and squeeze them. In a blender or food processor, combine all the ingredients and puree until smooth, or leave somewhat lumpy for texture.
If you want a milder flavor, add more olive oil to taste. Serve as a side dish or a dip. Enjoy.

4.141 Maxi Mac & Cheese
Total Time: 40 min, Servings: 4
Ingredients
Cooking Spray
Butter (Melted), 3 tbsp
Tortilla Chips (Finely Crushed), 1 Cup
2 Cup Macaroni, Uncooked
2 Cup Half-And-Half
1 Pound Velveeta Cheese
Instructions
Set aside a 2-quart "casserole dish" o"baking dish" that has been sprayed with the nonstick cooking spray on the inside.
Drizzle the (melted) butter and over tortilla chips & toss to coat. Remove from the equation.
In a saucepan of salted water, cook macaroni according to package directions until just cooked. (Subtract 1 to 2 minutes from the cooking time indicated.) On the Pit Boss, the pasta will continue to cook.
In a colander, drain the macaroni. Return to the burner and stir in the half-and-half. Warm over a low heat setting.
Stir in the cubed cheese until it is completely melted, about 5 minutes.
Return the drained macaroni to the saucepan & stir gently till all clumps are gone, and the macaroni is covered in the cheese sauce.
Pour the macaroni & cheese into the casserole dish that has been prepared.
Evenly sprinkle the greased tortilla chips on top.
When ready to prepare, preheat the oven to 350°F with the lid covered for 15 minutes.
Bake for 35 - 40 mins, or when the cheese sauce is bubbling & the tortilla chip topping is golden brown, with the casserole dish firmly on the grill grate.
Remove from the oven and set aside to cool little before serving. Enjoy.

4.142 Beer-Braised Cabbage along With Bacon
Total Time: 45 min, Servings: 4
Ingredients
Bacon (bulk unsliced), 1/4 pound
Yellow onion (diced), 1 cup
Apple (diced small), 1 cup
Green cabbage, 2 pound
Salt
Ground black pepper
Beer (light), 12 ounce
Instructions
When ready to cook, heat Pit Boss grill to 325 degrees F with the lid closed for 10-15 mins.
Preheat a big heavy pot/Dutch oven over moderate flame on the stovetop. Cook until the bacon is crisp (about 5 mins). Transfer to a paper towel-lined plate.
Return the saucepan to a medium-low heat setting. Cook for about 5 minutes, or till it gets golden brown, after adding the onion. Stir in the apple before adding the cabbage. Stir in a sufficient amount of salt and a pinch of black pepper for 3 minutes.
Over medium-high heat, pour in the beer & bring to a boil. Cover and transfer the pot to the Pit Boss right away.
Bake for 10 minutes at 325 ° F (160 ° C). Remove the top and continue to simmer for another 10-15 minutes, or until the cabbage is soft as well as the liquid has evaporated.
Toss in the saved bacon with the cabbage. Enjoy.

4.143 Southern Grilled Comfort Sweet Potato Fries
Total Time: 55 min, Servings: 2
Ingredients
Sweet potatoes, 2 whole
Olive oil, extra-virgin
Brown sugar, 1 tbsp
Salt
Black pepper
Butter, 1 tbsp
Southern comfort, 1 tsp
Toasted marshmallows, 1 tbsp
Instructions
Preheat the oven to High for 15 minutes with the lid covered when you're ready to cook.

Slice the potatoes (sweet) while this is going on. Your potato should be cut in half and then into tiny wedges. The simpler it is to cook a smaller wedge.

To soften the sweet potatoes, place them in a saucepan of hot water for 3-5 minutes. This way, you won't have to cook the potatoes all day.

Remove the potatoes from the water and blot them with such a paper towel before sprinkling them with oil.

Season with a little of salt & pepper and a sprinkle of brown sugar. Mix thoroughly.

Grill the potatoes that have been seasoned.

Cook the potatoes for 15-20 minutes on high, then turn them & cook for another 10-fifteen min.

Sauce:

Melt the butter in a skillet over medium heat. When the butter is golden brown, add the Southern Comfort and marshmallows to the pan and swirl to combine.

Remove the fries from the grill and glaze them. Enjoy.

4.144 Sheet Pan Roasted Vegetables

Total Time: 35 min, Servings: 4

Ingredients

Head Purple Cauliflower (Stemmed & Cut Into 2" Florets), 1 Small

Head Yellow Cauliflower, (Stemmed & Cut Into 2" Florets), 1 Small

Butternut Squash, 4 Cup

Oyster/Shiitake Mushrooms (Rinsed & Sliced), 2 Cup

Olive Oil, 3 tbsp

Kosher Salt, 2 tsp

Ground Black Pepper (Freshly)

Chopped (Flat-Leaf) Parsley, 1/4 Cup

Instructions

Preheat Pit Boss to 450°F and cook for 15 minutes with lid covered until ready to cook.

Combine all of the veggies in the large mixing basin.

Sprinkle olive oil over the top, then season with kosher salt & freshly ground black pepper.

Toss the veggies with your hands until they are uniformly covered.

Arrange the vegetables on 1 or 2 half-sheet pans or the baking sheets, leaving some space between them. (If they are overcrowded, the veggies will steam rather than roast, and the crispy texture will be lost.)

Cook for fifteen min on the Pit Boss using the sheet pans. Open & stir, then close the top and simmer for another 5 to 15 minutes, or until the veggies are golden around the edges.

Garnish with parsley & serve right away. At room temperature, the veggies are equally excellent. Enjoy.

4.145 Buffalo Blue Cheese Grilled Corn

Total Time: 30 min, Servings: 8

Ingredients

Butter, 1/2 cup

Hot sauce, 1/2 cup

Ear's corn, 8 pieces

Celery salt

Crumbled blue cheese, 1 cup.

Instructions

Preheat the oven too high for 15 minutes with the lid covered when you're ready to cook.

While the grill is heating up, combine the butter & hot sauce inside a small oven-proof pot and set on the grill grate to melt the butter. To mix the ingredients, whisk them together. Remove from the oven and keep warm.

Arrange the corn on the grate cook for 3 to 5 minutes each side, rotating as required with tongs until the corn is gently browned in patches.

Place the corn on a plate, a (disposable) foil pan, or a rimmed baking sheet.

Brush the corn on both sides with butter & spicy sauce mixture, working over the pan.

Lightly season using celery salt, then top with crumbled blue cheese. Serve right away. Enjoy.

4.146 Grilled Veggie Sandwich

Total Time: 1 hour, Servings: 4

Ingredients

Chickpeas, 1/2 cup

Tahini, 1/3 cup

Garlic (minced 0, 1 tbsp

Olive oil, 2 tbsp

Kosher salt, 1 tsp

Lemon juice, 4 tbsp

Eggplant (sliced into strips), 1 small.

Zucchini (sliced into strips), 1 small.

Yellow squash (sliced into strips), 1 small.

Portobello mushroom, 2 large

Olive oil

Lemon juice

Salt n pepper

Ricotta cheese, 1/2 cup

Garlic (minced), 1 clove

Ciabatta buns (for serving), 4 wholes.

Instructions

Preheat oven to 180°F and leave top closed for about 15 minutes when ready to cook.

Drain & rinse the chickpeas, then lay them out on a sheet tray to make the hummus. Place tray on grill grate & smoke for 15-20 minutes, or until desired degree of smoke is achieved.

Combine the smoked chickpeas, garlic, tahini, olive oil, salt, & lemon juice within bowl of a food processor and process until well combined but not entirely smooth. Place in a dish and set aside.

Preheat the grill to High (400-500°F).

Combine the zucchini, eggplant, squash, & portobellos in a mixing bowl with the olive oil & lemon juice, salt, & pepper. Place the vegetables, gill side up, straight on the grill grate. Cook until grill marks appear and the vegetables are soft (10 to 15 mins for sliced veggies, 20 to 25 mins for mushrooms).

In a separate bowl, mix the garlic, lemon juice, ricotta, salt, & pepper while the vegetables are cooking.

Open the ciabatta buns by cutting them in half. On one side, spread hummus, and on the other, ricotta. Stack the grilled vegetables and add tomatoes and basil on top. Enjoy.

4.147 Grilled Corn on Cob with some Parmesan and Garlic

Total Time: 35 min, Servings: 6

Ingredients

Butter (melted), 4 tbsp.

Garlic (minced), 2 cloves

Salt n pepper

Fresh corn, 8 ears

Shaved parmesan, 1/2 cup

Parsley (chopped), 1 tbsp.

Instructions

Preheat the Pit Boss to 450°F & cook for 15 minutes, covered, until ready to use.

Combine the garlic, butter, salt, and pepper in a medium mixing bowl.

Peel the silk off the corn husks and discard it. The corn should be massaged with half of the "garlic butter mixture."

Fold husks in half & place on grill grate right away. Cook for 20 to 25 minutes, stirring occasionally, or till corn is tender.
Take the husks off the grill & throw them away. Serve the corn with the remaining "butter, Parmesan, & parsley" on a serving dish.

4.148 Cast Iron Potatoes

Total Time: 1 hour 10 min, Servings: 4
Ingredients
Butter (cut into cubes), 4 tbsp.
Potatoes peeled & cut into 1/8" slices, 2 1/2 pounds.
Sweet onion (thinly sliced), 1/2 large.
Salt
Black pepper
Mild cheddar/jack cheese (grated), 1 1/2 cup.
Milk, 2 cups
Paprika
Instructions
Butter the interior of a cast-iron skillet and arrange half of potato slices on the bottom. Half of the onions should be on top. Salt & pepper to taste.
Sprinkle 1 cup of cheese and half of the butter over the potatoes & onions. On top, layer the leftover potatoes & onions. Dot the remaining butter on top.
Into the skillet, pour the milk. Aluminum foil should be securely wrapped around the skillet.
When ready to prepare, preheat the Pit Boss to 350°F with the cover closed for fifteen min.
Bake for about 1 hour, or till potatoes are fork-tender.
Take off the foil and sprinkle the remaining half cup of cheese on top. Bake for another 30 minutes, or till the cheese is gently browned (uncovered). Serve immediately with a paprika dusting on top.

4.149 Bacon Green Baked Bean Casserole

Total Time: 1 hour 10 min, Servings: 4
Ingredients
Green beans (fresh), 1/2 pound
Cream of mushroom soup, 1 can
Red bell pepper (diced), 1/4 cup.
Fried onions, 2/3 cup
Milk, 1/2 cup
Worcestershire sauce, 1/2 tsp
Black pepper, 1/2 tsp
Bacon, 8 slices
Instructions
Combine the beans, milk, soup, black pepper, Worcestershire sauce, 2/3 cup onions, 6 pieces crumbled bacon, & red bell pepper in a mixing dish. Fill a 1-half quart casserole dish halfway with the mixture.
When ready to prepare, preheat the Pit Boss to 350°F for 15 minutes with the lid closed.
Bake for 35 to 40 minutes, just until the filling is heated and bubbling.
Cook for 5 - 10 mins more, or till the onions are crisp & beginning to brown, on top of the remaining onions & the last 2 pieces of crumbled bacon. Serve and have fun!

4.150 Pico De Gallo Smoked

Total Time: 40 min, Servings: 4
Ingredients
Diced Roma tomatoes, 3 cups.
Jalapeño (diced), 1.
Red onion (diced), 1/2
Cilantro (finely chopped), 1/2 bunch.
Lime (juiced), 2.
Salt
Olive oil
Instructions
Preheat Pit Boss to 180°F and cook for 15 minutes with lid covered until ready to cook. If Super Smoke is available, use it for the best flavor.
Spread the chopped tomatoes out on a smaller sheet pan in a thin layer. Put the sheet pan straight on the grill for 30 min of smoking.
Toss all items in a medium bowl with lime juice, salt, & olive oil to taste after the tomatoes are done. Serve and have fun.

4.151 Baked Potato Soup Smoked

Total Time: 1 hour 15 min, Servings: 6
Ingredients
Russet potatoes, 6 large
Bacon, 12 ounces
Butter, 4 tbsp
Onion (diced), 1 small.
Flour, 1/4 cup
Milk, 4 cups
Chicken stock, 1 can
Onion powder, 1 tsp
Garlic powder, 1 tsp
Salt, 2 tsp
Sour cream, 1 cup
Instructions
Preheat the Pit Boss to 375°F for 15 minutes with the lid closed when ready to cook.
Use a fork to poke holes in the potatoes and lay them immediately on the grill grate. 1 hour of cooking Cook the bacon on the baking sheet for around 20 minutes simultaneously; remove, cool, & cut into 1/2" slices.
Remove the potatoes from the oven and leave to cool for fifteen min. Peel potatoes well and chop them into 1" pieces. Remove from the equation.
In a big Dutch oven, melt the butter. When the butter is melted and bubbling, add the onion & cook until it is transparent about 5-7 minutes.
Cook for 1 minute with the flour in the butter and onion combination before gradually adding the milk & chicken stock, half cup at a time. Add the onions powder, garlic powder, & 2 tsp salt once all of the liquid has been absorbed. Using a potato masher, mash the potato chunks into the soup until fully integrated but still chunky. Toss in the sour cream & 3/4 of the bacon, saving a little amount for decoration.
Add extra ingredients to the soup and serve it warm. Enjoy.

4.152 Brussels (Smoked & Shredded) Sprout Salad

Total Time: 50 min, Servings: 6
Ingredients
Sweet potato (peeled & cut into ½" cubes), 1.
Parsnips (peeled & cut ½" thick on bias), 2.
Shallots (sliced ¼" thick), 4
Olive oil, 4 tbsp
Kosher salt
Black pepper, freshly ground.
Oranges (halved), 2
Crumbled goat cheese, 4 ounces
Champagne vinegar, 2 tbsp
Brussels sprouts (shaved), 1 pound.
Pomegranate seeds, 3/4 cup
Fresh mint (chopped), 3 tbsp.
Instructions
Preheat Pit Boss to 450°F and cook for 15 minutes with lid covered until ready to cook.
On a baking sheet, combine the sweet potatoes, parsnips,

shallots, & 2 tablespoons olive oil, season with salt & pepper, and toss to coat. In a single layer, spread out the ingredients. Put the baking sheet on grill & cook for 30 minutes, or until the veggies are

golden and crisp. Allow to cool to room temp. On a wire rack. While the veggies are cooking, lay the orange cut side on the grill & cook for about 15 minutes, or until tender and slightly caramelized. Remove the chicken from the grill, cool, and squeeze the juice into the measuring cup, saving 5 tablespoons for the vinaigrette.

To make the vinaigrette, combine the goat cheese, 5 tbsp orange juice, and the vinegar in a food processor or blender and pulse until smooth. Blend in the remaining two tbsp of oil at low speed until incorporated. To taste, season with salt & pepper.

In a large mixing bowl, combine shaved Brussels sprouts & roasted veggies. Toss the salad with the vinaigrette to coat it. Taste and season with additional

salt if necessary. To serve, decorate with pomegranate seeds and mint leaves. Enjoy.

4.153 Asparagus Grilled Along with Wild Mushrooms & Fried Shallots

Total Time: 45 min, Servings: 4
Ingredients
Asparagus (ends trimmed), 2 bunch.
Olive oil (extra-virgin)
Butter, 2 tbsp
Olive oil, 2 tbsp
Mixed wild mushrooms, 4 cups
White wine, 1/4 cup
Lemon (juiced), 1 whole.
Shallot (sliced into rings), 1 large.
Flour, 1/4 cup
Canola oil, 1 cup
Instructions

Preheat the grill to High (or 500 ° F if using the Timberline grill) for 10 - 15 minutes with the lid covered when ready to cook.

In the meantime, cut the thick and woody ends off the asparagus and combine with 2 tablespoons extra virgin olive oil in a mixing dish. Toss the asparagus in the mixture to coat it completely.

Melt 2 tbsp butter & 2 tbsp olive oil in a moderate pan over medium-high heat.

Add the mushrooms to the pan when the butter begins to crackle and foam, toss to coat, distribute evenly in 1 layer (when there

are too many mushrooms in the pan, they will not acquire enough color - if your pan is just too small, cook the mushrooms in stages), and season with salt to taste.

Cook until the mushrooms are well browned on one side, then turn the pan & brown the mushrooms on the other side. Add some wine to the pan after the mushrooms just browned a little more and simmer until it has evaporated. Set the mushrooms aside after sprinkling them with lemon juice.

Heat the high-heat oil in a saucepan or cast-iron skillet over medium-high heat for about five min. In the meantime, put the cut shallots in the flour & toss to coat evenly. Get rid of any surplus flour.

Place one tester shallot in the heated oil and cook until it begins to bubble & sizzle vigorously. Stir in the remaining shallots and sauté until golden brown (about 1-2 minutes), careful not to overheat.

Remove from the oil, drain on paper towels, and season with sea salt right away. Remove from the equation.

Arrange asparagus on the grate immediately. Cook for 5 minutes with the lid closed, or till one side has developed color. Cook for a few minutes more after turning the asparagus, making cautious not to overcook it.

Arrange the asparagus on a serving dish, drizzle with lemon juice, and season with salt. Serve immediately with the mushrooms and fried shallots on top. Enjoy.

4.154 Corned Baked Beef Au Grautin

Total Time: 1 hour 5 min, Servings: 6
Ingredients
Butter (softened), 2 tbsp.
Heavy cream, 1 1/2 cup
Whole milk, 1/2 cup
All-purpose flour, 2 tbsp
Garlic (minced), 4 cloves
Kosher salt, 1 tsp
Black pepper
Russet potatoes, 3 pounds
Yellow onion (thinly sliced), 1 medium.
Corned beef brisket flat (fat cap at least ¼" thick), 1 pound
Instructions

When you're ready to cook, fire up the Pit Boss grill. Until the fire has formed, smoke with lid open (4 - 5 minutes). Preheat the grill to 450 ° F (500 ° F when

using a WiFIRE equipped grill) for 10 - 15 minutes with the lid closed.

Coat the base of a 9" cast iron pan with melted butter. Whisk together flour, milk, cream, minced garlic, salt, & some freshly ground black pepper for taste in a separate basin.

In a pan, combine 1/3 of the potatoes, onions, & corned beef. 1/3 of the cream mixture should be poured over the potatoes. Repeat the process twice more, finishing with the cream mixture.

Cover with foil & bake for thirty min in the Pit Boss. Remove the foil and bake the potatoes for another 20 minutes, or until golden brown & bubbling.

Sprinkle the grated cheese over the potatoes & bake for another 3 to 5 minutes, or until the cheese is melted. Enjoy.

4.155 Smoked 3-Bean Salad

Total Time: 35 min, Servings: 6
Ingredients
Great northern beans (drained & rinsed), 1 can (15 oz)
Kidney beans (drained & rinsed), 1 can (15.5 oz)
Olive oil, 1/4 cup + 1/2 tbsp
Salt n pepper
Shallot (shaved), 1 medium.
Garlic (minced), 1 clove
Red wine vinegar, 2 tbsp
Dijon mustard, 1 tsp
Flat-leaf parsley (chopped & fresh), 1 tbsp, add more for garnish.
Instructions

Preheat Pit Boss to 180°F and cook for 15 minutes with lid covered until ready to cook. If Super Smoke is available, use it for the best flavor.

Spread drained and washed beans straight on the grill grate from a sheet tray.

Fire the beans for about 15 - 20 minutes, or when the appropriate quantity of smoke flavor has developed. Remove the Pit Boss from the oven and set it aside.

Preheat the Pit Boss to 500°F and cook for 15 minutes with the top covered.

Season green beans with salt and pepper to taste and toss with 1/2 tbsp olive oil.

Arrange green beans on the grill and cook for 10 mins, or until tender & charred.

Take the Pit Boss out of the oven and store it in the refrigerator to cool.

Make the dressing while some green beans are cooling. In a small bowl, combine the shallot, garlic, vinegar, and Dijon mustard. Slowly drizzle in 1/4 cup olive oil while whisking until well-integrated. Season with salt & pepper and chopped parsley.

Toss all the beans in a separate dish with the dressing. Season with salt n pepper to taste and serve in a serving dish. If desired, top with additional chopped parsley. Enjoy.

4.156 Grilled Artichokes Along with Sauce Gribiche

Total Time: 1 hour, Servings: 4
Ingredients
Globe artichokes (simmered, cut & cooled), 3 large.
Mayonnaise, 1 cup
Whole milk yogurt, 1 cup
Dill pickle (finely chopped), 2 tbsp.
Flat-leaf parsley (chopped), 2 tbsp.
Capers (drained), 2 tbsp
Shallot (finely chopped), 1 tbsp.
Chopped thyme, 1 tsp.
Hard boiled eggs, 2 media
Lemon (juiced)
Salt n pepper
Olive oil (extra-virgin), 3 tbsp
Panko breadcrumbs (toasted), 1 cup
Instructions
Simmer artichokes in gently (salted water) for 30 mins in a big saucepan. Allow to cool before slicing in half.
When ready to prepare, preheat the oven to 350 ° F & cook for 10 - 15 mins with the lid covered.
To prepare the gribiche sauce, in a mixing bowl, whisk together the mayonnaise, pickles, yogurt, parsley, shallots, capers, thyme, eggs, lemon juice, & salt n pepper to taste. Stir until everything is well combined.
Brush the artichoke with olive oil, season with salt n pepper, & cook them cut side down for 15 minutes, or until they are a deep golden brown.
Transfer to a plate, remove the choke, top with breadcrumbs, and serve with the gribiche sauce. Enjoy.

4.157 Fingerling Grilled Potato Salad

Total Time: 1 hour, Servings: 4
Ingredients
Scallions, 10 wholes
Olive oil (extra-virgin), 2/3 cup
Fingerling potatoes (cut in half lengthwise), 1 1/2 pound.
Pepper
Kosher salt (divided), 2 tsp + more as needed.
Rice vinegar, 2 tbsp
Lemon juice, 2 tsp
Jalapeño (sliced), 1 small.
Instructions
Peel the potatoes or clean them well with a vegetables brush if preferred.
Place a pencil / chopstick from either side of a potato lengthwise; these will act as cutting guides.
Cut each potato crosswise into "thin slices" with a sharp knife, being careful not to cut all of the way through the bottom. Your knife should be prevented from cutting too deeply by the pencils. Carry on with the additional potatoes in the same manner.
Slice the "parmesan cheese" into 2-inch-thick pieces. Each slice should be cut into very thin slices.
Place the potatoes cut side up in a roasting tray. Drizzle the melted butter over them. Using the parmesan cheese thin slices, pierce each slice or every slice in the potato. You'll be able to fit fewer cheese slices in each potato if your slices are thicker.
Season with Pit Boss Veggie Rub liberally. Pour a small amount of cream over each potato for a little more richness.
When ready to prepare, increase the temp to High & preheat for fifteen min with the lid closed.
Place the baking pan on the grill and cover it with foil. Bake for 60 min or till potatoes are cooked.
Remove the foil and evenly sprinkle the cheese over the tops, then bake for another 5 minutes, just till the cheese is melted & brown.
Add chives and your choice toppings to the potatoes. Enjoy.

4.158 Christmas Brussel Sprouts

Total Time: 1 hour 5 min, Servings: 6
Ingredients
Thick-Cut Bacon, 1/2 Pound
Onion (Diced), 1 Medium
Fresh Brussels Sprouts, 2 Pound
Olive Oil, 2 tbsp
Salt n Pepper
Instructions
Preheat the oven to 350 degrees F and leave the lid covered for 10 - 15 minutes when ready to cook.
Cook for 15-20 minutes, or till bacon is gently browned, directly on the grill grate. Remove off the
grill and place on a dish lined with paper towels.
Cut onion in half, then cut into 14-inch moons and place in big mixing basin. Add brussels sprouts to bowl after slicing them in half lengthwise.
Add the saved bacon to the bowl, cut into 12-inch pieces.
Drizzle olive oil over the top and season with salt n pepper. Pour into the baking pan after tossing to coat.
Preheat the grill to 375 degrees Fahrenheit and set the baking pan on it. Cook for 30 minutes, stirring halfway through.

4.159 Cheesy Baked Accordion Potatoes

Total Time: 1 hour 20 min, Servings: 4
Ingredients
Baking potato, 4 large
Parmesan cheese, 1/4 pound
Butter (melted), 4 tbsp.
Pit Boss veggie rub, 1 as needed.
Heavy cream, 2 tbsp
Shredded cheddar cheese, 1/2 cup
Chives (freshly minced), 2 tbsp
Instructions
Peel the potatoes or clean them well with the vegetable brush if preferred.
Place a pencil / chopstick from either side of a potato lengthwise; these will act as cutting guides.
Cut every potato crosswise into thin slices with a sharp knife, taking care of not cutting via the bottom. Your knife should be prevented from cutting too deeply by the pencils. Carry on with the leftover
potatoes in the same manner.
Slice the parmesan cheese into 2-inch-thick pieces. Each slice should be cut into very thin slices.
Place the potatoes cut side up in a roasting tray. Drizzle the melted butter over them. Using the parmesan cheese thin slices, pierce each slice or every other slice in the potatoes. You'll be able to put fewer cheese slices in each potato if your slices are thicker.
Season with Pit Boss Veggie Rubs liberally. Pour a small amount of cream over each potato for a little more richness.
When ready to prepare, increase the temp to High & preheat for fifteen min with the lid closed.

Place the baking pan on the grill and cover it with foil. Bake for 60 min or till potatoes is cooked.
Remove the foil and evenly sprinkle the cheese over the tops, then bake for another 5 minutes, or till the cheese melt & brown.
Add chives and your choice toppings to the potatoes. Enjoy.

4.160 Smoked Potato Salad
Total Time: 55 min, Servings: 4
Ingredients
Small new potatoes, 2 pounds
Olive oil, 2 tbsp
Pure kosher sea salt, 1 tbsp
Black pepper, 1/2 tsp
Mayonnaise, 3/4 cup
Sriracha, 3 tbsp or more to taste
Chopped parsley, 1 tbsp.
Chopped chives, 1 tbsp.
Instructions
Preheat Pit Boss to 225°F and cook for 15 minutes with lid covered until ready to cook. If Super Smoke is available, use it for the best flavor.
Season potatoes with salt n pepper after tossing with olive oil. Set the potatoes on a sheet pan and place it straight on the grill grate for 15 - 20 minutes to smoke.
Remove it from the Pit Boss, raise the temp to 450°F, & preheat for fifteen min with the lid closed.
Return the potatoes to the grill & cook for another 20 - 25 minutes, or till they are soft.
When they're done, set them aside to cool.
Combine the mayonnaise & Sriracha in a mixing bowl while the potatoes are boiling, adjusting the quantity to taste. Toss the potato with the "Sriracha mayonnaise", parsley, and chives once they've cooled. Enjoy.

4.161 Grilled Peach Salsa
Total Time: 30 min, Servings: 6
Ingredients
Peaches (halved), 4
Olive oil (extra-virgin), 4 tbsp
Salt
Heirloom tomato, 4
Cilantro leaves (minced), 1 bunch
Jalapeño (minced), 1
Lime (juiced), 2.
Garlic (minced), 2 cloves
Instructions
Preheat the grill to 500°F and close the cover for 15 minutes when ready to cook.
Drizzle olive oil over the "cut side" of the peaches & season with salt. Place the peaches cut side down along the grill's perimeter. Cook for around 20 minutes until grill marks appear. It's preferable to choose peaches that aren't too ripe and are still firm.
When the peaches are cool enough to handle, remove them from the grill & dice them. Combine minced cilantro, diced tomatoes, jalapeño, lime juice, garlic, and olive oil in a large mixing basin. Season with salt and pepper to taste. If necessary, add extra lime juice.
Serve with some chips or a side dish of your choice. Enjoy.

4.162 Smoked Loaded Roasted Potato Salad
Total Time: 1 hour 20 min, Servings: 4
Ingredients
Bacon, 8 Slices
Yukon Gold Potato (Scrubbed & Cubed)
Eggs, 4 Large
Sour Cream, 1 Cup
Mayonnaise, 1/2 Cup
Pickle Relish, 1/4 Cup
Mustard
Pit Boss Prime Rib Rub, 2 tsp
Distilled White Vinegar
Shredded Cheddar Cheese, 1 1/2 Cup
Scallions, 4
Paprika
Parsley (Chopped)
Instructions
Scrub the potatoes with a vegetable brush under the cold running water if you like your potato salad to have skin.
When ready to prepare, preheat the Pit Boss to 350°F for 15 minutes with the lid closed.
Arrange the bacon pieces perpendicular to the grill bars on the grill grate. Place the eggs & potatoes on on the grill grate. Make an ice bath in a pan or a bowl.
Meanwhile, prepare the dressing: Combine the mayonnaise, sour cream, pickle relish (if using), Pit Boss Prime Rib, mustard seasoning, and vinegar in a mixing dish. Taste the dressing and adjust the seasoning as required with additional vinegar, mustard, or salt and pepper. The dressing should have a lot of taste. Combine the cheese & scallions in a mixing bowl. Remove from the equation.
Cook the bacon for 20 to 25 minutes, or until golden brown; it will be crispy as it cools. Move it to the paper towels to drain with tongs, then crumble.
When bacon is done, check the eggs: Remove 1 egg from grill & place it in the cold water to stop it from cooking. Check for doneness by peeling and slicing in half: There should be no rawness in the middle of the yolk. If one of the eggs is cooked through, place the others in ice water to chill briefly before peeling and slicing.
Raise the grill's temperature to High and bake the remaining potatoes for another 20 - 30 minutes, or till they're soft but not mushy. Allow to cool on a wire rack for a few minutes.
If preferred, peel the potatoes while they are still warm or leaving the skins on. Cut the potatoes into cubes and place them in a large mixing basin. Add the chopped eggs and crumbled bacon. Sprinkle the dressing over potato mixture & gently toss to incorporate with a rubber spatula. Season to taste once more.
Serve immediately bowl & top with parsley and paprika. Serve immediately or cover & chill. Enjoy.

4.163 Grilled Asparagus & Spinach Salad
Total Time: 20 min, Servings: 8
Ingredients
Apple cider vinegar, 4 ounces
Pit Boss apricot bbq sauce, 8 ounces
Asparagus (ends trimmed & cut into thirds), 2 bunch.
Olive oil, 3 ounces
Pit Boss beef rub, 2 ounces
Baby spinach, 24 ounces
Candied pecans, 4 ounces
Feta cheese, 4 ounces
Instructions
To make the salad dressing, whisk together apple cider vinegar & Pit Boss Apricot BBQ Sauce.
When ready to prepare, preheat the Pit Boss to 350°F for 15 minutes with the lid closed.
Toss asparagus with the Pit Boss Beef Rub and olive oil.
Place the asparagus in Pit Boss grilling basket & place it on the grill grate.
Cook for around ten min on the grill. Once the asparagus is

done, remove it from the pan.
Arrange the heated asparagus on top of a spinach bowl. Toss in the candied pecans, feta cheese, and salad dressing before serving. Enjoy.

4.164 Sugar Snap Grilled Peas & Smoked Bacon

Total Time: 35 min, Servings: 4
Ingredients
Sugar snap peas (ends trimmed), 2 pounds.
Olive oil (extra-virgin), 2 tbsp
Salt n pepper
Bacon, 1 pound
Butter, 2 tbsp
Shallot (thinly sliced), 2 media.
Garlic (minced), 1 clove
Bourbon, 1/4 cup
Maple syrup, 2 tbsp
Instructions
Preheat the Pit Boss to 350°F for 15 minutes with the lid closed when ready to cook.
Toss the peas with olive oil in a medium bowl & season with some salt n pepper to taste.
Cover the barbecue grate with a grill mat or tray to keep peas from falling through.
Put the peas on grill grate and cook for 10 minutes, or until cooked but still brilliant green.
Cook bacon slices next to peas on the grill for 15-20 minutes, or till fat is rendered & slightly crunchy.
Melt butter in a skillet over medium-high heat while the bacon & peas simmer.
Add the shallot & garlic and heat until the shallot and garlic are soft and cooked through. Cook until the bourbon has been reduced by half. Toss in the maple syrup and season with salt n pepper to taste. Remove from the equation.
Take the bacon from the griddle and cut it into 1/2-inch pieces.
Combine the bacon, grilled sugar snap peas, & maple bourbon mixture in a mixing bowl. Enjoy.

4.165 Grilled Fingerling Potato Salad

Total Time: 30 min, Servings: 6
Ingredients
Scallions, 10 Whole
Fingerling Potatoes (Sliced in Half Horizontally), 1 1/2 Pound
Pepper
Extra-Virgin Olive Oil (Divided), 2/3 Cup
Kosher Salt (Divided), 2 tsp plus Add More If Required
Lemon Juice, 2 tsp
Rice Vinegar, 2 tbsp.
Jalapeño (Sliced), 1 Small
Instructions
Preheat your Pit Boss to 450 ° F and cook for fifteen min with the lid covered.
Brush the scallions with oil before placing them on the grilled pan.
Cook for 2 - 3 minutes, or until browned on the edges. Remove it from the fire and set it aside to cool.
Remove the scallions from the heat & set them aside to cool.
After brushing the potatoes fingerlings with olive oil, season them with pepper and salt (reserving the 1/3 cup of oil for some later use). Place the cut-edge down on the grill for 4 - 5 minutes, or until fully cooked.
Combine the leftover olive oil (1/3 cup), 1 tsp salt, lemon juice, & rice vinegar in a mixing bowl. Add the potatoes, scallions, & jalapeño slices after that.
Garnish with a sprinkle of salt and pepper. Have fun with it.

4.166 Bacon Salad with Beet (Roasted)

Total Time: 1 hour, Servings: 4
Ingredients
Spinach (torn into the bite-size portions)
Champagne vinaigrette, 1/4 cup
Raw beets (thinly sliced & peeled), 2 media.
Ripe pears (sliced), 2 media.
Avocados (diced), 2 large.
Red leaf lettuce
Bacon, 8 slices
Raw pecans or walnuts, 1/4 cup
Instructions
Warm the Pit Boss to 400°F & keep the lid covered until ready to cook for 15 minutes.
Arrange beets on a foil-lined (baking sheet) and top with bacon. Cook for 25 minutes on a baking sheet directly on the grill grates (though preheating).
Coat the beets with the bacon grease that has been condensed.
Cook for a further 15 minutes, or until the beets are tender and the bacon gets crispy, spreading it out evenly.
Add the walnuts/pecans & continue to roast for another 5 minutes. Using a spoon, remove the nuts and place them on the paper towels to cool & drain.
Once the bacon has been cooled to the touch, roughly chop it into medium pieces.
Toss the avocado, beets, almonds, bacon, peas, & lettuce together in a large salad dish. Toss with a sprinkle of champagne vinaigrette before serving. Enjoy.

4.167 Wedge Grilled Salad

Total Time: 20 min, Servings: 2
Ingredients
Mayonnaise, 1 cup
blue cheese, 4 ounces
Buttermilk, 1/4 cup
Garlic (minced), 1 clove
Pepper n salt
Parsley flat leaf (chopped), 2 tbsp.
Bacon, 2 strips
extra-virgin Olive oil, One tbsp.
Romaine (sliced in longitudinally in half), 1 head.
black pepper, 1 pinch
Kosher salt, 1/4 tsp.
heirloom tomatoes (chopped), 2.
blue cheese (crumbled), 8 ounces
scallion (sliced), 1.
black pepper (Freshly ground)
Instructions
Mix together all the dressing ingredients in a small dish and put aside.
Heat the Pit Boss to about 400°F with lid covered for at least 15 minutes when ready to cook.
Place the "bacon strips" directly on the grill grate & cook for 10 to 15 minutes, or until the fat has rendered and the bacon is crisp.
Toss romaine lettuce with olive oil and season with salt and pepper. Cook for 5 to 7 minutes cut side down, on the grate after the bacon, until slightly browned and grill marks appear. Remove the "bacon" from the grill and thinly slice it.
Toss the grilled Romaine with the dressing on a platter or in a serving dish. On top are tomatoes, parsley, chopped bacon, (sliced) scallions, blue cheese, and black pepper. Enjoy.

4.168 Beet (Roasted) & Bacon Salad

Total Time: 1 hour, Servings: 4
Ingredients
Champagne vinaigrette, 1/4 cup
Avocados (diced), 2 large.
Raw pecans or walnuts, 1/4 cup
Ripe pears (sliced), 2 media.
Raw beets (thinly sliced & peeled), 2 media.
Eight slices bacon
Red leaf lettuce, 1 head or baby
Spinach (torn into the bite-size pieces)
Instructions
Heat the Pit Boss to about 400°F & keep the lid covered for fifteen min until ready to cook.
Arrange beets on a foil-lined baking pan with bacon on top. Cook it on a baking sheet directly on the grill grate for 25 minutes (though preheating).
Coat the beets with the bacon grease that has been condensed.
Cook for another fifteen min, or until the beets are soft and the bacon gets crisp, in a single layer.
Add the walnuts / pecans and roast for another 5 minutes. Using a spoon, remove
the nuts and place them onto the paper towels to cool and drain.
Once the bacon has cooled to a touch, roughly chop it into medium-sized pieces.
Toss the almonds, beets, bacon, pears, lettuce, and avocado in a large salad dish. Toss with a sprinkling of champagne vinaigrette to coat. Enjoy.

4.169 Roasted Carrots with Pomegranate Relish and Pistachio

Total Time: 40 min, Servings: 6
Ingredients
Coriander, 1 tsp.
Olive oil (extra-virgin), 2 tbsp.
Cumin, 1/2 tsp
Rainbow carrots, 2 bunch
Kosher salt, 2 tsp.
Garlic clove (finely & grated chopped), 2.
Lime (zested), 1
Fennel seed, 2 tsp
Sugar, 1 tsp
Mint (Chopped), 1/4 Cup
Chopped Pistachios, 1/2 Cup
Salt
Italian Flat-Leaf Parsley (Chopped), 1/4 Cup
Olive Oil (Extra-Virgin), 1/3 Cup
Pomegranate Seeds, 1/2 Cup
Lime (Juiced), 1
Instructions
Preheat the Pit Boss to 450°F & cook for 15 minutes with the lid covered until ready to use.
Rinse the carrots thoroughly to remove the dirt but keep the skins on. Combine the sugar, spices, and salt in a small cup. Toss the carrots in 2 tablespoons olive oil to evenly coat them, then add the spice mixture & garlic. Toss to coat evenly.
Place on a large sheet tray and cook on the Pit Boss for 30 minutes, turning once. Remove the "carrots" from the grill immediately after piercing them with a fork. Last but not least, grate the "lime zest" over the top.
To make the Pistachio & Pomegranate Relish, whisk together olive oil (1/3 cup), pistachios, lime juice, pomegranate seeds, spices, and a generous sprinkle of salt. Season with salt
 and pepper to taste, and if necessary, add additional seasoning.
When ready to serve, place the carrots on a serving dish. Place a large portion of the Pomegranate and Parsley Relish in the center of the carrots and serve the rest on the side. Have fun with it.

4.170 Grilled Wedge Salad

Total Time: 20 min, Servings: 2
Ingredients
Crumbled blue cheese, 8 ounces.
Scallions (sliced), 1.
Olive oil (extra-virgin), 1 tbsp
Kosher salt, 1/4 tsp.
Mayonnaise, 1 cup
Buttermilk, 1/4 cup
Blue cheese, 4 ounces
Garlic (minced), 1 clove
Heirloom tomatoes (chopped), 2.
Fresh ground black pepper
Chopped flat-leaf parsley, 2 tbsp.
Romaine (sliced in half), 1 head.
Lengthwise core kept intact.
Pepper n salt
Bacon, 2 strips
Black pepper, 1 pinch
Instructions
Mix all of dressing ingredients in a small dish and put aside.
Heat the Pit Boss to 400 degrees F with the
cover covered for at least 15 minutes when ready to cook.
Cook for 10 - 15 minutes, or until the fat has rendered and the bacon is crisp, by placing the bacon strips flat on the grill grate.
Toss romaine lettuce with olive oil and season with some pepper and salt. Cook for 5 to 7 minutes, cut side down, close to the bacon on the grill grate, until gently browned and grill marks appear.
Remove bacon from the grill and thinly slice it.
Drizzle the dressing over the grilled Romaine on the plate or in the serving bowl. On top are tomatoes, sliced scallions, chopped bacon, parsley, blue cheese, and black pepper. Enjoy.

4.171 Sherry Root Vegetables Roasted

Total Time: 1 hour 20 min, Servings: 8
Ingredients
Red onion, 1 medium
Turnips, 2 wholes
Fennel bulb, 1 whole
Olive oil (extra-virgin), 3 tbsp.
Dry sherry, 1/4 cup
Red skin potatoes, 4 small
Garlic, 1 head
Veggie rub Pit Boss, 2 tsp
Golden beets (diced & trimmed large), 2 wholes.
Yukon gold potatoes cut or halved into wedges, 4 small.
Carrots, 2 cups
Parsnips, 2 wholes
Thyme leaves 2 whole fresh or dried thyme, 1 tsp.
Instructions
Arrange the chopped veggies on a large sheet tray.
Using a serrated knife, cut approximately half an inch off the top of the garlic head to show the clove tops, leaving the "garlic skin" together on each clove. Place the garlic cloves on the aluminum foil square, drizzle
with 1 tablespoon olive oil, and wrap the foil across the garlic loosely. On a sheet plate, combine the remaining veggies.
Drizzle the remaining olive oil over the veggies. In a mixing dish,

combine the dry sherry, 2 tablespoons Pit Boss Veggie Rub, and the thyme. To combine, whisk everything together.
Heat the Pit Boss approximately 500°F with the lid covered for at least 15 minutes when ready to cook.
Cook for 60 - 90 mins, occasionally stirring until the veggies are soft and beginning to brown.
Squeeze the garlic cloves onto the veggies while stirring to combine. Remove the papery garlic husks and discard them. Serve immediately. Enjoy.

4.172 Whole Pickles (Smoked)
Total Time: 1 hour 15 min, Servings: 8
Ingredients
Kosher salt, 1/2 cup
Pink peppercorns, 1/2 tsp
Coriander seeds, 1 1/2 tsp.
White vinegar, 1/2 quart
Sugar, 1/4 cup
Mustard seeds, 1 tsp
Black peppercorn, 1 tsp
Celery seed, 1 1/2 tsp.
Garlic (peeled), 8 cloves.
Summer shandy rub (leinenkugel's Pit Boss), 3 tbsp
Fresh dill, 1 bunch
Water, 1 quart
Cucumbers, 12 small
Instructions
Preheat the Pit Boss according to the manufacturer's directions when you're ready to cook. Heat the oven to 180°F for at least five min with the cover closed.
On a baking sheet, combine the celery seeds, Kosher salt, coriander seeds, mustard seeds, peppercorns, & garlic cloves. Place the baking sheet directly on the grill grate and smoke for around 90 minutes, occasionally mixing the spices.
Bring the water and vinegar to a boil in a medium saucepan. Whisk in the sugar, summer shandy rub, and smoked herbs after removing the pan from the heat. After thoroughly mixing to dissolve the salt, add the fresh dill.
Arrange the cucumbers in a plastic container. Cover the cucumbers completely with hot brine. Allow it cool completely before covering and storing in the fridge.
Pickles will be made in a short amount of time, and they will taste better after a day or three. Enjoy.

4.173 Rosemary and Thyme-Infused Crushed Potatoes along with a Cream
Total Time: 1 hour 20 min, Servings: 6
Ingredients
Russet Potatoes, 4 1/2 Pound
Water, 1 1/2 Cup
Fresh Thyme, 3 Sprig
Heavy Cream, 1 Pint
Fresh Rosemary, 2 Sprig
Sage Leaves, 6
Black Peppercorn, 6 Whole
Kosher Salt
Ground Black Pepper
Garlic Clove, Peeled & Chopped 2
Unsalted Butter, Softened 2 Stick
Instructions
Heat the Pit Boss to about 350°F and keep the cover covered for 15 minutes until ready to cook.
To prepare mashed potatoes, peel and clean the potatoes before cutting them under one cube. Cook for 1 hour or until fork tender in a safe oven dish with 1/2 cup water.
While the potatoes are boiling, add the spices, peppercorns, milk, & garlic cloves to a small saucepan. Place on grill, cover, and steep for 15 minutes.
Remove the herbs and garlic from the cream and return it to the saucepan and keep it warm on the heat.
Drain the potatoes and rice them in a large stockpot using a food mill or a potato ricer. Slowly pour in 2/3 of the milk, followed by one stick of butter and a teaspoon of salt. As needed, add additional cream, salt, and butter to obtain the desired consistency.
Immediately serve or keep warm in a slow cooker set to the lowest setting or above a water bath. Enjoy.

4.174 Broil Cajun Pit Boss
Total Time: 1 hour 30 min, Servings: 8
Ingredients
Red potatoes, 2 lbs.
Olive oil, 2 tbsps.
Corn ears (cut each into thirds), 6.
Old bay flavoring
Shrimp (along with tails), 3 lbs. Large
Kielbasa smoked sausage, 2 lbs.
Butter, 2 tbsps
Instructions
Preheat Pit Boss to 450°F and cook for 15 minutes with lid covered until ready to serve.
Drizzle half of the oil so over potatoes & season with Old Bay sauce to taste. Place immediately on the grill grate. Roast the veggies for 20 minutes or until they are tender.
Drizzle the remaining olive oil and over corn & season with Old Bay seasoning. Place the kielbasa & corn on the grill grate after the potatoes. An additional fifteen minutes of roasting is necessary.
Drizzle the shrimp with Old Bay sauce. Cook for yet another ten min, or till hot pink & cooked through, over the same grill grate as the other items.
Remove everything from the barbeque grill and place
it in a large mixing basin. After adding the butter, season with Elder Bay sauce to suit. Serve
immediately after flipping to coat. Have fun with it.

4.175 Roasted Peach Salsa
Total Time: 35 min, Servings: 6
Ingredients
Fresh Peaches, 6 Whole
Jalapeño, 2 Whole
Tomatoes, 3 Fresh
Garlic, 2 Cloves
Onions (Green), 2 Whole
Cilantro, 1/2 Cup
Lime Juice, 1 tsp.
Apple Cider Vinegar, 5 tsps.
Black Pepper, 1/4 tsp.
Salt, 1/2 tsp
Instructions
Preheat the Pit Boss to 375 degrees Fahrenheit with the lid covered for 15 minutes until ready to cook.
Place the peaches (halved), tomatoes (halved), & jalapenos on on the grill grate (whole). Close the lid & roast for 8-10 minutes, or until the tomatoes and jalapenos have blistered and the skin has cracked.
Take the fruit off the grill and lay it away to cool until it is easily handled.
Remove the skins off the tomatoes & peaches. Remove the skin, seeds, and roots from the jalapenos.
Coarsely chop peeled jalapenos, tomatoes, peaches, & onions in a food mill.
Pulse in the ingredients left until they reach the desired consistency. Use short pulses for a chunkier salsa and big pulses

for a finer salsa.
Serve immediately or transfer to jars to chill until ready to use. In the fridge, it will keep for approximately a week. Have fun with it.

4.176 Macaroni Salad (Smoked)
Total Time: 3 hours 20 min, Servings: 4
Ingredients
Uncooked macaroni, 1 lb.
Bell pepper, 1 diced
Red onion (small), 1/2
Shredded carrot, 1/2 cup
Vinegar (white wine), 3 tbsps.
Black pepper
Sugar, 2 tbsps.
Salt
Instructions
Bring a large pot of the salted water to a boil over medium heat and cook pasta according to package directions. Cook until the pasta is al dente, then drain and rinse under cool water.
Heat the grill to smoke about 15 minutes with the lid covered when you're ready to cook.
Place a sheet plate on the grill grate and lay the cooked spaghetti out on it. Cook for 20 minutes, then take from the heat and place in the fridge to cool.
While the spaghetti is cooling, make the dressing. Mix all of ingredients in a medium mixing cup.
When the pasta has cooled, combine it with the diced vegetables and dressing in a large mixing dish.
Wrap in plastic wrap and chill for 20 minutes before serving. Have fun with it.

4.177 Baked Garlic Duchess Potatoes
Total Time: 1 hour 30 min, Servings: 8
Ingredients
Potatoes (Yukon Gold), 12 media size.
Salt
Egg yolk, 5 large
Melted butter, 10 tbsps.
Heavy cream, 1/2 cup
Garlic cloves, 2 minced.
Sour cream, 3/4 cup
Black pepper
Instructions
Place the potatoes in a large saucepan halfway filled with water. Season with salt and pepper. It comes to a boil over medium heat.
Lower heat to low & simmer for 25-35 minutes, or until potatoes readily glide through a filet knife. Drain the water and set it aside to cool.
Heat the Pit Boss to about 450 ° F for 15 minutes with the lid closed when ready to cook.
Mix the egg yolks, garlic, milk, butter, pepper, & sour cream in a large mixing basin. Season with salt.
Using just a ricer or food mill, cut potatoes and transfer them to a bowl with the egg mixture.
Carefully fold in the egg mixture, being careful not to overcrowd it.
Transfer to a 3-quart baking dish and bake for 30–40 minutes, until at lightly browned & puffed. Have fun with it.

4.178 Mini Quiches Breakfast (Baked)
Total Time: 30 min, Servings: 8
Ingredients
Cooking spray
Yellow onion, 1/2 diced.
Olive oil (extra-virgin), 1 tbsp.
Eggs, 10
Fresh spinach, 3 cups
Shredded mozzarella, swiss or cheddar cheese, 4 ounces
Fresh basil, 1/4 cup
Black pepper, 1/2 tsp.
Kosher salt, one tsp.
Instructions
Spray a 12-cup muffin pan liberally with cooking spray.
In a small skillet, heat the oil. Cook, stirring often, for approximately 7 minutes, or till the onion is softened. Cook for 1 minute more, or till the spinach has cooked.
Allow the mixture to cool on a cutting board before cutting it to break up the spinach.
Preheat the grill at 350 ° F with the lid closed for 15 minutes when ready to cook.
In a large mixing basin, whisk the eggs until foamy. In a mixing dish, combine the cooled onions & basil, spinach, cheese, 1/2 tsp pepper, and 1 tsp salt. To combine, whisk everything together. Distribute the egg mixture evenly among the muffin cups.
Place the sheet on the grill and cook for 18-20 minutes, or until the eggs have plumped up, cooked, & are beginning to brown.
Serve immediately or let cool fully on a chopping board before keeping in an airtight container for up to four days. Have fun with it.

4.179 Baked Savory & Sweet Baked Yams
Total Time: 1 hour 30 min, Servings: 6
Ingredients
Olive oil (extra-virgin), 3 tbsp
Yams, 3 media sized.
Goat cheese
Honey
Pecans pieces, 1/2 cup
Brown sugar, 1/2 cup
Instructions
Preheat oven to 350 degrees ° F & cook for 15 minutes with the lid covered.
Rinse the yams and poke tiny holes in them while the Pit Boss warms up. To keep the yams warm, wrap them in the wrap.
Bake for about 1 hour, or until a knife pierces the yam and it is soft. You don't want to overcook yams & make them too mushy since you want to slice them into circles.
When the yams have cooled enough just to handle, cut them into quarter-inch pieces. Brush each piece with olive oil and place on a sheet tray.
Dust each serving with brown icing sugar. Using a teaspoon, spread the appropriate amount of cheese over all of the pieces... Then, on top of that, add chopped pecans. Finally, drizzle honey over each piece.
Depending on your preference, add additional icing sugar & honey to the yams.
Place the foil tray back in the Pit Boss & bake for another 20 minutes with the cover closed. Have fun with it.

4.180 Scalloped Smoked Potatoes
Total Time: 1 hour 10 min, Servings: 6
Ingredients
Softened butter, 2 tbsps
Milk, 1/2 cup
Heavy cream, 1 cup
Garlic (chopped), 2 cloves.
Flour, 2 tbsp.
Russet potatoes (peeled & finely sliced), 4.

Black pepper
Kosher salt
White cheddar (finely grated), 1/2 cup.
Cheddar cheese (shredded), 1/2 cup
Instructions
Heat your Pit Boss to 375°F & cook for 15 minutes with the lid covered after the timer has been set.
Butter the sides & bottom of a stainless-steel skillet (9 inches).
Toss to combine milk, cream, & garlic in a mixing bowl.
Arrange a layer of potato (1/4th part) in a skillet, season with salt and pepper, and
cover with sauce mixture (1/4th piece). Rep the process three times more.
Grill the potatoes for 50 minutes.
Sprinkle both pieces of cheese evenly over the potatoes & simmer for 10 minutes, or until fork-tender.
Remove the burgers from the grill and serve them. Have fun with it.

4.181 Baked Spinach Creamed

Total Time: 45 min, Servings: 4
Ingredients
Shallot (finely chopped), 1.
Butter, 2 tbsp
Garlic cloves, 2
Heavy cream, 1 ½ cup
Chili pepper flakes, 1 tsp.
Ground nutmeg, 1 tsp.
Black pepper
Salt
Sour cream, 3/4 cup
Frozen spinach package (thawed & drained) 10 oz.
Romano cheese, 1/2 cup
Parmesan cheese, 1/2 cup
Panko breadcrumbs, 1/2 cup
Instructions
In a frying pan over medium heat, melt butter and stir-fry garlic & shallot. Cook for around 3 minutes. After introducing the chili flakes, cook for the next 2 minutes.
Heat the nutmeg & cream together in a saucepan. To taste, season it with salt and pepper.
Season with salt and pepper and stir throughout the sour cream & spinach. Take the pan out of the oven and stir in the cheeses.
Pour the mixture into a baking dish & sprinkle the panko on top.
Heat the grill approximately 375 ° F with the lid closed for 15 minutes when ready to cook.
Bake for another 25 - 30 minutes, straight on the barbeque grate, until the surface becomes golden brown & bubbling. Have fun with it.

4.182 Baked Pickles along with Buttermilk Dip

Total Time: 30 min, Servings: 4
Ingredients
Dill pickle spears, 1 jar (16 ounces)
Egg, 2 big
All-purpose flour, 1/3 cup
Hot sauce, 1 tsp
Chile powder (chipotle), 1/2 tsp
Ancho chile powder, ½ tsp
Dried oregano, ½ tsp
Pure salt (jacobsen salt co.), 1/4 tsp
Kosher salt
Black pepper, 1/4 tsp
Panko breadcrumbs, 1 cup
Grated parmesan cheese, 1/2 cup
Mayonnaise, 1/2 Cup
Buttermilk, 2 Tbsp
Parsley (Fresh Sliced), 1 Tsp
Jacobsen Salt, 1/2 Tsp
Kosher Salt
Garlic Powder. 1/4 Tsp
Garlic Salt, 1/4 Tsp
Onion Powder, 1/4 Tsp
Black Pepper, 1/4 Tsp
Instructions
Preheat oven to 450°F and cover for 15 minutes when ready to cook.
Place the cooling rack on top of the baking sheet and coat it with cooking spray.
Drain the pickles, spread them out on paper towels, and pat them dry.
Whisk together eggs, flour, pepper, oregano, hot sauce, chile powders, garlic powder, and salt in a normal mixing basin.
Combine the breadcrumbs and Parmesan in a large mixing basin. Remove the pickles from the egg mixture, let the excess drip out, and transfer to the breadcrumb mixture. Toss to evenly coat. Place the pickles in a separate layer on a cooling rack that has been prepared.
Place the baking sheet directly on the grate and cook for 10 minutes, and till the pickle's tops are crisp & golden brown.
To make the dip (buttermilk), combine all of the dip ingredients in a blender and mix until smooth. Season with pepper and salt to taste. Enjoy.

4.183 Loaded & Baked Potato Salad

Total Time: 50 min, Servings: 6
Ingredients
Russet Potatoes, 3 Pound
Salt & Pepper
Olive Oil, 1/4 Cup
Slab (Slice into Lardons Bacon), 1 Pound
Cheddar Cheese (Sliced), 1 Cup
Scallions (Lightly Sliced), 4
Sour Cream
Mayonnaise, 1/2 Cup
Chives (Chopped), 2 Tbsp
Dry Mustard, 1/2 Tbsp
Salt & Pepper
Instructions
Use a brush to scrub the potatoes under cold water. Season potatoes with pepper
and salt and drizzle with olive oil.
Preheat oven to 450°F and cook for 15 minutes with the lid covered. Place potatoes directly on the grate and bake for 35-40 minutes, or until cooked.
Place the bacon lardons in a cast-iron skillet or other safe dish and place them directly on the grate with the potatoes later. For around 30 minutes, bake until the fat has rendered and the lardons are crispy.
Remove the lardons from the grill grate, drain and remove the grease, and set the bacon aside.
When the potatoes are cooked, take them from of the grill & let them cool for 15 minutes at room temperature. Place in the refrigerator to chill completely. Make the dressing while the potatoes are chilling. Combine sour chives, cream, mayonnaise, salt n pepper, & dry mustard in a normal mixing bowl.
Once the potatoes have cooled completely, cut them into one-inch pieces. Toss the lardon, potatoes, and cheese together in a large mixing basin. Pour the dressing over the top and toss to combine. If required, top with more cheese and sliced onions. Enjoy.

4.184 Seasonal (Roasted) & Pickled Vegetables
Total Time: 1 hour, Servings: 8
Ingredients
Sweet Potatoes, 2
Potatoes, 3
Red Onion Skinned, 1
Zucchini, 2
Fresh Squash Summer, 2
Fresh Carrots, 4
Mushrooms (Cut Button), 8 Oz
Fresh Thyme, 2 Tbsp
Rosemary, 2 Tbsp
Dried Basil, 1 Tsp
Minced Garlic, 3 Tsp
Olive Oil, 1/4 Cup
Balsamic Vinegar, 2 Tbsp
Salt & Pepper
Instructions
Chop all of the veggies according to the ingredient list.
Preheat the grill when you're ready to cook. Until the fire is ready, smoke with
the lid open (4-5 mins). Preheat the oven to high and cook for 10-15 minutes with the lid covered.
In a separate dish, combine garlic, rosemary, thyme, basil (can use), balsamic vinegar, salt, olive oil, & pepper; set aside. Toss the cut veggies in a large mixing basin with the vinegar, oil, and herb combination.
Stir until each veggie is well covered. Using aluminum foil, line a baking/roasting pan tray with sheets of baking/roasting pan tray & lightly spray with a cooking spray.
Evenly distribute the veggies in the pan and drizzle with the remaining vinegar, oil, and herb combination. You may also season with more salt or pepper at this point. Cook for 40 minutes on the grill. Serve and take pleasure in it.

4.185 Roasted Creamy Brussel Sprouts
Total Time: 50 min, Servings: 4
Ingredients
Trimmed & split brussels sprouts, 2 pounds.
Olive oil
Salt & pepper
Cooked & diced bacon, 2 oz.
Butter, 1 tbsp
Onion (excellently diced), 1.
Flour, 1 tbsp
Whole milk, 3/4 cup
Chicken rub (Pit Boss), 2 tbsp
Grated gruyere cheese, 4 oz
Salt & pepper
Instructions
Preheat the oven too high for 15 minutes when ready to cook. Season Brussels sprouts
with salt and pepper and tosses with olive oil. Place immediately on the grate after spreading on the baking sheet. Cook for 15–20 minutes, till golden brown.
In a bigger cast-iron frypan, cook a piece of bacon till crispy on the heat. Remove the bacon from the pan and set it on a paper towel (paper).
Melt the butter in the bacon fat and sauté the onions until they are transparent. Toss the onions with the flour and stir for 1 - 2 minutes, or until lightly browned. Pour in the milk and whisk until it is completely smooth. Grill for 4 mins on low, or until the sauce covers the back of a spoon. Mix in the Pit Boss Chicken Rub well. Stir in the cheese until it has melted into sauce. Stir in the roasted bacon to the sauce. Season to taste with salt and pepper. Place sprouts on a serving plate and cover with cheese sauce. Enjoy.

4.186 Roasted Jalapeño Poppers
Total Time: 45 min, Servings: 2
Ingredients
Bacon middle cut, 8 slices
Cream cheese, 2 cups
Cheddar cheese (sharp), 2 oz
Chopped green onions, 1/2 cup.
Freshly squeezed juice of lime, 2 tsp
Sliced seeded tomato, 4 tbsp.
Chopped cilantro, 4 tbsp.
Kosher salt, 1/2 tsp
Garlic clove minced tiny, 2.
Instructions
Preheat the oven to 350°F for 10 - 15 minutes once you're ready to cook. Place two bacon slices directly on the grate and cook for 10 to 15 minutes, flipping halfway through, until cooked through and crispy. Remove yourself from the grill grate, but do not turn it off. When the bacon is cold enough to handle, thickly slice it and set it aside.
Combine green onions, cream cheese, cheddar cheese, salt, garlic, lime juice, tomatoes, cilantro, & diced bacon in a stand mixer bowl. Mix on the moderate speed with a paddle until everything is incorporated. Transfer the mixture to a bag (piping).
Cut the tops off the jalapeños and use a small knife to remove the seeds and ribs (paring). Pipe the mixture onto each pepper so that it rises a quarter-inch beyond the pepper's top. Replace the tops on each pepper.
Roll out the leftover 6 bacon pieces with a rolling pin until they are 1/8" thick. Each component should be cut in half. Half a bacon slice should be wrapped around each pepper and secured with a toothpick.
Place the peppers in a Pit Boss Jalapeno Popper Tray. Place the tray directly on the grate and cook for 30 - 40 minutes, or until the peppers are soft, the bacon is crispy, and the cheese is melted. Enjoy.

4.187 Whole Pickles Smoked
Total Time: 1 hour 15 mins, Servings: 8
Ingredients
Kosher salt, 1/2 cup
Pink peppercorns, 1/2 tbsp
Black peppercorn, 1/2 tbsp
Celery seed, 1 1/2 tbsp
Coriander seeds, 1 1/2 tbsp
Mustard seeds, 1 tbsp
Garlic clove (peeled), 8.
Water, 1 quart
White vinegar, 1/2 quart
Sugar, 1/4 cup
Leinenkugel's (Pit Boss) summer shandy rub, 3 tbsp
Fresh dill, 1 bunch
Cucumbers, 12 small
Instructions
Preheat the "Pit Boss" according to the
manufacturer's instructions when you're ready to cook. Heat the oven approximately 180 ° F for 5 minutes with the lid closed.
In a baking dish, combine the garlic cloves, coriander, celery seeds, peppercorns, mustard seeds, & Kosher salt.
Put the baking sheet on on the grill and smoke for 90 minutes, tossing spices occasionally.
Bring the water & vinegar to a low simmer in a normal saucepan. Stir in the cinnamon, smoked cloves, & summer shandy rub after removing the pan from heat. After removing the salt, stir in the fresh dill.
Place the cucumbers in a plastic bag. Put the hot brine out

over cucumbers & coat them completely. Allow it cool completely before covering and storing in the fridge.
The pickles would be ready in a few hours; however, they will have a stronger flavor after a day or so. Have fun with it.

4.188 Mango Coleslaw Grilled
Total Time: 20 mins, Servings: 6
Ingredients
Mangoes, 2 ripe
Pit Boss chicken rub, 1 tbsp
Shaved red cabbage, 1/2 head.
Shaved green cabbage, 1/2 head.
Chopped cilantro, 1/2 cup.
Olive oil, 2 tbsp
Fish sauce, 1 tbsp
Lime juice, 1 tbsp
Brown sugar, 1 tbsp
Zested lime, 1
Instructions
Heat the "Pit Boss" to 450°F with the lid covered for 15 minutes when ready to cook.
Remove the pit & meat from the mangoes by cutting them in half. Brush the chicken with a light layer of Pit Boss Chicken Rub.
In a Pit Boss, cook for five min with the mangoes. On the other hand, cook for yet another 5 minutes. Take the steak from the grill & cut them into thin slices.
In a big mixing bowl, combine sliced mangoes, cabbage, and cilantro. Toss everything around.
In a small cup, mix together the olive oil, brown sugar, lime zest, fish sauce, and lime juice to make the dressing. To coat the slaw, toss it in the dressing.
Place the slaw in the serving dish and, if preferred, top with chopped cilantro. Have fun with it.

4.189 Thyme-Infused" Mashed Potatoes & Rosemary with Cream
Total Time: 1 hour 20 mins, Servings: 6
Ingredients
Pound russet potatoes, 4 halves
Cup water, 1 half 1/2
Heavy cream, 1 pint
Fresh rosemary, 2 sprigs
Sprig (for garnish) fresh thyme, 3
Sage leaves, 6
Whole black peppercorn, 6
Clove garlic (peeled & chopped), 2.
Softened unsalted butter, 2 sticks.
Kosher salt
Black pepper ground
Instructions
Heat the "Pit Boss" to 350°F with the lid covered for 15 minutes when ready to cook.
Prepare the potatoes by slicing and washing them before cutting them into 1" cubes for mashed potatoes. In an oven-safe dish with 1-1/2 cup water, cook for 1 hour or until fork-tender.
While the potatoes are cooking, mix the spices, milk, peppercorns, & garlic cloves in a small saucepan. Place on the grill, cover, & let too steep for 15 minutes.
Drain the milk, remove the herbs & garlic, & place it in a pot on the stove to keep warm.
Drain the potatoes, then rice them using a potato ricer or food mill in a large stockpot. 2/3 of the milk should be carefully poured in, followed by one stick of butter & a tsp. As needed, add additional milk, butter, & salt to obtain the desired consistency.

Serve right now or keep warm inside a slow cooker on low or in a water bath. Have fun with it.

4.190 Stone Fruit Grilled along with Cream & Berries.
Total Time: 25mins, Servings: 4
Ingredients
Peaches (Halved), 2
Apricot (Halved), 2
Nectarine (Halved), 1
Vinegar (Balsamic), 1/2 Cup
Honey, 3 Tbsp
Orange Peel, 1 Tbsp
Cream, 2 Cup
Fresh Raspberries, 1/2 Cup
Blueberries, 1/4 Cup
Instructions
Preheat the "Pit Boss" to 400°F with the lid covered for 15 minutes when ready to cook.
Grill the apricots, nectarines, & peaches on both sides of the grill for 3 to 4 minutes each. Grill marks & a smokey scent are preferred.
In a mixing bowl, combine all of ingredients for the balsamic reduction. In a pan over medium heat, combine the balsamic vinegar, 2 tbsp sugar, and orange peel. Allow the sauce to boil until it has (thickened) to a medium consistency.
In a mixing dish, whisk cream & 1 tbsp. Honey until soft peaks form.
Arrange roasted stone fruits on a plate with berries and balsamic reduction drizzled on top. On the side, there's whipped cream.
Have fun with it.
Add a spoonful of whipped cream to the edge. Have fun with it.

4.191 Cauliflower Roasted
Total Time: 45 mins, Servings: 4
Ingredients
Fresh head cauliflower, 1
Olive oil (extra-virgin), 2 tbsp
Garlic clove, 2
Smoked paprika, 1 1/4 tbsp.
Salt, 1/2 tbsp
Black pepper, 1/2 tbsp
Parmesan cheese, 1 cup
Instructions
Heat the oven to almost 180°F with the lid covered for 15 minutes once you're ready to cook. Use Super Smoke if it's available for the greatest flavor.
Arrange the cauliflower florets on a baking pan and chop them into moderate pieces. To burn the sheet tray, place it on the grill for 20 minutes.
While the cauliflower is cooking, put all of the ingredients in a mixing dish, except the Parmesan cheese.
After 20 minutes, cut the cauliflower. Preheat the grill to about 450 °F and cook with the lid covered for 15 minutes.
While the grill is heating up, combine the cauliflower with spice mixture and return it to the foil tray.
Return to the Pit Boss & cook for another ten min, or
until a nice golden-brown color has emerged.
In the last few minutes of cooking, sprinkle the parmesan on each slice and cover till the cheese is melted. Have fun with it.

4.192 Smoked Deviled Eggs

Total Time: 45 mins, Servings: 4
Ingredients
Peeled & Cooked Hard-Boiled Eggs, 7
Mayonnaise, 3 Tbsp
Diced Chives, 3 Tbsp
Brown Mustard, 1 Tbsp
Apple Cider Vinegar, 1 Tbsp
Pepper & Salt
Hot Sauce
Crumbled Cooked Bacon, 2 Tbsp
Paprika
Instructions
Preheat the "Pit Boss" to 180°F with the lid covered for 15 minutes when ready to cook. Use Super Smoke if it's available for the greatest flavor.
Place cooked and peeled eggs straight on the grill grate and smoke for 30 minutes.
Take the eggs from the grill & place them on a plate to cool. After slicing the eggs lengthwise, toss the egg yolks into a large zip-top bag.
Add chives, mustard, salt, vinegar, chili sauce, mayonnaise, and pepper to the bag. Close the bag and use your hands to knead all of the ingredients
together until smooth.
Squeeze the yolk mixture into one of the bag's corners, breaking off a small corner. Fill the yolk mixture into the hardboiled egg whites. The deviled eggs are topped with paprika and crumbled bacon. Refrigerate until ready to serve. Have fun with it.

4.193 Smoked Hummus with Roasted Vegetables

Total Time: 45 mins, Servings: 4
Ingredients
Chickpeas, 1 half cup
Tahini, 1/3 cup
Minced garlic, 1 tbsp
Extra-virgin olive oil, 6 tbsp
Salt, 1 tbsp
Lemon juice, 4 tbsp
Sliced red onion, 1.
Butternut squash, 2 cups
Cut into florets cauliflower, 2 cups.
Fresh brussels sprouts, 2 cups
Portobello mushroom, 2 wholes
Salt
Black pepper
Instructions
Preheat the grill to about 180°F and cover it for 15 minutes until you're ready to cook.
To make the hummus, rinse and drain the chickpeas, then spread them out on a sheet tray. Place the tray on the grill brace and smoke for 15-20 minutes, or until the desired level of smoke is reached.
In the bowl of a food processor, mix the lemon juice, salt, garlic, smoked chickpeas, olive oil, and tahini. Process until thoroughly blended but not smooth. Put everything in a dish and put it aside.
Preheat the grill to high and add the steaks.
Drizzle olive oil over the veggies and spread them out on the sheet tray. Grill the veggies on a foil sheet for 15-twenty minutes, or until lightly browned and fully cooked.
To serve, spread hummus on a plate or dish and top with roasted veggies.
Drizzle with olive oil and serve with pita bread. Have fun with it.

4.194 Deviled Eggs Smoked

Total Time: 45 mins, Servings: 4
Ingredients
Cooked & peeled hard boiled eggs, 7.
Mayonnaise, 3 tbsp
Diced chives, 3 tbsp.
Brown mustard, 1 tbsp
Apple cider vinegar, 1 tbsp
Hot sauce
Pepper & salt
Crumbled cooked bacon, 2 tbsp.
Paprika
Instructions
Preheat the Pit Boss to about 180°F for 15 minutes with the lid closed when ready to cook. Use Pro Smoke if it's available for the greatest flavor.
Place cooked and peeled eggs on the grill dish right away and smoke about 30 minutes.
Remove the eggs from the grill & place them on a cooling rack. After slicing the eggs lengthwise, squeeze the yolks into a small zip-top bag.
Combine mayonnaise, chives, mustard, vinegar, chili sauce, salt, and pepper in a plastic bag. Close the bag and use your hands to knead all of the ingredients together until completely smooth.
Squeeze the yolk mix into one of the bag's corners, breaking off a small corner. Fill the yolk mixture into the hardboiled egg whites. The deviled eggs are topped with paprika and crumbled bacon. Refrigerate until ready to serve. Have fun with it.

4.195 Brussels Shredded Sprout Salad Smoked

Total Time: 50 mins, Servings: 6
Ingredients
Sweet potato (skinned & cut into half-inch cubes), 1.
Parsnips (stripped & cut half an inch wide on the bias), 2.
Sliced shallots, 4 1/4-inch-thick.
Olive oil, 4 tbsp
Halved oranges, 2
Crumbled goat cheese, 4 ounces
Kosher salt
Black pepper (freshly ground)
Champagne vinegar, 2 tbsp
Shaved brussels sprouts, 1 pound
Pomegranate seeds, 3/4 cup
Fresh chopped mint, 3 tbsp
Instructions
Preheat the Pit Boss to 450°F for 15 minutes with the lid closed when ready to cook.
Toss the sweet potato, parsnips, shallots, 2 tablespoons olive oil, salt, and pepper in a baking dish to coat. Arrange the ingredients in a single layer. Preheat the grill to high and cook the baking sheet for 30 minutes, or until the veggies are brown and crisp. Allow cooling on a wire rack to room temperature.
While the veggies are cooking, grill the oranges cut side down for about 15 minutes, or until tender and gently browned. Remove the chicken from the grill, cool, and pour the juice into a measuring cup, reserving 5 tablespoons for the vinaigrette.
To create the vinaigrette, in a blender or food processor, mix the goat cheese, five tablespoons orange juice, and the vinegar and pulse until smooth. When everything is blended, add the remaining 2 tbsp of oil on low speed. Season with salt and pepper to taste.
Combine the trimmed Brussels sprouts and roasted veggies in a large mixing cup. Toss the salad with enough vinaigrette to coat it completely. If required, season with more salt. Garnish

with pomegranate seeds and mint leaves before serving. Have fun with it.

4.196 Buck Grapefruit Cocktail Grilled
Total Time: 20 mins, Servings: 4
Ingredients
Grapefruit, 4 Halved
Turbinado Sugar, 1/2 Cup
Vodka, 12 Ounce
Squeezed Lemon Juice (Freshly), 1 Half Ounce
Smoked Pit Boss Simple Syrup, 3 Ounce
Fresh Mint Leaves, 8 Sprig
Ginger Beer, 12 Ounce
For Garnish Grapefruit, 2 (Sliced into Half Inch Sets)
Instructions
Preheat the Pit Boss to 500°F with the lid covered for 15 minutes when ready to cook.
Sprinkle turbinado sugar on both sides of the grapefruit and place on a Pit Boss that has been
warmed. 3 minutes per side on the grill, or until grill marks form. Take the steaks off the grill and set them aside until they're cool enough to handle.
Squeeze the juice from the grilled grapefruit and drain it (you should end up with about 16 ounces of juice).
In a pitcher, aggressively stir together the grapefruit juice, bourbon, lemon juice, Pit Boss Smoked Syrup, and one mint leaves sprig.
After adding a scoop of ice, vigorously shake for 30 seconds. Strain into six rocks glasses filled halfway with ice and top with ginger beer.
To serve, garnish with a grilled grapefruit slice and a sprig of mint. Have fun with it.

4.197 Pumpkin Chocolate Chip Cookies
Total Time: 20 mins, Servings: 8
Ingredients
Flour, 2 cups
Baking powder, 1 tbsp
Baking soda, 1/2 tbsp
Salt, 1/2 tbsp
Ground cinnamon, 1 tbsp
Ground nutmeg, 1/4 tbsp
Pumpkin pie spice, 1/2 tbsp
Ground ginger, 1/2 tbsp
Butter, 1/2 cup
Sugar, 1 cup
Canned pumpkin, 1 cup
Eggs, 1
Vanilla extract, 1 tbsp
Chocolate chips, 2 cups
Instructions
Preheat the Pit Boss according to the manufacturer's directions when you're ready to serve. Preheat the oven to 350 ° F and bake with the lid covered for 10 to 15 minutes.
Combine the ginger, baking powder, salt, baking soda, cinnamon, nutmeg, pumpkin spice, and flour in a bowl and set aside.
In a separate dish, cream the butter until light and creamy. Combine the honey, pumpkin puree, egg, & vanilla essence in a large mixing bowl.
Stir in the dry ingredients until they are thoroughly mixed with the liquid ingredients. Gently fold in the
chocolate chips.
Drop spoonfuls of dough onto a parchment-lined baking sheet.
Bake for about ten min on the Pit Boss, or until the cookies are gently browned. Before serving, reheat the dish. It is something to be proud of.

4.198 Cold Smoked Cheese
Total Time: 2 hours 5 mins, Servings: 8
Ingredients
Cheese of any kind: Provolone, Cheddar, Mozzarella
Instructions
Preheat the Pit Boss to 165°F and close the lid for fifteen min until ready to cook.
Transfer the contents of the half-size pan to the full-size pan. Fill a half-size pan halfway with ice and push it to the tip.
In a half-size pan, place the cheese on toothpicks or a cooling rack to allow air to flow and prevent sticking. To cook, place the pan on the grill.
Smoke the cheese for an hour. On the grill, turn the cheese over. After adding more ice to the melting water surrounding the pan, continue to smoke for another hour.
Remove the cheese from the grill by wrapping it in parchment paper. Refrigerate for 2 to 3 days to let flavors to come together. As a result, the smoke fragrance would be mellowed.
After 2 to 3 days, remove from the freezer, unwrap, peel, and serve with your favorite cracker, pickled veggies, and wine. Have fun with it.

4.199 Tomatoes Roasted
Total Time: 3 hours 5 mins, Servings: 2
Ingredients
Ripe tomatoes, 3 large
Kosher salt, 1/2 tbsp
Coarse ground black pepper, 1 tbsp
Sugar, 1/4 tbsp
Basil or thyme, 1/4 tbsp
Olive oil
Instructions
Line a rimmed baking sheet with parchment paper.
Preheat the Pit Boss to 225°F with the lid covered for 15 minutes when ready to cook.
After cutting the stem end of the tomatoes, slice them into half-inch-thick slices.
Combine the sugar, pepper, salt, & basil or thyme in a shallow mixing cup.
Pour olive oil into the well of a dinner plate.
Brush one side of each tomato slice with olive oil and place it on the baking sheet. Sprinkle the seasoned mixture on top of the tomato slices.
Place the pan on the grill plate right away and roast the tomatoes for about 3 hours, or until the fluids have dried up and the edges have constricted. Remove it off the grill and enjoy it.

4.200 Squash Butternut Macaroni plus Cheese
Total Time: 55 mins, Servings: 2
Ingredients
Butternut squash, 1 medium
Uncooked macaroni, 2 cups
Yellow onion, 1 small
Chicken broth, 1/2 cup
Milk, 1 cup
Pepper
Salt
Cheese grated, 1 cup.
Instructions
Turn on the Pit Boss grill, set the temperature to 225 ° F, and preheat for 10 -15 minutes with the lid covered once you're ready to cook.

Prick butternut squash with a fork several times and place on grill grate. Cook for 40 minutes to an hour, or until the veggies are soft. After the meat has been cooked, scoop it out and discard the seeds.

Cook elbow macaroni according to package directions. Drain and set aside the water.

In a medium pan, sauté the chopped onion until aromatic and brown. Combine broth, milk, salt, onions, and butternut squash in a food processor. Puree the ingredients until it is thick and creamy. Season with salt and pepper to taste.

Combine cooked pasta, pureed sauce, and shredded cheese in a large mixing bowl. Stir to melt the cheese, then gradually add milk until you get the desired consistency. Before serving, reheat the dish. Have fun with it.

4.201 The Max Burgers

Total Time: 32 mins, Servings: 4
Ingredients
Ground Beef (80% Lean), 3 Pound
Garlic (Minced), 3 Clove
Kosher Salt
Black Pepper (Finely Ground)
Bacon Jam, 1/2 Cup
Caramelized Onions, 1/2 Cup
Sharp Cheddar Cheese (Shredded), 2 Cup
Canola Oil
Kaiser Rolls (Split), 8
Salted Butter (Softened), 1/4 Cup
Instructions

In a large mixing basin, gently combine the ground meat, garlic, salt, and pepper.

Cover your work surface with a thick sheet of plastic wrap. Fill the plastic wrap with the ground beef mixture. Flatten the ground beef evenly on the plastic wrap with a rolling pin to make a 1/2-inch-thick rectangle.

Cut the ground beef rectangle into Sixteen equal-size squares with a pizza wheel. Equal amounts of (bacon jam), caramelized onions, and cheddar cheese should be spread on the 8 squares closest to you. Grasp the farthest-away side of the plastic wrap & fold the top 8 hamburgers over the ones closest to you. Remove the plastic wrap off the burgers' tops. With the pizza wheel, cut through the score markings to make 8 square burgers.

Form each square burger into a circular patty with your hands, sealing the edges of each burger to keep the stuffing in. Before cooking, chill the burgers for at least 1 hour.

When ready to cook, preheat the Pit Boss to 500°F with the lid closed for fifteen min.

Brush the grill grates liberally with canola oil. Season the burgers to taste with Salt and pepper. Place patties on Pit Boss and cook for 12 to 14 minutes, rotating once, until internal temperature reaches 160°F. If preferred, top the burgers with more cheese in the last few minutes of cooking.

Take the burgers off the grill, cover loosely with foil, and set aside for 5 -10 minutes before serving.

While the burgers are resting, butter the cut sides of the buns. Grill till golden, cut side down. Assemble the burgers, topping them
as desired. Enjoy.

4.202 London Broil Grilled Along with Blue Cheese Butter

Total Time: 1 hour 10 mins, Servings: 4
Ingredients
Soy Sauce, 1/4 Cup
Water, 1/4 Cup
Onion (Coarsely Chopped), 1 Small
Garlic (Minced), 1 Clove
Red Wine Vinegar, 2 tbsp
Extra-Virgin Olive Oil or Vegetable Oil, 2 tbsp
Ketchup, 1 tbsp
Worcestershire Sauce, 1 tsp
Black Pepper (Freshly Ground), 1 tsp
Sugar, 1 tsp
London Broil Steak (Top Round), 1 (2 Lb)
Pit Boss Beef Rub
Butter (Softened), 8 tbsp
Scallion (Minced), 1
Crumbled Blue Cheese, 1/4 Cup
Worcestershire Sauce, 1 tsp
Black Pepper, Freshly Ground
Instructions

To make the marinade, whisk together the water, soy sauce, onion, garlic, red wine vinegar, ketchup, oil, Worcestershire sauce, pepper, and sugar in a small mixing bowl.

Put the marinade over the meat in a big, resealable plastic bag. Refrigerate for a minimum of 6 hours and up to 24 hours. Take the steak out of the fridge and let it aside to come to room temp.

To make the Blue Cheese Butter, combine butter, scallion, blue cheese, Worcestershire sauce, and pepper in a small mixing bowl. Using a wooden spoon, combine the ingredients. If not used right away, cover and chill.

Now cut the steak from marinade and wipe it dry with paper towels after it has reached room temperature.

Season with Beef Rub on all sides.

When ready to cook, preheat the Pit Boss to 180°F with the lid closed for fifteen min.

Smoke the steak for 60 minutes by placing it straight on the grill grate.

Arrange the meat on a serving dish. Preheat the grill to 500 degrees Fahrenheit with the lid covered.

When the grill is hot, return the steak to it and cook for 15 to 20 minutes, or until the required internal temperature is attained, 130°F for medium-rare.

Allow the meat to rest for 3 mins before slicing thinly on a diagonal. Serve with a dollop of Blue Cheese Butter on top. Enjoy.

4.203 Filet Mignon Smoked with Sweet Pepper Relish & Baked Ricotta

Total Time: 2 hours 30 mins, Servings: 4
Ingredients
Filet Mignon Steaks, 32 Ounce
Rosemary (Chopped), 1 tbsp
Chile De Árbol (Thinly Sliced), 1 1/4 tsp
Lemon Zest, 2 tbsp
Black Pepper, 1 tbsp
Kosher Salt, 2 tbsp
Olive Oil (Extra-Virgin), 1 tbsp
Whole Milk Ricotta, 1 Cup
Fresh Thyme, 4 1/2 tsp
Fresh Parsley, 1 tbsp
Kosher Salt
Black Pepper
Bell Peppers (Mixed Colors), 4 Whole
Red Onion (Sliced), 3 Cup
Salt
Red Wine Vinegar, 1 tbsp
Fresh Oregano, 2 tbsp
Instructions

Rub rosemary, diced Chile, lemon zest, and black pepper into filets. Refrigerate for about 4 hours or up to 24 hours before serving.

Take the filets out of the fridge and set them out to come to

room temp. Drizzle with olive oil & season with Salt.
When you're ready to cook, fire up the Pit Boss grill according to the manufacturer's directions. Preheat for 10 - 15 minutes with the lid closed.
Place on a hot grill for 30 minutes of smoking.
Assemble the ricotta while the steaks are cooking. Combine ricotta, olive oil, 1 teaspoon thyme, parsley, 12 teaspoon salt, and 14 teaspoon peppers in a large mixing bowl. Mix well, then pour into an 8-inch cast-iron skillet. Top with the remaining thyme and the sliced chile. Drizzle with extra virgin olive oil.
After 30 minutes, increase the temp to 225 ° F. & cook until an instant-read thermometer put into the thickest portion of the meat reads 120 ° F.
Remove the steaks from the grill and place them on a plate to rest. Raise the temperature to be high & warm for 10-15 minutes with the lid covered. Grill the
ricotta for 30 minutes or until it is gently browned.
Prepare the relish while the steaks are resting. Brush the bell peppers lightly with olive oil and lay next to the ricotta on the grill grate. Cook until faintly charred, about 15-20 minutes.
Remove the stems, seeds, and membranes from the peppers and discard them. Place the peppers in a medium bowl, thinly sliced lengthwise. Over medium-high heat, heat a sauté pan. Pour in the olive oil.
Add onions, thyme, salt, and pepper when the pan is heated. Cook for 5 minutes, or until the vegetables are soft. Return the pan to heat and pour the onion mixture over the
peppers. Reduce by half by adding vinegar. Pour the sauce over the peppers and onions and mix well. Toss in the oregano. Season with Salt and pepper to taste.
Return the filets to the grill and sear for 5 minutes per side on High.
Remove from the grill and set aside for 5 minutes to cool. Slice the peppers against the grain and serve on top of them. Serve with baked ricotta and lemon wedges on the side. Enjoy.

4.204 Cheesesteak Sandwich Grilled
Total Time: 25 mins, Servings: 4
Ingredients
Green Bell Pepper (Sliced), 1
Red Bell Pepper (Sliced), 1
Yellow Bell Pepper (Sliced), 1
Yellow Onion (Sliced into Rounds), 1 Large
Salt n Pepper
Strip Slices (New York), 1 (1-1/2 Lb)
Pit Boss Beef Rub
Canola Oil, 1 tbsp
Hoagie Rolls, 4
Provolone Cheese, 4 Slices
Instructions
Preheat the Pit Boss to 500°F and cook for 15 minutes with the lid covered when ready to cook.
Preheat the grill by placing a cast iron griddle straight on the grate.
Season the peppers & onions with Salt & pepper to taste. Pit Boss Beef Rub is used to season the strip steak slices.
Drizzle 1 tbsp canola oil over the cast iron griddle. Season with salt and onions.
Cook onions for 5 minutes, or until they are transparent. Add the peppers and simmer for another 10 minutes, or until softened & cooked through.
While the peppers & onions are cooking, fry
the seasoned steak strips for 3 minutes on each side, straight on the grill grate next to the skillet, until nicely browned and cooked through.
To toast the buns, place them cut side down on top grill grate. Transfer the steak to the grill to assemble the sandwiches when it's done. Top each mound of steak with a heaping of peppers and onions, followed by a slice of provolone.
Put the cover on and wait for the cheese to melt. Transfer each mound on the buns with two spatulas and serve immediately. Enjoy.

4.205 Pit Boss BLT Burgers
Total Time: 55 mins, Servings: 6
Ingredients
Ground Chuck (80% Lean), 2 Pound
Pit Boss Beef Rub
Mayonnaise, 1/2 Cup
Pit Boss BBQ 'Que Sauce, 1/3 Cup
Pickle Juice, 1
Pastrami (Sliced), 1 Pound
Cheese (Sharp Cheddar), 8 Slices
Hamburger Buns, 8
Your Desired Toppings: Tomatoes, Lettuce, Red Onions, Etc.
Instructions
When you're ready to cook, turn on the Pit Boss's Smoke setting. Form 8 equal-sized patties out of ground beef and season with Pit Boss's Beef Rub. Place the chicken straight on the grate, cover, & smoke for 30 minutes.
Make the fry sauce while the burgers are cooking. Combine the mayo, BBQ sauce, & pickle juice in a small bowl. Combine all ingredients in a mixing bowl, cover, and chill till ready to use.
Take the burgers off the grill and turn up the heat to 450 ° Fahrenheit Return the burgers to grate after allowing the grill to warm for 10-15 minutes.
Cook burgers for 4-5 mins on one side before flipping. Add the pastrami on the grill in 8 separately portioned heaps when you flip the burgers. Cook for another 4-5 minutes with the lid closed.
Carefully lay the pastrami on top of the burgers, followed by a piece of cheese. You may even toss the buns on the grill to toast them if desired. Close the lid and heat until the cheese has melted & the burgers are done to your liking. 175 degrees F is the recommended interior temp for a well-done burger.
Place the burgers with pastrami on the bottom bread. Slather the top bun with fry sauce, then top with your favourite burger toppings and serve. Enjoy.

Chapter 5: Seafood Recipes

5.1 Pit Boss Baked Rainbow Trout

Total Time: 20 mins, Servings: 2
Ingredients
2 tbsp Olive Oil (divided)
2 Whole cleaned, gutted with heads and tails on Rainbow Trout.
1/2 tsp Fresh Dill.
1/2 tsp Fresh Thyme
1 tsp Pure Kosher Sea Salt by Jacobsen Salt Co.
1/2 Large Onion (sliced)
1. Thinly slice large lemon.
Black Pepper (Freshly grounded) 1 tsp.
Instructions
When you're prepared to cook, preheat your Pit Boss at 400°F. Also, keep the lid shut for at least 15 mins.
1 tbsp olive oil should be used to grease a 9X13 inch baking dish.
Place the fish in the baking dish and drizzle with the remaining olive oil.
Season the fish with salt, dill, and thyme on both the interior and exterior.
Stuff the fish with lemon and onion pieces, then season with salt and pepper. Also, a slice of lemon should be placed on each fish.
Bake for at least ten mins in a Pit Boss and pour hot water (2 tbsp) onto a dish.
Continue baking for another 10 mins, or until the fish flakes easily with a fork, and then serve.

5.2 Sweet & Spicy Sriracha Salmon

Total Time: 40 mins, Servings: 4
Ingredients
Soy Sauce, 1/4 Cup
2 tbsp Brown Sugar
1 tbsp Rice Vinegar
1 tbsp Sriracha
1 tbsp Grated Ginger
1 tbsp Garlic (Minced)
1 tsp Chipotle Pit Boss Rub
1/2 tsp Sesame Oil
1/2-2 lbs. Wild-Caught Salmon Skin-On Fillet
2 tbsp Scallions (Chopped)
2 tbsp Sesame Seeds (Lightly Toasted)
Instructions
In a big zipper bag, combine the soy sauce, brown sugar, sriracha, vinegar, garlic, sesame oil, and ginger. Add some salmon (about 4 oz. per) to equally marinate and coat in the fridge for at least 1 hr. Take it out of the zipper bag (Salmon). Remove the marinade from the equation.
Set the temp. Preheat your Pit Boss to 450°F and keep it covered for 10-15 mins.
Place the salmon on the grill, skin side down, for at least 8-10 mins for medium-well.
Remove the salmon from the grill and top with toasted sesame seeds and scallions.
Serve with brown or white rice, or quinoa and grilled baby bok choy. Enjoy.

5.3 Smoked Chilean Sea Bass

Total Time: 45 mins, Servings: 4
Ingredients
Marinade
Grapeseed or canola oil, 1/4 Cup
Lemon (Juiced), 1
Clove Garlic (Crushed), 1
Fresh oregano, 1 tbsp.
Blackened Saskatchewan rub Pit Boss, 1 tsp.
Fresh thyme, 1 tbsp
Main
Skin Off Striped Sea Bass or Fresh Chilean Fillets 4 (6 Oz)
Pure Irish Kerry gold Butter 8 tbsp
Chicken Rub Pit Boss
Lemon (for garnish) 4 slices.
Instructions
To make the marinade, combine all of the marinade ingredients in a big (resealable) bag and thoroughly mix them. Place the sea bass in the refrigerator for at least 30 mins after adding it to the marinade. At the very least, turn it once.
Set the temp to at least 325°F (and preheat) and bake for 15 mins with the lid closed.
Place the butter on a baking pan large enough to keep the fillets flat and melt it completely under the grill.
After removing the fish from the marinade, place it on a clean, flat surface. Fill the container with the marinade and butter. The fillets should be generously seasoned with Pit Boss Chicken Rub.
After putting the fillets in the pan with the butter mixture, return them to the grill. Cook for 30 mins, basting the fillets once or twice with the hot butter mixture.
Remove the fish from the Pit Boss after its internal temp reaches 160°F. As a garnish, fresh thyme and lemon slices may be used.

5.4 Grilled Shrimp Cocktail

Total Time: 15 mins, Servings: 2
Ingredients
Main
Shrimp along with Tails (Deveined), 2 lb.
Olive oil, 2 tbsp.
Old Bay Seasoning, 1 tsp.
For Garnish, Italian Parsley (Chopped)
Cocktail Sauce
Ketchup, 1/2 Cup.
Prepared horseradish, 2 tbsp.
Lemon juice 1 tbsp.
Some kosher salt
Black Pepper (grounded)
Hot Sauce.
Instructions
Preheat your Pit Boss at 350 deg Fahrenheit. Also, shut the lid for approximately 15 mins.
Rinse the shrimp in a colander and pat dry with paper towels. In a large mixing cup, combine the shrimp, Old Bay Seasoning, and oil. If not using seasoning, season with 1 tsp salt and 1/2 tsp black pepper (freshly ground). Toss until the shrimp are

uniformly cooked, then transfer to a baking dish that can be used on the grill.

Place the shrimp-filled baking sheet on the grill & cook for 5-7 mins, or until the shrimp are opaque.

To make the cocktail sauce, combine ketchup, lemon juice, and horseradish in a mixing bowl. Season with salt and pepper to taste, as well as spicy sauce if preferred.

Toss the fried shrimp with the cocktail sauce in a bowl. Chopped Italian parsley is sprinkled over the shrimp and sauce.

5.5 Grilled Salmon with Smoked Avocado Salsa
Total Time: 40 mins, Servings: 6
Ingredients
3 Avocados (Halved and Pitted).
Pit Boss Fin and Feather Rub, 1 tbsp.
Salmon fillet (Skin On), 3 lbs.
1/2 Red Onion (Diced).
Clove Garlic (Minced), 2.
Jalapeño pepper (Seeded & Minced), 1.
Cilantro (Roughly Chopped), 1/4 Cup.
1 Lime (Juiced).
1 tsp Salt.
1 tbsp Olive Oil.
Instructions
When you're prepared to cook, set your Pit Boss grill on smoke. Place the avocados on the grill grate, cut side up, and let them smoke for at least 10 mins. Take the steaks from the grill and put them aside to cool.

Preheat the grill at 450 deg Fahrenheit for 10-15 mins with the lid covered.

Place the fish and butcher paper on the grill straight immediately and cook for 15-20 mins, or until the internal temp of the thickest portion of the salmon reaches 155 deg F.

While the salmon is being cooked, make the salsa. Dice the smoked avocados into medium chopped pieces and combine them with the other ingredients in a shallow cup.

After taking the salmon from the grill, place it on any serving plate. On top, there's an avocado sauce.

5.6 Grilled Shrimp Brochette
Total Time: 40 mins, Servings: 6
Ingredients
Extra-large Shrimp (Peeled & Deveined), 1 lb.
Whole Jalapeños (Fresh), 6
8 oz Block Monterey Jack Cheese.
Bacon, 1 lb.
Meat Church the Gospel All-Purpose Rub, 2 tbsp.
Some Oil
Instructions
Set the shrimp aside after splitting them in half. After removing the seeds, slice the jalapenos into thin slivers. Slice the cheese into slivers about the same size as the peppers. Cut the bacon pieces in half.

Stuff a jalapeño slice and a piece of cheddar inside each shrimp. Secure the filled shrimp in a 1/2-piece of bacon with a toothpick.

After assembling all of the shrimp, season lightly with Meat Church, the all-purpose gospel rub.

Preheat the Pit Boss to 425°F for 15 mins with the lid closed.

Brush a little coating of oil over the grill grate, then place the shrimp immediately on it. Cook for approximately 20 mins, turning halfway during the cooking time. The bacon should start to crisp up, and the shrimp should become yellow.

Remove the steaks from the grill and let to cool for at least 10 mins.

5.7 Kimi's Simple Grilled Fresh Fish
Total Time: 50 mins, Servings: 2
Ingredients
Soy Sauce, 1 cup
Olive Oil (Extra-Virgin), 1/3 Cup
Garlic (Minced), 1 tbsp.
Lemons (Juiced), 2.
Fresh Basil
Fresh fish (should be in Portion-Sized Pieces), 4 lb.
Instructions
Combine all your ingredients for the sauce and marinate the fish for 45 mins.

Grill the marinated fish on the Pit Boss until it reaches a core temp of 140-145°F. Serve immediately and enjoy.

5.8 Bacon-Wrapped Shrimp
Total Time: 25 mins, Servings: 6
Ingredients
Jumbo Shrimp (large), 10.
Olive Oil (Extra-Virgin), 1/4 Cup.
Lemon Juice, 2 tbsp.
Lemon Zest, 1 tbsp.
Garlic (Minced), 1 tsp.
Salt 1 tsp.
Black Pepper, 1/2 tsp.
Flat-Leaf Parsley (Chopped), 1 tsp.
Strips Bacon, 10.
Instructions
Under cold running water, scrub the shrimp well and wipe dry with paper towels. Put the mixture in a resealable plastic bag or a cup.

To make the marinade, combine all of the ingredients in a mixing bowl. Combine the olive oil, lemon zest, lemon juice, salt, garlic, parsley, and pepper in a small container with a tight-fitting lid and shake vigorously until well combined. After pouring the sauce over the shrimp, chill for 30-60 mins.

30 mins before you want to cook the shrimp, preheat the Pit Boss grill. Smoke will develop before the fire is lit, so keep the lid open (4-5 mins). Preheat the grill to 400°F and bake with the lid covered for 10 to 15 mins.

Cook the bacon strips in a diagonal pattern on the grill grate for 10-12 mins or partially cooked but still flexible. Each strip should be a half-width cut. Turn the grill on.

Remove the shrimp from the marinade and discard it. Wrap a piece of bacon around the body of each shrimp and secure it with a toothpick. Cook for 4 mins on each side, turning once while cooking.

5.9 BBQ Roasted Salmon
Total Time: 35 mins, Servings: 4
Ingredients
Honey, 1 cup.
Mustard (Whole-Grain), 3 tbsp
Ketchup, 1 cup.
Brown Sugar (dark), ½ cup.
Cider Vinegar, 1 tsp.
Thyme Leaves (Finely Chopped), ½ tsp
Kosher Sea Salt (Pure) by Jacobsen Salt Co., 1/8 tsp.
Black Pepper (Freshly Ground), 1/8 tsp.
Salmon Fillets (Skin-On), 4, 6oz Each.
Instructions
Combine all sauce ingredients in a large mixing bowl, preferably 1 day before cooking the salmon.

The sauce should be sprayed on both sides of the salmon fillets. Every remaining sauce should be
preserved.

Preheat Pit Boss to 350°F for 15 mins with lid closed when ready to cook.
Place the fillets on the grill skin-side down and cook for 15 mins. Allow 3-5 mins for the fish to rest. Serve with more sauce on the side.

5.10 Vodka Brined Smoked Wild Salmon

Total Time: 55 mins, Servings: 4
Ingredients
Brine
Brown Sugar, 1 cup.
Black Pepper, 1 tbsp.
Coarse salt, 1/2 cup.
Vodka, 1 cup.
Main
1 Wild Caught Salmon (1-2 Lb.)
Lemon Wedges, 1.
Capers
Instructions
In a shallow mixing cup, combine brown sugar, pepper, salt, and alcohol.
Seal a clean resealable bag with the fish. Pour the marinade over the fish and give it a good massage. Before serving, chill it for 2-4 hrs.
Drain the bag's contents, clean it, then wipe it dry using paper towels.
Preheat the Pit Boss to 180°F with the lid closed for 15 mins when ready to cook. Use Super Smoke if it's available for the greatest flavor.
Smoke the salmon skin-side down for 30 mins.
Increase the grill temp to 225°F and cook the salmon for another 45-60 mins, or until the thickest part of the fish reaches 140°F and flakes easily when pressed with a finger or fork.
Serve with lemons and capers.

5.11 Grilled Swordfish with Corn Salsa

Total Time: 45 mins, Servings: 4
Ingredients
Ears Corn, (Husked), 4.
Olive oil, 2 cups.
Salt & pepper.
Cherry Tomatoes, 2 ozs.
Red Onion, (Diced), 1.
Chile, Serrano (Chopped), 1.
Lime (Juiced), 1.
4 Whole Swordfish Fillet
Instructions
Preheat the grill to high for 15 mins, then shut the cover.
Season the corn with salt and pepper after drizzling it with olive oil. After 12-15 mins on the grill, the corn should be cooked through and nicely browned. Allow time for the dish to cool before serving.
Remove the kernels from the corn once it has cooled and place them in a medium mixing cup. In a mixing bowl, combine the cilantro, tomatoes, serrano, red onion, and lime juice. Toss to combine and season to taste with salt.
After coating fish steaks with olive oil, season them with salt and pepper.
Cook for 18 mins on the grill grate, or until the fish is opaque and flakes readily when poked with a fork. (If you like your tuna or salmon rare, cook it for a shorter period.)
Serve the grilled swordfish with a heaping of corn salsa on top.

5.12 Pit Boss Cajun Broil

Total Time: 90 mins, Servings: 8
Ingredients
Olive oil, 2 tbsp
Red Potatoes, 2 lbs.
Old Bay Seasoning
Corn Ears (Each cut into 1/3), 6.
Kielbasa Sausage (Smoked), 2 lbs.
Shrimp (with Tails, Deveined), 3.
Butter, 2 tbsp.
Instructions
Preheat the Pit Boss to 450 deg Fahrenheit and cook for around 15 mins with the lid covered.
Drizzle half of the olive oil over the potatoes and season with Old Bay seasoning to taste. Place immediately on the grill grate. Roast the veggies for 20 mins, or until they are tender. Drizzle the rest of the olive oil over the corn and
season with old bay seasoning. Place the corn and kielbasa on the grill grate next to the potatoes. 15 mins of roasting
Season the shrimp with old bay seasoning. Cook it directly on the grill grate with the other items for 10 mins or become brilliant pink and cooked through.
After removing the grill, transfer everything to a large mixing bowl. After adding the butter, season it with additional old bay seasoning to enhance flavor. Toss to coat, and serve immediately.

5.13 Grilled Whole Steelhead Fillet

Total Time: 35 mins, Serving: 6
Ingredients
Salmon fillet or steelhead (Skin-On), 2-3 Lb.
Montana Mex - Sweet Seasoning, 2 tbsp.
Montana Mex - Jalapeño Seasoning Blend, 1 tsp.
Montana Mex Mild Chile Seasoning Blend, 1tsp.
Montana Mex - Avocado Oil, 2 tbsp.
Freshly Grated Ginger, 2 tbsp.
Lemon (Thinly Sliced), 1.
Instructions
Coat the fish evenly with all three dry spices,
grated ginger, avocado oil, and thinly sliced lemon.
Preheat the Pit Boss to 380°F for 15 mins with the lid closed.
Place the fish skin-side down on the grill and cook for at least 20 mins.
Take the fillet from the grill and put it aside to rest for 5 mins.

5.14 Fried Halibut Fish Sticks

Total Time: 45 mins, Servings: 4
Ingredients
Olive Oil (Extra-Virgin)
Halibut, 1-1/2 lbs.
1/2 Cup All-Purpose Flour
Salt, 1-1/2 tsp.
Black Pepper (grounded), 1 tsp.
Large Eggs, 2.
Panko Breadcrumbs, 1-1/2 Cup
Dried parsley, 2 tbsp.
Dill Weed (Dried), 1 tsp.
Instructions
Preheat the grill on high for 15 mins with the lid covered when you're ready to make the dish. Set the temp to 500°F if feasible for the best results.
Heat enough extra-virgin olive oil in a Dutch grill to cook fish within the grill (approximately 10 mins).
All fish fillets should be rinsed and dried. Cut the fillets into 1-inch strips.
In a mixing bowl, combine the all-purpose salt, flour, and pepper.
In a separate dish, beat some eggs.
In a third bowl, combine the parsley, panko, and dill.
The fish fillets should be floured first, then dipped in eggs, and

lastly in the panko mixture.
Heat the oil and fry the fish sticks for 3-4 mins, or until they reach a temp of 130 deg Fahrenheit (internal temp).
Serve with a side of fries.

5.15 Tuna Burgers
Total Time: 50 mins, Serving: 4
Ingredients
Tuna (Steak), 2 lbs.
2 Eggs.
Soy Sauce 1 tsp.
Green Bell Pepper (Diced), 1.
White or yellow onions, 1.
Pit Boss Saskatchewan Rub (Blackened), 1 tbsp.
Pit Boss Fin and Feather Rub, 1 tbsp.
Olive Oil (Extra-Virgin)
Instructions
In a large mixing bowl, combine eggs, tuna, Worcestershire or soy sauce,
green bell pepper, tomato, Saskatchewan Rub (Blackened), and Fin & Feather Rub.
Lubricate your hands with olive oil before making tuna patties.
Preheat the Pit Boss to 500°F for 15 mins with the lid closed.
Cook patties for 10-15 mins at the grill's edges (the hottest area on the grill). Flip the burgers halfway through the cooking time.
Remove the steaks from the grill and top with your desired toppings.

5.16 Baked Salmon Cakes
Total Time: 80 mins, Servings: 4
Ingredients
Salmon, 2 lb.
Salt
Black Pepper (Ground)
Small Onion (Diced), 1/2.
1 Celery, Stalks
Bell Pepper (Red), 1.
Dill (Fresh or Dried), 1 tbsp.
Lemon Zest, 1 tsp.
Black Pepper, 1/2 tsp.
Sea Salt (Coarse), ¼ tsp.
Breadcrumbs, 1-1/2 tbsp.
Large Eggs, 2.
Olive Oil (Extra-Virgin), 4 tbsp.
Instructions
Preheat the Pit Boss to 275°F for 15 mins, then shut the lid.
Season the salmon fillets with salt and pepper before placing them straight on the grill grate. Cook until the internal temp of the chicken reaches 120 deg Fahrenheit. Remove the steaks from the grill and place them on a cooling rack.
Split the chilled salmon fillets with a fork in a large mixing cup. In a mixing bowl, combine the celery, carrots, dill, bell pepper, lemon zest, salt and pepper, eggs, and breadcrumbs. Mix thoroughly.
Make six 2" deep patties with the salmon mixture. Preheat the grill to 375°F and shut the lid for 10-15 mins.
When the oil is heated, add the patties to the cast iron pan in batches. Cook for 10-12 mins, or until golden brown on both sides, flipping halfway through.

5.17 Grilled Blackened Saskatchewan Salmon
Total Time: 45 mins, Servings: 4
Ingredients
Salmon Fillets, 1.
Dressing of Zesty (Italian)
Saskatchewan Rub of Pit Boss (Blackened)
Lemon Slices

Instructions
After coating the salmon with Italian seasoning, season it with the "Saskatchewan Rub of Pit Boss (Blackened)."
Preheat the Pit Boss to 325°F and keep the lid closed for fifteen mins.
Cook the salmon on the grill for 20 to 30 mins, or until it reaches an internal temp of 145°F and flakes easily. Remove the fish from the heat. On the side, serve with lemon wedges.

5.18 Smoked Seafood Ceviche
Total Time: 1 Hr 20 mins, Servings: 4
Ingredients
Sea Scallops (Shucked), 1 lb.
Shrimp (Peeled & Deveined), 1 lb.
Canola Oil, 1 tbsp.
Lime (Zested & Juiced), 1.
Lemon Juice, 1.
Orange (Juiced), 1
Garlic Powder, 1 tsp.
Onion Powder, 1 tsp.
Salt, 2 tsp.
Black Pepper, 1/2 tsp.
Avocado (diced), 1.
Red Onion (Diced), 1/2.
Cilantro (Finely Chopped), 1 tbsp.
Red Pepper Flakes, 1 Pinch.
Instructions
In a mixing dish, combine the scallops, shrimp, and canola oil. When you're ready to make the dish, preheat the grill to 180 deg F and leave the lid covered for 15 mins.
Place the shrimp and scallops on the grill to smoke for approximately 45 mins. While the other ingredients are smoking, prepare them and combine them in a large mixing bowl.
Raise the heat to 325°F and steam the shrimp and scallops for an additional 5 mins to ensure that they are fully cooked.
Allow scallops and shrimp to cool slightly before slicing them in half widthwise and mixing them in with the rest of the ingredients in the meal.
To enable the flavors to blend, chill the Ceviche for approximately 2-3 hrs. Serve with corn chips as a side dish.

5.19 Prosciutto Wrapped Grilled Shrimp with Peach Salsa
Total Time: 30 mins, Servings: 4
Ingredients
Shrimp (Peeled & Deveined), 2 lb.
Prosciutto Ham, 8 slices.
Toothpicks
2 Peaches (Diced)
Balsamic vinegar, 2 tbsp.
Honey, 2 tbsp.
Serrano (Chopped), 1 Chile.
Basil (Fresh Chopped), 1 tbsp.
Salt
Black Pepper
Instructions
Under cold running water, thoroughly rinse the shrimp and wipe dry with paper towels. Wrap a piece of prosciutto around each shrimp and fasten
with a toothpick if necessary.
Peach Salsa: In a mixing bowl, combine peaches, 1 tbsp sugar, butter, 1/2 serrano pepper, basil, and salt and pepper. Add additional sugar, chile, butter, salt, and pepper to taste.

Set the temp to High and warm for 15 mins while keeping the lid closed.
Cook the "prosciutto-wrapped" shrimp for 4-6 mins on each side or until opaque on the grill grate.
Toss the shrimp with a little peach salsa and serve right away. Garnish with jalapeño slices for extra heat.

5.20 Smoked Salmon Flatbread
Total Time: 25 mins, Servings: 4
Ingredients
Pizza Dough, 1.
Creme Fraiche, 1/4 Cup.
Ricotta Cheese, 1/4 Cup.
Salt
Black Pepper
Chives (Chopped).
Smoked Salmon
Capers (Drained)
Olive Oil (Extra-Virgin).
Instructions
When prepared to cook, preheat the grill on high for approximately 15 mins with the lid covered.
In the meanwhile, roll out the pizza dough.
Place the dough on the grill grate. Cooking time is just around 3 mins each side.
Using crème fraiche, cover the crust. Add the ricotta cheese after that. If desired, season with chives and salt and pepper.
Top the crust with any remaining smoked salmon flakes. Finish with chives and capers. Drizzle a little olive oil on top if desired.

5.21 Teriyaki Salmon
Total Time: 1 Hr 10 mins, Servings: 2
Ingredients
Soy Sauce, 1 cup.
Brown Sugar. 6 tbsp.
Clove Garlic, 4.
Ginger (Minced), 1 tbsp.
Orange (Juiced), 2
Orange Zest, 2.
Salmon Fillets (6oz.), 4 Pieces.
Sesame Seeds, 1 tbsp.
Scallions (Chopped)
Sesame Seeds (Toasted)
Instructions
Combine everything in a saucepan except the sesame seeds and the fish. Bring to a boil, then reduce to a syrupy consistency (about a 50% reduction).
In a dish, combine the sesame seeds and fish and marinate for 60 mins.
Remove the salmon from the marinade and bring the sauce to a boil in a saucepan.
Preheat the grill to high heat with the lid covered for 10-15 mins. Place the salmon fillets on the grill grate, skin side up.
Cook the salmon for 3-5 mins each side, or until done to your liking, brushing it with the "Teriyaki Sauce" as needed.
Remove the salmon from the pan after it's cooked to your liking and sprinkle with sliced scallions and toasted sesame seeds.

5.22 Baked Tuna Noodle Casserole
Total Time: 1 Hr 30 mins, Servings: 4
Ingredients
Wheat Pasta Box 13.25oz, 1.
Yogurt, 2 cups.
Almond Milk, 1 cup.
Ground Mustard, 1 tsp.
Celery Salt, 1/2 tsp.
Button Mushrooms (Sliced), 1 cup.
Tuna (Cooked), 10 oz.
Peas (Canned), 1 Cup.
Cheese (Colby/Cheddar), 1 Cup.
Instructions
Brings a large kettle of salted water to a boil under high pressure. Follow the package directions for cooking the pasta. Drain and put aside the water.
In a medium mixing bowl, combine the sugar, yogurt, ground mustard, and celery salt. Next, combine the mushrooms, salmon, peas, and cooked pasta in a large mixing bowl. Half of the cheese should be folded in at this point.
Fill a greased 13" x 9" baking dish halfway with the mixture and top with the remaining cheese.
When prepared to cook, preheat the Pit Boss to 350°F with the lid closed for 15 mins.
Place the casserole dish directly on the grill grate and cook for 45 mins, or until the cheese has melted and the casserole is fully cooked.

5.23 Grilled Mussels with Lemon Butter
Total Time: 1 Hr 5 mins. Servings: 4
Ingredients
Mussels (Debearded, Washed), 2 lb.
Water, 5 quarts.
Salt, 1/3 Cup.
Garlic (Minced), 2 Cloves.
White Wine, 1/3 Cup.
1 Lemon Juice.
Parsley (Chopped), 3 tbsp.
French Country Bread, 1 loaf.
Instructions
Until you're all set to cook, preheat the Pit Boss grill to 375 deg Fahrenheit (190 C). Preheat for 10-15 mins with the lid closed.
To remove any dirt or barnacles, scrub the mussels well under running water.
Clean mussels should be soaked for 15 mins in a large dish with 5 quarts of water (5 L) and 1/3 cup salt (91 g).
Drain, clean, and repeat the soaking procedure 2 or more times to purge and remove all sand.
Melt the butter in a sauté pan (over moderately high heat). Cook for 1 min, or until the garlic smells good. Bring the wine to low heat and keep it there. Toss the mussels in the pan with a little lemon juice to coat them.
Cover with a tight-fitting lid and transfer to the grill. Allow for a steaming time of 8-10 mins for the mussels. Remove any mussels that haven't opened off the grill and discard.
Transfer to a serving dish, sprinkle with chopped parsley and serve with sliced bread on the side.

5.24 Mahi-Mahi Shish Kabobs
Total Time: 25 mins, Servings: 4
Ingredients
Mahi-Mahi, 1 Fillet.
Zucchini, 1.
Red Onion (Sliced), 1 Cup.
Baby Carrots, 1 Cup.
Green Beans (Flat), 1 Cup.
Olive Oil (Extra-Virgin), 1 Cup.
Pit Boss Veggie Rub, 1 tsp.
Pit Boss Blackened Saskatchewan Rub, 1 tsp.
Basil Leaves, 1 tsp.
Instructions
Mahi-mahi should be cut into 15 squares.
Combine all of the ingredients in a small container. Pit Boss

skewers should be strung with ingredients.
When preparing to cook, preheat the Pit Boss to 500°F and keep the lid closed for 10-15 mins.
Cook the kabobs for approximately 8 mins on the grill.

5.25 Baked Whole Fish in Sea Salt
Total Time: 40 mins, Servings: 4
Ingredients
Branzino, 3 lb (1/2 Each)
Thyme Sprigs, 10.
Lemon (Thinly Sliced, medium-sized), 1.
Sea Salt, 5 Cup.
Egg White, 10.
Olive Oil
Lemon Juice, 1.
Instructions
When preparing to cook, preheat the Pit Boss on High with the lid covered for approximately 10-15 mins.
The gills and fins of the fish should be cut. The cavity should be filled with thyme and lemon slices. After beating the egg whites to soft peaks, fold in the sea salt.
Place the fish directly on the grill and roast for approximately 30 mins, or until an internal temp of 135-140°F is reached when a thermometer is pushed through the salt crust and into the meat. Remove the fish from the grill and allow it to cool for 10 mins.
Slap the crust open with a wooden spoon to remove any remaining salt from the fish's skin.
Remove the skin of the fish and cover it in olive oil and lemon juice.

5.26 Smoked Salmon Salad
Total Time: 50 mins, Servings: 2
Ingredients
Olive oil, 2 tbsp.
White Balsamic Vinegar, 1/2 a tbsp.
Lime (Juiced), 1/2 Whole.
Hot Sauce, 1 tsp.
Honey, 1 tsp.
Salmon Fillets
Jicama (Fresh)
Cucumber
Cans Black Beans, 15 Oz (Rinsed & Drained)
Cherry Tomatoes (Sliced)
Sweet Peppers
Instructions
In a large mixing cup, combine white
balsamic vinegar, olive oil, spicy sauce, lime juice, and honey. After marinating the salmon in the marinade, chill it for at least 60 mins.
Preheat the grill to 325°F and keep the lid covered for approximately 10-15 mins until ready to cook.
Cook the fish directly on the grill grate for 25 mins.
Take the fish from the grill and put it aside to rest for 10 mins.
Pull the salmon into pieces with your fingers, then arrange the "salad" components before adding the fish.
Serve the salad with the dressing ingredients drizzled on top.

5.27 Honey Balsamic Salmon
Total Time: 35 mins, Serving: 2
Ingredients
Salmon Fillet (Medium), 1.
Pit Boss Fin & Feather Rub
Balsamic vinegar, ½ cup.
Minced garlic, 1 tbsp.
Honey, 2 tbsp.

Instructions
The Pit Boss Fin & Feather should be rubbed together. Rub the fillet all over.
To make the glazing, follow these steps: In a small pan, combine the garlic, vinegar, and honey. Simmer over medium heat for 10 to 15 mins, or until the liquid has been reduced by half. When the glaze coats the back of a spoon, it's ready to use. Coat the salmon fillet with glaze with a brush (basting).
Preheat the Pit Boss to 350°F and keep the lid closed for approximately 15 mins.
Preheat the grill and place the salmon fillet on it. Grill the salmon for 25 to 30 mins, or until opaque and flaky when flaked with a fork.
Serve immediately on a dish or plate. If required, bring any leftover glaze to a boil and pour over the fish.

5.28 Grilled Tuna Salad with Smoky & Spicy Mayo
Total Time: 45 mins, Servings: 6
Ingredients
Tuna, Steak, 2.
Pit Boss Salmon Shake
Olive oil, 2 tbsp.
Celery (Diced), 2 tbsp.
Green Onion (Thinly Sliced), 2 tbsp.
Parsley (Minced), 1 tbsp.
Mayonnaise, 2/3 Cup.
Chili Powder, ¼ tsp.
Capers (Drained), 2 tbsp.
Grain Mustard, 1 tbsp.
Pepper
Lemon Juice (fresh)
Instructions
Set the Pit Boss to the "Smoke" setting.
On both sides, season tuna steaks with the Salmon Shake. Place the tuna steaks on the grill to smoke.
Cook the tuna steaks for 30 to 60 mins in the smoker. How much smoke you want to taste is entirely up to you.
Once they've stopped burning, remove them from the grill, turn the heat up to high, and preheat for 10 to 15 mins with the lid closed.
Drizzle some olive oil on both sides of the tuna.
Grill the tuna for 6 to 8 mins, rotating halfway through (according to your liking).
After the tuna has cooled, carefully flake it apart and mix with the celery, parsley, and green onion.
Mix in the mustard, mayonnaise, capers, and chipotle chili powder, seasoning to taste. Give it a gentle swirl to combine.
Lemon juice may be added to taste. Have fun with it.

5.29 Grilled Fresh Fish
Total Time: 25 mins, Servings: 2
Ingredients
Firm White Fish Fillet (1): Sea Bass, Cod or Halibut
Pit Boss Fin & Feather Rub
Lemons, 2.
Instructions
When prepared to cook, preheat the Pit Boss to 325°F with the lid covered for 15 mins.
Set aside for 30 mins to marinade the fish with Feather Rub and Pit Boss Fin. Lemons may be sliced into two halves.
Place the fish and lemons on the grill grates (cut side down). Cook for 10 to 15 mins, or until the fish is flaky and the thickest part reaches 145 deg Fahrenheit. Make sure you don't overcook the meal.
Serve with "grilled lemons" on the side.

5.30 Roasted Yellowtail with Potatoes, Mushrooms & Italian Salsa Verde
Total Time: 40 mins, Servings: 2
Ingredients
Yellowtail Fillets, 4.
Olive oil, 4 tbsp.
Salt n Pepper
Baby Potatoes, 1 lb.
Oyster Mushrooms, 1lb.
Parsley (Chopped), 1/2 Cup
Mint, 2 tbsp.
Cilantro (Finely Chopped)
Oregano (Chopped), 1 tbsp.
Clove Garlic (Minced), 2.
Lemon Juice.
Salt.
Red Pepper Flakes.
Instructions
Preheat the grill to a high temp (above 4500 F) while keeping the lid closed for 10-15 mins.
On the grill, heat a cast-iron pan for 10 to 15 mins.
Season the fillets with salt and pepper after drizzling olive oil over them. Toss the mushrooms and potatoes with olive oil and season with salt and pepper to taste. Cook the potatoes for 8-10 mins in a heated cast-iron skillet before adding the oyster mushrooms. Place the fish fillets skin side down on the grill grate adjacent to the cast iron simultaneously as the mushrooms.
Cook for 6 mins on the skin line, then turn and cook for an additional 2-4 mins.
Combine all of the salsa Verde components and season to taste with salt and lemon juice while the potatoes and fish are cooking. On a serving dish, arrange the mushrooms and potatoes, top with the fillets and sprinkle with salsa Verde.

5.31 Smoked Albacore Tuna
Total Time: 10 mins, Servings: 4
Ingredients
Kosher Salt, 1 Cup.
Brown Sugar, 1 Cup.
1 Orange (Zested)
1 Lemon (Zested)
Albacore Tuna Fillets, 6 (8 Oz).
Instructions
In a small dish, combine the sugar, salt, and citrus zest. Layer the brine and fish in a container, making sure that if the fillets are stacked, there is enough brine between them so that they don't touch. Refrigerate for 6 hrs to brine the meat.
Drain the fillets of any leftover brine. Chill for 30-40 mins on an oiled cooling rack after completely drying.
Preheat the Pit Boss to 180°F with the lid closed for 15 mins. Use Super Smoke if it's available for a greater flavor.
Remove the fillets from the fridge and place them straight on the grill for 3 hrs.
Raise the temp. Preheat the grill to 225°F and cook for another hr, or until the fish is a light brown color and readily flakes with a fork.
Remove the steaks from the grill and serve immediately, or put them aside to cool. It can keep for up to a week in the fridge.

5.32 Smoked Crab Legs
Total Time: 45 mins, Servings: 4
Ingredients
Crab Legs, 4.
Butter (Melted), 4 tbsp.
Pit Boss Texas Spicy BBQ Sauce, 1/2 Cup
Salt n Pepper
Pit Boss Fin and Feather Rub, 1 tbsp.
Instructions
When prepared to cook, preheat the Pit Boss to 250°F and keep the lid closed for 15 mins.
Place the crab legs on the grill grate and smoke for 20 mins. While the crab is cooking, make the sauce. In a medium mixing cup, combine Pit Boss Texas Spicy BBQ sauce, melted butter, salt and pepper, and "Pit Boss Fin and Feather Rub."
After 20 mins of preparation, spray the crab legs with the BBQ sauce mixture. Cook for a further 10 mins, saving the remaining sauce for dishing. Remove the crab legs off the grill and serve with melted butter and a variety of barbecue sauces.

5.34 Cajun Smoked Shrimp
Total Time: 30 mins, Servings: 4
Ingredients
Olive Oil (Extra-Virgin), 1/4 Cup.
Lemon (Juiced), 1
Clove Garlic (Minced), 2.
Cajun Seasoning, 1 tbsp.
Kosher Salt, 1 tsp.
Raw Shrimp (Peeled & Deveined), 2 lb.
Instructions
Because marinating takes time, plan ahead of time. In a large resealable bag, combine all of the ingredients and gently toss to coat all of the shrimp. The shrimp may be covered and marinated for 3-4 hrs if needed.
When prepared to cook, preheat the Pit Boss to 500°F with the lid covered for approximately 15 mins.
Skewer the shrimp and place them on the hot grill immediately. Cook for 3-4 mins each hand, or until the flesh is opaque.

5.35 Seared Lemon Garlic Scallops
Total Time: 15 mins, Servings: 4
Ingredients
U20 Scallops, 12.
Kosher Salt.
Black Pepper.
Butter, 1 tbsp.
Olive oil, 1 tbsp.
Butter (Melted), 4 tbsp
Clove Garlic (Minced), 1.
Lemon (Juiced), 1.
Parsley (Chopped), for Garnish.
Lemon Zest, for Garnish.
Instructions
Preheat the Pit Boss to 500°F and leave the lid closed for 15 mins. Preheat the grill for 20 mins, directly on it, using a cast iron pan.
Remove the frill if it is still intact. Pat the scallops dry with a paper towel. Season with a liberal pinch of salt and a sprinkling of black pepper.
Heat the pan with olive oil and butter until the grill is hot. Place the scallops in the frypan and cook until the
butter has melted. Cover and cook for 2 mins, or until one side is seared and browned.
While the scallops are cooking, combine the melted garlic and butter in a small container after turning the scallops and spooning a few tbsps. Of garlic butter over the top, cook for another min.
Remove off the grill, sprinkle with parsley and lemon zest, and drizzle with additional garlic butter if desired.

5.36 Smoked Lobster Scampi
Total Time: 45 mins, Servings: 2
Ingredients
Lobster Tail, 1.
Handful Pasta (Angel Hair), 1.
Butter, 2 tbsp.
Garlic (Minced), 1 tsp.
Lemon Juice, 1/2 tsp.
Parmesan Cheese (Grated), 2 tsp.
Tomato Pesto (Sun-Dried), 2 tbsp.
Fresh Parsley
Instructions
Set the temp to 180°F and warm for 15 mins with the lid closed. To expose the skin, cut the top portion of the lobster on both sides with kitchen shears. Cook the lobster on the grill (directly) for 20-25 mins, depending on its size.
While the lobster cooks, prepare the pasta according to the package directions.
After 20-25 mins, take the lobster from the grill and remove the flesh of the tail. The meat should be chopped into pieces.
While the pasta is cooking, melt the butter over high heat. Add the lobster pieces and garlic and cook until the butter has become a tan color. Before adding the parmesan and lemon, toss a couple of times in the pan. Remove from the equation.
Until the pasta is done, toss 1 tbsp sun-dried tomato pesto onto the end of a dish or plate. Toss the "lobster scampi" on top of the spaghetti and serve. Serve with a garnish of parsley.

5.37 Simple Glazed Salmon Fillets
Total Time: 35 mins, Serving: 2
Ingredients
Center cut Salmon Fillets (Skin On), 4 (6-8 Oz).
Pit Boss Fin and Feather Rub
Mayonnaise, 1/2 Cup.
Dijon Mustard, 2 tbsp.
Fresh Lemon Juice, 1tbsp.
Tarragon (Fresh Chopped) or Dill, 1 tbsp.
Lemon Wedges.
Instructions
Season the fillets with Pit Boss Fin and Feather Rub.
Making the Glaze: Combine the mustard and mayonnaise in a small mixing cup. In a mixing dish, combine the dill or tarragon and lemon juice.
The glaze should be applied to the fleshy surface of the fillets.
Preheat the Pit Boss to 350°F for 15 mins with the lid closed.
Place the salmon fillets on the grill grate skin-side down. Grill the salmon for 25-30 mins, or until opaque and flaky when flaked with a fork.
Serve immediately with sliced lemons and (minced) dill on a plate or in bowls.

5.38 Garlic Salmon
Total Time: 35 mins, Servings: 4
Ingredients
Salmon Fillet (Skin On), 1 (2-3 lb.).
Pit Boss Fin and Feather Rub
Olive Oil, 1/4 Cup.
Garlic (Minced), 2 tbsp.
Parsley (Minced), 1/2 tbsp.
Lemon Wedges.
Instructions
Line a baking sheet with butcher paper or parchment. Place the salmon fillet skin side down on the baking sheet and season with Feather Rub and Pit Boss fin.
In a small bowl, combine the garlic, olive oil, and parsley. Remove from the equation.
When ready to cook, preheat the Pit Boss to 500°F with the lid closed for 15 mins.
Place the baking sheet on the grill and brush the "garlic mixture" over the fish.
Cook until the fish flakes easily or the internal temp reaches 140 deg Fahrenheit (about 20-25 mins).
Before serving with lemon wedges, remove the pan from the grill and spritz with any leftover garlic mixture.

5.39 Smoked Salmon Candy
Total Time: 3 Hrs 10 mins, Servings: 4
Ingredients
Gin, 2 Cup.
Brown Sugar (Dark), 1 Cup.
Kosher Salt, 1/2 Cup.
Maple Syrup, 1 Cup.
Black Pepper, 1 tbsp.
Salmon, 3 lb.
Vegetable Oil.
Brown Sugar (Dark).
Instructions
In a large mixing bowl, combine all of the cure components. Cut the fish into 2- oz pieces and place it in the cure.
Refrigerate overnight, covered.
When preparing to cook, preheat the Pit Boss to 180°F and keep the lid closed for 15 mins.
Vegetable oil should be brushed on the foil. Place the salmon on foil and sprinkle with more brown sugar.
Place the foil on the grill grate. Cook the salmon for 3 to 4 hrs in the smoker, or until it is fully done.
Serve hot or cold.

5.40 Grilled Texas Spicy Shrimp
Total Time: 18 mins, Servings: 6
Ingredients
Main
Jumbo Shrimp (Peeled & Deveined), 2 lb.
Olive oil, 3 tbsp.
Salt
(Ground) Black Pepper
Cilantro (Finely Chopped), 1/2 Cup.
Sauce
Olive oil, 1 tbsp.
Onion, (Finely Diced), 1.
Clove Garlic (Minced), 2.
Jalapeño Pepper (Seeded & Minced), 1 whole.
Pit Boss Texas Spicy BBQ Sauce, 1 Cup.
Instructions
Clean the shrimp by rinsing them in cold water, draining them, and patting them dry with paper towels. In a mixing bowl, combine all of the ingredients.
Toss the shrimp with 2 tsp oil and season to taste with salt and pepper. Set aside the sauce while you're preparing it.
1 tbsp oil, cooked in a skillet over medium heat to create the sauce Before the garlic, onion, and jalapeño pepper soften, sauté them. Stir in the barbecue sauce and keep it heated while the shrimp cooks.
Preheat the Pit Boss to 450°F and leave the lid closed for 15 mins.
Grill the large shrimp in a grilling basket or directly on the grill. Cook shrimp for 2-3 mins each hand, or until they are opaque, solid, and cooked through.
In a heated sauce, toss the fried shrimp with the chopped cilantro. Toss gently to coat and
serve.

5.41 Grilled Saké Shrimp
Total Time: 2 Hrs 10 mins, Servings: 4
Ingredients
Shrimp with Tails (Deveined), 24 Large.
Japanese sake, 1/2 cup.
Soy Sauce, 3 tbsp.
Lemon Juice (fresh), 1 tbsp.
Scallions, 1.
1 Piece inch fresh Ginger (peeled & sliced into coins).
Clove Garlic (Minced), 1.
Sesame Oil, 1 tbsp.
Sugar, 1 tsp.
Wedges of lemon, 1.
Instructions
The shrimp should be washed and drained.
In a large mixing bowl or plastic container, combine the soy sauce, sake, scallion, lemon juice, garlic, ginger, sugar, and oil to create the marinade (resealable).
To coat the shrimp, swirl or massage the bag. Refrigerate the marinade for approximately 2 hrs, stirring the bag occasionally to disperse it.
Preheat the Pit Boss to 450°F and leave the lid closed for 15 mins.
Drain and pat the shrimp dry before threading three shrimp onto each of the eight skewers. Cook the shrimp skewers and lemon wedges for 3-4 mins each hand on the grill, turning once, or until opaque and cooked through.

5.42 Pit Boss Smoked Mussels By Dennis The Prescott
Total Time: 35 mins, Servings: 4
Ingredients
Butter, 1/4 Cup.
Clove Garlic (Minced), 4.
Apple Cider, 1 Cup.
Mussels (Debearded & Washed), 3 lb.
1 Bunch of Chives (Fresh)
1 Bunch of Tarragon (Fresh)
1 Bunch of Basil (Fresh)
1 Bunch of Flat-Leaf Parsley (Chopped).
Clove Garlic (Chopped), 1.
Lemon Juice, 1/2 whole.
Salt & Pepper
Olive Oil (Extra-Virgin)
Lemon Wedges, 2 whole.
Crusty Bread
Instructions
Preheat the grill to 350°F and keep the lid covered for 15 mins. In a cast-iron (or grill-safe) pan, melt the butter over medium heat. After the butter has melted, add the garlic and sauté for 30 seconds (careful not to burn it), add the apple cider, and bring it to a low boil. Cover the mussels with a tight-fitting lid and place them in the Pit Boss. Cook for a further 8–10 mins, or until the mussels have opened.
While the mussels are cooking, make the salsa verde. Fresh herbs and garlic in a food processor (or strong blender) (finely chopped). After adding the lemon juice, season it with salt and pepper. Drizzle the olive oil into the blender in a slow, steady stream while it's on low until it's thick and beautiful.
To accompany those delicious wood-fired mussels, serve with lemon wedges, salsa verde, and crusty bread.

5.43 Smoky Crab Dip
Total Time: 25 mins, Servings: 6
Ingredients
Mayonnaise, 1/3 Cup.
Sour cream, 3 oz.
Smoked paprika, 1 tsp.
Cayenne Pepper, ¼ tsp.
Crab Meat (Lump), 1-1/2 lb.
Salt & Pepper
Scallions (Chopped)
Butter Crackers.
Instructions
Preheat the grill to 350°F and keep the lid covered for 15 mins.
Gently combine all of the ingredients in a large mixing bowl, except the crackers, crab meat, and garnish scallions, until thoroughly combined. Next, fold in the crab flesh gently but completely, careful not to break it up too much.
Season to taste with salt and pepper, then transfer to a " grill-safe serving dish."
Bake for 20-25 mins, or until golden and bubbling on top.
Serve immediately with butter crackers and sliced scallions as a garnish.

5.44 Pit Boss Crab Legs
Total Time: 45 mins, Servings: 4
Ingredients
Crab Legs (Thawed & Halved), 3 lb.
Butter (Melted), 1 Cup.
Lemon Juice Fresh, 2 tbsp.
Clove Garlic (Minced), 2.
Pit Boss Fin and Feather Rub or Old bay seasoning, 2 tbsp.
Lemon Wedges
Italian Parsley, (Chopped)
Instructions
If the crab legs are too large to fit in the pan (roasting), curl them or chop them down at the joints with a hefty knife. To open the shells, split them lengthwise. Preheat the grill to 350°F. Place the roasting pan in the grill.
Combine the lemon juice, sugar, and garlic in a mixing bowl. Roll the crab legs in the paste to coat them completely. Use "Pit Boss Fin & Feather Rub" or "Old Bay Seasoning" to season the crab legs.
When preparing to cook, preheat the Pit Boss to 350°F and keep the lid closed for at least 15 mins.
Cook the crab legs for 20-30 mins (depending on the size of the crab legs) or until fully done, basting once or twice with the butter sauce from the bottom of the pan.
Place the crab legs on a wide plate and divide the sauce and any leftover fluids among four dipping bowls.

5.45 Swordfish with Sicilian Olive Oil Sauce
Total Time: 25 mins, Servings: 4
Ingredients
Olive Oil (Extra-Virgin), 1/2 Cup. Plus 2 tbsp for Oiling the Fish.
Lemon (Juiced), 1 Whole
Clove Garlic, (Minced), 2.
Fresh Parsley (Finely Chopped), 3 tbsp.
Fresh Oregano (Finely Chopped), 1 tbsp or 1 tsp Dried Oregano.
Brined Capers, Drained, 1 tbsp. (optional)
Halibut, swordfish, Tuna, 4 (6 To 8 Oz) or Salmon Steaks, 1" Thick
Salt n Pepper
Instructions
Melt 1/2 cup olive oil in a saucepan over low heat.
2 tbsp lemon juice & 2 tbsp hot water Add the parsley, garlic, oregano, capers (if using), and season to taste with salt and

pepper. It's critical to keep things warm.
When prepared to cook, preheat the Pit Boss to 400°F with the lid closed for 15 mins.
After coating the fish steaks with 2 tbsp olive oil, season them with salt and pepper.
Place the fish on the grill and cook for 18 mins, or until opaque and flaky when pressed with a fork.
Drizzle the "warm" olive oil sauce over the fish steaks on a plate or in individual serving bowls. The leftover sauce should be served on the side. Enjoy.

5.46 Grilled Shrimp Tacos with Garlic Cilantro Lime Slaw

Total Time: 29 mins, Servings: 4
Ingredients
Olive Oil, 1/4 Cup.
Water, 1/4 Cup.
Oregano (Chopped), 1/4 Cup
Cilantro Leaves, 1/2 Cup.
Clove Garlic, 3.
Pure Kosher Sea Salt by Jacobsen Salt Co., ½.
2 Lime (Juiced)
Yogurt (Greek), 1/2 Cup
Raw Shrimp (Peeled & Deveined), 1 lb.
Chili Powder, 1 tsp.
Ground Cumin, 1 tsp.
Ground Cayenne Pepper, 1/4 Tsp
Shredded Cabbage, 3 Cup.
Corn Tortillas, 8 Small
Avocado (Sliced), 2.
Cilantro (Chopped)
Lime (Cut into Wedges)
Instructions
Pulse all of the sauce ingredients, except the Greek yogurt, until smooth in a food processor. Add the Greek yogurt and pulse to combine until the mixture is nearly smooth. Taste and make any necessary changes.
When preparing to cook, preheat the grill on high for at least 15 mins with the lid covered.
Pat the shrimp dry with paper towels and season with the seasonings. Grill the shrimp for approximately 5-8 mins, turning once or twice, until cooked through.
Toss the cabbage with part (but not all) of the sauce until it is covered to your liking. There must be enough sauce to weigh down the cabbage slightly. Any leftover salsa may be used to top tacos or in other recipes.
Spread a couple of tbsps of avocado on each tortilla, top with a few pieces of coleslaw, seafood, lime wedges, and cilantro, and serve.

5.47 Oysters Traegefeller

Total Time: 30 mins, Servings: 2
Ingredients
Butter, 1 tbsp.
Shallot (Finely Chopped), 1.
Collard Greens (Fresh), 2 Cup.
Clove Garlic (Minced), 3.
Pernod, 1/4 Cup.
Cream, 1/2 Cup.
BBQ Chips (Crushed), 1 Cup.
Parmesan Cheese, 1 Cup.
Bacon, 3 Slices.
12 Oysters
Rock Salt
2 Wedges of lemon.
Salt & Pepper
Instructions
Melt the butter in a medium saucepan over medium-high heat. Cook for 3 mins, or until the shallot and collard greens are wilted. 1 min, or until the garlic is aromatic.
Cook until the liquid has been reduced by half by deglazing it with Pernod. Simmer for another 3 mins, or until the liquid coats the back of the spoon.
In a small cup, combine crushed crispy bacon pieces, potato chips, and melted Parmesan cheese.
Set the Pit Boss to 500o F when you're all
set to cook. Preheat for 10-15 mins with the lid closed.
On each oyster, spoon 1 heaping tsp collard mixture, followed by a couple of tsps of potato chip mixture.
Season a baking pan generously with rock salt. Put the oysters in the salt to keep them from toppling over.
Cook immediately on the grill for 10-15 mins, until the sheet tray is bubbling and golden brown. On the side, serve with lemon wedges.

5.48 Spicy Shrimp Skewers

Total Time: 25 mins, Servings: 4
Ingredients
Shrimp (Peeled & Deveined), 2 lb.
Thai Chiles, 6.
Clove Garlic, 6.
Pit Boss Winemaker's Napa Valley Rub, 2 tbsp.
Sugar, 1 tsp.
White vinegar, 1/5 tbsp.
Olive Oil. 3 tbsp.
Instructions
If using bamboo skewers, soak them in cold water for 1 hr before grilling.
In a mixing dish, place the shrimp and put it aside. Combine the remaining ingredients in a blender and blend until a coarse-textured paste is formed. Make careful to decrease the number of chiles to taste if you prefer a milder heat.
Toss the shrimp with the chile-garlic mixture and set it aside to marinate for approximately 30 mins.
Remove the shrimp from the refrigerator and thread them onto bamboo or metal skewers.
Preheat the Pit Boss to 450°F and leave the lid closed for 15 mins when ready to cook.
Grill it for 2 to 3 mins each side, or until the shrimp are pink and firm to the touch.

5.49 Salmon (Balsamic Glaze)

Total Time: 45 Mins, Serving: 2
Ingredients
Fresh Black Pepper 1 Tbsp
Sugar 1 Tbsp
Balsamic Vinegar 2 Cup
Salt
Grand Marnier 1 Tbsp
Salmon Fillet 2 Pieces (8 Oz)
Instructions
Set aside the freshly ground black pepper and sugar.
In a small, thick-bottomed pan, pour the balsamic vinegar. Bring to a gentle boil over medium heat. Reduce the heat to maintain a steady simmer and reduce the balsamic vinegar until it resembles syrup or coats the back of a spoon. Allow cooling. Toss in a Grand Marnier and season with salt to taste.
When prepared to cook, raise the temp to be high and heat the grill for ten to fifteen mins. Season the salmon evenly with the sugar and pepper mixture, then place flesh-side down on the hot grill at the right front, if possible, to achieve a good sear. When they're seared, move them to the middle of the grill and cook for ten to fifteen minutes, or until they reach an internal temperature of 145°F. Enjoy with a sprinkling of glaze.

5.50 Scallops (Bacon-Wrapped)
Total Time: 40 Mins, Serving: 8
Ingredients
Dry-Packed, large Deep-Sea Scallops 24
Butter (1/2 Cup)
Salt
Fresh Black Pepper
Minced, Clove Garlic 1
Slices Thin-Sliced Bacon 12, Cut In Partial Diagonally
For Serving, Lemon Slices
Instructions
If the small, curved-shaped muscle is still connected to each scallop side, remove it. Dry the scallops thoroughly on paper towels (towels), then transfer them to a regular bowl.
In a small pan, melt the butter, add the garlic, and simmer for 1 min. Allow cooling slightly before pouring over the scallops. Season with pepper and salt and toss gently to coat.
Wrap a slice of bacon around each scallop and secure with a toothpick.
Preheat the Pit Boss to 400°F. Close the cover for fifteen mins after preparing to cook.
Place the scallops directly on the grill grate to assemble. Grate for 15 to 20 mins, or until the scallops are thick and the bacon has begun to crisp. If necessary, flip the scallops bacon-side down and stir them periodically to crisp the bacon. Don't overcook the food.
Transfer the scallops to a serving dish and garnish them with lemon wedges.

5.51 Albacore Tuna (Grilled) with Tomato-Potato Casserole
Total Time: 30 Mins, Serving: 8
Ingredients
Tuna Steaks 6, oz 6
Entire Lemon Zest 1
Finely Chopped Chile De Árbol 1
Thyme 1 Tbsp
Fresh Parsley 1 Tbsp
Instructions
Season the fish with lemon zest, thyme, chile, and parsley. Refrigerate for at least 4 hrs after covering.
Remove the fish from the refrigerator thirty mins before grilling to allow it to come to room temp.
Season the front and back of the fish with pepper and salt. Grill for 2 to 3 mins on each side (on the cast iron with the grill dish afterward), rotating once or twice. The tuna must be well-seared while remaining rare.

5.52 Salmon (Cedar-Plank) with Salsa (Mango)
Total Time: 50 Mins, Serving: 4
Ingredients
Seeded, Chopped & Peeled Entire Mango 2
Chopped Red Onion 1/2
Delicately Chopped Tiny Cucumber 1
Lime Juice Cup 1/4
Honey 2 Tsp
Chopped & Seeded Entire Habanero Pepper 1/2
Finely Sliced Cilantro 1/4 tbsp
Entire Cedar Planks 1
Salmon Fillet 1/2 lb (8 Oz)
Olive Oil
Salmon Shake (Pit Boss)
Instructions
In a mixing bowl, combine the onion, cucumber, mango, lime juice, chili pepper, and honey and toss to combine. Taste for seasoning, and if necessary, add more lime juice, chile, or honey. Stir in the cilantro gently. If not used right away, cover and chill.
Preheat the grill to 350°F and cook for ten to fifteen mins with the lid covered.
Drain a piece of wood. Oil (olive) on each side of the salmon, then top with Salmon Shake (Pit Boss). Place the board with the skin side down.
Place the plank with the salmon directly on the grill and cook for 25 to 30 mins, or until the salmon is thick and flakes easily with a fork. Serve with salsa (mango).

5.53 Shrimp Scampi
Total Time: 20 Mins, Servings: 3
Ingredients
Blackened Sriracha 2 tsp rub seasoning
Divided, Cubed Butter 1/2 cup
Chili pepper flakes 1/2 tsp
Chopped garlic cloves 3
For serving, to taste, lemon slices,
lemon, zest & juice 1
Cooked Linguine
Sliced parsley 3 tbsp
deveined and peeled shrimp 1 1/2 lbs.
For serving, baguette (toasted)
Instructions
Preheat the Pit Boss grill to a medium-high setting. If you're using a charcoal or gas grill, set the temp to medium-high.
Place 1/2 butter on the grate and cook for 60 seconds, or until the Blackened Sriracha, chili flakes, and garlic are aromatic.
Place the shrimp in the pan and cook for 120 seconds, stirring periodically, until opaque.
Place the remaining butter, lemon juice and zest, and parsley in a mixing bowl. Toss the shrimp in the butter (lemon), remove it from the grill and place it in a bowl.
Serve immediately with baguette and fresh lemon slices (toasted). If desired, serve over spaghetti, zucchini noodles, or linguine.

5.54 Tacos (Shrimp) with Crema (Lime)
Total Time: 25 mins, Servings: 4
Ingredients
Shredded cabbage 1/4
Sliced cilantro 2 tsp
Corn tortillas
Lime slices 1/2
Mayonnaise 1/4 cup
Blackened sriracha rub (Pit boss)
Minced bell pepper (red) 1/4
Peeled and stripped shrimp 1 lb.
Sour cream 1/4 cup
Oil (Vegetable) 2 tsp
Sliced onion (white) 1/2
Instructions
In a regular bowl, place the shrimp. Sprinkle with oil after seasoning with Sriracha Rub (Pit Boss) (vegetable). Pitch by hand to ensure adequate coating, then put aside.
In a small mixing dish, combine the sour cream, lime juice, and mayonnaise. Sriracha rub may be added to taste (Blackened). Set aside.
In a small mixing dish, combine the onion, cilantro, jalapeno, and red bell pepper. Set aside.
Preheat the grill (Pit Boss) on medium heat. Preheat a cast-iron skillet over medium heat.
Place tortillas on the grill to warm on both sides, then turn off the burner underneath.
Transfer the shrimp to the hot grill and cook for 4 to 6 mins, turning periodically until opaque. Extra Blackened Sriracha

may be used to make extremely spicy shrimp.
Assemble tacos by layering shrimp, pepper mixture, shredded cabbage, and sauce. Serve with lime slices on the side.

5.55 Lime Shrimp (Spicy & Grilled)
Total Time: 40 Mins, Servings: 4
Ingredients
Chili paste 2 tsp
Cumin 1/2 tsp
Chopped cloves garlic 2
Juiced big lime 1
Powder paprika 1/4 tsp
Flake's pepper (red) 1/4 tsp
Salt 1/2 tsp
Instructions
Combine the olive oil, lime juice, chili powder, paprika, pepper, salt, garlic, pepper flakes, and
cumin in a mixing bowl.
Pour it into a resealable bag, toss out the coat, add the shrimp, and marinate for thirty mins.
Start the grill on "smoke" and leave the lid open until the fire in the burn pot is ready (three to seven mins). Preheat the grill to 400°F.
Then, skewer the lime shrimp, place them on the grill grate, and cook for approximately 2 mins on each side until done. Remove the shrimp from the grate after it has reached done and enjoy.

5.56 Shrimp (Garlic & Pesto Bruschetta)
Total Time: 28 Mins, Servings: 12
Ingredients
Baguette bread slices 12
Pepper flakes (chili) 1/2 tsp
Powder of garlic 1/2 tsp
Chopped cloves garlic 4
Olive oil 2 tbsp
Smoked paprika 1/2 tsp
Parsley leaves tsp 1/4
Pesto
Salt
Pepper
Jumbo shrimp 12
Instructions
Start the grill on "smoke" and leave the lid open until the fire in the burn pot is ready (three to seven mins). Preheat the grill to 350°F. Place the baguette slices on a baking sheet lined with foil. Brush each side of the baguette slices with a mixture of chopped garlic and olive oil. Place the saucepan in the grate and bake for about ten to fifteen mins.
Add a splash of olive oil, garlic powder, shrimp, chili powder, salt pepper, and smoked paprika to a frying pan and cook on medium-high heat for nearly five mins (till the shrimp becomes pink). Make sure you whisk the mixture regularly. Remove the pan from the heat when it becomes pink. Allow five mins for the baguettes to cool before spreading a pesto layer on top of each, seasoning with a shrimp, and serving.

5.57 Tartar Sauce (Homemade) & Salmon Cakes
Total Time: 35 mins, Servings: 4
Ingredients
Dry breadcrumb 1/2 cups 1
Chopped capers tbsp 1/2
Dill pickle relish cup 1/4
Eggs 2
Divided mayonnaise, 1/4 cup 1
Grainy mustard 1 tbsp
Olive oil tbsp 1/2
Diced delicately red pepper 1/2
Sweet rib rub (Pit boss) 1/2 tbsp
Flaked cooked salmon 1 cup
Instructions
In a large mixing bowl, combine the eggs, salmon, breadcrumbs, 14 cup of mayonnaise, Sweet Rib Rub, bell pepper, and mustard. Allow fifteen mins for the breadcrumbs to absorb the liquid.
Set the Pit Boss grill to "smoke" mode. Adjust the temp to 350 deg Fahrenheit after it has been started.
Combine the leftover mayonnaise, chopped capers, and dill pickle relish in a small bowl. Set aside.
Preheat the grill by placing a baking sheet on the grate. When the baking sheet is hot, drizzle the olive oil into the pot and put rounded tbsp of the salmon mixture onto the baking sheet. Using a spatula, press the ingredients into a flat patty. Grill for three to five mins, then flips and grill for another one to two mins. Remove the steaks from the grill and serve with tartar sauce.

5.58 Smoked Tuna Belly Tacos
Total Time: 30 Mins, Servings: 4
Ingredients
3 lb Ahi Tuna Belly
3 Tbsp Olive Oil
1/4 Cup Pit Boss Chicken Rub
12 (4 Inch) Flour Tortillas
3 Tbsp Chopped Cilantro, For Garnish
1 1/2 Inch Ginger, Grated
3 Tbsp Seas1d Rice Vinegar
1 Tbsp Honey
1/8 Tsp Crushed Red Pepper
1/2 Tsp Salt
1/4 Tsp Freshly Ground Black Pepper
1/4 Tsp Fish Sauce
1 Large Fresh Pineapple, Cored, Peeled And Thinly Sliced
1 Head Cabbage, Shredded
2 Large Carrots, Grated
Instructions
When prepared to cook, preheat the Pit Boss to 500°F with the lid covered for 15 mins.
Brush your tuna using a thin coating of the olive oil before sprinkling it with Chicken Pit Boss Rub. Allow tuna to rest for 10 mins while you make the coleslaw.
To make the coleslaw, combine the following ingredients in a mixing bowl. Combine ginger, vinegar, salt, pepper, pepper flakes, honey, & fish sauce in a mixing bowl.
Toss the pineapple, cabbage, & carrots in a wide mixing bowl. Toss everything together with the dressing.
Cook your fish for around 3 mins from all sides directly on your grill grate.
Remove your fish from Pit Boss & set it aside to cool for 5 mins until slicing thinly.
Assemble your tacos by layering the fish, coleslaw, & cilantro on top. Enjoy!

5.59 Sweet Grilled Shrimp & Spicy Sausage Skewers
Total Time: 40 Mins, Servings: 6
Ingredients
24 Shrimp, Peeled And Deveined
1/2 Cup Apple Cider Vinegar
1 Tsp Dijon Mustard
1 Tsp Onion Powder
2 Clove Garlic, Minced
3 Tbsp Honey

1/4 Cup Canola Oil
1 Tsp Dried Thyme
Salt And Pepper
8 Italian Pork Sausage, Regular Or Spicy

Instructions

Vinegar, mustard, salt, pepper, onion powder, honey, thyme, garlic, & canola oil should all be mixed. Toss in the shrimp & let it aside for 30 mins to marinate.

Sausage links should be sliced in 1/2 lengthwise & into 2" chunks.

Set the temp to high & warm for around 15 mins with the lid covered.

On your skewers, alternate the shrimp & sausage. Place shrimp on the grill & cook for 8-10 mins, until it has done.

Remove the steaks from the grill & serve. Enjoy!

5.60 Smoked Trout Dip

Total Time: 4 hrs, Servings: 4

Ingredients

1 Quart Water
1 Cup Salt
1/2 Cup Brown Sugar
1 Whole Lemon Zest
4 Whole Bay Leaves
1 Tbsp Black Peppercorn
2 lb Trout
1/2 Cup Cream Cheese
1/2 Cup Sour Cream
1 Clove Garlic
1/2 Tbsp Parsley, Chopped
1/2 Tbsp Chives, Chopped
1/2 Tbsp Fresh Chopped Dill
1 Tbsp Lemon Juice
Salt And Pepper

Instructions

Combine water, bay leaves, salt, lemon zest, brown sugar, & peppercorns in a small saucepan. Bring to your boil on medium-high heat, constantly stirring, until the salt & sugar are completely dissolved. Remove from the heat & let aside for 15 mins to steep. To cool, pour the mixture into cold water. When the mixture is cold, pour it on the fish, cover, & chill for 2 hrs.

Remove the fish from the brine and discard brine. Fillets should be rinsed and dried. To make the pellicle, spread them out over a cooling rack & chill overnight. This makes it easier for smoke to stick on the fillets.

Prepare grill to 180°F & preheat for around 15 mins. Smoke the fillets straight on your grill grate for around 1-2 hrs, or unless the fish starts to flake.

In a medium bowl, mix cream cheese, lemon juice, herbs, sour cream, plus salt & pepper while the fish is smoking. Stir in flaked, smoked fish till the trout is broken up into very tiny pieces. Serve with some crackers and your favorite dipping veggies.

5.61 Pit Boss Salmon with Balsamic Glaze

Total Time: 45 Mins, Servings: 2

Ingredients

1 Tbsp Freshly Ground Black Pepper
1 Tbsp Sugar
2 Cup Balsamic Vinegar
1 Tbsp Grand Marnier
Salt
2 Pieces (8 Oz) Salmon Fillet

Instructions

Set aside some sugar & freshly ground pepper.

In a heavy-bottomed, small sauce pan, pour some balsamic vinegar. Bring to your gentle boil over medium heat. Reduce your Balsamic vinegar till it becomes like syrup or coats the spoon back, adjusting the temp to keep a consistent simmer. Allow cooling. Toss in some Grand Marnier & season with a sprinkle of salt for taste.

Set the thermostat to high & prepare your grill for 10-15 mins. Season your salmon with some pepper & sugar mixture equally and put on your hot grill, ideally towards the front, for a nice sear. Move everything to the middle of your grill once they've been seared & cook for around 10-15 mins, or till they hit a core temp of 145°F. Serve heated with the glaze drizzled over the top.

5.62 Bacon-Wrapped Scallops

Total Time: 30 Mins, Servings: 8

Ingredients

24 Jumbo Dry-Packed Scallops
1/2 Cup Butter
Salt
Freshly Ground Black Pepper
1 Clove Garlic, Minced
12 Slices Bacon Thin-Cut
Lemon Wedges

Instructions

If the tiny crescent-shaped muscle on the edge of every scallop is still connected, it should be removed. Transfer your scallops to a small bowl after carefully drying them on the paper towels.

In a medium saucepan, melt the butter, then add the garlic & simmer for 1 min. Allow it cool for a few mins before pouring over your scallops. Season to taste with salt & pepper, then toss lightly to coat.

Using a toothpick, attach every scallop with a slice of bacon. Preheat Pit Boss at 400°F for around 15 mins with lid covered.

Place the scallops on your grill grate immediately. Grill for 15–20 mins, or unless the scallops are opaque & your bacon is crisping. Flip the scallops onto their side, if preferred, and turn them periodically to crisp your bacon. Don't overcook the food.

Serve the scallops with some lemon wedges on a serving dish.

5.63 Grilled Albacore Tuna with Potato-Tomato Casserole

Total Time: 30 Mins, Servings: 8

Ingredients

6 (6 Oz) Tuna Steaks
1 Whole Lemon Zest
1 Thinly Sliced Chile-De-Árbol
1 Tbsp Thyme
1 Tbsp Fresh Parsley

Instructions

Season your fish with some Chile, thyme, lemon zest, & parsley before cooking. Refrigerate for almost 4 hrs after covering.

Take your fish out of the refrigerator for around 30 mins until cooking.

Season your fish from both sides using salt & pepper. Cook for 2-3 mins from each side, turning once, maybe twice. However, the tuna must be thoroughly seared.

5.64 Cedar-Plank Salmon with Mango Salsa

Total Time: 50 Mins, Servings: 4

Ingredients

2 Whole Mango, Seeded & Chopped, Peeled
1/2 Red Onion, Diced
1 Small Finely Diced Cucumber
1/4 Cup Lime Juice
2 Tsp Honey
1/2 Whole Seeded & Chopped Habanero Pepper

1/4 Tbsp Finely Chopped Cilantro
1 Whole Cedar Planks
1/2 lb Salmon Fillet
Olive Oil
Pit Boss Salmon Shake
Instructions
Blend the mango, lime juice, onion, cucumber, chile pepper, and honey in a wide mixing bowl & whisk to combine. Season to taste with additional lime juice, chile, or honey, if preferred. Stir in some cilantro gently. If not used right away, cover & chill.
Preheat the grill to 350°F & leave the lid covered for 10-15 mins. The plank should be drained. Season the fish from both sides using olive oil & Salmon Pit Boss Shake. Place over the plank. Place the plank firmly on your grill grate with your salmon & roast for 25-30 mins, or unless the salmon becomes opaque & flakes readily with the fork.

5.65 Shrimp (Bacon Wrapped)
Total Time: 15 Mins, Servings: 4
Ingredients
Strip bacon 8
Melted butter shortening style, cup 1/4
Chopped clove garlic 1
Juice of lemon, 1 tsp
Salt
Pepper
Jumbo (veined & stripped) shrimp
Instructions
Start the grill (Pit Boss) on "smoke" and keep the lid open until the fire in the burn pot is ready (three to seven mins). Preheat the grill to 450 deg Fahrenheit.
Take one bacon slice and wrap it around each shrimp piece, securing it with a toothpick.
In a mixing bowl, whisk together the shortening, lemon juice, and garlic. Each side of each shrimp should be brushed with sauce.
Place on the grate and cook for 11 mins.
Remove the bacon shrimp from the grill, serve, and enjoy.

5.66 Salmon (Cedar-Plank)
Total Time: 40 mins, Servings: 4
Ingredients
Sugar (brown) 1/4 cup
Olive oil tbsp 1/2
Competition seasoning (smoked) of Pit boss
Skin off salmon fillets 4
Instructions
Allow 1 day for the cedar plank to soak in water (untreated) before grilling. Remove and clean once you're ready to grill. Turn on the grill. Raise the temp to 350°F.
Combine the Lemon Pepper, oil, garlic, and herb seasoning, as well as the brown sugar, in a small bowl. Rub gently on the fish fillets.
Place the plank over an indirect heat source, then place the salmon on the plank and grill for 15 to 20 mins, or until the salmon is cooked through and flakes easily with a fork. Remove from the heat and serve right away.

5.67 Salmon (Glazed) Honey-Soy
Total Time: 15 Mins, Servings: 4
Ingredients
Paste of chili 1 tsp
Sliced chives
Garlic cloves grate 2
Fresh chopped ginger 2 tbsp
Honey 1 tsp
Juice of lemon 2 tbsp
Skin eliminated of salmon fillets 4
Sesame oil 1 tsp
Low sodium sauce of soy 2 tbsp
Instructions
Start the grill on smoke and keep the lid open until the fire in the burn pot is ready (three to seven mins). Preheat the grill to 400°F.
Place the salmon in a large resealable plastic bag, then top with the other ingredients (excluding the chives). Wrap the bag in plastic wrap and toss gently
to coat the salmon. Refrigerate the marinade for 20 mins.
Now, place the salmon on a smooth pan or directly on the grilles and cook for nearly three minutes, then flip and grill for another three minutes. Turn off the grill, remove the saucepan from the grill, plate, and top with chives.

5.68 Grilled Oysters by Journey South
Total Time: 50 Mins, Servings: 4
Ingredients
2 Medium Onion
1 Medium Red Bell Pepper
5 Tbsp Extra-Virgin Olive Oil
2 Lemons
3 Tsp Dried Thyme
3 Dried Bay Leaves
5 Tbsp Garlic, Minced
3 Tbsp Pit Boss Chicken Rub
3 Tbsp Worcestershire Sauce
5 Tbsp Hot Pepper Sauce
1/4 Cup White Wine
4 Butter, Sticks
12 Whole Oysters On The 1/2 Shell
Italian Blend Cheese
Instructions
When prepared to cook, preheat the grill on high for around 15 mins with the lid covered.
In a cast-iron skillet, heat the olive oil on medium heat. Place the onion & bell peppers in a hot skillet.
Lemon juice is poured into a sauté pan. Mix in thyme, garlic, bay leaves, & Chicken Rub Pit Boss.
Sauté the veggie combination for approximately 5-7 mins, or unless the onions become transparent & the peppers have softened.
Combine both Worcestershire sauce & spicy sauce in a mixing bowl. Add butter & white wine. Continue to cook for the next 15 mins.
Clean & shuck your oysters, leaving them within shell bottom while your sauce simmers.
Place your oysters over the Pit Boss & pour the sauce over them. 5 mins in the grill.
Serve with some Italian cheese on top. Enjoy!

5.69 Smoked Trout
Total Time: 2 Hrs 10 Mins, Servings: 6
Ingredients
8 Rainbow Trout Fillets
1 Gallon Water
1/4 Cup Salt
1/2 Cup Brown Sugar
1 Tbsp Black Pepper
2 Tbsp Soy Sauce
Instructions

Clean & butterfly your fresh fish.
To make the brine, combine water, salt, soy sauce, brown sugar, & pepper in a mixing bowl and whisk to dissolve both sugar and salt. Refrigerate the fish for 60 mins after bringing.
When prepared to cook, preheat the Pit Boss to 225°F with the lid covered for 15 mins.
Take the fish out of the brine & pat them dry. Bases on the trout thickness, cook it straight on your grill grate for approximately 1-2 hrs. When the fish becomes opaque & begins to flake, this is done. Serve warm or chilled. Enjoy!

5.70 Sweet Mandarin Salmon
Total Time: 15 Mins, Servings: 2
Ingredients
1 Whole Lime, Juiced
1 Tsp Sesame Oil
1 1/2 Cup Mandarin Orange Sauce
1 1/2 Tbsp Soy Sauce
2 Tbsp Fresh Chopped Cilantro
Freshly Cracked Black Pepper
1 Whole Salmon Side
Instructions
Preheat the Pit Boss to 375°F & shut the lid for 15 mins.
To make the glaze: Mandarin sauce, cilantro, lime juice, soy sauce, sesame oil, & black pepper should all be combined.
Cut your salmon fillets into 4 pieces. Brush with some glaze & put on your barbecue grate.
Cook for 15-20 mins, or unless your salmon hits a core temp of 155°F. Brush your salmon with some glaze again midway through the cooking time.
Remove your salmon from Pit Boss &, if wanted, serve with the leftover glaze. Enjoy!

5.71 Roasted Stuffed Rainbow Trout with Brown Butter
Total Time: 30 Mins, Servings: 2
Ingredients
8 Tbsp Butter
Lemon, Juiced
2 Whole Rainbow Trout, Cleaned
2 Tbsp Salt
2 Tsp Chipotle Pepper
4 Whole Oranges, Sliced
6 Whole Bay Leaves
8 Sprig Thyme Sprigs
2 Clove Garlic, Chopped
Instructions
Preheat the grill to 400°F (260°C.) & cook for around 10-15 mins with the lid covered.
In a medium sauce pan on medium-high heat, melt the butter. When the butter has fully melted, it will froth & milk solids would start to brown. Remove from the heat once all of the foam has subsided & the butter has become golden brown. Pour in a little lemon juice to stop the browning process.
Lay down a strip of foil with each end 3" larger than your fish. Season your fish with salt & chipotle powder after drizzling some brown butter over the outside & cavities. Fold the foil in a package & fill the cavity through the rest of the ingredients.
Cook for 15 mins or unless the core temp reaches 145°F by placing the packet straight on your grill grate.

5.72 Roasted Cod with Meyer Lemon-Herb Butter

Total Time: 30 mins, Serving: 2
Ingredients
4 tbsp Salted Butter (softened)
Zested and juiced lemon 1/2 Meyer.
1 clove garlic Chopped.
1 tbsp. Assorted Herbs (Finely minced), for example, Parsley Basil, Chives.
Salmon Shake 2 Pit Boss.
Instructions
When it's time to cook, raise the temp to be high and preheat your grill. Close the lid for at least 15 mins.
Combine the butter, lemon juice, and zest, the Pit Boss Salmon Shake, herbs, and garlic to make the com lb butter. If you're not going to use it straight away, put it in the fridge.
Grease a heatproof baking bowl with 1 tbsp butter.
Place the fish fillets in a single layer in the baking dish. Do the same with the Com lb butter pieces.
Bake it for at least 12-15 mins, or until the fish is done.
Enjoy the dish by sprinkling some sauce over the portions.

5.73 Roasted Halibut with Tartar Sauce
Total Time: 1 hr 15 Mins, Servings: 2
Ingredients
1 Cup Mayonnaise
1/2 Cup Chopped Pickles
1 Tbsp Chopped Capers
1/2 Tbsp Parsley, Chopped
1/2 Tbsp Dijon Mustard
1/2 Medium Lemon, Juiced
6 Pieces Thick-Cut Halibut Fillets
Olive Oil
Sea Salt
Instructions
To let the flavors mingle, make your tartar sauce almost 1 hr ahead of the time. Combine mayonnaise, lemon juice, capers, dill pickles, & mustard in a mixing bowl. Mix. Toss in some herbs & season to taste with salt.
Set the temp to high & warm for 15 mins with the lid covered. Halibut fillets should be placed on the sheet tray. Drizzle with some olive oil, season liberally with some sea salt, and completely cover the olive oil fillets using your hands. Allow for 5 mins of resting time.
Place your fillets immediately on your grill grate. Cook over high heat till the fish becomes opaque.
Reduce the temp to 180°F & cook the salmon for another 3-5 mins. Place the fish over a serving platter and top with some lemon wedges & tartar sauce.

5.74 Roasted Cod with Meyer Lemon-Herb Butter
Total Time: 25 Mins, Servings: 2
Ingredients
4 Tbsp Salted Butter
1/2 Meyer Lemon, Zested & Juiced

1 Clove Garlic, Minced
1 Tbsp Chopped Herbs Fresh
2 Tsp Chicken Pit Boss Rub
2 lb Cod Fillets
Instructions
Set the Pit Boss to 450°F & preheat for around 15 mins with the lid covered.
Combine butter, garlic, herbs, lemon juice, lemon zest, & Chicken Pit Boss Rub in a mixing bowl. If you aren't going to use it straight away, keep it refrigerated.
Oil a heatproof baking dish with a tbsp of butter. In your baking dish, arrange the fish fillets into a thin layer.
Dot with pieces of the corn lb butter in an equal layer. Roast for 12-15 mins on your Pit Boss, or unless the salmon has cooked through.
Over each plate, spoon some butter sauce out from your baking dish.

5.75 Grilled Trout with Citrus & Basil
Total Time: 20 Mins, Servings: 4
Ingredients
6 Whole Trout
2 Tsp Blackened Saskatchewan Pit Boss Rub
10 Sprig Fresh Basil
2 Lemons, Cut In 1/2
Extra-Virgin Olive Oil
Instructions
Preheat your Pit Boss at 450°F for 15 mins with the lid covered when.
Season the trout's central cavity with Blackened Pit Boss Saskatchewan. Place 2 basil sprigs into each cavity, followed by 4 lemon halves.
The fish should then be tied closed with the Butcher's twine & rubbed with some olive oil.
Cook the fish for 5 mins from all sides on your hot grill.

5.76 Seared Bluefin Tuna Steaks
Total Time: 15 Mins, Servings: 2
Ingredients
3 Whole Tuna, Steak
Olive Oil
Salt And Pepper
Soy Sauce
Sriracha
Instructions
Brush both sides of the tuna steaks with olive oil & season with sea salt & ground pepper.
When prepared to cook, increase the temp to high & preheat for 10-15 mins with the lid closed.
Grill the tuna steaks for 2-3 mins from each side.
Remove the tuna from the grill & set it aside to cool.
Cut into 1/2-inch to 3/4-inch pieces. Serve with some Soy Sauce & Sriracha sauce combination.

5.77 Grilled Crab Legs with Herb Butter
Total Time: 35 Mins, Servings: 2
Ingredients
12 Tbsp Butter
3 Tbsp Chopped Herbs Fresh
4 lb King Crab Legs
3 Whole Lemons
Instructions
Preheat your Pit Boss at 375°F for 15 mins with the lid covered. In a large sauce pan, combine the butter, herbs, garlic, & a sprinkle of salt. To melt the cheese, place it on the grill for around 5 mins. Remove the pan from the grill & stir.
Split your crab legs down the middle and spread herb butter on the flesh, saving 1/4th for dishing. Using the crab clusters, combine them in a wide mixing bowl with the herb butter, reserving 1/4 for serving.
Put your crab legs on your grill grate. Grill for 5-10 mins, or unless the shell is hot & starting to brown slightly.
Crab legs should be served with some lemon wedges & the herb butter that has been set aside.

5.78 Chinese Shrimp with Sweet Sherry

Total Time: 2 Hrs 5 Mins, Serving: 4
Ingredients
4 lbs Jumbo Shrimp
1 cup Soya Sauce
1 cup Teriyaki Sauce
1 cup Sweet Sherry
1 cup Olive Oil
1 clove Minced, Garlic
1 tsp Ginger Freshly Grated
Chicken Pit Boss Rub 1 tsp.
Instructions
First, cut the shrimp on the back side of the shell, removing the heads & black veins.
Wipe the shrimp with a wet paper towel and set it aside.
In a very shallow pan or a reasonable-sized bag, combine the remaining ingredients and stir well.
Add the shrimp and marinate in the refrigerator for at least 2-4 hrs.
Set the temp of your Pit Boss at 500 deg Fahrenheit and preheat it. For at least 415 mins, the lid must be closed.
Remove the shrimp from the marinade and thread them onto presoaked wooden or metal skewers at the top.
Place the shrimp immediately on the grill. Also, heat it for at least 3 mins with the lid closed.
After flipping the shrimp over, shut the cover. Cook for a further 3 mins or until the shrimp are opaque.
Now you may take the Pit Boss out of the grill since your dinner is ready.

5.79 Grilled Sriracha Salmon with Avocado Pineapple Salsa
Total Time: 30 Mins, Servings: 4
Ingredients
2 Tbsp Soy Sauce
1 Tbsp Rice Vinegar
2 Tbsp Sriracha
1 Tbsp Toasted Sesame Oil
1/4 Cup Pure Maple Syrup
3 Clove Garlic, Minced
1 Tbsp Grated Ginger
1 Lime Zest
1 Pinch Sea Salt
1 Pinch Freshly Ground Black Pepper
1 (3 Lb) Salmon Side

1 1/2 Cup Pineapple, Diced 1/2 Inch
1 Diced Avocado
1/2 Cup Red Onion, Finely Diced
1/4 Cup Cilantro, Finely Chopped
2 Tbsp Fresh Squeezed Lime Juice
1/2 Tbsp Apple Cider Vinegar
Sea Salt
Freshly Ground Black Pepper
Cilantro
Radishes, Thinly Sliced
Zucchini, Thinly Sliced
Jasmine Rice, Cooked
Instructions
To make the marinade, whisk together soy sauce, vinegar, sriracha, lime zest, sesame oil, garlic, ginger, maple syrup, & a sprinkle of salt & pepper in a wide mixing bowl.
Pour the marinade over the salmon in a big freezer bag. Refrigerate for 2 hrs after covering.
Set the temp to high & shut the lid for around 15 mins before cooking.
Using parchment paper, line a big baking sheet. Place your salmon on the baking sheet. Brush the fish top with some marinade to give it an additional layer of flavor, then place it on the grill.
To make the salsa, put the red onion, pineapple, avocado, & cilantro in a wide mixing bowl. Squeeze in some lime juice, then add vinegar & season for taste with some salt & pepper.
Serve grilled salmon with salsa, additional sriracha, & steamed rice, garnished with cilantro & radishes, plus zucchini.

5.80 Pit Boss Jerk Shrimp
Total Time: 25 Mins, Servings: 8
Ingredients
1 Tbsp Brown Sugar
1 Tbsp Smoked Paprika
1 Tsp Garlic Powder
1/4 Tsp Thyme, Ground
1/4 Tsp Cayenne Pepper
1 Tsp Sea Salt
1 Lime Zest
2 lb Shrimp in Shell
3 Tbsp Olive Oil
Instructions
In a wide mixing dish, combine the spices,
salt, & lime zest. Drizzle some olive oil over the shrimp in a large mixing bowl. Toss in some spice mix, making sure that each shrimp has kissed with sweetness.
Preheat the grill to 450°F & cook for around 15 mins with the lid covered.
Cook your shrimp for around 2-3 mins each side on your grill, till firm, opaque, & cooked through.
Lime wedges, mint, fresh cilantro, & Hot Pepper Caribbean Sauce are served on the side.

5.81 Whole Vermillion Red Snapper
Total Time: 25 Mins, Servings: 6
Ingredients
1 Whole Scaled & Gutted Vermilion Red Snapper
4 Clove Chopped Garlic
1 Whole Thinly Sliced Lemon
2 Sprig Rosemary Sprigs
Sea Salt & Black Pepper
Instructions
Set the thermostat to high & warm for 10-15 mins with the lid covered.
Garlic should be stuffed into the fish cavity. Then, season your fish with salt, rosemary, pepper, & lemon juice.
Fish should be cooked directly on your grill grate. Cook for around 20 mins to 25 mins. Serve.

5.82 Grilled Ahi Tuna Sliders
Total Time: 25 Mins, Servings: 4
Ingredients
1 Tsp Sesame Oil
1 Tsp Soy Sauce
1 Tsp Red Pepper Flakes
1 Tsp Crushed Garlic
1 Tsp Onion Powder
2 (8 Oz) Sushi Grade Tuna Yellowfin Filets
1 Large Peeled Pineapple
3 Tbsp Brown Sugar
12 Small Slider Buns, For Serving
2 Tbsp Mayonnaise
Lettuce, For Serving
1 Medium Sliced Avocado
Fresh cilantro,
Instructions
Whisk together garlic, sesame oil, pepper flakes, soy sauce, & onion powder in a large dish. Refrigerate the mixture after pouring it on the tuna fillets.
Set the Pit Boss to 450°F & preheat for around 15 mins with the lid covered.
To sear your fillets, put them on the grill till grill marks appear, then turn & cook for 3-5 mins longer in the middle. Be careful you don't overcook it. When it comes to tuna, medium-rare-medium is ideal.
While your tuna continues cooking, coat the pineapple into brown sugar & put it immediately on your grill unless grill marks appear.
Remove both pineapple & fish from your grill. Next, slice your tuna & assemble the sliders in the following order: bottom bun, avocado, mayonnaise, lettuce, grilled pineapple, tuna, & top bun.

5.83 Grilled Clams in Garlic Butter
Total Time: 18 Mins, Servings: 6
Ingredients
24 Clams, Littleneck
8 Tbsp Butter
3 Clove Garlic, Minced
2 Tbsp Parsley, Minced
2 Tsp Pernod Liqueur
6 Lemon Wedges
Instructions
Scrub your clams under cool running water
to eliminate those that do not close or maybe have cracked shells.
When you're prepared to cook, fire up your Pit Boss & warm it to 500°F, lid closed.
Place the heatproof skillet or casserole big enough to contain your clams over the grill with the butter, Pernod, garlic, parsley, & lemon wedges juice. Grill your clams for 5-8 mins, or till they open, straight on your grill grate. Those that don't open should be discarded.
Transfer your opened clams onto the pan plus the butter using tongs, being careful don't spill any clam fluids.
Serve with some lemon wedges in a small serving dish along with the clams & butter.

5.84 Citrus Salmon

Total Time: 25 mins, Servings: 2
Ingredients
2 Tbsp Softened Butter.
1/2 tsp Lemon Zest
1 tsp Lemon Juice
2 tsp Fresh Sliced dill
1/2 tsp Salt
Black Pepper
4 (8 Oz) Skin-On, Salmon Fillets
1 Lemon Thinly cut.
Instructions
When you're prepared to cook, preheat your Pit Boss at 350°F and shut the lid for almost 15 mins.
Combine the lemon zest, dill, softened butter, and lemon juice in a mixing bowl.
Using the butter dilled with lemon and 1 lemon slice, generously cover the fish fillets.
Place the salmon fillets on a hot grill, skin-side down, and cook until done. Cook for 15-20 mins for medium-rare salmon, or until it (salmon) is done to your liking. Garnish with dill.

5.85 Grilled Soy-Ginger Yellowtail Collar

Total Time: 30 Mins, Servings: 4
Ingredients
1/4 Cup Soy Sauce
2 Tbsp Grated Ginger
1 Medium Lemon
3 Tbsp Avocado Oil Montana Mex
1/2 Tsp Cracked Black Pepper
1 lb Yellowtail Collar
Instructions
In a mixing bowl, combine all your ingredients except the fish. After that, add your fish and turn it to coat it. Cover & marinate for 1-2 hrs in the refrigerator.
When prepared to cook, set the Pit Boss to 400°F & preheat, lid covered for 15 mins.
Cook for around 10 mins on your grill grate. Cook for additional 8 mins on the other side.
Remove from the grill & serve right away.

5.86 Cedar Plank Salmon with Sweet Thai Chili Sauce Glaze

Total Time: 155 Mins, Servings 4
Ingredients
4 pacific salmon
¼ Cups of soy sauce
¼ Cups of red wine
3 Tbsp rice vinegar
¼ Cups of brown sugar
¼ Cups of Thai Sweet Chili Sauce
cedar plan
Instructions
Place the salmon pieces into a Ziploc bag that may be used to store food. Pour on the salmon chunks a mixture of soy sauce, rice vinegar, red wine, & brown sugar. Refrigerate the marinated salmon for 1 or 2 hrs after sealing the bag.
Presoak the wood plank into the water while your fish is marinating.
Put the plank on the Pellet Grill, pat dry, & put the fish chunks on the board.
Shut the lid & set the temp to 200 deg Fahrenheit. Set aside for around 1 hr.
When the hr is up, brush 1/2 Thai Sweet Chili sauce over your salmon pieces.
Before bringing the grill temp to 350 Deg F, smoke your fish for the next hr & baste using the leftover Thai Sweet Chili sauce. Leave your planked salmon over the grill for another 15 mins with its lid down. When the core temp of fish hits 130 deg F, it is ready.

5.87 Smoked Sesame Crusted Halibut with Tahini Mayonnaise

Total Time: 90 Mins, Servings: 5
Ingredients
For Halibut:
1 & ½ lb. halibut fillet
½ Cup of sesame seeds, toasted
½ tsp flakes of kosher salt
1 Tbsp of vegetable oil
1 tsp of sesame oil
½ Cup of pickled ginger
For Mayonnaise:
2 egg yolks
2 Tbsp of lemon juice
¼ Cup of tahini paste
1 Tbsp of soya sauce
1 & ½ Cup of vegetable oil
Instructions
In the mortar & pestle, smash the sesame seeds along with some kosher
salt. You may also utilize some spice grinders, however, avoid over-processing. The final product should be gently crushed seeds rather than powder.
Mix vegetable oil & sesame oil and spread it all over your fish steaks.
Cover your fish pieces in sesame seeds, pressing them on the fish's surface.
Close the cover on the Pellet Grill & put the sesame-coated fish on the bottom rack. Preheat the grill to 225°F & smoke your fish for around 2-3 hrs.
Inside a blender, combine the first 4 ingredients for tahini mayonnaise. Increase the speed to higher and gradually drizzle into the oil. As you sprinkle within the oil, the dressing would emulsify and thicken into a rich, creamy mayonnaise.
To serve, top your smoked sesame coated halibut with both tahini mayo & pickled ginger.

5.88 Pit Boss Grilled Shrimp Scampi

Total Time 15 mins, Servings 6
Ingredients
1 lb raw shrimp colossal
½ cup melted salted butter
¼ cup white wine dry
½ tsp fresh garlic chopped
1 tbsp lemon juice
½ tsp garlic powder
½ tsp salt
Instructions
Preheat the grill to 400°F and place a skillet inside.
Melt the butter, add the garlic, white wine, & lemon juice, and

mix well. Carefully pour all liquids into the pan & heat for around 3-4 mins.
Sprinkle each shrimp with garlic powder & salt, then gently put them in the pan.
Close the cover and cook for around 10 mins on the grill. If you use smaller shrimp, the cooking time will be reduced.
Remove the skillet from the heat & enjoy while it's still hot!

5.89 Smoked Buttery Shrimp
Total Time: 40 mins, Servings: 4
Ingredients
15 shrimp
½ Cup butter (aka- 1 stick)
1 clove minced garlic
2 Rosemary sticks
1 Tbsp seasoning
¼ squeezed lemon
Instructions
Rinse Devein, de-shell, & shrimp as required.
Season to taste.
Melt butter in a mixing bowl. Add the minced garlic after the butter has melted.
Place 3 rows of shrimp in foil pan.
Toss the shrimp in the butter and garlic mixture. Put rosemary between the shrimp & squeeze 1 lemon into your pan.
Preheat the smoker to 275°F and add pecan wood. Put the pan over your grill for around 20-25 mins. When the shrimp is done, they will turn a bright orange hue.

5.90 Grilled Salmon in Foil
Total Time 30 mins, Servings: 3
Ingredients
1 Open Sockeye Salmon
1 Butter Stick
2 Tbsp chopped dill
2 Tbsp chopped thyme
1 Tbsp Powder Garlic
1 Tbsp Lemon Pepper
1 Tbsp Salt
1 Zucchini
1 Squash Yellow
1 Diced Red Pepper
1 Diced Yellow Pepper
1 Cup Chopped Broccoli
1/2 Cup Sliced Onion
Instructions
Preheat your grill to 375°F.
To make the butter, combine the garlic powder, thyme, dill, softened butter, & salt in a mixing bowl until thoroughly combined & creamy.
Put the vegetables and every fillet over a big piece of Al foil.
Lemon pepper & sea salt are used to season the vegetables and fish.
Apply the butter mix to the tops of the fillets.
Place the foil over the grill & close it.
Cook the fish until it reaches a core temp of 135-140°F. It should take approximately 15 mins to complete this task.
Allow sitting for 5-10 mins after removing from your grill.

5.91 Honey Smoked Tilapia with Cajun Spice Rub
Total Time 2 hr 20 min, Servings: 6
Ingredients
12 Tilapia fillets
1 Cup of Honey
Cajun blackening Black Magic spice Rub
Cooking Oil

Instructions
On the baking sheet, spread your tilapia fillets out. Brush the fillets with small cooking oil to prevent them from sticking to the smoker's grill grates.
Apply a little amount of heated honey to every fillet. You don't need much.
Season the fillets with the Spice rub.
As required, season with more salt & pepper.
Set up your Smoker Preheat your smoker at 275 deg Fahrenheit. Set up charcoal on the grill for indirect grilling.
To prevent your fish from adhering to grill grates, brush them with oil.
Use pieces of wood straight into a smoker's firebox, chips in the smoker box.
Smoking Tilapia
Put your tilapia fillets within the smoker after the smoke has started to appear.
Cook the tilapia within the smoker till they hit a core temp of 145°F.
Remove them from your smoker & serve right away.

5.92 Lemon Herb-Grilled Salmon
Total Time: 45 mins, Servings 4
Ingredients
1 & ½ lbs Salmon
½ tbsp Lemon Zest
1 tbsp Juice Lemon
1 tbsp butter unsalted
½ tsp Salt
½ tsp Black Pepper Ground
2 tsps Dill Freshly Chopped
1 tsp Parsley Freshly Chopped
Lemon slices
Instructions
Preheat the grill to 325 deg Fahrenheit & cook for around 5 mins with the lid covered.
Combine the sea salt, lemon zest, dill, parsley, unsalted butter, lemon juice, & black pepper in a mixing bowl.
Slather the mix over your salmon fillet & garnish with a lemon.
Enable a 10-min marinating period to allow the ingredients to soak.
Place your salmon fillets on the heated grill grate.
Cook for 20-25 mins, or unless the salmon hits a core temp of 145°F & flakes readily, or until done to your liking.
Serve with some lemon slices & a garlic butter dip, if desired.

5.93 Whole Red Snapper - Stuffed, Sauced and Smoked
Total time: 1 hr 25 mins, Servings: 5
Ingredients
For Stuffed Portion
1 red snapper
Salt & black pepper
2 sliced limes
2 red onion slices
2 slices orange
6 thyme sprigs
6 oregano sprigs
5 smashed garlic cloves
6 thyme sprigs
6 fresh oregano sprigs
4 garlic cloves
2 red onion thin slices
1 peeled/chunked orange
1.5 limes juice & zest
Kosher salt
Black pepper cracked

White pepper coarse ground
1 pinch flakes of red pepper
⅛ cup olive oil
⅛ cup white wine dry
Dash of hot sauce
Instructions
Stuff fish:
Season the red snapper, on the inside, with salt & pepper.
Make an angle incision below the gills along the fish side with a knife & do so each inch & a 1/2 corresponding to the initial cut on both fish sides.
Using lime slice, stuff every slit into the fish's sides.
Fill the red snapper cavity with the remaining ingredients from the filled portion.

5.94 Smoked Clams Casino
Total Time 60 Mins, Servings: 8
Ingredients
24 Clams Cherryst1
8 oz 2 sticks Butter
8 oz Bacon Crispy
1 Bell Pepper
¼ cup Garlic Chopped
1 cup Panko Breadcrumbs
½ cup Parsley Chopped
½ cup scallions Sliced
½ tbsp Chili Flakes Crushed
Instructions
Using the cold water, rinse & scrub the exterior of every clam. Fill a big saucepan or dish with some cold water & salt after the clams get clean. Allow the clams to purge within water for approximately 2 hrs gently. Allow butter to soften while the clams are purging slowly.
Preheat your grill at 325 deg Fahrenheit.
1-inch slices of raw bacon, chopped in 1-inch pieces, sauté till crispy. Remove the bacon & place it on the paper towel to absorb any excess liquid. In bacon fat, sauté your scallions, chopped bell pepper, & garlic. Allow cooling at room temp.
With the melted butter, combine the sautéed vegetables, crispy bacon, & pork king excellent breadcrumbs. Then add the remaining spices & parmesan Parmesan, then stir to combine.
Drain the clams & pat them dry after they've been purged. Cook for approximately 25 mins on your pellet grill. Remove your clams off the grill with care. Once the clams have cooled, remove them from shells & cut them into medium chunks. A few large pieces are OK, but they must be diced equally throughout.
Preheat the grill at 400 deg Fahrenheit.
In a large mixing bowl, combine chopped clams and casino butter mix. After that, break shells apart & rinse away any shell pieces. Fill 24 shells with a generous tbsp of the casino butter. Combine the leftover pork king excellent breadcrumbs & parmesan cheese into a mixing bowl, then sprinkle on top of the clams.
Cook your clams over sheet pan into the grill at 400° for around 10-15 mins, till the crumbs are brown & the butter starts the bubble out the edges.

5.95 Smoked Salmon and Brine Recipe
Total Time: 15 hrs 10 mins, Servings: 8
Ingredients
3 lbs. Salmon
¼ cup of sugar
¼ cup of kosher salt
3 cups of soy sauce
2 & 1/2 cups of water
½ cup of white wine dry
½ tsp powder onion
½ tsp powder garlic
½ tsp flakes of red pepper
1 tsp sauce tabasco
Instructions
In a mixing bowl, whisk together the wine, onion, sugar, water, soy sauce, kosher salt, & pepper, garlic powders, & Tabasco sauce to completely combine, then dissolve some sugar & salt.
Pour a bit of brine into the base of your pan. Place your smoked salmon into the pan & pour the remaining brine over it to completely coat it. Freeze for at least 8 hrs before serving. After brining for 8 hrs, take the salmon out from brine, shake off any excess brine, & drain over a rack. After that, set it into the front of the fan to dry & produce a glossy skin known as a pellicle. The pellicle adheres to a fish & provides a sticky base for smoke to cling to. This might take 4 hrs & is very important to complete. You may simply keep it simple and do this by leaving it open in the fridge. The chilly, flowing air is quite effective.
For simpler handling, cut the fish into thirds. Because salmon may stick, place it immediately on the rack coated with oil. If you don't want to chill the salmon before making the pellicle, wrap it in Al foil approximately the length of your fish to allow this smoke to circulate inside your smoker, then put it over a smoker rack.
It's time to start smoking the fish. Fill a water tray with water & smoke your salmon for around 6 hrs using wood alder chips. On your gas grill, start at 100 deg for around 2 hrs, then 140 deg for 2 hrs & lastly 175 deg for the last 2 hrs. If you prefer, baste with some brine mixture every time its heat is increased.
Allow about an hr of resting time after removing your salmon from the smoker and refrigerate or eat! After that, you may store it for almost 8-10 days.

5.96 Grilled Shrimp Foil Packets
Total Time: 25 Mins, Servings: 4
Ingredients
1 & 1/2 lb. peeled & deveined large shrimp
2 cloves minced garlic
2 thinly sliced andouille sausages
2 corn ears
1 lb. chopped potatoes red bliss
2 tbsp. olive oil extra-virgin
1 tbsp. seasoning Old Bay
Kosher salt
black pepper Freshly ground
2 tbsp. parsley freshly chopped
1 sliced lemon
4 tbsp butter
Instructions
Preheat the grill to higher heat to 400°. Cut 4 12-inch-long sheets of foil. Over foil sheets, equally distribute the sausage, corn, shrimp, garlic, & potatoes. Drizzle with some oil, then season with Bay seasoning, salt & pepper for taste. To mix, gently toss everything together. Each combination should be garnished with lemon, parsley, & butter.
To fully cover the meal, fold the foil packs crosswise over the shrimp boil mix. Then, to seal both top & bottom edges, roll them together.
Place foil packs on the grill & cook for 15-20 mins, or till cooked through.

5.97 Smoked Prawns Recipe
Total Time: 55 Mins, Servings: 4
Ingredients
16 peeled & deveined jumbo prawns
Seasoning Blend
2 tbsps powder chili
2 tbsps salt
1 tbsp powder garlic
2 tsps black pepper ground
¼ tsp bay leaf ground
½ cup butter melted
2 tsps lemon juice
2 tsp oregano dried
1 tsp parsley dried
Instructions
Preheat the smoker at 135 deg Celsius.
Combine the chili powder, pepper, garlic powder, salt, & bay leaf into a bowl. Season all sides of your shrimp with the spice mixture.
Combine the oregano, lemon juice, melted butter, & parsley into a mixing bowl.
To smoke, toss wood chips over hot coals.
In a smoker, place your shrimps. Cook for around 25-30 mins, brushing each 5-10 mins with some lemon-butter mix.
When completely cooked, shrimp will become orange in color.
Take the shrimp out of the smoker & serve right away.

5.98 Sweet Chili Lime Pit Boss Grilled Crappie Recipe
Total Time: 25 Mins, Servings: 5
Ingredients
1 lb panfish filets
3 limes Juice
½ cup of olive oil
¼ cup of Honey
1 tsp chili powder chipotle
½ tsp garlic powdered
Instructions
Fill a bag 1/2way with the fillets.
Combine the chipotle powder, olive oil, honey, lime juice, & garlic into a mixing bowl. To mix the marinade components, whisk them together. Pour some marinade on the fish into the bag & close it firmly. Massage your fillets lightly to coat fish with some marinade evenly.
Freeze for around 30 mins before serving.
Grill your fish for around 15 mins at 325° on the Pit Boss Grill. To keep the fish from adhering to the grill grates, we use a Pit Boss Grilling Basket gently sprayed with non-stick cooking spray.
On wild & brown rice, serve your fish.

5.99 Lemon Herb Cedar Plank Salmon Recipe
Total Time: 35 Mins, 6 servings
Ingredients
2-2.5 lb salmon fillet
salt
½ cup melted butter
3 finely minced garlic cloves
2 tbsp dill fresh
1 tbsp minced capers
1 large lemon zest
1 tsp of salt
black pepper ground
2 presoaked cedar planks
1 large asparagus bundle
1-2 tbsp olive oil
to season salt
1/2 lemon zest
Instructions
Presoak your cedar boards for almost 30 mins; however, ideally 4 hrs. When you're ready to cook the meal, preheat the grill. If you are using a grill, warm it for around 10 mins on 'smoke' mode. Preheat your grill at 450 deg Fahrenheit if using a traditional grill.
To make your butter topping, follow these steps: Melt some butter in a wide mixing bowl. Finely chop the garlic & capers, then combine with some fresh dill, salt, lemon zest, & a pinch of black pepper into melted butter. Put the bowl within the refrigerator for almost 10-15 mins after mixing all of the ingredients. Then, it's time for the butter to solidify into the spread.
Prepare your salmon by grilling it with/without the skin. Remove skin with a sharp knife. You may cook the fish whole or chop it into serving pieces. Before placing the salmon over the presoaked wood planks, gently season it over with some salt.
Remove the hard edges of your asparagus & wash it. Drizzle some olive oil over the asparagus over the flat tray. Salt & lemon zest to taste are added.
It's time to fire up the grill! Then increased the temp to 'grill' (approximately 425F) for the next 15 mins till the salmon looked ready. If using the traditional grill, cook the salmon for 20-22 mins on a low/medium heat at 450°F with its lid covered, till the edges become golden. Next, on low heat, grill your asparagus for around 10 mins, turning once or twice.
With the asparagus side & a couple of lemon wedges, your salmon may be served just off the plank.

5.100 Grilled Salmon Burger with Chipotle Mayo
Total Time: 20 Mins, Servings: 4
Ingredients
Salmon Burgers
Minced Scallions, 2 Whole
Seeded & Minced Jalapeno Pepper, 1
Pit Boss Chicken Rub, 1/2 tbsp
Salt
Black Pepper
Garlic, 1 Clove
Salmon, Skin & Pin Bones Removed, 2 Pound
Minced Cilantro Leaves, 1/2 tbsp
Chipotle Mayo
Mayonnaise, 1/2 Cup
Chipotle Peppers in Adobo Sauce, 2 Whole and 1 tbsp Sauce
Lime Juiced, 1/2
Pepper
Salt
For Serving
Pickled Red Onion
Butter Lettuce
Brioche Buns, Halved
Dill Pickles
Instructions
In a food processor, mix jalapeno, Cilantro, scallions, garlic, Pit Boss Chicken Rub, salt & pepper. Pulse a few times to incorporate. Scrape down the bowl's sides, then pulse once or twice more.
Finely chop salmon and pulse it 2 to 3 times in the food processor bowl.
Remove the salmon mixture from the food processor and divide it into 5 patties, each weighing about 6 ounces.
Refrigerate the patties for 10 to 15 minutes after placing them on a sheet pan.
Once ready to cook, preheat the Pit Boss to 500°F for 15 minutes with the lid closed.

Cook the salmon patties for 4 minutes on each side, turning once directly on the grill grate.

To make the Chipotle Mayo, in a small bowl, combine chipotles, mayonnaise and adobo sauce, salt & pepper, lime juice. Combine all ingredients in a large mixing bowl and chill until ready to use.

To make the burgers, put the salmon burger on the bottom bun & top with pickled red onions, lettuce, chipotle mayo, pickles or any toppings you like. Enjoy.

5.101 Baja-style Grilled Fish Tacos

Total Time: 30 Mins, Servings: 4
Ingredients
Main
Limes, 2
Pit Boss Veggie Rub
Skinless White Fish like Monkfish Cod or Halibut, 1 Pound
Marinade
Dijon Mustard, 2 tsp
Ground Black Pepper, 1/2 tsp
Salt, 1/2 tsp
Minced Garlic, 2 Clove
Olive or Vegetable Oil, 1/2 Cup
For Serving
Diced Red Onion
Pickled Jalapeno Slices
Cilantro Leaves
Shredded Cabbage
Diced Avocado
Salsa or Pico De Gallo
8 Corn Tortillas
Sour Cream
Instructions
Squeeze the juice from one lime. Cut the remaining lime into wedges and put them aside until ready to
serve.

To make the marinade, Mustard, combine lime juice, salt & pepper in a small mixing dish. Whisk in the oil slowly, then add the garlic.

Put the fish in a reclose able bag, pouring the marinade over it, and chill for 1 hour.

When ready to cook, preheat the Pit Boss to 400°F with the lid closed for 15 minutes.

Remove fish from marinade and wipe dry with paper towels to remove any excess marinade. Season both sides liberally with Pit Boss Veggie Rub.

Put the fish on the grill grate & cook until it is opaque and readily flakes when pushed with a fork. (You don't have to turn it.)

Transfer to a chopping board and chop into small pieces.

Heat the tortillas on Pit Boss for approximately 5 minutes in the meanwhile. On a big plate, arrange the fish, tortillas, and recommended accompaniments. Serve with the lime wedges that were set aside as a garnish. Serve right away.

5.102 Grilled Salmon Tacos with Smoked Tomato Salsa by Daniel Seidman

Total Time: 1 Hr 10 Mins, Servings: 2
Ingredients
Salt, 1 tbsp
Tomato, 1 Pound
Extra-Virgin Olive Oil
Powder of Ancho Chile, 1/2 tbsp
Smoked paprika, 1/2 tbsp
Brown Sugar, 1/2 tbsp
Garlic Powder, 1/2 tbsp
Black Pepper ground, 1/4 tbsp
1 Jalapeno medium size
1 Peeled & Halved small red onion
Dried Oregano Leaves, 1/4 tbsp
Cabbage Head, 1 Whole
Cilantro, 1/2 Whole
Limes, 3 Whole
Extra-Virgin Olive Oil, 2 tbsp
Instructions
Combine ancho chili powder, garlic powder, salt, smoked paprika, oregano, brown sugar and cracked pepper in a bowl to create the spice rub. Combine all ingredients in a mixing bowl and put them aside.

When ready to cook, preheat the Pit Boss to 275°F for 15 minutes with the lid closed.

Cut an "X" in the bottom of tomatoes & brush the veggies for the salsa (tomatoes, red onion, jalapeno) with olive oil & salt.

Cook for approximately 30 minutes on the grill. When they have softened and are starting to char, they are done. We're not attempting to blacken the veggies; rather, we're attempting to provide a smokey taste.

Remove the veggies from the pan and set them aside to cool till they are ready to handle. Remove the peel from the tomatoes and, if preferred, the seeds and membrane from the jalapeno.

Place them in the bowl of a food processor with the onion and Cilantro and pulse until all is coarsely chopped. Squeeze in lime and sprinkle in 1-2 tbsp olive oil, then pulse until you have the texture you want. Season with salt & pepper to taste. Place in a bowl and put aside until ready to serve, or keep in the refrigerator.

To make the cabbage, thin slice half a head of green cabbage & season with salt and the juice of 1 lime. Keep refrigerated until ready to serve.

Raise the grill's temperature too high.

Place the salmon flesh side down on a cutting board and lightly score the skin with a sharp knife. Drizzle olive oil over the fish and liberally apply the spice rub. This should be done on both sides of the fish.

Once the grill is hot, put the salmon skin side down on the grill and shut it.

Cook for approximately 20 minutes, or until the salmon reaches a temperature of 125°F on the inside (for medium-rare). When the fish is done, use a large spatula to sensibly remove it from the grill and place it on a serving plate. Allow for at least 5 minutes of resting time before serving.

To serve the tacos, wrap a stack of heated tortillas in foil and let everyone pull out bits of salmon with their fingers. With a squeeze of lime, top with cilantro leaves, smokey salsa, cabbage slaw, and a squeeze of lime. Enjoy.

5.103 Roasted Wild Salmon with Pickled Cauliflower Salad

Total Time: 1 Hr 10 Mins, Servings: 6
Ingredients
Head of Cauliflower and Cut into Florets, 1
Golden Raisins, 1/2 Cup
8 Pieces of sliced Jarred Peppers Pepperoncini
Large Red Bell Pepper, 1
Red Wine Vinegar, 3/4 Cup
Sugar, 1/3 Cup
Small Onion, 1
Peppercorns, 2 tbsp
Thyme Leaves, 2 tbsp
Dried Bay Leaves, 3 Whole
thinly sliced garlic, 3 Clove
Dried oregano, 2 tbsp
Fresh parsley, 1 tsp of
Extra-Virgin Olive Oil, 3/4 Cup

Skin-On Salmon Fillet, Sooner Wild-Caught, 3 Pound (2 Lb)
Fresh Dill, 1 tsp
Lemon Juice, 3 tsp
Black Pepper
Salt
Instructions
Boil a big pot of salted water for the pasta. Cook for 2–4 minutes, or until cauliflower is soft. Transfer the cauliflower to a basin of cold water using a slotted spoon. Carry on with the bell peppers.
Drain veggies and combine with pepperoncini, raisins and onions in a mixing bowl. In a small pan over medium-high heat, heat the oil and garlic. Cook until the mixture is aromatic.
Add vinegar, peppercorns, sugar, bay leaves and bring to a boil. Cook for 1-2 minutes, or until the sugar has dissolved. Combine oregano and thyme in a bowl and pour over veggies. Toss everything together. Allow resting for 10 minutes at room temperature before chilling.
When ready to cook, preheat the oven to 375°F with the lid covered for 15 minutes.
Combine garlic, olive oil, dill, parsley and lemon juice in a small bowl. Brush the mixture all around salmon and season to taste with salt and pepper.
Place the salmon directly on the grill grate & roast for 20-25 minutes, or until an instant-read thermometer placed in the thickest part of the flesh registers 145°F and the meat readily flakes. Remove the grill from the heat.
Serve immediately with a salad of pickled cauliflower. Enjoy.

5.104 Chinese Jumbo Shrimp
Total Time: 2 Hr 5 Mins, Servings: 4
Ingredients
Jumbo Shrimp, 4 Pound
Soy Sauce, 1 Cup
Olive Oil, 1 Cup
Teriyaki Sauce, 1 Cup
Pit Boss Chicken Rub, 1 tsp
Minced Garlic, 1 Clove
Sweet Sherry, 1 Cup
Freshly Grated Ginger, 1 tsp
Instructions
Cut the shrimp down the back of the shell using a sharp knife. Remove the black veins and the heads of the shrimp.
Using a wet paper towel, wipe the shrimp and put them aside. In a deep pan or gallon-size resealable bag, combine the remaining ingredients and stir thoroughly. Add the shrimp and marinate in the refrigerator for 2 to 4 hours.
When you're ready to cook, preheat the Pit Boss to 500°F with the lid covered for 15 minutes.
Thread the shrimp onto pre-soaked wooden skewers or metal, removing them from the marinade.
Place the shrimp firmly on the grill grate and cook for approximately 3 minutes with the lid closed.
Flip the shrimp, cover, and simmer for another 3 minutes, or until the shrimp are opaque.
Remove the meat from the Pit Boss and serve it right away. Enjoy.

5.105 Bacon Wrapped Shrimp
Total Time: 25 Mins, Servings: 6
Ingredients
Bacon, 10 Strips
Jumbo Shrimp, Deveined & Peeled, 1 1/2 Pound
Cheesy Grits, For Serving
Marinade
Extra-Virgin Olive Oil, 1/4 Cup
Chopped parsley, 1 tbsp

Fresh Lemon Juice, 2 tbsp
Lemon Zest, 1 tbsp
Salt, 1 tsp
Minced garlic, 1 tsp
Black Pepper, 1/2 tsp
Instructions
Rinse the shrimp well under cold water and pat dry with paper towels.
Place in a resealable bag or a mixing bowl.
To make the marinade, whisk together the olive oil, lemon juice, lemon zest, garlic, salt, pepper, and parsley in a small container with a tight-fitting lid.
Pour the sauce over the shrimp & chill for 30 minutes to an hour. When ready to cook, preheat the Pit Boss to 400°F for 15 minutes with the lid closed.
Place the bacon strips on the grill grate in a diagonal pattern and cook for 10-12 minutes, or till partly cooked but still flexible. Cut every strip in half across the width. Turn on the grill.
Drain the shrimp and throw away the marinade.
Using a toothpick, secure a piece of bacon from around the body of each shrimp.
Cook for 4 minutes on each side of the grill, flipping once. If preferred, serve over cheesy grits. Enjoy.

5.106 Smoked Fish Chowder
Total Time: 1 Hr 15 Mins, Servings: 4
Ingredients
Skin-On Salmon Fillet, Rather Wild-Caught, 12 Ounce (2 Lb)
Husks, 2 Corn
Hot Sauce, 2 tsp
Sliced Bacon, 3 Slices
Feather Rub and Pit Boss Fin
Cream Cheese, 8 Ounce
Condense Cream of Potato Soup, 4 Can
Whole Milk, 3 Cup
Thinly Sliced Onions, 3 pieces
Instructions
Preheat the grill to 180°F and shut the cover for 15 minutes when ready to cook.
Season salmon with Feather rub and Pit Boss Fin as required. Place the salmon on the grill grate skin-side down. 30 minutes of smoking.
Preheat the grill to 350 degrees Fahrenheit.
Cook for 30 minutes or until salmon readily flakes with a fork. (The precise time will vary depending on the fillet thickness.) The fish does not need to be turned. Transfer salmon to a wire rack to cool using a big thin spatula. Remove the outer layer of the skin. (The salmon may be prepared and chilled up to a day
ahead of time, covered in plastic wrap.) Set aside after breaking into flakes.
On the grill grate, arrange the bacon and corn slices. (While you're doing this, the salmon will be roasting.) Roast the corn and bacon together for 15 minutes, or till the corn is cooked through and fried in places and the bacon is crisp.
Meanwhile, in a big saucepan or Dutch oven on the stovetop, bring the cream of potato soup and milk to a boil over medium heat. Whisk in the cream cheese in a slow, steady stream. With long strokes of a chef's knife, chop the bacon into small pieces and slice the corn from the cobs.
Stir in the green onions and add to the soup. Add the salmon and mix well. Heat for 5-10 minutes on low heat. To taste, add the spicy sauce. Add additional milk if the chowder is too thick. Serve right away. Enjoy.

5.107 Roasted Clambake

Total Time: 1 Hr 20 Mins, Servings: 6
Ingredients
Small Potatoes, 8 pieces
Red Potatoes, 1 piece
Quartered Yellow Onion, 2 pieces
In Shell, 16 Clams
Unshocked, 16 Mussels
Ears Fresh Corn, 4 Pieces
Italian Sausage, 4 Mild
White Wine, 1 Cup
Garlic Smashed, 3 Clove
2 Whole Lobster, In the Shell
Butter Melted, 1/2 Cup
French Bread, 1 Loaf
Instructions
In a strong disposable aluminum foil turkey roaster, arrange the onions, potatoes, clams, corn, mussels and sausages in the order indicated.
Pour in the wine and submerge garlic cloves in it.
Arrange the lobster tails on top, shell-side down.
Smother the lobster halves in butter & nestle the lemon quarters into the pan.
Use heavy-duty aluminum foil to cover the pan completely.
When ready to cook, increase the temperature to high & preheat for 15 minutes with the lid closed.
Place the veggies and shellfish in the pan immediately on the grill grate.
Bake for 60-70 minutes, or even the potatoes are tender. (If they're done, everything else is probably done as well.)
Remove foil from the pan with care & place the veggies and fish on a wide plate.
Drizzle some cooking liquids over everything.
Serve with melted butter & French toast right away. Enjoy.

5.108 Smoked Salmon Sandwich

Total Time: 1 Day 3 Hrs, Servings: 4
Ingredients
Salmon, 4 Pound
Brown Sugar, 1 Cup
Juniper Berries, 1 tbsp
Salt, 1 5/8 Cup
Crushed Leaves, 4 Bay
Black Pepper, 1 tsp
Sugar, 1/2 Cup
Red onion, 2 pieces
Red Wine Vinegar, 3/4 Cup
Mayonnaise, 1/2 Cup
Tarragon Dried Leaves, 1 tsp
Fresh parsley, 1 tsp
Fresh, Dill or Dried, 1 tsp
Chives, 1 tsp
4 Ciabatta Loaf or Rolls
Heirloom Tomato, 2 Medium
Greens Fresh, 1 Cup
Instructions
Smoked Salmon: Thoroughly clean the salmon, removing any pin bones & scales.
Combine the salt, crushed juniper berries, brown sugar, bay leaves & black pepper in a mixing bowl.
Cover the counter with a large piece of plastic wrap. 2/3 of the cure mixture should be spread on top of the plastic; then, the salmon should be placed skin-side down. Spread the leftover cure on top of the fillet, then gently wrap the plastic wrap around the fillet, tucking the ends in to encapsulate the salmon cure.
Arrange the salmon on a sheet pan and cover it with a second sheet pan. Put something heavy on the top of the sheet pan to properly spread the weight over the salmon fillets. Allow for a 24-hour cure time.
Remove salmon side from plastic wrap after 24 hours and rinse the leftover cure. Lay the salmon flat on a cooling rack on the top of a sheet pan after patting it dry. Allow it to rest in the fridge overnight to create the pellicle. This will make it easier for the smoke to stick to the fish.
When ready to cook, preheat the oven to 180ºF with the lid covered for 15 minutes.
Place the salmon fillets on the grill skin-side down. Smoke for 1-3 hours, or until a thermometer placed into the thickest section of the salmon reads 150 degrees Fahrenheit. Keep a careful eye on the temperature to ensure it does not get beyond 160ºF. Remove the salmon from the pan and put it aside.
In a normal saucepan over medium-high heat, mix sugar, vinegar and salt while the salmon is cooking. Cook, constantly stirring, until the salt & sugar have melted, then pour over the cut onions. Refrigerate for at least 1 hour before serving.
Combine mayonnaise, herbs, and salt & pepper in a small bowl.
Spread herb mayo on both sides of the ciabatta bread before assembling the sandwich. Smoked salmon, spring greens, pickled red onion and tomatoes are layered together. Enjoy.

5.109 Baked Halibut Fish Sticks with Spicy Coleslaw

Total Time: 35 Mins, Servings: 4
Ingredients
Mayonnaise, 1/2 Cup
Salt, 1 tbsp
Sour Cream, 1/2 Cup
Black Pepper
Dill Seed, 2 tbsp
Sriracha, 2 tbsp
White Wine Vinegar, 2 tbsp
Sugar, 1 tbsp
Shredded Cabbage, 1 Head
Carrot, Peeled, Shaved Thin, 1 piece
Halibut, Skin Removed, 1 1/2 Pound
Extra-Virgin Olive Oil
All-Purpose Flour, 1/2 Cup
Eggs, 2
Panko Breadcrumbs, 1 1/2 Cup
Dried dill, 1 tsp
Black Pepper, 1 tsp
Dried parsley, 2 tbsp
Instructions
In a small mixing bowl, whisk together sour cream, mayonnaise, salt, dill seed, sugar, pepper, sriracha, and vinegar.
In a medium mixing bowl, combine the cabbage and carrots, then fold in mayonnaise mixture even well covered. Remove from the heat and set aside until ready to eat.
When ready to cook, increase the temperature to high & preheat for 15 minutes with the lid closed.
Preheat a dutch oven with just enough olive oil to cook fish inside the grill (approximately 10 minutes).
Rinse and pat dry all fish fillets. Fillets should be cut into 1" strips. Combine the all-purpose flour, salt, and pepper in a mixing basin.
Beat the eggs in a separate dish.
Combine the panko, parsley, and dill in a third bowl.
Dip the fish fillets in the flour, then the eggs, and finally the panko mixture.
10. Heat the Oil and fry fish sticks for 3-4 minutes, until and unless they reach an internal temperature of 140ºF. Enjoy.

5.110 Grilled Soft-Shell Crabs
Total Time: 35 Mins, Servings: 8
Ingredients
Soft-Shell Crabs, 8 Whole
Lemons Juiced, 2 Whole
Chopped Basil, Parsley Chives or a mixture, 3 tbsp
Cajun Seasoning, 1/3 Cup
Worcestershire Sauce, 2 tbsp
Extra-Virgin Olive Oil, 1/2 Cup
Tartar Sauce, For Serving
Instructions
Clean the crabs by rinsing them under cold running water & patting them dry with paper towels. Fill a big resealable bag halfway with the mixture.
To make the marinade, combine the following ingredients in a mixing bowl. Combine the herbs, lemon juice, half of the Cajun spice & Worcestershire
sauce in a small mixing bowl. Stir in the olive oil in a slow, steady stream. Refrigerate for 1 hour after pouring the marinade over the crabs.
Remove the crabs from the marinade and drain them.
Season the crabs lightly with the remaining Cajun spice.
When ready to cook, preheat the Pit Boss to 500°F for 15 minutes with the lid closed.
Place the crabs nonstop on the grill grate and cook, rotating once, until they become orangish-pink and are no longer "squishy" when pushed with a finger, approximately 16 to 20 minutes total, depending on size.
Arrange on a tray or plates & serve with tartar sauce of your choice. Enjoy.

5.111 Smoked Albacore Tuna Niçoise Salad
Total Time: 4 Hrs 10 Mins, Servings: 6
Ingredients
Brine
Kosher Salt, 1 Cup
Brown Sugar, 1 Cup
Large Orange, 1
Medium Lemon, 1
Albacore Tuna Fillets, 6 (8 Oz)
Potatoes
Potatoes, 1/2 Pound
Olive Oil, 1/4 Cup
Salt, 1 tbsp
Black Pepper, 1/2 tbsp
Dressing
Dijon Mustard, 1 tbsp
Garlic, 1 Clove
Red Wine Vinegar, 1/3 Cup
Salt, 1 tsp
Black Pepper, 1/4 tsp
Chopped parsley, 2 tbsp
Chopped Tarragon, 2 tbsp
Lemon Juice, 1 tbsp
Extra-Virgin Olive Oil, 1 Cup
main
Eggs, 6
Green Beans, 1/2 Pound
Head Butter Lettuce, 1
Castelvetrano Olives, Halved and Pitted, 1/4 Cup
Thinly Sliced Fennel, 2 Bulbs
Cherry halved Tomatoes, 1/2 Cup
Radish Sprouts
Instructions
To make the brine, mix the sugar, salt & citrus zest in a small dish. In a container, layer the fish & brine, ensuring that there's brine between each fillet if fillets are stacked, so they don't touch. Refrigerate for 6 hours after soaking in brine.
When ready to cook, preheat the Pit Boss to 180°F with the lid closed for almost 15 minutes. If Super Smoke is available, use it for the best taste.
Remove the fillets from the brine and rinse off any excess liquid. Place on a chilling rack in the refrigerator for 30-40 minutes after patting dry.
Take the fillets out of the fridge and put them immediately on the grill grate, cooking for around 3 hours.
Raise the temperature on the Pit Boss to 225°F and cook for another hour, or even the fish has become a light brown color and flakes easily with a fork.
Remove the pan from the grill and set it aside to cool to room temp.
While the tuna is chilling, preheat the Pit Boss to 375°F for 15 minutes with the lid closed.
Toss fresh potatoes in olive oil and season with salt and pepper. Cook for 20-30 minutes on the grill, or until potatoes are cooked, on a half sheet pan. Allow cooling to room temp after removing from the grill. When cool, cut in half and put away.
To make the dressing in a blender, mix the Dijon mustard, red wine vinegar, garlic, salt, parsley, pepper, Tarragon, & lemon juice until smooth. When the mixture is smooth, gently drizzle in the olive oil while the blender is set on medium-high. There should be no separation in the emulsion. Set aside the dressing.
To make the eggs, place them in a medium-sized pot with just enough water to cover them. Bring to a boil over medium-high heat & simmer for 7 minutes. Remove the eggs from the heat and put them in cold water to cool. Eggs should be peeled, sliced in half, and set aside.
To make green beans, start by filling a medium pot halfway with water and bringing it to a boil. Cook for 5 minutes after adding the green beans. Green beans
should be strained and placed in cold water to chill. Reserve.
To Assemble the Salad: Arrange olives, potatoes, fennel, green beans, cherry tomatoes, smoked albacore tuna, halved eggs, and radish sprouts on top of broken butter lettuce leaves in the bottom of a bowl. Serve with a drizzle of dressing. Enjoy.

5.112 Sweet Smoked Salmon Jerky
Total Time: 5 Hrs 30 Mins, Servings: 6
Ingredients
Water, 2 Quart
Maple Syrup, 2 Cup
Kosher Salt, 3/4 Cup
Morton Tender Home Meat, 1 Cup
Dark Brown Sugar, 4 Cup
Salmon Fillet, Skinned & Pin Bones Removed, 1 (2-3 Lb)
Instructions
Combine two quarts of water, curing salt (if used), salt, brown sugar, and 1 cup maple syrup in a large nonreactive mixing basin. To combine the salts and sugar, mix with a long-handled spoon.
Slice the salmon into 1/2-inch-thick slices on the cutting board with a sharp, serrated knife, keeping the short side parallel to you. To put it another way, make the cuts from top to bottom. (If the fish is frozen, this is much simpler.) Cut each strip into 4- or 5-inch lengths crosswise.
Place the pieces in the brine and weigh them down with a plate or ice bag. Chill for 12 hours after wrapping in plastic wrap.
When ready to cook, preheat the Pit Boss to 180°F for 15 minutes with the lid closed. If Super Smoke is available, use it for the best taste.
Drain and discard brine from the salmon strips. Arrange the salmon strips on the grill grate in a single layer. Smoke the jerky for 5 to 6 hours, or until it is dry but not rock-hard. Whenever you bite into it, you want it to give. Brush salmon strips on both

sides with the leftover cup of maple syrup and 1/4 cup of warm water halfway through the smoking time.
While the jerky is still heated, transfer to a resealable bag. Allow the jerky to rest at room temperature for an hour. Squeeze any air out of the bag and store the jerky in the refrigerator. Enjoy.

5.113 Slow Roasted Wild Salmon with Cheesy Scalloped Potatoes
Total Time: 2 Hrs 15 Mins, Servings: 4
Ingredients
Breadcrumbs, 1/2 Cup
Parsley Minced, 1/4 Cup
Chives Chopped, 3 tbsp
Lemon Juice, 1
Skin-On Salmon Fillet, If possible Wild-Caught, 1 1/2 Pound (2 Lb)
Salt
Black Pepper
Butter, 2 tbsp
Small diced onion, 1
Garlic Minced, 2 Clove
Heavy Cream, 3 Cup
Whole Milk, 1 Cup
Fresh Thyme, 4 Sprig
Bay Leaves, 2 Dried
Salt, 2 tsp
Black Pepper, 1/2 tsp
Russet Potatoes, Peeled & Thinly Sliced, 4 Pound
Cheddar Cheese, 1 1/2 Cup
Instructions
Preheat the Pit Boss to 250°F and cook the salmon for 15 minutes with the lid covered.
Combine bread crumbs, chives, parsley and lemon juice in a mixing dish.
Season the salmon with salt & pepper, then top with the bread crumb mixture.
Smoke the salmon for 30-40 minutes, or until it reaches a temperature of 140°F on the inside. Serve with potatoes as a side dish.
For the Scalloped Potatoes, set the temperature to High and warm for 15 minutes with the lid covered. Preheat the grill with a Dutch oven pan.
In a heated Dutch oven, melt the butter and add the onion. Cook until the onions become a golden color. Cook for 30 seconds after adding the garlic to the Dutch oven.
In a Dutch oven, combine the heavy cream, thyme, milk, potatoes, bay leaf, salt and pepper. Bring to a low boil, then reduce to low heat.
Cook until the potatoes are nearly cooked, approximately an hour, covered in the Dutch oven. To keep the potatoes from sticking to the bottom of the pan, stir them periodically.
Remove and discard the bay leaves and thyme sprigs. Sprinkle cheese on top of the potato mixture in a baking dish.
Return the baking dish to the Pit Boss and continue to bake until the sauce has thickened and is bubbling around the edges.
Allow it cool before slicing to the desired size. Serve alongside salmon. Enjoy.

5.114 Crab Cakes
Total Time: 25 Mins, Servings: 4
Ingredients
Main
Wheat Bread, 5 Slices
Large Red Bell Pepper, Seeded & Diced, 1/4
Garlic Minced, 2 Clove
Chopped Basil or Parsley, 3 tbsp
Chili Sauce
Eggs, 2
Salt. 1/2 tsp
Freshly Cracked Black Pepper, 1/4 tsp
Olive oil, 1 tbsp
Fresh Crab Meat, 2 Cup
Whole Wheat Flour
Non-stick Cooking Spray
Fresh parsley chopped, for Serving
Red Pepper Sauce
Small Red Peppers, 5
Garlic Chopped, 2 Clove
Diced Red Onion, 3 tbsp
Salt, 1/2 tsp
Freshly Black Pepper, 1/4 tsp
Olive oil, 1 tbsp
Water, 1/4 Cup
Instructions
Preheat Pit Boss to 450°F and cook for 15 minutes with lid covered until ready to cook.
In a food processor, combine the red bell pepper, bread, garlic, and basil (or parsley) and pulse for 20
seconds to create the crab cakes. Place in a mixing basin.
Whisk together the chili sauce, salt, eggs, black pepper, and oil in a separate bowl. Add it to the bread mixture, along with the crab meat, and gently fold everything together, taking care not to break up crab meat too much.
If the batter is too wet, add a tablespoon of whole wheat flour. Now add a little water if it's too dry.
Form the mixture into tiny disks/patties and put on a foil-lined baking sheet coated with non-stick cooking spray.
Cook for 8-10 minutes on the Pit Boss, or until the crust is golden brown.
To make the sauce, heat a little oil in a skillet and add the sweet peppers, garlic, and onion. Salt & pepper to taste. Over medium-low heat, sauté for 5 minutes.
Puree until smooth in a food processor with 1 tbsp oil & 1/4 cup water.
Toss the crab cakes with red pepper sauce and a sprinkling of fresh chopped parsley while they're still warm. Enjoy.

5.115 Grilled Crawfish with Spicy Garlic Butter
Total Time: 1 Hr 15 Mins, Servings: 4
Ingredients
Pound Crawfish, Live
Kosher Salt
Butter unsalted, 1 1/2 Cup
Hot Sauce, 1/4 Cup
Cayenne Pepper, 1/4 tsp
Garlic Minced, 6 Clove
Salt & Pepper
Parsley Chopped, 1 3/4 Cup
Instructions
Place the crawfish in a big saucepan of boiling salted water. Cook for approximately a minute and a half. In a dish filled with cold water, shock the crawfish.
Cut the whole length of the crawfish through the shell on the belly side. This will aid in the even cooking of the meat. Remove the sack behind the eyes as well as the vein throughout the body. Rinse the dish well.
In a food processor, combine the butter, spicy sauce, cayenne, and garlic. Blend until completely smooth. Place in a cast iron pan and season with salt & pepper to taste. Remove from the equation.
When ready to cook, increase the temp to high & preheat for 15 minutes with the lid closed.
Place the crawfish on the grill immediately. Grill, turning and stirring with tongs a few times until the shell becomes brilliant

red and the flesh is opaque approximately 10 minutes.
If you have space, put cast iron skillet with buttered next to the crawfish or on the top rack to melt during the final 5 minutes of cooking.
Transfer the crawfish to a huge mixing bowl and set it aside. Mix with spicy garlic butter & chopped parsley after seasoning with salt and pepper. Serve right away. Enjoy.

5.116 Grilled White Fish Steaks with Basil Orange Pesto

Total Time: 35 Mins, Servings: 4
Ingredients
Fresh Basil, 2 Cup
Flat-Leaf Parsley, 1 Cup Chopped
Toasted Walnuts, 1/2 Cup
Orange Juiced, 1
Orange Zest, 2 tsp
Olive Oil, 1/2 Cup
Parmesan Cheese, 1 Cup
Salt
Black Pepper
Fish Steaks, 4 White
Coarse Sea Salt, 1/2 tsp
Black Pepper, 1/2 tsp
Instructions
Preheat the oven too high for 15 minutes with the lid covered when you're ready to cook.
Meanwhile, prepare the pesto by combining the basil, walnuts, parsley, orange juice, and orange zest in a blender jar or food processor and blending until finely chopped. Slowly pour in the olive oil while the machine is running till the mixture is mixed.
If it seems overly thick, thin it down with a tablespoon or two of water. Scrape into a mixing dish and add the Parmesan cheese. Season to taste with salt & pepper as required.
Run cold water over the fish steaks and wipe them dry with paper towels; after that, season with salt and finely powdered black pepper on both sides after brushing with olive oil.
Place the fish steaks on the grill grate in an even layer. Grill, rotating once with a thin-bladed metal spatula, for 15 - 20 minutes, or until the salmon is opaque and breaks into pieces when pressed with a fork.
If preferred, insert an instant-read meat thermometer probe into the side of the fish, aiming for a temperature of 140-145°F.
Arrange the steaks on a serving dish. Drizzle with pesto and, if preferred, serve with orange wedges as well as fresh basil. Enjoy.

5.117 Baked Halibut Sandwich with Smoked Tartar Sauce

Total Time: 40 Mins, Servings: 4
Ingredients
Mayonnaise, 1 Cup
Chopped Pickles, 1/2 Cup
Chopped Capers, 1 tbsp
Parsley Chopped, 1/2 tbsp
Dijon Mustard, 1/2 tbsp
Lemon Juice, 1/2
6 Thick-Cut Halibut Fillets
Salt & Pepper
Brioche Burger Buns, 6
Heirloom Tomato, 2
Romaine Lettuce Heart
Instructions
When ready to cook, preheat the Pit Boss grill to 180 °F (with Super Smoke activated if using a WiFIRE equipped grill) for 10 to 15 minutes with the lid closed.

In a small dish, combine all tartar sauce ingredients; spread on a shallow sheet pan and put immediately on the grill grate. Smoky for 20-30 minutes at 180 degrees F, or until tartar sauce has acquired the appropriate level of smoke flavor. Place in the refrigerator until the halibut is ready.
Preheat the grill to 450 °F with the lid covered for 10-15 minutes. Season the fillets with salt & black pepper before placing them on a baking sheet. Cook 7-10 minutes, or until temp reaches 145 ° F, on a sheet tray direct on the grill grate.
To toast the brioche buns, place them cut side down on the grill grate for almost 3 minutes.
To assemble the sandwich, apply some tartar sauce on every side of the bread, then arrange the fillet, sliced tomato, and lettuce on the bottom bun in the order chosen. Finish with a top bun and eat.

5.118 Pit Boss Smoked Salmon

Total Time: 4 Hrs 15 Mins, Servings: 6
Ingredients
Salmon Fillet, 1 (2 to 3 Lb)
Kosher Salt, 1/2 Cup
Brown Sugar, 1 Cup
Ground Black Pepper, 1 tbsp
Instructions
Take out all of the pin bones from the fish.
Combine salt, sugar, and black pepper in a small bowl. Place a wide sheet of plastic wrap at least six inches taller than the fillet on a level surface. Half of the mixture should be spread on top of the plastic, and the fillet should be placed skin-side down on top of the cure. Spread the remaining 1/2 of the cure equally over the top of the
fillet. Fold the plastic's edges up and firmly wrap it around the object.
In the bottom of a flat, rectangular baking dish or hotel pan, place the wrapped salmon fillet. On top of the fillet, place a second
similar pan. To weigh down the top pan, place a couple of cans or anything heavy within it, ensuring sure the weight is spread evenly.
Place the weighted salmon in the refrigerator for 4-6 hours to cure.
Rinse the cure well after removing the salmon from the plastic wrap. Pat dries the skin side down on a wire rack on a sheet tray. Allow the salmon to dry overnight on the sheet tray in the refrigerator. This enables a sticky coating known as a pellicle to develop on the salmon's surface. The pellicle aids in the adhesion of smoke to the fish.
When ready to cook, preheat the Pit Boss to 180°F with the lid closed for almost 15 minutes. If Super Smoke is available, use it for the best taste.
Place salmon skin side down on the grill grate and smoke it for 3 to 4 hours, or when the internal temperature reaches 140°F. Warm or cold, this dish is delicious.

5.119 Smoked Whitefish Salad

Total Time: 16 Hrs, Servings: 4
Ingredients
Salt, 1/2 Cup
Brown Sugar, 1/3 Cup
Cold Water, Quart
Vodka
Whitefish, Gutted, Skin-On, 1 Whole
Celery Diced, 1/2 Cup
Red Onion, 1/2 Cup
Lemon Juice, 1 tbsp
Fresh Dill, Roughly Chopped Including Stems, 1 1/2 tbsp
Mayonnaise, 3/4 Cup

Sour Cream, 1/4 Cup
Ground Black Pepper, 1/2 tsp
Instructions
Make the brine: In a large shallow container, such as a roasting pan, brown sugar, combine salt, water & vodka (if using).
Toss in the fish, cover, and chill for 8-12 hours. Removed fish from the brine and thoroughly rinse it under cold running water, both inside and out. Using paper towels, pat dry. Remove the brine and discard it.
When ready to cook, preheat the oven to 180°F with the lid covered for 15 minutes.
Put the fish on the grate of the grill. 2 or 3 foil balls should be tucked into the cavity to increase the interior's exposure to smoke.
Smoke the fish for 3-4 hours, and until it flakes readily when pressed with a fork and reaches 150°F inside. Allow cooling before wrapping in plastic wrap and storing in the refrigerator.
Salad: Remove the skin from the fish and flake it; discard any pin bones.
Combine the celery, lemon juice, red onion, dill, sour cream, mayonnaise and pepper in a large mixing bowl. To mix, gently stir with a rubber spatula.
To serve, pile the salad over lettuce or radicchio leaves and serve with bagels, crackers, bagel chips, or cocktail pieces of bread.

5.120 New England Clambake
Total Time: 1 Hr 15 Mins, Servings: 4
Ingredients
Red Onion, 2
Garlic Smashed, 4 Clove
Lemons, 2
Corn, 4 Ears
New Potatoes, 1/2 Pound
Chorizo, Olympia Provisions, 1 Pound
Clams Littleneck, 1 Pound
Mussels Debearded, 1 Pound
Lobster Tails, Thawed, 4
White Wine, 1 Cup
Old Bay Seasoning, 2 1/2 tbsp
Kosher Sea Salt, 1 tsp
Parsley Chopped, 1 Bunch
Chopped Tarragon, 1/2 Bunch
Butter Melted, 8 Ounce
Lemon Wedges, 6 Whole
Instructions
When ready to cook, turn on the Pit Boss, adjust the temperature to 400 ° F (205 degrees C), and preheat for 10 to 15 minutes with the lid closed.
In a large cast-iron saucepan, layer the onions, garlic, corn, lemons, potatoes, chorizo (cut diagonally into 1-inch-thick slices), mussels, clams and lobster in this order: garlic, onions, corn, potatoes, lemons, chorizo (cut diagonally into 1-inch-thick slices), clams, mussels, and lobster. Season with old bay & salt after pouring in the wine.
Place the saucepan immediately on the grill grate, covered. Cook approximately 15 minutes with the lid closed.
Reduce the heat to 300 degrees F (150 degrees C) and continue to simmer for another 10-15 minutes, or until potatoes are soft, the lobster is cooked through, and the mussels & clams have opened.
Strain the liquid into a little sauce pan using a fine mesh strainer. Season to taste with salt and set aside.
Transfer the contents of the saucepan to a big piece of butcher paper or parchment to serve. Pour the remaining cooking liquid over the clambake and top with Tarragon and parsley.
Serve with melted butter ramekins and lemon wedges. Enjoy

5.121 Grilled Oysters with Mignonette
Total Time: 30 Mins, Servings: 2
Ingredients
Rock Salt, 4 Cup
Unsalted butter, 4 tbsp
Oysters, 18 Large
Garlic Minced, 2 Clove
Lemon Wedges, 12
Kosher Salt
Mignonette
Minced Shallot, 2 tbsp
Ground Black Pepper, 1/2 tsp
Red Wine Vinegar, 1/4 Cup
Instructions
Select a shallow serving plate large enough to accommodate all of the oysters. To make a 1/2-inch foundation, pour the salt onto the plate. This will help to keep the oysters steady while being served.
Before preparing the oysters, double-check that they are fully closed. Oysters that aren't edible should be discarded. To remove any grit from the surface of the oysters, wash and gently brush them. This will keep the grit out of the oyster once it has been shucked.
Stabilize the oyster in the opposite hand, the one holding the knife with a thick glove or dish towel. Locate the hinge on each oyster using an oyster knife or a very strong paring knife. Push the tip of the blade into the oyster until it feels firm, then place the point of the knife in hinge. To gently open the oyster, spin the knife firmly to provide torquing pressure.
Remove the oyster's top shell. Remove oyster from its shell using the point of the knife, keeping the fluids intact. Place each loose oyster on a baking sheet in its half shell.
When ready to cook, preheat the Pit Boss to 450°F with the lid closed for 15 minutes.
Melt the butter in a small saucepan over
medium-low heat. Cook, constantly stirring, until the garlic is aromatic but not browned, approximately 1 minute. Turn off the heat.
To make the Mignonette, combine the Shallot, red wine vinegar, & 1/2 teaspoon ground black pepper in a mixing bowl. Remove from the equation.
Spoon 1 tsp of the garlic butter sauce over each half-shelled oyster. Place each oyster carefully on the grill grates, making sure they don't slide. Close the cover and simmer for
3-4 minutes, or until the oysters' edges have come away from the shell. To preserve the liquids and butter in the shells, gently remove with tongs. To balance them, place them directly on rock salt. Serve immediately with lemon wedges for squeezing over the oysters and Mignonette. Enjoy.

5.122 Cider Hot-Smoked Salmon
Total Time: 1 Hr 25 Mins, Servings: 4
Ingredients
Wild Salmon Fillet, Bones Removed, 1 1/2 Pound
Apple Juice, 12 Ounce
Juniper Berries, 4 Pieces
Star Anise, 1 Piece
Bay Leaf Crumbled, 1 Piece
Kosher Salt, 1/2 Cup
Brown Sugar, 1/4 Cup
Pit Boss Saskatchewan Rub, 2 tsp
Coarse Black Pepper, 1 Teaspoon
Instructions
Wash the salmon fillet with cold running water and run a finger over the flesh portion of the fillet to check for pin bones. If you feel a bone, use kitchen tweezers or needle-nose pliers to remove it.

Place the cider, star anise, crushed juniper berries & bay leaf in a resealable plastic bag. Place the bag in a dish or pan in the freezer with the salmon fillet. Allow for at least eight hours of rest time or overnight.

Take the salmon out of the bag and toss the cider mixture away. Using paper towels, thoroughly dry the fish. Make the remedy: Combine the brown sugar, kosher salt & Pit Boss rub in a small mixing bowl.

Spoon half of the mixture onto a shallow plate or baking dish. Place the salmon fillet on top of the cure, skin-side down. Sprinkle the remaining cure over the top, covered with plastic wrap & chill for 1 to 1-1/2 hours. If you leave it any longer, the fish will get excessively salty.

Drain the salmon and pat it dry with paper towels after removing it from the cure. On top of the fillet, season with black pepper.

When you're ready to cook, preheat the oven to 200 ° F for approximately 10-15 minutes.

Place the salmon on the grill grate skin-side down. Cook approximately 1 hour, or until the fish flakes readily when pushed with a finger or fork, or the internal temperature reaches 150 degrees in the thickest section of the fish.

Set aside to cool somewhat. Remove the skin from the fillet by turning it over; it should come off in a single piece.

If not serving right away, chill the salmon fully before wrapping it in plastic wrap and storing it in the refrigerator for up to 2 days. Transfer to a serving plate and top with any or all of the recommended side dishes. Enjoy.

5.123 Grilled Lobster Tails
Total Time: 35 Mins, Servings: 2
Ingredients
Lobster Tails, 2 (8-10 Oz)
Butter, 8 tbsp
Paprika, 1 tsp
Garlic Salt. 1/4 tsp
Lemon Juice, 2 tbsp
Chopped parsley, 2 tbsp
Bay Seasoning, 1/4 tsp
Ground Black Pepper, 1/4 tsp
Instructions
To prepare the lobster, use kitchen shears to cut along the center of the rough shell toward the tail.

Gently pry the flesh from the shell with your fingertips, keeping it connected at the base of the tail. Place the meat on top of the split shell and lift it.

Cut a slit along the center of the meat to allow it to butterfly open on top.

Arrange the lobster tails on a baking sheet with a rim.

In a medium saucepan over medium heat, melt the butter. Lemon juice, garlic salt, paprika, Bay Seasoning, parsley and pepper are whisked in.

Brush each lobster tail with approximately a tbsp of the butter mixture. The leftover butter mixture should be kept warm.

When ready to cook, preheat the Pit Boss to 500°F for 15 minutes with the lid closed.

Place the lobster tails immediately on the grill grate after removing them from the baking sheet. Cook until the flesh is white and opaque, about 25 to 30 minutes.

Arrange the lobster tails on a plate and top with the butter mixture you set out. Enjoy.

5.124 Red Curry Salmon with Avocado Creme
Total Time: 23 Mins, Servings: 4
Ingredients
Avocado, Peeled and Pitted, 1
Garlic, 1 Clove
Brown Sugar, 2 tbsp
Cilantro Leaves, 1/4 Cup
Lime Juice, 2 tbsp
Coconut Milk, 5 tbsp
Salt, 3/4 tsp
Thai Curry Paste Red, 1 tbsp
Salmon Fillets, 4 (5 Oz)
Extra-Virgin Olive Oil, 2 tbsp
Medium Lime, 1
Cayenne Pepper, 1 Pinch
Instructions
To make the Avocado Crema, mix the avocado, lime juice, garlic, coconut milk, Cilantro, and 1/4 tsp salt in a blender or food processor. Pulse until the mixture is completely smooth. The texture should be thick yet spreadable, comparable to cake batter. 1 tbsp or 2 of coconut milk or water to thin it down if required, and pulse to
integrate. Cover and place in the refrigerator until ready to serve.

When you're ready to cook, preheat the Pit Boss to 500°F with the lid covered for 15 minutes. Preheat the grill grate by placing a 12" cast iron pan on it.

Combine red curry paste, brown sugar, cayenne pepper & 1/2 tsp salt in a small bowl.

Rub the brown sugar mixture into the flesh of each salmon fillet equally on both sides.

Pour 1 tablespoon of oil into the Pit Boss's cast iron pan. Cook until the underside of 2 of salmon fillets is crisp and just starting to blacken approximately 4 minutes.

Cook for another 4 minutes on the other side, or until the fish is firm to the touch. Remove the cast iron pan from the oven.

Swirl in the leftover tbsp of oil to coat the pan. Repeat the cooking procedure with the remaining 2 salmon fillets.

Marinate lime wedges by tossing them into the clean pan after the salmon has completed cooking or putting them in during the final minute of cooking.

Cook for thirty seconds on one side of the limes. Cook for another 30 seconds on the other side.

To serve, split the salmon fillets among separate dishes and top each with 2 tablespoons avocado crema.

Garnish with fresh Cilantro and a squeeze of lime. Enjoy!

5.125 Teriyaki-Glazed Cod with Ginger-Scallion Ramen
Total Time: 1 Hr, Servings: 4
Ingredients
Dressing
Rice Wine Vinegar, 2 tbsp
Fresh Lime Juice, 2 tsp
Vegetable Oil, 4 tbsp
Soy Sauce, 1 tbsp
Freshly Grated Ginger, 2 tsp
Honey, 1 tsp
Sesame Oil, 1 tbsp
main
Dried Ramen Noodles, 2 (3 Oz)
Red Bell Pepper, 3 tbsp
Non-stick Cooking Spray
Toasted Black & White Sesame Seeds, 1 1/2 tbsp
Thinly Sliced Scallions, 3
Skinless Cod Fillets, 1 1/2 Pound
Teriyaki Glaze

Soy Sauce, 1/2 Cup
Brown Sugar, 1/4 Cup
Mirin, 1/2 Cup
Japanese Sake, 1/4 Cup
Instructions
To make the dressing, mix the rice wine vinegar, lime juice, soy sauce, ginger, and honey in a container with a tight-fitting cover.
Shake vigorously until the sugar is completely dissolved. Shake in the vegetable & sesame oils until they are emulsified.
Meanwhile, prepare the ramen according to package instructions in boiling water. Save the seasoning packets for another use or discard them.
Drain the noodles and rinse them under cold running water before draining them again. In a medium mixing bowl, combine all of the ingredients.
If the dressing has split, shake it again. Toss the noodles in half of the dressing to coat them.
Toss in the scallions & red bell pepper, adding additional dressing if necessary.
Sprinkle sesame seeds on top. Cover and chill until ready to serve. The salad may be presented at room temp as well.
When ready to cook, preheat the Pit Boss to 350°F for 15 minutes with the lid closed.
Prepare the teriyaki glaze while the grill warms up. In a medium saucepan over medium heat, bring the soy sauce, brown sugar, mirin, and sake to a boil. Reduce the heat to low and cook the sauce for approximately 15 minutes, or until it coats the back of a spoon. Remove from the equation.
Spray a rimmed baking sheet with non-stick cooking spray and line it with aluminium foil. Arrange the fish on foil-lined baking sheet and use a basting brush to brush the teriyaki glaze over the fillets.
Place the baking sheet on the grill grate immediately.
After 10 minutes of cooking, coat the fish with the glaze once more. Glaze the fish once more until it's opaque & cooked through, approximately 5 minutes longer, then take it from the grill.
Arrange the fish fillets on plates with ginger-scallion ramen on the side. Enjoy.

5.126 Smoked Salmon Potato Bake
Total Time: 4 Hrs 40 Mins, Servings: 4
Ingredients
Salmon Fillets, 1 Pound
Gold Potatoes & Thinly Sliced, 1 Pound
Olive oil, 2 tbsp
Pit Boss Chicken Rub, 2 tbsp
Ground Black Pepper, 1/2 tsp
Cubed White Bread, 2 Cup
Scallions & Thinly Sliced, 2
Eggs, 6
Milk, 1 1/2 Cup
Butter, Softened
Dry Mustard, 1 tsp
Salt, 1/2 tsp
Sour Cream
Lemon Wedges
Red Onions
Capers
Instructions
Season the salmon fillets using Pit Boss Chicken Rub and set them aside for 3 hours in the fridge, uncovered.
When ready to cook, preheat the Pit Boss to 180°F for 15 minutes with the lid closed. If Super Smoke is available, use it for the best taste.
Place the salmon on the grill grate (skin-side down if it has skin). Smoke the fish for 2 hours, or until it readily flakes with a fork.
(The precise time will vary depending on the fillet thickness.) The fish does not need to be turned. Move salmon to a wire rack to cool using a big, thin spatula. If not used right away, cover the fish in plastic wrap and put it in the refrigerator. (This dish may be prepared 2-3 days ahead of time.) Remove any skin or discolored areas before breaking into flakes.
Raise the temperature of the Pit Boss to 400°F.
Brush a rimmed baking sheet with olive oil and place the potato slices in a single layer on the pan. Roast for 15-20 minutes, or until the potatoes are soft and gently browned. Allow potatoes to cool before transferring them to a large mixing dish. Combine the salmon, onions and bread cubes in a mixing bowl. Using a rubber spatula, carefully stir the mixture. Butter a 9x13 inch baking pan, ideally non-stick, generously. Fill the baking pan halfway with the bread & potato mixture. Whisk together the eggs, dill, milk, Mustard,
black pepper and salt in a separate large mixing basin. Pour over the bread and potato mixture equally. Allow to rest for 30 min before baking, or refrigerate for up to 1 day. (Before baking, cover and bring to room temperature.)
When fully prepared to bake the casserole, preheat the Pit Boss to 350°F for 15 minutes with the lid closed.
Bake the casserole for 45 minutes to an hour, or until the egg mix is set and the top is gently browned. (If you stick a knife in the middle, it should come out clean.) Allow 15 minutes for cooling before serving. Using a sharp knife, cut the dough into squares. Sour
cream, lemon wedges, chopped red onions and capers should be served separately in separate dishes. Enjoy.

5.127 Potato Crusted Salmon with Lemon Butter Sauce
Total Time: 29 Mins, Servings: 2
Ingredients
Potatoes, 4 Cup
Flour, 2 tbsp
Chives Chopped, 2 tbsp
Salt & Pepper
Vegetable Oil, 1/2 Cup
Salmon Fillet, 32 Ounce (8 Oz)
Dijon Mustard, 1/4 Cup
Lemon Juice, 1
Cream Whipping, 2 tbsp
White wine, 3 tbsp
Garlic Chopped, 1/4 tsp
Butter, 2 tbsp
Salt
Pepper
Instructions
Mash the potatoes with chives & flour in a medium bowl and season with salt and pepper. Season the salmon fillets with Pit Boss Salmon Shake on a work surface.
Brush each fillet with a thin coating of Mustard. Press the chopped potatoes onto the tops of each fillet in an even layer.
Place a 10-12-inch cast iron pan on grill grate and warm to 450°F, high, for 10 to 15 minutes with the lid covered.
Once the grill is hot, pour the oil into the pan and cook it for approximately 5 minutes. Place the salmon fillets in the oil, potato side down, with care.
Cook, occasionally stirring, until golden brown, approximately 8 minutes. Cook for 1 minute more after flipping the fish. Move the salmon to plates using a slotted spatula. Remove any excess oil using blotting paper.
In a small saucepan, lemon juice, combine white wine, garlic, cream, salt, and pepper to make the lemon butter sauce. Reduce to half its original volume by heating over high heat. Remove from the heat and add the butter in a swirling motion.

Serve the salmon warm with the lemon butter sauce and grilled asparagus, if desired. Enjoy.

5.128 Smoked Steelhead Breakfast Sandwich
Total Time: 2 Days 15 Mins, Servings: 2
Ingredients
Kosher Salt, 1 1/2 Cup
Sugar, 1 Cup
Steelhead Fillet, 2 Pound
Red Onion, 1
Tomatoes Sliced, 2
Chopped Dill
Cream Cheese
Capers drained, 1 Jar
Bagels, 6
Lemon Thinly Sliced, 1 Whole
Instructions
In a mixing dish, combine the salt & sugar. 1/3 of the cure should be spread over the base of a glass baking dish that is just bigenough to accommodate the fish.
Place the fillet of steelhead on top of the cure. Apply the leftover cure on the top of the fish, fully covering it. Refrigerate the fish for 24 to 48 hours after covering the dish with plastic wrap.
Rinse the fish under cold water to remove the cure. Using paper towels, pat the fish dry on all sides.
Place it on a wire rack over a sheet pan, skin side down. Allow the fish to dry in the refrigerator, uncovered, for 4 hours or until it feels sticky.
When you're ready to cook, fire up the Pit Boss according to the manufacturer's directions. Preheat the oven to 165 degrees Fahrenheit with the lid covered for 10-15 minutes.
Place the fish in the Pit Boss. Place a pan of ice on the grill if you're smoking fish on a hot day.
Smoke the Steelhead for about 12 hours, or until the skin is bronzed with smoked and the fish feel semi-firm & leathery.
Remove from the grill and chill for at least 4 hours before serving.
When ready to serve, cut the fish into paper-thin slices on a diagonal using a long, slender, and extremely sharp knife.
Spread cream cheese on bagels and top with a tomato slice, capers, red onion, fresh dill & lemon. Enjoy.

5.129 Smoked Creole Jambalaya
Total Time: 1 Hr 15 Mins, Servings: 4
Ingredients
Shrimp, Chopped Peeled and Deveined, 20
Chopped Tomato, 2 Cup
Andouille Sausage, 5 Ounce
Chicken Thighs, Diced, Boneless, 4 Ounce
Green or Bell Pepper Red, 1/4 Cup
Creole Seasoning, 1 tbsp
Onion Chopped, 1/4 Cup
Bay Leaves, 3
Celery Finely Chopped, 1/4 Cup
Garlic, 3 Clove
Worcestershire Sauce, 1 tsp
Hot Sauce, 1 tsp
Chicken Stock, 3 Cup
Rice Short Grain, 3/4 Cup
Salt & Pepper
Instructions
Set the Pit Boss to Smoke mode.
On a large baking sheet, spread out the chopped shrimp and diced chicken. Place the chopped tomatoes on a second baking sheet.
Place both baking sheets on the Pit Boss, along with andouille sausage, and smoke for 30 minutes.
Turn the heat to high and remove the meats and tomatoes from the Pit Boss. Place a dutch oven or a big pan on grill grate and cover the lid for 10 to 15 minutes to warm.
Slice Andouille sausage and mix it with the chicken & shrimp with the Creole spice once the meat has smoked.
Pour a few teaspoons of olive oil into Pit Boss pan, then add the chopped onion, pepper, and celery and cook for approximately 5 minutes.
Combine the garlic, bay leaves, smoked tomatoes, Worcestershire & spicy sauces in a mixing bowl. Stir in the rice, then gradually pour in the broth.
Cook, stirring periodically, until rice absorbs the liquid and becomes soft, approximately 15 minutes.
Add the shrimp, chicken, and sausage when the rice is barely soft. Cook for another 10 to 20 minutes, or until the meat is done.
Season with salt, pepper, and Creole spice to taste. Serve and have fun!

5.130 Smoked Salt Cured Lox
Total Time: 21 Hr 30 Mins, Servings: 8
Ingredients
Kosher Salt, 1 Cup
Sugar, 1 Cup
Cracked Black Pepper, 1 tbsp
Lemon Zest, 1 Whole
Orange Zest, 1 Whole
Packaged Dill, Chopped with Stems, 1 Whole
Salmon Fillet, 2 Pound
Instructions
Combine salt, black pepper, sugar, lemon zest, orange zest & dill in a mixing bowl.
Cut the fish in half lengthwise. Coat the whole meat of the fish with the salt-sugar mixture. Sandwich the two slices flesh to flesh and cover thoroughly with the salt sugar mixture.
Place firmly wrapped plastic wrap in gallon zip-top bag. Squeeze as much air out as you can. Place the wrapped salmon in a baking dish with something heavy on top, such as a pot of water or a foil-wrapped stone. Refrigerate for a minimum of 10 hours. After 10 hours, turn the weight over and place it back on top. Refrigerate for a further ten hours.
Remove from refrigerator, unwrap, and rinse with cold water to remove any leftover salt. Allow 1 hour on the counter after patting dry.
When ready to cook, preheat the grill to 180°F with the lid covered for 15 minutes.
Transfer the fish to a baking pan. Fill a second baking pan halfway with ice and put the baking pan with the salmon on top of it.
Place on the grill for 30 minutes to smoke. Remove from the grill and thinly slice.
Arrange bagels, capers, cream cheese, dill, sliced tomatoes, lemon wedges, and red onion on a platter. Enjoy.

5.131 Tandoori Shrimp
Total Time: 35 Mins, Servings: 6
Ingredients
Jumbo Shrimp, 2 Pound
Cajun Rub, 1 1/2 tsp
Plain Yogurt, 1 Cup
Squeezed Lime Juice, 1/2 Cup
Heavy Cream, 1/4 Cup
Onion diced, 1/2
Ginger, 1 Inch
Chili Powder, 2 tsp
Garlic chopped, 3 Clove

Ground Coriander, 1 tsp
Ground Cumin, 1 1/2 tsp
Turmeric, 1/2 tsp
Instructions
In a big resealable plastic bag, place the shrimp.
Stir the lime juice and the Pit Boss Cajun Rub in a mixing bowl. Freeze for 15 min after pouring the sauce over the shrimp.
Meanwhile, in a blender jar, blend the yogurt, onion, cream, garlic, chili powder, ginger, cumin, turmeric and coriander until the mixture is pretty smooth.
If desired, mix in a few drops of red and orange food coloring to mimic the vibrant hue of genuine tandoori. Remove the shrimp from the lime juice mixture. Marinade for 1-2 hours in the bag with the yogurt marinade. Thread the shrimp on thin metal after removing them from the marinade.
When ready to cook, preheat the oven to 450 degrees Fahrenheit with the lid covered for 10-15 minutes.
Place the shrimp skewers direct on the grill grate and cook for 3 to 4 minutes on each side, rotating once with tongs or until firm and pink.
Brush them with melted butter on both sides as they cook.
Slide the shrimp off skewers onto a tray or serving plates using the tines of a fork. Sliced red onions, lime wedges & cilantro sprigs serve as garnish.

5.132 Smoked Trout Hash
Total Time: 2 Hrs 30 Mins, Servings: 4
Ingredients
Water, 1 Quart
Salt, 1 Cup
Brown Sugar, 1/2 Cup
Ice Water, 1 Quart
Lemon Zest, 1
Bay Leaves, 4
Eggs, 4
Trout, 2 Pound
Black Peppercorn, 1 tbsp
Red Beets, 1/2 Cup
Extra-Virgin Olive Oil, 1 tbsp
New Potatoes, 1/2 Cup
Green Onions, 2
Instructions
Combine water, brown sugar, salt, lemon zest, pepper corns and bay leaves in a medium saucepan. Bring to a boil over medium-high heat, constantly stirring, until the salt and sugar are completely dissolved. Remove from heat and let aside for 15 minutes to steep. To cool, pour the mixture over cold water.
When the mixture is cold to the touch, pour it over the fish, cover, and chill for 2 hours.
Remove the fish from the brine and discard it. Clean the fillets by rinsing them and patting them dry. To make the pellicle, spread them out on a cooling rack and chill overnight. This makes it easier for the smoke to stick on the fillets.
Preheat the Pit Boss grill to 165 degrees Fahrenheit when ready to cook. Allow 10-15 minutes for the oven to preheat.
Directly place the fillets on the grill grate & smoke for almost 2 hours, or until the salmon starts to flake.
Preheat the oven to 375 degrees Fahrenheit for 10-15 minutes with the lid closed.
In a cast-iron skillet, heat the oil over medium-high heat. Cook for 10 minutes or until beets is nearly soft. Stir in the fresh potatoes and continue to simmer until both the beets and the potatoes are golden brown.
Cook until flakes, smoked fish and green onions are warmed through, approximately 4 minutes.
In the hash, make four wells and break an egg into each well. Transfer the pan to the Pit Boss and cook for 5-6 minutes, or until the whites are set but the yolks are still runny. Enjoy.

5.133 Cold-Smoked Salmon Gravlax
Total Time: 1 Hr 19 Mins, Servings: 6
Ingredients
Kosher Salt, 1 Cup
Sugar, 1 Cup
Red Onion, Sliced
Ground Black Pepper, 1 tbsp
Sushi-Grad Salmon Fillet, 2 Pound
Fresh Dill, 2 Bunch
Cream Cheese
Capers, Drained
Lemons
Instructions
Combine the salt, sugar, and black pepper in a mixing dish and whisk well. Turn the salmon skin side up on a work surface and massage with approximately half the salt mixture.
Line the bottom of baking dish big enough to accommodate the salmon with half of the dill. Place the salmon fresh skin side down on a dill bed.
Rub the remaining salt mixture all over the salmon's top and sides, then sprinkle with the remaining dill. Cover with plastic wrap, then put in the refrigerator for 2 days to cure with a weight on a small baking dish with cans of beans on top.
Take the salmon out of the fridge and rinse it under cold water before patting it dry with paper towels. Allow 1 hour to sit at room
temp on the counter.
Prepare oven to 180ºF and preheat for 15 min when ready to cook. If Super Smoke is available, use it for the best taste. Place the fish on a baking sheet. Fill a second baking pan halfway with ice and put the baking pan with the salmon on top of it. Place on the grill for 30 minutes to smoke.
Remove from the grill and thinly slice. Capers, dill, red onion, cream cheese & lemon are served on the side. Enjoy.

5.134 Smoked Shrimp and Grilled Dungeness Crab Cocktail
Total Time: 1 Hr 50 Mins, Servings: 2
Ingredients
Dungeness Crab, 2
Olive Oil, 1 Cup
Garlic, 6 Clove
Lime Juice, 6 tbsp
Cilantro, 1/2 Cup
Raw Shrimp, 1/2 Pound
Clamato, 2 Cup
Ketchup, 1 Cup
Hot Sauce, 2 tsp
Salt, 2 tsp
Onion, 1 Cup
Instructions
Remove the triangle tab from the crab's belly. Remove the shell. Crab innards and gills should be cleaned, washed, and drained. Allow to air dry.
In a small dish, combine the olive oil, garlic, 3 tbsp of lime juice, & 1/4 cup of Cilantro. Marinade for 60 minutes, dividing the marinade between the shrimp and crab.
When ready to cook, preheat the oven to 180ºF with the lid covered for 15 minutes.
Place the shrimp straight on the grill grate and smoke for 30-40 minutes, or until bronzed and firm with smoke.
Remove from the grill and set aside to cool. Raise the grill's temperature too high and preheat it.
Place the crab on the grill grate immediately. Cook crab legs for 4 minutes on each side, or until the flesh is barely opaque. Baste the crab with the remaining marinade regularly.

In a separate dish, mix the clamato, ketchup, lime juice, salt, onion, spicy sauce, and Cilantro while the crab cooks.
Cut 2/3 of the shrimp should be cut into tiny pieces. Remove all of the crab's flesh. Stir the shrimp & crab into the cocktail sauce to mix.
Serve in tiny cups with the remaining grilled shrimp on top. Enjoy!

5.135 Jalapeño Candied Smoked Salmon

Total Time: 5 Hrs, Servings: 4
Ingredients
Hot Water, 1/2 Cup
Jalapeno Chopped, 2 Whole
Red Pepper Flakes, 1
Soy Sauce, 1/4 Cup
Sugar, 1/4 Cup
Garlic Powder, 2 tbsp
Ground Black Pepper, 2 tbsp
Cold Water, 8 Cup
Salmon Fillet, 1 Whole
Brown Sugar, 1 Cup
Jalapeno, 2 Whole
Dijon Mustard, 3 tbsp
Instructions
Make the brine by combining hot water, red pepper flakes and jalapenos in a small pot. To get the appropriate level of heat, add jalapenos and red pepper flakes.
Bring a pot of water to a boil, then soak the jalapenos in it for 5 minutes. Stir in the other brine ingredients, except the cold water, until the sugar has dissolved.
Fill the container halfway with cold water. Pour the brine into a large unsellable bag and add the salmon after it is no longer heated.
Depending on the thickness of the fillet, chill the salmon in brine for 3-4 hours.
Remove the salmon from the brine, clean it, and pat it dry when ready to smoke.
Glaze: In a blender, combine brown sugar, jalapenos, and Dijon mustard and pulse until the jalapenos are completely mixed. Toss the fish with the glaze.
When ready to cook, preheat the Pit Boss to 180°F for 15 minutes with the lid closed.
Smoke the salmon for almost 30 mins with the skin side down. Raise the temp to 225 degrees Fahrenheit. Cook the fish for 45 to 1 hour.
Remove the steaks from the grill and serve. Enjoy.

5.136 Smoked Lobster Rolls

Total Time: 1 Hr 10 Mins, Servings: 2
Ingredients
Lobster Tails, 4
Old Bay Seasoning, 1/4
Lemon Juice, 3 1/2 tsp
Butter Melted, 2 tbsp
Stalk Celery, 1
Fresh parsley, 1 tbsp
Mayonnaise, 1/4 Cup
Green Onion, 1
Salt And Pepper
4 Roll
Instructions
Cut a slit through the middle of each lobster tail's hard shell to the tail fan using kitchen shears. Gently remove the flesh from the shell with a scoop around
the shell.
Melt the butter in a small bowl and combine Old Bay Seasoning and 1/2 teaspoon lemon juice.

Preheat the Pit Boss to 185 degrees Fahrenheit when ready to cook. Preheat for 10-15 minutes with the lid closed.
Put the lobster tails straight on the barbecue grate and brush some seasoned butter into each lobster's broken shell. Smoked the lobster tails for approximately 1 1/2 hours, or until an instant-read thermometer reads 135 to 140 degrees Fahrenheit and the flesh becomes opaque.
Meanwhile, prepare the lobster mayo sauce by combining mayonnaise, 1 tbsp lemon juice, chopped parsley, diced celery, green onion, pepper and salt in a mixing bowl.
Allow lobsters to rest for 5 mins after taking them from the grill before removing the flesh from the shells and chopping them into pieces.
Gently incorporate the lobster flesh into the mayonnaise mixture.
If preferred, butter and toast the buns on the Pit Boss before stuffing them with lobster mayo mixture. Enjoy.

5.137 Grilled Lobster with Lemon Garlic Butter

Total Time: 35 Mins, Servings: 4
Ingredients
(1-1/2 Lb) Live Lobsters, 4 Whole
Lemons Sliced, 2 Whole
Flat-Leaf Parsley
Lemon Garlic Butter
Butter, 3/4 Cup
Flat-Leaf Parsley, 2 tbsp
Minced Shallot, 1 tbsp
Garlic Minced, 2 Clove
Lemon Zest, 1 tbsp
Lemon Juice, 1 tbsp
Sea Salt, 1/2 tsp
Cracked Black Pepper, 1/2 tsp
Instructions
Fill a large stockpot halfway with water and bring it to a quick boil. Dispatcher the lobster in batches if required. To dispatch the lobster, first put the point of a sharp cook knife in the rear of the lobster, right below its head, and swiftly slice through the head.
Place the lobster head first in the boiling water, then cover with a lid. Cook for 2 mins, or until deep red, then chill in an ice bath for 5 minutes to halt the cooking process.
Split the lobster in half with a very sharp knife. Remove the tomalley from the body and throw it away.
Combine the softened butter, minced Shallot, parsley, lemon zest, minced garlic, and lemon juice in a medium mixing bowl. Season with freshly cracked pepper and a pinch of sea salt. Whisk everything together until it's completely smooth. Remove from the equation.
Preheat the grill to 425° F (215° C) with the lid covered for 15 minutes when ready to cook.
When the grill is hot, put the lobster's flesh side down on the grill and cook for 4 mins. Turn the lobster halves over and pour approximately 2 tsp compound butter over each side. Brush the meat with a brush as the butter starts to melt. Cook for 4-5 minutes, or until cooked through & melted butter has been applied.
Garnish with sliced lemons and serve right away. Enjoy.

5.138 Smoked Chilean Sea Bass by Doug Sheading

Total Time: 45 Mins, Servings: 4
Ingredients
Marinade
Canola or Grapeseed Oil, 1/4 Cup
Large Lemon, 1
Garlic Crushed, 8 Clove

Fresh oregano, 1 tbsp
Thyme, for garnish, 1 tbsp
Saskatchewan Rub, 1 tsp
main
Fillets Fresh Chilean, 4 (6 Oz)
Kerry gold Irish Butter, 8 tbsp
Pit Boss Chicken Rub
Lemon, 4 Slices
Instructions
To make the marinade, combine all of the ingredients in a big resealable bag and thoroughly mix them.
Toss the sea bass with the marinade and refrigerate for 30 mins, turning at minimum once.
When ready to cook, preheat the Pit Boss to 325°F with the lid closed for 15 min.
Set the butter in a baking dish big enough to hold the fillets flat and place it on the grill to melt fully.
Place the fish on a clean, flat plane after removing it from the marinade. Pour the marinade and butter into the pan. Pit Boss Chicken Rub should be generously applied to the fillets.
Return the fillets to the grill after placing them in the pan with butter mixture. Cook for approximately 30 minutes, basting the fillets with the hot butter mixture once or twice.
When the core temperature of the fish reaches 160°F, remove it from the Pit Boss. Fresh thyme & lemon slices may be used as a garnish. Enjoy.

5.139 Coconut Shrimp Jalapeño Poppers
Total Time: 1 Hr 5 Mins, Servings: 6
Ingredients
Shrimp, Peeled & Deveined, 8 Whole
Pit Boss Chicken Rub, 1/2 tsp
Olive Oil
Jalapeños, 6 Whole
Cream Cheese, 8 Ounce
Chopped Cilantro, 2 tbsp
Unsweetened Coconut Flakes, 1/2 Cup
Slices Bacon, 12
Instructions
Preheat the Pit Boss to 425°F for 15 mins with lid closed when ready to cook.
Rinse the shrimp and season with Pit Boss Chicken Rub.
Sprinkle shrimp with olive oil & cook for approximately 5 minutes on each side on the Pit Boss, or until they are opaque. Withdraw the shrimp and set them aside to cool.
Lower the temperature of the Pit Boss to 350°F.
In the meanwhile, start popping those poppers. Discard the stems & seeds from the jalapenos after cutting them in half.
Cut the shrimp into small pieces. Softened cream cheese, diced shrimp, 1/2 tsp Pit Boss Chicken Rub, and tbsp chopped cilantro are combined in a mixing bowl.
Fill each pepper half with a good quantity of the filling. Add a sprinkling of coconut on top.
Wrap a piece of bacon around each filled pepper and put it on a foil-lined baking pan.
Cook the peppers for approximately 45 minutes on the Pit Boss, or even bacon fat has drained, and the cream cheese has become golden. Enjoy.

5.140 Chicken, Andouille & Roasted Potato Gumbo
Total Time: 3 Hrs 45 Mins, Servings: 6
Ingredients
Andouille Sausage, and cut into slice 2 Inch, 1 Pound
Red Potatoes, 1 Pound
Butter, 1/2 Cup
Onion, 1
Red Bell Pepper, 1
Container Chicken Broth, 1 (48 Oz)
Garlic Minced, 2 Clove
Cajun Seasoning, 2 tsp
Ground Red Pepper, 1/8 tsp
Sliced Celery, 1 Cup
All-Purpose Flour, 1 Cup
Small Potatoes, 1 Pound
Olive Oil
Boneless Chicken Breasts, 2 Pound
Salt & Pepper
Instructions
Preheat the Pit Boss to 425°F for 15 minutes with the lid closed when ready to cook. Allow a cast-iron Dutch oven to warm on the grill for 20 minutes.
In a Dutch oven, brown sausage for 10 mins, stirring every 2 minutes. Remove the sausage from the pan, drain it, and wipe it dry with paper towels.
Reduce the temperature of the grill to 375°F. Return the cast iron pot to the grill and let it warm once more.
Add onion, celery, bell pepper, Cajun spice, garlic and ground red pepper to melted butter in a cast iron saucepan. Cook for 10 minutes, stirring periodically. Cook for another 10 mins with the lid covered after adding the flour.
Whisk in the chicken broth in a slow, steady stream. Combine the chicken and brown sausage in a large mixing bowl. Cook for 1 hour in a covered Dutch oven.
Halve the potatoes and place them on a baking pan. Toss with a drizzle of olive oil and a pinch of salt and
pepper to coat. Remove from the equation.
After 1 hour, remove the lid from the grill and stir the gumbo. Place the potatoes next to the gumbo on the grill. Cook for another hour on both.
Remove the gumbo and potatoes from the grill. Remove chicken from the gumbo & shred it using two forks into big pieces, then return it to the gumbo.
To serve, pour gumbo over baked potatoes in serving dishes. Enjoy.

5.141 Tuna Steak with Baby Bok Choy and Carrots
Total Time: 35 Mins, Servings: 2
Ingredients
Carrots, 6 Whole
Olive Oil
Salt & Pepper
Tuna Steak, 2 Whole
Bell Peppers, 2 Whole
Lime Juice, 1 tbsp
Cilantro Chopped, 1/2 Cup
Grated Ginger, 1 tsp
Honey, 3 tbsp
Soy Sauce, 2 tbsp
Jalapeño, Thinly Sliced
Sesame Seeds
Garlic Minced, 1 Clove
Wasabi Paste 1/4 tsp
Balsamic vinegar, 2 tbsp
Instructions
Peel & trim carrots; quarter them. Seal all but an inch of the top of a resealable bag with carrots to allow steam to escape. Cook the carrots for 2 minutes in the microwave. This will enable you to cook on the grill more quickly.
When you're ready to cook, turn on the Pit Boss's Smoke setting. Smoke the tuna steaks for 10 minutes on the grill. Remove the grill from the heat.
Preheat the oven to 450 degrees Fahrenheit for 10-15 minutes. Season tuna steaks with salt and black pepper after drizzling

with olive oil. After that, the carrots are cooled, spread out all of the veggies on
the pan and sprinkle with olive oil, season with salt and pepper to taste.
Arrange the tuna on the grill grate in the center. Cook the tuna for 3 minutes on each side. When you turn the tuna over, toss in the veggies.
In a mixing dish, whisk together the sauce ingredients while the tuna is cooking.
To create the carrot glaze, combine honey and balsamic vinegar. Toss the heated carrots in the glaze or brush on the glaze during the final minute of cooking.
Slice tuna steak into pieces, exposing the lovely pink center, and serve with the sauce and veggies on the side. Finish with a sprinkling of sesame seeds that have been toasted. Enjoy.

5.142 Alder Smoked Scallops with Citrus & Garlic Butter Sauce

Total Time: 50 Mins, Servings: 4
Ingredients
Large Sea Scallops, 2 Pound
Kosher Salt
Ground Black Pepper
Salted Butter, 8 tbsp
Garlic Minced, 1 Clove
Small Orange, 1
Worcestershire Sauce, 1/4 tsp
Fresh Chopped Parsley, 1 1/2 Teaspoon
Flat-Leaf Parsley
Instructions
Rinse the scallops well under cold water and pat dry with paper towels. Remove any
abductor muscle tissue tags you discover on the scallops' sides.
Season the scallops with salt and black pepper and place them on a baking pan with a cooling rack.
When ready to cook, preheat the Pit Boss to 165°F with the lid closed for 15 mins. If Super Smoke is available, use it for the best taste.
Place scallops on the baking sheet on the grill grate & smoke for 20 mins.
Make your sauce while your scallops are smoking. In a medium saucepan over medium heat, melt the butter. Add a sprinkle of salt, Worcestershire sauce, garlic, half of an orange's zest and juice, and parsley. Cook for 5 minutes on low heat. Keep yourself warm.
Remove the scalloped baking sheet from the grill & put it aside. Preheat the oven to 400 degrees Fahrenheit with the lid closed. Optional: Preheat the
grill with an oyster pan. Searing the scallops in these hefty iron pots is a wonderful idea.
Return the scallops to the grill on the baking sheet with butter sauce, saving some for Serving. Roast for 10 to 15 minutes, or until slightly opaque and soft. The length of time will be determined by the thickness of the scallops. Don't overcook the food. Brush each compartment gently with olive oil if using an oyster pan to avoid sticking. Place a dollop of butter sauce over each scallop, saving some for dishing.
Toss the scallops with a bit more orange zest, fresh parsley, and warm citrus & garlic butter sauce just before serving. Enjoy.

5.143 Smoked Salmon Veggie Dip

Total Time: 3 Hrs 45 Mins, Servings: 4
Ingredients
Brine
Water, 1 1/2 Quart
Salt, 1 1/2 Cup
Brown Sugar, 1 Cup
Juniper Berries, 1 tbsp
Leaves Crushed, 4 Bay
Black Pepper, 1 tbsp
main
Salmon Side, 1 (3-4 Lb)
Cream Cheese, 1/2 Cup
Chopped Chives, 1/2 tbsp
Sour Cream, 1/2 Cup
Chopped parsley, 1/2 tbsp
Lemon Juice, 1 tbsp
Chopped dill, 1/2 tbsp
Crackers or Vegetables
Salt & Pepper
Instructions
Combine 1-1/2 quarts water, brown sugar, salt, bay leaves, juniper berries and pepper in a medium pot. Bring to the boil over medium-high heat, constantly stirring, until the salt and sugar are completely dissolved. Remove from the heat and set aside for 15 minutes to steep.
To chill, pour the mixture over 1-1/2 cups of cold water. Pour the mixture over the salmon after it has cooled to the touch, cover, and chill for 2 hours.
Remove the fish from the brine and throw away the
brine. Fillets should be rinsed and dried. To make the pellicle, spread them out on a cooling rack and chill overnight. This makes it easier for the smoke to stick on the fillets.
When ready to cook, preheat the Pit Boss to 165°F with the lid closed for 15 min. If Super Smoke is available, use it for the best taste.
Smoke the fillets straight on the grill grate for 2-3 hours or until the fish starts to flake.
In a separate bowl, mix cream cheese, herbs, sour cream, lemon juice, salt & pepper while the salmon is smoking.
Stir in 1 pound of flakes and smoked salmon until the salmon is broken up into tiny pieces.
Serve with a cracker or your favorite dipping veggies. Enjoy.

5.144 Roasted Halibut in Parchment

Total Time: 30 Mins, Servings: 4
Ingredients
Halibut Fillets, 4 (4 Oz)
Kosher Salt & Black Pepper
Extra-Virgin Olive Oil
Lemons, Preferably Meyer, 2 Large
Ears Corn, 2 Large
Large Asparagus Spears, 16
Cherry Tomatoes, 8 Ounce
Chopped Assorted Herbs, 2 Tablespoon
Instructions
Preheat the Pit Boss to 425°F for 15 minutes with the lid closed when ready to cook.
Cut four 18-inch-long pieces of paper towels or Pit Boss butcher paper. On a piece of paper, place a fish fillet in the middle. Drizzle with olive oil after seasoning with a sprinkle of salt and pepper. Arrange 3 lemon slices on top of the fillet, gently overlapping them to cover the fish. Drizzle a little olive oil over the fish and season with a tiny sprinkle of salt and pepper.
Fold the top edges of the paper down to form a 1-inch seal, then continuing to fold down firmly over the fish and veggies. To keep steam from escaping, twist the open ends of the paper in opposing ways. Set the packets on a baking sheet after repeating the procedure with the rest of the ingredients and paper.
Freeze for 4 hours if not cooking right away.
Place the baking tray on Pit Boss & bake for 15 minutes, or until the packets are gently browned and puff up.

Place each packet on a tray and set it aside to cool for 5 minutes. Cut an X in the middle of each package using sharp scissors, then gently peel back the paper and sprinkle with herbs.
Serve right away. Enjoy.

5.145 Roasted Halibut with Spring Vegetables
Total Time: 35 Mins, Servings: 4
Ingredients
Halibut Fillets, 4
Oyster, King Trumpet 1/2 Pound
Butcher Paper
Carrots, 1 Pound
Feather Rub & Pit Boss Fin, 2 tbsp
Asparagus Ends, 1 Pound
Salt & Pepper
Butter, 2 tbsp
White Wine, 1/2 Cup
Instructions
Use Pit Boss Fin & Feather Rub to season the halibut fillets.
To make the packets, start with four 20-inch-long pieces of parchment paper. Fold it in half and then open it up again.
Divide the asparagus, carrots & mushrooms among the four paper sheets and dot a little butter on top of each. Salt & pepper to taste. Place a halibut on the top of each packet's veggies.
Wrap over so that the two ends touch and the food are enclosed. Make tiny, overlapping diagonal folds over the filling, starting at each end of the middle crease and closing the package firmly. Pour a little amount of wine into each package before completing the last fold, then seal fully.
When ready to cook, increase the temperature to high & preheat for 15 minutes with the lid closed.
Arrange all 4 packets on a sheet tray & grill them. Cook for 7-10 minutes, or until the fish reaches a temperature of 145°F. Remove the packet from the grill and then put it on a serving platter.
Cut open each package with a knife or scissors and fold the edges back. If preferred, finish with a squeeze of lemon juice. Enjoy.

5.146 Grilled Halibut Fillets with Lemon and Butter Sauce
Total Time: 30 Mins, Servings: 2
Ingredients
Lemon and Butter Sauce
White Wine, 1/2 Cup
Fresh Thyme, 2 Sprig
Shallot Thinly Diced, 1
Lemon Juiced, 1/2
Ground White Pepper, 1/2 tsp
Heavy cream, 1 tbsp
Stick Butter, 1
Kosher Salt, 1 tsp
main
Halibut Fillets, 4
Feather Rub & Pit Boss Fin
Unsalted butter, 2 tbsp
Instructions
Preheat the Pit Boss to 425°F for 15 minutes with the lid closed when ready to cook. Preheat the grill by placing a cast iron pan on the grate.
In a small saucepan over medium to high heat, combine the wine, shallots, thyme, and lemon juice. Reduce the liquid by half by bringing it to a simmer.
Reduce the heat to low and stir in the heavy cream. Add the butter in small increments, constantly beating with a wire whisk after every addition (this must be taking about 3-4 minutes to add all the butter). Consistently beat the sauce; it should never boil.
Season with salt & pepper to taste, then strain via a fine mesh strainer to remove any particles. Return the strained sauce to the saucepan and keep it heated until it's time to serve.
Rub Fin & Feather Rub on the halibut. In a heated cast iron pan, melt the butter. Sear the halibut fillets in the pan with the butter
until they reach a temperature of 140°F, approximately 4-5 minutes on each side.
Take the steaks off the grill and serve with a warm lemon butter sauce. Enjoy.

5.147 Grilled Surf & Turf
Total Time: 1 Hrs 20 Mins, Servings: 2
Ingredients
Steak, 2" Thick, 1
Kosher Salt
Pepper
Coffee Rub
Live Lobsters, 1 (1-1/2 Lb)
Butter, 8 tbsp
Fresh parsley, 2 tbsp
Red Chile Flakes, 1 1/2 tsp
Garlic, 4 Clove
Lemon Zest, 1 Whole
Salt & Pepper
Instructions
Preheat the Pit Boss to 225°F for 15 minutes with the lid closed when ready to cook.
Season steaks with salt, pepper, and Coffee rub to taste. Cook for 45-60 minutes, or until the temperature reaches 125°F, directly on the grill grate. Remove the steaks from the pan and set them aside to rest.
Preheat the grill by turning it up to high.
Before dispatching the lobster, place it in the fridge for 5-10 minutes. Remove from the freezer and put on a cutting board on a cloth.
Push a sharp chef's knife directly through the cross on the lobster's head right below the eyes until it hits the cutting board; this will immediately kill it. Extract the stomach & digestive tract that goes through the tail of the lobster by splitting it lengthwise.
To make garlic herb butter, mix butter, chili flake, parsley, lemon zest, garlic, salt & pepper in a small bowl.
Brush the cut sides of lobster with garlic herb butter & put them cut side up on grill grate. If you don't flip them while they're cooking, you'll lose the tomalley and liquids. 8-12 minutes on the grill, or until the meat is opaque and the shell is brilliant red.
Grill steaks for 4-6 minutes on each side, or until internal temperature reaches 135°F for medium-rare, immediately on grill grate next to lobster. Allow 5 minutes for the steaks to rest before slicing.
If preferred, serve the steak and lobster with additional garlic herb butter, hot sauce and lemon wedges. Enjoy.

5.148 Jamaican Jerk Grilled Halibut with Pico De Gallo
Total Time: 35 Mins, Servings: 4
Ingredients
main
Halibut Steaks, 4 (6 Oz)
Vegetable Oil, 1/4
Marinade
Orange Juice, 1/2 Cup
Pineapple Juice, 1/4 Cup

Rum, 1/4 Cup
Jamaican Jerk Rub, 1 tbsp
Brown Sugar, 1 tbsp
Vegetable Oil, 1/4 Cup
Pico de Gallo
Red Or Yellow Tomato, 1 Large
Onion Diced, 1 Sweet
Jalapeño, 1
Garlic Minced, 1 Clove
Cilantro Leaves, 1/2 Cup
Lime Juiced, 1/2
Salt

Instructions

Rinse the halibut steaks in cool water.

Place the fish in a shallow glass baking sheet or a resealable plastic bag big enough to contain it in one layer. juice, brown sugar, and Jamaican jerk spice in a mixing dish. Whisk in the vegetable oil slowly. Pour the mixture over the fish and flip it to cover all sides. Refrigerate for no more than 2 hours after covering.

To make the Pico de Gallo, combine the tomato, onion, jalapeno, garlic, cilantro, and lime juice in a mixing dish. To taste, season with salt, jalapeno and lime juice.

When ready to cook, preheat the Pit Boss to 500°F with the lid closed for 15 minutes.

Brush the grill grate well with vegetable oil to prevent the fish from sticking. Take the fish steaks out of the marinade and wipe them dry with paper towels. More Jamaican jerk spice on both sides of the steaks Arrange the steaks on the grill grate at an angle. 6–8 minutes on the grill Turn the fish with a spatula & cook for another 6 minutes, or until it flakes easily with a fork. Remove from the grill and serve with Pico de Gallo on the side. Enjoy.

5.149 Grilled Salmon Steaks with BBQ Corn Salad

Total Time: 45 Mins, Servings: 4
Ingredients
Salmon Fillets, 4
Slices Bacon, 4
Ears Corn, 3
Big Game Rub, 2 tbsp
Olive Oil, 4 tbsp
Cherry Tomatoes, 1/4 Cup
Salt & Pepper
Black Beans, 1/2 Cup
Cilantro Chopped, 4 tbsp
Scallions Sliced, 4
Lemon Juiced, 1/2

Instructions

Generously season salmon steaks with Big Game Rub.

When ready to cook, adjust temperature to Hot & preheat, lid covered for 15 minutes.

Cook for 10-15 minutes, or until fat is drained and bacon is crispy, directly on the grill grate. Remove the steaks from the grill and put them aside. Season corn liberally with salt and black pepper after rubbing it with olive oil. Cook for 15-20 minutes, or until the outside is gently browned and the corn is cooked through, right on the grilled grate next to bacon.

To make the corn salad, add lemon juice, corn kernels, black beans, cherry tomatoes, cilantro, chopped bacon, scallions, olive oil, and salt & black pepper in a mixing bowl. Toss everything together. Place aside until the salmon is ready to eat.

Place the salmon steaks firmly on grill grate & cook for 4-5 minutes on each side, or until an immediate read thermometer reads 145°F.

Arrange salmon steak on a dish and top with salad. Enjoy.

5.150 Spicy Asian BBQ Shrimp

Total Time: 40 Mins, Servings: 4
Ingredients
Jumbo Shrimp, 1 Pound
Green Onions, 1
Garlic Minced, 6 Clove
Sesame Oil, 1/2 tsp
Jalapeño Minced, 1 tsp
Kosher Salt, 1 tsp
Grated Ginger, 2 tsp
Jalapeño Minced, 1
Canola Oil, 3 tsp
Ginger Minced, 2 tbsp
Onion Diced, 1/2 Cup
Soy Sauce, 1/3 Cup
Brown Sugar, 1/4 Cup
Rice Vinegar, 1 tbsp
Tomato Paste, 2 tbsp

Instructions

In a large bowl, combine the green onion, shrimp, garlic, jalapeño, ginger, oil and salt. To coat the shrimp, carefully combine all ingredients. Let the shrimp marinate while you make the sauce.

For the Sauce: Fry the canola oil in a small saucepan. Add ginger, garlic, jalapeño, sauté and onion for about 3 minutes. Bring to a boil with soy sauce and brown sugar. Cook for approximately 8 minutes, covered, over medium-low heat, or until onion is soft. Allow cooling slightly before transferring to a blender. Process in the remaining sauce components until a smooth purée emerges.

When ready to cook, increase the temp to High & preheat for 15 minutes with the lid closed.

Using metal skewers, spear the shrimp. Place the shrimp skewers firmly on grill grate & cook for 3 to 5 minutes on each side, or until pink and opaque.

Brush the shrimp skewers with the prepared sauce after removing them from the grill. Enjoy.

5.151 Tuna Tacos with Lime & Cilantro Cream

Total Time: 45 Mins, Servings: 4
Ingredients
Olive Oil, 1/2 Cup
Orange Juice, 1/4 Cup
Cilantro, Chopped
Taco Seasoning, 1 tbsp
Garlic Minced, 2 Clove
Lime Juice, 3/8 Cup
Jalapeño, Sliced Rings
Tuna Steak, 1 Pound
Cilantro, 1/3 Cup
Garlic Chopped, 1 Clove
Sour Cream, 1 Cup
Corn Tortillas
Diced Roma Tomatoes
Shredded Cabbage
Jalapeño Diced, 1 tsp
Diced Red Onion
Lime

Instructions

Marinade: In a jar with a tight-fitting cover, lime juice, combine orange juice, taco seasoning, olive oil and chopped garlic cloves. Shake vigorously.

In a big resealable bag, pour the marinade over the tuna steaks. Freeze for 4 hours after sealing the bag.

Lime and Cilantro Cream: In a blender, combine sour cream, cilantro, lime juice, garlic & jalapenos until smooth. Refrigerate until ready to serve, covered.

Start the Pit Boss, adjust the timer to 400 °F and heat it up, lid closed for 10-15 minutes.
Pat tuna steaks dry with paper towels after draining. Organize steaks straight on the grill grate & grill till the tuna is fried to your liking, about 10-twenty minutes. Flip once midway through.
Remove off the grill and set aside to rest for few minutes.
Slice the tuna steaks thinly and serve with the toppings. Enjoy.

5.152 Baked Steelhead
Total Time: 30 Mins, Servings: 4
Ingredients
Steelhead Fillet, 1
Unsalted Butter, 3 tbsp
Italian Dressing, (16 Oz) Bottle
Shallot Minced, 1/2
Garlic Minced, 2 Clove
Pit Boss Saskatchewan Rub
Lemon, 1
Instructions
When you're ready to cook, fire up the Pit Boss according to the specified rules. Preheat the oven to
350 ° F with the lid covered for 10-15 minutes.
Melt butter in a little cast iron pan inside the Pit Boss while it's preheating. Toss the fillet in the Italian dressing to coat evenly. Pit Boss Shake to cover the dressing, apply a thin coating of blackened Saskatchewan. Garlic and shallots should be minced.
Carefully remove the butter from the pre-heated grill, as cast iron will be very hot. Add the shallots and garlic and mix well.
Cover the middle top of fillet with a thick coating of the mixture. Place thin slices of lemon on top of the butter mixture. Place the steelhead on the grill & cook for 20-30 minutes, until flaky but not overcooked.
Take the fillet off the grill. Enjoy.

5.153 Pan-Seared Halibut with Green Garlic Pesto
Total Time: 15 Mins, Servings: 4
Ingredients
Green Garlic Pesto
Green Garlic, 1 Cup
Toasted Pine Nuts, 1/3 Cup
Extra-Virgin Olive Oil, 2/3 Cup
Parmesan Cheese, 2/3 Cup
Ground Black Pepper
Sea Salt
main
Canola oil, 4 tbsp
Instructions
Preheat the Pit Boss to 500°F and cook for 15 minutes with the lid covered when ready to cook.
Preheat a cast iron pan on the lowest level of the grill as it warms up.
To make the Green Garlic Pesto, pulse together the green garlic, Parmesan cheese, and pine nuts in a food processor until a coarse pulp form. Turn on the machine and pour in 2/3 cup olive oil in a slow, steady stream until the mixture is smooth but not runny. If
required, add additional oil. Salt & black pepper to taste. Remove from the equation.
Season both sides of the fillets with salt & black pepper after the grill has achieved 500°F. Open the grill and pour 4 tablespoons of high-temperature oil into the iron pan.
When the oil begins to shimmer & smoke slightly, carefully put the fillets in the oil (taking caution not to overcrowd the pan) with the top of the fish down initially. Close the lid as soon as possible.
Cook the fillets for 4 mins on first side, or until a beautifully browned and somewhat crisp layer form, then open the grill and flip the fish over carefully. Close the lid as soon as possible. Cook for another 1-2 minutes until the salmon is opaque on both sides and cooked through.
Take the iron pan from the grill & place the fish on a cutting board to rest.
To serve, put the fish on a tray or dish, crispy side up, and top with a spoonful of Green Garlic Pesto. Serve with additional pesto on the side. Enjoy.

5.154 Smoked Shrimp and Grits
Total Time: 45 Mins, Servings: 4
Ingredients
Quick Grits, 1 Cup
Cheddar Cheese, 1 Cup
Cilantro Chopped, 1/4 Cup
Olive Oil, 1/2 Cup
Garlic, 1 Clove
Pepper, 1/2 tsp
Lemon Juice, 1/4 Cup
Pound Shrimp
Green Bell Pepper, 1
Red Onion, 1/2
Ounce Mushrooms, Sliced
Salt, 1 tbsp
Instructions
In a large cast-iron large frying pan, bring 4 cups saltwater to a boil. Remove from the heat and whisk in grits slowly, breaking up any lumps.
Return to the fire and cook, stirring periodically, until the sauce has thickened (about 8-10 mins). Cover and keep heat by stirring in the cheddar.
In a mixing bowl, combine the olive oil, garlic, lemon juice and pepper. Stir in the shrimp to evenly coat
them. Allow 5 minutes for the mixture to get to room temperature.
Begin the Pit Boss grill on the Smoke with both the lid open till the fire is created while the shrimp marinates (4 to 5 minutes). Preheat the oven too high for 10-15 minutes the lid closed.
Remove the shrimp from the marinade and discard it. Alternate the mushrooms, onion, peppers and shrimp on the skewers.
Once the grill is hot, cover the lid and cook the kabobs for 4-5 minutes on each side, or until the shrimp becomes pink.
When the kabobs are done, remove the kabob's contents and place them on the grits. Serve with cilantro as a garnish. Enjoy.

5.155 Smoked Seafood Paella
Total Time: 1 Hr 30 Mins, Servings: 6
Ingredients
Chicken Broth, 8 Cup
Saffron Threads, 1 tsp
Extra-Virgin Olive Oil, 4 tbsp
Sliced Dried Chorizo, 1/2 Pound
Diced Onion, 1 Medium
Garlic Minced, 2 Clove
Short-Grain Rice, 2 Cup
Frozen Peas, 1 Cup
Shrimp In Shell, 2 Pound
Mussels, Clams, 1 Pound
Lemons, 2
Flat-Leaf Parsley, 3 tbsp
Instructions
When you're ready to cook, fire up the Pit Boss according to the manufacturer's directions. Preheat the oven to 400 ° F and cook for 10-15 minutes with the lid covered.
For smaller versions, place two racks on the grill or one big rack

on the lowest point. In a medium pot with oven-safe handles, combine the stock and saffron.
Place on the grill to warm while you prepare the paella, stirring once, maybe twice to ensure that the saffron mixes in the stock. Preheat the grill and place the paella dish on it.
Add the chorizo, olive oil and onion to the pan and swirl to spread the oil evenly.
Cook, covered, for 10-15 minutes, or until onions are transparent, stirring twice throughout the process.
Add the garlic, mix thoroughly, cover, and simmer for 3 minutes. Mix in the rice and a sprinkle of salt, making sure that each grain is well coated in olive oil. Distribute the rice gently over the pan's bottom.
Using a spoon, pour in just enough stock to cover the rice in a thin veil. Stirring is not allowed. Allow 15 minutes for the rice to cook after closing the grill.
Almost all of the stock should have been absorbed by the rice. Arrange the pears on top of rice, then top with the seafood. Ensure the mussels & clams are put with seams down, so the fluids flow into the paella as they open.
Pour a thin layer of stock and over rice and cover with a lid. Cook for another 15-20 minutes, or until the rice has absorbed all of the liquid, and the clams & mussels have opened.
The rice has a slight crunch. If it is still too hard, add a bit more saffron broth and continue to simmer with the top down for a few minutes more.
Any clams or mussels that don't open should be discarded.
Finish with a sprinkle of extra-virgin olive oil and lemon parsley, and wedges.
In the pan, serve family style. Enjoy.

5.156 Spicy Crab Poppers

Total Time: 50 Mins, Servings: 8
Ingredients
Jalapeño, 18 Whole
Canned Corn, 1 Cup
Lump Crab Meat, 1/2 Cup
Cream Cheese, 8 Ounce
Scallions Minced, 2
Old Bay Seasoning, 1 1/4 tsp
Instructions
Remove the ribs and seeds from each by cutting it lengthwise through the stem.
To make the filling, whisk together the corn, cream cheese, scallions, crab meat & Old Bay Seasoning in a mixing bowl. Add the scallions and mix well. Fill the jalapeno halves with the filling, mounding it slightly.
Place the poppers on a foil-lined or parchment-lined baking sheet. When you're ready to cook, turn on the Pit Boss grill to Smoke and leave the lid open till the fire is ready (4-5 minutes). Preheat the oven to 350 °F and bake for 10 to 15 minutes with the lid covered.
Roast the jalapenos for 25–30 minutes, or until softened as well as the filling is hot & bubbling.
Allow it cool for a few minutes before serving. Enjoy.

5.157 West Coast Cioppino Fries

Total Time: 35 Mins, Servings: 6
Ingredients
Butter, 2 tbsp
Shallot Minced, 2 tbsp
Clams Littleneck, 4 Ounce
San Marzano Tomato, 1 Cup
Garlic Minced, 2 Clove
White Wine, 1/2 Cup
Halibut, 4 Ounce
Mussels Debearded, 4 Ounce
Shrimp, 4 Ounce
Cleaned Squid Bodies 4 Ounce
Chicken Stock, 1 Cup
Tomato Paste, 2 tbsp
Bay Leaf, 1
Parsley Chopped, 1 tbsp
Corn-starch, 2 tbsp
Sprig Thyme, 2
Water, 1 tbsp
Crispy Fries, 4 Cup
Instructions
When you're ready to cook, fire up the Pit Boss according to the specified rules. Preheat the oven to 325 degrees Fahrenheit with the lid covered for 10-15 minutes.
In a dutch oven, melt the butter over medium heat. Sauté for 1 minute with the garlic and shallot.
Toss in the clams and mussels to coat. 1 minute of sautéing
Pour in the white wine and cook for 1 minute, stirring gently.
Combine the remaining seafood, chicken stock, tomato puree, thyme, tomato paste, and bay leaves in a large mixing bowl. Bring to a low simmer, then cover and grill.
Grill for 10-15 minutes, or until all seafood is well cooked.
Replace the cover on the stovetop burner and turn it back on. Combine the corn starch & water in a slurry and stir into the cioppino.
Reduce to low heat and continue to boil until the sauce has thickened to a gravy consistency. Remove the bay leaves and thyme sprigs, and taste for seasoning, adding salt and black pepper as required.
Arrange fries on a serving plate and top with cioppino. Serve with chopped parsley on top. Enjoy.

5.158 Stuffed Lobster Tail

Total Time: 30 Mins, Servings: 4
Ingredients
Lobster Tails, 4
Butter, 1/2 Cup
Onion Diced, 2 Cup
Lump Crab Meat, 1 Pound
Garlic Minced, 3 Clove
Chopped Tarragon, 1 tbsp
Lemon Wedges
Parsley Chopped, 1/4 Cup
Lemon Juice, 1/4 Cup
Old Bay Seasoning, 2 tsp
Butter Crackers, 4 Cup
Instructions
In a big bowl or saucepan, make an ice water bath. Remove from the equation.
In a big saucepan or stockpot, bring many inches of salty water to a boil over high heat. Cover and blanch the lobster tails for 1-2 minutes. Allow the tails to cool in the ice water bath. Drain well, then use kitchen shears or a fresh pair of tin snips to remove the soft "belly shell."
Take the tail meat out of the shells and put them aside. Each part of tail meat should have the digestive tract removed from

the top. Combine the meat with shrimp or crabmeat in bite-size pieces. Remove from the equation.

Make the stuffing: In a large pan over medium heat, melt the butter. Cook until the garlic and onions are tender and transparent. Combine the parsley, tarragon, Old Bay, and lemon juice in a mixing bowl. Allow cooling after removing the skillet from the heat. Combine the leftover tail meat & crabmeat or shrimp in a mixing bowl. Stir in the cracker crumbs carefully to mix. (Add the crackers just when you're ready to cook; otherwise, they'll become soggy.)

Fill the leftover tail shells with the filling and put them on the rimmed baking sheet, mounding them liberally. Use crumpled aluminum foil to support the shells upright if they are "tippy."

When you're ready to cook, set the Pit Boss to Smoke and leave the lid open till the fire is ready (4-5 minutes). Preheat the oven to 425 degrees Fahrenheit with the lid covered for 10-15 minutes.

Place the baking sheet with the filled tails on grill grate and cook for 15-20 minutes, or until the filling is crispy and golden brown. Serve with lemon slices on the side.

5.159 Roasted Garlic & Clam Pizza
Total Time: 35 Mins, Servings: 4
Ingredients
Olive Oil, 1/4 Cup
Garlic Chopped, 3 Clove
Pizza Dough, 1 Pound
Flour
Cornmeal
Jacobsen Pure Kosher
Clams Chopped, 2 Can
Mozzarella Cheese, 2 Cup
Parmesan Cheese, 2 tbsp
Fresh Oregano, 1/4 tsp
Baby Arugula, 2 Cup
Red Pepper Flakes
Instructions
When you're ready to cook, fire up the Pit Boss grill. Until the fire has been created, smoke with the lid open (4 to 5 minutes). Preheat the oven to 450 °F and bake for 15 to 30 minutes with the lid covered. In the middle of the grill, place a pizza stone or an inverted rimmed baking sheet.

In a small dish, combine the garlic & 1/4 cup olive oil. On a lightly floured, knead the dough approximately 6 times.

Roll into a 12-inch circle and stretch. Place the dough on a cornmeal-dusted pizza peel or the other inverted baking sheet.

Brush the dough with half of the garlic oil and season with salt. Drizzle 2 tablespoons of the saved clam juice as well as the remaining garlic oil over the mozzarella & clams on the crust. Season with parmesan, oregano and salt & pepper to taste.

Place the pizza on a pizza stone or baking sheet that has been warmed. Bake for 13-15 minutes, or until the crust is lightly golden.

Drizzle the arugula with olive oil & lemon juice just before serving the pizza. Slice the pizza in half and
top each half with arugula and red pepper flakes. Enjoy.

5.160 Caribbean Curry Grilled Lobsters with Garlic Lime Asparagus
Total Time: 35 Mins, Servings: 8
Ingredients
Butter Softened, 1 Cup
Garlic Minced, 3 Clove
Minced Ginger, 1 tbsp
Lime, 1
Curry Powder, 1/2 tsp
Ground Turmeric, 1/2 tsp
Cayenne Pepper, 1/4 tsp
Cilantro Leaves, 2 tbsp
Diced Chives, 2 tbsp
Sea Salt
Live Lobsters, 4 (1-1/2 Lb)
Lime Wedges
Fresh Cilantro
Asparagus
Bunch Asparagus, 1
Olive Oil, 2 tbsp
Garlic Minced, 2 Clove
Lime 1
Instructions
Make a huge stockpot filled halfway with salted water to a quick boil. Make an ice bath for yourself.

Make the curry butter first. Combine the garlic, butter, ginger, cilantro, spices, chives, lime juice and zest, and a sprinkle of sea salt in a medium mixing bowl and stir thoroughly. Depends on how soft the butter is, it may take a few minutes. The mixed butter should be smooth, velvety, and easy to work with. (Hints: Compound butter freezes well, and it's always

handy to have a variety of tastes on hand for the next dish.) Double the butter recipe and keep it in the fridge with your next lobster grilling day.)

It's time for lobster. Using in batches, 1 or 2 lobsters at a time, put the lobster on a cutting board and quickly cut down through the head with the point of a chef's knife just below where the claws connect (it's frightening, but you can do it!). Transfer to the stockpot and simmer for 2 minutes with the cover on. Take to the ice bath to chill after 2 minutes. At this stage, the lobsters will be ruby red, but the flesh will still be transparent. Cook the remaining lobsters in the same manner. Cut via the body & tail of each lobster with a sharp knife and a firm hand to create two halves. Place each lobster under cold running water for a few seconds to clear the tomalley (green parts).

Toss asparagus, olive oil, garlic, and lime zest together in a large mixing basin. Remove from the equation.

When ready to cook, preheat the Pit Boss to 425°F with the lid closed for 15 min.

When the grill is hot, put the lobster's flesh side down on the grill and cook for 4 mins. Place the asparagus on the grill grates to cook with the lobster at the same time. Turn the lobsters after 4 minutes and pour approximately 2 tablespoons additional compound butter over each crustacean. Cook for 8-10 mins, or until well cooked and melted butter-coated.

Garnish with lime wedges, fresh cilantro, and a sprinkling of sunlight.

5.161 BBQ Oysters
Total Time: 16 Mins, Servings: 4
Ingredients
Unsalted Butter, 1 Pound
Meat Church, 1 tbsp
Green Onions, 1 Bunch
Garlic Minced, 2 Clove
12 Oysters
Seasoned Breadcrumbs, 1/4 Cup
Pepper Jack Cheese, 8 Ounce
Pit Boss BBQ Sauce
Green Onions, 1/2 Bunch
Instructions
Preheat Pit Boss to 375°F and cook for 15 minutes with lid covered when ready to cook.

To make the compound butter, combine the following ingredients in a mixing bowl. Combine the butter, garlic, onion, and Meat Church Rub in a large mixing bowl.

Place the butter on plastic wrap or parchment paper to keep it from sticking. Make a log out of it by rolling it up and tying each end with butcher's twine. To solidify, place in the refrigerator for an hour. This butter may be used to improve the taste of any grilled meat. You may also substitute the compound butter with high-quality butter.

Shuck the oysters, retaining as much liquid as possible in the shell. Breadcrumb the oysters and put them immediately on the Pit Boss. 5 minutes in the oven You'll want to check for the oyster's edge to begin to curl slightly.

Place a tablespoon of compound butter in each oyster after 5 minutes. Add a sprinkle of pepper jack cheese once the butter has melted.

After a total of 6 mins on the grill, remove the oysters. Add a spray of Heat BBQ Sauce & Pit Boss Sweet, a couple of chopped onions on the tops of the oysters. Allow cooling almost 5 mins before serving.

5.162 A.J. Allmendinger's Blackened Salmon
Total Time: 25 Mins, Servings: 4
Ingredients
optional cayenne pepper, 1 tbsp
garlic minced, 2 cloves
olive oil, 2 tbsp
sweet rib rub, 4 tbsp
salmon fillet, 2-pound
Instructions
It all begins with the rub. Sweet, savory, and spicy flavors are required for blackened salmon seasoning. All of those notes are covered with our pit boss sweet rib rub with cayenne pepper, resulting in a wonderful crust.

After applying the rub, just grill for 5 minutes on each side over high heat. If you want your salmon to have a little more char, open the flames broiler plate & cook on direct heat.

Note: For this recipe, new England fruit apple hardwood pellets are suggested.

Get your pit boss grill going. Adjust the timer to 350°F after it's started.

Remove the salmon's skin and discard it. Brush both sides of the salmon fillets with olive oil, then season with chopped garlic, cayenne pepper, and sweet rib rub.

Cook the salmon for 5 mins on one side of the grill. Cook for the next 5 min on the other side, or until salmon reaches a temp of 145°F. Remove the skewers from the grill & place them on a serving platter.

5.163 Shrimp scampi
Total Time: 20 Mins, Servings: 3
Ingredients
Blackened sriracha rub, 2 tsp
Butter, 1/2 cup
Chili pepper flakes, 1/2 tsp
Garlic cloves, 3
Lemon wedges
Lemon juice, 1
Linguine, cooked
Parsley chopped, 3 tbsp
Shrimp, 1 1/2 lbs
Toasted baguette
Instructions
Shrimp scampi prepared in a flash! For quick prep and clean-up, this simple and delicious shrimp scampi is cooked entirely on the pit boss griddle. In garlic and chili butter with a kick from black sriracha, the shrimp are grilled in minutes. Finish with fresh parsley and lemon, then serve with grilled bread or pasta for a meal you'll want to make again and again.

Pit boss grills charred sriracha seasoning is used in this dish.

Preheat your pit boss griddle to a medium-high setting. Set the grill to medium-high heat when using a gas or charcoal grill. Melt half of the butter on the griddle and cook the garlic, black sriracha, & chili flakes for 1 minute, or until fragrant.

Add the shrimp and cook for 2 minutes, stirring periodically, until opaque.

Combine the leftover butter, parsley, lemon zest, and juice in a mixing bowl. Remove the shrimp from the grill and move to serving dish after tossing them in the lemon butter.

Serve immediately with toasted bread & lemon wedges. If preferred, serve over spaghetti, linguine, or zucchini noodles.

5.164 Shrimp tacos with lime crema
Total Time: 20 Mins, Servings: 4
Ingredients
Cabbage shredded, 1/4
Cilantro chopped, 2 tsp
Corn tortillas
lime wedges, 1/2
Mayonnaise, 1/4 cup
Pit boss sriracha rub blackened
red bell pepper, 1/4
shrimp, 1 lb
Sour cream, 1/4 cup
Vegetable oil, 2 tsp
White onion, 1/2
Instructions
In a medium mixing dish, place the shrimp. Drizzle with veg oil after seasoning with pit boss black sriracha rub. Set aside after tossing by hand to coat thoroughly.

Combine mayonnaise, fresh lime juice and sour cream in a small mixing dish. Season with blackened sriracha to taste. Remove from the equation.

Combine the jalapeno, red bell pepper, onion & cilantro in a small mixing dish. Remove from the equation.

Preheat your pit boss versatile skillet at medium-high heat. Preheat a cast-iron pan over medium heat if using a grill.

Warm each side of the tortillas on the grill, then switch off the burner underneath.

Place the shrimp on the heated grill and cook for 4–6 minutes, or until opaque, turning periodically. Season with more blackened sriracha for hotter shrimp.

Assemble tacos with shredded cabbage, pepper mixture, shrimp & sauce drizzled on top. Warm lime wedges are served on the side.

5.165 Smoked salmon dip with grilled artichoke and cheese
Total Time: 12 Hrs 50 Mins, Servings: 12
Ingredients
Artichoke hearts, 28 oz
Blackened sriracha rub
Brown sugar, 1/2 cup
Cream cheese, 8 oz
Breadcrumbs, 1/2 cup
Garlic powder, 1 tbsp
Italian cheese, 1 cup
Mayonnaise, 1 cup
Olive oil, 2 tsp
Kosher salt, 1/4 cup
Onion powder, 1 tbsp
Parsley chopped, 2 tbsp
Parmesan cheese, 1/2 cup
Salmon, fillet, 1 1/4 lbs
White pepper, 1/2 tsp
Sour cream
Instructions

Combine the brown sugar, garlic powder, salt, white pepper and onion powder in a small mixing basin. This will produce twice as much cure as you need, so store the other half in a cover with plastic wrap for subsequent use when smoking fish. Spread a thin layer of the cure over a cover of plastic wrap on a tray. Place the salmon on top of the cure, skin-side down, and cover with a few tablespoons of cure. Wrap the salmon with plastic wrap after gently pressing the cure on top of the meat.

Chill for 8 hours or overnight in the refrigerator.

Remove the salmon from the freezer and rinse it in cold water to remove the cure.

Pat salmon dry with a paper towel and place skin side down on a wire rack. Dry for two hours at room temperature or until the salmon has a yellowish gleam.

Preheat your pit boss silver series, Lockhart, to 250 ° F. Set your grill to low, indirect heat if you're using a gas, charcoal, or another kind of grill.

Place the fish on the top shelf of the upper cabinet. Smoke for 2 hours, then raise the grill temp to 350°F to keep a cabinet temp of 225°F and smoke for another 1–2 hours, or until the salmon achieves a temp of 145°F.

Remove the salmon from the refrigerator and put it aside for 15 minutes to rest before flaking it apart. After grilling, set aside 12 cups to serve on top of the dip.

Drain the artichokes and thread them onto metal skewers while the salmon is resting.

Drizzle with blackened sriracha and place on the grill. 2-3 minutes on the grill, or until browned.

Remove off the grill, let it cool somewhat before chopping coarsely. Remove from the equation.

Mix shredded Italian cheese, breadcrumbs, grated parmesan, and parsley in a mixing dish. Remove from the equation.

In a cast iron pan, combine cream cheese, mayonnaise, and sour cream. For 5 mins, stir regularly with a wooden spoon till the mixture is smooth.

Gently incorporate flakes of salmon & grilled artichoke hearts into the dip, then top with breadcrumb mixture.

Brush with olive oil, then cover the grill lid & bake for 20 - 25 minutes, or until the dip bubbles around the
edges and the cheese caramelize on top.

Remove the dip from grill and top with the saved salmon and parsley. Serve with crackers, bagel chips, or crusty toast while still warm.

5.166 Grilled Shrimp with Cajun dip
Total Time: 25 Mins, Servings: 4
Ingredients
Garlic clove, 1
Sour cream, 1 cup
Mayonnaise, ½ cup
Olive oil, 2 tbsp
Shelled & deveined shrimp, ½ lb
Lemon juice, 1 tsp
Hickory bacon rub
Scallions
Instructions
Grilled shrimp with a creamy & spicy Cajun dip will take your celebration up a notch (or two). This savory appetizer is bursting with strong Cajun flavors with the perfect amount of spice and smokiness. The entire dish is put on the pellet grill and cooked until it's bubbling and sticky. Serve over garlicky Texas toast, tortillas, or vegetables, and dig down.

It is suggested that you use fruit pellets hardwood for this recipe.

Also, Pit boss bacon rub spice is used in this recipe.

Preheat your pit boss grill to 350 degrees Fahrenheit. Set the grill to medium heat if you're using a gas or charcoal grill.

Combine mayonnaise, Cajun spice, sour cream, lemon juice, garlic, spicy sauce, and hickory bacon in a glass mixing bowl. Whisk everything together until it's completely smooth.

Cajun shrimp: mix shrimp, Cajun-style spice, olive oil and hickory bacon seasoning together in a small dish. Remove from the equation.

Pour the dip into a cast-iron ramekin or a small dutch oven & cover with foil. After that, cook for 10-15 mins on a hot grill or until the dip starts to bubble around the edges. Place a cast-iron pan on the grill and add the shrimp at the same time. Cook for 3 to 5
minutes on each side, or till shrimp are opaque.

Remove the dip from the grill & top with scallions and spicy shrimp. Enjoy with garlic toast squares when still warm.

5.167 Blackened Catfish
Total Time: 40 Mins, Servings: 4
Ingredients
Cajun seasoning, ½ cup
Granulated garlic, 1 tsp
Ground thyme, 1 tsp
Unsalted butter, 1 stick
Cayenne pepper, ¼ tsp
Onion powder, 1 tsp
Pepper, 1 tsp
Skinless catfish, 4 (5-oz.)
Ground oregano, 1 tsp
Smoked paprika, 1 tbsp
Instructions
With this classic grilled, blackened catfish, you can channel the flavors of the bayou. The mildness of the catfish provides the ideal backdrop for the Smokey and spicy creole tastes. Complete with a slice of lemon for added flavor, then serve with rice, beans, and coleslaw for a full-fledged Cajun seafood feast.

On the barbecue, how to create blackened catfish

It all begins with the rub. Intense sweet, savory, and spicy Cajun spices are required for blackened catfish flavoring. Apply generously all over the fish, then cook for 3 to 5 minutes on each side over high heat. The meat should have a black crust and be beautiful and flaky.

Remember to use a cast-iron skillet.

Your crust will get a lovely, buttery sear in the cast iron skillet. While this method allows you to fry your catfish directly on the grill grates, grilling it in butter in a cast-iron pan brings the taste of the fish to a whole other level.

It is suggested that you use mesquite wood pellets for this recipe.

Mix the Cajun spice, onion powder, smoked paprika, ground oregano, ground thyme, granulated garlic, and cayenne pepper in a small bowl.

Season the fish with salt & set aside for 20 minutes to rest.

Preheat your pit boss to 450 degrees Fahrenheit. Set the grill to medium-high heat if you're using a gas or charcoal grill. Preheat the grill by placing a cast iron pan on it.

While the grill is heating up, lightly coat the catfish fillets with the spice mixture. Swirl half of the butter into the hot cast iron pan to coat it; add additional butter if necessary. Cook the fillets in a heated skillet for 3-5 minutes, or until a brown crust. Cook for another 3-5 minutes, or until the salmon flakes apart when gently pushed with your finger.

Remove the fish from the grill and top it with fresh parsley. Enjoy with lemon wedges on the side.

5.168 Cedar plank salmon
Total Time: 40 Mins, Servings: 4
Ingredients
Brown sugar, 1/4 cup
Olive oil, 1/2 tbsp
Pit boss smoked seasoning
Salmon fillets, 4
Instructions
Salmon is favorite seafood since it lacks the fishy odor that some people find off-putting. Because salmon cooks fast, particularly on your pellet grill or smoker, it's a popular date night or weekday meal.
Because the woodblock shields the delicate skin from direct heat while also adhering to your grill grates, this cedar plank salmon dish infuses cedar wood flavor and crisps the fish's skin without overcharging it.
On the grill, how to prepare cedar plank salmon
Before grilling, soak the untreated wood board in water for 24 hours. Remove the pan and clean it down when you're ready to grill. Grill the salmon for 15-10 min at 350°F, or until it is cooked through and readily flakes with a fork.
Note: For this recipe, England apple hardwood pellets are suggested.
This dish calls for smoked seasoning from a competition.
Before grilling, soak the undiagnosed cedar plank in water for 24 hours. Remove the pan and clean it down when you're ready to grill.
Light your grill. Then, preheat the oven to 350 degrees Fahrenheit.
Combine the brown sugar, lemon pepper, oil, herb and garlic seasoning in a small bowl. Rub the salmon fillets liberally with the mixture.
Put the plank indirect heat and grill the salmon for 15-20 minutes, or until it is cooked through it and flakes readily with a fork. Remove the pan from the heat & serve right away.

5.169 Seared Ahi Tuna Steak
Total Time: 1 Hr, Servings: 2
Ingredients
Soy sauce, 1/2 cup
Large sushi ahi tuna steak, 1
Lime juice, 1/4 cup
Rice wine vinegar, 2 tbsp
Sesame oil, 2 tbsp
Sriracha sauce, 2 tbsp
Sweet heat rub, 4 tbsp
Water, 2 cups
Instructions
This seared ahi tuna steak is a show-stopping seafood appetizer or special occasion meal! It's ideal for cooking on the pellet grill, and it'll give you restaurant-quality results at home. This dish will make your mouth swim and is ideal for an anniversary or birthday supper for a special someone.
Get your pit boss up and running. Set the temp to 400°F after it's started. Setup for heat over direct heat if you're using gas or charcoal.
Combine the water, lime juice, soy sauce, 1 tbsp sesame oil, rice wine vinegar, sriracha sauce, and mirin in a glass baking dish. With the whisk, mix the marinade until everything is thoroughly combined. Place the ahi steak in the marinade and refrigerate it for 30 minutes in the baking dish with the ahi steak. After 30 minutes, turn the ahi steak over and marinate for another 30 minutes, allowing the ahi to completely marinade on both sides.
Drain the marinade from the tuna steak and wipe it dry on all sides with paper towels once it has finished marinating. Put the sweet heat, rub it onto a plate and liberally massage the remaining tbsp of sesame oil over both sides of the tuna steak, then carefully put the tuna steak into seasoning on the dish, rotating to coat equally on all sides.
Place the ahi steak on the hottest area of the grill and insert a temp probe into the part of the steak. Grill the ahi tuna steaks for 45 seconds on each side, or until opaque and grill marks appear on the exterior. Allow the steak to cook for 45 seconds on the opposite side or until the exterior is just cooked through. The internal temperature of the ahi tuna steak should be about 115°F.
When the steak reaches 115°F, remove it from the grill and slice and serve immediately. The steak should be chilly and cherry pink on the inside.

5.170 Salmon cakes and homemade tartar sauce
Total Time: 30 Mins, Servings: 4
Ingredients
Breadcrumb, 1 1/2 cups
Pickle relish, 1/4 cup
Eggs, 2
Capers, 1/2 tbsp
Mayonnaise, 1 1/4 cup
Mustard grainy, 1 tbsp
Red pepper, 1/2
Boss sweet rib rub, 1/2 tbsp
Olive oil, 1/2 tbsp
Cooked salmon, 1 cup
Instructions
Combine the salmon, 14 cup mayonnaise, eggs, red bell pepper, breadcrumbs, sweet rib rub, and mustard in a large mixing dish. Then allow the mixture to rest for 15 minutes to allow the breadcrumbs to absorb the liquid.
Set your pit boss to "smoke" mode. Set the temp to 350 degrees Fahrenheit after it's started.
Combine the leftover mayonnaise, chopped capers and dill pickle relish in a small bowl. Remove from the equation.
Preheat the grill by placing the baking sheet on it. Put olive oil over the baking sheet once it's heated, then place rounded teaspoons of the salmon combination onto the sheet pan. With a spatula, press the
ingredients into a flat patty. Allow for 3-5 mins of grilling time, then turn and cook for another 1-2 minutes. Remove from the grill & serve with the tartar sauce you set beforehand.

5.171 Grilled Mango Shrimp
Total Time: 15 Mins, Servings: 4
Ingredients
Olive oil, 2 tbsp
raw tail-on, deveined & thawed shrimp, 1 pound
Instructions
Heat your pit master grill to 425 degrees Fahrenheit. Using cold water, rinse the shrimp. Season liberally with mango magic seasoning and olive oil in a mixing bowl. In a large mixing basin, toss everything together
well.
Thread numerous shrimp onto a skewer until they are barely touching one another. Rep with the remaining skewers and shrimp.
Grill the shrimp for 2-3 minutes on each side, or until they are pink and opaque throughout. Remove from the grill and serve right away.

5.172 Mango Thai Shrimp
Total Time: 25 Mins, Servings: 4
Ingredients
Brown sugar, 2 tbsp
1 pinch (optional) red pepper flakes
Sriracha hot sauce, 1 tsp
Mango magic seasoning, 2 tbsp
Rice wine vinegar, 1/2 tbsp
Raw tail-on, deveined & thaw shrimp, 1 pound
Soy Sauce, 2 tbsp
Chili sauce, 1/2 cup
Instructions
Heat your grill to 425 ° F. Using cold water, rinse the shrimp. Place all of the items mentioned above in a bowl. Allow for a 2- to 4-hour marinate time.
Thread numerous shrimp onto skewer till they are barely touching one another. Rep with the remaining skewers and shrimp.
Grill the shrimp for 2 to 3 mins, or until they are pink and opaque throughout. Remove from the grill and serve right away.

5.173 Crab Stuffed Mushrooms
Total Time: 4 Hrs 15 Mins, Servings: 4
Ingredients
Cream Cheese, 1
Porcini Mushroom Caps, 12
Lemon juice, 1 tbsp
Lemon zest, 2 tsp
Imitation crab, 1/2 (2 oz)
Parmesan cheese, 1/2 cup
Parsley, 2 tbsp
Panko bread crumbs, 3/4 cup
Chop steak rub, 1 tsp
Instructions
Mix the cream cheese, breadcrumbs, imitation crab, 14 cup parmesan cheese, lemon juice, lemon zest, parsley, and pit boss chophouse steak flavor in a large mixing basin. Mix until everything is well mixed.
Fill the mushroom caps with a big rounded spoonful of the filling and gently push it in with a spoon. Top with the outstanding 14 cups of parmesan cheese after all of the mushrooms have been packed.
Warm your pitmaster grill to 350 degrees Fahrenheit. Grill the mushrooms for 5 minutes, or until the cheese is bubbling and golden well as the mushrooms are soft.
Enjoy while it's still hot.

5.174 Fish Tacos
Total Time: 20 Mins, Servings: 12
Ingredients
Black pepper, 1 tsp
Oregano, 1 tsp
Codfish, 1 1/2 lbs
Cumin, 1/2 tsp
Cayenne pepper, 1/4 tsp
Paprika smoked, 1 1/2 tsp
Garlic powder, 1 tsp
Salt, 1/2 tsp
Instructions
Preheat the oven to 350 ° F.
Combine paprika, oregano, cumin, garlic powder, cayenne pepper, salt & pepper in a mixing bowl. Drizzle over the cod.
Cook the fish for approximately 5 minutes on each side on a hot grill. If desired, toast the tortillas over an open flame.
Cut the fish into bite-size pieces, crush the avocado, split the tomatoes, and distribute them equally among the tortillas. Red onion, jalapenos, sour cream, lettuce & cilantro go on top. Enjoy a spritz of lime juice.

5.175 Lemon Smoked Salmon
Total Time: 1 Hr 5 Mins, Servings: 4
Ingredients
Dill, fresh
Salmon, 1 1/2 - 2 lbs
Lemon, 1
Instructions
Salmon is one of the most popular foods to smoke, and for a valid reason. The taste of smoked salmon is refined and magnificent. By adding a cedar wood plank & smoking it with a slice lemon on top, the recipe enhances that taste. As a consequence, salmon is a delectable and versatile component that can be eaten on its own or utilized in a number of recipes.

5.176 New England Lobster Rolls
Total Time: 40 Mins, Servings: 4
Ingredients
Butter, 1/2 cup
Hot dog bun(s), 4
Lemon, 1
Lobster tail, 4
Mayo, 1/4 cup
Pepper
Instructions
Preheat your grill on "smoke," with the lid open, until a fire in the burn pot is created (3-7 minutes). Preheat the oven to 300 °
Cut the tail shell in half with kitchen shears to reveal the flesh. Season with salt and pepper after adding the butter. Place the tails flesh side up on the grill & cook for 35 minutes, or until the shell has become red
as well as the meat is white.
Remove the meat from the shell and remove it from the grill. Season the meat with pepper and toss it in bowl with lemon juice, mayo and rind. Stir to blend, then divide equally among hot dog buns.

5.177 Grilled Lobster Tails
Total Time: 20 Mins, Servings: 3
Ingredients
Black pepper
Chives chopped, 2 tbsp
Garlic minced, 1 clove
Lobster tail, 3 (7-ounce)
Butter, 3/4 stick
Lemon, sliced
Salt, kosher
Instructions
With these wonderfully buttered grilled lobster tails,
you can get your surf on. The lobster tails are brushed with delicious garlic, chives and butter sauce before being cooked to excellence on a pit boss wood pellet barbecue for additional depth and flavor. This dish is perfect for a summer night with friends or for a special holiday meal.
Recommendation for wood pellets
Our maple mix wood pellets are a great option for this recipe because of the delicate & sweet tastes of maple hardwood.
Preheat your grill on "smoke," with the lid pen, until a fire in the burn pot is created (3-7 minutes).
Preheat the grill to 350 degrees Fahrenheit.
In a small mixing bowl, combine the butter, chives, chopped garlic, and black pepper. Wrap the dish in plastic wrap and put it aside.

Flow the tails down the center of the softer bottom of the shell in a butterfly pattern. Make sure you don't cut all the way through the flesh. Drizzle tails with olive oil & season to taste with salt and pepper.
Grilled lobsters cut side down for 5 minutes, or until shells are brilliant red. Toss the tails with a good spoonful of herb butter and serve. 4 minutes more on the grill, or even the lobster flesh is opaque white.
Remove the pan from the heat and top with additional herb butter & lemon wedges.

5.178 Garlic Shrimp Pesto Bruschetta
Total Time: 25 Mins, Servings: 12
Ingredients
Bread baguette, 12 slices
Garlic powder, 1/2 tsp
Salt
Chili pepper flakes, 1/2 tsp
Olive oil, 2 tbsp
Paprika smoked, 1/2 tsp
Pesto
Garlic minced, 4 cloves
Parsley leaves, 1/4 tsp
Pepper
Shrimp jumbo, 12
Instructions
Preheat your grill on "smoke," with the lid open, until a fire in the burn pot is created (3-7 minutes). Preheat the oven to 350 degrees Fahrenheit. Place the baguette pieces on a foil-lined baking sheet. Coat
both ends of the baguette slices with a mixture made from olive oil and minced garlic. Bake for approximately 10-15 minutes with the pan within the grill.
In a pan, combine a splash of olive oil, chili powder, the shrimp, garlic powder, salt and pepper, smoked paprika, and cook for approximately 5 minutes over medium-high heat (until the shrimp is pink). Make careful to stir often. Remove the pan from the heat after it has become pink. Allow 5 minutes for the baguettes to cool before spreading a layer of pesto on each one, topping with a shrimp and serving.

5.179 Scallops Wrapped in Bacon
Total Time: 30 Mins, Servings: 4
Ingredients
Lemon juice, 3 tbsp
Scallop, 12
Pepper
Instructions
Preheat your grill on smoke with lid open till a fire in the burn pot has formed (3-7 minutes).
Preheat the oven to 400 degrees Fahrenheit. Cut bacon rashers in half & wrap every half around a scallop, securing it with a toothpick.
Drizzle the scallops with lemon juice and arrange them on baking pan.
Place the bacon on the grill and cook for 15-20 mins, or until crisp. Remove from the grill and serve.

5.180 Grilled Spicy Lime Shrimp
Total Time: 40 Mins, Servings: 4
Ingredients
Chili paste, 2 tsp
Red flakes pepper, 1/4 tsp
Garlic minced, 2 cloves
Lime juiced, 1 large
Cumin, 1/2 tsp
Paprika powder, 1/4 tsp
Salt, 1/2 tsp
Instructions
Combine lime juice, garlic, olive oil, chili powder, paprika, salt, cumin, pepper, & red pepper flakes in a mixing bowl.
Pour the mixture into a bag, add shrimp, toss
to coat, and set aside for 30 minutes to marinate.
Preheat your grill on "smoke," with the lid open, until a fire in the burn pot is created (3-7 minutes). Preheat the oven to 400 degrees Fahrenheit. Next, thread the shrimp onto skewers, put them on the grill, and cook for approximately two minutes on each side, or until done. Remove the shrimp off the grill after they're done and eat.

5.181 Cedar Smoked Salmon
Total Time: 1 Hr 15 Mins, Servings: 6
Ingredients
Black pepper, 1 tsp
Cedar plank, 3
Garlic minced, 1 tsp
Olive oil, 1/3 cup
Onion, 1 tsp
Parsley minced, 1 tsp
Rice vinegar, 1 1/2 tbsp
Salmon, 2
Sesame oil, 1 tsp
Soy sauce, 1/3 cup
Instructions
Immerse the cedar planks for an hour or longer in warm water.
Combine the olive oil, sesame oil, rice vinegar, chopped garlic and soy sauce in a mixing bowl.
Toss in the salmon & let aside for 30 minutes to marinate.
Preheat your grill on smoke with the lid open till a fire in the burn pot has created (3-7 minutes).
Preheat the grill to 225 degrees Fahrenheit.
Arrange the boards on top of the grate. It's time to bring in the fish after the boards begin to smoke & crackle a bit.
Drain the marinade and season the fish with onion powder, parsley, and black pepper before discarding it.
Place the salmon on the planks and cook until the internal temperature reaches 140°F.
Remove off the grill and set aside for 10 minutes before serving.

5.182 Honey-soy Glazed Salmon
Total Time: 11 Mins, Servings: 4
Ingredients
Chili paste
Chives chopped, 1 tsp
Garlic cloves, 2
Ginger, 2 tbsp
Honey, 1 tsp
Lemon juice, 2 tbsp
Salmon fillets, 4
Sesame oil, 1 tsp
Soy sauce, 2 tbsp
Instructions
Preheat your grill on smokes with the lid open till a fire in the burn pot has formed (3-7 minutes). Preheat the oven to 400 degrees Fahrenheit.
Place the salmon in a large cover with plastic wrap, along with the other ingredients (excluding the chives). Close the plastic bag & toss the salmon evenly to coat it. Refrigerate the marinade for 20 minutes.
After the salmon has marinated for 20 minutes, put it on a flat pan or directly on the grill grates, cook for 3 minutes, and then turn and grill for another 3 minutes. Turn the grill off, take the pan from the grill, plate, and top with chives.

5.183 Blackened Catfish Tacos

Total Time: 1 Hrs, Servings: 3
Ingredients
Catfish
Cabbage
Grilla Grills Rub
Tortillas
Shredded Cheese
Lemon
Tartar Sauce
Onion diced, 1
Lemons juiced, 2
Cream cheese, 1
Wasabi paste, 3 tbsp
Cucumber diced, 1
Mayo, 1 cup
Pickle relish, 1/4 cup
Instructions
To begin, use Grilla Grills All Purpose Rub on both sides of the catfish fillet. While you're making the sauce, put the seasoned fillets put it in the fridge. To begin, finely chop 1 white onion, then place it in a mixing dish. Mix one piece of cream cheese & one cup of mayonnaise in a mixing bowl and stir until thoroughly mixed. Add three tablespoons of wasabi paste or sauce to a quart of dill pickle relish.

Roll two lemons gently on your cutting board, squeeze the juice into the cup, and avoid the seeds.

Finally, toss in your diced cucumber and season with a pinch of AP Rub or salt and black pepper to suit. Set away from your combination in the refrigerator until you're ready to serve it.

Preheat your Grilla to 350 ° F, and grease your grill grates to protect your fish from sticking. There's no need to turn your fish once it's on the grill. Simply let them set until one side is scorched, then return to check on them after approximately 10 minutes.

After you've removed your fish from smoker, it's time to assemble your tacos! Cut a piece of fish and put it in your tortilla, then top with purple cauliflower for crunch, your preferred shredded cheese, and a dab of tartar sauce to complete. Enjoy.

5.184 Cajun Crab Stuffed Shrimp & Jicama Corn Salad Recipe

Total Time: 30 Mins, Servings: 4
Ingredients
Stuffed shrimp
Lime zest
Red onion
Lump crab meat
Lime juice
Minced Garlic Seasoning
Jalapeno
Bacon
Ritz Crackers
Red onion & jalapeno
Instructions
Chop the cartilage from the crab. Wrap the items with bacon and serve. Grill till golden brown.

Mayonnaise, tiger sauce, chili sauce, Creole mustard, lemon zest, scallions, lemon juice and salt, minced garlic, chopped capers, minced celery, salt & black pepper Chill all of the ingredients together. Salad with jicama and corn.

Jicama, corn on the cob diced Lime juice, lime zest, black beans, cumin, carrots, cilantro, basil, scallions, lime juice, bell pepper, red pepper & corn on the cob should be grilled.

Rinse the black beans well. Chill the ingredients after mixing them.

5.185 Grilled Seafood Delight with Kickin Corn Maque Choux

Total Time: 55 Mins, Servings: 4
Ingredients
Alaska Salmon Filets, 1 ½ pound
Cream 4-6 tbs, 1/3 cup
Jalapeno pepper-diced, 2
Alaska Prawns, 1lb
Unsalted butter
Alaska crab legs, 6
Bell pepper, ¾
Red onion, 1
Blackening seasoning, 3 tbs
Lime, 1
Fresh corn, 5
Bell pepper, ¾
Fresh dill, 1 tbs
Salt
Black pepper
Olive oil
Water, ¼ cup
Instructions
Reduce the cream by 12 percent in a pot on the grill. Remove the husk from the corn and de-silk it. Using a little coating of olive oil, salt, & crushed black pepper, lightly coat the corn. Cook for 20-30 minutes on the grill. Remove the corn from the comb.

2 tbs butter in a separate skillet, melt over medium heat, chopped onions and diced peppers, sauté until soft. Cook for another 1-2 minutes after adding the corn, a sprinkle of cayenne, and the cream. Remove from the equation.

Snow Crab, Prawns, and Blackened Salmon Cut salmon fillets into 6 4–6-ounce pieces, blot dry, and season on both sides with a little salt & blackening spice. 12 tbs olive oil & 2 tbs butter, heated on medium-high (On the grill, use a cast-iron skillet.)

Sauté salmon until it's two-thirds done on one side, then turn it (internal temp should be about 140 degrees when done, allow to rest.) Grill the shrimp until done, seasoning them with blackening seasoning. Use the flesh from the legs of snow crabs, separated into one piece for each leg. Season with the same seasoning as the shrimp on the grill.

Remove everything except a little amount of butter and oil from the skillet. Return Corn Maque Choux to skillet with 14 cup water and 1 teaspoon blackening seasoning to taste. To taste, add lime zest and a dash of lime juice.

Heat until all of the water has evaporated. Serve Salmon, Prawns, and Snow Crab with Kickin Corn Maque Choux. Dill and parsley should be sprinkled on top.

5.186 Grilled Mahi Fish Tacos with Creamy Chipotle Sauce Recipe

Total Time: 1 Hr, Servings: 8
Ingredients
Mahi Mahi, 2 to 3 lb.
Corn tortillas, 8
Grilla AP Rub, 3 tbsp
Tomato chopped, 1
Limes, 2
Cabbage shredded, ¼ head
Chipotle Sauce
Dried dill, ¼ tsp
Mayonnaise, ½ Cup
Dried oregano, ½ tsp
Ground cumin, ¼ tsp
Greek yogurt, 1/3 Cup
Salt & pepper

Instructions
Make the chipotle sauce first. In a blender, purée all of the ingredients until smooth. Keep it refrigerated until you're ready to use it. Preheat the Grilla, Silverbac or Kong to 300° F. Dry your fish with a paper towel before applying the rub. Cook the fish for 5 to 7 minutes on each side of the Grilla Grills. If your fish is thick, you may need additional time.
Serve the fish with cabbage, onion, tomato, and a large dollop of chipotle sauce with a squeeze of lemon juice on warm tortillas.

5.187 Grilled Salmon with Honey Sriracha Lime Glaze
Total Time: 40 Mins, Servings: 4
Ingredients
Salmon, 4-6 pieces
Honey, ¼ Cup
Olive oil, 1/3 Cup
Grilla AP Rub, ¼ Cup
Lime juice, 2 tbsp
Sriracha, 2 tbsp
Instructions
Pat the salmon dry with a paper towel. Brush the fish
using olive oil and season with salt and pepper. Preheat the Grilla Grill at 300°F. Place the fish flat-side up on the grill. Flip the fish once the grill marks appear. This should only take 5 to 8 minutes for each side to prepare. Lift one side of fish with a spatula to inspect for grill marks. As the fish cooks, it will become more delicate, so proceed with caution.
Begin coating the glaze on the fish after it has been flipped. The fish is done when it feels firm and has grill marks on both sides. If you want your salmon to be rarer, remove it from the grill sooner. You don't want to overheat it, but the glazing will help salvage any portions that are dry.
Serve the salmon with the remaining honey sriracha salmon glaze on the side.

5.188 Grilled Shrimp Bruschetta with Balsamic Glaze
Total Time: 30 Mins, Servings: 3
Ingredients
Tomatoes, 6
Bell pepper diced, ½
Basil, ¼
Garlic minced, 4 cloves
Balsamic vinegar, 1 tbsp
Salt, ¼ tsp
Mozzarella shredded, 1 Cup
Grilla AP Rub 1 tbsp
Black pepper, ¼ tsp
Extra virgin olive oil, ¼ Cup
Butter, 1/3 Cup
French baguette, 1
Shrimp, 15-20
Instructions
Toss tomatoes, basil, garlic, balsamic vinegar, bell pepper, salt & pepper in a large mixing basin. Refrigerate for 30 minutes after covering with plastic wrap. To make the balsamic glaze, combine all of the ingredients in a pan and cook over medium heat, continues to pull to dissolve the sugar. Bring to the boil, then lower to a low heat setting. Cook until the glaze has been reduced by half. The back of a spoon should be thoroughly coated with glaze. Remove from the oven and set aside to cool.
Preheat the Grilla Grill from 275°F to 300°F. If you have a set of Cook Grates, you may use these to grill the bread.

To increase surface area, cut bread into 12-inch slices with a little bias. Clean your shrimp and remove the tails if they haven't previously been deveined and cleaned. Toss with the remaining 14 cup olive oil as well as rub in a plastic bag and shake thoroughly. While you grill the bread, let it rest for approximately 20 minutes.
Brush each side of the bread with melted butter just before placing it on the Grilla. You don't want to burn over or the bread, so grill each side until it's gently toasted. Remove the cooked bread from the grill and put it aside.
You have a few choices for grilling the shrimp.
Thread them onto a few skewers and cook them directly on the grill grates.
Place a piece of foil on the counter and fry them there.
Preheat the grill and cook them in a cast-iron pan.

5.189 Lemon Ginger Grilled Shrimp Recipe
Total Time: 2 Hrs 30 Mins, Servings: 8
Ingredients
Jumbo shrimp, 3 lbs
Olive oil, ½ Cup
Sesame oil, 2 tsp
Lemon juice, ¼ Cup
Onion chopped, 1
Garlic peeled, 2 cloves
Ginger, 1
Cilantro, 2 tbsp
Grilla AP Rub, 3 tbsp
Skewers, 12 to 15
Instructions
To save time and effort, combine the olive oil, garlic, ginger, lemon juice, cilantro, & rub in a blender or food processor and mix until smooth. A little quantity of this mixture should be set aside for final brushing. Take the remaining sauce and pour it into a bowl with the shrimp. Toss to coat, then cover and chill for 1-2 hours. Preheat the Grilla to around 250° F. Using skewers, thread the shrimp onto the skewers. To keep them secure, thread them between the tail & head region. To allow for skewer flipping, keep them all set down in the same direction. Remove any leftover marinade and discard.
Grill the shrimp for 3-4 minutes on each side or until they are opaque. Brush with the remaining sauce. If you want your shrimp to be more colorful, add 1 tbsp of BBQ sauce to the mix.

5.190 Lobster Tails and Herb Butter Recipe
Total Time: 55 Mins, Servings: 2
Ingredients
Lobster Tails
Fresh Basil, ½ Cup
Olive Oil
Butter, 1 lb
Grilla Grills Rub, 1 tbsp
Instructions
Breaking the lobster tails in two is the first step. Place the lobster on your cutting board upside down and cut through the center
with a sharp chef's knife. After you've cracked open the initial layer, gradually crack the remainder of it open.
Pour one stick of butter into a mixing basin once it has melted. 12 cup fresh sliced basil + 1 tablespoon Grilla Grill's Rub - add more to taste if you want a stronger flavor. Combine all ingredients in a mixing bowl and put them aside.
Preheat the Kong to 275°F. Consider using a burner for cooking the lobster over indirect heat since it will cook faster. Apply a coating of olive oil from each
lobster tail before putting it on the grill using a brush. Apply a

coating of oil to the grates in which each tail will fall as well. Put lobster tail flesh-side down on a baking sheet and bake for 5 minutes. You'll want to stay nearby and check on them every minute or so. When the shells acquire a beautiful reddish-orange hue, and the flesh turns milky white, the tails are done. Finish with a dollop of herb butter and serve.

5.191 Quick Hot Smoked Salmon
Total Time: 5 Hrs. 30 Mins, Servings: 2
Ingredients
Fillet of Salmon
KOSHER salt 1 cup
Brown Sugar, 2 cups
Instructions
To create a dry brine, combine the salt and brown sugar.
Add the brine to the salmon's flesh side (just enough to uniformly coat the fish). Allow the fish to cure for 1-2 h at room temperature in the brine.
Preheat the Grilla Grills to 225 ° F.
Wipe away any extra moisture after the salmon has cured for 1-2 hours, but keep the brine on.
Place the salmon skin side down on a piece of foil in the smoker.
Smoke for 1 hour or until your internal temperature reaches 140 degrees.
Set aside for 10 minutes before serving.
The salmon will keep for 7 days in the refrigerator.

5.192 Red Snapper Los Grilla
Total Time: 2 Hrs 30 Mins, Servings: 8
Ingredients
Filets of Red Snapper, 4
Medium Onions, 2
Ancho Chili Powder, 1 tsp
Olive Oil, 1/3 Cup
Lime, 1
Salt, 1 tsp
Black Pepper, 1 tsp
Ponzu Sauce, 1/4 Cup
Chopped Cilantro, 3 tsp
Lime Zest, 1/2 tsp
Cumin, 1/2 tsp
Minced Garlic, 1 tsp
Instructions
After zesting your lime, slice it into slices. Break apart your onions after slicing them into extremely thin rings. The onions & lime slices will serve as a bed for the fish to cook on.
In a mixing bowl, combine all of the ingredients with olive oil. This combination should be thoroughly mixed. You'll want to whisk it once more immediately before applying it. You should be able to baste the fish approximately three times with this baste.
Preheat your grill to 350 degrees Fahrenheit. Place the fish in the basket and apply a thin layer of basting on it.
Return every 15 minutes or so to re-baste the fish. The thickness of fish will influence the cooking time. If your fillets are thinner, they will cook in approximately 30 minutes. Allow another 15-20 minutes if they are extremely thick. I don't always prepare Red Snapper and other firm-fleshed fish according to a schedule. Instead, I cook until the meat is firm.
Squeeze the flesh of fish with your index finger. It's finished when it feels solid and thick.

5.193 Swine Life's Smoked Parmesan Crusted Salmon
Total Time: 40 Mins, Servings: 4
Ingredients
Salmon, 1 pound
Chopped parsley, 2 tbsp
Melted butter, 2 tbsp
Parmesan, 1/4 cup
Mississippi Grit
Minced garlic, 2 tbsp
Grilla Grills rub
Instructions
To begin, preheat the Silverbac to 400 ° F. After that, place the salmon skin down on a chopping board to remove the skin. To remove the skin off the base of the salmon, gently work a fillet knife along the base of the fish.
Then, on both sides of the salmon, apply a medium coating of Mississippi Grit of your choice. Then sprinkle a small coating of Grilla Beef rub on top.
In a mixing dish, combine the Parmesan, melted butter, chopped parsley & minced garlic. Fill a foil boat with salmon. Spread the parmesan mixture
evenly over each piece of fish.
Place the fish on the Grilla Grills Silverbac, which has been warmed to 400 degrees, in a foil boat. Cook for 20 minutes, or until the temperature reaches 145 degrees.
This dish is guaranteed to become a family favorite, from the butter melting and slightly browning underneath the fish to the amazing parmesan garlic topping.

5.194 Sugar Cured Salmon
Total Time: 50 Mins, Servings: 3
Ingredients
Skinned salmon, 3 lbs
Grilla BBQ Sauce, 1/3 Cup
Sea salt, 1 ½ Cup
Grilla AP Rub, 2 tbsp
Brown sugar, 3 Cup
Instructions
To create your remedy, combine salt and brown sugar in a dish and massage together. Choose a pan or baking dish that is large enough to hold your salmon. At bottom of the bowl, sprinkle about a 14-inch layer of brown sugar. Put the salmon on top of this cure layer. Take the rest of the cure and wrap it around the fish. All sides of the salmon, including the top, should be covered. Refrigerate this dish for 4-6 hours after covering it.
Grab the plate from the fridge and place it on the counter. You'll see that all of the formerly dry brown sugar has become moist and muddy. This is the moisture content of the salmon after it has been dehydrated. You'll notice that the salmon's flesh is considerably firmer now.
Preheat the Grilla Grill at 275°F. Lower the temperature to 225°F and slow-smoke the fish for a more Smokey taste. Cook at 300 ° if you want a more grilled taste.
Take the fish from the cure and rinse off any excess cure gently before patting dry with paper towel.
Place the fish flat-side down on the Grilla. If you want, you may keep the fish flat-side down & then never flip it. This will reduce the likelihood of your fish breaking apart. It also produces excellent grill marks on one side while leaving the other side undercooked. This method is effective in ensuring that everyone receives their preferred kind of salmon. Some people like it less done, while others love a little char.
Around almost 15-20 minutes, if you're cooking at 275 to 300 °, your salmon will be almost done. Brush the meat with BBQ sauce at this stage. You may also use whatever glaze you

choose, from plain honey to teriyaki sauce. The sugar cure prepares the fish to complement almost any taste combination.

Remove the fish from the Grilla after it has reached the desired firmness. There's no need to wait for it to rest; you can plate it right away.

5.195 Tequila Lime Shrimp Tacos with Pineapple Pomegranate Salsa

Total Time: 1 Hr, Servings: 4
Ingredients
Tequila, 2 tbsp
Zest & juice, 4 limes
Crushed red pepper
Kosher salt, 2 tsp
Louisiana hot sauce, 1 tbsp
Extra virgin olive oil, 1/2 cup
Garlic cloves, 2
Ginger minced, 1 tsp
Pineapple, 1
Brown sugar, 1/4 cup
Napa cabbage, 1 cup
Alabama Gulf Shrimp, 2 lbs
Pomegranate, 1
Cilantro leaves, 2 tbsp
Corn tortillas, 6
Pineapple juice, 1/4 cup
Instructions
In a basin of room temperature water,
soak 6 wooden skewers.
Heat the grill to medium.
In a large mixing basin, whisk together the first 8 items until emulsified.
Peel the shrimp and remove the veins. Set aside after tossing in the marinade till thoroughly covered.
Cut the pineapple into ½-inch broad rings after removing the peel and core.
Brush both sides of each pineapple ring with brown sugar and cook until caramelized (2-3 mins per side).
Cut the pomegranate in half and beat the remaining sides with a wooden spoon over a big basin until all seeds fall out.
Toss the grilled pineapple with pomegranate seeds in a mixing dish.
Stir in the pineapple juice & cilantro until thoroughly combined.
Arrange shrimp evenly on skewers and cook for 2 minutes on each side.
Pour the leftover marinade into a medium bowl and put it on the grill's hottest section, bringing it to a boil. Allow to thick and decrease by 1/3 before turning off the heat.
Heat tortillas for approximately 30 seconds on each side of the grill. To assemble, spread Napa cabbage equally on tortillas. Drizzle approximately a spoonful of the reduced marinade over each. 1 skewer of shrimp and a heaping spoonful of pineapple pomegranate salsa on top of each.

5.196 BBQ Salmon with Bourbon Glaze

Total Time: 50 Mins, Servings: 4
Ingredients
Jim Beam Bourbon, 1 Cup
Minced garlic, 1/2 tsp
Blues Rub Seasoning, 2 Tbsp
Brown Sugar, 1/2 Cup
Worcestershire Sauce, 3 tsp
Ketchup, 1 Cup
Lemon Juice, 1 Tbsp
Apple Cider Vinegar, 1/4 Cup
Salt
Black Pepper, 1/2 tsp
Yellow Mustard, 1 Tbsp
Olive Oil, 1 Tbsp
Instructions
Preheat the grill to 350°F. I cook using a pellet grill.
To eliminate any moisture from your skinless salmon fillet, carefully dry it with a paper towel. Set aside after brushing every side with olive oil and dusting with Blues Hog Rub Seasoning. Incorporate the remaining ingredients in a mixing dish and well combine.
Place the salmon on grill for about 5 mins, just long enough for an outside crust to form. Cover the surface of the salmon liberally with the glaze mixture
and cook for about 10 minutes.
Cook for yet another 5-10 minutes after reglazing the top side and gently turning it over to glaze the other side. To avoid overcooking the salmon, choose how long
you would like to cook it based on thickness of fillet.
Recoat the top, then turn it over and recoat again. Check the interior temperature at this point; it should be 145 degrees F. Continue to grill until the temperature reaches this point. Serve and enjoy once the temperature has been achieved.

5.197 Smoked New England clam chowder

Total Time: 2 Hrs 30 Mins, Servings: 8
Ingredients
Clams Chopped, 4 Can
Whipping Cream, 2 Cup
Butter, 3 tbsp
Russet Potatoes, 1 Pound
Bacon, 6 Slices
Onion, 1
Stalk Celery, 2
Flour, 1/3 Cup
Bay Leaves, 2 Whole
Oyster Crackers
Clam Juice, 2 Cup
Fresh thyme, 1 tbsp
Salt & Pepper
Hot Sauce
Instructions
Drain the clams but save the liquid; put aside.
Prepare oven to 180°F and preheat for 15 min when ready to cook. If the clams haven't been cut, chop them up and put them out in a thin layer in a small foil pan or deep baking sheet. Place the clams on grill grate for 30 minutes to smoke.
Add the cream to the pan, along with 1 cup of the saved clam juice, and continue to smoke for another 30 minutes. Remove from the equation.
Preheat the Pit Boss to 325 degrees Fahrenheit. In a big heavy pot or Dutch oven, combine the butter and bacon. Cook until the butter has melted & the bacon is sizzling and releasing its fat.
Add the onion & celery and simmer, stirring periodically, for 5 to 10 minutes, or until softened. Salt & pepper to taste. (Don't forget to account for the saltiness of the bacon.)
Add the flour & cook for 5-8 minutes, constantly stirring, so the flour does not burn. Toss in the potatoes, clam juice from a bottle, bay leaves, and fresh thyme. Bring the mixture to a boil, then reduce to low heat and simmer until the potatoes are cooked. (Once the liquid boils, the potatoes will need 12-15 minutes to cook.)
Simmer for at least 5 minutes after adding the smoked clam & cream combination. Stir in a tiny quantity of instant potato flakes if the chowder is too thin. If it's too thick, thin it out with additional clam juice until it's a perfect consistency.
Season to taste, adding more salt & black pepper if necessary.

Remove the bay leaves and any fir stalks before serving, and mix in the parsley. Serve with oyster crackers and spicy sauce as a garnish. Enjoy! Cook times may vary based on the temperature of the oven and the ambient temperature.

5.198 Bourbon Bacon Stuffing

Total Time: 1 Hr 10 mins, Serving: 8
Ingredients
Butter, 1/2 Cup
Bacon, 1/2 Pound
Celery, 2 Stalk
Fresh Rosemary, 1 tbsp
Bourbon, 1/2 Cup
Thyme Leaves, 1 tbsp
Onion, 1 Large
Garlic, 1 Clove
4 Egg
Pumpernickel Bread, 1 Loaf
Chicken Stock, 1 Quart
Instructions
In a big, deep pan, fry the bacon until it is uniformly browned over medium heat. Using paper towels, absorb any excess liquid. Set aside the leftover bacon fat in a separate dish.
Melt the butter in the same skillet over medium heat. Cook, occasionally stirring, until the onion, diced celery, garlic, rosemary, and thyme are soft and translucent, approximately 5 minutes. Stir in the bacon fat that has been set aside.
In a large mixing bowl, put the pumpernickel bread cubes. Combine the eggs & onion mixture in a mixing bowl. Toss to distribute the ingredients properly.
In a mixing dish, combine the chicken stock plus bourbon. Put the chicken stock combination over bread mixture and adjust the consistency as needed. Mix all the ingredients evenly with your hands.
Grease a 9x13-inch baking dish lightly and pour the stuffing mixture equally into it.
Begin the Pit Boss in Smoke with the lid open till it fire is created when you're ready to cook. Preheat the oven to 350 °F and bake for 10 minutes with the lid covered.
Cooked for 45 minutes in the Pit Boss with the stuffing. Warm the dish before serving. Enjoy!

5.199 Baked Peach Cobbler

Total Time: 60 mins, Serving: 8
Ingredients
Yellow Peaches, 3 Pound
Butter, 2 tbsp
Sugar In Raw, 1 tbsp
Pit Boss Smoked Syrup, 1/4 Cup
Flour, 2/3 Cup
Cinnamon
Sugar, 1/2 Cup
Egg, 1 Whole
Salt to taste
Baking Powder, 3/4 tsp
Unsalted Butter, 1/2 Cup
Vanilla, 1/2 tsp
Instructions
Bring the Pit Boss to 350°F and heat for 15 minutes when you're ready to cook. 2 tablespoons melted butter inside a cast iron skillet Blend pear in Smoked Simple Syrup in a normal bowl and put in the preheated cast iron pan.
Now combine cinnamon, flour, baking powder, & salt in a small basin; put aside. Blend the butter and half a cup of sugar in a separate dish. Combine the egg and vanilla essence in a mixing bowl.
Now mix in flour mixture gradually. Spread the batter over top

of the peaches and finish with a sprinkling of raw sugar. Preheat the grill to 350°F and bake the cast iron for 40 - 45 minutes. * Have fun! Cooking times will vary
based on the temperature of the set and the ambient temperature.

5.200 Smoked Brisket Pot Pie

Total Time: 1 Hr, Serving: 8
Ingredients
Carrots, 2 Whole
Garlic, 1 Clove
Frozen Peas, 1/2 Cup
Cornstarch
1 Egg
Salt & Pepper
Beef Stock, 2 Cup
Butter, 2 tbsp
Yellow Onion, 1 Whole
Chopped Brisket, 2 Cup
Pearl Onions, 1 Cup
Frozen Pastry Dough, 1 Sheet
Instructions
In a medium stockpot, melt the butter. Add the carrots to the heated butter and cook for 10 to 15 minutes, until gently browned.
Cook for 5 to 7 minutes, or until the onion is soft and transparent. Sauté for another 30 seconds, or until the garlic is aromatic.
Combine the peas, onions, and chopped brisket in a mixing bowl. Bring the beef stock to a low simmer.
Simmer until the liquid has thickened enough just to cover the slotted spoon and has been reduced. Unless the sauce does not thicken, add a corn-starch slurry until it does. To taste, season with salt.
Fill an oven-safe baking dish halfway with the brisket mixture. Make incisions in the top of the pastry dough to allow air to escape.
In a separate bowl, whisk together the egg and brush the egg wash over the pastry.
Set the Pit Boss to 350°F and preheat for 15 minutes with the lid covered when you're ready to cook.
Bake for 45 minutes, or until the top is gently browned and bubbling, straight on the grill grate.
Allow 10 minutes for cooling before serving. Enjoy!

5.201 Baked Eggs in Bacon Nest

Total Time: 40 mins, Serving: 4
Ingredients
Eggs, 6 Whole
Bacon, 6 Strips
Pepper, 1/4 tsp
Salt, 1/4 tsp
Instructions
Once ready to cook, preheat the oven to 375 ° F and cook for 10-15 minutes with the lid covered.
Cook for 15 minutes upon that grill grate with bacon slices immediately on it. Move to a towel to absorb excess moisture. Using cooking spray, generously coat a muffin tin. One piece of bacon is used to line each muffin cup, and then one egg is cracked into each cup. Season salt and pepper to taste in each cup.
Cook for 15-10 min on the grill till the bacon gets crisp, the whites are barely set, and the yolk still is runny. Enjoy!

5.202 Sweet Smoked Salmon Jerky
Total Time: 5 Hrs 30 mins, Serving: 6
Ingredients
Kosher Salt, 3/4 Cup
Water, 2 Quart
Dark Brown Sugar, 4 Cup
Maple Syrup, 2 Cup
Salmon Fillet, 1 (2-3 Lb)
Morton Tender, 1 Cup
Instructions
Combine 2 quarts of water, salts, curing salt (if used), brown sugar, and 1 cup maple syrup in a large non - reactive mixing basin. To absorb the salts and sugar, stir with such a long-handled spoon.
Cut the salmon into 1/2-inch-thick slices on a cutting board with a sharp, sharp blade, keeping the short side perpendicular to you. To put it another way, making your cuts from top to bottom. (If the fish is frozen, this is much simpler.) Cut each strip into 3 - 5-inch lengths crosswise.
Place the strips inside the brine and weigh them down with just a plate or ice bag. Freeze for 12 hours after wrapping in plastic wrap.
Once ready to cook, preheat the Pit Boss to 180°F for 15 minutes with the lid closed. If Super Smoke is available, use it for the best taste.
Drain and remove the brine from the salmon strips. Organize the salmon strips on the grill grate in a single layer. Smoke the jerky for 5 to 6 hours, or until it is dry, but just not rock-hard. As you bite into it, you want it to give.
Brush the salmon strips on both sides with the leftover cup of maple syrup and 1/4 cup of warm water midway through the smoking time.
Whereas the jerky is still heated, move to a resealable bag. Allow the jerky to rest at room temperature for an hour. Squeeze any air out of the bag and store the jerky in the refrigerator. Enjoy!

5.203 Prosciutto Wrapped Dates with Marcona Almonds
Total Time: 15 mins, Serving: 8
Ingredients
Marcona Salted Almonds, 1 Container
Prosciutto, 8 Ounce
Limes, 2
For Serving Flake Salt
Medjool Dates, 24 Whole
Olive Oil, 2 tbsp
For Serving Honey
Instructions
Preheat the Pit Boss to 400°F for 15 minutes with the lid closed when ready to cook.
Preheat the grill by placing a big cast iron pan on it. Slice a slit lengthwise through the top within each date with a tiny paring knife. Get rid of the pit. Replacing the pits with 1–2 Marcona almonds, press the dates together with your fingertips to seal them.
Cut the prosciutto lengthwise into 24 pieces. Wrap each date by placing one from the bottom of just a strip of prosciutto and rolling the prosciutto around it to cover it, leaving a little of the date visible on either end.
In a hot cast iron pan, pour 2 tablespoons of olive oil. Put the dates in pan and heat, rotating as required, until the prosciutto is seared on both sides, approximately 2 - 3 minutes total. Carefully remove the skillet from the grill after the prosciutto is crispy.
Squeeze the limes over the pan to soak the citrus zest into olive oil and over to the dates. On a serving plate, arrange the dates. Serve some flake salt, a drizzle of extra virgin olive oil, and honey. Enjoy!

5.204 Sweet Smoked Salmon
Total Time: 3 Hrs 10 Mins, Servings: 4
Ingredients
Salmon Side, 1 (3-4 Lb)
Kosher Salt, 1/2 Cup
White Sugar, 1/2 Cup
Ground Black Pepper, 1 tsp
Brown Sugar, 1/2 Cup
Rub
Paprika, 1/4 Cup
Pure Sea Salt, 1 tbsp
Garlic Powder, 1 tbsp
Brown Sugar, 1/3 Cup
Instructions
Take out all of the pin bones from the fish.
Combine white, brown sugar, sugar, black pepper and kosher salt in a small bowl.
Cover a long, wide baking sheet with a layer of tin foil. Cover the tin foil layer with a layer of plastic wrap. 1/3 of the mixture of the curing ingredients should be sprinkled over tin foil. Place the salmon fillet on the top of cure mixture, skin side down, and distribute another third of the cure mixture over the flesh side of the fish.
Place the next salmon fillet on top of the first, flesh side down. Place another piece of plastic wrap on top of each fillet, followed by another foil layer, and wrap up the ends to enclose the salmon and cure firmly in the plastic and foil wrap. Refrigerate the whole baking sheet and cover it with another baking sheet. Place a heavy object on the top of the baking pan to equally distribute the weight over the salmon fillets.
Place the weighted salmon in the refrigerator for 12-24 hours to cure. Erase the salmon from foil and thoroughly rinse the cure off the fillets. Using paper towels, pat dry.
In a small dish, combine the rub ingredients. Apply the rub on flesh side of salmon fillets & gently pat it in. Shake off any excess rub, then put the fillets flat on a baking sheet in a dry and cool location for 1 hour to rest.
When ready to cook, preheat the Pit Boss to 180°F with the lid closed for almost 15 minutes. If Super Smoke is available, use it for the best taste.
Smoke the salmon fillets for 1-3 hours, or until a thermometer set into the thickest portion of the fish reads 140°F. Keep a careful eye on the grill temperature to ensure it does not get beyond 180°F. If required, place a tray of ice next to the salmon on the grill to lower the temperature.
Remove the fish from the grill and thinly slice it. Serve with your favorite toppings. Enjoy.

Chapter 6: Appetizers Recipes

6.1 Baked Garlic Bread

Total Time: 30 Mins, Servings: 4
Ingredients
1 Baguette
1/2 Cup Softened Butter
1/2 cup Mayonnaise
4 Tbsp Minced Italian Parsley
6 Clove Minced Garlic
Chile Flakes
Salt
1 cup Mozzarella Cheese
1/2 cup Parmesan Cheese
Instructions
When ready to cook, preheat the Pit Boss to 190°C and cover with a fifteen-minute lid.
Place the baguette on the chopping board and cut it in half (lengthwise).
In a mixing bowl, combine mayonnaise, butter, garlic, salt, chili flakes, and parsley. Mix everything up well.
Spread the butter mixture on the bread halves and sprinkle with parmesan and mozzarella cheese.
Place the baguette on the grill. Cook for 15 to 25 mins on the grill. Serve immediately.

6.2 Lynchburg Bacon

Total Time: 30 Mins, Servings: 4
Ingredients
Bacon 1 Lb
Tennessee Whiskey 1 Cup
Apple Juice
Poultry Rub & Pit Boss Pork 1 Tbsp
All-Purpose Flour, 3/4 Cup
Brown Sugar,1/3 Cup
1 Tsp Ground Black Pepper
Instructions
Separate the bacon pieces and place them in the large resealable bag.
In a mixing bowl, combine the apple juice/whiskey, Poultry Rub, and Pit Boss Pork. Pour the apple juice/whiskey over the bacon slices, pushing the bag down to ensure that every piece is covered.
Set aside for more than thirty mins.
On the wax paper sheet, sift the brown sugar, black pepper, and flour. After that, transfer it to the other resealable bag.
Drain your bacon and add it to the flour mixture, a few pieces at a time.
Shake the bag to coat each piece evenly; then place in a single layer on the baking pan.
When you're ready to cook, preheat the Pit Boss to 190°C and shut the lid for fifteen mins.
Bake your bacon for 20- 25 mins, or until it becomes golden brown and crunchy. Enjoy.

6.3 Chorizo Armadillo Eggs

Total Time: 60 Mins, Servings: 8
Ingredients
4 Oz Cream Cheese
1/2 Cup Shredded Cheddar Cheese
1 Minced coriander
Six, Halved Jalapeño
12 Lb Ground Pork
12 Tbsp Poultry Rub & Pit Boss Pork
Instructions
When you're ready to cook, preheat the Pit Boss to 160°C and shut the lid for fifteen mins.
In a stand mixer bowl, combine the cheddar, cilantro, cream cheese, and beat with the paddle attachment until thoroughly combined. After cutting the jalapeño in half again, spoon the cheese mixture into each half.
Fill the 14 (0.25) thick discs with 1/4 cup of flattening & chorizo. Cover the jalapeno cheese-stuffed jalapeno with the sausage and shape it into an egg shape in the middle. Repeat with any remaining jalapenos.
Season the chorizo balls with the Poultry & Pork rub.
Place the chorizo balls directly on the grill grate and cook for thirty mins, turning once, until the color changes to lightly browned and cooked through.

6.4 Bison Summer Sausage & Smoked Wild Boar

Total Time: 4 Hrs 10 Mins, Servings: 4
Ingredients
1/2 Lb Ground Wild Boar
1/2 Lb Ground Wild Bison
1 Tbsp Morton Tender
1 Tbsp Kosher Salt
Meat Cure
1/2 Tsp Mustard Seeds
1/2 Tsp Black Pepper
1/2 Tsp Garlic Powder
Instructions
Combine all ingredients in a small bowl but be careful not to overmix. Place the mixture in the refrigerator for the night.
Form the meat into a log and wrap it with plastic wrap. Smooth out the log by turning the plastic tight ends (use the hands). Unwrap carefully to maintain a smooth form.
When you're ready to cook, set the Pit Boss to 107 degrees Fahrenheit and shut the lid for fifteen mins.
Place directly on the grill grate and cook for 3 to 4 hrs. Remove it from the grill and set it aside to cool for 1 hr at room temperature.
Once it has cooled, wrap it in plastic wrap, keep it cold, or slice and serve.

6.5 Southwestern Filled Peppers

Total Time: 55 Mins, Servings: 6
Ingredients
6 Large Red Bell Pepper
1 Lb Ground Beef
1 Diced Onion
12 Garlic Chopped
12 Tbsp Pit Boss Cajun Rub
Tomato Salsa, 2/3 Cup
12 Cup Cooked Rice

1 Cup Drained & Rinsed Black Beans
1 Cup Ears Fresh Corn
Grated Colby & Monterey, 1 1/2 Cup
Jack Cheese
Instructions
Rinse each pepper coarsely under cold running water. Using a knife, cut each in half lengthwise and remove the ribs and seeds.
To make the stuffing, follow these steps: Brown the ground beef in a large frying pan and break it up with a spoon (wooden).
Sauté the garlic and onion for 12 to 3 mins. Cook, occasionally stirring, until the salsa, Pit Boss Cajun Rub, black beans, corn, and rice are well combined, about five mins. Fill each pepper half with the filling.
Set the temperature to 175°C and cook for ten to fifteen mins with the lid covered.
Arrange the peppers, filled side up, on a grill grate, evenly spaced between the rungs.
After that, bake for around 40 mins.
Drizzle the grated cheese over the peppers evenly, then bake for 5 mins.

6.6 Paprika Chicken Grilled along with Jalapeño Salsa

Total Time: 60 Mins, Servings: 6
Ingredients
Main
6 Whole Chicken Legs
12 Tbsp Olive Oil
1 Tbsp Smoked Paprika
1 Tsp Ground Coriander
1 Zested Lime
Sea Salt, 1 1/2 Tsp
1 Tsp Cracked Black Pepper
Jalapeño Salsa
4 Med Jalapeños
4 Clove Peeled Garlic
6 Sprig Cilantro
12 Green Onions
1 Tbsp Lime Juice
12 Tbsp Pure Maple Syrup
1/2 Cup Distilled White Vinegar
1 Tsp Sea Salt
Instructions
Get your chicken ready. In a large mixing bowl, combine the chicken, smoked paprika, olive oil, lime
zest, coriander, pepper, and sea salt. Cover it with plastic wrap and marinate for 4 hrs in the refrigerator.
When you're ready to cook, set the Pit Boss to 175°C and shut the lid for fifteen mins.
Arrange the chicken directly on the grill grates, skin side up. Cook for 40-45 mins, or until it is properly grilled.
While the chicken is cooking, make the jalapeno salsa. Place the peppers directly on the grill grates (next to the chicken) and cook for 25-30 mins. Remove the stems from the jalapenos and mix with the other salsa ingredients and peppers until smooth.
Serve the chicken with jalapeno salsa, which is hot and spicy.

6.7 Bacon Cheddar (Smashed) Baby Potatoes

Total Time: 1 Hr 10 Mins, Servings: 6
Ingredients
12 Lb Potatoes
Olive Oil, 1/3 Cup
1 Tsp Garlic Powder
1 Tsp Onion Powder
1 Tbsp Smoked Paprika
1 Tbsp Dried Chives
12 Cups Chopped Cheddar Cheese
1 Lb Crumbled Cooked Bacon
1 Chopped Bunch Spring Onion
Sour Cream, 1/4 Cup
Instructions
Boil or microwave young potatoes until fork soft, then set aside to cool to room temperature.
Combine the garlic powder, olive oil, paprika, chives, and onion powder in a mixing bowl. In a big mixing Bowl. Toss in the potatoes to coat. Place the potatoes on a cookie sheet coated with baking release paper. To flatten the potatoes, smash them with the spatula.
When you're ready to cook, preheat the Pit Boss to 230°C and shut the lid for fifteen mins.
Grill the potatoes for 20 to 30 mins, turning once, until golden and crispy. Bacon, onions, and cheddar cheese are added to the mix. Cook for another ten mins on the grill.
Remove off the grill and top with more green onions and sour cream. Now take pleasure in it.

6.8 Cooked Taco Skillet Dip

Total Time: 55 Mins, Servings: 10
Ingredients
12 Tbsp Vegetable Oil
1 Diced Red Onion
Kosher Salt
12 Lb Ground Beef
12 Tbsp Taco Seasoning
Fifteen Oz Roasted Tomatoes with their Juices
Fifteen Oz Rinsed & Drained Black Beans
4 Oz Diced Green Chiles
Green Onions, sliced
1/2 Cup White Rice
Instructions
When you're ready to cook, set the Pit Boss to 200°C and shut the lid for fifteen mins. On the grate of the grill, Preheat the 12-inch cast-iron skillet. While the grill is getting ready to cook,
When the grill reaches 200°C, turn it off. In a skillet, combine the onion, oil, and 1/2 tsp salt. Cook, whisking once or twice, until the onions are soft, about ten mins.
Cook for 15 to 20 mins, bling the meat with the back of a wooden spoon until it is browned. Combine the taco seasonings in a mixing bowl.
Combine the beans, tomatoes, green chiles, rice, and 1/2 of a tomato can of water in a mixing bowl. Make sure the rice is well submerged in the liquid by whisking it in.
With a tightly fitting cover, cook for 20 to 25 mins, or until the rice is fully cooked, covered in the skillet.
Remove the lid and pour the cheese over the top of the dip. Return the pan to the grill, uncovered, until the cheese has melted.
Season with a generous dollop of crema and a sprinkling of green onions, if preferred. It's great with corn chips.

6.9 Red Onion Jam, Duck Confit, & Goat Cheese Crostini

Total Time: 50 Mins, Servings: 6
Ingredients
12 Tbsp Butter
3 Sliced Red Onions
12 Minced Garlic clove
Sugar, 1/4 Cup
Pepper
Freshly Cracked Black & Sea Salt
Dry Red Wine, 1/4 Cup

1 Tbsp Apple Cider Vinegar
1 Zested Lemon
4 Prepared Duck Confit Legs
1 Sliced Thin Baguette
1/2 Cup Crushed Herb Goat Cheese
Olive Oil
Pomegranate Arils, 1/4 Cup
Instructions
When you're ready to cook, set the Pit Boss to 175°C and shut the lid for fifteen mins.
Reduce the heat to low and melt the butter in a 3-quart pan. Once the butter has melted, add the garlic, onions, and sugar, followed by the sea salt. Whisk well, cover, and simmer for 20-30 mins, or until softened and caramelized. Please remove it from the heat and whisk in the red wine, vinegar, and lemon zest.
Bakery release paper should be used to line the cookie sheet. Place the duck legs on a grill with the skin side up. Cook for 8 to 10 mins, or until the skin starts to crisp and the flesh easily falls apart with a fork. 12 forks are needed to chop the meat.
Meanwhile, drizzle each baguette slice with olive oil and season with salt, pinch, and pepper. Place on a grill and cook until grill marks appear, and the bread becomes golden.
With red onion jam, chopped duck, goat cheese, grilled baguette, and pomegranate, assemble the crostini.

6.10 Cooked Teff Flatbread along with Zhoug Sauce

Total Time: 15 Mins, Servings: 4
Ingredients
Flatbread
Teff Flour, 1 1/2 Cup
Water, 1 3/4 Cup
Salt, 1/2 Tsp
1 Egg
Olive Oil
Zhoug Sauce
4 Med Chopped Garlic
12 Bunch Chopped Fresh Cilantro
12 Stemmed & Seeded Jalapeño
1 Tsp Kosher Salt
1 Tsp Ground Cardamom
1 Tsp Ground Cumin
1/2 Tsp Red Pepper Flakes
Additional-Virgin Olive Oil, 3/4 Cup
Lemon Juiced, 3/4 Cup
Instructions
In a glass container, combine the 1-3/4 cup water and the teff flour. Allow warming overnight, loosely covered.
When you're ready to cook, set the Pit Boss to 175°C and shut the lid for fifteen mins. While the grill preheats, place the cast iron pan directly on the grate. Whisk the egg and salt into the fermented teff mixture. Lightly oil the cast iron pan. Once the oil is hot, put a little amount of batter into the skillet and quickly flip it around.
Cook till it has firmed up on both sides. Serve right away.
In the bowl of a food processor, combine all the ingredients and process until smooth.

6.11 Pit Boss Mandarin Wings

Total Time: 35 Mins, Servings: 2
Ingredients
1 Bottle Mandarin Orange Sauce
Pit Boss Chicken Rub
Pit Boss Beef Rub
12 Lb Flats & Drumettes Separated Chicken Wings
Instructions
Coat chicken wings with mandarin sauce. Drizzle the wings with Pit Boss Chicken Rub and Pit Boss Beef Rub. Marinate for 30 mins.
When you're ready to cook, set the Pit Boss to 175°C and shut the lid for fifteen mins.
Place straight wings on the grill grate and cook for thirty mins.

6.12 Bacon-Wrapped Chicken Wings

Total Time: 1 Hr 30 Mins, Servings: 6
Ingredients
12 Lb Chicken Wings
Twenty-4 Oz Beer
12 Tsp Red Pepper Flakes
1 Lb Bacon
Pit Boss Cajun Shake
Instructions
The tips of the wings should be cut off and put aside.
Cut the skin tab between the drumette and the flat to keep the wing straight and easy to cover.
Place the wings in a large mixing Bowl and top with the red pepper flakes and beer. Refrigerate it for 1 day before grilling. Remove the wings from the brine and pat them dry. Add a good shake of Pit Boss's Cajun on the top.
Wrap each wing with a slice of bacon.
When you're ready to cook, preheat the grill to 230°C.
Place the wings directly on the grill grate, cover the top, and cook for around thirty mins. Cook for another thirty mins, or until the bacon is crispy and the chicken is cooked through.

6.13 Grilled Shrimp Cocktail

Total Time: 15 Mins, Servings: 2
Ingredients
Main
12 Lb Shrimp with Tails
12 Tbsp Olive Oil
1 Tsp Old Bay Seasoning
Minced Italian Parsley
Cocktail Sauce
1/2 Cup Ketchup
12 Tbsp Prepared Horseradish
12 Tbsp Lemon Juice
Ground Black Pepper
Kosher Salt
Instructions
When you're ready to cook, set the Pit Boss to 175°C and shut the lid for fifteen mins.
Rinse the shrimp in a colander and pat dry. In a large mixing Bowl, combine the shrimp, oil, and Old Bay Seasoning. Toss until shrimp are well coated, then place on a cookie sheet that will fit.
Place the cookie sheet with the shrimp on the grill and cook until opaque, about five to seven mins.
Combine horseradish, lemon juice, and ketchup in a cocktail sauce. Season with salt and pepper.
Combine the cocktail sauce and grilled shrimp in a mixing bowl. Italian parsley, minced, is used to season the shrimp and sauce.

6.14 Grilled Shrimp Brochette

Total Time: 40 Mins, Servings: 6
Ingredients
1 Lb Peeled & deveined Additional-Large Shrimp
6 Whole Fresh Jalapeños
8 Oz Jack Cheese (Block Monterey)
1 Lb Bacon
12 Tbsp Gospel All Purpose Rub

Oil
Instructions
Set aside the Fillet Shrimp that has been opened. Slice your jalapenos into small slivers once cored. Slivers of cheese-like slivers should be cut (as the peppers). Cut your bacon pieces in half.
1 jalapeno slice and 1 cheese slice should be placed into each shrimp. Half a slice of bacon should be used to cover the loaded shrimp.
After the shrimps have been cooked, gently coat them with the Gospel (All-Purpose Rub).
When you're ready to cook, preheat the Pit Boss to 210°C and shut the lid for fifteen mins.
Lightly oil your grill grate, then place shrimp directly on it. Cook for about 20 mins, flipping halfway through. The color of the shrimp should become pink, and the bacon should crisp up.
Allow it to rest for 10 mins after removing it from the grill.

6.15 Roasted Garlic Herb Fries
Total Time: 60 Mins, Servings: 4
Ingredients
4 Whole Russet Potatoes
1 Tsp Salt
12 Tbsp Avocado Oil
1 Tsp Minced Rosemary
1 Tsp Chopped Thyme
12 Minced Garlic clove
12 Tsp Flake Salt
1 Tsp Chopped Parsley
Instructions
When you're ready to cook, preheat the Pit Boss to 210°C and shut the lid for fifteen mins.
Cut potatoes into fries and put immediately in a frost
water bath with 1 tsp salt for 15 to 13 mins.
In a bowl, combine the rosemary, oil, garlic, and thyme. Remove the potatoes from the freezing water and thoroughly dry them.
Toss the potatoes in the oil mixture and arrange them in a single layer on 12 to 3 parchment-lined cookie sheets. Drizzle the flake salt over the fries.
Place cookie sheets on the grill and roast for thirty mins, then flip the fries and cook for another fifteen mins, or until golden and crispy. Serve with a parsley garnish.
Enjoy it now with your favorite dipping sauce.

6.16 Grilled Prosciutto Covered Asparagus
Total Time: 30 Mins, Servings: 6
Ingredients
12 Bunch Asparagus
Salt & Pepper
4 Oz Prosciutto
Olive Oil
1 Med Zested Lemon
12 Tbsp Divided Balsamic Vinegar
3 Tbsp Toasted Pine Nuts
Instructions
When you're ready to cook, set the Pit Boss to 200°C and shut the lid for fifteen mins.
Clean and dry the asparagus. Cut the bottom third of the asparagus stalks off and discard.
Cover 4 to 5 stalks with prosciutto and place on a baking sheet. Add salt, olive oil, lemon zest, and pepper to the asparagus.
Place the cookie sheet on the grill and heat. After five mins, turn the asparagus and drizzle with 1 tbsp balsamic vinegar.
Return to the grill and cook for another five to eight mins, or until the prosciutto is crispy and the asparagus is fully cooked.

Toss the asparagus with pine nuts and any remaining balsamic vinegar.

6.17 Pit Boss Smoked Guacamole
Total Time: 55 Mins, Servings: 6
Ingredients
Seven Whole Seeded & Peeled Avocados
1 Whole Poblano Pepper
4 Whole Husked Ears Corn
Chopped Cilantro, 1/4 Cup
Chopped Tomato, 1/4 Cup
Chopped Red Onion, 1/4 Cup
12 Tbsp Lime Juice
1 Tsp Cumin
1 Tbsp Minced Garlic
Chile Powder
Pepper & salt
Instructions
When you're ready to cook, set the Pit Boss to 90°C and shut the lid for fifteen mins.
Place avocados cut side up on the grill grate and cook for 10 mins.
Remove the avocados from the Pit Boss and raise the temperature to 230°C.
Place the corn and poblano pepper on the grill grate in a straight line. Cook for around 15 to 20 mins.
Slice scorched corn from cobs and put it aside.
Wrap the poblano pepper in plastic wrap and wait 10 mins before removing the peel. Put the pepper into the corn kernels after dying it.
In a large mixing bowl, lightly mash smoked avocados (leaving a few pieces). Combine the corn, peppers, and any other ingredients in a mixing bowl.

6.18 Sweet Potato (Grilled) Planks
Total Time: 25 Mins, Servings: 6
Ingredients
Five Large Sweet Potatoes
1 Tbsp Canola Oil
1 Tsp Salt
1 Tsp Pepper
1/2 Tsp Onion Powder
Instructions
Clean and peel your sweet potatoes before cutting them into eighths (lengthwise).
Season with salt, oil, onion powder, and pepper.
When ready to cook, set the Pit Boss to 250°C and cook for fifteen mins with the lid closed.
Place the sweet potatoes on the grill.
Transfer them to the center of the grill and cook for another 15 to 20 mins.

6.19 Baked Artichoke Dip
Total Time: 1 Hr 15 Mins, Servings: 8
Ingredients
Ten Peeled Garlic clove
1/2 cup Parmesan Cheese
Olive Oil
1/2 cup Asiago Cheese
1/2 cup Fontina Cheese
1/2 Cup Provol1 Cheese
8 Oz Cream Cheese
1/2 cup Mayonnaise
1 Can Artichokes
1 Can pepper
Instructions

When you're ready to cook, preheat the grill to 175°C for 15 mins. Garlic cloves should be placed in a small grill-safe pan with enough olive oil to cover them. Place it on the grill and cook for 35 to 40 mins. When the garlic is smooth enough to be pressed with a fork, it is ready. Remove it from the grill and set it aside to cool.

After the oil and garlic have cooled, separate them, and keep them separate to use in future recipes. Place garlic in a Bowl and smash with a fork until it forms a smooth paste.

Combine the asiago, parmesan, fontina, and provolone cheeses in a mixing bowl. 1/2 cup of the cheese mixture should be saved for seasoning the dip.

Combine the cheese, mayonnaise, cream cheese, artichokes, and garlic in a mixing bowl. Mix thoroughly, then season with pepper and salt.

Place the mixture in a grill-safe dish and season with 1/2 cup of the saved cheeses. Preheat the grill to 175°C and cook the dip for 60 mins.

With crackers and a sliced baguette, serve the dip.

6.20 Honey & Sage Skillet Cornbread
Total Time: 40 Mins, Servings: 6
Ingredients
1 cup All-Purpose Flour
1 cup + 3 Tbsp St1 Ground
1 Tbsp Baking Powder
Yellow Cornmeal
1/2 Tsp Baking Soda
12 Tbsp Granulated Sugar
1/2 Tsp Kosher Salt
Minced Fresh Sage, 1/4 Cup
1 Large Lightly Beaten Egg
1 cup Milk
4teen oz. Cream Corn
1/2 Cup Softened Unsalted Butter
Butter, flaky salt & honey
Instructions
When ready to cook, preheat the grill to 200°F and cook for fifteen mins with the lid
covered.
1 cup cornmeal, flour, baking powder, baking soda, salt, chopped sage, and sugar are combined in a wide mixing bowl. Stir everything together well.
In a 2nd dish, lightly beat the egg before adding the creamed corn and milk. Stir thoroughly, but don't overmix.
Fold all your wet ingredients into your dry ingredients.
Melt the butter in the cast iron pan over medium heat; then, evenly sprinkle the skillet with 3 tbsp additional cornmeal. Place the butter in the skillet and spread it out with the spatula or spoon.
Transfer the batter to the skillet and put it on the bottom rack of the Pit Boss (which has been warmed). Cook for around 25 mins.
Remove it from the grill and set it aside for 10 mins before cutting. Serve with honey, flaky salt, and butter while still hot.

6.21 Pit Boss Fries along with Chipotle Ketchup
Total Time: 30 Mins, Servings: 4
Ingredients
Chipotle Ketchup
In Adobo Sauce, 4 Can Chipotle Peppers
1 Tbsp Olive Oil
1 Tsp Onion Powder
1 Tsp Garlic Powder
1 Cup Tomato Ketchup
1 Tbsp Sugar
1 Tbsp Cumin
1 Tbsp Chili Powder
1 Lime Juice
Main
6 Yukon Gold Potatoes (Cut into Thick Strips)
12 Tbsp Melted Butter
1 Tbsp Pit Boss Beef Rub
Finely Chopped Flat-Leaf Parsley, 1/4 Cup
Instructions
Mince the chipotle peppers and combine them with the other chipotle ketchup ingredients in a bowl.
Refrigerate the mixture for 1 hr to allow the flavors to meld.
When you're ready to cook, preheat the Pit Boss to 225°C and shut the lid for fifteen mins.
Toss the potatoes in the Bowl with the Pit Boss Beef Rub and melted butter, then toss to coat.
Place the fries on a baking sheet and bake for 10 to 15 mins.
Remove the fries from the grill, place them in a mixing dish, and toss with parsley.

6.22 Smoked Nuts (Diva Q's Savory)
Total Time: 1 Hr 5 Mins, Servings: 4
Ingredients
Main
12 Tbsp Melted Clarified Butter
1 Tsp Toasted Sesame Oil
12 Cup Mixed Nuts
Cholula Chipotle Hot, 1 1/2 Tsp
Sauce
Worcestershire Sauce, 1 1/2 Tsp
1 Tsp Salt
Instructions
Combine all the ingredients in a bowl, except the salt, and spread in a single layer onto an oiled Al (disposable) pan.
When you're ready to cook, set the Pit Boss to 125°C and shut the lid for fifteen mins.
Smoke the nuts for about an hr, turning them
every fifteen mins. When they're done, remove them from the grill and season with salt.
When chilled, store in an airtight container.

6.23 Pit Boss Chex Party Mix
Total Time: 1 Hr 15 Mins, Servings: 8
Ingredients
6 Tbsp Butter
12 Tbsp Worcestershire Sauce
Seasoned Salt, 1 1/2 Tsp
Garlic Powder, 3/4 Tsp
1/2 Tsp Onion Powder
3 Cup Corn Chex Cereal
3 Cup Rice Chex Cereal
3 Cup Wheat Chex Cereal
1 Cup Salted Mixed Nuts
1 Cup Bite-Size Pretzels
1 Cup Minced Garlic
Instructions
When ready to cook, preheat the grill to 125°C and shut the cover for ten to fifteen mins.
Melt butter in a large roasting pan on the grill. Combine Worcestershire sauce and toppings in a mixing bowl. Slowly mix in the remaining ingredients until they are evenly covered.
Cook for 1 hr at 125 degrees C, whisking every fifteen mins.
To cool, place it on a paper towel. It should be kept in an airtight container.

6.24 Buffalo (Baked) Chicken Dip

Total Time: 40 Mins, Servings: 6
Ingredients
Eight-oz Softened cream cheese
1/2 cup Sour cream
1/2 cup Mayonnaise
12 tbsp dry ranch seasoning
1 tsp Kosher salt
1/2 cup Red hot sauce
12 cup shredded cooked chicken
1 cup shredded mozzarella cheese
1 cup shredded cheddar cheese
1/2 cup blue cheese
4 strips Crumbled cooked bacon
Chips, crostini & crackers
Vegetables
Instructions
When you're ready to cook, set the Pit Boss to 180°C and shut the lid for fifteen mins.
In the medium bowl of a stand mixer, add sour cream, cream cheese, ranch, mayonnaise, salt, spicy sauce, and beat until thoroughly mixed.
Combine mozzarella, shredded chicken, and cheddar cheese in a mixing bowl. Transfer to an oven-proof dish and top with crumbled bacon and blue cheese.
Place the dish on the grill grate and cook for 20 to 30 mins, or until the top color becomes golden brown and the dip begins to bubble.
Serve with crackers, chips, and crostini as a side dish.

6.25 Sweet Cajun Wings (Grilled)

Total Time: 45 Mins, Servings: 4
Ingredients
12 Lb Chicken Wings
Pit Boss Cajun Shake
Poultry Rub & Pit Boss Pork
Instructions
Pit Boss Cajun Shake and Pit Boss Sweet Rub should be used to coat the wings.
When you're ready to cook, preheat the Pit Boss to 175°F and shut the lid for fifteen mins.
Cook for about thirty mins, or until the skin is brown and the center is moist.

6.26 Potato Skins(Baked) along with Pulled Pork

Total Time: 1 Hr 15 Mins, Servings: 6
Ingredients
Main
4 Baker Style Potato
Salt
Vegetable Oil
4 Russet Potatoes
12 Tbsp Melted Butter
Canola Oil
3 Cup Pulled Pork
4 Tbsp Pit Boss Sweet & Heat BBQ
Sauce
1 cup Mozzarella Cheese
1 cup Cheddar Cheese
Minced Green Onion
Sour Cream
Minced Bacon
Instructions
When you're ready to cook, preheat the Pit Boss to 230°C and shut the lid for fifteen mins.
Rub the potatoes with canola oil and season equally with salt.
Place the potatoes on the grill grate and cook for 45 mins.
Cut the potatoes in half, leaving 1/4 inch of skin on the potatoes. Brush the insides of the skins with melted butter and place them on the baking pan. Return it to the grill and cook for another 5–6 mins.
Combine the Pit Boss Sweet, Hot BBQ Sauce, pulled pork, cheddar cheese, and mozzarella cheese in a large mixing bowl.
Stuff the skins with the mixture and place them back on the Pit Boss with the lid closed, waiting for the cheese to melt. Bacon, sour cream, and chopped onions go on top.

6.27 Deep Dish Supreme Pizza (Baked)

Total Time: 45 Mins, Servings: 4
Ingredients
1 Oz Pizza Dough
Additional Virgin Olive Oil
1/2 Cup Pizza Sauce
12 cup Mozzarella Cheese
1 Tsp Fresh Oregano
Parmesan Cheese
1 Tsp Fresh Basil
Italian Sausage (Lb Mild)
1 1/2 Green Bell Pepper
12 Tbsp Diced Onion
1 1/2 Red Bell Pepper
Fresh Mushrooms
Black Olives
Sliced Pepperoni
Instructions
When ready to cook, preheat the grill to high and shut the cover for fifteen mins.
Using more virgin olive oil, coat the ten to twelve-inch cast-iron pan. Place the dough in the skillet and press it out from the bottom and around (up) the sides.
To construct the pizza, spread sauce over the dough top and add all spices. Drizzle with basil and oregano and top with grated parmesan and mozzarella.
Cook for 25 to 30 mins.
Allow it to rest for five to ten mins before slicing.

6.28 Ultimate Loaded Nachos

Total Time: 45 Mins, Servings: 4
Ingredients
1 Bag Tortilla Chips
1/2 Cup Fresh Salsa
1 Lb Cooked & Sliced Kielbasa Sausage
1 Cup Cooked Chicken Breast (Shredded)
1 Lb Cooked & Cubed Tri-Tip
Sliced Scallions, 1/4 Cup
1 Small Sliced Jar Jalapeños
Sliced Black Olives, 1/4 Cup
Cheddar Cheese, 1 1/2 Cup
1/2 Cup Sour Cream
1/2 Cup Guacamole
Cilantro, 1/4 Cup
Instructions
When you're ready to cook, preheat the Pit Boss to 190°C and shut the lid for fifteen mins.
On the large platter, equally, distribute the tortilla chips. Sprinkle the salsa, chicken, tri-tip, and Kielbasa sausage on the chips. Jalapenos, scallions, cheese, and olives are used to season nachos.
Place the tray on the grill and cook for ten to fifteen mins, or until the cheese melts and the nachos are well cooked.
Serve with guacamole, cilantro, and sour cream on the side.

6.29 Onion Dip
Total Time: 1 Hr 20 Mins, Servings: 8
Ingredients
1 Tbsp Butter
1 Tbsp Vegetable Oil
12 Large Sweet Onion
Sugar, 1 1/2 Tsp
1 Tsp Garlic Salt
1 Tsp Black Pepper
1/2 Tsp Dried Thyme
1/2 Cup Beef Bouillon
1 Tbsp Worcestershire Sauce
1 Tbsp Bourbon
Sour Cream, 1 1/2 Cup
8 Oz Cream Cheese
12 Tbsp Chives
Instructions
When you're ready to cook, preheat the grill to 250 degrees and shut the cover for fifteen mins.
In a disposable foil skillet, place the butter and vegetable oil on a grill grate. Whisk in the sugar, chopped onions, pepper, thyme, and garlic salt after the butter has melted.
Combine the Worcestershire sauce, bourbon, and beef bouillon in a mixing bowl.
Returning to the pan over the grill, grate and cook the onions, stirring occasionally and adding more sauce if needed, until they are tender and golden brown. Allow for full cooling of the onions.
While the onions are cooking, whisk together the cream cheese and sour cream in a large mixing Bowl until smooth.
Whisk in the cooled onions and chives if preferred. Add additional salt and pepper to taste.
Cover and chill until ready to serve. It goes well with potato chips or crudites.

6.30 Smoked Trout
Total Time: 2 Hrs 10 Mins, Servings: 6
Ingredients
8 Rainbow Trout Fillets
1 Gallon Water
Salt, 1/4 Cup
1/2 Cup Brown Sugar
1 Tbsp Black Pepper
12 Tbsp Soya Sauce
Instructions
Fresh fish should be washed.
1-gallon water, soy sauce, brown sugar, pepper, and salt, whisked together until sugar and salt are dissolved. Brine your fish for 1 hr in the refrigerator.
When you're ready to cook, set the Pit Boss to 120°C and shut the lid for fifteen mins.
Remove the fish from the brine and pat it dry. Place the fish on the grill grate for around 12 hrs. When the fish becomes opaque and starts to flake, it is finished.

6.31 Spicy Bacon covered Chicken Skewers (Grilled)
Total Time: 3 Hrs 20 Mins, Servings: 6
Ingredients
1/2 Cup Ranch
1/2 Tsp Garlic Powder
12 Tbsp Chili Sauce
1/2 Tsp Dried Oregano
16 Oz Cubed Chicken Breast
1 Sliced Red Onion
1 Sliced Green Bell Peppers
8 Strips Sliced Bacon
Instructions
In a large mixing bowl, combine the garlic powder, ranch dressing, Chile sauce, and oregano. Toss in the cubed chicken and toss to coat thoroughly. Now marinate the chicken for up to 3 hrs in the fridge.
Set the temperature to high and cook for fifteen mins with the lid covered.
Begin assembling the Pit Boss skewers by threading the onion wedge, pepper, bacon slice, and chicken onto the skewers. Continue to alternate chicken and bacon until the bacon is evenly distributed among the chicken pieces. Add the onion wedge and pepper to the end of each skewer. If you want to cook quickly, don't overcrowd the skewer. Repeat with the remaining skewers.
Place the skewers on the grill grate, with the foil piece beneath the skewer's end makes turning easier and prevents them from burning.
Bake for about five mins on each side, rotating a quarter of the way through for a total of 20 mins. Take out the skewers.

6.32 Bacon Onion Ring
Total Time: 1 Hr 10 Mins, Servings: 6
Ingredients
16 Slices Bacon
12 Sliced Vidalia Onion
1 Tbsp Chili Garlic Sauce
1 Tbsp Yellow Mustard
1 Tsp Honey
Instructions
Continue wrapping the bacon around the solitary onion ring until all the bacon is gone.
To prevent the bacon from unraveling during the cooking process, do the following: Place the skewer next to the bacon-covered onion slice.
When you're ready to cook, preheat the grill to 200°C and cook for ten to fifteen mins with the lid covered.
Meanwhile, blend yellow mustard and chili garlic sauce in a mixing dish until well combined; add honey.
Place the skewers on the grill grate and cook for 1 hr and 30 mins, rotating after 45 mins.

6.33 Chicken Wings (Tandoori)
Total Time: 1 Hr 30 Mins, Servings: 4
Ingredients
1/2 cup Yogurt
1 Minced Scallions
1 Tbsp Chopped Cilantro Leaves
12 Tsp Minced Ginger
1 Tsp Masala
Salt, 1 1/2 Tsp
1 Tsp Ground Black Pepper
Chicken Wings, 1 1/2 Lb
12 Tbsp Mayonnaise
12 Tbsp Cucumber
12 Tsp Lemon Juice
1/2 Tsp Cumin
Cayenne Pepper, 1/8 Tsp
Instructions
In a blender jar, combine the scallions, yogurt, ginger, cilantro, salt, garam masala, and pepper. Blend until smooth. Place the chicken on top and cover all the wings with the sauce; knead the bag. Refrigerate it for four to eight hrs. Remove the excess marinade wings and the marinade itself.
Set the temperature to 180°C and cook for ten to fifteen mins with the lid covered. Brush and oil the grill grate.
Arrange the wings on the grill grate. Cook for 45- 50 mins, or

until the skin becomes brown and begins to crisp. To keep the wings from sticking to the grill grate, flip them once or twice while cooking.
Meanwhile, combine all the sauce ingredients and chill until ready to serve.
Once the wings are fully cooked, transfer them to a dish or platter. It's best served with a yogurt sauce.

6.34 Brown Sugar Bacon Bites (BBQ)
Total Time: 40 Mins, Servings: 2
Ingredients
1/2 cup Brown sugar
1 tbsp. Ground fennel
12 tsp Kosher salt
1 tsp ground black pepper
One-lb Diced pork belly
Instructions
Fold the Al foil strip (12 x 36) in half and fold the ends to create a rim. Using a fork, poke holes in the final piece of foil. A few bacon fats would be removed, and the bacon would begin to crisp due to this.
When you're ready to cook, preheat the grill to 175°C and cook for fifteen mins with the lid covered.
In a mixing dish, combine the ground fennel, brown sugar, black pepper, and salt. To mix the ingredients, whisk them together.
Toss the diced pork belly in the mixture until it is well covered. Transfer the pork to a foil-lined baking sheet.
Place it on the grill and cook for 20 to 30 mins, or until the pieces are crispy, bubbling, and glazed.

6.35 Hasselback Potatoes (Roasted)
Total Time: 2 Hrs 30 Mins, Servings: 6
Ingredients
6 large Russet potatoes
1 lb Bacon
1/2 cup butter
Black pepper
Salt
1 cup Cheddar cheese
3 Scallions
Instructions
To chop potatoes, place 12 wooden spoons on any potato side. Cut potato into thin chips, leaving about one-fourth fixed on the bottom.
Freeze the bacon slices for about thirty mins before cutting them into small pieces. Please place them in the cracks between the other pieces.
Place the potato in a large cast-iron pan. Hard butter pieces are used to season the potato. Season with salt and pepper.
When ready to cook, preheat the Pit Boss to 175°F and cook for fifteen mins with the lid closed.
Place the cast iron directly on the grill grate and cook for 2 hrs. Extra butter should be added to the potatoes, and melted butter should be drizzled every thirty mins.
In the final ten mins of cooking, drizzle with cheddar and return to the grill to melt. Garnish with chives.

6.36 Old Fashioned Cornbread
Total Time: 35 Mins, Servings: 4
Ingredients
1 cup All-purpose flour
1 cup Cornmeal
1 tbsp Sugar
12 tsp baking powder
1/2 tsp Salt
3 tbsp Butter
1 cup Milk
1 Egg Lightly beaten
Instructions
In a mixing dish, combine the cornmeal, flour, baking powder, salt, and sugar.
Melt the butter in a saucepan. Remove the pan from the heat and whisk in the egg and milk.
Whisk together the milk-egg mixture and the dry ingredients. Make sure you aren't overmixing it.
Spread the batter evenly in a greased 8/9-inch square baking pan.
When you're ready to cook, preheat the Pit Boss grill to 190 degrees Celsius.
Cook for 25-35 mins, or until the cornbread begins to pull away from the pan edges and the top begins to brown. Cut into wedges or squares.

6.37 Smoked Olives
Total Time: 30 Mins, Servings: 4
Ingredients
1 Lb Mixed Olives
1 Quart Additional-Virgin Olive Oil
1 Orange Zest
1 Lemon Zest
1/2 Tbsp Red Pepper Flakes
1/2 Tbsp Dried Fennel Seed
3 Dried Bay Leaves
4 Thyme Sprigs
4 Rosemary Sprigs
Instructions
Once you're ready to cook, turn your Pit Boss grill to the smoke setting and leave it there.
Place the olives on the grill after removing them from the roasting pan. Smoke for about 20 to 30 mins.
Once the olives are required for smokiness and coolness, remove them from the grill. Mix olive oil, smoked olives, lemon zest, orange-red pepper flakes, bay leaves, fennel, thyme, and rosemary once cold. Make sure the olives are completely submerged in the airtight container.

6.38 Breakfast Mini Quiches (Baked)
Total Time: 35 Mins, Servings: 8
Ingredients
1 Tbsp Additional-Virgin Olive Oil
Cooking Spray
1/2 Yellow Diced Onion
3 Cup Fresh Spinach
Ten Eggs
4 Oz Mozzarella Cheese (Shredded Cheddar)
Fresh Basil, 1/4 Cup
1 Tsp Kosher Salt
1/2 Tsp Black Pepper
Instructions
With the cooking spray, coat a 12-cup muffin tin generously with cooking spray.
In a small pan over medium heat, warm the oil. Cook, often stirring, until the onion is softened, about 7 mins. Cook for another min or so until the spinach has wilted.
Transfer it to a cutting board to cool, then mince the mixture.
When you're ready to cook, preheat the grill to 175°C and shut the cover for fifteen mins.
In a mixing dish, whisk the eggs until foamy. Combine the cooled onions and cheese, spinach, basil, 1 tsp salt, and 1/2 tsp pepper in a mixing bowl. To mix the ingredients, whisk them together. Divide the egg mixture evenly between the muffin

cups.
Place the tray on the grill and bake until the eggs become brown, puff up, and are set, about 18-20 mins.
Serve right away or keep refrigerated for up to 4 days in an airtight container.

6.39 Jalapeño Poppers (Coconut Shrimp)

Total Time: 60 Mins, Servings: 6
Ingredients
8 Shrimp Peeled & Deveined
1/2 Tsp Pit Boss Chicken Rub
Olive Oil
6 Whole Jalapeños
8 oz Softened Cream Cheese
12 Tbsp Chopped coriander
1/2 Cup Unsweetened Coconut Flakes
12 Slices Bacon
Instructions
When you're ready to cook, preheat the Pit Boss to 218°C and cover it for fifteen mins.
Rinse your shrimp and season them with the Chicken Rub (Pit Boss).
When using olive oil, Sprinkle the shrimp with salt and pepper and cook for about five mins on each side on a Pit Boss.
Allow the shrimp to cool before serving.
Reduce the Pit Boss's temperature to 176°C.
Cut the jalapenos in half and remove the seeds and stems.
Shrimp should be minced. Combine the minced shrimp, melted cream cheese, 2 tbsps chopped coriander, and 1/2 tsp Pit Boss Chicken Rub in a mixing bowl.
Fill each pepper half with a generous amount of the filling. With a drizzle of coconut oil, season to taste.
Place each filled pepper on a foil-lined baking sheet and top with a bacon piece.
Cook the peppers on the Pit Boss for 45 mins, or until the bacon fat has rendered and the cream cheese has become golden.

6.40 Bloody Mary Wings (Grilled)

Total Time: 1 Hr 20 Mins, Servings: 6
Ingredients
12 Lb Chicken Wings
Mix 12 Cup (Pit Boss Smoked) Bloody Mary
3 Tbsp Pit Boss Bloody Mary
Cocktail Salt
Instructions
When ready to cook, preheat the Pit Boss to 175°F and cook for fifteen mins with the lid closed.
Top the wings evenly with the Cocktail Salt (Bloody Mary) and put them directly on the grill grate. Cook for about thirty mins, often turning until the wings are crispy and golden.
Remove the wings from the grill and put them in the Al skillet with the Bloody Mary mix (Smoked). To coat the wings, whisk them together.
Return to the grill for another thirty mins, whisking halfway through.
Transfer the chicken wings to a serving dish or plate.

6.41 Beef Satay

Total Time: 20 Mins, Servings: 6
Ingredients
12 Lb Flat Iron Steak (Black)
1 Bottle Carne Asada Marinade
12 Minced Garlic clove
12 Chopped Scallions
Crushed Peanuts, 1/4 Cup
Peanut Sauce
12 Limes
Instructions
Using a fine knife, cut your steak into one-third-inch pieces.
Place the meat in the Carne Asada marinade and mix in the scallions and garlic. Place in a large mixing bowl or a resealable plastic bag. Refrigerate it for one hr.
Remove your meat from the marinade, removing any onion/garlic bits. Thread each piece onto the bamboo skewer.
When you're ready to cook, turn the Pit Boss too high and shut the lid for fifteen mins.
Grill your satays for 3 to 4 mins on each side, turning once.
Meanwhile, pour the peanut sauce into a dish and set it on one end of the plate. Arrange the satays on the plate and sprinkle with the minced peanuts. Serve with lime wedges on top.

6.42 (Adobo Skewers) Honey Lime Chicken

Total Time: 35 Mins, Servings: 6
Ingredients
4 Diced Chicken Breast
1 Tbsp Vegetable Oil
12 Tsp Minced Garlic
Onion Powder 12 Tsp
Rice Vinegar, 3/4 Cup
Soy Sauce, 1/4 Cup
Honey 3 Tbsp
Juiced Lime Two
Black Pepper
Salt
Pit Boss Skewers Eight
Instructions
Combine all the ingredients, including the chicken, in a large mixing bowl.
Cover the mixture and place it in the refrigerator for the night.
When you're ready to cook, turn the Pit Boss too high and shut the lid for fifteen mins.
Place the marinated chicken on skewers and cook it on the Pit Boss. Irregularly flipping till done (around 12 to 15 mins).
It's best served with grilled limes.

6.43 Chinese Jumbo Shrimp

Total Time: 2 Hrs 5 Mins, Servings: 4
Ingredients
4 Lb Jumbo Shrimp
1 cup Soy Sauce
1 cup Teriyaki Sauce
1 Cup Sweet Sherry
1 cup Olive Oil
1 Clove Minced Garlic
1 Tsp Freshly Grated Ginger
1 Tsp Pit Boss Chicken Rub
Instructions
Cut the shrimp with the back of a shell. Remove the heads and

black veins from the shrimp.
Wipe the shrimp with a wet paper towel and put it aside.
Combine leftover items in a small pan and stir well. Place the shrimp in the refrigerator for 2-4 hrs to marinate.
When you're ready to cook, preheat the Pit Boss to 260°C and cover it with the lid for fifteen mins.
Thread the shrimp onto the wooden skewers after removing it from the marinade (pre-soaked).
Place the shrimp directly on a grill grate, cover with a lid, and cook for 3 mins.
Cook for a further 3 mins after flipping the shrimp and closing the cover.
Serve it straight off the Pit Boss. Now sit back and relax.

6.44 Smoked Hummus along with Roasted Veggies
Total Time: 55 Mins, Servings: 4
Ingredients
Chickpeas, 1 1/2 cup
Tahini, 1/3 cup
1 tbsp minced garlic
6 tbsp. Additional-virgin olive oil
1 tsp Salt
4 tbsp. Lemon juice
1 Sliced red onion
12 cup Butternut squash
12 cup Fresh brussels sprouts
12 cup Cauliflower (cut into florets)
12 Portobello mushroom
Black pepper
Salt
Instructions
When ready to cook, preheat the grill to 90°C and shut the cover for fifteen mins.
Rinse and drain the chickpeas before placing them on the sheet tray for the hummus. Place the tray on the grill grate and smoke for 15 to 20 mins.
In a food processor bowl, mix tahini, smoked chickpeas, olive oil, garlic, lemon juice, and salt. Process until thoroughly blended but not completely smooth. Transfer to the bowl and set aside.
Raise the grill's temperature too high.
Sprinkle olive oil over the vegetables and put them on the sheet tray. Place the sheet pan on the grill for 15 to 20 mins, or until it's gently browned and fully cooked.
Season the hummus with roasted veggies and place it on a serving platter/bowl.
Serve with pita bread and a drizzle of olive oil.

6.45 Venison Tater Tot Casserole (Baked)
Total Time: 50 Mins, Servings: 4
Ingredients
12 Lb Ground Venison
12 Can Canned Peas
12 Can Mushroom Soup Cream
Twenty-8 Oz Frozen Tater Tots
Instructions
Cook ground venison in medium sautés pan over medium heat until browned. Drain the excess fat and set aside the venison.
Combine peas, soup, and venison in a 13x9-inch pan. Toss with tater tots before serving.
When you're ready to cook, preheat the Pit Boss to 175°F and shut the lid for fifteen mins.
Place the casserole dish on the grill grate and cook for about thirty mins. Enjoy it while it's still warm.

6.46 Sweet Potato Fries (Roasted)
Total Time: 45 Mins, Servings: 4
Ingredients
4 Sweet potatoes
3 tbsp. Additional-virgin olive oil
1 tbsp. Salt
1 tsp Black pepper
1 cup Mayonnaise
In adobe sauce, 12 chipotle peppers
12 Juiced limes
Instructions
When ready to cook, increase the temperature to high and cook for fifteen mins with the lid covered.
Toss your sweet potatoes with salt, pepper, and olive oil before placing them on the sheet pan. Place the sheet pan on the grill grate and cook for 20 to 30 mins, stirring sporadically until the potatoes are crispy and golden.
While the potatoes are cooking, puree the chiles, lime juice, and mayonnaise in a blender until smooth.

6.47 Spicy Cashews & Smoked Sweet
Total Time: 1 Hr 5 Mins, Servings: 6
Ingredients
3 Tbsp Sambal Oelek
1 Tbsp Pit Boss Smoked Simple Syrup
1 Zested Lemon
1/2 Tbsp Chopped Rosemary
1 Tsp Red Pepper Flakes
1/4 Tsp Cayenne Powder
1 Lb Cashews
Instructions
When you're ready to cook, preheat the Pit Boss to 107 degrees Celsius and cover it for fifteen mins.
In a small bowl, combine simple syrup, sambal oelek, rosemary, lemon zest, cayenne, and red pepper flakes. Toss the cashews in the mixture to coat them.
Spread the cashews evenly on the sheet pan and place them directly on a grill grate. Cook the nuts for 1 hr, stirring them occasionally.
Remove it from the grill and set it aside to cool. Now it's time to serve.

6.48 Grilled Corn Salsa
Total Time: 45 Mins, Servings: 6
Ingredients
4 Large Corn Husks
4 Chopped Tomato
1/2 Cup Finely chopped Cilantro
1 Garlic Powder 1 Tsp
1 Tsp Onion Powder
1 Diced, Seeded, & Grilled Jalapeño
1 Juiced Lime
Black Pepper
Salt
Instructions
When you're ready to cook, turn the Pit Boss too high and shut the lid for fifteen mins.
Place the corn on the grill and cook until it is fully roasted. Remove the husk and remove the kernels off the cob.
Combine the corn with the other ingredients and chill until ready to serve.

6.49 Smoked Seafood Ceviche
Total Time: 1 Hr 20 Mins, Servings: 4
Ingredients

1 Lb Shucked Sea Scallops
1 Lb Peeled & Deveined Shrimp
1 Tbsp Canola Oil
1 Lime Juiced & Zested
1 Lemon Juice
1 Juiced Orange
1 Tsp Garlic Powder
1 Tsp Onion Powder
12 Tsp Salt
1/2 Tsp Black Pepper
1/2 Tsp Diced Avocado
1/2 Diced Red Onion
1 Tbsp Finely Chopped Cilantro
1 Pinch Red Pepper Flakes
Instructions
In a mixing dish, combine the scallops, canola oil, and shrimp. When you're ready to cook, preheat the grill to 90 degrees Celsius and shut the cover for fifteen mins.
Arrange the scallops and shrimp on the grill, then smoke them for 45 mins. In the meanwhile, prepare all the ingredients and combine them in a large mixing bowl.
Switch your grill up and cook for another five mins once the scallops and shrimp are d1 with smoking.
Allow the shrimp and scallops to cool before cutting them in half (widthwise) and mixing them with the other ingredients in a medium mixing bowl.
Refrigerate the Ceviche for 12 to 3 hrs to enable the flavors to meld. It's great with corn chips.

6.50 Prosciutto Covered Grilled Shrimp along with Peach Salsa
Total Time: 40 Mins, Servings: 4
Ingredients
12 Lb Peeled & Deveined Shrimp
8 Slices Prosciutto Ham
12 Diced Peaches
Toothpicks
12 Tbsp Balsamic Vinegar
12 Tbsp Honey
1 Serrano Chopped Chile
12 Tbsp Fresh Chopped Basil
Black Pepper
Salt
Instructions
Clean the shrimp in cold water and pat it dry using paper towels. Wrap a slice of prosciutto around each shrimp in a spiral.
Add 1 tbsp vinegar, peaches, half of a serrano pepper, honey, basil, salt, and pepper in a mixing dish. Add more vinegar, Chile, honey, salt, and pepper if desired.
When ready to cook, increase the temperature to high and cook for fifteen mins with the lid covered.
Arrange the prosciutto-covered shrimp on the grill grate and cook for 4 to 6 mins on each side.
Warm prawns seasoned with peach salsa are delicious. Serve with jalapeño slices on top.

6.51 BBQ Bacon-Wrapped Water Chestnuts
Total Time: 40 mins, Serving: 6
Ingredients
Brown Sugar, 1/3 Cup
Spicy BBQ Sauce, 1/3 Cup
Water Chestnuts, 2 Can
Bacon, 1 Pound
Mayonnaise, 1/3 Cup
Instructions
When you're ready to cook, fire up the Pit Boss grill. Until the fire has created, smoke with lid opened. Preheat the oven to 350 °F and bake for 10 minutes with the lid covered.
Use aluminum foil to cover a rimmed baking sheet. Each slice of bacon should be cut into thirds or half. Wrap a slice of bacon big enough to surround each water chestnut and fasten it with a toothpick.
Place the bacon-wrapped chestnuts on the prepared baking sheet in a single layer. Preheat oven to 350°F and bake until 20 minutes. Turn on the grill.
In a mixing bowl, combine the mayonnaise, sugar, & Pit Boss Spicy BBQ Sauce. Return the chestnuts to the grill for another 10 minutes of baking in the sauce. Transfer to a serving dish. Enjoy!

6.52 Roasted Habanero Wings
Total Time: 7 Hrs, Serving: 4
Ingredients
Onion, 1 Medium
Chicken Wings, 4 Pound
Green Onions, Cup
Vegetable Oil, 1/4 Cup
Garlic Clove, 2 Clove
Hot Sauce, 2 tbsp
Allspice, 1 1/2 tsp
Dried Thyme, 1/2 tsp
Habanero Pepper
Black Pepper, 1 tsp
Salt, 1 1/2 tsp
Soy Sauce, 2 tbsp
Ground Cinnamon, 1/2 tsp
Instructions
Remove the tips of wings & discard or preserve them for stock making. To make drumette and flat portions, cut their wings in half.
To prepare the marinade, combine all of the ingredients in a mixing bowl. In a food processor, blend the onion with green onions until they have the consistency of a thick paste. Mix the oil, hot pepper sauce, soy sauce, salt, and all of the spices, as well as 1/2 or all of habanero pepper, depending on your preferred level of heat. Combine all ingredients in a food processor and process until smooth. Set aside a portion of such marinade for basting.
Set the wings inside a deep baking dish, then pour the marinade on them, turning with tongs to evenly cover the wings with sauce. Cover and chill the wings. Allow for at least six hours of marinating time, or possibly overnight, flipping each wing at least 2 times.
Once ready to cook, preheat the Pit Boss to 350°F for 15 minutes with the lid closed.
Cook the wings straight on a grill grate for 30 min, then baste with reserved marinade and turn them.
Cover and simmer for another 10 mins, or when the wings become brown and crispy and now have achieved an internal temp 165 degrees Fahrenheit.
Serve immediately with the leftover green onions as a garnish. Enjoy!

6.53 BBQ Brisket Hot Dog
Total Time: 15 min, Serving: 4
Ingredients
Beef Brisket, 1/2 Pound
Hot Dogs, 6 Whole
Hot Dog Buns, 6 Whole
Onion, 1
Jalapeño, 2 Whole
Heat BBQ Sauce & Pit Boss Sweet, 1/2 Cup
Cheddar Cheese, 1/2 Cup

Instructions

When you're ready to cook, fire up the Pit Boss as per the manufacturer's directions. Preheat the grill to 450 degrees F for 10-15 minutes with the lid closed.

Place hot dogs straight on the grill grate & cook for 7-10 minutes, or until warmed through it and lightly browned, rotating periodically.

To keep the brisket slices moist, wrap them in aluminium foil with some BBQ sauce. Place next to hot dogs mostly on grill grate & cook till warmed through, approximately 5-7 minutes.

To serve, put the hot dog on the bun, top with the brisket, extra Barbecue sauce, cheddar cheese, onion, and jalapenos, and serve. Enjoy.

6.54 Grilled Oysters

Total Time: 40 mins, Serving: 2
Ingredients
Oysters, 18 Medium
Chopped Parsley
Garlic, 2 Clove
Butter, 8 tbsp
Rock Salt
Dried Oregano, 1 tsp
Parmesan Cheese, 1/4 Cup
Instructions

On a serving plate, sprinkle approximately 1/2 inch of rock salt. Once the oysters are cooked, this will help keep them level. Begin with oysters that have fully closed their shells but are still living. Throw away any oysters that are open; this indicates that they are dead, and you just want them to become as clean as possible. Keep the oysters on ice inside a dish in the lower fridge till you're ready to eat them. To avoid grit getting into the oysters after you open them, wash and gently brush them with water before shucking.

Begin by slicing the onion with just an oyster's knife or even a strong paring knife. To make it simpler to grip and protect your hand, wrap the oysters in a towel. Place the knife's tip in the oyster's "hinge." Wiggle and push the knife more into the oyster till it feels secure. To softly pop open the oyster, apply spinning pressure to the knife.

Gently move around the oyster with the knife to fully open it, careful not to damage the fluids. Make careful not to cut the oyster flesh. Gently pull the shell open until it bursts to open fully. The top shell should be removed and discarded. To release the oyster, run your knife beneath it, but leave this in the lower shell.

In a small saucepan, melt the butter. Sauté for 2 to 3 minutes with the minced garlic and dry oregano. Turn off the heat. Fill each oyster with a tablespoon of the butter mixture.

When ready to cook, increase the temperature to High & preheat for 15 minutes with the lid closed.

Place the oysters upon this grill grate, placing them between bars to keep them from spilling. Grill for 8 to 10 minutes, or when the oyster flesh edges curl slightly, the fluids are bubbling.

Carefully move the oysters to the prepared serving plate using tongs.

Garnish with grated parmesan & chopped parsley just before serving. Allow cooling somewhat before eating since the shells and fluids will be extremely hot. Enjoy!

6.55 Smoked Hummus with Roasted Vegetables

Total Time: 50 mins, Serving: 4
Ingredients
Tahini, 1/3 Cup
Chickpeas, 1 1/2 Cup
Olive Oil, 6 tbsp
Lemon Juice, 4 tbsp
Red Onion, 1
Butternut Squash, 2 Cup
Cauliflower, 2 Cup
Garlic, 1 tbsp
Salt, 1 Teaspoon
Portobello Mushroom, 2 Whole
Black Pepper
Brussels Sprouts, 2 Cup
Salt to taste
Instructions

Preheat the grill to 180°F and shut the cover for 15 minutes when ready to cook.

Drain & rinse the chickpeas, then lay them out on a sheet pan to make the hummus. Place tray on grill grate & smoke for 15-20 minutes, or until the desired amount of smoke is achieved. Add smoked chickpeas, tahini, ginger, olive oil, salts, and lemon juice in the bowl and stir and process until thoroughly combined but not entirely smooth. Place in a dish and set aside.

Preheat the grill and raise the temperature to high.

Drizzle the vegetables using olive oil and lay them out on a sheet pan. Roast the vegetables on a sheet pan on the grill for 15-20 minutes, or until gently browned & cooked through.

To serve, spread hummus on a serving plate or bowl & top with roasted vegetables.

Garnish with pita bread and a drizzle of olive oil. Enjoy!

6.56 Buffalo & Pork Stuffed Poblano Peppers

Total Time: 60 mins, Serving: 4
Ingredients
Olive Oil, 2 tbsp
Poblano Pepper, 6 Medium
Fresh Parsley, 1/4 Cup
Vegetable Oil, 2
Ground Buffalo, 1/2 Pound
Salt, 3/4 tsp
Red Pepper Flakes
Tomato Sauce, 8 Ounce
Ground Pork, 1/2 Pound
Yellow Onion, 1 Medium
Garlic, 1 tbsp
Black Pepper, 1/2 tsp
Rice, 2 Cup
Instructions

Preheat the Pit Boss on High for 15 minutes with the lid covered when you're ready to cook.

Drizzle olive oil over all but one of the poblano peppers, then adds salt and pepper. Toss to coat completely.

Roast peppers for 10 mins, or when the surface is brown and blistered, directly on the grill grate. Remove the steaks from the grill and put them aside to cool.

Preheat a cast-iron pan on the grill for 20 minutes with the lid covered.

Chop parsley, onion, and leftover poblano pepper and mince garlic.

Halve the peppers lengthwise. With a spoon, scrape out the ribs and seeds.

Add the onions and diced poblano pepper, followed by the oil. Cook for 3 minutes or until soft. Pork, garlic, buffalo, salt, parsley, black pepper, and pepper flakes are added to the pan.

Cook, tossing with just a huge wooden spoon to break down the lumps, till the beef is browned, approximately 6 minutes. Stir in the rice & tomato sauce well.

Remove from fire and season with salt and pepper to taste. Reduce the grill's temperature to 350 ° F.

Stuff the peppers with rice mixture and bake them in a skillet. Put a pan on grill & cook peppers for 25 to 30 minutes, or till

very tender and filling is cooked through.
Take off the grill and set aside for 10 minutes aside. Enjoy!

6.57 Smoked Sweet & Spicy Cashews
Total Time: 1 Hrs 5 mins, Serving: 6
Ingredients
Pit Boss Smoked Simple Syrup, 1 tbsp
Red Pepper Flakes, 1 tsp
Cashews, 1 Pound
Lemon Zested, 1
Sambal Oelek, 3 tbsp
Fresh Chopped Rosemary, 1/2 tbsp
Cayenne Powder, 1/4 tsp
Instructions
Preheat Pit Boss to 225°F and cook for 15 minutes with lid covered until ready to cook. If Super Smoke is available, use it for the best taste.
Mix sambal oelek, rosemary, lemon zest, red pepper flakes, simple syrup, and cayenne in a small bowl. Toss the cashews in the mixture to coat them.
Spread cashews on such a sheet tray & set just on grill grate immediately. Cook approximately 1 hour, stirring once in a while.
Remove from the grill and set aside to cool. Enjoy!

6.58 Roasted Sweet Potato Fries
Total Time: 45 mins, Serving: 4
Ingredients
Olive Oil, 3 tbsp
Salt, 1 tbsp
Mayonnaise, 1 Cup
2 Limes Juices
Black Pepper, 1 tsp
Peeled Sweet Potatoes, 4 Whole
In Adobo Sauce Chipotle Peppers, 2
Instructions
Preheat the Pit Boss to 400°F for 15 minutes with the lid closed when ready to cook.
Whisk the sweet potatoes in olive oil and season with salt and pepper before spreading them out on a sheet pan.
Put a sheet pan straight upon that grill grate to cook for 20 minutes, till the potatoes are golden and crispy, turning periodically.
Puree the mayonnaise, chiles, & lime juice in a blender until smooth, whereas the potatoes are
cooking.
Drizzle chipotle mayo over the fries or serve on the side for dipping. Enjoy!

6.59 Bourbon BBQ Chicken Kabobs
Total Time: 25 mins, Serving: 4
Ingredients
Pit Boss Texas BBQ Sauce, 1/2 Cup
Chicken Breasts, 3 Pound
Bourbon, 1/4 cup
Garlic, 1 tsp
Onion Powder, 1 tsp
Pit Boss BBQ Sauce apricote, 1/2 Cup
Honey, 2 tbsp
Instructions
In a 2 quarts resealable bag, combine most of the ingredients & marinate
as in refrigerator overnight.
Thread skewers with marinated chicken pieces.
Once ready to cook, preheat the Pit Boss to 450°F for 15 minutes with the lid closed.
For a beautiful char, place the skewers in front of the grill. After that, transfer them to the middle of the grill & cook for another 8 to 10 minutes, or until the chicken reaches a temp of 165°F. Enjoy!

6.60 Journey South Oyesters
Total Time: 50 mins, Serving: 4
Ingredients
Olive Oil, 5 tbsp
2 Lemons
Dried Thyme, 3 tsp
Red Bell Pepper, 1 Medium
Onion, 2 Medium
Dried Bay Leaves, 3
Garlic, 5 tbsp
Hot Pepper Sauce, 5 tbsp
Butter, 4
Italian Blend Cheese
White Wine, 1/4 Cup
Worcestershire Sauce, 3 tbsp
Pit Boss Chicken Rub, 3 tbsp
Oysters On Half Shell, 12 Whole
Instructions
Once ready to cook, preheat the grill on high for 15 minutes with the lid covered.
In a cast-iron pan, heat the olive oil over medium heat. Place the onion & bell peppers in a hot pan.
Squeeze lemon juice into a sauté pan. Mix in the bay leaves, thyme, garlic, & Pit Boss Chicken Rub.
Sauté the vegetable combination for approximately 5-7 minutes, or until the onions are transparent and the peppers have softened.
Stir in the spicy sauce and Worcestershire sauce. 4 sticks of butter, and a glass of white wine. Continue to cook for another 15 min.
Clean & shuck the oysters, leaving those in the bottom of the shell while the sauce simmers.
Arrange the oysters on the Pit Boss and drizzle with the sauce.
5 minutes in the oven
Serve with a dollop of Italian cheese on top. Enjoy!

6.61 Baked Potato Skins with Pulled Pork
Total Time: 1 Hr 15 mins, Serving: 6
Ingredients
Salt to taste
Russet Potatoes, 4
Canola Oil
Mozzarella Cheese, 1 Cup
Butter, 2 tbsp
Vegetable Oil
For Serving Sour Cream
Potato, 4 Whole
For Serving Chopped Green Onion
For Serving Chopped Bacon
Cheddar Cheese, 1 Cup
Heat BBQ Sauce & Pit Boss Sweet, 4 tbsp
Pulled Pork, 3 Cup
Instructions
Preheat Pit Boss to 450°F and cook for 15 minutes with lid covered until ready to cook.
Drizzle canola oil over the potatoes and season equally. Put the potatoes straight on a grill grate, then cook for 30 min, or until a fork pricks them in the centre and they are tender.
Halve the potatoes and empty the insides, retaining 1/4 inches of potato skin on the outside. Place the skins on a baking pan and brush the insides with melted butter. Return to the grill & cook for a further 5 to 6 minutes, or until lightly browned.

Combine all Pit Boss Sweet and Heat BBQ Sauce, pulled pork, mozzarella cheese, and cheddar cheese in a mixing bowl.
Load the skins with mixture and return to the Pit Boss, lid closed, for just long enough for the cheese to melt.
Toss with chopped onions, bacon, and sour cream before serving. Enjoy!

6.62 BBQ Brown Sugar Bacon Bites
Total Time: 35 mins, Serving: 2
Ingredients
Fennel, 1 tbsp
Pork Belly, 1 Pound
Brown Sugar, 1/2 Cup
Kosher Salt, 2 tsp
Ground Black Pepper, 1 tsp
Instructions
To make a rim, fold a 12" × 36" sheet of aluminium foil in half & crimp the edges. Poke holes inside the bottom of the foil with a fork. This will render part of the bacon fat and the bacon bits will crisp.
Once ready to cook, preheat the oven to 350°F for 15 minutes with the lid closed.
Mix the ground fennel, brown sugar, salt, & black pepper in a large mixing basin. To mix, stir everything together.
Toss up diced pork belly inside the mixture until well coated. Place the pork slices on a foil-lined baking sheet.
Place on the grill and cook for 20-30 minutes, or when the pieces become crispy, glazed, and bubbling. Enjoy!

6.63 Roasted Potatoes by Doug Scheiding
Total Time: 2 Hrs 30 mins, Serving: 6
Ingredients
Bacon, 1 Pound
Russet Potatoes, 6 Large
Salt to taste
Cheddar Cheese, 1 Cup
Scallions, 3 Whole
Butter, 1/2 Cup
Black Pepper
Instructions
Place two wooden spoons on each side of the potato to chop it. Slice potato into shrill chips, leaving approximately 1/4" of the bottom intact.
Freeze the bacon slices for approximately 30 minutes before cutting them into tiny stamp-sized pieces. Place them between each slice in the crevices.
In a big cast iron pan, place the potato. Hard butter slices should be placed on top of the potato. Salt & pepper to taste.
Once ready to cook, preheat the Pit Boss to 350°F for 15 minutes with the lid closed.
Cook for two hours with the cast iron straight on the grill grate. More butter on top of the potatoes, then baste every 30 minutes with melted butter.
Sprinkle with cheddar cheese in the final 10 minutes of grilling and return to the grill to melt.
Toss using chives or scallions to finish. Enjoy!

6.64 Everything Pigs in a Blanket
Total Time: 35 mins, Serving: 4
Ingredients
Dried Minced Onion, 1 tbsp
Sesame Seeds, 2 tbsp
Pillsbury Crescent Rolls, 8 Ounce (8 Oz)
1 Egg
Salt, 1 tsp
Poppy Seeds, 2 tbsp
Garlic, Minced, 2 tsp
Dijon Mustard, 1/4 Cup
Instructions
Preheat your Pit Boss around 350 degrees F for 10 minutes with the lid covered when you're ready to cook.
Combine poppy seeds, dried minced garlic, dried minced onion, salt, and sesame seeds in a large mixing bowl. Remove from the equation.
Cut each crescent roll dough triangle in thirds lengthwise, resulting in three tiny strips of each roll.
Rub the dough strips with Dijon mustard. Roll up the tiny hot dogs on one end of the dough.
Arrange them on a prepared baking sheet, seam side down. Brush using egg wash and then season with the seasoning mix.
Bake for 12 to 15 minutes in a Pit Boss until golden brown.
Serve with your favourite mustard or dipping sauce. Enjoy.

6.65 Pit Boss Fries with Chipotle Ketchup
Total Time: 25 mins, Serving: 4
Ingredients
Olive Oil, 1 tbsp
In Adobo Sauce Chipotle Peppers, 2 Can
Garlic Powder, 1 tsp
Tomato Ketchup, 1 Cup
Cumin, 1 1 tbsp
Sugar, tbsp
Onion Powder, 1 tsp
Chili Powder, 1 tbsp
Lime juice
Main
Pit Boss Beef Rub, 1 tbsp
Butter, 2 tbsp
Flat-Leaf Parsley, 1/4 Cup
Yukon Gold Potatoes, 6 Whole
Instructions
Split the chipotle peppers, then put them in a mixing bowl with the other chipotle ketchup ingredients.
Chill the mixture for at least 1 hour to let the flavours meld.
Once ready to cook, preheat the Pit Boss to 450°F for 15 minutes with the lid closed.
In a mixing bowl, combine the potatoes, melted butter, and Pit Boss Beef Rub, stirring to coat.
Arrange the fries on something like a baking sheet, then bake for 10 minutes, or until they are crispy to your liking. Take the fries from the grill, then toss with parsley in a mixing bowl.
Serve by the handful, with lots of chipotle ketchup on the side.

6.66 Whole Roasted Cauliflower with Garlic Parmesan Butter
Total Time: 50 mins, Serving: 4
Ingredients
Salt & Pepper
Butter, 1/2 Cup
Chopped Parsley, 1/2 tbsp
Head Cauliflower, 1 Whole
Garlic, 2 Clove
Olive Oil, 1/4 Cup
Parmesan Cheese, 1/4 Cup
Instructions
Preheat Pit Boss to 450°F and cook for 15 minutes with lid covered until ready to cook.
Drizzle olive oil over the cauliflower and season generously with salt and black pepper.
Place the cauliflower inside a cast iron pan on a grill grate & cook for 45 minutes, or until lightly golden and soft in the middle.

In a separate dish, mix the softened butter, parmesan, garlic, and parsley while the cauliflower is heating.
Sautee the cauliflower with melted butter mixture during the final 20 minutes of cooking.
Take the cauliflower from the grill and, if preferred, sprinkle with more parmesan and parsley. Enjoy!

6.67 Grilled Watermelon with Lime & Smoked Chili Salt
Total Time: 25 mins, Serving: 2
Ingredients
Olive Oil, 2 tbsp
Kosher Salt, 2 tbsp
Lime juice, 2
Watermelon, 1/2 Whole
Red Pepper Flakes, 1/4 tsp
Instructions
Once ready to cook, preheat the Pit Boss to 500°F with the lid covered for 15 minutes.
Drizzle olive oil over watermelon slices and put immediately on the grill grate. 15 to 20 minutes on the grill, turning once until grill marks appear.
In a spice grinder, mix salt & red pepper flakes while the watermelon is cooking.
Remove the watermelon from grill and drizzle with lime juice. Serve with a pinch of chili salt. Enjoy!

6.68 Pit Boss English Muffins
Total Time: 25 mins, Serving: 2
Ingredients
Instant Yeast, 2 Packet
Large Egg, 2
Kosher Salt, 3 tsp
Semolina Flour, 6 tbsp
Whole Milk, 3 1/2 Cup
Bread Flour, 9 Cup
Honey or Sugar, 4 tbsp
Butter, 6 tbsp
Instructions
In the bowl of an electric mixer fitted with the paddle attachment, combine the milk, yeast, sugar, butter, egg, bread flour, and kosher salt, and beat on low for 1 to 2 minutes. Increase the speed to medium and mix for 2 min, or when the dough is glossy and drifts away from the bowl's sides. Allow the sticky dough to rise for 90 minutes in a lightly oiled basin, covered with a kitchen towel.
Once ready to cook, preheat the Pit Boss to 325°F for 15 minutes with the lid closed.
Place the dough on a lightly greased board and divide it into 15 balls. Set aside for 5 min before shaping. Sprinkle semolina flour on a sheet pan lined with parchment paper.
Gently form the dough into 3-to-4-inch round discs and put on a prepared sheet pan, covering with just a kitchen towel till ready to bake.
Place 4–6 muffins directly on the prepared grill pan and cook for 8 to 9 minutes with the lid closed.
Turn these English muffins over with a spatula and gently push down if the centres have risen more than edges. Cook for another 7 - 10 minutes, or until golden brown on the surface and cooked through in the middle (at least 200°F).
Allow cooling somewhat before separating with a fork. Enjoy!
Notes: Place the fork prongs mostly on the side of the muffin closest to the centre and remove. Please continue to work your way around the muffin, then split it with your hands. If you cut them with a knife, you'll lose all of the lovely pockets within. These will
keep in the freezer for a long time. If frozen, keep them whole and thaw before separating with a fork & toasting.

6.69 Grilled Burrata Salad with Ripped Croutons
Total Time: 60 mins, Serving: 6
Ingredients
Asparagus, 20 Stalk
Tomatoes, 20 Whole
Butter, 3/4 Cup
Avocado Oil, 1/2 Cup
French Bread, 1 Half Loaf
Truffle Oil, 2 tbsp
Burrata Rounds, 3 Whole
Flake Salt & Pepper
Arugula, 4 Cup
Garlic Salt, 1 tsp
Balsamic Reduction, 4 tsp
Instructions
Once ready to cook, preheat the Pit Boss to 500°F with the lid covered for 15 minutes.
Whisk the tomatoes & asparagus with a generous quantity of salt and black pepper, and avocado oil. Place the tomatoes & asparagus on a grill grate once the grill is hot and cook for 20 mins, or when the asparagus is ready as well as the tomato are blistered.
Cut the Garlic bread in silver dollar-sized (or bigger) chunks. Place the bread on a sheet pan and toss it with butter & garlic salt. Put the sheet pan upon that highest grill level and toast the bread for 20 minutes, or until brown.
Arrange the arugula upon this bottom of the serving plate and sprinkle with the truffle oil. Arrange the asparagus and tomatoes on the dish in a circular pattern. Intersperse the burrata rounds about the dish, then top with bunches of broken bread croutons. Finish with a sprinkling of flake salt and a drizzle of balsamic reduction across the whole dish.

6.70 Smoke Blended Salsa
Total Time: 25 mins, Serving: 6
Ingredients
Sweet Onion, 1 Medium
Garlic, 2 Clove
Salt, 1 tsp
Lime juice, 2
2 Tomato
RO*TEL Original Green Chilies & Diced Tomatoes, 2 Can
Honey, 2 tsp
Cilantro Leaves
Ground Cumin, 1/2 tsp
Instructions
Once ready to cook, preheat the grill on high for 15 minutes with the lid covered.
Halve your tomatoes & jalapenos as your Pit Boss starts heating up. The onion should be quartered. Place the tomatoes, jalapenos, & onion cut side down on the grate & grills for 5-10 minutes after it has been warmed.
After grilling, place all of the ingredients inside the base of either a mixing bowl or a decent blender & pulse to mix for 30 seconds or until all of the ingredients have been finely diced, and the salsa has reached the required consistency. Season to taste and adjust seasonings as needed. Serve with tortilla chips or tacos. Enjoy!

6.71 Grilled Fruit Skewers with Yogurt Sauce
Total Time: 36 mins, Serving: 2
Ingredients
Brown Sugar, 1/2 Cup
Peeled Green Apples, 1

Nectarines, 2
Vanilla Yogurt, 8 Ounce
Orange Juice, 1
Water, 1/4 Cup
Ground Cinnamon, 1 tsp
Persimmon, 1
Instructions
Soak wooden skewers in water for a period 30 mins before using.
Combine the brown sugar, cinnamon, 1/4 cup water, & orange zest in a small saucepan. Over medium heat, bring to a boil. Remove from the heat and let it reach room temperature before serving.
Once ready to cook, preheat the Pit Boss to 275°F for 15 minutes with the lid closed.
Cut the fruit into 1" chunks & thread two pieces of each fruit variety onto each skewer.
Grill the skewers for 6 minutes, turning them a 1/4 turn every 1-½ minutes, till the fruit is warmed and lightly browned.
Make careful to brush each round with brown sugar syrup.
Prepare the dipping sauce whereas the fruit is cooking. In a serving dish, combine the yoghurt, orange juice, plus 1 tablespoon brown sugar syrup.
Serve the skewers with dipping sauce on a serving dish. Enjoy!

6.72 Roasted Tingle Wings
Total Time: 40 mins, Serving: 6
Ingredients
Cayenne Pepper Sauce, 1 tbsp
Pit Boss Blackened Saskatchewan Rub, 2 tbsp
Honey, 1/2 Cup
Water, 1/4 Cup
Spicy BBQ Sauce, 1/2 Cup
Jalapeño, 3 Whole
Worcestershire Sauce, 1 tbsp
Instructions
To make the sauce, combine all of the ingredients in a blender, except the wings, and blend until smooth.
Pour the mixture into such a covered container and toss the wings around in it to fully coat them. Marinate for a minimum of 1 hour and up to 24 hours.
Preheat the oven to 350 ° F and cook for 10-15 minutes with the lid covered.
Cook for 30 minutes, or until wings achieve a core temperature of 165 ° F, directly upon that gill grate. Enjoy!

6.73 Smoked Stuffed Avocado Recipe
Total Time: 45 mins, Serving: 8
Ingredients
Leftover Pulled Pork, 3 Cup
Avocados, 6 Whole
Quail Eggs, 8 Whole
Tomato Salsa, 1 Cup
Monterey Jack Cheese, 1 1/2 Cup
Chopped Cilantro, 1/4 Cup
Instructions
Preheat the oven to 375 ° F and leave the lid covered for 10 minutes until ready to cook.
Remove the pits from avocados and, if necessary, part of the avocado from the centre.
Combine the pork, cheese, salsa, and cilantro in a mixing dish.
Place the pork cream on top of the avocados & cook them. Cooking time is 25 minutes.
Form a divot or "nest" for quail egg with a spoon. Carefully break the quail eggs into "nest" and cook for 5 - 10 minutes more, or when the egg is done to your liking.
Take the burgers off the grill & serve. Enjoy!

6.74 Smoked Venison Holiday Jerky
Total Time: 4 Hrs 20 mins, Serving: 6
Ingredients
Apple Cider Vinegar, tsp
Venison, 2 Pound
Granulated Garlic, 1 tsp
Soy Sauce, Cup
Worcestershire Sauce, Cup
Salt, 1 tsp
White Pepper, 2 tsp
Star Anise, 2 tsp
Ground Nutmeg, 1 tsp
Brown Sugar, 1 tbsp
Ground Cinnamon, 2 tsp
Ground Cloves, 1 tsp
Instructions
Slice the venison into 1/4-inch-thick slices using a sharp knife. Any excess fat as well as connective tissue should be removed.
In a mixing bowl, whisk together all of the ingredients except the venison. Then toss in the venison slices and stir well.
Pour the contents of the dish into a big resealable bag and close it tightly, pressing out that much space as possible. Refrigerate overnight to marinate.
Once ready to cook, preheat the Pit Boss to 165°F with the lid covered for 15 minutes. If Super Smoke is available, use it for the best taste.
Arrange the meat upon that grill grate in a single layer. Add a pinch of white pepper, ground cinnamon, ground clove, star anise, and nutmeg to taste.
Smoke the jerky for 4 hours, or until it is dry and still chewy and pliable when bent.
Move to either a cooling rack after removing from the Pit Boss. Allow 1 hour for cooling. Refrigerate in an airtight container or a resealable bag. Enjoy!

6.75 Grilled Hummus
Total Time: 60 mins, Serving: 4
Ingredients
Garlic, 1 Head
Olive Oil, 1/4 Cup
Salt to taste
Pita Bread
Pepper
Chickpeas, 1 Can
Tahini, 1 1/2 tbsp
Lemons, 2 Small
Instructions
Preheat the Pit Boss to 375°F (180°C) for 15
minutes with the lid closed when ready to cook.
Cut the top of the garlic bulb off, exposing the garlic cloves. Wrap in foil after pouring a little quantity more olive oil over top. Place the garlic head covered in foil just on grill grate. 30 minutes on the grill After 30 minutes, add the halved lemons and bake for additional 10 min.
Reserve half of chickpea liquid for the dip and drain the remainder. In a blender, puree chickpeas. Toss in the tahini paste.
Remove the garlic & lemons from the grill and set aside to cool.
Remove the garlic wrapper and press 4–6 cloves into blender. Squeeze two lemon halves into blender, being careful not to let the seeds fall in.
Pour in ¼ cup (100 mL) olive oil into a blender. Pulse all of the ingredients together until smooth. Season to taste with salt and pepper. Paprika or cumin may be used as well.
Toss pita bread with hummus and serve. Enjoy!

6.76 Grilled Oysters with Mignonette
Total Time: 30 mins, Serving: 2
Ingredients
Main
Oysters, 18 Large
Unsalted Butter, 4 tbsp
Rock Salt, 4 Cup
Kosher Salt
Lemon Wedges, 12 Medium
Garlic, 2 Clove
Mignonette
Red Wine Vinegar, 1/4 Cup
Minced Shallot, 2 tbsp
Ground Black Pepper, 1/2 tsp
Instructions
Select a shallow serving plate large enough to accommodate all of the oysters. To make a 1/2-inch foundation, put the salt onto plate. This will help to keep the oysters
steady while being served.
Before preparing the oysters, double-check that they are fully closed. Oysters that aren't edible should be discarded. To remove any grit from the surface of the oysters, wash and gently brush them. This will keep the grit out of the oyster once it has been shucked.
Stabilize the oyster there in hand opposite one that holding the knife with a strong glove or dish towel. Identify the "hinge" on every oyster just use an oyster cutter or a very strong paring knife. Wiggle a tip of knife into oyster till it feels firm, then fit the point of knife in the hinge. To gently open this oyster, spin the knife firmly to provide torquing pressure.
Remove the oyster's top shell. Remove the oyster from it's own shell using the point of the knife, keeping the fluids intact. Place each loose oyster on either a baking sheet in its half shell. Once ready to cook, preheat the Pit Boss to 450°F with the lid covered for 15 minutes.
Melt the butter in a small saucepan over medium-low heat. Cook, stirring constantly, until the garlic is aromatic but not browned, approximately 1 minute. Turn off the heat.
To make the Mignonette, red wine vinegar, combine the shallot, and 1 tbsp finely ground black pepper in a mixing bowl. Remove from the equation.
Spoon 1 teaspoon of garlic butter sauce over each half-shelled oyster. Place each oyster carefully on a grill grates, making sure they don't slide. Close the cover and simmer for 3 - 5 minutes, or until the oysters' edges have come away from shell. To preserve the liquids & butter in the shells, gently remove with tongs. To balance them, place them directly upon this rock salt. Serve immediately with lemon wedges for squeezing over the oysters and mignonette. Enjoy!

6.77 Baked Brie
Total Time: 25 mins, Serving: 6
Ingredients
Honey, 1/3 Cup
Pecans, 1/4 Cup
Brie Wheel, 16 Ounce (16 Oz)
Sliced Apple
Crackers
Instructions
Preheat the Pit Boss to 350°F for 15 minutes with the lid closed when ready to cook.
Use parchment or aluminium foil to cover a rimmed baking sheet. Slice the brie's top—the white rind—off with a sharp serrated knife. (Leave the rind intact on a sides and bottom.)
Arrange the brie on a prepared baking sheet, cut side up, and sprinkle with honey. Add nuts to the top.
Bake for 8 to 10 minutes, or until the brie is soft & oozing but not melted. Allow to cool for a few minutes before transferring to a serving dish.
Garnish with crackers and apple wedges, cut. If desired, drizzle with additional honey. Enjoy!

6.78 Holiday Smoked Cheese Log
Total Time: 1 Hr 10 mins, Serving: 8
Ingredients
Shredded Cheddar Cheese, 3 Cup
Cream Cheese, 16 Ounce
Bacon, 8 Slices
Chopped Pecans, 1 Cup
Worcestershire Sauce, 1 tbsp
Hot Sauce, 1 tsp
Green Onion, 2
Instructions
Mix the heavy cream (room temp) and also
the cheddar cheese in a mixing bowl with a hand blender or a big spoon.
Combine the Worcestershire sauce & spicy sauce in a mixing bowl. Recombine the ingredients.
Toss in the cooked & crumbled bacon, as well as the green onions. Mix until everything is well mixed.
Refrigerate for 4 hours, or when the cheese mixture is hard enough to shape, by covering the bowl using plastic wrap. Form into a log then sprinkle the toasted nuts on top.
Wrap with plastic wrap. To keep the cheese log from becoming too mushy while it's smoking, freeze it overnight.
Preheat the Pit Boss to 180 degrees Fahrenheit the following day for 10-15 minutes.
Remove the frozen cheese log from the freezer & unwrap it. Place on a sheet pan & smoke for 60 minutes. Try to ensure it doesn't get excessively soft by keeping an eye on it.
Transfer the mozzarella log to either a serving dish or serve with crackers of your choice. (Refrigerate the cheese for a couple of hours if it's too soft.)

6.79 Double-Decker Pulled Pork Nachos with Smoked Cheese
Total Time: 60 mins, Serving: 4
Ingredients
Cheese, 8 Ounce
Leftover Pulled Pork, 2 Cup
Cilantro
Pepper Jack Cheese, 8 Ounce
Tortilla Chips
Black Olives
Jalapeño
Instructions
Preheat the Pit Boss to 165 degrees Fahrenheit when ready to cook. Preheat for
10-15 minutes with the lid closed.
Place the frozen cheese on a rack upon top of an ice-filled pan. To help the cheese smoke more rapidly, chop it into smaller pieces, maybe 2 to 4 chunks per block.
Smoked the cheese for 45 minutes and then set them aside to cool. Set aside the shredded cheeses (approximately 1 cup of each).
Preheat the Pit Boss to 350° and cook for 10 minutes with the lid covered.
Arrange the tortilla chips on a large baking sheet and sprinkle with shredded, smoked cheeses equally. Cook for approximately 10 minutes, or when the cheese melt and bubbling, on the Pit Boss barbecue grate.
Take the pan off the Pit Boss and begin putting together the double-decker nachos. Build the nachos with a bottom layer

of cheesy chips, a layer of pulled pork, and a coating of cheesy chips on top. Add your favourite nacho toppings to finish it off. Warm the dish before serving.

6.80 Smoked Homemade Crackers

Total Time: 30 mins, Serving: 4
Ingredients
Flour, 3 Cup
Sugar, 2 tsp
Olive Oil, 4 tbsp
Poppy Seeds, 1 tbsp
Dried Garlic, 1 tbsp
Coarse Salt, 2 tsp
Salt, 2 tsp
Toasted Sesame Seeds, 1 tbsp
Water, 1 Cup
Dried Onions, 1 tbsp
Instructions
Preheat the oven at high for 15 minutes with the lid covered when you're ready to cook.
Combine sugar, flour, & salt in a mixing bowl.
Mix in the water and oil until a soft, sticky dough forms. If there is flour mostly in
bottom of the bowl, drizzle in a little water until it is completely mixed.
Place the dough on a floured board and roll it out to a thickness of 1/8 inch. If the dough starts to shrink as you roll it, cover it and let it aside for 5 minutes before rolling again.
In a small dish, combine the remaining spices.
Sprinkle the spice over cracker dough after brushing it with a little water.
Split the crackers in squares and place them on a baking sheet lined with parchment paper, allowing space across each cracker.
Place the baking sheet upon this grill grate & cook for 10-15 min, or until the cracker are crisp and the edges have started to brown. Start serving with cheese and meat on the side. Enjoy!

6.81 Smoked Cajun Chicken Wings

Total Time: 1 Hr 5 mins, Serving: 6
Ingredients
Baking Powder, 1 tbsp
Garlic Powder, 1/2 tsp
Dried Thyme, 1/2 tsp
Dried Oregano, 1/4 tsp
Kosher Salt, 1/4 tsp
Ground Black Pepper, 1/4 tsp
Chicken Wings, 3 Pound
Butter, 1/4 Cup
Worcestershire Sauce, 1 tbsp
Hot Sauce in Louisiana Style, 1/4 Cup
Cayenne Pepper, 1/8 tsp
Cumin, 1/4 tsp
Onion Powder, 1/2 tsp
Paprika, 1 tsp
Instructions
Rub: Combine thyme, baking powder, garlic powder, paprika, onion powder, oregano, salt, cumin, pepper, & cayenne in a small
bowl.
Clean the chicken wings by rinsing them and patting them dry using paper towels. Toss the wing in a large mixing basin with the rub to evenly coat them.
Place a cooling rack in a baking pan coated with aluminum foil. Arrange the wings inside a single layer, leaving a little gap between them. Refrigerate the baking sheet with the wings for eight hours to overnight.
Once ready to cook, preheat the oven to 180°F with the lid covered for 15 minutes.
Cook the wings for 30 mins in the smoker.
Raise the temperature of the grill to 350°F after 30 minutes & roast for 50 minutes.
In a small sauce pan, mix hot sauce, butter, and Worcestershire sauce while the wings are on the grill. Bring to a low simmer over moderate heat and stir until everything is well mixed.
Turn the heat down to low & keep the wings warm until they're done.
Place the wings in a large mixing basin. Toss in the sauce to coat the wings completely.
Serve warm with carrot and celery sticks, ranch, parmesan, or other preferred dipping sauces on a plate. Enjoy!

6.82 Roasted Buffalo wings

Total Time: 40 mins, Serving: 4
Ingredients
Main
Corn-starch, 1 tbsp
Chicken Wings, 4 Pound
Kosher Salt
Pit Boss Chicken Rub
Buffalo Sauce
Frank's Red-hot Sauce, 1/2 Cup
Unsalted Butter, 6 tbsp
Spicy Mustard, 1/4 Cup
Instructions
Preheat the Pit Boss to 375°F for 15 minutes with the lid closed when ready to cook.
Dry the chicken wings with just a paper towel while the grill is heating up. In a large mixing bowl, combine the corn-starch, wings, Pit Boss Chicken Rub, and salt to taste. Cover both sides of chicken wings with the mixture.
Put the wings mostly on grill when it's hot & cook for thirty minutes total, rotating halfway during the cooking time.
After 35 minutes, check the interior temperature of the wings. Internal temperature must be at least 165 degrees Fahrenheit. Internal temperature of 175-180°F, on the other hand, will provide a superior texture.
To make the Buffalo Sauce, mix together Franks Red Hot, mustard, and butter in a saucepot. Combine all ingredients in a mixing bowl and cook on the burner until well heated. Whereas the wings are cooking, keep the sauce warm.
Remove the wings from the grill and put them in a medium mixing basin. Turn the wings with tongs to cover them with the buffalo sauce.
Return to the grill for a further 10-15 minutes to let the sauce to solidify. Wings should be served with a ranch and blue cheese dressing. Enjoy!

6.83 Smoked Jalapeño Poppers

Total Time: 1 Hr 15 mins, Serving: 4
Ingredients
Bacon, 6 Slices
Jalapeño, 12 Medium
Cream Cheese, 8 Ounce
Grated Cheese, 1 Cup
Poultry Rub and Pit Boss Pork, 2 tbsp
Instructions
Preheat Pit Boss to 180°F and cook for 15 minutes with lid covered until ready to cook. If Super Smoke is available, use it for
the best taste.
Cut the jalapenos lengthwise in half. With a tiny spoon or

paring knife, scrape away any seeds or ribs. Combine melted cream cheese, Pit Boss Pork and Poultry Rub, and shredded cheese in a mixing bowl. Fill each side of jalapenos with the mixture. Wrap the bacon around the cheese and fasten with a toothpick.

Arrange the jalapenos on a baking sheet with a rim. Place on the grill for 30 minutes to smoke.

Raise the grill flame to 375°F and cook for another 30 minutes, or until the bacon is grilled to your liking. Warm it up and enjoy it!

6.84 Coconut Shrimp Jalapeño Poppers

Total Time: 60 mins, Serving: 6
Ingredients
Pit Boss Chicken Rub, 1/2 tsp
Cream Cheese, 8 Ounce
Chopped Cilantro, 2 tbsp
Olive Oil
Bacon, 12 Slices
Jalapeños, 6 Whole
Shrimp, 8 Whole
Coconut Flakes, 1/2 Cup
Instructions
Preheat the Pit Boss to 425°F for 15 minutes with the lid closed when ready to cook.
Rinse the shrimp and season with Pit Boss Chicken Rub.
Spray the shrimp using olive oil & cook for approximately 5 minutes each side on the Pit Boss, or until they are opaque.
Peel the shrimp and set them aside to cool.
Lower the temperature of the Pit Boss to 350°F.
In the meanwhile, start popping those poppers. Discard the stems & seeds from the jalapenos after cutting them in half.
Cut the shrimp into small pieces. Softened cream cheese, diced shrimp, 1/2 tsp Pit Boss Chicken Rub, and 2 teaspoons chopped cilantro are combined in a mixing bowl.
Fill each pepper half with a good quantity of the filling. Add a sprinkling of coconut on top.
Wrap a piece of bacon around each filled pepper and put on such a foil-lined baking pan.
Cook the peppers for approximately 45 minutes on the Pit Boss, or when the bacon fat completely rendered or the cream cheese has become golden. Enjoy!

6.85 Reuben Dip

Total Time: 40 mins, Serving: 8
Ingredients
Cooked Corned Beef, 12 Ounce
Swiss Cheese, 3 Cup
Sauerkraut, 16 Ounce
Butter, 2 tbsp
Mayonnaise, 1/4 Cup
Thousand Island Dressing, 1/2 Cup
Breadcrumbs, 1 Cup
Instructions
Mix the sauerkraut, corned beef, plus 2 cups Swiss cheese in a large mixing basin.
Whisk together all the Thousand Island Dressing as well as the mayonnaise. Combine the cheese and meat in a mixing bowl. Fill a greased baking dish or saucepan with the mixture. The remaining cheese should be sprinkled on top.
Toss the breadcrumbs & butter together and sprinkle over the dip. When you're ready to cook, fire up the Pit Boss grill. Until the fire has created, smoke with lid open.
Preheat the oven to 350°F and cook the Reuben Dip about 35-40 minutes. Served with crackers / cocktail breads as an accompaniment. Enjoy!

6.86 Smoked Dry Rub Wings

Total Time: 1 Hr 15 mins, Serving: 8
Ingredients
Main
Brown Sugar, 1/4 Cup
Salt, 1/4 Cup
Dried Thyme, 1 tsp
Garlic, 4 Clove
Chicken Wings, 2 Pound
Red Pepper Flakes, 1 tbsp
Rub
Granulated Onion, 1/2 tsp
Chipotle Chile Pepper, 1/4 tsp
Brown Sugar, 1/4 Cup
Garlic Powder, 1/4 tsp
Smoked Paprika, 1/4 tsp
Pit Boss Rub, 1/4 tsp
Instructions
To make the brine, whisk together the brine ingredients in a large mixing basin or container with 4 cups water till the brown salt and sugar have dissolved.
Place the wings in the brine. Allow the wings to brine for 24 hours, covered and refrigerated.
Take the wings out of the brine, clean them, and pat them dry. Once ready to cook, preheat the Pit Boss to 180°F with the lid covered for 15 minutes. If Super Smoke is available, use it for the best taste.
To make the rub, combine all of the dry rub ingredients in a small dish. Rub both sides of the wings with rub.
Smoke the wings for 30 to 45 minutes on the grill grate. Remove the steaks from the grill.
Preheat the grill to 450°F with the lid covered for 15 minutes. Return the wings to the grill & cook for 3-5 minutes on each side, or until golden brown and crisp.
Take the wings off the grill & serve right away. Enjoy!

6.87 Smoked & Loaded Baked Potato

Total Time: 1 Hr 10 mins, Serving: 4
Ingredients
Bacon, 8 Slices
Russet Potatoes or Yukon Gold, 6
Sour Cream, 1 Cup
Melted Butter, 1/2 Cup
Green Onions, 1 Bunch
Cheddar Cheese, 1 1/2 Cup
Salt & Pepper
Instructions
Preheat Pit Boss to 375°F and cook for 15 minutes with lid covered when ready to cook.
Poke potatoes with just a fork before placing them directly on the grill. 1 hour of cooking
Cook bacon on even a baking sheet upon that grill for approximately 20 minutes at the same time; remove, cool, and crumble.
Remove the potatoes from the oven and allow it to cool approximately 15 min.
Cut each potato in half lengthwise to get long halves. To create a boat, scoop off approximately 70percent of the potato with a tiny spoon, leaving a layer of potato skin.
Reserve any leftover potato in a dish. Extra potato should be lightly mashed with only a fork; add the butter, sour cream, and 1/2 cup cheese; add salt and pepper.
Fill the potato skins with the potato mixture, then top with more cheese and bacon.
Return to the grill for another 10 mins or until warmed through it and then cheese has melted. Serve with additional sour cream and green onions as a garnish. Enjoy!

6.88 Roasted Potato Poutine
Total Time: 55 mins, Serving: 6
Ingredients
Vegetable Oil or Olive Oil
Beef Gravy or Cup Chicken
Scallions, 2 tbsp
Russet Potatoes, 4 Large
Pit Boss Rib Rub
Yellow or White Cheddar Cheese Curds, 1 1/2 Cup
Ground Black Pepper
Instructions
Preheat the oven to high for 15 minutes with the lid covered when you're ready to cook.
Peel the potatoes and cut them into fries, wedges, or whatever form you like.
Coat the potatoes with oil in a large mixing basin. Season using Pit Boss Prime Rib rub liberally.
Spread the potatoes in a single layer on a rimmed baking sheet, cut sides down.
Grill for 15 min, then flip the potatoes with a spatula to the other sliced side. Continue to roast for another 15 to 20 minutes, or when the potatoes are soft and golden brown.
Simmer the gravy on either the stovetop or even in a heat-proof pan using your Pit Boss while the potatoes are cooking.
Put the potato in a big shallow bowl such as on a serving plate to construct the poutine. Place the cheese curds over top and spread them out evenly. Pour the heated gravy over the potatoes & cheese curds in an equal layer.
Sprinkle with black pepper and thinly sliced scallions before serving. Serve right away. Enjoy!

6.89 Grilled Sweet Potato Planks
Total Time: 25 mins, Serving: 6
Ingredients
Canola Oil, 1 tbsp
Pepper, 1 tsp
Onion Powder, 1/2 tsp
Salt, 1 tsp
Sweet Potatoes, 5 Large
Instructions
Peel and wash the sweet potatoes, after this cut them into eighths lengthwise.
Toss them in a bowl with a little pepper, oil, salt, and onion powder.
When you're ready to cook, preheat the Pit Boss to 500°F with the lid covered for 15 min.
Arrange the sweet potatoes on the grill immediately. Note that putting them or at front and also very back of grill will give them a nice sear.
After they've developed excellent grill marks, transfer them to the middle of the grill and cook for another 20 minutes. Serve.

6.90 Smoked Beet-Pickled Eggs
Total Time: 50 mins, Serving: 4
Ingredients
Red Beets, 1
Beet Juice, 1 Cup
Granulated Sugar, 1/3 Cup
Boiled Eggs, 6 Hard
Onion, 1/4
Apple Cider Vinegar, 1 Cup
Star Anise, 1
Cardamom, 3
Instructions
Preheat the Pit Boss grill to 275 degrees Fahrenheit when you're ready to cook. Preheat for 10 minutes with the lid closed.
Directly on the grill, set the peeled boiled eggs & smoke for 30 minutes.
Place the smoked eggs in the bottom of a quart-size glass jar with cooked/chopped beets.
Combine the vinegar, sugar, onion, cardamom, beet juice, and anise in a medium sauce pan.
Bring to a boil, and then reduce to a low heat and simmer, uncovered, until the sugar dissolves as well as the onions are transparent (about 5 minutes).
Take the pan from the oven and set it aside to cool for several minutes.
Pour the onion and vinegar mixture over eggs & beets mostly in jar, thoroughly covering the eggs.
Using the jar lid, secure the jar. Refrigerate for up after one month before serving. Enjoy!

6.91 Smoked Asparagus Soup
Total Time: 55 mins, Serving: 4
Ingredients
Olive Oil, 1 tbsp
Yellow Onion, 1/2
Butter, 1 tbsp
Raw Asparagus, 2 Stalk
Asparagus Spears, Pound
Salt & Pepper
Garlic, 2 Clove
Cream, 1 1/2 Cup
Chicken Stock, 1 1/2 Cup
Instructions
Preheat the grill to 180°F and shut the cover for 15 minutes when ready to cook. If Super Smoke is available, use it for the best taste.
Season 1 pound of asparagus using salt and pepper after drizzling it with olive oil. Smoke for 20-30 minutes, directly on the barbecue grate. Flavor along way to decide the amount of smoke, and withdraw sooner if necessary.
Melt 1 tablespoon butter inside a saucepan
over medium heat. Sauté the onion and garlic for a couple of minutes, or until the onion is transparent.
Take the asparagus from grill and chop it into 1-inch pieces. Add the asparagus, onions, and stock to the pan, along with the cream. Bring to a low boil, then reduce to a low heat.
Remove from the heat and purée until smooth in a blender / immersion blender.
Season to taste with salt & pepper before serving. Salt and pepper to taste, pepper, and smoked paprika, if preferred, and top on fresh shaved asparagus. Enjoy!

6.92 Roasted Red Pepper White Bean Dip
Total Time: 45 mins, Serving: 4
Ingredients
Olive Oil, 4 tbsp
Garlic, 4 Whole
Red Bell Pepper, 2
Leaf Parsley, 3 tbsp
Fresh Dill, 3 tbsp
Cannellini Beans, 2 Can
Salt, 1 1/2 tsp
Lemon Juice, 4 tsp
Instructions
Roasting the red peppers and garlic.
Once ready to cook, preheat the oven to 400 °F (205 degrees C) with the lid closed for approximately 15 min.
Peel the garlic husk's outer layers away. Remove the top of the garlic bulb to reveal each clove. Apply olive oil to the top of garlic head and massage it's in. Wrap the garlic cloves in foil to fully encase it. On the Pit Boss, place the garlic head and

two bell peppers (washed and dried).

Roast the peppers for approximately 40 minutes as well as the garlic for approximately 25-30 mins. Every 10 minutes rotate pepper peppers a quarter turn till the surface is blistered & browned.

Remove the peppers from the grill and place them in a mixing dish. Leave the bowl covered in plastic wrap for 15 minutes. The steam may loosen the skins, allowing them to slide off like a barbecued drumstick.

Remove the skin of the pepper. Cut the stems off and dig out the seeds, and you're good to go.

Allow the garlic to cool before removing the separate cloves as required.

Take a dip: Combine the roasted red peppers, 4 garlic cloves, lemon juice, dill, olive oil, parsley, drained & rinsed beans, and salt in a blender.

Puree the dip until it is smooth and silky. You may have to scrape along the edges of the blender a few times. If it's not mixing well or seems to be overly thick, add additional olive oil/lemon juice. (If you think it needs additional acid or brightness, add additional lemon juice.) Enjoy!

6.93 Baked Breakfast Mini Quiches

Total Time: 30 mins, Serving: 8
Ingredients
Olive Oil, 1 tbsp
Cooking Spray
Black Pepper, 1/2 tsp
10 Eggs
Shredded Cheddar Cheese, 4 Ounce
Fresh Basil, 1/4 Cup
Yellow Onion, 1/2
Spinach, 3 Cup
Kosher Salt, 1 tsp
Instructions
Lightly coat a 12-cup muffin pan with cooking spray.
Warm the oil in a small pan over medium heat. Cook, often turning, until the onion is softened, approximately 7 minutes. Cook for another minute or until the spinach has
wilted.
Allow cooling on a cutting board before chopping the mixture to break up the spinach.
Once ready to cook, preheat the grill to 350°F with the lid covered for 15 minutes.
Whisk the eggs in a large mixing basin until foamy. Combine the cooled onions & spinach, cheeses, basil, 1 teaspoon salt, and 1/2 teaspoon pepper in a mixing bowl. To mix, stir everything together. Evenly distribute the egg mixture amongst these muffin cups.
Place the dish on the grill & bake for 18 to 20 minutes,
or when the eggs have swelled up, complete set, and are starting to colour.
Serve right away, or cool completely on such a wire rack before storing in a sealed jar for up to four days. Enjoy!

6.94 The Dan Patrick Show Grilled Bloody Mary Wings

Total Time: 1 Hr 20 mins, Serving: 6
Ingredients
Chicken Wings, 2 Pound
Smoked Mary Mix, 2 Cup
Pit Boss Mary Cocktail Salt, 3 tbsp
Instructions
Preheat the Pit Boss to 350°F for 15 minutes with the lid closed when ready to cook.
Sprinkle the Bloody Mary Cocktails Salt equally over the wings and put them immediately on the grill grate. Simmer for 30 minutes, often stirring, until brown and crispy.
Remove the wings from the grill and place them in an aluminum pan with the Smoky Bloody Mary Mix. Coat the wings with the sauce.
Return to the grill, covered, for another 30 minutes, stirring halfway through. If the pan begins to dry out, add a splash of liquid.
Arrange the wings on a dish or platter to serve. Enjoy!

6.95 Competition Style BBQ Pulled Pork

Total Time: 10 Hrs 25 mins, Serving: 8
Ingredients
Meat Injector
Bone-In Pork Butt, 1 (8-10 Lb)
Apple Juice, 2 3/4 Cup
Poultry Rub & Pit Boss Pork, 1 Cup
Butcher Barbeque Pork Injection, 1/4 Cup
Instructions
Preheat Pit Boss to 225°F and cook for 15 minutes with lid covered until ready to cook. If Super Smoke is available, use it for the best taste.
Trim extra fat from the meat as the grill warms up.
Combine half of the Pit Boss Pork and Poultry Rub, 2 cups fruit juice, & butchers pork injection in a small dish. Using an injector, thoroughly infuse pork butt throughout.
Apply a coat of Pit Boss Meat & Poultry Rub to the pork. Allow 20 minutes for the meat to rest.
Cook the meat for 4-1/2 and 5-1/2 hours on the barbecue. Verify the temp of the pork after 4-1/2 hours. This should be around 155- and 165-degrees Fahrenheit. If not, wait 30 minutes and check again.
Wrap the pork in the second layer of big heavy aluminium foil when the temperature hits 155-165°F. Place the pork inside a foil packet using 3/4 cup of the saved apple juice and return to the grill.
Increase the temperature of the grill to 250°F & cook for the next 4 hours. After 3 hours, check the interior temperature. In the thickest portion of the pork, the temperature should be between 204°F and 206°F. Check the temperature of the pork every 30 min until it reaches 204-206°F. Depending on the amount of pork, the total cooking time must be between 8 and 10 hours.
Remove the pork from the grill & open the foil package for 10 minutes to allow the
steam to escape. Re-seal the bag and set it aside for 40-45 minutes to an hour.
After resting, drain a liquid out of foil and use a fat separator to remove the fat from the broth. Pull the flesh away from the bone. Toss the removed meat with 2 cups of broth. If required, add more broth to reach the appropriate moisture level. Enjoy!

Chapter 7: Desserts Recipes

7.1 Grilled Stone Fruit with Berries & Cream

Total Time: 25 mins, Servings: 4
Ingredients
2 Peaches (Halved)
2 Apricot (Halved)
1 Nectarine, (Halved)
Balsamic Vinegar, 1/2 Cup
Honey, (Divided), 3 tbsp
Orange Peel, 1 tbsp.
Cream, 2 Cup.
Fresh Raspberries, 1/2 Cup.
Blueberries, 1/4 Cup.
Instructions
When prepared to cook, preheat the Pit Boss to 400°F with the lid covered for 15 mins.
Cook the apricots, nectarines, and peaches on the grill for 3-4 mins on each side. The grill mark and a little smokey flavor are perfect.
In a mixing bowl, combine all the ingredients for the balsamic reduction. In a small saucepan over low heat, combine the balsamic vinegar, 2 tbsps sugar, and the orange peel. Allow the sauce to cook until it has thickened to a medium consistency.
Meanwhile, in a mixing dish, beat cream and 1 tbsp honey until soft peaks form.
Arrange the stone fruits on a dish, top with berries, and sprinkle with balsamic reduction. On the side, there's whipped cream. Serve with a dollop of whipped cream on top.

7.2 Dutch Baby with Bourbon Apples

Total time: 50 mins, Servings: 4
Ingredients
4 small Cored & sliced apples (like honey crisp)
Bourbon, 1/4 cup
Brown sugar, 1/2 cup.
Butter (unsalted), 1 stick (divided)
Cinnamon (ground), 2 tsp.
3 eggs.
Flour (all-purpose) 2/3 cup
White sugar, 1/2 cup.
Milk, 3/4 cup.
Instructions
Preheat your "Pit Boss grill" to 400 degrees Fahrenheit and place a cast iron or another heat-resistant pan within.
In a blender or food processor, combine the eggs, milk, cinnamon, flour, and white sugar. Blend until the mixture is completely smooth.
Apply 4 tsp butter to the pan once the grill is hot and swirl it around until it is completely melted. Pour the ingredients into the pan and cook for 20 mins, then lower the temperature to 300F and cook for another 5-7 mins, or until golden and fluffy. Remove the Dutch baby from the grill and eat it straight from the pan until it deflates.
In a large saucepan pan over low heat, melt the remaining butter, and add the apple pieces. Cook for 5 mins, or until the sauce slightly thickens. Cook until the brown sugar and bourbon has dissolved, and the sauce has thickened. On top of the Dutch boy, place the apples.

7.3 Christmas Shortbread Cookies

Total Time: 52 mins, Servings: 24
Ingredients
Butter, 8 oz.
Corn starch, 1/4 cup.
Flour (all-purpose), 3/4 cups.
Peppermint extract (for mint glaze), 1/4 tsp.
Powdered sugar (for mint glaze), 2 cups.
Vanilla extract, 1 tsp.
Milk (for mint glaze), 4 tbsp.
Instructions
Preheat oven to 350°F. Line two sheet pans with parchment paper.
In a mixing dish, place the soft butter. Stir everything together with a wooden spoon or spatula until it's lovely and smooth. Combine the sugar and vanilla extract in a mixing bowl. Hand-mix until frothy and thoroughly combined.
Combine flour and cornstarch in a mixing bowl. Stir until all the flour is incorporated. Turn the dough out onto a lightly floured board and roll it into a ball.
Roll out the dough to a thickness of 3/8 inch on a lightly floured work surface. Keep the dough on the surface, and lightly sprinkle the rolling pin with flour. Cut out the required shapes and place them on the baking sheets. Reroll each scrape until the dough is gone.
Refrigerate the cutouts for at least 1 hr.
When ready to bake, set the grill to smoke mode, wait for the fire to catch, and warm to 350 degrees Fahrenheit (177 degrees Celsius). Bake for 12 to 14 mins, or until the edges are just beginning to turn golden. Allow cooling completely before frosting.
In a mixing dish, combine milk, peppermint essence, and powdered sugar for the mint glaze. Blend until completely smooth. It's best if the glaze is thick yet pourable.
Dip the tops of the cookies into the glaze to glaze them. Allow any remaining glaze to run back into the basin. Flip the cookie right side up as soon as possible. Allow 15-30 mins for the glaze to dry before serving. Enjoy.

7.4 Maple Bacon Donuts

Total Time: 45 mins, Servings: 8
Ingredients
Powdered Sugar, ½ - 1 Cup.
Maple Syrup, 1/4 Cup.
Extract (Maple), 2 tsp.
Heavy Cream, 2 tbsp.
(Glazed) Yeast Doughnuts, 12.
Instructions
Set the temperature to High and warm for approximately 15 mins, keeping the lid closed.
In a medium saucepan, combine the syrup, powdered sugar, and maple flavoring and steam until the mixture comes to a steady boil. Cook for 3-5 mins, stirring occasionally.
Reduce the heat to low and whisk in the (heavy) cream. Add additional powdered sugar/cream as needed to get the

desired texture. (Add more powdered sugar if you want a frosting-like covering; more cream if you want a glaze-like finish.)

On the grill, place bacon strips. Cook it on the grill for approximately 5-7 mins with a hand (until crisp).

Allow cooling on a platter before crumbling or cutting.

Grill doughnuts (don't wipe the grate after cooking the bacon; the oil will keep the doughnuts from sticking). Grill each hand for 3-5 mins, or until the glaze is bubbling and the doughnuts have grill marks.

When the doughnuts are still delicious, transfer them to a serving plate. Apply the glaze directly on top. Serve immediately with a sprinkling of "crumbled bacon" on top.

7.5 Baked Dutch Baby
Total Time: 35 mins, Servings: 6
Ingredients
Flour (All-Purpose), 3/4 Cup.
4 Eggs
1 Egg Yolk
Milk, 3/4 Cup.
Sugar, ½-1 tbsp.
Ground Nutmeg, 1/8 tsp.
Vanilla Extract, 1 tsp.
Butter, 4 tbsp.
Fruit (Fresh)
Powdered Sugar
Instructions

When you're prepared to cook, preheat the Pit Boss to 500°F and keep the lid closed for approximately 15 mins.

In a food processor or a normal bowl, mix the eggs, rice, sugar, milk, nutmeg, and vanilla. Blend until the mixture is completely smooth.

In a heated Dutch oven, melt the butter. As soon as the butter has melted, pour it into the pan (be careful not to burn it).

On the Pit Boss, bake for 20 mins, or until brown and fluffy.

Reduce the temperature of the grill to 300°F and continue to roast for another 5 mins. Slice the pancake into wedges after removing it from the grill.

Serve with jams, honey, powdered sugar, cinnamon sugar, or fresh fruit on top as soon as possible.

7.6 Maple Bacon Pull Apart
Total Time: 55 mins, Servings: 8
Ingredients
Bacon (Sliced), 12 Slices.
Biscuits Homestyle (Canned), 2 Can
Maple Syrup, 1 Cup.
Brown Sugar, 1 Cup.
Butter, 1 Cup.
Water, 1/2 Cup
Cinnamon (Ground), 2 tsp
Instructions

When prepared to cook, preheat the Pit Boss on High for approximately 15 mins with the lid closed.

On 1 hand, fry the bacon for 5-8 mins, depending on thickness, then turn and cook for another 5-8 mins. Set aside the crumbled bacon.

Remove the biscuits from the can, cut each 1 into four halves, and peel each half in half.

Combine the honey, butter, brown sugar, and water in a saucepan; bring to a boil, then lower heat, and simmer for 1 min. Blend in the cinnamon well. Toss biscuit quarters with bacon crumbles and sugar until evenly coated.

Preheat the grill to 350 degrees Fahrenheit and place the pan on it. Cook, covered, for 30-35 mins, or until the biscuits are done.

Place the pan on the serving plate after removing it from the grill.

Warm the dish before serving.

7.7 Donut Bread Pudding
Total Time: 55 mins, Servings: 8
Ingredients
Sixteen Cake Donuts
Raisins (Seedless), 1/2 Cup
Five Eggs,
Sugar, 3/4 Cup.
Heavy Cream, 2 Cup.
Vanilla Extract, 2 tsp.
Ground Cinnamon, 1 tsp.
Butter (Melted & Slightly cooled), 3/4 Cup.
Ice Cream
Instructions

Gently butter a baking pan. Arrange the donuts in an equal layer in the tub. To use, sprinkle the raisins (dried apricots) over the end. Drizzle the butter over the whole surface in an equal layer.

In a large mixing basin, whisk together the eggs, sugar, milk, cinnamon, and vanilla to create the custard. Whisk in the butter until it is completely combined. Over the doughnuts, pour the glaze. Allow for a 10- to 15-min stay, pushing doughnuts into the custard as desired. Wrap foil around the bowl and secure it with a rubber band.

Set the Pit Boss to Smoke when you're all set to cook, and keep the lid open until the fire is ready (4-5 mins). Preheat the oven to 350°F and bake with the lid covered for 10 to 15 mins.

Bake for 30-40 mins, or until the custard in the bread pudding is set. Remove the foil and bake for a further 10 mins to lightly brown the top.

Allow for a few mins of cooling before cutting into squares. Drizzle with melted ice cream if desired.

7.8 Grilled Season Fruit with Gelato
Total Time: 15 mins, Servings: 2
Ingredients
2 whole Apricots
2 whole Peaches (Fresh)
2 whole Plums (Fresh)
Turbinado Sugar, 3 tbsp.
Honey, 1/4 Cup.
Gelato
Instructions

When preparing to cook, preheat the grill on high for approximately 15 mins with the lid covered.

Remove the pit from each fruit slice and cut it in half. Apply honey on the cut side, and then sprinkle sugar on top.

Place the fruit cut side down on the grill before grill marks form. Remove the fruits from the grill and serve them with gelato scoops. Drizzle with honey if desired.

7.9 Dark Chocolate Brownies with Bacon-Salted Caramel
Total Time: 50 mins, Servings: 8
Ingredients
8 Strips Bacon
Kosher Salt, 1/2 Cup.
1 whole Brownie Mix
1 Jar Caramel Sauce
Instructions

Cook some bacon strips (6 - 8) till extremely crisp, around 25 mins at 350 degrees, to create the bacon salt. Allow cooling before pulsing in a food processor until thinly chopped. In a

mixing basin, combine 1/2 cup kosher salt. Before you may use it, keep it refrigerated.
Preheat the oven to 350°F and keep the lid covered for approximately 10-15 mins until prepared to cook.
Prepare the brownies according to the package directions and place them in a greased baking pan. Drizzle approximately 2 tbsps caramel sauce over the brownie batter. Toss in 1 tsp bacon salt into the mix. Directly on the Pit Boss grill (preheated).
Bake the brownies for 20-25 mins, or until the batter begins to firm up. Remove it off the grill and drizzle with 2 tbsps caramel sauce and a sprinkle of bacon salt. Return the brownies to the grill for 20-25 mins more, or until a toothpick inserted in the center comes out clean.
Drizzle (another) layer of caramel on top of the warm brownies and, if preferred, sprinkle with bacon salt. Allow brownies to cool completely before cutting into squares. Clean the knife between each slice to prevent the brownies from adhering to it.

7.10 Baked Cast Iron Berry Cobbler
Total Time: 50 mins, Servings: 6
Ingredients
4 cups Berries
Sugar, 12 tbsp.
Cup Orange Juice
Flour, 2/3 Cup.
Baking Powder, 3/4 tsp.
Salt, 1 Pinch.
Butter, 1/2 Cup.
Sugar (Raw), 1 tbsp.
Instructions
When prepared to cook, preheat the grill to 350°F (180°C) with the lid covered for approximately 15 mins.
In a 10" cast iron / other baking pans, combine the berries, 4 tbsp sugar, and orange juice.
In a shallow mixing cup, combine the baking powder, flour, and salt.
In a separate bowl, cream together the butter and granulated sugar. In a separate bowl, whisk together the egg and vanilla extract until well combined.
Over the berries, pour the batter and sprinkle with raw sugar.
Preheat oven to 350°F and bake cobbler for 35-45 mins. Allow it cool for a few mins before serving with whipped cream.

7.11 Baked Molten Chocolate Cake
Total Time: 40 mins, Servings: 4
Ingredients
Flour (All-Purpose)
4 Ounce Butter.
Chocolate (Bittersweet), 6 Ounces.
2 Eggs
2 Egg Yolk
Sugar, 1/2 Cup.
Salt, 1 Pinch.
Instructions
Preheat the oven to 450°F and keep the lid covered for approximately 15 mins until prepared to cook.
4 (6-ounce) ramekins oiled and floured. Remove any excess flour. On the baking sheet, keep the ramekins.
Melt the butter and chocolate in a double boiler at low pressure. Whisk the eggs, yolks, sugar, and salt together at high speed in a medium mixing cup until thick and pale.
Stir in the chocolate until smooth, then incorporate the flour and egg mixture.
Fill the ramekins halfway with the mixture and bake for 20 mins, or until the edges are hard, but the centers are still wet.

Allow 1 min for each to cool before covering with an inverted dessert pan. Carefully turn each over, then put aside for 10 seconds before unmolding.
Serve immediately with Maple Ice Cream and Candied Bacon.

7.12 Caramelized Bourbon Baked Pears
Total Time: 40 mins, Servings: 4
Ingredients
Pears (Fresh), 3 Whole.
Brown Sugar, 1/4 Cup.
Bourbon, 1/4 Cup.
Butter (Melted), 2 tbsp
Vanilla Extract, 1 tsp
Salt, 1/2 tsp.
Instructions
Preheat the oven to 325°F and keep the lid covered for approximately 15 mins until all set to cook.
Remove the skins and cores from the pears. Arrange the vegetables in a greased baking dish.
In a shallow mixing cup, combine the bourbon, brown sugar, vanilla, butter, cinnamon, and salt. Pour the whiskey mixture over the pears.
Preheat the grill, cover the baking dish, and bake for 30 to 35 mins, or until the pears are soft.
Drizzle the caramelized bourbon mixture over the pears on a serving dish.
While still heated, serve over vanilla ice cream.

7.13 Smoked Whipped Cream
Total Time: 7 hrs 40 mins, Servings: 4
Ingredients
Heavy Cream, 3 Cup.
Sour Cream, 1/2 Cup.
Powdered Sugar, 6 tbsp.
Vanilla Extract, 1/2 tbsp.
Instructions
Preheat the oven to 180°F and keep the lid covered for 15 mins until ready to prepare.
Pour heavy cream into an oven-safe dish or pan. It is not recommended to use cast iron.
Cook for 20 mins on the Smoke setting on the Pit Boss grill with the cream. For a superior smoke taste, smoke for 40 mins.
Remove the cream from the Pit Boss and put it away to cool at room temperature for 60 mins. Refrigerate for at least 6 hrs before serving.
In a mixing dish, combine all the ingredients and fold in the whipped cream. Only whisk the cream until stiff peaks form.
Serve it with your favorite fruits or desserts.

7.14 Croissant S'mores on the Grill
Total Time: 25 mins, Servings: 6
Ingredients
Six Croissants
Twenty-five large Marshmallows (Regular)
8 Ounce Chocolate
Instructions
When prepared to cook, preheat the grill on high for approximately 15 mins with the lid covered.
Place cut-side down croissant pieces on the grill for 1 min of toasting. (Keep an eye on them since they will rapidly toast.)
To create a (toasty) croissant s'mores sandwich, remove the s'mores from the grill and stack marshmallows and chocolate squares, finishing with the other half of the croissant.
Before the chocolate melts and the marshmallows become golden, toast the sandwiches on the grill for 30 seconds to 1

min.
Remove the s'mores from the grill while they're still warm and sticky and serve immediately.

7.15 Marbled Brownies with Amaretto & Ricotta
Total Time: 35 mins, Servings: 4
Ingredients
Ricotta Cheese, 1 Cup.
Eggs,
Amaretto Liqueur, 1 tbsp.
Sugar, 1/4 Cup.
Cornstarch, 2 tsp.
Vanilla Extract, 1/2 tsp.
1 Brownie (Mix)
Instructions
Set aside a nonstick baking pan that has been sprayed with cooking spray and brushed with softened butter.
Whisk together the egg, amaretto, cornstarch, sugar, and vanilla in a medium mixing cup.
Prepare the "brownie mix" according to the package directions. Spread the brownie mixture evenly on a prepared dish. Drop the ricotta mixture dollops into the batter at random. Move the plastic knife through the ricotta mixture to make the brownies appear marbled.
Preheat the oven to 350°F and keep the lid covered for approximately 15 mins until prepared to cook.
With brownie batter in the pan, bake for 25 to 30 mins on a grill directly. Put a bamboo skewer/toothpick in the middle of the brownies to see if they're done: the batter should never be sticky.
On a wire cooling rack, chill the brownies completely. The squares should be removed.

7.16 Baked Irish Creme Cake
Total Time: 1 Hr 20 mins, Servings: 4
Ingredients
Pecans (in pieces), 1 Cup.
1 Cake Mix Yellow (Boxed)
Vanilla Pudding (Instant Package), 1 (3.4oz).
Eggs, 4 Large.
Water, 1/2 Cup.
Vegetable Oil, 1/2 Cup.
Cream Liquor (Irish), 1 Cup.
Butter, 1/2 Cup.
Sugar, 1 Cup.
Instructions
Spread butter & flour on a 10" Bundt dish. Pecans should be scattered over the bottom of the pan.
Using an electric mixer, combine the pudding mix, yellow cake mixes, water, eggs, oil, and Irish Cream liquor in a large mixing basin. Fill the container with the mixture and pour it on top of the nuts.
When prepared to cook, preheat the Pit Boss to 325°F with the lid closed for approximately 15 mins.
In a Bundt pan on Pit Boss, bake for 60 mins, or until a toothpick inserted in the center comes out clean. Remove from heat and put aside for 10 mins to cool.
While the cake is cooling, bring the water, butter, and sugar to a boil. Cook for 5 mins, stirring constantly. Remove the pan from the heat and add the Irish cream liquor to it.
Using a bamboo skewer, poke holes in the cooled cake. Using a pastry brush, drizzle the glaze over the cake. Allow the glaze to sink into the cake for a few mins.

7.17 Baked Bourbon Monkey Bread
Total Time: 60 mins, Servings: 6
Ingredients
Pillsbury Buttermilk Grands Biscuits, 3 Can.
Sugar, 1 Cup.
Ground Cinnamon, 3 tsp.
Butter (Unsalted), 1 Cup.
Brown (dark) Sugar, 1 Cup.
Bourbon, 1 tbsp.
Instructions
When prepared to cook, preheat the Pit Boss to 350°F with the lid covered for approximately 15 mins.
Each biscuit should be quartered. In a Ziploc container, combine sugar and cinnamon, then add quartered biscuits. To coat, toss in the cinnamon sugar.
Pour the biscuit dough into a Bundt pan coated with nonstick cooking spray.
In a small saucepan, combine the brown sugar, butter, and bourbon. Over medium heat, cook until the sugar has dissolved.
In a Bundt pan, combine the biscuits and butter mixture.
Cook it in the center of the grill for 40 mins, or until it's a deep golden brown.
Allow cooling on the counter for 5-10 mins before putting out onto a serving dish.

7.18 Baked Gluten-Free Banana Bread
Total Time: 55 mins, Servings: 4
Ingredients
2 bananas
Brown Sugar, 1/2 Cup.
Milk, 1/2 Cup
Coconut oil, 1 tbsp.
Eggs,
Vanilla Extract, 2 tsp.
Flour (Gluten-Free), 3/4 Cup.
Almond Flour, 3/4 Cup.
Baking Powder, 2 tsp.
Kosher Salt, ½ tsp.
Ground Cinnamon, 1 tsp.
Dark Chocolate Chunks, 3/4 Cup.
Instructions
Preheat the oven to 350°F and keep the lid covered for approximately 15 mins until prepared to cook.
A 9 x 5-inch loaf pan should be gently greased.
Toss together the brown sugar, mashed bananas, coconut oil, milk, egg, and vanilla in a large mixing dish.
Whisk together baking powder, flour, salt, and cinnamon in a separate large mixing basin.
In a mixing basin, whisk together the wet and dry ingredients until smooth. With a spatula, fold in the "chocolate chunks" until they are equally distributed.
Fill the loaf pan halfway with batter and bake for 50-55 mins, or until a toothpick inserted in the middle comes out clean.
Allow the bread to cool in a pan on a wire rack for ten mins before inverting onto the rack and cooling for another 30 mins before slicing.

7.19 Baked Carrot Sheet Cake with Cream Cheese Frosting
Total Time: 40 mins, Servings: 8
Ingredients
Flour, 2 Cup.
Baking Soda, 2 tbsp.
Salt, 1/2 tsp.
Ground Cinnamon, 2 tsp.
Vegetable Oil, 3/4 Cup.
Sugar, 2 cups.
Eggs, 3 Large.

Buttermilk, 3/4 Cup.
Vanilla Extract, 1/2 tsp.
Carrots (Grated), 2 Cup.
Pineapple (in chunks or crush), 1 Can.
Coconut Flakes (Large), 1 Cup.
Cream Cheese, 12 Ounce.
Butter (Softened), 3/4 Cup.
Powdered Sugar, 16 Ounce.
Coarsely Pecans (Chopped), 1 Cup
Ground Nutmeg

Instructions

In a sister, combine baking soda, flour, cinnamon, salt, cooking oil, and sugar. Using an electric mixer, blend the eggs, vanilla, and buttermilk. Slowly drizzle in the flour mixture while the motor is set to medium.

In a blender, combine 8 ounces pineapple, carrots, and flakes coconut. Using nonstick cooking spray, coat a foil tray and pour the cake batter into it.

When prepared to cook, preheat the grill to 350°F with the lid covered for approximately 15 mins.

Cook for 25-30 mins, or until a toothpick put in the middle of the cake comes out clean, directly on the grill.

When making the icing, remove the cake from the oven and put it aside to cool.

To prepare the frosting, beat together cream cheese and butter in a mixer fitted with a paddle attachment until smooth. Incorporate powdered sugar gradually until the mixture is light and fluffy. Blend in the vanilla extract until well combined.

Sprinkle some cream cheese icing on top of the carrot cake after it has cooled. Before serving, toss with chopped pecans and nutmeg.

7.20 Baked Apple Turnover

Total Time: 55 mins, Servings: 4
Ingredients
Flour (All-Purpose), 1/2 Cup.
Butter, 3/4 Cup.
Cold Water, 6 tsp.
3 Apples
Sugar, 3 tbsp.
Brown Sugar, 3 tbsp.
Ground Cinnamon, 1/4 tsp.
Corn Starch, 1/2 tbsp.
Salt, 1/4 tsp.
Milk.
Turbinado Sugar, 1 tbsp.

Instructions

In a large mixing basin, whisk together the flour and butter until it resembles cornmeal, then add the water.

After mixing the dough, cover it in plastic wrap and refrigerate it for 30 mins.

As dough chills, peel, core, and dice the apples, then combine them with brown sugar, butter, cornstarch, cinnamon, and salt.

When prepared to cook, preheat the Pit Boss to 325°F with the lid closed for approximately 15 mins.

Roll chilled dough into a 1/4" thick round on a lightly floured cutting board. Place the apple mixture in the center. Invert the corners and fold them inward.

Wipe the tart's top with milk and sprinkle it with "Turbinado sugar."

Place it on a parchment-lined "sheet pan" or directly on the grill with the parchment paper.

Bake the turnovers for at least 25 to 30 mins.

Serve with a dollop of whip cream or a scoop of vanilla ice cream on the side.

7.21 Pumpkin Pie with Bourbon Whipped Cream

Total Time: 60 mins, Servings: 6
Ingredients
1 Pie Crust Frozen (Thawed)
Pumpkin (Canned), 15 Ounces.
4teen Ounce Condensed Milk (Sweetened)
Pumpkin Pie Spices, 1/2 tsp.
Vanilla Extract, 1/2 tsp.
Salt
2 large Eggs,
Heavy Cream, 1 Cup.
Powdered Sugar, 2 tbsp.
Bourbon, 1/2 tbsp.

Instructions

Keep the "pie crust" refrigerated till all set use. In a mixing cup, combine the cream, pumpkin, pumpkin pie spices, vanilla, and salt, ideally using a hand mixer. Whip in the eggs until well combined. The filling should be poured into the pie shell.

When prepared to cook, preheat the Pit Boss to 425°F with the lid closed for approximately 10-15 mins.

Preheat the oven to 350°F and bake the pie for at least 15 mins.

Reduce oven temperature to 350°F and bake for an additional 35–40 mins, or until a thin knife inserted in the middle of the custard comes out clean.

Whip the cream with a hand mixer or an eggbeater until soft peaks form. Before fully mixing, whisk in the sugar, whiskey, and 1/2 tsp vanilla essence. Butter may be made by overwhipping (bourbon-flavored). Serve with puff pastry.

7.22 Triple Chocolate Cast Iron Cookie

Total Time: 35 mins, Servings: 4
Ingredients
Butter (Softened), 1 Cup
Vanilla Extract, 1 tsp.
Sugar, 1/2 Cup.
2 Eggs
Flour, 1/4 Cup.
Baking Soda, 1 tsp.
Kosher Salt, 2 tsp.
Brown Sugar, 1/2 Cup.
Chocolate Chips, 1 Cup.
Chocolate (dark) Chips, 1/2 Cup.
Chocolate (white) Chips, 1/2 Cup

Instructions

Before the fire is ready, turn on the "Pit Boss grill" to smoke and keep the lid open (4-5 mins). Preheat the oven to high, cover, and set aside for 10-15 mins to warm up.

In a mixing dish, combine the vanilla, butter, and sugars. Crack the eggs into the mixture one by one. "Combine the wet and dry ingredients."

Form into large balls and cook in a cast-iron pan. Bake for 15 mins on warm in the Pit Boss.

7.23 Baked Honey Cornbread Cake

Total Time: 50 mins, Servings: 6
Ingredients
Vegetable Oil, 2/3 Cup.
Buttermilk, 1/2 Cup.
4 large Eggs (Lightly Beaten)
Butter (Melted), 5 tbsp.
Mayonnaise, 1/2 Cup.
Honey, 2 tbsp.
Flour, 3 Cup.
Baking Powder, 2 tbsp.
Salt, 1 tsp.

1 Cornmeal
Granulated Sugar, 1/2 Cup.
Instructions
When you're ready, start preparing. Preheat
the Pit Boss to 350°F with the cover closed (10-15).
In a medium mixing bowl, combine the buttermilk, cooking oil, melted butter, eggs, mayonnaise, and honey.
Combine the sugar, flour, baking powder, cornmeal, and salt in a large mixing basin.
To combine the wet and dry ingredients, gently fold them together, taking care not to overmix. Next, coat a 9x13" baking dish with cooking oil.
Pour the mixture into the prepared baking dish and bake for 35-40 mins, or until the top of the cornbread starts to brown and crack.
Before slicing, remove the meat from the Pit Boss and let it cool fully. Cornbread cake may be served with butter and honey.

7.24 Strawberry Rhubarb Cobbler

Total Time: 45 mins, Servings: 6
Ingredients
Sugar, 5/8 Cup
Tapioca (Quick), 2 tbsp.
Salt, 1 Pinch.
Rhubarb (Fresh), 4 Cup
 Fresh Strawberries, 1/2 Cup.
Orange Liqueur, 1 tbsp.
1 Egg (Beaten)
Cream, 1/4 Cup.
Vanilla Extract, 1/2 tsp.
Almond Extract, 1/4 tsp.
Flour, 1 Cup.
Baking Powder, 1/2 tsp.
Cinnamon, 1/2 tsp.
Salt, 1/4 tsp.
Chilled Butter, 4 tbsp.
Instructions
Butter liberally a 2-quart baking dish or casserole, as well as 6 ramekins or individual gratin plates.
In a large mixing basin, whisk together the tapioca, sugar, and salt to fill. Then, with a rubber spatula, fold in the strawberries (hulled and quartered), rhubarb (diced and trimmed), and orange liqueur, if using.
In a mixing basin, whisk together the egg, salt, vanilla, and almond extracts to make the topping. In a mixing cup, combine the sugar, flour, cinnamon, baking powder, & salt. To blend, combine all the ingredients in a mixing bowl. Using the pastry cutter, cut some butter into flour mix unless coarse crumbs form. Toss the flour with a fork, then whisk in the milk and egg mixture until well combined.
Fill the prepared (baking) dish or ramekins with the fruit and its juices. Make an equal layer of batter on top. Sugar may be sprinkled on top if desired.
Warm the Pit Boss to 350°F and preheat for 10 to 15 mins with the top covered.
Place the (baking) dish or ramekins directly on the grill and bake for 30 to 35 mins, or until the filling has bubbled and the topping has become golden brown. Allow for a few mins of cooling before serving.

7.25 Smoked Cherry Bourbon Ice Cream

Total Time: 2 Hrs 40 Mins, Servings: 4
Ingredients
1 Pound Fresh or Frozen Whole Cherries, Pitted
1 Tbsp Water
10 Tbsp Sugar
3 Tbsp Bourbon
1 Cup Milk
1 cup Heavy Cream
Salt
6 Egg Yolk
1 Vanilla Bean, Split Lengthwise
Instructions
When prepared to cook, preheat the grill to 180°F with the lid covered for 15 mins. If Super Smoke is available, use it for the best taste.
Place fresh cherries on your grill grate using a sheet tray. For around 30 mins, smoke your cherries. Then, remove the steaks from the grill & put them aside.
In a small saucepan, combine the cherries, water, sugar & bring to a simmer on medium heat. Cook for 10 mins or until the liquid has condensed to a syrupy consistency. Take the pan off the heat, add the bourbon, and put it aside.
In a small saucepan, combine the milk, cream, egg yolks, sugar, salt, & vanilla bean, then bring to your boil, stirring continuously. Cook till the sauce has thickened to the point where it coats the back of a spoon.
Remove the pan from the heat and pour the contents into a heatproof dish set across the ice bath. Allow cooling fully.
In the ice cream machine, churn the ice cream base as per the manufacturer's directions.

7.26 Smoked Irish Coffee Pie

Total Time: 60 Mins, Servings: 6
Ingredients
16 Ritz Crackers
12 Oreo Cookies
4 Tbsp Unsalted Butter
1 1/2 Cup Heavy Cream
1/2 Cup Sugar
2 Tbsp Bailey's Irish Cream
3 Tbsp Coffee, Instant
4 Tbsp Lindt Excellence 70% Cocoa Bar
5 Egg Yolk
Instructions
When prepared to cook, preheat the grill to 180°F with the lid covered for 15 mins. If Super Smoke is available, use it for the best taste.
To prepare the crust, blend the ritz, Oreos, & melted butter in the food processor. Then, use hands to press the mix on the bottom & edges of an 8-inch pie plate.
Take cream to your simmer in a small saucepan. Remove the pan from heat & stir in some Irish Cream, sugar, & instant coffee. Whisk everything together unless the sugar has completely dissolved.
Fill a small baking dish halfway with pie filling & put it immediately on your grill grate. 10 mins of smoking. Remove the steaks from the grill & put them aside.
Preheat your grill at 325 degrees Fahrenheit.
To melt the chocolate, put it in a metallic bowl and set it on the double boiler.
Whisk egg yolks in a different dish, then gently pour in some cream mix while whisking. Whisk in the melted chocolate slowly. To prevent the yolks from curdling, ensure the cream & chocolate are only warm, without hot.
Pour the mixture into the pie crust that has been made. Cook @ 325°F for around 30-35 mins or straight on your grill grate unless the center is set. Place on the cooling rack & set aside to cool fully. Serve with a dollop of whipped cream on top. Enjoy!

7.27 Pit Boss Chocolate Chip Cookies

Total Time: 50 Mins, Servings: 8
Ingredients

Unsalted Butter 1 Cup
Brown Sugar 1 Cup
Granulated Sugar 1/2 Cup
Eggs 2
Vanilla 2 Tsp
All-Purpose Flour 3 Cup
Baking Powder 1 Tsp
Baking Soda 1/2 Tsp
Jacobsen Salt 2 Tsp
Dark Chocolate Chips 1 & 1/2 Cup
Instructions
When prepared to cook, preheat the Pit Boss to 350°F with the lid covered for 15 mins.
In the stand mixer, combine the butter & both sugars, then beat on low speed for around 3-4 mins, or unless the mixture lightens in color & the sugar has completely absorbed into this butter.
Add the eggs, waiting till the 1st is well mixed before moving on to the next, and the vanilla extract.
Combine all dry ingredients in a wide mixing bowl & whisk thoroughly. Decrease the frequency to medium-low & add flour mix in three parts, mixing well after each addition.
Remove the stand mixer bowl & add chocolate chips. Hand-mix using the spatula till evenly combined.
Line 2 half-sheet sheets using parchment paper & divide out all the cookie dough with a scoop, putting four cookies on every sheet pan. Keep them piled high to provide a chewy, doughy inside with a baked outside. If preferred, add a pinch of sea salt.
Bake all sheet trays straight on your grill grate for around 30-35 mins, or unless lightly browned. Allow 10 mins for them to set up at room temp after removing them from your grill. Enjoy!

7.28 Flourless Chocolate Cake with Raspberry Sauce
Total Time: 55 Mins, Servings: 6
Ingredients
1 As Needed Cooking Spray
3 Tbsp Unsweetened Cocoa Powder
3/4 Cup Unsalted Butter
12 Ounce Semisweet Chocolate, Such as Guittard, Coarsely Chopped Or In Small Pieces
1/2 Tsp Salt
1 Tsp Vanilla Extract
6 Whole Eggs, Room Temperature
1 1/2 Cup Granulated Sugar
Raspberry Sauce
2 Cup Fresh Raspberries or Frozen Raspberries, Thawed
2 Tbsp Granulated Sugar
1 Tsp Fresh Lemon Juice
Instructions
When prepared to cook, preheat the Pit Boss to 325°F with the lid closed for 15 mins.
Spray 8 tiny ramekins. Dust with some cocoa powder.
Melt the butter in a wide saucepan on low heat. Whisk in chocolate & salt until completely melted. Remove the pan from heat & add the vanilla extract.
In the stand mixer, whisk together the eggs & sugar. 3-4 mins on medium, or unless light & fluffy. Instead, the hand mixer may be used.
Stir your chocolate into the egg mix until it is evenly distributed.
Pour all cake batter into a pan that has been prepared.
Place that pans on your grill grate & bake for 35-40 mins.
To make the raspberry sauce, combine the following ingredients in a blender. In a food processor, combine the raspberries, sugar, & lemon juice. Blend for around 30 seconds, or till you get a smooth purée. Remove all seeds from the sauce by straining them. Taste and adjust with additional lemon juice & sugar if necessary.
Drizzle some raspberry sauce over the cake in the small dish. Serve right away.

7.29 Traditional Baked Pumpkin Pie
Total Time: 1 Hrs 55 Mins, Servings: 6
Ingredients
2 1/2 Cup Flour
1 3/4 Tsp Salt
6 Tbsp Unsalted Butter, Cubed
3/4 Cup Vegetable Shortening
1/2 Cup Cold Water
3/4 Cup Sugar
1 1/2 Tsp Cinnamon
1/2 Tsp Ground Ginger
1/4 Tsp Ground Cloves
1/4 Tsp Ground Nutmeg
2 Eggs
15 Ounce Pumpkin Puree
12 Ounce Milk, Evaporated
Instructions
In the food processor, pulse the flour & salt until well mixed & aerated.
Add the cold butter & shortening next. Pulse 3 to 4 times till the texture resembles a pea-sized hazelnut mixture. Drizzle in some cold water while the mixer is running.
Stop pulsing after the mixture has come together and begun to retain its form, & finish by mixing with hand to integrate all of the flour in one dough ball. Refrigerate until hard, then divide into two discs and cover in plastic wrap.
Make a circle of dough that might fit in a pie plate with an overhang. To make a decorative edge, pinch its edges together. Prepare the filling and pour it into the shell. Place on the baking sheet with a foil tent over it.
Set the temperature to High & warm for 15 mins with the lid covered. Preheat the oven to high and bake for around 15 mins.
Reduce the oven temperature to 350 degrees Fahrenheit & bake for around 40 mins.
Allow it cool for one hr before storing it in the refrigerator overnight.

7.30 Baked Cherry Bourbon Pie
Total Time: 1 Hr 30 Mins, Servings: 8
Ingredients
Crumble
1/2 cup Old Fashioned Oats
1/4 Cup All-Purpose Flour
1/4 Cup Brown Sugar
1/4 cup Sliced Almonds
1/2 Tsp Salt
1/4 Cup Unsalted Butter, Chilled
Filling
3/4 Cup Sugar
3 Tbsp Cornstarch
6 Cup Frozen Sweet Cherries, Thawed And Drained
2 Tbsp Bourbon
1 Tbsp Fresh Orange Juice
1 Tbsp Orange Zest
main
1 Whole Store Bought Or Homemade Pie Dough
Instructions
When prepared to cook, preheat the Pit Boss to 350°F with the lid covered for 15 mins.
To make the crumble, combine the oats, almonds,
brown sugar, flour, & salt in a wide mixing bowl. Mix in the cold butter with your fingertips until it resembles crumbs. Refrigerate

for a few hrs.
Filling Ingredients: Whisk together the sugar & cornstarch in a wide mixing bowl. Combine the cherries, whiskey, orange juice, & zest in a mixing glass. Using a spatula, gently fold the pieces together.
Roll out pie dough sufficient to cover the pie pan, either from scratch or from a shop. The edges should be crimped.
Fill each pie crust with the filling. Place the crumble on top of the filling in the Pit Boss.
Bake for around 60 mins, or until the filling is bubbling & the crust & crumble topping become golden brown. Allow time for the pie to cool.

7.31 Baked Bread Pudding by Doug Scheiding
Total Time: 1 Hr 25 Mins, Servings: 8
Ingredients
3 Cup Sugar
2 1/2 Tbsp Vanilla
6 Eggs
2 cup Heavy Cream
1/2 Cup Water
6 Cup Bread, Challah
12 Ounce White Chocolate
Butter
1/2 Cup Light Brown Sugar
3/4 Cup Butter, Softened
1 cup Coarsely Chopped Pecans
Cinnamon
5 Tbsp Bourbon
1 Pinch Salt
Instructions
Combine sugar, vanilla, eggs, heavy cream, & water in a wide mixing bowl. Toss in the bread to coat.
In a medium saucepan, combine both white chocolate & heavy cream, then heat till chocolate becomes melted. Allow it to cool somewhat before pouring on the bread mix. Toss to mix, keeping track not to over-break the bread. Allow 30 mins for the ingredients to rest before pouring into a generously greased Dutch oven. Any leftover liquid should be poured on top of the bread mixture.
Combine butter, brown sugar, & pecans in a mixing bowl. Sprinkle nuts on bread mix, then a thin sprinkling of cinnamon. Start your Pit Boss grill & adjust the temperature to 325°F. Preheat for around 10-15 mins with the lid closed.
Place the Dutch oven on your grill grate & cook for 50-60 mins, or until the sauce has thickened and is boiling.
To make the bourbon glaze, mix the butter, sugar, & bourbon in a medium saucepan & heat to a boil. Decrease the heat to low and cook for 2 mins. Remove from the fire & season with some salt. If desired, add more butter/bourbon.
Well before serving, drizzle the glaze over the bread pudding.

7.32 Baked Cherry Cheesecake Galette
Total Time: 30 Mins, Servings: 6
Ingredients
1 Pound Cherries, Thawed and Drained If Using Frozen
1/4 Cup Plus 1 Tbsp Sugar
1 Tbsp Orange Zest
1/2 Tbsp Lemon Zest
1 Tsp Coriander
1 Tsp Cornstarch
1 Pinch Salt
1 Refrigerated Pie Crust
Egg Wash (1 Egg Plus 1 Tbsp Water, Milk or Cream)
Granulated Sugar
Vanilla Ice Cream, For Serving
Cream Cheese Filling
8 Ounce Cream Cheese, Softened
1 Egg
1 Tsp Vanilla
1/4 Cup Sugar
Instructions
When prepared to cook, preheat the Pit Boss to 350°F with the lid covered for 15 mins.
Combine cherries, sugar, salt, orange, cornstarch, coriander, & lemon zest in a wide mixing bowl.
To make cream cheese filling, whisk together vanilla, sugar, cream cheese, & egg in a different dish.
Stretch pie dough using the rolling pin till it is 1" bigger in diameter over a sheet pan.
In the middle of pie crust, spread cream cheese filling, leaving a 1" border all-around borders. Over cream cheese, pile some cherry mix.
Fold your pie dough's edges up & on the filling in tiny pieces. Egg washes the edges & sprinkle the leftover granulated sugar on top.
Bake your galette for 15-20 mins, till the crust becomes golden brown & cheesecake filling is set straight on your grill grate.
Serve the galette with some ice cream while it's still warm.

7.33 Holiday Brownie Pie
Total Time: 1 Hr 25 Mins, Servings: 8
Ingredients
1 1/4 Cup Flour
1/4 Tsp Salt
1/3 Cup Vegetable Shortening, Plus More as Needed
1/2 Cup Salted Butter, Softened
3 Ounce Unsweetened Chocolate, Chopped
3 Whole Lightly Beaten Egg
1 & ½ Cup Sugar Granulated
½ Cup Flour All-Purpose
1 Tsp Vanilla
2 Cup Chocolate Pieces Mint Flavored
1 Cup of Chocolate Chips
Whipped Cream
Instructions
Combine flour & salt in a mixing bowl. Cut in the shortening with the pastry blender till the bits are pea-size.
Sprinkle some cold water on a portion of the mix; toss softly using a fork. The wet dough should be pushed to the edge of a bowl.
Using 1 tbsp cold water at a time, wet the dough till it is completely moistened.
Make a ball out of the dough. Using your hands to flatten the dough on a floured surface.
Prepare the puff pastry & roll it out. Trim & crimp the edge of a pie dish with pastry.
To assemble: Melt butter & chocolate in a small pot over medium heat, stirring constantly. Allow 20 mins for cooling.
Combine the eggs, flour, sugar, & vanilla in a wide bowl. Combine the chocolate mix & chocolate pieces in a mixing bowl. Pour into a pie dish lined with puff pastry.
Preheat the oven to 350°F and leave the lid covered for 10-15 mins.
Bake for around 55 mins, or unless the filling has uniformly puffed & slightly cracked around the edges.
Cool completely on a wire rack. Serve using a dollop of whipped cream on top.

7.34 Grilled Stone Fruit with Berries & Cream
Total Time: 25 Mins, Servings: 4
Ingredients
2 Peaches, Halved
2 Apricot, Halved

1 Nectarine, Halved
1/2 cup Balsamic Vinegar
3 Tbsp Honey, Divided
1 Tbsp Orange Peel
2 Cup Cream
1/2 Cup Fresh Raspberries
1/4 Cup Blueberries
Instructions
Set the Pit Boss to 400°F & preheat for 15 mins with the lid covered.
Place 3-4 mins per side on the grill for nectarines, apricots, & peaches. Grill marks & a mild smokey flavor are ideal.
For Balsamic Reduction, follow these steps: Add the balsamic vinegar, honey, & orange peel to a skillet over medium heat. Allow boiling until the sauce has thickened to a moderate consistency.
Meanwhile, beat cream & honey in a dish till soft peaks appear.
Place stone fruits grilled on a dish, then top with berries & balsamic reduction. Whipped cream is served on its side.

7.35 Baked Pear Tarte Tatin
Total Time: 55 Mins, Servings: 6
Ingredients
2 1/2 Cup All-Purpose Flour
2 Tbsp Sugar
Butter, Chilled
8 Tbsp Cold Water
1/4 Cup Granulated Sugar
1/4 Cup Butter
8 Whole Bartlett Pear
Instructions
Preheat the oven to 350°F & leave the lid covered for 10-15 mins.
To make the crust: Pulse flour & sugar together in the food processor to combine. Pulse in a little amount of butter. When it resembles cornmeal, add some water and stir till the dough comes together.
Form a circle out of the dough, cover it with plastic wrap, & chill it.
Make caramel sauce while your dough cools. Add granulated sugar & butter to the saucepan. Cook for a few mins, until the butter & sugar has become a rich caramel color.
Fill a cake pan halfway with caramel. Then, arrange pear slices into a fan configuration on top of caramel while it's still hot.
Roll out the cold pie dough in a large circle to fit the pan. Cover your pan with pie dough after pricking it using a fork. Allow for shrinking while trimming the crust.
Place pears on your grill & cook for 45 mins, or till soft. Most of the liquid would evaporate & thicken as the pears soften.
Put a plate on the pie & turn it over while the pan remains hot. Lift this plate slowly. Allow for 3 mins of resting time.
Serve warm with a dollop of whipped cream on top.

7.36 Crème Brûlée
Total Time: 60 Mins, Servings: 2
Ingredients
1 Quart Heavy Whipping Cream
1 Pieces Vanilla Bean, Split and Scraped Or 1 Tsp Of Vanilla Extract
6 Large Egg Yolk
1 Cup Sugar
Instructions
When you're all set to cook, fire up your Pit Boss grill. Till the fire has created, smoke with its lid open. Next, preheat the oven to 325°F with the lid covered for around 10-15 mins.
In a medium-high-heat saucepan, combine the vanilla bean, cream, & scraped seeds. Bring the water to a boil. Leave too steep after removing from the heat. Remove and discard each vanilla bean from the pot.
Whisk egg yolks & sugar in a mixing dish until the mixture begins to brighten in color. Slowly drizzle in the cream, stirring constantly.
Put the ramekins in a wide roasting pan & pour the mix into 6 ramekins. Fill the pan with boiling water until it reaches midway through the sides of the ramekins.
Put the water bath pan on your grill & bake for 40-45 mins, till the Crème Brûlées slightly jiggle in the middle.
Refrigerate your ramekins for almost 2 hrs & till 2 days after removing them from the roasting pan.
Allow 20 mins for Crème Brûlée to get to room temperature before touching on tops.
Over of every ramekin, evenly sprinkle sugar. Melt your sugar until it caramelizes and produces a crispy top.
Allow for some time of resting time before serving your Crème Brûlée.

7.37 Smoked Sweet Potato Soufflé by Diva Q
Total Time: 1 Hr 30 mins, Servings: 4
Ingredients
Sweet Potatoes, 4 Large.
Brown Sugar, 3/4 Cup.
Pit Boss Simple Smoked Syrup, 1 cup.
3 Eggs.
Heavy Cream, 1/4 Cup.
Butter, 7 tbsp.
Vanilla Extract, 1 tbsp.
Fresh Thyme, 1 tbsp.
Pit Boss Chicken Rub, 1 tsp.
Pecans, 1 Cup.
Brown Sugar, 1 Cup.
Flour, 1/2 Cup.
Salt, 1/2 tsp.
Bourbon, 2 tbsp.
Instructions
Preheat the oven to 350°F and keep the lid covered for approximately 15 mins until prepared to cook.
Prick each sweet potato with a fork and place it immediately on the grill grate. It should be grilled for approximately 60 mins, or until the potatoes are tender. Allow for a cooling time of 15 mins.
Potatoes should be cut in half, and the flesh scraped out using a spoon. Then, by hand, mash sweet potatoes until smooth, then press through a "fine mesh sieve."
In a large mixing bowl, combine the sugar, sweet potatoes, eggs, Pit Boss Quick Syrup, butter, milk, thyme, vanilla, and the "Pit Boss Chicken Rub."
In a greased 9x9 glass baking dish, pour the potato mixture (buttered).
To create the topping, in a large mixing bowl, add brown sugar, pecans, Pit Boss simple syrup, butter, salt, flour, and bourbon (optional). Using the frosting, cover the casserole.
Bake at 350°F for 30 mins, or until golden brown on top.
If preferred, garnish with toasted marshmallows, nuts, and fresh thyme sprigs. Before eating, reheat the food.

7.38 Tarte Tatin
Total Time: 1 Hr 20 mins, Servings: 6
Ingredients
Flour (All-Purpose), 2 Cups.
Salt, 1 tsp
Butter, 1 Cup.
Cold Water, 5 tbsp.
Unsalted Butter, 1/4 Cup.

Granulated Sugar, 3/4 Cup.
10 Apple granny smith (in Wedges),
Instructions
When prepared to cook, preheat the Pit Boss to 350 degrees F with the lid covered for approximately 10 to 15 mins.
To create the crust, mix the salt and flour in a food processor. Add a little bit of butter at a time, pulsing after each addition. Add water and mix until the dough comes together until it resembles cornmeal. Form the dough into a circle, cover it in plastic wrap, and refrigerate it.
Preheat the grill as the dough cools, butter and sugar in a pie dish or a 10" round cake pan. Allow for caramelization.
Remove the sugar from the grill after it has caramelized and become a deep amber color. Then, in a fan form, cover the caramel with "apple wedges."
Make a circle out of the pie dough that is large enough to cover the whole dish. After pricking the plate with a fork, cover it with the pastry dough. When trimming the crust, keep in mind that it will shrink.
Place the apples on the grill for 55 mins or until tender. Allow for a 3-min rest period. While the pan is still moist, place a plate over the pie and flip it over.
Serve hot, topped with whipped cream or ice cream.

7.39 Oatmeal Chocolate Chip Cookies
Total Time: 20 mins, Servings: 8
Ingredients
Brown Sugar, 3/4 Cup.
Sugar, 1/2 Cup.
Butter (Softened), 1 Cup.
Vanilla, 1 tsp.
Eggs, 1.
Rolled Oats, 2 Cup.
Flour (All-Purpose), 1/2 Cup.
Baking Soda, 1 tsp.
Salt, 1 tsp.
Chocolate Chips (Semisweet), 3/4 Cup.
Instructions
When you're all set to cook, preheat the Pit Boss to 350°F with the lid covered for approximately 10-15 mins.
Cream the sugars and butter together in a large mixing bowl until smooth. Whisk the egg and vanilla extract together in a separate dish until light and frothy.
In a mixing basin, combine the oats, pasta, baking soda, and salt. Toss in some chocolate chunks.
Drop the dough onto a parchment-lined baking sheet in a rounded heaping spoonful, spacing them approximately 2" apart.
Bake for 10 to 12 mins, or until golden brown. Allow cooling for a few mins before transferring to a wire rack to cool completely.

7.40 Baked Cherry Cobbler
Total Time: 50 mins, Servings: 8
Ingredients
Flour (All-Purpose), 1/2 Cup.
Sugar, 51 tsp.
Baking Powder, 1/2 tsp.
Salt, 3/4 tsp.
Unsalted Butter (Cold), 8 tbsp.
Sour Cream, 1/2 Cup.
Cornstarch, 3 tbsp.
Cherries (Pitted), 5 Cup.
Lemon Juice
1 Lemon Zest.
1 Orange Zest.
Vanilla Extract, 1/2 tsp
Turbinado Sugar
Whipped Cream
Instructions
In a medium mixing cup, combine sugar, flour, baking powder, and salt to make the topping with a cookie cutter or two knives, cut in the chilled butter until the mixture resembles peas and ground-up crackers.
Fold in the sour cream until it is evenly distributed (be careful not to "over mix" or overwork the dough).
In a mixing dish, combine cornstarch, sugar, and salt to create the filling. Lemon juice, cherries, citrus zest, and vanilla should be set aside.
Finish with the cobbler topping and the "cherry filling" in the baking dish. On top, "turbinado sugar" should be sprinkled.
Start Pit Boss according to the manufacturer's instructions when you're all set to cook. Preheat the oven to 350 degrees F and bake with the lid covered for 10-15 mins.
Bake for 35-45 mins, or until the cobbler topping is finely colored and bubbling immediately on the grill. The mixture should have thickened to the consistency of syrup.
Serve with a dollop of whipped cream on top.

7.41 Holiday Roasted Apple Pudding
Total Time: 1 Hr 25 mins, Servings: 6
Ingredients
Sweetened Cranberries (Dried), 1/2 Cup.
Ginger (Candied & Finely Diced), 1 tbsp.
Apple Cider (Hot), 1/4 Cup.
Cream Cheese (Softened), 6 Ounces.
Brown Sugar (Firmly Packed), 3 tbsp.
Butter (Softened), 2 tbsp.
Vanilla Extract, 1/2 tsp.
Ground Cinnamon, 1/2 tsp.
Ground Nutmeg, 1 Pinch.
Walnuts (Chopped), 1/4 Cup.
Apple (Crisp, Baking), 6 Large.
Walnuts, Halves.
Instructions
In a shallow heatproof dish, pour the hot apple cider over the cranberries and ginger if using. Allow 30 mins for the apple cider to soak before draining and storing it.
Set the oven to 350 degrees Fahrenheit and warm for 10 to 15 mins with the lid closed.
In a medium mixing bowl, beat together the
brown sugar, cream cheese, vanilla, butter, cinnamon, and nutmeg until smooth. 1/4 cup chopped walnuts, leftover cranberries, and ginger are added to the mixture.
Starting at the stem and moving down, core the apples, leaving the bottom half intact. (If you puncture a hole in the rim by accident, use a marshmallow to patch it up.) Remove 1/2 inch of skin from the equator of the apple to prevent it from breaking during roasting. The filling should be stuffed into the apples.
Arrange apples vertically in a compact baking dish. Pour the apple cider that has been put aside into the dish's foundation. Roast apples for 45-60 mins, occasionally basting with apple cider. Warm walnut halves should be placed on top of the dish.

7.42 Grilled Plums with Brown Sugar Balsamic Reduction
Total Time: 25 mins, Servings: 4
Ingredients
Black Plum, 10 Whole.
Balsamic Vinegar, 1/2 Cup.
Brown Sugar, 1/2 Cup.
Instructions

Plums should be rinsed (halve & pit them).
Set the oven to High (450o F) and preheat for 15 mins when ready to cook.
Cook the plums for 10 mins on the grill grate, cut side down.
Meanwhile, reduce the "balsamic vinegar" by boiling it with sugar (brown) in a saucepan over medium heat until thickened and reduced by half, about 5-10 mins.
Brush the plums with the balsamic and brown sugar reduction and roast for another 2 to 5 mins. Plums soften somewhat but remain firm.
Serve the plums softly drizzled with any leftover balsamic reduction.

7.43 Grilled Peaches & Cream Popsicle
Total Time: 15 mins, Servings: 4
Ingredients
Honey, 10 tbsp.
Peaches (Halved), 4 Whole.
Yogurt (Plain), 1 Cup.
Vanilla Bean (Split & Scraped), 1 Whole.
Cream, 1 Cup.
Instructions
When prepared to cook, preheat the oven to 4500 degrees Fahrenheit with the lid covered for 10 to 15 mins.
Drizzle 2 tbsp honey over the cut side of the peaches and cook them cut side down.
Cook for 10 mins total, or until grill marks appear. Place the steaks in a blender once they have been removed from the grill. After pureeing until smooth, set aside.
Combine the sugar, cream, residual butter, and "vanilla beans" scraped off the vanilla bean in a medium mixing cup. Whisk the ingredients together to combine them.
Fill popsicle molds half, full of peach puree and half full of chocolate, leaving a little space at the end.
Insert a popsicle stick into each popsicle and freeze for at least 4 hrs.

7.44 Carrot Souffle
Total Time: 1 Hr 10 mins, Servings: 4
Ingredients
Cooking Spray
Carrots (Fresh), 1 lb.
Sugar, 1 tbsp.
Butter (Softened), 1/2 Cup.
Eggs, 3.
Vanilla Extract, 1 tsp.
Flour, 1/4 Cup.
Baking Powder, 1 tsp
Ground Cinnamon, 1/2 tsp.
Ground Nutmeg, 1/4 tsp.
Salt, 1/8 tsp.
Powdered Sugar
Instructions
Set aside a cooking mist-coated glass or Al pie dish that measures 8 to 9 inches in diameter.
Carrots should be peeled and sliced into 1" pieces. Bring a (sauce) pan of water and 1 tbsp sugar to a boil over high pressure. Cook, often stirring, for 20 to 25 mins or until the carrots are very soft.
Drain and place the carrots in a mixing dish. Using a hand mixer, mash until smooth. Incorporate the butter into the mixture. In a mixing bowl, whisk together the eggs and vanilla extract. Toss the carrot mixture with the baking powder, flour, nutmeg, cinnamon, and salt until thoroughly combined. Fill the pie dish with the prepared filling.
When you're ready to start cooking, Preheat the Pit Boss to 350 degrees Fahrenheit and leave the lid covered for 10 to 15 mins.
Preheat oven to 350°F and bake for 50–60 mins, or until golden brown on top and a toothpick inserted in the middle comes out clean. Allow cooling somewhat before dusting with powdered sugar, if desired. It's great hot, cold, or at room temperature. Any leftovers should be stored in the fridge.

7.45 Baked Pear & Fig Upside Down Cake
Total Time: 1 Hr 20 mins, Servings: 6
Ingredients
Butter
Butter Unsalted (at room temp), 13 tbsp.
Brown Sugar, 1/2 Cup.
Pear (Cut In 1/8" Thick Slices), Length Wise, 1 Whole.
Figs (Cut in 1/2), 4 Whole.
Granulated Sugar, 3/4 Cup.
Eggs, 3 Whole
Vanilla, 1 tsp.
Cake Flour, 1/2 Cup.
Baking Powder, 3/4 tsp.
Baking Soda, 1/4 tsp.
Sour Cream, 1/2 Cup.
Salt, 1/4 tsp.
Instructions
When you're ready to start cooking, Preheat the Pit Boss to 350 degrees F and leave the lid covered for approximately 10 to 15 mins.
Butter a 10-inch cast-iron pan or a conventional cake pan.
In a mixing dish, combine the butter and brown sugar. In the bottom of a cast iron tub, sprinkle the brown sugar and butter mixture over the fruit.
In a stand mixer, cream together the butter and sugar until light and fluffy. Pound for another min after adding the eggs and vanilla essence. In a mixing cup, combine the baking powder, sifted rice, and baking soda. Add the sour cream and mix well.
Pour the mixture over the fruit and place the pan immediately on the grill grate. Preheat the oven to 350 degrees Fahrenheit and bake for 35–45 mins.
Allow the cake to rest for 10 mins. Loop a knife around the corners of the cake to remove the sides. Invert the cake onto a serving platter (cake must be warm while inverted onto the plate).
Cut into slices and serve.

7.46 Lava Cake (Chocolate) and Whipped Cream (Smoked)
Total Time: 60 mins, Servings: 4
Ingredients
Whipping Cream, 1 Pint.
Butter (Melted), 1/2 Cup.
1/2-Sweet Chocolate, 1 Cup.
Powdered Sugar, 1/4 Cup.
Eggs, 2 Large.
Egg Yolk, 2.
Flour, 6 tbsp.
Bourbon Vanilla, 1 tbsp.
Cocoa Powder
Instructions
When preparing to cook, preheat the grill to 180°F and leave the lid covered for approximately 15 mins.
Pour the cream into a shallow-rimmed Al baking pan. Allow 30 mins for the cream to flame in the Pit Boss pan. Half-fill a large mixing bowl with smoking cream and put it aside for later use. Preheat the grill to 375 degrees Fahrenheit.
1 tbsp melted butter, brush over 4 tiny "soufflé cups" Melt the chocolate and the remaining sugar in a heat-proof dish over

boiling water, stirring continuously. Combine the sugar (powdered) and vanilla essence in a separate dish. Whisk the eggs and egg yolks in a steady stream. Completely combine the flour in a separate basin.

Half-fill the "soufflé cups" with batter. On a Pit Boss, bake it for 13 to 14 mins, or until the sides are done.

Remove the cream from the fridge (chilled, smoked) and whisk in the "bourbon vanilla extract" until light and frothy. Whip until stiff peaks form, then sprinkle with confectioners' sugar.

Serve with whipped cream, confectioners' sugar, and chocolate powder.

7.47 Baked Cast-Iron Cookie with Smoked Bourbon Whip

Total Time: 35 mins, Servings: 4
Ingredients
Mascarpone, 8 Ounce.
Sugar, 11 tbsp.
Whipping Cream, 1/2 Cup.
Bourbon, 4 tbsp.
Orange Zest
Butter (Softened), 1 Cup.
Brown Sugar, 1/2 Cup.
Vanilla Extract, 1 tsp.
Egg, 2.
Flour, 1/4 Cup.
Baking Soda, 1 tsp.
Kosher Salt, 2 tsp.
Chocolate Chips, 2 Cup.
Instructions
Preheat the Pit Boss grill to 400 degrees F with the lid covered for approximately 10-15 mins.
Smoke the mascarp1 for 10 mins on high in a Pit Boss. Whip all of the ingredients until stiff peaks form.
To create the cookie, combine the vanilla, butter, and sugars in a mixing bowl. Smash the eggs into the mixture one by one. Combine the "dry ingredients" with the "wet ingredients." It's best to roll in chocolate chips.
In a Pit Boss, bake for 15 mins on high. With a dollop of whipped cream on top.

7.48 Kodiak Cakes Candied Bacon Crumble Brownies

Total Time: 1 Hr 20 Mins, Servings: 6
Ingredients
Big Bear Brownie (Kodiak Cakes) 1 Box.
Eggs, 2.
Butter (Melted), 1 Stick.
Coconut Oil, 2 tbsp.
Water, 2 tbsp.
Cooked Bacon, 2 Cup.
Almonds (Chopped), 1/2 Cup.
Sugar, 1/2 Cup.
Instructions
When ready to cook, preheat the Pit Boss to 300°F with the lid covered for approximately 15 mins.
Brush nonstick frying oil into an 8-inch "baking pan."
In a medium mixing cup, pour the brownie mix from the "Kodiak Cake." In a mixing dish, combine the melted butter, eggs, coconut oil, and water. Mix slowly and gently, being careful not to overmix. Pour into a tightly packed pan.
Bake for 45 mins on the grill grate with brownies in the center. While the brownies are baking, assemble the bacon crumble. Melt the honey/sugar in a medium saucepan over high heat. Toss in the bacon and almonds. Stir for a few mins, or until the sugar is completely dissolved. Remove the pan from the heat and let it cool.
Remove the brownies from the grill and place them on a cooling rack to cool completely. Candied bacon crumbs may be sprinkled on top of brownies.

7.49 Baked Rhubarb Cobbler

Total Time: 55 mins, Servings: 8
Ingredients
Flour (All-Purpose), 1/2 Cup.
Sugar, 3 tbsp.
Baking Powder, 1/2 tsp.
Salt, 1/2 tsp.
Chilled Butter, 8 tbsp
Sour Cream, 1/2 Cup.
Rhubarb (Fresh), 1 lb.
Brown Sugar, 1 Cup.
Salt
Lemon (Juiced), 1/4 Whole.
Lemon Zest, 1 tsp.
Vanilla, 1 tsp.
Sugar (Raw), 2 tbsp.
Instructions
Preheat the oven to 350°F and keep the lid covered for approximately 15 mins until ready to cook.
In a medium mixing cup, combine the salt, baking powder, sugar, and rice. Break-in cold butter with a pastry cutter / 2 knives until the fat and flour are pea sized.
Gently stir in the sour cream until everything is well combined (make sure not to overwork or overmix the dough).
In a shallow cup, combine the sugar, chopped rhubarb, lemon juice, salt, vanilla, and lemon zest. Toss to combine and pour into a baking dish of your choosing (8x8 works great).
Spoon the "biscuit dough" on top of the rhubarb in dollops until it's all gone. On top, "raw sugar" should be sprinkled.
Cook it on the grill for 35 mins, or until the "biscuit topping" is finely browned and the cobbler is boiling.
Serve it with a dollop of whipped cream on top.

7.50 Baked Peach Cobbler

Total Time: 55 mins, Servings: 8
Ingredients
2 tbsp Butter (Melted)
3 lb Yellow Peaches (pitted & sliced)
Simple Pit Boss Syrup Smoked, 1/4 Cup.
Flour, 2/3 Cup.
Baking Powder, 3/4 tsp.
Cinnamon
Salt
1/2 Cup Unsalted Butter
1/2 Cup Sugar.
1 Egg Whole.
1/2 tsp Vanilla.
1 tbsp Sugar (raw).
Instructions
Set the Pit Boss to 350°F and warm it for at
least 15 mins before you're ready to cook. Coat the inside of the cast-iron pan with 2 tbsps melted butter.
In a medium bowl, toss the peaches with some Simple Syrup (Smoked) and place them in the (prepared) cast iron pan.
Set aside a small bowl containing baking powder, flour, salt, and cinnamon.
In a separate dish, cream together the butter and 1/2 cup sugar. In a mixing dish, combine the vanilla essence and the egg.
Slowly pour in the flour mixture. Finish with a sprinkle of raw sugar on top of the battered peaches.
Preheat the grill to 350 degrees Fahrenheit and roast the cast-

iron skillet for 35 to 45 mins. Have a good time. Cooking periods will vary depending on the temperature of the oven and the temperature of the air.

7.51 Chocolate Chip Cookies
Total Time: 30 mins, Servings: 4
Ingredients
1/2 Cup Flour,
1 tsp Baking Soda
1/2 tsp Salt
1/2 Stick Butter (Softened)
1 Cup Brown Sugar (Firmly Packed)
1/2 Cup Sugar
2 Egg, Whole
1 tsp Vanilla Extract,
2 1/2-sweet Chocolate Chips Cup.
1/2 Cup Walnuts/Pecans (Optional).
Instructions
Combine baking soda, flour, and salt in a large mixing basin. Beat the butter in a separate dish until it becomes frothy. Add the (brown) sugar, eggs, sugar, and vanilla at this point.
Slowly incorporate the "flour mixture." Fold the "chocolate chips" and almonds into the dough with care.
Using a spoon, place a tbsp of dough in an Al foil pan.
Preheat the oven to 350°F when you're ready to start. To prevent sticking, bake it for approximately 17 mins in the oven. To make each batch of cookies, start with new foil sheets.

7.52 Smoked Roasted Apple Pie
Total Time:1 Hr 20 mins, Servings: 6
Ingredients
8 Cups Apples (peeled, cored & lightly sliced),
1 tbsp Lemon Juice
Sugar, 3/4 Cup
1 tsp Cinnamon,
Nutmeg, 1/4 tsp
2 Whole Pie Crust Frozen (Thawed),
Apple Jelly, 1/4 Cup
2 tbsp Whipping Cream Heavy,
Instructions
In a large mixing basin, combine the lemon juice, apples, cinnamon, flour, sugar, and nutmeg.
Cut two 11-inch rounds from the pie crust dough. Fill a 9" pie dish with 1 circle, preferably glass (make sure not to spread the dough). Using the "apple jelly," apply it to the surface. Toss in the "apple mixture" into the pan.
To wet the crust's edge, use apple juice. Push the ends of the top crust together to seal them. Trim the pastry and flute the sides if necessary. Make several small slits on the top crust with a paring knife. Apply a little layer of cream to the top of the pie using a pastry knife.
Preheat the oven too high for 15 mins before you start cooking. Preheat the oven to 350°F and bake for 50–60 mins, or until the apples are tender and the crust is golden brown. Place the cake on a wire rack to cool. Serve warm or at room temperature. Have a good time. Cooking times may vary depending on the oven temperature and the ambient temperature.

7.53 Cast Iron Pineapple Upside Down Cake
Total Time: 55 mins, Servings: 6
Ingredients
Butter (Melted), 1/4 Cup
1 Cup Brown Sugar
Twenty Ounce Pineapple (Sliced),
Six Ounce Maraschino Cherries,
1 Whole Cake Mix Yellow (boxed)
Vegetable Oil
Eggs
Instructions
When you're ready to cook, preheat the
Pit Boss to 350°F and leave the lid closed for approximately 10-15 mins.
In a 12" cast-iron skillet, melt the butter. Brown sugar should be sprinkled on top of the melted butter. Place the pineapple slices on the brown sugar and push them in as much as possible. Place a cherry in the middle of each pineapple slice and gently push it into the (brown) sugar.
Prepare cake batter according to package directions, replacing as much "water" as feasible for the pineapple juice mixture and adding oil and eggs as required. In the cast-iron skillet, pour the batter over the pineapple and cherries.
Cook it on the grill for approximately 20 mins using the cast-iron pan. Rotate the pan 1/2 turn to ensure that it cooks evenly. Continue to cook for another 20 mins, or until a toothpick inserted in the middle comes out clean.
To loosen the cake, run a knife along the sides of the pan. Flip the pan over with a (heatproof) serving dish on top.
On top of the cake, place the tray. Allow 5 mins for the (brown) sugar to trickle down the sides of the cake. Allow for the chilling time of 30 mins.

7.54 Super Bowl Sundae (Smoked)
Total Time: 1 Hr
Cooking Time: 1 Hr
Serving: 4
Ingredients
1 Heavy Cream Cup
2 1/2-&-1/2 Cup
2 Tsp Bourbon
1 Tbsp Vanilla Extract
Sugar (Granulated) Cup, 2/3
Salt
4 Unpeeled, Divided Lengthwise, Ripe and Firm Bananas
1 Tsp Cinnamon
2 Tbsp Maple Syrup
Instructions
Set the temperature to 180°F and warm for 15 mins with the lid covered.
In an Al roasting pan, combine the heavy cream and 1/2-and-1/2. Smoke the pan for 45 mins in a Pit Boss.
When the cream mixture has smoked, remove it from the grill and add the salt, vanilla, sugar, and bourbon. Cool in the fridge for 1 hr after mixing until completely dissolved.
Pour into an ice cream machine until it reaches a smooth-serve consistency. Place it in a plastic container and place it in the freezer for at least 1 hr, or until you're ready to collect the banana splits.
Raise the temperature to be high and preheat the oven.
Line a baking sheet with Al or parchment foil and place the bananas cut side up on the sheet. Drizzle with maple syrup and a pinch of cinnamon. Place a baking sheet on the grate and cook for ten to fifteen mins, or until the bananas are golden. Remove bananas from the grating and make banana sundaes with your favorite toppings.

7.55 Grilled Apple Pie
Total Time: 60 mins, Servings: 4
Ingredients
Apples, 5 Whole.
Sugar, 1/4 Cup.
Cornstarch, 1 tbsp.
Pie Crust (Refrigerated), 1 Whole.

Peach (Pre-Servings), 1/4 Cup.
Instructions
When you're ready to start cooking, Preheat the Pit Boss on high for approximately 15 mins with the top closed. Combine the sugar, apples, and cornstarch in a medium-sized mixing basin; put aside.
Remove the pie crust from the package and unroll it. Fill a pie pan that hasn't been filed with the mixture. Using the back of a spoon, spread pre-Servings thinly across the crust. Arrange the apple slices in an equal layer in the pie dish. Fold the crust gently over the filling.
Place a (baking) sheet on the grill upside down to create a raised surface. To remove the grill from the heat, place the pie plate on top of it. (This will prevent the pan's bottom from overcooking.)
Remove off the grill and put aside for 10 mins to cool before serving. Have a good time. Cooking times may vary depending on the oven temperature and the ambient temperature.

7.56 Baked Apple Bourbon Crisp
Total Time: 1 Hr 45 mins, Servings: 6
Ingredients
Butter, according to need.
Brown Sugar (Firmly Packed), 1/2 Cup.
Flour, 1/2 Cup.
Oats (Old Fashioned), 1/2 Cup.
Walnuts, 1/4 Cup.
Ground Cinnamon, 3 tsp.
Salted Butter (chilled & cut in 1/2 Inch Cubes), 1 Stick.
Granny Smith / Apples honey crisp (Peeled & Lightly Sliced), 3 lb.
Sweetened Cranberries (Dried), 1/2 Cup.
Honey, 1/4 Cup.
Bourbon, 1/2 tbsp.
Lemon Juice (Fresh), 1 tbsp
Vanilla, 1 tsp.
Salt, 1 Pinch.
Instructions
Butter the interior of a well-seasoned 12" cast iron pan and set it aside.
In a food processor, combine the flour, brown sugar, almonds, cinnamon, walnuts, and butter to make the topping. Set aside the mixture after pulsing it until it's crumbled but still clumpy.
In a large mixing basin, combine the cranberries, strawberries, butter, brown sugar, lemon juice, whiskey, vanilla, cinnamon, and salt. To combine, carefully mix everything.
Pour the fruit mixture into the greased pan. In an equal layer, pour the topping over the fruit.
Preheat the oven to 350°F and keep the lid covered for approximately 15 mins until ready to cook.
Bake for 60 mins, or until the fruit is warm and bubbling and the topping is golden brown.
Allow cooling for approximately 30 mins. Serve with a scoop of vanilla ice cream on the side.

7.57 Blueberry Bread Pudding
Total Time: 1 Hr 10 mins, Servings: 4
Ingredients
Eggs, 5
Sugar, 3 Cup
Milk, 1/2 Cup.
Vanilla, 1/2 tsp.
Cinnamon, 1 tsp
Salt, 1 Pinch.
Bread, 5 Cup.
Blueberries, 3 cups.

Instructions
Beat the eggs in a large mixing bowl. Combine the milk, sugar, cinnamon, cocoa, and salt in a mixing bowl.
2 cups bread & blueberries in another large mixing bowl (200 g).
Place the "egg mixture" on top of the "bread-blueberry mixture" and leave aside for 30 mins to let the flavors merge.
Meanwhile, prepare a muffin pan by lining it with muffin liners. When you're ready to cook, turn the Pit Boss grill on Smoke and leave the lid open until the fire is ready (for about 4-5 mins).
Fill prepared cups halfway with the "bread-blueberry" mixture; evenly sprinkle the remaining cup of blueberries on top, gently pressing them into the pudding with the back of a spoon.
On top, streusel with sugar.
With the pan directly on the grill, smoke for approximately 30 mins.
Preheat the oven to 350°F and bake the pudding for 25 mins, or until firm and golden brown on top.
Allow it cool completely before dusting powdered sugar on top. Serve hot with "whipped cream" (sweetened) or "vanilla ice cream," if desired.

7.58 Funfetti Ice Cream Sandwich
Total Time: 10 min, Servings: 8
Ingredients
Flour, 1/2 Cup.
Baking Powder, 1 tsp
Baking Soda, 1/2 tsp.
Salt, 2/3 tsp.
Sugar, 1 Cup
Butter, 1 Cup.
Egg, 1.
Vanilla, 1 tsp.
Milk, 2 tbsp.
Sprinkles (Multi-Colored), 3/4 Cup.
Ice Cream
Instructions
When you're ready to cook, preheat the Pit Boss to 350°F and leave the lid closed for approximately 10 to 15 mins.
In a mixing bowl, combine the salt, rice, and baking soda. Using an electric mixer, cream the sugar and butter together until light and fluffy. Whisk together the egg and vanilla essence in a separate dish.
Before adding all the flour, stir in 1/2 cup of the flour mixture at a time. Mix in the honey and sprinkles until everything is evenly distributed.
Place 2 tbsp dough on a prepared cookie sheet, spacing them 4" apart. Flatten the dough with the base of a sugar-dusted glass to keep it from sticking.
Place the cookie sheet on the grill and cook for 8 mins, or until thoroughly browned on both sides. Remove the cookies from the grill and place them on a cooling rack.
Fill 2 cookies halfway with ice cream, wrap the edges in sprinkles, and enjoy straight away.

7.59 Baked Walnut Pumpkin Cookies
Total Time: 30 mins, Servings: 6
Ingredients
Flour (All-Purpose), 2 Cup.
Baking Powder, 1 tsp
Baking Soda, 1/2 tsp.
Salt, 1/2 tsp
Ground Cinnamon, 1 tsp.
Ground Nutmeg, 1/4 tsp.
Pumpkin Pie Spices, 1/2 tsp.
Butter, 8 tbsp.
Sugar, 1 Cup.

Pumpkin Puree, 1 Cup.
Egg, 1.
Vanilla Extract, 1 tsp.
Walnuts (Chopped), 1 Cup.
Instructions
Preheat the oven to 325°F and keep the lid covered for approximately 15 mins until ready to cook.
Set aside a mixture of baking powder, flour, salt, baking soda, nutmeg, pumpkin spice, and cinnamon.
Butter should be beaten in a separate cup. Combine the pumpkin puree, honey, vanilla essence, and egg in a mixing bowl. Slowly and steadily stir in the flour mixture. Combine the walnuts and fold them in.
Spoon dough onto Al foil and place
spoonful on the grill grate. Preheat the oven to 350°F and bake for 18 mins.

7.60 Pound Cake
Total Time: 1 Hr 10 mins, Servings: 8
Ingredients
Butter, 1/2 Cup.
Cream Cheese, 8 Ounces.
Sugar, 3 cups.
Eggs, 6.
Bourbon Vanilla, 3 tsp.
Lemon Zest, 1 tbsp.
Fresh Strawberries
Whipped Cream
Instructions
In a large mixing basin, cream together the cheese, butter, and sugar. Add the eggs one at a time, whisking in between each addition. Combine the vanilla and lemon zest in a mixing bowl.
To make the cake rise, pour approximately half of the mixture into prepared loaf pans.
When you're ready to cook, light the grill before it catches fire, and smoke while keeping the lid open (4-5 mins). Preheat the oven to 325°F and bake for 10-15 mins with the lid closed.
In loaf pans, cook it on the grill for 60-75 mins. After 45 mins, if the cake is golden brown, lightly cover with foil and continue baking until a toothpick inserted in the middle comes out clean.
Cool for approximately 10 mins in the pan before transferring to a wire rack to cool completely.
Serve with sliced fresh strawberries and a dollop of smoky whip cream.

7.61 Brownie Pudding of Bread (Baked)
Total Time: 50 Mins, Serving: 6
Ingredients
4 Egg
3 Tsp Extract of Vanilla
1 Pinch Salt
1/2 Cup Chocolate Chips (Bittersweet)
4 Cup Leftover Brownies
1 Cup Heavy Cream
1/2 Cup Sugar
Larger Coconut Flakes, 1/4 Cup
2 Butter Stick
2 Cup Sugar (Brown)
1/2 Tsp Salt
1 Tsp Baking Soda
Cream (Whipped)
Candied Pecans or Walnuts, 1/4
Instructions
Preheat the oven to 350°F and cook for 15 mins with the lid closed.

To make the bread pudding, whisk together the sugar, eggs, vanilla, heavy cream, and salt in a small bowl. Whisk everything together well. Combine chocolate chips and brownies in a mixing bowl.
Pour the mixture into a greased 9 x 13 baking pan and sprinkle with coconut flakes.
Place baking pan on the grill grate and cook for 45 mins, or until sides are slightly browned and puffed, and center is just set.
To make the caramel sauce, combine sugar, salt, and butter in a normal saucepan over medium-high heat.
Bring the mixture to a boil and simmer until an instant-read thermometer registers 275°F. Remove from heat immediately and stir in vanilla and baking soda. It would bubble up and emit steam if you used to care.
Serve with caramel sauce, candied walnuts, and whipped cream.

7.62 French Toast of Raspberry Casserole (Baked)
Total Time: 60 Mins, Serving: 4
Ingredients
Loaf One, Challah Bread One, Cut into Slices, 3/4
8een Raspberries (Fresh) Oz
8 Egg (Large)
1 Tsp Salt (Kosher)
2 Tsp Extract of Vanilla
2 Cup Entire Milk
1 1/2 Tsp Ground Cinnamon
Sugar, 3/4 Cup
Instructions
In a 3-quart baking dish, arrange raspberries and bread in an even layer.
In a large mixing basin, combine 1/2 cup sugar, salt, and 1 tsp cinnamon. Combine the vanilla, milk, and eggs in a mixing bowl.
Pour an egg mixture equally over the bread and fruit, pressing down to immerse each item completely.
Cover and let aside for 1 hr at room temperature.
Start the Pit Boss according to the grill's directions whenever you're ready to cook. Preheat the oven to 350°F and bake for ten to fifteen mins with the lid closed.
1/4 cup residual sugar and 1/2 tsp cinnamon Drizzle a little on top of the casserole.
Place the casserole on a hot grill and bake for 45 to 1 hr, or until golden brown on top.
Allow ten mins before serving to allow flavors to meld. Serve with maple syrup and a dusting of powdered sugar.

7.63 Watermelon and Pineapple Creamsicles (Grilled)
Total Time: 25 Mins, Serving: 8
Ingredients
1/2 Sliced Entire Watermelon
1/2 Sliced Entire Pineapple
1/2 Cup Sugar
2 Fresh Entire Squeezed Lime Juice
1 Cup Heavy Cream
Instructions
When ready to cook, set the grill (Pit Boss) on Smoke and follow the grill's instructions.
Grill the melons and pineapple for 15-20 mins. Remove the watermelon from the grill and remove the rind. Transfer to a mixer after cutting into 1 piece.
Strain after pureeing until smooth. Repeat with the pineapple, this time keeping them separate. Add 12 cups sugar to each juice, 1 lime juice to each, and 12 cups of cream. Stir until the sugar is completely dissolved.

Fill a popsicle mold 1/4 full of pineapple, 1/2 full with watermelon, and 1/4 full with pineapple. Place the molds in the freezer for 1 hr, or until they are partially frozen. Then, add a popsicle stick and return to the freezer for the night or until completely frozen.
To get rid of it, run warm water around the outside of the mold and slowly remove a pop.

7.64 Bananas Foster
Total Time: 20 Mins, Servings: 4
Ingredients
Banana nectar. 1/3 cup
4 Quartered bananas
Brown sugar, 3/4 cup
Butter, 1/4 cup
1/2 tsp Ground Cinnamon
Dark rum, 1/3 cup
Ice cream (Vanilla)
Instructions
Preheat the Griddle (Pit Boss) to medium-high heat. Heat a cast-iron frypan if using a charcoal or gas grill.
Place a big frypan on the grill and melt the butter in it. Mix in the cinnamon and brown sugar until the sugar is completely dissolved.
Place the bananas and banana nectar in a bowl. To coat, mix well.
Put the rum in when the bananas begin to soften and become brown. Mix, then light a sauce with a softer stick. Boil the sauce for 2 mins once the flames have died down.
Divide the bananas into four bowls/scoops of vanilla ice cream, then pour the sauce over the top. Serve right away.

7.65 Vegan Pumpkin Muffins of Apple (Gluten-Free)
Total Time: 45 Mins, Servings: 12
Ingredients
All-purpose flour (gluten-free), 1.5 cups
1 cup Almond milk
2 tbsp Avocado oil
1 tsp baking powder
1/2 tsp baking soda
1/2 cup Brown sugar
1 tsp Ground cinnamon (also more for apples)
1 batch Flax egg (1 tbsp flaxseed meal, 2.5 tbsp water)
Gluten-free oats, 1/3 cups (also more for topping)
2 Peel, dice & core granny smith apple
Pumpkin puree, 3/4 cup
Salt, 1/4 tsp
1 tsp Vanilla extract
1 tbsp Vegan butter
Instructions
Preheat the grill to 350 degrees Fahrenheit.
In a large mixing bowl, prepare the flax egg and put it aside.
In a heated frypan, melt vegan butter and add cinnamon and apples to taste. Cook until the vegetables are tender (3 to 4 mins).
In a mixing dish, combine the vanilla essence, avocado oil, almond milk, brown sugar, and pumpkin puree, along with the egg (flax).
In a shifter, combine the baking soda, cinnamon, salt, baking powder, and flour. Sift the dehydrated ingredients into a bowl gradually. Slowly blend the ingredients as you add them.
Combine the apples and oats in a mixing bowl and stir until well combined.
Fill each muffin liner or pan halfway with the muffin mixture, then sprinkle additional oats over the top.
Bake for 25-30 mins on the grill, or until a toothpick inserted in the center comes out clean. 12 mins before the end of the cooking time, turn the pan.

7.66 Beaver Tails
Total Time: 25 Mins, Servings: 8
Ingredients
2 tbsp Melted butter
2 tbsp Ground cinnamon
1 Egg
2 1/2 cups All-purpose flour
1/2 cup warm milk
1/2 tsp salt
1 tsp Sugar
1/2 tsp Vanilla
1-liter Vegetable oil
Warm water, 1/4 cup
2 1/2 tsp Instant active yeast
Instructions
Combine sugar, yeast, milk, and water in a small basin. Allow sitting for about 10 mins, or until bubbling.
Pour the flour into the second bowl and create a well in the center. Combine the butter, salt, vanilla, egg, and sugar in a mixing bowl. Combine all of the ingredients in a mixing bowl and stir until the dough is soft. Knead the dough for about 5 mins before placing it in a basin (greased). Wrap in a cloth and leave aside for almost 60 mins, or until the dough has doubled in size.
1 hr later, prepare the grill to 450°F. Fill a cast-iron pan halfway with vegetable oil and place it on the grill's grates. To prevent grease flare-ups, keep the flame broiler closed. Heat the oil to 350 degrees Fahrenheit.
While you're waiting for the oil to heat up, puff down the dough and divide it into eight little balls; make a circle out of each dough piece (flat). Cook the dough for about 1 min on each side in the hot oil, or until golden brown.
Sprinkle with cinnamon sugar right away, or top with your favorite toppings. Enjoy.

7.67 Banana Trifle (Smoked)
Total Time: 35 Mins, Servings: 8
Ingredients
Cream cheese
Whip cream
Brown sugar
Condensed milk
Bananas
White sugar
Instructions
In a mixing dish, combine cream cheese, sweetened condensed milk, pudding, rum extract, white sugar, and whip cream.
Brown sugar, cinnamon, and butter are combined in a cast-iron pan under the flaming broiler. Continue to stir until bubbles appear. 8 to 10 bananas, chopped into the sugar mixture. Remove from the heat as soon as possible.
In jars, layer bananas, wafers (vanilla), and cream (mason). Continue in this manner until the jar is full. Drizzle with cinnamon and serve immediately or chill in the refrigerator for up to 24 hrs before serving. The longer the wafers cool, the smoother they will become.

7.68 Pie (Blueberry)
Total Time: 35 Mins, Servings: 8
Ingredients
1 Can of blueberry pie filling
1 Deep 9" pie shell

Instructions
Preheat the grill to 400 degrees Fahrenheit.
Using a fork, prick the bottom of the pie filling. Pour the mixture into the pie crust.
Bake for 30 mins on the grill, turning halfway through.
Enjoy it while it's still warm.

7.69 Chocolate Chip Cookies (Mint)
Total Time: 25 Mins, Servings: 24
Ingredients
1/2 cup Melted butter
1 Mix of chocolate chip cookie packet
Food coloring 8-10 drops
1/2 tsp Extract mint
Instructions
Preheat the grill to 350 degrees Fahrenheit.
Follow the instructions of the Chocolate Chip Cookie mix and add the mint essence and green food coloring. Stir until everything is well mixed.
Drop dough balls about the size of 2 tbsps into the saucepan on a baking sheet coated with parchment paper (parchment).
Bake for 10-12 mins on the grill. Allow it to
cool for a few mins before removing it from the pan.

7.70 Cheesecake Frypan Brownie
Total Time: 40 Mins, Servings: 2
Ingredients
1 Brownie mix box
1 packet Cheese cream
2 Egg
1/2 cup Oil
1 Can of blueberry pie filling
1/2 cup Sugar
1 tsp Vanilla
Warm water, 1/4 cup
Instructions
Combine each brownie ingredient & mix. In a distinct bowl, combine sugar, cream, vanilla, cheese, and egg & mix until soft. Grease frypans & pour into brownie batter. Top up with cherry pie filling and cheesecake, using a knife (sharp) to blend to give out a mottled look.
Put in the Grill at 350F & bake for around 30 mins.
Let it cool down for around 10 mins & enjoy.

7.71 Cookies of Peanut Butter
Total Time: 25 Mins, Servings: 24
Ingredients
1 Egg
1 cup Peanut butter
1 cup Sugar
Instructions
Start the grill on high heat with the lid open until the fire in the burn pot is ready (3-7 mins). Increase the heat to HIGH. In a mixing dish, combine all the ingredients. Drop tbsp dough portions onto a greased baking sheet and bake for 15-20 mins in the grill. Allow 5 mins for cookies to cool on the baking pan.

7.72 Pumpkin Pie (Pit Boss)
Total Time: 1 Hr 15 Mins, Servings: 6
Ingredients
1 tsp Ground cinnamon
Ground cloves, 1/4 tsp
2 Egg (large)
1/2 tsp Ground ginger
1 Evaporated milk
1 Deep 9" pie shell
1 Can of pumpkin pie
1/2 tsp Salt
Sugar, 3/4 cup
Instructions
Start the grill on the smoky side with the lid open until the fire in the burn pot is ready (3-7 mins). Preheat the oven to 400 degrees Fahrenheit. In a small bowl, combine the cinnamon, salt, ginger, cloves, and sugar. In a large mixing basin, whisk together the eggs, pumpkin, and sugar-spice mixture. Mix in the evaporated milk slowly. Pour into a pie crust after everything is combined.

7.73 Grilled Banana Split with Vanilla Bourbon Ice Cream
Total Time: 1 Hr 15 mins, Servings: 4
Ingredients
1 Cup Heavy Cream.
2 tsp Bourbon
1 tbsp Extract the seeds from the bean of 1 vanilla or Vanilla Extract.
Granulated Sugar (Divided), 2/3 Cup.
4 Whole Bananas (Firm, split lengthwise & unpeeled)
Nuts (Chopped), for serving
Cream (Whipped), for serving
Maraschino Cherries (4 or more), for serving
Instructions
When you're ready to cook, preheat the Pit Boss to 180°F and keep the lid closed for 15 mins. Use the "super smoke" if it's available for the best taste.
Combine heavy cream and 1/2-and-1/2 in an iron roasting pan. Place them in the Pit Boss for 45 mins to smoke.
Remove the grill from the smoking cream mixture and stir in the whiskey, vanilla, 2/3 cup sugar, and salt. Stir until all the sugar has dissolved, then refrigerate for 1 hr.
Place the ingredients in an ice cream maker and process until a soft-serve consistency is achieved. After that, place it in a plastic container and place it in the freezer for at least 1 hr, or until it's ready to connect the banana splits.
Preheat the Pit Boss to 450°F with the top covered for 15 mins while the ice cream is building up. Coat the bananas with 1 tbsp sugar and cook them directly on the grill grate for 5-7 mins, or until they are lightly caramelized.
Place the bananas in a serving dish after removing them from the Pit Boss. Ice cream, cherries, almonds, and any other tasty sauces or toppings are optional.

7.74 Chewy Coconut Gluten-Free Cookies
Total Time: 25 Mins, Servings: 8 people
Ingredients
2 Large Eggs
4 Tbsp Sugar
1 Cup Unsweetened Coconut Flakes
1 Pinch Kosher Salt
1/2 Cup Chopped Semisweet Chocolate
5 Tbsp Butter, Melted and Cooled to Room Temperature
Sea Salt, For Serving
Instructions
Set the Pit Boss to 375°F and preheat for 15 mins with the lid covered.
Using parchment paper, line a baking pan.
Whisk together the eggs & sugar in a mixing dish until well combined. The salt, chocolate, coconut flakes, and butter are then added. Stir until the mixture is light and fluffy.
Allow 20 mins for the batter to rest so that the coconut may absorb part of the liquid & swell.

Place the piles on the tray & form a pyramid with them. Place the tray under the grill for 10-15 mins, or until browned on top. Enjoy with a pinch of sea salt!

7.75 Grilled Mango with Lime and Coconut
Total Time: 30 Mins, Servings: 2
Ingredients
4 Whole Ripe Mangoes
3 Tbsp Maple Syrup
1 Cup Coconut Flakes
4 Cup Coconut Yogurt
3 Tbsp Lime Zest
1 Tsp Chile Powder
Instructions
Set the Pit Boss to 500°F & preheat for 15 mins with the lid covered.
Mango cheeks are peeled & sliced into cheeks, then brushed with maple syrup.
On your Pit Boss grill, cook the mango until golden brown. Toast the coconut flakes in a frying pan on the grill until they are light golden brown.
In a wide bowl, combine the mango cheeks, coconut yogurt, coconut flakes, lime zest, & Chile powder. Enjoy!

7.76 Grilled Seasonal Fruit with Gelato
Total Time: 15 Mins, Servings: 2
Ingredients
2 Whole Seasonal Fruits: Apricots, Peaches or Plums
3 Tbsp Turbinado Sugar
1/4 Cup Honey
Your Favorite Gelato, For Serving
Instructions
Set the Pit Boss to 450°F and preheat for 15 mins with the lid covered.
Remove the pit from the fruit before slicing it in half. Brush honey on the cut side & sprinkle sugar on top.
Place the fruit straight on your grill unless grill marks appear.
Remove the fruits from your grill & serve with gelato scoops. If desired, drizzle with some honey.

7.77 Baked Caramel Pecan Brownie
Total Time: 55 Mins, Servings: 6
Ingredients
3/4 Cup Pecans, Halves
1/4 Cup Butter
Cup Brown Sugar
3/4 Cup Heavy Cream
1 Cup All-Purpose Flour
1/2 Cup Cocoa Powder
3/4 Tsp Baking Soda
1/2 Tsp Salt
6 Tbsp Butter, Melted
3 Large Eggs
6 Ounce Chocolate, Chopped
Instructions
To prepare Pecan-Caramel Sauce, roast the nuts in a skillet on medium-high heat. Pecans should be toasted for 5 mins, stirring periodically. Toss the nuts with butter & brown sugar. Stir till the brown sugar & butter have melted and mixed.
Remove the pecans from the heat and slowly pour in heavy cream. Return to the heat & whisk until all the creams have been incorporated. Remove the pan from the heat & put it aside.
To make the brownies, whisk together the baking soda, flour, brown sugar, cocoa powder, & salt in a wide mixing bowl. Mix in the eggs, melted butter, & cream well. Fold in some milk chocolate chunks. Over caramel pecan mix, pour some brownie batter.
Preheat your Pit Boss at 325°F for 15 mins with the lid covered. Cook the brownies within Pit Boss for around 35-40 mins, till a toothpick inserted in the middle, comes out clear.
Place the pan on your grill grate & cook for around 35-40 mins, till a toothpick inserted in the middle comes out clear.
Allow cooling for almost 10 mins after removing from the grill.
Serve with some ice cream while it's still warm.

7.78 Baked Coffee Cake
Total Time: 60 Mins, Servings: 8
Ingredients
1/2 Cup Unsalted Butter, Softened
1 Cup Sugar
2 Eggs
2 Cup Flour
1 Tsp Baking Soda
1 Tsp Ground Cinnamon
1/2 Tsp Salt
1 Cup Sour Cream
1 1/2 Tsp Vanilla Extract
1/2 Cup Sugar
1/4 Cup Brown Sugar
2 Tbsp Flour
1 Tbsp Vanilla Extract
1/2 Tsp Ground Cinnamon
1 Tbsp Butter, Melted
Instructions
When ready to cook, preheat the Pit Boss to 325°F with the lid covered for 15 mins.
Lightly spray a cake pan using cooking spray, then line using parchment paper and spray all parchment.
Cream the sugar and butter together in the mixer till light & creamy. Scrape the edges of the basin between every addition as you add all eggs.
Sift the flour, cinnamon, baking soda, & salt in a wide mixing bowl.
Whisk the vanilla extract & sour cream in a medium bowl.
In three portions, alternate wet & dry flour with sour cream mixes in the sugar mix, scraping that bowl after every addition. To make crumble topping, combine all the ingredients in a large mixing bowl. Combine all crumble ingredients into a small mixing dish. Pour half of the batter into the cake pan & top with half of the crumb mix. Pour in the rest of the batter & top with the remaining crumbs.
Place the pan straight on your grill grate & bake for 45-60 mins, till the toothpick inserted in the middle of the cake falls out clean.
Allow cooling after removing from your grill grate. Then, cut into slices & serve. Enjoy!

7.79 Baked Peach Cobbler Cupcakes
Total Time: 45 Mins, Servings: 8
Ingredients
2 Large Peach
3/4 Cup Sugar
2 Tsp Lemon Juice
1/2 Tsp Ground Cinnamon
Yellow Cake Mix, Boxed
1 Can Vanilla Icing
Instructions
A kettle of water should be brought to a boil. Cut a shallow across the bottom of the peaches by turning them upside down. To loosen the skin of peaches, place them in hot water for around 1 min.
Drain the same peaches & rinse with some cold water into a

colander.
Filling: Dice the peaches & put them in a wide baking dish. Peaches should be cooked on medium heat. Add the sugar, lemon, & cinnamon as it begins to sizzle. Cook for around 10-15 mins over medium heat, or unless the bulk of the peach juice has evaporated, leaving the thick syrup.
Allow cooling in a bowl.
Preheat your Pit Boss at 350°F for 15 mins with the lid covered.
Cupcakes: Prepare the cake mix according to the package instructions and bake in a cupcake tray lined with liners.
Bake the cupcakes for around 13-16 mins, till golden brown once the grill has been warmed.
After the cupcakes completely cooled, put some peach cobbler mix into the center using the piping bag.
Using your favorite vanilla frosting, ice the cake. Enjoy!

7.80 Baked Strawberry Shortbread
Total Time: 25 Mins, Servings: 6
Ingredients
1 Quart Fresh Strawberries
5 Tbsp Sugar
2 Tsp Grand Marnier
2 Cup All-Purpose Flour
1 Tbsp Baking Powder
1/4 Tsp Salt
1/4 Tsp Ground Cinnamon
2 Tbsp Butter
2 Tbsp Vegetable Shortening, Plus More as Needed
1/3 Cup Milk
Whipped Cream
Instructions
Combine fresh strawberries & sugar for taste in a mixing dish. If used, mix into Grand Marnier, gently smashing berries to unleash their juices. Cover & chill.
In a large bowl, sift together the flour, sugar, salt, baking powder, & cinnamon. Using the pastry blender, knife, chop the butter & shortening into dry ingredients until the mix decreases to clumps. In the middle, form a well & pour in some milk. Stir unless everything is well mixed. Don't overmix the ingredients.
Dump your shortcake mix over a lightly floured cutting board. To get the dough, gently knead it. Cut rounds out from a biscuit cutter after patting into a thick round. Place on the baking sheet that hasn't been buttered. Brush some melted butter over the shortcakes.
Set the temp to High & warm for around 15 mins with the lid covered.
Close the cover and place that pan with shortcakes on your grill grate. Bake for around 10 mins, or unless the shortcakes are beautifully browned & have risen. Allow cooling somewhat before cutting in half using a knife. Replace the shortcakes after dividing the strawberries among the bottom halves. Finish with a dollop of whipped cream.

7.81 Baked Gluten-Free Banana Bread
Total Time: 1 Hr 15 Mins, Servings: 4
Ingredients
2 Bananas
1/2 Cup Brown Sugar
1/2 Cup Milk
Cup Oil, Coconut
1 Egg
2 Tsp Vanilla Extract
3/4 Cup Gluten-Free Flour
3/4 Cup Almond Flour
2 Tsp Baking Powder
1 1/2 Tsp Kosher Salt
1 Tsp Ground Cinnamon
3/4 Cup Dark Chocolate Chunks
Instructions
Preheat the oven to 350°F for 15 mins with the lid closed.
Grease a loaf pan lightly.
Toss together bananas, brown sugar, egg, coconut oil, milk, & vanilla in a wide mixing dish.
Whisk baking powder, flour, salt, & cinnamon in a different wide mixing bowl.
In a separate bowl, whisk together the wet and dry ingredients till fully combined. Fold in chocolate pieces gently.
Transfer the mixture to the loaf pan & bake for 50-55 mins, till a toothpick inserted into the middle comes out clean.
Allow your bread to cool for 10 mins in the wire rack before inverting onto the rack & cooling for the next 30 mins before slicing.

7.82 Baked Apple Pear Crisp
Total Time: 1 Hr 15 Mins, Servings: 6
Ingredients
1 1/2 Cup All-Purpose Flour
1 cup Old Fashioned Oatmeal (Not Quick-Cooking or Instant)
3/4 Cup Brown Sugar
1 1/4 Cup Sugar
16 Tbsp Butter
1/4 Tsp Salt
5 Pound Diced Apples and Pears
1 Whole Lemon Zest
1 Whole Lemon, Juiced
2 Tsp Ground Cinnamon
1/2 Tsp Ground Nutmeg
Instructions
Spray a baking dish using cooking spray.
To prepare the topping, combine flour, oats, brown sugar, butter, granulated sugar, & salt in a wide mixing bowl of a stand mixer.
Mix over low speed till butter become peas-sized & the mix becomes crumbly. Set aside
if you're not using an electric mixer.
To make the fruit, combine the lemon zest, apples, & lemon juice in a wide mixing bowl.
Using a wooden spoon, mix in the cinnamon, sugar, & nutmeg. Place the fruit mix into the pan that has been prepared. Evenly distribute the filling on the fruit.
Preheat your Pit Boss at 350°F for 15 mins with the lid covered.
Bake for around 50-60 mins, or unless the top becomes beautifully browned & fruit is boiling & tender, straight on your grill grate.
Serve with whipped cream while still warm.

7.83 Baked Apple Pie with Cheddar Cheese
Total Time: 60 Mins, Servings: 8
Ingredients
2.833 cup All-Purpose Flour
1/4 cup Cheddar Cheese
1 Tsp Salt
1 Tbsp Sugar
1 1/8 Cup Butter
7 Tbsp Ice Water
10 Apples
1 Tbsp Ground Cinnamon
1 Orange Zest
1/2 Lemon, Juiced
1 Tsp Ginger, Minced
1/3 Cup Brown Sugar
1 Lemon Zest
1 Egg, Beaten With 1 Tbsp Water

1 Tbsp Raw Sugar
Instructions
Combine flour, sugar, shredded cheddar, & salt in the food processor bowl. To mix, pulse a few times. Drop in small chunks of chilled butter while the machine is running till all your butter has been added & the result looks fine cornmeal.
Add cold water till dough forms cohesive. It's possible that you won't need all of the water.
Roll out the dough onto the floured board into two large circles.
Using a fork, puncture the bottom of the pie plate.
Preheat your Pit Boss at 350°F for 15 mins with the lid covered.
Combine flour, sliced apples, brown sugar, cinnamon, ginger, lemon juice, lemon zest, orange zest, & butter in a mixing bowl. Toss well to coat & place in prepared pie plate.
Place the remaining pie dough over apples, crimp its edges, cut holes in the top to allow air to escape, brush with some egg wash, & dust with sugar.
Cook for around 40 mins, or unless the crust becomes golden brown, straight on your grill grate. Allow cooling.
When ready for serving, place cheddar over each pie & reheat until melted.

7.84 Grilled Honey Bourbon Peaches

Total Time: 35 Mins, Servings: 8
Ingredients
1/8 Cup Honey
3 Tbsp Bourbon
2 Tbsp Butter
6 Whole Peach
Instructions
When prepared to cook, preheat the grill on high for 15 mins with the lid covered. If possible, raise the temperature to 500°F for best results.
Combine the bourbon, honey, & butter in a pot on heat. Set aside after the cheese has melted.
Remove the stones from the peaches & coat them with some honey-bourbon sauce.
Put the peaches on your grill till grill marks appear.
Remove off the grill &, if desired, top with some whipped cream.

7.85 Baked Chocolate Brownie Cookies with Egg Nog

Total Time: 35 mins, Servings: 6
Ingredients
Bar bittersweet chocolate (finely chopped), 16 Ounce
Unsalted Butter, 4 tbsp
4 Eggs
Granulated Sugar, 1 Cup
Vanilla Extract, 1 tsp.
Flour, 1 Cup.
Baking Powder, 1/2 tsp
Semisweet Chocolate Chips, 1 Cup
Instructions
When prepared to cook, preheat the Pit Boss to 350°F with the lid covered for approximately 15 mins.
Line Stack 2 baking sheets on top of the parchment paper.
Combine the finely chopped chocolate and butter in a heatproof dish; place over a pan of barely boiling water and often stir until the chocolate is completely melted and smooth. Allow it to cool to room temperature.
Whisk together the sugar, eggs, and vanilla extract in a medium mixing cup.
Sift together the flour and baking powder in a shallow mixing cup. Whisk the melted chocolate mixture into the egg mixture with a rubber spatula until it is completely combined.
With a spatula, gently fold the flour mixture into the batter in 3 batches. Stir in the "chocolate chips" until all the flour has been incorporated.
Scoop 1/2 tsp of dough onto parchment-lined baking sheets. Bake for 10-12 mins or until the edges are firm. Make sure the potatoes aren't overcooked.
Allow the baking sheets to cool completely before removing them from the oven.

7.86 Mom's Best Baked Pumpkin Bread

Total Time: 1 Hr 15 Mins, Servings: 8
Ingredients
1 Cup Pumpkin, Canned
2 Eggs
2/3 Cup Vegetable Oil
1/2 Cup Sour Cream
1 Tsp Vanilla Extract
2 1/2 Cup Flour
1 1/2 Tsp Baking Soda
1 Tsp Salt
1/2 Tsp Ground Cinnamon
1/4 Tsp Ground Nutmeg
1/4 Tsp Ground Cloves
1/4 Tsp Ground Ginger
Butter
Instructions
Whisk together the sour cream, vegetable oil, pumpkin, eggs, & vanilla in a wide mixing bowl.
Combine the nutmeg, cloves, flour, salt, cinnamon, baking soda, & ginger in a different bowl. Incorporate the dry & wet ingredients in a mixing bowl and whisk to combine. Do not overmix the ingredients.
Preheat oven to 350°F. Butter the insides of 2 loaf pans. Stir in 1 or maybe more extra ingredients as desired.
Dust the greased surfaces with some flour, then tap off any excess. Evenly divide all batter among the 2 pans.
Preheat your Pit Boss at 350°F for 15 mins with the lid covered. Place the loaf pans on your grill grate immediately. Bake for around 45–50 mins, till a toothpick stabbed in the middle comes out clean. When lightly pushed with the finger, the loaf top should bounce back.
Before slicing your loaves, allow them to cool completely. Allow 10 mins for loaf pans for cooling completely before gently turning out your pumpkin bread. If not eating straight away, cover in plastic wrap.

7.87 Pumpkin Chocolate Chip Cookies
Total Time: 20 Mins, Servings: 8
Ingredients
2 cup Flour
1 Tsp Baking Powder
1/2 Tsp Baking Soda
1/2 Tsp Salt
1 Tsp Ground Cinnamon
1/4 Tsp Ground Nutmeg
1/2 Tsp Pumpkin Pie Spice
1/2 Tsp Ground Ginger
1/2 Cup Butter
1 Cup Sugar
1 Cup Pumpkin, Canned
1 Egg
1 Tsp Vanilla Extract
2 cup Chocolate Chips
Instructions
When you're ready to cook, fire up the Pit Boss as per the manufacturer's directions. Preheat the oven to 350°F and bake for 10-15 mins with the lid covered.
Set aside a mixture of flour, pumpkin spice, baking powder, cinnamon, nutmeg, salt, baking soda, & ginger.
Beat the butter in a separate dish until light & fluffy. Mix in the sugar, egg, pumpkin puree, & vanilla extract.
Gradually mix all dry ingredients in the wet components until they are completely combined. Fold in chocolate chunks gently.
Spoon dough over a parchment-lined baking sheet with spoonful.
On your Pit Boss, bake for approximately 10 mins, or unless the cookies become gently browned. Warm the dish before serving.

7.88 Baked Chocolate Coconut Brownies
Total Time: 45 Min, Servings: 4
Ingredients
1/2 Cup Gluten-Free Or All-Purpose Flour, Such As Bob's Red Mill
1/4 Cup Unsweetened Alkalized Cocoa Powder
1/2 Tsp Sea Salt
4 Ounce Semisweet Chocolate, Coarsely Chopped
3/4 Cup Unrefined Coconut Oil
1 cup Raw Cane Sugar
4 Eggs
1 Tsp Vanilla Extract
4 Ounce Semisweet Chocolate Chips (Optional)
Instructions
When prepared to cook, preheat the Pit Boss to 350°F with the lid covered for 15 mins.
Line a baking pan using parchment paper & grease it.
In a wide mixing bowl, combine the cocoa powder, flour, & salt.
Melt both chopped chocolate & coconut oil in a microwave. Allow cooling slightly before serving.
Combine the eggs, sugar, & vanilla extract in a mixing bowl. Whisk until everything is thoroughly mixed.
Fold in chocolate chips after whisking within flour mix. Pour into a pan that has been prepared.
Place on grill & bake for 20-25 mins, till a toothpick inserted into the middle of brownies falls out clean. This will result in a gooey brownie. If you like the drier brownie, bake for another 5-10 mins.
Allow the brownies to cool fully before cutting them into squares. Keep at room temp for around 3 days in the airtight container.

7.89 Double Chocolate Chip Brownie Pie
Total Time: 60 Mins, Servings: 8
Ingredients
1 1/2 Cup Semisweet Chocolate Chips
1 cup Butter
1 cup Brown Sugar
1 Cup Sugar
4 Whole Eggs
2 Tsp Vanilla Extract
2 cup All-Purpose Flour
2/3 Cup Unsweetened Cocoa Powder
1 Tsp Baking Soda
1 Tsp Salt
3/4 Cup White Chocolate Chips
3/4 Cup Nuts (Almonds, Pecans, Peanuts, Etc.)
1 Whole Hot Fudge Sauce, 8oz
2 Tbsp Guinness Extra Stout
Instructions
Spray the Nonstick cooking spray into the interior of a pie dish. When you're all set to cook, preheat your grill at 350°F (180°C) with the lid covered for 15 mins.
In the microwave, melt chocolate chips. Combine the brown sugar, butter, & granulated sugar in a mixing bowl. Add the eggs & the vanilla extract. Melt the chocolate chips and add them in.
Sift cocoa powder, baking soda, flour, & salt on wax paper. Lift the paper's corners & gently pour the butter mix into them.
Mix until your dry ingredients have combined. In a large mixing bowl, combine the remaining chocolate chips, chocolate chips, & nuts. Place the dough within the pie pan that has been prepared.
Place this brownie pie over the grill & cook for 45 to 50 mins, or unless the center is set. Midway through cooking, rotate your pan. Cover the top using Al foil if the edges start to brown.
Heat some fudge sauce within the microwave. Pour in the Guinness and mix well.
Allow your brownie pie to cool for around 20 mins after it's finished. Then, cut into wedges & serve with some fudge sauce on the side.

7.90 Baked Pumpkin Pie
Total Time: 55 Mins, Servings: 6
Ingredients
4 Ounce Cream Cheese
15 Ounce Pumpkin Puree
1/3 Cup Cream, Whipping
1/2 Cup Brown Sugar
1 Tsp Pumpkin Pie Spice
3 Large Eggs
1 Frozen Pie Crust, Thawed
Instructions
Preheat your Pit Boss at 325°F for 15 mins with the lid closed.
Combine cream cheese, milk, sugar, puree, & spice in a mixing bowl. Incorporate one egg into the mix. Fill the pie shell halfway with the mixture.
Bake for around 50 mins, or until the sides are brown and the pie is hard around the edges with some movement in the center. Allow cooling before adding the whipped cream.

7.91 Baked Pumpkin Cheesecake
Total Time: 9 Hrs, Servings: 6
Ingredients
4 Tbsp Butter
2 Cup Cookie, Crushed
2 (8 Oz) Package Cream Cheese
1 Pint Sour Cream

2 Eggs
1 cup Sugar
1/2 Tsp Vanilla Extract
1/2 Can (30 Oz) Pumpkin Pie Filling
1 Cup Whipped Cream
Instructions
Set the temperature to High & warm for 15 mins with the lid covered.
In a large mixing basin, melt the butter. Mix broken cookies with some melted butter till all the crumbs are covered & no liquid remains in the base of your bowl. In a springform pan, press the crumb mix.
Bake this crust on Maximum for 10 mins with the lid covered in the springform pan straight on your grill grate. Remove the steaks from the grill & put them aside. Reduce your grill's temp to 325°F.
In a wide mixer, beat cream cheese till smooth as the grill heats up. Once everything is thoroughly combined, add the sugar & continue to stir. Add the sour cream after the sugar has been incorporated. Then add pumpkin pie filling, vanilla extract, & eggs.
Pour the cheesecake mix over the crushed cookie crust after it has been well mixed and smoothed. To even this batter and remove air bubbles, lightly tap the pan over the counter.
Cook your cheesecake for around 45 mins to an hr and a half. Then, place your cheesecake in the refrigerator for almost 8 hrs once it's finished.

7.92 Baked Chocolate Soufflé with Smoked Whipped Cream

Total Time: 60 Mins, Servings: 4
Ingredients
1 Pint Cream, Whipping
9 Tbsp Butter
220 G Semisweet Chocolate
1 1/4 Cup Powdered Sugar
2 Large Eggs
2 Egg Yolk
6 Tbsp Flour
1 Tbsp Bourbon Vanilla Extract
Powdered Sugar
Cocoa Powder
Instructions
Set the temperature at 180°F & preheat for 15 mins with the lid covered.
To make Whipped Cream, combine the following ingredients in a mixing bowl. In a deep Al baking pan, pour the cream. Place this pan on your grill for around 30 mins to smoke.
Place your smoked cream in a large bowl & chill until ready to use.
Preheat your grill at 375 degrees Fahrenheit with the lid covered.
1 tbsp of melted butter, brushed over 4 tiny soufflé cups
In a dish set over boiling water, melt chocolate & the remaining butter till smooth.
Add the powdered sugar and mix well. Next, continuously whisk in the eggs & egg yolks. Finally, whisk in the flour until it's fully combined.
Pour the batter into the soufflé cups that have been prepared. Bake for around 13-14 mins, or unless the sides are set, on your grill.
Remove the cooled cream from the fridge, add some bourbon vanilla, then whisk until light and fluffy.
Whip in the confectioners' sugar till the whipped cream makes firm peaks.
Top soufflés with whipped cream & a dusting of confectioners' sugar & chocolate. Enjoy!

7.93 Baked Soft Gingerbread Cookie

Total Time: 25 mins, Servings: 8
Ingredients
Flour (all-purpose), 3/4 Cup.
Baking Soda, 1/2 tsp.
Ground Cinnamon, 1/2 tsp
Kosher Salt, 1/4 tsp.
Ground Ginger, 1/2 tsp.
Ground Cloves, 1/4 tsp.
Brown Sugar, 1/3 Cup.
Granulated Sugar, 1/2 Cup plus 4 tbsp.
Butter (Softened), 3/4 Cup
1 Egg
Molasses, 1/4 Cup.
Instructions
When preparing to cook, preheat the Pit Boss to 325°F and keep the lid covered for at least 15 mins.
Set aside the baking soda, flour, salt, cinnamon, cloves, and ginger in a medium-size mixing basin.
In the stand mixer bowl, cream together the granulated sugar (1/2 cup), brown sugar, and butter until light and fluffy. Mix in the molasses and egg at a medium speed, scraping down the sides of the bowl as needed.
Combine the dry ingredients in a separate container and blend at low speed until thoroughly combined. Blend for another 30 seconds after scraping down the edges.
Coat 1 tbsp of dough into a ball, then roll it in the remaining 4 tbsps of sugar.
Place the dough balls on a parchment-lined baking sheet, spaced a couple of inches apart.
Cook on a baking sheet directly on the grill for approximately 10 mins, or until gently browned but still fluffy in the center.
Remove it from the grill and place it on a cooling rack to cool. Enjoy yourself.

7.94 Baked Summer Berry Cheesecake

Total Time: 1 Hrs 30 Mins, Servings: 8
Ingredients
12 Crushed Graham Crackers or Your Favorite Cookies
1/4 Cup Brown Sugar
1/8 Tsp Cinnamon
5 Tbsp Butter, Softened
2 1/2 Pound Cream Cheese
1/2 Cup Sour Cream
1 Cup Sugar
6 Whole Eggs
1 Tbsp Vanilla
1/4 Cup Water
2 Cup Fresh Raspberries
1 cup Blueberries
1 cup Blackberries
2 Tsp Lemon Juice

1 Pinch Salt
2 Tbsp Butter
Instructions
Preheat the oven to 300°F & cook for around 10 mins with the lid covered. When you're all set to cook, fire up your Pit Boss grill. Till the fire has created, smoke with the lid open.
Combine the brown sugar, Graham crackers, & cinnamon in a mixing bowl using a paddle attachment. Mix on moderate speed until everything is well combined. Next, mix at a lower speed until all butter is absorbed.
In a buttered pan, press your crust in the bottom.
Stir cream cheese in a mixing dish till it is creamy & soft.
Beat in the sour cream till it is soft & thoroughly combined. Add sugar & continue to beat for another 3 mins. Toss in the eggs & whisk to combine. Finally, blend in the vanilla extract.
Pour the mix into the pan that has been prepared. Bake for about 1-2 hrs in a water bath in a preheated Pit Boss. Refrigerate the cheesecake for almost 8 hrs once it's finished.
To prepare berry compote, combine water and sugar in the nonreactive pan. Bring to the boil and cook for 1 min, or till sugar is completely dissolved. Next, combine the lemon juice, berries, & salt in a mixing bowl. Bring to the boil, then stir in the butter till it is completely dissolved. Allow it to cool before serving.
Serve with a berry compote on the side.

7.95 Gluten-Free Baked Fruit Crisps
Total Time: 50 Mins, Servings: 6
Ingredients
2 Cup Gluten-Free Rolled Oats
1 Cup Gluten-Free Flour
1/2 Cup Almond Flour
3/4 Cup Brown Sugar, Firmly Packed
1 Tsp Ground Cinnamon
1/2 Tsp Kosher Salt, Plus More As Needed
1/4 Tsp Ground Nutmeg
3/4 Cup Cold Unsalted Butter, Cut into 12 Pieces
3 Pound Mixed Apples and Pears, Peeled, Cored and Diced
1/2 Tsp Vanilla Extract
1 Pinch Salt
3 Tsp Raw Cane Sugar
Creme Fraiche or Whipped Cream, For Serving
Instructions
When prepared to cook, preheat the Pit Boss to 350°F with the lid covered for 15 mins.
Prepare the baking sheet by lining it with parchment paper & placing eight coquettes on it.
To make Crisp Topping, combine the following ingredients in a mixing bowl. In a wide mixing bowl, combine the cinnamon, salt, brown sugar, oats, flours, and nutmeg.
Add butter & chop it into pea-sized pieces using a fork. Keep it refrigerated until you're all set to use it.
In a small bowl, combine the vanilla, fruit, & a sprinkle of salt, then taste. Only use cane sugar for sweetening if required.
Fill every ramekin with fruit, then top with the crisp topping. Then, directly on your grill grate, place a sheet pan in the ramekins.
Bake for 30-40 mins, or unless the tops become golden and bubbling. Allow 20 mins for cooling.
Top with the dollop of whipped cream to serve.

7.96 Scones with Vanilla Bean Glaze
Total Time: 38 Mins, Servings: 2
Ingredients
2 cup Flour
1/2 Cup Sugar
1 Tsp Baking Powder
1 Tsp Salt
1 Small Box Vanilla Instant Pudding
1/2 Cup Chilled Butter, Cut into 1/2" Cubes
1 Egg
1 Tbsp Vanilla
Cup Half-And-Half
2 Tbsp Butter, Softened
1 cup Powdered Sugar
1 Tbsp Vanilla Extract
1 Tbsp Smoked Heavy Cream
Instructions
Preheat the Pit Boss at 375°F with the lid covered.
Using parchment paper, line the baking sheet. Combine the baking powder, flour, sugar, & salt in a mixing bowl.
Using a pastry cutter, cut in the chilled butter till it looks coarse meal. In a separate bowl, combine all dry pudding mix and the milk.
In the middle of dry ingredients, make the well & pour in vanilla essence, egg, & all but half-and-half.
Mix the dough with your hands until all dry ingredients become combined.
Form your dough in small circles on the floured board, then slice into triangles. Brush all triangles with half-and-half on the parchment-lined baking sheet.
Bake for around 6-8 mins in your Pit Boss, or unless golden brown. Remove from the oven and set aside to cool.
To create the glaze, combine the sugar and butter in a mixing bowl and mix until crumbly. Next, mix in the vanilla & smoked cream until completely combined.
Serve scones with glaze drizzled on top. Enjoy!

7.97 The Dan Patrick Show Smoked Super Bowl Sundae
Total Time: 2 Hrs, Servings: 4
Ingredients
1 cup Heavy Cream
2 Cup Half-And-Half
2 Tsp Bourbon
1 Tbsp Vanilla Extract
2/3 Cup Granulated Sugar
Salt
4 Bananas, Ripe but Firm, Unpeeled and Split Lengthwise
1 Tsp Cinnamon
2 Tbsp Maple Syrup
Instructions
Set the temperature to 180°F & preheat for around 15 mins with the lid covered.
In an Al roasting pan, combine both heavy cream & half-and-half. Smoke for around 45 mins with the pan in your Pit Boss.
Remove cream mix from your grill after it has smoked, then add the vanilla, sugar, bourbon, & salt. Stir till the sugar is completely dissolved, then refrigerate for 1 hr.
Fill the ice cream machine halfway with the mixture and process until it achieves the soft-serve consistency. After that, put it into a plastic container & freeze it for almost 1 hr, or till ready to construct banana splits.
Raise the heat to high & preheat the oven.
Place bananas on the baking sheet lined with parchment paper or Al foil. Cinnamon is sprinkled on top, & maple syrup is drizzled on top. Place the baking sheet on your grill grate & cook for 10-15 mins, or unless the bananas start to turn brown.
Remove the bananas from your grill. Enjoy!

7.98 Baked Brownie Bread Pudding

Total Time: 55 Mins, Servings: 6
Ingredients
4 Egg
3 Tsp Vanilla Extract
1 Pinch Salt
1/2 Cup Bittersweet Chocolate Chips
4 Cup Leftover Brownies, Cut into 1" Cubes
1 cup Heavy Cream
1/2 Cup Sugar
1/4 Cup Dried Coconut Flakes
2 Stick Butter
2 cup Brown Sugar
1/2 Tsp Salt
1 Tsp Baking Soda
Whipped Cream
1/4 Candied Walnuts or Pecans
Instructions
Set the oven to 350°F & preheat for 15 mins with the lid covered.
To make bread pudding, whisk together sugar, eggs, heavy cream, vanilla extract, & salt in a mixing bowl. Ensure that everything is well combined. Combine brownies & chocolate chips in a mixing bowl & stir to combine.
Sprinkle coconut flakes over the top of the batter in a baking pan.
Cook for around 45 mins, or unless the sides are gently browned & puffy, the center has barely set by placing the baking pan straight on your grill grate.
To make the caramel sauce, melt the butter with the sugar and salt in a small saucepan.
Bring the mix to a boil & simmer until it reaches 275°F on an immediate thermometer. Remove the pan from the heat & quickly whisk in the vanilla & baking soda. It will boil up & emit steam, so proceed with care.
Whipped cream, Caramel sauce, & candied walnuts go well with bread brownie pudding.

7.99 Baked Raspberry French Toast Casserole

Total Time: 60 Mins, Servings: 4
Ingredients
1 Challah Bread, 1 Loaf, Cut into 3/4" Slices
18 Ounce Fresh Raspberries
8 Large Egg
1 Tsp Kosher Salt
2 Tsp Vanilla Extract
2 cup Whole Milk
1 1/2 Tsp Ground Cinnamon
3/4 Cup Sugar
Instructions
Arrange bread & raspberries equally in a baking dish.
In a wide mixing bowl, stir together sugar, cinnamon & salt. Add the eggs, milk, & vanilla and stir to blend.
Pour egg mixture evenly on bread & fruit, push down to completely immerse all items.
Cover & leave at room temp for 1 hr.
When you're all set to cook, fire up the Pit Boss as per the manufacturer's directions. Preheat the oven to 350°F and bake for 10-15 mins with the lid covered.
Combine leftover sugar & cinnamon. Sprinkle evenly on the casserole.
Put the casserole on the prepared grill & bake till golden brown, approximately 45 mins to 1 hr.
Leave for 10 mins before serving. Dust with some powdered sugar & serve with maple syrup.

7.100 Grilled Pineapple & Watermelon Creamsicles

Total Time: 25 Mins, Servings: 8
Ingredients
1/2 Whole Watermelon, Sliced
1/2 Whole Pineapple, Trimmed & Sliced
1/2 Cup Sugar
2 Whole Lime Juice Fresh
1 cup Heavy Cream
Instructions
When you're all set to cook, turn your Pit Boss on the Smoke and follow the instructions over the grill.
Cook for around 15-20 mins on your grill with the watermelon & pineapple. Remove the watermelon from the grill & remove the rind. Transfer to the blender after cutting into one piece.
Strain after pureeing till smooth. Continue with pineapple but keep them separate. Sugar, lime juice, & cream are added to every juice. Whisk till the sugar is completely dissolved.
Fill every popsicle mold 1/4 with pineapple, 1/4 with watermelon, and ¼ full of pineapple. Freeze the molds for 1 hr, or till they are partially frozen. Put the popsicle stick within the freezer overnight till it is well frozen.
To release the pop, pour hot water on the mold and peel it away gently.

Chapter 8: Cocktail Recipes

8.1 Pit Bossade Cocktail
Total Time: 15 Mins: Servings: 2
Ingredients
2 lemons, sliced
2 Tbsp Pit Boss Smoked Simple Syrup
3 Oz bourbon
2 Oz lemon juice
2 Oz Pit Boss Smoked Simple Syrup
2 Sprig fresh mint for garnish
Instructions:
Set the Pit Boss to 500°F & preheat for around 15 Mins with the lid covered when you're all set to cook.
To make your grilled lemons, combine all the ingredients in a large mixing bowl. Put lemon slices on the grill after brushing them with Smoked Pit Boss Simple Syrup. Cook until caramelized marks form on the surface. Remove the steaks from the grill and put them aside.
Combine the bourbon, lemon juice, & Simple Syrup in the mixing glass.
Shake well and pour into a tall glass filled with clean ice.
Serve with grilled lemon & mint as garnish. Enjoy!

8.2 Smoked Hibiscus Sparkler
Total Time: 40 Mins, Servings: 4
Ingredients
1/2 Cup Water
1/2 Cup Sugar
2 Tbsp Dried Hibiscus Flowers
1 Bottle Sparkling Wine
Crystallized Ginger, For Garnish
Instructions
Set the Pit Boss to 180°F & preheat for around 15 Mins with the lid covered when you're all set to cook.
Fill a small baking dish halfway with water & put it on your grill grate. Smoke this water for around 30 Mins or till you get the desired smoke taste.
In a medium saucepan, combine the water, sugar, & hibiscus flowers. Take to a low simmer & boil until the sugar has dissolved on medium heat.
Remove all hibiscus flowers & place the simple syrup in a small jar in the fridge to cool.
In the base of the champagne glass, pour some smoked hibiscus syrup & cover with some sparkling wine.
Garnish with some pieces of crystallized ginger. Enjoy!

8.3 Smoked Ice Mojito Slurpee
Total Time: 10 Mins, Serving: 2
Ingredients
1 Cup White Rum
1/2 Cup Fresh Squeezed Lime Juice
1/4 Cup Pit Boss Smoked Simple Syrup
12 Fresh Mint Leaves
4 Sprig Fresh Mint, For Garnish
4 Lime Wedges, For garnish
Instructions
Set the Pit Boss to 180°F & preheat for around 15 Mins with the lid covered when you're all set to cook. If the Super Smoke is available, use it for the best taste.
To make smoked ice, use the following ingredients. In a metal high-sided pan, pour some water. Place the pan on the grill and let it smoke for around 30 Mins.
Remove the smoked water from the grill & pour it into an ice cube tray. Place in the freezer till completely frozen.
In a blender, combine the rum, Simple Syrup, lime juice, mint leaves, & smoked ice.
Pour in glasses after the mixture has reached the slushy consistency.
Serve with the lime wedge & mint sprig as garnish. Enjoy!

8.4 Smoked Mexican Hot Chocolate
Total Time: 50 Mins, Servings: 2
Ingredients
1/8 Tsp Cayenne Pepper
1/2 Tsp Ground Cinnamon
1/2 Tsp Smoked Paprika
2/3 Cup Heavy Cream
4 Cup Milk
1/2 Cup Sugar
1/4 Cup Cocoa Powder
1/8 Tsp Salt
1 3/4 Bittersweet Chocolate, Finely Chopped
1/2 Tsp Vanilla Extract
Instructions
Once all set to cook, preheat the grill to 180°F with the lid covered for 15 Mins.
Smoke the cayenne pepper now for around 30 Mins in the heatproof pan. Smoke for the next 5 Mins after adding the cinnamon & paprika into the pan.
Scald the cream, milk, & sugar in a small saucepan. Whisk in some cocoa & salt after some time.
Stir in all smoked spices, bittersweet chocolate, & vanilla when the mix is heated.
Combine all ingredients in a mixing bowl & serve with some marshmallows or whipped cream. Enjoy!

8.5 Smoked Barnburner Cocktail
Total Time: 50 Mins, Servings: 2
Ingredients
16 Oz Fresh Raspberries
1/2 Cup Pit Boss Smoked Simple Syrup
1 1/2 Oz Smoked Raspberry Syrup
3 Oz Reposado Tequila
1 oz Lime Juice
1 oz Lemon Juice
2 Grilled Lime Wheel, For garnish
Instructions
Set the Pit Boss to 180°F & preheat for around 15 Mins with the lid covered when you're all set to cook. If the Super Smoke is available, use it for the best taste.
To make Raspberry Syrup, combine all the ingredients in a blender and blend until smooth. Smoke for around 30 Mins with fresh raspberries over the grill mat. After all, raspberries have just been smoked, set aside a bunch for garnish & combine the rest with Simple Syrup in a wide sheet pan.
Smoke for around 45 Mins using a sheet pan over your grill grate. Remove from the grill & set aside to cool. Remove particles by straining through the fine mesh screen. Refrigerate the syrup till you're set to use it.
In a small mixing glass, combine raspberry syrup, lime juice, lemon juice & tequila with ice. Shake well & pour on ice cubes. Smoked raspberries & lime wheel serve as garnish. Enjoy!

8.6 Smoked Mulled Wine
Total Time: 1 hr 10 Mins, Servings: 10
Ingredients
2 Bottle Red Wine
1/2 Cup Whiskey
1/2 Cup White Rum
1/2 Cup Honey
1 Cinnamon Stick
2 Pods Star Anise
4 Whole Cloves
1 (3 In) Orange Peel
Instructions
Set the Pit Boss to 180°F & preheat for around 15 Mins with the lid covered when you're all set to cook. If the Super Smoke is available, use it for the best taste.
Combine wine, cloves, whiskey, rum, star anise, cinnamon stick, honey, & orange peel in a small baking dish. Stir until everything is fully blended.
Place this dish over your grill grate & smoke for around one hour, or till the mix is heated.
Remove these from your grill and remove all mulling spices. Cinnamon sticks, orange zest, anise, or a mixture of the three may be a garnish. Enjoy!

8.7 Smoked Cold Brew Coffee
Total Time: 2 hrs 15 Mins, Servings: 8
Ingredients
12 Oz Coarse Ground Coffee
Heavy Cream or Milk
Sugar
Instructions
Fill the plastic container halfway with coffee grinds & gently pour some water on the top. Add the rest of the grinds & pour further water in the circular motion on the top.
Using the back of the spoon, press the grinds into water. Refrigerate for 18-24 hours after covering and transferring to a refrigerator.
Remove from the refrigerator & strain using mesh strainer & a dual layer of the cheese cloth into some clean container.
Set the Pit Boss to 180°F & preheat for around 15 Mins with the lid covered when you're all set to cook. If the Super Smoke is available, use it for the best taste.
Fill a small baking dish halfway with cold brew & put it straight on your grill grate. Now smoke for around 1-2 hours, based on how much smoke you want.
Remove from the grill and chill in the ice bath. Drink straight up, with cream, sugar, & in your popular coffee recipe. Enjoy!

8.8 Game Day Micheladas
Total Time: 5 Mins, Servings: 2
Ingredients
2 Tbsp Cajun Seasoning
2 Tbsp Kosher Salt
2 Limette, In Keile Geschnitten
6 Oz Clamato
6 Oz Pit Boss Smoked Bloody Mary Mix
12 Oz Modelo
Instructions
In a medium bowl, combine the Cajun seasoning & kosher salt. Dip your pint glass into the Cajun salt mixture after running a lime wedge over the rim.
In your pint glass, combine Clamato & Bloody Mary Mixture. Serve with the lime wedge & a splash of Modelo. Enjoy!

8.9 Smoked Pineapple Hotel Nacional Cocktail
Total Time: 40 Mins, Servings: 2
Ingredients
2 Pineapple
1/2 Cup Water
1/2 Cup Sugar
3 Fluid Oz White Rum
1 1/2 Fluid Oz Lime Juice
1 1/2 Fluid Oz Pineapple Syrup
1 Fluid Oz Apricot Brandy
2 Dash Angostura Bitters
Instructions
To make the syrup, preheat the Pit Boss to 180°F & cook for around 15 Mins with the lid covered. If the Super Smoke is available, use it for the best taste.
Remove the pineapple's ends and discard them. Slice the pineapple in thick slices. Don't bother about your skin; it won't harm you if you keep it on. Smoke all pineapple slices for approximately 15 Mins from all sides on your grill.
While your pineapple continues smoking, mix the sugar into water in the saucepan on low heat, stirring frequently. Place the syrup into a large mixing basin and put it aside.
Once the pineapple has done cooking, slice every slice into 8 or more wedges, then toss to cover & cover with some simple syrup.
Allow the mix to macerate within the refrigerator for almost 4 hours, stirring occasionally.
Using the fine-mesh strainer, pour the syrup into a clean bowl & crush the pineapple using a spoon to extract the juice. The syrup may be stored in a container and kept in the refrigerator for almost four days.
To prepare the drink, start by combining the following ingredients. In a cocktail shaker/mixing glass, combine the apricot brandy, lime juice, rum, pineapple syrup, & bitters. Fill with some ice cubes & shake till they are completely frozen.
Fill a frosty cocktail glass halfway with ice and strain it. Serve with the lime wheel as a garnish. Enjoy!

8.10 Smoked Plum and Thyme Fizz Cocktail
Total Time: 1 hr 5 Mins, Servings: 2
Ingredients
6 Fresh Plums
4 Fluid Oz Vodka
1 1/2 Fluid Oz Fresh Lemon Juice
2 Oz Smoked Plum and Thyme Simple Syrup
4 Fluid Oz Club Soda
2 Slices Smoked Plum, For Garnish
2 Sprig Fresh Thyme, For garnish
Plum and Thyme Simple Syrup
8 Sprig Thyme
2 Cup Pit Boss Smoked Simple Syrup
Instructions
Set the Pit Boss to 180°F & preheat for around 15 Mins with the lid covered when you're all set to cook. If the Super Smoke is available, use it for the best taste.
Remove your pit from the plums & cut them in half. Smoke for around 25 Mins by placing the plum pieces on your grill grate. Simple Syrup with Plums & Thyme: Remove the plums from your grill after 25 Mins & quarter them. 1 cup Simple Syrup, plums, & thyme sprigs 45 Mins should be enough time to smoke the combination. Remove the meat from the grill, drain it, and set it aside to cool. Refrigerate any leftovers for almost one month.
In a wide mixing glass, combine the vodka, lemon juice, smoked plum & thyme syrup.
Shake in the ice. Strain over fresh ice, top with some club soda, then garnish with some thyme sprig & a plum slice. Enjoy!

8.11 Smoked Hot Toddy
Total Time: 40 Mins, Servings: 2
Ingredients
16 Oz Lemonade
2 Mint Tea Bag
2 Peach Tea Bag
2 Green Tea Bag
8 Oz High West Double Rye
2 Lemon Slice, For Garnish
2 Cinnamon Stick
Instructions
Set the Pit Boss to 500°F & preheat for around 15 Mins with the lid covered when you're all set to cook.
Fill a small baking dish halfway with lemonade & put it immediately on your grill grate. Cook for 20-30 Mins, or till its temp reaches 200°F.
Pour your lemonade off the grill in a glass. For 2–4 Mins steeping tea bags into hot lemonade. Take out the tea bags & add the whiskey.
If preferred, garnish with some lemon slices & cinnamon stick. Enjoy

8.12 Smoked Kentucky Mule
Total Time: 6 Mins, Servings: 2
Ingredients
4 Oz High West Whiskey
1 Oz Lime Juice
1 Oz Pit Boss Smoked Simple Syrup
8 Oz Ginger Beer
2 Sprig Fresh Mint, For Garnish
2 Lime Wedge, For garnish
Instructions
Pour lime juice, whiskey, & Simple Syrup into a glass filled with ice. To blend, stir everything together.
Finish with a splash of ginger beer. Stir it again, then top with mint & a slice of lime. Enjoy!

8.13 Smoked Sangria
Total Time: 55 Mins, Servings: 6
Ingredients
1 (750 Ml) Medium-Bodied Red Wine
1/4 Cup Grand Marnier
1/4 Cup Pit Boss Smoked Simple Syrup
1 Cup Fresh Cranberries
1 Whole Apple, Sliced
2 Whole Limes, Sliced
4 Cinnamon Stick
Soda Water
Instructions
Set the Pit Boss to 180°F & preheat for
around 15 Mins with the lid covered when you're all set to cook. If the Super Smoke is available, use it for the best taste.
Combine the red wine, Simple Syrup, Grand Marnier, & cranberries in a small dish and put it immediately on your grill grate.
Smoke for around 30-45 Mins, or till the liquid absorbs desired quantity of smoke. Remove off the grill & set aside to cool.
Place the mix in a big pitcher after it's been cooled. In the pitcher, combine sliced apples, cinnamon sticks, limes, & ice.
If desired, top with some soda water. Enjoy!

8.14 Smoky Mountain Bramble Cocktail
Total Time: 35 Mins, Servings: 2
Ingredients
Smoked Blackberry Simple Syrup
16 Oz Blackberries
2 Cup Sugar
10 Smoked Blackberries
3 Oz Vodka
1 1/2 Oz Alpine Distilling Preserve Liqueur
1 1/2 Oz Lemon Juice
1 Oz Smoked Blackberry Syrup
Instructions
Set the Pit Boss to 180°F & preheat for around 15 Mins with the lid covered when you're all set to cook. If the Super Smoke is available, use it for the best taste.
To create a Simple Syrup, follow these steps: Smoke the blackberries for around 15-20 Mins on your grill mat.
In a medium saucepan, combine water & sugar, then cook on medium heat till sugar dissolves. Remove from fire & macerate some blackberries into simple syrup.
Strain via a mesh strainer & keep for almost 14 days in an airtight container.
To prepare the drink, start by combining the following ingredients. In a cocktail shaker, muddle 4-5 smoked blackberries. Combine the vodka, lemon, Preserve Liqueur, & blackberry syrup in a mixing glass. Shake vigorously with ice. Pour into the old-style glass with a dual strain.
Serve with a blackberry & lemon twist as a garnish. Enjoy!

8.15 Smoked Pomegranate Lemonade Cocktail
Total Time: 50 Mins, Servings: 2
Ingredients
Pomegranate Ice Cubes
32 Oz POM Juice
2 Cup Pomegranate Seeds
3 Oz Vodka
8 Oz Lemonade
Lemon Wheel, For Garnish
Fresh Mint, For Garnish
Instructions
When you're all set to cook, preheat the Pit Boss to 225°F with the lid covered for around 15 Mins. If the Super Smoke is available, use it for the best taste.
For Ice Cubes Smoked Pomegranate, use the following ingredients. In a wide sheet pan, combine POM juice & pomegranate seeds. Smoke for around 45 Mins on your Pit Boss. Remove the grill from the heat and set it aside to cool.
Fill ice molds with POM juice (smoked) and place them in the freezer.
Place these frozen pomegranate cubes in the mason jar until all set to serve. Over ice cubes, pour the vodka & lemonade.
Serve with the lemon wheel & fresh mint as garnish. Enjoy!

8.16 A Smoking Classic Cocktail
Total Time: 1 hr 5 Mins, Servings: 2
Ingredients
2 Bottle Angostura Orange Bitters
10 Sugar Cubes
8 Oz Champagne
Lemon Twist
Instructions
Set the Pit Boss to 180°F & preheat for around 15 Mins with the lid covered when you're all set to cook. If the Super Smoke is available, use it for the best taste.
To make the Orange Bitters, combine the following ingredients in a small mixing bowl. Combine Angostura orange bitter,

water, & Four sugar cubes in a medium saucepan.
Smoke for around 60 Mins using a skillet over your grill grate.
Return the smoked bitter into the bottle after cooling.
In every Champagne flute, place sugar cube & soak it into smoked bitters.
In the flute glass, combine champagne & lemon twist. Enjoy!

8.17 Grilled Hawaiian Sour
Total Time: 30 Mins, Servings: 2
Ingredients
2 Whole Pineapple, Trimmed and Sliced
1/2 Cup Palm Sugar
3 Oz Bourbon
2 Oz Grilled Pineapple Juice
2 Oz Pit Boss Smoked Simple Syrup
10 Oz Lemon Juice
2 Grilled Pineapple Chunk, For Garnish
2 Pineapple Leaf, For garnish
Instructions
Set the Pit Boss to 350°F & preheat for around 15 Mins with the lid covered when you're all set to cook.
For Pineapple Juice with Grilled Pineapple: Sprinkle palm sugar over pineapple slices. Cook for around 8 Mins each side, directly on your grill grate.
Remove off the grill & set aside to cool. Some pieces should be set aside for garnish. To extract the juice, run the remaining pineapple slices via centrifugal juicer.
To prepare the drink, follow these steps: In the cocktail shaker with ice, combine the bourbon, simple syrup, pineapple juice, & lemon juice. Shake the bottle vigorously. In a cold coupe glass, strain twice. Serve with some grilled pineapple chunks & pineapple leaf as a garnish. Enjoy!

8.18 Grilled Applejack O'Lantern Cocktail
Total Time: 40 Mins, Servings: 2
Ingredients
2 Orange, Sliced
12 Oz Dogfish Head Punkin Ale
1 Oz Pit Boss Smoked Simple Syrup
2 Oz Apple Brandy
1 Oz Lemon Juice
1 Oz Orange Juice
Instructions
When you're all set to cook, preheat the Pit Boss to 500°F with the lid covered for around 15 Mins.
For grilled oranges, follow these instructions: Cook for 20-30 Mins, or till the fruit starts to caramelize, by placing orange wheels straight on the barbecue grate. Remove off the grill and set aside to cool.
In the chilled Collin glass, combine all your ingredients. Serve with a half-grilled orange wheel dotted with 3 cloves as a garnish. Enjoy!

8.19 Grilled Grapefruit Buck Cocktail
Total Time: 20 Mins, Servings: 4
Ingredients
Grilled Grapefruit Juice
4 Grapefruit, Halved
1/2 Cup Turbinado Sugar
12 Oz Vodka
1 1/2 Oz Freshly Squeezed Lemon Juice From 1 Lemon
3 Oz Pit Boss Smoked Simple Syrup
8 Sprig Fresh Mint Leaves
12 Oz Ginger Beer
2 Grapefruit Sliced into 1/2 Inch Rounds, For Garnish
Instructions
When you're all set to cook, preheat the Pit Boss to 500°F with the lid covered for around 15 Mins.
Place your sliced grapefruit over the preheated Pit Boss & coat all sides using turbinado sugar. Grill for 3 Mins on each side or till grill marks appear. Remove the steaks from the grill and put them aside until they are cool to the touch.
To obtain juice from grilled grapefruit, squeeze it.
In the pitcher, combine the vodka, lemon juice, grapefruit juice, Simple Syrup, & mint leaves. Stir aggressively with the cocktail spoon.
Whisk vigorously for around 30 seconds after adding a scoop of ice.
Top with some ginger beer & pour into Six rocks glasses packed with ice.
Serve with a grapefruit slice & a sprig of mint as a garnish. Enjoy!

8.20 Grilled Jungle Juice
Total Time: 35 Mins, Servings: 8
Ingredients
1 Pineapple, Trimmed and Sliced
3 Orange, Sliced
5 Limes, Sliced
1 Lb Fresh Strawberries
1/4 Cup Granulated Sugar
1 Bottle Pineapple Juice
Oz Cranberry Juice
Oz Sparkling Water
1 Bottle Tito's Vodka
1 Bottle Silver Tequila
1 Bottle White Rum
1 Bottle Triple Sec
Instructions
Set the temp to 350°F & preheat for around 15 Mins when you are all set to cook.
Shake off any extra sugar before tossing the citrus segments with it.
Cook your citrus slices, pineapple spears, & strawberries straight on your grill grate for around 10-20 Mins, or till grill marks appear.
Remove the fruit slices as they complete cooking to avoid overcooking. Allow cooling before serving.
Add your chilled grilled fruit to the jungle juice container, accompanied by all the liquids. Mix everything well. Enjoy!

8.21 Smoked Margarita
Total Time: 20 Mins, Servings: 2
Ingredients
24 Whole Lime Wedges, Slit in Center
1 Cup Turbinado Sugar
3 Cup Fresh Squeezed Grilled Lime Juice
6 Cup Silver Tequila
3 Cup Cointreau
1 & ½ Cup Smoked Pit Boss Simple Syrup
1 Cup Bloody Mary Pit Boss Cocktail Salt
Lime Wedge, For Garnish
Instructions
When you are all set to cook, preheat the Pit Boss to 500°F with the lid covered for around 15 Mins.
Limes should be halved, dipped in turbinado sugar, & placed on a hot grill.
Grill for around 5 Mins, or till char appears. Remove these limes from your grill and squeeze their juice.
In the pitcher, combine tequila, Cointreau, lime juice, & Simple Syrup. To blend, stir everything together.
Place the Bloody Mary Cocktails on the grill. In a dish large enough to accommodate the edge of the glass, sprinkle salt.

Run one lime across the rim of each glass, then dip its rim into the salt & fill with some ice.
Pour in the margarita mix & top with a slice of lime. Enjoy!

8.22 Bacon Old-Fashioned Cocktail
Total Time: 25 Mins, Servings: 2
Ingredients
16 Slices Bacon
1/2 Cup Warm Water (110°F To 115°F)
1500 ML Bourbon
1/2 Fluid Oz Maple Syrup
4 Dash Angostura Bitters
2 Fresh Orange Peel
Instructions
To cook bacon, follow these steps: Preheat the Pit Boss to 325°F for 15 Mins with the lid closed when ready to cook.
Place the bacon on the cooling rack, which fits in the baking sheet pan. Cook for around 15-20 Mins in the Pit Boss, or till bacon has browned & crispy. Save the bacon for the later day. Allow the fat to cool somewhat before using it to infuse your bourbon.
In the glass or sturdy plastic container, combine warm liquefied bacon fat using the full contents of the bottle of your bourbon.
Stir well with a fork. Allow it to rest for some hours on a counter, stirring occasionally.
Place the bourbon fat mix in the freezer after 4 hours. The fat would solidify after approximately one hour, & you can scoop this out using a spoon if you want to eliminate all the fat; fine strain the mix via a sieve.
Combine the ingredients in the mixing bowl with ice & whisk until well chilled. In a glass, strain over new ice & garnish with saved bacon & orange peel.

8.23 Grilled Peach Mint Julep
Total Time: 60 Mins, Servings: 2
Ingredients
2 Whole Peach
4 Oz Whiskey
2 Cup Sugar
4 Tbsp Pink Peppercorns
20 Whole Fresh Mint Leaves, Plus More for Garnish
2 Lime Wedge, For Garnish
4 Oz Bourbon

Instructions
To make the Whiskey Peaches, slice the peach into pieces and soak them in whiskey for 4-6 hrs into your refrigerator.
Simple Syrup with Pink Peppercorns: Combine sugar, water, & pink peppercorns in a small pan.
Set the Pit Boss to 180°F & preheat for around 15 Mins with the lid covered when you're all set to cook. If the Super Smoke is available, use it for the best taste.
Cook syrup for around 30 Mins on your grill or till desired smoke taste is achieved. Then, remove the steaks from your grill.
Preheat the Pit Boss to 350°F. Cook the whiskey peach pieces directly on your grill grate for 10-12 Mins, or till softened & grill marks appear.
To prepare a julep, combine the following ingredients in a mixing glass. Mint leaves & whiskey peaches are muddled with Simple Syrup Pink Peppercorn.
Over the rim of your glass, strew crushed ice. Stir with the bourbon on crushed ice. 1 mint & fresh lime for garnish. Enjoy!

8.24 Grilled Peach Smash Cocktail
Total Time: 15 Mins, Servings: 2
Ingredients
2 Peach, Sliced and Grilled
10 Fresh Mint Leaves
1 1/2 Oz Pit Boss Smoked Simple Syrup
4 Oz Bourbon
2 Mint Sprig, For garnish
Instructions
Set the Pit Boss to 375°F & preheat for around 15 Mins with the lid covered when you're all set to cook.
Brush the peach slices with Simple Syrup & slice them into 6 pieces. Cook 10-12 Mins, or till peaches are softened & grill marks appear directly on your grill grate.
Put Three grilled peach pieces, Five mint leaves, & Simple Syrup in a wide mixing glass
Muddle the ingredients to unleash the mint oils & peach juices.
Pour in the bourbon & the crushed ice.
Mix thoroughly and strain into a stemless wine glass. Finish with a sprinkling of ice cubes. Serve with peach & a sprig of mint as a garnish. Enjoy!

8.25 Pit Boss Old Fashioned
Total Time: 1 hr 10 Mins, Servings: 2
Ingredients
2 Orange
2 Cup Cherries
3 Oz Bourbon
1 Oz Pit Boss Smoked Simple Syrup
8 Dash Bitters Lab Apricot Vanilla Bitters
Instructions
Set the Pit Boss to 180°F & preheat for around 15 Mins with the lid covered when you're all set to cook. If the Super Smoke is available, use it for the best taste.
Slice the entire orange in wheels while the Pit Boss warms up.
Place the cherries on the wide sheet pan in your Pit Boss & cook them. Place orange slices on your grill grate immediately.
Before taking from the grill, smoke the cherries for around 1 hour & oranges for almost 25 Mins, based on flavor. Allow time for the oranges & cherries to cool.
Pour the bourbon first, then the Simple Syrup & bitters into the glass. Stir in the ice for around 45 seconds or till the drink has been well diluted.
Fill the new glass halfway with ice and strain the contents. For garnish, skewer an orange wheel & add a cherry. Enjoy!

8.26 Smoked Grape Lime Rickey
Total Time: 55 Mins, Servings: 4
Ingredients
1/2 Lb Red Grapes
1/2 Cup Plus 1 Tbsp Sugar
1/2 Cup Water
1 Lime, Sliced
2 Limes, Halved
1 Tbsp Sugar
1 L Lemon Lime Soda
Instructions
Set the Pit Boss to 180°F & preheat for around 15 Mins with lid covered when you are all set to cook.
Rinse the grapes well before placing them in a small baking tray. Stir sugar into the water till sugar

dissolves. Pour the wine over the grapes.
Smoke a baking dish straight on your grill grate for 30-40 Mins, or till the grapes become tender.
Remove this baking dish from your grill & pour the whole contents into a blender. Puree till smooth on high, filter through some fine mesh sieve.
Increase the temp of the Pit Boss to 350°F.
Place all lime slices & halves immediately on your grill grate after tossing them with sugar. Cook for around 15–20 Mins, or till grill marks appear on the surface. Remove the slices from the grill and put them aside. When the lime halves have cooled enough, juice them.
Fill the pint glass halfway with ice to start the cocktail. Add 1 & 1/2 oz. Lime juice, 1 & 1/2 oz. Grape syrup & a splash of soda. Serve with a lime slice (grilled) as a garnish. Enjoy!

8.27 Grilled Blood Orange Mimosa
Total Time: 20 Mins, Servings: 4
Ingredients
3 Blood Orange, Halved
2 Tbsp Granulated Sugar
1 Bottle Sparkling Wine
Thyme Sprigs, For Garnish
Instructions
Set the Pit Boss to 375°F & preheat for around 15 Mins with the lid covered when you're all set to cook.
Dip the sliced side of all orange halves into sugar and set it on your grill grate once the grill has heated.
Grill for around 10-15 Mins, or till grill marks appear on the oranges.
Remove this from your grill and set it aside to cool to room temperature.
Once the oranges are cool enough, juice them and filter them juice thru a fine sieve to remove any pulp.
Fill every glass with sparkling wine & orange juice.
Serve with the sprig of thyme as a garnish. Enjoy!

8.28 Smoked Jacobsen Salt Margarita
Total Time: 1 day 5 Mins, Servings: 2
Ingredients
Kosher Sea Salt
3 Cup Jacobsen Co. Honey
6 Oz Tequila
4 Oz Fresh Squeezed Lime Juice
1/2 Cup Jacobsen Salt Co. Cherrywood Smoked Salt or Smoked Kosher Salt
2 Oz Simple Syrup
2 Tsp Orange Liqueur
Instructions
Take salt (kosher sea) and put it out over a tray if producing your smoked salt.
Set the Pit Boss to 165°F & preheat for around 15 Mins with the lid covered when you are all set to cook. If the Super Smoke is available, use it for the best taste.
Place your salt tray straight on your grill grate & smoke for approximately 24 hrs, stirring every 8 hrs. Please remove it from the grill after it's been smoked for around 24 hrs & use it in all your desired meals. Use Smoked Salt (Jacobsen Salt) if you wish to bypass the extensive smoking session.
Syrup de base: In a medium saucepan, combine the honey & water. Cook for approximately 20 Mins on low heat, stirring occasionally.
Ice should be added to the cocktail shaker. Combine the tequila, simple syrup, lime juice, & orange liqueur in a mixing glass. Cover & shake for approximately 30 seconds, or until well combined and cooled.
On a dish, sprinkle smoked salt. To rim all edges of a cold rocks glass, press that rim in the salt. In a glass, strain the margarita. Enjoy!

8.29 Smoked Apple Cider
Total Time: 35 Mins, Servings: 2
Ingredients
32 Oz Apple Cider
2 Cinnamon Sticks
4 Whole Cloves
3 Star Anise
2 Pieces Orange Peel
2 Pieces Lemon Peel
Instructions
Set the Pit Boss to 225°F & preheat for around 15 Mins with the lid covered when you're all set to cook. If the Super Smoke is available, use it for the best taste.
In a small baking dish, combine the clove, lemon, cinnamon stick, cider, star anise, & orange peel.
Smoke for around 30 Mins by placing straight on your barbecue grate. Remove from the grill, filter into four cups, and serve.
To serve, garnish via an apple piece & cinnamon stick. Enjoy!

8.30 Smoked Arnold Palmer
Total Time: 10 Mins, Servings: 4
Ingredients
4 Black Tea Bags
8 Medium Lemon, Juiced
1 Cup Smoked Pit Boss Simple Syrup
1 Lemon, Cut into Wheels for Garnish
Instructions
In the heat-safe bowl, place tea bags.
Bring water to a boil and pour it on the tea bags. Allow 5 Mins for tea to steep.
Remove your tea bags & allow the tea completely to cool before serving.
Lemons should be juiced. Toss some lemon juice into the iced tea.
In a mixing bowl, combine the lemon tea and Simple Syrup. Refrigerate the mixture until it is fully cold.
Serve into the glass on ice after it has cooled. Serve with the lemon wheel as a garnish. Enjoy!

8.31 Smoked Berry Cocktail
Total Time: 30 Mins, Servings: 2
Ingredients
1/2 Cup Strawberries, Stemmed
1/2 Cup Blackberries
1/2 Cup Blueberries
8 Oz Bourbon or Iced Tea
2 Oz Lime Juice
3 Oz Simple Syrup
Soda Water
Fresh Mint, For Garnish
Instructions
Set the Pit Boss to 180°F & preheat for around 15 Mins with the lid covered when you're all set to cook. If the Super Smoke is available, use it for the best taste.
Wash your berries well before spreading them out on a dry cookie sheet & grilling them. 15 Mins of smoking berries
Transfer the berries to the blender when they have been removed from the grill. Puree your berries till smooth, then pour out the seeds using a metal mesh sieve.
Pour berry puree into the base of your glass to make a layered drink. Then, using a spoon, pour bourbon and iced tea in the glass, followed by lime juice & soda water, simple syrup, plus

ice. Finish with the sprig of mint & a few additional berries as a garnish.
Carry on with the same procedure for three additional servings. Enjoy!

8.32 Pit Boss French 75 Cocktail
Total Time: 15 Mins, Servings: 2
Ingredients
2 Lemon, Thinly Sliced
3 Oz Gin
1 Oz Fresh Lemon Juice
1 Oz Pit Boss Smoked Simple Syrup
6 Oz Champagne
Instructions
When preparing to cook your grilled lemon, preheat the Pit Boss to 500°F with the lid covered for around 15 Mins.
Place the lemon straight on your grill grate after brushing with Simple Syrup. Grill for 15 Mins from each side, or till caramelized marks form.
In a wide mixing container with ice, combine the lemon juice, gin, & Simple Syrup. Shake vigorously before straining into the Champagne flute.
Finish with a splash of champagne & lemon as garnish. Enjoy!

8.33 Smoke Screen Cocktail
Total Time: 40 Mins, Servings: 2
Ingredients
4 Whole Lemons
4 Oz Ransom Whiskey
1 1/2 Oz Pit Boss Smoked Simple Syrup
Instructions
When you are all set to cook, preheat the Pit Boss to 500°F with the lid covered for 15 Mins.
To make the lemon juice, combine all the ingredients in a blender and blend until smooth. 1 lemon, cut in half, placed on your grill. To make the garnish, cut the remaining lemon into thick wheels & set them on your grill.
Cook for around 15 Mins, or till one side of the lemons has grill marks. Remove all lemon wheels and set them aside. The split lemon should give juice.
Shake rapidly in the shaker glass, having ice to mix Ransom Whiskey, lemon juice, & Simple Syrup. Fine strain in the cooled coupe glass with a lemon wheel as a garnish. Enjoy!

8.34 Seeing Stars Cocktail
Total Time: 5 Mins, Servings: 2
Ingredients
4 Oz Siete Leguas Blanco Tequila
1 1/2 Oz Lime Juice
1 Oz Giffard Blue Curacao
1 Oz Watermelon Juice
1 Oz Pit Boss Smoked Simple Syrup
2 Watermelon Slice, For garnish
Instructions
Combine all the ingredients in the shaker with ice. Fine filter into a rock glass full of ice and rimmed with the smoked salt.
Serve with a slice of watermelon as a garnish. Enjoy!

8.35 Maui Waui Cocktail
Total Time: 35 Mins, Servings: 2
Ingredients
4 Fresh Strawberries
Sugar
1 Oranges
1 Tbsp Pit Boss Smoked Simple Syrup
2 Oz Water
1 Cup Agave
2 Oz Pineapple Juice
2 Oz Orange Juice
3 Slices Kiwi Fruit
Ice
2 Oz Rum
Italian Cherry
Instructions
When you're all set to cook, fire up the Pit Boss as per the manufacturer's directions. Preheat the grill to
325°F and cook for 10-15 Mins with the lid covered.
Half the strawberries & roll them into granulated sugar. Cook for around 15-20 Mins straight on the grill. Remove the steaks from the grill and put them aside to cool.
Cut the orange in wheels for the Orange Agave. Coat sliced orange wheels into Simple Syrup & cook until the exterior has a faint sear. Reduce the temp to smoke & leave aside for 10-15 mins to cool.
Agave nectar thinned with water. For 45-60 Mins, steep the charred chard oranges into agave over smoke, stirring every 10 Mins.
In a small sheet pan, combine equal parts orange juice & pineapple juice. Put a sheet pan over your grill grate straight & smoke for 45 Mins. Remove the steaks from the grill & put them aside to cool.
Combine the burned kiwi slices, orange agave, & grilled strawberries in a wide mixing glass. Lightly muddle. Combine ice, rum, & smoked juice in a cocktail shaker. Shake well & strain twice over ice.
On the skewer, skewer the grilled pineapple & Italian cherry. Enjoy!

8.36 Smoked Hot Buttered Rum
Total Time: 35 Mins, Servings: 4
Ingredients
2 Cup Water
1/4 Cup Brown Sugar
1/2 Stick Butter, Melted
1 Tsp Ground Cinnamon
1/4 Tsp Ground Nutmeg
Ground Cloves
Salt
6 Oz Rum
Instructions
Set the Pit Boss to 180°F & preheat for around 15 Mins with the lid covered when you're all set to cook. If the Super Smoke is available, use it for the best taste.
Combine water within all your ingredients except the rum in a wide baking dish & set immediately on your grill grate. 30 Mins of smoking.
Remove the steaks from your grill & throw them into the blender pitcher. Process until the mixture is foamy.
In four glasses, pour rum. Divide the heated butter mixture among the 4 glasses equally.
Add cinnamon stick & grated nutmeg to the top. Enjoy!

8.37 Smoky Paloma Cocktail
Total Time: 15 Mins, Servings: 2
Ingredients
2 Grapefruit, Sliced
4 Tbsp Jacobsen Salt Co. Cherrywood Smoked Salt
4 Oz Cazadores Tequila Reposado
2 Oz Soda Water
1 1/2 Oz Grapefruit Juice
1 Oz Simple Syrup

Instructions
When you are all set to cook, preheat the Pit Boss to 500 degrees Fahrenheit with the lid covered for around 15 Mins.
Grill the grapefruit slices till gently browned, about 10 Mins.
Place the Jacobsen salt into a small dish. For coating, the rim of your glass wet this with some grapefruit juice and then dip this in salt.
Inside a tumbler full of ice, combine all your ingredients except for the grapefruit slices & mix thoroughly. Enjoy with the grilled grapefruit slices as a garnish!

8.38 Spiced Cider Brew Cocktail
Total Time: 30 Mins, Servings: 2
Ingredients
8 Lemons, To Yield 1 Cup Grilled Lemon Juice
2 Bottle (750ml) Bottle Rye Whiskey
2 Quart Fresh Apple Cider
2 Cup Pit Boss Smoked Simple Syrup
6 Oz Fernet-Branca
2 Tsp Angostura Bitters
Cinnamon Sticks
Orange Peel Twists, For Garnish
Dry Ice (Optional)
Instructions
When you are all set to cook, preheat the Pit Boss to 500°F with the lid covered for around 15 Mins.
To make the lemon juice (grilled), combine the following ingredients in a small bowl. Lemons should be sliced in half & placed on your grill grate. Cook for approximately 20 Mins, or till grill marks appear & the sugars begin to caramelize. Juice, filter, and set aside to chill.
Combine all your ingredients in the punch bowl & maybe a large container, except for the peel twists of orange & dry ice, in the punch bowl. Cover and chill for around 1-4 hours into the refrigerator.
Serve with some ice blocks & orange peel twists as a garnish. Enjoy!

8.39 Smoked Bloody Mary Cocktail
Total Time: 5 Mins, Servings: 2
Ingredients
2 Lemon, Cut into Wedges
Pit Boss Bloody Mary Cocktail Salt
Ice
3 oz Vodka
8 oz Tomato Juice
8 oz Pit Boss Smoked Bloody Mary Mix
Instructions
After wetting it with the lemon slice, dip pint glass rim with Cocktail Salt (Bloody Mary Pit Boss).
Fill this glass with the tomato juice, ice, vodka, & Bloody Mary Mixture in a 1:1 ratio.
Garnish with bacon, shrimp, olives, crab legs, lime wedges, lemon wedges, and any garnishes of your choosing. Enjoy!

8.40 Smoked Irish Coffee
Total Time: 20 Mins, Servings: 2
Ingredients
10 Oz Hot Coffee
1/2 Cup Heavy Cream
1 Tbsp Sugar
2 Oz Irish Whiskey
Freshly Grated Nutmeg, For Garnish (Optional)
Instructions
Set the Pit Boss to 180°F & preheat for around 15 Mins with the lid covered when you're all set to cook. If the Super Smoke is available, use it for the best taste.
Put the coffee & cream in different small baking pans and put them on your grill grate together. Smoke for around 10-15 Mins, or unless the liquids have taken on a faint smoky taste.
Remove the cream from the grill & set it aside to cool. Once the cream has cooled, add some sugar & beat until soft peaks form in the stand mixer.
Pour some whiskey into all your glasses of steaming coffee.
If desired, garnish with some whipped cream & grated nutmeg. Enjoy!

8.41 Ryes and Shine Cocktail
Total Time: 35 Mins, Servings: 2
Ingredients
2 Lemon, Cut into Wheels for Garnish
6 Tbsp Granulated Sugar
2 Oz Rye
1 Oz Bourbon
3 Oz Lemon Juice
1 Oz Pit Boss Smoked Simple Syrup
6 Dash Fernet-Branca
Instructions
When you are all set to cook, preheat the Pit Boss to 325°F for around 15 Mins with the lid closed.
Coat all sides of lemon wheels using granulated sugar. Cook for around 15 Mins from all sides, or till grill marks appears, directly on your grill grate.
In a shaker, combine the rye, lemon juice, bourbon, Simple Syrup, & Fernet-Branca. Shake until somewhat diluted.
Serve neat in a new glass with a lemon wheel as a garnish. Enjoy!

8.42 Strawberry Basil Daiquiri
Total Time: 25 Mins, Servings: 2
Ingredients
4 Strawberries, Stemmed
6 Tbsp Granulated Sugar, Divided
6 Basil Leaves
3 Oz White Rum
2 Oz Lime Juice
1 Oz Pit Boss Smoked Simple Syrup
2 Fresh Basil Leaves, For Garnish
2 Lime Slice, For garnish
Instructions
Set the Pit Boss to 375°F & preheat for around 15 Mins with the lid covered when you're all set to cook.
Coat granulated sugar after cutting strawberries in half. Cook for around 15-20 Mins on the grill grate. Remove from the heat & set aside to cool.
In a wide shaking tin, gently mix granulated sugar & basil leaves. Muddle in the strawberries once more.
In a mixing glass, combine the lime juice, white rum, & Simple Syrup. Ice should be added to the shaker.
Fill a frozen glass halfway with the ingredients & garnish with huge basil leaf & sliced lime.

8.43 Smoked Bloody Mary with Grilled Garnishes
Total Time: 1 hr 30 Mins, Servings: 4
Ingredients
5 Roma Tomatoes, Sliced into 1/4" Rounds
Salt And Pepper
2 Tbsp Pit Boss Beef Rub
10 Slices Bacon
1 Jar Asparagus, Pickled
1 Jar Green Beans, Pickled

1 Jar Pepperoncinis
1 Jar Cocktail Onions Vermouth Soaked
2 Tomatoes Cherry
1 Jar Olives Mixed
2 Fresh Mushrooms
2 Grilled Shrimp
1 Grilled Lobster Tail
4 Stalks Celery
Bamboo Skewers
3 Cup Tomato Juice
3 Tbsp Worcestershire Sauce
2 Tsp Prepared Horseradish
5 Tsp Hot Sauce
1 Whole Lemon, Juiced
2 Whole Lemon Wedges
Pit Boss Bloody Mary Cocktail Salt
Ice
1 1/2 Fluid Oz Vodka
Instructions
When you are all set to cook, preheat the grill to 275°F with the lid covered for around 15 Mins.
Remove the stems & quarter the tomatoes.
Place your tomatoes on the metal rack on top of a baking pan.
Season with some salt, pepper, & Beef Rub to taste. On your grill, place this baking pan & rack with the tomatoes.
For Smoked Bacon, cook the bacon straight on your grill grate beside the tomatoes for approximately 60 Mins, or till crisp. Crispy bacon will hold up to being used as the garnish into the drink.
Remove the bacon & tomatoes from the grill after almost 1 hour. Remove the skins from the tomatoes & put them aside for cooling.
Increase the temp of the grill to high & preheat it.
Using olive oil, brush the skewers & set them straight on your grill. 5 Mins each side on the grill, or till grill marks appear. Remove them from the grill and put them aside for cooling.
To make your Bloody Mary Mix, pulse peeled tomatoes in the food processor till smooth.
Combine tomato juice, spicy sauce, horseradish, Worcestershire sauce, and 1 full lemon juice.
Season to taste with some salt & black pepper.
Pulse once more to blend
Rub a lemon slice over the rim of your pint glass, and dip it in Bloody Mary Pit Boss Cocktail Salt.
Fill glass with some vodka, ice cubes, & Bloody Mary Mix.
Gently stir
To make the Bloody Mary (Smoked), garnish with a lemon & a lime slice on every rim.
Toss the cocktail with grilled, pickled veggie skewers, smoked bacon, & celery stick.

8.44 Strawberry Mint Julep Cocktail
Total Time: 5 Mins, Servings: 4
Ingredients
2 Oz Pit Boss Smoked Simple Syrup
16 Large Strawberries, Stemmed
1/4 Cup Fresh Mint Leaves
12 Oz Bourbon
2 Large Strawberries, Sliced Lengthwise into 6 Slices, For Garnish
6 Sprig Fresh Mint, For garnish
Instructions
In an intermediate pitcher, combine Simple Syrup, Mint, whole strawberries, & bourbon.
Muddle until the strawberries & mint are evenly distributed.
Pour the contents into glasses in an equal layer. Fill the glass with some crushed ice until it overflows.
Put a straw into each glass & strawberry slice on top. Enjoy!

8.45 Sunset Margarita
Total Time: 55 Mins, Servings: 2
Ingredients
4 Oranges
2 Cup Plus 1 Tsp Agave
1/2 Cup Water
1 Oz Burnt Orange Agave
3 Oz Reposado Tequila
1 1/2 Oz Fresh Squeezed Lime Juice
Jacobsen Salt Co. Cherrywood Smoked Salt
Instructions
Preheat the Pit Boss to 350°F with the lid covered for around 15 Mins.
Cut an orange into half & coat the cut side into agave syrup. Grill for around 15 Mins, or till grill marks appear, with the cut side downwards on your grill grate.
Slice the second orange & brush all sides with some agave while your orange halves are roasting. Cook for around 15 Mins, or till grill marks appear, by placing slices straight on your grill grate adjacent to those halves.
Remove the orange halves off your grill grate & set them aside to cool. Juice half of them and filter when they've cooled.
In a small bowl, whisk together water & agave nectar. Remove the orange pieces from your grill and toss them into the agave mix, saving some garnish.
Lower the grill temp to 180°F & put the agave & oranges in a small dish straight on your grill grate. Do 40 Mins of smoking. Remove the pan from the heat & strain the contents.
To make the cocktail, rim the glass with Smoked Jacobsen Salt. In a cocktail glass, combine tequila, orange juice, lime juice, & burned orange agave syrup. Add the ice & give it a good shake.
Over fine ice, strain it into rimmed glass. Serve with the orange slice as a garnish. Enjoy!

8.46 Smoked Salted Caramel White Russian
Total Time: 30 Mins, Servings: 4
Ingredients
16 Oz Half-And-Half
Salted Caramel Sauce
6 Oz Vodka
6 Oz Kahlúa
Instructions
Set the Pit Boss to 180°F & preheat for around 15 Mins with the lid covered when you're all set to cook. If the Super Smoke is available, use it for the best taste.
Fill a small baking dish halfway with half-and-half & put it immediately on your grill grate. Next, pour some water into a small baking dish & set it beside the half-and-half over the grill. For 20 Mins, smoke both half-and-half & water. Leave to cool after removing from your grill.
Refrigerate the half-and-half till ready to be using. Fill ice cube pans halfway with smoked water & place within freezer till frozen.
Into 4 glasses, divide the ice cubes (smoked). Pour the caramel sauce (salted) into the glass and swirl it around.
Fill every glass with vodka & Kahla, then top with some smoked half-and-half.

8.47 Grilled Frozen Strawberry Lemonade
Total Time: 20 Mins, Servings: 4
Ingredients
1 lb Fresh Strawberries

1/2 Cup Turbinado Sugar
8 Lemon, Halved
1/4 Cup Cointreau
1/4 Cup Simple Syrup
2 Cup Ice
1 Cup Tito's Vodka
Instructions
When you are all set to cook, preheat the grill on high for around 15 Mins with the lid closed.
Place your lemon halves immediately on your grill grate after dipping them into turbinado sugar. Place your strawberries beside the lemons after tossing them with leftover sugar.
Cook till grill marks appear on both lemons & strawberries, approximately 15 Mins for lemons & 10 Mins for strawberries. Remove from the heat & set aside to cool.
Using a strainer, extract the juice from grilled lemons, removing any seeds & pulp. Fill the blender pitcher halfway with water. Remove the stems from the grilled strawberries & combine them with the lemon juice into the blender pitcher. Add simple syrup, 2 ice, vodka, & Cointreau.
Transfer in 4-6 glasses after pureeing till smooth. If desired, garnish with some grilled strawberries & lemon slices. Enjoy!

8.48 Smoked Eggnog
Total Time: 1 hr 10 Mins, Servings: 4
Ingredients
2 Cup Whole Milk
1 Cup Heavy Cream
4 Egg Yolk
Cup Sugar
3 Oz Bourbon
1 Tsp Vanilla Extract
1 Tsp Nutmeg
4 Egg White
Whipped Cream
Instructions
Prepare ahead of time since this dish needs chilling time.
Preheat the Pit Boss at 180°F with the lid covered for 15 Mins. If the Super Smoke is available, use it for the best taste.
Fill the baking dish halfway with milk & cream, then smoke for around 60 Mins on your Pit Boss.
Meanwhile, beat your egg yolks in a bowl of the stand mixer till they brighten in color. Slowly add sugar & beat till sugar melts fully.
Add the smoked milk & cream to an egg mix, with some bourbon, vanilla, & nutmeg, then whisk to mix.
Within the bowl of the stand mixer, whisk your egg whites until soft peaks form.
While the mixer is still running, slowly drizzle in sugar & continue to beat till firm peaks form.
Gently incorporate your egg whites in the cream mix, then whisk everything together completely.
Allow for flavor melding by chilling the eggnog for another few hours. Finish with a sprinkling of nutmeg & a dollop of whipped cream over the top.

8.49 Zombie Cocktail Recipe
Total Time: 50 Mins, Servings: 2
Ingredients
Fresh Squeezed Orange Juice
Pineapple Juice
2 Oz Light Rum
2 Oz Dark Rum
2 Oz Lime Juice
1 Oz Pit Boss Smoked Simple Syrup
6 Oz Smoked Orange and Pineapple Juice
2 Grilled Orange Peel, For Garnish
2 Grilled Pineapple Chunks, For garnish
Instructions
Set the Pit Boss to 180°F & preheat for around 15 Mins with the lid covered when you're all set to cook.
Smoked Orange & Pineapple Juice: In a wide sheet pan, combine equal parts orange juice & pineapple juice, then smoke for around 45 Mins. Remove from the grill & set aside to cool. Measure out three oz juice & store the rest in the fridge for later use.
In a wide mixing glass, combine lighter and darker rums, smoked orange plus lime juice, pineapple juice, & Simple Syrup.
Add ice, mix, & pour into the Tiki glass over fresh ice.
Serve with grilled pineapple & orange peel as garnish.

8.50 The Old Orchard Cocktail
Total Time: 25 Mins, Servings: 2
Ingredients
2 Apple, Sliced
2 Tbsp Granulated Sugar
1 Tsp Cinnamon
3 Oz Rye Whiskey
1 1/2 Oz Pit Boss Smoked Simple Syrup
1 Oz Fresh Lemon Juice
4 Oz Angry Orchard Hard Cider

Instructions
When you are all set to cook, preheat the Pit Boss to 500°F with the lid covered for around 15 Mins.
Toss the apple slices with cinnamon & granulated sugar.
Cook for around 20-25 Mins with apple slices straight on your grill grate. Remove from the heat & set aside to cool.
Combine whiskey, Simple Syrup, & lemon juice in the shaker.
To combine flavors, add ice & shake for around 15 seconds.
Strain into a beer glass over fresh ice & top with Orchard Cider (Angry).
Serve with the baked apple-cinnamon piece as a garnish. Enjoy!

8.51 The Trifecta Cocktail
Total Time: 5 Mins, Servings: 2
Ingredients
16 Fresh Mint Leaves
1 Oz Pit Boss Smoked Simple Syrup
3 Oz Bourbon
Instructions
Mint leaves & Simple Syrup should be lightly muddled.
Fill the glass halfway with some crushed ice & add your bourbon.
Stir till the outside of the cup becomes frosted. To make the ice dome, top with additional crushed ice. If preferred, garnish with mint leaves & bitters.

8.52 Pit Boss Boulevardier Cocktail
Total Time: 1 hr 5 Mins, Servings: 2
Ingredients
4 Oranges
1/2 Cup Honey
1500 ML Rye Whiskey
1 1/2 Oz Campari
1 1/2 Oz Sweet Vermouth
2 Tbsp Granulated Sugar
3 Oz Grilled Orange Infused Rye
Instructions
When you are all set to cook, preheat the Pit Boss to 350°F with the lid covered for around 15 Mins.

2 oranges, split in half and honeyed on the cut side. Remove the peels from the leftover orange & set them on your grill. The cooking time is 20-25 Mins.
Remove off the grill and set aside to cool. Cook for 20-30 Mins, or till black grill marks emerge, by placing orange halves directly on your grill grate. Remove the orange halves & set them aside to cool.
Fill a rye whiskey bottle halfway with orange halves & soak for 10-12 hours. The orange taste will get sweeter & more intense as they soak longer.
In a medium mixing glass, combine all ingredients & whisk till diluted. Into a new coupe glass, strain & serve neat.
Serve with orange peel as a garnish.

8.53 Pit Boss Gin & Tonic
Total Time: 55 Mins, Servings: 2
Ingredients
1/2 Cup Berries
2 Orange, Sliced
4 Tbsp Granulated Sugar
3 Oz Gin
1 Cup Tonic Water
2 Sprig Fresh Mint, For garnish
Instructions
Set the Pit Boss to 180°F & preheat for around 15 Mins with the lid covered when you're all set to cook. If the Super Smoke is available, use it for the best taste.
To make your smoked berries, combine all the ingredients in a large mixing bowl. On the sheet pan, spread mixed berries & set immediately on your grill grate. Remove from your grill after 30 Mins of smoking.
Preheat your grill to 450°F and cook all orange slices for around 15 Mins with the lid covered.
Place these orange slices immediately on your grill grate after tossing them with some granulated sugar. Cook for around 5 Mins, flipping once, or till grill marks appear on these slices.
Fill a glass with gin, ice, & berries, now top with some tonic water. Garnish with the orange wheel & fresh mint leaf.

8.54 Pit Boss Paloma Cocktail
Total Time: 35 Mins, Servings: 2
Ingredients
4 Grapefruit, Halved
Pit Boss Smoked Simple Syrup
10 Stick Cinnamon
3 Oz Reposado Tequila
1 Oz Lime Juice
1 Oz Pit Boss Smoked Simple Syrup
Grilled Lime, For Garnish
Cinnamon Stick, For Garnish
Instructions
Set the Pit Boss to 350°F & preheat for around 15 Mins with the lid covered when you're all set to cook.
Cut Two grapefruits in half to make grapefruit juice. In every grapefruit half, place one cinnamon stick & drizzle with a Simple Syrup. Place on the grill grate & cook for around 20 Mins, or till the edges begin to brown & grill markings appear. Remove from the heat and set aside to cool.
Squeeze and filter the juice when the grapefruits fully cooled. The juice would give 10-12 oz.
Combine the lime juice, tequila, Simple Syrup, & grapefruit juice in a medium mixing glass.
Shake in the ice. In a glass, the strain on ice.
To serve, garnish with a lime slice & cinnamon stick.

8.55 Smoked Raspberry Bubbler Cocktail
Total Time: 50 Mins, Servings: 2
Ingredients
2 Cup Fresh Raspberries
Pit Boss Smoked Simple Syrup
8 Oz Sparkling Wine
Instructions
Set the Pit Boss to 180°F & preheat for around 15 Mins with the lid covered when you're all set to cook. If the Super Smoke is available, use it for the best taste.
Raspberry Smoked Syrup: 1 cup of fresh raspberries, smoked for around 30 Mins on the grill mat.
Set aside a few raspberries for garnish once they've been smoked. Fill a wide sheet pan halfway with Simple Syrup and set aside. Return that to your grill grate & smoke for around 45 Mins. Leave to cool after removing from the heat. Refrigerate till ready to utilize after straining.
In the base of the champagne flute, pour smoked raspberry syrup, then cover using white sparkling wine & champagne.
Serve with some smoked raspberries as a garnish. Enjoy!

8.56 Smoked Sangaree Cocktail
Total Time: 5 Mins, Servings: 2
Ingredients
4 Oz Paul Beau Vsop Cognac
2 Oz Quinta Do Noval Black Port
1/2 Oz Pit Boss Smoked Simple Syrup
6 Dash Angostura Bitters
Instructions
Combine all your ingredients in a mixing bowl and whisk in ice. Fill a cold coupe with the mixture.
Serve with the orange twist laced with a whole clove as a garnish. Enjoy!

8.57 Smoked Spring Tea Cocktail
Total Time: 20 Mins, Servings: 2
Ingredients
2 Lemon, Sliced
2 Tbsp Sugar
3 Oz Vodka
6 Oz Lapsang Souchong (Smoked Tea)
3 Oz Lemonade
2 Sprig Fresh Mint, For garnish
Fresh Edible Flowers, For Garnish
Instructions
Set the Pit Boss to 500°F & preheat for around 15 Mins with the lid covered when you're all set to cook.
To make the lemon garnish, combine the following ingredients in a small bowl. Sugar your lemon slices & place them straight on your grill grate. Caramelize lemons for 15-20 Mins, or till golden.
For the drink, combine the following ingredients: Combine all your ingredients in the shaker having ice & shake vigorously before straining over fresh ice.
Serve with the grilled lemon slices, mint sprigs, & edible flowers as garnish. This drink may also be made into the pitcher. Enjoy!

8.58 Smoky Scotch & Ginger Cocktail
Total Time: 1 hr 5 Mins, Servings: 2
Ingredients
1 Oz Ginger Syrup
1/2 Oz Brandied Cherry Juice
1/2 Oz Agave Nectar
4 Oz Scotch
1 1/2 Oz Lemon Juice

2 Slices Grilled Lemon, For Garnish
2 Cherry, For garnish
Instructions
Set the Pit Boss to 180°F & preheat for around 15 Mins with the lid covered when you're all set to cook. If the Super Smoke is available, use it for the best taste.
Put the cherry juice, ginger syrup, & agave nectar into a small dish & place it directly on your grill grate for making ginger smoked cherry syrup.
Smoke for around 60 Mins, or till the taste of the smoke has permeated the mixture. Leave 30 Mins to cool after removing from the grill.
Shake with some ice the scotch, ginger smoked cherry syrup, & lemon juice in the shaker tin. Strain into the glass with ice & a lemon wheel (grilled) & cherry for garnish. Enjoy!

8.59 Smoking Gun Cocktail
Total Time: 50 Mins, Servings: 2
Ingredients
2 Jar Cocktail Onions Vermouth Soaked
3 Oz Vodka
1 Oz Dry Vermouth
Instructions
Set the Pit Boss to 180°F & preheat for around 15 Mins with the lid covered when you're all set to cook.
Pour the jar of vermouth-soaked cocktail onions over a wide sheet pan to produce the onion vermouth (smoked). Do 45 Mins of smoking. Remove from the grill and put them aside to cool.
In a medium mixing glass, combine vodka, liquid from smoked onions, & dry vermouth. Shake well before straining into a cold martini glass.
On the skewer, skew cocktail onions (smoked) as a garnish. Enjoy!

8.60 Smoking Jacket Cocktail
Total Time: 5 Mins, Servings: 2
Ingredients
6 Oz Extra Brut Champagne
1/2 Oz Pit Boss Smoked Simple Syrup
6 Oz Guinness Extra Stout
Instructions
In the chilled glass, combine the Champagne & Simple Syrup. Pour the Guinness over the base of your bar spoon, carefully layering it over top of a Champagne. There is no garnish.

8.61 Pit Boss Smoked Daiquiri
Total Time: 40 Mins, Servings: 2
Ingredients
2 Limes, Sliced
2 Tbsp Granulated Sugar
3 Oz Rum
1 Oz Pit Boss Smoked Simple Syrup
1 1/2 Oz Lime Juice
Instructions
Preheat the Pit Boss to 350°F for around 15 Mins with the lid covered when you are all set to cook.
Place fresh lime slices immediately on your grill grate after tossing them with some granulated sugar. Cook for around 20-25 Mins, or till grill marks appear. Remove off the grill & set aside to cool.
Combine the rum, Simple Syrup, & lime juice in a medium mixing glass. Shake your mixing glass with ice in it. Fill a cold glass halfway with the contents.
Serve with a lime wheel as a garnish.

8.62 Pit Boss Grilled Tiki Cocktail
Total Time: 60 Mins, Servings: 2
Ingredients
4 Lemons
1 Cup Sugar
1 Pineapple, Fresh
Cup Palm Sugar
2 Peach
4 Oz Spiced Rum
2 Oz Brandy
2 Oz Peach Liquor
Instructions
To prepare a Lemon Syrup, combine all the ingredients in a large mixing bowl. 4 lemons, peeled and placed in a basin with sugar. Leave 30 Mins for the lemon oil from the peels to start to dissolve the sugar.
Set the temp to high & warm for around 15 Mins with the lid covered when you are all set to cook. If possible, raise the temperature to 500°F for best results.
Peeled lemons should be cut in half & placed on your grill. Cook for approximately 8 Mins, or until the lemons have developed a faint sear. Remove the lemons from the grill & set them aside to cool.
Remove the lemon juice when the lemons have cooled. Toss both lemon peel & sugar mixture with lemon juice. Stir until all the remaining sugar has dissolved. Remove the lemon peels & keep the lemon syrup refrigerated until ready to use.
To make grilled fruit, combine all the ingredients in a large mixing bowl. Remove the pineapple's outer peel & crown. Using a knife, cut the pineapple into horizontal slices. Sprinkle palm sugar over pineapple slices. Cook pineapple slices for around 8 Mins on each side directly on your grill grate. Remove from the oven and set aside to cool for almost 5-10 Mins.
Peaches should be cut in half & the pit removed. Lightly dust using palm sugar. Place peaches on your grill grate & cook till grill marks appear, approximately 5 Mins based on peach ripeness.
To prepare the drink, follow these steps: In a big pitcher, put 4 huge scoops of the ice. Combine the rum, brandy, lemon syrup, peach liquor, & grilled fruit in a wide mixing glass. To completely combine the ingredients, stir them together. Allow 15 mins for the mixture to dilute.
Garnish with more caramelized peaches, grilled pineapple chunks, lemon twist, & fresh mint in 4 glasses on ice.

8.63 Robert Palmer Cocktail
Total Time: 15 Mins, Servings: 2
Ingredients
2 Orange, Sliced
4 Oz Chilled Breakfast Tea
3 Oz Dewar's Aged 12 Years Scotch
1 1/2 Oz Lemon Juice
1 Oz Pit Boss Smoked Simple Syrup
Instructions
When you are all set to cook, preheat the Pit Boss to 500°F with the lid covered for around 15 Mins.
10 Mins on the grill, till lightly charred orange slices
In the tumbler full of ice, combine all your ingredients except for orange slices & mix thoroughly. Enjoy with the orange slice as a garnish!

8.64 Pit Boss Cocktail
Total Time: 25 Mins, Servings: 2
Ingredients
2 Lime, Sliced
4 Tbsp Granulated Sugar
3 Oz Blanco Tequila
1/2 Oz Lime Juice
1/2 Oz Lemon Juice
4 Oz Pit Boss Smoked Simple Syrup
Instructions
Set the Pit Boss to 500°F & preheat for around 15 Mins with the lid covered when you're all set to cook.
Place fresh lime slices immediately on your grill grate after tossing them with some granulated sugar. Cook for 15–20 Mins, or till grill marks appear.
Fill the mixing glass halfway with ice & add Blanco tequila, lemon juice grilled, lime juice, & Simple Syrup. To mix the flavors, give it a good shake.
Strain over fresh ice & serve with a lime wheel as a garnish.

8.65 Maipole Cocktail
Total Time: 5 Mins, Servings: 2
Ingredients
6 Oz Maibock Or IPA
6 Oz Club Soda
1 1/2 Oz Grapefruit Juice
1 Oz Pit Boss Smoked Simple Syrup
2 Slices Grapefruit, Halved
Jacobsen Salt Co. Cherrywood Smoked Salt
Instructions
Fill a frosty pilsner glass halfway with ice & add all the ingredients.
Half a grapefruit wheel coated with smoked cherrywood salt may be used as a garnish.

8.66 Strawberry Mule Cocktail
Total Time: 25 Mins, Servings: 2
Ingredients
8 Grilled Strawberries, Plus More for Serving
3 Oz Vodka
1 Oz Pit Boss Smoked Simple Syrup
1 Oz Lemon Juice
6 Oz Ginger Beer
Fresh Mint Leaves
Instructions
Set the Pit Boss to 400°F & preheat for around 15 Mins with the lid covered when you're all set to cook.
Cook for 15 Mins, or till grill marks emerge, by placing strawberries straight on your grill grate.
In the cocktail shaker, combine grilled strawberries, vodka, Simple Syrup, & lemon juice. Shake the bottle vigorously.
With some crushed ice, strain twice into a new glass.
Garnish with more grilled strawberries & fresh mint or a splash of ginger beer.

8.67 In Pit Boss Fashion Cocktail
Total Time: 25 Mins, Servings: 2
Ingredients
2 Whole Orange Peel
2 Whole Lemon Peel
3 Oz Bourbon
1 Oz Pit Boss Smoked Simple Syrup
6 Dash Bitters Lab Charred Cedar & Currant Bitters
Instructions
Preheat the Pit Boss at 350°F for around 15 Mins with lid covered when you are all set to cook.
Cook for 20-25 Mins, or till the orange and lemon peel are gently caramelized, directly on your grill grate.
In a medium mixing glass, combine the bourbon, Simple Syrup, & bitters, then stir on ice. Stir till the ingredients are properly diluted & the glass is cooled.
On fresh ice, strain into the new glass & garnish with a grilled orange and lemon peel.

8.68 Pit Boss 'Que Cocktail
Total Time: 25 Mins, Servings: 2
Ingredients
2 Oranges, 1 Cut in Half And 1 Sliced
1 Oz Pit Boss 'Que BBQ Sauce
1 Oz Water
2 Oz Lemon Juice
1/2 Oz Honey
4 Oz Whiskey or Bourbon
1 Hefeweizen Beer
Instructions
When you are all set to cook, preheat the Pit Boss to 500°F with the lid covered for around 15 Mins.
Place the orange halves & orange slices straight on your grill grate & cook till grill marks appear, 15-20 Mins for the halves & approximately 10 Mins for the slices. Slices should be saved for garnish.
Juice & set aside once the halves have cooled enough.
Set aside BBQ Sauce Pit Boss 'Que & water.
Fill 2-pint glasses halfway with ice and set aside. Fill each with lemon juice, honey, orange juice, bourbon, & sauce water BBQ combination, then stir well.
Some beer & orange slices complete each drink.

8.69 Home Team Cocktail
Total Time: 5 Mins, Servings: 2
Ingredients
4 Oz Buffalo Trace Bourbon
1 1/2 Oz Lemon Juice
1 Oz Pineapple Juice
1 1/2 Oz Pit Boss Smoked Simple Syrup
2 Whole Egg
2 Oz Root Beer
Instructions
Shake all the ingredients in the shaker glass, except for the root beer. Add ice & shake once more.
Fine filter into the frosty fizz glass with root beer.

8.70 Garden Gimlet Cocktail
Total Time: 50 Mins, Servings: 2
Ingredients
2 Cup Honey
4 Lemons, Zested
4 Sprig Rosemary, Plus More for Garnish
1/2 Cup Water
4 Slices Cucumber
1 1/2 Oz Lime Juice
3 Oz Vodka
Instructions
Set the Pit Boss to 180°F & preheat for around 15 Mins with the lid covered when you're all set to cook. If the Super Smoke is available, use it for the best taste.
In a small pan, thin one cup honey with water to produce smoked lemon & honey rosemary syrup. Add rosemary sprigs with lemon zest.
Smoke for 45-60 mins with the pan placed on the barbecue grate. Remove from the heat, strain, & set aside to cool.

Muddle your cucumbers with smoked lemon & honey rosemary syrup in the cocktail shaker.
Add the vodka, lime juice, & ice after muddling. Shake well and pour into the coup glass twice.
Garnish with some rosemary sprigs.

8.71 Honey Glazed Grapefruit Shandy Cocktail
Total Time: 25 Mins, Servings: 2
Ingredients
4 Grapefruits
4 Tbsp Honey
Granulated Sugar
2 Oz Bourbon
1 Oz Pit Boss Smoked Simple Syrup
4 Oz Honey Glazed Grilled Grapefruit, Juiced
2 Bottle Ballast Point Grapefruit Sculpin
Instructions
Set the Pit Boss to 375°F & preheat for around 15 Mins with the lid covered when you're all set to cook.
To make the honey-coated grapefruit, cut a grapefruit in half & coat this with honey.
Slice the remaining grapefruit on wheels. Coat the wheels into granulated sugar till they are completely covered.
Cook for around 20-30 Mins with grapefruit halves & wheels on your grill grate. Remove all wheels from your grill & put them aside.
Fill the measuring cup halfway with grapefruit halves. This should make roughly 2 oz of juice.
In the shaker, combine the bourbon, grapefruit juice, & Simple Syrup, next top with some ice. Shake vigorously for around 10-15 seconds.
Strain into the glass, fill with some ice, then top up with beer. Serve with the grapefruit wheel as a garnish.

8.72 Grilled Strawberry Bourbon Lemonade
Total Time: 25 Mins, Servings: 8
Ingredients
1 Pint Fresh Strawberries, Washed, Stemmed and Sliced
1 Cup Turbinado Sugar, Divided
16 Lemon, Halved
1 Cup Granulated Sugar, Plus More as Needed
1/2 Cup Honey
2 Sprig Mint, Plus More for Garnish
1 Cup Bourbon
Fresh Strawberry Slices, For Garnish
Lemon Slices, For Garnish
Instructions
Set the Pit Boss to 400°F & preheat for around 15 Mins with the lid covered when you're all set to cook.
Toss your sliced strawberries in turbinado sugar & arrange those in an equal layer in the foil-lined oven-safe pan. A few strawberries should be saved for garnishing.
Strawberries should be roasted for approximately 10 Mins, or till they soften & begin to exude juices. Remove from the oven and set aside to cool.
Meanwhile, immerse all lemon halves into the remaining turbinado sugar. In an oven-safe dish, combine any leftover turbinado sugar & granulated sugar, as well as honey, water, & mint sprigs.
Place your lemons on your Pit Boss & cook till they're tender and starting to brown, approximately 5-10 Mins. Place your sugar, honey, & mint in the grill pan & cook, stirring regularly, till the sugar has fully dissolved (approximately 5 Mins).
Remove the lemons & simple syrup from the grill & set them aside to cool. Squeeze the lemons into a pitcher via the sieve to capture all seeds & pulp. Blend & puree all cooled strawberries till smooth in the blender or with an immersion blender.
Fill your lemonade pitcher halfway with strawberries. Stir in bourbon, simple syrup, & more water until everything is well combined. Taste your lemonade and, if necessary, add additional sugar & water.
Pour in glasses after adding some ice. Serve with strawberry slices, lemon slices, & mint
leaves as garnish.

8.73 Smoked Pumpkin Spice Latte
Total Time: 55 Mins, Servings: 4
Ingredients
1 Small Sugar Pumpkin
Olive Oil
1 Can Sweetened Condensed Milk
1 Cup Whole Milk
2 Tbsp Pit Boss Smoked Simple Syrup
1 Tsp Pumpkin Pie Spice
Pinch Of Salt
Cinnamon
Whipped Cream
Shaved Nutmeg
8 Oz Smoked Cold Brew Coffee
Instructions
Preheat grill to 325°F with lid covered for around 15 Mins when you are all set to cook.
Cut the sweet pumpkin in half & scrape out all the seeds. Brush the cut side of these pumpkin halves with some olive oil & place them on the baking sheet.
Cook for 45 Mins, or till the flesh becomes soft, on a sheet tray straight on your grill grate. Remove from the heat & set aside to cool.
Scoop out the flesh of the pumpkin after it has cooled enough & mash till smooth.
Put 3 tbsps of a pumpkin puree into the separate dish and save the rest for the next time.
Toss all pumpkin puree with the condensed sweetened milk, pumpkin pie spices, whole milk, Simple Syrup, & salt. To mix the ingredients, whisk them together.
Pour your cold brew on ice, add your pumpkin creamer spice to taste, and garnish with some cinnamon, whipped cream, & shaved nutmeg, if preferred.

8.74 Cran-Apple Tequila Punch with Smoked Oranges
Total Time: 30 Mins, Servings: 2
Ingredients
6 Cup Apple Juice, Chilled
6 Cup Light Cranberry Cocktail
1 Cup Cranberries, Fresh or Thawed
3 Large Oranges, Halved
1 Cup Sugar, For Rimming Glasses
2 Tbsp Lemon Juice
2 Cup Reposado Tequila
1 Cup Orange-Flavored Liqueur, Such as Grand Marnier or Cointreau
2 Bottle Sparkling Wine (Such as Prosecco) Or Sparkling Water
Instructions
1 cup of apple & cranberry juices combined, then poured in ice cube tray. Place some cranberries in every cube if the molds are large enough. Freeze for a minimum of 6-24 hrs.
Set the Pit Boss to 180°F & preheat for around 15 Mins with the lid covered when you're all set to cook. If the Super Smoke is available, use it for the best taste.
Place orange halves on your grill & smoke for around 15 Mins. Remove the oranges from your grill & juice them. Keep the orange juice aside.

Place your sugar on the flat platter when prepared to serve. Fill a dish with lemon juice which will fit over each glass rim.
To make a sugar rim, carefully dip the glass rim within lemon juice, next within sugar. Before usage, turn your glass up & leave it to dry for some time.
In a wide mixing bowl, combine the leftover cranberry cocktail, apple juice, & orange juice, as well as the orange liqueur, tequila, & sparkling wine, well before serving. Taste and adjust the amount of every ingredient to your liking.
Place some ice cubes into each glass once you are about to serve, now pour punch on the top. Place all ice cubes within the punch bowl.

8.75 Dublin Delight Cocktail
Total Time: 25 Mins, Servings: 2
Ingredients
2 Orange, Sliced
3 Fluid Oz Teeling Whiskey
1 1/2 Fluid Oz Pit Boss Smoked Simple Syrup
6 Dash Aromatic Bitters
6 Fluid Oz Guinness Beer
2 Amarena Cherry, For garnish
Instructions
Set the Pit Boss to 450°F & preheat for around 15 Mins with the lid covered when you're all set to cook.
Cook for 20-25 Mins with orange slices straight on your grill grate. Remove off the grill & set aside to cool.
Whiskey, Simple Syrup, & bitters should all be combined in a medium mixing glass. Shake with ice. Pour into an ice-filled beer glass & top with some Guinness.
Serve with Amarna cherry & an orange slice on top.

8.76 Grilled Piña Colada
Total Time: 25 Mins, Servings: 4
Ingredients
1 Whole Pineapple, Peeled, Cored and Cut into Spears
15 Oz Coconut Milk
7 1/2 Oz Dark Rum
2 Oz Light Rum
5 Cup Ice
Instructions
In the blender pitcher, combine coconut
milk, grilled pineapple, & both rums. Blend in the ice till it is completely smooth.
Pour the contents of the blender into 4 glasses & top with the leftover grilled pineapple.

8.77 Bulldog Margarita
Total Time: 1 day 25 Mins, Servings: 6
Ingredients
Sea Salt
7 Limes
3 Oranges
2 Cup of Tequila
½ Cup of Grand Marnier
2 Cups of Smoked Simple Pit Boss Syrup
6 Bottles Corona Beer
Instructions
Set the Pit Boss to 165°F & preheat for around 15 Mins with the lid closed once ready for cooking.
Begin by adding sea salt that you want to smoke. Spread this out on the baking sheet & smoke this for 24 hrs on the Pit Boss, stirring after 8 hrs. Allow it cool before storing it in the jar of your liking.
Place Five limes & One orange on your counter & roll these back & forth using your palm while exerting pressure. Once you juice each citrus, it will yield extra liquid. The leftover lime & orange should be used later.
In a big measuring cup, juice both limes & orange, then add the Grand Marnier, tequila, & Simple Syrup. Combine all the ingredients.
In a small bowl, pour smoked salt. Swipe the outside of your glasses rim with juiced limes. Invert the glass into your smoked salt till the rim becomes completely coated. Repeat for every glass.
To decorate your glass rim afterward, cut a lime & an orange in slices. Set the Pit Boss to 450°F & preheat for around 15 Mins with the lid covered when you're all set to cook.
For around 5 Mins on all sides, grill your lime & orange slices.
In the blender, combine ice and margarita liquid to cover all ice.
Blend with additional margarita or ice mix till you reach the desired consistency.
Pour your frozen margarita in a glass with a rim of smoked salt, then open the Corona & drop it into the glass, drowning it in your margarita.
On the glass rim, a place previously cooked citrus segment. To every glass, repeat the instructions.

8.78 Smoked Lemonade with Pit Boss Simple Syrup
Total Time: 15 Mins, Servings: 6
Ingredients
16 Whole Lemons, Cut in Half
1/2 Cup Turbinado Sugar
3 Cup Pit Boss Smoked Simple Syrup
3 Cup Water
1 Cup Vodka
Lemon Slices, For Garnish
Instructions
Set the Pit Boss to 500°F & preheat for around 15 Mins
with the lid covered when you're all set to cook.
Cut side downward, dip lemons into turbinado sugar. Place the lemons on your grill grate & cook for 5-10 Mins, or till grill marks appear & the sugar caramelizes. Remove the steaks from the grill and put them aside for cooling.
Squeeze the juice from the lemon halves in a small bowl after they have cooled enough. Pour fresh lemon juice into a big pitcher via a sieve.
Add water, simple syrup, & vodka (if used). To blend, stir everything together. Taste & modify with additional sugar, lemon juice, & water till the lemonade is balanced.
Toss in some ice & serve. If desired, garnish with some lemon slices & mint.

8.79 Burnt Orange Julep Cocktail
Total Time: 1 hr 5 Mins, Servings: 2
Ingredients
2 Orange
Brown Sugar
1 1/2 Oz Agave
2 Bunch Mint
4 Oz Bourbon
4 Dash Angostura Orange Bitters
Instructions
When you are all set to cook, preheat the Pit Boss to 500°F with the lid covered for around 15 Mins.
Oranges candied: Cut oranges in wheels and covered completely in some brown sugar.
Cook for 15 Mins from all sides, straight on your grill grate, till grill marks appear. Remove the wheels from the grill & put them aside to cool. 2 wheels are set aside for garnish.
To produce the burned orange agave, follow these steps:

Reduce the temp of the grill to 200°F. Combine your candied oranges with agave syrup in a shallow pan & put immediately on your grill grate. Cook for 30-45 Mins, or until done to your liking.

To make the drink, fill a mixing pan halfway with burned orange agave & 5 to 6 mint leaves. Muddle the ingredients to unleash the mint oils.

Shake gently with bourbon, bitters, & crushed ice. Pour everything into a copper mug or glass and top it over with broken ice.

Serve with orange wheel & mint as garnish. Enjoy!

8.80 Cannonball Cocktail
Total Time: 40 Mins, Servings: 2
Ingredients
4 Limes
4 Oz Banks 7 Golden Age Rum
1 1/2 Oz Grilled Lime Juice
1 1/2 Oz Pit Boss Smoked Simple Syrup
Cayenne Powder, For Garnish
Instructions
When you are all set to cook, preheat the Pit Boss to 500°F with the lid covered for around 15 Mins.

To make the lime juice, combine all the ingredients in a blender and blend until smooth. Place two limes on your grill, cut in half.

To make the garnish, slice a lime into thick wheels & set it on your grill. Cook for around 15 Mins, or till one side of the limes has a good grill mark. Remove your lime wheels and set them aside.

Lime halves should be juiced.

Shake rapidly in the shaker glass along with ice to combine Banks Seven Age Rum Golden, lime juice, & Simple Syrup. Pour it into a frosty coupe glass with a stiff strain.

Serve with a lime wheel & cayenne pepper as a garnish. Enjoy!

8.81 Elite 8 Punch Cocktail
Total Time: 35 Mins, Servings: 2
Ingredients
4 Whole Oranges, Halved
Agave
3 Oz B&B French Brandy
1 Oz Bourbon
3 Oz Grilled Orange Juice
1 Oz Pit Boss Smoked Simple Syrup
1 Oz Lemon Juice
4 Dash Bitters
2 Bottle Redd's Apple Ale
Grilled Orange Peel, For Garnish
Grilled Lemon Peel, For Garnish
Instructions
Set the Pit Boss to 350°F & preheat for around 15 Mins with the lid covered when you're all set to cook.

Brush the halved oranges using agave & set face down straight on your grill grate for orange juice (grilled). Grill for around 20-30 Mins, or till browned on the edges. Allow cooling before extracting the juices.

Toss all thin peels of lemon & orange into granulated sugar & grill them. Place on the grill & cook until the oils have caramelized & the edges have roasted.

Combine all your ingredients in the shaker glass, except for the Apple Ale. Shake in the ice.

Pour on ice, top with some Apple Ale, then serve with grilled orange & lemon peel for garnish. Enjoy!

8.82 Fig Slider Cocktail
Total Time: 25 Mins, Servings: 2
Ingredients
2 Peach, Halved
4 Oranges
Honey
Sugar
2 Tsp Orange Fig Spread
1 Oz Fresh Lemon Juice
4 Oz Bourbon
3 Oz Honey Glazed Grilled Orange Juice
Instructions
When you are all set to cook, preheat the Pit Boss to 325°F with the lid covered for around 15 Mins.

Cut the peach in half & remove the pit. One of your oranges should be halved. Glaze the cut sides of the peaches and oranges with honey & cook them straight on your grate till honey caramelizes & the fruit gets grill marks.

Cut the other orange in wheels & cover both sides using granulated sugar. Cook 15 Mins from all sides, or till grill marks appear, straight on your grill grate.

Add lemon juice, grilled peaches, the spread of orange fig, bourbon, & honey-glazed orange juice to a mixer tin.

To combine the juices & fig spread, firmly shake the container. Using clean ice, strain the mixture. Serve with an orange wheel as a garnish.

8.83 Weizen Up Cocktail
Total Time: 5 Mins, Servings: 2
Ingredients
10 Oz Hefeweizen Beer
1 1/2 Oz Lemon Juice
1 Oz Pit Boss Smoked Simple Syrup
1/2 Oz Giffard Crème De Banane
2 Lemon Slice, For garnish
Instructions
In a frosty pilsner glass, combine all your ingredients, now add ice. Serve with a lemon slice as a garnish.

8.84 Brush Fire Cocktail
Total Time: 10 Mins, Servings: 2 people
Ingredients
2 Sprig Smoked Sage, For Garnish
4 Oz Maker's Mark Bourbon
2 Oz Grapefruit Juice
1 Oz Pit Boss Smoked Simple Syrup
Instructions
Preheat the grill to 400°F & seal the cover for around 15 Mins before cooking.

Place the sage sprig on your grill grate at the grill's hottest place. Cook for some time, or till that sage is gently browned & crisp on the edges. Remove the steaks from the grill & put them aside.

Fill a chill copper mug halfway with crushed ice and stir to combine.

Serve with smoked sage, which has been roasted on Pit Boss as a garnish.

8.85 Batter Up Cocktail
Total Time: 1 hr 10 Mins, Servings: 2
Ingredients
2 Whole Nutmeg
4 Oz Michter's Bourbon
3 Tsp Pumpkin Puree
1 Oz Pit Boss Smoked Simple Syrup
2 Large Egg

Instructions
Set the Pit Boss to 180°F & preheat for around 15 Mins with lid covered when you are all set to cook smoked nutmeg. If the Super Smoke is available, use it for the best taste.
Place the entire nutmeg on the sheet pan and cook it. Keep 1 hour of smoking. Remove off the grill & set aside to cool.
Combine all the ingredients in the shaker with no ice & mix vigorously. Shake well with ice, then pour into a frosty highball glass.
Serve with shredded smoked nutmeg as a garnish.

8.86 Grilled Peach Sour Cocktail
Total Time: 25 Mins, Servings: 2
Ingredients
2 Peach, Sliced
2 Tbsp Sugar
1 1/2 Oz Pit Boss Smoked Simple Syrup
4 Oz Bourbon
6 Dash Bitters Lab Apricot Vanilla Bitters
2 Sprig Fresh Thyme, For garnish
Instructions
When you are all set to cook, preheat the Pit Boss to 325°F for around 15 Mins with the lid closed.
Put peach slices immediately on the grill grate after tossing with some granulated sugar. Cook for around 20 Mins, or till grill marks appear on the surface. Remove off the grill & set aside to cool.
Muddle the peaches with Simple Syrup into a tin. During the muddling process, these peaches should produce around an oz of juice. After that, add the other ingredients & mix well.
Over new ice, pour the ingredients in glass & garnish using fresh thyme.

8.87 Blackberry Bourbon Smash
Total Time: 15 Mins, Servings: 8
Ingredients
8 Limes, Halved
1/3 Cup Sugar
12 Oz Blackberries
2 Sprig Thyme
1 Cup Smoked Pit Boss Simple Syrup
1 Quart Soda Water
2 Oz Bourbon
Instructions
When you are all set to cook, preheat the Pit Boss to 500°F with the lid covered for around 10-15 Mins.
Cut sides of limes should be dipped in some granulated sugar & placed on your grill grate. Cook for 10 Mins, or till grill marks appear.
Remove off the grill and set aside to cool. When the limes are cool enough, juice them & set them aside.
Combine fresh blackberries and sugar in a mixing bowl. Lightly smash the blackberries with the glass rim or fork to release juice.
Add thyme sprigs to the mix. Leave 30 Mins for blackberries to soak in this sugar. Take your thyme sprigs out.
Lime juice & Simple Syrup should be mixed. Mix in all blackberries that have been crushed. Pour in club soda & whisk well.
Taste and adjust with extra club soda, as necessary. This combination may be served as an alcoholic or non-alcoholic beverage.
Fill the Collins glass halfway with ice for making Blackberry Smash. Next, pour blackberry-limeade into the glass, followed by your preferred bourbon.
Stir to combine, then top with the thyme sprig.

8.88 Bloody Mary with Grilled Garnishes
Total Time: 25 Mins, Servings: 2
Ingredients
6 Large Shrimp
10 Stalk Asparagus
2 Tbsp Extra-Virgin Olive Oil
Salt And Pepper
3 Oz Mezcal
8 Oz Pit Boss Smoked Bloody Mary Mix
8 Oz Tomato Juice
4 Stalk Celery, For Garnish
10 Whole Stuffed Olives on A Skewer, For Garnish
2 Small Lime Wedge, For Garnish
2 Small Lemon Wedge, For garnish
Instructions
Set the Pit Boss to 450°F & preheat for around 15 Mins with the lid covered when you're all set to cook.
With salt, olive oil, & pepper, season your shrimp & asparagus. Cook your shrimp for around 4 Mins on each side & your asparagus for around 5 Mins overall on your grill grate.
Place fresh bacon pieces beside asparagus on your grill grate & heat till the fat has rendered & the bacon becomes crispy.
Cocktail Ingredients: Fill the pint glass using tomato juice, ice, mezcal, & Bloody Mary Mixture into a 1:1 ratio. Serve with some shrimp, asparagus, lemon wedge, celery, olives, bacon, & lime wedge on the side.

8.89 Grilled Rabbit Tail Cocktail
Total Time: 35 Mins, Servings: 2
Ingredients
1 1/2 oz Lemon Juice
4 Oz Apple Brandy
1 Oz Orange Juice
1 Oz Pit Boss Smoked Simple Syrup
Instructions
Preheat the Pit Boss to 350°F for around 15 Mins with its lid closed when you are all set to cook.
Cook for around 20-25 Mins, or till grill marks form, by placing lemon halves straight on your grill grate. Remove off the grill and set aside to cool. When the lemons are cold enough, juice them, then chill & save the juice.
Mix all your ingredients into a big thermos & top with a little ice, using proportions given above & considering the consumption rate & size of the tailgate crew.
Guests may pour themselves from thermos utilizing 6 to 8 oz glasses, garnishing every drink with the apple slice.

8.90 Smoked Roasted Apple Pie
Total Time: 1 hr 20 Mins, Servings: 6
Ingredients
8 Cup Apples, Peeled, Cored and Thinly Sliced
1 Tbsp Lemon Juice
3/4 Cup Sugar
1 Tsp Cinnamon
1/4 Tsp Nutmeg
2 Whole Frozen Pie Crust, Thawed
1/4 Cup Apple Jelly
2 Tbsp Heavy Whipping Cream
Instructions
In a wide mixing bowl, combine the flour, cinnamon, lemon juice, apples, sugar, & nutmeg.
Make two 11-inch rounds out of the dough (pie crust). Fill the 9" pie dish, ideally glass, with one circle. Add some apple jelly to the surface. Add this apple mix to the pan.
Pour apple juice to a crust's edge. Seal all edges of the top crust by pushing them together. If desired, slice the pastry &

trim the edges. Using a knife, make numerous tiny slices on the top of the crust. Using a pastry brush, lightly coat the surface of the pie with cream.

Preheat the grill too high for around 15 Mins once you're all set to cook. Bake for around 50–60 Mins, or till the apples become soft & the crust becomes golden brown. Allow cooling on the wire rack.

8.91 Beer & Smoke Cocktail

Total Time: 35 Mins, Servings: 2
Ingredients
2 Tsp HP Original Sauce
1/8 Oz Valentina Hot Sauce
1 Tsp Maggie Seasoning Sauce
24 Oz Mexican Lager
3 oz Lime Juice
Instructions
When you're all set to cook, fire up your Pit Boss grill. Till the fire has built, smoke with its lid open.
In a small oven-safe dish, combine 12 pieces of spicy sauce, Original Sauce HP, & Maggi Seasoning. Smoke for around 30 Mins by placing the dish straight on your grill grate.
Remove off the grill & set aside to cool. In a frozen sal-de-gusano & salt rim pint glass full of ice, mix all your ingredients.

8.92 Smoke and Bubz Cocktail

Total Time: 50 Mins, Servings: 2
Ingredients
16 Oz POM Juice
2 cup Pomegranate Seeds
6 Oz Sparkling White Wine
2 Lemon Twist, For Garnish
2 Tsp Pomegranate Seeds
Instructions
Set the Pit Boss to 180°F & preheat for around 15 Mins with the lid covered when you're all set to cook. If the Super Smoke is available, use it for the best taste.
To make the Pomegranate Juice, combine all the ingredients in a blender and blend until smooth. In a small sheet pan, combine POM juice & pomegranate seeds. Smoke for around 45 Mins on your Pit Boss. Remove the grill from the heat, pour off the seeds, & set aside to cool.
In the base of the champagne flute, pour some pomegranate juice.
To serve, garnish with white wine, pomegranate seeds, & lemon twist.

8.93 Grilled Watermelon Punch

Total Time: 25 Mins, Servings: 4
Ingredients
2 Small Seedless Watermelon
3/8 Cup Olive Oil
Salt And Pepper
1/4 Cup Pit Boss Smoked Simple Syrup
4 whole Lime, Juiced
Soda Water
Lime Wedge, For Garnish
Instructions
When you're all set to cook, fire up your Pit Boss as per the manufacturer's directions. Preheat your grill to 450°F & bake for 10-15 Mins with the lid closed.
Drizzle some olive oil over watermelon slices & season with some salt. Cook for 10 Mins, or till grill marks appear, straight on your grill grate.
Remove off the grill & chill within the refrigerator. Except for two slices of watermelon which should be saved for garnish; every watermelon must be skinned.
In a blender, combine the lime juice, trimmed watermelon, & Simple Syrup. Puree till completely smooth.
Fill a pitcher halfway with watermelon juice & ice. Fill halfway with some soda water & mix well.
Garnish with the lime slice & watermelon slice in the Collins glass.

8.94 Grilled Melancholy Fix Cocktail

Total Time: 15 Mins, Servings: 2
Ingredients
2 Whole Cantaloupe
1 cup Turbinado Sugar
1/2 Oz Pit Boss Smoked Simple Syrup
1/2 oz Lime Juice
2 Oz Cantaloupe Juice
Jacobsen Salt Co. Cherrywood Smoked Salt
3 Oz Reposado Tequila
Instructions
When you are all set to cook, preheat the Pit Boss to 500°F with the lid covered for around 15 Mins.
Cantaloupe should be halved & the seeds should be scooped out. Then, one cantaloupe halves should be cut into wedges. Remove all rind from its other half & cut into cubes. Puree the cantaloupe in the blender & filter via a mesh sieve. Set aside the liquid.
Place melon slices on a hot grill after coating them with turbinado sugar. Put 3 Mins on each side on the grill, or till grill marks appear. Remove the wedges from the grill, quarter them into triangles, & put them aside.
Combine Simple Syrup, smoked salt, lime juice, cantaloupe juice, & tequila in the cocktail shaker. Put 10 seconds in the shaker, then pour into a dual rocks glass.
Fill glass with crushed ice till it is overflowing.
Serve with a piece of cantaloupe as a garnish. Enjoy!

8.95 Pig in a Hammock

Total Time: 50 Mins, Servings: 4
Ingredients
3 Strips Bacon
3 Whole Bananas
12 Oz Pure Maple Syrup
8 Oz Water
1 Pinch Salt
6 Oz Bourbon
8 oz Fresh Lemon Juice
8 Dash Angostura Bitters
Instructions
When you're all set to cook, preheat the Pit Boss to 350°F with the lid covered for around 15 Mins.
Put bacon on the sheet pan into the center of your grill & cook for around 20 Mins, or till desired crispness has been achieved. Remove from the oven and set aside to cool.
Preheat the Pit Boss to 500°F & cook for around 15 Mins with the cover closed.
Cook around 5 Mins on each side till grill marks emerge after peeling bananas & placing them straight on your grill grate. Remove off the Pit Boss & put it aside.
In a medium saucepan, bring maple syrup, water, & salt to a simmer. Add a couple of the scorched bananas to that saucepan into half-moons. Cook for around 15 Mins before straining into a heat-resistant container. Make sure to scrape out all syrup off these bananas. Remove the bananas and place the syrup in the fridge to cool.
In the cocktail shaker, combine bourbon, lemon juice, burnt maple/banana syrup, & Angostura Bitters. Shake for around 10 seconds after adding ice. Repeat with the rest of the 3 drinks,

straining in the coupe glass.
Serve with crispy bacon as a garnish. The 3rd banana should be sliced into slices & placed on top of every drink.

8.96 Smoked Texas Ranch Water
Total Time: 1 hr 5 Mins, Servings: 4
Ingredients
3 Whole Limes
1 Tbsp Pit Boss Blackened Saskatchewan Rub
12 Oz Blanco Tequila
24 Oz Topo Chico or Other Sparkling Mineral Water
8 Slices Jalapeño (Optional)
Instructions
Set the Pit Boss to 225°F & preheat for around 15 Mins with the lid closed when you're all set to cook.
Slice 2 limes in halves and coat with some Blackened Saskatchewan Sauce. Place the 4 lime halves over your grill grate's edge and let them smoke for 1 hour. Remove the steaks from the grill and put them aside for cooling.
Pour the rub over a dish. Cut the 3rd lime into wedges & rub the rims of four cocktail glasses with the lime, then flip the glasses inverted & into this rub for salting the rims.
Pour tequila, Topo Chico, juice of a lime, & lime wedge into every glass over many ice cubes. Add slices of jalapeno to every glass if utilizing.
Combine all ingredients in a mixing bowl and serve.

8.97 Smoked Blood Orange & Rosemary Spritz
Total Time: 1 hr 10 Mins, Servings: 2
Ingredients
1 cup Granulated Sugar
1 Cup Water
4 Sprig Rosemary
4 Large Blood Oranges, 1 Sliced in Rounds And 1 Halved
2 Oz Blood Orange Juice
2 Oz Rosemary Simple Syrup
3 oz Aperol
2 Slices Grilled Blood Orange, For Garnish
2 Sprig Rosemary, For garnish
Instructions
When you are all set to cook, preheat the Pit Boss to 185°F with the lid covered for around 15 Mins. If the Super Smoke is available, use it for the best taste.
Dissolve both water and sugar in the saucepan; now add fresh rosemary & grill.
On the barbecue grates, place your blood orange pieces & halves. Smoke for around 1 hour, or till they've begun to sear & simple syrup has taken on a lovely smokey hue. Remove the pan from the grill & set it aside to cool fully.
Set aside some cooled orange segments for decoration. Orange halves should be juiced, then strained, and the sediments discarded.
To make the drink, fill the cocktail shaker halfway with ice. Combine the blood oranges juice, simple syrup, rosemary, & Aperol in a mixing bowl. Shake & pour in your favorite wine glass, now top fresh prosecco. Serve with an orange slice & rosemary sprig for garnish.

8.98 Red, White, and Blue Summer Breeze Drink

Total Time: 35 Mins, Servings: 3
Ingredients
1 cup of water
1 cup of sugar
1 cup of fresh strawberries
¼ cup of Harvest Rum Wilderness Trail
¼ cup of Blue Curacao
Fresh Juice, 1 lime
Instructions
Bring some water to your boil with some sugar. Refrigerate and save for later. Lime & strawberry should be halved. Grill on low heat. Combine the strawberries & rum in a muddle, then add simple syrup. Combine the lime juice, blue curacao, & simple syrup in a mixing glass. Fill glass halfway with shaved ice, then pour the cooled mix on both sides at once.

8.99 Smoked Lemon Sweet Tea
Total Time: 25 mins, Servings: 6 - 8
Ingredients
8 bags black tea
5 cups of boiling water
2 cups of ice
9 lemons
3 cups of sugar
3 cups of water
Instructions
In a temp-safe pitcher, put your tea bags. 4 cups of water, brought to your boil, poured on teabags. Allow 5-10 mins for steeping. Remove the tea bags from the pitcher & put them aside for cooling.
Set the Pit Boss on smoke mode & turn this on. Inside a small metal pan, combine sugar & water. Cook, stirring periodically, for approximately 45 Mins, or till the mix has reduced to a sticky, simple syrup. Allow cooling after removing from

your grill.
Preheat the Pit Boss at 450 degrees Fahrenheit and turn on a flame broiler. Set the fire to high on a gas grill.
Cut your lemons in halves and roast them over flame broiler for approximately 7 Mins, or till browned. Remove the steaks from the grill and put them aside for cooling.
In a large mixing bowl, squeeze the lemons. For removing seeds & pulp from lemon juice, pour it via a metal strainer in a tea pitcher.
Pour the chilled simple syrup in the pitcher & swirl till the tea & lemons are well combined. Refrigerate till ready to serve with 2 glasses of ice.

8.100 Smoked Ice Recipe & Cocktail
Total Time: 2 hr 15 Mins, Servings: 1
Ingredients
2 & ¼ water
½ tsp sugar
4 dash Cherry Bitter
2 oz Bourbon
smoked ice cube large
smoked cherries
1 orange
Instructions
Combine the sugar, bitters, & bourbon in big rocks glass & stir well.
Toss in an ice cube smoked.
Serve with an orange slice & smoked cherry as garnish.

Chapter 9: Baked Goods Recipes

9.1 Sausage and Pesto Lasagna

Total Time: 1 Hr 40 mins, Serving: 8
Ingredients
Italian Sausage, 1 1/2 Pound
Olive Oil, 2 Tbsp
Pinch of Kosher Salt
Mozzarella Cheese Shredded, 4 Cup
Basil Tomato Sauce for Pasta, 2 Jars
Whole Milk, 15 Ounce
Fresh Black Pepper
Whisked Egg, 1 Large
Pesto Prepared, 1/2 Cup
Parmesan Cheese Grated, 3/4 Cup
Lasagna Noodles, 1 Pack
Instructions
Set the Pit Boss to 400°F, then preheat for 15 minutes with the lid covered when you're ready to cook.
Warm the olive oil in a large pan over medium heat. Add the sausage to the pan and distribute it over the bottom, letting this brown before flipping it. Cook, constantly stirring, until the chicken is fully cooked, approximately 4 - 5 minutes. Remove a few tablespoons of tomato sauce to cover the bottom of the lasagna pan. Combine the sausage and tomato sauce in a saucepan and cook for 15 minutes, or until the flavors have melded. If required, season with salt.
Making the cheese filling while the sauce is simmering. Combine 3 cups mozzarella, ricotta, and 1/2 cup grated Parmesan cheese in some kind of a medium mixing basin. To mix, stir everything together. If necessary, season with a sprinkle of salt & freshly ground pepper. Incorporate the egg into the mixture by stirring it in.
In a small mixing bowl, combine the leftover cup of mozzarella as well as the other 1/4 cup of Parmesan. Remove from the equation.
Spread the saved tablespoons of sauce over the base of a 9x13 or 8x12 inch cake pan to start assembling the lasagna. Place four lasagna noodles crosswise on a baking sheet, enabling them to overlap slightly if required. (If the noodles you're using don't span the whole length of the pan, start by layering three noodles lengthwise.)
Spoon half of the ricotta cheese mixture over the noodles in spoonsful. To produce a reasonably uniform coating, distribute it out uniformly with a spoon or even your hands if necessary. 1/3 of meat sauce should be poured over cheese and distributed evenly with a spatula.
Repeat with a third of the meat sauce, the leftover ricotta mixture, the pesto, and another layer of noodles. Add the last layer of noodles, followed by the remaining sauce, making sure the noodles are well coated.
Top lasagna with the remaining mozzarella & Parmesan cheeses.
Wrap a piece of aluminium foil around the pan and secure it.
Put this on a baking tray and cook for 45 minutes on the Pit Boss. Lift one corner of the foil and cut into the lasagna with a knife. If the noodles are readily punctured, remove the cover and bake for another 10 minutes, or until bubbling. Whether not, covering it again and simmer for 5–10 minutes more before testing to see if it's done.
Allow 10 minutes for lasagna to cool before slicing. Serve right away. Enjoy!

9.2 Baked Apple Bourbon Crisp

Total Time: 1 Hr 15 mins, Serving: 6
Ingredients
Main
For Serving, Ice cream
Butter
Topping
Flour, 1/2 Cup
Brown Sugar, 1 Cup
Walnuts, 1/4 Cup
Oats, 1/2 Cup
Salted Butter, 8 Tbsp
Cinnamon, 1 1/2 Tsp

Filling
Thinly sliced Granny Smith, 3 Pound
Dried Cranberries, 1/2 Cup
Brown Sugar, 1/2 Cup
Honey, 1/4 Cup
Bourbon, 2 1/2 Tbsp
Lemon Juice, 1 Tbsp
Ground Cinnamon, 1 1/2 Tsp
Vanilla, 1 Tsp
Pinch of Salt
Instructions
Butter the interior of a 12" cast iron pan that has been well-seasoned and put aside.
To make the topping, mix the flour, walnuts, oats, cinnamon, brown sugar, and butter in the bowl of a food processor. Pulse the mixture until it's crumbly but still clumpy, and then put it aside.
To make the filling, mix the brown sugar, cranberries, honey, whiskey, apples, lemon juice, vanilla, cinnamon, and salt in a large mixing bowl. To mix, carefully stir everything together.
Fill the greased pan halfway with the fruit mixture. Pour the topping over the fruit in an equal layer.
Once ready to cook, preheat the Pit Boss to 350°F with the lid covered for 15 minutes.
Bake for approximately 60 minutes, just until the fruit gets hot and bubbling and the coating is golden brown.
Set aside for cooling for at least 30 mins. Sprinkle with ice cream on the side. Enjoy!

9.3 Pit Boss Fries with Chipotle Ketchup

Total Time: 25 mins, Serving: 4
Ingredients
Chipotle Ketchup
Olive Oil, 1 Tbsp
Onion Powder, 1 Tsp
In Adobo Sauce Chipotle Peppers, 2 Can
Garlic Powder, 1 Tsp
Chili Powder, 1 Tbsp
Lime juice
Tomato Ketchup, 1 Cup
Sugar, 1 Tbsp

Cumin, 1 Tbsp
Main
Gold Potatoes, 6 Whole Yukon
Finely Chopped Parsley, 1/4 Cup
Melted Butter, 2 Tbsp
Beef, 1 Tbsp
Instructions
Cut the chipotle peppers, and then put them in a mixing bowl with the other chipotle ketchup ingredients.
Chill the mixture for at least 1 hour to let the flavors meld (making it one day ahead of time is even better if you can swing it).
Once ready to cook, preheat the Pit Boss to 450°F for 15 minutes with the lid closed.
In a mixing bowl, combine the potatoes, melted butter, and Pit Boss Beef Rub, stirring to coat.
Arrange the fries on even a baking sheet & bake for 10 mins, or until they are crispy to your liking. Take the fries from the grill and toss the parsley in a mixing bowl.
Serve by the handful, with lots of chipotle ketchup on the side.

9.4 Baked Honey Cornbread Cake
Total Time: 50 mins, Serving: 6
Ingredients
Buttermilk, 2 1/2 Cup
Vegetable Oil, 2/3 Cup
Large Egg, 4
Mayonnaise, 1/2 Cup
Honey, 2 Tbsp
Melted Butter, 5 Tbsp
Sugar, 1 1/2 Cup
Baking Powder, 2 Tbsp
Cornmeal, 1
Salt, 1 Tsp
Flour, 3 Cup
Instructions
When you're ready to cook, fire up the Pit Boss according to the package directions. Preheat the oven to 350 degrees F with the lid covered (10-15 minutes).
Mix the buttermilk, vegetable oil, melted butter, eggs, mayonnaise, & honey in a medium mixing bowl.
Remove from the equation.
In a large basin, mixing combines sugar, flour, baking powder, cornmeal, and salt.
Gently fold the wet and dry ingredients together to blend, being careful not to over mix. Using cooking spray, cover a baking dish of 9x13-inch.
Pour the mixture into a baking dish, then bake for 35 mins, or until cornbread begins to color and crack on top.
Remove the meat from Pit Boss and cool before slicing. With butter and honey, serve cornmeal cake. Enjoy.

9.5 Baked Salmon Cakes
Total Time: 50 mins, Serving: 4
Ingredients
Salt & Pepper
Salmon Fillets, 2
Small Onion, 1/2
Bell Pepper, 1 Medium
Dried Dill, 1 Tbsp
Olive Oil, 3 Tbsp
Stalk Celery, 1
Lemon Zest, 1 Tsp
Sea Salt, 1/4 Tsp
Italian Breadcrumbs, 1 1/2 Tbsp
Black Pepper, 1/2 Tsp
Large Eggs, 2

Instructions
Preheat the Pit Boss to 275°F and shut the cover for 15 minutes before cooking.
Salt and pepper the salmon fillets and put them immediately on a grill grate. Cook till the temperature reached 120 degrees Fahrenheit. Remove the steaks from the grill and put them aside to cool.
In a large mixing basin, break up the chilled salmon fillets using a fork. Combine the onions, celery, lemon zest, dill, salt, pepper, bread crumbs, bell pepper, and eggs in a mixing bowl. Mix thoroughly.
Form the salmon batter into 6 patties, each about 2 inches in diameter.
Preheat the Pit Boss to 375°F and cook for 15 minutes with the lid covered.
Preheat the grill grate by placing a frying pan on it.
Pour olive oil into the cast iron pan that has been warmed. When the oil is heated, add the patties in batches to cast iron pan. Fry for 13 mins, or until golden brown on both sides, turning halfway through. Enjoy!

9.6 Baked Mac & Cheese with Jerky Dust
Total Time: 35 mins, Serving: 6
Ingredients
Yellow Onion, 1 Medium
Butter, 4 Tbsp
Garlic, 2 Clove
1 1/2 Cup Whole Milk
Flour, 5 Tbsp
Heavy Cream, 2 1/2 Cup
Thyme, 3 Sprig
Bay Leaves, 2 Whole
Black Peppercorn, 1 Tbsp
Rosemary, 1 Sprig
Shredded Cheese, 1 Pound
Elbow Noodles, 1 Pound
Panko Breadcrumbs, 1 Cup
Salt to taste
Smoked Paprika, 1/2 Tbsp
Beef Jerky, 4 Ounce
Parmesan Cheese, 1/4 Cup
Melted Butter, 4 Tbsp
Instructions
Preheat the Pit Boss to 350°F for 15 minutes with the lid closed when ready to cook.
Melt the butter in a wide pot over medium-high heat. Sauté for 5 mins or until the onion is transparent and soft. Sauté for another 30 seconds after adding the garlic. With a wooden spoon, mix in the flour well. Cook the roux for 1 min or until it smells nutty. Stream in the milk and cream while whisking. Continue whisking until all of the flour clumps are gone.
Tie cheesecloth over herbs and black peppercorns with thread. Drop into the cream mixture and cook for 20 mins or until the liquid has thickened. Remove the cheesecloth with the herbs and throw it away.
Remove from the fire and whisk in the Gruyere until completely melted. Season with salt. Remove from the heat and set aside until the noodles are done.
Bring a big saucepan of salted water on the stove. Boil for 4–6 minutes, or until the noodles are al dente. Rinse and drain the pasta.
Stir into the cheese sauce to combine.
Mix Parmesan cheese, panko, melted butter, and paprika in a small bowl. Transfer the mixture to a big cast-iron skillet. Stir everything together well. Top all shredded jerky "dust" and spread the mixture over mac and cheese.
Bake 20 minutes, till cheese sauce starts bubbling & the top is gently browned in a cast-iron skillet straight on the grill grate.

Take the burgers off the grill, then serve. Enjoy!

9.7 Strawberry Rhubarb Cobbler

Total Time: 50 mins, Serving: 6
Ingredients
Filling
Cooking Tapioca, 2 Tbsp
Salt to taste
Sugar, 1/2 Cup
Orange Liqueur, 1 Tbsp
Strawberries, 2 1/2 Cup
Freshly Rhubarb, 4 Cup
Cobbler Dough
Heavy Cream, 1/4 Cup
Beaten Egg, 1 Large
Almond Extract, 1/4 Tsp
Vanilla Extract, 1/2 Tsp
Sugar, 2 Tbsp
Flour, 1 Cup
Baking Powder, 1 1/2 Tsp
Salt, 1/4 Tsp
Butter, 4 Tbsp
Cinnamon, 1/2 Tsp
Instructions

Oil a 2-quart casserole dish, as well as 6 ramekins or individual gratin plates, generously. Remove from the equation.

To make the filling, mix the sugar, tapioca, as well as salt in a large mixing basin. To mix, stir everything together. Mix in the rhubarb, strawberries, and orange liqueur, if using, using a rubber spatula. Remove from the equation.

To make the topping for the cobbler, whisk together the egg, cream, vanilla, and almond extracts in a mixing bowl. Mix the flour, baking powder, sugar, cinnamon, and salt in a mixing dish. To blend, stir everything together. Add the butter and work it into flour mixture with a pastry blender until coarse crumbs appear. Toss the flour with a fork and whisk in the milk & egg mixture until barely incorporated. Remove from the equation.

Pour the fruit as well as its juices into a serving bowl or ramekins that have been prepared. Dollop batter on top in an equal layer. Sprinkle with more sugar if desired.

Once ready to cook, preheat the Pit Boss to 350°F for 15 minutes with the lid closed.

Place the baking dish and ramekins straight just on grill grate & bake for 30 to 35 minutes, or until the mixture is bubbling as well as the topping turns golden brown. Allow to cool for a few minutes before serving. Enjoy!

9.8 Pit Boss English Muffins

Total Time: 25 mins, Serving: 2
Ingredients
Warm Milk, 3 1/2 Cup
Honey Or Sugar, 4 Tbsp
Instant Yeast, 2 Packet
Large Egg, 2
Softened Butter, 6 Tbsp
Bread Flour, 9 Cup
Semolina Flour, 6 Tbsp
Kosher Salt, 3 Tsp
Instructions

In the bowl of an electric mixer fitted with the paddle attachment, combine the yeast, milk, sugar, bread flour, butter, egg, and kosher salt, and beat on low for 1 to 2 minutes. Increase the speed to medium and mix for 2 min, just until the material is glossy & pulls away from the bowl's sides. Allow the sticky dough to rise for 90 minutes in a lightly oiled basin, covered with a kitchen towel.

Once ready to cook, preheat the Pit Boss to 325°F for 15 minutes with the lid closed.

Place the dough on a lightly oiled board and divide it into 15 balls. Set aside for 5 mins before shaping. Sprinkle semolina flour on a sheet pan lined with parchment paper.

Gently form the dough into 3-to-4-inch round discs and put on the ready sheet pan, covering with just a kitchen towel till ready to bake.

Place 4–6 muffins directly on the prepared grill pan and cook for 8 to 9 minutes with the lid closed.

Turn the English muffins out with a spatula and gently push down if the centers have risen more than the edges. Cook for another 8–10 minutes, or until golden brown on the surface and cooked through in the middle (at least 200°F).

Allow cooling somewhat before separating with a fork. Enjoy!
Notes: Place the fork prongs just on the side of the muffin closest to the center and remove. Continue to work your way around the muffin, then split it with your hands. If you cut them with a knife, you'll lose all of the lovely pockets within. These will keep in the freezer for a long time. If frozen, keep them whole and thaw before separating with a fork & toasting.

9.9 Yellow Layer Cake with Smoked Candied Bacon

Total Time: 1 hr 45 mins, Serving: 6
Ingredients
Cake
Vanilla Pudding, 1 Whole Box
Yellow Cake, 1 Whole Box
Chocolate Pudding, 1 Whole Box
Milk, 1 Cup
Large Eggs, 4
Melted Butter, 12 Tbsp
Candied Bacon
Cold Bacon, 1 Pound
Brown Sugar, 3 Tbsp
Maple Syrup, 2 Tbsp
Frosting
Powdered Sugar, 4 Cup
Butter, 2 Cup
Cocoa Powder, 1 Cup
Milk, 3 Tbsp
Vanilla Extract, 1 Tbsp
Instructions

Preheat the Pit Boss to 350°F for 15 minutes with the lid closed when ready to cook.

To create the yellow cake, whisk together the remaining ingredients inside a stand mixer, next add the eggs, milk, and butter in a slow, steady stream. Blend until completely smooth. Coat three 6.5-inch round pans using non-stick cooking spray, then divide the batter evenly between them. Simmer for approximately 30 minutes until it's golden and well cooked. Allow cooling fully.

Preheat the Pit Boss to 375°F and prepare the candied bacon while the cakes cool. In a large mixing bowl, combine the bacon, syrup, and sugar and whisk until the bacon is evenly covered. Place the bacon strips immediately on the grill, cook for 25 minutes, or until fully cooked. Allow it to cool fully on such a cooling rack prior to cutting into tiny pieces, with the exception of a few larger pieces for garnish.

To make the topping, together cream the butter & sugar until fluffy & light. Then mix in the chocolate and vanilla for another 3 minutes. 1 spoonful at a time, stir in the milk until the desired consistency is achieved.

Frost the top layer of the cake and top with candied bacon. Add additional icing and bacon to the second layer. End with last layer as well as a thin coating of frosting to cover the whole cake. After 30 minutes in the refrigerator, apply a second coat

of icing.
Place complete pieces of candied bacon half an inch the edge of the cake as a garnish. Enjoy!

9.10 Salt Crusted Baked Potatoes
Total Time: 1 Hr 15 mins, Serving: 4
Ingredients
Canola Oil, 3 Tbsp
Potatoes, 6 Russet
Butter
Kosher Salt, 1 Tbsp
Cheddar Cheese
Sour Cream
Bits of Bacon
Fresh Chives
Instructions
Toss the potatoes in oil and season well with salt in a large mixing basin.
Once ready to cook, preheat the Pit Boss to 450°F with the lid covered for 15 min.
Bake the potatoes straight upon this grill grate for 30-40 mins, or until tender when poked with a fork in the middle. Serve with a heaping helping of your favorite toppings. Enjoy.

9.11 Ultimate Pit Boss Cookie
Total Time: 40 mins, Serving: 8
Ingredients
Brown Sugar, 1 Cup
Broken Pretzels, 1 Cup
Unsalted Butter, 1 Cup
Granulated Sugar, 3/4 Cup
Paste of Vanilla Bean, 1 Tsp
Flour, 3 Cup
Baking Soda, 1 Tsp
Eggs, 2
Spice of Apple Pie, 1/2 Tsp
Toffee Bits, 1/2 Cup
Caramel Bits, 1 Bag or (11 Oz)
Chocolate Chips, 1 Cup
Smoked Salt of Cherrywood, 1 Tsp
Milky Chocolate Chips, 1 Cup
Instructions
Preheat Pit Boss to 275°F and cook for 15 minutes with lid closed until ready to cook.
Place pretzel pieces straight on a grill grate using a sheet tray. 25 minutes of smoking Remove the pretzels from the grill and set them aside to cool.
Preheat the Pit Boss to 375°F and cook for 15 minutes with the lid covered.
In the bowl of a stand mixer equipped with a paddle attachment, place the sugar. Mix in the butter for approximately 5 minutes on medium speed in a mixing bowl. Halfway through, scrape down the edges of the basin. The solution should be light and frothy in color.
With the motor running, add the vanilla paste then eggs one at a time, ensuring that each is well mixed before adding the next for 5 to 7 minutes. Scrape the bowl's sides halfway through.
Mix all the flour, baking soda, and apple pie spice in a separate medium basin. Add the Jacobson smoked salt to the mix.
With the motor running at low speed, gently add all of the dry components to an egg mixture in stages, careful not to overwork. Next, mix in the remaining ingredients until they are barely mixed in the mixer.
Take the dough from the mixing bowl and divide it using a spatula to ensure uniform size. Mold dough into balls then places it 3 inches apart on a parchment-lined baking sheet.
Bake for 10 to 12 minutes, turning pan halfway through the cooking time, firmly on the grill grate.
The edges of the cookies should be golden brown, with just a soft, gooey middle. Place cookies on a wire rack to cool for 10 minutes.
Serve warm or keep for up to five days in an airtight jar. Enjoy!

9.12 Baked Caramel Pecan Brownie
Total Time: 1 Hr 5 mins, Serving: 6
Ingredients
Pecans, 3/4 Cup
Butter, 1/4 Cup
Heavy Cream, 3/4 Cup
Flour, 1 Cup
Brown Sugar, 1.833 Cup
Cocoa Powder, 1/2 Cup
Salt, 1/2 Tsp
Melted Butter, 6 Tbsp
Baking Soda, 3/4 Tsp
Chopped Chocolate, 6 Ounce
Large Eggs, 3
Instructions
To make the Pecan-Caramel Sauce, roast the nuts in a 9-inch cast-iron skillet over medium-high heat. Pecans should be toasted for 5 mins, stirring periodically. Toss the nuts with 1/4 cup butter & 1/2 cup brown sugar. Stir until the brown sugar and butter have melted and mixed.
Remove the pecans from the heat and slowly pour in 1/2 cup of heavy cream. Return to the heat and whisk until all of the creams are incorporated. Remove the pan from the heat and put it aside.
To make the brownies, whisk together the cocoa powder, baking soda, flour, brown sugar, and salt in a large mixing basin. Mix in the melted eggs, butter, and cream well. Fold in the milk chocolate chunks. Pour the brownie batter over the caramel pecan mixture.
Once ready to cook, preheat the Pit Boss to 325°F for 15 mins with the lid closed. Cook the brownies in the Pit Boss for 35-40 mins, or until a toothpick inserted in the middle comes out clean.
Set the cast iron pan just on the grill grate & cook for 35-40 mins, or until a toothpick inserted in the middle comes out clean.
Remove the steaks from the grill and leave them to cool for at least 10 min. Serve with ice cream while it's still warm. Enjoy.

9.13 Baked Candied Bacon Cinnamon Rolls
Total Time: 55 mins, Serving: 6
Ingredients
Cream Cheese, 2 Ounce
Brown Sugar, 1/3 Cup
Cinnamon Rolls, Pre-Made
Bacon, 12 Slices
Instructions
Preheat the Pit Boss to 350°F for 15 minutes with the lid closed when ready to cook.
Dredge 8 of the bacon slices in brown sugar, ensuring both sides are covered.
Arrange the browned sugared bacon slices, as well as the other bacon pieces, on a cooling rack set on a big baking sheet.
Cook the bacon for 15-20 mins on the Pit Boss, or until the fat has rendered, but the bacon is still flexible. Then, reduce the temperature to 325°F in the Pit Boss.
Unroll and open the cinnamon buns. Place 1 slice of browned sugared bacon on top of the unwrapped rolls, then wrap back

up while the bacon is still heated. Carry on with the rest of the rolls in the same manner.

Spray an 8" × 8" cake pan or baking dish with non-stick cooking spray and place cinnamon rolls in it. Preheat the oven to 325°F and bake the cinnamon rolls for 10 mins, or until brown. Halfway through the cooking period, rotate the pan half a turn.

In the meanwhile, soften the cream cheese and combine it into the supplied cream cheese frosting. Finally, cook the bacon and crumble it into cream cheese icing.

Drizzle warm cinnamon buns with icing. Warm it up and enjoy it!

9.14 Homemade Turkey Gravy

Total Time: 3 Hrs. 20 mins, Serving: 8
Ingredients
Onion, 2 Large
Turkey Neck, 1
Celery, 4
Garlic, 8 Clove
Chicken Broth, 4 Cup
Carrots, 4 Large
Flour, 1 Cup
Thyme Sprigs, 8
Black Pepper, 1 Tsp
Salt, 1 Tsp
Butter Sticks, 1
Instructions
Preheat the Pit Boss to 350°F and cook for 15 minutes with the lid covered when ready to cook.

Combine the turkey neck, carrot, onion, garlic, celery, and thyme in a large roasting pan. Season with salt and 4 cups chicken stock.

Place the turkey upon this rack in the roasting pan in the Pit Boss and cook.

Cook for 3 to 4 hours, or until the breast reaches 160 degrees Fahrenheit. After being removed from the grill, the turkey would continue to cook until it reaches an internal temperature of 165°F.

Pour the meat juices into such a saucepan and reduce to low heat.

In a bigger pot, mix the butter (cut in 8 pieces) & flour until golden brown. This takes approximately 8 minutes of continuous stirring.

Finally, mix the drippings into the roux and bring to a boil. Season to taste with salt & pepper and serve immediately. Enjoy.

9.15 Baked Soft Gingerbread Cookie

Total Time: 25 mins, Serving: 8
Ingredients
Baking Soda, 1/2 Tsp
Flour, 1 3/4 Cup
Ground Cinnamon, 1/2 Tsp
Ground Ginger, 1 1/2 Tsp
Ground Cloves, 1/4 Tsp
Molasses, 1/4 Cup
Kosher Salt, 1/4 Tsp
Brown Sugar, 1/3 Cup
Granulated Sugar, 4 Tbsp plus 1/2 Cup
1 Egg
Butter, 3/4 Cup
Instructions
Preheat the Pit Boss to 325°F for 15 minutes
with the lid closed when ready to cook.

In a medium mixing bowl, whisk together cinnamon, flour, salt, baking soda, ginger, & cloves.

Whisk together all t1/2 cup granulated sugar, brown sugar, and butter in the bowl of a stand mixer until light and fluffy. Mix in the molasses and egg at medium speed, scraping down all sides of the bowl as needed.

In a separate dish, add the dry ingredients and mix at low speed until well mixed. Scrape down the edges and blend for another 30 seconds.

Roll one tablespoon of dough into a ball, then roll in the remaining four tablespoons of sugar.

Put dough balls on such a parchment-lined baking tray, spacing them apart by a couple of inches.

Cook for approximately 10 minutes, until gently browned but still tender in the middle, on a baking tray directly here on the grill grate.

Remove the burgers from the grill and let them settle on a cooling rack. Enjoy!

9.16 Smoked Pumpkin Soup

Total Time: 2 Hrs. 15 mins, Serving: 6
Ingredients
Pumpkin, 5 Pound
Butter, 3 Tbsp
Onion, 1
Garlic, 2 Clove
Brown Sugar, 1 Tbsp
Paprika, 1 Tsp
Ground Cinnamon, 1/4 Tsp
Ground Nutmeg, 1/8 Tsp
Ground Allspice, 1/8 Tsp
Apple Cider, 1/2 Cup
Chicken Broth, 5 Cup
Whipped Cream, 1/2 Cup
Parsley
Instructions
Split the pumpkin in quarters using a strong knife. Remove the seeds & stringy threads using a spoon. If desired, break the seeds from the fibers and reserve the seeds for roasting.

Once ready to cook, preheat the Pit Boss grill to 165 degrees Fahrenheit with the lid covered.

Place the pumpkin quarters immediately on the grill grate, skin-side down. 1 hour of smoking

Preheat the oven to 300°F, then roast the pumpkin for 90 minutes, or until it is soft and easily punctured with a fork. Allow cooling before removing the pumpkin meat from the skin.

Inside a 4-quart pan or stockpot, melt the butter on medium heat.

Cook the onion for approximately 5 minutes, or until tender and transparent.

Combine the smoked paprika, nutmeg, brown sugar, cinnamon, & allspice in a large mixing bowl. Put the apple cider right away and simmer for a few minutes until the solution is reduced & syrupy.

Combine the pumpkin with chicken broth in a mixing bowl. Allow 20 minutes for the soup to boil.

Puree the soup in a blender or with a hand-held immersion blender until smooth. Season to taste with salt and pepper. If

the sauce is too thick, add additional chicken broth.
To serve, ladle the soup in bowls and top with heavy cream. If preferred, garnish with just a sprig of parsley.

9.17 Baked Potato Skins with Pulled Pork
Total Time: 1 Hr 15 mins, Serving: 6
Ingredients
Salt to taste
Russet Potatoes, 4
Potato, 4
Vegetable Oil
Canola Oil
Pulled Pork, 3 Cup
Heat BBQ Sauce and Pit Boss Sweet, 4 Tbsp
Melted Butter, 2 Tbsp
Mozzarella Cheese, 1 Cup
Green Onion, Chopped
For Serving Sour Cream
Cheddar Cheese, 1 Cup
For Serving Bacon, Chopped
Instructions
Preheat Pit Boss to 450°F and cook for 15 minutes with lid covered until ready to cook.
Drizzle canola oil over the potatoes and season equally. Put the potatoes straight on a grill grate, then simmer for 30 min, or until a fork pricks them in the center and they are tender.
Halve the potatoes and empty the insides, retaining 1/4 inch the potato peels on the outside. Place the skins on a baking pan and brush the insides with melted butter. Please return to the grill & cook for a further 5 to 6 minutes, until it's golden brown.
Combine the pulled pork, mozzarella cheese, Pit Boss Sweet & Heat BBQ Sauce, and cheddar cheese in a mixing bowl.
Cover the skins with mixture and return to the Pit Boss, lid closed, for just long enough for the cheese to melt.
Toss with chopped onions, bacon, and sour cream before serving. Enjoy!

9.18 Pulled Pork Enchiladas with Smoke-Roasted Red Sauce
Total Time: 60 mins, Serving: 4
Ingredients
Tomatoes, 1 1/2 Pound
Garlic, 1 Head
Large Onion, 1
Cumin, 2 Tsp
Hot Sauce
Chili Powder, 2 Tsp
Flour Tortillas, 6 Whole
Pulled Pork, 3 Cup
Monterey Shredded Jack Cheese, 1 Cup
Cheddar Cheese, 1 Cup
Instructions
Preheat Pit Boss to 375°F and cook for 15 minutes with lid covered when ready to cook.
Remove the top of the garlic head and cover it in aluminum foil. Directly on the barbecue grate, set the tomatoes & wrapped garlic on a vine and onion halves. Cook, occasionally stirring, for 10 mins, or until tomato skins completely split and the onion & garlic have softened.
Take the tomatoes from the vine and peel the garlic foil away. Add the tomatoes & onions to a blender; now press the softened garlic out from its peel. Let the steam escape by holding the lid at an angle. In a blender, combine the cumin, salt, chili powder, and hot sauce. Blend till the sauce has reached a silky consistency. If the sauce is too thick, thin it out with a tbsp of water until it reaches the appropriate consistency.
Spread a thin layer with sauce over the bottom of something like a 9x13 baking dish. In a large mixing bowl, combine 1/4 cup enchilada sauce with pulled pork. To mix, gently toss with a spoon.
Place about 1/3 cup of a pulled pork mixture, including a couple of tablespoons of cheese, in each tortilla. Place the tortilla throughout the baking dish seam-side down. Continue with the rest of the tortillas and meat till the pan is filled.
Top with shredded cheese and the leftover enchilada sauce. Place the pan straight just on the grill grate & bake for 25 minutes, just until the sauces are bubbling as well as the cheese is fully melted. Enjoy!

9.19 Baked Deep Dish Supreme Pizza
Total Time: 45 mins, Serving: 4
Ingredients
Pizza Dough, Ounce
Olive Oil
Pizza Sauce, 1/2 Cup
Parmesan Cheese
Fresh Oregano, 1 Teaspoon
Mozzarella Cheese, 2 Cup
Italian Sausage, Pound
Fresh Basil, 1 Tsp
Bell Pepper, 1 Half Red
Bell Peppers, 1 Half Green
Onion, 2 Tbsp
Mushrooms
Black Olives
Sliced Pepperoni
Instructions
Once ready to cook, preheat the grill on high for 15 mins with the lid covered.
Coat a cast iron pan using extra virgin olive oil, 10-12 inches in diameter. Fill the pan halfway with dough and push it out through the bottom and up the edges.
To construct the pizza, pour the sauce over the dough and top with all of the toppings. Next, sprinkle oregano and basil on top of the mozzarella plus fresh grated Parmesan.
Bake for 25-30 minutes, or until the cheese and sauce are bubbling, and the crust is lightly browned.
Allow for 5-10 mins to rest before slicing. Enjoy!

9.20 Baked Cornbread Sausage Stuffing
Total Time: 1 Hr 20 mins, Serving: 6
Ingredients
Chopped Pecans, 1 1/4 Cup
Cornbread, 10 Cup
Breakfast Sausage, 1 Pound
Sweet Onion, 2 Cup
Celery, 1 1/2 Cup
Minced Parsley, 1/2 Cup
Butter, 3/4 Cup
Minced Sage, 2 Tbsp
Minced Thyme, 1 Tbsp
Salt, 2 Tsp
Paprika, 1 Tsp
Minced Rosemary, 1 Tbsp
Black Pepper, 1 1/2 Tsp
Chicken Broth, 1 1/2 Cup
Milk, 1 1/2 Cup
Whole Eggs, 2
Instructions
Arrange the cornbread cubes in such a single layer on two rimmed baking pans and air-dry overnight, stirring periodically. In a large mixing bowl, place the dry cornbread squares. Toss

in the pecans.
In something like a large cast iron pan, sauté the sausage over medium-high heat on the stovetop. With a wooden spoon, crumble sausage until it is browned and cooked thoroughly. Don't mix the sausage into the cornmeal and pecans.
Melt the butter in the skillet without wiping it out. Cook, occasionally stirring, until the onion & celery has softened, approximately 8 to 10 minutes.
Add the parsley, thyme, rosemary, salt, pepper, sage, & paprika and stir to combine. Don't stir as you pour the sauce over the cornmeal. Combine the parsley, sage, rosemary, thyme, salt, pepper, and paprika in a large mixing bowl. Don't stir as you pour the sauce over the cornmeal.
In a mixing bowl, whisk together the eggs and milk. Next, add chicken broth to the pot.
Put the egg mixture over the cornbread mixture and gently fold everything together. If necessary, add additional chicken broth; the mixture should be wet but not soggy.
Grease a 9" × 13" baking sheet or a big casserole dish with butter. Fill the dish with the filling mixture.
Once ready to cook, preheat the oven to 325°F with the lid covered for 15 minutes.
Place the baking dish just on the grill grate and simmer the stuffing for 50 to 60 minutes, or until it is gently browned & slightly crusty on top.
Remove from the oven and set aside to cool slightly before serving. Enjoy.

9.21 Spicy Bacon Wrapped Grilled Chicken Skewers
Total Time: 3 Hrs 20 mins, Serving: 6
Ingredients
Garlic Powder, 1/2 Teaspoon
Ranch, 1/2 Cup
Chili Sauce, 2 Tablespoon
Chicken Breast, 16 Ounce
Sliced Onion, S1 Whole Red
Dried Oregano, 1/2 Teaspoon
Sliced Bacon, 8 Strips
Sliced Bell Peppers, 1 Whole Green
Instructions
Combine ranch dressing, oregano, garlic powder, & chili sauce in a large mixing basin. Toss in the cubed chicken and toss well to coat. Let the chicken marinate for 1 to 3 hours in the refrigerator.
When ready to cook, increase the temperature to High & preheat for 15 minutes with the lid closed.
Begin constructing Pit Boss skewers by sliding an onion wedge, a pepper, a piece of bacon, and then chicken. Alternate the bacon and chicken until the bacon is woven across the chicken pieces. Finish with such a pepper or onion wedge on each skewer. To ensure quick and uniform grilling, do not overcrowd the skewer. Rep with the remaining skewers.
Arrange the skewers on a grill grate with a piece of foil beneath the skewers' ends to protect them from burning as well as to make rotating them easier.
Cook for 5 minutes each side, quarter-turning halfway through, for such a total of 15 min, or when the chicken reaches a temperature of 165°F. Take out the skewers. Enjoy!

9.22 Bacon Onion Ring
Total Time: 1Hr 10 mins, Serving: 6
Ingredients
Honey, 1 Tsp
Vidalia sliced Onion, 2 Whole
Bacon, 16 Slices
Sauce Chili Garlic, 1 Tbsp
Yellow Mustard, 1 Tbsp
Instructions
Wrap a slice of bacon around each onion ring until all of the bacon is gone. Some onion slices are thicker than others, necessitating two sections of bacon to form a ring.
To prevent the bacon from unraveling during cooking, poke a fork through the bacon-wrapped onions slice.
Once ready to cook, preheat the oven to 400 °F and cook for 15 minutes with the lid covered.
In a small mixing bowl, combine the chili garlic sauce & yellow mustard; stir in the honey.
Place the skewer here on the grill grate & cook for 90 minutes, turning halfway through. Enjoy!

9.23 Oktoberfest Pretzel Mustard Chicken
Total Time: 40 mins, Serving: 4
Ingredients
Dijon Mustard, 3 Tbsp
Pretzel Sticks, 1/4 Pound
Brown Ale or Apple Cider, 3 Tbsp
Chicken Breasts, 4 Boneless
Fresh Thyme, 1 1/2 Tsp
Honey, 1 Tbsp
Instructions
Blend the pretzel pieces in a hand blender or crush them by hand in such a plastic baggie until they're the consistency of panko breadcrumbs.
Place the crumbs in a shallow, wide basin.
Combine honey, beer or cider, thyme and mustard in a separate shallow bowl.
Place a wire rack on top of a sheet tray and coat it with cooking spray. Place each chicken breast on the wire rack after dipping it in the mustard sauce and dredging it in pretzels crumbs to coat evenly. Using cooking spray, gently coat the tops of each chicken breast.
Once ready to cook, preheat the Pit Boss to 375°F with the lid covered for 15 minutes.
Prepared pan on the Pit Boss to bake for 20 to 25 minutes, just until the chicken breasts are completely cooked, and an instant-read thermometer reads 165 degrees Fahrenheit.
Set aside for 5 minutes to allow the chicken to cool. If desired, garnish with fresh thyme. Enjoy!

9.24 Rosemary and Thyme-Infused Mashed Potatoes with Cream
Total Time: 1 Hr 20 mins, Serving: 6
Ingredients
Water, 1 1/2 Cup
Russet Potatoes, 4 1/2 Pound
Heavy Cream, 1 Pint
Fresh Thyme, 3 Sprig
Leaves, 6 Sage
Rosemary, 2 Sprig
Black Peppercorn, 6 Whole
Unsalted Butter, 2 Stick
Kosher Salt
Chopped & peeled garlic, 2 Clove
Black Pepper
Instructions
Preheat the Pit Boss to 350°F for 15 minutes with the lid closed when ready to cook.
Peel and wash the potatoes before cutting them into 1-inch cubes for the mashed potatoes. Simmer for 60 minutes or till

fork tender inside an oven-safe dish about 1-1/2 cups water.
In a small saucepan, mix the cream, herbs, peppercorns, and garlic cloves, whereas the potatoes boil. Put on the grill, cover, and let for 15 minutes to steep.
Strain the cream to exclude the herbs & garlic, then return it to a saucepan & keep it heated on the fire.
Drain, and then rice the potatoes in a large stockpot with a potato ricer and food mill. First, 2/3 of cream should be poured slowly, followed by 1 stick of butter and a spoonful of salt. Then, to get the correct consistency, add additional cream, butter, and salt as needed.
Serve warm or keep warm inside a slow cooker on to the lowest setting or over a water bath. Enjoy!

9.25 Baked Granola

Total Time: 1 Hr 20 mins, Serving: 6
Ingredients
Brown Sugar, 1/2 Cup
Honey, 1/2 Cup
Butter, 1/2 Cup
Vanilla Extract, 2 tsp
Pinch of Salt
Ground Cinnamon, 2 tsp
Oats, 5 Cup
Almond Extract, 1/2 tsp
Toasted Wheat Germ, 1/2 Cup
Unsalted Sunflower Seeds, 1 Cup
Dried Fruit (Such as Raisins, Cranberries, Cherries, Blueberries, Pineapple, etc.), 2 Cup
Salted Mixed Nuts, 1 Cup
Instructions
In a small saucepan, mix the honey, butter, brown sugar, & salt. Over medium-low heat, bring the mixture to a simmer. Cook, stirring periodically, for 5 mins.
Remove the pan from the heat, then whisk in the almond extract, vanilla, and cinnamon. Allow cooling slightly before serving.
Lightly grease a rimmed baking sheets bottom and sides.
In a large mixing bowl, mix the sunflower seeds, oats, wheat germ, and roughly chopped nuts.
Drizzle the heated syrup over the oats. Grease your hands and thoroughly combine the ingredients. Place the mixture on the baking sheet that has been prepared.
Once ready to cook, preheat the grill to 300°F with the lid covered for 15 mins.
Bake the granola for 1 hour or until gently browned. Allow cooling before chopping into pieces in such a large mixing basin.
Add the coconut & dried fruit and mix well. Keep the container sealed. Enjoy!

9.26 Apple & Bourbon Glazed Ham

Total Time: 1 Hr 15 mins, Serving: 6
Ingredients
Apple Jelly, 1 Cup
Large Ham, 1
Bourbon, 2 tbsp
Fresh Lemon Juice, 2 tsp
Dijon Mustard, 2 tbsp
Cider or Apple Juice, 2 Cup
Ground Cloves, 1/2 tsp
Instructions
Preheat Pit Boss to 325°F for 15 minutes with lid closed when ready to cook.
Place the ham straight on a grill grate once the grill is hot. The cooking time is 30 minutes.
Melt the apple jelly in a small pot over medium-low heat in the meanwhile. Remove from the heat and put aside the mustard, bourbon, lemon juice, apple juice, and crushed cloves.
Glaze the ham with apple bourbon mixture after 30 minutes. Cook for another 30 minutes, or until an internal temperature of 135°F is reached when a thermometer is put into the thickest portion of the meat.
Remove the ham from the grill and set it aside for 20 minutes to rest before serving. If preferred, reheat the leftover sauce, then serve with ham. Enjoy!

9.27 Asian BBQ Chicken

Total Time: 1 day 1 Hr, Serving: 4
Ingredients
Whole Chicken, 1
Whole Ginger Ale, 1
Pit Boss Asian BBQ
Instructions
Clean the chicken by rinsing it in cold water & patting it dry using paper towels. Apply Pit Boss Asian Barbecue rub all over the chicken, being careful to get some on the interior as well. Cover and chill overnight for 24 hours in a big bag or dish.
Once ready to cook, preheat the Pit Boss to 375°F for 15 minutes with the lid closed.
Take a couple of large gulps of ginger ale from the can. Place the soda can on a firm surface. Remove the chicken from the refrigerator and put it on top of the Coke can. To keep the chicken upright, the base of the can, as well as the legs of the bird, should create a tripod.
Place the chicken in the middle of the heated grate and cook for 40 to 1 hour, until the skin is lightly browned and also the internal temperature of the chicken reaches 165°F on an instant-read thermometer.
Remove chicken off the throne. Enjoy!

9.28 Baked Garlic Duchess Potatoes

Total Time: 1 Hr 30 mins, Serving: 8
Ingredients
Egg Yolk, 5 Large
Medium Potatoes, 12
Salt to taste
Heavy Cream, 1.24 Cup
Sour Cream, 3/4 Cup
Minced Garlic, 2 Clove
Black Pepper
Melted butter, 10 tbsp
Instructions
Fill a big saucepan halfway with water and add the potatoes. Season with salt & pepper. Over medium-high heat, bring to a boil.
Reduce heat to low and cook for 25 to 35 minutes, till a paring knife smoothly glides into potatoes. Drain and set aside to cool.
Once ready to cook, preheat the Pit Boss to 450°F for 15 minutes with the lid closed.
In a large mixing bowl, whisk together the egg yolks, cream, garlic, sour cream, cream, butter, & pepper. Season with salt & pepper.
Peel potatoes and press flesh into the basin with egg mixture using a ricer or food mill. Carefully fold in egg mixture, taking care not to over mix it.
Bake for 30–40 minutes in a 3-quart baking dish, just until lightly browned and slightly puffed. Enjoy!

9.29 Baked Sweet and Savory Yams by Bennie Kendrick

Total Time: 1 Hr 30 mins, Serving: 6
Ingredients
Yams, 3 Medium size
Olive oil, 3 tbsp
Honey
Goat Cheese
Brown Sugar, 1/2 Cup
Chopped Pecans, 1/2 Cup
Instructions
Preheat the oven to 350°F and leave the lid covered for 15 minutes when ready to cook.
While the Pit Boss heats up, wash the yams, then poke several holes all over them. Finally, wrap the yams in foil to keep them warm.
Bake for 45-60 minutes, or until the meat is tender when pierced with a knife. Since you would like to reduce each yam into rounds, you don't want to overcook them and make them too soft.
When the yams are cool enough to handle, cut them into 1/4" circles. Place each round on a sheet tray and lightly coat with olive oil.
Sprinkle brown sugar on top of each serving. Next, put an adequate amount with goat cheese on every round using a teaspoon. After that, sprinkle chopped pecans on top. Finally, sprinkle each circle with Bee Local honey.
Add additional brown sugar + honey to taste, depending on how sweet you prefer your yams.
Return your sheet tray to the Pit Boss & cook for just another 20 minutes with the lid closed. Enjoy!

9.30 Chorizo Cheese Stuffed Burgers

Total Time: 60 mins, Serving: 2
Ingredients
Sliced Lettuce
Pit Boss Rib Rub, 4 Ounce
Chorizo, 12 Ounce
Ground Beef, 2 Pound
Cheddar Cheese, 2 Slices
Sliced Tomatoes
Sliced Red Onion
Brioche Burger Buns, 4 Whole
Instructions
In a mixing bowl, combine 2 pounds of 80/20 ground beef with Pit Boss Prime Rib Rub.
Form eight 1/4-pound patties from the ground meat. Make the foundation of one burger by laying 1/4 of the cheese slice, 3 oz. Chorizo, with some 1/4 cheese slice. To bind the two parties together, place another patty on top and squeeze the edges all the way around at the burger.
Continue until all four patties are cooked.
Once ready to cook, preheat the oven to 325°F and cook for 15 minutes with the lid covered.
Cook the burgers for 15 minutes on each side of the Pit Boss. Garnish each burger with a piece of Cheddar cheese and melt it if desired. Remove from the Pit Boss and cover with foil to rest for 10 minutes.
While the burgers are resting, spray the brioche buns using melted butter and toast them on the grill for 30-45 seconds. Remove the buns from the grill and put the burger together with the toppings. Enjoy!

9.31 Venison Meatloaf by Nikki Boxler

Total Time: 1 Hr 30 mins, Serving: 4
Ingredients
Ground Venison, 2 Pound
Onion, 1
Beaten egg, 1
Salt to taste
Black Pepper
Breadcrumbs, 1 Cup
Worcestershire Sauce, 1 tbsp
Milk, 1 Cup
Onion Soup Mix, 1 Ounce
Ketchup, 1/4 Cup
Brown Sugar, 1/4 Cup
Apple Cider Vinegar, 1/4 Cup
Instructions
Set the Pit Boss grill & preheat it to 350 degrees F when you're ready to cook.
Coat a loaf pan using non-stick cooking spray. Combine the ground venison, egg, breadcrumbs, Worcestershire sauce, salt & pepper, onion, milk, and onion soup package in a large mixing basin using your hands. Take care not to over mix the ingredients.
Combine the ketchup, brown sugar, and apple cider vinegar in a small bowl. Half of the glaze should be applied to the pan's bottom and sides. Place the meatloaf on top of the sauce and cover with the remaining sauce.
Cook for 1 hour & 15 mins, until the temperature, reaches 165 degrees F, immediately on the grill grate.
Allow cooling somewhat before slicing. Enjoy!

9.32 Old Fashioned Cornbread

Total Time: 35 mins, Serving: 4
Ingredients
Cornmeal, 1 Cup
Flour, 1 Cup
Sugar, 1 tbsp
Lightly Beaten Egg, 1
Salt, 1/2 tsp
Butter, 3 tbsp
Baking Powder, 2 tsp
Milk, 1 Cup
Instructions
Combine the flour, sugar, cornmeal, baking powder, & salt in a mixing dish.
In a small saucepan, melt the butter. Remove the pan from the heat and add the milk and egg. (Be careful not to overheat the mixture, or the egg may curdle.)
Stir together the dry ingredients as well as the milk-egg combination. Do not over mix the ingredients.
Pour the batter into an oiled 9-inch square baking sheet or pie dish and spread evenly.
When you're ready to cook, fire up the Pit Boss grill & preheat it to 375 degrees F.
Bake the cornbread for 25 to 35 mins or until it, starts to peel away from the edges of the pan as well as the top begins to brown. For serving, cut into cubes.

9.33 Greek Chicken Pizza

Total Time: 40 mins, Serving: 6
Ingredients
Olive Oil
Chicken Breasts, 3
Feather Rub and Pit Boss Fin
Oregano
Pizza Dough
Olive oil, 3 tbsp
Spinach, 1 Cup
Feta Cheese, 1/4 Cup
Medium-sized Sliced Tomatoes, 2
Kalamata Olives, 2 Ounce
Instructions
Lightly coat the chicken breasts with olive oil on both sides. Season with Pit Boss Fin and Feather Rub on both sides.
Once ready to cook, preheat the Pit Boss to 375°F for 15 mins with the lid closed.
Place the chicken breasts straight on the grill grate & cook for about 20 minutes, turning midway through, or until an instant-read thermometer reads 165 degrees F on the inside.
Remove the chicken from the pan and set it aside to rest for about 10 minutes. Then, across the grain, finely chop the chicken breasts.
Preheat the Pit Boss to 400 ° F, or High, for 10 minutes with the lid closed.
In the meanwhile, layout the pizza dough to the desired thickness.
Drizzle with olive oil and season using fresh oregano on both sides.
Cook the top side of the pizza dough first, right on the grill grate. Then, on each side, cook for 5 minutes.
Remove the dough from the Pit Boss when it has done cooking and on top, sprinkle some olive oil.
Arrange olives, sliced chicken, tomatoes, spinach, and feta cheese on the pizza dough in an even layer. Enjoy! Serve.

9.34 Baked Chicken Pot Pie

Total Time: 50 mins, Serving: 4
Ingredients
Butter, 2 tbsp
Small Onion, 1
Stalk Celery, 1
Flour, 2 tbsp
Turkey Stock or Chicken, 2 Cup
Milk or Cream, 1/2 Cup
Dry Sherry, 2 tsp
Frozen Peas & Carrots, 1 1/2 Cup
Pit Boss Pork and Poultry Rub, 1/2 tsp
Dried Thyme Leaves, 1/4 tsp
Turkey or Cooked Skinless Chicken, 4 Cup
Salt & Pepper
Frozen Puff Pastry, 1 Sheet
For Dusting Flour
1 Egg
Instructions
Preheat the Pit Boss to 400°F for 15 minutes with the lid closed when ready to cook.
In a large pan over medium heat, melt the butter. Cook, occasionally stirring, for 5 mins, until the onions are yellow. Toss with flour and toss to coat.
Gradually pour in the chicken stock, stirring to remove any lumps. Bring the milk or cream to a low boil. Allow boiling for a few minutes until the liquid has thickened slightly and coats the back of a spoon. Add the dry sherry to the mix.
Heat for 10 minutes with the Pit Boss Pork and Poultry Rub, thyme, carrots and peas, and chicken. Season with salt to taste.
Spray a cast iron pan and fill it halfway with pot pie filling.
On some kind of lightly floured countertop, unfold the puff pastry sheet. Allow defrosting for a few minutes.
Crimp any overhanging puff pastry onto the top of cast iron. To allow the steam out, make many tiny holes in the middle and gently brush with egg wash.
Bake for 30 mins, or when the puff pastry becomes golden brown and the filling is boiling. Serve right away. Enjoy!

9.35 Baked Coffee Cake

Total Time: 60 mins, Serving: 8
Ingredients
Main
1/2 Cup Unsalted Butter, Softened
1 Cup Sugar
2 Eggs
2 cup Flour
1 Teaspoon Baking Soda
1 Teaspoon Ground Cinnamon
1/2 Teaspoon Salt
1 cup Sour Cream
1 1/2 Teaspoon Vanilla Extract
Crumble
1/2 Cup Sugar
1/4 Cup Brown Sugar
2 Tablespoon Flour
1 Tablespoon Vanilla Extract
1/2 Teaspoon Ground Cinnamon
1 Tablespoon Butter, Melted
Instructions
Once ready to cook, preheat the Pit Boss to 325°F with the lid covered for 15 minutes.
Cooking spray an 8x8-inch cake pan, then cover with parchment paper and spray the parchment. Remove from the equation.
Cream the sugar and butter together in the mixing bowl until light and creamy. Scrape the sides of the basin between each addition as you add the eggs in a bowl.
Mix all the flour, cinnamon, baking soda, and salt in a medium mixing basin.
Mix all the sour cream & vanilla extract in a small bowl.
In three portions, alternate wet and dry flour and sour cream mix in the sugar mixture, wiping the bowl after each application.
To make the crumble topping, combine all of the crumble ingredients in a small bowl. Pour half of the batter into the cake pan and top with half of the crumb mixture. Pour in the rest of the batter and top with the remaining crumbs.
Cover the lid directly upon this grill grate and bake for 45 to 60 minutes until a toothpick inserted in the middle of the cake comes out clean.
Allow cooling after removing from the grill grate. Cut into slices and serve. Enjoy!

9.36 Baked Breakfast Mini Quiches

Total Time: 30 mins, Serving: 8
Ingredients
Cooking Spray
Basil, 1/4 Cup
Kosher Salt, 1 tsp
Black Pepper, 1/2 tsp
Olive oil, 1 tbsp
Spinach, 3 Cup
10 Eggs
Yellow Onion, 1/2
Shredded Mozzarella, 4 Ounce

Instructions
Coat a 12-cup muffin tray with non-stick cooking spray.
Warm the oil in a pan skillet over medium heat. Cook, turning regularly until the onion is softened, about 7 minutes. Cook for another minute or until the spinach has wilted.
Allow cooling on a cutting board before chopping the mixture to break up the spinach.
Once ready to cook, preheat the grill to 350°F with the lid covered for 15 min.
Whisk the eggs in a large mixing basin until foamy. Combine the cooled onions & basil, spinach, cheese, 1 tsp salt, and 1/2 tsp pepper in a mixing bowl. To blend, stir everything together.
Evenly distribute the egg mixture among the muffin cups.
Place the tray upon this grill and bake for 18 to 20 minutes until the egg has swelled up, has set, and therefore are beginning to color.
Leave to cool on even a wire rack before serving, or store in a sealed jar for up to four days. Enjoy.

9.37 Dark Chocolate Brownies with Bacon-Salted Caramel

Total Time: 50 mins, Serving: 8
Ingredients
Bacon, 8 Strips
Caramel Sauce, 1 Jar
Brownie Mix, 1 Whole
Kosher Salt, 1/2 Cup
Instructions
Cook a few slices of bacon (6 - 8) until extremely crisp for bacon salt: It should take about 25 minutes at 350 degrees. Allow cooling before pulsing until finely minced in a food processor. Combine half a cup of kosher salt in a mixing bowl. Keep it refrigerated until you're ready to use it.
Preheat the oven to 350 ° F and leave the lid covered for 10 minutes when ready to cook.
Follow the box directions for making the brownies and pour them onto a prepared pan. Using around 2 teaspoons of the caramel sauce, drizzle it over the brownie batter. Add about 1 teaspoon of bacon salt to the mixture. Place directly just on preheated Pit Boss grill grate.
Prepare the brownie for 20-25 minutes, or until the batter begins to firm up. Take from grill and top with 2 tablespoons additional caramel sauce and a pinch of bacon salt. Return the brownies to grill for another 20-25 mins, or until a tester inserted in the centre comes out clean.
If you want a little more caramel, drizzle an additional layer on top of the warm brownies and finish with a pinch of bacon salt. Allow for thorough cooling before cutting the brownies into squares. To keep the brownies from sticking to the knife, clean it between each slice. Enjoy!

9.38 Baked Peach Cobbler Cupcakes

Total Time: 45 mins, Serving: 8
Ingredients
Sugar, 3/4 Cup
Peach, 2 Large
Lemon Juice, 2 tsp
Mix yellow cake
Ground Cinnamon, 1/2 Teaspoon
Vanilla Icing, 1 Can

Instructions
A kettle of water should be brought to a boil. Make a small shallow X around the bottom of the peaches by turning them upside down. To loosen the skin of peaches, place them in hot water for 1 minute.
Drain the peaches and rinse with cold water in a colander.
Remove the skin of the peaches.
Filling: Dice the peaches and lay them in a large baking dish. Peaches should be cooked over medium heat. Add the sugar, lemon, and cinnamon after it begins to sizzle. Cook for 10-15 minutes over medium heat or until the majority of the peach juice has evaporated, producing a thick syrup.
Allow cooling in a basin.
Preheat the Pit Boss to 350°F for 15 minutes with the lid closed when ready to cook.
Cupcakes: Prepare the cake mix according to the package directions and bake in a cupcake tray lined with liners.
Bake cakes for approximately 13-16 minutes, till light golden brown, when the grill has been prepared.
After the cupcakes have cooled, put the peach cobbler filling into the centre with a piping bag.
Using your favorited vanilla frosting, ice the cake. Enjoy!

9.39 Baked Donut Holes

Total Time: 30 mins, Serving: 6
Ingredients
Corn-starch, 2 tbsp
Flour, 1 Cup
Baking Powder, 1 tsp
Ground Cinnamon
Salt to taste
Baking Soda, 1/4 tsp
Cup Sugar
Buttermilk, 1/2 Cup
Butter, 7 tbsp
Vanilla Extract, 1 tsp
Eggs, 1 Large
Ground Cinnamon, 1/2 tsp
Cooking Spray
Instructions
Once ready to cook, preheat the grill to 350 degrees Fahrenheit with the lid covered for 15 minutes.
Incorporate the dry ingredients (flour, a pinch of ground cinnamon, baking powder, corn-starch, baking soda, and salt) in a medium mixing bowl and whisk to combine.
Mix the wet ingredients (buttermilk, half cup sugar, egg, butter, and vanilla) in a separate bowl and whisk well until the egg is completely absorbed.
Put the wet mixture in to dry and whisk just until incorporated with just a rubber spatula, being careful not to overmix.
Cooking sprays a tiny muffin tin and scoop 1 tablespoon of batter inside each muffin.
Bake for 15-20 minutes, till a toothpick, came out clean, with the muffin pan right on the grill grate. Remove off the grill and set aside to cool for 5 minutes. Then, remove the muffins from the tin and place them on a sheet tray.
1 tbsp icing sugar & 1/2 tsp cinnamon in a small bowl
Toss the doughnut holes in the cinnamon sugar after dipping them in the melted butter. Fill the doughnut holes with chocolate sauce, curd, or your favorited jam, if preferred. You are welcome to mix the sugar mixture too. (We used lemon curd and a mixture of cardamom, caster sugar, and lemon zest to fill our doughnut holes.) Play with them, have fun, and enjoy yourself

9.40 BBQ Pulled Pork Pizza

Total Time: 1 Hr. 15 mins, Serving: 6
Ingredients
Dry Yeast, 2 Active
Water, 1 1/2 Cup
Olive Oil, 1/4 Cup
Salt, 1 tsp
Sugar, 2 tsp
Heat BBQ Sauce & Pit Boss Sweet, 2 Cup
Cornmeal, 2 Cup
Flour, 4 Cup
Pulled Pork, 1 Pound
Sliced Red Onion
Finely Chopped Cilantro
Mozzarella Cheese, 3 Cup
Pit Boss Rib Rub
Instructions
To make the dough, fill a basin halfway with warm water, then add the yeast & stir gently. Allow to sit for 5 mins or until it foams up. Combine the sugar, oil, and salt in a mixing bowl. Mix in the flour until the dough resembles a ball.
Place dough in a large mixing bowl that has been lightly oiled. Allow dough to double in size by covering this with plastic wrap, then letting it sit for at least an hour (approximately one hour). Knead the dough four to five times on a lightly floured board. Allow 15 minutes for resting.
While the dough is resting, warm the Pit Boss to 450 degrees F (500 degrees when using a WiFIRE-enabled grilling) with the lid closed for 10-15 minutes.
Cornmeal should be liberally applied to your work surface. Divide dough in half then rolls out into circles on top of cornmeal to a thickness of about 1/4 inch.
1 cup Pit Boss Sweet Heat BBQ sauce, equally distributed on each round of pizza dough. To each pizza, add 1/2 cup of cheese. Chop the pulled pork into small pieces and spread it on top of the cheese.
Apply a thin application of Pit Boss Prime Rib Rub to the pizzas. Using a pizza peel or the bottom surface of a sheet pan, transfer pies to the grill.
Cook the pizza for 25 minutes, rotating it every 5 minutes. Remove the pizza from the oven and set aside for 5 min before slicing. Sliced red onion & chopped cilantro go on top. Enjoy.

9.41 Baked Cinnamon Rolls

Total Time: 1 Hr. 20 mins, Serving: 8
Ingredients
Main
Active Dry Yeast, 1/2 Ounce (2 Packets)
Eggs, 1 Large
Cane Sugar, 1/3 Cup
Salt, 2 tsp
Flour, 5 Cup
Warm Water, 1 Cup
Warm Milk, 1 Cup
Butter, 1/2 Cup
Cinnamon, 2 tbsp
Brown Sugar, 1 Cup
Cream Cheese Icing
Butter, 1/2 Cup
Cream Cheese, 4 Ounce
Pinch of Salt
Vanilla, 1/2 Teaspoon
Powdered Sugar, 2 Cup
Milk, 1 tsp
Instructions
In a mixing basin or even the base of the stand mixer, combine the yeast, 1 teaspoon sugar, and warm water. To blend, stir everything together. Allow 5 minutes for the yeast to prove; it should begin to bubble, indicating that yeast is alive.
Over the yeast mixture, sprinkle the flour, salt, and the remaining 1/3 cup sugar. Stir for thirty seconds with a dough hook or maybe a wooden spoon. Combine the heated milk and the egg in a mixing bowl.
Knead the dough again on a medium-low setting or by hand on a floured surface until it is extremely soft, adding up with one additional cup of flour until it is soft to the touch and no longer sticky.
Cover the bowl with only a thin layer of oil, then place mixture dough in it, stirring to coat the dough uniformly. Allow 45 minutes to prove by covering the bowl with only a clean towel and placing it in a warm position in the kitchen. By this time, the dough will still have about doubled in size.
Mix the sugar, softened butter, & cinnamon in a small mixing dish.
On a floured work area, punch down all dough, then roll it out into a rectangle.
Cover the dough with cinnamon butter mixture and roll it up like a log.
Divide the dough into 2-inch-thick rolls. Cover rolls with a kitchen towel and place in a greased baking dish but rather cast-iron skillet. Allow the rolls to rise until they have doubled in size.
Once ready to cook, preheat the oven to 325°F with the lid covered for 15 minutes.
Put the baking dish and cast iron directly just on the grill grate & bake the rolls for about 20 minutes, until lightly browned.
In the stand mixer fitted with just a paddle attachment, combine cream cheese and butter. Combine all ingredients in a medium-sized mixing bowl and stir until well blended. Slow the amount too low and carefully drizzle in the powdered sugar. Mix in the vanilla, a bit of salt, and the milk until everything is well combined.
Whereas the rolls still are warm, remove them from the grill, then spread icing on top. Enjoy!

9.42 Baked Dutch Baby

Total Time: 30 mins, Serving: 6
Ingredients
Flour, 3/4 Cup
Eggs, 4
Egg Yolk, 1
Milk, 3/4 Cup
Sugar, 1 1/2 tbsp
Ground Nutmeg, 1/8 tsp
Vanilla Extract, 1 tsp
Butter, 4 tbsp
Fresh Fruit
Powdered Sugar
Instructions
Once ready to cook, preheat the Pit Boss at 500 degrees for

15 minutes with the lid closed.

Sift the eggs, sugar, milk, nutmeg, flour, & vanilla in a food processor or a conventional basin with a hand whisk. Blend until completely smooth.

Melt the butter in the hot Dutch oven. Add the butter to the pan as fast as the butter has melted (be careful not to burn it). Bake for 20 minutes on the Pit Boss until the pancakes are brown and puffy.

Reduce the temperature of the grill to 300 °F & bake for a further 5 minutes. Then, remove the pancake from the grill and slice it into wedges.

Serve immediately, adding preserves, syrup, powdered sugar, fresh fruit, or cinnamon sugar. Enjoy!

9.43 Baked Venison Casserole Tater Tot
Total Time: 50 mins, Serving: 4
Ingredients
Venison, 2 Pound
Tater Tots, 28 Ounce
Mushroom Soup cream, 2 Can
Peas, 2 Can
Instructions
In a big sauté pan using medium-high heat, brown venison. Remove any excess fat from the venison and leave it aside.

Combine the venison, peas, and soup in a 13x9-inch baking dish. Serve with tater tots on the side.

Preheat the Pit Boss to 350°F for 15 minutes with the lid closed when ready to cook.

Heat for 30 minutes by placing the casserole dish on the grill grate. Then, enjoy while it's still hot!

9.44 Baked Asparagus Pancetta Cheese Tart
Total Time: 50 mins, Serving: 8
Ingredients
Eggs, 4 Whole
Heavy Cream, 1 Cup
Sheet Puff Pastry, 1 Whole
Parmesan Cheese, 4 tbsp
Goat Cheese, 1/4 Cup
Thin Asparagus Spears, 8 Ounce
Pancetta, 8 Ounce
Chopped Chives, 1 tbsp
For serving Parmesan Cheese
For Serving Lemon Zest
Instructions
Once ready to cook, preheat the Pit Boss to 375°F with the lid covered for 15 minutes.

Put the puff pastry on such a half sheet tray, then cut a 1-inch border around the perimeter, being vigilant not to cut it all way through. Then Prick the puff pastry in the centre with a fork.

Put the sheet tray around the grill grate to bake for 20 minutes until the pastry is swelled up and begun to brown.

In a separate bowl, whisk together the cream, 3 eggs, cheeses, and chives while the pastry bakes. To thoroughly combine the ingredients, whisk them together.

Take each sheet tray from the grill and fill the puff pastry with the egg mixture. Next, arrange the asparagus spears onto the top of the beaten egg and top with the pancetta that has been cooked.

In a small dish, whisk the remaining egg and brush the egg wash over the pastry.

Cook for just another 15 minutes on the grill grate or until the egg batter is barely set.

Finish with shaved Parmesan, lemon zest, and additional chopped chives. Enjoy!

9.45 Baked Cast Iron Berry Cobbler
Total Time: 60 mins, Serving: 6
Ingredients
Berries, 4 Cup
Sugar, 12 tbsp
Orange Juice, Cup
Flour, 2/3 Cup
Baking Powder, 3/4 tsp
Pinch of Salt
Butter, 1/2 Cup
Sugar, 1 tbsp
Instructions
Once ready to cook, preheat the grill to 350°F (180°C) with the lid covered for 15 minutes.

Combine the berries, 4 tablespoons sugar, and orange juice in a 13.3-inch (25-cm) cast iron or even another baking pan.

Combine the flour, baking powder, and salt in a small mixing dish. Remove from the equation.

Cream the butter & granulated sugar together in a separate bowl. Mix in the egg plus vanilla essence until everything is well combined. Fold in flour mixture gradually.

Pour the batter over the berries, then sprinkle with raw sugar. Preheat the oven to 350°F and bake the cobbler for approximately 35-45 minutes. Allow it to cool somewhat before serving with whipped cream. Enjoy!

9.46 Baked Strawberry Shortbread
Total Time: 25 mins, Serving: 6
Ingredients
Grand Marnier, 2 tsp
Sugar, 5 tbsp
Fresh Strawberries, 1 Quart
Baking Powder, 1 tbsp
Flour, 2 Cup
Butter, 2 tbsp
Salt, 1/4 tsp
Ground Cinnamon, 1/4 tsp
Whipped Cream
Milk, 1/3 Cup
Vegetable Shortening, 2 tbsp
Instructions
Combine the strawberries and sugar to taste in a mixing dish (1 to 2 tablespoons is usually enough to sweeten the berries). If used, mix in the Grand Marnier, gently smashing a few berries to extract their juices. Cover and chill until ready to serve.

In a mixing basin, sift together the 2 cups flour, baking powder, sugar, salt, & cinnamon. Using a fork, pastry mixer, or knife, cut melted butter & shortening into dry ingredients till the mixture is compressed to pea-size clumps. In the middle, make a well and pour it into the milk. Stir until everything is well mixed. Do not overmix the ingredients.

Pour the shortcake mixture onto a lightly floured cutting board or countertop. To mix the dough, gently knead it. Cut rounds out from a biscuit cutter and an upended glass after patting it into 1/2" thick round. Place on a baking sheet that hasn't been buttered. Brush the melted butter over the tops of the shortcakes.

Adjust the timer to High and warm for 15 minutes with the lid covered when ready to cook.

Close the cover and place the pan with shortcakes just on the grill grate. Bake for 10 min, until the shortcakes are beautifully browned and have risen. Allow cooling somewhat before cutting in half with just a knife. Replace the tops of the shortcakes after dividing the strawberries between the bottom half. Finish with a dollop of sweetened whipped cream. Serve and have fun!

9.47 Banana Bacon Pancakes

Total Time: 25 mins, Serving: 6
Ingredients
Vanilla Extract, 1/2 tsp
Eggs, 1 Large
Buttermilk, 1 Cup
Flour, Cup
Butter, 2 tbsp
Sugar, 2 tbsp
Cornmeal, 2 tbsp
Baking Soda, 1/2 tsp
Baking Powder, 1 tsp
Cooked Bacon, 6 Slices
Salt, 1/2 tsp
Vegetable Oil
2 Bananas
Instructions
Once ready to cook, preheat the grill to 350 degrees Fahrenheit with the lid covered for 15 minutes.
Mix egg, buttermilk, and vanilla in a mixing basin. Whisk everything together well. In a separate bowl, whisk together the melted butter and the egg yolks.
Sift the flour, baking powder, sugar, baking soda, cornmeal, and salt in a separate large mixing basin. To combine the ingredients, whisk them together.
In the middle of dry mixture, make another and pour within wet ingredients.
Whisk the batter until it is reasonably smooth. If you over-mix the batter, the pancakes will become tough. Combine the bananas & crumbled bacon in a mixing bowl.
Using non-stick cooking spray, lightly coat the griddle. Place the griddle just on grill and heat it (about 5 minutes). 1/4 cup batter should be poured onto the griddle.
Heat the first side of the pancake until the bottom begins to appear bubbly, golden, & firm enough just to move.
Cook for another minute or so on the other side. Serve. Enjoy!

9.48 Baked Halibut Fish Sticks with Spicy Coleslaw

Total Time: 35 mins, Serving: 4
Ingredients
Black Pepper
Sour Cream, 1/2 Cup
Mayonnaise, 1/2 Cup
Salt, 1 tbsp
Sugar, 1 tbsp
Dill Seed, 2 tbsp
White Wine Vinegar, 2 tbsp
Sriracha, 2 tbsp
Peeled Carrot, 1 Large
Shredded Cabbage, 1
Dried dill, 1 tsp
Olive Oil
Halibut, 1 1/2 Pound
Dried parsley, 2 tbsp
Black Pepper, 1 tsp
Panko Breadcrumbs, 1 1/2 Cup
Large Eggs, 2
Flour, 1/2 Cup
Instructions
In a small bowl, mix mayonnaise, salt, pepper, sour cream, dill seed, sriracha, sugar, & vinegar.
Combine the cabbage & carrots in a medium mixing basin, then fold in mayonnaise mixture till the cabbage & carrots are evenly covered. Remove from the heat and set aside till ready to eat.
Set the temperature at High and warm for 15 minutes with the lid covered when ready to cook.
Preheat a dutch oven with just enough olive oil and cook fish inside the grill for approximately 10 minutes.
Rinse and pat dry all fish fillets. Fillets should be cut into 1" strips.
Combine the all-purpose flour, salt, and pepper in a mixing basin.
Separate the eggs and beat them in a separate dish.
Combine the parsley, panko, and dill in a third bowl.
Fish fillets should be dipped in flour first, then eggs, and finally panko.
Place the fish sticks in the oil and fry for 3 minutes, or till they reach a temperature of 140°F on the inside. Enjoy!

9.49 Salted Apple Cheesecake Galette

Total Time: 1 Hr., Serving: 6
Ingredients
Granulated Sugar, 1/3 Cup
Ground Cinnamon, 1/2 tsp
Apple Pie, 1 (21 Oz)
Cream Cheese, 8 Ounce
Corn-starch, 2 tbsp
Heavy cream, 2 tbsp
Large Egg, 1
Frozen Pie Crust, 1
Vanilla Extract, 1/2 tsp
Heavy Cream
Flour, 2 tsp
Caramel Sauce, 1/2 Cup
Turbinado Sugar, 2 tbsp
Coarse Sea Salt, 1/2 tsp
For Serving Ice Cream
Instructions
Preheat the oven to 350°F for 15 minutes with the lid closed when ready to cook.
Set aside the apple filling in a medium bowl with the cinnamon.
Mix cream cheese & sugar together in a mixer until frothy. Continue to mix in the egg, whipping cream, corn-starch & vanilla until smooth.
On a floured piece of parchment paper, roll out the pastry dough into a flat circle.
Put cream cheese filling just on the pie with a spatula, keeping a 2-inch (5.08cm) border around the edge. On top of cream cheese, sprinkle the apples and cinnamon.
Fold the crust over edge of the pie all the way around. Using heavy cream, brush the pie's edge, then sprinkle little turbinado sugar. 1/4 cup (60ml) salted caramel drizzled over the top
Place a Galette just on a grill, parchment paper still attached to the pie. Bake for 30 minutes, then check for doneness on the crust. If the apples aren't golden, bake for another 10 minutes on the grill or until the crust is beautifully browned and the apples are bubbling.
Remove off the grill and set aside to cool. Drizzle with the leftover caramel and, if preferred, a pinch of sea salt. Served with ice cream on the side. Enjoy!

9.50 Baked Green Bean Casserole with Pulled Pork

Total Time: 1 Hr. 15 mins, Serving: 6
Ingredients
Green Beans, 2 Pound
Kosher Salt
Olive oil, 2 tbsp
Cremini Mushrooms, 1 Pound
Butter, 6 tbsp
Fresh Thyme, 4 Sprig

Flour, 2 tbsp
Whole Milk, 1 1/4 Cup
Heavy Cream, 1 Cup
Garlic, 4 Clove
Parmesan Cheese, 1/2 Cup
Black Pepper
Leftover Pulled Pork, 1 Pound
Crispy Fried Onions, 3/4 Cup
Instructions
Preheat the Pit Boss to 375°F for 15 minutes with the lid closed when ready to cook.
Cook green beans in a big saucepan of boiling salted water, working in batches, until brilliant green and halfway tender, approximately 3 minutes each batch. Drain and set aside to cool. Trim the ends of the stems.
In a large skillet, heat 1 tablespoon of oil over medium-high heat. Cook, occasionally stirring, until half of the mushrooms are golden brown, approximately 2 minutes. Toss and cook for another 3 minutes, or until both sides are browned.
2 tbsp butter, 2 sprigs thyme, 2 tbsp butter Cook for another 4 minutes, turning periodically until the butter has browned and the mushrooms appear dark brown and soft. Transfer to a dish and season with salt. Repeat with the remaining salt, butter, and oil, as well as the mushrooms and thyme.
Inside a big saucepan over medium heat, melt the remaining 2 tablespoons of butter. Cook, whisking regularly until the roux is lightly browned and nutty smelling, approximately 4 minutes.
In a separate bowl, whisk together the milk and cream.
Increase the heat to medium-low and cook, frequently whisking, until the sauce is thick and boiling, approximately 5 minutes. Remove the pan from the heat and stir in the garlic and parmesan cheese. Salt & pepper to taste.
In a 2-quart baking dish, layer green beans, pulled pork, & mushrooms. Pour the sauce over the top.
Cover firmly with foil and bake for 25-30 minutes, or until sauce is bubbling. Uncover and bake for another 15-20 minutes, or until the top and sides of the dish are gently browned.
Sprinkle with fried onions & bake for another 3 minutes, until either onion becomes slightly darker and aromatic. Allow 10 minutes for the sauce to solidify before serving. Enjoy!

9.51 Baked Venison Meatloaf with Potato Puree
Total Time: 1 Hr. 20 mins, Serving: 8
Ingredients
Breadcrumbs, 1 Cup
Ground Pork, 1 Pound
Ground Venison, 2 Pound
Onion, 2 tbsp
Milk, 1 Cup
Salt, 3 tbsp
Ground Sage, 1/2 tsp
Thyme, 1/2 tbsp
Black Pepper, 1 tbsp
Chives, 1/2 tbsp
Minced parsley, 1/2 tbsp
Peeled Russet Potatoes, 1 1/2 Pound
Peeled Parsnips, 1 1/2 Pound
Heavy Cream, 3/4 Cup
Kosher Salt, 2 tbsp
Ground Black Pepper, 1/4 tsp
Butter, 1/4 Cup
Instructions
Preheat the Pit Boss to 325°F for 15 minutes with the lid closed when ready to cook.
In a large mixing bowl, thoroughly combine all meatloaf ingredients. Make it into a loaf and cook on the grill.
Cook for 1 hour & 15 minutes, then check its internal temperature; it should be 160 degrees Fahrenheit. Cook for another 15 minutes or until the desired temperature has been achieved.
Before slicing, remove the steak from the grill and let it rest for 10 minutes.
Prepare the potato puree while the meatloaf is cooking. Fill a big saucepan halfway with water and add the potatoes and parsnips. Bring to the boil and simmer for 10 to 15 minutes, or until fork-tender.
Return the potatoes and parsnips to the saucepan after draining. Mash in the salt, butter, and pepper. Season with salt to taste.
Serve the meatloaf with mashed potatoes. Enjoy!

9.52 Baked Cherry Pie
Total Time: 1 Hr. 45 mins, Serving: 8
Ingredients
Salt, 1 tsp
Sugar, 1 tbsp
Butter, 8 Ounce
Flour, 2 1/2 Cup
Beaten Egg, 1
Frozen Cherries, 5 Cup
Ice Water, 8 tbsp
Almond Flour, 3 tbsp
Granulated Sugar, 1 1/2 Cup
Instructions
Combine flour, sugar, and salt in a mixing bowl. Using a pastry cutter or just a food processor, cut in the butter a bit at a time. Add the water in small increments until dough forms, taking care not to overdo it.
Refrigerate the dough for at least 30 min after forming it into a disc.
Combine the cherries, granulated sugar, and almond flour in a saucepan. Bring to the boil, then reduce to low heat and simmer for 10 minutes. The liquid should start to evaporate and solidify into a syrup.
Remove the dough from the refrigerator and set it aside for 5 minutes to rest.
Roll out 1/2 of the dough into a circle big enough to fit the pie pan.
Prick it with a fork and place it on the pan. Place parchment paper over the top of the dough and a weight on top to keep it in place.
Preheat the Pit Boss to 350°F for 15 minutes with the lid closed when ready to cook.
Bake the pie crust for 10 minutes on the grill. Remove the parchment paper & weight and bake for another 5 minutes. Remove the pie from the Pit Boss and fill it with the filling.
Roll the remaining 1/2 dough disc into a circle, then cut into 1/2-inch strips to make the lattice pie top. Place 4 to 7 parallel pieces of pie dough over the pie filling, leaving approximately 1/2 inch to 34 inches between each strip. Every other strip should be folded back. Perpendicular towards the parallel lines lay 1 long strip of dough. Over the perpendicular strip, unfold the folded strips. Fold the parallel strips that run under the perpendicular strip over the perpendicular strip. Place a second perpendicular piece of dough on top of the first, leaving some space between them. Over the second strip, unfold all folded parallel strips. Continue weaving over top of the pie till the weave is complete. Trim extra dough from all sides of the pie.
Fold the rim of a shellback over the lattice strips, then fasten with a crimp. Egg washes the lattice, then sprinkle fine sugar on top.
Return the pie to the Pit Boss & bake for another 30 to 45 minutes, until the crust is light brown.
Allow cooling completely before cutting. Enjoy!

9.53 Baked Pretzel Bites & Beer Cheese Dip

Total Time: 55 mins, Serving: 8
Ingredients
Pretzel Dough
Dry Yeast, 1 Packet
Sugar, 1 tbsp
Warm Water, 1 1/2 Cup
Unsalted Melted Butter, 2 tsp
Flour, 4 1/2 Cup
Salt, 2 tbsp
Main
Kosher Salt
Water 1 tbsp with 1 Egg Yolk Beaten
Baking Soda, 2/3 Cup
Water, 10 Cup
Vegetable Oil
Beer Cheese
Cream Cheese, 8 Ounce
Cheddar Cheese, 1/2 Cup
Gruyere Cheese, 1/2 Cup
Bottle Beer, 1/2 Cup (12 Oz)
Onion Powder, 1/2 tsp
Kosher Salt, 1/2 tsp
Black Pepper, 1/4 tsp
Instructions
To make the pretzel dough, combine water, sugar, and salt in a stand mixer basin, then sprinkle dried yeast on top. Allow to rest for 4 - 5 minutes, or until the top begins to froth.
Add butter and flour to the bowl with the hook attachment, then mix on low until thoroughly mixed. Then, on medium speed, mix for approximately 5 minutes, or until the dough is creamy and pulling away from the sides.
Remove the dough from the bowl and coat it with veg oil spray. Return the dough to the bowl, cover it with a towel or plastic wrap, and let it rise until it doubles in size.
Bring 10 cups of water to boil, then add some baking soda as the dough rises. Divide the dough into four pieces and roll each into a rope when it is ready.
Each rope should be cut into 1-inch sections. Drop 15 pretzel bits at a time into boiling water for about 30 seconds. Using a slotted spoon, remove each one and put it on a parchment-lined sheet tray.
Once ready to cook, preheat the Pit Boss to 350°F with the lid covered for 15 minutes.
Egg washes the pretzel bits and season in Jacobsen Sea Salt. Bake pretzel bits for 20 mins on a sheet pan in the Pit Boss.
To make the cheese sauce, mix white cheddar, cream cheese, Gruyere cheese, onion powder, beer, salt, and pepper in a medium mixing bowl. Pour into a small cast-iron skillet.
Bake for 20 minutes, until the cheese, is melted and the top is golden brown, right upon this grill grate beside the pretzels.
Serve the beer sauce with the heated pretzel bits. Enjoy!

9.54 Baked German Pork Schnitzel with Grilled Lemons

Total Time: 40 min, Servings: 2
Ingredients
Garlic Powder, 1 tsp
Pinch of salt
Lemon, 2 Whole
Black Pepper
Pork Chops, 16 Ounce
2 Eggs
Paprika, 1 tsp
Flour, 1/2 Cup
Panko Breadcrumbs, 1 Cup
Instructions
Adjust the timer to High and warm for 15 minutes with the lid covered when ready to cook.
Place pork chops between two sheets of plastic wrap, one on top of the other. Using a meat mallet, pound them to a thickness of 1/4 to 1/8 inch. Season both sides with a liberal amount of salt and pepper.
In a bowl, combine the garlic powder & paprika. Whisk the eggs in a separate dish. Place the breadcrumbs in a third bowl.
One by one, coat pork cutlets in flour, brushing off any excess, and now in eggs, and last in breadcrumbs. Place the breaded pork fillets on a wire rack over just a baking sheet that has been gently greased.
Simmer for 15 min before flipping and baking for an additional 5 minutes. Place sliced lemons on the grill grate flesh face down as you uncover the grill to turn the pork.
Remove from the grill and top with grilled lemon slices. Enjoy!

9.55 Mini Sausage Rolls

Total Time: 40 Mins, Servings: 4
Ingredients
4 Egg Yolk, Beaten
Ground Sage
3/4 Cup Distilled White Vinegar
3/4 Cup Dry Mustard
1/2 Cup Honey
2 Pound Sausage, Uncooked
17 1/2 Ounce Frozen Puff Pastry
1 Small Onion, Diced Small
Instructions
Make the mustard: In a small mixing dish, mix the mustard and vinegar. To develop the tastes, seal with aluminium foil and let at room temperature overnight. Mix the honey & egg yolks to the mustard mixture in a small heavy pot. Cook, whisking continuously until the sauce has thickened, approximately 7 minutes. Allow cooling before refrigerating until ready to serve.
Put the sausage as well as onion in a wide mixing dish and stir well. Fold each sheet of frozen puff pastry - there must be two per box - into an 11 by 10-1/2" rectangle on a freshly floured work surface.
Cut each rectangle in three strips, each 3-¼ inches wide, using only a pizza cutter either knife. Wash your hand and form a

tube-like shape out of part of the sausage. Place one of several puff pastry strips in the middle.

Wrap the dough across the sausage and use a little beaten egg to seal the seams. Using the leftover sausage and puff pastry, repeat the process. Place all of the rolls on the work area, seam side down, and gently brush the tops with the egg. Cut the rolls into 1-1/2-inch-long pieces and place them on a parchment-lined rimmed baking sheet. Between each roll, leave approximately an inch. When cooked, preheat the grill to 350°F with the lid covered for 15 minutes.

Prepare the sausages for approximately 30 min, or until the dough is golden brown and the sausage gets cooked through. Serve with honey mustard on the side.

9.56 Baked Creamed Spinach

Total Time: 45 Mins, Servings: 4
Ingredients
Garlic, 2 Clove
Chopped Shallot, 1
Heavy Cream, 1 1/2 Cup
Butter, 2 tbsp
Red Pepper Flakes, 1 tsp
Black Pepper
Ground Nutmeg, 1 tsp
Panko Breadcrumbs, 1/2 Cup
Salt
Sour Cream, 3/4 Cup
Frozen Spinach, 2 (10 Oz) Package
Romano Cheese, 1/2 Cup
Parmesan Cheese, 1/2 Cup
Instructions

Melt butter inside a saucepan over medium heat and cook onion and garlic. Simmer for about 2 min. Cook for another 2 minutes after adding the chili flakes.

Bring the cream and nutmeg to a boil. Season with salt to taste.

Season with salt and pepper after adding the spinach and sour cream. Remove the pan from the heat and whisk in the cheeses.

Fill a baking dish halfway with the mixture and top the remaining panko.

Once ready to cook, preheat the grill to 375°F with the lid covered for 15 minutes.

Bake for 25-30 minutes, until the top, is golden and bubbling, straight on the grill grate. Enjoy!

9.57 Baked Pork Belly Mac and Cheese

Total Time: 3 Hrs. 30 mins, Serving: 6
Ingredients
Brown Sugar, 4 tbsp
Salt, 4 tbsp
Pork Belly, 3 Pound
Elbow Macaroni, 1 Pound
Black Pepper, 1/2 tsp
Butter, 3 tbsp
Olive oil, 1 tbsp
Garlic, 1 tbsp
Onion, 1/2 Whole
Whole Milk, 1 1/2 Cup
Flour, 3 tbsp
Cayenne Pepper, 1/4 tsp
Ground Nutmeg, 1/2 tsp
Shredded Cheddar, 3 Cup
Instructions

Pork Belly: Mix salt, sugar, & black pepper in a large mixing bowl. Coat pork belly evenly with the mixture. Allow resting in the fridge overnight, covered.

Set the thermostat to High and warm for 10 minutes with the lid covered when ready to cook.

Put the pork belly in a baking dish and broil the pan. Cook for 30 minutes on high, or until a little color has formed. Reduce the heat to 250°F and cook for another 1-2 hours, or until the pork belly becomes tender.

Allow the pork belly to cool to room temperature before serving. When cold enough yet to handle, wrap in plastic and refrigerate until completely cooled.

Bring a big saucepan of salted water on the stove for the macaroni and cheese. Cook until the noodles are soft. Drain and set aside. Over medium-high heat, boil another large saucepan. Combine the olive oil, butter, & onion in a mixing bowl. Cook until the vegetables are soft.

When the onion is soft, add the garlic and cook until fragrant. In a separate bowl, sift in the flour and mix to combine. Cook the roux until it smells like popcorn and becomes a golden-brown color.

Stir add the entire milk while whisking. Make sure any lumps are worked out. Simmer, occasionally stirring, until the mixture has thickened. Remove the pan from the heat and add the cheese, nutmeg, & cayenne pepper. Stir in the noodles until everything is well combined.

The pork belly should be cut into large pieces or slices and warmed thoroughly on the grill.

To serve, place the macaroni and cheese in a bowl, then top with the pork belly. Enjoy!

9.58 Caramelized Bourbon Baked Pears

Total Time: 40 Mins, Servings: 4
Ingredients
Butter, 2 tbsp
Salt, 1/2 tsp
Brown Sugar, 1/4 Cup
Ripe Pears, 3 Whole
Bourbon, 1/4 Cup
Vanilla Extract, 1 tsp
Instructions

Preheat the oven to 325°F with the lid covered for 15 minutes when ready to cook.

Pears should be peeled and cored. Place them in a baking dish that has been greased.

Mix the brown sugar, butter, bourbon, cinnamon, vanilla, and salt in a small bowl. Over the pears, pour the bourbon mixture. Put the baking dish on the grill grate, cover the lid, and bake the pears for 30-35 minutes, or until fork-tender.

Place the pears on a serving dish and drizzle the caramelized bourbon mixture over them.

Over vanilla ice cream, serve warm. Enjoy!

9.59 Ultimate BLT Salad

Total Time: 35 Mins, Servings: 4
Ingredients
Kosher Salt, 1 1/2 Teaspoon
Country Bread, 1 Loaf
Bacon Lardons, 8 Ounce
Butter, 3 tbsp
Chopped shallot, 1 tbsp
Black Pepper, 1/4 tsp
Heirloom Tomato, 4
Apple Cider Vinegar, 1/4 Cup
Black Pepper, 1/4 tsp
Mayonnaise, 3/4 Cup
Sugar, 1/8 tsp
Parmesan Cheese, 1/2 Cup
Romaine Lettuce Heart, 2
Buttermilk, 1/2 Cup

Instructions
When you're ready to cook, fire up the Pit Boss as per the manufacturer's directions. Preheat the oven to 375 ° F and bake for 15 minutes with the lid covered.
In a cast-iron pan, put bacon lardons (slab bacon sliced into matchsticks approximately 1/2-inch thickness by 1 inch long) immediately on the grill grate. Cook, stirring periodically, for 15-20 minutes, or until fat is reduced & lardons are crispy. Drain and discard the fat, and put aside the lardons.
Toss 1-inch pieces of French bread with melted butter before serving. Put it out on a baking tray and add salt and pepper. Cook for 10-15 minutes, or until the bread is crisp & lightly browned, directly on a grill grate.
Combine shallot & vinegar inside a small bowl and set aside for 5 minutes. To emulsify, whisk in the buttermilk. Mix in the parmesan cheese, mayonnaise, salt, sugar, and pepper. Remove from the equation.
Toss lettuce, bacon, tomatoes (cut into wedges), and croutons in a large mixing
basin. Toss in the dressing to coat.
Put on a serving dish and sprinkle with more grated parmesan cheese, if desired. Enjoy!

9.60 Beer-Braised Cabbage with Bacon
Total Time: 45Mins, Servings: 4
Ingredients
Apple, 1 Cup
Yellow Onion, 1 Cup
Bacon, 1/4 Pound
Salt to taste
Green Cabbage, 2 Pound
Beer, 12 Ounce
Black Pepper
Instructions
Once ready to cook, preheat the Pit Boss grill to 325 °F (160 degrees C) with the lid closed for 15 minutes.
Heat a big heavy saucepan or Dutch oven on medium heat on the stovetop. Cook until the bacon is crispy (about 5 mins). Transfer to a paper towel-lined plate.
Return the saucepan to a medium-low heat setting. Cook for 5 mins, or until golden brown, after adding the onion. Stir in the apple before adding the cabbage. Stir in a large amount of salt and a pinch of black pepper for 3 minutes.
Over medium-high heat, pour in the beer, then bring to a boil. Cover and transfer the pot to the Pit Boss right away.
Cook for 10 minutes at 325 °F (160 degrees C). Remove the cover and continue to simmer for another 10-15 minutes, or until the cabbage is soft and the fluid has evaporated.
Stir in the cabbage and the bacon that has been set aside. Enjoy!

9.61 Lynchburg Bacon
Total Time: 30 mins, Servings: 4
Ingredients
Flour, 3/4 Cup
Tennessee Whiskey, 1 Cup
Bacon of country style, 1 Pound
Poultry Rub and Pit Boss Pork, 1 tbsp
Ground Black Pepper, 1 tsp
Brown Sugar, 1/3 Cup
Instructions
Place the bacon pieces in a big resealable bag and separate them.
In a small bowl, combine the Pit Boss Pork and Poultry Rub and the whiskey (or apple juice). Drizzle whiskey over bacon pieces and massage the bag to cover them evenly.
Allow at least thirty minutes for preparation.
Mix all the flour, brown sugar, and black pepper on wax paper. Fill a separate resealable bag with the mixture.
Rinse the bacon and add a couple of slices at a time to the flour mixture.
Shake the bag to coat each piece evenly, then spread them out on a baking sheet in a single layer.
Set the Pit Boss to 375°F, then preheat for 15 minutes with the lid covered when you're ready to cook.
Bake the bacon for 20 to 25 minutes, or until golden brown and crisp. Enjoy!

9.62 Baked Cranberry Chicken
Total Time: 1 Hr. 15 min, Servings: 4
Ingredients
Black Pepper, 1/4 tsp
Butter, 4 tbsp
Chicken Breasts, 6 Whole
Salt, 1/2 tsp
Sliced Celery, 1/2 Cup
Onion, 1/2 Cup
Pit Boss Que Sauce BBQ, 1 Cup
(16 Oz) Cranberry Sauce, 1 Can
Instructions
Season the chicken with salt and pepper. In a large pan, melt butter and brown the chicken on both sides. Place the mixture in an oiled 9x13x2 baking sheet.
In the chicken & butter drippings, cook onions and celery until soft. Combine the cranberry with barbecue sauces in a mixing bowl. Cook for another 2-3 minutes after thoroughly mixing. Pour over the chicken in an equal layer.
Preheat the Pit Boss to 350°F for 15 minutes with the lid closed when ready to cook.
Bake for 1-1/2 hours at 350°F, uncovered, till the chicken juices flow clear. Every 15 min of baking time, spoon sauce over the chicken.
Place the chicken pieces on a serving dish and pour the sauce over them all. Enjoy!

9.63 Baked Tuna Noodle Casserole
Total Time: 1 Hr. 30 mins, Servings: 4
Ingredients
Ground Mustard, 1 Teaspoon
Whole Milk Yogurt, 2 Cup
Wheat Pasta, 1 Whole
Almond Milk, 1 Cup
Grated Colby & Monterey Jack Cheese, 1 Cup
Sliced Mushrooms, 1 Cup
Celery Salt, 1/2 tsp
Peas, 1 Cup
Tuna, 10 Ounce
Instructions
Over high heat, put a pot of water to a boil. Cook the pasta according to the package instructions. Drain the water and put it aside.
Combine yogurt, ground mustard, milk, & celery salt in a medium mixing basin. In a large mixing bowl, combine the mushrooms, tuna, peas, and cooked pasta. Half of the cheese should be folded in.
Fill an oiled 13" x 9" baking sheet halfway with the mixture and top with the remaining cheese.
Preheat the Pit Boss to 350°F for 15 minutes with the lid closed when ready to cook.
Cook for 45 minutes, or until warmed completely and cheese has melted, by placing casserole dish on grill grate. Enjoy!

9.64 Baked Macaroni & Cheese

Total Time: 1 Hr. 35 mins, Servings: 8
Ingredients
Paprika
Salt, 1 tbsp
Water, 5 Quart
Grated Cheddar Cheese, 1 1/2 Cup
Butter, 12 tbsp
Milk, 2 Cup
Dry mustard, 1 tsp
American Cheese, 2 Pound
Salt to taste
Black Pepper
Flour, 1/2 Cup
Breadcrumbs, 2 Cup
Elbow Macaroni, 2 Pound
Instructions
Inside a large stockpot on high heat, heat 5 quarts of water to boil. Take 1 teaspoon of salt to the mixture.
Toss in the macaroni and mix well. Cook for 2 minutes shorter than the package's suggested time. To prevent the spaghetti from sticking, stir it occasionally.
Drain well and place in a large bowl, and mix.
In a pot over medium heat, melt 8 tablespoons of butter. Whisk continuously as you slowly add the flour plus mustard. Continue whisking for another 2 minutes, taking care not to let the mixture brown. Finally, whisk in 1-1/2 cups milk in a steady stream till the batter is smooth.
Reduce heat to moderate and whisk in the Velveeta a quarter at a time until it is completely melted and integrated.
If the melty cheese is too thick, add additional milk. Season with salt to taste.
With just a spatula or a wooden spoon, carefully mix the cheese sauce into the pasta.
Butter a baking pan/casserole dish and evenly distribute the macaroni and cheese. On top, grate the cheddar cheese.
In a saucepan, melt the remaining butter. Stir in the breadcrumbs to coat them with butter. Dust the top of macaroni and cheese with paprika and equally distribute the breadcrumbs. Set the Pit Boss to 350°F and preheat for 15 minutes with the lid covered when you're ready to cook.
Bake for 45-60 mins, or until the mac and cheese are hot & bubbling as well as the breadcrumbs become golden brown. Halfway through the baking time, flip the pan 180°. Serve immediately. Enjoy!

9.65 Baked Cheesy Corn Pudding

Total Time: 35 mins, Servings: 6
Ingredients
Whole Kernel Corn, 15 1/4 Ounce
Butter, 3 tbsp
Cheddar Cheese, 1 Cup
Garlic, 3 Clove
Cream Cheese, 8 Ounce
Kosher Salt, 1 tbsp
Parmesan Cheese, 1 1/2 Cup
Breadcrumbs, 1/2 Cup
Black Pepper, 1/2 tbsp
Rosemary, 1 tbsp
Thyme, 1 tbsp
Instructions
Preheat the oven to 350 degrees Fahrenheit and cook for 15 minutes with the lid covered.
3 to 4 minutes over medium heat, cook the garlic with butter in a wide saucepan. Combine the cheddar cheese, cream cheese, 1 cup parmesan cheese, corn, and salt & pepper in a large mixing bowl. Put it into a baking dish once the cheese has melted.
Mix the leftover bread crumbs, 1/2 cup parmesan cheese, and fresh herbs in a separate dish. Over the cheese and corn, evenly distribute the bread crumb mixture.
Cook for 25 minutes, until the butter, is bubbling, in a baking dish on the grill. Warm the dish before serving. Enjoy!

9.66 Tin Foil Dinner

Total Time: 1 Hr. 10 mins, Servings: 4
Ingredients
Fish Sauce, 1 tsp
Worcestershire Sauce, 1 tbsp
Small Red Onion, 1
Pit Boss Veggie Rub, 1 tbsp
Garlic, 1 Clove
Green Bell Pepper, 2
Stew Meat, 1 Pound
Russet Potatoes, 2 Whole
Butter, 8 tbsp
Thyme, 4 Sprig
Salt & Pepper
Instructions
Once ready to cook, preheat the Pit Boss to 350°F with the lid covered for 15 minutes.
In a medium mixing bowl, place the stew meat. Combine the fish sauce with Worcestershire sauce in a large mixing bowl. Salt, pepper, & Pit Boss Veggie Rub to taste. Re-mix to ensure equal distribution.
4 pieces of foil, torn and spread out on every flat surface
Distribute the potatoes equally among the four pieces of foil, then add the bell pepper, potato, onion, garlic, and stew meat, finishing with thyme. 2 tablespoons butter on top of each packet
Fold the foil in half and firmly wrap it around the object.
Transfer the packets to a sheet pan and cook them. Simmer approximately 45 minutes to 1 hour, or till potatoes are soft & stew meat is cooked through.
Remove the package from the grill, open it, and sprinkle fresh basil if desired. Enjoy!

9.67 Cast Iron Potatoes

Total Time: 1 Hr. 10 mins, Servings: 4
Ingredients
Paprika
Potatoes, 2 1/2 Pound
Black Pepper
Salt to taste
Milk, 2 Cup
Jack Cheese, 1 1/2 Cup
Butter, 4 tbsp
Sweet Onion, 1/2
Instructions
In a cast-iron pan, butter the interior and arrange half of the sliced potatoes on the bottom. Half of the onions should be on top. Salt & pepper to taste.
1 cup of cheese and half of the butter should be sprinkled over potatoes and onions. On top, layer the leftover potatoes and onions. Dot the remaining butter on top.
Fill the skillet with milk. Aluminum foil should be firmly wrapped around the skillet.
Once ready to cook, preheat the Pit Boss to 350 degrees Fahrenheit with the lid covered for 15 minutes.
Heat for 60 minutes, or until potatoes are fork-tender.
Remove the paper and sprinkle the other 1/2 cup grated cheese over the top. Bake for another 30 minutes until the mozzarella is gently browned (uncovered). Serve immediately with a paprika dusting on top.

9.68 Baked Bacon Green Bean Casserole

Total Time: 1 Hr., Servings: 6
Ingredients
Worcestershire Sauce, 1/2 tsp
Crispy Fried Onions, 2/3 Cup
Mushroom Soup cream, 1 Cup
Green Beans, 1 1/2 Pound
Milk, 1/2 Cup
Black Pepper, 1/2 tsp
Red Bell Pepper, 1/4 Cup
Bacon, 8 Slices
Instructions
Mix beans, soup, black pepper, Worcestershire sauce, 2/3 cup onions, milk, 6 pieces crumbled bacon, and red bell pepper in a mixing dish. Fill a 1-1/2 quarts casserole dish halfway with the mixture.
Preheat the Pit Boss to 350°F for 15 minutes with the lid closed when ready to cook.
Cook for 35 to 40 minutes until the stuffing is heated and bubbling.
Sauté for 5 to 10 minutes longer, just until the onions turn crisp and starting to brown, on top of the leftover onions and the final 2 pieces of crumbled bacon. Serve and have fun!

9.69 Baked Bourbon Monkey Bread

Total Time: 1 Hr., Servings: 6
Ingredients
Butter, 1 Cup
Bourbon, tbsp
Sugar, 1 Cup
Buttermilk Biscuits, 3 Can
Brown Sugar, 1 Cup
Ground Cinnamon, 3 tsp
Instructions
Preheat the Pit Boss to 350°F for 15 minutes with the lid closed when ready to cook.
Each biscuit should be quartered. Combine sugar & cinnamon in a Ziploc bag, then add quartered biscuits. Toss in the cinnamon sugar to coat.
Dump the biscuit dough into such a Bundt pan that it has been sprayed with non-stick cooking spray.
Mix the butter, brown sugar, & bourbon in a small saucepan. Cook till the sugar is dissolved over medium heat.
And over biscuits inside the bundt pan, pour the butter mixture.
Cook for 40 minutes, until it's dark golden brown, in the middle of the grill.
Allow it cool for 5-10 minutes on the counter before turning out across a serving platter. Enjoy!

9.70 Smoked Baked Potato Soup

Total Time: 1 Hr. 15 mins, Servings: 6
Ingredients
Onion, 1 Small
Bacon, 12 Ounce
Russet Potatoes, 6 Large
Butter, 4 tbsp
Milk, 4 Cup
Flour, 1/4 Cup
Onion Powder, 1 tsp
Sour Cream, 1 Cup
Chicken Stock, 1 Can
Salt, 2 tsp
Garlic Powder, 1 tsp
Instructions
Preheat the Pit Boss to 375°F for 15 minutes with the lid closed when ready to cook.
Use a fork to poke holes in the potatoes and put them immediately on the grill grate. 1 hour of cooking Cook bacon on some kind of baking sheet for approximately 20 minutes simultaneously; remove, cool, and cut into 1/2" slices.
Remove the potatoes from the oven and leave to cool about 15 min. Peel potatoes well and chop them into 1" pieces. Remove from the equation.
In a big dutch oven, melt the butter. When the butter is melted and bubbling, add onion and cook until it is transparent about 5-7 minutes.
Cook for 1 minute with the flour in the butter and onion combination before gradually adding the milk & chicken stock, 1/2 cup at a time. Add the garlic powder, onion powder, and 2 tsp salt after the liquid has been absorbed.
Place the potato chunks in the soup and mash them with just potato masher until they're mostly mashed but still lumpy. Toss in the sour cream & 3/4 of bacon, saving a little amount for decoration.
Serve the soup hot, garnished with extra toppings. Enjoy!

9.71 Not Your Mama's Meatloaf

Total Time: 2 Hr. 15 mins, Servings: 6
Ingredients
Meatloaf
Milk, 1 Cup
Breadcrumbs, 1 Cup
Onion, 2 tbsp
Ground Sausage, 1/4 Pound
Ground Beef, 2 Pound
Salt, 2 tsp
Ground Sage, 1/2 tsp
2 Egg
Glaze
Apple Juice, 1/2 Cup
BBQ Sauce, 1 Cup
Instructions
Once ready to cook, preheat the Pit Boss to 225°F with the lid covered for 15 minutes. If Super Smoke is available, use it for the best taste.
Combine the breadcrumbs, milk, onion, sage, and salt in a mixing bowl. Toss in the beaten eggs. Mix in the ground meat and ground sausage well. Form the ingredients into a loaf, compressing it as firmly as possible.
Place the meatloaf on a wire rack on the grill to cook. Cook for 2 hours, or until an internal temperature of 160°F is reached.
To make the glaze, whisk together the Pit Boss' Que Sauce and the apple juice. During the final 20 minutes of cooking, glaze the meatloaf.
Allow 10 minutes for the meatloaf to rest before slicing. Enjoy!

9.72 Baked Breakfast Sausage Casserole

Total Time: 1 Hr. 15 mins, Servings: 8
Ingredients
Olive oil, 1 tbsp
Green Bell Peppers, 2 Medium
Yellow Onion, 1 Medium
Kosher Salt, 3 tsp
Thick-Cut Bacon, 1 Pound
Breakfast Sausage 1 Pound
Shredded Hash Browns, 2 Pound
Cheddar Cheese, 3 Cup
Eggs, 10 Large
Milk, 1/2 Cup
Black Pepper, 1 tsp
Instructions
Set the Pit Boss to 350°F & preheat for 15 minutes with the lid covered when you're ready to cook. Put a cast-iron pan about

one side of the grill and let it warm with the lid covered while the grill preheats.
1 tbsp olive oil Combine the chopped peppers, onion, & 1 teaspoon salt in a mixing bowl. Cook until soft, approximately 20 minutes, whisking every 5 - 8 minutes with the lid covered.
Place the bacon on a grill at the same time & cook until crispy, approximately 25 to 30 minutes. Bacon should be drained on paper towels before being chopped into bite-size pieces.
Remove the peppers & onions from the pan after they're done cooking & add the sausage. Sauté the sausage until it is crumbled and just cooked through, approximately 8 to 10 mins total, raising the grill cover to stir this every few minutes.
Mix the hash browns/tater tots, bacon, cooked sausage, onions, cooked peppers & salt, pepper, and 1-1/2 cup cheese in a large mixing dish. Mix well and pour into a 9x13-inch baking dish.
Whisk together 2 teaspoons salt, eggs, milk, & 1 tsp freshly ground black pepper in a separate basin. Allow 5 minutes for the eggs to soak into other ingredients after pouring the egg mixture equally over other ingredients in the baking dish. The remaining cheese should be sprinkled on top.
Wrap the dish in foil and place it on the grill. Remove the cover & bake for another 10 min, or when the mixture is set, the potatoes are browned, as well as the cheese is bubbling. Enjoy!

9.73 Baked Winter Squash Au Gratin
Total Time: 1 Hr., Servings: 8
Ingredients
Garlic, 4 Clove
Salt & Pepper
Heavy Cream, 2 Cup
Gruyere Cheese, 3 Cup
Yellow Potatoes, 3
Butter, 2 tbsp
Squash Seeded, 1 Acorn
Butternut Squash, 1
Instructions
Set the Pit Boss to 375°F and preheat for 15 minutes with the lid covered when you're ready to cook.
Cook the cream in a small saucepan, stirring continuously, till it reaches a low simmer. Season with salt, pepper, garlic, and shredded Gruyere. Stir until the cheese is completely melted.
Tbsp butter, greased a 9x13 inches baking sheet Combine potatoes, butternut, and acorn squash in a large mixing basin. Add the cheese sauce and mix well. Place the mixture in the baking dish that has been prepared and broil it.
Cook for 45 minutes, or till potatoes & squash is soft when pierced with a fork. Allow 10 minutes to cool before serving after removing from the grill. Enjoy!

9.74 Baked Queso Blanco Dip
Total Time: 40 mins, Servings: 6
Ingredients
Green Chiles, 2 Can
American Cheese, 1 Pound
Heavy Cream, 12 Ounce
Mozzarella Cheese, 1/2 Pound
Cumin, 1 tbsp
Chili Powder, 1 tsp
Pit Boss Chicken Rub, 1 tbsp
Red Pepper Flakes, 1/2 tsp
Cherry Tomatoes
Chopped Cilantro,
Tortilla Chips
Sliced Jalapeños
Instructions

When you're ready to cook, fire up the Pit Boss according to with manufacturer's directions. Preheat the grill to 450 degrees F for 10 to 15 minutes with the lid closed.
Over medium heat, bring cream to just a simmer. Slowly whisk in the cheese in stages, being careful to thoroughly integrate the first batch before moving on to the next.
Add the green chilies and spices after all of the cheese has melted. Taste and season to taste, adding extra Pit Boss Chicken Rub if necessary.
Fill a cast-iron skillet with the cheese mixture and put it immediately just on the grill grate. Cook, occasionally stirring, for 15-20 minutes, or until the cheese mix is bubbling.
If preferred, garnish fresh tomatoes, jalapenos, cilantro, and a pinch of chili powder. Serve with tortilla chips of your choice. Enjoy!

9.75 Baked Corned Beef Au Grautin

Total Time: 1 Hr, Servings: 6
Ingredients
Flour, 2 tbsp
Heavy Cream, 1 1/2 Cup
Butter, 2 tbsp
Whole Milk, 1/2 Cup
Kosher Salt, 1 tsp
Garlic, 4 Clove
Russet Potatoes, 3 Pound
Black Pepper
Corned Beef Brisket Flat, 1 Pound
Yellow Onion, 1 Medium
Instructions
When you're ready to cook, fire up the Pit Boss grill. Until the fire has been created, smoke with the lid open (5 minutes). Preheat the grill to 450 °F for 10 to 15 minutes with the lid closed.
In a 9-inch fry pan, smear melted butter all across the bottom. Whisk gently cream, flour, salt, minced garlic, milk, and freshly ground black pepper for taste in a separate basin.
In a pan, combine 1/3 of onions, potatoes, and corned beef. 1/3 of cream mixture should be poured over the potatoes. Repeat the process twice more, finishing with cream mixture.
Wrap in foil and bake for 30 minutes in the Pit Boss. Remove the foil and bake the potatoes for another 20 minutes, until lightly browned and bubbling.
Put some grated cheese on top of potatoes & bake for an additional 3 to 5 minutes, or until the cheese has melted. Enjoy!

9.76 Skillet S'Mores Dip with Candied Smoked Pecans
Total Time: 40 mins, Servings: 4
Ingredients
Candied Smoked Pecans
Salt, 1 tsp
Sugar, 1/2 Cup
Brown Sugar, 1/2 Cup
Ground Cinnamon, 1 tbsp

1 Egg
Wasser, 1 tsp
Cayenne Pepper, 1/4 tsp
Main
Marshmallows, 10 Large
For Serving Graham Crackers
Butter, 1 tbsp
Chocolate Chips, 2 Cup
Pecans, 1 Pound
Instructions
Set the Pit Boss to 300°F & preheat for 15 minutes with the lid covered when you're ready to cook.
To make the candied smoked pecans, whisk together the salt, sugars, cinnamon, and cayenne pepper in a small bowl. Mix thoroughly.
Stir together egg white & water in a medium mixing basin until foamy. It should take approximately 5 minutes to complete this task.
Place pecans in a large mixing bowl. Toss the pecans in the egg white mixture as well as the sugar mixture to coat them.
Place pecans straight on the grill grate after spreading them out on a parchment-lined sheet pan. Pecans should be smoked for 25 to 30 minutes, stirring often.
Allow cooling after removing from the grill. If required, break apart and cut coarsely. Remove from the equation.
Set the Pit Boss temperature to 400° & warm for 15 minutes, lid covered, for the S'mores Dip.
While the grill warms up, place a cast iron pan immediately on the grill grate.
Once the iron pan is heated, add the butter and allow it to melt fully. To coat the pan, swirl it around.
Toss in the chocolate chips after this top with marshmallows. Cook for 6 - 8 minutes, or until the marshmallows are gently toasted and the chocolate has melted. Remove the grill from the heat.
Garnish with graham crackers for dipping and a spoonful of candied pecans on top. Enjoy!

9.77 Baked Cheesy Accordion Potatoes

Total Time: 1 Hr 20 mins, Servings: 4
Ingredients
Baking Potato, 4 Large
Parmesan Cheese, 1/4 Pound
Butter, 4 tbsp
Pit Boss Veggie Rub, 1
Heavy Cream, 2 tbsp
Cheddar Cheese, 1/2 Cup
Minced Chives, 2 tbsp
Instructions
Peel the potatoes if preferred, or just clean them well for a vegetable brush.
Place a pencil and chopstick on each side of a potato lengthwise; they will act as cutting guides.
Chop each potato diagonally into thin slices with a sharp knife, taking care not to break all of the ways through the bottom. Your knife should be prevented from cutting too deeply by the pencils. Carry on with the leftover potatoes in the same manner.
Parmesan cheese should be cut into 2" broad pieces. Each slice should be cut into extremely thin slices.
Place the potatoes cut-side up in a baking dish. Drizzle the melted butter over them. Using the parmesan cheese thin slices, pierce each piece or every slice inside the potatoes. You'll become able to put fewer cheese slices in each potato if your slices are thicker.
Season with a liberal amount of Pit Boss Veggie Rub. Pour a little amount of cream through each potato for a little more richness.

Adjust the timer to High and warm for 15 minutes with the lid covered when ready to cook.
Place the baking pan on the grill and cover it with foil. Bake for 60 min or until potatoes is cooked.
Remove the foil and evenly sprinkle the cheese over the tops, then bake for another 5 minutes, just until the cheese melt & brown.
Potatoes should be garnished with chives and your preferred toppings. Enjoy!

9.78 New England Clambake

Total Time: 1 Hr, Servings: 4
Ingredients
Garlic, 4 Clove
2 Lemons
Red Onion, 2 Medium
4 Ears Corn
Tails, 4 Lobster
New Potatoes, 1/2 Pound
White Wine, 1 Cup
Clams, 1 Pound
Mussels, 1 Pound
Chorizo, 1 Pound
Bay Seasoning, 2 1/2 tbsp
Parsley, 1 Bunch
Kosher Sea Salt, 1 tsp
Chopped Tarragon, 1/2 Bunch
Lemon Wedges, 6 Whole
Butter, 8 Ounce
Instructions
Begin the Pit Boss, adjust the timer to 400 ° F (205 degrees C), and warm for 15 minutes with the top closed.
Place the onions, lemons, garlic, corn, chorizo (cut diagonally into 1-inch-thick slices), clams, potatoes, mussels, and lobster in a big cast iron saucepan in this order: onions, lemons, garlic, corn, chorizo (cut diagonally into 1-inch-thick slices), clams, potatoes, mussels, and lobster. Sprinkle with the old bay as well as a salt after pouring in the wine.
Place the saucepan immediately on the grill grate, covered. Cook approximately 15 min with the lid closed.
Reduce the heat to 300 degrees F (150 degrees C) and continue to simmer for another 10-15 minutes, until the potatoes are soft, the lobster is cooked through, and the mussels & clams have opened.
Using a fine-mesh strainer, drain the liquid into such a small sauce pan. Season to taste with salt and set aside.
Pour the mixture of the saucepan onto a big piece of parchment paper or butcher paper to serve. Pour the remaining cooking liquid over the clambake and top with parsley & tarragon.
Serve with melted butter ramekins and lemon wedges. Enjoy!

.79 Roasted Steak Fries with Homemade Ketchup

Total Time: 35 mins, Servings: 8
Ingredients
Garlic, 3 Clove
Olive Oil, 2 tbsp
Yellow Potatoes, 5 Large
Melted Butter, 1 tsp
Black Pepper, 1 tsp
Kosher Sea Salt, 2 tsp
Onion Powder, 1 tsp
Instructions
Thoroughly wash the potatoes. Toss the potatoes with olive oil, butter, smashed garlic, onion powder, salt, and pepper after cutting them into eighths.

When you're ready to cook, fire up the Pit Boss as per the manufacturer's directions. Preheat the oven to 500 degrees Fahrenheit with the lid covered for 15 minutes.

To create excellent grill markings, place the wedges on the hottest areas of the grill, which are usually the front and rear. To obtain markings on both sides, turn.

Bring them to the middle of the grill once they've been seared and cook for another 10 minutes. Serve immediately with a side of homemade ketchup. Enjoy!

9.80 Baked Ziti with Italian Sausage
Total Time: 50 mins, Servings: 6
Ingredients
Parmesan Cheese, 1/4 Cup
Spaghetti Sauce, 1 Jar
Salt & Pepper
Red Pepper Flakes, 1 Pinch
Mozzarella Cheese, 2 Cup
Italian Sausage, 1 Pound
Ziti, 1 Pound
Garlic, Minced, 1 tsp
Instructions
Set the thermostat to High (450F), then preheat the oven with the lid closed when ready to cook (15 minutes).

In a large mixing bowl, combine the cooked pasta, red pepper flakes, spaghetti sauce, garlic, salt, and black pepper to taste. Toss. In a large mixing bowl, combine the sausage, spaghetti, and cheese.

Using non-stick cooking spray, cover a 9 x 13 x 2 inches baking dish.

Put half of pasta mixture into the baking dish you've prepared. 1/2 of the mozzarella should be sprinkled on top. Fill the dish with the remaining pasta, level down the top, and top with the remaining mozzarella.

Cook for 20 minutes in a Pit Boss until the cheese is light brown and bubbling.

Remove from the oven and top with parmesan cheese. Enjoy!

9.81 Baked Bacon-Weaved Honey Bourbon-Glazed Meatloaf
Total Time: 1 Hr 15 mins, Servings: 6
Ingredients
Olive Oil
Celery, 1 Stalk
Mushrooms, 4 Ounce
Peeled Carrot, 1 Whole
Red Onion, 1/2
Grated Garlic, 2 Clove
Ground Beef, 3 Pound
1 Beaten Egg
Thyme Leaves, 4 Sprig
Worcestershire Sauce, 2 tsp
Cooked Bacon, 6 Slices
Heat BBQ Sauce and Pit Boss Sweet
Pepper, 1/2 tsp
Salt, 1 1/2 tsp
Condensed Tomato Soup, 1/2 Cup
Breadcrumbs, 1 Cup
Thin Bacon, 1 Pound
Instructions
Once ready to cook, preheat the Pit Boss to 225°F with the lid covered for 15 minutes. If Super Smoke is available, use it for the best taste.

In a bowl, combine carrots, celery, mushrooms, and onions, and sprinkle with olive oil. To soften the veggies, cover the bowl using plastic wrap, then microwave for approximately 2 minutes.

Allow veggies to cool before mixing them with ground beef, thyme, egg, Worcestershire sauce, breadcrumbs, bacon, salt, garlic, pepper, and tomato soup in a large mixing bowl.

Place the loaf on either a wire rack above a foil-lined baking tray.

Use the bacon to weave your bacon weave on a big piece of foil paper.

Flip the meatloaf over and place the weave over top of it, with the parchment on top. Remove the parchment paper from the pan.

Cook the meatloaf for 45 minutes on the grill. Take the meatloaf from the grill and raise the temperature to 325 degrees Fahrenheit. Allow Pit Boss to warm for 10 minutes with lid closed.

When the grill reaches temperature, return the meatloaf to it and cook for approximately an hour, or until an instant-read thermometer reads 160 degrees F.

Coat the meatloaf using barbecue sauce to caramelize during the final 15 minutes (after it gets about 140°F).

Before slicing, remove the steak from the grill and let it aside for 15 minutes. Enjoy.

9.82 Guinness Shepherd's Pie
Total Time: 1 Hr 45 mins, Servings: 4
Ingredients
Fresh Thyme, 1 tsp
Tomato Sauce, 1 1/2 Cup
Russet Potatoes, 6
Garlic, 4 Clove
Onion, 1
Ground Beef,
Cheddar Cheese, 1 1/2 Cup
Vegetables, 4 Cup
Guinness Stout, 1 Cup
Worcestershire Sauce, tbsp
Butter, Sticks
Salt & Pepper
Cup of Milk
Instructions
For the potatoes, bring a big saucepan of water to the stove. Allow this to heat while you prepare the meat combination.

Cook the onion and garlic in a large skillet. Cook until the meat or lamb is browned. The grease should be removed.

Toss in the veggies and tomato sauce. Cook, often stirring, for 4-5 minutes.

Toss in the Guinness, thyme, Worcestershire sauce, and season to taste with salt and pepper. Boil till the liquid has thickened and reduced by half (about 15 minutes).

Cook the potatoes for 15-20 minutes, or until tender but not mushy, in boiling water. Drain and set aside to cool. Using the milk, butter, and salt and black pepper to taste, mash the potatoes.

Split the meat mixture into two plates after the meat mixture has finished cooking and the potatoes have been mashed. The cheese is placed on top of the mashed potatoes.

Preheat the Pit Boss at 350 °F and cook for 10 minutes with the lid covered.
Bake for 30-45 minutes, or until cheese has melted and potatoes are golden brown. Serve immediately. Enjoy!

9.83 Baked Apple Turnover
Total Time: 60 mins, Servings: 4
Ingredients
Apples, 3
Butter, 3/4 Cup
Flour, 2 1/2 Cup
Cold Water, 6 tsp
Brown Sugar, 3 tbsp
Sugar, 3 tbsp
Milk
Salt, 1/4 tsp
Corn-starch, 1 1/2 tbsp
Ground Cinnamon, 1/4 tsp
Turbinado Sugar, 1 tbsp
Instructions
Incorporate the flour and butter in a large mixing basin till it resembles cornmeal, and add the water and stir to combine.
Cover the dough with plastic wrap and chill for 30 minutes once they've been mixed.
Peel, core, slice the apples while the dough is chilling, then mix them with the brown sugar, sugar, corn-starch, cinnamon, and salt.
Preheat the Pit Boss to 325°F for 15 minutes with the lid closed when ready to cook.
Roll out cold dough to 1/4" inch thick round with a lightly floured cutting board. In the middle, place the apple mixture. Fold the corners inward.
After that, brush the tart's top using milk and instead sprinkle this one with Turbinado sugar.
You may either move it to a parchment-lined sheet pan or place the paper straight on the grill.
Preheat the oven to 350°F and bake the pie for 25 minutes.
Serve with vanilla ice cream or whip cream. Enjoy!

9.84 Grilled Mussels with Lemon Butter
Total Time: 60 mins, Servings: 4
Ingredients
Mussels, 2 Pound
Water, 5 Quart
Salt, 1/3 Cup
Garlic, 2 Clove
White Wine, 1/3 Cup
Lemon Juice, 1 Whole
Chopped Parsley, 3 tbsp
Country Bread, 1 Loaf
Instructions
Begin the Pit Boss grill & change the heat to 375 °F
 when you're ready to cook (190 C). Close the cover and preheat for 10-15 minutes.
Scrub mussels well under running water to eliminate any debris and barnacles.
For approximately 15 minutes, soak clean mussels inside a big basin with 5-quart (5 L)
water + 1/3 cup (91 g) salt.
To purge & remove all sand, drain, rinse, and repeat the soaking procedure two more times.
In a frying pan over medium heat, melt the butter. Cook for 1 minute or until garlic is aromatic. Bring the wine to a low simmer. Toss the mussels with the lemon juice in the pan to coat.
Transfer on the grill and cover with a tight-fitting lid. Allow 8-10 minutes for the mussels to steam. Remove the mussels from the grill & discard those that haven't opened.
Serve immediately plate and top with chopped parsley. With sliced bread on the side. Enjoy!

9.85 BBQ Brisket Breakfast Tacos
Total Time: 40 mins, Servings: 6
Ingredients
Flour Tortillas
10 Eggs
Green Bell Pepper, 1
Olive Oil, 1/2 tsp
Yellow Bell Pepper, 1
Cheddar Cheese, 2 Cup
Beef Brisket, 4 Pound
Milk, 1/2 Cup
Salt & Pepper
Instructions
Begin the Pit Boss grill & adjust the heat to 375 °F when you're ready to cook. Preheat for 10 minutes with the lid closed.
Warm leftover beef in the grill with a second layer of foil.
Preheat the grill about 10 mins after coating the interior of just a cast iron pan with oil. When the pan is heated, add the diced peppers and cook, occasionally turning, until they are done to your liking.
Mix all the milk, eggs, salt, and pepper to taste while the peppers are cooking. Scramble the scrambled eggs in the skillet. When the eggs are nearly done, add the cheese to the skillet.
Remove the eggs and brisket from the grill. Serve eggs inside a tortilla with beef on top. If desired, top additional salsa or guacamole. Enjoy!

9.86 Sourdough Pizza
Total Time: 42 mins, Servings: 4
Ingredients
Flour, 1 1/4 Cup
Olive Oil, 1 tbsp
Sourdough Starter, 1 1/2 Cup
Kosher Sea Salt, 1 tsp
Instructions
When you're ready to cook, fire up the Pit Boss. Until a fire is created, smoke with the lid opened (4-5 minutes). Preheat oven to 450 °F and bake for 15 minutes with lid closed.
Combine the sourdough starter, Jacobsen salt, one tablespoon of oil, and 1-1/4 cup flour in a mixing bowl. To create a pizza dough consistency, add additional flour a bit at a time as required.
Let the dough settle for 30 minutes before spreading it out. To avoid sticking, roll out the dough into a circle with a little quantity of flour.
Place the pizza on such a pizza stone. Preheat the oven to 350°F and cook the crust for about 7 minutes.
Take the crust from grill and brush over any residual oil to keep the toppings from soaking in. Return the pizza to the grill and sprinkle with preferred toppings; bake till the crust is golden brown, and the cheese has melted.

9.87 Baked Brie
Total Time: 23 mins, Servings: 6
Ingredients
Sliced Apple
Honey, 1/3 Cup
Brie Wheel, 16 Ounce (16 Oz)
Crackers
Pecans, 1/4 Cup
Instructions

Once ready to cook, preheat the Pit Boss to 350°F for 15 minutes with the lid closed.
Using parchment or aluminium foil, line on rimmed baking sheet. Slice the brie's top—the white rind—off with a sharp serrated knife. (Leave the rind intact upon this sides and bottom.)
Drizzle the honey over the brie, cutting side up, just on prepared baking sheet. Add nuts to the top.
Bake for 8 to 10 minutes, or until the brie is soft & oozing but not melted. Allow cooling for a few minutes before transferring to a serving dish.
Served with crackers and apple wedges, cut. If desired, drizzle with additional honey. Enjoy!

9.88 Holiday Breakfast Strata
Total Time: 45 mins, Servings: 4
Ingredients
Cheddar Cheese, 1 Cup
Breakfast Sausage, 1 Pound
Bread, 6 Slices
Mustard, 1 tsp
Worcestershire Sauce, 1 tsp
Pepper, 1/4 tsp
Salt, 1/2 tsp
Half-&-Half, 3/4 Cup
Whole Milk, 1 1/2 Cup
Ground Nutmeg, 1 Pinch
4 Beaten Egg
Instructions
Begin the Pit Boss grill & change the temperature to 350 ° F when you're ready to cook. Preheat for 10 minutes with the lid closed.
Remove the crust of the bread and cut it into 3/4-inch-thick slices to fit in the base of a 9-by-13-inch baking pan. Drain any extra grease from the sausage after browning it.
Combine mustard and sausage in a mixing bowl. Spread the meat equally over the bread and top with cheese.
Pour remaining ingredients over cheese and sausage (eggs, half-&-half, salt, milk, nutmeg, pepper, & Worchester shire sauce).
Bake for 25 minutes on the Pit Boss. Warm the dish before serving. Enjoy!

9.89 Baked Cheesy Parmesan Grits
Total Time: 1 Hr 30 mins, Servings: 8
Ingredients
Chicken Stock, 4 Cup
Butter, 3 tbsp
Salt, 3/4 tsp
Quick Grits, 1 Cup
Cheddar Cheese, 1 Cup
Pepper
Monterey Jack Cheese, 1/2 Cup
Whole Milk, 1/2 Cup
Large Eggs, 2
Instructions
Once ready to cook, preheat the Pit Boss to 350°F for 15 minutes with the lid closed.
Butter an 8-inch baking dish or just a 10-inch cast-iron skillet.
In a medium saucepan, heat the butter, chicken stock, & salt to a boil. Whisk in the grits gradually.
Reduce heat to medium and simmer, often stirring, until the mixture thickens slightly approximately 8 minutes. Remove the pan from the heat.
Stir in the cheeses until they are completely melted. Season with salt and pepper to taste.
In a small bowl, whisk together the milk and eggs. Gradually incorporate the mixture into the grits.
Into the greased cast iron pan, pour the cheese grits. Bake for 1 hour or until grits is firm to the touch.
Remove the steaks from the grill and set them aside for 10 minutes before adding. Enjoy!

9.90 Double-Decker Pulled Pork Nachos with Smoked Cheese
Total Time: 60 mins, Servings: 4
Ingredients
Cilantro
Cheese, 8 Ounce
Jack Cheese, 8 Ounce
Jalapeño
Black Olives
Tortilla Chips
Pulled Pork, 2 Cup
Instructions
When you're ready to cook, fire up the Pit Boss & adjust the timer to 165 degrees Fahrenheit. Preheat for 10-15 minutes with the lid closed.
Place the frozen cheese on such a shelf on top of an ice-filled dish. To help the cheese smoke more rapidly, chop it into smaller pieces, maybe 2 to 4 chunks per block.
Allow 40 - 60 minutes for the cheeses to smoke before serving. Set aside the shredded cheeses (approximately 1 cup of each).
Preheat the Pit Boss to 350 degrees Fahrenheit with the lid covered for 10 minutes.
Place the tortilla chips on a wide baking sheet and equally distribute the shredded smoked cheeses. Cook for 10 mins, until the cheese melt and bubbling, on the Pit Boss barbecue grate.
Start assembling the double-decker nachos by removing the pan from Pit Boss. Build the nachos with a bottom layer of cheesy chips, a layer of pulled pork, and a top of cheesy chips on top. Add your favorite nacho toppings to finish it off. Warm the dish before serving.

9.91 Artichoke & Spinach Dip
Total Time: 1 Hr 20 mins, Servings: 6
Ingredients
Lemon Juice, 1 tsp
Garlic, 2 Clove
Artichokes, 6 Large
Olive Oil, 2 tbsp
Butter, 2 tbsp
Chopped Shallot, 1 Medium
Salt to taste
Frozen Spinach, 10 Ounce (10 Oz)
Cream Cheese, 8 Ounce
Paprika, 3/4 tsp
Salt, 1 tsp
Heavy Cream, 1 Cup
Parmesan Cheese, 1/4 Cup
Mozzarella Cheese, 1 Cup
Ground Black Pepper, 1/2 tsp
Instructions
Preheat the Pit Boss to 500 degrees Fahrenheit. Preheat for 10 minutes with the lid closed.
Each artichoke's stem & top third should be removed. Garlic should be stuffed in the centre and between several of the leaves. Spray with olive oil and season with salt and lemon juice.
Roast artichokes for 45 minutes directly just on the grill grate.
Remove artichokes from the grill after they've softened and cooked through. Reduce grill temp to 350 ° F. Allow the

artichokes to cool.

Extract the artichoke hearts next. Leaves should be peeled back and discarded. Scrape out the hairy top of the heart with a spoon and discard. The artichoke's heart will be the only thing left. Cut the meat into tiny pieces and set aside.

Using a clean dishtowel, preferably paper towels, squeeze out as much moisture as possible from the spinach.

In a large skillet over medium heat, melt butter and cook shallots until tender, about 3-5 minutes. Stir in the paprika and simmer for 30 seconds, or until fragrant.

Combine spinach, cream cheese, cream, artichoke hearts, salt, and pepper in a large mixing bowl. 8-10 minutes, occasionally stirring, until warmed through it and slightly reduced. Mix in the mozzarella and Parmesan cheeses, then transfer to an oven-safe baking dish.

Warm the baking dish on the grill until all of the mozzarellas have melted. Stir in additional grated parmesan cheese and serve.

Remove from the grill so if cooked and serve with sliced bread, crackers, or pita chips. Enjoy!

9.92 Pumpkin Chocolate Chip Cookies
Total Time: 20 mins, Servings: 8
Ingredients
Baking Powder, 1 tsp
Flour, 2 Cup
Salt, 1/2 tsp
Baking Soda, 1/2 tsp
Ground Nutmeg, 1/4 tsp
Ground Cinnamon, 1 tsp
Pumpkin Pie Spice, 1/2 tsp
Sugar, 1 Cup
Ground Ginger, 1/2 tsp
Butter, 1/2 Cup
1 Egg
Chocolate Chips, 2 Cup
Vanilla Extract, 1 tsp
Pumpkin, 1 Cup
Instructions
When you're ready to cook, fire up the Pit Boss as per the manufacturer's directions. Preheat the oven to 350 ° F and bake for 10 minutes with the lid covered.

Set aside a mixture of flour, baking soda, pumpkin spice, cinnamon, nutmeg, baking powder, salt, & ginger.

Beat the butter in a separate dish until light and fluffy. Mix in the sugar, pumpkin puree, egg, and vanilla extract.

Gradually mix all dry ingredients into wet components until they are completely combined. Fold in chocolate chunks gently.

Spoon dough onto a parchment-lined baking sheet in spoonfuls.

On the Pit Boss, bake for approximately 10 minutes or until the cookies are gently browned. Warm the dish before serving. Enjoy!

9.93 Bacon Weaved Stuffed Turkey Breast
Total Time: 1 Hr 20 mins, Servings: 8
Ingredients
Pit Boss Chicken Rub, 4 tbsp
Stuffing Mix, 14 Ounce
Celery, 1/2 Cup
Chopped Sage, 2 tbsp
Thick-Cut Bacon, 20 Strips
Apple Cider, 2 Cup
Dried Cranberries, 1/2 Cup
Instructions
To make the stuffing, combine all of the stuffing ingredients in a large mixing dish and toss to combine.

Make a bacon weave & arrange it on a cutting board in a 5x5 arrangement.

Butterfly each of the turkey breasts with a long, thin knife. Close each breast after filling it with a good quantity of stuffing.

Wrap the turkey breast in the prepared bacon weave and fasten it using toothpicks. Rep with the other breast.

Begin the Pit Boss grill & adjust the temperature at 375 °F when you're ready to cook. Preheat for 10 minutes with the lid covered.

Place the breasts on a baking tray, seam side down. Place immediately on the grill.

Place the bacon-wrapped turkey breasts on the Pit Boss and cook for 45 minutes to an hour, or till an instant-read thermometer inserted into the stuffing registers 165 degrees F. Cover the bacon with foil if it becomes too dark. Cut and savor!

9.94 Baked Pear, Bacon & Brown Butter Stuffing
Total Time: 1 Hr 20 mins, Servings: 6
Ingredients
Bacon, 1/2 Pound
Brioche Loaf, 1
Yellow Onion, 1
Peeled Ripe Pear, 4
Celery, 3 Stalk
Fresh Thyme, 1 tsp
Salt to taste
Garlic, 2 Clove
Rosemary Sprigs, 1
Large Egg, 4
Salt & Pepper
Chicken Broth, 1 3/4 Cup
Butter, 4 tbsp
Instructions
Preheat the oven to 225 degrees Fahrenheit and cook for 15 minutes with the lid covered.

Place the bread directly just on grill grate after spreading it out on a sheet pan. Bake for 30-45 minutes, or until the bread is toasty and dry. Place the bread in a large mixing basin.

Cook the bacon in inches pan over medium heat till the fat has drained out and that the bacon has gently browned. All except 1 tablespoon of bacon grease should be removed.

Season the celery, onions, and pears in the bacon skillet with salt. Cook for 8-10 minutes, or until the vegetables are tender and fragrant. Cook for another 1-2 minutes after adding the rosemary, thyme, and garlic.

Place the vegetable mixture in the same bowl as the bread.

In a large pan, melt the butter over medium-high heat until it foams up. Cook, constantly stirring with a heat-resistant spatula, until the mixture smells nutty well as the milk solids start to brown. Serve the veggies and bread with browned butter.

Preheat the grill at 350 degrees Fahrenheit with the lid covered for 15 minutes.

Combine the eggs plus chicken broth in a mixing dish with the other ingredients. Salt & pepper to taste. To avoid breaking the bread, gently toss in.

Cover with foil and transfer to a 2-quart casserole. Cook for 45 minutes, or until the casserole is cooked through and the top is gently browned, immediately on the grill grate. Enjoy!

9.95 Western Breakfast Casserole
Total Time: 55 mins, Servings: 8
Ingredients
Milk, 1 Cup
Whole Eggs, 6
Bread, 6 Slices

Ground Mustard, 3/4 tsp
Salt, 3/4 tsp
Chorizo, 6 Ounce
Black Pepper, 3/4 tsp
Ground Turkey, 6 Ounce
Onion, 1/2 Whole
Red Bell Pepper, 1/2 Whole
Cooked Bacon, 4 Slices
Anaheim Chile, 1/2 Whole
Baby Spinach, 1 Cup
Cheddar Cheese, 1 Cup
Cheese, 1 Cup
Swiss Cheese, 1 Cup
Instructions
Preheat the oven to 350 ° F and leave the lid covered for 15 minutes when ready to cook.
Using non-stick cooking spray, coat a 9" by 13" baking pan. Inside the bottom of the container, arrange the bread cubes inside a single layer. Set aside the ground mustard, eggs, salt, milk, & black pepper that have been whisked together.
Sauté the chorizo & ground turkey in a pan on the heat until fully done.
Sauté the onion & peppers in the pan until they are soft. Sauté for another minute with the garlic and fried bacon, then add the spinach and simmer until it wilts.
Half of the meat and vegetable combination, half of egg mixture, and half of cheeses are layered on top of the toast. Continue the layers once again until all ingredients are already utilized.
Cover & bake at 350°F for 35-40 minutes, or until well cooked, uncovering for the final 5-10 minutes to allow the cheese to golden slightly on top. Enjoy!

9.96 Baked Parker House Rolls
Total Time: 2 Hrs 15 mins, Servings: 8
Ingredients
Oil
Warm Water, 1 Cup
Dry Yeast, 1/2 Ounce
Salt, 2 tsp
Cane Sugar, 6 tbsp
Warm Milk, 1 Cup
Eggs
Sesame Seeds, 2 tbsp
Garlic Flakes, 1 tbsp
Flour, 5 Cup
Melted Butter, 4 tbsp
Sea Salt Flakes, 1 tbsp
Poppy Seeds, 2 tbsp
Instructions
In a mixing basin and the base of such a stand mixer, combine the yeast, two teaspoons of cane sugar, and warm water. Stir to mix. Allow 5 minutes for the yeast to prove; it should begin to bubble a little, indicating that yeast is alive.
Over the yeast mixture, sprinkle the flour, salt, and the remaining 6 tablespoons of sugar. And use a dough hook or a wooden spoon, whisk for 30 seconds. Combine the heated milk and the egg in a mixing bowl.
Knead the dough again on a medium-low setting or by hand on a floured surface until it is extremely soft, adding up to one additional cup of flour until it is nice and supple and no longer sticky.
Cover the bowl with just a thin layer of oil and put the dough in it, rotating to uniformly coat the dough with the oil. Allow 45 minutes to prove by covering the bowl with such a clean towel and placing it in a warm area in the kitchen. The dough will nearly double in size throughout this process.
Place the dough on a floured surface and punch it down. Cut the dough into half, then into 12 evenly sized for each half. Tuck the seams within each slice of dough in with your hands, then put the dough on a lightly floured board.
Put your fingers around at the piece of dough, then roll this in a circular pattern to form a smooth, even ball. Alternatively, roll the dough across your palms to form a spherical ball. Carry on with the rest 20 pieces in the same manner.
Using a tablespoon of melted butter, grease a 9x13" baking pan. Create rows of four pieces of dough through and 6 pieces of dough down in the pan by equally placing the dough balls. Let the dough rise for another 30 minutes in a warm place, covered with a clean cloth.
Set the Pit Boss to 325°F and warm for 15 minutes with the lid covered, whereas the dough is proving. Brush the bread with the remaining two tablespoons of butter and season with flake salt, seeds, and garlic flakes.
Prepared pan just on a grill, cover, and cook for 15 minutes, or until the rolls are golden brown on top and fully cooked. When the dough is baked and the bottom is gently browned, you must peel apart two pieces.
Allow 30 minutes for cooling before serving. The rolls may be prepared ahead of time and kept in a sealed jar, then warmed just before serving. Enjoy!

9.97 BBQ Chicken Baked Potato
Total Time: 1 Hr 10 mins, Servings: 4
Ingredients
Garlic, 2 Clove
Russet Potatoes, 4
Chicken Breasts, 2
Olive Oil, 2 tbsp
Salt & Pepper
Poultry Rub and Pit Boss Pork
Worcestershire Sauce, 2 tsp
Pit Boss Apricot Barbeque Sauce
Sour Cream
Butter
Chopped Chives
Cheese for serving
Instructions
Begin the Pit Boss & adjust the timer to 500 degrees F. Preheat for 10 minutes with the top covered.
Clean the potatoes and use a fork or a skewer to make numerous holes in them. Grill for 1 hour - 1 hour thirty minutes on the grill before they're tender.
Meanwhile, massage the chicken with minced garlic, drizzle with olive oil & Worcestershire sauce, and season with Pit Boss Pork and Poultry Rub.
Place the chicken on the grill after potatoes have now been cooking for approximately 30 minutes.
Allow the chicken to simmer for 20 minutes, or until an instant-read thermometer reads 165 degrees on the inside.
When the chicken is done, remove it from the pan and put it aside to allow the fluids to redistribute before slicing. Keep an eye just on potatoes and remove them when they're done.
Remove the chicken breasts from the pan. Add a liberal quantity of Pit Boss Apricot Barbecue Sauce to the mixture.
Slice open cooked potatoes and stuff them with your preferred toppings, seasoning generously with salt and black pepper.
To serve, garnish each potato with a mound of barbecue chicken as well as a sprinkling of chives. Enjoy!

9.98 Baked Sweet Potatoes
Total Time: 1 Hr 15 mins, Servings: 8
Ingredients
Sweet Potatoes, 8 Medium

Maple Syrup, 1/4 Cup
Butter, 1 Cup
Ground Cinnamon, 1/2 tsp
Instructions
To make the Maple-Cinnamon Butter, follow these steps: Whip the maple syrup, butter, & cinnamon together in a mixing basin using a wooden spoon. (Alternatively, you may use a hand mixer or just a stand mixer to combine the ingredients.) Place in a medium bowl, cover, then refrigerate until ready to serve.
Adjust the Pit Boss to 375°F when ready to cook, place the sweet potatoes here on the grill grate, and bake until tender, about 1 to 1-1/2 hours based on the size of potatoes. Cut a split throughout the middle of each one and fluff the ends with a gentle squeeze.
With the Maple-Cinnamon Butter, serve immediately. Enjoy!

9.99 Twice Baked Potatoes
Total Time: 1 Hr 25 mins, Servings: 8
Ingredients
Russet Potatoes, 8 Medium
For Garnish Chives
Minced Chives, 2 tbsp
Salt & Pepper
Hot Milk, 2 Cup
Cooked Bacon, 6 Strips
Cheddar Cheese, 2 Cup
Butter, 12 tbsp
Instructions
Set the Pit Boss to 450°F and preheat for 15 minutes with the lid covered when you're ready to cook.
Rinse the potatoes with cold water and dry them with paper towels. With a fork, poke numerous spots.
Place the potatoes straight upon this grill grate, then bake for 1 hour and 30 min, or until they are fully cooked.
Move the potatoes to something like a baking tray using oven mitts. Allow 10 minutes for the potatoes to cool somewhat.
Reduce the temperature of the grill to 375°F.
Cut the potatoes lengthwise in half and scoop out the meat into a dish, leaving a 1/4-inch shell.
Whip the potatoes for 30 seconds on low speed in a mixer. Add the boiling milk & melted butter in a slow, steady stream. Increase the rate to medium-high & whip for 1 1/2 to 2 minutes, just until the potatoes appear fluffy and smooth.
Combine the chives & bacon in a mixing bowl. Season to taste with salt and pepper.
Fill the hollowed-out mashed potatoes to the brim with whipped potato filling on even a large baking sheet. Using a liberal sprinkle of cheese, top each potato half.
Cook for 20 minutes at 375 degrees F, or until lightly golden and cheese has melted.
Remove off the grill and, if wanted, garnish with chives. Enjoy!

9.100 Glazed Ham
Total Time: 2 Hrs 15 mins, Servings: 8
Ingredients
Orange Juice, 2 Cup
Kurobuta Bone-In Ham, 1 Whole
Butter, 4 tbsp
Chicken Stock, 2 Cup
Ground Ginger, 1 tbsp
Ground Cloves, 1 tbsp
Orange Zest, 1 tbsp
Black Pepper, 1 tbsp
Kosher Sea Salt, 1 tbsp
Rosemary, 1 tbsp
Instructions
Preheat the oven to 350 degrees Fahrenheit when ready to cook (about 10-15 minutes).
Remove the ham from the fridge and blot it dry as you wait for the grill to heat up.
Combine orange juice & chicken stock in a stock pot.
Combine clove, melted butter, rosemary, orange zest, ginger, salt, and pepper in a separate small bowl. This will create a paste, which you should massage all over the ham.
Cover the ham and place it in the stock pot. Place the stock pot just on a grill when it's ready.
Simmer for 2 hours with the lid closed before checking. The interior temperature should be 145 degrees Fahrenheit.
If you want to obtain some nice color on the exterior of the ham, you may place it directly on the grill grates. Cut into slices and serve. Enjoy

9.101 Donut Bread Pudding
Total Time: 50 mins, Servings: 8
Ingredients
Sugar, 3/4 Cup
Raisins, 1/2 Cup
Cake Donuts, 16
Eggs
Vanilla Extract, 2 tsp
Heavy Cream, 2 Cup
Ice Cream
Butter, 3/4 Cup
Ground Cinnamon, 1 tsp
Instructions
Butter a 9-by-13-inch baking pan lightly. In the pan, layer the doughnuts in an equal layer. If used, scatter the raisins over the top. Drizzle the butter in an equal layer.
To make the custard, combine all of the ingredients in a mixing bowl and whisk. Whisk together the vanilla, sugar, cream, eggs, & cinnamon in a medium mixing basin. Add the butter and whisk to combine. Pour the glaze over the doughnuts. Allow it to rest for 10 minutes, pressing the donuts back into the custard as needed. Wrap foil around the dish.
Begin the Pit Boss to Smoke with lid open till the fire is created when you're ready to cook. Preheat the oven to 350°F and bake for about 15 minutes with the lid covered.
30–40 mins, until the mixture is set, bake the bread pudding. Remove the paper and bake for another 10 minutes, or until the top is gently browned.
Allow it cool for a few minutes before slicing into squares. If desired, drizzle with melting ice cream. Enjoy!

9.102 Baked Bacon Caramel Popcorn
Total Time: 50 mins, Servings: 6
Ingredients
Salt, 1/2 tsp
Popcorn Kernels, 1 Cup
Bacon, 1 Pound
Unsalted Butler, 2 Stick
Kentucky Bourbon, 1/4 Cup
Brown Sugar, 2 Cup
Vanilla, 2 tsp
Baking Soda, 11 tsp
Instructions
Set the Pit Boss to 350°F, then preheat for 15 minutes with the lid covered when you're ready to cook.
Cook for 20 minutes, or till the fat is reduced and bacon is gently browned, directly upon this grill grate. Remove the meat from the grill and cut it into 1/2-inch pieces. Remove from the equation.
Pop popcorn kernels in either a popcorn maker while the grill cools. Set aside popped kernels & bacon inside a large mixing

basin.

Combine butter, salt, and sugar in a medium saucepan. Bring the mixture to a boil, reduce to low heat, and continue to simmer until an instant-read thermometer registers 275°F. Remove from heat immediately and mix in the whiskey, vanilla, and baking powder. Even though it will rise to the surface & emit steam, proceed with care.

Reduce the heat to 225°F and then let the grill cool for 10 minutes.

Toss the bacon and popcorn in the caramel sauce to coat. Popcorn should be spread out on a big sheet pan lined with parchment paper.

Place the sheet tray straight upon that grill grate & cook for 15 minutes at 225°F, keeping an eye on it, so the caramel doesn't burn.

Remove the popcorn from the grill and place it on a parchment-lined counter. Allow it cool for thirty min or until the caramel has hardened. Enjoy!

9.103 The Dan Patrick Show pull-apart Pesto Bread

Total Time: 40 mins, Servings: 8
Ingredients
Butter, 1/2 Cup
Sourdough Baguette, 1
Blend Cheese, 1 1/2 Cup
Pesto Sauce, 1 Cup
Instructions

When you're ready to cook, fire up the Pit Boss grill. Until the fire has been created, smoke with the lid open (4-5 minutes). Preheat the oven to 350 °F and bake for 10-15 minutes with the lid covered.

Make 1" diagonal slices into the bread with a serrated knife, keeping the base crust intact. To create diamonds, turn the bread over and make diagonal slices in the other direction.

Put the bread on a wide piece of foil that will wrap around the whole loaf. Fill the gaps in the bread with melted butter. Put the pesto into crevices with a spoon, then push the cheese into each crack with a fork.

Wrap the loaf in foil and place it on a baking sheet by folding it up the edges. Put the baking sheet upon this grill grate immediately.

Bake for 15 minutes, then remove the foil and continue to bake for another 10 minutes. Remove the skewers from the grill & place them on a serving platter. Enjoy!

9.104 Smoked & Loaded Baked Potato

Total Time: 1 Hr 10 mins, Servings: 8
Ingredients
Sour Cream, 1 Cup
Bacon, 8 Slices
Russet Potatoes, 6
Melted Butter, 1/2 Cup
Thinly sliced Green Onions, 1 Bunch
Salt & Pepper
Cheddar Cheese, 1 1/2 Cup
Instructions

Set the Pit Boss to 375°F, then preheat for 15 minutes with the lid covered when you're ready to cook.

Potatoes should be poked with a fork before being placed directly on the grill. 1 hour of cooking

Cook bacon on something like a baking sheet, mostly on the grill, for approximately 20 minutes at the same time; remove, cool, and crumble.

Remove the potatoes from the oven and leave to cool approximately 15 min.

Cut each potato in half lengthwise to make long halves. To create a boat, scoop off approximately 70% of potato with a tiny spoon, leaving a thick coat of potatoes near the skin.

Place any leftover potato in a dish and set aside. The extra potato should be lightly mashed with just a fork; add the butter, sour cream, and 1/2 cup cheese; add salt and pepper. Fill the potato skins with the potato mixture, then top with more cheese and bacon.

Return to the grill for another 10 mins or until warmed through this, and cheese must have melted. Serve with additional sour cream and green onions as a garnish. Enjoy.

9.105 Baked Pumpkin Pie

Total Time: 60 mins, Servings: 6
Ingredients
Brown Sugar, 1/2 Cup
Pumpkin Puree, 15 Ounce
Cream Cheese, 4 Ounce
Pie Crust, 1 Frozen
Whipping Cream, 1/3 Cup
Eggs
Spice of Pumpkin Pie, 1 tsp
Instructions

Preheat the Pit Boss to 325°F for 15 minutes with the lid closed when ready to cook.

Combine cream cheese, sugar, puree, milk, and spice in a mixing bowl. Incorporate an egg into the mixture one at a time. Fill the pie shell halfway with the mixture.

Cook for 50 minutes, or until the sides are brown and the pie is hard around the edges with some movement in the centre. Allow cooling before adding the whipped cream. Serve and have fun!

9.106 Baked Wood-Fired Pizza

Total Time: 32 mins, Servings: 4
Ingredients
Pizza Dough
All-Purpose Flour, 2 Cup
Kosher Salt, 1 tsp
Active Dry Yeast, 2 1/2 tsp
Warm Water, 2/3 Cup
Granulated Sugar, 1/2 tsp
Oil, 1 tbsp
Main
Fine Cornmeal, 1/4 Cup
Grilled sliced Portobello Mushroom, 1 Large
Pickled Artichoke Hearts, 1 Jar
Fontina Cheese, 1 Cup
Parmigiano-Reggiano Cheese, 1/2 Cup
Minced Roasted Garlic
Olive Oil, 1/4 Cup
Banana Peppers
Instructions

Combine the heated yeast, water, and sugar in a glass basin. Allow to sit for 10 minutes or until the mixture begins to froth. Mix 1-3/4 cup sugar, flour, and salt in a mixer. In a mixing bowl, combine the yeast and the oil. Slowly drizzle the liquid into the dry ingredients as gradually raising the mixer's speed until everything is well mixed. It's important that the dough be smooth or just not sticky.

Make the dough on either a floured surface for 5 to 10 minutes, gradually adding the leftover flour required to keep the dough from sticking.

Make a ball out of the dough. In a large mixing bowl, drizzle a thin coating of olive oil. Cover this dough ball with just a little quantity of olive oil before placing it in the basin. Allow to rise for 60 minutes or till doubled in size in a warm area.

Set the Pit Boss to 450°F and heat for 15 minutes with the lid covered when you're ready to cook.
While the grill is heating up, put a pizza stone on it.
On a floured board, punch down the dough, then roll it into a 12-inch circle.
On the pizza peel, evenly spread the cornmeal. Arrange the toppings in the following sequence on the pizza peel: Parmigiano-Reggiano, fontina, roasted garlic, portobello, artichoke hearts, olive oil, and banana peppers.
Slide the constructed pizza from pizza peel to prepared pizza stone & bake for 10 to 12 minutes, just until the base is light brown. Enjoy.

9.107 Bacon Chili Cheese Dogs
Total Time: 55 mins, Servings: 2
Ingredients
Stewed Tomatoes, 1 Can
Onion, 1 Medium
Tomato Paste, 1 tbsp
Garlic, 2 Clove
Tomato Sauce, 1 Can
Ground Beef, 1 Pound
Chili Powder, 1 tsp
Bacon, 4 Slices
Cracked Black Pepper, 1/2 tsp
Smoked Paprika, 1/2 tsp
Cumin, 1 1/2 tsp
Ground Nutmeg, 1/8 tsp
Beef Hot Dogs, 4
Salt & Pepper
Worcestershire Sauce, 1 tsp
Thinly Sliced Jalapeño
Cheddar Cheese, 1/2 Cup
Butter
Hot Dog Buns, 4
Yellow Mustard, 2 tbsp
Sour Cream
Instructions
When you're ready to cook, fire up the Pit Boss as per the manufacturer's directions. Preheat the oven to 350 ° F and bake for 10-15 minutes with the lid covered.
Place the bacon inside a pot and simmer for approximately 20 minutes on the Pit Boss or when the fat has rendered. All except 1 tablespoon of the bacon fat should be poured away.
Cook, occasionally stirring, until the onions are transparent, approximately 5 minutes. Cook, breaking up the ground beef with a spoon & stirring periodically, till the beef is browned, approximately 10 minutes longer.
Bring to heat, then add tomato paste after draining most of the fat. Cook for a further 2-3 minutes, or until the color changes from brilliant red to rust.
Simmer for 15 minutes, or until thickened, with tomato sauce, stewed tomatoes, cumin, smoked paprika, black pepper, Worcestershire sauce, chili powder, nutmeg (optional), and mustard. If necessary, season with salt.
Add the hot dogs to the grill while the chili is cooking to produce some beautiful grill marks.
Remove the chili and dogs from the grill once they've finished cooking, and place the greased buns on top to toast gently.
Assemble your chili dogs, slathering each with bacon chili and topping them with cheddar cheese, sour cream, and jalapenos. Enjoy!

9.108 BBQ Pulled Pork Breakfast Burrito with Smoked Hot Sauce
Total Time: 2 Hrs 10 mins, Servings: 2
Ingredients
Olive Oil, 4 tbsp
Garlic, 1/2 Clove
Hot Peppers, 30
White Onion, 2
Black Pepper, 2 tsp
Salt, 6 tsp
Water, 2 Cup
Sugar, 4 tsp
Pulled Pork, 1 Cup
Sour Cream, 1/2 Cup
White Vinegar, 1/2 Cup
Eggs
Flour Tortillas, 2
Cheddar Cheese, 1/2 Cup
Salt & Pepper
Instructions
When you're ready to cook, fire up the Pit Boss according to the manufacturer's directions. Preheat the grill to 225 degrees F for 5 minutes with the lid closed.
Toss peppers, garlic, & onion (quartered) with olive oil, salt, and pepper (appropriate mix, stems & the desired number of seeds removed). Place on just a sheet tray and spread out. Smoke for 2 hours on a sheet tray straight on the grill grate.
Remove the steaks from grill and place them in a blender. Puree the water, sugar, and vinegar until smooth.
Fill a wide stock pot halfway with the ingredients and bring to boil over medium heat. Cook for around 30 minutes, or until the sauce has thickened.
To cool, move to a container and place in the refrigerator.
To make the burrito, follow these steps: Heat the pulled pork & put it in the tortilla's centre. Season scrambled eggs with salt and black pepper on a non-stick pan. On top of the pulled pork, scramble the eggs.
Cheese, sour cream, and smoked sauce go on top. Enjoy your burrito in a roll!

9.109 Pit Boss Baked Corn Dog Bites
Total Time: 50 mins, Servings: 6
Ingredients
Milk, 1 Cup
Dry Yeast, 4 tsp
Granulated Sugar, 1/4 Cup
Flour, 2 Cup
Yellow Cornmeal, 1/2 Cup
Baking Soda, 1 tsp
Mustard Powder, 1/2 tsp
Vegetable Oil, 1/4 Cup
Cayenne Pepper, 1/2 tsp
Kosher Salt, 1 tbsp
Beef Frankfurters, 15
1 Beaten Egg
Minced Garlic, 1 tsp
For Serving, Mustard & Ketchup
Instructions
In a mixing dish, combine the yeast, milk, and sugar. Put down for 5 minutes or until foam appears.
1 teaspoon salt, all-purpose flour, baking soda, cayenne pepper, corn meal, mustard powder, oil,
Mix with only a spoon until well mixed, then knead into such a dough with your hands.
Place dough in a bowl, cover with plastic wrap, and leave aside for 45 minutes, or until the dough has doubled in size.
Set the Pit Boss to 375°F and preheat for 15 minutes with the lid

covered when you're ready to cook.
Remove the dough from the bowl and cut it into 15 equal pieces.
To roll out, Use a rolling pin the piece of dough into 3" × 3" pieces on a floured work area.
Put a hot dog in the centre of the dough sheet. To create 15 tiny corn dog bites, roll this in the dough & seal the edges.
Brush corn dog pieces lightly with beaten egg and place on a baking sheet lined with parchment paper. Add the remaining salt and dry minced garlic to each mouthful.
Place sheet tray on grill grate & bake for 30 minutes, or until golden brown.
Serve with ketchup, mustard, or your favorite dipping sauce. Enjoy!

9.110 Baked Heirloom Tomato Tart
Total Time: 50 mins, Servings: 4
Ingredients
Puff Pastry, 1 Whole Sheet
Heirloom Tomatoes, 2 Pound
Kosher Salt, 1/2 tbsp
Ricotta Cheese, 1/2 Cup
Eggs
Salt & Pepper
Thyme Leaves, 1/2 tsp
Red Pepper Flakes, 1/2 tsp
Thyme, 4 Sprig
Instructions
Once ready to cook, preheat the grill to 350°F with the lid covered for 15 minutes.
Put the puffed pastry on such a parchment-lined sheet pan and cut it 34 percent of the way through, 12 inches from the edge.
Season the tomatoes with salt and pepper. Place on a paper towel-lined sheet tray.
Combine the ricotta, red pepper flakes, thyme leaves, 4 eggs, salt, and black pepper in a small mixing dish. Whisk everything together until it's smooth. Pour the ricotta mixture evenly over puff pastry, stopping 12" from the edge.
The final egg should be whisked into a small bowl. Brush the pastry's exposed edges with the egg wash.
Bake for 45 minutes, turning halfway through, with the sheet tray immediately on the grill grate.
Remove off the grill once the sides are brown and the liquid from tomatoes has gone and set aside to cool for 5-7 minutes before adding. Enjoy!

9.111 Pork Belly Bourbon Baked Beans
Total Time: 6 Hrs 15 mins, Servings: 8
Ingredients
Salt & Pepper, 2 tbsp
Apple Cider Vinegar, 1/2 Cup
Apple Juice, 2 Cup
Pork Belly, 3 Pound
Bourbon, 1/2 Cup
Brown Sugar, 3/4 Cup
Kidney Beans, 2 (16 Oz)
Pinto Beans, 3 (16 Oz)
Yellow Onion, 1/2 Cup
Yellow Mustard, 2 tbsp
Pit Boss 'Que Barbeque Sauce, 2 Cup
Instructions
Season the pork belly on both sides with Pit Boss Pork and Poultry Rub.
Set the Pit Boss to 180°F, then preheat for 15 minutes with the lid covered when you're ready to cook. If Super Smoke is available, use it for the best taste.
Put the prepared pork belly fat-side down upon that grill grate and cover the lid once the grill is smoking. 2 hours of smoking
Mix apple juice, apple cider vinegar, 1/2 cup brown sugar, and bourbon in a large Dutch oven. During 2 hours of smoking, remove the pork belly from grill and put it in the Dutch oven. Return to the grill, covering the Dutch oven with lid, and raise the temperature to about 275°F. Cook for another 2 hours, or when the pork is soft and readily shredded with a fork.
Remove any extra liquid from Dutch oven and put it aside. Remove any extra fat from the pork belly before shredding it. Combine the beans, BBQ sauce, mustard, 1/4 cup brown sugar, and 1/2 cup of the cooking liquid that has been set aside.
Bring to the grill and cover with the lid. Cook for another 2 hours. Usually like our beans thicker, but if you prefer a thinner sauce, feel free to add more BBQ sauce as needed. Serve with your favorite Barbeque food as a side dish. Enjoy!
We prefer our beans rich, but if you're after a thinner sauce, please add more BBQ sauce as needed. Serve with your favorite BBQ food as a side dish. Enjoy!

9.112 Baked Potatoes & Celery Root Au Gratin
Total Time: 1 Hr 30 mins, Servings: 2
Ingredients
Fresh Ground Black Pepper
Sliced Leeks, 2 Large
Butter, 5 Tablespoon
Kosher Salt
Shredded Gruyere 1 Cup
Celery Root, 2 Whole
Small Yukon Gold Potatoes, 5
Minced Sage, 1 tbsp
Cream, 2 Cup
Instructions
Preheat Pit Boss to 400°F for 15 minutes with lid closed when ready to cook.
1 tablespoon softened butter, melted in a 9x13 baking sheet. Melt the leftover butter in a medium pan over medium heat. Cook, often turning, for approximately 5 minutes, until the leeks are softened, adding a liberal sprinkle of salt and pepper.
Allow cooling after removing from the heat. In a large mixing basin, combine the potato & celery root pieces. 1 cup cheese, cream, leek mixture, chopped sage, 1 teaspoon of salt, and 1/2 teaspoon pepper. To coat, gently stir.
In the prepared pan, put a layer of potato & celery root slices that are slightly overlapping. Repeat the process two more times for a total of 3 levels of potatoes. Pour the extra cream from the bowl over gratin, then scatter the other cup of cheese over the top.
Cap the dish firmly using foil and bake for 45 minutes on the grill. Remove the cover and bake for another 30 to 45 minutes, or when the top is brown, and bubbling, as well as the potatoes, are soft when poked. Allow for a 10-minute rest period before serving. Enjoy!

9.113 Baked Sweet Potato Hash
Total Time: 50 mins, Servings: 4
Ingredients
Oyster Mushrooms, 8 Ounce
Olive Oil, 2 tbsp
Unpeeled Sweet Potatoes, 2 Medium
Pinch of Salt
Red Onion, 1/2 Large
Garlic, 1 Clove
Eggs
Thyme Leaves, 2 tsp
Smoked Paprika, 1/2 tsp

Chopped Herbs, 2 tbsp
Goat Cheese, 1/4 Cup
Ground Black Pepper
Instructions
Once ready to cook, preheat the Pit Boss to 450°F with the lid covered for 15 minutes.
Place a fairly big cast iron / grill-proof pan right on a grill grates to warm while heating up.
Once the grill is hot, add the oil, mushrooms, sweet potatoes, onions, and a large sprinkle of salt to the pan. Cook for 10 min, stirring once while cooking, after stirring to coat the veggies.
Combine the minced garlic, paprika, thyme leaves, and a sprinkle of black pepper in a mixing bowl. Cover the grill lid and cook for another 10 minutes, just until the potatoes are completely browned, or the onions are tender.
Make 5 pockets out of the vegetables and break one egg into each one. Cook for another 10 minutes on the grill grate or until the white is barely set.
Add chopped herbs, goat cheese, and paprika to the top. Enjoy!

9.114 Green Bean Casserole

Total Time: 30 mins, Servings: 6
Ingredients
Green Beans, 4 Can
Small Onion, 1
Butter, 1/2 Stick
Cheddar Cheese, 1 Cup
Sliced Mushrooms, 1/2 Cup
Pepper
Lawry's Salt, 1 tsp
Mushroom Soup Cream, 2 Can
Crispy Fried Onions, 1 Can
Instructions
Set the Pit Boss to 375°F, then preheat for 15 minutes with the lid covered when you're ready to cook.
In a cast-iron pan, melt the butter and cook the onions and mushrooms, turning periodically until tender.
Stir in the drained green beans & creme of mushroom soup until everything is well combined.
Sprinkle using seasoned salt and black pepper, then top with fried onions and shredded cheddar cheese.
Preheat oven to 350°F and bake for 30 min. Warm it up and enjoy it!

9.115 Gyros

Total Time: 1 Hr 15 mins, Servings: 6
Ingredients
Chopped Garlic, 3 Clove
Thinly sliced Onions, 1 Medium
Veal Or Ground Lamb, 1 Pound
Dried Oregano, 1 tbsp
Souvlaki Seasoning, 2 tbsp
Ground Beef, Pound
Marjoram, 1 tbsp
Pita Bread
Tzatziki Sauce
Cayenne Pepper, 1/4 tsp
Instructions
Using non-stick cooking spray, coat a loaf pan. Aluminum foil a brick or just a heavy container from the pantry; put the bread pan and the block aside.
Inside the mixing bowl, add the onion and garlic and pulse until finely chopped. Scrape into just a colander rather than a mesh strainer and press on the sediments for 15 minutes to drain. The blender bowl should not be washed.
Carefully transfer Souvlaki Rub, beef, lamb, marjoram, oregano, and cayenne to the food processor bowl. Return to the bowl with the drained onion-garlic combination and pulse until a paste form.
In the prepared loaf pan, press firmly. If preferred, cook the beef until it reaches this stage, now cover it using plastic wrap and refrigerate for a few hours or overnight.
Begin the Pit Boss grill, adjust the timer to 325F, and warm for 15 minutes with the lid closed.
In a water bath, simmer the gyro meat until it reaches 165 degrees Fahrenheit, about 70 to 75 minutes.
Take from water bath with care, drain & discard any excess fat and place on even a cooling rack.
To compress the meat, place the foil-covered block on top of it. Remove the meat first from the loaf pan after 15 minutes and slice thinly with just an electric blade or a keen serrated knife.
Build the gyros using the above-mentioned serving components, ending with tzatziki sauce.

9.116 Smoked Mushrooms

Total Time: 1 Hr 10 mins, Servings: 4
Ingredients
Blackened Saskatchewan Rub, 1 tsp
Apple Cider Vinegar, 1/2 Cup
Mushrooms, 1 Pound
Soy Sauce, 1/2 Cup
Instructions
Place the mushrooms in a big Ziploc bag after cleaning them. Rub in the apple cider vinegar and soy sauce.
Mix thoroughly and marinate for at least two hours in the refrigerator.
Begin the Pit Boss grill, adjust the timer to 350 degrees F, and warm for 15 minutes with the lid closed.
Warm up the cast iron skillet on the grill for 20 minutes.
Slowly pour in the mushrooms & marinade into a cast-iron skillet.
Cook for 15 minutes uncovered, then cover and cook for another 30 minutes, or until mushrooms are cooked.
Remove the pan from the grill and set it aside for Five minutes before adding. Enjoy!

9.117 Orange & Maple Baked Ham

Total Time: 2 Hrs 15 mins, Servings: 2
Ingredients
Dijon Mustard, 1/8 Cup
Maple Syrup, 1/3 Cup
Orange Juice, 2/3 Cup
Orange Marmalade, 1/3 Cup
Ground Cinnamon, 1/2 tsp
Apple Cider Vinegar, 1 1/3 tbsp
Ham, 2/3
Ground Cloves, 1/8 tsp
Instructions
Begin the Pit Boss grill, adjust the timer to 325 degrees F, and warm for 15 minutes with the lid closed.
Meanwhile, prepare the glaze: Combine the maple syrup, orange juice, mustard, marmalade, cinnamon, vinegar, and cloves in a small saucepan.
Heat over medium heat, constantly whisking to incorporate all of the ingredients. Removing the pan from the heat & set aside.
In a large roasting pan coated with aluminium foil, place the ham. Cook for about 1.5 hours on the grill using the pan.
Open the grill and brush the ham with the saved glaze. Cook for another 30 minutes, or until an internal temperature of 135 degrees F is reached when a thermometer is put into the thickest portion of the meat.

Before serving, remove the ham from the grill and let it rest for 20 minutes.
If preferred, reheat the leftover sauce & serve with ham. Enjoy!

9.118 Bacon Weave Mac n' Cheese

Total Time: 1 Hr 20 mins, Servings: 8
Ingredients
Mustard Powder, 1 tbsp
Butter, 3 tbsp
Elbow Macaroni, 1/2 Pound
Flour, 3 tbsp
Bacon, 15 Slices
Bay Leaf, 1 Whole
Milk, 3 Cup
Chipotle Chile Powder, 1/4 tsp
Smoked Paprika, 1/2 tsp
Cheddar Cheese, 8 Ounce
1 Egg
Pit Boss BBQ Sauce
Salt & Pepper
Instructions
Cook the pasta to al dente in a big saucepan of boiling, salted water, following the package instructions.
Melt the butter in a separate saucepan, whereas this pasta is cooking. Mix in the flour & mustard for approximately five minutes, scraping off any lumps as you go.
In a large mixing bowl, combine the milk, chipotle chili powder, bay leaf, and paprika. Discard the bay leaf after 10 minutes of simmering. Temper the egg by whisking a little amount of the heated milk mixture into eggs and then adding the eggs to the milk mixture. Season with salt and pepper and stir in the cheese.
In a 2-quart casserole dish coated with foil, mix the macaroni noodles into the mixture. Refrigerate for at least 4 hours to allow the flavors to meld.
Put the macaroni cheese upturned on such a large baking tray once it has been set up. Weave the bacon over the top, interlacing the pieces as much as possible.
Once ready to cook, preheat the Pit Boss to 350 degrees F for 10 minutes with the lid closed.
Put your macaroni and cheese just on the grill grate & smoke for 1/2 an hour before cooking for 1 hour at 350 degrees. During the final 10 minutes of cooking, brush with Pit Boss Regular BBQ Sauce. Enjoy!

9.119 Baked Sage & Sausage Stuffing
Total Time: 60 mins, Servings: 4
Ingredients
Herb Seasoned Stuffing, 14 Ounce
Butter
Onion, 1/2 Cup
Sage-flavored Sausage, 1 Pound
Sweetened Cranberries, 1/2 Cup
Celery, 1/2 Cup
Butter, 6 tbsp
Chicken Broth, 2 Cup
Instructions
In a big frying pan, brown the sausage, breaking it up with a wooden spoon.
Cook until the onion & celery are softened. Get rid of any extra fat. In a large mixing basin, combine all of the ingredients. If using, sprinkle the filling mix and cranberries.
Heat the chicken broth on low heat, then add the butter and stir until it melts. Toss in the bread/sausage mixture & toss gently to combine.
Using butter, grease a 3-quart casserole or baking sheet. The mixture should not be compressed, or it will become thick.
Preheat the Pit Boss to 350°F for 15 minutes with the lid closed when ready to cook.
Cover and bake the filling for 40 - 45 minutes, or uncover for the final 20 minutes if you want a crunchier texture.
Remove the steaks from the grill and serve. Enjoy!

9.120 Smoky Crab Dip
Total Time: 25 mins, Servings: 6
Ingredients
Mayonnaise, 1/3 Cup
Cayenne Pepper, 1/4 tsp
Sour Cream, 3 Ounce
Butter Crackers
Smoked Paprika, 1 tsp
Salt & Pepper
Lump Crab Meat, 1 1/2 Pound
Chopped Scallions
Instructions
Begin the Pit Boss and adjust the timer to 350 degrees F when you're ready to cook. Preheat for 15 minutes with the lid closed.
Meanwhile, carefully combine all of the ingredients in a large mixing bowl, except for the garnish scallions, crackers, and crab meat, until well mixed. Fold in crab meat gently but thoroughly, taking care not to split it up too much, though.
Season with salt and pepper to taste, then transfer to such an oven-safe baking tray.
Bake for 20 minutes, or until the top is bubbly and brown.
Serve warm toasted butter crackers and extra chopped scallions on top. Enjoy!

9.121 Baked Game Day Hatch Chile and Bacon Hot Dish
Total Time: 55 mins, Servings: 6
Ingredients
Unsalted Butter, 2 tbsp
Flour, 1/4 Cup
Chicken Soup cream, 2 Can
Whole Milk, 2 Cup
Onions, 2 Medium
Boneless, 1 Pound
Chopped Hatch Chiles, 1/2 Cup
Dried Thyme, 1/4 Teaspoon
Salt & Pepper
Chopped Smoked Bacon, 1 Cup
Frozen Tater Tots, 1 Pound
Instructions
Set the Pit Boss to 400°F & preheat for 15 minutes with the lid covered when you're ready to cook.
Melt the butter in a pan over medium heat, then whisk in the flour.
Dilute this chicken soup with the milk in a separate dish before pouring it into the pan. Continuously whisk the mixture until it thickens.

Combine the chicken, thyme, chiles, onions, salt, and pepper in a large mixing bowl. Allow for a 10- to 15-minute simmer, and when the chicken is thoroughly cooked.

Season with salt and pepper after folding in the smoky bacon. Fill a 2-1/2 quarts casserole dish halfway with the mixture. Toss the tater tots on top of the mixture.

Preheat oven to 350°F and bake for 30–35 minutes, or until golden brown. Serve immediately. Enjoy!

9.122 Steak Fries with Horseradish Creme

Total Time: 35 mins, Servings: 6
Ingredients
Garlic, 3 Clove
Olive Oil, 2 tbsp
Potatoes, 5
Butter, 1 tsp
Black Pepper, 1 tsp
Kosher Sea Salt, 2 tsp
Onion Powder, 1 tsp
Instructions
Toss the potatoes in the butter, olive oil, onion powder, smashed garlic, salt, and pepper after thoroughly washing them and cutting them into eighths.

Set the Pit Boss grill under smoke with the lid open until the fire is formed when you're ready to cook (4 to 5 minutes). Preheat the oven to 450 ° F (high) for 15 minutes with the lid closed.

To create excellent grill markings, match up the wedges at the front and the rear of the grill, then flip them to just get grill grates on both sides.

Move them to the middle of the grill once they've been seared and continue cooking for another ten minutes. Serving platter with horseradish mayo. Enjoy!

9.123 Strawberry Basil Daiquiri

Total Time: 25 mins, Servings: 2
Ingredients
Basil Leaves, 6
Granulated Sugar, 6 tbsp
Strawberries, 4
Lime Juice, 2 Ounce
Lime Slice, 2
White Rum, 3 Ounce
For Garnish Basil Leaves, 2
Pit Boss Smoked Syrup, 1 Ounce
Instructions
Set the Pit Boss to 375°F, then preheat for 15 minutes with the lid covered when you're ready to cook.

2 tablespoons of granulated sugar, cut strawberries in half Sauté for 20 minutes directly on the grill grate. Remove from the heat and set aside to cool.

In a shaking pan, gently mix 1 tablespoon granular sugar and basil leaves. Muddle in the strawberries once more.

In a mixing glass, combine the white rum, lime juice, & Pit Boss Smoke Simple Syrup. Ice should be added to the shaker.

Fill a chilled glass halfway with the ingredients and garnish with a big fresh basil leaf with sliced lime. Enjoy!

9.124 Tuscan Meatloaf

Total Time: 1 Hr 40 mins, Servings: 6
Ingredients
Onion, 1
Eggs
Red Bell Pepper, 1
Olive Oil, 2 tbsp
Minced Garlic, 3 Clove
Green Bell Pepper, 1
Parmesan Cheese, 1 Cup
Milk, 1/2 Cup
Italian Herbs, 1 tbsp
Italian Breadcrumbs, 2/3 Cup
Ground Black Pepper, 1 tbsp
Salt, 1 tsp
Ground Pork, 1 Pound
Marinara Sauce, 1 1/2 Cup
Ground Beef, 1 Pound
Italian Sausage, 1/2 Pound
Instructions
In a saucepan, cover 4 of the eggs with 1 inch of cold water and bring to a boil over medium-high heat for 6 minutes.

Transfer to a bowl of ice water. Peel, then set aside.

Meanwhile, in a frying pan, saute the onion and bell peppers in olive oil over medium heat until softened.

Add the garlic and cook for 1 to 2 minutes more, then let cool. Beat the remaining two eggs in a large mixing bowl. Add the herbs, milk, breadcrumbs, parmesan, and salt and pepper.

Add meats & half of the onion and pepper mixture. Combine with your hands, being carefully not to over-mix.

Roll the meat out into an 8/5-inch rectangle between the sheets of the wax paper. Allocate the outstanding onion/pepper mixture lengthwise down the centre of the meat.

Lay 3 to 4 of the hard-cooked eggs end to end on top of the onion/pepper mixture. Bring the sides of the meat rectangle up over the eggs and vegetables and pinch all the seams closed. Put seam-side down on a rimmed baking sheet or in a loaf pan.

When prepared to cook, start Pit Boss grill and set the temp to 350F. Preheat, lid closed, for 10-15 mins.

Bake the meatloaf for about 1 hour, or until an instant-read meat thermometer inserted in the middle of the loaf reads 165F.

If desired, pour the marinara sauce over the top of the meatloaf and bake for 10 to 15 minutes more. Let cool slightly before slicing and serving. This is also excellent when served cold.

9.125 Sweet Potato Marshmallow Casserole

Total Time: 1 Hr 10 mins, Servings: 6
Ingredients
Vanilla, 1 tsp
Unsalted Butter, 1/2 Cup
Sweet Potatoes, 5 Large
Brown Sugar, 1/2 Cup
Unsalted Butter, 1/4
Kosher Salt, 1 tsp
Mini Marshmallows, 1 Bag
Cracked Black Pepper, 1 tsp
Instructions
Preheat the oven to 375 degrees Fahrenheit and cook for 15 minutes with the lid covered.

Using a fork, pierce the yams' skin a few times. Place inside the Pit Boss on a baking sheet and otherwise foil pan and roast for 50 minutes, or until very tender.

Remove the yams from the grill and place them on a plate until they are cool enough to handle. While the potatoes are cooling, combine 1/2 cup melted butter, brown sugar, vanilla, salt, and pepper in a stiff whisk.

Sweet potatoes should have their skins removed and mashed until smooth. Transfer to something like a cast iron pan after folding in the butter mixture.

Cook for 15-20 minutes on the grill using cast iron. Remove from grill and top with the leftover 1/4 cup butter and marshmallows.

Return to the Pit Boss for another 15 minutes, or until the

marshmallows become golden. Enjoy!

9.126 Scalloped Potatoes with Bacon & Chipotle Cream

Total Time: 1 Hr 20 mins, Servings: 4
Ingredients
Mexican Cheese, 3 Cup
Whipping Cream, 2 Cup
Vegetable Oil
Russet Potatoes, 4 Large
Green Onion, 2
Salt & Pepper
Smoked Paprika
Bacon, 3 Slices
Bacon, 3 Strips
Chipotle Peppers, 7 Ounce
Instructions
When you're ready to cook, fire up the Pit Boss grill & adjust the timer to 350 degrees Fahrenheit. Preheat for 15 minutes with the lid closed.
Blend the adobo chiles inside a blender or small food processor till creamy paste forms. 2 tablespoons are set aside; the remainder will be used later.
To make the chipotle cream, follow these steps: In a medium saucepan on the stovetop, bring the cream to a boil. 1 tablespoon chipotle paste, whisked in, then taste. If you want a hotter taste profile, add more. If using, mix in the green onions.
To keep the potatoes from changing color, peel them and place them in cold water.
Grease a 10 to 12 inches cast iron skillet generously. Working by one potato at that same time, use the slicing disc of a mixing bowl, a mandolin (cutter), or even a sharp knife to slice it thinly.
Season the potato slices with salt and black pepper there at the bottom of the pan, now top with some chipotle cream and cheese. Continue layering the potatoes, chipotle cream, and cheese with the leftover potatoes till you have chipotle cream, 4–6 layers of potatoes, & cheese. Wrap foil around the dish.
Cook the potato for 30 mins in the pan on the grill grate. Then, to promote browning, remove the foil.
Simmer for yet another 30 mins, until the potatoes are golden brown and soft. Lay the bacon slices perpendicular to bars upon its grill grate at the same time.
Remove the bacon after 20 to 25 minutes, when it is gently browned and crisp. Allow cooling before crumbling and setting aside.
Place the scalloped potatoes on even a flat wire rack and set them aside to firm up for 15 to 20 minutes. If desired, sprinkle with crumbled bacon and smoked paprika. Enjoy!

9.127 Pit Bossed Lasagna

Total Time: 1 Hr 20 mins, Servings: 6
Ingredients
Red Onion, 1 Medium
Italian Sausage, 1 1/4 Pound
Lasagna Noodles, 9 Whole
Italian Ground Sausage, 3/4 Pound
Crushed Tomatoes, 2 Can
Garlic, 3 Clove
Chicken Stock, Cup
Tomato Paste, 2 Can
Basil, 2 tsp
Parsley, 7 tbsp
Kosher Sea Salt, 3/4 tsp
Fennel, 3/4 tsp
Parmesan Cheese, 10 tbsp
Whole Egg, 1
Ground Black Pepper, 1/4 tsp
Mozzarella Cheese, 4 Cup
Ricotta Cheese, 15 Ounce
Instructions
Drain the noodles after cooking them according to the package instructions.
Cook both types of sausage & onion at high temperature for 8-10 mins, or till meat isn't any longer pink and crumbles, on the stovetop. Garlic should be added. Cook for a further minute. Remove any extra grease and set aside.
Bring crushed tomatoes, chicken stock, tomato paste, 3 tablespoons parsley, fennel, basil, 1/2 teaspoon Jacobsen salt, & pepper to a boil in a separate saucepan. Reduce the temperature. Cook for 30 minutes, uncovered, stirring periodically.
Set aside a small bowl containing ricotta cheese, the egg, and leftover parsley and salt.
Preheat the Pit Boss to 375ºF for 15 minutes with the lid closed when ready to cook.
Using a little quantity of sausage grease, grease a cast iron pan. Start layering the Lasagna. Begin by putting around 1/3 cup tomato sauce on the table. 3-4 Lasagna noodles should be layered on top of the sauce. Half of the cooked sausage should be added first, followed by a third of the ricotta cheese mixture. 1 cup cheddar cheese plus 2 tsp parmesan cheese are sprinkled on top.
Cover and bake for 20-25 minutes on the Pit Boss, or until golden and bubbling. Allow 15 minutes to rest before serving. Enjoy!

9.128 Tarte Tatin

Total Time: 1 Hr 10 mins, Servings: 6
Ingredients
Cold Water, 5 tbsp
Butter, 1 Cup
Salt, 1 tsp
Unsalted Butter, 1/4 Cup
Granny Smith Apples, 10
Granulated Sugar, 3/4 Cup
Flour, 2 Cup
Instructions
Set the Pit Boss and adjust the timer to 350 degrees F. Preheat for 10 minutes with the top covered.
To make the crust: Pulse flour & salt inside a food processor to combine. Pulse in a little amount of butter at a time. When it resembles cornmeal, add water and stir until the dough comes together. Form a circle out of the dough, cover it with plastic wrap, and chill it.
Set a pie dish or a 12" round cake pans upon this grill while the dough cools; butter and sugar the pie dish. Allow it to caramelize.
Remove the sugar from the grill after it has caramelized and become a dark amber color. Cover the caramel with apple slices in a fan configuration.
Make a circle with the pie crust large enough just to fit the pan. Cover with a lid with pie dough after pricking it with a fork. Allow for shrinking while trimming the crust.
Place the apples just on the grill and cook for 55 minutes or until they are tender. Allow for 3 minutes of resting time. Put a plate over the pie and turn it over while the pan is still hot.
Warm, with ice cream rather than whipped cream on top. Enjoy!

9.129 Smoked Trout Hash

Total Time: 2 Hrs 30 mins, Servings: 4
Ingredients
Ice Water, 1 Quart
Water, 1 Quart
Lemon Zest, 1
Brown Sugar, 1/2 Cup
Black Peppercorn, 1 tbsp
Trout, 2 Pound
Red Beets, 1/2 Cup
Olive Oil, 1 tbsp
Bay Leaves, 4
New Potatoes, 1/2 Cup
Eggs
Green Onions, 2
Salt, 1 Cup
Instructions
Mix water, brown sugar, salt, bay leaves, lemon zest, and peppercorns in a medium saucepan. Bring to the boil over medium-high heat, constantly stirring, until the salt and sugar are completely dissolved. Turn off the heat and set aside for 15 minutes to steep. To cool, pour the mixture over cold water. When the mixture is cold to the touch, pour it over the fish, cover, and chill for 2 hours.
Remove the fish from the brine and discard it. Clean the fillets by rinsing them and patting them dry. To make the pellicle, spread them out on such a cooling rack & chill overnight. This makes it easier for the smoke to stick on the fillets.
When you're ready to cook, fire up the Pit Boss grill & set the temperature to 165 degrees Fahrenheit. Allow 10-15 minutes for the oven to preheat.
Smoke the fillets directly just on the grill grate for 1 1/2-2 hours, or until the fish starts to flake.
Preheat the oven to 375 degrees Fahrenheit for 10-15 minutes with the lid closed.
Inside a cast iron skillet, heat the oil over medium heat. Cook for 10 minutes or until beets is nearly soft.
Cook until both the beets and the potatoes are starting to color.
Cook until flakes, smoked fish and green onions are warmed through, approximately 4 minutes.
In the hash, make four wells and break 1 egg through each well.
Transfer the pan to the Pit Boss and cook for 5-6 minutes, or until the whites are set but the yolks are still runny. Enjoy!

9.130 Thanksgiving Sausage Leek Stuffing

Total Time: 50 mins, Servings: 8
Ingredients
Celery, 1 Cup
Butter, 1 Stick
Bread, 16 Cup
Onion, 2
Granny Smith Apples, 2
Kosher Salt, 1 tbsp
1 Leek
Flat Leaf Parsley, 2 tbsp
Italian Sausage, 1 Pound
Black Pepper, 1 tsp
Sweetened Cranberries, 1 Cup
Chicken Stock, 2 Cup
Instructions
Once ready to cook, preheat the oven to 300 degrees Fahrenheit with the lid covered for 15 minutes.
Bake the bread cubes for 7 minutes inside a single layer on something like a sheet pan. Transfer the bread chunks to a large mixing basin.

Raise the temperature of the Pit Boss to 350 degrees Fahrenheit.
Meanwhile, heat the butter in a large sauté pan. Add the onions, leeks, apples, celery, salt, parsley, and pepper. Sauté for approximately 10 minutes over medium heat or until the veggies are softened. Toss in with the bread cubes.
Cook the sausage in the same sauté pan over medium heat for 10 minutes, or until browned as well as cooked through, breaking it up with a fork as it cooks. Combine the bread cubes & veggies in a mixing bowl.
Mix inside the chicken stock or the cranberries or pecans, then pour into a 9 inches baking dish. Bake for 30 minutes, or until the top is browned and the centre is heated. Warm the dish before serving.

9.131 Baked Blueberry French Toast Casserole

Total Time: 8 Hrs, Servings: 8
Ingredients
Vanilla Extract, 1 tsp
Cream Cheese, 12 Ounce
Milk, 2 Cup
Beaten Eggs
Fresh Blueberries, 1 Cup
Powdered Sugar, 1/2 Cup
Maple Syrup, 1/2 Cup
Sour Cream, 1 Cup
Salt to taste
For Serving Maple Syrup
For Serving Whipped Cream
French Bread, 1
Instructions
Grease a 9x13-inch baking dish lightly. Half of the bread cubes should be placed in the dish.
Using a handheld mixer, mix the softened cream cheese, sour cream, and powdered sugar in a separate dish. Using a rubber spatula, evenly spread over the bread cubes.
Blueberries should be sprinkled over the cheese mixture, and the remaining bread pieces should be placed on top.
Combine the eggs, syrup, milk, vanilla extract, and salt in a large mixing basin. Pour the mixture over bread cubes.
Refrigerate overnight, covered with foil. 30 minutes before baking, extract the bread cube ingredients from the refrigerator.
Preheat Pit Boss to 350°F for 15 minutes with lid closed when ready to cook.
Bake for 30 minutes with the closed baking dish on the grill grate.
Remove the foil & cook for another 30 minutes, until the loaf is golden and firm in the middle.
If desired, top with syrup & whipped cream. Enjoy!

9.132 Game Day Cheese Dip

Total Time: 28 mins, Servings: 6
Ingredients
Swiss Cheese, 1 3/4 Cup

Fresh Horseradish, 2 tsp
Dijon Mustard, 2 tsp
Mayonnaise, 1/2 Cup
Cream Cheese, 8
Scallions, 3
Slices Bacon, 8
Instructions
When you're ready to cook, fire up the Pit Boss. Until a fire is created, smoke with the lid opened (4-5 minutes). Preheat oven to 400 °F and bake for 15 minutes with lid closed.
Mix cream cheese, dijon mustard, mayonnaise, swiss cheese (except for topping cheese), horseradish, scallions, and crumbled bacon in a mixing bowl.
Fill a deep small casserole/baking dish halfway with water. Add another 1/4 cup of swiss cheese to the top of the dip.
Put the casserole dish upon its Pit Boss grill grate, then cook for 15 to 18 minutes, or until brown and bubbling around the sides. Add sliced scallions on top. Enjoy!

9.133 Pit Boss Baked Protein Bars
Total Time: 40 mins, Servings: 6
Ingredients
Vanilla Protein Powder, 1 Scoop
Honey, 2 tbsp
Apricots, 1 Cup
Rolled Oats, 1 Cup
Vanilla Extract, 1 tsp
Frozen Cherries, 2 Cup
Instructions
Preheat the Pit Boss to 350°F for 15 minutes with the lid closed when ready to cook.
Add cherries, apricots (revived in boiling water for a few minutes then drained), honey, vanilla protein powder, & vanilla to the bowl of a food processor. Pulse approximately 10 to 20 times to break up the fruit and combine all of the ingredients.
Combine the oats and fruit combination in a separate bowl. Place the mixture in a loaf pan and silicone mold and broil it.
Preheat oven to 200°F and bake for 20–25 minutes.
Allow it to cool fully before slicing into 8 pieces. Enjoy!

9.134 Grilled Vegetables with Lemon Herb Vinaigrette
Total Time: 35 mins, Servings: 4
Ingredients
Lemon Juice, 2 tbsp
Dijon Mustard, 2 tbsp
Ground Black Pepper, 1/4 tsp
Kosher Salt, 1/2 tsp
Garlic, 1 Clove
Honey, 1 tsp
Red Wine Vinegar, 1/4 Cup
Chives, 1 tsp
Fresh Dill, 1 tsp
Baby Bell Peppers, 1 Whole Bag
Olive Oil, 1/2 Cup
Baby Squash, 2 Whole Packages
Baby Red Onions, 1 Whole Bag
Baby White Onions, 1 Whole Bag
Baby Carrots, 2 Bunch
Cherry Tomatoes, 1 Whole Carton
Snow Peas, 1 Pound
Baby Eggplant, 1 Whole
Black Pepper
Kosher Salt
Ears Fresh Corn, 1 Can
Instructions
Preheat the oven to high for 15 minutes once you're ready to cook. To preheat the grill, set your Pit Boss grill bag on it.
To make the Lemon Herb Vinaigrette, combine all of the ingredients in a mixing bowl and whisk until smooth. In a small mixing bowl, whisk together the red wine vinegar, garlic, honey, salt, dijon mustard, black pepper, dill, lemon juice, and chives.
While whisking, it gradually drizzles in the olive oil. Shake the dressing until it is emulsified in a sealable container. Remove the item from circulation.
Season with salt & black pepper after tossing the veggies in olive oil. Place all of the veggies in the Pit Boss Grill Basket, cover, and cook for 5 minutes.
Open the grill and toss the veggies around a little. Grill for another 5-10 minutes with the lid closed. Mix with Lime Herb Vinaigrette after removing from grill.
Let it chill in the fridge before serving hot, or chill and serve cold. Enjoy! *Cook times may vary based on the temperature of the oven and the surrounding environment.

9.135 Drunken Peach Cobbler
Total Time: 1 Hr 10 mins, Servings: 6
Ingredients
Brown Sugar, 1/2 Cup
Peeled Large Peaches, 6
Ground Cinnamon, 1/2 tsp
Bourbon, 1/8 Cup
Flour, 3 Cup
Corn-starch, 2 tbsp
Sugar, 4 tsp
Butter, 4 tbsp
Butter, 2 Stick
Vegetable Shortening, 4 tbsp
Milk
Cold Water, 5 tbsp
Salt, 1/2 tsp
Instructions
Melt the butter in a big pot.
Mix sugar, corn starch, and cinnamon in a separate basin.
Cook, stirring continuously until the peaches have thickened in the sugar mixture.
Remove from the fire and stir in the bourbon. Allow cooling after stirring.
To make the dough, combine all of the dry ingredients in a mixing bowl. Mix in the butter or shortening until the mixture resembles coarse grain.
Mix with a little amount of cold water. Refrigerate for at least 150 minutes after wrapping in plastic wrap.
Cut the dough in two once it has cooled, one slightly bigger than the other.
Make an 11-inch-diameter circle out of the larger piece. Use inches cast iron skillet to cook it in. Allow for a little excess around the edges of the dough.
Cut the leftover dough into 1-inch-wide ribbons by rolling it out into a big rectangle.
Fill the bottom dough with the peach mixture.
Make a lattice top dough one strip at one time. Pinch the excess bottom crust together to seal it. Milk should be brushed on the top.
Begin the Pit Boss, adjust the timer to 350°F, shut the lid, and warm for 10-15 minutes before grilling.
Bake for 35 to 40 minutes, or until peaches are bubbling and the crust is lightly browned. Enjoy!

9.136 Baked Artichoke Dip with Homemade Flatbread

Total Time: 50 mins, Servings: 8
Ingredients
Spinach, 10 Ounce
Artichoke Hearts, 14 Ounce
Pepper Jack Cheese, 1 Cup
Kosher Salt, 1/2 tsp
Parmesan Cheese, 1 1/2 Cup
Mayonnaise, 1 Cup
Cake Flour, 1 Cup
Extra-Virgin Olive Oil, 1 1/2 tbsp
Milk, 1/2 Cup
Baking Powder, 1/4 tsp
Instructions
Begin the Pit Boss grill & adjust the heat to 350 ° F when you're ready to cook. Preheat for 15 minutes with the lid closed.
To prepare the dip, combine the following ingredients in a mixing bowl. In a large mixing bowl, combine spinach, artichokes, parmesan, jack cheese, and mayonnaise.
Place the mixture in a cast-iron dish that has been greased and placed in the Pit Boss. Cook until the cheese has melted and the dip is well cooked.
To make the flatbread, combine 1/2 cup parmesan, salt, flour, and baking powder in a large mixing basin.
Stir in the milk & olive oil till a smooth dough form. On a floured surface, knead the dough until it becomes smooth and thus no stickier, applying flour as needed.
Form the dough into yet another rectangle and dust both sides with flour. Divide the dough into 12 equal rectangles using a pizza cutter.
Bake the dough for 23-28 minutes, or until golden brown, on a baking sheet under the grill.
Remove the bread from the grill and coat it with the artichoke dip. Enjoy!

9.137 Artichoke & Spinach Dip

Total Time: 1Hr 20 mins, Servings: 6
Ingredients
Olive Oil, 2 tbsp
Garlic, 2 Clove
Salt to taste
Frozen Spinach, 10 Ounce Package
Lemon Juice, 1 tsp
Chopped Shallot, 1 Medium
Artichokes
Butter, 2 tbsp
Cream Cheese, 8 Ounce
Paprika, 3/4 tsp
Salt, 1 tsp
Parmesan Cheese, 1/4 Cup
Heavy Cream, 1 Cup
Black Pepper, 1/2 tsp
Mozzarella Cheese, 1 Cup
Instructions
Preheat the Pit Boss to 500 degrees Fahrenheit. Preheat for 10 minutes with the lid closed.
Each artichoke's stem & top third should be removed. Garlic should be stuffed in the centre and between several of the leaves. Drizzle using olive oil and season with salt and lemon juice.
Roast artichokes for 45 minutes directly just on the grill grate.
Remove artichokes from grill after they've softened and cooked through. Reduce grill heat to 350 ° F. Allow the artichokes to cool.
Extract the artichoke hearts next. Leaves should be peeled back and discarded. Scrape out the hairy top of the heart with a spoon and discard. The artichoke's heart will be the only thing left. Cut the meat into tiny pieces and set aside.
Using a clean dishtowel, preferably paper towels, squeeze out as much moisture as possible from the spinach.
In a large skillet over medium heat, melt butter and cook shallots until tender, about 3-5 minutes. Stir in the paprika and simmer for 30 seconds, or until fragrant.
Combine artichoke hearts, cream cheese, spinach, cream, salt, and pepper in a large mixing bowl. 8-10 minutes, occasionally stirring, till warmed through it and slightly reduced. Mix in the mozzarella and Parmesan cheeses, then transfer to an oven-safe baking dish.
Warm the baking dish on the grill until all of the mozzarellas have melted. Stir in additional grated parmesan cheese and serve.
Remove from the grill once ready to eat and serve with sliced bread, crackers, or pita chips. Enjoy!

9.138 Baked Maple and Brown Sugar Bacon

Total Time: 1 Hr 10 mins, Servings: 4
Ingredients
Brown Sugar, 1/2 Cup
Cold Bacon, 1 Pound
Maple Syrup, 1/2 Cup
Instructions
Once ready to cook, preheat the Pit Boss to 300°F with the lid covered for 15 minutes.
Set a wire rack on top of a foil-lined rimmed baking sheet. On the wire rack, arrange the bacon strips inside a single layer.
Drizzle each strip of bacon with hot maple syrup on both sides with a pastry brush and then equally sprinkle brown sugar.
Place the baking sheet on the grill & cook the bacon for 60-120 minutes, or until it is crisp and browned.
Allow for some cooling time before consuming the bacon. Enjoy!

9.139 Baked S'Mores Donuts

Total Time: 40 mins, Servings: 8
Ingredients
Sugar, 1/3 Cup
Flour, 1 Cup
Baking Soda, 1/4 tsp
Powdered Sugar, 2 Cup
1 Egg
Buttermilk, 3/4 Cup
Butter, 2 tbsp
Marshmallows, 24
Whole Milk, 1/4 Cup
Vanilla Extract, 1 1/2 tsp
Chocolate Bars, 4
Instructions
Preheat the Pit Boss to 350°F for 15 minutes with the lid closed when ready to cook.
Coat the donut pans with non-stick frying spray.
In a large bowl, combine sugar, flour, & baking soda.
Buttermilk, egg, melted butter, and vanilla should all be whisked together in a separate dish.
With a spatula, mix the solid and liquid ingredients until just incorporated. Fill a piping bag halfway with the mixture.
Fill the oiled donut pans halfway with batter. Preheat oven to 350°F and bake for 25 minutes, or till donuts are puffy and a toothpick inserted in the centre comes out clean. Allow cooling completely in the pans.
In a medium saucepan, combine the milk and vanilla extract. Warm over medium heat until the desired temperature is reached.
Whisk the confectioners' sugar into the milk mixture until it is

completely mixed. Take the glaze off the heat and place it over a basin of warm water to cool.

Donuts should be dipped in glaze and put on such a cooling rack over a baking sheet or foil. Allow for a 5-minute rest period.

Donuts should be cut in half. To create a s'more sandwich, sandwich halved marshmallows and several bits of chocolate between both the two sides of a doughnut.

Grill the s'more sandwiches for 4–5 minutes, or until the marshmallows & chocolate have melted.

9.140 Baked Cherry Cobbler
Total Time: 40 mins, Servings: 8
Ingredients
Sugar, 51 tsp
Flour, 1 1/2 Cup
Salt, 3/4 tsp
Baking Powder, 1 1/2 tsp
Sour Cream, 1/2 Cup
Unsalted Butter, 8 tbsp
Frozen Cherries, 5 Cup
Corn-starch, 3 tbsp
1 Lemon Zest
Lemon Juice
Vanilla Extract, 1/2 tsp
Whipped Cream
Turbinado Sugar
Orange Zest, 1
Instructions
To make the topping, whisk together sugar, baking powder, flour, and salt in a medium mixing basin. Cut in the chilled butter with a pastry cutter with two knives till the consistency is reached peas and broken up crackers.

Stir in the sour cream until it barely mixes whole (be careful not to over mix or overwork the dough).

To make the filling, combine sugar, corn starch, & salt in a mixing bowl. Set aside the citrus zest, lemon juice, cherries, & vanilla.

Place the cherry filling inside a baking dish and top with the cobbler topping. Turbinado sugar should be sprinkled on top. When you're ready to cook, fire up the Pit Boss according to the manufacturer's directions. Preheat the oven to 350 °F and bake for 10 minutes with the lid covered.

Bake 35-45 minutes until the cobbler topping is gently colored and the cobbler is bubbling, directly mostly on the grill grate. The fluid should have thickened into a syrup-like consistency.

Serve with a dollop of whipped cream on top. Enjoy!

9.141 Sopapilla Cheesecake by Doug Scheiding
Total Time: 50 mins, Servings: 8
Ingredients
Cream Cheese, 24 Ounce
Butter, 2 tbsp
Vanilla, 2 tsp
Granulated Sugar, 2 Cup
Crescent Rolls Pillsbury Butter Flake, 2 Can
Cinnamon
Butter, 1/2 Cup
Instructions
Set aside a 9x13" baking dish that has been coated with 2 tablespoons melted butter.

Set the Pit Boss to 350°F, then preheat for 15 minutes with the lid covered when you're ready to cook.

Mix heavy cream, 1 - 1-1/2 cups sugar, and vanilla in a mixer. With the paddle attachment, mix for 60 - 90 seconds on high.

Remove the crescents from the refrigerator. One can be opened and placed in a greased 9x13 inch rectangle metal pan or a glass dish. Make sure the spaces on the lower side of crescents are filled up.

To make the mozzarella mixture level, place it on top of the crescent layer with a spatula.

Open the second crescent can and place it on top of a cream cheese layer, filling up the gaps in crescents to cover the centre.

Pour 1/2 cup melted butter on top of the last crescent layer. Begin with the sides, then the centre.

After that, coat the whole pan with 1/4 cup - 1/2 cup sugar and a light, even sprinkling of cinnamon.

Place the pan directly on the grill grate & bake for 30 to 35 minutes, or until the top is golden brown and crusty.

Remove off the grill and set aside for 10 minutes to cool. This enables the cheesecake to firm, making it easier to divide. This dessert is delicious hot or cold. Enjoy!

9.142 Braised Collard Greens & Bacon
Total Time: 2 Hrs 15 mins, Servings: 4
Ingredients
Smoked Ham, 3/4 Pound
Chopped Sweet Onions, 2 Medium
Chopped Smoked Bacon, 12 Slices
Garlic, 6 Clove
Collard Greens, 3 Pound
Apple Cider Vinegar, 1/3 Cup
Sugar, 1 tbsp
Pepper, 3/4 tsp
Salt, 1 tsp
Chicken Broth, 3 Container
Instructions
Once ready to cook, preheat the Pit Boss to 165°F with the lid covered for 15 minutes. If Super Smoke is available, use it for the best taste.

For 10 minutes, smoke the collard greens. Remove the collard greens off the grill and raise the heat to 375°F.

Preheat the grill for 15 minutes with the Dutch oven on it.

Cook bacon until nearly crisp in a hot Dutch oven. Add the onions and cook for another 8 minutes. Sauté for another minute with the ham and garlic.

In a large mixing bowl, combine the collard greens, broth, and the other ingredients. Cook for 2-1/2 hrs, or till desired tenderness has been achieved.

Enjoy while it's still hot!

9.143 Baked Bread Pudding by Doug Scheiding
Total Time: 1 Hr 25 mins, Servings: 8
Ingredients
Vanilla, 2 1/2 tbsp
Sugar, 3 Cup
Heavy Cream, 2 Cup
Eggs
Bread, 6 Cup
Water, 1/2 Cup
Light Brown Sugar, 1/2 Cup
White Chocolate, 12 Ounce
Butter
Coarsely Chopped Pecans, 1 Cup
Cinnamon
Pinch of Salt
Bourbon, 5 tbsp
Butter, 3/4 Cup
Instructions
Combine 1 1/2 cups (200 ml) whipping cream, 2 cups sugar (200 g), 6 eggs, 2 1/2 teaspoons vanilla, and 1/2 cup (50 ml) water in a large mixing basin. Toss in the bread (dry, cut in 1/2-inch (2 cm) cubes).

In a small saucepan, mix white chocolate and half a cup (250 ml) heavy whipping cream and heat till chocolate is melted. Allow it to cool somewhat before pouring over the bread mixture. Toss to mix, taking care not to over-break the bread. Allow 30 minutes for the ingredients to rest before pouring into a generously greased 4 - 5 quarts dutch oven. Any leftover liquid should be poured on top of the bread mixture.

Combine butter, brown sugar, and pecans in a small bowl. Sprinkle nuts on top of the bread mixture, then a thin sprinkling of cinnamon.

Begin the Pit Boss grill & change the heat to 325 degrees F when you're ready to cook (160 C). Preheat for 10-15 minutes with the lid closed.

Place the dutch oven on the grill grate & cook for 50-60 minutes, or until the sauce has thickened and is boiling.

To make the bourbon glaze, mix the sugar, butter, and bourbon in a shallow saucepan and heat to a boil. Reduce heat to low and cook for 2 minutes. Remove from the fire and season with salt. If desired, add more butter or bourbon.

Just before serving, drizzle the glaze over the bread pudding. Enjoy!

9.144 Easy Garlic Cheese Bombs

Total Time: 60 mins, Servings: 6
Ingredients
Pizza Dough
Sugar, 1 1/2 tbsp
Salt, 1 tbsp
Instant Yeast, 2 tsp
Bread Flour, 4 1/2 Cup
Main
Water
Lukewarm Water, 15 Ounce
Olive Oil, 3 tbsp
Mozzarella Cheese, 1 Pound Block
Parmesan Cheese, 1 tbsp
Garlic Salt, 2 tsp
Marinara Sauce
Butter, 4 tbsp
Parmesan Cheese, 1 tbsp
Butter, 4 tbsp
Instructions
In a food processor, combine flour, sugar, salt, and yeast for the pizza dough. Pulse 3-4 times until the ingredients are uniformly distributed.

15 oz of lukewarm water and olive oil. Run the food processor for approximately 15 seconds or until the mixture forms a ball that rides across the bowl just above the blade. Continue processing for another 15 seconds.

Transfer the dough ball to a lightly floured and knead it by hand once or twice until it forms a smooth ball. Divide the dough into three equal pieces and put each in a One-gallon resealable plastic bag. Allow rising for at least 24 hours in the refrigerator.

Take the dough from the refrigerator at least 2 hours before baking and roll into balls, gradually gathering dough toward this bottom and pressing tight. Each one should be floured well and placed in a separate sized mixing basin. Cover firmly with plastic wrap & set aside to rise until approximately doubled in volume at room temperature.

Roll out the pizza dough into a 1/4-inch-thick rectangle. Cut into 2-inch-thick strips. Then repeat to make 2x2 squares.

In the middle of each dough square, place one slice of mozzarella cheese. Using a little amount of water, wet the edges and fold them up firmly. Put the cheese balls on a cardboard baking sheet, seam-side down.

Mix the softened butter, garlic salt, and Parmesan cheese in a small bowl.

Brush the butter mixture over each cheese ball.

Once ready to cook, preheat the Pit Boss to 350°F with the lid covered for 15 min.

Bake for 20 minutes, until the sheet tray is light brown, directly upon that grill grate. Serve with marinara or a dipping sauce of your choice.

9.145 Baked Cherry Cheesecake Galette

Total Time: 30 mins, Servings: 6
Ingredients
Main
Sugar, 1/4 Cup + 1 tbsp
Cherries, 1 Pound
Lemon Zest, 1/2 tbsp
Orange Zest, 1 tbsp
Corn-starch, 1 tsp
Coriander, 1 tsp
Pie Crust, 1 Refrigerated
Egg Wash
Water; cream or milk, 1 tbsp
For Serving Vanilla Ice Cream
Granulated Sugar
Pinch of Salt
Cream Cheese Filling
1 Egg
Sugar, 1/4 Cup
Vanilla, 1 tsp
Cream Cheese, 8 Ounce
Instructions
Once ready to cook, preheat the Pit Boss to 350°F with the lid covered for 15 min.

Mix the cherries, orange, 1/4 cup sugar, coriander, corn-starch, salt, and lemon zest in a medium mixing basin.

Make the cream cheese filling, whisk cream cheese, sugar, vanilla, and egg in a separate dish altogether.

Stretch the pie dough with just a rolling pin till it is 1 inch bigger in diameter on a sheet pan.

In the middle of the pie crust, layer the cream cheese filling, leaving a 2 inches border around the borders. On top of cream cheese, pile the cherry mixture.

Fold the pie dough's edges up and then over the filling in tiny pieces. Egg washes the edges and sprinkle the remaining granulated sugar on top.

Bake each galette for 15 minutes, till the crust is lightly browned and the cheesecake mixture has set, directly here on the grill grate.
Serve the galette with ice cream while it's still warm. Enjoy

9.146 Pit Boss Duck Poppers
Total Time: 35 mins, Servings: 2
Ingredients
Crushed Red Pepper, 1/4 tsp
Garlic, 1 tsp
Boneless Duck Breasts, 2 (6 Oz)
Onion Powder, 3 tsp
Bacon, 12 Strips
Salt to taste
Jalapeño, 3
Pepper
Balsamic Vinegar, 1/2 Cup
Salt, 1 tsp
Olive Oil, 1/4 Cup
Instructions
Cover the duck with plastic wrap, then pound this out to a 1/4-inch thin piece, then divide it lengthwise into three pieces.
Garlic, jalapenos, onion powder, and cream cheese
are mixed. Fill each strip with duck with 1 spoonful of cheese mixture and wrap it up. Freeze for 1 hour after wrapping every duck ball with such a bacon strip.
When ready to cook, preheat the Pit Boss to 325 degrees Fahrenheit with the lid covered for 10 minutes.
Cook the duck poppers for 15 minutes on the grill or when the bacon is completely cooked.
Make the sauce in the meanwhile. Combine the crushed bell pepper, extra virgin olive oil, salt, balsamic vinegar, and onion powder in a mixing bowl.
Dish them hot with a side of dipping sauce.

9.147 Spring Frittata
Total Time: 35 mins, Servings: 6
Ingredients
Chives, 2 Tablespoon
Chopped Mushrooms, 1 Cup
Heavy Cream, 1/4 Cup
Eggs
Salt & Pepper, 1/4 tsp
Mozzarella Cheese, 1/2 Cup
Butter, 2 tbsp
Diced Ham, 1/2 Cup
Red Bell Pepper, 1/4 Cup
Asparagus Spears, 4
Instructions
When you're ready to cook, fire up the Pit Boss grill, then adjust the timer to 350 degrees Fahrenheit. Preheat for 10 minutes with the lid closed.
Mix the cream, eggs, and salt and pepper in a medium mixing bowl. To mix the ingredients, whisk them together. If using, stir in the chives. Add the cheese and mix well. Remove from the equation.
Melt some butter in a pan oven-proof pan with butter on the stovetop, ideally non-stick or even well cast iron. 5 minutes until the asparagus, mushrooms, and red bell pepper are soft. Add the ham and mix well.
Distribute the ingredients equally over the skillet's bottom. Spread the egg mixture over the veggies and meat in an equal layer. Cook the frittata in the pan on the grill grate for 15 to 20 minutes, or until firm in the middle and gently browned on the bottom. Allow 5 minutes for the frittata to rest preceding cutting into wedges & serving.

9.148 Grilled Meat Lover's Pizza
Total Time: 30 mins, Servings: 4
Ingredients
For Serving Red Pepper Flakes
Cornmeal or Semolina Flour
Homemade Pizza Dough or store made, 1 Pound
Ground Beef, 4 Ounce
Garlic, 2 Clove
Spicy Sausage, 4 Ounce
Cooked Bacon, 4 Ounce
Canadian Bacon, 4 Ounce
Pepperoni, 6 Ounce
Mozzarella Cheese, 1 1/2 Cup
Parmesan Cheese
Pizza Sauce, 1/3 Cup
Instructions
Set the Pit Boss to 500°F, then preheat for 15 minutes with the lid covered when you're ready to cook. While the grill warms up, put a pizza stone immediately on the grate.
Form the dough into some kind of flat circle and gradually press it down until it is reasonably thin. Transfer to a semolina flour or cornmeal-dusted pizza peel.
Sprinkle the garlic on top of the sauce, nearly to the edges. The other ingredients should be placed on top of the shredded mozzarella.
Toss with Parmesan cheese to taste, then place to a pizza stone to bake for 15 to 20 minutes, just until the dough is puffy, crisp, and blistered. Serve immediately with a sprinkle of red pepper flakes.

9.149 Baked Honey Glazed Ham
Total Time: 2 Hrs 20 mins, Servings: 8
Ingredients
Cloves, 20 Whole
Butter, 1 Stick
Kurobuta Half Boneln Ham, 1 (6-8 Lb)
Honey, 1 Cup
Dark Corn Syrup, 1/4 Cup
Instructions
Once ready to cook, preheat the Pit Boss to 325°F with the lid covered for 15 min.
Make a ham score. Place the ham in a foil-lined pan, smear it with melted butter, and then stud it with whole cloves.
Mix the darker corn syrup & honey in a mixing bowl. If necessary, warm to blend. Pour 3/4 of glaze over the ham and grill for 1 1/2 to 2 hours, or until it reaches 140°F.
Every 20 minutes, baste the ham with the remaining honey glaze.
Remove off the grill and set aside for a few minutes to cool.
Cut into slices and serve. Enjoy!

9.150 Spicy Asian Brussels Sprouts
Total Time: 20 mins, Servings: 4
Ingredients
Asian BBQ Rub, 1 tbsp
Vegetable Oil, 2 tbsp
Thai Chile Sauce, 1/4 Cup
Brussels Sprouts, 2 Cup
Instructions
Set the temperature on the Pit Boss grill to 350 degrees Fahrenheit. Allow 10-15 minutes for the grill to heat up.
On a prepared cookie sheet, place the half Brussel sprouts inside a single layer. Drizzle the oil over the top, then toss to coat.
Place the cookie sheet on a grill and evenly coat the Brussel sprouts with an Asian Barbecue rub. Cook for 7-10 min with the

lid closed.
Return the brussels sprouts to the grill for 3-4 minutes more, or until crisp-tender, tossing them throughout the Thai Chili Sauce. Serve right away. Enjoy!

9.151 Stuffed Cabbage Rolls
Total Time: 1 Hr 15 mins, Servings: 6
Ingredients
Cooked Brown Rice or White Rice, 1 Cup
Pork Sausage, 1/4 Pound
Ground Beef, 1 1/4 Pound
Chopped Onion, 1 Small
Cabbage, 1
Parsley, 2 tbsp
Garlic, 2 Clove
Cajun Rub, 1 1/2 tbsp
1 Egg
Tomato Soup, 10 3/4 Ounce
Salt & Pepper
Chives
Sour Cream
Tomatoes, 14 1/2 Ounce
Instructions
Thaw the cabbage after freezing it overnight (the leaves may wilt).
Using a paring knife, gently remove the core and pull the leaves anywhere without breaking them. The outermost, deep green leaves should be discarded because they are not very delicate as the milder ones. You'll need 6 to 10 leaves for this recipe. (Save the rest of the cabbage for another dish.)
Gently shave off the thick centre vein of each leaf, moving toward the bottom, with your knife almost parallel to a cutting board. Remove the leaves and set them aside.
Meanwhile, put the meat, pork, rice, onion, garlic, parsley, egg, and Pit Boss Cajun Rub in a large mixing bowl and mix thoroughly.
Mix the crushed tomatoes with tomato soup in a separate bowl. Season with salt to taste.
On your work surface, place a leaf. Form a sausage-like log out of a part of the meat mixture, approximately 1-1/4 inch thick and 2-1/2 inch long, and put it towards the bottom of a leaf. Roll up from the ground, folding the 2 sides over the log's ends. Place in a single layer, seam-side down, in a baking dish. Rep until you've used up all of the meat.
Cover the cabbage rolls firmly with foil after pouring the tomato sauce combination over and around them.
When you're ready to cook, fire up the Pit Boss grill & adjust the timer to 350 degrees Fahrenheit. Preheat for 10 minutes with the lid closed.
Oven the cabbage rolls until approximately 1 hour, or when the meat filling reaches 160 degrees inside. If preferred, top with sour cream & chives.

9.152 Grilled Quadruple Cheese Pizza
Total Time: 30 mins, Servings: 6
Ingredients
Thyme, 1/8 tsp
Parmesan Cheese, 1 1/2 Cup
Cream, 8 Ounce
Fresh Oregano, 1/2 tsp
Garlic, 2 Clove
Basil, 1/8 tsp
Butter, 2 tbsp
Pizza Dough, 1
Cornmeal
Cheddar Cheese, 1 Cup
Mozzarella Cheese, 1 Cup
Cheese, 1 Cup
Black Pepper, 1 Dash
Instructions
Begin the Pit Boss grill & change the temperature to 500 °F when you're ready to cook. Preheat for 10 minutes with the lid closed.
Melt butter inside a small saucepan over low heat on the stovetop. Once the butter has melted, add the garlic and cook until it is brown. Whisk in the cream until the butter and cream are no longer separated. Add the cheese and seasonings and stir until the cheese is completely melted. Continue to simmer for another 10-15 minutes on low heat.
Place the stretched-out or tossing pizza dough on such a cornmeal-dusted pizza peel. When a peel isn't available, the back of just a baking sheet may be utilized.
Cover the dough with the appropriate quantity of sauce. On top of the sauce, sprinkle the cheese and slide the pizza straight onto the grill grates. Cook approximately 10 minutes before serving.
Remove the pizza from the grill and set it aside to cool for 5 minutes before slicing. Enjoy!

9.153 Baked Garlic Parmesan Wings
Total Time: 50 mins, Servings: 4
Ingredients
Parmesan Cheese, 1 Cup
Chicken Wings, 5 Pound
Unsalted Butter, 1/2 Cup
Garlic, 10 Clove
Garlic, 10 Clove
Butter, 1 Cup
Chopped Parsley, 3 tbsp
Pit Boss Chicken Rub, 3 1/2 tbsp
Instructions
Set the Pit Boss to 450°F and preheat for 15 minutes with the lid covered when you're ready to cook.
Combine the wings with Pit Boss Chicken Rub in a large mixing basin.
Sauté for 20 minutes with the wings directly upon this grill grate. Cook for another 20 minutes after flipping the wings.
Check the interior temperature of the wings; the finishing temperature should be between 165°F and 180°F.
To create the garlic sauce, mix the butter, garlic, and leftover rub in a medium saucepan and simmer over medium heat on the stovetop where the chicken is cooking. Cook, stirring periodically, for 8 - 10 mins.
Remove the wings from the grill and put them in a large mixing basin. Combine the wings, garlic sauce, Parmesan cheese, and parsley in a mixing bowl. Enjoy!

9.154 Mini Apple Pies
Total Time: 50 mins, Servings: 6
Ingredients
Vanilla Ice Cream
Honey, 2 tbsp
Apple Pie Spice, 1/2 tsp
Honeycrisp or Pink Lady, 7 Whole Apples
Rum Extract, 1/4 tsp
Coarsely Chopped Pecans, 1/4 Cup
Pie Crust, 1 Refrigerated
Coconut Oil, 2 tbsp
For Serving Cream of Whipped Coconut
Unsalted Melted Butter, 1 tbsp
Cinnamon
Caramel Sauce
Instructions
Preheat the Pit Boss to 375 degrees Fahrenheit. (We used apple-flavored pellets, but pecans would also be delicious)
Remove the tops of four apples and slice them in half.

Carefully remove the interior portion of each apple using a melon baller.

To stand erect, you may have to cut the bottom equally. To make the apple pie filling, dice the three remaining apples into tiny pieces.

To create the apple pie filling, combine chopped apple chunks, nuts, apple pie spice, honey, and rum extract in a large mixing bowl.

Over medium heat, heat the coconut oil and sauté the apple combination for 2 minutes. Remove the pan from the heat.

Fill hollow apples with apple pie filling that has been made ahead of time.

Split pie crust into 1/4" strips using only a pizza cutter and arrange in a lattice pattern over the top of every apple. With a knife, trim the extra pie crust around the edges.

Brush the tops of the pie crusts with melted butter, then sprinkle with cinnamon-coconut sugar.

Place the apples in a baking dish with a high wall. Fill the bottom of the dish with approximately 1/4 cup of water, just enough to covers the bottoms of apples. Bake for 20-25 minutes, covered with foil. Return to the oven for another 20 minutes after removing the foil. When the crust edges are golden brown, and the apples are tender to slice, the apples are done.

Enjoy fresh coconut whip cream, clear caramel sauce, and vanilla ice cream while it's still warm!

9.155 Baked Pimento Bacon Mac & Cheese

Total Time: 1 Hr 10 mins, Servings: 6
Ingredients
Yellow Onion, 1
Flour, 5 tbsp
Garlic, 2 Clove
Diced Pimento Peppers, 1/4 Cup +1 tbsp
Heavy Cream, 2 1/2 Cup
Butter, 4 tbsp
Bay Leaves, 2
Parmesan Cheese, 1/4 Cup
Panko Breadcrumbs, 1 Cup
Fresh Thyme, 3 Sprig
Whole Milk, 1 1/2 Cup
Sprig Rosemary, 1
Gruyere Cheese, 1 Pound
Black Peppercorns, 1 tbsp
Elbow Macaroni, 1 Pound
Salt to taste
Smoked Paprika, 1/2 tbsp
Chopped Parsley, 1 tsp
Crumbled Cooked Bacon, 1/4 Cup
Butter, 4 tbsp
Instructions
Once ready to cook, preheat the Pit Boss to 350°F with the lid covered for 15 min.

Inside a wide stock saucepan over medium heat, melt the butter. Sauté for 5 minutes, or until onion and peppers are transparent and soft. Sauté for another 30 seconds after adding the garlic. With a wooden spoon, mix in the flour well. Cook the roux for 1 minute or until it smells nutty. Stream in the milk and cream while whisking and whisk until the flour clumps are gone.

Cheesecloth is wrapped around herbs and black peppercorns and tied with string. Drop into the cream mixture and cook for 15 to 20 minutes, or until the liquid has thickened. Remove the cheesecloth with the herbs and throw it away.

Remove from the fire and whisk in the Gruyere until completely melted. Season with salt. Remove from the heat and set aside until the noodles are done.

Bring a big saucepan of salted water on the stove. Cook for 6 to 8 minutes, or until the noodles are al dente. Rinse and drain the pasta. Stir into the cheese sauce to combine. Fill a big cast iron pan halfway with the ingredients.

Mix Parmesan cheese, panko, melted butter, and paprika in a small mixing dish and whisk well. Over the macaroni and cheese, sprinkle the mixture.

Cook 15 to 20 minutes, till melty cheese is bubbling & the top is gently browned, in a cast-iron skillet directly upon this grill grate.

Take from the grill and top on bacon and parsley before serving. Enjoy!

9.156 Italian Herb & Parmesan Scones

Total Time: 35 mins, Servings: 8
Ingredients
Italian Seasoning, 1 tbsp
Garlic Salt, 1/2 tsp
Baking Soda, 1 tsp
Baking Powder, 2 tsp
Parmesan Cheese, 1 Cup
2 Eggs
Olive Oil, 1/4 Cup
Buttermilk, 1 1/2 Cup
Flour, 2 1/2 Cup
Instructions
Sift the flour, garlic salt, baking powder, Italian seasoning, soda, and half a cup of cheese in a large mixing basin. In the middle, dig a well.

Mix over eggs, buttermilk, & olive oil in a smaller mixing dish.

Pour the batter into a well throughout the dry ingredients and whisk just until everything is incorporated. It will have a lumpy appearance.

muffin cups, oiled, sprayed using cooking spray or lined with paper liners

Using a spatula, evenly distribute the batter among the cups. Sprinkle the leftover Parmesan cheese on top of the muffins.

When you're ready to start cooking, Preheat the oven to 400 ° F and bake for 10 minutes with the lid covered.

Place the muffin pan on the grill grate & bake for 20 mins, unless a toothpick inserted inside the middle comes out clean. Allow cooling in the muffin pan for a few minutes before removing. Heat adding butter or olive oil, if desired. Enjoy!

9.157 Baked Artichoke Dip

Total Time: 1 Hr 15 mins, Servings: 8
Ingredients
Olive Oil
Garlic, 10 Clove
Asiago Cheese, 1/2 Cup
Parmesan Cheese, 1/2 Cup
Provolone Cheese, 1/2 Cup
Fontina Cheese, 1/2 Cup
Sliced Vegetables or Sliced Baguette, For Serving
Cream Cheese, 8 Ounce
Kosher Salt
Artichokes, 1 (14 Oz)
Black Pepper
Mayonnaise, 1/2 Cup
Instructions
Once ready to cook, preheat the Pit Boss to 350°F with the lid covered for 15 min.

In a medium oven-safe pan, place the garlic cloves with enough oils to cover them.

Sauté for 30 - 40 minutes on the grill. Garlic is ready when it is soft enough to be readily pierced with a fork. Remove off the grill and set aside to cool.

Split the garlic & oil once they have cooled, and save the garlic oil to use in future recipes. In a bowl, crush the garlic with just a fork once it becomes a homogeneous paste. If it seems to be dry, drizzle in a little garlic oil.
Combine the Parmesan, Asiago, fontina, and provolone cheeses in a mixing bowl. Set aside half a cup of the cheese mixture to use as a garnish for the dip.
Combine the cheese, mayonnaise, cream cheese, garlic, and artichokes in a mixing bowl. Season with salt to taste.
Fill an oven-safe dish halfway with the mixture and top over 1/2 cup of the saved cheeses.
Preheat the grill to 350°F and bake the dip for 60 minutes.
The dip may be served with baguette slices, crackers, or sliced veggies. Enjoy!

9.158 Baked Green Chile Mac & Cheese by Doug Scheiding

Total Time: 2 Hrs 10 mins, Servings: 8
Ingredients
Unsalted Butter, 6 tbsp
Mozzarella Cheese, 8 Ounce
Half-And-Half, 2 1/2 Cup
Elbow Macaroni Noodles, 16 Ounce
Heavy Whipping Cream, 2 Cup
Prime Rib Rub, 2 tbsp
Cream Cheese, 8 Ounce
Roasted Green Chile, 16 Ounce
Cheddar Cheese, 24 Ounce
Instructions
Once ready to cook, preheat the Pit Boss to 165°F with the lid covered for 15 min.
Place 16 ounces shredded cheddar cheese and 8 ounces shredded mozzarella cheese on a small pan or cookie sheet on the grill grate. 30 to 40 mins of smoking. Remove the steaks from the grill and put them aside.
Raise the temperature of the Pit Boss to 300°F and add the butter to a large disposable aluminium half pan. After the butter has completely melted, remove your pan from the grill. Combine the noodles, whipping cream, half-and-half, 16 oz cold smoked cheddar, all the smoked cream cheese & mozzarella cheese broken into tiny pieces, in a skillet. Stir in the green chilies to fit (12 ounces for mild, 16 ounces for spicy), and season with salt and pepper.
Preheat the grill to high and bake the pan for 2 h, stirring every twenty minutes. If the macaroni and cheese seem to be drying out, add a splash of half-and-half and toss to mix.
Sprinkle the leftover (unsmoked) cheddar cheese and a little sprinkling of Pit Boss Prime Rib Rub during the final 20 minutes of cooking. Serve immediately. Enjoy.

9.159 Pit Boss Cowboy Beans

Total Time: 3 Hrs 10 mins, Serving: 8
Ingredients
Bacon, 6 Slices
Salt & Pepper
Pork Steaks, 2 Pound
Mexican Chorizo Sausage, 4 Whole
1 Onion
Garlic, 3 Clove
Pinto Beans, 5 Can (15.5 Oz)
Serrano Chiles or Jalapeños, 2 Whole
Hot Sauce, 1
Diced Tomatoes with Chiles or 1 Salsa
Chicken Broth, 1
Ground Cumin, 1 Pinch
Cilantro, 1/2 Cup
Mexican Beer, 1 Bottle (12 Oz)

Instructions
When you're ready to cook, fire up the Pit Boss as per the manufacturer's directions. Preheat the grill to 185°F for 5 minutes with the lid closed.
Coat the country-style spare ribs with salt and black pepper on both sides.
For one hour, smoke pork ribs.
Raise the grill temp to 325 degrees F once you've finished smoking. Continue cooking the pork after the grill has reached the desired temperature. Arrange the chorizo & bacon on the grill grate at the same time. Transfer all of the meat to chopping board after 25 minutes. Discard any bones from pork ribs before chopping them into bite-sized pieces. The chorizo should be cut into 1/4-inch pieces, and the bacon should be diced.
In a large Dutch oven, place all of the meat. Combine the garlic, onion, pinto beans, jalapenos, beer, tomatoes, cumin, and a sprinkle of oregano in a large mixing bowl. To mix, stir everything together. Whereas if the mixture seems to be too dry, add 1 cup of chicken broth as well as water at a time. Return the Dutch oven to the grill, covered.
Bake for 1 to 2 hours, whisking once in a while. Remove the cover when the beans appear to be too soupy. If they seem to be dry, add a splash of chicken stock or water.
Stir inside the cilantro during the final 15 minutes of simmering. Season to taste with salt & pepper as required. Serve with a side of spicy sauce. Enjoy!

9.160 Baked Cauliflower Tots

Total Time: 35 mins, Serving: 6
Ingredients
Panko Breadcrumbs, 1/2 Cup
Cauliflower, 1 Head
Kosher Salt, 1 tsp
2 Eggs
Parmesan Cheese, 1/4 Cup
Cheddar Cheese, 3/4 Cup
Garlic Powder, 1/2 tbsp
Chopped Chives, 3 tbsp
Canola Oil
Onion Powder, 1/2 tbsp
Instructions
A big saucepan of salted water should be brought to a boil. Cook the cauliflower
florets in boiling water for 5 to 7 minutes or until they are soft.
Strain the florets and immediately put them in an ice bath to chill. When the cauliflower is cold enough to handle, strain it again and put the florets in the mixing bowl. Pulse till the cauliflower looks rice. To get a uniform texture, process fresh florets in batches.
Place the cauliflower rice on the double piece of cheesecloth and roll it up. Squeeze off excess water (as much as you can) and add cauliflower rice to just a large mixing bowl.
Mix in the other ingredients until well combined. If the mixture appears too wet or dry, add another egg or even more panko breadcrumbs till it holds together.
Place the cauliflower mixture on a sheet tray in the desired form. Refrigerate the sheet pan for 30 minutes to allow the tots to cool.
Set the Pit Boss to 375°F and preheat for 15 minutes with the lid covered when you're ready to cook.
Brush the heated grill grate using canola oil after cleaning it with a grill brush. Arrange the tots around the sides of the grill grate.
Cook until the tots are gently browned, about 10 to 15 minutes. Avoid the urge to move them about too much and too soon. Remove them one by one as they complete for the best effect.

Serve with dipping sauces of your choice. Enjoy!

9.161 Irish Soda Bread
Total Time: 1 Hr, Serving: 8
Ingredients
Baking Soda, 1 1/4 tsp
Flour, 3 1/2 Cup
Cornmeal
Salted Butter
Sugar, 1 1/2 tsp
Buttermilk, 1 Cup
Salt, 1 tsp
Instructions
Set the Pit Boss to 400°F, then preheat for 15 minutes with the lid covered when you're ready to cook.
Set aside an 8-inch round cake pan that has been lightly dusted with cornmeal.
Remove a big piece of wax paper from the package and place this in your work area.
In a large sifter, toss to combine sugar, baking soda, salt, and sift onto wax paper. Carefully pull off the wax paper sides and re-sift the flour mixture into the sifter. Sift again into a big mixing basin.
Flour the work surface lightly.
One cup of buttermilk poured into a well in the centre of flour mixture there in the bowl. Using a wooden spoon, stir the mixture. As when the carbon bubbles produced when the buttermilk touches the dry ingredients deflate, work swiftly and carefully. The dough will be shaggy; if it seems to be dry, add a bit more buttermilk.
Turn out onto a floured surface and knead for 20 - 30 seconds, just strong enough to catch the dough pieces together with floured hands. (It will resemble biscuit dough rather than bread dough.)
Pour towards the prepared pan and shape into a flattish circle. Cut a deep cross inside the top of loaf using a sharp knife, together with all way to the other side of the bread. Place this in the Pit Boss for bake as soon as possible; if it sits for too long, this will deflate.
Bake for 40 - 50 minutes, just until the bread is golden and hollow when tapped on the bottom with your knuckles.
Take the pan from the oven and place this on a serving plate to cool. Cut the bread in half just before serving, now slice each half in thin slices.
Serve with a pat of butter. Wrap leftovers in plastic wrap/foil firmly. This bread is excellent for toasting. Enjoy!

9.162 Veggie Flat Bread
Total Time: 60 mins, Serving: 4
Ingredients
Onion, 1/2
Olive Oil, 3 tbsp
Pizza Dough, 1 Pound
Garlic, 2 Clove
Tomatoes, 1/2
Red Bell Pepper, 1/4
Black Pepper
Dried Oregano
Instructions
Follow the package's instructions for thawing the dough. Coat a cake pan with non-stick spray, then press the dough into the pan to create a crust. 2 tbsp. olive oil drizzled over the dough Spread the garlic, onion, & red pepper over the dough, leaving the crust exposed.
Drizzle the remaining olive oil over the tomatoes over top of the crust. Add oregano and pepper to taste.
When you're ready to cook, fire up the Pit Boss grill. Until the fire has created, smoke with lid open. Preheat the oven to 450°F and bake for 10 minutes with the lid covered.
The cooking time is 30 minutes. The crust must be golden and sturdy to the touch. Enjoy!

9.163 Baked Green Bean Casserole with Crispy Shallots
Total Time: 1 Hr, Serving: 10
Ingredients
Unsalted Butter, 2 tbsp
Green Beans, 3 Pound
Kosher Salt, 1 tbsp
Olive Oil, 2 tbsp
Mixed Mushrooms, 1/2 Pound
Shallot, 1/4 Cup
Rice Flour, 3/4 Cup
Pinch of Salt
Sliced Shallot, 8 Whole
Sherry Cooking Wine, 1/2 Cup
Almonds, 1 Cup
Parmigiano Reggiano, 1 Cup
Vegetable Oil or Canola, 4 Cup
Chicken Stock, 2 Cup
Instructions
Adjust the timer to High and warm for 15 minutes with the lid covered when ready to cook.
Bring 2/3 full water to a boil in a large stockpot over high heat. Make an ice bath in a big tub. Add 1 tbsp of salt to the boiling water. Put 1/2 of green beans once the water has risen to a rolling boil. Cook for approximately 2 minutes, or until the pasta is al dente. Remove the beans with a colander and chill in an ice bath. Take the peas from water and lay them out to dry on paper towels. Rep with the rest of the green beans. To remove the water, put fresh green beans on some kind of clean dish towel and wrap them up.
To create the sauce, follow these steps: In a small saucepan, melt butter and olive oil. Put the shallots and mushrooms, along with a large sprinkle of salt, and simmer, turning occasionally, for approximately 5 minutes, or until the mushrooms are tender.
2 minutes after sprinkling the rice flour on top, toss to coat all mushrooms & cook-off raw flour flavour.
Stir in the sherry and reduce it, then gradually add the stock, letting it thicken and ensure there are still no lumps, approximately 3 minutes.
Combine the cream and Parmigiano-Reggiano- Season with salt and pepper to taste. Mix the green beans and the sauce in a mixing bowl. Fill a large oven-safe
serving dish with the mixture. Almonds should be sprinkled on top.
Bake for 30 minutes on the Pit Boss until the mixture is boiling and the almonds are golden.
Fry the shallots, whereas the green beans will be on the grill. Heat the oil in a large saucepan and Dutch oven to 350 degrees Fahrenheit.
In a small basin, whisk together the rice sifted flour with a fork. The shallots should be sliced into 1/8" rings. Shake off any excess rice flour from the shallots in a strainer before tossing them in the flour.
In batches, fry the shallots until golden brown, approximately 30 seconds to a minute. Using paper towels, absorb any excess liquid.
Garnish the dish with fried shallots when it's done. Enjoy!

9.164 Baked Otium House Rolls
Total Time: 45 mins, Serving: 4
Ingredients

Warm Water, 1 Cup
Dry Yeast, 1 Whole Packet
Kosher Salt, 1 1/2 tsp
Garlic, 1 Clove
Sugar, 1/4 Cup
Whole Egg, 1
Unsalted Butter, 1/4 Cup
Butter
Chopped Thyme, 1 tbsp
Butter, 1/4 Cup
Flour, 3 Cup

Instructions
Inside a kitchen aid medium bowl, combine all of the dry ingredients. For 10 minutes, activate yeast in water. Combine all ingredients in a mixing bowl and beat with just a dough hook for 10 min, starting on low and increasing too medium-high.
Form into tiny balls and put in a cast iron pan that has been greased. Allow 1 hour for proofing.
Warm the oven to high (450°F+), cover, and leave for 10-15 minutes to preheat.
With a wash brush, clean the area. Cook on high for 25 minutes, brush every 5 minutes. Warm it up and enjoy it!

9.165 Baked Meat Bagel
Total Time: 60 mins, Serving: 4
Ingredients
Ground Pork, 2 Pound
Butter, 1 tbsp
Onion, 1 Large
Tomato Paste, 2/3 Cup
Salt & Pepper
Smoked Paprika, 1 tsp
Garlic Powder, 1 tsp
Whole Egg, 2
Sliced Tomatoes
Sliced Avocado
Iceberg Lettuce
Instructions
Preheat oven to 400° degrees F and leave the lid covered for 15 minutes when ready to cook.
Using parchment paper, line a baking dish.
Over medium heat, sauté the onions in butter until they are transparent. Leave to cool before incorporating into the meat.
Incorporate the sautéed onions with the other ingredients in a mixing bowl and stir to combine.
Make 6 equal pieces of meat and roll them into balls. To make a bagel shape, indent the centre and flatten slightly.
Place the meat bagels on a parchment-lined sheet pan. Cook for 40 minutes on the grill or until an instant reading thermometer placed in the thickest portion of the meat registers 165 degrees F.
Allow cooling after removing from the grill. Fill with toppings like tomato slices, onions, lettuce, and avocado, then slice like a normal bagel. Enjoy!

9.166 Baked Maple Venison Sausage Quiche
Total Time: 55 mins, Serving: 4
Ingredients
Green Chiles, 4 Ounce (4 Oz)
Whole Egg, 12
Ground Venison, 2 Pound
Baking Powder, 1 tsp
Monterey Jack Cheese & Grated Colby, 1 1/2 Cup
White Onion, 1 Whole
Cottage Cheese, 16 Ounce

Instructions
In a wide sauté pan at medium-high heat, brown ground venison. Remove any extra fat from the venison and put it aside.
In a large baking basin, whisk together the eggs. Stir in the remaining ingredients one at a time. Fill one 13x9 oven and a 9x9 pan with the mixture.
Preheat the oven to 350 °F and leave the lid covered for 10-15 minutes until ready to cook.
Cook for 45 minutes, or until a knife stabbed into the middle comes out clean, directly on the grill grate. Allow 10 minutes for cooling before serving. Enjoy!

9.167 Baked Cheesy Garlic Fries
Total Time: 30 mins, Serving: 4
Ingredients
Red Pepper Flakes, 1/2 tsp
Olive Oil, 2 tbsp
Gold Potatoes, 4 Yukon
Garlic, 1 tbsp
Salt, 1 tsp
Onion Powder, 2 tsp
Chopped Chives
Pepper, 1 tsp
Sour Cream
Cheddar Cheese, 2 Cup
Instructions
Each potato should be cut into eight wedges. Mix the red pepper flakes, garlic, onion powder, oil, salt, and
pepper in a large mixing basin. Whisk the potato wedges in the dressing to coat them.
Set the temperature to 500°F and warm for 15 minutes with the lid covered when ready to cook.
Cook the wedges for 8 mins on a hot grill. Top the cooked potatoes with cheddar cheese on an oiled cast iron pan or griddle.
Return the cheesy potatoes to the grill for another 5 mins, just until the cheese has completely melted. Serve hot with soured cream on the side, garnished with chives, and enjoy!

9.168 Brule
Total Time: 1 Hr, Serving: 2
Ingredients
Sugar, 1 Cup
Vanilla Extract, 1 tsp
Egg Yolk, 6
Whipping Cream, 1 Quart
Instructions
When you're ready to cook, fire up the Pit Boss grill. Until the fire has been created, smoke with the lid open. Preheat the oven at 325 °F (160 degrees C) with the lid closed for 10 minutes.
In a normal heat saucepan, combine the vanilla bean, cream, and scraped seeds. Bring the water to a boil. Allow to steep after removing from the heat (about 15 minutes). Pick and remove one vanilla bean from the pot.
Mix egg yolks & 1/2 cup (100 g) sugar in a mixing dish until the mixture brightens in color. Slowly drizzle in the cream, stirring constantly.
Put the ramekins inside a large grill pan and pour the sauce into 6 (8 ounces) ramekins. Fill the pan with boiling water until it reaches halfway up both sides of the ramekins.
Place the water bath pan on the grill and bake for 40 to 45 minutes, or until the Crème Burles still jiggle in the middle.
Refrigerate the ramekins for at least 2 hours and up to 2 days after removing them from the roasting pan.
Allow 20 minutes for the Crème Brûlée to get to room temperature before touching the tops.
On top of each ramekin, evenly sprinkle the remaining 1/2 cup (100 g) sugar. Melt the sugar with a torch in a circular motion

until it caramelizes and produces a crispy top.
Allow for a few minutes of resting time before serving the Crème Brûlée. Enjoy!

9.169 Baked Blueberry Slab Pie
Total Time: 1 Hr 15 mins, Serving: 8
Ingredients
main
Flour, 5 Cup
Granulated Sugar, 1/4 Cup
1 Egg
Coarse Sugar, 1/4 Cup
Kosher Salt, 1 tsp
Ice Water, 8 tbsp
Unsalted Butter, 2 Cup
For the Filling
Corn-starch, 2 tbsp
Lemon Zest, 2 tsp
Blueberries, 10 Cup
Granulated Sugar, 1/2 Cup
Vanilla Extract, 1 tsp
Pinch of Salt
Instructions
To create the pie dough, mix the flour, granulated sugar, and salt in a food processor & pulse a few times until combined. Pulse in the cooled butter pieces for approximately ten pulses until the mixture forms a coarse meal.
Pulse 3 times with 8 teaspoons of cold water. When you squeeze the dough between your fingers, it should stay together but not be sticky. If it's crumbly, add a spoonful of water at a time until it's smooth, pounding twice after this addition.
Turn the dough onto a flat surface and pull it together with your hands as soon as it holds together. There should be obvious butter striations.
Make two rectangles out of the dough by dividing it in half. Refrigerate the rectangles for at least two hours or even overnight, wrapped individually in plastic wrap. Allow 30 minutes for the dough to come to room temperature before rolling it out
To make the filling, combine the blueberries, corn-starch, lemon zest, granulated sugar, vanilla, and salt in a large mixing basin. Allow resting while rolling out the dough.
Roll-off 1 dough rectangular into a 22- x 18-inch rectangle on a lightly floured surface, approximately 1/8 inch thick.
Unroll the dough onto the top of a lined baking sheet after wrapping it around the rolling pin. Squeeze the
dough into the pan's bottom and sides gently. With scissors or even a knife, trim the edges, leaving a 1/2" overhang. Freeze while stretching out the lattice crust dough.
Make a 22 × 18-inch rectangle out of the remaining dough rectangle. Mark six 1-inch gaps along the short edges of the dough using a ruler.
Cut six 1 x 22" strips from the dough using a flute pastry roll, a pizza cutter, or a knife. Re-roll this dough into an 18-inch square using the leftovers. Mark 1-inch gaps along with the dough once again, then cut (6) 1 x 18-inch strip from it.
For the lattice, you'll only need 5 within each size strip, but you'll have an additional in case one breaks. If the dough gets so hot at any stage throughout the process, place it in the refrigerator before proceeding.
Put the blueberry mixture into cooled bottom crust & spread this out evenly to create the lattice crust. 5 longer strips should be placed lengthwise over the pie, evenly spaced.
Fold every other strip in half and place a short strip all over the unfolded strips perpendicularly. Fold back the opposite strips each time to make a total of five strips of dough equally over the top.
Trim any lattice strip overhangs. To ensure that the lattice strips bake together, pinch them into the dough, mostly on the rim of the baking sheet.
One teaspoon of water was used to beat the egg. Brush the beaten egg mixture over the lattice crust and sprinkle with coarse sugar. Refrigerate the dough for 10 min before baking if it is too warm.
Once ready to cook, preheat the Pit Boss to 400°F with the lid covered for 15 minutes.
Put the slab pie straight on the grill grate, cover, and bake for 45 minutes until the surface is golden well as the filling is bubbling if the topping is browning too fast, tent the pie with aluminum foil.
Before slicing and serving, move the baking sheet to just a wire rack and allow the pie to cool by at least 1 hour. Enjoy!

9.170 Ultimate Game Day Dip

Total Time: 40 mins, Serving: 6
Ingredients
Main
Cream Cheese, 1 Pound
Mayonnaise, 1 Cup
Cheddar Cheese, 1 Cup
Parmesan Cheese, 1/2 Cup
Jalapeños, 6
Chopped Bacon, 8 Slices
Chopped Scallions, 1/2 Cup
Vegetables or Chips, For Serving
Topping
Panko Breadcrumbs, 1 Cup
Parmesan Cheese, 1/2 Cup
Butter, 1/4 Cup
Instructions
Preheat the Pit Boss to 350°F for 15 minutes with the lid closed when ready to cook.
Mix cream cheese & mayonnaise in the mixing bowl and beat with the paddle attachment till smooth. Combine the rest of the ingredients for the dip in a mixing bowl.
Pour the mixture into a cast-iron skillet & smooth the top. To make the topping, combine all of the ingredients and put on top of the dip. Cook for 20-30 minutes, or until the top is gently brown and the dip is bubbling, directly on the grill grate. Mix cream cheese & mayonnaise in the mixing bowl and beat with the whisk attachment
until smooth. Combine the rest of the ingredients for the dip in a mixing bowl.
Serve with dipping chips, crostini, or vegetables. Enjoy.

9.171 Pit Boss Potatoes Au Gratin
Total Time: 1 Hr 20 mins, Serving: 6
Ingredients
Whole Milk, 1/2 Cup
Flour, 2 tbsp
Heavy Cream, 1 1/2 Cup
Salt, 1 tsp
Garlic, 4 Clove
Ground Black Pepper

Cheddar Cheese, 1 Cup
Butter, 2 tbsp
Russet Potatoes, 4 Whole
Instructions
Once ready to cook, preheat the Pit Boss to 500 degrees Fahrenheit with the lid covered for 15 minutes.
Heavy whipping cream, milk, flour, chopped garlic, salt, and ground black pepper for taste are whisked together in a mixing bowl.
Slice the potatoes as thinly as possible and as evenly as possible. Softened butter should be smeared all across the bottom of just a baking dish. Place 1/3 of potatoes in the baking dish's bottom. 1/3 of the cream mixture should be poured over the potatoes. Repeat the process twice more, finishing with a cream mixture.
Wrap in foil and bake for 30 minutes on the Pit Boss.
Remove the foil and continue baking for a further twenty minutes, or until the potatoes are light brown and bubbling. Put the mozzarella on top of potatoes, then bake for an additional 3 to 5 minutes or until the cheese has melted. Enjoy!

9.172 Pizza Bites
Total Time: 1 day 20 mins, Serving: 6
Ingredients
Sugar, 1 1/2 tbsp
Pepperoni, 8 Ounce
Olive Oil, 3 tbsp
Lukewarm Water, 15 Ounce
Pizza Sauce, 1 Cup
Pinch of salt
Kosher Salt, 2 tsp
Bread Flour, 4 1/2 Cup
Instant Yeast, 2 tsp
Mozzarella Cheese, 1 Cup
Egg, 1 Whole
Instructions
In a food processor, combine flour, salt, sugar, & yeast for the pizza dough. Pulse 3–4 times until the ingredients are uniformly distributed. Combine the olive water and oil in a mixing bowl. Run the food processor for approximately 15 seconds, or until the mixture forms a ball which always rides across the bowl just above the blade. Continue processing for another 15 seconds. Transfer the dough ball to a lightly floured surface & knead it by hand once or twice until it forms a smooth ball. Divide the dough into three equal halves and put each one in a 1-liter zip-top bag. Allow at least 1 day for the dough to rise in the refrigerator. Take the dough from the refrigerator at least 2 hours before baking and roll into balls by collecting dough towards the bottom and pressing tight. Each one should be floured well and placed in a separate sized mixing basin.
Cover firmly with plastic wrap, then
set aside to rise until approximately doubled in volume at room temperature.
Preheat the grill to 350°F for 15 minutes with the lid covered when ready to cook.
Remove the dough from the fridge after the first rise and set it aside to come to room
temperature. On a level surface, roll out the dough. Cut the dough into 18-inch-long strips that are 3 inches broad.
Pepperoni should be sliced into strips.
Combine the mozzarella, pizza sauce, and pepperoni in a medium mixing basin.
1 TBSP pizza filling, approximately halfway down the length of the dough, spooned onto the pizza dough every two inches.
Brush the egg wash around the pizza filling using a pastry brush. Fold the half of the dough that isn't filled with pizza filling over the other half filled with pizza filling.
With your fingertips, gently press down between each pizza bite. Cut around each filling with a ravioli or pizza cutter, forming a rectangle and sealing the dough in.
Place each pizza slice on a cookie sheet lined with parchment paper. Allow for 30 minutes of rising time after covering with a kitchen towel.
Preheat the grill to 350°F with the lid covered for 10-15 minutes when ready to cook.
Brush the bites with the remaining egg wash, season with salt, and put on the sheet tray immediately. Bake
for 10-15 minutes, or until golden brown on the outside.
Remove off the grill and place on a serving platter. Enjoy with a side of additional pizza sauce for dipping.

9.173 Baked Cornbread Turkey Tamale Pie
Total Time: 60 mins, Serving: 6
Ingredients
Ears Corn, 2
Turkey, 2 Cup
Black Beans, 15 Ounce
Yellow Bell Pepper, 1
Bell Pepper, 1
2 Jalapeño
Cilantro, 2 tbsp
Cumin, 1/2 tsp
Green Onions, 1 Bunch
Chipotle Sauce, 7 Ounce
Paprika, 1/2 tsp
Flour, 1 Cup
Sugar, 1 tbsp
Salt, 1/2 tsp
Cheddar Cheese, 1/2 Cup
Enchilada Sauce, 15 Ounce
Cornmeal, 1 Cup
Baking Powder, 2 tsp
Butter, 3 tbsp
Buttermilk, 1 Cup
1 Egg
Instructions
To make the filling, put all of the ingredients in a mixing bowl. Place in the middle of a 10-inch pan that has been coated with butter.
To make the cornbread topping, whisk together the salt cornmeal, sugar, flour, baking powder in a mixing dish. In a small saucepan, melt the butter. Remove the butter from heat and whisk in the milk & egg. If the mixture becomes too heated, the egg may curdle.
Stir the milk-egg mixture into the dry ingredients until everything is well combined. Don't over mix the ingredients.
To make Tamale Pie, start by putting together the following ingredients. Fill a butter-greased 10-inch pan halfway with shredded turkey filling. Smooth the cornbread topping to the edges of the pan.
Preheat the oven to 375°F with the lid covered for 15 minutes when ready to cook.
Cook for 45-50 minutes, or until the cornbread is lightly browned and cooked through, directly on the grill grate. Enjoy!

9.174 Gluten-Free Baked Fruit Crisps
Total Time: 50 mins, Serving: 6
Ingredients
Gluten-Free Flour, 1 Cup
Brown Sugar, 3/4 Cup
Kosher Salt, 1/2 tsp
Vanilla Extract, 1/2 tsp
Pinch of Salt
Whipped Cream or Creme Fraiche

Pears & Mixed Apples, 3 Pound
Ground Nutmeg, 1/4 tsp
Ground Cinnamon, 1 tsp
Gluten-Free Oats, 2 Cup
Almond Flour, 1/2 Cup
Unsalted Butter, 3/4 Cup
Cane Sugar, 3 tsp
Instructions
Once ready to cook, preheat the Pit Boss to 350°F with the lid covered for 15 minutes.
Prepare a baking sheet by lining it with parchment paper and placing eight 1 cup coquettes on it.
To make the Crisp Topping, combine the following ingredients in a mixing bowl. In a large mixing basin, mix the oats, brown sugar, flour, salt, cinnamon, and nutmeg.
Add the butter and chop it into pea-sized pieces using a pastry mixer or fork. Keep it refrigerated until you're ready to use it.
Chef's Note: Because this recipe produces a double batch of crisp topping, I can prepare this crowd-pleaser whenever I discover excellent stone fruit and berries at the market.
In a medium bowl, combine vanilla, the fruit, and a sprinkle of salt, and taste. Only use the cane sugar to sweeten if required.
Fill each ramekin with fruit to the top, and then top with two tablespoons of crisp topping. Directly on the grill grate, place a sheet pan with ramekins.
Bake for 30 to 40 minutes, or when the tops are golden and bubbling. Allow 20 minutes for cooling.
Top with just a dollop of crème Fraiche / whipped cream to serve. Enjoy!

9.175 Pit Boss Wheat Bread
Total Time: 1 Hr 30 mins, Serving: 4
Ingredients
Flour, 2 Cup
Olive Oil
Cornmeal
Salt, 1 1/4 tsp
Dry Yeast, 1 1/4 Ounce Packet
Whole Wheat Flour, 1 Cup
Water, 1 1/2 Cup
Instructions
Set aside a big mixing bowl that has been oiled. Mix the yeast, flour, and salt in a second mixing bowl.
Form a claw with your fingers by pulling your sleeve upwards to your elbow. Combine the dry ingredients in a large mixing bowl and stir until thoroughly mixed.
Mix in the water until everything is well combined. The dough would be somewhat stringy, moist, and fuzzy.
Cover the dough with plastic wrap after placing it in the greased mixing bowl.
Let the dough rise for 2 hours at room temperature (about 70 degrees), just until the surface bubbles.
Flour the top of the dough and turn it out onto a lightly floured work surface. Fold the dough twice over on itself with greased hands. Allow the dough to settle for 15 minutes after covering it loosely with plastic wrap.
Wheat bran, cornmeal, or flour may be used to dust a cleaned lint-free cotton towel. Form the dough into a ball with greased hands and put it, seam side down, just on a towel.
Cover the dough with a second towel and dust the top with cornmeal, wheat bran, or flour. Allow the dough to rise until it has doubled in size and no longer springs back when pressed with a finger.
Meanwhile, preheat the Pit Boss grill to 450 degrees Fahrenheit. Preheat for 10-15 minutes with the lid closed.
Place a covered 6 – 8-quart iron Dutch pan on the grill grate, ideally one that is enameled.

Remove the entire towel, slip your hand under the bottom towel to hold the dough, and gently tip the dough into the prepared pot; seam side up.
Remove the towel from the room. If the dough seems uneven, stir the dish a couple of times; it will straighten up as it bakes.
Heat the bread for thirty min with the cover on the pot. Remove the cover and heat the bread for another 15 to 30 minutes, or until it is beautifully browned and hollow when tapped on the bottom with your knuckles.
Allow cooling on a wire rack. Using a serrated knife, slice the vegetables. Enjoy!

9.176 Cider-Glazed Baked Holiday Ham
Total Time: 2 Hrs 15 mins, Serving: 6
Ingredients
Ham, 1 Large
Apple Cider, 4 Cup
Maple Syrup or Honey, 1/4 Cup
Ground Nutmeg, 1 Pinch
Dijon Mustard, 1/4 Cup
Thick Slice of Apples, 3
Bourbon, 1/4 Cup
Ground Cinnamon, 1/2 tsp
Ground Cloves, 1/4 tsp
Instructions
Once ready to cook, preheat the Pit Boss to 325°F with the lid covered for 15 minutes.
To make clean-up simpler, prepare a roasting pan using heavy-duty foil.
To make a natural roasting rack, arrange apple slices inside the bottom of a roasting pan. Place the ham on top of apple slices and cover with the remaining 1 cup apple cider.
Bake for 1-half hours with the roasting pan straight on the grill grate.
In a small saucepan, mix the remaining 3 cups of apple cider & bourbon & bring to a boil over medium heat for the glaze. Simmer until the liquid has been reduced by one-third. Combine the mustard, cinnamon, honey, cloves, and nutmeg in a mixing bowl.
Glaze ham using apple cider combination as required (use any leftover for serving) then continue cooking
for the next 30 min or until an internal temperature of 140°F is reached when a thermometer is put into the thickest section of meat.
Remove the ham from the grill and set it aside for 20 minutes to rest before serving
If preferred, reheat the leftover sauce & serve with ham. Enjoy!

9.177 Baked Thanksgiving Shepherd's Pie
Total Time: 1 Hr 10 mins, Serving: 6
Ingredients
Kosher Salt, 1 tsp
Flour, 2 tbsp
Canola Oil, 2 tbsp
Garlic, 2 Clove
Chopped Onion, 1 Cup
Chicken Broth, 1 Cup
Chopped Rosemary, 2 tsp
Leftover Turkey, 1 1/2 Pound
Green Beans, 1 Cup
Mashed Potatoes, 2 Cup
Chopped Thyme, 1 tsp
Worcestershire Sauce, 1 tsp
Tomato Paste, 2 tsp
Black Pepper, 1/2 tsp
Leftover Gravy, 1 Cup
Leftover Stuffing, 1 Cup

Instructions
Set the Pit Boss to 400°F, then preheat for 15 minutes with the lid covered when you're ready to cook.
In a medium sauté pan, heat canola oil over medium-high heat. When the oil begins to shimmer, add the onion & cook for 3 to 4 minutes, or until softened and gently browned. Stir in the garlic until everything is well combined. Salt & pepper to taste.
Continue to sauté for another minute after sprinkling the onions with flour and tossing to coat. Combine the leftover gravy, tomato paste, Worcestershire sauce, chicken stock, rosemary, and thyme in a large mixing bowl. To mix, stir everything together. Bring to the boil, then turn off the heat. Cover and cook for 10-12 minutes, even the sauce, has slightly thickened.
Combine the remaining turkey, green beans, and stuffing in an 11x7-inch glass baking dish and distribute evenly.
Starting from around edges to form a seal to avoid the contents from bubbling up, top with mashed potatoes and smooth with just a rubber spatula. Bake for 25 minutes, or until the potatoes start to brown, directly just on the grill grate. Before serving, chill for at least 10 min on a cooling rack. Enjoy!

9.178 Pull-Apart Dinner Rolls
Total Time: 30 mins, Serving: 8
Ingredients
Vegetable Oil, 1/3 Cup
Salt, 1/2 tsp
1 Egg
Cooking Spray
Sugar, 1/4 Cup
Warm Water, 1/4 Cup
Dry Yeast, 2 tbsp
Flour, 3 1/2 Cup
Instructions
Once ready to cook, preheat the Pit Boss to 400°F with the lid covered for 15 min.
Warm water, oil, yeast, and sugar are combined there in a mixing bowl. Allow for 10 minutes of resting time, or until foamy and bubbly.
Mix in the egg, salt, plus two cups of flour using a dough hook until well mixed. 1/2 cup at a time, add the remaining flour (dough will be sticky).
Set aside a cast iron pan that has been sprayed with cooking spray.
Using cooking spray, coat your hands and roll the dough into the 12 balls.
Put in the preheated frypan and set aside for 10 minutes after shaping. Bake for 10 - 15 minutes in a Pit Boss, or till tops are gently brown. Enjoy!

9.179 Pit Boss Baked Rainbow Trout
Total Time: 30 mins, Serving: 2
Ingredients
Rainbow Trout, 2 Whole
Fresh Dill, 1/2 tsp
Olive Oil, 2 tbsp
Onion, 1/2 Large
Ground Black Pepper, 1 tsp
Fresh Thyme, 1/2 tsp
Kosher Sea Salt, 1 tsp
Sliced Lemon, 1 Large
Instructions
Once ready to cook, preheat the Pit Boss to 400°F with the lid covered for 15 minutes.
1 tbsp oil greased a 9x13" baking dish
Place the trout in the baking dish and drizzle with the remaining olive oil. Dill, thyme, and salt are used to season the interior and exterior of the fish. Fill every fish with onion & lemon slices, then season with pepper. On each fish, place a lemon slice.
Bake for 10 minutes in the Pit Boss. Fill the baking dish with 2 tablespoons of boiling water. Continue baking for another 10 minutes or until the salmon flakes easily with just a fork. Enjoy!

9.180 Ultimate Baked Garlic Bread
Total Time: 30 mins, Serving: 4
Ingredients
Butter, 1/2 Cup
1 Baguette
Italian Parsley, 4 tbsp
Chile Flakes
Parmesan Cheese, 1/2 Cup
Garlic, 6 cloves
Salt to taste
Mayonnaise, 1/2 Cup
Mozzarella Cheese, 1 Cup
Instructions
Once ready to cook, preheat the Pit Boss to 375°F with the lid covered for 15 minutes.
Cut the baguette in half lengthwise on a chopping board. Combine butter, parsley, mayonnaise, salt, garlic, and chili flakes in a mixing bowl. Mix thoroughly
Top baguette halves with butter mixture, then mozzarella with Parmesan cheese.
Preheat the grill and place the baguette on it. Cook for 25 to 30 minutes on the grill. Warm the dish before serving. Enjoy!

9.181 BBQ Baked Beans
Total Time: 1 Hr 20 mins, Serving: 6
Ingredients
Yellow Onion, 1
Pork & Beans, 4 Can
Dry Mustard, 2 tbsp
Onion Powder, 1/2 tbsp
Black Pepper, 1 tbsp
Ketchup, 1 Cup
Bacon, 1 Pound
Green Bell Pepper, 1
Kosher Salt, 1/2 tbsp
Garlic Powder, 1/2 tbsp
Instructions
In a chilly sauté skillet over medium heat, place the bacon. Cook until the fat has rendered and the bacon is crispy. Remove the grease from the bacon, saving 2 tablespoons, and put the bacon aside.
Return the saved fat to the pan, along with the onion and pepper. Sauté for 10 minutes or until onions and peppers are transparent. Remove the pan from the heat and put it aside.
Once ready to cook, preheat the Pit Boss to 350°F with the lid covered for 15 min.
Add beans, cooked bacon, onions and peppers, and the remaining ingredients in a 9x13 inch casserole dish. To mix, stir everything together well.
Place the casserole immediately on the grill grate, covered with aluminum foil. Cook, stirring periodically, for 1 hour, and when the sauce got thickened and deepened somewhat in color.
Before serving, remove the steaks from the grill & set them aside for 20 minutes to rest. Enjoy!

9.182 Cornish Game Hens
Total Time: 1 Hr 10 mins, Serving: 4

Ingredients
Sage or Rosemary, 4 Sprig
Pit Boss Chicken Rub
Cornish Game Hens, 4
Butter, 4 tbsp
Instructions
Wash the Cornish game chickens inside and out with cool running water. (Giblets aren't typically included with game chickens, so look for them before washing.) If you discover giblets, you may freeze these for chicken stock.)
Using paper towels, thoroughly dry the area. Knot the legs together along with the butcher's thread and tuck the wings under the backs.
Melted butter should be rubbed all over each fowl. Pit Boss Chicken Rub is used to season the chicken. Place a twig of rosemary in each hen's major cavity.
Set the Pit Boss to 375°F, then preheat for 15 minutes with the lid covered when you're ready to cook.
Roast the chickens for 50–60 minutes, or until the juices flow clear, as well as the core temperature of the thigh, reaches 165°F when measured with an instant-read meat thermometer.
Allow the chickens to settle for 5 min on a dish or platters.
Before serving, garnish with a rosemary sprig. Enjoy

9.183 Peach Tart

Total Time: 1 Hr 20 mins, Serving: 6
Ingredients
Crust
Flour, 1 Cup
Almonds, 1/2 Cup
Ice Water, 8 tbsp
Salt, 1/2 tsp
Sugar, 1 tbsp
Butter, 1 tbsp
Filling
Raspberries, 1/2 Cup
Yellow Peaches, 2
Granulated Sugar, 2 tbsp
Lemon Zest, 1 tbsp
Corn-starch, 2 tsp
Lemon Juice, 1
Main
Topping
Egg Yolk, 1
Butter, 2 tbsp
Almonds, 1/4 Cup
Sugar, 2 tbsp
Instructions
Place the roasted, cooled almonds inside the food processor to create the crust. Pulse until the mixture is coarse. Pulse in the flour, sugar, and salt to mix. Pulse in the butter till it looks like peas and carrots. To solidify, add approximately 1/4 cup of hot water while pulsing.
Once ready to cook, preheat the Pit Boss to 350°F with the lid covered for 15 min.
If your grill permits it, shift the bottom rack from the searing position to the cooking position. Reduce the grill temp to 325°F using a different model.
Place the dough on a floured board and flatten it into a disc. Place on a parchment-lined sheet tray and set aside.
In a medium mixing bowl, combine all of the filling ingredients and 1 tbsp of flour; stir to coat. Fill the middle of the dough with the filling and spread it out, leaving at least 1-two inches of crust visible. Fold the crust's edges over the filling with care.
Using a whisked egg yolk, brush over top of the crust.
Pulse the almonds & sugar for topping together in the mixing bowl. Slowly drizzle in the butter while the engine is running. Place the mixture in a mixing basin and put it aside.
Sprinkle the crumbled almonds over the top.
Bake for 1 hour, or until the crust is golden brown as well as the filling is thickened and is bubbling, directly upon this grill grate.
Serve the tart with ice cream while it's still warm. Enjoy!

9.184 Baked Strawberry Rhubarb Pie

Total Time: 50 mins, Serving: 6
Ingredients
Salt, 1 tsp
Flour, 2 1/2 Cup
Chilled Butter, 1 Cup
Ice Water, 8 tbsp
Strawberries, 3 Cup
Sugar
Unsalted Butter, 3 tbsp
Sugar, 17 tbsp
Rhubarb, 2 Cup
"Minute" Tapioca, 3 tbsp
1 Egg
Instructions
Combine salt, flour, and sugar in a mixing basin. Mix half of the butter with a fork or even a pastry cutter until it becomes a coarse meal. Work in the remaining butter until the dough is smooth and elastic.
Drizzle 6-8 tbsp water in small increments, mixing and tossing after each addition. When there is still a little amount of dried flour throughout the bowl, stop adding water. The dough should not be overmixed, or it will turn firm.
Split the dough in half, roll it into a disc, and cover it in plastic wrap. Refrigerate for 30 minutes to let flavors meld.
In a large mixing basin, combine the rhubarb and strawberries. Combine the sugar and tapioca in a separate bowl. Combine the strawberries & rhubarb with the tapioca. Allow for 15 minutes of resting time.
Once ready to cook, preheat the oven to 375°F with the lid covered for 15 minutes.
Roll one of the dough rounds into a circle big enough to fit a 10-inch pie plate using a rolling pin. Cut the extra dough around the pan and place it on the dish. Using a fork, prick the bottom.
On top of the pie dough, place a sheet of parchment paper. Place additional dried rice or beans on top of parchment paper to hold it in place. Bake for 15 minutes on the Pit Boss.
Remove the pie from the grill and toss out the parchment paper as well as the rice/beans. Strawberry rhubarb filling should be used to fill the pie. Dot butter all over the top of the filling.
Place the second pie crust on top of the filling and roll it out. Cut off any extra dough and press the edges together to seal. Make several slits at the top with a knife.
Apply an egg wash to the top of the cake. Sugar should be sprinkled on top.
Place the pie on the grill & bake for 45 minutes. The pie shell must be golden brown in color and cooked through in the middle. Enjoy!

9.185 Tater Tot Bake

Total Time: 20 mins, Serving: 4
Ingredients
Salt & Pepper
Frozen Tater Tots, 1 Whole
Green Onion, 1/4 Cup
Cheddar Cheese, 1 Cup
Sour Cream, 1 Cup

Bacon, 1/2 Cup
Instructions
Prepare Pit Boss to 375 °F for 10 minutes with lid closed.
To make clean-up easier, line a baking tray with aluminum foil and put frozen potato tots on top.
Season to taste using Pit Boss Veggie Shake either salt & pepper.
Sauté the tater tots for about 10 minutes on a preheated grill grate with the baking sheet on top.
Drizzle sour cream on tater tots that have been fried.
Over the top of tater tots, scatter the cheese, bacon pieces, and green onions.
Increase the heat to high and cook for another 5 minutes, or until the cheese has melted. Serve immediately. Enjoy!

9.186 Baked Pig Candy
Total Time: 1 Hrs 10 mins, Serving: 4
Ingredients
Maple Syrup, 1/2 Cup
Thin Sliced Bacon, 1 Pound
Chipotle Chile Powder, 3 tbsp
Light Brown Sugar, 2 Cup
Instructions
Once ready to cook, preheat the Pit Boss to 250°F with the lid covered for 15 minutes.
On such a large disposable, shallow aluminum pan, arrange the bacon pieces in a single layer. Maple syrup should be brushed on each bacon piece. Brown sugar is liberally sprinkled on top, followed by chipotle powder.
Place the lid on the grill & cook for approximately 1 hour, or when the bacon has soaked some brown sugar and seems to be crispy. Take the bacon from the pan and arrange it on a wire rack placed over some rimmed baking sheet in a single layer. Allow it to sit for a few minutes until the bacon is completely dry. Refrigerate for up to 1 week
in an airtight jar with parchment paper among layers. Enjoy

9.187 Pulled Pork Stew
Total Time: 2 Hrs 5 mins, Serving: 4
Ingredients
Chicken Stock, 2 Cup
Roasted Red Peppers, 15 Ounce
Salsa Verde, 16 Ounce
Pulled Pork, 1 Pound
Sliced Avocado
Ground Cumin, 1 tsp
Black Beans, 15 Ounce
Salt & Pepper
Instructions
Preheat the oven to 375 ° F and bake for 10 minutes with the lid covered.
In a large mixing bowl, combine the black beans, fire-roasted tomatoes, salsa verde, cumin, shredded pork, and chicken broth. To taste, season with salt.
Cook for 1 hour on the Pit Boss, stirring after twenty minutes. After 60 minutes, cover the Dutch oven with a lid and continue it to cook for another hour.
Avocado, Fresh herbs, and sour cream may be added to the stew towards the end. Enjoy while it's still hot!

9.188 Baked Buffalo Cauliflower Bites
Total Time: 55 mins, Serving: 4
Ingredients
Olive Oil, 2 tbsp
Hot Sauce, 2 tbsp
Sour Cream, 1/4 Cup
Salt & Pepper
Sriracha, 1 tbsp
Cauliflower, 1 Head
Ranch Dressing, 1 Cup
Lemon Juice, 1/2 tsp
Salt, 1 tsp
Butter, 1 tbsp
Heavy Cream, 1/4 Cup
Instructions
Adjust the timer to 350°F and preheat for 15 minutes with the lid covered when ready to cook.
Spread cauliflower florets on a sheet pan and toss with salt & olive oil. Cook for 25-35 minutes, till cooked through and gently browned, directly upon that grill grate.
Mix Cholula, Sriracha, lemon juice, and melted butter while the cauliflower is cooking. Mix thoroughly.
Toss the cauliflower with the spicy sauce combination once it has been removed from the grill. Return to the grill for yet another 5 minutes after spreading on the baking sheet.
To make the Ranch Sauce, whisk together the sour cream, ranch, heavy cream, salt, and pepper in a separate bowl.
Buffalo cauliflower should be served with ranch dressing. Enjoy!

9.189 Butternut Squash Macaroni and Cheese
Total Time: 55 mins, Serving: 2
Ingredients
Yellow Onion, 1 Small
Milk, 1 Cup
Salt to taste
Cheese, 1 Cup
Chicken Broth, 1/2 Cup
Macaroni, 2 Cup
Butternut Squash, 1 Medium
Pepper
Instructions
Start the Pit Boss grill, adjust the timer to 225 degrees F, and warm for 10 minutes with the lid closed.
Prick butternut squash several times with a fork and put on grill grate. Cook for 40 minutes, or until the vegetables are soft.
Scoop out the meat and toss the seeds once it's cooked.
Cook elbow macaroni as directed on the box. Drain the water and put it aside.
Sauté chopped onion in a medium pan until aromatic and golden. In a food processor, combine broth, milk,
salt, onions, and butternut squash. Puree until the mixture is smooth and creamy. Season to taste with salt and pepper.
Pour the blended sauce over the cooked noodles and sprinkle the shredded cheese over the top. Whisk to melt the cheese, then add milk until the desired consistency is achieved. Warm the dish before serving. Enjoy!

9.190 Baked Loaded Tater Tots
Total Time: 45 mins, Serving: 6
Ingredients
Black Beans, 1 Can
Frozen Tater Tots, 2 Pound
Jalapeños, 1
Leftover Queso, 1 Cup
Red Onion, 1
Sour Cream, 1/2 Cup
Leftover Chili, 1 1/2 Cup
Chopped Cilantro, 1/2 Cup
Instructions
Once ready to cook, preheat the Pit Boss to 375°F with the lid covered for 15 minutes.
Using a sheet tray, spread freezing tots out and put directly

upon this grill grate.
Cook until tots are crispy, about 20 to 25 minutes.
Warm queso, chili, and beans go on top. Return to the grill for another 15 minutes.
Remove from the grill and serve the cilantro, red onion, sour cream, and jalapeno on the side. Enjoy!

9.191 Pit Boss Baked Focaccia
Total Time: 55 mins, Serving: 4
Ingredients
Warm Water, 1 Cup
Instant Yeast, 1 tbsp
Salt, 1 tsp
Sea Salt
Olive Oil, 3 tbsp
Flour, 2 1/2 Cup
Sugar, 1 tsp
Fresh Thyme, 1 tbsp
Grated Parmesan, 2 tbsp
Instructions
In the bowl of a stand mixer, combine the yeast, water, sugar, salt, flour, and oil and mix for 60 seconds. You may alternatively use a food processor to combine the flour, sugar, salt, and yeast in a mixing bowl, then process while slowly pouring in the warm water and olive oil. Mix until everything is well mixed as well as a ball form.
If necessary, gently roll the sticky dough out lightly and put it in a 12" cast iron pan that has been well-oiled. Drizzle additional olive oil over the topping of the dough. Allow rising in a warm place for 45 minutes, covered with plastic wrap as well as a kitchen towel.
Just after the dough has risen, push it to the pan's edges and cover it once more. Allow for a 15-minute rising time.
Once ready to cook, preheat the Pit Boss to 375°F with the lid covered for 15 minutes.
Uncover the dough, then push it into divots around the sides of the pan with your fingers.
Drizzle the olive oil and herbs, then top with Parmesan & flaky salt.
Bake it for 30 minutes on the Pit Boss, or until lightly browned & cooked through. Allow cooling somewhat before slicing and removing from cast iron. Enjoy!

9.192 Funfetti Ice Cream Sandwich
Total Time: 9 mins, Serving: 8
Ingredients
Baking Powder, 1 tsp
Baking Soda, 1/2 tsp
Sugar, 1 Cup
Butter, 1 Cup
Vanilla, 1 tsp
1 Egg
Salt, 2/3 tsp
Ice Cream
Flour, 2 1/2 Cup
Milk, 2 tbsp
Multi-colored Sprinkles, 3/4 Cup
Instructions
When you're ready to cook, fire up the Pit Boss as per the manufacturer's directions. Preheat the oven to 350 °F and bake for 10 minutes with the lid covered.
Stir to combine salt & baking soda in a mixing basin. Cream the sugar and butter together with an electric mixer until light and creamy. In a separate bowl, whisk together the egg and vanilla extract.
1/2 cup at that same time until all of the flour has been combined. Mix in the milk plus sprinkles until everything is well mixed.
Drop 2 tablespoons of dough onto a prepared cookie sheet, spacing them 4 inches apart. To keep the dough from sticking, flatten it with the bottom of a sugar-dusted glass.
Put the cookie sheet on the grill and cook for 8 minutes, or until the sides are gently browned. Remove the cookies from the grill and set them aside to cool.
Sandwich your ice cream over two cookies, wrap the edges in sprinkles, and enjoy right away. Enjoy!

9.193 Green Bean Casserole Circa 1955
Total Time: 40 mins, Serving: 6
Ingredients
Mushroom Soup Cream, 1 Can
Soy Sauce, 2 tsp
Black Pepper, 1/2 tsp
Green Beans, 1 1/2 Pound
Milk, 1/2 Cup
Red Bell Pepper, 1/4 Cup
Worcestershire Sauce, 1/2 tsp
Crispy Fried Onions, 1.334 Cup
Instructions
Combine the soy sauce, beans (trimmed and boiled until soft, or 2 16 oz. cans), soup, Worcestershire sauce, milk, black pepper, 2/3 cup onion rings, and red pepper, if using, in a mixing bowl. Fill a 1-1/2 quarts casserole dish halfway with the mixture.
Once ready to cook, preheat the grill to 375°F with the lid covered for 15 minutes.
Cook the casserole for 25 to 30 minutes, and when the filling is heated and bubbling. Cook for another 5 to 10 minutes, and until the onions become crisp and start to brown.

9.194 Pretzel Rolls
Total Time: 1 Hrs 20 mins, Serving: 4
Ingredients
Quick-Rise Yeast, 1 Packet
Salt, 1 tsp
Hot Water, 1 Cup
Sugar, 7 tsp
Baking Soda, 1/4 Cup
Bread Flour, 2 3/4 Cup
Caraway Seeds, 1/2 tsp
Celery Seed, 1/2 tsp
Cornmeal
Coarse salt
Water, 8 Cup
Egg White, 1 Whole
Instructions
In a hand blender or standing beater fitted with a dough hook, mix bread caraway seeds, flour, salt, 1 tsp sugar, 1 packet yeast, and celery seeds.
Pour hot water slowly into the machine while it is running, adding just enough water to create a smooth, elastic dough. Kneading takes 1 minute. (Alternatively, you may need this by hand for several minutes.)
Grease a medium mixing bowl. Toss the dough into the basin and flip to coat it. Cover bowl using plastic wrap, then a cloth, and let the dough rise in a warm, draft-free location for 35 minutes.
A big baking sheet should be floured. Punch dough down & knead until smooth on a lightly floured surface. Cut each piece into eight pieces. Make a ball out of each piece of dough.
Put dough balls on a baking sheet, gently flattening each one. Cut an X in the top center of every dough ball with a serrated knife. Cover with a cloth and then let dough ball rise for

approximately 20 minutes, or until fully doubled in volume.
Begin the Pit Boss with Smoke with the lid open until a fire has been created when you're ready to cook (4-5 minutes). Preheat the oven to 375 degrees Fahrenheit (190 degrees Celsius) with the lid closed for 10 minutes.
Another baking sheet should be greased, and cornmeal sprinkled. In a big saucepan, bring water to a boil. Mix in the baking soda and sugar. Cook for 30 seconds on each side with 3 rolls (or as many as will fit nicely in the pot).
Transfer rolls to baking sheet using a slotted spoon, X side up. Continue with the remaining rolls. Egg white glaze should be applied to the rolls. Using coarse salt, liberally season the rolls. Bake the rolls for 20 to 25 minutes, or until they are golden brown. Cool for 10 minutes
on wire racks. Rolls may be served warm or even at room temp. Enjoy!

9.195 Baked Rhubarb Cobbler
Total Time: 50 mins, Serving: 8
Ingredients
Baking Powder, 1 1/2 tsp
Butter, 8 tbsp
Flour, 1 1/2 Cup
Brown Sugar, 1 Cup
Salt to taste
Lemon Zest, 1 tsp
Raw Sugar, 2 tbsp
Lemon juice, 1/4 Whole
Fresh Rhubarb, 1 Pound
Sugar, 3 tbsp
Salt, 1/2 tsp
Sour Cream, 1/2 Cup
Vanilla, 1 tsp
Instructions
Once ready to cook, preheat the oven to 350°F with the lid covered for 15 minutes.
Sift the flour, sugar, baking powder, and salt in a medium mixing basin. Cut in the soft butter with a pastry cutter as well as two knives until the fat & flour are now the sizes of peas.
Stir in the sour cream until it barely comes all together.
Combine the chopped rhubarb, lemon juice, sugar, salt, lemon zest, and vanilla in a small bowl. Toss to coat, then pour into a baking dish of choice (8x8 works great).
Place dollops of biscuit dough over the top of the rhubarb until all of the dough is gone. Raw sugar should be sprinkled on top. Cook for 35 minutes, or until the cookie topping is golden brown and the cobbler is bubbling, directly upon that grill grate.
Serve with a dollop of whipped cream on top. Enjoy!

INDEX OF RECIPES

(Adobo Skewers) Honey Lime Chicken	285
3 Ingredient Pot Roast	26
3-2-1 BBQ Beef Cheeks	37

A

A Classic Smoking Cocktail	194
A Smoking Classic Cocktail	324
A.J. Allmendinger's Blackened Salmon	266
Albacore Tuna (Grilled) with Tomato-Potato Casserole	236
Alder Smoked Scallops with Citrus & Garlic Butter Sauce	260
Ancho-Chile Chicken Legs (Smoked BBQ)	174
Ancho-Chili Smoked BBQ Chicken Legs	129
Andouille, Chicken & Potato Roasted Gumbo	158
Anytime Pork Roast	91
Apple & Bourbon Glazed Ham	101
Apple Cider Smoked	194
Apple Juice BBQ Brined Pulled Pork	116
Applejack O'Lantern Cocktail Grilled	194
Applewood Smoked Bacon.	111
Apricot Pork Tenderloin	89
Apricot-Sauced Roasted Ham	86
Artichoke & Spinach Dip	366
Arugula Pesto & Smoked Chorizo	86
Asian BBQ Chicken	131
Asian-Style Grilled Beef Skewers	23
Asian-Style Grilled Rib-Eye Steak	37
Asian-Style Pork Tenderloin	92
Asparagus Grilled & Honey-Glazed Carrots	194
Asparagus Grilled & Spinach Salad	182
Asparagus Grilled Along with Wild Mushrooms & Fried Shallots	212
Asparagus Roasted	195

B

Baby Back Ribs Smoked	79
Baby Carrots Grilled & Fennel with Spanish sauce (Romesco)	186
Baby Carrots Grilled and Fennel with Romesco	191
Bacon & Brie Mac & Cheese	93
Bacon & Cheese & Brie Mac	86
Bacon Asparagus (Wrapped)	186
Bacon Cheddar (Smashed) Baby Potatoes	278
Bacon Cheesy Malibu Chicken	164
Bacon Chili Cheese Dogs	118
Bacon Dog Grilled	82
Bacon Explosion	119
Bacon Green Baked Bean Casserole	211
Bacon Jalapeño Chicken	141
Bacon lattice turkey	142
Bacon Old-Fashioned Cocktail	326
Bacon Onion Ring	89
Bacon Pork Pinwheels (Kansas Lollipops)	110
Bacon Roasted & Wrapped Beef Tenderloin	68
Bacon Salad with Beet (Roasted)	215
Bacon Stuffed Smoked Pork Loin	107
Bacon Stuffed Weaved Turkey Breast	168
Bacon Weave Mac n' Cheese	374
Bacon Weave Smoked Country Sausage	101
Bacon Weaved Stuffed Turkey Breast	367
Bacon with Roasted Beans (Green)	181
Bacon Wrapped Shrimp	248
Bacon-Draped Introduced in Pork Loin Roast	73
Bacon-Rubbed Smoked Ribs Applewood	98
Bacon-Wrapped Chicken Stuffed Breast	154
Bacon-Wrapped Chicken Wings	178
Bacon-Wrapped Scallops	238
Bacon-Wrapped Shrimp	227
Bacon-Wrapped Skewers	151
Bacon-wrapped turkey legs	143
Bacon-Wrapped Water Chestnuts BBQ	84
Bagel Breakfast Sandwich	117
Baja-style Grilled Fish Tacos	247
Baked Apple Bourbon Crisp	311
Baked Apple Pear Crisp	316

Baked Apple Pie with Cheddar Cheese	316
Baked Apple Turnover	302
Baked Apricot Glazed Chicken Thighs	138
Baked Artichoke Dip	280
Baked Artichoke Dip with Homemade Flatbread	379
Baked Asparagus Pancetta Cheese Tart	354
Baked Bacon Caramel Popcorn	118
Baked Bacon Green Bean Casserole	361
Baked Bacon-Weaved Honey Bourbon-Glazed Meatloaf	48
Baked Ballpark Mac and Cheese	113
Baked BBQ Chicken Potato	169
Baked Bean Casserole with the Pulled Pork	105
Baked Blueberry French Toast Casserole	377
Baked Bourbon Monkey Bread	301
Baked Bread Pudding by Doug Scheiding	305
Baked Breakfast Mini Quiches	297
Baked Breakfast Sausage Casserole	109
Baked Brie	293
Baked Brownie Bread Pudding	321
Baked Buffalo Cauliflower Bites	393
Baked Candied Bacon Cinnamon Rolls	98
Baked Caramel Pecan Brownie	315
Baked Carrot Sheet Cake with Cream Cheese Frosting	301
Baked Cast Iron Berry Cobbler	300
Baked Cast-Iron Cookie with Smoked Bourbon Whip	309
Baked Cauliflower Tots	385
Baked Cheesy Accordion Potatoes	363
Baked Cheesy Corn Pudding	360
Baked Cheesy Garlic Fries	387
Baked Cheesy Parmesan Grits	366
Baked Cherry Bourbon Pie	304
Baked Cherry Cheesecake Galette	305
Baked Cherry Cobbler	307
Baked Cherry Pie	356
Baked Chicken Pot Pie	179
Baked Chocolate Brownie Cookies with Egg Nog	317
Baked Chocolate Coconut Brownies	318
Baked Chocolate Soufflé with Smoked Whipped Cream	319
Baked Cinnamon Rolls	353
Baked Coffee Cake	315
Baked Cornbread Sausage Stuffing	347
Baked Cornbread Turkey Tamale Pie	389
Baked Corned Beef Au Gratin	46
Baked Corned Beef Au Grautin	362
Baked Cranberry Chicken	133
Baked Creamed Spinach	208
Baked Crispy Chicken Thighs with Buffalo Sauce	170
Baked Deep Dish Supreme Pizza	89
Baked Donut Holes	352
Baked Dutch Baby	299
Baked Eggs in Bacon Nest	125
Baked Game Day Hatch Chile and Bacon Hot Dish	127
Baked Garlic Bread	277
Baked Garlic Duchess Potatoes	218
Baked Garlic Parmesan Wings	140
Baked German Pork Schnitzel with Grilled Lemons	105
Baked Gluten-Free Banana Bread	301
Baked Granola	349
Baked Green Bean Casserole with Crispy Shallots	386
Baked Green Bean Casserole with Pulled Pork	355
Baked Green Chile Mac & Cheese by Doug Scheiding	385
Baked Halibut Fish Sticks with Spicy Coleslaw	249
Baked Halibut Sandwich with Smoked Tartar Sauce	252
Baked Heirloom Tomato Tart	372
Baked Honey Cornbread Cake	302
Baked Honey Glazed Ham	382
Baked Irish Creme Cake	301
Baked Loaded Tater Tots	393
Baked Mac & Cheese with Jerky Dust	343
Baked Macaroni & Cheese	360
Baked Maple and Brown Sugar Bacon	379
Baked Maple Venison Sausage Quiche	387
Baked Meat Bagel	387
Baked Molten Chocolate Cake	300
Baked Otium House Rolls	386

Baked Parker House Rolls	368
Baked Peach Cobbler	124
Baked Peach Cobbler Cupcakes	315
Baked Pear & Fig Upside Down Cake	308
Baked Pear Tarte Tatin	306
Baked Pear, Bacon & Brown Butter Stuffing	367
Baked Pickles along with Buttermilk Dip	219
Baked Pig Candy	393
Baked Pimento Bacon Mac & Cheese	384
Baked Pit Boss Potato Torte	183
Baked Pork Belly Mac and Cheese	106
Baked Potato Skins with Pulled Pork	98
Baked Potato Soup Smoked	211
Baked Potatoes & Celery Root Au Gratin	372
Baked Potatoes Salt Crusted	187
Baked Pretzel Bites & Beer Cheese Dip	357
Baked Prosciutto-Wrapped Chicken Breast with Spinach and Boursin	126
Baked Pumpkin Cheesecake	318
Baked Pumpkin Pie	318
Baked Queso Blanco Dip	362
Baked Raspberry French Toast Casserole	321
Baked Rhubarb Cobbler	309
Baked S'Mores Donuts	379
Baked Sage & Sausage Stuffing	374
Baked Salmon Cakes	229
Baked Salt-Crusted Potatoes	202
Baked Savory & Sweet Baked Yams	218
Baked Soft Gingerbread Cookie	319
Baked Spinach Creamed	219
Baked Steelhead	263
Baked Strawberry Rhubarb Pie	392
Baked Strawberry Shortbread	316
Baked Summer Berry Cheesecake	319
Baked Sweet & Savory Yams	204
Baked Sweet and Savory Yams by Bennie Kendrick	350
Baked Sweet Potato Hash	184
Baked Sweet Potatoes	368
Baked Thanksgiving Shepherd's Pie	390
Baked Tuna Noodle Casserole	230
Baked Venison Casserole Tater Tot	354

Baked Venison Meatloaf with Potato Puree	356
Baked Walnut Pumpkin Cookies	311
Baked Whole Fish in Sea Salt	231
Baked Winter Squash Au Gratin	184
Baked Wood-Fired Pizza	370
Baked Ziti with Italian Sausage	48
Banana Bacon Pancakes	83
Banana Trifle (Smoked)	313
Bananas Foster	313
Batter Up Cocktail	337
BBQ Bacon-Wrapped Water Chestnuts	90
BBQ Baked Beans	391
BBQ Beef Ribs	28
BBQ Beef Sandwich	62
BBQ Beef Short Ribs	35
BBQ Beef Short Ribs with Pit Boss Prime Rib Rub	43
BBQ Beef Tamale Casserole	24
BBQ breakfast sausage not so fatty	142
BBQ Brisket Breakfast Tacos	49
BBQ Brisket Competition Style	66
BBQ Brisket Hot Dog	43
BBQ Brisket Reuben	35
BBQ Brisket Sandwich Along with Special Sauce	59
BBQ Brisket with Pit Boss Coffee Rub	32
BBQ Brown Sugar Bacon Bites	89
BBQ Burnt Ends	32
BBQ Chicken Bacon Ranch Sandwich	132
BBQ Chicken Baked Potato	368
BBQ Chicken Drumsticks	154
BBQ Chicken Legs	137
BBQ Chicken Nachos	161
BBQ Chicken Sandwich	137
BBQ Chicken Thighs	174
BBQ Chicken Tostada	140
BBQ Chicken Wings with Spicy Honey Glaze	138
BBQ Dragged Pork and Pork Belly Bánh Mì	104
BBQ dry rubbed turkey drumsticks	142
BBQ Game Day Chicken Wings and Thighs	137
BBQ Half Chicken with Alabama White Sauce	173

BBQ Halved Chickens	157
BBQ Meatball Onion Bombs	53
BBQ Oysters	265
BBQ Paleo Pork Spareribs	110
BBQ Pork Belly Tacos	111
BBQ Pork Chop Seared	82
BBQ Pulled Pork Breakfast Burrito with Smoked Hot Sauce	119
BBQ Pulled Pork Pizza	103
BBQ Pulled Pork Sliders	94
BBQ Pulled Pork with Sweet & Heat BBQ Sauce	111
BBQ pulled turkey sandwiches	149
BBQ Quick Ribs	120
BBQ Rib Sandwich	108
BBQ Roasted Salmon	227
BBQ Salmon with Bourbon Glaze	274
BBQ Spareribs with Classic Wedge Salad	95
BBQ Spareribs with Spicy Mandarin Glaze	97
BBQ Spatchcocked Chicken	128
BBQ St Louis Fashion Ribs with Homemade BBQ Sauce	122
Beantown Chicken Wings Grilled	161
Beaver Tails	313
Beef Pot Roast	39
Beef Satay	32
Beef Short Ribs Braised Along with Creamy Grits	172
Beef Stew Old-Fashioned	70
Beef Tenderloin with Tomato Vinaigrette	35
Beer & Smoke Cocktail	339
Beer Brined Corned Beef	47
Beer Can Chicken Roasted	167
Beer-Braised Cabbage along With Bacon	209
Beer-Braised Cabbage with Bacon	107
Beer-Braised Chicken Tacos with Jalapeño Relish	176
Beer-Braised Corned Beef & Irish Vegetables	29
Beer-brined turkey	148
Beet (Roasted) & Bacon Salad	216
Beginner's Smoked Beef Brisket	34
Belly Bourbon Beans of Pork (Baked)	123

Big Game Day BBQ Ribs	96
Big Game Roast Chicken	162
Bison Summer Sausage & Smoked Wild Boar	277
Blackberry Bourbon Smash	338
Blackened Catfish	267
Blackened Catfish Tacos	271
Blistered Curry Cauliflower	202
Bloody Mary Flank Steak	41
Bloody Mary Wings (Grilled)	285
Bloody Mary with Grilled Garnishes	338
Blue Cheese & Peppercorn Butter over Beef Tenderloin Steaks	27
Blueberry Bread Pudding	311
Blueberry Sausage (Grilled)	76
Bologna Smoked.	84
Boneless stuffed turkey breast	134
Bourbon Bacon Stuffing	124
Bourbon BBQ Chicken Kabobs	175
Bourbon Glazed Ham & Apple	81
Bourbon-Braised Beef Short Ribs	56
Braised Alarm Chili	67
Braised Beef Short Ribs with Mashed Potatoes	55
Braised Beer Chicken Stew	139
Braised Brunswick Stew	50
Braised Butter Green Beans	183
Braised Cincinnati Chili	47
Braised Collard Greens & Bacon	380
Braised Italian Meatballs	171
Braised Mediterranean Beef Brisket	31
Braised Pork Chile Verde	97
Brats in Beer	123
Breakfast Brisket Hash Recipe	36
Breakfast Mini Quiches (Baked)	284
Breakfast Mini Quiches Baked	205
Breakfast Pizza Grilled	88
Breakfast Strata Holiday	85
Brie stuffed turkey burgers	135
Brined Smoked Brisket	27
Brisket Tacos with Smoked Cilantro Cream	56
Broccoli Rabe (Grilled)	184
Broccoli Rabe Grilled	194
Broil Cajun Pit Boss	217
Brown Sugar Bacon Bites (BBQ)	284

Brown Sugar Bacon Bites BBQ	81
Brownie Pudding of Bread (Baked)	312
Brush Fire Cocktail	337
Brussels (Smoked & Shredded) Sprout Salad	211
Brussels Shredded Sprout Salad Smoked	222
Buck Grapefruit Cocktail Grilled	223
Bucket O' Chicken Baked	162
Buffalo & Pork Stuffed Poblano Peppers	105
Buffalo (Baked) Chicken Dip	282
Buffalo Blue Cheese Grilled Corn	210
Buffalo Chicken Dip Baked	159
Buffalo Chicken Thighs	138
Bulldog Margarita	336
Burnt Orange Julep Cocktail	336
Butternut Roasted Squash Soup	205
Butternut Squash	189
Butternut Squash Macaroni and Cheese	393

C

Cabbage Braised-Beer with Bacon	83
Cajun Brined Maple Smoked Turkey Breast	136
Cajun Brined Smoked Turkey Breast	175
Cajun Broil Pit Boss	78
Cajun Chicken Wings Smoked	167
Cajun Crab Stuffed Shrimp & Jicama Corn Salad Recipe	271
Cajun Smoked Shrimp	232
California Club Chicken	141
Cannonball Cocktail	337
Caramelized Bourbon Baked Pears	300
Caribbean Curry Grilled Lobsters with Garlic Lime Asparagus	265
Carne Asada Tacos	171
Carolina Pulled Pork Sandwiches (Smoked)	121
Carrot Souffle	308
Carrots along with Pistachio & Pomegranate Relish Roasted	208
Casserole Green Bean	182
Cast Iron Pineapple Upside Down Cake	310

Cast Iron Potatoes	211
Cauliflower Roasted	221
Cauliflower Whole Roasted with Garlic Parmesan Butter	199
Cedar plank salmon	268
Cedar Plank Salmon with Sweet Thai Chili Sauce Glaze	243
Cedar Smoked Salmon	270
Cedar-Plank Salmon with Mango Salsa	238
Chardonnay Chicken with Roasted Root Vegetables	175
Cheesecake Frypan Brownie	314
Cheesesteak Sandwich Grilled	225
Cheesy Baked Accordion Potatoes	213
Chef's Brisket	32
Cherry BBQ Steak Skewers	45
Cherry Smoked Bomb Chicken	158
Chewy Coconut Gluten-Free Cookies	314
Chicken Cordon Bleu Baked	150
Chicken Fajita Skewers Grilled	161
Chicken Lollipops	156
Chicken Roasted with Wild Rice & Mushrooms	151
Chicken Smoked with Apricot BBQ Glaze	168
Chicken Wings (Tandoori)	283
Chicken, Andouille & Roasted Potato Gumbo	259
Chile Chicken Thighs	138
Chili-Lime Corn (Grilled)	191
Chimichurri Sauce	188
Chimichurri Smoked Rib-Eyes	46
Chinese Jumbo Shrimp	248
Chinese Shrimp with Sweet Sherry	241
Chipotle Honey Wings	140
Chipotle Ketchup with Pit Boss Fries	183
Chipotle-Lime Poultry Bowls with Guacamole	173
Chocolate Bark Brisket	69
Chocolate Chip Cookies	310
Chocolate Chip Cookies (Mint)	314
Chopped Grilled Pork along with Pineapple-Mango Salsa	79
Chorizo Armadillo Eggs	277
Chorizo Cheese Stuffed Burgers	40
Christmas Brussel Sprouts	213

Christmas Shortbread Cookies	298
Cider Brew Cocktail Spiced	195
Cider Hot-Smoked Salmon	253
Cider-Glazed Baked Holiday Ham	390
Cinnamon Almonds Roasted	193
Citrus Brined Pork Roast with Fig Mostarda	96
Citrus Salmon	243
Classic Beef Chili	45
Classic Sausage Stuffing	103
Cocktail Batter Up	197
Cocoa Crusted Grilled Flank Steak	33
Cocoa-Crusted Pork Tenderloin	100
Coconut Shrimp Jalapeño Poppers	259
Coffee Break Smoked Beef Jerky	25
Cold Brew Coffee Smoked	192
Cold Smoked Cheese	223
Cold-Smoked Salmon Gravlax	257
Competition BBQ Chicken Thighs	174
Competition Style BBQ Pork Ribs	97
Competition Style BBQ Pulled Pork	103
Competition-Style Spareribs	122
Cooked Potato Skins along with Pulled Pork	80
Cooked Taco Skillet Dip	278
Cooked Teff Flatbread along with Zhoug Sauce	279
Cookies of Peanut Butter	314
Corn Dog Bites (Baked)	121
Corn Grilled on the Cob with Garlic and Parmesan	192
Corn on The Cob Grilled	194
Corn Salad Mexican Street	199
Corn Salsa (Grilled)	188
Corned Baked Beef Au Grautin	212
Corned Beef Hash	51
Cornish Game Hens	391
Crab Cakes	251
Crab Stuffed Mushrooms	269
Cran-Apple Tequila Punch with Smoked Oranges	335
Crème Brûlée	306
Croissant S'mores on the Grill	300
Crushed Cheddar Baby Potatoes Bacon	181
Cuban Sandwich Cubano	119

D

Dan Patrick Display Chorizo Armadillo Eggs	74
Dark Chocolate Brownies with Bacon-Salted Caramel	299
Deep Dish Supreme Pizza (Baked)	282
Deli-Style Grilled Turkey Breast	175
Deviled Eggs Smoked	222
Diablo Grilled Chicken Thighs	133
Diva Q's Herb-Crusted Prime Rib	30
Donut Bread Pudding	299
Double Chocolate Chip Brownie Pie	318
Double Decker Tacos from Pit Boss BBQ	83
Double-Decker Pulled Pork Nachos with Smoked Cheese	114
Drunken Peach Cobbler	378
Dry brine Pit Boss turkey	146
Dry Brined Texas Beef Ribs by Doug Scheiding	44
Dry Rub Wings Smoked	169
Dublin Delight Cocktail	336
Duck Confit, Red Onion Jam, and Goat Cheese Crostinis	127
Dutch Baby with Bourbon Apples	298

E

Easy Garlic Cheese Bombs	381
Egg Cups & Grilled Ham	85
Elite 8 Punch Cocktail	337
Espresso Beef Tenderloin (Coriander & Rubbed)	27
Everything Pigs in a Blanket	102

F

Fall Vegetables (Roasted)	189
Fall-off-the-bone BBQ Ribs	100
Famous Chef Curtis' Chimichurri Sauce	209
Fennel with Romesco & Grilled Baby Carrots	203
Fig Slider Cocktail	197
Filet Mignon Smoked with Sweet Pepper Relish & Baked Ricotta	224

Fingerling Grilled Potato Salad	213
Fish Tacos	269
Flank Steak Matambre	50
Flat Iron Steaks	65
Flourless Chocolate Cake with Raspberry Sauce	304
French Onion Dip (Grilled)	191
French Pit Boss Dip Sandwich	61
French Toast of Raspberry Casserole (Baked)	312
Fried Halibut Fish Sticks	228
Frypan Potato Cake	189
Funfetti Ice Cream Sandwich	311

G

Game Day Cheese Dip	377
Game Day Micheladas	323
Garden Gimlet Cocktail	334
Garlic & Herb Roasted Prime Rib	66
Garlic and Herb Stuffed Prime Rib Roast	50
Garlic BBQ Chicken	159
Garlic Duchess Potatoes Baked	204
Garlic Fries (Cheesy & Baked)	185
Garlic Herbed Potato Wedges	181
Garlic Parmesan Grilled Filet Mignon	30
Garlic Salmon	233
Garlic Shrimp Pesto Bruschetta	270
Glazed Cajun Meatloaf	57
Glazed Ham	369
Gluten-Free Baked Fruit Crisps	320
Gluten-Free Mashed Potato Cakes	198
Gochujang BBQ Pork Ribs Marinated	110
Goddess Green Chicken Legs	156
Grass-fed Beef Burgers	43
Greek Chicken Pizza	178
Green Bean Casserole	194
Green Bean Casserole Baked with Pulled Pork	207
Green Bean Casserole Circa 1955	394
Green Beans Roasted with Bacon	200
Green Beans Southern	198
Green Chile Potatoes Mashed	199
Grilled Ahi Tuna Sliders	242
Grilled Albacore Tuna with Potato-Tomato Casserole	238
Grilled Apple Pie	310
Grilled Applejack O'Lantern Cocktail	325
Grilled Artichokes Along with Sauce Gribiche	213
Grilled Asian Chicken Burgers	176
Grilled Asian lettuce wrap turkey burger	147
Grilled Asparagus & Spinach Salad	214
Grilled Bacon Cheeseburger	48
Grilled Bacon Chicken Lettuce Wraps	170
Grilled Bacon Dog	89
Grilled Bacon-Wrapped Hot Dogs	31
Grilled Balsamic & Blue Steak	53
Grilled Banana Split with Vanilla Bourbon Ice Cream	314
Grilled Beef Back Ribs	52
Grilled Beef Sliders	69
Grilled Beer Cabbage	185
Grilled Blackened Saskatchewan Salmon	229
Grilled Blood Orange Mimosa	327
Grilled Breakfast Pizza	92
Grilled Burrata Salad with Ripped Croutons	201
Grilled Butter Basted Porterhouse Steak	41
Grilled Butter Basted Rib-Eye	38
Grilled Cabbage Steaks with a Bacon Vinaigrette	181
Grilled Carne Asada Burrito with Smoked Pico	55
Grilled Carne Asada Skirt Steak	37
Grilled Carne Asada with Grilled Peppers & Onions	33
Grilled Chicken Alfredo Pizza	131
Grilled Chicken and Roasted Beet Salad	179
Grilled Chicken Fajitas	141
Grilled Clams in Garlic Butter	242
Grilled Cleveland Polish Boy	56
Grilled Combination Pizza	123
Grilled Corn on Cob with some Parmesan and Garlic	210
Grilled Corn Salad	199
Grilled Corn Salsa	207

Grilled Corn with Honey Butter & Smoked Salt	188
Grilled Crab Legs with Herb Butter	241
Grilled Crawfish with Spicy Garlic Butter	251
Grilled Double Burgers with Texas Spicy BBQ Sauce	55
Grilled Duck Breasts	168
Grilled Fingerling Potato Salad	215
Grilled Flank Steak with Chilean Salsa	38
Grilled Fresh Fish	231
Grilled Frozen Strawberry Lemonade	330
Grilled Fruit Skewers with Yogurt Sauce	291
Grilled German Sausage with a Smoky Pit Boss Twist	75
Grilled Grapefruit Buck Cocktail	325
Grilled Greek Chicken with Garlic & Lemon	136
Grilled Halibut Fillets with Lemon and Butter Sauce	261
Grilled Ham & Egg Cups	91
Grilled Hawaiian Sour	325
Grilled Hellfire Chicken Wings	163
Grilled Honey Bourbon Peaches	317
Grilled Hummus	292
Grilled Italian Meatballs	71
Grilled Italian Meatballs (Polpette)	99
Grilled Jungle Juice	325
Grilled Korean Short Ribs	41
Grilled Lemons on Aked German Pork Schnitzel	83
Grilled Loaded Chicken Tacos	157
Grilled Lobster Tails	254
Grilled Lobster with Lemon Garlic Butter	258
Grilled Loco Moco Burger	46
Grilled Mahi Fish Tacos with Creamy Chipotle Sauce Recipe	271
Grilled Mango Shrimp	268
Grilled Mango with Lime and Coconut	315
Grilled Meat Lover's Pizza	382
Grilled Melancholy Fix Cocktail	339
Grilled Mussels with Lemon Butter	230
Grilled New York Style Pepperoni Pizza	94
Grilled Oysters	288
Grilled Oysters by Journey South	239
Grilled Oysters with Mignonette	253
Grilled Paprika Chicken with Jalapeño Salsa	126
Grilled Peach & Bacon Salad with the Maple Vinaigrette	199
Grilled Peach Mint Julep	326
Grilled Peach Salsa	214
Grilled Peach Smash Cocktail	326
Grilled Peach Sour Cocktail	338
Grilled Peaches & Cream Popsicle	308
Grilled Piña Colada	336
Grilled Pineapple & Watermelon Creamsicles	321
Grilled Pit Boss Whole Corn	195
Grilled Plums with Brown Sugar Balsamic Reduction	307
Grilled Pork Chops with Pineapple-Mango Salsa	90
Grilled Prosciutto Covered Asparagus	280
Grilled Quadruple Cheese Pizza	383
Grilled Rabbit Tail Cocktail	338
Grilled Rib Eyes with Hasselback Sweet Potatoes	25
Grilled Ribeye Shish Kabobs with Chimichurri Sauce	37
Grilled Ribeye Steak Sandwich	54
Grilled Rib-Eye Steaks by Doug Scheiding	40
Grilled Rib-Eye with Green Butter	53
Grilled Saké Shrimp	234
Grilled Salmon Burger with Chipotle Mayo	246
Grilled Salmon in Foil	244
Grilled Salmon Steaks with BBQ Corn Salad	262
Grilled Salmon Tacos with Smoked Tomato Salsa by Daniel Seidman	247
Grilled Salmon with Honey Sriracha Lime Glaze	272
Grilled Salmon with Smoked Avocado Salsa	227
Grilled Santa Maria Tri-Tip	26
Grilled Seafood Delight with Kickin Corn Maque Choux	271
Grilled Season Fruit with Gelato	299
Grilled Seasonal Fruit with Gelato	315
Grilled Shrimp Brochette	227

Grilled Shrimp Bruschetta with Balsamic Glaze	272
Grilled Shrimp Cocktail	226
Grilled Shrimp Foil Packets	245
Grilled Shrimp Tacos with Garlic Cilantro Lime Slaw	235
Grilled Shrimp with Cajun dip	267
Grilled Sirloin Steaks	40
Grilled Skirt Steak Bulgogi Bowls	36
Grilled Skirt Steak with Peach Salsa	63
Grilled Soft-Shell Crabs	250
Grilled Southern Pimento Cheeseburger	44
Grilled Soy-Ginger Yellowtail Collar	243
Grilled Spicy Lime Shrimp	270
Grilled Sriracha Salmon with Avocado Pineapple Salsa	241
Grilled Sriracha Wings	138
Grilled Steak	44
Grilled Steak for Two with Cocoa Rub	45
Grilled Stone Fruit with Berries & Cream	298
Grilled Strawberry Bourbon Lemonade	335
Grilled Sugar Snap Peas & Smoked Bacon	114
Grilled Surf & Turf	261
Grilled Sweet Cajun wings	130
Grilled Sweet Potato Casserole	198
Grilled Sweet Potato Planks	296
Grilled Swordfish with Corn Salsa	228
Grilled Texas Spicy Shrimp	233
Grilled Thai Beef Skewers	40
Grilled Thai Chicken Burgers with Papaya Slaw	164
Grilled Tomahawk Steak	34
Grilled Triple Cheeseburger	39
Grilled Tri-Tip with Garlic Mashed Potatoes	54
Grilled Trout with Citrus & Basil	241
Grilled Tuna Salad with Smoky & Spicy Mayo	231
Grilled Vegetables with Lemon Herb Vinaigrette	378
Grilled Veggie Burgers along with Lentils & Walnuts	206
Grilled Veggie Sandwich	210

Grilled Wagyu Burgers	43
Grilled Watermelon Punch	339
Grilled Watermelon with Lime & Smoked Chili Salt	291
Grilled Wedge Salad	216
Grilled White Fish Steaks with Basil Orange Pesto	252
Grilled Whole Steelhead Fillet	228
Grilled Zucchini Squash Spears	196
Guinness Shepherd's Pie	49
Gyros	62

H

Ham Glazed	87
Harvest Vegetables (Grilled)	189
Hasselback Potatoes (Roasted)	284
Hawaiian BBQ Baked Beans	107
Hawaiian Pulled Pig	104
Hawaiian Sour Grilled	191
Heirloom Carrots Roasted	196
Herb Roasted Turkey	179
Hickory Smoked Prime Rib	52
Holiday Breakfast Strata	91
Holiday Brownie Pie	305
Holiday Ham Cider (Glazed & Baked)	78
Holiday Prosciutto-Wrapped Pork Tenderloin	112
Holiday Roasted Apple Pudding	307
Holiday Smoked Cheese Log	113
Home Team Cocktail	334
Home-Cured Bourbon Bacon	110
Homemade Smoked Ketchup	208
Homemade turkey gravy	144
Honey & Sage Skillet Cornbread	281
Honey Balsamic Salmon	231
Honey Glazed Grapefruit Shandy Cocktail	335
Honey Glazed Pineapple Grilled	198
Honey Grilled Garlic Wings	159
Honey Lime Chicken Adobo Skewers	132
Honey Smoked Tilapia with Cajun Spice Rub	244
Honey-Glazed Roasted Pork Loin	124
Honey-soy Glazed Salmon	270
Hot & Fast Smoked Baby Back Ribs	124

Hot Buttered Rum Smoked	195
Hot turkey sandwich	143
Hummus (Smoked) with Roasted Vegetables	206

I

In a Blanket Everything Pigs	82
In Pit Boss Fashion Cocktail	334
Injected drunken smoked turkey legs	144
Irish Soda Bread	386
Italian Grilled Chicken Saltimbocca	158
Italian Herb & Parmesan Scones	384

J

Jalapeño Beef Jerky	25
Jalapeño Candied Smoked Salmon	258
Jalapeno Cheddar Smoked Sausages	109
Jalapeño Poppers (Coconut Shrimp)	285
Jamaican Jerk Grilled Halibut with Pico De Gallo	261
Jerked Jamaican Chicken Legs	162
Journey South Oyesters	289

K

Kansas City Hot Fried Chicken	133
Kimi's Simple Grilled Fresh Fish	227
Kodiak Cakes Candied Bacon Crumble Brownies	309
Korean BBQ Short Ribs	32

L

Lava Cake (Chocolate) and Whipped Cream (Smoked)	308
Leftover BBQ Sandwich	52
Leftover Pit Boss Turkey Soup	153
Lemon Chicken Breast	180
Lemon Ginger Grilled Shrimp Recipe	272
Lemon Gremolata	197
Lemon Herb Cedar Plank Salmon Recipe	246
Lemon Herb Chicken	166
Lemon Herb-Grilled Salmon	244
Lemon Pepper Tenderloin (Grilled)	121
Lemon Smoked Salmon	269
Lime Shrimp (Spicy & Grilled)	237
Loaded & Baked Potato Salad	219
Loaded Reuben Fries with Fontina Cheese	36
Loaded Tater Tots (Baked)	190
Lobster Tails and Herb Butter Recipe	272
Loin Smoked Pork	77
London Broil Grilled Along with Blue Cheese Butter	224
Lynchburg Bacon	75

M

Macaroni Salad (Smoked)	218
Machaca Mexican Shredded Beef	171
Mahi-Mahi Shish Kabobs	230
Maipole Cocktail	334
Mandarin Chicken Breast	168
Mango Coleslaw (Grilled)	183
Mango Coleslaw Grilled	221
Mango Thai Shrimp	269
Maple Bacon Donuts	298
Maple Bacon Pull Apart	299
Maple Bacon Pull-Apart	104
Maple Baked Ham	122
Maple Bourbon Drumsticks	153
Maple smoked thanksgiving turkey	135
Marbled Brownies with Amaretto & Ricotta	301
Marcona Almonds with Prosciutto Roofed Dates	78
Marinated Beef Ribs	23
Marshmallow Casserole Sweet Potato	182
Mashed Potatoes (Roasted)	190
Mashed Red Potatoes	204
Maui Waui Cocktail	328
Maxi Mac & Cheese	209
Mayo and herb-roasted turkey	144
Meatloaf Cupcake Bites	43
Meaty Beer Beans	113
Mexican Grilled Skirt Steak Tacos	36
Mini Apple Pies	383
Mini Quiches Breakfast (Baked)	218
Mini Sausage Rolls	106

Moink Burger Smoked by Scott Thomas	80
Mom's Best Baked Pumpkin Bread	317
Moroccan Ground Meat Kebabs	52
Muffaletta Sandwich (Pit Boss Smoked)	73
Mustard Pork Chops with Peach Relish	91
Mustard Wings Smoked	156

N

Nashville hot turkey melt	145
New England Clambake	253
New England Lobster Rolls	269
New Potatoes Roasted	196
Not Your Mama's Meatloaf	34
NY Grilled Steak Along with Cornbread Salad	64

O

Oatmeal Chocolate Chip Cookies	307
Oktoberfest Pretzel Mustard Chicken	131
Old Fashioned Cornbread	284
Old-Fashioned Roasted Glazed Ham	76
Onion Dip	283
Onion Ring of Bacon	81
Orange & Maple Baked Ham	373
Oysters Traegefeller	235

P

Pan-Seared Halibut with Green Garlic Pesto	263
Paprika Chicken Grilled along with Jalapeño Salsa	278
Parmesan Chicken Sliders along with Pesto Mayonnaise	154
Parmesan Roasted Cauliflower	193
Party Mix Pit Boss Chex	193
Pastrami Short Ribs	71
Peach & Basil Grilled Chicken Recipe	139
Peach Sour Cocktail Grilled	197
Peach Tart	392
Pepper and onion turkey burger sliders	143

Peppercorn Steaks Grilled with Mushroom Cream Sauce	60
Pernil	112
Peruvian Roasted Chicken with Green Sauce	165
Pickle Brined Chicken Sandwich	163
Pico De Gallo (Smoked)	188
Pico De Gallo Smoked	192
Pie (Blueberry)	313
Pig in a Hammock	339
Pineapple Skewers & Sticky Teriyaki BBQ Pork	79
Pinwheels Bacon Pork (Kansas Lollipops)	74
Pit Boss Bacon-Wrapped Filet Mignon	42
Pit Boss Baked Corn Dog Bites	371
Pit Boss Baked Focaccia	394
Pit Boss Baked Protein Bars	378
Pit Boss Baked Rainbow Trout	226
Pit Boss BBQ 44958 Chickens	131
Pit Boss BBQ Chicken Breasts	132
Pit Boss BBQ Chicken Salad	136
Pit Boss BBQ Double Decker Taco	32
Pit Boss BLT Burgers	225
Pit Boss Boulevardier Cocktail	331
Pit Boss brined smoked turkey	146
Pit Boss Cajun Broil	92
Pit Boss Chex Party Mix	281
Pit Boss Chocolate Chip Cookies	303
Pit Boss Cocktail	334
Pit Boss Cowboy Beans	385
Pit Boss Crab Legs	234
Pit Boss Crispy Orange Chicken Wings	141
Pit Boss Duck Poppers	382
Pit Boss English Muffins	291
Pit Boss Filet Mignon	42
Pit Boss French 75 Cocktail	328
Pit Boss Fries along with Chipotle Ketchup	281
Pit Boss Fries with Chipotle Ketchup	200
Pit Boss Frito Pie	68
Pit Boss Gin & Tonic	332
Pit Boss Grilled Shrimp Scampi	243
Pit Boss Grilled Tiki Cocktail	333
Pit Boss Jerk Shrimp	242
Pit Boss Mandarin Wings	127

Pit Boss Mushrooms Smoked	196
Pit Boss NY Strip Steak	51
Pit Boss Old Fashioned	326
Pit Boss Paloma Cocktail	332
Pit Boss Pork Chops	91
Pit Boss Potatoes Au Gratin	185
Pit Boss Prime Rib Roast	51
Pit Boss Pulled Pork Sandwiches	115
Pit Boss 'Que Cocktail	334
Pit Boss Roasted Easter Ham	93
Pit Boss Salmon with Balsamic Glaze	238
Pit Boss Smash Burger	36
Pit Boss Smoked Coleslaw	190
Pit Boss Smoked Daiquiri	333
Pit Boss Smoked Deviled Eggs	149
Pit Boss Smoked Guacamole	280
Pit Boss Smoked Mussels By Dennis The Prescott	234
Pit Boss Smoked Salami	57
Pit Boss Smoked Salmon	252
Pit Boss Smoked Sausage	75
Pit Boss Smoky Meatball Subs	26
Pit Boss Tri-Tip Roast	42
Pit Boss Ultimate Thanksgiving Sandwich	150
Pit Boss Wheat Bread	390
Pit Bossade Cocktail	322
Pit Bossed Lasagna	376
Pizza Bites	389
Plain Smoked Ribs	76
Pomegranate Lemonade Cocktail Smoked	192
Pork Belly Bourbon Baked Beans	372
Pork Chops Pit Boss	85
Pork Chops with Mustard and Peach Relish	87
Pork Loin Injected Bacon-Draped Roast	92
Pork Roast Anytime	87
Pork Spareribs BBQ Paleo	77
Pork Tenderloin and Lemon Pepper Grilling	85
Pork Tenderloin Asian-Style	88
Pork Tenderloin of Cocoa Crusted	81
Porterhouse Grilled Steak Along with Creamed Greens	71
Pot Smoked Roast Brisket	70
Potato Crusted Salmon with Lemon Butter Sauce	255
Potato Salad (Smoked)	187
Potato Skins(Baked) along with Pulled Pork	282
Potato Wedges with Garlic and Herbs	186
Potatoes & Smoked Sausage	82
Pound Cake	312
Pretzel Rolls	394
Prosciutto Covered Grilled Shrimp along with Peach Salsa	287
Prosciutto Stuffed Chicken Roasted	149
Prosciutto Wrapped Dates with Marcona Almonds	120
Prosciutto Wrapped Grilled Shrimp with Peach Salsa	229
Pull-Apart Dinner Rolls	391
Pulled Enchiladas Pork with Smoke-Roasted Red Sauce	99
Pulled pig from Hawaii	83
Pulled Pork Enchiladas with Smoke-Roasted Red Sauce	347
Pulled Pork Mac & Cheese	77
Pulled Pork Stew	393
Pumpkin Chocolate Chip Cookies	223
Pumpkin Pie (Pit Boss)	314
Pumpkin Pie with Bourbon Whipped Cream	302

Q

Quick Hot Smoked Salmon	273
Quick Ribs BBQ	85

R

Ratatouille Salad (Grilled)	189
Red Curry Salmon with Avocado Creme	254
Red Mashed Potatoes	187
Red Onion Jam, Duck Confit, & Goat Cheese Crostini	278
Red Onion Salad and Broccoli (Roasted)	190
Red Pepper White Roasted Bean Dip	207
Red Snapper Los Grilla	273

Red, White, and Blue Summer Breeze Drink Recipe	340
Rendezvous Ribs Smoked	87
Reuben Dip	295
Reuben Sandwich	24
Reverse Seared Bone-In Pork Chops	76
Reverse Seared Filet Mignon with Red Wine Reduction	54
Reverse Seared NY Strip Steak	51
Reverse Seared Rib-Eye Caps	34
Rib-Eye Grilled with Hasselback Sweet Potatoes	74
Ribs Smoked Beef Pastrami	58
Roast Chicken & Pimenton Potatoes	177
Roast Citrus Chicken	169
Roast Pork Loin along with Mango Salsa	78
Roasted Asparagus	202
Roasted Beans (Green) with Bacon	182
Roasted Broccoli with Parmesan	188
Roasted Buffalo Wings	168
Roasted Carrots with Pomegranate Relish and Pistachio	216
Roasted Cauliflower & Broccoli Salad with Bacon	201
Roasted Chicken Enchiladas	152
Roasted Christmas Goose	130
Roasted cider brined turkey breast	148
Roasted Citrus-Herb Turkey	165
Roasted Clambake	249
Roasted Cod with Meyer Lemon-Herb Butter	240
Roasted Creamy Brussel Sprouts	220
Roasted Crispy Potatoes	201
Roasted Garlic & Clam Pizza	265
Roasted Garlic Herb Fries	182
Roasted Garlic Wings	137
Roasted Habanero Wings	287
Roasted Halibut in Parchment	260
Roasted Halibut with Spring Vegetables	261
Roasted Halibut with Tartar Sauce	240
Roasted Ham with Apricot Sauce	93
Roasted Hasselback Potatoes	204
Roasted herbed turkey breast	147
Roasted Honey bourbon glazed turkey	148

Roasted Jalapeño Poppers	202
Roasted Mushrooms with Sherry and Thyme	195
Roasted Mustard Crusted Prime Rib	38
Roasted New Potatoes	185
Roasted Olives	191
Roasted Parmesan Cauliflower	183
Roasted Peach Salsa	217
Roasted Pork Loin Honey-Glazed	75
Roasted Pork Tenderloin with Herbs and Garlic	97
Roasted Pork with Balsamic Strawberry Sauce	108
Roasted Potato Poutine	296
Roasted Potatoes by Doug Scheiding	290
Roasted Prime Rib with Mustard and Herbs De Provence	25
Roasted Red Pepper White Bean Dip	296
Roasted River Potatoes by Chef Timothy Hollingsworth	188
Roasted Root Vegetables	206
Roasted Rosemary Orange Chicken	129
Roasted Santa Maria Tri-Tip	29
Roasted Serrano Wings	128
Roasted Sheet Pan Chicken	133
Roasted Smoke Chicken along with Herb Butter	153
Roasted Steak Fries with Homemade Ketchup	363
Roasted Stuffed Rainbow Trout with Brown Butter	240
Roasted stuffed turkey breast	145
Roasted Sweet Potato Fries	201
Roasted Teriyaki Wings	132
Roasted Tin Foil Dinners	128
Roasted Tingle Wings	166
Roasted Wild Salmon Along with Cauliflower Pickled Salad	205
Roasted Wild Salmon with Pickled Cauliflower Salad	247
Roasted Yellowtail with Potatoes, Mushrooms & Italian Salsa Verde	232
Robert Palmer Cocktail	333
Romaine Caesar Salad (Grilled)	189
Romaine Caesar Salad Grilled	205
Root Vegetables Roasted	184

Rosemary & Mashed Thyme-Infused Potatoes with Cream	203
Rosemary and Thyme-Infused Crushed Potatoes along with a Cream	217
Rosemary and Thyme-Infused Mashed Potatoes with Cream	348
Rosemary Prime Rib	30
Rosemary Roasted Pork Collar	101
Ryes and Shine Cocktail	329

S

Salmon (Balsamic Glaze)	235
Salmon (Cedar-Plank)	239
Salmon (Cedar-Plank) with Salsa (Mango)	236
Salmon (Glazed) Honey-Soy	239
Salmon cakes and homemade tartar sauce	268
Salt & Pepper Beer-Braised Beef Ribs	23
Salt Crusted Baked Potatoes	345
Salt-Crusted Baked Potatoes	192
Salt-Crusted Prime Rib	67
Salted Apple Cheesecake Galette	355
Sausage & Pesto Lasagna	200
Sausage and Pesto Lasagna	342
Sausage Pepper Skewers	106
Sausage Stuffing (Classic)	82
Scalloped Potatoes with Bacon & Chipotle Cream	376
Scalloped Smoked Potatoes	218
Scallops (Bacon-Wrapped)	236
Scallops Wrapped in Bacon	270
Scones with Vanilla Bean Glaze	320
Seared Ahi Tuna Steak	268
Seared BBQ Pork Chop	89
Seared Bluefin Tuna Steaks	241
Seared Lemon Garlic Scallops	232
Seasonal (Roasted) & Pickled Vegetables	220
Secret Ingredient BBQ Beef Short Ribs	23
Seeing Stars Cocktail	328
Sheet Pan Roasted Vegetables	210
Sherry Root Vegetables Roasted	216
Short Rib Braised Sandwich	60
Short Rib Chili	64

Shrimp	256
Shrimp (Bacon Wrapped)	239
Shrimp (Garlic & Pesto Bruschetta)	237
Shrimp Scampi	236
Shrimp tacos with lime crema	266
Simple Glazed Salmon Fillets	233
Simple Smoked Ribs	102
Skillet S'Mores Dip with Candied Smoked Pecans	362
Skillet-Roasted Game Bird	177
Skirt Steak Quesadillas Grilled	63
Skirt Steak with Corn & Avocado Salsa	46
Slow Roasted Wild Salmon with Cheesy Scalloped Potatoes	251
Slow Smoked and Roasted Prime Rib	42
Slow Smoked Rib-Eye Roast	41
Smoke and Bubz Cocktail	339
Smoke Blended Salsa	291
Smoke n Grill Flank Steak	68
Smoke Roasted Chicken	159
Smoke Salsa Roasted	195
Smoke Screen Cocktail	328
Smoked & Loaded Baked Potato	295
Smoked 3-Bean Salad	212
Smoked Albacore Tuna	232
Smoked Albacore Tuna Niçoise Salad	250
Smoked Apple Cider	327
Smoked Arnold Palmer	327
Smoked Asparagus Soup	296
Smoked Baby Back Ribs	88
Smoked Bacon Cheese Ball	116
Smoked Baked Potato Soup	361
Smoked Barnburner Cocktail	322
Smoked BBQ Ribs	96
Smoked Beef Back Ribs	55
Smoked Beef Cheek Tacos	29
Smoked Beef Pastrami	58
Smoked Beet-Pickled Eggs	296
Smoked Berry Cocktail	327
Smoked Blood Orange & Rosemary Spritz	340
Smoked Bloody Mary Cocktail	329
Smoked Bloody Mary with Grilled Garnishes	329
Smoked BLT Sandwich	87
Smoked Bologna	90

Smoked bourbon & orange brined turkey	147
Smoked Bourbon Jerky	41
Smoked Bratwurst with Homemade Mustard	93
Smoked Brisket	29
Smoked Brisket Pot Pie	125
Smoked Brisket with Pit Boss Coffee Rub	53
Smoked Buffalo Fries	178
Smoked Burgers	28
Smoked Buttery Shrimp	244
Smoked Cajun Chicken Wings	294
Smoked Carolina Burger	48
Smoked Cherry Bourbon Ice Cream	303
Smoked Chicken along with Jalapeno Salsa Verde	166
Smoked Chicken Leg & Thigh Quarters	136
Smoked Chicken Lollipops along with BBQ Champagne Sauce	166
Smoked Chicken Tikka Drumsticks	128
Smoked Chicken with Chimichurri	180
Smoked Chilean Sea Bass	226
Smoked Chilean Sea Bass by Doug Sheading	258
Smoked Chili Rib Eye Steaks	39
Smoked Chorizo & Arugula Pesto	93
Smoked Citrus & Polenta Pork Tenderloin	114
Smoked Clams Casino	245
Smoked Classic Porchetta	95
Smoked Coffee Break Beef Jerky	70
Smoked Cold Brew Coffee	323
Smoked Corned Beef & Cabbage	30
Smoked Corned Beef Brisket	44
Smoked Crab Legs	232
Smoked Creole Jambalaya	152
Smoked Deviled Eggs	180
Smoked Ditch Chicken	139
Smoked Dry Rub Wings	295
Smoked Dry Rubbed Baby Back Ribs	116
Smoked Eggnog	331
Smoked Fish Chowder	248
Smoked German Rouladen	57
Smoked Grape Lime Rickey	326
Smoked Hibiscus Sparkler	322
Smoked Homemade Crackers	294
Smoked Hot Buttered Rum	328
Smoked Hot Toddy	324
Smoked Hummus along with Roasted Veggies	286
Smoked Hummus with Roasted Vegetables	222
Smoked Ice Mojito Slurpee	322
Smoked Ice Recipe & Cocktail	341
Smoked Irish Coffee	329
Smoked Irish Coffee Pie	303
Smoked Italian Lasagna Recipe	112
Smoked Jacobsen Salt Margarita	327
Smoked Jalapeño Poppers	294
Smoked Kentucky Mule	324
Smoked Korean Wings	170
Smoked Lemon Sweet Tea	340
Smoked Lemonade with Pit Boss Simple Syrup	336
Smoked Loaded Roasted Potato Salad	214
Smoked Lobster Rolls	258
Smoked Lobster Scampi	233
Smoked Longhorn Brisket	43
Smoked Longhorn Cowboy Tri-Tip	42
Smoked Macaroni Salad	200
Smoked Margarita	325
Smoked Mexican Hot Chocolate	322
Smoked Midnight Brisket	38
Smoked Moink Burger by Scott Thomas	40
Smoked Mulled Wine	323
Smoked Mushrooms	373
Smoked New England clam chowder	274
Smoked Nuts (Diva Q's Savory)	281
Smoked Olives	187
Smoked Packed Avocado Recipe	84
Smoked Paleo Beef Jerky	27
Smoked Pasta Salad	202
Smoked Pastrami Burgers	59
Smoked Pastrami Sandwich	65
Smoked Peppered Beef Jerky	44
Smoked Peppered Beef Tenderloin	58
Smoked Pickles	185
Smoked Pineapple Hotel Nacional Cocktail	323
Smoked Pit Boss Coleslaw	197

Smoked Pit Boss Pulled Pork	100
Smoked Plum and Thyme Fizz Cocktail	193
Smoked Pomegranate Lemonade Cocktail	324
Smoked Porchetta with Italian Salsa Verde	118
Smoked Pork Loin along with Apples and Sauerkraut	73
Smoked Pork Loin with Sauerkraut and Apples	109
Smoked Pork Spareribs	115
Smoked Pork Tenderloin	86
Smoked Porterhouse Steak	31
Smoked Pot Roast	55
Smoked Potato Salad	214
Smoked Prawns Recipe	246
Smoked Pumpkin Soup	203
Smoked Pumpkin Spice Latte	335
Smoked Raspberry Bubbler Cocktail	332
Smoked Rendezvous Ribs	117
Smoked Rib-Eyes with Bourbon Butter	33
Smoked Ribs BBQ	79
Smoked Ribs with the Coconut Rum BBQ Sauce by Journey	114
Smoked Roasted Apple Pie	310
Smoked Salmon and Brine Recipe	245
Smoked Salmon Candy	233
Smoked salmon dip with grilled artichoke and cheese	266
Smoked Salmon Flatbread	230
Smoked Salmon Potato Bake	255
Smoked Salmon Salad	231
Smoked Salmon Sandwich	249
Smoked Salmon Veggie Dip	260
Smoked Salt Cured Lox	256
Smoked Salted Caramel White Russian	330
Smoked Sangaree Cocktail	332
Smoked Sangria	193
Smoked Sausage & Potatoes	102
Smoked Sausage Pancake Sandwich	102
Smoked Scalloped Potatoes	209
Smoked Scotch Eggs	150
Smoked Seafood Ceviche	229
Smoked Seafood Paella	263
Smoked Sesame Crusted Halibut with Tahini Mayonnaise	243
Smoked Shrimp and Grilled Dungeness Crab Cocktail	257
Smoked Shrimp and Grits	263
Smoked Spatchcocked Cornish Game Hens	137
Smoked Spring Tea Cocktail	332
Smoked Steelhead Breakfast Sandwich	256
Smoked Stuffed Avocado Recipe	91
Smoked Sweet & Spicy Cashews	289
Smoked Sweet Potato Soufflé by Diva Q	306
Smoked T-Bone Steaks	50
Smoked Teriyaki Jerky	59
Smoked Texas BBQ Brisket	30
Smoked Texas Ranch Water	340
Smoked Texas Spicy Drumsticks	137
Smoked Texas-Style Beef Brisket	63
Smoked Tri-Tip	31
Smoked Trout	239
Smoked Trout Dip	238
Smoked Trout Hash	257
Smoked Tuna Belly Tacos	237
Smoked turkey	146
Smoked turkey (bacon-wrapped turkey breast)	134
Smoked turkey jerky	144
Smoked turkey legs	142
Smoked turkey legs with brown butter and bourbon glaze	147
Smoked turkey with fig BBQ sauce	146
Smoked Venison Holiday Jerky	292
Smoked Whipped Cream	300
Smoked Whiskey Burgers	60
Smoked Whitefish Salad	252
Smoked wild turkey jerky	145
Smoked Wings	169
Smoking Gun Cocktail	333
Smoking Jacket Cocktail	333
Smoking' Thai Curry Chicken	127
Smoky Crab Dip	234
Smoky Fried Chicken	174
Smoky Ham & Bean Soup	86
Smoky Mountain Bramble Cocktail	324
Smoky Paloma Cocktail	328
Smoky Scotch & Ginger Cocktail	332

Smothered Pork Chops	108
Sopapilla Cheesecake by Doug Scheiding	380
Sourdough Pizza	365
Southern Grilled Comfort Sweet Potato Fries	209
Southwest Wild Turkey Egg Rolls	154
Southwestern Filled Peppers	277
Southwestern Stuffed Peppers	26
Spareribs Sweet Peach	74
Spatchcocked Chicken with Toasted Fennel & Garlic	129
Spatchcocked Chile-Lime Rubbed Chicken	129
Spice BBQ Beef Short Ribs	69
Spiced Cider Brew Cocktail	329
Spice-Rubbed Pork Tenderloin	109
Spicy Asian BBQ Shrimp	262
Spicy Asian Brussels Sprouts	382
Spicy Bacon covered Chicken Skewers (Grilled)	283
Spicy Bacon Covered Grilled Chicken Skewers	81
Spicy Bacon Wrapped Grilled Chicken Skewers	99
Spicy BBQ Whole Chicken	141
Spicy Cashews & Smoked Sweet	286
Spicy Crab Poppers	264
Spicy Mandarin Glaze with BBQ Spareribs	73
Spicy Pork and Sweet Roast	84
Spicy Shrimp Skewers	235
Spicy Smoked Chili Beef Jerky	24
Spring Frittata	382
Squash Butternut Macaroni plus Cheese	223
St. Louis BBQ Ribs	115
Stand Pineapple Chicken	155
Steak Fries with Horseradish Creme	375
Steak Sweetheart with Lobster Ceviche	65
Sticky Grilled Ginger Chicken Thighs	161
Sticky Teriyaki BBQ Pork & Pineapple Skewers	88
Stone Fruit Grilled along with Cream & Berries.	221
Strawberry Basil Daiquiri	329
Strawberry Mint Julep Cocktail	330
Strawberry Mule Cocktail	334
Strawberry Rhubarb Cobbler	303
Strip Steak Along with Bacon-Onion Jam	70
Stuffed Bacon-Wrapped Chicken Thighs	155
Stuffed Balsamic Chicken	139
Stuffed Jalapenos	190
Stuffed Lobster Tail	264
Stuffed Pork Crown Roast	95
Stuffing Turkey Bacon Balls	155
Sugar Cured Salmon	273
Sugar Snap Grilled Peas & Smoked Bacon	215
Sunday Supper Beef Roast	35
Sunset Margarita	330
Super Bowl Sundae (Smoked)	310
Supreme Pizza Baked Deep Dish	80
Sweet & Spicy Sriracha Salmon	226
Sweet and Spicy Beef Sirloin Tip Roast	39
Sweet and Spicy Pork Roast	90
Sweet Baked Potato Casserole along with Marshmallow Fluff	204
Sweet Braised & Sour Brisket	172
Sweet Cajun Wings	175
Sweet Cajun Wings (Grilled)	282
Sweet Chili Lime Pit Boss Grilled Crappie Recipe	246
Sweet Grilled Potato Planks	182
Sweet Grilled Shrimp & Spicy Sausage Skewers	42
Sweet heat Cajun spatchcock turkey	142
Sweet Mandarin Meatloaf	28
Sweet Mandarin Salmon	240
Sweet Potato (Grilled) Planks	280
Sweet Potato Fries (Roasted)	286
Sweet Potato Marshmallow Casserole	375
Sweet Potato Roasted Fries	187
Sweet Potato Roasted Steak Fries	184
Sweet Potatoes Marshmallow Hasselback	207
Sweet Smoked Salmon	276
Sweet Smoked Salmon Jerky	250
Sweetheart Steak	31

Swine Life's Smoked Parmesan Crusted Salmon	273
Swordfish with Sicilian Olive Oil Sauce	234

T

Tacos (Shrimp) with Crema (Lime)	236
Tandoori Chicken Burgers	152
Tandoori Chicken Wings	130
Tartar Sauce (Homemade) & Salmon Cakes	237
Tarte Tatin	306
Tater Tot Bake	392
T-Bone Grilled Steaks Along with Bloody Mary Steak Sauce	67
Tenderloin Apricot Pork	80
Tenderloin Pork	77
Tenderloin Smoked Pork	79
Tequila Lime Chicken Thighs	140
Tequila Lime Shrimp Tacos with Pineapple Pomegranate Salsa	274
Tequila-Lime Wings Roasted	163
Teriyaki Beef Jerky	35
Teriyaki Salmon	230
Teriyaki-Glazed Cod with Ginger-Scallion Ramen	254
Texas-style turkey	134
Thai Chicken Skewers	152
Thanksgiving BBQ Turkey	149
Thanksgiving Sausage Leek Stuffing	377
Thanksgiving Shepherd's Pie Baked	160
Thanksgiving smoked turkey	135
The Dan Patrick Show Grilled Bloody Mary Wings	297
The Dan Patrick Show pull-apart Pesto Bread	370
The Dan Patrick Show Smoked Super Bowl Sundae	320
The Grilled Chicken Challenge	126
The Max Burgers	224
The Old Orchard Cocktail	331
The Old-fashioned Orchard Cocktail	196
The Perfect Smoked New York Strip Steak	39
The Trifecta Cocktail	331
Three Ways BBQ Chicken Wings	167

Thyme-Infused" Mashed Potatoes & Rosemary with Cream	221
Tin Foil Dinner	33
Tomatillo Braised Chicken	134
Tomatoes Roasted	198
Traditional Baked Pumpkin Pie	304
Traditional smoked thanksgiving turkey	145
Triple Chocolate Cast Iron Cookie	302
Tuna Burgers	229
Tuna Steak with Baby Bok Choy and Carrots	259
Tuna Tacos with Lime & Cilantro Cream	262
Turkey Cornbread Tamale Pie Baked	160
Turkey Jalapeño Meatballs	156
Turkey Lettuce Wraps Smoked	150
Turkey Sliders with Chipotle Tartar Sauce	164
Tuscan Meatloaf	64
Twice Baked Potatoes	369
Twice Cut Grilled Pork Chop with Sweet & Sour Peaches	123

U

Ultimate Baked Garlic Bread	391
Ultimate BLT Salad	107
Ultimate Game Day Dip	388
Ultimate Loaded Nachos	28
Ultimate Pit Boss Cookie	345
Ultimate Scratch Gravy	157
Ultimate Smoked Turkey	170

V

Vegan Pumpkin Muffins of Apple (Gluten-Free)	313
Vegetables Pan Roasted Sheet	181
Veggie Flat Bread	386
Venison Meatloaf by Nikki Boxler	350
Venison Tater Tot Casserole (Baked)	286
Vietnamese Beef Jerky	24
Vietnamese Chicken Wings	151
Vodka Brined Smoked Wild Salmon	228

W

Wagyu Tri-Tip	38
Watermelon and Pineapple Creamsicles (Grilled)	312
Watermelon Grilled	197
Wedge Grilled Salad	215
Weekend Pasta Along with Braised Slow Meat Sauce	61
Weizen Up Cocktail	337
West Coast Cioppino Fries	264
Western Breakfast Casserole	117
Whiskey Bourbon BBQ Cheeseburger	49
White Chicken Chili	160
Whole Chicken	130
Whole Pickles (Smoked)	217
Whole Pickles Smoked	220
Whole Red Snapper - Stuffed, Sauced and Smoked	244
Whole Roasted Cauliflower along with Garlic Parmesan Butter	196
Whole Roasted Cauliflower with Garlic Parmesan Butter	290
Whole Roasted Chicken	133
Whole Smoked Chicken	129
Whole Vermillion Red Snapper	242
Wrapped Asparagus in Grilled Prosciutto	76

Y

Yellow Layer Cake with Smoked Candied Bacon	344
Yogurt-Marinated Chicken Thigh & Beef Tenderloin Kabobs	127

Z

Zombie Cocktail Recipe	331

Made in the USA
Columbia, SC
13 December 2023